ALSO BY HARRIET EVANS
FROM CLIPPER LARGE PRINT

Going Home
A Hopeless Romantic
The Love of Her Life
I Remember You
Love Always
Happily Ever After
Not Without You

A Place for Us

Harriet Evans

W F HOWES LTD

This large print edition published in 2015 by
W F Howes Ltd
Unit 4, Rearsby Business Park, Gaddesby Lane,
Rearsby, Leicester LE7 4YH

1 3 5 7 9 10 8 6 4 2

First published in the United Kingdom in 2014
by Headline Review

A CIP catalogue record for this book is available
from the British Library

ISBN 978 1 47128 292 8

Typeset by Palimpsest Book Production Limited,
Falkirk, Stirlingshire
Printed and bound by
www.printondem...   ...rough, England

This book is r...   ...dy materials

For Bea and Jockey with love

PART I

THE INVITATION

The family – that dear octopus from whose tentacles we never quite escape nor, in our inmost hearts, ever quite wish to.

Dodie Smith, *Dear Octopus*

MARTHA

The day Martha Winter decided to tear apart her family began like any other day.

She woke early. She always did, but lately she couldn't sleep. This summer sometimes she'd been up and dressed by five: too much to think about. No point lying in bed, fretting.

On this particular morning she was awake at four thirty. As her eyes flew open, and memory flooded her body, Martha knew her subconscious must understand the enormity of what she was about to do. She sat up and stretched, feeling the bones that ached, the prick of pain in her knee. Then she reached for her old silk peacock-feather-print dressing gown and quietly crossed the bedroom, as always stepping over the board that creaked, as always silently shutting the door behind her.

But David wasn't there. She could count on the fingers of both hands the nights they'd spent apart, and this was one. He'd gone to London to see about that exhibition, and Martha meant to put

3

her plan into action today, before he came back; told her she was wrong.

In late August the sun still rose early over the hills above Winterfold, the heavy trees filtering the orange-rose light. *Soon*, they'd whisper, as the wind rushed through the leaves at night. Soon we will dry up and die; we will all die some time. For it was the end of summer, and the Plough was in the western sky. Already, she could feel the chill in the evening air.

Was it because autumn was on its way? Or her eightieth birthday? What had prompted this desire to tell the truth? She thought perhaps it was this exhibition next year. 'David Winter's War', it was to be called. That was why he said he'd gone to London, to meet up with the gallery, go through his old sketches.

But Martha knew that was a lie. She knew David, and she knew when he was lying.

That was what had started this all off. Someone in a gallery in London deciding the time was right for a show like this, little knowing what damage they would do. So innocuous, thinking the past was dead and buried and couldn't hurt anyone. 'Didn't David Winter do some rather good stuff on bombed-out London?' 'David Winter? The Wilbur cartoonist?' 'Absolutely.' 'Gosh, no idea, old chap. Where was he from?' 'East End, I think. Could be interesting. Not just cartoon dogs and all that.' 'Good idea. I'll write and ask him.' And then plans were laid and events put in motion and slowly, inexorably, the truth would come out.

Martha made herself a pot of tea, every morning, singing to herself. She liked to sing. She always used the same mug, Cornish pottery, blue and cream stripes, her gnarled fingers hooked round its scalding.middle. She had time to drink tea now, gallons of the stuff, and she liked it strong. 'Thrutchy,' Dorcas had called it. A good Somerset word, that: Martha had learned it during the war. Evacuated out of Bermondsey aged seven in 1939 – four kids in one room, where life and death was seemingly as random as swatting a fly or missing it – one day she'd simply been shoved on to a train and the next morning woken up in a strange house with a view of nothing but trees out of the window. She might as well have been on the moon. Martha had gone downstairs, crying, and there she'd seen Dorcas, sitting at a table like this. 'Cup of tea, my dear? Nice and thrutchy, it is.'

A long time ago. Martha drained her first mug of tea, then spread her pens out, and the smooth creamy paper. Readying herself for the moment when she felt able to write.

So many years now in this gentle, honest house, every inch of it made with care, refashioned with love. They had been here for forty-five years. At first Martha had thought she'd never be able to take it on. It was a mess when they saw it; green paint covering the original Arts and Crafts wooden

5

panelling, rotten floorboards, the garden one large compost heap of mouldy, brown mulch.

'I can't do this,' she'd told David. 'We don't have the money.'

'I'll make the money, Em,' he'd told her. 'I'll find a way. We have to live here. It's a sign.'

The children had bounced up and down, holding on to their parents' arms, little Florence like a monkey, gibbering with excitement, Bill peering out of windows, shouting, 'There's a huge dead rat up here, and something's tried to eat it! Come up!' Even Daisy's face had lit up when she saw the space Wilbur would have to run around.

'But do you have the money?' she'd asked, worried. Daisy heard too much, Martha knew it.

And David had swept his daughter into his arms. 'I'll make the money, little one. I'll make it. For a house like this, wouldn't it be worth it?'

Martha always remembered what Daisy said next. She'd struggled to be put down on the ground again, crossed her arms and said, 'Well, I don't like it here. It's too pretty. Come on, Wilbur.'

She'd run off into the house again, and Martha and David had looked at each other and laughed.

'We have to live here,' she'd said, feeling the bright sunshine on her head, the children shouting happily behind her.

David had smiled. 'I can hardly believe it. Can you?'

'Shall we tell them why?'

Her husband had kissed her, and stroked her cheek. 'No, I think not. Let's keep it our secret.'

They had money now, of course, but not then. David was the creator of Wilbur the dog and Daisy, the little girl who thought she understood him. Every home had a Wilbur tea towel, pencil case, a book of cartoon strips. But back then Wilbur was in the future and the Winters had nothing much, except each other. Only Martha and David knew what they'd gone through to get to the moment where they stood on the lawn that hot day in 1967 and decided they'd buy Winterfold.

She had forgotten nothing, nothing that had happened before, or afterwards. The secrets every family acquires, some small – little indiscretions, tiny jokes. Some big, too big for her to bear any more.

The morning sun was above the trees now. Martha moved around the kitchen, waiting for the tea to brew. She'd learned the art of patience long ago; learned that having babies slows you down, takes your dreams of your own career and slowly chips away at them. She had wanted to be an artist too, as much as her husband. But each pregnancy tied her firmly to her home; each night lying awake on her side, feeling the movement, back aching, breath short, and nothing to do but wait for the baby to come. And then you grew older and slower and those babies grew up and left you. You could hold them close but one day they would leave, as sure as the sun rising in the morning.

Bill was still here, she told herself, but he was

different, not the man she'd thought he'd become. He was nearly eight when they moved to Winterfold. Daisy and Florence would spend all day out in the garden, or in the tree house in the woods, collecting friends, dirt, stories to tell. But Bill would usually remain inside, playing Meccano, or battleships, or reading his book. Occasionally he would come into the kitchen or the sitting room, his sweet, serious face hopeful: 'Hello, Mother. Are you all right? Can I give you a hand with anything?'

And Martha, in the middle of mending a plug or stuffing up a mouse hole, for there was always something to do in this house, would smile, knowing what he knew: that Bill had saved up his visit to her, counting down the minutes, because he wanted to be with her all the time, but knew he couldn't. It was sissy, and Daisy already taunted him about it, not to mention the boys at school. So if she felt she could get away with it Martha would give him a hug and something to do: washing up, chopping vegetables. Both of them pretending he didn't want to be there, that he was only trying to be helpful. Where was he now, that serious, brown-eyed boy who'd broken her heart with love every day?

At least he was still here. Her daughters weren't. After Bill came Daisy, and the moment they'd handed her to Martha that first time Martha had looked into her green eyes, just like her own, and known her. She could translate perfectly her

8

furious, shifting expressions, her love of solitude, her little plans. Daisy was the only thing Martha and David had ever fundamentally disagreed about, in six decades. People didn't understand her. But she'd proved them wrong, hadn't she?

'Daisy? Oh, yes, she's very well. We don't hear from her so much these days. She's very busy and the area she's in has extremely poor communication. She sends a message, from time to time. But we're so proud of her.' It was a neat little speech, she knew: Daisy had come good. Daisy wasn't who everyone thought she was. Whereas Florence . . . Martha often felt Florence was like a giraffe in a family of eels. She loved her, was so proud of her, in awe of her intellect and her passion and the way she'd become, against all the odds, spectacularly her own person – but sometimes she wished she wasn't so . . . *Florence.*

Bill, Daisy, Florence. Martha told herself she loved all her children equally, but in the secret part of herself she had a little rhyme: Bill was her first baby, Daisy was her first girl and Florence was David's. She knew it sounded awful. But it kept coming back to her, this little rhyme. She'd find herself chanting it under her breath while she weeded the garden, walked into the village, brushed her teeth. Like a song stuck in her head, as though someone were playing it while she slept every night. She found she was terrified someone might look into her heart, and see what she had done. But the time for secrets was over. It was

9

coming. It was all coming to her, and soon it would all come out.

Would anyone want to come back after the truth was out? There was a set programme of entertainment in place at Winterfold, which never varied in the detail. Their Christmas drinks party was the biggest night in the diary for miles around: mulled wine served from a huge, two-foot-high pot on the Aga, Martha's famous gingerbread cut into stars and hung with ribbons on the huge Christmas tree, which stood in the sitting room, by the French windows, as it had done for years and would continue to do. The Valentine's Day drinks, where the children handed round heart-shaped sandwiches and the guests drank too much sloe gin, and more than one amatory mistake had been made late at night walking back down to the village (the teenage Bill, alighting from the bus late one night returning from another party, swore he'd seen Mrs Talbot from the post office kissing Mrs Ackroyd, the landlady of the Green Man, on the other side of the bus shelter). Fireworks every year on Guy Fawkes Night, a hugely popular Easter egg hunt, and there was always a summer party in August, around which people planned their holidays: an awning on the lawn and paper lanterns stretching along the driveway.

Nothing changed, not even after the disastrous summer party of – was it 1978 or '79? which had passed into local legend. The truth was no one knew why, or could have explained how it was different, at Martha and David's. Their house was lovely, the food was delicious, the company was always warm and fun. All Martha had ever wanted was to make it clear that you were welcome. Whoever you were. Whether you were the television actress who lived in the mansion at the top of the hill, or the postman who stopped to chat to Mr Winter about cricket every day in summer. That there was no 'gang'. All she and David had ever wanted to do was to make a home, a place unlike their past. To give their children a childhood that would stay with them. To work hard together. Be happy.

A blackbird bounced through the herbs in her garden, acid-yellow beak pecking at the cocoa soil. He looked up with a bright, glassy-eyed stare at Martha as she sat by the window, pen poised, and she met his gaze until he darted into a hedge. She took another sip of tea, delaying for just a second. Savouring the final moments of stillness. For she knew that the moment she began to write, something would be set in motion, a time bomb waiting to go off. She would post the invitations and then the party would happen and she, Martha, would finally be able to tell them all what she had done. And it would never be the same after that.

A single tear dropped on to the worn kitchen table. She sat up straight, and said to herself, 'Come on, old girl. It's time.'

Carefully her pen scratched across the surface, lines cross-hatching and curling till they formed something, a house, a long low house: the roof, the wooden buttresses, the old front door. Underneath, in her beautiful italic script, she wrote:

David & Martha Winter
request the pleasure of your company at
a party to celebrate Martha's 80th Birthday

There will be an important announcement.
We ask that you please be there.

Drinks with friends Friday 23rd November
2012 7 p.m.
Family only lunch 1 p.m. Saturday 24th
November
Winterfold, Winter Stoke, Somerset
R.S.V.P.

DAVID

I t was a mistake. He shouldn't have come back. David Winter sat alone in the corner of the pub, trying not to look as obviously out of place as he felt. Returning to the old neighbourhood was one thing. Meeting here – he'd been crazy to suggest it, but he hadn't known where else to go. The old Lyons Corner House was a bank, the other old places round here all gone or so gentrifed they weren't actual pubs any more.

He flexed his aching hands in and out and checked his watch again, blinking hard. Some days he felt better than others. And some days the black cloud felt as if it were swallowing him whole in its pillowing softness, so that he was ready to float away with it. He was so tired. All the time. Ready to lie down and go. And yet he couldn't, not yet.

Seventy years ago, when he was a boy, the Spanish Prisoners had been the roughest pub in the whole area, and that was saying something. They said the Ripper had drunk there, once upon a time. That a barmaid was murdered and buried beneath the bar. The clichés weren't funny here, they were true. Every kind of Bill Sikes was to be

13

found at the Spanish Prisoners – and Nancys too, women like his mother. There was nothing David didn't know about that, about dark corners, terrified women, fear that sank into your bones so deep you didn't know if you'd ever shake it off the rest of your life, ever be free of its shadow.

The Spanish Prisoners had stunk of tobacco, of piss and sweat, of mould and sewage, and stout. There were men there who could recall sheep being driven down Islington High Street to Smithfield Market, who remembered the old Queen's death, who'd had sons killed in the Boer War. Davy Doolan had collected the pennies whenever his mother played piano and waited to help her husband home. If he decided to come home, that was. The pub was a vast Georgian box on the outside, London stock brick, big windows, and it was a mystery how inside it was such a dark warren of a place. You had to be fearless, or dying of thirst, to go in there.

Now, in 2012, it was unrecognisable – a gleaming temple to the religion of coffee and microbreweries – and David wished his hands weren't so damned painful that he couldn't whip out a notebook there and then and start drawing. The wood shone, glass sparkled. The list of beers was as long as David's arm; he hadn't known where to begin, and in the end had plumped for an orange juice. The barman had a beard, tortoiseshell-frame glasses and when he walked past David after his shift ended, David had noticed, with his cartoonist's eye for detail, that he was wearing shorts, socks and slip-on loafers, carrying a canvas printed bag. Before that, though, he'd presented David with a minuscule glass of hand-pressed Valencian orange juice and said politely, 'Four pounds, please.'

Four pounds for a glass of orange juice? He thought how Martha would laugh if she saw him, for the first time practically, baulk at the expense of something. But Martha wasn't here, and he couldn't tell her about this. He had to carry on with this fiction for his visit to London. And he hated it, hated lying to his wife.

It wasn't entirely fiction: there was to be an exhibition of his early East End work. When the call came through, he had agreed, hadn't he? With a weary acceptance: time was running out. A fortnight after the gallery had rung him to suggest the idea, David had finally taken out the drawings, hidden away for decades in hard, cloth-backed folders in the cupboard in his study. He'd waited till Martha was out; gritted his teeth, and at first it had been fine. Then, suddenly, it had been too much, looking at them again, the weight of what he carried. He'd simply put his head on the desk and cried, like a little child. And he couldn't stop crying, had to tell Martha he was going to bed, another headache. He knew then, knew it meant he had to ring her up, beg her to see him again.

'Davy?'

The tap on his arm made David jump; he looked up in shock. 'Don't get up.'

'Of course—' he struggled to stand, his breathing rapid, every gulp an effort. 'Of course I will. Cassie, my dear.' He put his hand on her shoulder.

They stared at each other, face to face after forty-four years.

She was the same height as he, tall for a woman; he'd loved that about her. And her eyes were cool and clear and grey, like they saw through you and were laughing at you. Her ash-blond hair was smooth, carefully twisted up on her head. She wore no wedding ring. She looked . . . classy.

'You're still tall,' he said. 'Tall and beautiful. I'd know you anywhere.'

She fiddled with the belt of her coat, never taking her eyes off him. 'I can't say the same about you, Davy. You look – well. I wouldn't have known you.'

He gave a faint smile. 'Let me get you a drink.'

'No, Davy. I'll get it. You sit down.'

She returned with a rum and Coke. 'Five pound eighty! Five pound eighty, Davy, what a racket!'

Her rueful smile relaxed him. He pointed. 'Four pounds, this was.'

'The world's gone mad.'

'Too right, Cassie.'

There was an awkward pause; she took a sip of her drink. David cleared his throat. 'So – you keeping well?'

'I'm all right, thanks.'

'Where you living?'

16

'Flat off the Essex Road. I came back, you see.'

'I'm glad,' he said, uncomfortably.

'It's not the same. Everyone's gone. It's bankers and lawyers round here mostly. Or younger people. I don't know anyone.' Beneath her heavy fringe her eyes filled with tears. 'Long way back to Muriel Street from where you are, isn't it?'

He nodded. He didn't belong here. He'd hoped he might walk around afterwards, but fear haunted these streets for him, the way it always had. Suddenly he wished he was at home, sitting in his sunny study, the sound of Martha singing in the kitchen, Daisy and Florence playing in the garden . . . He blinked. Daisy was gone, wasn't she? And Florence . . . Cat was still there, yes? No, Cat had gone too. They'd all gone.

'You got any more kids? I'm sorry. I don't know – anything about you.' He gave an embarrassed half-laugh.

'You know I didn't want us to stay in touch,' she said. 'Look, we got our own lives. No. I haven't got any kids, Davy. We never had any, me and Terry.' Her watery eyes were fixed on him again. 'You understand what I mean.'

His hand covered hers. 'I do, Cassie.'

'What I don't understand is why you wanted to see me,' she said. 'After all this time.'

David shifted in his seat. 'I'm dying,' he said. He smiled at her, trying to ignore the pain that was always there. Her grey eyes widened.

'Davy. That true? Cancer?'

17

He loved the vowels. *Kainsa*. That London voice. He'd lost it deliberately, couldn't wait for it to melt away. 'No. My heart.' He clenched his fist, in and out, like the doctor had showed him. 'The muscle's dying. It doesn't want to work any more. One day I'll just – phut. Then that's it.'

Her tears fell then, little black circles staining the newly waxed wood tables. 'Oh, Davy.'

He hadn't told Martha. Only his son, Bill, knew. As Cassie put her arms round him and drew his head on to her heaving shoulder, as she cried softly and silently, it occurred to David she was the only link he had to where he'd come from. He'd tried for years to put it away, to push forward towards the golden life he'd promised himself he and Martha deserved, only to be obsessively seeking it out again now. He thought of the meeting he'd had that morning with his gallery in Dover Street.

'I mean there's a few I wonder if we need to show. Sensitivity and all that. Do we want to include this one?' Jeremy, the director of the gallery, had slid the watercolour, pen and ink towards him.

David had looked at it and as he always did with everything he drew, squeezed his arms against his sides, a little *aide-mémoire* to help him recall what it was, why he'd done it, how, what it had been like. In fact, he remembered the scene well, a bombed block of flats out in Limehouse. He'd walked there, the morning after a bad night. V2 rockets had come to London when the war was almost over, and they were worse than the bombs of the Blitz. You only heard them, flying towards you, if you were out of their path. If they were headed right for you you never knew, until it was too late.

David didn't sleep much, since the bomb that hit their street. He'd dream about pulling Mum out of the wreckage, his sister too, running away with them somewhere safe. Not to the shelters but far away, out of the city, out where there were trees and no dead people, and no dad, coming at him, huge and black, stinking of stout and that smell men got.

He'd woken up early that morning. Walked and walked as he liked to do. He could walk for hours, no one was bothered where he was, after all. He'd gone along the canal to Limehouse, past the bombed-out warehouses, the abandoned boats, the muck. A girl asleep on a bench, lipstick smudged, greenish tweed skirt twisted around her legs. He wondered if she was one of those kinds of girls and he'd have stopped to draw her but a policeman came past on a bicycle and shoved him along. He kept on walking, and walking, because John, a boy down the street, had told him there was a bad lot there.

The sketches he produced that morning of the scene in Victoria Court became the painting he'd seen that morning, nearly seventy years later, in the white, hushed gallery in Mayfair. But he could still remember how it felt, all those years later. Women sobbing, hair coming loose from their scarves. Men dazed, picking through the rubble. It was very quiet, otherwise. There was one wall standing, against the road, and he'd squatted and sketched, a parody of a still-life scene of the corner of a room.

Flaps of yellow wallpaper printed with ribbons, fluttering in the morning breeze. The side of a cup, a packet of rice, a tin plate, blue paint scratched off. And a child's arm, probably a toddler, the cotton sleeve of its shirt frayed where it had become detached from the body with the force of the explosion. The small pink fingers, curled up.

'Of course it stays in,' he'd said.

Jeremy had hesitated. 'David, I think it's wonderful. But it's very dark.'

'War is very dark,' David had said, the pain almost sending him under. 'Either we do this or we don't. If you want cheeky urchins playing in rubble, forget it.' He had bowed his head, remembering, remembering, and the other men were silent.

Now, as he hugged Cassie, he realised he didn't know her any more, and that he had to do what he'd come here for. He sat back and patted her hand.

'Don't cry, dearest. Let me tell you why I wanted to meet.'

She wiped her nose. 'Fine. Make it good. You bastard, making me cry, after all these years. You're the one who ran out on me, Davy.'

'Don't start that. Didn't I help you?'

'You saved my life,' she said. 'And my little girl's, later. I know it, I'll always know it. Davy . . .' she gave a big sigh, '. . . I wish it was all different, don't you?'

'I don't know,' he said. 'Maybe. Maybe not. I'd never have gone to Winterfold if it hadn't been like this. I'd never have met Martha. And had the children.'

'Give me their names, then? All of them?'

'Bill, he's the eldest.'

'Where's he?'

'Oh, Bill never went far. Lives in the village, he's a GP. Pillar of the community, you might say. Married to a nice girl, Karen, much younger than him. Second marriage; he's got a grown-up daughter, Lucy. Then there's Daisy . . . she's – well, we don't see her so much any more. She's in India. A charity worker. Very dedicated. Raises money for these schools in Kerala.'

'Blimey. How often does she come home?'

'It's sad. She doesn't, really.'

'Never?'

'Not for years now. She has a daughter, too. Cat. Lives in Paris. We raised her, after Daisy . . . left.'

Cassie seemed fascinated by this. 'She ran out on her own kid?'

'Yes. But . . . it's hard to explain Daisy. She was – she's difficult to understand. We're very proud of her.'

It was such an easy lie, once you got used to it.

21

He kept thinking of Daisy these days. Wondering what had gone wrong with her, whether it was his fault, something in his genes.

'And – the other one, Davy, so what's she called?'

'Florence. Florence is the baby. But she's very tall too.'

Her eyes met his. 'Just like her father.'

'Just like her father and we're very close. She's . . .' he hesitated, '. . . very academic. She's a professor, Cassie. Of art history. Lives in Florence.'

'Lives in Florence and she's called Florence?'

He smiled. 'It's true. She—'

A languorous waiter came over to ask them if they wanted food, and broke the spell. David looked at his watch and said no, and Cassie slid her purse into her handbag. She clicked her tongue. 'So tell me what you want.'

David took a deep breath, ignoring the fluttering pain in his chest. 'I want you to come to Winterfold. Meet them all. Before I die.'

She laughed. It took him by surprise, big belly laugh, a touch of hysteria, and it went on and on, until the fellow drinkers turned round to see what the two old people in the corner found to laugh about.

When she stopped laughing, she swallowed, and drained the rest of her rum and Coke.

'No,' she said. 'Absolutely not. You got your nice life down there, I got mine. That's the deal we made. I wish it were different but it's not. Forget it about the past, Davy.'

'But we need to straighten everything out. I want it all done before . . . I don't know how long I've got. It could be months, it could be a years, but—'

She gripped his wrist, her eyes bright. 'Davy, you always said I was cleverer than you. Didn't you? So listen to me. Leave the past alone. Forget you saw me. All right?'

'But doesn't family mean anything to you, anything at all?' David tried to hold on to her grip, but she pulled her hand away from him and stood up.

'Yes, my dear, it does. It means pain, and misery, and suffering, and you're mixed up with it enough. Take the time you've got and just enjoy it,' she said, fixing her big bright scarf, not looking at him. Her voice wavered, but she finished firmly, 'Let it be, Davy. God bless you, my love.'

KAREN

Karen Winter sat at the bar while the girl in front of her held her fingers, scraping at her cuticles. Outside, rain fell steadily out of a metallic sky, turning the golden Bath stone a dirty sand. People hurried past the nail bar, the fogged-up windows blurring their figures into smears of dull colour. Karen stared blankly up at the music channel on the screen above her head, eyes following the video, not registering any of it.

The invitation had arrived that morning, as she was on her way out. What did it mean? What the hell was Martha on about? Had she guessed? Was it a threat? Karen wasn't normally one for introspection: she acted first, thought later. When her stepdaughter, Lucy, stayed with them she alternately drove Karen up the wall and made her laugh with her amateur dramatics, staying in bed till all hours, sighing over her phone, frantically texting, scribbling her every last thought into a book she called a Journal, which Karen thought was pretty pretentious. Then she'd flop into the kitchen at midday and say she hadn't slept well because things were 'on her mind'. Karen, who was only ten years older than Lucy, always wanted to retort: *Can't you unload the dishwasher at the same time as having things on your mind?* Karen was a devotee of motivational self-help books and knew the main principle of effective living as outlined in *The 7 Habits of Highly Effective People* was the Character Ethic. Lucy needed the Character Ethic. She, Karen, had it and – well, anyway.

She sighed. Coralie looked up. 'OK, miss?'

'Sure.' Karen shrugged. The nail bar was warm, tiny, crowded; it hummed with the easy chatter of women in salons. She could hear snatches of conversation: M&S were having a sale on clothes, some child wouldn't eat pasta, someone was going to Menorca on a package deal. 'Didn't sleep much last night,' she added, for no particular reason.

'Oh dear. That's bad. Why?' Coralie slapped Karen's hands, slicking them with cream, and rubbed each one in turn.

Karen's fingers itched to scratch her face, a habit of hers since she was little, when she felt awkward. She inhaled slowly, watching Coralie deftly plumping the glossy blob of undercoat on to her nail. 'Oh, family business.'

'Oh. Family.' Coralie coughed. 'Huh.'

Karen smiled. 'My mother-in-law's having a party. Could do without it. You know?'

'Sure. I know.' Coralie rolled her eyes. 'Where do they live?'

'They're just south of here. It's called . . . Winterfold.' She looked at Coralie, expecting her

25

to recognise it, and then smiled. Why the hell should she? The way people said 'Winterfold' in hushed tones, same as 'the Queen' or 'the National Trust'. But the Winters were famous, they had a sort of sheen to them. Their parties were legendary, they knew everyone for miles around, and it was all because of Martha. She had a cupboard full of woollen rugs for picnics in summer, for God's sake. She made sloe gin, she pickled green tomatoes, she sewed bunting for birthdays. She remembered anniversaries, and brought round lasagnes to new parents. Didn't stop to coo, just handed it over and left. She didn't want to be your best friend, she just made you feel welcome, gave you a drink, and she listened.

Karen's only attempt to create something similar, her and Bill's New Year's Eve drinks party the previous year, had been a disaster. Susan Talbot, who ran the village shop-cum-post office, and therefore apparently had to be kept sweet otherwise she'd close it down and then Winter Stoke would be plunged back into the Middle Ages, had leaned too close over Karen's Swedish candle display, which she'd re-created from a magazine article, and Susan's hair had caught alight. It had ruined the atmosphere. Thirty people was too many in a house their size and the smell of burned hair wouldn't leave, even after they opened all the doors and windows.

It was somehow symptomatic of her and Bill, she thought. They didn't 'entertain' well. At least his daughter brought a bit of life into the house, even if she was messy and loud and bouncy, like Tigger. Lucy made Bill smile. People seemed to drop by when she was staying. She was the exact combination of her grandparents: warmth radiated off her like David, she could knock up a meal from baked potatoes and a packet of ham and turn it into a delicious little winter supper and the wine would flow, noise and laughter flowering in the house like a desert after rain . . . Karen had bought Susan vouchers for a proper salon experience at Toni & Guy by way of apology, and Susan had been deeply offended. Karen knew that if Lucy had been responsible for the Swedish candle disaster she'd have had everyone laughing in seconds and more drinks flowing, and sent Susan Talbot home warm with attention and grateful for her free haircut.

Afterwards, in bed, Karen had said angrily to Bill, 'I'm sure your parents never have a sodding cock-up like that at one of their parties. It's just us.'

Bill had laughed. 'You weren't there for the Summer Party Disaster.'

'What?'

'Oh, it was years ago. Our dog, Hadley . . .' He'd begun to smile, then said, 'Actually, it was awful. But everyone stayed till three, in the rain. There was a conga, I seem to remember. Funny, isn't it?'

No, it wasn't funny. Karen, dying to know what had happened, had simply turned over and pretended to go to sleep. Of course. They'd had a party and it'd gone horribly wrong but of course that was all part of the fun, wasn't it? Those Winters!

Maybe that was when the sinkhole started to form under their marriage, and no one saw it, of course. Karen hated herself for being mean about her in-laws, but she couldn't help it. Winterfold was only a house, for God's sake, not a cathedral. They were only a family.

'It's my mother-in-law's eightieth. They have a beautiful house,' she told Coralie. 'Near here. Yes . . . they're having a family party.'

Coralie looked blank. 'Fine. Why don't you want go?'

Karen's cheeks twitched. 'Because . . . we're so different. I don't fit in there.' She didn't know Coralie's surname or where she lived but it was easier to say it to her than him. She'd been married to Bill for four years now, she knew every mole and freckle on his slim body, she knew how he liked his eggs done and what he meant when he said 'Hmm' any one of fifteen ways, and yet she didn't know how to tell him that. *I don't fit in.*

'Fit in?'

Coralie's supple fingers pressed the tiny bones in Karen's hand. She jumped. 'Like . . . I don't belong there. Oh, it doesn't matter.'

'You feel stupid with them. I know.' Coralie took the clear nail varnish off the rack, shook it. Karen stared at it.

'Something like that.' She thought of the look

28

on Martha's face if she could hear her. Did she know that was how Karen felt? Did Bill? Or his crazy sister, Florence the crackpot? Florence barely acknowledged Karen; it was like she didn't exist. Karen laughed softly to herself. She remembered the first time she'd met Bill and he'd told her he had a sister who studied art history.

'Just . . . looks at paintings all day? For real? That's her *job*?'

'Yes, I'm afraid so,' Bill had said, like she'd said something funny, and she'd flushed. This quiet man who was – what – ten years older than she, and yet so handsome in a strange way, so intriguing, polite. He'd been so easy to tease, back then. She'd wanted to talk to him just to hear his soft voice, see the light in his eyes when he looked at her. But she'd made a fool of herself, even that first time.

Funny to think of it now, really, the first time she'd met him. She remembered thinking: this guy's a bit older than me but he could be the father of my kids. She'd felt instantly, completely, like she'd found someone safe, calm, funny, kind. But she'd got his age wrong: he was seventeen years older, almost old enough to be her dad. He had a twenty-year marriage behind him, and a teenage daughter. She'd got a lot of things wrong, hadn't she? And now she was paying, she supposed. Paying to not fit in.

Karen heard her phone buzz with a text message; she glanced down into her bag, hands trapped, then, with her heart racing, looked up again, trying to seem calm.

Suddenly, she said, 'Can I change my mind about my colour? I don't want clear any more.'

'Fine. What colour you want?'

Coralie gestured at the wall behind her, where the bottles of polish were stacked in multicoloured rows, like sweets. Karen nodded. 'Fifth Avenue, please. Third along from the end.'

Coralie reached round and plucked the third bottle off the shelf, then checked the base. 'Yes,' she said, impressed. 'Is Fifth Avenue. How you know that?'

'I just know,' Karen shrugged.

'Bright, sexy red.' Coralie pulled one of Karen's slim, tanned hands towards her, unscrewed the white lid. 'You going out tonight?'

'No,' said Karen. 'We're staying in.'

'Aha!' Coralie smiled. 'You want to look good, huh? A night in with hubby.'

'Something like that.' Karen tried to smile.

FLORENCE

'**D**ear me,' Florence Winter said, hurrying along the road, shoving the invitation back into her capacious yet overstuffed straw bag. 'What does it mean?'

She felt upset. Out of the blue here it was, this extraordinary message slapping on to the cold stone tiles of her apartment floor while she was having her coffee. Years ago her brother, Bill, would joke that was why she'd gone to study in Italy, to drink as much coffee as she liked. He didn't make that joke any more – she'd lived there for twenty years. Besides, these days you had to search high and low for a decent *tabacchi*, everything in Florence was either Irish-themed pubs – the Italians were mad about them, perplexingly – or soulless *pizzerie* serving an ever-changing carousel of Japanese, American, French or German tourists.

Nowadays Florence felt less disloyal about admitting the worst tourists were often the English. They were either bellicose, obese, annoyed at being in this culturally heavy but entertainment-lite hole, or by contrast desperate to prove they were Italian, waving their arms around and saying *grazie mille* and *il conto, per favore*, as if that made them Italian, as if every waiter couldn't speak English like a native because that was the only way of getting ahead these days. It depressed her, either shame at her homeland or sadness at the world she inhabited. Florence the city, once the noble flower of the Renaissance, was becoming a ghost-town, a history-theme-park shell filled with moving shoals of visitors, shepherded along by pink umbrellas and microphones. And still she loved it, with all her heart.

When she was a little girl, many years ago, she'd asked her father why they'd named her Florence.

'Because we came here on our honeymoon. We were so happy.' David had told her solemnly. 'I made your mother promise if we ever had a baby girl we'd call her Florence, to remind us every day how much in love we were.'

'Why didn't you call Daisy that then? She came first.'

Her father had laughed. 'She wasn't a Florence. You were.' And he'd kissed her on the head.

When Florence was a little girl her birthday treat was to go up to London for the day with her father: he was her favourite person in the world. They always followed the same programme. First to the National Gallery to look at the Italian Rennaissance paintings, paying particular attention to her father's favourite, *The Annunciation* by Fra Filippo Lippi. Florence loved the story of the chaste monk who ran off with the golden-haired

32

nun, and she loved David's quiet, rapt expression as he gazed at the handsome angel with his thick curls, the graceful arc of Mary's bowed head as she received news of her destiny. 'The most beautiful piece of art in the world,' her father would say, every time, visibly moved.

Then they would walk five minutes up to Jermyn Street, and have lunch at the same old-fashioned English restaurant, Brights, where the waiters were all terribly ancient and formal, and the tablecloths snowy white linen. Florence always felt so grown up, drinking a ginger beer out of a huge crystal goblet and eating a steak the size of her head, having proper conversations with her father. Not talking about Wilbur, for once; everyone always wanted to ask him about that silly dog. When she was out with Pa they always wanted to know if she was Daisy. Florence hated that, though not as much as Daisy would have, if she'd known.

She could ask him anything at those lunches, so they didn't talk about boring things like Daisy's moods or the girls at school or Games. They'd talk about things he'd seen on his travels, because he'd been everywhere when he was younger.

'Before you married Ma and she had all of us.'

'Ma came too. We were both artists, we wanted to see the world. Then we had all of you. And then we moved to Winterfold. We didn't want to go away much after that.'

Florence didn't really understand why they'd moved to Winterfold, when they could have lived

33

in London. She wanted to live in London, but whenever she asked her father about growing up there, she got the same response. 'I never liked London very much.'

He never talked directly about his childhood. Never said, 'Your granny had blue eyes', or, 'We lived on this or this road'. Only oblique references to events that happened to him. Florence worshipped her father and wanted to know everything possible about him so she'd draw him out, as much as she could. Hear about Mr Wilson, the art teacher at school who'd let David stay late, given him sugar paper and pastels to take home. The boy in the next road over who was born without a nose – Pa swore it was true. The time one summer's morning he caught the train to Bath, then walked for hours until he saw Winterfold, how he'd promised to come back there one day. He loved walking, back then. He'd walk into town and go to concerts at the National Gallery during the war. All the paintings had been taken away, to a cave in Wales, but people played the piano there instead. Once, the air raid sirens sounded, and he had to stay there for hours, hidden in the basement with all the others: local office workers, young lovers meeting at lunchtime, posh old men. Everyone was very scared, they sang songs, and one of the posh old men gave David a piece of fudge.

Years later, Florence was back at the National Gallery, giving an oft-delivered lecture to some students in front of Uccello's *The Battle of San Romano*. Her mind wandered and she found herself working out that her father would have been really quite small during the Blitz, no more than nine or ten. The idea of him drifting freely around town at that age, in the middle of a war too, seemed appalling to her. When she'd mentioned it to him later on, he'd smiled. 'I was grown-up for my age. You had a sheltered childhood, Flo.'

'I'm glad,' she'd said, never happier than when she was safely cocooned away with a book or several books, undisturbed by dogs or family or Daisy's special treatment.

And he'd said, 'Well, that's good, isn't it?'

Florence sometimes wondered now if her childhood had been too sheltered. She was nearly fifty, and felt she should have a better grip on life, yet more and more it seemed to her that life was veering away from her, like a runaway train. The little girl who was too tall for her bigger sister's cast-offs, who only wanted to read and look at pictures was now a professor employed at the British College of Art History in Florence, author of two books, contributor to several more, a visiting professor at the Courtauld Institute of Art in London, and an occasional voice on the radio: she'd been on Melvyn Bragg's *In Our Time* last year, only they'd cut most of what she said. (When Florence was nervous, she tended to ramble, and it was often impossible to prune the tangled mess of her original point.)

Alone in her apartment, writing or thinking on her own, everything was always clear. It was talking aloud, interracting with people that tripped her up: it was reality she found difficult.

When Florence had last been back in the UK in July, she had been invited to dinner at the house of her Courtauld colleague, Jim Buxton. Jim was an old boyfriend of hers from Oxford, still a good, dear friend. He was married to Amna, a professor of Islamic Studies at UCL, who spent much of the year in far-flung places like Tashkent, spoke at least six different languages and was, frankly, terrifying to Florence. They lived in Islington, not far from the centre of town, but due to several mishaps including broken spectacles and a flapping boot sole, Florence arrived late, and flustered. When Jim introduced her to the other guests, one of them – a well-known editor at Penguin called Susanna – half stood up, shook her hand and said, 'Oh, the *famous* Professor Winter! We heard you on the radio, talking about Masaccio. I agreed with you broadly but for your interpretation of the *Expulsion of Adam and Eve*. It's simplistic to merely say that— oh!'

For Florence, still holding her cloth book bag, which passed for a handbag, had simply cut a deep bow (so that her change slid out of her pockets) and backed out of the room, the boot sole folding under and nearly tripping her up. She went to the downstairs bathroom, and sat on the lavatory for five minutes. She knew she'd have to apologise when she emerged, could see enough to know that she should explain about the broken spectacles meaning she'd got on the wrong bus, and the unglued boot sole severely impeding her journey, but she couldn't ever work out a way to apologise gracefully for something so that the moment was forgotten.

When she emerged, they'd all gone into the dining room so she'd taken her seat and the other guests pretty much ignored her, but Florence didn't mind. She almost preferred it that this Susanna person *thought* she was totally crackers, that they all did. It meant she didn't have to bother with entangling herself in social situations.

The next day she'd gone to see Jim in his office.

'I'm sorry about last night, Jim, about stowing away in your lav. I was in a bit of a flap when I arrived. So was my boot. Ho ho.'

And Jim had said with a smile, 'Don't worry. Susanna's awful. It rather made the evening, I thought.'

Yes, more and more this idea haunted her, the question she couldn't escape. What was that missing piece, the one she knew existed but couldn't ever see? What if she'd wasted the last twenty years staring at the same paintings, working on the same ideas, and coming to no worthwhile conclusions? Just shuffling opinions around and about from one journal to another book to yet another set of students, in the same way a banker got paid for moving money about? She loved Florence, but had she stayed out here for one reason, and one reason only, for a man who barely cared if she was there or not?

No, she told herself, in her more buoyant moments. He did care. He *did*.

Florence hurried over the Ponte Santa Trìnita, barely glancing at the tourists thronging the Ponte Vecchio, crammed with tiny shops like a pantomime set. She was able to block out the modern world, almost too effectively; if Lorenzo the Magnificent had appeared on horseback cantering over the bridge and asked in his best Renaissance Italian if she'd like to accompany him to his palazzo for some wild boar, Florence would not have been surprised.

She was so absorbed in imagining what Lorenzo de Medici would wear on a normal day out and about in the city – and he *did* go out and about, that was why he'd been such a great leader; truly *Il Magnifico* – that, as she turned the corner leading to the College Florence wasn't looking where she was going. She felt herself trip on something and then stumble, hurtling to the ground with the curiously drunken sensation of lost gravity.

'*Attento!* Signora, please take care!' said an angry voice, one that set her heart thumping as she lay on the cobbles, arms and legs waving in the air like an upturned beetle. '*É molto—* oh, it's you. For God's sake watch where you're going, can't you?'

Florence scrambled to her feet, by herself, as

Peter Connolly disentangled the leather straps of her bag from his leg with such force she nearly yelped. 'Oh dear,' she said, looking down at the ground. 'Where are my glasses?'

'I've no idea.' He was rubbing his foot, glaring coldly at her. 'That bloody hurt, Florence. You—' He stopped, looking around.

The arriving students watched them curiously; Byronic, slightly eccentric but still impressive Professor Connolly, the one who'd written the unlikely bestseller about the Renaissance that made the Medici into a bawdy soap opera, and got a BBC TV series out of it – he was famous, their mums watched him! And that weird Professor Winter, mad hair awry, searching for her glasses. The plastic frames were cracked and frequently the sharp wire arms of the glasses slid out if she leaned forward, but she never even noticed. Someone had seen her singing Queen to herself the previous week as she walked past the Uffizi. Singing really loudly.

Florence's head was spinning. She looked at Peter, flustered, and pushed her hair out of her eyes. He was so different these days, ever since that damned book had come out and he'd started to listen to the siren call of Fame. All smart and stylish, in a televisually approved rumpled academic sort of way. So very far from the curly haired, slightly hopeless man she'd once known and loved – loved so much that she—

'Here.' Professor Connolly pulled her bag back

up so it was slung over her shoulder and not hanging off her wrist.

'Ha-ha! Oh, unhand me, Professor Connolly!' Florence said loudly, putting her hand to her breast, and dropping several items on the ground in the process. She had thought this would sound hilarious, but as so often when some witticism came out of her mouth it hung there in the air, sounding completely awful. She looked mad, as always, a crazy old hag whom no one had ever loved or could possibly ever in the future love, especially not Professor Connolly, to whom of all people she had once so hoped to cleave herself.

The professor bent down and picked something off the kerb.

'You dropped this.' He glanced down, nosily. 'Nice invitation. Is this your family? Curious way of asking people to a party. What does that bit at the end mean?'

Florence gently took it out of his hand, biting her lip.

'Thank you. It's from my parents. I have no idea what it means. I'll have to go home for it, I suppose.'

'Leaving Florence again, Florence?' He gave a small smile. 'I must say, we are becoming practised in the art of missing you.' He rocked on his feet, and tipped his imaginary hat to her.

'Why, did you – did you need me for something, Pe— Professor?'

He gave her a look of complete astonishment. 'Goodness, no. Why would you think that?'

Another slight, another little barb, but she was equal to it. She knew his little secret, and she was glad to carry it safe until such time as he felt the need to make use of her again. Florence bowed her head, as though she were a lady bidding farewell to a knight.

'Then, Peter, I must bid you farewell, for now, yet not for ever,' she said, though this too came out all wrong. He had walked towards the revolving doors, not even saying goodbye. She hobbled towards the entrance, and as she did glanced down at the invitation, and the strangeness of it struck her again. Ma wanted them all back.

Why? Was it Dad? Was it about Daisy?

And Florence suddenly realised, though she had not considered it until this very moment, that she knew why.

JOE

Joe Thorne leaned his weight on to the smooth oak bar, crossed his arms and looked around him. Mid-morning, mid-week, he would have hoped the pub would be, well – not crowded exactly, but at least hosting a few old regulars with a pint, maybe a couple of early patrons for lunch. But no. The eponymous tree outside cast only gloom into the room. It was too early in the season for a roaring log fire. The bowls of sweetly salty pork crackling that Joe himself had roasted and stripped that morning stood on the bar, untouched. The barrels were full, the glasses gleaming.

And the place was empty.

Sheila Cowper, the landlady, appeared in the doorway of the Snug. 'Don't stand there with your arms folded, Joe,' she said briskly, whipping him lightly with a tea towel. 'No one'll want to come in if they look in and see you growling at them like an angry bear. Go and cut up that bread like I asked you an hour ago.'

'Oh, what's the point,' said Joe gloomily, though he obeyed her, stomping back into his tiny kitchen.

He took a newly baked loaf of sourdough,

weighing it in his hands. Joe loved bread, loved its smell, its texture. He loved the springy smoothness of newly formed dough, how you could thump the base of a freshly baked loaf, hard, and get a pleasing drum-like sound, how homemade bread had love and care baked into it, like a new life. Joe started cutting slim, even slices, his strong fingers working the knife. Who am I making this for? he found himself wondering. What is the point?

Six months ago Joe had left Yorkshire, Jamie, and home, to come and work for Sheila. She'd spent fifteen years in London working as a manager in various restaurants and returned home to Winter Stoke the previous year with some cash in her pocket, and the dream of rejuvenating the Oak Tree. She wanted to make it the best place to eat in Somerset, at the same time turning it back into a proper local pub. 'Better than the Sportsman in Whitstable, better than the Star at Harome. I want it to get a Michelin star,' she'd told him and he'd found his heart beating faster. He believed this woman, and though he'd never met her before he was sure she could do it. And Joe, with his training and his track record, had been a shoe-in. At the interview he'd made her pork belly with fennel, accompanied by homemade char sui buns and a cabbage remoulade, and sea-salted caramel three-some – ice cream with popcorn, toffee pot, and compote with marshmallows. He was a bit over sea-salted caramel himself, but it was all the rage and he'd known from their phone conversation that she'd like it. Joe could pretty much tell what people wanted to eat.

It was because he trusted Sheila that he'd taken the job. He couldn't turn it down, it was too good an opportunity to miss and it was time to leave Yorkshire. If it wasn't for Jamie he'd have done it years ago. He'd been there all his life apart from his training. Yes, his restaurant had a Michelin star, but he'd learned all he was going to there. The head chef was a psychopath, the old cliché, and it was a joyless place to work, more about assemblage and timings than baking with care, making food with love. Joe cooked to make people happy, not to hear them faint with admiration over his use of nasturtiums in salads or sumac-flavoured sorbets or any of the other silly things you had to do these days to be a 'hot young chef', whatever that meant.

Joe didn't want any of that. He wanted to work in a place rooted in the community. He wanted to see old blokes chatting about their experiences in the war over a pint, to have lonely people come in for a read of the paper and a friendly face. A place for dates, anniversaries, weddings, funerals. Family. In his mind's eye he saw this happy group of punters round the bar, perhaps even singing songs of an evening, while Joe served up delicious, lovingly prepared meals, food that'd bring people together, make them happy. And Joe's food was the best there was . . .

But it wasn't working out that way, not at all. Six months on, everyone still went to the Green

Man at the other end of the high street. The Green Man had Sky Sports, velour carpets and piles of fag butts outside the door that no one ever seemed to sweep up. It served pickled onion crisps and rancid old pasties, and there was a fight most Saturdays. It was a dump. But it seemed the residents of Winter Stoke and the surrounding countryside would rather take their chances there. The Oak had been closed for so long it was hard to change habits.

Sheila had a few months left, still, but if things hadn't picked up by Christmas she'd as good as told Joe they'd each be out of a job. She'd have to sell, and Joe would be cast out into the metaphorical snow, and he'd have to go back to his mother's in Pickering. The way things were going here, especially in the last couple of weeks, that didn't seem too bad a prospect. He missed home, his mum and sister, more than he'd thought he would. Most of all he missed Jamie.

Sometimes when Joe thought about Jamie he was almost ready to pack it in and drive back then and there to Yorkshire. Like when he thought about his crazy, curly blond hair, the dark little smudges under his eyes he got when he was tired or upset, the little red birthmark above his lip and the things he said that cracked Joe up. 'I'm going to live on the moon when I'm older, Dad. You can come and visit me in the long whooshing tube I'll have built by then, all right?'

The more Joe tried not to think about his son

the worse he felt. He knew now that looking at pictures of him on his phone didn't bring him closer. Sometimes it just made him sadder. He was supposed to see him once a month, but often it didn't happen: Jemma had booked a holiday to Turkey, Jamie's best friend had a birthday party, a school outing would be getting back too late for Jamie to travel all the way down to Somerset, or for Joe to pick him up and take him to his mum's in Pickering, which is what he sometimes did. The thing was, Joe knew it wouldn't ever get better, because Jamie wouldn't ever live with him full time, of course he wouldn't, he had to be with his mum. But Joe missed him, as though there was a clamp on his heart that made him wince when he thought about him, pepper in his nostrils that made his eyes water, dry bread in his throat that made him swallow, bow his head, say a prayer for him and whatever he was doing. Playing in break time? Drawing at one of those little tables, messing around with toy dinosaurs on the floor, dancing to 'Telephone', that Lady Gaga song he'd made up all the actions to?

'Joe? Joe!' Sheila's voice penetrated his train of thought.

'I've nearly done it.' Joe blinked, wiping his forehead on his arm. 'Nearly there.'

'No. Not that. Mrs Winter's here for you.'

He flinched, instantly recalled to the present. The knife slipped, and he pushed it away, against his knuckle. It fell on to his left hand, sliding across his finger and cutting open the flesh. Everything seemed to happen almost in slow motion: Joe felt and, most disturbing of all, saw the flash of hard white bone beneath, watched almost with disinterest as the long thick line suddenly turned red, and his hand started to throb, black-red blood gushing out – and there was so much of it, dripping crimson on to his kitchen whites.

Sheila yelped. 'What's— Oh, Joe dear, what've you done?'

Joe held up his dripping finger. He wrapped a cloth around it. Now it really hurt. He smiled, feeling slightly stunned. 'Stupid idiot. I'm sorry. You gave me a fright. Mrs Winter . . . she's outside?'

'Sure, but it's OK, I'll tell her—'

'No.' Joe tightened the knot on the cloth. 'Don't turn away anyone who's come in, much less one of that lot.' He followed Sheila outside.

'Hello, Joe,' said Martha Winter. 'Lovely to see you.' She glanced down at the bloody cloth. 'My goodness. What have you done to your finger?'

'Nothing. Perk of the job.' The finger throbbed again, an aching thrum. 'How can I help you?'

'You're sure you're all right?' He nodded, and she looked at him a little quizzically. 'Well, I wanted to talk to you. I wondered if you'd be able to do the food for a party we're having in November. It's drinks on the Friday, so I'd need canapés for about fifty.'

Her husky, accentless voice was soothing. 'Right then.' Joe started mentally calculating how much canapés for fifty would cost. 'I can do that.'

Martha cleared her throat. 'And then lunch on the Saturday.' She paused. 'That's the main event.'

'How many on the Saturday?'

'Just family. Seven of us. I think.'

The Winters were kind of famous round these parts. Joe had always imagined there were loads of them. He said curiously, 'I thought there were more of you than that.'

'There were, around twenty,' Martha said. 'But I've murdered them all and buried them in the garden.'

'Makes the catering easier,' Joe said, and they both smiled, shyly, at each other.

'David says you're a wonderful chef.'

'He's a nice man.' David Winter came in sometimes for a whisky. Joe liked him a lot. He was one of the few people around here Joe had actually had a proper conversation with.

'He's a very nice man and he takes his food seriously.'

'I know that,' he said. 'I've never seen someone eat a pie that fast.'

A shadow crossed her smiling face; she said, 'Anyway, he says I need to hire you smartish for this party. He thinks you'll be off soon.' She leaned forward on the bar with her elbows. 'Give us a chance, won't you?'

Joe stiffened. 'I never – I'm liking it very much here, Mrs Winter.'

'Don't go all formal on me again, will you?' she begged. 'I only meant I know how hard it is. When I first came here I didn't know anyone. I was just a mouthy Cockney and I thought it was the back end of beyond. An awful place.'

He didn't believe she was ever a Cockney. 'You're from London?'

'Yes, Bermondsey. But when the war came I was evacuated, and . . .' She waved her hand. 'Never mind. I know what you're going through. We're nice people round these parts. Give it time.'

Joe's head spun, the finger throbbing so hard he felt it might suddenly burst. 'Yes, of course.' He tried to concentrate, and picked up a pen from the bar, holding it uselessly in his right hand. 'I'd better do you a quote.'

'You're left-handed? Oh dear, that's bad,' she said. 'So am I, so's David. All the best people are. My granddaughter Cat, too. She lives in Paris.' She added, suddenly, 'You'd like her. She's coming back for this party. At least I hope she is. I haven't seen her for a very long time.'

He tried to nod and winced; the pain was really bad. She was right. No. Left! It seemed funny suddenly. 'That's nice for you. What were . . .' He blinked suddenly; a throb of exquisite pain from his finger ran through his body. 'Excuse me.'

'Joe, it does seem to be bleeding rather a lot,' Martha said. She took his hand, and the feeling of skin, of her warm flesh holding his, was almost intoxicating. Her green eyes stared at him appraisingly, and he felt quite light-headed. 'I think we'd better take you to Bill's surgery, just to be sure,' she said.

'No, I don't want – uh, don't worry,' Joe gripped the rail of the bar firmly in his strong hand, but everything was rocking, suddenly. He swallowed. 'I'll be right as rain, I just need to—'

Martha swam before him. The floor seemed to be rising up, his eyes unbearably heavy. Something was pressing down on his head, and as he sank down he saw her face, shaken out of its calm, her mouth open in a small O, before everything, slowly, went black.

CAT

lways late. Always needing to be somewhere else. Cat hurried out of the Marché, past the endless cyclamen in gaudy reds, the knotty geraniums with their fading flowers, the bushes with zesty, citrus-coloured berries. Working at the flower market you were always aware of the changing seasons: every year she dreaded the arrival of winter, standing outside all day and slowly freezing to death. But in the first week in September it was still summer: the tourists were still jamming the tiny streets of the Île de la Cité, moving so slowly they might be zombies, heads down, eyes fixed on their phones.

Cat strode across the slim pedestrian bridge at the foot of Notre-Dame, weaving her way in and out of the crowds. The usual troupe of jazz musicians on the bridge was playing a wistful, lilting version of 'There's a Small Hotel'. She slowed down for a split second. It was one of Gran's favourite songs. She'd sing it in the evenings, wandering round the kitchen, mug of tea in hand. Gran was always singing.

'Hello, English girl!' one of the musicians

called as she hurried past them. Cat rolled her eyes. All these years here and, *English girl,* when her French was probably better than theirs. But in Paris you were Parisian, you were French, not that you went around yelling about it, that would be so very, very *outré,* but there were certain things, a particular finesse, attitude to life . . . Cat consoled herself with the knowledge that she passed for French these days. She was slim, French-girl slim, not through effort: she just didn't eat very much. Her dark eyes were partly hidden by her treacly brown-black mane of hair. She was wearing the only expensive thing she owned, a pair of glossy red Lanvin ballet flats, which Olivier had bought her, back when things were still good between them. She had tried to sell them on eBay, a few months ago: she finally got so desperate she had to have the money, and it was ridiculous to have shoes worth £300 when she couldn't afford a sandwich at lunch. But there was an olive oil stain on one shoe, a remnant of a Luke-based accident, and the seller had rejected them when Cat, eternally honest, had pointed this out. She was glad, for they were beautiful: a glossy, coral red, they made her happy in a way she hadn't thought possible. Like all fashionistas, even lapsed ones, Cat despised the handbag culture, the stamping of labels on everything: look, my sunglasses say GUCCI in huge letters, therefore I must have money. But looking down at these beautiful red shoes always made her smile, even if it was a particularly bad day and the smile merely a tiny one. It surprised – and cheered – her, to discover this capacity for pleasure still existed within her. She thought it must have been entirely stamped out.

Cat strode quickly along the main street of the Île Saint-Louis, her rangy frame weaving nimbly around the shuffling crowds gaping in at the windows of the *boulangerie*, the *fromagerie*. She could see them queuing up for Berthillon, the old-fashioned *glacier* with its gleaming marble tabletops. Cat loved Berthillon, she knew it was hopelessly touristy to do so, but sometimes when she was in particular need of a treat, when the fog settled over the two little islands, and the bleakness of her situation seemed particularly acute, she would wish more than anything that she could just treat herself, run over the bridge at lunchtime and order a tiny cup of molten, black chocolate, served with yellow cream in a smooth little silver jug. But finances didn't stretch to that, hadn't for over a year now since Olivier's money stopped all together.

She popped into the convenience shop around the corner from the apartment, to buy Vermouth. It was eyewateringly expensive, but this was the Île Saint-Louis, of course it was eye-wateringly expensive, and it was for Madame Poulain. No expense spared was very much Madame Poulain's motto, though she kept track of everything she

53

gave Cat to the nearest cent, and nothing was bought for Madame Poulain that Cat might share. This was made very clear, always had been: Cat shopped at Lidl or Franprix. She smiled as she waited to pay, catching sight of the rows of Dijon mustard. That was why Paris was civilised, despite its many annoyances. In a tiny convenience store you could still find five different types of *moutarde de Dijon: mais bien sûr.*

'*Bonsoir, Madame.*'

'*Ah, bonsoir, Catherine. Ça va?*'

'*Ça va bien, merci, Madame. J'ai pris le Vermouth. Je vous offre un verre?*'

'*Oui, oui.*' The old woman gave a great guffaw in her wing-back chair as Cat gingerly put the tissue-wrapped bottle down on the great old sideboard. If she asked the question she most desperately wanted to right away Madame Poulain would get angry. If she waited just a minute she would be pleased.

Cat drew in a short breath, took a glass off the shelf and said,

'Your medicine, Madame: all's OK for me to pick it up tomorrow, yes?'

'Sure.' Madame Poulain stubbed out her cigarette. 'Tell them to check it this time. I'm sick of the wrong dosage. I am ill. It must be correct.' She lit another cigarette. 'Can you make me the drink before you run off again? I mean, of course I know you're so *terribly* busy but . . .'

54

'Sure,' said Cat, trying not to smile. The first time she'd come to Madame Poulain's apartment, overlooking the Seine south towards the Latin Quarter, she had been overawed: the vast airy space, the wooden beams, the old shutters with their carved iron handles and the fretwork on the balcony. Then, as now, the only items on the old mahogany dresser (from Vichy, acquired in shady circumstances by her father, a coward and a traitor, about whom Madame Poulain was only able to speak by expectorating heavily into her ashtray afterwards) were menthol cigarettes, an ashtray, and cough syrup. Which, Cat had often thought since, pretty neatly summed up her landlady.

'Was it busy today?' Madame Poulain stretched out in the chair, flexing her long, claw-like hands.

'The market was crowded. But we were not busy. Henri is worried.'

'He should be worried. Now this fool is in charge we are all doomed. That I should live to see Socialism annihilated in this way. When I was a child we would have called that man a Fascist. Ha!' Madame Poulain dissolved into a fit of coughing, which consumed her for some time. Cat fetched her a glass of water, and poured her Vermouth, all the while anxiously listening for other signs of life in the apartment. She could hear nothing.

Eventually Madame Poulain's hacking subsided and she shoved aside the proffered glass of water, grasping the Vermouth. Cat passed her her pills and she swallowed each one laboriously after much sighing, followed by raspy gagging. It was the same every night, had been for these last three. Olivier had hated Madame Poulain, the couple of times he'd met her. Said she was a fake, a phoney. Her family were collaborators. How he knew this Cat had no idea, but Olivier's biggest *bête noire* was phoneys. One of his many ironies.

Don't think about Olivier. One . . . two . . . three . . . Cat looked around the room, counting objects to distract herself. She knew what to do, now. When Olivier barged into her thoughts as he did so often, she had a rotating carousel of images with which to distract herself, otherwise . . . Otherwise she'd go mad, get so angry she'd smash something. She thought of Winterfold. The Christmas when she and Lucy made the snowman with a beach-bucket-shaped head, covered in sand from the previous summer in Dorset. The walk into the village on an autumn day when the leaves were quince yellow. Her uncle Bill with the waste-paper basket on his head, trying to find his way from one end of the sitting room to the other. Sitting up in bed in her cosy, sunny room on summer mornings peering out of the window at the peach, violet, turquoise sunrise creeping over the hills behind the house. The patchwork cushion Gran had made her, her name in blue hexagons, and Lucy's rage that she didn't get one. 'She lives here, she has everything!' she'd shouted. She was three years younger than Cat.

It had seemed such a big gap sometimes; now it would be nothing at all, she supposed.

All these things she didn't know. What was Lucy like, still the same? Cat often wondered. She was going to be a famous writer and live in a turret, that was always her aim. Was Southpaw's leg still bad, and *did* Gran still sing all day, giving you that quick, catlike smile if you corrected her lyrics? And was the patchwork cushion still there? Resting on the old wicker chair, waiting for her to come back?

Yet it was all so clear to her. She remembered every creaking stair, every mark on every wooden pillar, every old, battered book on the shelf opposite the chair: *Ballet Shoes* next to *Harriet the Spy* and *The Story of Tracy Beaker*, a much-too-young birthday present from her father.

She had cut them all off, and now she couldn't go back. Years and years of feeling like this had changed her personality, she knew. She was a different Cat now, the one she had always secretly feared becoming. When a door banged now, she jumped.

'How's Luke?' she asked finally, when Madame Poulain was more settled.

'Asleep. Curled up in the warmth. You spoil him. Like they always say, the English spoil their pets and ignore their children. He's your pet, hmm?'

Since Madame Poulain seemed to feed Luke on nothing but biscuits while Cat was at work this was not something Cat felt equal to tackling at that moment. She could not risk an argument, any shift in the status quo. She was, as ever now the day was drawing to a close, so tired she felt she might slide on to the floor. She rubbed her face; it was a little sunburned and suddenly she longed for winter. For crisp cool days, for cosy evenings inside, not this dried-out, strung-along warmth.

'I'm just going to go and check on him,' she said, getting up. 'Then I'll make you an omelette, yes?'

'Well . . .' To Madame Poulain, any display of concern for another living thing was a waste of cigarette-smoking time. 'Go, then. And – oh, before that – your grandmother rang.'

Cat turned round. Her heart started to thump, hard, in her chest. 'Gran rang, here? Did she say why?'

'She wants to know why you have not replied to the invitation.'

Cat cleared her throat. 'I . . . What invitation?'

'I said that too. The French post. This man will break the country. I do not—'

'Madame Poulain, please,' Cat's desperation, just this once, nearly broke through, 'has there been an invitation?'

'The strangest thing, today there it was. As I told your grandmother when she rang. And I said that I would pass it along to you, the moment you arrived home.' Madame Poulain slid one bony hand down the side of the chair, like a child sitting on secrets. 'They don't know, hmm? They don't know your little lie to them, do they?' She handed the creamy card to Cat, who held it in between her fingers as though it were something magical.

'Not a lie . . .' she said, in a faint voice. The address, in Martha's familiar elegant hand. It wasn't a lie when you simply hadn't told them, was it?

That writing: Cat knew it better than anyone's. Who else had written her those endless stories, dotted with jewel-like, tiny illustrations? Who had stuffed notes into her lunchbox for Cat to find, sitting by herself underneath the scratched and slimy benches in the playground, chin resting on her scabbed knees?

Gran used to sit at the kitchen table every morning, teapot next to her, slim, poised frame perfectly still as she gazed out of the window into her garden, making plans for the day ahead, scribbling little ideas and plots and jokes on to her pad, and notes. These notes, which Cat would find hidden behind her sandwiches, she would usually scrunch up and throw away, embarrassed in case they'd find them again.

Your grandma writes you love notes?

You baby.

Your mum's a hippy, everyone knows that. She freaked out and ran away and that's why you have to live with your grandma!

Hippy! Hippy! Hippy! Cat's a hippy!

Memories, sensations, long-buried, threatened to wash over her. The envelope paper was thick, heavy, cold, and Cat's fingers trembled; she fumbled with the glue, wanting to tear it open, wanting to know

59

what was inside and yet at the same time dreading its contents. Madame Poulain watched her, head curving around the wing of the chair like a gargoyle.

'The letter opener is on the dresser, Catherine. Don't tear. Don't be so foolish.'

Oh, shut up, you hateful, awful, loathsome, vile, horrific old woman. Shut up or I will hurt you. I will smash your head in with your precious Sèvres vase and I'll watch you die and laugh as you do.

She was no longer shocked at how easily thoughts like this slid into her head. She read the invitation, the hand-drawn letters, the plea contained within them, and then looked up, staring at nothing, as the voices that screamed at her from rising to sleeping climbed to a fever pitch. Home to Winterfold. Could she even think about going, this time? What would she tell them about what had happened to her since she left England? How could she start? And how would she get there? She had no money. She had not been able to afford a Métro *carnet* last week, let alone a Eurostar home. Home.

She let the card drop to the floor, as her fingers twisted restlessly around in her lap, and Madame Poulain took her silence for surrender. 'I would love that omelette. If you are not going to check on Luke why don't you make me one?'

'Yes, of course.' *Everything is all right,* Cat said to herself, going into the kitchen, and when Madame Poulain gave a little grunt of curiosity she realised she had said it out loud, in English, to herself. *Everything is all right.*

LUCY

'*L*ucy!* The meeting. Are you coming?'
Deborah called over her shoulder as she
passed. The sound of her low voice,
suddenly so alarmingly close by, as ever had the
effect of freezing Lucy to her very marrow.

'Sure, sure. Just a minute.'

Lucy hesitated, scribbled one more line in her
notebook, then leaped up from her desk. *Don't
sweat. Don't talk too much. You always talk too much,
just shut up and don't say anything for once! Except
when you have to. Then be brilliant and incisive. Like
Katharine Graham. Or Nancy Mitford. Or Gran. Be
like Gran.* Propelling herself forward in haste, Lucy
collided against Lara, the newly promoted junior
fashion writer, with a hard, deadening *thwack*. She
ricocheted back towards her desk, catching her
thigh on the sharp grey metal of her filing cabinet.

'Oh, please watch where you're going, OK, Lucy?'
Lara didn't break stride, simply carried on walking,
the corridor her own runway, her curious loping
gait aping a catwalk model. She turned her head
slightly and gestured downwards. 'These are new,
you know? I could have been carrying a coffee.'

61

Lucy, wincing with pain, looked at Lara's retreating feet, as she was supposed to. Of course Lara had the new hightops exclusive to Liberty, which *Grazia* had featured this week. Of *course* she did: hightops were everywhere. Lucy didn't think she could walk in them, but she'd probably have to get some. Trainers with heels? What was the point of that? No point at all. Like putting tights on a giraffe. But after one year on the Features desk at the *Daily News* Lucy knew what to expect. The men didn't have to do anything, just show up in a crappy suit, but if you were a woman you had to follow each new trend obsessively. You'd never heard of BB cream and suddenly it was everywhere and if you didn't use it you might as well be saying 'I hate myself and I am a loser'. So Lucy glanced anxiously down at her little blazer as Lara rounded the corner, tossing her blond hair, and disappeared. Was the cropped blazer over yet? Would anyone tell her if it was or would she suddenly be dragged outside, forced to rip it from her body and burn it in an oil drum, surrounded by a circle of angry, jeering fashion policewomen?

'*Lucy!*'

'Coming, I'm sorry, Deborah!' Lucy jogged along the corridor, ignoring the stabbing pain in her leg. Outside was a bright, blustery day, puffy clouds scudding over the churning Thames. She wished she was outside, walking in Embankment Gardens, maybe. Watching a blackbird pick at the soil. At Winterfold, the trees over the valley would be starting to turn. Pale green at first, barely noticeable. Then mustard yellow, then in a few weeks fiery orange, chilli red, hot pink.

She hurried into the breakout area and sat down. The Topshop batik-print dress was slightly too small and cut into her legs – everything was slightly too small for Lucy. She stared at her chicken-skin thighs, wondering whether she should go down there this weekend, stay with Gran.

The invitation was stiff in her pocket, and she could feel it, digging into her hip. Lucy had always thought she was up to speed with Gran's plans but this had come out of the blue, that very morning. When she'd rung her dad, to pump him for information, he'd been useless. Would Florence and Cat return for this strange-sounding party? Would Daisy?

Deborah cleared her throat and the others put down their phones. 'Right – everyone here?' She scanned the room, eyes resting on Lucy, then looking away. 'Wow, Betty, I love your scarf. Is it Stella McCartney?'

'Yes, it's so cute, isn't it? I love her palette.'

The others cooed agreement, Lucy joining in late, and half-heartedly with a blank, 'Nice.'

Exactly one year ago today, Lucy had joined the *Daily News* as Features Assistant. She'd spent the previous day, Sunday, in bed going through her finances, or rather lack of finances. This was the other thing she didn't understand about working here. She could barely pay for her rent, let alone scarves from Stella McCartney. How did the other girls afford it? The bags from Marc Jacobs, the sandals from Christian Louboutin, the Ray-Bans? In an effort to keep up last month Lucy had bought a pair of blue what were called 'Rey Sans' sunglasses from a knock-off stall on Leicester Square which she had worn triumphantly back to the office, only to be chided by Deborah for supporting fashion piracy.

'Agreed. Lovely note of colour, Betty. Very visual. OK, let's crack on.' Deborah cleared her throat and crossed her legs, brushing an imaginary speck of something off her long, slim calf. Lucy knew this was because she'd noted Lara's hightops and had to let Lara know she eschewed hightops (this was the one area Deborah and Lucy agreed on) in favour of heels – in this case Jimmy Choo holographic leather with heels three inches high.

'Ideas meeting. It was shit last week, we got virtually nothing we can use.' Her voice was toneless and low, and Lucy found herself as ever leaning slightly forward to hear what Deborah was saying. 'I really hope you're all on better form this week. Trends and fashion first. *Stylist* has a great piece on autumn layering, what have we got?'

'What about colour blocking?' said Betty. 'It's really hot right now. I saw these great pictures of Gwyneth Paltrow on the school run—'

'Great. Lucy, write it down.'

'Winter coats,' said Suzy, Deputy Fashion Editor. 'There's some big statement pieces from—'

'No, done to death already, Suzy. Way too late for that.' Deborah smoothed a strand of glossy fine black bobbed hair slowly between her fingers. Suzy's face froze, her mouth a tiny O. 'What else?'

'Eyebrows,' Lara said, as Suzy began tapping at her BlackBerry, muttering angrily. 'They're massive? We could do a feature on how to do them properly. You know, eyebrow make-up, Cara Delevingne. Bushy is back. Throw away the tweezer. Lauren Hutton, Brooke Shields.'

'That's good.' Deborah clapped her hands briskly. 'What else?'

Relieved, everyone started babbling. 'Travel hotspots for 2013. Iran is going to be huge.' 'Sherry is back.' 'Grilled chicken is going to be a thing next year.' 'Butt lifts.' 'Foot jewellery.' Lucy scribbled it all down, different words but the same ideas every week. It wasn't an ideas meeting, more like a random word generator. She often thought she could stand up and say, 'Fossilised dinosaur bones hollowed into clogs will be massive in 2013,' and they'd all nod, those Identikit girls with their blond centre partings and platinum-diamond-whose-fiancé-earns-the-most engagement rings, then look panicked they hadn't heard about dinosaur bone clogs.

'There's some stuff here.' Deborah tapped at her phone again. 'Thanks, everyone. Now, features. Did anyone have anything—'

'I had some ideas.' Lucy heard her voice, far too loud, too high, the words floating above the circle and hanging there. 'I mean – sorry, Deborah. I interrupted you.'

'Right. Of course.' Deborah pursed her lips and leaned forward, as though confidentially imparting a secret. 'Girls,' she murmured. 'It's one year today since Lucy joined the Features desk. We had a talk last week and she mentioned she had some ideas. Didn't you, Lucy?'

This wasn't an exact representation of their conversation, which had started with Lucy asking for a promotion or at least a pay rise, and ended with Deborah telling her that if she was one hundred per cent brutally honest she didn't see Lucy's future in Features.

Lucy had become used to that sad sense of alienation that defines office life in the early years of one's career, the gentle deflation of your hopes and dreams to workaday reality. She'd been a waitress, an envelope stuffer, a PA, a temp, a junior reporter on the *Bristol Evening Post* before being made redundant, and now she was here, and she knew she was lucky, very lucky.

Southpaw had told her about the job. He still did a few cartoons a month for the *Daily News* and when he did, the front cover had a huge blue rosette with 'New Wilbur Inside!' in big gold letters, and the circulation rose each time by at least ten thousand copies. Lucy didn't want to think about how she'd got the job – she'd interviewed twice, supplied references, seen four different people, but she couldn't ever escape the lingering suspicion she was there because she was David Winter's granddaughter. She stuck out like a sore thumb, she knew it. Aside from her grandfather, she was unconnected to the things that mattered, completely separate from this strange world of trendy London where people operated at a higher level of consciousness than her, a bit like Scientology. They knew about pop-ups and new margarita flavours and YOLO, while Lucy was rereading Frances Hodgson Burnett books and planning day trips to Charleston, Chatsworth and Highclere. In addition, and most damningly, she knew, she was a size fourteen. She was, to them, fat.

Her gaze shifting around the circle, from one expectant face to another, Lucy cleared her throat and opened her notebook. Trying to sound casual, she said, 'What about a jokey piece on how to get more Twitter followers? I tweeted a photo of a dog jumping in the air on the beach, and about thirty more people followed me. But when I'm tweeting about that No More Page 3 campaign no one pays any attention.'

'That's a nice idea, Lucy. Very sad, though, because we ran something similar in August. I think you were on holiday.'

There was a pause. Someone cleared their throat.

'Or . . . Top Tens. Top Ten on how to get over being dumped.' A snigger. Lucy could feel a red flush starting on her breastbone, prickling up her neck. 'I was dumped last year. It was awful. How you get over it. Because *He's Just Not That Into You* is a great book.' She paused, feeling the red blotchy blush rise higher. 'My stepmother gave it to me and I thought I'd hate it, but actually it was brilliant.'

Lucy was sure that those weeks, after she found out Tom was seeing Amelia and everyone had known for months except her, had left her with a Pavlovian fear of her dad's new house. She'd go there every weekend and lie in bed crying until she felt like a zombie, face puffy, synapses vanished so that she was unable to hold a sensible conversation without either trailing off and staring across the room, or weeping. One Saturday morning her stepmother Karen had left the book outside her bedroom door with a note: 'Hope this helps. Karen.' As so often with Karen, Lucy was sure it was meant kindly but at the time, it didn't feel particularly kind.

Deborah's voice was icy. 'No, not this time. Anything else?'

Betty laughed nervously – half in sympathy. Betty was nice, but the laugh was sad. The others crossed their legs, enjoying the show, Lucy knew it. She breathed in, then stared down at the list on the notebook.

Twitter followers The dreaded number 267
– how most people just have 267 followers
Getting Dumped Big feature about turning
our lives around and seeing the positive

<u>Eyebrows</u> Why is there always one really long hair that you haven't noticed in your eyebrows?

And, at the bottom:

The invitation this morning. A piece about our family? Something about Southpaw?

'Well, eyebrows.' She looked up. 'Do you ever suddenly notice there's one really long eyebrow hair, about an inch long, and it'll suddenly waggle out of place and stick right up like . . . a pubic hair?'

In the silence that followed Lucy heard the rush of the air conditioning vents, the clicking of someone's hard drive.

'I don't think that's . . . No,' Deborah said. 'Let's leave this. We're really looking for something a bit meatier than that.' Lucy opened her mouth. 'OK, thanks, Lucy, was there anything else?' And, like the owner of a pet shop, throwing a blanket over a squawking parrot, she turned to the rest of the group, and the meeting continued.

Back at her desk, Lucy tore out the page of her notebook. She stared at it then, angrily, threw it in the bin. The line 'A piece about our family?' seemed to burn into her eyes. She thought about going back to her damp cold flat tonight, taking out the thick cream card and propping it up on her desk in her bedroom. Those words, in Gran's beautiful, blank script: 'An important announcement.'

What was it all about? What was going on there?

Lucy's heart ached, as it always did when she thought of Winterfold. It was home, though she'd never lived there, it was her weak spot. Winterfold was the happy place people talked about finding in psychobabble articles about mindful relaxation, which the *Daily News* ran at least once a week. 'Go to your happy place.' Lucy was always there, that was the trouble. Wondering when the air would start to smell of autumn, as it always did by half-term. The sloes thickening, ripe for picking in late October on the bushes by the river, that first frost, the hunter's moon.

When her parents divorced and sold the messy Victorian villa in Redland in Bristol where Lucy had grown up she hadn't minded that much. When Cat was upset about Daisy, her mum, or worrying about some mean girl at school, or about life in general (Cat used to do that a lot), Lucy, the younger one, was the bracing dose of common sense. When her dad was at his lowest and she'd moved in with him for a few months after university, she'd held his hand, helped him paint the tiny little almshouse he'd bought in the village, listened to him witter on about his patients and watched *The Godfather* trilogy with him on a loop. She was all right when she was there, at Winterfold. It was the one place she felt truly safe, truly happy.

Lucy muttered something to herself, then stood

up and walked over to the corner office. She knocked on the door.

'Yes?' Deborah looked up. 'Oh. Lucy. Yes?'

'Can I have a word?'

'*Another* word?' Deborah pulled at one of her delicate gold cluster earrings.

Lucy ran a hand through her short messy curls. 'Yes. I'm sorry about earlier. I've got an idea, though, a much better one. You told me to think big.'

'This isn't about diets again, is it?'

Lucy had written a pitch last month called 'The Myth of Diets: Why 85% of All Weight Lost Through Dieting Goes Back on After 6 Months'. Deborah had practically choked on her soy latte. 'Jesus, if people knew that was the truth half our ad revenues would vanish. Are you mad? Women like reading about diets, OK?'

Feeling Deborah's coolly appraising gaze on her, Lucy sucked in her stomach. 'It's not about diets. You know, that exhibition of South— of my grandfather's is opening next year. I want to write a piece about our family. I think – it might be interesting.'

Deborah didn't sit up exactly, but she stopped gazing over Lucy's shoulder. 'What kind of article?'

'Um – what it was like to grow up with my grandfather.' She hoped she wasn't blushing. 'How wonderful he is. Our family. The house. You know they live in this lovely house and—'

'I know about the house,' Deborah said. 'Yup. It'd make for some nice photos. This is a good idea, Lucy. Warm reminiscence. The *Daily News* family.

"As our beloved cartoonist celebrates X years in the business with an exhibition of landmark paintings showing our city at war, *Daily News* features assistant Lucy Winter tells us about life with the grandfather who created the nation's favourite cartoon strip."' She nodded. 'I like it. All the family there? Any skeletons I should know about?'

'My mum's a herbalist called Clare who lives in Stokes Croft.' Lucy said, deadpan. 'In Bristol. So . . . I don't think so.'

Deborah laughed but she sounded a little impatient. 'I mean your grandfather's family.'

'Right.' Now she had got this far, Lucy suddenly found she didn't know what to say. 'My aunt Daisy – well, maybe it's not really a mystery.'

'What about your aunt Daisy?' Deborah's tone was, for her, almost flippant.

'Uh – well, I'm never sure if it's serious or not. I've always thought it was a bit strange.' She glanced at Deborah, feeling suddenly uneasy: was she really the right person to be talking to about this stuff? But it was too late now. 'My aunt sort of . . . disappeared twenty, thirty years ago. Out of the blue. Left her baby with my grandparents when she was just five weeks old and took off.'

'What do you mean, "disappeared"? Did she die?'

'No. It's weird. I mean, she's still alive. My grandmother gets emails from her. Now and then.'

'If your grandmother gets emails – where does she think she's gone, then?' There was a note of

72

impatience in Deborah's voice. *What kind of family doesn't know where their own daughter is?*

Lucy tried to explain, but as she didn't really understand it herself, it was hard to know how to put it. 'I think she was . . . always a bit difficult.' She remembered having a teenage tantrum about not being allowed to go to Katie Ellis's party and her dad yelling at her once: 'Oh God, Lucy, don't be like *Daisy*,' as if that was the worst thing a person could be. And Lucy had seen Daisy all of four times in her life. She didn't really know her. 'She's very cool. Um – well, I think she got pregnant very young, and it was all a bit much for her?' Almost appealing to Deborah for her agreement, she held her hands slightly open, racking her brains for a way to try to explain it. 'We don't talk about it, you know what families are like, the strangest things happen and people act like it's not even a big deal. Do you know what I mean?' Her shoulders slumped; of course not.

But Deborah said, 'Oh, tell me about it. My mother never knew who her father was, grew up believing he was dead, in fact, and one evening she and my dad are sitting there – I'm at university by this point – and there's a knock at the door and there's this man and he says hi there, I'm your father, and I've been looking for you for ten years.'

'What?' Lucy's eyes bulged. In the year she'd worked for her she'd learned nothing about Deborah, other than that she was from Dorking but said 'near Guildford' and that she'd asked

73

Lucy to order her loads of *Fifty Shades*-style erotica to take on holiday that summer. 'Oh my goodness. What happened next?'

Deborah shook her head and crossed her legs, briskly, as if she was regretting saying anything at all. 'It's not important. I'm just saying, I agree, families are strange. Go on. What happened to – what's your aunt's name? Don't tell me. She was murdered?'

'Er – no. Daisy. She ran off to India to work in a children's school and my grandparents raised the baby. Cat, my cousin. And that's basically it. She stayed in India. She helped build a school; I think she got some award for it. She's been back home four, five times since. Usually to ask for money.' Lucy frowned at the clearest memory she had of her thin, wrinkly-tanned aunt Daisy, so pretty and exotic and strange, and yet familiar in the old safe surroundings of Winterfold. She'd come back for Dad's unexpected wedding to Karen (which took place so hastily, Lucy had been gloomily convinced that news of a pregnancy would come soon afterwards, but no such announcement was ever made), and everyone was surprised to see her, Lucy remembered that much. She seemed to be permanently half there, half eager to join in and yet always on the edge of leaving. She had a silver elephant she always carried in her pocket. And big green eyes, too big in her gaunt face; she really was the thinnest person Lucy had ever seen. She clearly had no idea how old Lucy was and kept asking her if she'd read *The Famous Five* and talking to her in a babyish voice. She had a row with Dad about money the day before the wedding. And she'd said something to Cat, Lucy was never sure what, but she found Cat crying afterwards in her room, hugging her old cushion on the bed, almost inconsolable, and since then Cat had hardly been back, and Lucy missed her so much, though Cat had become so cool, so distant she'd never dream of saying any of that to her.

'Daisy usually has some argument with my dad, or my grandparents,' she finished. 'She leaves and says she's never coming home again.'

'So she's broken off contact with all of you?'

'It's not really like that.' Lucy didn't want to exaggerate. 'She wasn't ever that close to Flo, my other aunt. Or Dad, I suppose. But she still emails Gran these days. It's strange because . . . we've always been a really happy family otherwise. It's like she came from somewhere different.'

As she said this she felt it had been true that they were a happy family once, but not now. Things were different, they were all sadder; she could not explain it.

Deborah's hands were pressed to her cheeks. 'Well, you're right, that is interesting. An article about growing up with your grandfather, the lovely house . . . and then this about Daisy. Very meaty – yes. I suppose your grandfather wouldn't mind?' She looked like a cat, about to pounce on a mouse.

Lucy said carefully, 'I didn't mean . . . I'm not sure I'd want to write about all of it.'

'Why not? Lucy, don't be contrary.'

'I was really thinking of a piece about our family, how jolly we are, what we get up to, Southpaw drawing us little pictures, you know?' Deborah's nostrils flared. 'Look,' Lucy tried to sound firm, 'my grandfather doesn't like people digging into his past. He wouldn't even let the man from the *Bath Chronicle* interview him about his new show. I don't think he's going to want you to publish an article about . . . Daisy, and stuff.'

Deborah's voice took on a gentler, honey-like tone. 'Of course. Look, Lucy, you don't have to be sensationalist about it. There are plenty of people in situations like that: you know, unfinished business. And you never know, you might find out more about her and think how happy your grandparents would be. We've got two million readers, there must be someone who knows something.' She cleared her throat, delicately. 'I'll be honest. I like you, Lucy. I want to help you. You know? I mean, don't you *want* to write it?'

'I could ask him,' Lucy said, hesitantly, trying to feel her way on this slippery ground. 'We've got a family reunion coming up – I don't know if Daisy'll be there. It just feels a bit funny . . .'

'Ask your grandparents. Or speak to her daughter. Though I don't know why you can't just email your aunt yourself, ask her if she's coming back for the reunion. That'd make the perfect hook for the piece. Imagine it. You must have an address for her somewhere.' The phone on Deborah's desk rang and she diverted it with a jab of one bony finger. 'When you were in here last week asking for a pay rise you told me you were positive this was what you wanted to do. I'm not asking you to write some hatchet job on your family. I'm just saying, think about digging around a bit, seeing if there's something there.'

Lucy nodded. 'OK.'

'You can write, Lucy.' Deborah shook her head so her hair fell into its perfect bobbed shape. She ruffled it with her fingers, and then put on some lip gloss. 'You're good at pitching, you made me believe you wanted a job writing for a newspaper. You aren't there yet.' She stood up, peculiarly gawky, and slung a long coat around her shoulders, rather like Cruella de Vil. 'I have to go, I have lunch with Geordie. Think about it, Lucy. G'bye.'

And she left, leaving Lucy alone in her large glass office, staring out of the window, wondering what she'd just got herself into. *You can write.* Lucy pulled out Gran's invitation, her mind racing. She had no idea what she'd do next, but she was sure about one thing: wherever Daisy was, she wasn't coming back for this party.

DAISY

March 1969

I hate this house.

We have been here for a whole year now and I know I hate it. I am nearly eight and I am not stupid, though everyone seems to think I am, because I don't like reading stories like baby Florence, and I don't like hanging round the kitchen with Ma like Billy Lily. He hates it when I call him that!

When we first saw this house I didn't understand it would be only us living there. I said to Daddy: but it's far too big! There's only five of us and the dogs! They thought that was so funny, Daddy and Ma, like I'd said something jolly amusing. Grown-ups never understand that you mean what you say.

They showed us around the garden and Flo and Bill were awfully keen on it. Because of the space and the woods. But, I *hate* it. I am scared out here. I wish we were back in Putney, where the houses were the same and everything is safe.

And it is too big for us, now we're in. Daddy is

78

so pleased with himself because he could afford to buy it, because of him having no money and a sad childhood. I heard him saying that to Ma. I listen to them all the time, when they don't know I'm there. I know all about his dad and how his mummy died too. All the wood is painted green (in the house). There's mice and rats everywhere and Wilbur is terrible at catching them. He hides under the sideboard or, once, in the games cupboard in the sitting room when they appear. There's wasps, too, under the roof. No one else has spotted the wasps yet. And a huge garden. Ma is cross all the time. She wants to draw and she can't draw because she doesn't have time because of the mice and the dogs and dropping us at school and making food and all of the housewife chores. Daddy is off in London having meetings and lunch with friends. He comes home late, he smiles, Ma hisses at him and she gets so cross. They shout but they also whisper things, and that's when I like listening, when they're in bed at night and they can't hear me pressed against the door.

Everything's different since we came here. And Florence is here. Since she came along everything's worse. We moved because of her. We had to leave Putney and our old house with the poppies and the corn wallpaper because of her. Everything was fine before she arrived. It was quiet and nice and I knew where we were, me and Bill, Daddy and Ma. Ma had time for me, for Wilbur. Now she's always cross.

The other thing is we don't have enough money to pay for the house. I worry about it all the time. I try to say it to Ma and Daddy: there's not enough money because you told me once Daddy gets £100 for a painting or a sketch and this house was £16,000. And Ma doesn't have any money. She is from a poor family too, though not as poor as Daddy's. We don't see her family very much. There wasn't room for them in Putney to come and stay but they stayed the night here last week and I hope they don't come again. Her sister speaks with a funny accent and she was mean to me. She told me to shut up when I wanted to talk some more about Wilbur. So before she went I put a piece of broken glass from the time I pretended Florence broke the glass – well I keep some of the pieces in my tree by the daisy bank at the back of the garden – and I put it in her handbag. So when she reaches in for her handkerchief she will slice her fingers. I hope she slices them right off.

So I have got three things that I want to do. One, move back to Park Street, Putney. Two, get rid of Florence. An accident like what happened to Janet, although that scares me, and I didn't mean for it to happen. Three, make everyone say that Wilbur is my special dog not the family's. They can have Crispin as their family dog and Wilbur can be mine. I drew some pictures of him doing funny things, and I put them up in my room. The first one is of Wilbur hiding with the snakes and ladders in the cupboard when he sees a mouse. The second is him jumping up like a bean pole on the other side of the table when he sees food held in the air. He looks so funny. The third is him walking behind me down the hill to school. He does it every day and then he walks back up to Winterfold and sits with Ma and waits for me to come home. I love Wilbur, more than anyone else in the whole world. He is a bit sandy, and he is a cross between a Labrador and a retriever, I think.

This is what I'm worried about most at the moment: just before the holidays, Janet Jordan at school laughed at him and said he was ugly and a mongrel. The next day Janet fell on the steps and hit her head and now she can't speak. At all.

I worry that I did that to Janet. I didn't make anything special happen like I do sometimes, but I thought a lot about it, I wanted her to die for being nasty to Wilbur. I really did. Sometimes I stare at things very very hard and I'm sure I move them just a bit with my thoughts, and I get so scared but I can't stop doing it. When I look at books late at night in the new room sometimes the colours jumble up and start to jump in front of my eyes like they're talking to me. And when I see myself in the mirror I think an evil person's talking to me, and sometimes he is. Then I think: so what? Janet wasn't nice, she laughed at me for being new, and having a pinafore on, and she was nasty to other girls, but she started being nice when she saw my house was big. She deserved it.

When Wilbur's with me, though, it's all all right. They are saying they might put poison down for the rats, and if Wilbur ate it it would kill him, so he has to get used to sleeping in here then. I like him being in here. I feel safe. We are friends. I draw him while he's lying there. I can't draw like Daddy but I try and match the way his back swishes in a curl, and how his legs fold under him, so neatly. Wilbur is very clever as well as being a bit silly sometimes. Mrs Goody says my drawings of him are very good, and I should hang them up in the classroom, but I don't want other people to see them and ooh and ah so I put them up in my room.

Daddy likes the drawings. 'Well done, Daze,' he says, looking at the picture of Wilbur in the games cupboard hiding from a rat. 'Lovely idea, that. Very funny.' But it's not funny at all, it's serious.

JOE

Ten days after his accident, Joe Thorne left the Oak Tree and, carefully carrying his package wrapped in brown paper under one arm, walked up to Winterfold. He couldn't help but be nervous. He'd mentioned he was doing this catering gig to a couple of people. 'Ooh, up at the Winters, are you? That's good,' Sheila had said. 'Listen here, Bob, Joe's going up to Winterfold.'

Bob, their one regular, had raised his eyebrows.

'Right then,' he'd said. And he'd almost looked impressed.

The early autumn sunshine was like misty gold, flooding the quiet streets as he strode past the war memorial and the post office. Susan Talbot, the post mistress, was standing in the doorway talking to her mother, Joan. Joe raised his bandaged hand at her and Susan smiled widely at him, waving enthusiastically. Joe felt bad about Susan. He wasn't sure why, just that she was always on at him. Last time she'd wanted him to lug some boxes around, then stay for a cup of tea, then the rest of it, and she'd gone a bit funny when, in the course of conversation (in truth, when she'd asked him outright) he'd said he wasn't really looking for a relationship. Not at the moment.

'No time for love?' Susan said. 'All work and no play . . .' She'd smiled brightly at him and he'd frowned, because he hated that look on her face like she was making the best of it. 'You want to be careful, Joe my dear. A good-looking chap like you, those lovely blue eyes and those cheekbones to die for all going to waste! Someone should enjoy them. You can't just coop yourself up in that flat night after night on your own.'

It had freaked him out, more than a little bit. The way she'd stared at him, as though she knew something.

Now he nodded at her in a friendly way and carried on, clutching the brown paper package under his arm so tight that he gave a tiny moan as his finger throbbed once more.

Bill Winter was a good doctor, that was for sure. The nurse at the hospital in Bath where Joe had ended up that day told him Bill had saved his finger and maybe his whole hand – Joe thought that was a bit dramatic, but they'd said if blood poisoning had set in it'd have been serious. Who'd want a chef who can't use a knife, whisk a sauce, knead dough? What would he have done? He'd have lost his job here, that was for sure. He'd have had to do something else, become a bartender, maybe. Besides, he wanted to help Jemma out with money, even if she said she didn't need it, didn't need anything, as she kept telling him. Not now she was with Ian.

Jemma had cancelled Jamie's last visit, a couple of weeks ago; something about *The Gruffalo* on stage and how he couldn't miss it, everyone in his class was going. Joe hadn't seen his son now for two months. Jamie had been down to stay in late July, just after the school holidays had started. It had been brilliant. They'd gone swimming in the river at Farleigh Hungerford. They'd camped out at Sheila's – Joe's rooms above the pub were tiny, and Sheila had a cottage with a long garden that stretched down to the woods, where you heard foxes fighting and owls hooting, and the strange, rustling sound of unknown creatures nearby. They'd made a fire, Joe cooked the Oak Tree's own delicious herby sausages and put them in his own rosemary and walnut bread rolls, slathered with mustard, and there the two of them had sat, out under the stars, munching away together and Joe couldn't remember ever feeling this happy. He'd made Sheila some treacly, creamy truffles to say thanks for the garden loan. He and Jamie had made a box out of cardboard and decorated it – the felt-tip marks where they'd overshot the cardboard were still on his kitchen table – blue, orange and green scribbles, made in a second – and now when Joe saw them every night, he felt the sharp pang of Jamie's absence. Sheila had cooed with delight when he gave her the box, the night after he'd got back from taking Jamie home to York.

'You shouldn't have, it were my pleasure, Joe. He's lovely. You must be very proud of him.'

'I am,' he'd said, swallowing hard. 'Nothing to do with me, though.'

'You're joking, aren't you? He's the spitting image of you, my dear, it's uncanny.' Then she'd looked and seen his expression. 'Oh, Joe. I promise you, he is. And he's welcome any time you want.'

He would always love Sheila for saying that, but being here was taking him away from his son, more and more. This restaurant, two hundred and fifty miles away from his son. Why had he thought he could do it? Why was he screwing everything up here? Why wasn't he back in York, or even Leeds, or back with Mum in Pickering, helping her out?

Jemma and Ian were getting married next year, and though he honestly wished them well and was glad for Jemma that she could have all the manicures she wanted, Joe was the one left behind. He'd never been right for her. He'd never really understood why she'd come over to him in the first place. She'd been way out of his league. He'd only been in the club because one of the chefs was leaving. It was a footballer's place, and she was the kind of girl you saw with footballers.

Joe's sister, Michelle, had warned him off her. 'She's trouble, Joe. She's after your money.'

Joe had said quietly, 'She knows I don't have any money.'

'You're her cute bit of action on the side before

she bags herself a millionaire,' she told him. Michelle was a realist. 'You don't understand women, OK? You're not that fat spotty kid with the knee-high socks and Mam's apron on, making brownies, any more, right, love? You're . . . ugh.' She'd closed her eyes and shuddered. 'You're a good-looking lad, and you're nice, OK? All my friends are after you. So just use your head.'

They'd only been dating a few months when Jemma told him she was pregnant. Joe was over the moon, but she wasn't. She was scared. He could see now that the game she was playing was to get herself some security, because she'd failed at school and her mum had nothing, and her dad, like his, was long gone. Jemma was like Michelle: she didn't have any qualifications, anything to give. The only thing she had was her body and her looks, and she'd used them to get him, someone who wouldn't hit her or cheat on her, but the moment she'd decided it'd be him she'd realised she didn't really love him anyway. She was nearly five months gone by that point.

If they'd been older and wiser, maybe it could have worked. If he'd been mature enough to see how young and scared she really was and how a lot of the crap she pulled was because she was frightened, and wanted to test him, maybe he'd have kept her. But she started going out again when Jamie was only a few weeks old, and coming back all hours, and he was working all hours too, and they were shouting when they were together,

her yelling at him because he was never around and didn't earn enough money, and the flat in Leeds was tiny and both of them were so tired all the time, they could only be vile to each other. She'd start shouting at him – completely wild, she'd get – and Joe would stare at his son, his tiny red wrinkled head, solemn mouth, beady black eyes that opened wide, the sudden smile when you picked him up. He'd wonder: could Jamie hear the terrible things his mum and dad were saying to each other? Was it damaging him, making him believe the world was full of anger and sadness?

One day he'd got back from the restaurant, at four in the morning, and they were gone. Just a note, and it said, 'Sorry Joe. I can't do this any more. You can see Jamie whenever. J. x PS You were lovely.'

It was fine to start with. He saw Jamie every weekend, some weekdays, took him out and about, to the park, to the playgroup at the church hall. He loved kids, and the mums were always friendly; Joe loved it. Then Jemma moved to York and it got a bit harder to see Jamie, but it was still OK. Joe kept on working, head down, not living much, going on the occasional date, the odd pint with an old mate. Really, just waiting for his weekends with Jamie, time he could make into bricks, a substantial bulk of memory.

Then, at Jamie's third birthday party, there was Ian Sinclair, a lawyer. Jemma had cut his hair and he'd asked her out, and now he was here, in her living room, snapping away with a massive expensive Nikon camera and his own present, a bright red sit-on truck for Jamie. Joe had turned up late with a Victoria sponge made by his mother, which Liddy had laboriously decorated all over with Smarties. It had got squashed on the bus. He'd stood at the back chatting to Jemma's neighbour Lisa, then tried to pick up Jamie but he'd wailed and screamed. Then he'd given him a bow and arrow set, and Jemma had practically stabbed him with it: 'What the hell is he going to do with that, Joe? Walk down Museum Gardens and shoot something? Are you serious?'

Ian Sinclair had handed round a train-shaped cake and given the grown-ups each a fondant fancy, both of which he'd ordered in from Bettys. Joe's present was rolled up in its plastic bag, put down the side of the sofa on the floor. On the way back from the toilet Joe caught side of his mum's squashed cake, abandoned untouched in the sterile brand-new kitchen, buttery grease blotting the now bent paper plates Liddy had carefully sandwiched it between. Joe ended up drinking too much with Lisa, the neighbour, then going back to her flat, where they had sex, he was fairly sure – he couldn't even remember and that made it worse somehow.

It got worse: the next day, as he was leaving, Jemma appeared on the pavement, shaking with rage.

'Things are changing, Joe. OK?' She jabbed her finger on the window of Ian's Jeep, which she used to drive Jamie to the childminder's. 'I'm sick of you hanging round like a dog that's lost its owner. He'll always be your son, don't you understand that?'

Joe could see Jamie, strapped into his car seat, watching his father, thumb in mouth, a little confused. His thick curls were stuck to his head; he still looked half-asleep. He reached forward and jabbed at the window with one small finger. 'Dad?'

'Go and get your own life,' Jemma hissed at Joe. 'Seriously.'

She was right, of course. But Joe didn't know what his own life looked like. His dad had left when he was five, and Michelle was eight, and he'd come back lots at the start, then not at all. Derek Thorne was a liar, and a gambler, who took money off their mother, and once hit her when he was drunk. The worst thing was, Joe remembered him pretty well. He'd always thought he was a brilliant dad, till the moment he'd upped and left. Joe didn't know where he'd gone, his mum never wanted to talk about it, his sister hated him, and that was it . . . it wasn't even dramatic. He'd just sort of faded away.

Now Joe saw that it could happen, very easily. How careful he had to be, to maintain his amicable relationship with Jemma and Ian. Because the memories of his times with Jamie were growing more and more precious. *He* was Jamie's dad, not

Ian, and nothing could change that. And he didn't want to be a dick about it; he wasn't some Fathers4Justice idiot. He didn't ever want to get in the way of Ian. Ian was the one who'd be there at night when he woke up, who'd hug Jamie when he was scared of monsters under the bed. He would do all that . . .

Joe stopped, halfway up the hill, breathing in the scent of fallen leaves, wood smoke, rain, and blinked back the sharp tears in his eyes. The memory of his son's wriggly, sturdy body against his when they hugged was exquisite pleasure mixed with aching pain in his heart. The smell of wood smoke in his hair, his head next to his father's in the tent at night that summer. His low, dry voice, the way he slept with his fists scrunched up tight – he'd always done that, ever since he was a baby. His gummy teeth, his babbling chatter about children at school, and how his best friend was a girl called Esme.

Joe knew he had to keep going, now he was in this situation. But he was already screwing it up, he felt. It was already maybe too late.

It was a ten-minute walk out to Winterfold. The lane grew steeper, winding up through the trees past the ruins of the old priory and then ending with a wooden gate, and there was the name of the house, carved into the low wall behind. *Winterfold.* Joe hesitated before unhooking the latch. Though he didn't care much about money or privilege he found he was nervous, walking up the gravel drive, as though he were entering another world.

The trees were dry, the dark olive-green leaves burnished with bright yellow. The branches rustled softly as Joe looked up to see Winterfold in front of him. The front door was right at the centre of an L, so the house seemed to hug you. The bottom half was golden-grey local Bath stone, sprinkled with white lichen, and it was topped by four great gables in wooden clapboard, two on either side, each with a dormer window, like eyes peering down. Wisteria twisted and turned along the edge of the lowest beam. Joe peered into one of the low leaded windows by the door, then jumped. Someone was moving around inside.

Joe went up to the great blackened oak door on to which were carved intricate repeating patterns of berries and leaves. The knocker was in the shape of an owl. It stared at him, unblinking. He knocked firmly and stepped back, feeling like Jack coming to see the giant in his home.

He waited for what seemed like ages, then reached forward to knock again and as the door opened he fell forwards, almost lurching into Martha Winter's arms.

'Well. Hello, Joe. It's lovely to see you. How's your hand?'

'It's much better.' He fumbled for the parcel under his arm. 'I bought you something, actually.

To thank you. They said if Dr Winter hadn't acted so fast I'd have lost the finger.'

'Come inside.' Martha unwrapped the bread, her fingertips running over the cracked, crusty surface. 'Tiger bread – it's my favourite, did you know that? No. Well, it's very clever of you. Joe, I didn't want anything. Anyone would have done the same. It's my son you should be thanking.'

'Yes,' he said. 'Of course.'

'You haven't been here before, have you? It's lovely in the afternoons, when the sun starts to come over the hill.'

Somehow she'd taken his coat off and it was hanging on the old carved row of hooks. He glanced left as they passed through the hall: a huge, light sitting room, lined with dark wooden cupboards, white-washed walls slit by black beams. The French windows were open and beyond them was the garden, a green mist splashed with reds, blues and pinks.

'It's been a great summer for gardeners. All the rain. The tree house is practically pulp, but we don't have any children running around these days sadly, so no use for it.' Martha pushed open the kitchen door and he followed her. 'I'm shutting the door behind us because David's in his study and he'll try to join us.'

'Oh. Would that be so bad?'

'He's got a deadline. He loves being distracted and he'll hear you and come in.' She ruffled her bob with her fingers. 'Do sit down, Joe. Would you like some tea? I was going to make a pot. Have a piece of gingerbread.'

Martha pulled out a large, carved wooden armchair, and slid a blue and white plate across the table towards him. Joe took a piece, gratefully – he was hungry all the time since the accident, and wondered if it might be some kind of delayed shock. He watched as she moved around the roomy kitchen. Behind her a large pair of wooden doors was folded back, leading through to the wood-panelled dining room. A jam jar of hot pink and violet-blue sweet peas stood on the sideboard. Liddy grew sweet peas back at home, obsessively trailing them through the trellis on the wall outside their little cottage. Joe breathed in, smelling their rich, heady scent. He looked around the room as she made the tea, thinking he ought to say something. Show he was engaged, keen, up for this job.

'Is that Florence?' he said, pointing to a watercolour on the wall.

Martha looked up, in delight. 'Yes. We did it on our honeymoon. Both of us together.'

'It's beautiful. I studied in Italy. My catering course – we were there for a term.'

'My daughter lives in Florence,' she said. 'How wonderful. Where were you?'

'In a village, middle of nowhere in Tuscany. It was great. What's she doing there then?'

'She's an art history professor. Mostly at the British College, but she teaches over here too.

She's very clever. Nothing like me. I studied art, but I'm no good at talking about it.'

'You're an artist too?'

Martha folded her arms and looked down at her wedding ring. 'Once, I suppose. David and I both had scholarships to the Slade. Those poor East Enders, they used to call us. Terribly posh children from the Home Counties, and us. The girl I shared a bedsit with was called Felicity and her father was a brigadier. Golly, she did go on about him.' She smiled, and her lips parted, enough to show the gap between her teeth. 'Now you'd just look it up on your phone, I suppose, but then, I had no idea what a brigadier was. After about a month, I asked David what it meant. He was the one person I could ask.'

'Did you know him from home?'

Martha suddenly snapped shut the recipe book next to her, and stood up. 'No. Different parts of London. But I'd met him before. Once.' Her voice changed. 'Anyway, I don't paint any more. Not really. When we moved here . . . everything else took over.' She smiled, a little mechanically. 'Here's your tea.'

She doesn't like talking about herself either.. 'When you were doing it though . . . what kind of stuff did you paint?' He corrected himself. 'Not stuff, sorry. Works.'

Martha laughed at that. '"Works" sounds so grand, doesn't it? Oh, everything. I started off doing pastiches, watercolours, copying famous paintings.

95

Used to sell them in Hyde Park on a Sunday. But latterly it was more . . . woodcuts. Prints. Nature and nurture.' Sun flickered into the room, reflected off a plane high, high above, and her green eyes flashed hazel-gold. 'But it was a long time ago. And having children isn't conducive to being the next Picasso, you know.'

'So, you've two children then?'

'Three.' She stood up and went over to the sink. 'There's Daisy too. She's the middle one. She lives in India. Works for a charity – literacy and schools in Kerala.'

Joe didn't say, *Wilbur and Daisy, I know all about her.* He somehow hadn't thought that little girl in the cartoons he devoured as a child was real. 'India. That's exotic.'

'Don't think it is, much, not with the work she does. But she's had some wonderful results out there.' Martha washed an apple, splashing water everywhere. 'Right. Do you want one of these?' He shook his head. 'Then shall we draw up a list? I had a few ideas, just a couple of suggestions.'

'Will she be there for your birthday?'

She stared at him blankly and sat down again. 'Who?'

'Daisy? Your daughter?' Joe said nervously, wondering if he'd already forgotten her name.

Martha started peeling the apple with a knife. 'This is a tense moment.' There was a silence as the silver cut through the shining green skin. 'I like doing this in one perfect ribbon, and lately my skills are starting to slip.' She added, almost as an afterthought, 'Daisy won't be there, no.'

'I'm sorry. I shouldn't have asked.' Joe fumbled to take his notepad out of his pocket, embarrassed.

'No, it's fine. There's no big drama with Daisy. She's always been a bit – difficult. She had a baby very young, an affair with a boy she met in Africa, building wells, I think it was. Nice young boy,' Martha screwed up her face as if trying to picture him. 'Giles, something. Isn't that terrible? Nice boy. Very Home Counties . . .'

She stopped as though recalling something. 'Anyway. She's out in India now and she really has made a difference. The area where she helped build the school in Cherthala has equal attendance rates for girls and boys now, and last year we – she, I should say, she did it all – raised enough money to ensure every school in the area is on the mains system for water. It'll save about five thousand lives a year. It's things like that – she's very driven, when she gets the idea in her head, you see.'

'You know a lot about it.' He was impressed.

'Well, we just – miss her. I'm interested in what interests her. And Cat – that's her daughter – it's sad, like I say.' Her eyes were shining.

'She's never seen her baby? Not once?'

The spiral of skin fell on the table. Martha sliced the creamy naked apple. 'Oh, a few times over the years. We raised Cat ourselves. Daisy's always seen

97

her when . . . you know, when she comes back. She loves being here.'

'When was the last time she came back?'

Martha looked thoughtful. 'Oh . . . I'm not sure. Bill's wedding to Karen? That was four years ago. She was a little difficult. Daisy has the zeal of the convert, do you know anyone like that? It annoys some people. Her brother . . . her sister too, come to mention it. It's just . . .' she began, then she stopped. 'Oh, nothing.'

Intrigued, Joe said, 'Go on. It's just what?'

Martha hesitated, and looked over her shoulder, towards the dining room, golden autumn light streaming in from the garden outside.

'It's just – oh, Joe, it's not the way you imagine they'll turn out when they're babies. When you hold them in your arms, that first time and look at them. And you see what kind of person they are. Do you know what I mean?'

Joe nodded. He knew exactly. He could still remember the moment right after the birth, as Jemma lay back, exhausted, and the midwife turned round from the station by the bed and, like a magician performing a magic trick, handed him this bundle in a towel, which made a mewling sound, a bit like a persistent ringtone. *Waah. Waah. Waah.*

'Your son!' she'd said brightly. And he'd stared at his round, purple face, and the eyes had opened so briefly and fixed on something near Joe's face, and what had crossed Joe's mind was, *I know you. I know who you are.*

'Yes,' he said after a moment. 'I knew what he was like the first time I held him. Right then just by looking at him. Like I could see his soul.'

'Exactly. That's all. It's not . . . it's not what I wanted for her.' Martha paused and her green eyes filled with tears. She shrugged. 'I'm sorry, Joe. I just miss her.'

'I'm sure you do.' Joe's heart went out to her. He sipped his tea and finished the cake and, for a few moments, they sat in companionable silence. He felt once again that strangely familiar sense of contentment in her presence. Like he'd known her for a long time.

'So then,' he said, putting down his mug. 'I had a few ideas. Want to talk them over?'

'Sure,' Martha said, brushing something off her cheek. She gave a quick smile. 'I'm so glad you're doing this, Joe.'

'Well, I'm glad to be doing it.' He grinned, almost shyly at her. 'I thought for the family lunch on Saturday we'd do a big tapas selection, loads of dips and meats. Go up to the smokery on the Levels together and get some sausages, salmon, pâté and the like. And then a suckling pig. Porchetta, fennel seeds, sage, a nice sort of event piece, and I can do loads of veg and all. Fruit salad and a big birthday cake for afters, and a huge cheese board, all as local as possible. How's that sound?'

'It sounds wonderful,' she said. 'I knew you'd get it.' She reached out and patted his good hand.

'My mouth's watering, just thinking about it. You can use herbs from our garden, that'd be a nice—' The door swung open behind them and she turned, half in irritation, half in amusement. 'David, darling, it's been ten minutes! Can't you – oh, *Lucy*! Hello!'

'Hi, Gran!' A tall curly haired girl bounded into the room, and threw her arms around Martha. 'Oh, it's nice to be back. Where's Southpaw?'

'What are you doing here?' Martha stroked her hair.

'Sorry to surprise you, I only decided – oh, sorry again. Didn't realise you were with someone.'

'I'm Joe,' said Joe, standing up. 'Nice to meet you.'

'Lucy. Hi.' She held out her hand, staring up at him and he shook it. She had big hazel eyes, a creamy complexion and a wide, generous smile. There was a gap between her teeth, like her grandmother's, and she blushed as she smiled at him, clamping one arm self-consciously over her chest.

'Oh, what a nice surprise,' said Martha. She hugged her granddaughter again, and kissed the top of her head. 'Lucy, Joe's the new chef at the Oak Tree. He's going to do the food for the party.'

'How exciting!' Lucy said, eagerly. 'My stepmother can't stop going on about you. Says you're the best thing to happen to the village since she got there.' She took some cake and sat down. 'Mm. Gran, it's so great to be here.'

'Right. Who's your stepmother?' Joe put another piece of gingerbread in his mouth.

'Well, I think she's got a crush on you, so watch out.' Lucy was shovelling down cake with aplomb. 'Karen Bromidge. D'you know who I mean? Thirties, small, looks like a kind of female Hitler in tight tops?'

'Lucy, don't be rude,' said Martha. 'Joe, are you all right?'

Joe was coughing, trying not to choke. 'Bit . . .' He couldn't speak. 'I—'

'Get him some water,' Martha said.

Lucy jumped up, ran the tap, handed him a glass and he tried to drink, breathing hard, feeling like an idiot. *Nice one.* She thumped him hard, on the back and he spluttered, then sat down again.

Lucy wiped the crumbs off her face and turned to Martha. 'So, Gran, what's the big idea?' she said. 'With this party, I mean. I got the invite. You sent it to my old address, by the way.'

'Darling, you keep moving. I don't have your new address. What was wrong with the old flat?'

'Domestic issues,' Lucy said succinctly. 'It was time.'

'You were only there three months.'

'This pigeon kept raping another pigeon on the roof outside.'

'What?'

Lucy swallowed the last of the cake. 'Every morning. This pigeon with a big fluffed-up neck would chase these other pigeons and they'd try and fly away and he'd fly after them. And I'd be lying in bed and there'd be this screaming cooing noise and you'd look out and feel really bad for the girl pigeons.'

'It's the circle of life,' Martha said. 'Draw the curtains.'

'There weren't any curtains.' Martha buried her face in her hands and laughed. Lucy ignored her. 'I'm living with Irene now. It's all right.'

'Who's Irene?'

'Irene Huang? Irene from Alperton? Gran, you met her when we had lunch in Liberty. She's a fashion blogger. Allegedly. She's actually pretty annoying. She leaves these notes on the fridge about her cat and his distressed bowels and how I must not, repeat not, feed him anything myself.'

'Lucy!' said Martha, as though she were eight. 'No bowels talk, please.'

Lucy shot her a look. 'It's germane.'

'It's not bloody germane to talk about some cat's guts.'

'The cat's called Chairman Miaow. Now that is germane. It's actually quite a great name. I was sucked in by the greatness of her cat's name and now it's too late.'

'Why did you want to live with her? Apart from the cat?' Joe asked, trying to breathe steadily, though he could still feel exactly where the ginger-bread had become stuck in his throat.

'She lives in Dalston. Dalston's the centre of everything these days.'

'Never heard of it,' said Martha.

'It's East London,' Joe told her. 'Very trendy.'

'Imagine the Greenwich Village of the fifties, today,' Lucy said.

'Oh. Right. How's the job? Lucy works on the *Daily News*,' Martha explained to Joe.

'The job?' Lucy said, brightly. 'It's great. Really great. Listen – I wanted to ask you something about it, in fact. Do you think—' There were footsteps in the hall; Joe saw how quickly Lucy flushed, and shrugged, saying quickly, 'Actually, never mind,' as the kitchen door banged open and David Winter stood on the threshold, holding the door back with his stick.

'Any chance of some tea, Em?'

'Of course.' Joe saw Martha look at him. 'What's up?'

'I'm having some trouble with Wilbur. Can you come and pretend to be chasing your tail?' He caught sight of Lucy and his face lit up. 'Lucy, darling, hello! This is much better. Come into the study, I need you to run around in a circle.' Lucy gave a throaty, delighted chuckle. 'And Joe, wonderful! Hello there, sir. Are you here to talk about the plans for the party?'

'Hello, David.' Joe stood up, and shook his hand. He felt faint. 'Yes. I think we've agreed on the menu.'

David leaned against the table. 'Well, that's marvellous. Now I shall take this piece of gingerbread and go back to my study. Lucy . . .?'

'I need to ask Gran something.' Lucy looked at her grandmother. 'Can Joe do it?'

'Joe, please come and run around in a circle pretending to be a dog, won't you?' David said, smiling, and Joe thought again that you'd do anything to please a man with a smile like that.

'Of course.'

'You know, it's easier to just show you on YouTube,' he said, when they were in David's study.

'On YouTube?' David sat heavily back in his chair, breathing hard. Joe glanced at him. There were dark grey circles under his brown eyes. 'That hadn't occurred to me. It's a terrific idea.' He lay back a little, and closed his eyes.

'You all right?'

'Bit tired, that's all. I don't sleep that well. I used to take sleeping pills. Can't any more.' He tapped his chest. 'Dodgy ticker.'

'I'm sorry.' Joe moved round next to him behind the large oak desk and began typing on the old computer balanced precariously on the corner, next to sheets of paper, a large mug filled with pencils, and a pile of thrillers in a large, wobbling tower. David stared into space, his hands sitting uselessly on his lap. 'This desk is a health and safety liability, David,' Joe said, for want of something else to say. David's fame made him nervous. He wasn't like the footballers or Big Brother rejects who came into the restaurant back in Leeds and ordered Cristal and then sat there fiddling with their phones. He was someone Joe really admired, had done all his life, and it was weird . . . and

104

strange. 'You'd never be allowed to work in my kitchen.'

'Ha,' David said. 'My life's work in here. All our paperwork too. It's a mess, and one day someone will have to sort it all out. Hopefully not me.' He sat up as Joe clicked on a video. 'Look at that, eh. Marvellous. How did you know what kind of dog Wilbur was? That's the exact spit of him.'

'I owned all your books, David,' Joe said, embarrassed. 'My uncle used to buy me the new one every Christmas. I knew Daisy and Wilbur better than I knew most of my family.'

'Really?' David looked absolutely delighted. 'That's wonderful! What was your uncle called?' He picked up a pencil, his thick red hands curling uselessly around it, until it slipped out of his grasp. 'Dammit. My hands are bad today. Having terrible trouble doing anything.'

'Alfred, and he's dead, so don't worry.' Joe put his hand on the older man's trembling fingers, immensely touched. 'David, everyone in my school had something from Wilbur.'

'Oh, well. Isn't that terrific, though?'

'Yes,' Joe grinned. 'Now, I'll leave you to get on.'

'No – oh, do stay and chat,' David said, sadly. 'I hate being in here all on my own. Especially days like this.'

'I'd best get back. Mrs Winter wants you to do some work.' Besides, Joe was already feeling he'd spent enough time in this house, getting into all their business. The way they pulled you all in, all of them, without stopping to ask you if you wanted to – it was crazy, charming, discombobulating. His head was throbbing. 'I've got to head back to the pub for evening service.'

'Well, this is awful news,' David said. 'Absolutely ruddy awful.' He plucked the gingerbread out of his jacket pocket. 'I might eat this then have a nap. Don't tell Martha. Deadline's later.'

Joe left then, shutting the door softly on David picking up his pencil again. He walked back towards the kitchen, and as he did he heard Martha's raised voice.

'No, Lucy. Absolutely not. I can't believe it. How dare they even ask you? How much has Southpaw done for them over the years?' There was a clank of something, a crack of china clashing. 'Oh, dammit. I've a mind to ring them up, give them hell.'

Joe hovered, not sure whether to go in; but he didn't want to eavesdrop.

'Please don't, Gran. It wasn't their idea, it was mine. Forget it.'

'Your idea!' Martha laughed. 'Lucy, after everything – absolutely not.'

Lucy's voice was thick. 'I wouldn't put anything in you didn't want, Gran. If it's a terrible idea of course I'll leave it. I just wondered why I can't simply email Daisy and ask her why she's—'

Martha's hissed reply was so soft Joe barely heard her. 'It'd be a pretty bad idea, that's all.' She looked up, as if she knew someone was outside. 'Is that

Joe, then?' Her voice was sharp. 'What are you doing, hanging around listening to us bicker?'

'Sorry.' Joe came in, scratching his head. Lucy was flushed. Martha put her hand on her soft hair, and stroked it.

'Forgive me, darling. I shouldn't have lost my rag. Joe, do you want some more tea? Or maybe a glass of wine. I could do with a glass of wine.'

Joe looked at the clock. 'I'd best be off soon. Let's just nail down the rest of the menu and then I'll go.'

Lucy pushed her chair out. 'I'll pop back to Dad's, dump my stuff. I'll see you back here for supper then, Gran? I'm sorry.' Her eyes were still bright, feverish, almost. She swallowed, then turned to Joe. 'Someone rang you. Oh, and your phone kept buzzing, someone's texting you.'

'Oh, that'll be my mum . . .' Joe began. Liddy texted him all the time. And then he looked down, saw the most recent text gleaming up at him before it faded away into black glass, and his mouth turned dry.

This is it, he thought. I've been found out.

See you later? I can get away. X

But Lucy was staring fretfully at her grandmother, and he couldn't be sure if she'd read it or not. His finger throbbed, as though darts of toxic poison were gushing into his body and he braced himself, but all Lucy said was, 'So, um. Maybe I'll see you at the pub some time, I hope?'

'Absolutely,' he said. 'Come down whenever. Tell

someone at the newspaper to come and review it. We need all the help we can get.'

She stared at him, thoughtfully. 'Maybe I will. Thanks, Joe.'

Lucy shrugged, and picked up her bag. 'I'd better get back to Dad,' she said, and as she left, she threw a swift, secretive smile at Joe. He genuinely didn't know what it meant.

FLORENCE

'*Pronto!*'

'Professor Lovell. You wanted to see me?'

George Lovell laid down his pen and gently placed the pads of his fingers together. He closed his eyes and inclined his head, very slightly. 'Yes. *Adesso, Signora.*'

Florence shut the door and sat down on one of the high-backed mahogany chairs which, common rumour had it, Professor Lovell had 'liberated' from an abandoned palazzo near Fiesole. 'In any case,' she said, 'I wanted to ask you if I may take some time off in November. Three days, I think.'

'I take it this is not part of your work for the Courtauld?'

'No, holiday. I'm visiting my parents.' Florence plunged her hands into the pockets of her skirt and smiled as engagingly as she could at him.

Professor Lovell sighed. His eyes rolled upwards until he was staring at the tufty overhang of his brow. She watched him and wondered how he held that position, totally motionless, like an owl.

'George?' Florence said after a few moments. 'Ah – George?'

'Florence. This, again. Again.'

She was taken aback. 'What again?'

'Going off in the middle of term.'

'What?' Florence cast her mind around. 'That? But that was two years ago, and it was an operation,' she said. 'I had a mole removed and it turned septic. You must remember.'

'Yes, the famous mole on your back,' said Professor Lovell, in a tone of voice that suggested he doubted the whole story.

'I got blood poisoning afterwards,' Florence said in what she felt was a mild tone. 'I nearly died.'

'I think that's exaggerating it somewhat, isn't it?'

Florence crossed her hands in her lap. She knew Professor Lovell of old and there was no point in contradicting him. She could still see the nuns in the hospital round her bed as she drifted in and out of consciousness. She could hear them anxiously wondering in Italian about the *signora* and whether she was Catholic and would she like prayers said over her body, for surely she was not long for this world. 'Again, I'm sorry about that.' There was no arguing with George when he was like this. 'It's my mother's eightieth birthday. I am owed the holiday, you know.'

'Hmm.' Professor Lovell nodded. 'That's as may be. Ahem. As may be. Professor Winter, Professor Connolly and I have been wondering.' At Peter's name, Florence smiled privately, for merely hearing his name spoken in public felt like a luxury. 'This was his idea, and perhaps it is appropriate to ask

110

you now whether you would you like to take some time off?'

Florence began to wonder whether George was losing his mind. 'Well – that's what I was asking for. Yes. Three days in November.'

'No, Florence.' The professor's hand came down on the old desk. 'I meant – a term or two. Give you some time to assess your options.' He wouldn't meet her eye. 'You're a busy woman, now you have this Courtauld job.' He said the word 'Courtauld' in the same way one might say 'tumour' or 'Nazi'.

Florence stared at him, bewildered. 'But, George – there's the paper on "Benozzo and Identity" to finish, for the conference in December, you can't have forgotten. And my book – I have a lot of reading to do on it. A lot.'

Professor Lovell gave a sardonic laugh. 'Your book? Of course.'

'It's not the same level as Peter's, of course . . .' Florence began, and George smirked. *Of course not.* 'But it's important none the less. And the spring lecture series – I really only want three days away next month, not two terms.'

'Right.' George Lovell sat back in his chair, hands on the armrests. There was a faint sheen of perspiration on his smooth, yellowing pate. 'Florence . . . How do I explain this clearly? We think it's time for you to take a step back. This is not a demotion, nor is it age-related. But we need lecturers with a more diverse approach to complement our syllabus, and to that end—'

111

'*What?*'

'To that end,' he repeated, ignoring her, 'Professor Connolly has appointed Dr Talitha Leafe to assist us in the Art History faculty. I know the pair of you will work extremely well together. She's extremely talented, very enthusiastic – her specialities are Filippo Lippi and Benozzo Gozzoli—'

Florence felt like Alice, tumbled down a hole and out into a world that made no sense. 'But – that's *my* speciality.' She pointed above him. 'Look! Look at the book behind you on the shelf! *Studies in Benozzo Gozzoli and Fra Filippo Lippi*, edited by Professor Florence Winter! That's why you employ *me*, George. You don't need this – Tabitha Leaf? *I'm*—'

'Ta*li*tha Leafe,' George broke in. 'Tally,' he added, unneccessarily.

Florence narrowed her eyes, trying to think clearly. So this was it. She knew they couldn't fire her on account of her age, because last year they'd tried to get rid of Ruth Warboys, an excellent Ancient Historian professor, and replace her with a twenty-four-year-old boy with slicked-back hair who had a Twitter account. Ruth had hired a lawyer and kicked them down the street, and the twenty-four-year-old had not been heard of again. Young blond WASP boys were right up Professor Lovell's alley, Florence knew: she and George had been at Oxford together and she remembered the time he'd turned up for a formal hall with a black eye, the result of some misread signals from a fellow choral society member at Queen's. George was peculiarly arrogant about his own chances. Florence had noticed unattractive men often were.

But young girls like this Talitha – *Talitha?* – Leafe, that wasn't his area of interest. It just didn't add up.

'We have discussed this at length, Professor Connolly and I. And we also feel the burden of your extra work at the Courtauld, not to mention your penchant for travelling to conferences, as well as your . . . your *behaviour*, well – it might all be compromising you a little.' Professor Lovell shifted in his chair.

'My behaviour?' Florence said, astonished.

'Come on, Florence. You must know what I mean by that.'

'No, I don't.' She screwed up her nose.

'You are a little – unpredictable. Particularly of late.' George tapped his Adam's apple. 'And you have become something of a talking point, with various insinuations . . . and so forth.'

'Insinuations?' Florence could feel a watery sensation flooding her body, making her head spin. 'Do elucidate, George, please. I'm afraid I have absolutely no idea what you mean.'

Professor Lovell bared his teeth with a smile that didn't reach his eyes. 'Come now, Florence. I'm afraid the facts about your workload speak for themselves.' He added, in what was clearly supposed to be a kindly tone, 'Perhaps you've simply taken too much on, my dear.'

'What about Peter taking on too much?' she demanded. 'Since the TV series, and that book, he's never here. And he makes mistakes. I don't make mistakes. You can hardly castigate *me* when your head of department has taken it upon himself to become a media personality, George.'

'That is an entirely different matter,' squeaked George. '*The Queen of Beauty* is an enormous hit. The value to us of Peter being a . . . a . . . "media personality", as you put it, is incalculable.'

'He didn't even get the date of the Bonfire of the Vanities right!' Florence said, trying to stop her voice from rising. 'He was on some silly BBC breakfast programme and he couldn't say when the most notorious event of the Renaissance took place!'

'A lapse,' George said, irritated. 'Live television, Florence. He got it right in the book, didn't he?'

'*Of course he got it right in the book!*' Florence shouted, and then stopped abruptly, and the two of them stared at each other, eyes wide.

Don't say it. Just leave it well alone. She bit her tongue.

'You may scorn it, but what Peter's doing is the future, Florence. Times are tough and your jetting off to London every two months to give up your best research to the Courtauld is not particularly collegiate, is it?'

As news of Florence's Courtauld appointment had come through, it emerged that Professor Lovell had applied for a similar post at the same time – but without success. His speciality – Holman

Hunt – was out of fashion. Florence loathed Hunt, and found it rather satisfying that George couldn't understand why no one else was as interested as he in hyperrealistic, moralising paintings of symbolic goats, fallen women, and ghastly pink and blue babies.

She could see very clearly what this was all about. They were scared of her, so the old boys' club was closing ranks. She reminded herself of what she did, in fact, know, the damage she could do if she just opened the hatch and gave her craziness full rein. She could hear the words forming.

You know I wrote most of Peter's book for him. You know if I were to tell anyone it'd be a scandal big enough to close down the College.

And yet she couldn't do it. She wasn't brave enough. Was she? She wished she had a coffee. She always thought better after coffee. She sat silently, almost slumped in her high-backed chair, listening to George's reedy, precise voice.

'This isn't immediate. We'd want to see a change come January 2013. Dr Leafe is getting married at Christmas, of course, and she starts here in the New Year. She would very much like to meet you, work out a way in which the two of you—'

Florence stood up abruptly. 'Is that the time? I have to go. Do forgive me. I have a meeting with . . .' She stared up at the ceiling, trying to sound calm, and steady. 'Rat controllers. I have rats. Well, George, I shall consider what you say, and get back to you.'

Professor Lovell stuck his fat lower lip out. 'I shall be in touch, if you are not.'

Florence put one trembling hand on the door and took a deep breath. 'Well, we shall talk anon, no doubt, though I warn you I intend to defend my own patch extremely vigorously. Incidentally, your desk has woodworm. Goodbye!'

She even managed a cheery nod as she exited.

She ran until she was out of breath. It was only when she reached the other side of the river that Florence stopped and realised she was shaking, head to toe. She disliked confrontation, almost as much as she disliked mice. She had eschewed teaching and become an academic for that very reason, only to find out too late that the world of academia was like fourteenth-century Florence, riven with internecine strife, internal politics and wordless betrayal. Increasingly these days it reminded her of growing up with Daisy, where she didn't know the rules and couldn't work out when the attack would come. At least the Florentines occasionally massacred each other at Mass, to clear the air. Much more straightforward than all this creeping aggression and stress, which ate away at her, like waiting for one of Daisy's little plots to explode.

Talitha Leafe. What kind of a name was that? With a thrill Florence wondered if this was a legitimate enquiry she could make of Peter.

'Oh, *Peter,*' Florence said aloud, scuffing one

worn shoe on the ancient cobbles. Every single moment of those few weeks that hot summer were imprinted in her mind, like an album of holiday photos, one she could flick through whenever she cared to, which was often. And she always felt quite the woman of the world when thinking about him, about what happened. She liked acting as though things were normal around him, in front of other people especially. The idea people might be gossiping about them thrilled her. *Professor Winter and Professor Connolly? Oh, yes. Apparently they had a fling a few summers ago. He was mad about her, I heard.* Yes, that was how she wanted people to think of her. Florence Winter: dashing, mysterious woman of letters, academic, passionate lover, brainy, vital woman of today.

Something touched her leg; Florence jumped, then realised it was her finger. Her skirt had a hole in the pocket. She scraped her nail on her naked skin. Her legs were hairy; she couldn't remember the last time she'd shaved them. Say if she were to meet Peter, right here, walking down the street as had happened that Tuesday in January. He'd been on his way to dinner with friends in the Oltrarno. Niccolò and Francesca, she'd remembered their names, looked up their address.

Say they'd got talking, then she asked him up for a glass of wine. They'd sit on the roof terrace, a tiny space no bigger than a picnic rug, looking out at the Torre Guelfa and the Arno. Say they'd laugh about George and his peccadilloes, the way they used to, before Peter started freezing her out, treating her like she was an embarrassment. Say then that he'd put his hand on her knee as she said something funny, and laughed. 'Oh, Flo.' He always used to call her Flo and it reminded her of home. 'I miss you. D'you miss me?'

'Sometimes,' she'd say, smiling just a little archly at him; she didn't want to seem girlish.

And say he simply took her hand and pulled her into the bedroom, peeling off her clothes one by one, and say they made love in the warm, terracotta-coloured chamber, the sound of the evening bells in the distance, the sheets rumpled, their faces rosy and glowing with pleasure . . . Say it were to happen, well, he wouldn't care, would he? He hadn't cared before. It had been so lovely, like that . . .

Florence peered up at the blue sky, framed by the black, shadowed buildings, her hands pressed to her burning red face, a secret smile playing on her lips.

Someone laughed and she looked up, almost surprised. Two Charlotte Bartlett-esque tourists, British, she knew it, were staring at her. She hurried on.

Florence lived on the top floor of an old palace, now divided into apartments, on the Via dei Sapiti. Her apartment had once been a prince's chamber and when she'd moved in ten years ago there had been several old pieces of furniture that no one had ever claimed and of which Giuliana, her land-lady, professed to know nothing. Florence liked to think they might have been there for centuries; that perhaps some scheming nobleman had hidden letters in the wedding chest, or a knife under the great wooden chair.

She closed the huge wooden door on the outside world, feeling quite light-headed. She needed coffee, that was it. She wandered into the tiny kitchen. It had a plug-in gas ring, an espresso maker, some dusty packages of pasta and tomato purée, and a vigorous, thickly scented basil plant which, against all odds, flourished on the window-sill. Like the Boccaccio story of Isabella and the pot of basil, which alas always reminded her of yet another awful Holman Hunt painting. It was so typical of someone like George. How could you live here, among this great art, and still admire Holman Hunt?

Florence set the battered Bialetti on the gas ring, and flung open the warped doors that led out to the terrace. She breathed in, as the golden evening sun fell on to her tired face. She could hear chil-dren playing in the street outside.

It was moments like this that she realised how much she loved it here. The sun, the smells, the feeling of being alive, of possibility. When she'd first arrived on a sabbatical, twenty years ago now, she hadn't intended to stay. But her brain worked here, like being plugged into the right socket. How she longed for Italy when she was back in England, where the damp and the grey seeped into her bones and made her feel wet, woolly, soggy. She didn't want to end up like Dad, claw-like hands, pale and gasping for sunshine, or like Ma, shut up, closed off. It was here she had discovered who she was.

Waiting for the coffeemaker to boil, Florence put the books she'd brought home on her desk, staring at the frieze of *The Procession of the Magi*, which she'd Blu-tacked up there herself many years ago. She shivered suddenly, thinking about her meeting with George. Florence was no good with instant reaction; she needed to go away and sift through the data presented to her.

'Think about it later,' she told herself. She'd leave if she had to. Why was she staying here, at this second-rate college, humiliated by men who weren't her intellectual equals? Why did she care so much?

But she knew the answer. Peter. She would always stay while he was here and she thought he might, one day, need her again. Sometimes she wondered if she'd deliberately made him into the engine that kept her pushing along and now it was too late to admit she was wrong. Florence stared at the pictures she'd pinned up, scanning them for something, some message. Her eye fell upon the only one in a frame – the reproduction of her father's favourite painting, *The Annuciation* by Fra Filippo Lippi, which they'd visited every year for her birthday. She gazed at the angel's calm, beautiful face. Something important, buried deep in her conscious, was tapping at the edges of her weary brain. A thought, a memory, something that needed to be salvaged. She looked at the boy again, at the shaft of light on Mary's womb.

What's going on?

The coffee pot rattled on the gas ring, the black liquid bursting like oil from the funnel. Florence poured the coffee and as she took the first scalding sip the doorbell rang, so shrill and unexpected she jumped, and the cup trembled, spilling half the contents on to the floor.

'Bugger,' Florence said, under her breath. She went over to the door, frowning; her fairly eccentric landlady had a habit of waiting until Florence had been back for half an hour, then stomping upstairs, demanding a translation of something, an explanation of something else, an argument with someone.

But it wasn't Giuliana, and as she opened the door her face froze.

'Florence. Hello. I thought you'd be in.'

'Peter?' Florence clutched the door. Had she conjured him up by thinking about him? Was he real? 'What are you doing here?' And she smiled, her eyes lighting up.

'I had to see you,' he said. 'Can I come inside?'

She knew him so well, every inch of him committed to memory for years now through intensive recall and daydreaming. It was often a surprise to her, as now, to note that he was wearing something she didn't recognise. Florence smiled at him as she held the door open, noting the squeak of his new shoes, the faint scent of aftershave. He had made an effort.

'I was just having some coffee.'

'Of course you were.' He gave a little smile.

She blushed; he knew her better than anyone.

Peter cleared his throat. 'I wanted to talk to you, Florence. Have you got anything to drink? I mean, some wine?'

'Absolutely.' Florence shoved her hands in her pockets, to stop herself fidgeting, and went into the kitchen. 'A lovely Garganega, delicious, just like the one we—'

Just like the bottle we had at Da Gemma that evening, when you had the lamb and I had veal. We did drink an awful lot, then we argued about Uccello and kissed afterwards for the first time, and you were wearing that tie with the tiny fleur-de-lis on it, and I had the blue sundress on.

'Sounds delicious. Thanks, Flo, old girl. Listen, I'm sorry to burst in on you like this . . .' Peter followed her into the kitchen. He hesitated. 'God, I haven't been here for a long time. Lovely place you have. As they say.'

He gave a little snort and she did too, almost unable to believe this was happening, that this was real time, instead of some elaborate fantasy she had constructed. *It's not, is it? Am I completely crackers?*

Part of her wasn't sure she should trust him. But she also knew he still felt something for her. She was sure of it. And even if he slapped her now, or told her he'd been married for ten years and wanted her to be godparent to his child, even if he urinated on the floor she could still say that he'd been here, still have some fresh memories to add to that photo album in her head. In fact, she thought wildly, as she ushered him out on to the tiny terrace with a soft push on his back, nothing she owned or thought or had meant as much to her as this, this moment right here.

Peter sat down, folding his gangly limbs into the chair. Florence watched him. Though his mind was the most precise she had ever come across, his body, like hers, seemed constantly to take him by surprise. She put the scratched old tumblers down on the rickety table, and handed him a bowl of olives. He took one, chewed it, threw the stone over into the street.

'Bloody tourists,' he said, as the babble of Japanese from below momentarily stopped. Florence handed him a glass. '*Salute*,' she said.

'*Salute*,' he answered, and he clinked his glass to hers. 'To you. Good to see you, Flo.'

'And you, Peter. We're quite the strangers, these days.'

'I looked for you yesterday. I wanted to ask you about an inscription in Santa Maria Novella.'

'Oh? You should have called me.' She wanted to sound beatific, happy, self-contained, a woman with her own life yet who would always, always be waiting for him.

'Yes. Perhaps I should have.'

There was silence then. Florence stuck her finger through the hole in her pocket again, arched her back and wondered if she could quickly excuse herself to shave her legs. Always be prepared. Her brother, Bill, the Boy Scout, lived by this motto and had tried to impress it upon his chaotic sisters, to little effect.

The bells from over the way rang out, a loud metallic clamour. The sound of a police car faded away in the distance. She breathed in the warm petrolic, pine scent of evening.

'I miss you, Peter,' she said, eventually. 'I'm sorry. I know there's other things going on but . . . I do. I wish—'

And she reached out, to touch his arm.

It was as though she had flicked a switch. Peter jerked his head up and swivelled towards her. 'This is what I mean, Florence. That's why I need to talk to you. It's got to stop.'

'Talk to me . . . about what?'

'You. *You* . . . and me. This lunatic idea you have that there is something between us.' His jowly face was suddenly taut, and he jabbed a forefinger at her. 'The hints, the insinuations you've been making to people. I know you told the chap from the Harvard Institute we'd had an affair. Dear God, Florence! And the Renaissance Studies seminar group. One of them asked me if it was true. I tell you, I will sue you for slander if this goes on.'

Florence tugged at her hair, hanging either side of her cheeks. 'I – what?'

'Do you deny it?'

'I have never told anyone, *anyone*, about our relationship. Peter, how could you?'

Peter's voice dripped scorn. 'It *wasn't* a relationship.' He sank the rest of the wine in one gulp. 'Florence, it was three nights. Four years ago. Don't be ridiculous. That's not a relationship.'

'*Four*,' Florence said, her voice shaking. 'It was four nights. And you said – you said you loved me.'

'No! I *didn't!*' Peter stood up, his face red with fury. 'When will you give up this pathetic fantasy of yours, Florence? I know what you do. You hint and you nod your head and smile, you say these half-sentences, and you make people believe it was something.'

'I have never done that!'

He wiped his mouth, looking at her with disgust. 'Florence, you told Angela that you'd seen my bedroom, but that you obviously couldn't say any more than that. You told Giovanni that we'd discussed getting *married*! But that you weren't keen and he wasn't to mention it! I get a phone call from him asking me if it's true! You *have* to stop this, it's . . .' He searched around, shaking his head. 'It's – it's rubbish! We had three – OK, OK, *four* nights. That's it. Understand?'

There was a terrible silence. 'You d-d-*did* say you loved me,' Florence said after a pause, her voice breaking.

Peter leaned over her. A white spot of spittle glistened on his lip. 'One sentence said after too much wine against five years of total indifference? You're building a case against me based on *that*? Doesn't hold up, Florence.' He waved his long, thin hands at her. 'Don't you mind how damned tragic it makes you look?'

Florence stood up, as though she were stretching. She took a deep breath, and patted his arm. 'Peter. Don't be horrible,' she said. She needed to recast herself. Needed to know this was going to be all right when he left. 'I'm sorry I've made you angry. Obviously some people have . . . got the wrong end of the stick, taken things I've said out of context.' She peeked down at him, then pushed her glasses along her nose. 'Now. What was it you wanted to discuss? Or was that the nub of it?'

'That – yes. And, well, there was something else. It is linked. It's all linked, as you will agree,' Peter said rather grandly, but he glanced at her uncertainly and Florence knew she had the power back, if only momentarily. He was scared of females, that indefinite group of humans with breasts and hormones and bleeding.

'Well, have some more wine,' she said, turning back into the kitchen. She picked up the bottle.

'For God's sake, Florence,' Peter said. His heavy brows suddenly shook with rage. 'Are you actually taking any of this in? Don't twist this all to suit your facts for once. Just listen.'

'Gosh, Peter, how cross you are,' she said, trying to keep her voice light, but suddenly she was afraid. 'Why are you being like this, is it b-because you're a big star these days? And you don't want to be reminded of your past mistakes? Mistakes, Peter. You have made mistakes, haven't you?'

'What does that mean?' He looked up, warily.

They'd never discussed what she'd done for him. Florence bit her tongue, but she was too upset now, and she couldn't stop the words pouring out.

'You know what it means. Remind me . . . how many weeks did *The Queen of Beauty* spend at Number One?'

127

'Shut up.'

'How much have your publishers offered you for your next book?' The questions flew out of her, bitterly, eagerly. 'What did you tell them when they said they wanted the next book to be *just as good as the last book*? Did you tell them you'd have to ask *me* to write another one? Did you tell them that?'

'I don't know what you're talking about,' he hissed, his eyes widening, his face going pale under his tan.

She laughed. She felt quite mad, and really didn't care any more.

'Jim asked me if I'd written it, you know? Out of the blue.'

'Jim?'

'Jim Buxton. At the Courtauld.'

'Oh, come off it. The man's a liar. And an idiot. What Jim Buxton knows about the Renaissance you could write on a matchstick.'

'He knows me. He said he could tell it was my writing, not yours.'

'That's because he wants to sleep with you, I expect. He's always been eccentric.' He looked at her, with disgust, and she almost laughed, it was cartoonish, his revulsion towards her.

'Jim's not—' Florence wrapped her long arms around her body. 'Nevertheless, he specifically asked me if I'd written any of it. Someone gave it to him for Christmas – he wanted me to understand he hadn't bought it himself. I thought that was quite funny. He said the writing style is quite obviously mine, if you're aware of my other work.'

Peter Connolly laughed. 'You're pathetic.'

'No, Peter, I'm not,' Florence told him smartly. She was feeling almost confident again. He couldn't push her around . . . he had to see how much he meant to her now, that she was willing to subjugate herself totally to his needs, already had done. 'You owe me so much, Peter, but you see, I don't mind.' She walked towards him; had she judged this right? 'I like it like that.' She stared up into his face, at the dark, clever eyes, the drooping mouth.

'Oh God,' he said.

'I know,' Florence replied. 'We're even now, don't you see? Darling, I'll do anything for you.'

He pushed her away. Actually shoved her, hard, in the breastbone, as if repelling her like a force-field, and Florence stumbled, catching hold of the rusty railings. 'God.' The revulsion on his face was horrible to see. 'You don't understand, do you? You don't get it.'

'What?' she said.

'What? I'm getting married in a few weeks. Didn't George tell you? Because before Tally arrives we'll need to reorganise the department, and you and I need to discuss how best to do that.' His voice took on a beseeching tone. 'Listen, we worked well together in the past . . . Which is why I thought a one- or maybe two-term sabbatical might be the answer for you. To get you and Tally both used to the situation.'

129

'Tally,' Florence said blankly.

'Dr Talitha Leafe. George said he'd told you.'

'You're marrying *her*?'

'Yes. Once again.' Peter glanced at her, wearily. He jangled his keys in his jacket pocket as if to say, *when will this be dealt with? When can I leave?*

'You can't,' she heard herself say.

'What?'

There was that voice again, pushing her, like a finger jabbing in the back when one is standing on the edge of the precipice. 'If you marry her . . . I'll – I'll tell everyone I wrote *Queen of Beauty*. I'll sue you, Peter. And the publishers.'

'You wouldn't.' He sat back, and laughed. Like he was so confident of his position at the top of the tree, and she some grubby little minion in the shadows. 'Don't be silly. Listen, Tally's at the Sorbonne at the moment. You'll meet her soon. You just need to get used to the idea, understand that some of your responsibilities will change . . . After our marriage she'll move to Florence, and of course George has very kindly done his best to be accommodating, and that means—' He broke off. 'Florence? Florence?'

For Florence had stood up, and walked to the huge old door. She turned and looked at him.

She opened the door, Peter staring at her all the while.

'No. You can't treat me like that,' she said, clearly. 'Not any more.'

'Oh, come on, you can't run off like you always

do—' Peter began, getting up, exasperated, but Florence went out, slamming the door behind her so hard that the whole building shook. She ran downstairs, past old Signor Antonini and his little wife, past Giuliana, wailing loudly in her kitchen to Italian pop. She ran through the old palazzo door, down the street, the balls of her feet bare on the hard old cobbles, her hands deep in her pockets, hair flying behind her. She passed out of the Porta Romana, the ancient gate south of the city. The sun had set now, and the heavens swelled into a deep lavender blue, clouds above her, gold stars pricking at the velvet sky.

As she ran the old memory resurfaced: the day Daisy had pinned her up against the wall and told her where she'd come from. Whispered this filthy, awful stream of stories into Florence's small head, lies about their dad, about the Winters, about everything Florence believed in.

Florence had run away then, too, through the woods at the front of the house that covered the hill and led down to the village. She'd tripped on the brambles twined into the trees, torn gashes in her spindly legs, but kept on going. She'd ended up at the church and sat in the graveyard, hiding behind one of the angels guarding the grave of a child who'd died years ago. She was nine. She'd never been this far away from home on her own before, and she didn't know how to get back.

It was Dad who'd found her, much later that

evening, feet drawn up under her chin, little voice piping out Gilbert and Sullivan songs to keep her teeth from chattering in the cold spring dusk. He'd crouched down, inky hand leaning on the angel.

'What have we got here, eh? Is that my little Flo?' His voice was light but a bit strained. 'Darling, we've been looking for you, you know. Mustn't run off like that.'

Florence had stared at the lichen blooming on the old stone. 'Daisy said you're not my mum and dad.'

David had stopped stroking her hair and looked down at her. 'She said what?'

'She said you're not my mum and dad, that my real mum and dad didn't want me, and that's why I'm here, and I'm not like any of the rest of you.'

David had shuffled closer to her, sideways, like a crab, then put his arm round her thin shoulders. 'Darling. Did you believe her? Is that why you ran off?'

Florence had nodded.

He'd been silent then and Florence was terrified, more afraid than at any time with Daisy. That he was going to say, *yes, it's true, I'm not your daddy.*

She could still remember that feeling now. The black hole of fear that the one person in the world she loved more than anyone else would be taken away from her. That Daisy would win, that she'd have been right.

Her father pulled her head close to his. She could hear him, breathing fast. She held her breath. *Please. Please don't let it happen. Please . . .*

But after a while he simply whispered in her ear, 'That's rubbish. You know you're much more my daughter than she is.' Then he sat back a little. 'Don't tell anyone your old dad said that, hmm?'

'Oh, no,' Florence said, giving a little secret smile, still looking down, but when she stole a glance up at him shortly after, she saw he was smiling too. Then he held out his hand. 'Come back with me? Ma's made a lemon cake and she's been so worried about you. We all have.'

She stood up, brushing the fresh black earth off her pinafore, her tights. 'Not Daisy. She hates me.'

'Wilbur's just died, she's sad about that. Let's be kind to her, though. She doesn't have what we have.' It was the only time he acknowledged it really and she always remembered it. 'Come on. It's time to go home, Flo.'

They trudged back up the road to Winterfold, and as they reached the drive her father had said, 'Let's keep this to ourselves, shall we? You pretend to Daisy she never said anything. And if she does ever say something, tell her to come and see me and I'll set her right.'

There was a tone in his voice then and she nodded. When Dad was angry he was scary, really frightening. Florence wondered if he ever said something to Daisy, because she left Florence alone for a month or two, until the next time, the wasps' nest, which nearly killed Florence, and which she knew she couldn't ever actually pin on Daisy. Daisy wasn't stupid. She'd always known exactly when to pounce.

Eventually Florence stopped running. She collapsed on to a graffitied bench in an old square, filled with bashed-up cars, staring at the cobbles below her. There was no one this time to come and pick her up, to tell her it was all a lie. No one who'd say, 'They're all wrong and you're right.'

She knew her dad hadn't told her the truth. She didn't know how or why, just knew. Daisy was never wrong about things like that and when she'd pinched Florence's arm and said: 'You were a bastard orphan and no one wanted you, little sister, so they picked you off the scrap heap otherwise you'd have been kept in a home,' Florence knew she was right. She didn't know how she'd found out: Daisy knew how to get into secret drawers, how to hear private conversations, how to twist and turn situations to get what she wanted from them.

It struck Florence then, sitting on this bench surrounded by empty Peroni bottles and cigarette butts, the night's chill cooling her sweating limbs, that it was all the same now. She'd been fooling herself again.

She wondered when she could go back to the flat, if Peter would still be there. She wondered how long it had been coming, this realisation that despite how she liked to run away, she'd got it all wrong. How long she'd been kidding herself about her life here, about living away from home. And as she sat with her head in her hands, she wondered if she'd always known that at some point, she'd have to go home and face the truth again. What came next she didn't know.

KAREN

'ello, love. Sorry I'm late. How are you?'
'Oh, hello, Bill.' Karen didn't look up from the couch where she was reading a magazine, or pretending to read. She raised an eyebrow and turned a page. 'How was your day?'

She didn't need to watch to see his little ritual every evening. She knew it off by heart. The way he carefully wound his scarf once around the banister. Always just once. He'd take off his coat, thumb precisely flicking the buttons out, one-two-three in a row. A little shake before deftly hanging it up with one finger. Then, the clearing of the throat and a rub of the hands. That hopeful, kind look on his face.

He wore that expression now. 'Good, thanks, my love. I'm sorry I'm late. Mrs Dawlish . . . she's very shaky since the fall. I paid her a quick visit to drop off the pills and ended up staying on for a cup of tea. And – how about you?'

'Crap. Annoying.' Karen ran one finger over the bridge of her nose up to her forehead.

'I'm sorry to hear that.' Bill picked up the post on the hall table, thumbing carefully through it. She watched him, in silence.

Their marriage was based on silence these days. More and more. What they didn't say was everything, and what they did, inconsequential.

After a minute or so Bill looked up from his credit card statement, his brow furrowed. She could tell he was trying to remember what she'd said, pick up the thread, carry on with the steps of the dance. 'So, what's up? Is it work?'

Karen shrugged. 'They're announcing the redundancies next month.'

His eyes flickered briefly to meet her gaze. 'Are you worried? Surely not. Your appraisal was great, wasn't it?'

She wasn't in the mood for him to be right. 'That was four months ago, Bill. It's a big company. Things change fast. You don't—' She pressed her hands to her cheeks. 'Never mind.' She sounded hysterical, she knew. Sometimes she felt as though she was going mad with it all. 'I can feel a headache coming on. I might go out for some fresh air in a bit. I said I'd drop round Susan's birthday card.'

'Oh, right.' He dropped the little pile of his post on to the bureau and stood behind her, then tweaked one of the cushions on the sofa. 'That's nice.'

'What's nice?' Karen had picked up the magazine again.

'You. Seeing Susan. I'm glad you two are friends again.'

'After I set fire to her hair, you mean?'

'Well, it's nice you have a friend in the village.'

She threw him a glance of amused contempt. 'You make it sound like it's a real achievement.'

Bill went into the kitchen. 'I didn't mean it like that.' He never picked a fight, and it drove her insane. She really wanted him to tell her to shut the hell up and stop being such a cow. To grab her by the shoulders, kiss her and tell her she was in need of a good seeing to. To sweep the damned letters off the stupid hall table and push up her skirt, bending her over the immaculate cream Next sofa, until they collapsed on to the floor, tangled, smiling, his hair ruffled, their warm bodies flushed with the sensation of nakedness. She wanted to see the man she'd fallen in love with, the sweetly awkward, fastidious and kind man who was late for their first date because he'd stopped to help a young mother whose car had broken down by the A36. Who lived to be useful to others, who made himself indispensable, who chuckled with hilarity like a toddler being tickled when he spoke to his daughter, who used to look at Karen as though she was a goddess come to life before his very eyes. Everything was always all right when Bill was in the room.

She blinked, staring into nothing, and then followed him into the kitchen.

'How was your day?' she said, guilt making her attentive. She smoothed her hand over his close-cropped hair.

Bill was rubbing his eyes, tired. 'Oh, all right. I

had Dorothy in again. She's in a bad way. Oh, I bumped into Kathy, she said she'd had Mum's invitation to the drinks on the Friday. Everyone seems excited about there being a party at Winterfold again. Very nice.'

Karen went over to the fridge. 'Supper's ready, in fact. Want a glass of wine?'

Bill shook his head. 'A cup of tea'd be nice first.'

'I'm not making tea. I'm opening wine.'

'Right, I'll put the kettle on then,' he said, imperturbably.

Karen poured herself a drink, her mind already running through the list she kept at the front of her thoughts. She had an early start tomorrow, 8 a.m. train from Bristol to Birmingham for a conference. Suit hanging in spare room. Sandwiches for train. Presentation locked and loaded on laptop. Rick's notes typed up – her boss emailed her all the time, and you had to transcribe it to make sure you'd got everything he'd said. Rick was exacting, to say the least, but Karen liked order. And she liked a challenge, relished it, in fact. Lisa, her best friend back home in Formby, was always saying Karen was born to have children.

'You're the most organised person I know,' she'd said, last time Karen was back home. 'You'd deal with the – Megan, leave it, OK? You'd deal with not being able to take your eye off them, getting everything ready in the morning, knowing how to get one into the bath and give the other his tea. *No! Niall!* You stop that, you little monster. I've had enough of you, I'm telling you. Honestly, Karen, you'd be great . . . any plans?'

Any plans? Any plans? She perfectly recalled Lisa's intense, slightly cultish expression, the one all mothers assume with childless people, like they *have* to understand exactly what it's like because they can have no concept of how wonderful and natural and fulfilling it is. She'd left soon after. But the truth was that what she couldn't forget, what she found more disturbing, was the warmth created by the mess and haphazardness of Lisa's life. Her bungalow near the sea, overflowing with broken toys and discarded clothing. Awful childish paintings stuck all over the place. Silly magnets on the fridge, 'World's Best Mum' and all of that. But it was a home, a safe, welcoming place, and as Karen set the little dining table she looked around her at the life she had created with Bill. She couldn't see how any number of armless dolls and pieces of Lego would make their cottage feel like home.

Karen's parents were divorced when she was ten. She and her mother were both neat freaks, and enjoyed nothing more than having a really good go at the oven. After her mother had been to Winterfold for the first time, just before Karen and Bill's marriage, Mrs Bromidge had grabbed Karen's arm on the way home.

'That fireplace!' she'd said. 'Doesn't it drive them up the wall? All those ashes? It's summer, they don't need to keep it burning, why don't they get a nice fire effect? Or get gas?'

Her daughter couldn't help but agree. Karen often thought the difference between her world and the Winters' was that she believed in gas fires and much of the time at Winterfold seemed to be spent lighting or replenishing the fire in the huge hearth of the sitting room. But she didn't say that to her mother. She had to be loyal to this strange family she'd chosen to enter. She made sure Bill's house had a gas fire, though.

New Cottages was a row of four almshouses down from the church, the house Bill had bought after his divorce. A couple of months before their wedding Karen had, with Bill's agreement, had the place redecorated, so it felt a bit more modern, a bit less like the home of people who wore nylon nighties and smelled of Yardley English Lavender perfume. She'd moved those possessions of hers that weren't already there over from her single girl's flat in Bristol. There wasn't really room for them. It was a tiny house. That first night, over a Chinese and some white wine, sitting on a rug on the new cream carpet because the new sofa hadn't arrived yet, Bill had said, 'If something or someone else comes along, well – we'll have to think about scaling up, won't we!'

He said it in that Bill way – gently joking, with a puckered brow, so that she could never quite tell how serious he was about it. And when, a year and a half later, she'd mentioned it: 'I've not been on the Pill for nearly a year, Bill, isn't it strange nothing's happening?' he'd just smiled and said,

'It'll take a while, I think. You're thirty-three, but I'm old. I'm fifty!' That was what he'd kept on saying. *It'll take a while*. Eventually, like so many things in their marriage, she'd given up. He was so closed-up, like a clam, like his mother. Karen liked Martha, always had. But she didn't know her. She just knew that behind that cool exterior there was something there, some secret storm. But did she ever show it? Course not.

She was getting more and more frustrated, trying anything to get a rise out of him. When, a year ago, Karen had thrown a tea mug at him and the splintering china cut his ankles, Bill said, 'That was a bit dangerous, Karen. Maybe don't do it again.' Six months ago, she'd stormed out, after a row about something so stupid she couldn't even remember it now. She hadn't come back till morning. He'd texted her the next day, at lunchtime.

Do you know where the torch is?

Why was he like this? How could he be so passive? It drove Karen mad. At first she'd tried to change him. Lately, she'd simply stopped trying.

They had dinner in silence, opposite each other at the tiny table. Bill ate methodically, lining up each morsel of food like a balancing act; Karen sometimes found it hypnotic. When the watery garlic butter burst through the meat of the chicken Kiev and landed on his napkin and not his shirt, she was almost disappointed.

She was silent because she'd got used to it. Before, she'd chattered away. Now, it was less effort, less disappointing, to just sit there and eat. Like those couples you saw on holiday, sitting there with nothing to say to each other. She'd think things instead. Wonder about this, or that, her mind racing, her heart pounding at how bad she could be if she pushed herself. It surprised her, she'd never thought she was the kind to have an over-active imagination, and she was in the middle of a mental conversation with him about their sex life when suddenly she heard Bill say, out of nowhere, 'I wonder if Daisy'll come to this thing.'

Karen blinked. 'What thing?'

Bill speared a single pea with one tine of his fork. 'Ma's party. Wonder if she'll even remember it's her own mother's eightieth birthday.'

Karen didn't know quite what to say. 'Course she will, she wouldn't forget a thing like that. Anyway, your mum's asked you to all be there, hasn't she? That odd invitation and everything.'

'I'm not sure. It's typical Ma. It's her strange sense of humour.'

Karen wasn't sure about that. She had the feeling it was more than having a slightly idiosyncratic sense of humour. 'OK then. Well, I'm sure she'll be there.'

Bill opened his mouth, then shut it, then said slowly, 'You don't know Daisy.'

He wants to talk about it. 'Well, I know what you

143

lot say about her. Or rather don't say about her. She obviously loves your mum, even if you and Florence don't like her much.'

'Of course I like her. She's my sister.'

'That's not the same thing.'

Bill sighed. 'I mean . . . there's something there. Despite everything she's done, I still love her. We're family.'

'What exactly did she do, though?'

He shrugged, a classic boy's slump of the shoulders. 'Nothing. She just isn't very . . .' He mashed a clump of peas against his knife. 'She's mean.'

A bark of laughter escaped Karen. 'Mean! What, she used to hide your things and call you Smelly? That's no excuse, Bill!'

'She called me Lily,' he said, staring at the plate. 'Billy Lily. 'Cause she was Daisy Violet and Florence's middle name's Rose, and she said I was the biggest girl of all.' He rubbed his eyes. 'But you're right, it's silly. She didn't do anything terrible—'

'I thought she stole the Guides' money from the bring-and-buy stall at the church fête and spent it on pot?'

'Oh, yeah.' Bill was stroking the bridge of his nose. 'How d'you know that?'

'Sources.' She tapped her nose. 'Lucy told me.'

'How does *she* know that?'

'Your daughter knows everything,' Karen said. 'And she told me Daisy nearly set the barn on fire

144

smoking a joint with some guy from the village when she was back from travelling.'

He stared at her for a second, almost debating whether to have the conversation or not. 'Well, I have to say she was a bit of a druggie before she took off. And she did stuff. I've often wondered . . .' He stopped.

'Wondered what?'

'It sounds rather hysterical if you say it out loud, I'm afraid. Events beyond my control. Although now she's turned into this angelic figure who saves orphans and raises all this money, we're not allowed to criticise her.' He laughed. 'Don't mention that to Ma, will you?'

'You lot are crazy,' Karen said, piling the plates together with a crash and almost throwing them on to the breakfast bar, which connected them with the kitchen. 'Why don't you ever talk about it? I mean, why did she leave in the first place? She never sees Cat. It's mad.' She could hear the Mersey in her voice, coming out the more she spoke. 'And Cat's mad too, while we're at it. Over in Paris and won't let anyone visit her, like she's a leper or something.'

'That's not true. Cat comes home.' She knew Bill was very fond of his niece. 'She's just busy, that's all.'

'She works in a flower market, how's that busy? She used to be some amazing fashion journalist mixing with all these designers and all sorts and now she's selling potted plants, Bill.' She knew she sounded cruel, but just for once she wanted to shake him out of his quiet, repressed complacency. 'She hasn't been home for over three years. Don't you have to wonder what that's about?'

But her husband merely shrugged. 'She had that chap, Olivier, he sounded like bad news. He went off to Marseilles. Had a dog, Luke. Left the dog behind, left Cat to look after him, from what Ma said. The whole thing was a bad business, poor old Cat.' Bill poured himself another glass of wine. 'He was a nasty piece of work.'

Karen found she wanted to scream. 'What does that mean? Was he abusive? What did she need to get over?'

'I don't know, Karen,' Bill said, and he looked sad. 'I feel rotten, that's the truth. Haven't been in touch. Things just slide, don't they?' He rubbed his forehead, staring blankly at the tablecloth. 'Did I tell you about Lucy?' He didn't wait for her answer. 'She wants to write some article about it for the paper. "David Winter's Family Secrets", something like that.'

Karen took a moment to digest this. 'That's what it'll be called?'

He hesitated; she saw the sadness in his face and felt a sharp pain in her heart. 'You know what these newspapers are like; they've learned nothing. They love picking over the bones of . . . things.'

Karen felt herself shivering in the warm room and gave herself a little shake, as Bill leaned forward, on his crossed arms. 'I don't want to

146

say no to her but I'm not sure about it. I don't think it's a good idea, raking it all up. It'll just upset Ma.'

'You say things like that, but I never really know what you mean, Bill,' Karen said. 'Raking what up?' She wished she could keep that note of impatience out of her voice. 'Daisy's selfish, if you ask me. So's Cat. They could come back and they don't. As for Florence, she's in another world. And Lucy – it's about time she got on with her career. She's always saying she wants to be a writer, make it big and all that, and she does nothing about it.' Bill and Lucy's closeness annoyed her now, as it always did when she got cross with Bill, and she wanted to hurt him. The way they laughed at the same stuff, the way his eyes lit up at a cutting she'd send him or a postcard or a cartoon from the *New Yorker*. Lucy had lived with him after the divorce, and their closeness excluded Karen. Lucy was full of life, a breath of fresh air, too big and clumsy for their small house. Karen wasn't part of their world, and she tried not to let it get to her but sometimes it crawled out: a nasty spiteful childish desire to hurt. 'You're the only one who seems to care about your parents. The way things are at the moment just leaves you shouldering everything down here.'

'I'm not shouldering anything.' He smiled sadly. 'I like being here. I like popping in on Ma and Pa. I'm not like the girls. I'm the boring one. I like a quiet life.'

Their eyes met and they stared at each other across the small table. There was a short silence. Karen knew she'd ruined the evening now; perhaps this was the moment to go. She stood up and crossed her arms. 'I'm sorry. I'm tired and it's been a long day. I'm working too hard. Do you mind if I pop out now, drop that card off?'

Bill stayed in his seat, looking down at the grain of the wood.

'Bill?'

After a moment he said, 'It's Susan, is it?'

Her voice trembled. 'Yes, it is.'

He glanced at her. 'Give her my love.'

'I will . . . I will.' Karen turned away, putting her coat on.

'I've been thinking.' Bill sat back, slowly. 'Maybe you need a break. After the party. Maybe we should go to Italy. Florence – we could see Florence. Or Venice. A mini-break in December, before Christmas. Karen? What do you think?'

Her heart was thumping so loud in her chest Karen felt sure he must be able to hear it. She rummaged in her pockets, then reached for her keys, buying time.

'Sure.'

He got up, and came over to her. 'I know things haven't been – I know things are difficult.' She nodded, slowly raising her chin so she was looking straight into his eyes. Her husband. His brown eyes, so solemn, so sweet and kind. A pang of memory shot through her, like a comet, streaking through the darkness, reminding her that she hadn't been wrong, that there had been something there, once. 'We deserve a break, both of us. We could get some practice making that baby,' he said softly, as if it was a secret.

Karen put her hands up to his and they were both still, forearms touching. She breathed in, then out, slowly, trying to suppress the wave of nausea that threatened to sweep over her. *You're a doctor,* she wanted to shout. *Haven't you noticed it's been over three years and nothing's happening in that department?*

Instead she shook her head.

'Maybe.'

'Oh.' He gave a small laugh, and his fingers grasped hers. They were warm: Bill was always warm. 'Maybe's better than nothing, I suppose.'

Karen said, 'I'd better go. Susan'll be—'

'I know,' he said. 'I think I'll probably be asleep when you get back. Long day.'

'Sure. Sure . . .'

Karen picked up the card so carefully propped up on the hall table – more post – and opened the door. Bill said softly under his breath, 'Night then.' And as she walked hastily away, shivering in the sharp autumn night, Karen knew she should have felt free, but she couldn't.

CAT

Cat

I cannot look after Luke that weekend in November. Luke is not my problem any more. You made that clear when you took him away from me. You can't now have it both ways.

If you go and see Didier at Bar Georges in the eleventh he will give you the envelope I meant to give you. Something to help you in it. I think you will find it beneficial.

Olivier

Cat read the email and slammed the laptop shut so hard the corrugated plastic roofing of the stall rattled in the rain. Water dripped off the roof and on to the edges of the ornamental lavenders, the sunny marigolds and geraniums. Tourists huddled miserably against the birdcages crammed with brightly coloured canaries who sang all day, an incessant cheeping noise that filled the air but which Cat had long ago stopped hearing.

She didn't have time to go to see Didier. But

she had to. He'd got her, again. She had to get back to Winterfold, and the price of the train ticket was, these days, beyond her reach. But even the thought of going back to the eleventh made her angry, and afraid. It was the idea that Olivier still had the power to drag her back to her old life.

Once, Cat had lived not far from the eleventh, before she met Olivier, and if she could have seen herself now she'd have been astonished at who she would become. She had had a year of unemployment sprinkled with gardening jobs after university, until the magical day when she'd heard she'd got the job as Editorial Assistant on *Women's Wear Daily*. It came after months of job applications, which had severely tested Cat, shy at the best of times, violently full of self-doubt and lanky awkwardness at the worst. When the letter arrived at Winterfold (she'd kept that letter, the one that brought her here. It seemed so quaint now, a *letter*) offering her the position, Cat had jumped up and down in the hallway, then clung to her grandmother, almost hoping Martha might beg her not to go. Even though all Cat had ever wanted to do was live in Paris and this job was more than she could ever dare to hope for, it still seemed too hard, too much to have to leave this place where she felt so safe, where she had been, she thought, so happy. She'd been away, to university in London, though that had been nothing, really, but extended periods where she always knew she was coming back to Winterfold. This was different. She was twenty-two, and this was the beginning of real life.

'I don't want to leave you both. I don't want to . . . do a runner. Like Daisy.' Saying her mother's name was always strange. The 'D' sang out, like a bell, and she felt as though strangers might turn and stare. 'Oh . . . it's *that* girl. Daisy Winter's daughter. Wonder how *she'll* turn out.'

But her grandmother had been surprisingly firm.

'You're not your mother, darling. You're nothing like her. Besides, you're not some recluse who's never left home. You've spent three years in London, you've got a degree, and we're so proud of you, darling girl. But I think this is the right thing to do. Don't be afraid of going. Just make sure you come back.'

'Of course I'll come back . . .' Cat had laughed, and she remembered that bit, how ridiculous it had seemed that she might not return to Winterfold, but at the same time she knew her grandmother was right. Her friends were all getting jobs, moving on, it was time for her to do the same.

She arrived in Paris in the spring of 2004, a little unsure, already homesick. She found an apartment not far from Café Georges, on a little *cité* behind Boulevard Voltaire. She had four window boxes, which she carefully tended, one tea trunk from home, which stood in as a coffee table, an IKEA bed, a chest of drawers her grandmother and

Uncle Bill brought over a fortnight later in the car, two hat stands from a market in Abbesses with wire strung between each for use as an open wardrobe, and a set of ten wooden hangers stamped 'Dior', acquired the same day. She loved playing house, her first proper grown-up home. It made her feel independent, for the first time in her life.

Her bare, beautiful flat was usually unoccupied, though. She was either in the office, or out with her boss taking notes at meetings with designers, visiting studios for private views or, during the bi-annual Fashion Week, dashing from show to show, sitting in the back row with the other penniless fashionistas, scribbling notes and trying to learn as much as she could. Her favourite part of her job, though, was calling on the individual ateliers and watching the stout, middle-aged Parisian seamstresses who had worked at Dior for years, seeing their flying fingers sewing the hundredth sequin of a thousand on to a shimmering, glittering fishtail train, pinning a tiny tuck-seam on a model's silk shirt, sliding butter-thick velvet through their machines, tidying, smoothing, finishing, their quick fingers transforming an inert piece of fabric into something magical.

Cat grew to find the world of fashion ridiculous but never this, the beating heart of the business. It was why she had always loved gardening with her grandmother, for she already knew that creating a beautiful vision to be enjoyed by others meant hard graft behind the scenes. Everything had to be perfect, even a seam that no one would see, because if it was to be done it must be worth doing. Her grandmother had always said there was only one rule to gardening: 'The more care you take, the greater the reward you'll reap.'

She sent Martha regular updates, letters and then emails. At first, Cat hardly went back, maybe because she loved the place too well, and a clean break seemed better than constantly revisiting, but then, as her life in Paris took root, the trips home became more spaced out. In the beginning, Martha had come to visit once a year; that had been wonderful. They'd shopped in Galeries Lafayette, walked in the Parc Monceau, strolled through the Marais.

Her grandmother had asked Cat once, as they wandered by the Seine, looking at the vintage prints and books for sale: 'Are you happy? Do you like it here? You know you can always come back, don't you?'

Cat had simply said, 'Yes, darling Gran. I love it here. It . . . it fits.'

Martha had said nothing, just smiled, but Cat had seen tears in her eyes, and thought she must be thinking about Daisy. Out of the ashes of nothing except her grandparents' love and her grandmother's insistence that Cat must make something of herself, she had fashioned this life, and when she told Martha that it fitted her, she knew it was true.

Then she met Olivier.

One sultry June day, in a *boulangerie* around the corner from her apartment. So Parisian, so romantic. 'We met in a *boulangerie* in Paris,' she told the girls in the office, smiling, her cheeks rosy with shy happiness. 'Olivier was buying croissants, I was buying Poilâne, we picked up the wrong bags – *voilà*.' Appearances can be deceptive – Oliver didn't eat bread, it transpired, he had been collecting the pastries for a friend. She only wondered when it was all over who the friend was. A girl, waiting in bed for him while he picked up someone else. He had said, 'I like your dress, English girl,' and Cat had turned to give him a sharp, colloquial put-down, and been arrested by his tousled black hair, his brown eyes, his beautiful pink mouth with the amused smile playing about it. He was a jazz trumpeter, played every week at the Sunset, and had his own group. They were trying to make it work. He was good, she could just tell.

She was ashamed – or a little proud, she didn't know afterwards which – to recall that they had slept together that very day. Yes, he had taken her out for coffee, and she had said she would buy him a glass of wine that evening, and so after work they had met in a little bar behind the Palais-Royal, in a cellar that was supposed to be part of Richelieu's old palace. They had both ordered a kir, picked at a plate of *saucisson* and cornichons, and after two drinks he had simply said, 'I do not want to drink any more. Will you come home with me?'

His apartment was tiny, the shutters flung open, the sound of people carousing, arguing, singing floating up from the street below all night, as they came together in a way she had never known she needed before. Cat was organised, controlled: she feared more than anything else being like her long-lost mother, a woman who had so little clue of how to live her own life she had had to leave everyone behind, go to the other side of the world to help people worse off than she was.

So at first, she was horrified to discover, three years after moving to Paris and establishing her life so beautifully, that everything had collapsed, like a pile of cards. That Oliver's strong, smooth hands, cupping her breasts and moving up her arms till his fingers twined with hers, his knee pushed between her legs, his lips on her neck, his words in her ear . . . filthy wet words that made her moan, that all this could quite simply, unman her – un-woman, in fact, although she had never felt more womanly, never felt so sensuous and sexy all her life. The rest of that summer was forever in her mind, an ache between her legs, where she wanted him inside her all the time. She grew pale and stringy: while her workmates were tanned from holidays, the sea, the outdoors, Cat was inside with Oliver, whole weekends lost in a haze of sex, sleeping, eating,

156

the whole cycle over again. She was so happy, she felt like a new person, reborn here in Paris with him. He had not known her as the spotty awkward thin teenager, the girl without a mother. He only saw her as the person she had remade herself into and he loved that person, or so he said, and so she loved him for it, even though all the time she kept wondering: *when will he find me out?*

Afterwards she would look back and see how short a time the happiness had actually lasted. By winter the signs were all there but she chose to ignore them. It made her sick, how stupid she had been. What was crazy was for how long she let it go on.

How foolish she'd been, she saw that now, too. In the New Year she'd given up her flat, moved in with Olivier. She had gone home for Bill's wedding in 2008. To everyone's sly enquiries, and Lucy's open enthusiasm, about this mysterious boyfriend, Cat was noncommittal. And they didn't ask more. She had been a low-key, sardonic person for so long now that her lack of cosy titbits about life with her French boyfriend didn't surprise anyone. 'Typical you,' her aunt Flo had said. 'You always were a dark horse, Cat.'

But I'm not, Cat had wanted to tell them. *I think I've made a terrible mistake.*

At the reception back at Winterfold, after the curious wedding in the Guildhall, she was trying to text Olivier, wondering what he'd want her to say. She felt something gripping her arm, and she jumped, scared. It was her mother, it was Daisy.

Cat looked down at Daisy's tiny, skeletal fingers, pressing into her arm.

'I'm just trying to send this text.' She was short. She hated this, being here, feeling so out of place.

Daisy had leaned forwards, skull-like face mirroring Cat's.

'Don't try and pretend I'm not your mother, Catherine. We're the same. I know it. I see it in you. We're exactly the same, so stop thinking you're better than me. You're not.'

The scent of lilies in the cool dining room; Karen's white dress, flashing in her peripheral vision; the hot sun outside, beating down on the yellowing grass. Her mother's voice, hoarse and silvery. 'I know what you're like, Cat. Stop fighting it and get on with it.'

Cat had removed Daisy's fingers from her arm. She'd leaned back, away from her thin, awful face. 'If I'm like you, God help me too,' she'd said, and walked towards the open door.

That had been the last time she'd seen her. Cat went back to Paris knowing she couldn't ever tell any of them what was really going on. She just had to make the best of it, because she was lucky, wasn't she? It was wonderful, wasn't it? She had such high expectations, because of her mother, because of everything, and she should just stop being so difficult, as Olivier said, and shut up.

And it was such a boring cliché. The gradual change, so that within months she had gone from glorious certainty in his love to absolute certainty that he despised her and that he was right to. The sudden absences, the unexplained behaviour, the hours she'd spend waiting for him, only to have him turn up angry at her, because he said she'd gone to the wrong place. She lost all confidence in her ability to make decisions. How often, when evening fell and she grew hungry, had she stood dithering in the hall about whether to start cooking for him? Was he nearly there, would he want some food? Or would he be back hours later, and shout at her for letting his meal go cold? 'How the fuck am I supposed to eat this . . . this shit, Catherine? You're so selfish, you couldn't wait another hour? What, OK, an hour and a half? So I met some friends – they're important contacts – I'm supposed to rush home because if I don't I'm not allowed any supper?' He always made it sound like he was right, and she always ended up apologising.

They acquired a dog, a wire fox terrier called Luke, after Olivier's English grandfather, a soldier who stayed on in Brittany. When Cat laughed at this – naming your pet after your grandfather seemed a crazy thing to her to do – Olivier slammed out of the apartment, and didn't come back till the following morning. At first, he was obsessed with Luke, as though he were a son, or a new best friend – taking him for walks in the

Tuileries Gardens, even once to a gig, where Luke sat obediently on a chair next to his trumpet case, Olivier exclaiming with pleasure when Luke did *un caca* on the parquet floor – but soon, as Cat was realising, as with everything in Olivier's life, the obsession waned, to be replaced with disinterest, annoyance and then downright contempt. Luke, still not quite a year old, did not understand why, when he trotted over to his master and stared hopefully at him, he was ignored or batted away with one big, hairy hand. '*Vas-y! Vas-y*, you stupid dog.'

It was through Luke that Cat started to realise what a mistake she'd made, but it was longer still before she saw that it wasn't her mistake – that he had hoodwinked her. She was worthless to him except as a pretty plaything and once that bored him she – like Luke – was of no use. On the day that changed everything, she had coffee with Véronique, an old, very dear friend from work. They had once been almost the same: girls with long brown hair and fringes who giggled together over male models at the shows, saw each other into cabs after one too many glasses of champagne, they had struggled up flights of stairs with each other's boxes, moving into tiny apartments, they had slept on each other's couches and shared lunches. But these days Véronique was almost a parody of everything Cat should have become. She had worked at *Women's Wear Daily* and was now at *Vogue*.

She had shiny, glossy hair, patent leather Marni sandals, a black Paul & Joe chiffon top finished off with a tailored pink blazer and matching baby-pink nails. Cat, who barely cared what she looked like these last few months, was in dirty jeans, pulled-back ponytail and blue Breton-striped top. She couldn't be bothered to dress. She felt sick all the time, a tight nausea at the back of her throat, she wasn't hungry and she couldn't sleep.

'What the hell is wrong with you?' Véronique had said immediately. When Cat had tried to explain, she'd shrugged her shoulders in horror. 'Why are you still there? Leave, for God's sake, Catherine! This man is . . . he's killing you, slowly. What if you have children with him?'

A tear had run slowly down Cat's cheek. She brushed it away.

'I know,' she said. 'I had a miscarriage six months ago. He was glad. I was too, after a while, and now . . .' She started crying, pressing the heel of her palm into her eyes, keening forwards and backwards, uncaring of who might see her.

After a while she said, 'Sometimes I wish he'd hit me. To prove it. Maybe I deserve it.'

Véronique leaned back, as if she'd been hit herself, and there was a silence.

She didn't leave him that day, nor that week, but once the words were out, it became something tangible. The look on Véronique's face – of complete bewilderment, pity, a tiny flicker of disdain was the closest she could come to describing it – was almost a wake-up call: the two of them had once been so close, not just in temperament but in stages of life.

When it was all over Cat could see how lucky she had been. She had got out before he'd sucked her further in. She had nothing else, and so much water had flowed under the bridge, the many bridges, that she could not, now, ever, ring up her grandmother and explain. Martha, who had been so proud of Cat, who had raised her to be like her, not like her mother.

The last time Cat saw Martha was before Christmas, a year ago, when she came over for lunch, for some Christmas shopping and 'to see you, darling, because I feel I don't know anything about your life now'.

They met in Abbesses, and ate *confit de canard* in a dark red bistro with views over the city. It was very different this time. There was so much Cat couldn't tell her grandmother, now. Something huge had happened to her, and somewhere along the way that had meant cutting everyone else out to try to cope with it.

Cat said as little about herself as she could. They walked around the shops in a desultory way until the time, which had dragged, abruptly came for Martha to leave if she was to make her train, and then she was gone. But Cat couldn't help but keep with her, the gloved hand on her arm. The whisper in her ear. 'We're always here when you need us, darling. Never forget that.'

Then the desire to blurt it all out had nearly overwhelmed Cat. To sob on her grandmother's shoulder, tell her about Olivier, about Luke, Madame Poulain, about how she had nothing, how she sometimes missed lunch, how she had taken two pieces of bread off the table for later. How she was doing everything wrong and couldn't just change one thing, needed to start again completely to have any hope of unpicking the tangled threads of her life.

But at the fatal moment Martha had, gently, for a split second, looked away, then at her watch, and –

'I must go, darling. Are you sure you're all right? Tell me, you will always tell me, won't you?'

'Yes, yes.' She had kissed her grandmother again, saw the tiny chink of light closing. 'Please don't worry about me. How can anyone be unhappy, living here?'

The scudding December clouds, the twinkling fairy lights golden in the gathering gloom, the soaring towers of Notre-Dame and the honk of the bateau-mouche below as Cat watched Martha hurrying towards the Métro, and she turned for home, alone again, knowing that something had changed. Too much water had passed under the bridge now, and she could never really go back. This was her life, whether she had chosen it or not.

The following afternoon, Cat opened the door of the Bar Georges, just off the rue de Charonne. Despite her misgivings about returning, she liked the eleventh; real Parisians lived there, families – it reminded her of a happier time in her life. She checked her watch, always making sure she wouldn't be late for Luke. Forty minutes. Twenty minutes here, twenty to get back.

She waved hello to Didier, the owner, and took a seat at the bar.

'*Ça va, Catherine?*' Didier was polishing coffee cups, and expressed no surprise at seeing her after three years. '*Un café?*'

'*Non, merci.*' Cat spoke in French. 'Didier, I had an email from Olivier yesterday. He said you have an envelope for me.'

Didier nodded. 'Yes.' He carried on polishing the cups.

'Well . . . can I have it?' Cat said, trying not to sound impatient.

'He's pretty sad, Catherine,' said Didier. 'You have been very cold.'

Cat closed her eyes, very slowly. 'Huh-uh,' she said. She nodded. *Don't get cross.* She pictured herself, like a woodlouse, rolling up into a tiny ball, no part of herself visible or vulnerable. *Think of what you have to do.*

Didier reached under the cold white marble bar. He produced a square brown envelope. Cat stared at it; it was thick. 'This is it?' she said, but she knew the answer. Her name was on the front, the handwriting she knew so well.

'Yes.'

'So, you saw him?' Cat asked.

'I was down in Marseilles, for the jazz festival. He asked me if I could help. I was glad to.' Didier slid the envelope across to her.

Cat didn't know whether to open it in front of Didier or not, though her hands were shaking. In the end, she stood up and, clutching the envelope, waved it in front of him. '*Merci, Didier. Au revoir.*'

'You don't care how he is?'

She stopped, and turned. 'Olivier?' She wanted to laugh. 'Um – yes of course. Does he care? About us?'

'Of course he cares,' Didier said, looking faintly disgusted. 'How can you say that?'

'Evidence suggests otherwise.'

'You are the one who left him.'

Cat stood perfectly still. 'I was pregnant,' she said.

'Yes, and—'

She cut across him. 'He nearly broke me.' She said it very quietly, so quietly she wondered if Didier would hear. 'He would have done the same to – to Luke.'

'He loved that boy. Like he loved that dog, and you—'

Cat shook her head. 'No, this is wrong, you are

165

wrong,' she said. Already she was terrified that Olivier was here somewhere, that he'd demand to see Luke, that he'd follow her home like before, that this was a trap. 'He chose his name. I let him call him after his stupid dog, don't you see how crazy that was? Don't you see I'd have done anything to keep the peace? To stop him . . .' And it didn't matter now, it didn't matter at all, but when she thought of any of it, it made her remember how low she had been. She had to leave. She had to get out of here, get back to her son now. She waved the envelope. *'Au revoir.'*

'C'est pour Luke,' she heard him call as she banged the door behind her, stepping out on to the narrow street.

Fingers fumbling, Cat pulled open the sticky glue, tearing into the thick paper. She felt ridiculous, desperate as she was, standing on the street unable to wait until she got home. Her hands rested on something smooth, not crinkly and rough as she'd expected. She pulled out . . . a piece of cardboard. Thick, corrugated, plump cardboard, with a heart drawn on it in a wobbling line of Biro, arrows shooting out of it, dripping with blood.

Underneath he'd written:

YOU DID THIS. I HOPE YOU ARE HAPPY.

Her first reaction was to laugh. How pathetic. Then anger gripped her, anger that he could yank her around like this, like a dog on a lead. She could hear him, laughing at her now. She looked up and around, as if expecting to see his dark face, leering out at her from an upstairs window. He'd always loved 'practical' jokes, tricking people. He was laughing at her stupidity, at how she thought she was free but she wasn't, because she'd still drop everything to collect a package from him.

She was like a dog, like a whipped dog; that's what he'd called her the day after Luke had run away, out into the street, never to be seen again. The old Luke. 'You're my dog now,' he'd said, and he'd gripped her by the throat, and pushed bread into her mouth until she gagged, and managed to break free.

Cat threw the cardboard into the gutter.

The voices in her head, calling out for her to do something stupid, go back to Didier and scream at him that his friend was a beast, that he had made her like this, he had ruined any chance he had with his son, were rising again. With a supreme piece of self-control she ignored them. She scuffed her shoes on the dirty streets, feeling with every scrape on the ground that she was somehow wiping Olivier from her feet. When she reached the Métro, she banged open the plastic ticket barrier, and walked downstairs on to the platform, hugged herself, pulling the thin cardigan around herself so no one else could see she was shaking.

★   ★   ★

After all that, she was early. She knew where she'd find them. Just before the Pont Marie, in the little Jardin Albert Schweitzer. As she approached, Simone, the mother of Luke's friend François, looked up from her magazine.

'*Bonjour, Catherine.*' Cat nodded, smiling.

'*Merci beaucoup, Simone.*'

Simone smiled, a little stiffly. She was one of the many people to whom Cat owed a huge debt, one she would never be able to repay. Using up their goodwill when Madame Poulain's was exhausted. Relying on the kindness of strangers, people to whom she could never fully explain her situation.

'Maman!' She looked up at the sound of his voice, the thudding steps, the feeling of hurtling towards happiness that was always, always the best part of her day. 'Mum, Mum, Maman!'

He threw himself into her arms, her little Luke. His thick dark hair, his hard little body, his babbling chat, his sweet, high-pitched voice, caught between English and French, all the time, as she was.

He was hers, all hers. And he was all that mattered.

'Maman, Josef eat a snail last week! He eat a snail!' She wrapped her arms around him, as tightly as she could, brushed her lips on to his forehead.

'Ate, my love.'

'Ate. Can we have pasta for tea?'

At the memory of her sad self standing on the pavement scrabbling to open an envelope that wasn't full of money, but a patronising pawn in

168

Olivier's little game, suddenly Cat felt something lifting up and away, and floating out over the road, out to the Seine, away with the churning river. Something that made her feel free. She said goodbye to Simone, and she and Luke crossed the road towards the bridge that would take them back across to the island. She clutched Luke's hand, so tightly that he shook her arm.

Everything was getting better. She saw it now. It could be good again, one day. She kissed his hand. It was a victory of sorts, for someone who'd had the fight knocked out of her a while ago.

That evening, Cat crept quietly out of the *chambre de bonne* and downstairs to the kitchen. Madame Poulain was out playing bridge, as she was every Tuesday evening: it was the one time of the week Cat had to herself. Free from the little room she shared with her son, sweltering in summer, freezing in winter, free from Madame Poulain's vermouth-soaked ramblings, free from the backaching work when she had to stay late at the market. Sometimes she watched boxed sets that Henri lent her – she was very into *Game of Thrones* at the moment – but it was strange, watching episode after episode of *Spiral* or *The Wire* on your own. Usually, she read. She made herself an omelette and salad and ate in a daze, staring out of the window at the dark of the Seine and the glistening lights of the Left Bank. Not really thinking; just letting her whirling brain slow down a little.

Then she curled up in the big armchair with a glass of wine and a green Penguin she'd been given by one of the booksellers on the river bank, a nice old chap she said good morning to whenever she crossed the bridge. More and more she found herself drawn to the novels of her childhood, the books that filled the upstairs shelves at Winterfold: Edmund Crispin, Georgette Heyer, Mary Stewart.

Cat was utterly absorbed when the phone rang, and she looked at the screen with annoyance: Henri was always ringing to check up on his mother.

But no. *Appel international.* International call. *'Allô?'*

A hesitant voice down the line: 'Cat? Oh, hello, Cat!'

Cat paused, her wine glass halfway to her mouth. No one ever called her on Madame Poulain's landline.

'Who's this?'

'It's Lucy. Oh good. Your mobile was switched off. I didn't even know if this number would work. I'm sorry, are you in the middle of something?'

Lucy's voice, the same as always: how could she not have recognised it straight away? Cat put the book down and said, cautiously, 'No, it's lovely to hear from you. How – how are you?'

'Good, good. Thanks.' Lucy hesitated. 'I think I'm living round the corner from BO Bee Man, though. That was partly why I rang, actually.'

'No way.'

'Way. He's got the T-shirt and everything.'

Incredulous, and yet wanting to believe it true more than anything, Cat asked, 'Is it black and yellow?'

'Sure is.'

BO Bee Man was a regular fixture of their seaside holidays in Dorset. He appeared on the beach at midday, clad always in black jogging bottoms, a black baseball cap, a black and yellow bumblebee-style T-shirt and big black specs. He was about twenty-five stone, and walked very slowly up and down the promenade. Lucy once claimed she saw him weeing on a chained-up dog, but Cat never believed this. Lucy was a bit of a fantasist.

Cat snuggled tighter into the chair. 'That is so random. Where do you see him?'

'On the way into work. He's got massive foam headphones. He listens to Bon Jovi and Guns 'n' Roses at full blast.'

At that, Cat couldn't help but laugh, the tightness in her throat releasing just a little. 'Please, *please* take a photo of him,' she said. 'You have to.'

'I'll try and catch him unawares. He usually walks past while I'm going down the Kingsland Road.'

'Dalston? What on earth are you doing round there, Luce?'

'Well, I live there,' Lucy said. 'It's lovely.'

'Get away. Dalston was like murder row when I lived in London.'

'How long have you been away?' Lucy said, sounding cross. 'Eight years? Dalston's like . . . it's the new Hoxton.'

'Don't I feel stupid,' Cat said mildly.

There was a pause.

'Listen,' Lucy said, sounding embarrassed. 'I won't keep you. I just wanted to know if you're coming back for Gran's thing next month.'

'Um – I hope so.' Cat hesitated.

'Oh.'

Cat could hear the disappointment in Lucy's voice, and she knew how much it must have meant for her to ring, and how much she missed her, and she said, 'I'm coming, yeah. Absolutely. I just need to book my ticket and – sort out a few things.'

'Oh, right!' She sounded so pleased, and Cat felt the warmth of being wanted, loved even, running through her veins. 'That's so great.'

'Thanks!' Cat said, almost gratefully. Then she added, curiously, 'Um, what was that strange stuff on the invite about, do you know?'

'Not sure.' There was a small silence. Cat wished there was a button she could press, to take her straight into the groove she and Lucy had once had, the easiness that seemed to pick up where they'd left off every time: holidays, bank holidays, Christmas. Clare, Lucy's mother, was often away, and so then Bill took Lucy to stay at Winterfold. Every summer there was Dorset as well, a cottage of an old friend of their grandparents on Studland Bay. They had so much fun, that was the thing. They were both only children and, though there were a few years between them, they loved being together, were more like sisters than cousins for a while. Lucy, bold and imaginative, invented the plays they put on, and the songs they sang. Cat could make anything, headdresses for a story about Greek gods, bushy leafy tails for *The Lion, the Witch and the Wardrobe*, and the one time when she really got in trouble: the summer of Cutting Up Her Mother's Dresses for Dolls' Clothes.

Martha had been furious – alarmingly, frighteningly furious – when she came into Cat and Lucy's room just after the school holidays had begun and found them crouched over Daisy's frocks, fixing pieces of fabric together with David's huge industrial-sized stapler. Cat had never seen her grandmother upset like this. The lines of her grandmother's sculpted, delicate features were drawn into a rictus of rage: nostrils flared, thin eyebrows arched, teeth bared, like a hissing, angry cat.

'This was her room. She left those dresses for you, Cat. When she left. You remember?'

'Course I don't remember. I was a month old.'

'Don't be cheeky.' She thought her grandmother might slap her. 'She left them for *you*, she said they weren't to be shared with anyone else and she certainly didn't mean for you to ruin them. How – how *could* you?' Martha had picked up the curved offcuts of useless fabric in handfuls, letting them fall through her fingers. 'The only things, the *only* things she gave you, she wanted to be yours, and you've ruined them. I can't – no, I can't.'

Glassy pools of tears wobbled in her cold eyes, and she had turned and walked out.

Cat had had to stay in her room for the rest of the day and night, alone, while Lucy slept in her father's room on the floor. The long Laura Ashley seventies floral robes, like a medieval princess might wear, the demure violet velvet sheath, the white lace confirmation dress, the printed silk sundresses, all in little pieces, were taken away and Cat never saw them again. The holidays passed as they always did, in a constant carousel of silly voices, funny dances, hidden treasure, songs they changed the lyrics to and sang over and over.

But something changed then too. The result of the episode with the ruined dresses was that Cat never really talked to her grandmother her about her mum any more.

After a pause, Lucy said, 'If I'm totally honest? Things are a bit weird down there. That invitation's only part of it.'

Fear clawed at Cat's stomach as she said, 'I thought it sounded a bit odd. The way it was worded.'

Lucy paused. 'Well, Gran must have something to tell us all, mustn't she?'

'Is she OK?'

'I think she is. I mean, she's going to be eighty.' Lucy drew in her breath. 'I think Southpaw's a bit crook these days.'

'Really? How? What's wrong? What's he . . .' But the words died on her mouth. *Come home and see for yourself.*

'It's not about him, really.'

175

'What's it about?' Cat said. She tried to keep her tone level, but she thought she might be shaking. She couldn't tell. She was scared, though. Lucy was like the gate back into Winterfold, into a world Cat had to keep shut out.

Lucy took a deep, ragged breath. 'Oh, Cat, I don't know. The more I think about it all . . . maybe I shouldn't say.'

She sounded miserable, and Cat felt a rush of sympathy for her.

'Hey, Luce,' she said. 'Don't tell me if you don't want.'

'It's about my dad. Dad and Karen. I'm worried about him. Well, about her, really.'

'What do you mean?'

'Something's going on.' Lucy clicked her tongue. 'I think – I heard her on the phone, last time I was down. Talking to someone. She's having an affair, I'm sure.'

'Oh, no, Luce.' Cat put down her drink. 'Really? Could it have been your dad?'

'Dad was in the bath. Singing along to *The Gondoliers*. And I know it wasn't him. You could just . . . tell.' Lucy's voice grew distant. 'She sounded really excited. Happy. She hasn't sounded like that for ages . . . Oh, poor Dad. I knew she'd do him wrong,' Lucy said, angrily. 'I bloody knew it, the moment I met her.'

'I liked Karen,' Cat said. 'Can't you – talk to her? Maybe you've got the wrong end of the stick. Do you have any idea who it might be?'

'No,' said Lucy. 'I thought it might be this guy Rick at work; she's always going on about him.'

'Who is he?'

'Her boss. And she said something about giving him HR problems with his work . . . how she didn't want him to get into trouble because of her. In this awful flirty voice. Yuck. It probably is him, you know . . . he's a creep. But . . . Oh, I don't know.' She gave a big swallowing sound. 'Just . . . I don't know what to do. And I feel as though if I could just talk to Dad, gently explain it . . .'

'Sometimes there isn't anything you can do, Luce,' Cat said. 'You've always worried too much about your dad. He'll be fine.'

It was the truth and, as so often with the truth spoken aloud, it hung in the air, like a sign written by a skywriter. They were both silent.

'You're right.' Lucy muttered. 'Look, I'm sorry. I didn't mean to ring you up and pour my guts out to you, you know, Cat. I just wanted to ask if you were coming back. And, you know, say hi and everything. How's . . .?' She hesitated. 'How's life?'

'It's good. How's things with you?'

'All right. I can't complain.' Lucy sounded flat. 'It's fine. I'm lucky to have a job, I keep telling myself that. And, yeah. You know. Flat has mice and my flatmate's cat won't catch them. Love life's a disaster. Except for this guy who's just started at the pub, you'd love him, I've already got a huge crush on him.' Lucy talked when she was nervous, Cat knew.

'He works at a pub in Dalston? Is he a hipster? Moustache? Weird rolled-up trousers?'

'No, Cat! The Oak, in Winter Stoke! Joe, he's the new chef. He's won a Michelin star before. He's gorgeous. And . . . shy. So shy you can't get him to say a word. He's got these dark blue eyes, and they look at you like—'

Cat interrupted. 'The Oak? The grottiest pub in the world? Why's he working there?'

'It's been completely done up. It's sad, though; no one's going there. I've told Joe I'll get Jeremboam Tugendhat to review it. He's the food critic at the *Daily News* and he's got a crush on me. Or rather, he's an old perv who likes taking young women out to lunch. I said I'd go with him in early December, that's the next slot he's got free. If he starts wrestling with my jeans I'll have Dad on speed dial and he can come and duff him up.'

Cat smiled, though she couldn't imagine her lovely uncle Bill dashing into a pub and punching someone's lights out. 'Are you going to ask Joe out?'

Lucy gave a shout of embarrassment. 'Not likely! He'd never go for me. I mean, he's really nice to me and all, but he's very sad. He misses his son. He's got a son. He doesn't say much either, that's the trouble. Anyway, enough of him, I'll keep you posted. Maybe I *should* ask him out . . . Don't know. So, how are things with you, Cat?' she said, not drawing breath. 'I wish I'd called you sooner. It's been too long. You know—'

'Oh,' Cat said hastily. 'Thanks. Things are good.' She knew how to deflect. Give just enough information away so they didn't think to ask about the important things she kept secret. 'It's still really warm. I love it here this time of year, less tourists, and Madame Poulain is better when the summer's over.'

'You and that crazy old woman, it's so funny. I never understand it.'

'Oh, I like to keep myself mysterious, Luce. I'm really a spy.'

'Ha! That's funny . . . actually, it is funny you should say that. 'Cause I do want to ask you something for an article.'

'So you're writing stuff for them, then? That's great.'

'Just this, so far. I have to actually produce something first.' Lucy stopped. 'Maybe it can wait till you're back next month. You're busy.'

Cat took another sip of wine. 'No, go on. I'm not doing anything.'

'Well . . . OK. I want to ask you about your mum.'

Cat said, 'What about my mum?'

There was a silence and she could hear Lucy, who never had an unexpressed thought, working out what to say next. 'Don't know if the phone's the best way to do it.'

She's still so young, Cat thought to herself. How can she be only three and a bit years younger than me? I feel like an old, old woman.

'I'm writing an article about Daisy and . . . oh, hold on, that's my other phone.' There was a muffled rustling sound and Cat stared intently at the wall opposite, squeezing her toes and blinking, as if she expected something else to happen, that by saying her mother's name some spirit might be invoked. She put her hand on her breastbone. 'Come on,' she said to herself, exhaling through the pain of it, the stress of the long day, of the constant battle to keep body and soul together, for herself, for Luke. But she couldn't think about her son now, no. She couldn't think about how much she feared she was simply repeating the mistakes of the past, that she was her mother, that she had become that person, just as Daisy had predicted.

'Are you still there?' Lucy's voice hissed. 'That was Irene. God, she's annoying. My flatmate, she's got this cat and—'

Cat interrupted. 'You're writing an article about my . . . mum?' It was one of the peculiarities of having seen your mother just four times in your life that Cat never knew how she should refer to Daisy. 'Mother' was too Victorian, 'Mum' too . . . too like someone who was your actual mum, which she definitely wasn't.

'Well, I offered to do something on Southpaw at work for this exhibition of his, and then they heard about Daisy and they got all interested in that. The whole Daisy and Wilbur thing and where she's gone. And . . . look, I thought I should ask you what you think before I go any further. If you'd talk about it . . . what it was like, having her as your mother.'

Cat had been told many times by well-meaning teachers and family friends that she was a lucky girl to be living in this beautiful house with her grandparents, surrounded by people who loved her. But she didn't have a mum. And it was little things that reminded her of it. It was rubbish, that saying: 'you can't miss what you don't have', because she did miss it, all the time, in loads of tiny different ways. Like when she saw Tamsin Wallis being kissed by her mum after Sports Day. On the field below the church that the vicar let them use every year. She remembered it clearly: Tamsin and Cat together, hand in hand, running over to her mum. Shouting 'Red Team won! We won!' And Tamsin's mother, smiling so hard, her spiky blond hair sticking up, her green earrings bobbing, her arms stretched so wide she could have caught fifteen Tamsins up. But she didn't, just one. Cat was left standing to the side, panting, while Julie Wallis gave her daughter a big hug, and then pushed her hair aside, kissed the dome of Tamsin's tanned forehead like she was the most precious thing in the world to her, which she was.

Now, Cat could see it. Now, she understood it. Then, it only bewildered her, when she went over and asked for the same from Julie Wallis, and she stared at her, sadly, then gave her a little kiss. 'Of course, Cat.' A tight small hug, a quick little lip brush, a pat on the back.

'What do you think?'

Cat realised the phone was slipping out of her hand, as she gazed unseeingly out into the night. She heard the sound of a door opening, then clicking shut; dread sound.

'What do I think about what?'

'Don't you wonder where she is?' Lucy's voice was loud down the crackling line. 'And how weird it is she never comes back?'

Cat could hear Madame Poulain coming up the stairs.

'What a stupid question,' she said, sounding much harsher than she meant. 'She was my mother.' She corrected herself. 'She is my mother, I can't change that, but that doesn't mean I don't think about it. Or that I want to talk about it to you so you can put it in some newspaper.'

'Oh, Cat. Listen, I only wanted to know—'

Cat held up her hand as if she could see her cousin. Rage bubbled through her. 'You're a real little gannet, aren't you? Grubbing around in stuff that's not your business. You never get in touch, never ask me how I am, now you pop up, all friendly, because you want something from me.'

'That's rubbish, Cat! You never email. This – I was glad to have an excuse to ring you.' Lucy's voice throbbed. 'You've cut us all off, just like your mum, so don't make out I'm the one who's betraying the family in some way.'

'There's a reason I don't come back. You don't understand—'

And the door opened with a bang; Madame Poulain flung her ancient purple umbrella on the floor. '*Les idiots!*'

Cat realised she was shaking. 'Grow up, Lucy,' she said, not caring how mean she sounded. 'Just grow up. I think I'd better go now. Bye.'

She slammed the phone back in its cradle, instantly regretting the words and turned away, trying to stop the painful tears squeezing the corners of her tired eyes.

'Can I have a tea, please, Catherine?' Madame Poulain dropped her coat on the floor and flopped on to the chair. 'Don't use those glasses, I'm worried you'll break them. A tea? Thank you so much.'

Cat set her shoulders, rubbed her eyes briefly. 'Of course, Madame,' she said. 'I hope you had a good evening?' She looked at her watch. Ten more minutes of fake conversation, then she could go upstairs, go to bed, lie down next to Luke and watch his warm soft body on the cot bed next to hers, rising and falling with each breath. Wait for sleep to wash over her, until grey morning slid into the tiny room and the whole thing began again.

As Cat made the tea, she prayed she wouldn't dream about her mother. She used to have those dreams: Daisy running towards her, on the beach in Dorset, hair flying behind her. She'd hold Cat tightly and whisper into her ear, 'I'm sorry. I'm back now and I'm never going away again. You're my little girl, no one else's.' She even knew where they'd live too – the tiny old schoolmistress's cottage next to the church, a gingerbread house with a thatched roof and roses round the door. Big enough for two, no one else.

MARTHA

Martha always enjoyed planning for Hallowe'en, even though now there was no one really to celebrate it with; very few trick or treaters these days, what with the children having grown up and the village increasingly full of second homes. When the children were small, they'd had a famous party; Halloween was a novelty then, an American import; now it was ubiquitous. She'd had a Chamber of Horrors room, where the children had to put on blindfolds and be escorted round the room by her. They were made to feel various ghoulish treasures: a slice of lemon stuck over a bottle which, when the guest inserted a cautious finger into the neck of the bottle, felt exactly like a dead man's eye socket, ghostly noises, rustling sounds made with newspaper, and a real skeleton David had acquired for life drawing: one dangled it in front of the blind victim, letting them feel the bones.

The children always screamed, always got hysterical, and then always ate huge amounts of chilli con carne, served with a golden cornmeal top, baked potatoes and cheese. For months the anticipation was rife in the village: what new horror would Mrs Winter have for them? Eight-year-olds would cluster around her when she walked into Winter Stoke. 'Mrs Winter, is it true you found a head on a spike?' 'Is it true you got a dead wolf and you're going to stuff it?' 'Is it true you captured a ghost, and you've got it upstairs in a room?'

'Yes,' she'd always answer, gravely, and they'd shriek with wriggling delight and rush away. 'Oh, it's even worse this year!'

She'd carried on doing the party with Cat and Lucy: Lucy loved it, but Cat got genuinely scared, the only one of all of them who did. Years before that, Daisy had loved it, of course. Hallowe'en was her favourite time of year.

It wasn't the same today, but Martha still always kept an old plastic cauldron filled with sweets from the petrol station by the door in case anyone came, and this year she was rewarded: Poppy and Zach, the vicar's children, came around about six, she dressed up as Hermione, he as some kind of amorphous zombie, his metallic silver and red face paint striped flesh coloured by the rain. Martha was vaguely amused: the austere, Victorian-era vicar who'd been here when they had first moved in hadn't allowed his grandchildren to celebrate Hallowe'en: it was pagan, not suitable in this quiet, traditional village that had changed so little over the years. Kathy's children were delightful, well-brought up and hopping with sugar and excitement. They said thank you very nicely for her sweets, as well they might; Martha never under-catered.

The rain was just starting again as she closed the door on them, smiling at their hoarse-with-excitement-howls. As they ran away towards their waiting father, Martha shivered. She went into the empty drawing room, and bent down, stiffly thrusting another log on to the fire. Resin crackled; something spluttered, and a ball of golden sparks leaped up, scattering over the great hearth. She stumbled back in shock, nearly catching her foot on the guard, and stood still for a moment, listening to the faint screams of the children echoing down the twisting dark lane, the eerie strength of the crackling wood, the sound of the wind at the windows. The clocks had gone back the previous Sunday, and now they were properly into winter. It had been a nasty autumn; wet, wild, sharp with sudden cold. Hurtful, as if to say, season of mists? What kind of sentimental idiot are you?

Her old tutor at art college, Mr McIntyre, had always made them sketch in winter, saying the bleakness was good for their artistic souls. He liked poetry and had made them read various poets, and often quoted John Donne: 'Whither, as to the bed's-feet, life is shrunk'. Life had shrunk. Well, if it was to come let it come. She had nothing to fear now, she kept telling herself. This thing she had been dragging around for so long would be gone soon.

She tried to concentrate only on the positive: her family would be together, everyone here, once again. Florence was coming back, Karen and Bill and Lucy all together again, and of course, her darling Cat – nearly four years away.

It was that falsely jovial, strange lunch with Cat the previous year in Paris that had made Martha realise that she had to change something. Cat needed her, so did Bill, and Florence, and Lucy and, oh – all of them. Once, they had been close, because of her. She'd kept them all together, like an invisible silk thread, binding herself to them, around them. But these last few years they weren't really a family any more and once they had been. Years had passed and changed them, and she knew she was the only one who could make it right again, and this is what the lunch would do. Beyond 24 November she saw nothing. She had no idea what the future after this might hold.

She didn't realise that she had fallen into a brown study, staring into the heart of the fire, but a sound across the hallway made her jump. A cry of pain.

'David?' Martha went into the study.

'It's nothing.' Her husband was leaning heavily on his desk, one fist pressing down on a mass of crumpled papers, standing in a curious position. He was facing the blank wall, away from the window.

'What's up?' Martha said in the doorway, unsure as to whether he wanted her to enter or not.

'Dammit,' David said. In profile he looked terrible; lines of pain deep as hatching etched around his mouth, across his sunken brow. Standing in this strange spot, turned towards the wall, she saw him clearly for the first time in a long while and, with a dart of fear, noticed how thin, how grey he was. 'It's nothing. Just the damn hands again – I get so tired, darling. I'm sorry.'

'They're awfully swollen.' She looked at him. 'Worse than ever. Oh, my sweet.'

'I can't do it.' It came out as a sob. 'They need something by Friday. Said I'd post it to them tomorrow.'

'It doesn't matter. They'll understand.'

'They won't.' He closed his eyes, slowly. 'It's over, Em. That article they want Lucy to write – it's a stab in the back. They're looking for any reason to get rid of me.'

'Darling, she's not writing it any more. I'd asked her not to. She rang me yesterday. Said she's spoken to Cat and she doesn't think it's a very tactful piece to write. You mustn't worry about that. You really mustn't.'

'Oh, but that's not fair. Poor Luce, she deserves a break.'

Martha couldn't help but laugh. 'Oh, my love. You're too kind. Forget about those vultures at the newspaper, too. It doesn't matter, does it?' She stared at the scratchy sketch on the paper in

189

front of him, and glanced at his kind, dark eyes, so full of pain, so sad. 'It's been a good long run at it. You can't keep killing yourself trying to get them two cartoons a week. It's not fair. It's not—'

'Please, Em,' he said. 'Just once more. Just this once.'

It was something in his voice, and in the hypnotic sound of the rain thrumming outside, enclosing them alone together around the green lamp under which lay a piece of creamy-white paper, glowing in the dark of the study.

Martha swallowed. 'This is the last time, darling. It's gone on too long. It's not fair on you, anyway. It's killing you. You're ill because you push yourself like this and, David, you really don't need to.'

'I'm dying anyway,' David said harshly.

'You're not. Not until I say you are.'

He smiled. 'Maybe working keeps me sane. Stops me thinking.'

Martha bowed her head, and sat down at the desk, picked up the steel-nibbed fountain pen, and then she began to draw. She didn't need to ask him what he had had in mind; over fifty years of marriage, she didn't need to be told.

David lowered himself into the chair opposite, looking over her shoulder as she carried on, sketching out swift, certain strokes.

'Thank you,' he said. 'My dear. What would I have done without you all these years.'

'You too, David.' She looked up, and reached out her hand. 'Look what you've done for me.'

'If people knew . . .'

'I think that's true of most families,' she said. 'Everyone has their secrets. We've had this place. We've had each other, and the children . . .'

'But, Em, don't you think that's the trouble with it all?' She looked up, startled. 'We've spent so long saying it has to be worth it and I'm – I'm not sure whether it was.' With great effort, David pulled himself out of the low chair and walked over to the window, looking out into the darkness, the silver rain dripping like a curtain over the bare branches of overhanging wisteria. 'You do everything. You've kept us all together these years, my darling, and I've done nothing. Nothing except—'

'Stop that.' Her voice rang out, louder than she meant it. 'Stop talking like that, David. Of course it was worth it. You dragged yourself out of that life, you saved yourself, and Cassie – you brought me back here again. You brought in money. You gave me our babies. You made me grateful, every day of my life.'

'Cassie . . .' He was still staring out of the window. 'She doesn't want to see me. Any of us.'

'What?'

He ignored her. 'Look what happened. Look how it turned out. All these lies we've told along the way. Look at us, we're miserable.'

'We're not.' She slammed her hand on the desk. 'We're old, and tired, and it's winter, and we have had some sadnesses to deal with. It'll be Christmas soon and all of this will be forgotten. You'll be happy again. I promise.'

'I don't know.' He looked so defeated, suddenly old, and she could feel her heart aching as she looked at him.

'David. You've made me so happy. You've made millions of people happy. I didn't do that.' She laid down the pen, pinched the bridge of her nose, breathed in. 'I'm no good at being spontaneous and carefree and making a mess and not caring what happens. You are. You always were. That's why people love you.'

They were very still in the study, the only sound the water outside and the moan in the chimney behind her.

'You had other things to do,' David said. His face was grey. 'You've done everything else.' The final word sounded like a sob. 'Darling, darling girl. I don't know what I'd do without you. Oh, Em.'

She stretched across the desk to take his hand. His rigid swollen fingers were immobile in her small, warm hand. She pressed his palm with the pad of her thumb. They stared at each other, David looking down, his breathing laboured, and after a few moments Martha picked up the pen again, and began drawing. He watched her.

'You're going to tell them about Daisy, aren't you?'

The figures were coming to life on the paper: a little girl dancing, a crazed, happy dog, and still she did not stop.

'Martha?'

'Yes,' she said quietly. 'I'll tell them then.'

'That she's dead? Everything?'

She started and the pen snagged on an invisible bump; the paper tore just a little, the ink bleeding out, black on white.

'Not everything,' she said, after a pause, and resumed her work.

PART II

THE PARTY

'Now, my bonny lad, you are *mine*! And we'll see if one tree won't grow as crooked as another, with the same wind to twist it!'
Emily Brontë, *Wuthering Heights*

DAISY

Wilbur is dead. We buried him last night, in the daisy bank. And I'm the only one who cares.

He was old, that's what Mr Barrow the vet said, but I don't think that's a reason for him to just die. Plenty of people are old, like Mrs White in the village who has – wait for it – white hairs on her chin. She is ninety-five, as she tells everyone every chance she gets. Stupid woman. Wilbur was the same age as me (I am twelve, in October). He wasn't old.

Ma was nice. She helped me bury him. We dug a big hole and wrapped him up, and we sang 'Abide with Me'. We burned candles. There were moths fluttering around in the evening light.

But the others weren't nice. Bill said it was stupid, a funeral for a dog, and he went to play guns in the wood. I always think this is funny because he's on his own – who does he hide from and who does he shoot? And when I crept up on him afterwards and fired one of his blanks, he jolly nearly peed his pants. I think he might have.

And Florence said she didn't like Wilbur because Wilbur used to jump up and scare her and she didn't want to come. She watched out of the window in our room. Scared, stupid, little pig. PIG.

And Pa? Pa was away, in London, for the night. Ma rang him to tell him. He didn't even care. Ma didn't say that, she said, 'Oh, Dad is very sad. He says to send his love.' But I know he didn't. Pa doesn't love me. He loves Florence, sort of loves Bill, but mainly Florence, because she likes paintings and she's a really vile little sneak, a swot, and the worst word I can think of and I'm not writing it down.

And Pa doesn't like me because he thinks I make trouble. I DON'T. I *gave him the idea for Wilbur* and he just doesn't care. All these years Wilbur has been with us, our family mainstay and support (I got that in a book about awful lives of kitchen maids in Victorian times) and my family doesn't care enough to come and watch him be buried, just me and Ma. Pa stole my ideas off me too. He knows what he did, he knows about my stories about Wilbur. And that's why he's famous now and he still didn't come.

It's not even all of that, it's that I think Wilbur understood me and I understood him. Because he was shaggy and clumsy (not like me, I'm not like that, I'm very careful about everything) and he was enthusiastic about everything, so sometimes he scared people but he was only being friendly. I think people who don't understand that about dogs are stupid.

198

Florence, I am writing your name down on my list I am keeping. I wish you would die. If Wilbur's dead you should definitely be dead too.

Florence doesn't belong here. She's not even one of us. Look at her. And look at me.

There is a wasps' nest in our room, underneath the roof. We used to have them when we first moved in, and now they're back. Last year there was a nest in the barn and Joseph, the gardener, was stung really badly. He had to go to hospital. I haven't told anyone about this one. The art of war isn't Bill's stupid stupid plastic gun with the babyish paper cartridges, it is planning.

I lie in bed at night and I can hear them humming, in the eaves. It's the wooden gables they like. Wasps like wood. Sometimes it's very faint, but sometimes it seems to get louder, as though they will burst out of the back of the nest, into my room. It keeps me awake. It scares me but I like being scared, too. I like the rushing feeling. I hate being bored. Really I hate it more than anything else.

I am going to make a list and plan out my life about what I want to do when I grow up. I can't wait to be a grown-up. I hate being here.

1. I will leave Winterfold, as soon as I can.
2. I will be rich.
3. I will have a husband. No children, I don't want any children.

4. People will be sorry when they have been horrible to me.
5. I won't come back, not even to see Ma.
6. I will be famous and everyone will have heard of me and be sorry they weren't nicer to me.
7. Florence, Verity, other girls at school who are my friends and then annoy me or won't talk to me any more, I will pay them back for it.
8. I will have another dog and I will call him Wilbur.
9. I will make everyone see the truth about Florence.

But to do that I have to tell her the truth first of all. What I know . . . how little she knows. You see yesterday I heard Ma and Pa arguing. In their room. I stood outside listening quite blatantly as I knew I could quite simply say, 'I'm on my way to the bathroom,' if they caught me.

What they said needs some thinking about as I am not sure I actually entirely understand it.

They don't argue like they used to when we came here. I think they have got used to this house and us all being here but I haven't.

Ma said, 'You said, when Florence came, you'd look out for her.'

Pa said, 'I am. You need to as well, Em. You said you'd send Daisy away to school if she didn't start behaving.'

Ma said, 'I don't want to. You of all people should know why.'

That's exactly what they said and I know two things. Florence is from somewhere else, and Pa wants to send me away.

I don't mean to be naughty, it just happens. I get bored, or angry, or I don't understand something, and then suddenly there's a broken glass, a smashed blackboard, a crying child. I want to feel remorse but I don't. Does Pa feel remorse, for Wilbur? Remorse is what Miss Tooth said I should feel when I flushed Verity's head down the lavatory after school. Verity is a coward, she screamed and cried. I don't cry. Verity's mother came to Winterfold, and shouted at my mother. She said I wasn't ever to go to Verity's house again. I don't care about that, Verity lives in a nasty house, she doesn't have colour television, and her father smells of BO. I hated going there for tea.

I sit in our room. It's the corner of the house. I can see Bill and Flo, playing some stupid game with Hadley, the new dog, and Bill's old swords in the meadow by the Daisy Bank, my Daisy Bank, mine *mine*. They should have asked me because it's *my* place and they're not allowed to play there, especially now that Wilbur is buried there. Everyone has one place for themselves. That's my place, my place where I can go. Flo is always in our room when I want to be by myself. She shouldn't be there too. I can see them there and it makes me very very very very angry. I can see Mummy in the garden deadheading the roses, with a scarf in her hair. It's a pretty scarf.

There's two more things I know: Hadley is dangerous. His father was destroyed for fighting. He has bitten people before. I don't like him. They got him when they found out Wilbur was dying.

And I can see the wasps, flying into the eaves. Just casually, one at a time, and they're building up their nest till there's more of them till one day when they'll blow the house apart.

I hate it here. I wish I could run away. Mummy is always asking me why I don't feel sorry. It's not a thing I can feel. I wish I could, I wish I was like them but I'm not. I have always known it.

FLORENCE

21 November 2012

Dear Professor Lovell,

It is with great sadness that I write you this letter. But since it has been made clear to me that my position at the British College is under threat, and in the <u>most pernicious of circumstances</u>, I am compelled to act.

My subject is nothing less than the most serious of academic crimes. <u>Plagiarism</u>.

I am writing to set down before you in detail the charge which I bring against our colleague Professor Peter Connolly. Namely that his book *The Queen of Beauty: War, Sex, Art and God in Renaissance Florence* (a Number One bestseller, translated into fifteen languages) contains whole sections of work written by, but uncredited to, me. I would estimate roughly 75% of the book is mine.

Please see the attached, a facsimile of a sample chapter on Medici portraiture with my notes to Prof. Connolly written on the page. The original is in a safe place and can be examined by you at any time. My colleague Professor Jim Buxton of the Courtauld Institute is prepared to stand as expert witness should these proceedings come to court. Believe me, it is extremely painful for me to even contemplate betraying the man I once

'Flo? Florence, don't you want some tea?'

'I'm just coming!'

'It's getting cold!'

'Honestly, Ma! I'll be with you as soon as possible.'

Florence smiled even as she heard herself – she'd be fifty next year, but it was funny how after only a day at home one reverted to type. Arching her back, she waggled her head, feeling the click of several bones in her neck and shoulders. She blinked intensely and stared at the screen, then deleted the last sentence.

Then she typed: 'I once thought Professor Connolly the finest of men, but he is no more than'

No. Don't give them anything on paper.

'. . . Believe me, Professor Lovell, I raise this accusation reluctantly. It is only the fact that my job and reputation are being impugned by you and Professor Connolly'

No. Too bitter, sounded like a revenge attack. And she wasn't bitter, was she?

I look forward to hearing from you. You will see that I am copying into this letter my colleagues at the Courtauld Institute, as well as Professor Connolly's literary agent, and his publishers.

Yours sincerely,

Professor Florence Winter, D.Phil(Oxon)

She saved the document, and opened her emails.

It was strange, working at her father's desk. There were his drawings, littering the floor, the walls, scraps of ideas pinned on to the cork board behind in his shaky hand, yellowing postcards and notes from friends and admirers. There was even a water-marked framed letter from 10 Downing Street: they all knew it off by heart. While the ancient internet cable grumbled into action Florence turned round to read it again.

Dear Mr Winter,

The Prime Minister very much enjoyed your cartoon in yesterday's *Daily News*, featuring Daisy and Wilbur throwing eggs at a protester. He is a great admirer of your work and asks me to pass on his very best wishes to you.

Yours, etc.,

And then a totally unreadable squiggle beneath. A letter meaning nothing – why had he enjoyed the cartoon? Bland, bland, David had said, and had it framed as an *aide-mémoire* – that was why he did the work, to keep sharp, to stop himself from becoming bland. 'Yours, etc.' had become a saying with all of them. A shorthand for glibness.

Coming home this time felt different. She'd emailed Daisy last week before she left. Signed it 'Yours, etc.' Of course, she hadn't heard anything back. On the flight back, Florence had begun to wonder why she was coming home at all, why she couldn't have just got out of it. Now she was here she knew something was brewing. Her mother was on edge: not that she'd ever confide in Florence. But Pa was so distant, wrapped up in his own thoughts, smiling as he listened to her talk but in a way that made her feel like a little girl again, chattering about something she'd read in a book.

She opened her emails, clicking her tongue with disdain at the attempt by one of her students to ask for another extension. 'No means no, Camilla,' Florence typed briskly. 'I don't care when ski season starts. I expect the essay in by Friday at the latest. FW' and pressed Send. In haste, and wanting to be finished, she almost missed the email nestling below it.

From: Daisy Winter
To: Florence Winter
Tue, Nov 20, 2012 at 11.30 PM
Flo,
Thanks for asking but I won't be coming

back for the reunion dinner. It's complicated.
Ma will explain why. Hope all's good with
you in Italy.
D x

Florence's heart skipped several beats. She peered
forwards, as if by getting closer to the pixilations
on the screen she would glean further information
about her sister. Where, why, who? Daisy, Daisy,
give me your answer do.

Six years ago, two years before Bill's wedding,
she'd come back. Some fundraising mission. She
could only pay a flying visit to Winterfold, one
night. Florence had scrambled to get there; luckily
she'd been going to Manchester for a conference
anyway. She didn't know why she was so keen to
see her older sister, who'd tormented her throughout
their childhood, but she was – curious, was that
it? Did she want Daisy's approval?

And Daisy was impressive when she talked about
it – had all the facts to hand about literacy and
clean water and female education. She made
Florence, as ever, feel rather inadequate. She'd
received a medal, though she didn't really like to
talk about it (Martha brought it up). She'd been
travelling a little, to see other projects. She said
she'd come back for Christmas, hopefully she'd
see Cat again?

In the end she couldn't come back over
Christmas, she'd said, because the school was
open over New Year. She sent paper lanterns in

the post, folded cream and red paper stars with tiny star-shaped holes that let the light through. Martha had hung them in the dining room on Christmas Day and they all drank a toast to Daisy, come good at last. No one said as much, but that was what they thought.

So when she returned that summer, two years later, for Bill and Karen's wedding, Florence was looking forward to seeing her again, hoping that perhaps things might continue on the same positive footing. She was happier than she'd ever been, her brief affair with Peter Connolly at its height and she felt the universe liked her, for the first time. That she wasn't the freak everyone said she must be behind her back. Daisy too – she wasn't the cruel child who Florence sometimes, in her darkest moments, thought might kill her. She was her sister! Her family! She was wrong, of course.

'Have you had your hair cut since I last saw you, Flo? Don't think you can have, can you?' she'd said, running a caressing hand through Florence's strawberry-brown and grey bob so that Florence stepped back in alarm. (She'd forgotten her sister always had rather invasive body language, hugging people she didn't know when she was little, stroking the teacher's arm at the Nativity play, clasping Dr Philips a little too tightly when he bandaged up Florence's arm after an accident with a frayed swing rope.)

The gulf was too wide for Florence to reach across to her sister. She seemed odd. At breakfast, the morning after the wedding, she was restless, shifting in her seat, constantly on the verge of speaking, long skinny fingers spearing holes in the bread roll on her plate. She ate nothing. Their father was due to go into hospital that day for a long-scheduled knee operation, and when Martha asked whether Florence could drive him in, Florence had had to explain, regretfully, that she'd be leaving after lunch that day for London, a conference on Piero della Francesca that began that evening. It was Jim Buxton's conference, and she had to attend. She tried to explain this, to find out if she might see Daisy in London again before she left, but Daisy, with the older sister's contempt for any achievement of the younger, gave a small laugh.

'You are funny, Flo. Enjoy the conference. Good for you! I'm out of here soon; I won't see you again. I have to raise some money for actual problems. You know, like wells so people can drink. And drainage so they don't, you know, *die*.' She'd blown her a kiss, careless, and got up and left the kitchen, slammed the door of her room, stayed there all day. That was the last time Florence had seen her.

As she stared at Daisy's email, Florence picked at her fingers, puckering her brow as she reread the email into meaninglessness. *It's complicated.*

'Flo! Your crumpet's almost cold!' The heavy door swung open and Florence's head jerked up, guiltily.

Martha paused on the threshold. 'What are you doing?'

'Nothing – nothing! Just – doing some work. Checking emails.'

Her mother's eyes narrowed and she plunged her hands into the pockets of the faded blue artist's smock she wore around the house. 'Are you now? Good-oh.'

'There. Just one more thing.'

Florence pressed Delete, and the opening word, 'Flo' collapsed before her eyes as the email was sucked into the virtual trash can. Watching it, Florence was reminded of the plastic crisp packets the three of them used to toast over the campfire, watching them warp and shrink. They used them as tokens, and whoever had the most usually got their way. She remembered trying to explain this to some girl at school. *We camp in the woods in summer and we have tokens made of crisp packets shrunk down in a hot oven. The person with the most tokens given to them by the others in thanks for actions performed gets to be the king or queen for the day.*

As with so many aspects of Winter family life, this was met with blank incomprehension by outsiders.

'What are you smiling about?' Martha said. Her voice was light but Florence thought she looked peculiarly unnatural, somehow, leaning against the door and watching her daughter.

'Just thinking about camping in the garden and the shrunken crisp packets.' Florence stood up. 'It's funny, being back this time. I keep remembering things I've forgotten. Maybe . . . maybe it's winter,' she finished lamely, looking outside at the driving rain. 'What a nasty day.'

'Yes, awful. There's so much water on the road you can't pass the lane in some places. Even this high up. Joe had dreadful trouble getting here this morning. He had to leave the car outside.'

'Joe?'

'Joe Thorne. He's the chef who's doing the catering on Friday and Saturday. He's awfully nice. Come and meet him and have some tea.' She tucked her arm into her daughter's. 'You've been working so hard since you got back here.'

'Yes, well. Something rather strange has come up at the College.'

Martha stopped. 'What's that?'

'A – oh, plagiarism, I'm afraid. It might end up in court,' Florence said. The words sounded fantastical, out loud. She was doing this. Wasn't she? Would she actually dare to send that letter to George Lovell? Seal it up, post it?

'Court? It's not anything to do with you, is it?' Martha patted Florence's hand. 'You never needed to steal anything, did you? Look! Florence is here!' she called out, as they entered the kitchen.

The kitchen was neater than usual, and Florence looked around and realised it must be the mark of a professional chef. Stacks of canapés in rows were laid out on the countertops amidst the everyday gentle chaos, while Radio 3 blared out

211

slightly too loudly in the corner (Martha was a little deaf, but refused to admit it). Her father sat in his chair doing the crossword, chewing his pencil, one swollen hand resting on his lap.

'Hello, darling,' he said with pleasure as Florence came in. 'You finished with the world of academia for today?'

She put her hand on his shoulder and sat down next to him. 'Yes. Thanks, Dad, I'm sorry to crowd you out of your study like that. Just a few things I had to . . . get to.'

David tapped her arm. 'Don't chew your hair, darling. What's up?'

It's just us. His smile was warm. Florence took a deep breath.

'Oh, Dad. I—'

The back door banged open and a tall, dark man came in. 'Shit. I – I mean, sugar. The – ah, can I just squeeze past you, please?' He reached behind Florence, unhooked the Aga door and took out a tray of tiny blind-baked tartlet cases, egg-yolk yellow, and flicked them on to a cooling rack, then slid another tray from the counter in and shut the door. 'Sorry about that. Minute longer, they'd have burned.' He wiped his hand on his apron. 'Hello, I'm Joe. You must be Daisy.'

There was a short silence.

'I'm Florence.' She shook his hand quickly. 'I – um, I'm the – I'm Florence. Yes.'

Blood rushed into Joe's face. 'I'm so sorry. I forgot. It's Florence.' He whispered to himself. '*Florence.*'

'It's fine, there's too many of us, don't worry,' Florence said. 'Nice to meet you. Ma's so pleased with what you've been doing.'

'Have a cup of tea, Joe,' David said, pushing the teapot over towards him. 'Martha's made some of her gingerbread. You'll like it. Even you, a professional chef. Sit down.'

'I've had it before and it was delicious.' Joe grabbed a mug off one of the hooks on the dresser, then pulled out a chair. 'I really am sorry,' he said, handing the plate to David, then Florence. 'I know you're Florence, you're the one who lives in Italy and you know everything about art.'

'Sort of,' Florence said, embarrassed. She was long used to being lined up next to her local hero brother and feline, exotic sister and told by strangers or her parents' friends, 'Oh, now you must be Florence. I hear you're the brains of the family!' or once, memorably, 'You've changed so much, dear. Oh, well,' by an old newspaper editor, just after he'd said to Daisy, 'My dear, you're ravishing. Have you ever thought of being a model?' So she changed the subject. 'You live here, don't you? Have you met the others?'

'Yes . . . most of them,' Joe said. 'Your brother – he sewed up my finger after I sliced it open a couple of months ago. Did a fine job.' He held up his hand and Florence stared at it, impressed.

'Good grief, that looks nasty.'

'Would have been a disaster for me if it hadn't been well done. I – I owe him a lot.' He gulped back the rest of his tea and stood up. 'Look, I have to get to the shops to pick up a couple of things I've forgotten. It was great to meet you, Florence.'

And he left, without even waving goodbye. Martha followed him out.

'Funny bloke,' said Florence, taking a sip of tea. 'Is he always like that?'

'Like what?'

'Shifty,' she said. 'Like he's just nicked your wallet, Pa.'

David was fiddling with the jar of pencils that always stood on the table. 'Don't be a snob, Flo. I think he feels uncomfortable here. For some reason.'

'I'm not being a snob!' Florence said. 'He was pretty odd, that's all. Like he thought we were about to arrest him or something.'

Her father put his hand over one eye, then sat back in his chair and said quietly, 'Oh, don't ask me. These days I just draw and have naps.'

'You?' she said, cheerily, though she watched the way he squinted, as if he couldn't make her out. 'Hardly!'

'I can't afford to do anything else, my darling.'

Florence gave him a sharp look. 'What does that mean?'

'What I say.' He wouldn't look at her.

'Pa,' she said, her heart thumping. 'Are you all right? You don't look all right.'

David laughed, and sat up a little.

'Charming child.'

'Sorry. I mean, since I've been back. You . . . you look rather grey.'

His face cleared. 'Not really, that's the honest truth.'

Florence took a deep breath. 'Oh.' She could feel her throat thickening, tears swimming into her eyes. 'How bad is it?'

David took his daughter's hand, and kissed it. 'Do you remember when we'd go to the National Gallery for your birthday?'

'Of course,' she said, alarmed that he'd think she'd ever forget.

'I'd like to take you back down to London some time.'

'Yes, Pa, I'd love that. We can look at *The Annunciation*, have lunch. Have a steak, go for a walk in Green Park, visit that cheese shop you like . . .' She spoke almost frantically.

They were alone in the warm, cluttered kitchen. He smiled. '"The most beautiful representation of motherhood in Western Art. Mary is every woman, alive or dead, at that moment."'

'I wrote that,' Florence said, surprised.

'I know you did,' said her father. He glanced up as Martha walked past the kitchen window, carrying a basket from the garden. She waved at Florence, shielding her head from the rain with her hand, and smiling. Joe Thorne climbed into his car, said something to Martha, then slammed the door. They could hear the engine, stalling and revving again as he turned around in the driveway.

215

'This might be the only chance we get,' David said urgently, his voice soft. She had to lean towards him to hear. 'Listen to me. I love them all but I love you in a way I didn't the other two. You know that, don't you? Always a special place for you. You were my golden girl. I saved you.'

'Pa?' Florence shook her head, her mouth dry. She peered into his glazed eyes. 'I don't understand. What are you talking about?'

'You must promise me you'll always remember I told you that. You were my favourite. Shouldn't say that. You'll understand one day. I'm so proud of you, my darling.'

'It's absolutely bucketing down out here!' she heard her mother call, from outside. Florence didn't move. She stared into her father's eyes, squeezed his hand gently. 'Dad – I wish you'd tell me what you mean.'

'Soon,' he said, nodding, and he was smiling, and the smile was what made her want to cry. 'Very soon.'

Outside, Joe drove down the drive. In a blur Florence heard Martha call loudly, 'Goodbye!'

It happened in slow motion. Florence looked up and saw, through the blur of rain, her mother wave, then drop the basket and shout, her hands pressed to her cheeks. Then the crash, the sound of splintering glass, someone screaming, someone shouting. Then, silence.

They stood up, Florence and David, struggling

from his chair, in time to see a slim figure, hair flying, running down the drive.

'Oh God,' said Florence. 'What—'

The figure was screaming. 'Luke! Luke! Oh my God, darling, *Luke!*'

There was a shattering crunch, as Florence dropped her mug of tea on the floor, and stared through the window.

A little boy stood in front of them, thumb in his wide-open mouth, face purple with yelling, and blood dripping from his forehead. He screamed, pulling at his black hair, smearing blood across his wet cheeks.

Behind him a woman came running towards him, her mouth also wide open, her eyes wide, white, wild. She caught him in her arms and he buckled to the ground, still wailing with pain.

'Luke!' she screamed, turning this way, that way, then crying out as she caught sight of them, framed in the window. 'Gran! Southpaw! Help me, Luke's, he's . . . he's hurt.' And she buried her face in his, sobbing, and stroking his hair.

CAT

She was ahead of herself, for once. For once! A miracle. The Eurostar had been on time. She had picked up the car without incident, though it was slightly unnerving, getting into a completely strange car when she hadn't driven for years, let alone on the left-hand side, strapping Luke in and then setting off along the Euston Road, easily one of the busiest roads in London. Thankfully, the Wednesday afternoon traffic was thin and she drove through the drizzling rain with almost a light heart. When they got to Richmond, she turned on the radio, sang along to a Blondie song. 'One Way or Another'. *One way or another.* She was coming back home. And, even though she hadn't planned it like this, she had Luke with her and perhaps, really, that was wonderful.

'What will we see, Maman? Will we see the Tiger who came to tea?'

Luke was incredibly excited. He had never been to London, to England, never been away from France. He still didn't properly understand that he was half-English, despite what she told him every night as she stroked his hair and soothed him to sleep in their little room. He was too little to understand that you could be from another country, too.

Once they were on the motorway, he dozed and a couple of times she turned around to check on him. His cheeks were flushed, his mouth in a pout; there was a scratch on his forehead, a line of little beaded scabs, the result of some convoluted dispute with Benoit over a ball at the nursery. He was here. Her son was here, with her.

The week before she was supposed to go, one night in their room when Cat was sitting up in her bed engrossed in a Ngaio Marsh, she suddenly heard a noise, and Luke's small hand burrowed under his duvet, out towards the edge of the bed, and found her hand. 'I want to come with you.'

'What?'

'To England.'

'Oh, Luke,' she'd said. The idea he might want to hadn't ever occurred to her, so busy was she planning, controlling everything to make his life as safe and warm as possible. 'Don't you want to stay with Josef? It's only two nights. It'll be fun.'

'I want to see the Queen. And I want to see the paper dogs.'

'The dogs Southpaw drew me, darling?' The words caught in her throat.

'The ones in the frame. I want to see them.' The little voice was clear in the darkness.

In the end, as big decisions often are, it was a

simple choice to make. Why on earth wouldn't she take him? He wasn't four yet, he didn't need a ticket. When she rang to confirm this, the operator told her they were offering discounted transfers on to a train the day before, as her train was overbooked. Gleefully, Cat said yes. She would get to Winterfold early and give them a real surprise, introduce her son, her secret, beloved, precious little boy, to her grandmother and grandfather. She would tell the truth at last. And somehow, the element of surprising them a day early took away the terror of reality. The fact that she didn't know where her mother was. The reason for this birthday dinner. And most of all, the fact that she had had this child, kept him a secret from her family for three years.

When she found she was pregnant, she was at the lowest point she'd been able to go. Olivier had stopped telling her what to wear, or lashing out at her in rage, driving her into a corner of fear so great she tiptoed around him, making him even more vicious, contemptuous of her. Now, he openly despised her. He barely came home by then, and when he did, bringing people back with him: musicians, artists, philosophers – it made Cat feel very bourgeois that she didn't understand how one could be in one's late twenties and have a job as a philosopher. They stayed up long into the night, talking, playing music, drinking beers, banging out rhythms on Cat's old trunk-cum-coffee table. She never joined them. She had a new job now, at the flower stall in the market on the edge of the Île de la Cité, and it meant getting up early. It paid virtually nothing but she'd taken it because she didn't know what else she could do, and Olivier made it clear he didn't want her hanging round the house during the day when he was sleeping off the excesses of the night before. She liked it, too, except the hours were long, the pay small, and the weather sometimes tough. But it wasn't a career. At night she would come home, exhausted, and fall into bed praying that she wouldn't be called upon to see the others he brought back with him, ridiculed as the 'fat English girl who lives with me'. 'She's pathetic, like my dog, panting and following me through the place.'

She heard him once, fucking a girl on the sofa, a lithe, smooth, ginger-haired thing of about eighteen who smiled patronisingly at her in the morning, and offered her a coffee as Cat staggered blearily out of bed in her baggy T-shirt and into the shower. After that she started wearing earplugs. She didn't really know what else to do. She had no spine, she had no will, no energy to fight.

She had had a miscarriage six months previously, and had gone straight back on the Pill. When she missed a period she thought nothing of it; she wasn't regular, her body was behaving in strange ways. When another month went by and she eventually did a test, she was astonished: how could this relationship, this awful toxic mess of humiliation and unhappiness have created something? Olivier did not want children, he had made that clear the last time. She didn't admit it to herself for a week or so, thinking perhaps it would go away, or that she would take the decision to get rid of it.

Cat had thrown herself into her relationship with Olivier thinking it would provide her with something she'd never had before: her own home, her own unit, and so it was ironic that it was finding out she was pregnant with his child that gave her the strength to break it off. She knew, though, if she was going to do it, she had to have thought it through. She had to carry on as though, to everyone else, everything was normal. Her grandmother came to visit: she told her nothing. She went out for drinks with Veronique: and said nothing. Here the seeds of secrecy were sown.

By the time she told Olivier, her exit plan was worked out. Her new boss at the flower stall, Henri, was always complaining about his elderly mother. Madame Poulain, it had been decided, needed a lodger, but she was so difficult it was impossible to persuade the procession of live-in helps to stay. It was not too arduous, so why was it so hard? She needed someone to help with her shopping, to collect her prescription and to make sure she took her pills (she had had cancer, and she now had a heart condition, and diabetes and osteoporosis. In the years to come Cat often had to remind herself of this, that for all Madame

Poulain's faults, she really had not been well). She needed someone to sit with her of an evening, an old-fashioned companion. No, she did not mind a baby. There was a *chambre de bonne*, and the infant would be out of the way there, and an excellent public nursery just across the river. All would be well. To Cat, desperate, it seemed like good luck from a movie, or a fairy story: she didn't consider how it might actually work.

So, when she was around four months pregnant, and starting to show, one beautiful spring day when Paris was coming alive with green and the trees were bursting with blossom, she packed everything she owned up in the coffee table trunk, kissed Luke the dog goodbye, her tears dropping on to his kinked, soft fur, stroked his ears and hugged him close to her, and then she left. She didn't tell Olivier where she was going, just said she was leaving. A week later, an *avocat*, a lawyer wife of someone with whom she'd worked at *Women's Wear Daily*, a specialist in family law, had written to Olivier, explaining Catherine Winter was pregnant and that he was the father and would be required to pay her child support.

She never received a penny, nor did she want to, but it did the trick: she turned from being a person of interest to Olivier, albeit briefly although it was always dangerous, into a sad bitch who was trying to get money out of him, thus allowing him to be the wronged party. The one mistake she made was in the naming of the baby. Two months after she moved out, Luke the dog had run away and was never seen again. Olivier, deciding to toy with her again, somehow managed to blame Luke's disappearance on her, and demanded that he chose the name if the baby was a boy. He picked Luke. Some sad way of reminding her of his ownership of her? What else could it be?

But in the grand scheme of things, Cat didn't care. She liked the name Luke and she had loved the other Luke. She simply couldn't get upset about Olivier's games any more, or so she told herself. And then, when Luke was a year old, Olivier moved to Marseilles. He saw his son a few times, peripatetically, if he was in town. He'd bring Luke presents – a stuffed wicker elephant that took up a corner of the tiny bedroom, some jazz records, once, a pair of shoes, which were too small, though new.

Cat wanted Luke to know he had a father, and to know his father loved him. And so she had to let Olivier see Luke when he was in town. On the last visit, when he was three hours late, unshaven, smelling rank and unwashed, Luke stared at him and said, 'You stink!' Then laughed. 'Stinky.'

She saw Olivier's eyes narrowing, the precursor to his anger. The little quiver of the bottom lip. The tone of his voice when he said, 'Don't say that again.' And she was afraid for her son, afraid of what loving his father might do to him.

Luke sometimes asked, 'Why doesn't my father live nearby?' But he never said anything else and their strange but safe little life continued, high up in the tiny back bedroom on the Île-Saint-Louis, the days she took one at a time turning into weeks, then months, and now her baby was three.

She found, since becoming a mother, she thought ceaselessly about her own mother. Cat knew where her father was – a charity worker living in Kent, with three children and a wife called Marie. He'd always kept in touch, assiduously enough to remove any sense of mystery about himself, and whenever she met him Cat found herself wondering how on earth she could be related to him. Winterfold was where she came from, not from this nice, kind, mild rangy man who wore wireless frames and had hair that stuck up in tufts.

When Cat had been nine, he'd taken her to the pantomime in Bath ('I think you should call me "Giles", don't you agree, Catherine?'), as a special Christmas treat. He had talked all through their pizza about world hunger, then sat cross-armed and perplexed through the pantomime, hissing at Cat when she shot her hand up to go on stage. ('No, Catherine, honestly – I think you'd better not. You are in my care, after all . . . Is that OK? I'm awfully sorry . . .') Cat had sunk down in her chair furiously, watching with envy as a little girl called Penelope and not her was chosen, then shot out of a joke cannon on a seesaw by Lionel Blair. Giles had refused to buy a programme or an ice cream, and then forgotten where he'd parked the car. Cat had come back and told her grandmother she thought he looked like an owl, but most of all he was very dreary.

She'd seen him since, lunches in London, and when she was at university she'd even stayed with him in Kent, but it was that encounter she remembered most clearly, and about which she often felt guilty; it occurred to her when she had Luke that it must have been quite a thing for Giles, leaving his (then very small) three children with his wife, a few days before Christmas, to drive from Kent to Somerset to take a cross little girl out for an expensive treat. She liked him for sending Christmas cards, for the fact that he'd always been clear about where he was ('Dear Catherine, this is to let you know we have moved, should you need to contact me. We are all well. Emma is . . .')

She could contact Giles if she wanted, but she didn't really want to. No, it was her mother who haunted her, who filled her dreams. All through the hot sweltering summer before Luke was born, Cat lay in her new little bedroom and thought about Daisy, tried to piece together what she knew about her. The only concrete evidence she had were the clothes her mother had left when she walked out, nearly thirty years ago. A dress for every year, every occasion, and she'd hung them all up in a row and just walked out of the house and kept on walking, and that had been that. 'Not to be shared' – somehow Cat felt sorry for her mother, so desperate that Cat should have her own things. She didn't understand that by leaving her like this she had ensured her daughter would have nothing but her own things. When Lucy came to stay Cat was so keen to share her toys that often Lucy, bored, would wander off into the garden. 'I don't care about your Sindy house, Cat. I want to play with this stick.' It was what had led Cat to cut up her mother's dresses for dolls' clothes, that fateful day. It seemed such a waste, having them hanging there, unworn. *She* wasn't ever going to wear them, no fear of that.

When she gave birth to Luke, at l'Hôpital Pitié-Salpêtrière, he was very small and they took him to the baby unit and kept him in an incubator. Cat was in a ward on the floor below. She couldn't sleep and so she walked the corridors at night slowly in her new bright yellow dressing gown, stomach still distended, very sore, feeling like a waddling duck. On the third day her hormones kicked in and a male nurse found her, sobbing brokenly into a wall, helpless with tiredness, with worry about this tiny baby who was so small she could hold him with one hand, why she wasn't producing enough milk to feed him, with how she would get him home from the hospital, the horrible, dark, nasty world he had come into and how she couldn't protect him from it.

The nurse sat her down on a plastic chair in the squeaky clean corridor, the only sound the faint mew of babies in the room next door. He patted her hand as she cried, tears dropping like rain on to the shining floor.

'Take it day by day,' he told her, and she only realised afterwards that he had spoken in English. 'Just day by day. Do not worry about the future. Do not worry about the past. Think of the day and what you have to do to get through, and it will be OK.'

And that's what she did. Every day. When she thought about the future, how Luke couldn't possibly grow up in a tiny room with his mother, how she had no money, how she had to tell her grandparents one day, how she had let all of this happen and screwed it up . . . When the walls of her life started to crowd too closely in on her, Cat focused on the immediate present. Get to the bank. Buy more vermouth for Madame Poulain. Put aside twenty euros a week for Luke's new shoes. Breathe. Just . . . breathe.

One day, she would like to try to pull herself out of this life. Start a gardening business, everything from window boxes for busy people to full-on self-sufficiency vegetable gardens. But how could she when she wasn't self-sufficient herself? Once, Cat had been a dynamic person, but that person was long gone and she did not know if she could find that Cat again, dust her down, put her on like a dress from Daisy's wardrobe she used to wear, before they were cut up.

When they got to Stonehenge, Cat woke Luke up, and they got out of the car. Luke was fascinated, standing as close as he could get to the stones behind the wire fence, staring intently around even as the drizzling rain misted everything in front of them.

'Where are they from, the stones?'

Cat screwed up her eyes. Being relatively close to her school, Stonehenge had cropped up frequently in day trips, but she could remember very little about it.

'That's a good question. No idea.'

'They are very big.' Luke peered at one of the signs. 'I can't read.'

'I think they put them on rollers and pulled them along.' He looked unconvinced. 'And I have a feeling they're from Wales. Somewhere like that. They weigh about two tonnes each.' So she did remember. They stared up at the huge monoliths – she'd forgotten quite how big they actually were. 'Good, isn't it?' She turned to him eagerly, smiling as he nodded and grinned.

They drove across Salisbury Plain. She pointed out the mysterious hillocks and mounds, graves of buried kings, the empty army tanks that hugged the narrow lay-bys, the sheep huddled on the hill-sides, and Luke stared out of the window, his nose and one finger pressed cold-cream white against the glass.

As they started the slow but steady climb up towards Winter Stoke Cat felt sick, dizzy, tired, adrenalin swamping her body so that she thought she might simply pass out at the wheel. She had been trying to downplay it in her mind, as though this wasn't the most important moment of her life since Luke was born. Coming back. Maybe even to see her mother again, for ever since her phone conversation with Lucy she felt sure this was about Daisy in some strange way. Whatever this was, there was no hiding any more. She had to keep reminding herself it was a good thing. Yet she was terrified.

Her thirteenth birthday! How could she have forgotten it, yet there it suddenly was, then the highlight of her – as she saw it – dreary life. December 1995. They went to Pizza Hut, in Bath. Gran, Southpaw, five of her best friends, Lucy too, then to the cinema to see *Goldeneye*. Lucy wasn't allowed to, being too young. She went back early to Winterfold with Gran in a right grump. Cat, Liza, Rachel, Victoria and – who else was there? How awful that she couldn't remember – they all came home to Winterfold for a sleepover, and Martha let them have half a glass of champagne each. Gran had the right idea about birthdays. They were giggly and emotional with excitement, and they stayed up late listening to Take That and crying about Robbie leaving, and as they were going to sleep Rachel, who was the really cool one, said, 'Wow, Cat, I'm really jealous of you, living here. Your gran is amazing.' Only she sort of muttered it into the bedclothes so Cat was never sure if the others heard, but she had heard it, and she smiled in the darkness. She could still remember how it made her feel, the idea this random girl – God knows what had happened to her – the idea anyone would be jealous of her, it was still a childishly lovely feeling.

The rain was still falling, soft yet heavy outside. Luke turned away from the window, sucking his thumb noisily, occasionally whispering to himself in French. At one point he called out, 'Mum! Maman! *Le grand cheval blanc*! *Le cheval!*'

'Shh,' she said, because he often had nightmares about lions and very big zebras, and she thought this was another one. 'It's OK, there's no white horse, darling.'

'Yes, yes, there is, Maman! *Look!*'

She turned swiftly and saw him pointing out of the passenger seat window, and she corrected her steering and looked to one side, remembering at the same time that of course, there were white horses everywhere round here. On the hillside, a tiny horse, prancing in the distance, bone white stamped into the green.

'Of course, I'm sorry. I'm stupid. They have them round here.'

'*Why*, though, Mummy? Maman?' Luke demanded.

'No idea. I'm sorry. I should have – we'll get a book while we're here. A book of British history. It'll explain about Stonehenge too. You'll be able to show everyone at school we've seen it. And the Westbury white horse.' Westbury – of course – where had that come from?

Memory led her further back, as they grew closer

to Winterfold. The hedgerows would be full of sloes now, the river Frome, below the house, swollen with autumn rains. The lichen silvery grey, the last of the autumn leaves on the roads, acid yellow and deep red. 'It's close. We're very near, Luke.' They drove along the vertiginous lane leading up to Winterfold. 'Mummy hasn't been here for ages,' she said, preparing to turn into the drive, a hard ball in her throat. 'You're going to meet—'

There was a loud smash, and a huge force, like a great weight pushing on her chest, thrusting her back. Her neck tore with pain, and she cried out. The car spun round so fast she didn't know what was happening. She remembered only the door flying open, glass everywhere, Luke screaming, and the deep, harsh bell of the blaring horn. She climbed out of the car, dazed, fingers fumbling at Luke's car seat, clicking, while he screamed, and blood was pouring down his forehead, ribbons of red. Was this Winterfold, had she come home? Why was this house so different, the windows so big?

'Luke—'

He darted away from her as she set him on the ground, and then her legs buckled with shock and she fell to her knees. She stood up, shaking, and ran down the lane, as though in her dreams once more. She yelled his name and when she reached the house she saw a little figure running ahead of her. Was that Luke? Who was it, was it her? There was blood on the gravel, she remembered the gravel; there was a tall man, covered in blood, holding him. It was Luke. Her grandparents were there. A woman was screaming, and the tall man turning to her and asking her something. But she couldn't hear him, and that's why she thought it must be a dream, because everything else went black.

MARTHA

They were lucky, the emergency switchboard operator said. An ambulance was just passing, on its way back from a nonurgent drop-off. Martha moved them inside, out of the rain, to wait. They gathered in the middle of the sitting room, Florence throwing a rug and cushions haphazardly on the floor. Luke cried and cried, his mother too, nestling his dark head in her arms, her blue jumper covered in blood. Occasionally, he would stare up at this room of adults, then close his eyes and cry again.

Martha watched, her jaw working with anxiety. Her mind wasn't functioning properly; she felt as though she had slammed into something herself. It was by now clear that Luke – this little person was called Luke, wasn't he? Hadn't Cat also had a *dog* named Luke? – was going to be all right. It was a scalp wound, but it was a nasty cut, and a nasty shock. It was *all* a shock. She peered at her granddaughter's face, so thin, grimy with mud, blood and tears. This was Cat. Cat was a *mother*. Martha, who knew what she would be eating for supper two days ahead, who could grasp any idea, had not planned for this.

'What the hell were you doing?' Cat shielded her son's head and glared behind Martha at the doorway.

'I'm so, so sorry,' Joe said, as he fell to his knees next to Luke. He rubbed his eyes, his voice hoarse. 'I don't know how it happened. I just didn't see you as I was backing out and—'

'You're a bloody lunatic, you shouldn't be driving.' Her voice throbbed. She kneeled and scooped Luke round so he was facing away from Joe, over her shoulder. Her cheeks each had a pink spot, bleeding out on her too-white skin. Martha remembered, when Cat was little, how passion used to take over her thin body, whether with anger or happiness. 'I mean, what the hell were you thinking? Don't you say: "Hmm, before I just reverse at twenty miles an hour down this drive and round a corner I might actually turn my head and look?"'

Joe said quietly, 'I wasn't concentrating. My mind wasn't there. It's no excuse.'

Cat shot him a look of pity tinged with disgust. Joe squatted beside her, twisting his fingers around and around. He squeezed Luke's shoulder gently and said quietly, 'Hey, little mate. I'm so sorry. You're going to be all right.'

Cat stared up at him, her grey eyes icy with fury. 'Get away from him. Leave us alone.'

Luke wriggled in her arms and turned round. 'What did you do with the car that was so bad, because you hurt my head when you did it.' He

235

hiccuped, with a little sob. 'It hurt my head and . . . *Maman, je ne comprends pas pourquoi nous sommes ici.*'

His mother squeezed him even more tightly against her. 'It's OK, sweet boy. The ambulance is on its way, they're going to . . .' As she spoke a siren sounded and flashing lights bounced off the walls of the sitting room. Luke stiffened in alarm.

'It's all right, Luke,' Joe said. 'Promise. Some nice people are here and they're going to look at your head, and I'll give you a cake afterwards.'

'Stop talking to him,' Cat said, standing up, lifting Luke with her and wincing, slightly. 'Just fuck off, why don't you?'

'Cat,' Martha said.

'Sorry, Gran.' Cat's hair flew into her eyes as she turned round to her grandmother. She pushed it away with one hand, tangling it into a cloud. 'But he nearly killed us. He shouldn't be—'

'Cat, I can't say enough how sorry I am.' Joe backed up against the French windows as she passed by him, and they heard the ambulance sirens coming up the hill, and Martha stiffened as she saw a police car turning into the drive. 'They always send the police if it's a road accident,' David said, reassuring, in her ear. 'He's going to be fine, Em. Don't worry.'

She wanted to pivot around then and take him in her arms, kiss his worn cheek, stroke his hot, thick hands. He was always behind her.

'She's really back,' she said, 'Isn't she?'

'Yes, she is,' David said, watching Joe approach the young policeman who climbed out of the car. Joe pointed at his bumper, shaking his head, jabbing his finger to his chest. 'Poor Joe. That poor lad.'

Later, when Jan and Toby, the paramedics, had gone, bearing biscuits and a Thermos of tea, leaving Luke with a little line of neat stitches below his hairline, Joe came up to Martha in the hallway, aimlessly brushing fluffy dust off a painting frame.

'I've given them a statement and they've gone. I've told them Cat's insurance mustn't be affected. I've put the samosas in the larder and the little cakes. What else can I do, Martha?'

'Just go, Joe,' Martha said, looking at him. 'Unless you want another cup of tea?' He shook his head, and she knew he wanted to be anywhere but here. 'Go and get some rest. Leave the car here and walk home, the fresh air'll do you good.' Cat appeared in the hallway, arms folded. Martha patted Joe's shoulder. 'You look shattered, my dear. I'll call you if they need you. I'm sure they won't.'

'I need to do the rest of the pastry cases. I'll bake them at home.' He didn't look at Cat. 'Mrs Winter, once again—'

'It was an accident, Joe, please. Of course it was. You look absolutely done in, you know.'

'Thanks.' He gave a faint glimmer of a smile. 'Not sleeping that well at the moment. I've got a lot on my mind. I blame myself for what happened.

I've had some news that has been a bit a shock – but it's no excuse.'

Martha looked at him with concern. There was something about Joe that reminded her of a small boy. Those sad eyes, that jaw that was so firm, closed shut for most of the time. The awkward, shy way he had of explaining things, the way his smile, when it came, was like a bear hug – it wrapped you in its warmth. 'Is everything OK?'

'Yes.' He pulled the keys off the dresser and Cat stood up, darting out of his way as though he'd hit her. 'I'd best be off. Leave you to it. I'll bring up the . . . Should I come back tomorrow?'

Martha gave a sharp laugh. 'You'd bloody better, Joe! Come on, it was an accident. Wasn't it, Cat?'

Cat stared at the floor. 'Sure.'

Martha opened the door and watched him wandering out down the lane, almost like a robot.

'Bye,' she called, but he didn't hear her. 'He's gone now.'

'Good riddance,' Cat muttered. Martha shut the door, and turned round, her hand on the latch, looking thoughtful.

'Who was dat?' said Luke, appearing from the living room.

'Yeah,' Cat said, rubbing her neck, and wincing. 'Who *was* that idiot?'

'The chef. He's doing the catering for this weekend. You poor thing. You'd have liked him, if you'd met him in different circumstances.'

'I doubt it.' Cat kissed Luke on the head. 'Darling

Gran. I'm so – this isn't how I wanted to come back. It was supposed to be a lovely surprise.' She gave a small, tentative smile and kissed Luke's head. 'I'm sorry. About all of this.'

Martha reached forward, and touched her grand-daughter's cheek. Her smooth, rose-pale cheek. Then she stroked Luke's head, feeling the thick hair, the shape of his skull. Her great-grandchild, his head in her hands. She closed her eyes briefly, as the enormity of the moment threatened to overwhelm her, then steeled herself.

'Don't ever, ever be sorry, my darling. Let's get a cup of tea for ourselves. Florence? Can you put the kettle on? And get the cake tin. It's in the larder by the tea bags.'

'You painted it!' Cat exclaimed, following her grandmother into the kitchen. Her face was pale, but she was smiling. She gave Luke a big hug and pulled him on to her knee. 'Oh, the blue chair's still there. And the bowl of limes . . . Oh, good-ness. Luke, this is where Mummy used to live.'

Luke nodded, looking around him and chewing his thumb, with a kind of dazed fascination mixed with extreme fatigue. Martha couldn't stop staring at him. He was her great-grandson.

'It used to be orangey, now it's sort of wattle and daub, isn't it? Very trendy,' Cat said.

Martha laughed. 'It hadn't been painted since I did it myself when we moved in. Florence was four and she stuck her foot in the paint tin, I remember. Orange footprints everywhere.'

'Really?' Florence said. 'Oh dear, I'm sorry. Did I really?'

'I'm afraid so, and it took forever to get off your foot, too. But you did make pretty foot-shaped flowers, on the tiles over there.' She pointed. 'This time I got someone in to do it. Very lazy.' She moved towards Luke, and stroked his cheek softly with one finger. 'And how are you feeling, Luke? You were very brave.'

'Yes, I was,' said Luke. 'I wanted to cry. But look at this.' He tapped his head purposefully, then frowned and burst into tears again. 'It hurts!' he wailed. 'Maman . . .' and he began to babble away in French, and Martha did not understand him.

David, who had been standing by the doorway, held out his hand. 'Luke, come with me, little one. I have something to show you. And there's cake in my study, too.'

Luke looked up at his great-grandfather questioningly, then nodded and ran over to him. He took his hand, and as they disappeared Cat sank down into Southpaw's carved wooden chair and stared into space.

'He'll draw him a little Wilbur cartoon about it, won't he?'

Martha thought of the last time David had tried to draw Wilbur, a pathetic, grotesque parody of the dog he used to scribble in one-two-three-four-five seconds for an eager child or an enthralled fan.

240

'He'll think of something, I'm sure.'

'I can't believe it,' Cat said. 'I still can't believe . . . we're here.' She squared her slim shoulders and said quietly, 'Gran, you must want to know what happened. Why I didn't – tell you about Luke. Who he is, and all that.'

'Well, I can guess he's your son, and his father had black hair, that's about it,' Martha said. 'What I want to know is why you didn't tell me.'

Cat said something so faint Martha couldn't hear.

Martha leaned in. 'I'm a little deaf. Say it again.'

She said, very softly, 'I lost myself.'

'What do you mean?'

'It sounds so . . . stupid, saying it out loud.' Cat said. 'My friend Véronique calls it the mist. Like I got caught in it, couldn't see out of it.'

Martha stood up and fetched the old teapot. She plucked the mugs off the dresser behind Cat as the door opened and Florence came in.

'There you two are. Pa's having a great time with Luke, you know. I'm going to make some coffee. Cat, love, coffee for you?'

Martha nodded approvingly at her, and handed Cat the mugs. 'I'll stick to tea. Oh, these old friends,' Cat said, looking at them. 'The Silver Jubilee, the Brane of Brittian . . . Leeds Castle . . .' Martha saw tears falling on to the wooden table.

'Why are you crying, darling?' she said, stroking her granddaughter's shoulders.

Cat bent forward, her head in her hands, and cried as though her heart was breaking, softly, sobs thrumming through her, rocking backwards and forwards. It was a good minute or so before she could speak. Florence tactfully busied herself at the sink with some washing up, while Martha sat beside her granddaughter, waiting till she raised her head. Suddenly she felt enormously guilty. She had done this. She had created this.

Then, quite clearly, she heard Daisy's voice.

She has to know, Ma. You have to explain what you've done.

It was so distinct she turned round. But no one was there. Martha shrugged, batting the invisible away. She gripped Cat's heaving shoulder.

'Darling, tell me what's wrong. Tell me why you're crying. Then I can help you.'

Cat looked up, and said softly, 'Everything is wrong. I shouldn't have come home. Seeing the mugs and Southpaw's sketches on the wall, and the owl on the door – I – I can't go back there, knowing that now.'

'Knowing what?'

'How much I hate it. I can't . . . We can't do it any more.'

She pressed her fingers to her face.

'You can stay here,' Martha said. 'You, and little Luke.' Her breath caught in her throat. 'You don't have to go back.'

Cat laughed. 'We can't stay here.'

'Yes, you can.' She whispered it in her ear.

'Darling you're home. You don't ever have to leave again.'

Only after she said it did she remember to whom she'd said it before, and why.

LUCY

The doorbell rang, ferociously, at seven a.m. Lucy tried to ignore it, as she did most mornings, then she sighed and let out a low growl of irritation, rolled out of bed and stamped down the hall. The rain had stopped, and as she opened the door a sharp wintry breeze flew into the damp flat.

'Package.' The grim-faced courier held out a box and a tiny BlackBerry, screen hopelessly scratched. 'Please sign.' Lucy drew a straight line, wondering if there was a piece to be written about signatures on courier deliveries, because she'd never once managed to sign something on one of the screens that even closely approximated to her name. The courier walked away without a word – they always acted as though she'd kept them waiting ten minutes, not ten seconds – and Lucy slammed the door, slightly louder than she should have.

'Post for you, Irene,' she growled, throwing the box outside her flatmate, Irene's, closed door. Irene was an obsessive eBayer and at least once a day, usually more, some piece of vintage fashion would arrive in Amhurst Road, ready to be exclaimed over, photographed, blogged about. Lucy really didn't understand how Irene could afford any of it, but she didn't want to be hauled away to prison as an accessory to identity fraud so she assumed a position of ask no questions, and longed for the day when she had a place of her own.

Lucy started making herself some coffee, then remembered she was trying not to drink coffee because of that article she'd read about how every cup shortened your life by 3.5 minutes. So she made herself some hot water with a slice of lemon, which was what Lara had at the start of each day, as she liked to inform the office in her blaring foghorn voice. 'It's amazing, it's really cleansing. It means you're not hungry for breakfast.'

She said it every morning.

The flat was on the ground floor of a draughty Victorian house in the heart of Hackney. Lucy's room was much bigger than Irene's and soon after Lucy moved in she'd understood why Irene had chosen the other. Lucy's was freezing, even in summer. It faced north-east and the sun never quite reached the huge, draught-magnetic grimy grey bay window. It smelled vaguely of cats and damp; Irene's room, however, smelled of cleaning products, plastic synthetic packaging materials and Gucci Envy.

Snuggling back under the still-warm duvet with her hot water and lemon, Lucy pulled her laptop up on to the bed and waited for it to power up, and as she did she gazed vacantly at the black screen. She wished she could shake this feeling of dread that seemed to have settled on her, like a cloud, somewhere just above her head, lately. She couldn't work out what was causing it.

It wasn't just the foreboding she felt when she thought about Gran's invitation, or her wild, panicked eyes when Lucy had asked her about that damned article. She wished she'd never mentioned it to Deborah. It wasn't just Southpaw's frail face and swollen hands, either. This time tomorrow she'd be in her dad and Karen's house. Karen would have brought croissants from Marks and Spencer. Dad would have something to show her; he always did. Some funny book, some article from a newspaper he'd cut out. And Karen . . . she'd be there, sipping coffee, just . . . staring at them.

It was always the same, but the last time she'd been back, nearly two weeks ago, she *knew* something was going on between them. Was it true? Had Dad found something out? Karen was snappy, not eating anything. Dad was behaving strangely, too. That kind, friendly Dad-style jollity she knew so well was turned up several notches. He only did that when he was feeling panicked: the more worried he was, the more sprightly he became. She'd lived with it for years. As a child, Lucy had always known if her mother was particularly bonkers, or feeling spiteful, when she got up in the morning. Dad would be making eggy bread in the kitchen, singing Gilbert and Sullivan at the top of his voice. Everything's fine here! Nothing to see!

'So, all was good up at Winterfold,' she'd said. 'Gran says the preparations are going well. She's polished all the silver.'

'Oh, yes!' Dad had said. 'More coffee, Karen? The party, hey! It's going to be great.'

Karen had looked up from her magazine. 'No, thanks.' She'd pushed her plate away, the croissant virtually untouched. 'I'm not feeling that well, actually.'

'Oh dear,' Bill had said, and then, 'Poor old thing. You've been working so hard lately, haven't you?'

Lucy saw her father watching Karen, and she didn't quite understand the look in his eyes, and was discomfited. 'Yes, much too hard,' Karen said. She arched her back and stood up, then said, too casually, 'I keep meaning to tell you, by the way. I'll be at the lunch, of course, but the drinks on the Friday night – I'm not sure I'll be able to make them. There's a conference call with the States at six thirty that day—'

'Oh, no!' Lucy, ever the Pollyanna, cried. 'Can't you tell them it's important?'

Karen was standing in the doorway. She rubbed her eyes, then looked over at her husband. 'I have, several times. Rick won't listen. I'll be there the next day.'

'But how sad you have to miss the drinks, those parties of Gran and Southpaw's are the best,' said

Lucy, who literally could imagine nothing better than a family gathering at Winterfold, the house full of people and light and laughter.

Her father said nothing throughout this. Then he got up too, went over to the sink and rinsed out the cafetière. 'That's a real shame, Karen,' and he started humming.

And I am right and you are right and all is right as right can be!

Lucy took a sip of her hot water, grimacing. The lemon was bitter, the water lukewarm in the chill of her room. The truth was, she couldn't bear the idea of upsetting her dad. He'd been like a sad old dog after he split up with her mum, padding around his new house in the village in his slippers, trying to invite people over for weird things like Korean Barbecue night. Karen had been good for him. And – Lucy forced herself to admit it – she liked her.

Karen was fun, when she didn't have that awkward look in her eyes. She liked *X Factor* and popcorn films; she could recite *The Proposal* and *The Holiday* off by heart but, like Lucy, she hated *Love Actually*, said it was way too saccharine, which is exactly what Lucy thought. And she was so clever, she had this amazing job. Lucy had once heard her on the phone to her boss, and Karen had said about fifteen things Lucy didn't even understand as sentences, let alone pieces of actual information. She'd been good for Dad. She'd relaxed him, when Lucy's mother, Clare, had wound him up with her intense moodiness and obsession with fads: tai chi, womb rebirth, Bikram yoga. Lucy had grown up with it and she'd seen how hard it was for him. Karen didn't take, take, take all the time, she just let him be himself, and in the beginning you could tell she just thought he was wonderful, looked at him like he was the voice of wisdom. Lucy sometimes felt Dad laboured under a yoke of Winter-ishness. Pretending everything was OK when it wasn't, keeping the mood of the room upbeat, happy, when it wasn't. He wanted the approval of his parents more than anything, and because he was nearby, handy, undramatic, he never seemed to get it. Which was stupid, Lucy thought. He was the best dad ever, and he was an amazing doctor, nothing too trivial for him. He cared about people: look at old Mr Dill's housemaid's knee, which had got so bad he couldn't walk. Dad went and saw him every day for two weeks and took him soup and just let him talk. Or Joe Thorne's finger: Joe had told Lucy in the pub last week that he'd have lost it, if it wasn't for her dad. No career, nothing. He'd saved that awful man Gerald Lang's life at the disastrous summer party, which had passed into Winter folklore. And there was the time he waded into the river and pulled out Tugie, Gran and Southpaw's final dog, who was obsessed with finding otters, while Lucy and Lucy's then boyfriend, Tom, just looked on, blankly.

Tom said afterwards, 'I would have gone in but I really didn't want to cramp your dad's style. I think he needed that.'

Yeah, right, Lucy had wanted to say. You're a twenty-five-year-old ex-rower who runs every day. My dad is nearing fifty and his knees click when he walks. Sure, that was really nice of you.

Oh, why hadn't she done anything?

A sound along the corridor, of creaking floorboards and mewling, suggested Irene was awake and about to come out to feed Chairman Miaow. Lucy snapped out of her reverie, looking around her. It was seven thirty-two. She ought to get up, get in the shower first, be at work early, ahead of the game, so when Deborah asked her for the fourth time what was happening with that article about Southpaw, she'd be able to say, 'I'm sorry. I still need to dig around a little more. Work out what angle to take. But I've had this idea for a piece on the Kardashians. The Oscars. Rihanna. Jennifer Aniston and her secret heartbreak.'

She'd rung her grandmother and told her she wasn't going to do it any more, and she'd meant it. Lucy's conversation with Cat had shaken her, not just because Cat was so . . . vicious. It was more than that. For the last few weeks Lucy had been buying time so she could decide whether she really should just give up the whole thing or carry on digging a little further, for her own sake, if no one else's. Even if she never showed the article to another living soul she felt she had to write it: because something wasn't right, that was for sure.

She scrolled quickly through her emails. The usual morning inbox junk. Discounts from The Outnet, celebrity gossip updates, a new pub around the corner from her was opening a microbrewery called the Dalston Hopster – even Lucy could see the lack of irony in that was almost appalling.

She almost missed the email from her mother, sent late the previous night, and Lucy's shoulders tensed in anticipation as she opened it.

Hi Darling

I'm off to India tomorrow, just to remind you. I find it hard to be in the country with the celebrations taking place this weekend. I feel excluded by your grandparents. This is a source of sadness to me.

In answer to your question, I have been in touch with Daisy myself. I wanted some advice on travelling alone, especially through Delhi. I have tried to contact her several times with no reply. I did remember however that she used another name when she went to Kerala: Daisy Doolan. Read this because even though it's four years old I think it is very interesting.

https://bitly.com/perssonch

She didn't tell your grandparents she'd been booted out, did she? What's happened to her, then? I'll let you know if she replies.

I'm away until the week before Christmas. Raymond has my schedule and the details of the ashram if you need to contact me in an emergency. Take care, darling, be well, be full of light and love.

Clare xx

Who was Raymond? Typical Mum. Lucy clicked on the link, and as she read slowly, her eyes opened wide, her jaw dropped.

'No,' she said to herself. 'She wouldn't do that. That's not right.'

Charity worker fired, sent home in disgrace

Local residents profess themselves shocked and saddened by the exit from the Sunshine Children's School of Daisy Doolan from the United Kingdom, who has done so much to aid school attendance and prosperity in this area and was rewarded only recently with a medal from the mayor (see picture). In 1982 when Miss Doolan arrived in Cherthala, literacy was already high but attendance was low and poverty was great. She raised 2 million rupees towards the building of the new school for girls and, as we know, five pupils have gone on to Bombay University to study a diverse range of subjects. Miss Doolan is said by the school's principal to have been embezzling money up to the sum of one million rupees over five years. She has been dismissed and police are anxious to trace her whereabouts. One colleague said she had left and gone back to England.

CAT

By Friday, it felt as though she had been at home for months. Had she really been away all that time? The only difference was that first night, seeing herself in the mirror of the upstairs bathroom, unchanged after all these years, same William Morris peacock wallpaper, same pig-shaped tooth mug, handle missing. Same carpet, same dust-encrusted bottles of ancient Body Shop Ice Blue Shampoo and Grapefruit Shower Gel. With the truth that only old familiar mirrors give you, she'd stared at her reflection, tired, strung out after a long day and nearly screamed. Instead she'd thought: I look like her. I look *exactly* like her.

That first night, Cat slept as though she'd been drugged; Luke too. It was the first night they'd been in different rooms and she was still worried that the cut on his head might wake him up, but the thought of putting him into his own room: that alone made coming home worthwhile. When she checked on him, he was fast asleep, arms flung outwards like he was running to hug someone, duvet tangled around his feet, cheeks flushed.

It was so strange, how easy it was to slip back into life here. As if it had been waiting for her, and her son, to come back into it. Easy, and terrifying at the same time. Had she changed? Was she a different person? Were they? She couldn't help asking herself this, as the day of the birthday lunch grew nearer, and then it was Friday.

'Apples, milk for Luke, bin bags. I'll be home in time for lunch. Luke?' She looked around. 'Luke?'

'He's with Southpaw.' Florence appeared in the kitchen, where Cat and her grandmother were sitting, and poured herself some more coffee. 'They're making something together. They're covered in paint.' She shrugged. 'It looks like a dragon.'

Cat stood up. 'It's so great. I've never seen him like this. He's shy around men.'

'Your grandfather is a childish man in many ways,' Martha said, smiling. She stood up slowly. 'Get some lemons, will you? Oh, and can you do me a favour?'

'Sure.' Cat hunted around in her purse, hoping against hope she might find some more English money in there.

'Can you pop into the Oak, and tell Joe I've found the extra champagne glasses in the attic and he doesn't need to bring any more up?'

'Oh, right. Sure.'

If Martha registered Cat's hesitation she didn't comment. She reached for a chocolate biscuit.

'Have this, darling, you're far too thin. Take your time. Lunch is all ready and Luke's fine.'

As she strode away from the house, down the hill to the village, Cat swung her arms in front of her, breathing in the damp, mulchy air. Luke *was* fine, in fact more than fine. Since he'd been here he hadn't stopped talking, a sort of French-English babble that he sang to himself as he ran around the sitting room, picking books off the shelves that lined the walls, asking Southpaw a hundred questions. His great-aunt Florence, too – he seemed fascinated by her and what she knew about things. 'Why is your hair so messy?' he'd asked – only he said *'messeee'* – the night before at dinner, and Florence had simply thrown her head back and roared with laughter.

Recalling it now, his pleasure at Florence's glee, the whole family together and the lightness of it, how silly it was, gave Cat a sharp pain in her chest. No matter how often she said to herself, 'It's just for the weekend, enjoy it,' she knew now that one of the reasons she'd never wanted to come back was simply that a part of her had always known she'd find it almost impossible, once she was here, to leave again.

To have been that person in Paris with that life seemed unreal, out here on this beautiful day, with the curling lane rolling away from her, the village in the distance, the gentle hue of ginger-brown leaves still dusting the top of the trees. The sky was a clean grey blue, wisps of cloud like lines of cotton wool. She breathed in again, clearing her mind. 'Three more days,' she said to herself, as she turned off and headed through the woods, her feet following the same old path across the stream she'd always taken. 'Forget about everything else. Be like Luke. Enjoy it.'

It was a little after twelve when Cat entered the pub with her shopping, cheeks flushed from the crisp damp wind whistling through the village. The door banged behind her and the lady behind the bar looked up, as did the only other people there, a couple in the corner who then fell back into conversation.

'How can I help you?' said the landlady.

Cat stared. 'Sheila? It's Cat! Winter! I heard you were back in Winter Stoke. Gosh, hello!'

Sheila stared back, then her eyes widened and she clapped her hands together. 'Well, I never. Cat, my dear! Come here, give me a kiss.' She hugged Cat. 'Well, I heard you were coming back for this party, but I didn't think it'd be true. You here to see Joe about tonight?'

'Oh—' Cat began.

But Sheila said firmly, 'He's nearly free anyway. *Joe!*' she called, sharply.

Cat's heart sank as the man in the far corner turned round and, seeing her, scrambled to his feet. The woman he was with stood up quickly. 'Cat!' she said, brightly.

Cat froze. 'Karen? Karen!' She'd seen her once,

and so long ago that it took Cat a moment to recognise her. She looked at her, and then at Joe. 'How are you?'

'I'm really well, Cat. It's great to have you back. I know they're all so pleased you've made it.'

Cat thought Karen didn't look well at all. She had yellow shadows under her eyes and she'd obviously been crying. She wrapped her shapeless black cardigan defensively around her and Cat, trying not to let her mind run ahead, smiled at her in a friendly way.

'Oh, thanks.' All she could think was, *Poor Lucy was right,* and she wished her cousin was there, wished their last words hadn't been angry ones. She laid a hand on the bar and gestured to Joe. 'Hi. I didn't mean to interrupt. Gran wanted me to give you a message.'

Joe glanced at Karen, who said, 'I was just in to talk to Joe about your grandmother's cake, actually! Bill's sorting it out this end, and we've had – oh, we've had a lot of fun with it, haven't we . . . Joe?' she ended, as though she weren't quite sure of his name.

Cat nodded. She glanced at Joe, and their eyes met.

He looked awful, she thought, even worse than he had on Wednesday. Maybe he just looked like that all the time. She remembered Lucy saying he was gorgeous, dark blue eyes, all of that. To Cat he looked like a man pushed almost past endurance. His face was grey and he hadn't shaved.

Black stubble prickled his jaw, and his eyes were bloodshot.

He rubbed his chin. 'How's your little lad?' he said. 'And the car – it's all sorted with the hire company? You'll let me know what I need to do?'

'Yes, thanks. And – Luke's fine. Thank you.'

'I wanted to give you something for him, actually. I haven't—'

'Honestly, it's fine.' Cat cleared her throat. 'Listen, I won't keep you. I just wanted to let you know Gran doesn't need the extra champagne glasses. She found the others in the attic.'

He nodded, still staring at her, but didn't say anything. 'Is that OK?' she said after a few seconds.

'Joe,' Sheila said, sharply. 'Answer her.'

He jumped. 'Sure. That's great. Thank you for letting me know. You must have enough on.'

'Me? I'm fine,' Cat said. 'Seriously, are you all right? You look like you're coming down with something.'

'I'll be off then,' Karen said chirpily to no one in particular. 'See you – all later then. Bye! Thanks for the drink, Joe.'

The door slammed heavily behind her. Joe flinched, then shook his head. 'I – Sorry. I'm just tired.'

Sheila said, 'He's not been sleeping. It's this party, is it, Joe?'

'Something like that.' Joe gave a small smile. His

phone buzzed with a text, but he slid it straight into his pocket, then looked up at her. 'Can I get you a drink?'

Despite herself, Cat suddenly felt sorry for him. He seemed totally alone, standing by the bar, his wide shoulders drooping, his jaw clamped so tight shut it was almost as though he was smiling. But this was the man who'd written off his own car and caused thousands of pounds worth of damage to her hire car, to say nothing of nearly killing her son in the process. And Karen – what was he up to, huddled away with Bill's wife in the middle of the day?

'No. Thank you. So you know Karen, do you?' she asked, a little too bluntly.

'Yes.' Joe picked up a beer mat, cracking the hard cardboard apart between his fingers. 'She's been kind to me since I came here.'

'Yes,' she said, uncertainly. 'Course.'

'It's strange. Moving far away from your – your family, not knowing anyone.' He stared out of the windows at the grey sky. 'When you want to belong. And you don't. I'm grateful to her.'

Cat, who had expected some glib reply, frowned. 'Yes. Of – course.'

He shook his head as though recalling himself to the present. 'Look, I got Luke this book anyway. I meant to drop it off today. Jamie loved it when he was his age.'

He disappeared behind the bar, and pulled a package out from beside the till. Dust rose up in the air, and it seemed horribly symbolic, falling there in the deserted pub.

'Oh . . .' Cat said, embarrassed. 'You didn't need to.'

'No, but I wanted to. Jamie and I read it all the time.' He handed her a paper bag, and she slid a long slim volume out of it, and looked dubiously at the front cover.

'"*Stick Man*",' Cat read. 'Right. "From the author of *The Gruffalo*". It looks great. Thank you. Never heard of *The Gruffalo*, but I'm sure it's a good one.'

Joe said softly, 'Sorry. You've never heard of *The Gruffalo*?'

'No. Um . . .' She didn't want to be rude. 'I'm sure it's a really good book. Looks great.'

'You have never heard of *The Gruffalo*?' He repeated this. 'Seriously?' He looked around him. 'Is this a wind-up? Maybe it's got another name in France. Look at the back. There's a picture of the Gruffalo.'

Cat, feeling annoyed, turned the book over. 'No. Sorry. There are lots of children's books, anyway, and—'

'I think it's really weird you've never heard of *The Gruffalo*, that's all. What kind of a country is it you live in that doesn't have *The Gruffalo*?'

'So you've said.' Cat put the book back in its bag.

'Let me give you some context,' Joe told her. 'It's like not having heard of Winnie-the-Pooh.'

'That's rubbish.'

'It is,' he said, insistently. 'It really is.'

'Well, I'll read him *Stick Man* tonight. Thanks.'

'Stick Man's an idiot, basically, always nearly getting burned on a fire or carried away by a bird. *The Gruffalo*, that's what you want. It's double bluff, it's genius.' He looked at her. 'Look. I'll give you my copy.'

'You've got your own copy? *That's* a bit weird, isn't it?'

He grinned, suddenly, and his face changed. 'That came out wrong. I mean for when Jamie comes to stay. My son. You can borrow it while you're here for the weekend. I'll bring it up some time.'

'This evening. The drinks.'

'Yes.' He stopped. 'Of course. Look, I'd best get on. If that's all?'

'Oh, yes.' She suddenly felt foolish, in the way. 'Thanks again for this. Um – see you later.' She raised her hand to Sheila. 'Lovely to see you again, Sheila,' and made to leave.

'Hey,' Joe called out. 'Listen. I'm sorry, again.'

Cat turned. 'Are you talking to me?'

'Yes.' Joe gripped his hair. 'I'm really sorry. I feel worse and worse, every time I think about his little face. Believe me, I'm so glad he's OK. It was bloody stupid.' He stared at the floor.

Sheila had gone into the back and there was no one else in the pub. Cat crossed her arms. 'Well, it was an accident. Wasn't it?' she said, gently smiling, but he looked at her seriously.

'Of course it was, Cat.'

'I was joking,' Cat said. 'I don't actually think you were trying to murder us.'

'Right.' Again he scratched at his scalp. 'I don't even understand when people are making jokes any more. This morning the guy from the brewery went "Boo" to me and I nearly punched him in the face.'

She laughed. 'You must have a lot on, with this party.'

'That's about all we have on. This place isn't keeping me busy. So the party, yes, I want it to be right. Impress everyone so they start coming here. It's – yeah, I suppose it's been on my mind a lot.'

She watched him. 'Is there anything I can do?'

He gave a shy smile. 'Just say ooh and ahh when it comes out and make out you've never eaten anything so delicious before. That's what you can do.'

Cat laughed. 'OK. Well, Gran says it's going to be amazing. She doesn't lie.'

'You live in Paris, though; you're a tough person to please.'

'Believe me, I'm not. I can't wait for a proper posh meal. I live on frozen foods and the odd croissant.' *And Henri and Madame Poulain's leftovers, and once I ate a baguette someone left untouched on a bench in the Tuileries Gardens. Basically, I don't eat much because we live on eighty euros a week. And then people compliment me on how slim I am.*

'Well, I hope you enjoy tonight. And lunch tomorrow. It's very important to your gran that it's all perfect,' Joe said, moving behind the bar.

She watched him, his easy strength as he lifted a crate of tonic bottles out of the way, almost like he could flick them with his finger. 'Thank you,' she said, trying not to sound defensive. 'I think I know what it's about, though.' She gave him a piercing look. 'It's pretty obvious, isn't it, when you think about it?'

He stopped unloading the bottles and their eyes met, again. Cat had the strangest feeling whenever she looked at him. As if she knew him from somewhere.

'Whatever. She's very glad you're back. She's missed you. And your granddad. He's not been well, has he?'

She shook her head, her heart pumping. 'I – I don't know.'

'He's a lovely man. Been wondering about him lately; wanted to ask someone in the family if he was OK.'

'You could always have asked Karen,' she said lightly.

There was a silence. 'Yes,' Joe said slowly. He bowed his head slightly, and their eyes locked again. 'Look, Cat—'

What would have happened next Cat didn't know, but the door opened again. 'Hello, Joe. Well, hello there, Cat!'

Cat turned round. 'Hello,' she said, warily. A

largish woman, older than she, sandy cropped hair and a big smile, plumped herself down next to Cat, who racked her brains wildly. Who was this?

'What can I do for you, Susan?' Joe said. Cat threw him a grateful glance.

'Anything you want, Joe, you know that!' Susan said, and gave an awkward titter. Joe smiled tightly. *Susan* . . . Cat racked her brains. *Susan Talbot. Post office. George and Joan Talbot's daughter.*

She put her hand on Susan's arm. 'Hello, Susan. Lovely to see you.'

'And you, my dear,' Susan chuckled, her eyes twitching in a slightly disconcerting way. 'I'm looking forward to the party tonight. You'll all be there. It's all anyone's talking about. Have to work out what I'm going to wear!' She gave a matronly, arch smile and grinned at Cat, folding her arms below her big bosom. 'I came in to get a bottle to take up with me tonight. You can help me with that, can't you, Joe?'

Joe nodded and bent down, taking out three different bottles. 'Of course. One of these any good?'

'You don't need to bring anything tonight,' Cat told Susan, who was watching Joe with a look in her eye that Cat didn't like. Susan had always been crazy. One of many tightly furled memories began to roll out in Cat's brain. When they'd been at school Susan had accused one of the teachers of being a pervert and he'd been sacked. It hadn't been true.

'No, no! I wouldn't hear of it! I want to do my bit, you're all like family to me! The Winters!' Susan took out her purse, looking at Joe from under her thick black eyelashes, so at odds with her blond complexion.

Cat caught Joe's eye, briefly. 'OK, well, I'd better be getting back.' She picked up the bag again. 'See you later, both of you. And – er . . .' she smiled at Joe, '. . . thanks again. So, I'll get started on this. We'll look forward to the other one. *The Gruffle.*'

'Something like that,' he said, and she wasn't sure if he was joking or not.

She left him dealing with Susan and strode home back up the hill, wishing Lucy would hurry up and arrive. She was less and less sure of everything the longer she was here.

KAREN

'I'm disappointed not to be going. Honest, Bill.'

Karen sat at the foot of the stairs, watching Bill pull his coat on, and trying to catch his eye.

He buttoned his coat. Still not looking at her, he said, 'I'm sure you are.'

'It's just . . .' she tugged the dressing gown tight around her, '. . . I still feel really rotten. Think it's best I stay in bed after my call's done. Rest up for tomorrow. I'll definitely be there, tomorrow.'

Bill didn't say anything. He went to open the door, one hand resting on the frame so it was still closed to. She swallowed, tasting metal in her mouth, feeling weak, wishing he'd speak. These last few days . . . just waiting for him to say something. Because she knew.

'OK?' she said. 'Are you listening to me?'

'Lucy's already up there. I'd better go. Goodbye, Karen,' he said.

'Look, Bill, I told you weeks ago I wouldn't be able to come and I'm sorry, I wish I could. So – you go, give them all my love, I'll see them tomorrow, yes?'

267

He met her imploring gaze then and she thought he was smiling because he agreed with her. For a brief, blissful couple of seconds she thought the world was right again, and then he held open the door and said, 'I think it's best you don't come tomorrow, Karen. I think you know that, too.'

Cold air was rushing into the stuffy house. 'What do you mean? Of course I'm coming.'

'Karen, don't treat me as though I'm stupid. I'm not stupid.'

Karen stayed where she was, afraid to move. 'I don't understand.'

'Yes, you do. Karen, I know all about you and him.'

The door was wide open; people walked past, looking into the house.

'Hello, Bill! Oh, Karen! See you up there, will we?'

Bill turned, with military precision, hand on the door again. 'Evening, Clover. On my way up. See you soon,' then closed the door and came towards Karen. He towered above her, sitting at the foot of the stairs. 'I've known about it for weeks.'

Karen swallowed. 'Who told you?'

'That's – that's all you've got to say to me?' His voice was thick with anger, and she realised, emotion. But Bill never got emotional. 'You're cheating on me, and all you care about is how I found out? Susan Talbot told me, that's who. Came in last month, to show me her verruca.' He gave an angry laugh. 'Halfway through she said there was something she thought I *had* to know.' His voice was cracking and she looked away, unable to bear the look on his face. All the seeds she'd sown, everything she'd done, it was all coming out now . . . and she had to take it. Nothing to do but sit here and accept it. 'That's how I found out my wife is – is . . .' Bill covered his face with his hands, '. . . sleeping with someone be-be-behind my back. Susan Talbot with her sock off whispering secrets into my ear.' He turned and stared at the empty bookcase, breathing heavily.

'It's not—' Karen began. It was all clichés, wasn't it? *It's not what you think.* How could she explain to him what it was? She'd slept with someone else, been doing it for months. Those were the facts.

I love you. And I know you don't love me. That's why.

She stood up, ignoring the wave of nausea that crashed over her. Holding on to the banister, she said, 'Yes. It is true.'

'Thank you,' said Bill. Almost as though he was pleased to be proved right. 'And is she right? Tell me who it is.'

'Bill—'

'*Tell me who the hell it is, Karen!*'

Karen backed away so she was standing at the other side of the sofa, hugging herself.

Bill said, 'I'm not going to hit you. Don't be ridiculous. Just say it. Say his name.'

'Joe,' she whispered. 'It's Joe Thorne.'

'I knew it.' Bill bowed his head. 'The . . . my God. I thought we had something. I know we've had our problems, I know we're different, but I thought you loved me.'

'I do,' Karen said quietly. 'Bill, I've always loved you. But you don't love me. You don't have room for me. I realised that a while ago.'

It was as though he hadn't heard her. 'How long's it been going on?'

'It's not – it's not "going on".' She folded her hands together. 'It was only a few times, the last time was September and then he – he broke it off. When he found out I was married.'

The night I said I was dropping off Susan's birthday card, in fact.

Your daughter happened to mention to him she had a stepmother called Karen Bromidge when they were both at Winterfold. He hadn't realised before then. So you can thank Lucy. Thanks, Lucy!

'He broke it off, not you.' Bill looked at the ground. 'He – oh God, Karen.'

'I never meant – I wasn't looking to – oh, Bill.' She knew how lame that sounded. 'We're similar. He's a good man.'

'A good man! Karen, your sense of good and bad is pretty questionable, if you don't mind me saying.'

'He—' Her eyes were full of tears. *A good man like you.* 'He understands . . . oh, things.' But she couldn't throw anything back at him, not now. 'He understands what it's like, here.'

'What, the awful life you both lead in this beautiful village with your lovely home and nice job? My heart bleeds.' Bill's eyes were dark with anger. 'You've always thought you're too good for us lot, Karen. That's the truth, isn't it?'

She laughed, crossing her arms. 'What on earth are you on about? That's bloody rubbish. If anything it's the other way round, Bill. I'm the one who's not good enough for the rest of you, and don't you love letting me know.'

Bill shook his head. 'You haven't got a clue. You think you're always right. Your point of view and no one else's. I've watched you give that bored little sneer when my family does something, if Lucy's a bit too eager or Ma talks about the garden or something.'

'I don't!' It was getting away from her, all of this.

'You do. You only see Flo as eccentric.' Bill's voice was quiet. 'She's wonderful underneath, the funniest person I know, but you've never bothered to find out. You think we're all snobs, but you're the one who can't get past the fact she doesn't use conditioner and she doesn't care about manicures. That makes you the snob, Karen.' Bill's face was pink. 'And if we talk about a book we've read or cinema or anything remotely cultured, I've seen you, Karen. With the big sigh as if you think we're all a bunch of idiots. You think anyone who's interested in anything intellectual is a loser.'

'No, Bill,' she said, not wanting to sound spiteful, unable to help it. 'I suppose just for once

271

occasionally it'd be nice if someone didn't want to talk about books or paintings or Radio 4. Just for once.'

'Ma and Pa had nothing when they were growing up. It's what they're interested in. Don't exaggerate.'

'I'm not. I'm bloody not.' Her voice shook.

Bill said angrily, 'So in that case I guess a man who cooks chicken and chips for a living's about your level then, isn't he?'

'He's a proper chef, you – you – idiot! And at least we'd talk about things! We'd laugh about things! We didn't sit there in silence doing nothing, saying nothing, night after night! He was there for me, when you're always out, Mr Dill this, Mrs Cooper that, Bill. You see your father at least twice a week, just when I'm back from work . . .'

His face got that pinched look she knew so well. 'Pa finds the evenings hardest. Especially if Ma's out. You don't understand.'

'Because you never tell me anything!' Karen's voice broke. 'You love being needed, Bill. But I'm right here. *I* need you, I'm your wife . . .'

She covered her face with her hands, furious with herself for crying, having not intended to.

For their third date, they'd driven over to the beach at Clevedon and sat on the beautiful old pier eating sandwiches he'd made, which tasted really strange. He'd pulled a rug out from his car and spread it over her knees. It had been chilly. They were silent a lot of the time, just smiling at each other.

Then he'd said, 'I've been practising chicken Kiev sandwiches all week. You – you – when we were talking last week, you mentioned it was your favourite meal when you were a little girl. I don't know how successful they've been, though.'

And Karen looked away from the grey sea, the endless white sky, and the wheeling seagulls, at the quiet, neat man next to her, and they both smiled at each other, and he'd taken her hand in his, under the blanket. 'I feel like a pensioner,' she'd said, happily.

'Well, for the first time in a long while, I don't,' he'd replied, and leaned over and kissed her, very calmly, and his hand squeezed hers tightly as he did. He'd stroked her cheek and said, 'You're the most beautiful thing I've ever seen, do you know that?'

Karen, who knew she was a good prospect with her full bling, favourite Karen Millen dress, heels and handbag combination on, had believed he thought it was true. She understood him, their world together, and then . . . then the doubts had set in, the loneliness, the need for attention, which had been her downfall. But she wasn't a child for wanting it, was she? For wanting someone to laugh with, talk to?

She scratched at her cheeks, furiously, staring at him, remembering it all. This was it, maybe for ever.

After a long pause Bill said, 'I can't believe how wrong I was about you.'

She swallowed back a sob. 'It's not just me, Bill. You're so distant. All the time, these days. You're shutting me out.'

He paced back and forth, two steps here, then there.

'I've had a lot on my mind lately.' She stared up at him. 'Nothing to do with you. It's—' He rubbed his eyes.

'Bill, tell me. Can't you tell me? Is it about this lunch tomorrow? Your mother's announcement?'

'It's not her. It's Pa.' He rocked on his feet, like a tired, small boy. 'Anyway, that's not what this is about, Karen. Don't try and turn this round.'

'I'm not doing that, Bill,' she said. She tried to think of the best way of making him see that this was exactly what she was talking about. 'I'm not. You are. It's like a sinkhole's opened up, right under our marriage. Been growing bigger and bigger for ages. I can see it. You can't. You've just blocked your eyes to it. To me. To how far apart we've grown. I – I don't know how else to put it.'

He blinked and said quietly, 'Is it over, then? With him? With us?'

'It's over with him.' She swallowed, praying she wouldn't start gagging, or worse. 'I think it is.' How could she finish this, how could she tell him the rest of it?

'Oh, no, he ended it? You poor thing.' His voice dripped contempt and it was horrible. Bill never teased, or was cutting. He was always gentle. 'Well, I'd love to stay, but I'm already late. I'll leave you to nurse your bruised ego. Maybe eat a few chocolates and watch a sad film eh?' He clenched his fists. 'Damn you, Karen! Now, of all times. Why did you have to—'

'It wasn't my choice. None of this is my choice.' She scratched her face again, feeling the ribbons of pain on her skin.

'Don't act like it's all a big surprise. You knew I knew. I've been watching you these last few days. You're like a cornered rat.'

'I am,' she said, frankly, and she saw the look of surprise in his eyes. 'I am, I'm trapped, Bill. Sit down. I have to talk to you properly. There's something else you need to know.'

DAISY

January 1983

She is still sleeping. If I just carry on maybe she'll stay asleep. I don't think it's sleep like adults sleep. It's a furious pause. Fists screwed up. Angry nasty little face wrinkled. Horrible bent knees and long feet curled against the chest in these nappies I can't get right. The pin is blunt and I keep forcing it through the damn nappy and then pricking her.

I can see clearly, then I can't. I can feel calm, then I can't. I am worried I will hurt her. I don't think she'd notice, that's what I tell myself. She is so tiny, so cross and small, she doesn't open her eyes except to stare, not focusing on anything. I don't want her to love me, I never did this for that. I could have got rid of her. I just wish she'd look at me.

Sometimes when I've tried to feed her and I can't, and I've given her some other milk and she won't drink it, I lie in bed crying very quietly so they won't hear, and she cries and cries too. She falls asleep eventually and I stare at her, small and red, splayed across my tummy. Her mouth flutters

276

open like a butterfly. She's so tiny. She felt massive inside me and now she's just so small.

I hate it here. I always did, and now I'm trapped. They think it's the making of me. I hate their condescension. Billy Lily at Christmas. 'Be the making of you, everyone should have a baby, Daisy!' What does he know about it? That disgusting self-centred hippy he's going out with, she's completely wrong for him and that's obvious, but everyone's so pleased Bill finally found someone who'd fuck him they don't care she's as ugly as sin, completely rude and stupid too. I really hate her.

And Florence. I can't even talk about Florence. I crawl with revulsion; I think I might be allergic to her. Whatever it is in my head, there's something there that reacts whenever I have to go near her. I hate how obvious she is. She doesn't . . . understand anything. I actually think she might be mentally disabled. I read an article about it. She is brilliant, I know, you all keep telling me, I know. But she is totally incapable of having a conversation. She can't even say hello without making fifteen different noises afterwards and pushing her glasses around her face. I hate her. I'm quite calm about it.

She was there at Christmas, poking this baby, stroking her face like some pervert, cooing over her. I want to say: You don't belong here, Florence. You aren't part of this family. Why don't you just get out?

But I'm the one who doesn't belong. I can tell that's what they all think. They don't really get the fact that I'm the one who belongs here, and she doesn't. So I have to go.

This thing here – I've thought about plonking her on Giles's doorstep. But I know he's terrified his girlfriend will find out we fucked. Straight after we'd done it he said: 'That was a mistake.' Nice, huh? Rolled off me and starts sweating in the tent. I could hear the hyenas outside, screeching and mating.

I didn't say anything. Just turned over and pretended to sleep. I remember the mattress was scratchy and a little piece of horsehair kept poking me in the neck all night. It kept me awake, burrowing into me, but I couldn't pull it out when I looked for it. And all that night this thing was taking root inside me, swallowing me up.

I'd done it before: with boys in the village like Len the farmer's boy or that man who came up to drop off Daddy's page proofs, a long drippy thing he was, a bit like Giles, now I come to think of it. I think I got too sure of myself, because Gerald Lang from up at the Hall really hurt me. If you act confident they love it, they're so scared. I'd tell them to meet me in the woods, then be waiting with my pants off and let them touch me there, and then they'd want to do it, even if they didn't, if you know what I mean? Because they'd think it wasn't manly to say no. I think men are pathetic. But Gerald didn't like it that he couldn't do it properly the first time.

He said could he meet me again. I said, yes. So we met at the back of the woods again and this time he was different, he kicked me, he bit my breasts and then he shoved up inside me, and I really did hurt for days and days, and I bled afterwards. He kept doing it after I'd shouted and when I bit him back he just bit me even harder. He told me I was a stupid cunt, kept saying it. I couldn't stop him. I just said: you're hurting me. Over and over.

The weird thing is he liked that.

So what is strange is: when he'd finished it, he stopped and was all normal again, and then he said: 'That'll teach you a lesson, girlie.'

Girlie. We'd grown up together. I was six months older than him, in fact. *Girlie.*

The next week I saw him in the street, and now I think about it, four or so years later, I realise it was rape, it was. And he waved. 'Hello, Daisy old girl, how are you?'

I don't understand the world, the way it works. More and more.

I think it is all part of the lessons I've learned. The one lesson that was wrong was Giles. It's lonely out here, dangerous too. During the day I'm a hero, at night I'm scared and don't know where to go. I thought it'd be good to do it again with someone who wasn't rough. And Giles wasn't rough, he was a drippy, sloppy, mush of a man.

Like a cold wet plate of boiled spinach. I thought it'd be nothing, and instead look what it did to me.

I don't see why I should give her a name. I don't want to give her anything, then she won't have any connection with me, and really? It'll be much easier that way.

Ma and Dad are treading on eggshells around me; they'll believe anything I say. If I say she's hungry, they try to pretend it's all right that she cries for hours because they don't want to interrupt Daisy when she might be doing something useful for once.

Actually I'm arranging the clothes in the wardrobe, bit by bit. All my favourite dresses, all together for once. It's childish but it *was* childish, how I had to give everything to Florence, to Caroline in the village, to everyone. I never had my own things. I never came anywhere except in the middle, people squeezing me on both sides.

It'll be light soon. She's crying again and I can't feed her. I keep trying and it's agony. They keep saying it'll get better but it doesn't. I don't understand any of this, why this is in the world and what I should do. I know now she'd be better off without me. I look at her in the cradle. She is so furious. Her mouth is wide, wide O. Purple, her face is purple. She smells. If I put this towel over her she's muffled and I really can't hear her.

It's quite nice, the sound blocked out.

I'm sitting on the edge of the bed rocking the cradle. If she'd just shut up I'll take the towel off.

She's quiet now. I lift the towel away. You know, it's strange, she's crying, but I don't hear it any more.

I look at my daughter's face like it's the first time. Who are you? Who are you, little baby? Did you really come out of me? I know she did, and I know she needs me, and the idea of that makes me start to cry again. Her face has changed, even in the night. She looks like Ma.

I realise how bad it is. How bad I've got. I can't stay here and I know it now, it's just being brave enough to leave.

So I write the note. These clothes are for her.

I look down at her in the cradle, and I touch her cheek. It's very, very soft. I think I'll always remember how it felt even when I don't remember how everything else felt these awful last few weeks.

I know when I shut the door behind her I won't be a mother any more. I can hitch to London and Gary has said he'll save me the ticket. I wish it wasn't so easy to be like this, sometimes.

I look at her as she sleeps. Bye-bye little girl. I'm sorry you're part of me. The thing I hope most for you is that you grow up to be absolutely nothing like me.

LUCY

Everyone agreed the Winters threw the best parties. Even though it might be, as tonight was, a cold evening, a swirling mist eddying along the lanes and roads, the kind of night that made you want to stay in, curl up on the sofa with a glass of wine, no one who was invited to Winterfold ever did.

It was a treat to make the journey up the hill to the house, and this time the arriving guests knew Martha had outdone herself. The sound of Ella Fitzgerald and babbled conversation floated out down the lane. Coloured plastic lanterns hung from the branches and hedgerows as you turned into the drive, and golden light poured from the windows into the drizzle. The front door was propped open, and inside one of the vicar's children took your coat, and someone else – Martha, elegant as ever in a midnight-blue and gold shot taffeta jacket, her dark green eyes smiling at you, or maybe clever, striking Florence, bright as a peacock in green and purple silk, smiling and chatting, or taciturn but friendly Dr Winter, Bill, who'd always looked after you so well, listened understandingly to your complaints about arthritis or your fears about cancer or your worries about your husband – one of them gave you a kiss and a glass of champagne, in a way that made you feel truly welcomed. You were ushered out of the cold, into the cheery sitting room, where the fire leaped in the great inglenook hearth lined with pretty blue and white tiles, and someone else offered you a tray stacked high with delicious-looking canapés. As the first, chalky-sharp gulp of champagne bubbled through you, you glanced round and saw an attractive, dark girl leaning against the wall and David, smiling next to her – was that really Cat, the prodigal granddaughter returned from Paris? And as you inhaled the atmosphere, of light in the winter's dark, warmth and security, you felt the sense of being pulled into the centre of something, a place you wanted to be.

The village was out in force. Kathy, the vicar, was over there, Sheila from the pub, even nervous new parents Tom and Clover, the pair always referred to as 'that sweet young couple in the village', had got a babysitter for once, Tom's hair standing on end, Clover flushed and sweet in a dress that showed too much of her large breasts. The Range Rovers, who never came to anything in the village, were there. That pompous ass Gerald Lang, of Stoke Hall, and his wife, Patricia, who hadn't been to a Winterfold party for years, after what happened to Gerald – even *they* were there. The biggest coup was the actress from the ITV cop drama and her director husband, who lived in the really big house further up the hill and never came to anything. But they, like you, were simply guests in this lovely home, enjoying themselves and you all had something in common, which was that a tiny part of you wished you could live there, become part of the family, have this life for yourself.

Though, increasingly, you felt, the Winters had their problems these days. You knew Daisy wasn't to be spoken of and the other daughter was, really, increasingly batty, wasn't she? And why was the son's new wife, a cold fish, mysteriously absent? Susan Talbot had been spreading rumours all week about Karen, and as you mingled more you discovered Cat had returned with a *son*, whom she'd apparently kept secret. And Bill was drinking too much and Lucy, his daughter, talked too much, and dear old David – he looked pretty done in, didn't he? Not well at all – and the birthday girl, Martha, wasn't herself, it couldn't be denied, distracted and mechanical in her responses to you, as though she were somewhere else entirely.

But though all of these things were true, when that nice Joe Thorne appeared, an hour or so into the party, carrying a birthday cake blazing with so many candles he seemed to be carrying a halo of fire and everyone sang 'Happy Birthday', Martha's face, bathed in the glow of the fire and the champagne and the atmosphere, seemed then to be lit from within with some kind of emotion. And you felt sure that, though of course things weren't easy for anyone, no matter how it looked from the outside, the Winters must, indeed, know themselves to be a lucky family.

Just as Lucy finished handing round another spread of canapés she saw Cat shushing a reluctant Luke out of the room and off to bed. Cat turned and raised her eyes at Lucy, mouthing: *This is really weird.*

Lucy had to admit it was. Kind of unreal, a dream, or a scene from a film, not as she'd expected, and she rubbed her eyes. It had been a long day. Cat had a son. Karen wasn't here. Everything else seemed unchanged: the twinkling lights and the Clarice Cliff platters worn with years of sausage rolls and washing up, the old lead crystal flutes, the same faces of people she had known all her life, some bent with age, the children dashing around through people's legs, Gran talking intently to Kathy, the vicar – she looked tired; Lucy thought she must be knackered. The punch bowl on the side, the fire burning – but everything felt different, this time. As she stood still and looked around the room, she wished she could go away now, and quickly scribble it all down so she'd remember, the sense of her world spinning, getting faster and faster, like a carousel before the music suddenly stops.

'Hello, old thing.' Florence put her hand on

Lucy's shoulder. 'Haven't spoken a word to you all evening. How are you, darling?'

Lucy kissed her aunt, shaking herself out of her haze of thoughts. 'I'm fine. Listen, have you seen Joe?'

'Handsome Joe?' Florence grinned. 'He is awfully nice.'

'Oh . . .' Lucy could feel herself blushing. 'Don't be embarrassing. I need to tell him something. Hey, that purple and green is fantastic on you, Flo. You should wear colours more often. You look like Cleopatra.'

Florence threw back her head and laughed. 'You do talk rubbish.' But she looked pleased and there was an undeniable glow about her this evening. 'I'm feeling pretty chipper, I have to say.'

'How so?'

Florence drained her drink. 'Lucy, well – I've been putting my house in order.'

'That sounds vague.' The sound of rattling glass sounded in the corner and, glancing over her aunt's shoulder, Lucy could see her father trying to push an empty champagne flute on to a tray, making too much noise.

'Yes, it does, doesn't it? But I've righted a wrong. Took rather a lot of courage to do it. No going back now.'

One of the things Lucy loved about Florence was she didn't seem to care about things that, to Lucy, were so important. 'Flo, you're being very mysterious.'

'Someone betrayed me. Sounds dramatic, but it's true.' Her face clouded, and she looked frightened, very young, suddenly. 'I've been a total fool. I've decided I'm not going to put up with it any more. God. I hope I haven't made a huge mistake.'

'What have you done?' Lucy said.

'I've done something for myself,' Florence said. 'I'll tell you about it sometime. You might even be able to help me, in fact.'

'How so?'

'Well . . .' Florence bit her lip. 'I don't want to say too much at the moment. Maybe I'll be calling on your journalistic connections at some point. My niece, the Fleet Street rising star.'

'Oh, I'm really not that,' Lucy said frankly. 'I couldn't—'

Someone shoved against her and Lucy jolted her glass, spilling champagne. She turned around to find her father, swaying slightly, fiddling with his phone.

'Hello there, Dad,' Lucy said. He glanced at her and grunted. 'Good party, isn't it?'

She handed her father a tray of tiny Florentines. Bill looked at them and then at her, as if trying to remember why he was there. His eyes were slightly glazed.

'You all right, William?' Florence gestured to her brother, and Lucy realised she, too, was not exactly sober. 'Look at those freckles. Do you remember in the summer we used to join the dots all over

287

your body with one of Dad's ink pens? When he was bigger he'd try and fight us off but Daisy was always stronger, wasn't she, Bill?'

Bill shrugged. 'She was freakishly strong.'

'Your sisters were stronger than you?' Lucy said.

'We were,' Florence laughed.

'Oh, I'm the joke of the family, aren't I?' Bill said. 'Big joke. That's me.'

'Oh, Bill, no, I only meant she—' Florence began, but he interrupted, heavily.

'Listen, Flo, I might head off. Not feeling so good and tomorrow'll be a long day.'

'I'll come with you,' Lucy said.

'No, you stay here, why don't you?' Bill squeezed his daughter's shoulder. 'Think Gran could do with the help. Anyway, like I said, Karen's not well, I said, didn't I? You can sleep in Cat's room, can't you? Stay here, that's best.'

Lucy gripped his arm. 'Oh.' She said softly, 'What's up, Dad? Everything OK?'

Bill said, 'It's fine, love.' He blinked and swayed a little. 'I shouldn't drink. I can't take it.'

'You can't,' Lucy said. 'Remember my birthday?'

'Well, that.' Her father stopped. 'Was different. That bar was very loud. I distinctly said just singles, and she kept giving me triple gins and tonics.'

'Rubbish,' said Lucy. She looked to her aunt for support, but Florence had wandered off. 'Dad – I'll come home with you.'

'No,' her father said roughly. 'I said, stay here.'

'I just meant I'll walk you home,' Lucy said,

feeling tears prick her eyes. 'Make sure you're all right. I won't come in—'

A voice behind said, 'Any more champagne, over here?' and both Lucy and her father turned.

'Oh, hello,' Lucy said, smiling. 'Dad, it's Joe.' She nudged his arm and beamed at Joe, who was staring at them both, bottle in hand, frozen still. She pulled at her floral shirtdress, awkwardly, wishing it weren't so tight. 'I – I—'

'Do I want more champagne?' her father interrupted, his voice a little too loud. 'Is that what you're asking?'

Lucy ignored her father. She said, brightly, 'I've got some good news, anyway. Keep forgetting to tell you. I'm sure I've got our restaurant guy to agree to review the Oak. He says December the seventh, and . . .' she trailed off, and looked at Joe, and then at her father, on either side of her, staring at each other.

'I hope you rot in hell for what you've done,' Bill said softly to Joe. He slammed his glass down on the table, where it rocked drunkenly from side to side, knocking over an empty plastic cup. Joe swept it up deftly in one hand as Bill strode out of the room, looking at no one, head down. There was a murmuring ripple of surprise around them as the heavy front door slammed shut.

It's starting, Lucy thought. She turned back to Joe, a polite smile fixed on her face, and when she saw his expression she knew. In that moment, she saw it perfectly clearly, almost everything. How could she have been so blind? Of course. He was looking at her intently, something like rage and anger written all over his face. He didn't even look ashamed, standing there holding the champagne bottle and the empty glass. Suddenly Lucy wished everyone would leave, that this was over. It suddenly seemed unbearably fake, all of it. And what she wanted now was the truth. She knew it now. That was why they were all there, all of them.

CAT

'So you're back, dear, for how long?'
'I hear you have a . . . son, how old is he?'
'And you're still working at the . . . plant stall, then?'

'It must be wonderful to live in Paris, dear.'

'Your grandmother's always talking about you, dear, she must be so pleased you're here.'

Hiding in the loo off the freezing cold cloakroom Cat wondered how long she could actually stay there. Until someone banged on the door, maybe? She wished she'd brought a glass with her, but she'd already drunk too much. Maybe she needed something to eat. Those canapés were delicious – Joe Thorne may have nearly killed her son and written off her hire car, but he knew how to make pastry and Cat, like any self-respecting Parisian, took pastry seriously.

She hadn't realised how hard it would be, this bit of coming back. Two days here and she was used to the shock of the familiar, but that was before the party. After an hour of questioning, of pecked cheeks and beady eyes, Cat was ready to hide upstairs.

She'd never had Lucy's ebullience; if someone asked Lucy something she didn't want to answer – like Clover, that mumsy airhead from the village: 'Do you have a boyfriend yet, Lucy?' (Cat got the feeling Clover was the kind of person who asked that question a lot) – Lucy just diverted attention: 'Oh, no chance, not at the moment. Are you watching *X Factor* or *Strictly*? I'm *Strictly* this year.'

Cat simply didn't know how to do it. So when Patricia Lang, who was very grand, fixed her with a stare and said, 'Why haven't you been back for so long, dear?' Cat had felt herself flushing with irritation. She had never liked Mrs Lang, and she loathed her husband, Gerald, who'd always reminded her of a kind of red-faced bullfrog. She remembered him of old. He gave her the creeps.

'Y'very like y'mother,' he'd slurred once, after Midnight Mass, to which he'd turned up obviously drunk, and then he'd slid his large, meaty hand across her ribs, and stomach, like he was measuring her for size. Cat, then thirteen, had dodged out of the way, grabbed his arm and bitten him, hard, on the fleshly ball of his palm, then kicked him in the shin. Then, surprised and slightly alarmed at the violence of her behaviour, had left him, hobbling and swearing softly in the porch, and run all the way home, in the dark. She'd never told anyone.

He must be fifty, or sixty now, but Cat realised she still loathed him. Wasn't it funny, these people you didn't think about for years? She'd looked round for him: Gran always said vaguely that it was no wonder he mostly never came to any of their parties after what had happened to him here, but could never be drawn on exactly what that was. Almost like it was a joke. She supposed he was a joke, in a way, a nasty, aggressive man who didn't realise he was a dinosaur. His wife, however, was more beady than ever, and Cat honestly hadn't known what to say. She'd blushed even more and then excused herself, to go to the loo.

Bang! Bang! Cat jumped out of her skin.

'Hello? Anyone in there?'

Cat ran the tap and dried her hands. 'Sorry, just coming.'

Opening the door, she saw Clover's large, moon-like face hovering in wait for her.

'Oh, I'm so sorry. I didn't realise – I wasn't sure – that's why I knocked, there was silence for *such* a long time you see, and I do need to – we've got a babysitter, and we have to get back to her! It's a rare night out for us!' She gave what Cat thought would be best described as a simpering smile and said, 'How often do you get to go out, Cat? In Paris?'

Cat said, 'Not much.'

'Yes. Of course.' Clover nodded as though Cat had enlightened her. 'And Luke's father, he . . .' she trailed off.

Cat let the half-question hang in the air. 'He, yes.'

'Ha, ha!' Clover laughed too loudly. 'Oh, well I think you're *very* brave. Tell me, did you breast-feed? Because I hear that in France breast-feeding is totally frowned on. It's such a shame. One of my NCT friends—'

'Great!' Cat said, patting her on the back. 'Lovely to see you again, Clover. I'll let you get off, isn't it awful weather. Goodbye!'

As Clover retreated, muttering something about playdates, Mrs Lang appeared from the kitchen doorway. 'Hello again, dear. I was just saying to Gerald that I must find out from Cat if—'

Cat couldn't take it any more. 'Thank you! Excuse me, have to check on something outside for Gran.' Recklessly, she drained the glass of wine on the sideboard, opened the door and escaped outside.

It was still raining, and the soft mist rolling off the lawn met the light from the house, fusing into a phosphorescent glow. Cat hurried around the terrace, past the living room and the silhouettes of the guests, framed by the windows, like pictures in a children's book. She stopped, and looked out across the valley. It was a black night, the rain blotting out the moon and stars.

I think you're very *brave.*

Cat had turned at the corner of the L by the kitchen and was wishing she had a cigarette for the first time in years when a low voice called out urgently, 'Hey? Who's there?' She started, and her hands shot into her mouth.

'It's Cat. Who is this?'

'Cat. It's Joe.'

Joe Thorne appeared from the darkness, and Cat pulled her fingers out of her mouth. 'Oh, thank goodness.' Relief, and adrenalin, and alcohol, made her sound almost ecstatically glad to see him. 'What are you up to?'

He stamped his feet gently on the mossy ground. 'Just wanted some fresh air. Thought it'd be OK to have a couple of minutes' break. The party's starting to wind down.'

Cat came and stood next to him, under the shelter of the porch. She said awkwardly, 'You must be exhausted.'

He nodded. 'Yes. It's been a good night, though. I hope your grandmother's enjoyed herself. I wanted her to be pleased.'

'I know she is. Very pleased.'

There was a small, awkward pause. The rain dripped softly on to the stones of the terrace.

'Luke absolutely loved *Stick Man*,' she began. 'And – er . . . I looked up *The Gruffalo*. It turns out I'm the only person who's never heard of it. I feel terrible.'

'Maybe it's banned in France. Anti-competitive. Perhaps they have their own *Gruffalo* knock-off.'

'I'm sure they have it. Sometimes I miss out on stuff, with Luke. It doesn't matter, we read every night and he loves it but we don't . . .' She looked down. 'Oh, well. We have a bit of a strange life there. That's why it's so lovely being here. Everyone together.'

He crossed his arms. 'Right.' Out of the corner of her eye, Cat stole a glance at him. He always looked so serious, so weary. Suddenly she wasn't sure if she wanted another drink or was wishing she hadn't drunk the last one so quickly.

'This is your idea of hell, isn't it?' she said.

'No, not at all.' He glanced back at the door. 'I suppose family things make me . . .' He trailed off.

'You like *Game of Thrones*, don't you?' she said, suddenly.

'How do you know that?'

'Saw the DVD in your bag yesterday when we were all in the kitchen.'

'Please don't say *Game of Thrones* reminds you of your family. Oh, my God.' He looked around in mock alarm. 'Winterfell. Winterfold. Are you . . . the Starks? Are you the Lannisters? Oh, no. Don't be the Lannisters.'

Cat put her hands over her mouth and laughed softly. 'No. Don't be silly. I just mean you have to take it all with a pinch of salt. Family. Otherwise it's . . . It's too much.'

He nodded. 'Yes. Well, *Game of Thrones* aside, family gatherings like this do make me feel . . . um. Very sad.'

She tried to help. 'You miss home.'

He laughed. 'Fat chance. My mother texts me every fifteen minutes. "Did you know Di Marsden got married? Did you hear Steve was on *Look North* with his rabbits?" No, Mam, I didn't. It's my son,' he said abruptly. 'It's him I miss.'

'Of course. He's called Jamie, isn't he?'

'Yes.'

'Where does he live?'

'In York, with his mum. That's a tactful way of asking the question, isn't it?'

'I've had practice, you can tell. When did you break up?' She stopped. 'Sorry, I'm being nosy. You don't have to say.'

Joe rubbed his fingers. She saw he had a long, thin new scar on his left hand. 'I don't mind. He was one. Just a baby really.' He was staring at the floor, and then his head snapped up and he said, firmly, 'She's with someone else now. A good guy. He can give Jamie everything he needs.'

'You're still his dad.'

'Yes. Of course I am. But maybe that stuff doesn't matter.'

'It does.' Cat moved away from him, retreating into the darkest corner of the porch. 'It shouldn't matter, but it does. He's your family.'

My mum's still my mum, she wanted to say, *part of me will always love her no matter what,* but she found it impossible. She rubbed her hands along her ribcage, as though comforting herself. 'What I mean is, you can't replicate blood. He's your son, doesn't matter if for a few years you don't see him as much, he'll always be your son. Even if you're away, you can always come back.'

'Like you did, you mean.'

'Like I did. But it took a while.'

297

Joe said quietly, 'Suppose sometimes that must be hard.'

Cat stamped her feet, moving further into the darkness. *Don't be nice to me.* 'I wasn't talking about me. I'm used to being on my own. I don't know my mum, or my dad really. Don't have any brothers and sisters. I just got on with it, I had to.'

She wanted to bat him away like she'd done with Mrs Lang, but he just said, 'You've had a time of it, haven't you?' and his voice was so kind.

Her eyes swam with tears. 'Oh, it's all right. That's the way it goes.' Cat swallowed, she had to move things along. 'Anyway, enough about me. Maybe she's better off without you.'

'Who?'

'Your ex.'

'I'm absolutely sure about that, Cat.' Joe gave a grim laugh.

'I didn't mean it like that.' Cat was mortified.

'I know what you meant. And it's true.'

'I meant you weren't right for each other. No point in making each other unhappy.'

'We did make each other unhappy. It's just the fact I couldn't push that all to the side and get on with it for Jamie's sake. He deserves two parents . . . who . . . you know what I mean?'

'No,' Cat said, shaking her head. 'No, no. It's not true. There's no way it would have been good for me to stay with Luke's dad. Not good for me, not good for Luke.'

There it was. Right there. The guilt, pushing

down on her all these years, just lifting off her shoulders and floating away into the night. It was true, and she shrugged to see it go.

'It's funny, being on your own, though, isn't it?' His face turned towards hers. 'You think you're OK, and then suddenly you realise how sunk into yourself you've got. You sit there brooding on all these things that don't really matter.'

'You shouldn't, Joe, it's not good for you.'

'I don't, not really. It's only evenings, bedtime. If I'm not working. I think about Jamie. I used to read him a story every night. Jemma didn't like reading him stories. I'd read him this book – over and over and over again he wanted it. *The Runaway Bunny*. I bet you've never heard of that one, either.'

She shook her head. 'No.'

'I'd love to see what books you have in France. Honestly. *The Runaway Bunny* is great.' His soft voice was warm in the darkness. 'You know, it's about this bunny who—'

'Who runs away?'

'No. He sets up an investment bank. Yes, he runs away.' He smiled and she thought how different he looked when he smiled. It changed his face.

'So this bunny—'

'I hate stories like this,' said Cat. 'Will it make me cry?'

'Probably. It makes me cry. Every time.'

'Why?'

'Because the bunny keeps saying, I'm going to

run away, and turn into a fish. And the mummy bunny says, if you turn into a fish I'll turn into a fisherman and catch you, because you're my little bunny. So he says if you turn into a fisherman I'll turn into a rock, really high up, so his mummy says she'll learn to be a mountain climber, and climb all the way up there . . . and you get the picture. Wherever the bunny goes, his mummy says, I'll always come and find you.'

'Right,' said Cat, embarrassed at how close to tears she was. She swallowed, then gave a half-laugh. 'This is stupid.'

'Well, it is,' Joe said. 'But it made me cry every time. It still does because . . . he's my lad, you see? And he must sometimes want me, when he's scared, or someone's being cruel to him, and I'm not there, because I've left him behind. You know, I thought it was for the right reasons, give his mum and her boyfriend some space, make a new life for myself, and now I just think . . . what the hell am I doing here?'

'Oh, Joe. Don't say that.'

He looked down at his glass. 'When all you want to do is make people happy by cooking up some nice grub and trying to be a good person.'

'I'm used to being on my own,' she said briskly. 'Believe me, I prefer it.'

'Oh. Right,' he said.

She laughed. 'You sound disappointed.'

He looked up, quickly. 'I—'

Blushing at her recklessness, Cat found herself

shaking her head. 'I wasn't . . . I didn't mean anything by it. Sorry.'

He moved forwards into the light, his figure casting a shadow over her face. Cat blinked, in the darkness, tilting her head up towards him.

'Look. I should go,' she said.

'Of course. Cat?' He was facing her.

'Yes?'

'I'm just glad we've cleared the air. I'm so sorry. I'm just glad . . . you don't hate me.'

She could see his shadow behind him on the kitchen door.

'You?' Her heart was thumping in her chest. She could feel her head, clearer than it had been for months, years, maybe. 'Why would I hate you?'

'For – you know. The business with the car.' Joe shook his head. 'I – oh, well, I won't keep on about it,' he said, under his breath.

They were inches apart now. 'I've forgiven you for that,' Cat said, staring straight at him, and she took his hand. 'Honestly.'

'Don't,' Joe said, but he didn't move away. 'Cat—' He broke off, gazing at her.

Cat could feel his bones, his fingers squeezing hers, a sweet, oddly old-fashioned gesture, and they stayed like that, pressed against each other, shivering in the cold, their warm hands knotted together.

'I'm going to anyway.' Cat closed her eyes, leaned forward, and kissed him.

His stubble brushed against her cheeks, his body

against hers, solid and tall; but she was almost as tall as he. She kissed him first, but then she felt his hand gripping her shoulder, his tongue firm in her mouth. He pushed her against the wall of the house, and she pushed against him frantically, feeling his weight on her body, the taste of him, the sound of his breath heavy in her ear . . .

Then suddenly, he broke away, shaking his head. 'Sorry. No.'

Cat laughed, her mouth still full of the taste of him. She felt drunk, reckless. 'What?'

'No.' He shook his head. 'I shouldn't have. Don't.'

He was staring at her as though he'd seen a ghost. She wanted to laugh. 'Fine.' Anger rose within her. 'What's your problem?'

'I – I shouldn't have done that. That's all.'

Cat was sobering up, rapidly. 'Are you with someone?'

'No.' He said. 'Yes. I don't know.'

'What on earth does that mean?'

He touched his fingers to his mouth, breathing hard. 'It means I shouldn't have kissed you. That's what it means.'

'*I* kissed *you*. I wanted to.'

'I wanted you to. But I can't.'

Cat put her hand on the wall of the house, steadying herself.

There was a short, heavy, silence.

'Karen,' she said, suddenly, seeing it clearly, the alcohol suddenly like acid in her stomach. 'Are you sleeping with Karen? Because Lucy told me she wondered if she might be . . . And when I saw you two in the pub I wondered if . . .' She trailed off. 'Oh God. Oh shit. Of course.'

Joe reached for her hand. 'Cat. It's complicated. I can't explain it.'

She pulled away from him, laughing. 'Wow! You really are a snake, aren't you? Here tonight . . . serving our drinks . . . chatting about children's books . . . sucking up to my grandparents. Oh, Joe's so wonderful. And you're . . . you're sleeping with *Karen*?' she hissed. 'You prick. What the hell are you doing here? My uncle, my cousin – why are you here? Why don't you just get out? Go away?'

'I wish I could.' He shook his head. 'I can't. Not yet.'

'I really don't think anyone'll miss you.'

'I'm thinking about it,' he said quietly. 'Honestly. Look—'

'Oh God,' Cat said again. She wiped her mouth on her sleeve. 'I'm so stupid. I can't believe it.'

'I should have stopped it. But you have no idea how much I wanted to kiss you.'

Cat could feel her eyes burning with unshed tears. She turned away. 'I'm going in. Don't *ever*—'

'*Shh.*' Joe gripped her arm, turning towards the garden, alert like an animal after the scent.

'Don't tell me to—' Cat began, but then she froze as his grip tightened, and she followed his gaze.

On the raised stone path beside the daisy bank and the vegetable patch a figure appeared, hurrying quietly through the rain, making no sound. Instinctively, Cat and Joe shrank out of sight under the porch, watching as she came closer. The rain was relentless now and it was impossible to see her clearly, until she rounded the edge of the vegetable patch and stopped. She turned back towards the dark woods.

'See you tomorrow, darling Daisy,' she called faintly, and she blew a kiss into the night air.

Cat held her breath, and found herself reaching for Joe's hand again, warm, wet, and strong, before pulling away, just as Martha looked almost straight at them, her eyes glinting in the dark. Then she turned back, towards the front of the house, and was gone.

DAISY

August 2008

I shouldn't have come back.

I didn't realise how much it would hurt.

I'm no good at being this person . . . oh, what kind of person is that, though? A sister who throws confetti and looks pleased for her brother. That's who.

So Bill marries again, and we all stand there and look happy. I find it bizarre, to be honest. I always thought he was either gay or just one of those celibate types, you know, you'd get them in detective novels, and our old vicar was like that. Just not the marrying kind, they used to say.

I'm not the marrying kind either, I suppose. Whenever I looked at Bill and that rat-faced girl who's got her grubby red claws into him, I wanted to laugh. It sounds so bloody silly, doesn't it, when people are scratching around in the dirt for food or children are dying from insect bites in their thousands, or women are being raped and murdered on a daily basis with no one so much as raising an eyebrow, and here's this . . . civilised behaviour in this Regency Guildhall on this sunny day. Everyone being respectable. My daughter is here. We smile and say, 'Hello, how are you?' like we're distant cousins at a family reunion.

She looks nothing like me and I'm glad. She doesn't look like her father either, but Giles was a drip so that's a relief. She looks like Ma; good for her. Ma is getting old. Southpaw's knee is busted, he can barely walk, and he looks done in. Bill has finally reached middle age, which is what he's been lurching towards as fast as he can since he was a child. Florence: oh dear. Florence is exactly the same but she keeps giggling and is wearing a floral Laura Ashley dress, which would be hilarious if it weren't so embarrassing. I suspect she's persuaded some idiot to screw her and that's what her tragic bucktoothed grinning is all about.

Oh God. I hate Bath, I hate being home and going down these paths again. I'm not this person. In Kerala I'm not this person, I'm just not. I get up in the morning and I know what needs doing, and no one looks at me, and sniffs out the stench of years of disappointment and fear they all smell here when they come near me. Since I've been here I keep telling myself I'll be back in Cherthala soon and I just need more time to make things work. Then I remember what I did, and how I can't go back there again.

I'm so stupid, so fucking stupid. I wanted things, I wanted more than I had. A nicer place, nicer clothes, money for a car. A couple of treats for myself, maybe? And people said I deserved those things. And, to be honest, really honest? I did deserve them, after all I've done for them. But I was silly about it. I have a trusting nature. I let the wrong people in, and they betrayed me, you see. I have lost everything these last couple of months, and now there's nothing I'm good at, nothing I can do.

Catherine is very thin. She has shadows under her eyes and she smiles in this shy way, as though she doesn't know if she's allowed to enjoy something or not. She has just started living with a boyfriend in Paris and she has a job in fashion. Which is funny because she seems to me to be a solitary person. I can't work her out. Never could. Fashion doesn't seem to suit her, I said to Ma, and she only said, 'That's a terrible pun, Daisy. Oh, darling, do you really not see why she's doing that job?'

Oh, darling. Course I don't because I don't understand anything.

If I could only get some help, something to calm me down, something to make everything distant and fuzzy again. I hate the idea of marriage too, how it chains you to someone else and you stand up there and actually admit to it, in a room full of people who supposedly love you. But then I hate the fact that they think they have a claim on me too.

I'm very tired, to be honest. Very tired of it all. I don't think anyone understands, either. I shouldn't have come back.

When Karen threw the bouquet – awful plastic gerberas – Lucy caught it, jumping up like some plump puppy. Everyone laughed and clapped, Karen kissed Lucy, and everyone was saying, 'Keep it in the family' and being jostled on the steps by the next lot of idiots going in to tie the knot. Well, I thought I might just walk off then. I went and stood by the entrance to some sports shop, opposite. These little oiks inside staring at trainers, they all turned when my family started cheering. I'm there in my smart dress, half in that world of light and confetti and smiling, half in this normal one, grey, sad, boring. The photographer lined them up, started shouting, 'Immediate family, please.' There they all were. Grinning, still, humming with something.

And no one looked for me, no one said, 'Where's Daisy?' I stood back against the racks of trainers outside and watched them all and they didn't even notice I wasn't there.

That's when I realised they wouldn't notice if I went. I watched them all, and I wanted to hurt them, to make them feel just a bit of pain the way I feel it, to make them hate themselves the way I hate myself. Most of all I just wanted to feel nothing. To know it's all over.

Saturday 24 November 2012

At exactly one p.m. the day after the party, Martha stood in the doorway of the sitting room, and rang the gong.

'Please go through to lunch,' she said, gesturing, and then she turned, walked through the kitchen, and the rest of the Winters followed her, in silence. Cat was the last one out of the room. As she put her hand on Luke's shoulder, propelling him through the kitchen, she looked up to find Joe's steady gaze on her, his hands mechanically drying a metal bowl.

She stared back at him, her tired, slightly hungover brain clicking over and over. Suddenly she wished she could close the door on the rest of her family, seating themselves carefully at the long oak table, chairs scraping, murmuring quietly, quiet panic on their faces. They all knew something was coming, like a twister over the plains. Somewhere, someone was having a perfectly nice, normal Saturday, a trip to the shops, maybe playing in the garden with their children on this unseasonably sunny, golden day.

The heavy crystal champagne flutes sparkled in the gleaming autumn sun; the untouched champagne in the glasses glowed like honey in a jar. Plump snowy linen napkins, glistening silver cutlery and the ancient Wedgwood dinner service, bought after David's first Wilbur syndication deal. The pattern on the plates – blue and white trim, yellow and coral at the centre – was vaguely Chinese, now worn to pastel, the china veined with a hundred tiny lines after years of family meals ladled on to it, of Christmas goose and baked potatoes on Bonfire Night and roast chicken on birthdays and fish pie on Fridays.

As she sat down, Cat noticed the great green vase of wintersweet at the centre of the table, the sparky yellow flowers like splashes of sunshine against the dark wood panelling. Her grandmother had taken her seat at the head of the table, facing down the room towards the kitchen doors. Southpaw was opposite her, staring down at his empty plate. Bill was unreadable, scanning the room. Florence was in her own world, it would seem, buttering the bread and pouring water, but there were bruised smudges below her eyes. Lucy was quiet, hands fidgeting in her lap. She looked scared, and young. Next to Southpaw sat Karen. Cat thought how pretty she was without make-up, a grave, boyish kind of beauty at odds with her usual coral lipstick, her boxy suits, her determined manner. Her small hands raked her cheeks, the nails leaving streak marks on the pale skin. She started, when

Martha stood up, and Cat turned round to see Joe in the doorway.

Martha tapped her glass. 'Luke,' she said, bending down a little, 'Joe's going to take you to the living room. He's made you a special pie and chips. You can watch *Ratatouille* while we have lunch.' Luke glanced at Cat, astonished that such a great bounty should befall him. Cat nodded, smiling, and kissed his dark hair as he bustled past her, hurrying to take Joe's hand.

As his hand rested on the handle, their eyes met again, and then the sliding doors were closed. Cat could hear Luke chattering to Joe, their feet clattering over the old kitchen tiles. Then there was total silence.

'We will eat shortly,' Martha said, and gestured to a giant rib of beef and bowls of vegetables, resting on the sideboard. She cleared her throat and shook her head, almost smiling. She leaned both hands on the table, shoulders hunched forward as she looked carefully at each of them from under her fringe.

'I have to tell you something, as you know. That's why I planned this . . . this birthday.' Her mouth twisted. 'It's a special birthday, you see. And it's time I was honest.'

'*No!*'

They all jumped, as David's voice cried out from the other end of the table. 'I don't want you doing this.' A paunch of skin quivered under his chin, his agitated mouth working, chewing his cheeks, his lips. He was gaunt, white. 'I've changed my mind.'

Martha got up swiftly. She went over to him, squeezing Karen's shoulder lightly as she passed, and Karen flinched with shock.

'My love,' Martha whispered in her husband's ear. 'You can't. It's gone too far.'

David's voice cracked. 'I don't want you putting yourself in the line of fire. It's for me to do, not you, Em.'

'No, it is for me to do,' she said quietly. 'For me.' She held his hand. 'My darlings. All I ever wanted was to give you all a home.' Her gaze swept the table. 'The thing is – I failed.'

'That's rubbish, Ma,' Bill said clearly, and Karen felt her heart clench.

'Is it?' His mother smiled at him. 'My sweet boy. You're the only one who's still here.' She held up her hand. 'I just want you all to understand a bit more. Understand why I did what I did. I've been trying for so long to make everything perfect. You know I was evacuated during the war. To a family, very much like this. To a house—' she smiled – 'a lot like this. And before that I'd lived in Bermondsey with a dad who was never home and a mum who tried to raise us, and I didn't have shoes, I didn't have enough to eat, I had lice and rickets and – more wrong with me than right.'

'Martha . . .' David looked up at her. 'No, love.'

'And then I met David and he made everything seem possible.' She watched her husband. 'He did.

We were from these grey worlds, both of us, and suddenly there was art, and music, and poetry, these things I'd never come across, and my mind worked when I approached them, it worked better than ever. There wasn't an opera I didn't know, a poem I couldn't recite, I lapped it all up, all of it. And when we got married, well, I gave up my idea of being an artist. I'm going to sit down again. I feel rather shaky.'

Martha walked back to her chair, along the length of the room.

'Women weren't supposed to think we could have both, back then. Do the job we loved, have the family we wanted. And it's a shame, because I loved doing it.' She lowered herself into her chair and stared blankly at the wintersweet. 'I really did. But that was what happened, then. You were all so tiny and you needed me, so much. Especially you, Flo.'

Florence looked down the table at her mother. 'Why me?' she said sharply, and Lucy watched her face change, saw something there she'd never seen before. *What does she know?*

'You were a surprise to me, that's all,' Martha said. 'A lovely surprise. But that's not what I'm talking about. I promised myself, when I packed away the easel and the hundreds of brushes I'd scrimped and saved for over the years, that I'd make the perfect family instead. I think that's what everyone wants to do, isn't it? They want to build a home, to lift up the drawbridge and keep themselves and their children safe at night.'

313

Karen gave a muffled sob, her fingers still pressed against her lips. Lucy closed her eyes, hugging herself.

Martha looked out over the dining room to the garden. Poised, calm. She spoke as though reciting lines from a script. 'I think we raised you well. I think we gave you everything, tried to keep you safe, to plant you in the world. But we tried so hard I think we went wrong, somewhere along the way. What seemed like small things grew and – they've overtaken us now.' She looked at Florence. 'We haven't been honest with you. All of you.'

She drank from the flute in front of her. They heard her throat working, the liquid fizzing in the glass.

'It begins with Daisy. It ends with her too. I don't really know how to say it.' She gave a small laugh, twisting her rings round her finger. 'Funny, after all these years of planning—'

'Ma,' Bill broke in, and his voice was hoarse. 'Where is Daisy?'

Martha and David looked at each other, across their children, across the table.

'She's here,' Martha said, after a pause. 'Daisy's here.'

There was a silence, heavy and pregnant with meaning.

'What do you mean?' Cat said, after a few moments. 'She's – here? Where – where is she?'

Martha looked desperately at her granddaughter. 'Darling. I'm so sorry.'

'Where is she?' Cat said again, turning her head.

Martha looked out at the sunny garden. In her clear, calm voice she said, 'I buried her there. In the daisy bank. Because we planted it together when she was small and she did like it there. We buried Wilbur there, too. And that's where I thought she'd like to be.'

'*Buried?*' Florence said, her voice shaking, and Bill said, at the same time, 'She's dead? She's . . . Daisy's . . .'

'Oh, no.' Lucy heard her own voice. 'No, Gran, you didn't.'

But Martha said, 'She killed herself. Here. A few years ago.'

'I don't believe it,' Karen murmured.

'She didn't want anyone to know. She just wanted to disappear back into her life again, you see. Gradually fade and leave you all with the idea she . . . didn't exist any more.'

'What?' Florence shook her head. 'Ma, you helped her? She did it . . . here?' She clenched and released her hands, resting on the old table, and then reached over to take her father's hand.

But David did not react, just stared into space. A plump tear rolled down his cheek, in a straight, glistening silver line.

Cat didn't move, couldn't speak. Her grandmother tried to take her hand too, but Cat sat back, hands tightly clasped together. She stared out again, into the garden, at the daisy bank.

Martha said, 'I repaid all the money. We gave it

all back. And more. I have all the records. Daisy
– did some good. She wasn't a . . .' Her smooth,
calm face cracked. 'She wasn't a bad person. She
tried her best.'

And Martha sank back into her chair again. Her
veined hands clutched the tablecloth, she stared
at them all and then, with something like surprise
on her face, she started crying.

MARTHA

Martha had only realised how bad things were when it was too late.

The day after Bill and Karen's marriage, Daisy said she didn't feel well. David had gone off in a taxi, first thing, for his long-awaited knee operation, the first return to normality after the half-romance of the peculiarly rigid wedding day.

'Don't let her push you around,' he'd said as Martha had helped him into the car. 'See you tomorrow. OK?'

She'd kissed him. 'I won't. She doesn't do that any more, David, honestly.'

He'd sighed and smiled. 'You always let her play you, darling. Don't do it. Be Martha. Be strong.'

Martha had brought Daisy a cup of tea, up to the old bedroom that had been first hers, then Cat's and, since Cat had left first thing that morning, back to Paris and her new life, Daisy's once more. She had heard their awkward goodbye. 'It was good to see you again, Catherine . . . If you're ever in India come and stay with me!' Daisy had said, and Cat, halfway to the car where Florence was waiting to drive her to London, had turned back.

317

'Oh, gosh.' She took a step forward, and Martha's stomach lurched. 'Really? I'd love to,' Cat had said, her mouth opening into a smile, her eyes shining. 'When can I come? Will I stay with you? Will we ride on some elephants?' Daisy looked at her, bemused, incredulous, a lazy half-smile playing on her face. Then, flushing with anger, Cat had shaken her head. 'I'm joking. You know, that's a very strange thing to say.' Her face was ugly. 'I'm not going to go to India to see you. You must know that by now, surely. That's all you have to say to me? You don't once ask me how I am or what my life's like? Don't you care?' She shrugged her slim shoulders, as though the simplicity of the question was too painful for an answer. 'Doesn't matter. Goodbye, Daisy.' She looked up at the house, festooned with wisteria like a wedding garland. 'Bye, house.' Martha felt then that she was saying goodbye for ever, and she was worried about Cat, and then, later, the moment was lost, after everything else; wasn't lodged in her mind. A rare slip, when she prided herself on always knowing when they needed her.

'You're the only person in this family I don't think I've tried to kill,' Daisy said to her mother, after Cat had left. She was sitting in bed, with the cup of tea. Martha sat down on the bed.

'You do say some silly things,' she said carefully, because Daisy never got hysterical. When she was born, she hadn't cried. A mewl as she came out and then – nothing. The cottage hospital thought the baby might be ill, at first. Martha knew she wasn't, though. Just calm, taking it all in. Her daughter had stared up at Martha, her eyes dark pools like liquid mercury, open from the start, not like Bill. She was always calm, on the surface, and you never knew what was coming next or what in particular had triggered it. One summer in Dorset, after she kicked over the sandcastle he'd spent hours on the beach making, normally gentle Bill had hit her really hard, *smack* in the face. Of course, Martha and David had punished him, but not too hard. She'd done it deliberately, for no other reason than that he'd been praised by passers-by, who'd admired its four towers and hand-crafted crenellations, and he had – unusually for Bill – enjoyed basking in the limelight, just this once. After the smack, and Bill's being sent to bed with no supper, Martha was on edge for the rest of the summer. What would Daisy do to him? Because she knew by now that Daisy wasn't like Bill, who blustered and cried, or Florence, who became hysterical and clingy. She was different. She was . . . not like the rest of them and that was all there was to it. She would sit very quietly and then go out and leave, and you never knew what was going on behind those now moss-coloured eyes, in that curious head of hers.

At first, they made something of a joke of it. 'Daisy? Oh, she'll either kill us or become Queen,' David used to say. But there were signs, little things

Martha noticed about her daughter that started to make sense, and the more they made sense the more Daisy frightened her. Florence, caught in her bedroom for ten minutes with the wasps' nest and the door apparently swollen shut with summer heat, and David running the chainsaw so that no one heard Florence's screams. And Florence's hysteria, the crazy things she'd said afterwards, the lies about Daisy. It wasn't true! The cuts and bruises on her arms that Florence whined about to Martha who, wanting Florence to grow up, wanting Daisy not to be bad, told her not to fuss about. The Girl Guides' bring-and-buy sale where the money vanished, and then Daisy was expelled from school for smoking pot, four months later. Martha still thought she was the only one who'd connected the two. Because Daisy took her time, she knew it by then. Just before the Christmas after the sandcastle incident Bill slipped on the floor of the bathroom on some Johnson's Baby Oil and broke his ankle.

And it was then Martha realised she was too afraid to talk to David about it, in case he confirmed her worst fears. She didn't know if he felt the same way. Every morning as the Winters sat at the breakfast table eating porridge or toast, Florence singing Latin verbs in the background, swinging her stockinged legs as she told everyone cheerfully what her day at school held, Bill carefully explaining the principle behind the latest Apollo mission by drawing careful sketches on the table for his father, Martha would watch Daisy in the middle of it all, eating carefully, watching, listening, but never betraying what she thought. A black hole in the heart of the family. Afterwards, clearing breakfast away, Martha would shake herself and laugh at her dramatic tendencies. Ridiculous!

Only she had made her daughter and when she looked at her, as she did that day in August, she knew her heart. She knew Daisy so well, because she'd seen her a few seconds after she was born, when they handed her to Martha, and the same expression was on her face then, as it was now, forty-seven years later. Calm, like Martha – everyone said she was like Martha – but something else too. 'She's a cool customer, this one,' the sister had said, looking at Daisy, tightly swaddled in her mother's arms. 'I've never seen a baby that didn't cry before.'

'What's wrong, pet?' Martha said to Daisy now. It was nearly lunchtime. She wondered whether Daisy would eat lunch, or stay here.

'I need to talk to you about something,' Daisy said. She fingered the blancmange-coloured tassels of the tattered bedspread. 'You won't like it.'

Martha tensed her shoulders, just slightly. 'Go on.'

'I've not been very happy lately, you know that, don't you?'

'Yes,' Martha said. 'What's up? Something's up, I can tell.'

Daisy shook her hair out of her face. Dark rings hung below her eyes. 'I can't speak for long.'

'Why?'

She swallowed. 'Just can't.' She put her hand on her mother's. 'Look. I got fired last month. I'm back for good.'

'Fired?' Martha was appalled. 'Darling, how come?'

Daisy rubbed her eyes. 'Long story. I stole some money. That's what they said, anyway. That's what they'll say if you ask them. But it's not true. I just borrowed bits from different bits. I'm the only one who knew where everything was. You see? It's fine.' She pinched the tip of her nose. 'But, yeah, it was for drugs. And – well, drugs.'

Martha kept quite still, not knowing how to react. She sensed this was the truth. 'Is that all?'

Daisy nodded. 'Yep. I've screwed up again. It's a real shame, because it was the one thing I did. In my life. You know.' She sounded almost cheerful. 'That's how it is, I guess. Only got myself to blame. It's just I wish I could swap myself for someone else sometimes. Just . . . *be* someone else, sometimes.'

A cloud passed over the window and Daisy looked up at her mother. *She's getting old.* Martha realised it then: her daughter was a middle-aged woman. Not a cruel, fascinating, beautiful little girl. She was past the age when anything she did could be put down to youth or inexperience, and it struck Martha like an arrow piercing her heart. She had made her like this. Hadn't she?

So she said what she'd always said, because she didn't know what else to say.

'You're a clever, talented girl,' Martha said. 'I'm so proud of you. You'll find something else, you can—'

'No.' Daisy broke in, her voice harsh for once. 'No. Look, I need your help.'

'All right,' said Martha, cautiously. It was usually money. Historically it would be a situation with a teacher at school, and once, picking her up from a police station in Bristol, where she'd been found wandering the streets after forty-eight hours absent from home. But usually, these days, it was money.

'I've been up all night, thinking about it,' Daisy said.

'I'm sure you have, darling. Are you sure you can't appeal? Go back and find—'

But she was cut off again. 'Ma, it's too late for that. It's too late. They don't want me back.'

'Can't you just try—'

'God, I hoped you'd understand. Listen. I'll probably be arrested if I go back to India, don't you realise that?'

'Oh.' Martha closed her eyes, briefly. 'I see.'

'I just need your help, one more time. I didn't sleep at all last night, going over it all. Can I have a couple of Southpaw's pills, the ones in the bathroom cabinet?'

David had been prescribed sleeping pills and painkillers to help with his knee, which was causing him more and more pain in the run-up to the operation. 'No, Daisy,' Martha said firmly. 'Absolutely not. I said last time was the final time. They're too strong.'

'OK, fine,' Daisy said. She took another sip of tea, then lay back and closed her eyes. Martha's hand reached out to Daisy's wrist, and she encircled it with her brown fingers. She was hot to the touch. 'I might have a sleep. Thanks, Ma. I won't want any lunch. Just leave me now.'

She seemed to be almost asleep, even then. Martha went out, shutting the door behind her, and stood on the landing outside her daughter's room for a moment, listening to the quiet, hoping Daisy would find some peace. She knew she'd found the wedding tough. Martha knew that seeing Cat was hard on Daisy, much as she pretended it wasn't.

Martha shook her head, swallowing back tears and, picking up the laundry basket outside Daisy's room, started folding up towels. She found herself humming a tune from *The Mikado* under her breath; it had been on the Proms the previous night as they were clearing up after the (modest) wedding breakfast. It had been a strange wedding, she thought to herself; her mind wandered. Thinking things over, trying to work out what was going on so she could act for the best. Karen's mother seemed nice – should they invite her down for the weekend in the autumn? Cat's life in Paris troubled her somehow – did she need to talk to her about it? Florence's behaviour was a little strange, but she seemed happy. Something was going on there, though, she knew.

When Martha went to the bathroom five minutes later, she wondered if she'd even hear Daisy snoring, as she was wont to. She even smiled at herself in the mirror while washing her hands. Perhaps Daisy was mellowing in her old age.

The prickling, uncertain feeling she could never entirely get rid of, that was what was bothering her, not her hip, not those headaches . . . And suddenly, with a small cry Martha flung open the bathroom cabinet. But she knew what she'd see even before that. The sleeping pills were open, and the bottle was empty.

Martha pushed open the bathroom door, kicking the towels and sheets out of the way, stumbling as her foot caught on a pillowcase. She fell to the floor, crying out, and then she remembered she was alone; Florence had taken Cat to the station, David was gone. Gone. She staggered towards Daisy's bedroom.

She knew before she opened the door what she would see. Daisy was lying on the bed, head pulled back, but she wasn't snoring. Her eyes were half-open, just like when she was a baby. Martha leaned over, her heart pounding so hard she couldn't hear anything else. She cried out her daughter's name, over and over again. She shook her, but she didn't move.

Then she saw the note, in Daisy's neat, tiny handwriting, splashed with tea.

Dearest Ma,

Don't be sad. I'd already taken the pills when you came in. I'm glad I got to talk to you before I started to go to sleep. I have only done what I wanted to do. I know how to do it, too, I've been planning it for a while. One of the reasons the charity sacked me was drugs; heroin. Heroin, yes I know. Some kind guy from an NGO got me hooked on the stuff a few years ago. You'd expect better from a charity worker, wouldn't you? But it's a good way to kill yourself if you know how to mix it, and with what. I've picked up a few things along the way, haven't I?

I'd run out of things to do, and I wasn't any good at any of the things I did do. Never was, we all know it don't we. And I hate being back here. Dad's a fake, it reminds me every time what a fake he is. You know I hate how he's lied about everything. Where he comes from. Where Florence comes from. She's his bastard, isn't she? I know she isn't yours. I remember that summer you went away, and you came back with a baby, and we were supposed to believe it. He had an affair, didn't he? He lied to you. I know she's his, he loves her more than me, more than Bill, you can see it.

I get these bits of rage when I can't see

straight and I want to – I don't know. Kill something. I suppose. I always felt I didn't belong here. But then, not anywhere. I tried so many places and I went as far away as I could and it's just I don't belong anywhere.

I can hear you singing 'The Sun Whose Rays' as I write this, and I wish you sang more. You used to all the time and now I think you're sad. Thank you for saying you wouldn't give me the pills. It makes it much clearer, doesn't it?

Ma, can you bury me here, next to Wilbur? In the garden. Wilbur was my friend, and he was my idea.

Tired now. Please make sure Catherine OK? She

There it ended.

She stood in the hot bedroom, and looked down at her daughter, face slack, limbs heavy, at rest at last.

Then Martha went into her bedroom and shut the door. She listened once again. Everything was silent. No one near, no one with her except Daisy. She sat on the edge of the bed, gazing out at her garden, at the neat rows of lettuce, the apple trees in the distant orchard. At the daisy bank, churned with mole holes. Then she stood up, and crossed herself, though she had no idea why, or what it would do to help her, and she went outside to the shed, and picked up a spade. *A time to be born,*

327

and a time to die, and I was there at both of them. I love you Daisy, and I will hold you close now, the way I never could before.

Martha had learned a lot from her years in the countryside during the war. She knew how to bury old folk and dead sheep, and she'd buried a few Winter dogs in her time. She'd done Hadley by herself, after he'd been put down after the summer party when he attacked someone. You had to dig a hole so deep nothing else could get to it. And as she was working all that long day, she tried to feel nothing, and when Florence came back from her day trip to London, flushed and happy and obviously up to something, Martha told her Daisy had left.

'She got an email from the orphanage about a grant that's come through,' she said, sitting at the kitchen table, sipping the stone-cold cup of tea, as though it connected her to something.

'So she just *left*?' Florence said. 'My God, she really does take the biscuit. She didn't even say goodbye!'

'You know Daisy,' said Martha. 'It must have been important.'

'That's rubbish. She was just sick of being here, that's all, and no one was paying her any attention. She never changes.' Florence looked at her watch. 'Well – I might just make a phone call!' Her face creased into a joyful smile. 'I have some work to do.'

Martha watched her bounce out of the room

into David's study. She followed her and stood in the doorway. 'You seem very jolly,' Martha said.

'Oh . . . It's nothing really!' Florence said, her mouth twitching. Then she frowned. 'Oh . . . Daisy's Yahoo is still open.'

'What?'

'Her email. Looks like . . .' Florence started clicking on the screen.

'Stop it,' Martha said, realising something. 'Let me. She didn't have time, she had to leave fairly suddenly.'

Florence, who was even more in another world than usual, stood up, and started scanning the bookshelves, humming to herself.

'Why are you singing that?' Martha sat down at the computer. She stared at the screen. If she logged out of Daisy's email, that was it – she'd never get back in again. This way . . .

'Singing what?'

'The Sun Whose Rays.'

Florence turned round. 'No idea. Were you playing it yesterday?'

Heart racing, blood thumping, Martha opened Daisy's account details. *You have about ten seconds. You have to appear calm. If you take too long this will start to look suspicious.* My account. Reset password online. She clicked on the link. What is your mother's maiden name? What is your date of birth?

Martha swallowed. 'I'm sorry you missed her,' she said. She had never wanted anything more than she wanted Florence to go away for just a minute. 'Love, can you put the kettle on?'

Florence gave her a curious glance but went into the kitchen, still humming. Martha sat down, changed the password to something she could remember: Daisy61, and closed down the application. When Florence returned, she stood up.

'I'd love some tea if you're making a pot,' Florence said.

Martha had stared at her. 'I'm not, no. See you later.'

She went upstairs smoothly, and locked Daisy's door.

The next morning, after Florence had left, Martha dragged her middle child down the twisting staircase, through the kitchen and outside to the garden. Though she had been painfully thin in life, in death Daisy was heavy and Martha was old, and she cried as she carried her, because it was undignified, and she had wanted it to be dignified, a proper end to the life of her baby, her baby girl whom she had somehow ruined, broken. She had favoured her too much or too little; she didn't know, but Daisy had never been right, and now that she could finally do something that her daughter wanted for her, it ought to be done properly. In the afternoon sunshine she rolled Daisy into the black sheeting they used on the lawn, and bound her up with plastic ties. Sometimes she had to stop, sometimes pain would overwhelm her and she would kneel beside her daughter, crying as quietly as she could, but then she would count to five. Stand up again, pretend she was doing something else. Something mundane.

The whole time, Martha had the unreal sense that someone would appear, would find out what she was doing, would stop her. But they didn't, and she was glad, because she knew it was what her daughter wanted. Before the last tie covered up Daisy's face, Martha steeled herself, stroked her daughter's forehead, then ran her finger along the bridge of her nose as she had done when she was tiny, to get her to close her eyes and sleep. She covered the body over with earth, and replaced the turf as best she could, trusting that no one would go out there for months, maybe. David wouldn't be able to walk far when he came home, and no one else was in the garden these days. Cat was gone and Bill had Karen, and Lucy was grown up. It was just Martha, and Daisy.

On sunny days Martha went out to the daisy bank, and sometimes she talked to her. Mostly, she just sat there, quite still, keeping her company. She knew enough to know it was ridiculous to think Daisy would want to hear her prattling on about life. She hadn't cared when she was alive, she wouldn't care now. Somehow that made some kind of sense to Martha.

MARTHA

It was Karen who broke the silence. She stood up, walked over to the sideboard, and poured Martha some red wine. 'Here,' she said, and then she crouched down beside her mother-in-law and handed her the glass. She pulled Martha's neatly pressed handkerchief out of her pocket and gave it to her, and Martha blew her nose, still crying, as Karen stroked her arm, her hand, the back of her neck. 'There, there,' Karen said, softly. 'It's all right. You did the right thing. You did the right thing.'

The others watched her without moving, rooted to their seats as though by some kind of magic. Martha's sobs hung in the heavy silent air, only the faintest rattle of chase-scene music from Luke's DVD echoing from the other side of the house.

Eventually Karen stood up again and went back to her seat. She spread her hands wide, and with a little laugh of strained near-hysteria, she said, 'You know, someone has to say something eventually.'

She turned to her husband, who wouldn't meet her glance. His eyes were full of tears.

'I gave her money,' said Florence, eventually. 'For her school. Last year. *And* she emailed me,' more loudly. 'A couple of days ago, Ma. Was – was that you?'

Martha nodded.

'You were emailing us all?' Florence said hoarsely. 'All that time?'

'Since . . . after Bill and Karen's wedding.' Martha wiped her nose and stuffed the handkerchief in her pocket. 'Not before. She did it all before.'

'What happened to the money?' Bill said.

'That's what you care about?' Martha turned to him. 'Honestly, Bill? I tell you this story and *that's* what you want to know?'

Bill said softly, 'I was just wondering, that's all. Ma, it must have been quite a lot.'

'The charity and the orphanages, they sacked her, for stealing. I sent them the money back, in her name, to apologise. And then I kept on sending them money, as though it was from her, from all of us.' Martha shrugged, her hands in her pockets. 'I thought that's what she'd want.'

'Daisy was out for herself—' Florence began, then stopped. 'I'm sorry.' She wiped her nose on her sleeve, and looked from her father to her mother. 'This is . . . Ma, this is crazy. Absolutely bloody crazy. Why didn't you tell anyone?'

Martha sat upright. This was the hardest bit of all. 'I wanted people . . . to . . . to think well of her. She wasn't like you two. She found things difficult.'

'I—' Florence exploded, her mouth open, but she closed it swiftly, shaking her head. 'We all find things difficult, you know, Ma. That doesn't mean – you lie, and steal, and cheat, and abandon people, and hurt people, and . . .' Her voice broke. 'That doesn't mean you do those things.'

'I know,' Martha said. 'I know that.' Her fingers touched her forehead, as if buying herself time. After a pause she looked up at her eldest grand-daughter. 'Cat?'

Cat shook her head, her lips clamped together, grimacing. She covered her face with her hands. David reached out to her, stroked her arm.

'My dear girl,' David said, his voice as faint as a whisper, but Cat said nothing.

'I don't know what to do,' Bill said, almost conversationally. 'I honestly don't know what we should do.'

'Well, I think we should call the police.' Florence looked around the table. 'It's illegal what you did, Ma, I'm sorry.'

'Oh, don't, Florence,' said Lucy, speaking for the first time.

Florence said, 'But someone's going to find out sooner or later. We can't just leave her there.'

'We can,' said David. 'You can bury someone on private ground.'

'Not like this!' Florence blinked, her eyes bulging. 'Bill, what is it? What's the term for it?'

'Disposing of a body and preventing lawful burial,' Bill whispered.

'Exactly. It's illegal. You could go to prison. Why – what?' Florence burst out laughing. 'This is crazy, it's just crazy . . .'

Lucy turned to her left and pointed her finger at her aunt. 'Oh, stop it,' she said. 'Have a heart, Florence, for God's sake. Stop it.' Florence shook her head in disbelief and Lucy paused, trying to think through what they should do next, what happened now. 'Does anyone know a lawyer? I think we need a lawyer.'

Karen said, 'I do.'

Lucy nodded. 'Great, Karen.'

Bill looked at his wife across the table. 'Who's that, then?'

But Karen looked sadly at her husband, and turned to Cat. 'Cat, love. This is a big shock to us all, isn't it? Why don't you say something?'

Cat, who was staring down at nothing, shook her head. Eventually, very softly, she whispered, 'I don't know what to say.'

Bill shuffled his chair closer to his niece. He put his arm around her. 'Cat, whatever it is that's happened, we're all here now, aren't we? It doesn't change the fact we're very glad you came back, and that you've brought Luke. He's part of our family, like you, me . . .' His eyes rested on Karen for a moment, then down at his place. The plate was broken, where he'd dropped the knife on it. He pushed the two cracked pieces together, carefully. 'Daisy – she was wonderful but she wasn't ever happy. Perhaps it's . . .' He trailed off.

335

'It's for the best?' Cat laughed. 'I don't know.' Her eyes filled with tears again. 'What was wrong with her? What's wrong with me?'

'Oh, sweetheart,' Florence said wretchedly. 'Nothing's wrong with you. You poor darling girl.' She stood up. 'I do think we have to call the police.'

'No.' Karen shook her head. 'Let them alone for just a day or two. Then we'll decide.'

Florence gave her a sharp look, but said nothing.

'Who made you the family spokesman, all of a sudden?' Bill asked his wife.

'Don't, Bill,' she said, brushing him aside with a tired gesture. She stood over him, so small and determined, right hand fiddling with her wedding and engagement rings, turning them over and over.

'Get out,' he said, suddenly. 'You shouldn't be here.'

Karen stared at him. 'Really, Bill? Now?'

'You two. Not now,' Martha said.

'Dad—' Lucy held out a placatory hand. 'Not now, Dad, if you're going to—'

He turned to her, and said, 'Don't worry, Lucy sweetheart.'

'But, Dad, please don't—'

'Lucy.' His voice was hard. 'Mind your own business.'

'It *is* my business!' Lucy shouted, her voice cracking. 'This is all my business, all our business.'

'No,' David cried, weakly. 'We mustn't turn on

336

each other. We're a family, goddammit. That's what I did it all for.'

But his soft voice was drowned out by the sliding of the doors. Karen stood up and Bill turned back to her, grabbing her wrist.

'All I ever wanted was to make you happy, to make a home with you, our own home away from all this. And what have you done? Why are you here?'

'You're right. I shouldn't be here,' Karen said. 'I've never belonged here. It's a shame 'cause I thought maybe I did, but you're right.' Her voice rose, and she didn't see the two figures standing in the open door. 'You're all so afraid of being honest with each other, telling the truth for once, being open about what's going on, and this is where it's got you!'

'You bloody *hypocrite*!' Bill shouted, and Martha watched in horror, as her son's expression changed so that he looked quite wild. He jabbed his hand behind him. 'She's pregnant, you know? Three months pregnant! And, by the way, I'm not the father. That idiot through there, Joe! *He's* the father, for God's sake, and *I'm* the one who's not been honest!'

Karen put one hand to her neck, rubbing it, her eyes huge in her small, white face. 'Bill, I told you yesterday. It could be his, it might not be. I said I always thought because nothing happened for years . . .' She shook her head. 'Not now. Let's not talk about it now, Bill.'

'Why not?' Bill drew himself up, tall, his trembling lips pushed together. 'Why can't we?'

'Dad, shut up,' Lucy said. 'Not now.'

'Of course I couldn't talk about it to you,' Karen said suddenly, tears glittering in her eyes. 'Four years together and nothing happened. I thought it must be me. You'd already had a kid. And I couldn't talk to you about it.'

'No.' He stared at her, agonised. 'You could.'

'Bill, I couldn't. I tried and I – you know I tried. You have time for everyone else, darling. Not me.' The words stuck in her throat. 'And the one time I didn't – I was reckless – I . . . the one time we didn't . . . Oh God. This is a mess. I . . .'

Karen put her hands over her face and began to softly sob.

'Mum, I finished the movie,' came a small voice. 'I don't like it here any more. I want to go home now.'

Luke and Joe stood in the doorway, as Karen pushed back the chair, which fell to the ground with a cracking thud and ran past them, not even looking at Joe.

'Karen,' Joe called, in a low voice. 'Where are you going? *Karen?*' He kept his hand on Luke's neck, propelling him towards his mother. Cat wrapped her arms around him and stared up at Joe.

'Go after her,' she said. Joe nodded, and left the room, his heavy footsteps thudding through the house. Seconds later, they heard the front door slam.

At the other end of the room Martha said, 'I'll repay you all the money, of course.'

'Don't be silly,' Florence interrupted her. She stood up, and went over to her mother. 'Oh, Ma. You're very brave to have told us. I don't know – I don't know why she was like that.'

Martha stared at her, and she put her hands to her cheeks. 'Flo. Oh, Florence, darling, you . . .' Her face was drained of colour, her eyes glassy. Her eyes darted towards David, then back at Florence. 'I don't know why either, darling. That's families for you. I had to tell you, you understand that, don't you?'

Bill came and stood next to Florence. 'Flo's right.' He kissed his mother's head. 'I'm sorry, Ma. I'm so sorry.'

'I just wanted everything to be out in the open. I wanted us to be . . . happy again.' She looked down the long table at her husband, and then screamed.

'David? *David!*'

Lucy, glancing at her grandfather, cried out. His head had fallen forwards, his mouth was wide open.

'Oh, no. *No, no!*' Bill ran over to his father and fell to his knees. He loosened his tie, patted his face. 'Lucy, call an ambulance.' Lucy ran out of the room. 'Tell them it's urgent.'

Martha had stumbled out of her chair, over to her husband. 'Urgent,' Bill shouted after his daughter, cradling David's head in his hands. 'Tell them it's urgent.' He turned to Cat, nodding at Luke. 'Get him out of here.'

Cat left and the others stared at each other, blind panic on their faces. A weak afternoon winter sun shone into the stuffy room. 'Help me,' Bill said to Florence, and the two of them lifted their father gently, terribly carefully, out of his chair and placed him on the worn carpet.

His face was grey, his mouth turned down, as though in ghastly mockery of a clown. He said, 'Violet's hat.'

'What's he saying?' Martha moved closer.

'Violet. Bury me with my old hat.'

'What?' Florence said, squeezing his head to her, as if by holding him tight she might make it better. 'What hat? The one on your door? Of course, Pa, darling, but don't be ridiculous.' She swallowed, to speak. 'You're going to be all right.'

He raised his hand to try to touch hers, but he was too weak.

'You're my girl,' he said. 'I'm so proud of you, Flo.'

Then his head rolled away. Florence gently cradled it, brokenly whispering to him.

Five minutes later David died, his head in Florence's lap, his hands folded on his chest. Martha, kneeling on the floor beside him, saw a movement out of the window. She looked up and caught sight of Cat in the garden, hand in hand with Luke, the shadow of the house falling over them. Suddenly they heard sirens, ringing out loudly in the lane up to the house. They all looked up, at each other, and then, instinctively, at Martha.

So Martha took David's warm hand in hers and gently closed his eyes. They needed her to be in control. She was. She was completely in control.

'He's tired,' she said, very calm. 'He's resting. He's been tired for a while. Don't let them in, not just yet. It's going to be fine. He just needs a bit more time.'

She could feel them all, all of them, staring at her. Then came the sound of the door knocker, thudding loudly through the still house.

PART III

THE PAST AND THE PRESENT

Does the road wind up-hill all the way?
Yes, to the very end.
Will the day's journey take the whole long day?
From morn to night, my friend.

Christina Rossetti, 'Up-Hill'

MARTHA

O ne day, many years ago, Martha had had a premonition of death.

She never tried to explain it to anyone else: it sounded too unlikely. They had had an early supper, and she was in the kitchen one evening, washing up, while David worked in his study. Cat was asleep upstairs; she must have been around twelve or so.

It was one of those still-light spring evenings, where the birds sing softly, the black earth is alive with promise, and the cool air is sweet. *Rhapsody in Blue* was playing on the radio. Martha loved Gershwin, and she was banging a wooden spoon on the sink in time to the piano, staring at nothing really in the soapy water, when suddenly she saw it, in front of her eyes.

She, and David. They were walking down the lane together, like the first time. David was wearing the hat Violet had given him, all those years ago; light was falling between the trees. They went towards it, gladly: it seemed to be sunshine. But the light fell on her, like a cloak, and suddenly changed. She stared up at the sky, but saw only a grey, heavy nothing, and she realised she didn't know where the light was coming from and so she started to shout, to call for help. The lane, the trees, the hedgerow, David: they all disappeared, and she saw only grey around her, like a plane, plummeting through clouds. She could hear him calling her, she could hear her own screams, could feel herself desperately running towards something, but nothing seemed to work, to change, and she was racing into the mist, into nothing . . .

Martha had started running then, through the house, to the study. She'd flung the door open, and it was only then she realised she was soaking wet: washing-up water all over her top, her hair, her cheeks. She was crying, shaking from head to toe.

'My love, what on earth's wrong?' said David, standing up.

'I . . .' Martha began, and then she felt stupid. *I have just seen how I'm going to die. I'm going to leave you.* She couldn't stop shaking now, and there was a sharp metallic taste in her mouth. She put her hands on her cheeks. 'I saw something awful while I was washing up. It sounds crazy. How . . . You and me.'

The music floated in from the kitchen, but otherwise the house was still. David walked around the desk and took her in his arms. 'Darling. Washing up can be dangerous, can't it? Goose walk over your grave?' He held her tight, and she rested her head on his shoulder, like she always did. She

346

loved him then, more than ever, if it were possible. He understood, he knew.

'Something like that. I can't explain it. It was terrifying.'

His hands, holding her close to him, patted her back, softly. 'Must have been.'

'I don't want to leave you. I don't want to be without you. Ever.'

'You won't,' he said, and there was laughter in his voice. 'Silly girl. I'm in the study drawing, and in twenty years' time I'll still be in the study, drawing.'

But Martha couldn't laugh. 'Promise?'

'Promise. You and me, remember? Just us.'

From the radio in the kitchen there came the clashing final bars, a drum roll, and then applause, and it broke the tension. They laughed.

'I feel silly,' Martha said, but the strength of that deadening terror was still with her, and she felt sick.

David pulled his battered old hat off its hook. 'I'm finished anyway. Let's go and sit outside and have a drink, darling,' he said. 'First outside of the year. No more ghosts tonight.'

Later that evening, he had suddenly said to her, as they sat on the steps by the French windows, 'I'd die if you left me, you know that, don't you?'

'David. Don't be dramatic.' She felt completely herself again, remote, amused, in control. How unlike her that earlier scene had been. How silly. He was the romantic one who cried at films, who had wept when the last of Cat's baby teeth came out and that was their final night of doing the Tooth Fairy, drawing chalk flowers and stars on the floor by the child's bed. He was the one who had brought them all here, who had brought Florence into the family, who had fought tooth and nail for his own life. She was the pragmatist who said the dog had to be put down, who wrestled with wiring.

A life without each other was too far away to think about; they had conquered everything when they were young, and so they were careless about the future. It held no fear for them. She dismissed the premonition from her mind, for many years. Neither of them ever considered the possibility that their time together might end. They never thought about it: the truth was, Martha knew he would never leave her.

DAVID

Martha had stood in the hallway that morning, mouth pursed into a worried bud, watching David as he put on his hat and picked up his battered old portfolio, which contained what he hoped was his best work yet.

'If he says no,' she said, 'you'll – well, you have to at least ask him if there's anything else you can do for him. Cartoons, or some other kind of work. You have to come back with something, David. He's known you for years; he can't throw you off entirely.'

'For goodness' sake, someone like Horace Wilson doesn't deal in favours, Martha. And neither do I.' His voice was raised. 'This meeting, it's very important. Let me handle it, please, will you?'

'You're the one who wanted us to move here.' Her voice was sharp, the Cockney she'd left behind sneaking away with her consonants, as it always did when she was cross. David had a tighter grip on it. He never let his past show through.

'We both wanted to come back here, Martha.'

349

'Dear God, David!' It was the same old argument they'd been having for months. 'You're the one who said it'll be fine. And there's damp in the dining room, we've got rats everywhere, I hate this paint, nothing keeps in this heat and we can't afford a refrigerator. Daisy needs new shoes, for God's sake. She crams her toes into the only ones she's got, she's walking like a cripple! All because of you and your bloody rewriting history complex.' Martha was close to him now, her green eyes glowing with fury. She pushed her hair out of her face. 'I gave up doing my job for this, David.'

He knew she was as good as he was. They both knew it. Somehow, this made him angrier. 'Daisy's a damned liar and she'll say anything to get you on her side.'

'Fine. Do whatever you want.' Martha had turned and walked back into the kitchen, slamming the green baize door on her way.

He should have kept his mouth shut. Martha wouldn't hear a word against Daisy. He stood there in the empty hall looking around him, wondering whether it was all worth it, but he told himself it had to be, he had to make it all right otherwise something else would have won. He wasn't sure what. As he fiddled one final time with his tie, he felt a wet nose nudging the fold of his knee, and he turned and crouched on the ground.

'You like it here, don't you, old fellow?' he said to Wilbur, who looked at him with dark solemn eyes, his lopsided pink tongue hanging crazily out of his mouth.

Wilbur gave a small, soft yelping bark. As if to say, 'You're all right with me.' David fondled his soft, warm ears, touching his cheek to his muzzle.

A voice beside him said quietly, 'Dad?' David jumped. Daisy was standing next to him: he never seemed to hear her approach. 'Dad, did you look at the drawings? Of Wilbur?'

'Oh. Darling, I didn't, I'm sorry.' He stood, picking up the portfolio.

Her small face got its pinched, dead-eyed look. 'Oh.'

'I'll look tonight.' He wished she'd leave; he wanted to look in the mirror, talk himself up a little. Daisy threw him off balance. In abstract he wanted to draw her closer to him, and yet in practice he frequently found himself wishing he could keep her at arm's length. 'What did you draw him doing, then?'

She curled a twine of straggling hair round one thin finger. 'Look, they're here.' She took a sheet of paper carefully out of a book of wild flowers on the sideboard. 'Look at this one. He's bouncing up and down so hard like he did the other day to catch the piece of meat that he hits his head on my hand and falls over. Then in the other one he's waiting for me to come back from school and making that strange noise that he makes. And in the other one he's chasing his own tail. And he's saying, "It's like a merry-go-round, but I'll just catch this tail and then I'll get off."' Her eyes shone as David laughed, and glanced at the drawing she held tightly in her hand. She was a funny little thing. He found himself dropping a kiss on her head. 'Do you like it?'

'Love it, darling. His nose looks very wet. I'll look at the rest of them later. Be nice to Florence.'

Her voice took on that wheedling, surprised tone. 'Daddy! Of course I will be, I always am nice to Florence, it's just—'

He patted her shoulder, and said goodbye. 'I'll miss my train.'

As he strode up the driveway he saw, as through fresh eyes, the gate hanging off its hinge, no post to attach it to. Wood pigeons cooed lazily in the trees above. David turned to look at the view of the valley sliding away from him and breathed in once again. He knew where he'd come from to get here. Anything was better than that.

'Come in, come in, old chap, sit down. Drink? June, get Mr Winter here a drink – what – G and T? Whisky?'

'Oh – whisky, please.'

'Wonderful, wonderful. Got that, dear? Right. David, jolly good to see you. How's that beautiful wife of yours?'

'She's very well. Says to say we must get you down to Winterfold some time.'

'I'd love that.' Horace Wilson slouched and slid his arms across the table, fingers touching. 'How is that house of yours? Pretty amazing place, I hear?'

'We're very happy with it.'

'You, in the deepest English countryside. It's really rather amusing. How long's it been now?' Horace pointed one long finger precisely in his ear, and wiggled it about in an explorative fashion.

'About a year now.' David put the portfolio on the table, fingers itching to open it. He didn't want to make small talk. He especially didn't want to discuss the house.

'Making the place your own, I hope.'

David found he was sweating. It was a close, oppressive day, thick cloud hanging heavy over London, trapping in the heat. The boardroom of the *Modern Man* magazine was dank, and reeked of stale cigarette smoke: a typical Soho office. 'Can't wait to see what you've got for me, old chap,' Horace said, lighting another cigarette and pushing his drink out of the way. 'Truth is we're up against it for next week's issue. Could be your lucky day.'

Delicately, David slid the sheets of sugar paper out. He had laboured all day and night for months on this project and it sounded pompous if one said it aloud, but put simply, it was the climax of everything he wanted to achieve as an artist. He'd ignored Martha, swatted away the children, walked unseeing around this crumbling, malfunctioning white elephant he'd taken on while winter rain dripped through the old roof and rodents gambolled in the kitchen.

Meanwhile, deadlines for his existing commissions came and went. The weekly cartoon for the *News Chronicle*, the illustrations for *Punch*, the funny little details he was supposed to sketch for the theatre column in the *Daily News* – he'd let them all down, these past weeks, chasing some ghost. He had known for some time he had to exorcise whatever it was that hung over him, even more so now he'd moved into Winterfold, and it had seemed to him this was the only way he knew how.

'I'll show you . . . I'm rather excited about them myself.' He cleared his throat. 'Right, here we go.'

'Jolly good.' Horace rubbed his hands together.

But his thin smile grew rigid as David spread the sketches over the table. 'As you know, I began this series when I was . . .' he swallowed, his voice high and formal, '. . . younger. It came about through my experiences in the war. I have always wanted to return to this subject, to explore the impact of the last twenty years on the bomb sites of London, and the people who still live there. So I went back to the East End, talked to the residents, drew the new landscapes that are springing up there alongside the craters that still haven't been filled in.'

'Right.' Horace wasn't really listening. He was scanning the drawings, fingers drumming the table. 'Let me have a look . . . Oh, I see. Pretty grim, David.'

354

'Yes, it was.'

Images started flashing in front of David's mind: falling masonry like rocks raining down from the sky, houses ripped apart like they were made of paper, bodies in the streets, rubble everywhere, and the sounds – screaming, whistling bombs, crying, agonised pleas for help, children hysterical with fear, the smell of shit, of piss, of terror and sand and fire.

Suddenly he was back there, curled up into the small shell shape his mother had told him to make, time and time again, crouching on the floor beside him in the kitchen. 'Like this, little one. He doesn't mean to hurt me. If you hide, though, he can't see you and he can't hurt you. So make yourself small. Like this.'

He couldn't stop these memories. They came like a stabbing pain in the heart and he couldn't stop them, he couldn't acknowledge them, would simply have to go on like he had always done when this happened . . .

'David?' The laconic voice recalled him to the present. 'I say, David!'

'Sorry.' David covered his mouth, trying to hide his panicky, laboured breathing. 'Miles away.'

Horace was giving him a curious look. 'Right. Listen, are you in town this evening? I'm rather keen on going to a club in Pimlico I think you'd like – it's got a—'

'No,' said David, louder than he had meant. 'I really just came up to show you these. I have to be back tonight. Work and . . . other business.' He hoped he sounded vague. As though the real reason he had to be home wasn't just because he hated being away from Martha, whether she was speaking to him or not. But that was the truth. He was only happy when he was with Martha, was only able to work when he could hear her low, clear voice singing around the house. She was his home.

'Well, what a shame.' Horace glanced again over the pen-and-ink drawings. He scratched his chin, jangling the glass of melting ice in his other hand and muttered something under his breath: David heard the word 'domesticated'.

'Listen,' Horace said after a moment. 'It's certainly an impressive collection, old bean. I'll give you that. You're rather . . . brave. I'd have thought you'd have learned your lesson with the dying industries lot you shoved my way last year.'

David stared at the sheets of paper, spread out over the table. 'This isn't some Sunday Hyde Park artist's stuff, Horace – this is my life's work. What happened there, it's all been forgotten. We build new things and make new homes and it all gets bulldozed over and we mustn't forget, that's all.' He could hear himself and how desperate he sounded and he tried to modulate his voice. 'You know I'd rather hoped you could see your way to something rather like that prisoner of war series you did with Ronnie Searle.'

'Ah, but he's – he's got the whole package. Wonderful chap. Anyway, it isn't what people want, these days, David.' Horace swilled the liquid in his glass around languorously. 'It's a hip, crazy world out there, everything's changing, old order gone, all of that and—'

'Exactly,' said David. 'I want to—'

A flash of anger lit up Horace Wilson's face. 'Do let me finish, old thing, will you? I'll be frank. We can offer you work, but it's got to be light entertainment, you savvy? We want to make people laugh. Give them a break from their dire little lives.'

David couldn't bear to look at the sketches, spread out in front of them. Instead, he saw the red electricity bill . . . Martha's face that morning . . . the gate that hung off the hinge. He saw his own ridiculous folly, how trying to pull himself out of the past had led them to this house, how stupid he was, wanting something he couldn't afford and didn't deserve. 'I got the wrong end of the stick, I'm afraid. Not clear what you were looking for in my mind and that's my fault.' He was talking, saying anything to hold Horace's attention, his nimble mind jumping over the conversational rubble to get to safety, away from the demons that pursued him.

He knew, without stopping to think, that this was the moment everything hinged on. 'How about dogs? They off the table too?'

'What do you mean?'

'We have a dog called Wilbur.' His mind was racing; he tried to sound calm, as though this was part of the plan. 'Wonderful chap. Mongrel.

Very affectionate, bit stupid, but wise in his way. You see?' He raised his chin, meeting Horace's eyes, smiling gently, as though they were both in on a joke he hadn't even thought of yet. 'My elder daughter, Daisy, got him for Christmas a few years ago, but he's all of ours, really. Now Daisy's very naughty and Wilbur gets her out of scrapes. But they're also rather sweet together. The other afternoon, for instance. I came into the kitchen. Hot day, I rather fancy a bottle of beer. I catch him chasing his tail, round and round . . .' He twirled his finger in the air, and Horace nodded. David knew he had him then.

'Daisy was watching him, nodding solemnly and I thought he was talking to her, saying something like, "It's like a merry-go-round, old girl. I'll just catch this tail and then I'll get off."' Horace laughed. 'And he appears at the other side of the table like a jumping bean at supper, bouncing in the air in case there's some spare food. He's jolly funny. Here,' David said, his heart beating hard, 'let me show you. Do you have any . . .' he looked around for paper, but there was none in the empty boardroom. 'Never mind.' He turned over one of the sketches, pulled his pen out of his pocket and swiftly drew the picture Daisy had shown him that morning, Wilbur, whirling round in a circle, and he added Daisy, brows drawn together, arms crossed, glowering at him in confusion.

'Something like this. A little girl and her dog. You call it "The Adventures of Daisy and Wilbur".

358

Have a page every week. How Wilbur helps the family and hinders at the same time. Hmm?' He rapidly traced his pen across the page again. Now he knew what he had to do, he was in control. 'Wilbur's waiting at the end of the lane for Daisy to come back from school.' He laughed. 'He does it every day. It's sweet. But he doesn't recognise her, keeps running up to the wrong people and licking them and they often . . . let's say they don't welcome the overtures. The young mother with the pram, she screams and says, "Leave my Susan alone!" Then there's the vicar. Wilbur likes chewing his waistcoat. And the barmaid at the Oak Tree, well. You can imagine what Wilbur goes for there, I'm sorry to say.'

Horace gave a snickering giggle. 'It sounds idyllic. You're a clever chap, David. I like it. I think we've got something there. Will your daughter mind?'

'Daisy? She's six. Don't worry.' David wanted to clear the other drawings up now, to stow them away, safe and sound. 'She'll love it. So – should I get something off to you in the next couple of days? I have a deadline but I can easily work with you to—'

'We want to get this rolling as soon as possible, you know,' said Horace. 'Come into the office with me and let's discuss the terms and all of that.'

'And these?' David gestured to the sketches, as he swept them up into his portfolio folder. 'Any interest in seeing these again?'

'Oh, gosh no. This way, please. June, would you fetch me another drink? David – another for you? Marvellous. Yes, I think this could be the start of something rather special.'

Afterwards, he walked out of the building, with a contract and a cigarette, and he thought he would go straight to Paddington but he didn't. He headed out of Soho and through Bloomsbury, up the leafy, wide climb of Rosebery Avenue towards the Angel.

He didn't know why after all these years, couldn't have explained it. He just kept on walking, getting closer and closer. He thought he was fine, to begin with. Merely an interested party revisiting an old place, but his stomach started to cramp and he winced when he saw the Clerkenwell fire station. How often after Mum died he'd stood there waiting for news, rather than go back home, like they might suddenly tell him she wasn't dead and it was all a mistake if he waited long enough. He'd hear the bells ringing and see them racing out at full pelt. By the end of the war he'd got so used to it he'd know already, just by the sounds of houses collapsing, where it was, whether their place was in danger.

The flashbacks started again as he crawled up and over the City Road, up to the backstreets near

Chapel Market. Rubble like rain, the sounds of the baby screaming, the bewildered faces of the tiny kids who'd huddle together, moving in a pack towards the shelter of the Angel tube station. And his stomach started knotting up again. No food, the whisky Horace had given him curdling the milky coffee he'd had for breakfast. Bile rose in his gullet, and his throat thickened, as if it had swollen shut. He kept on walking, past the Lyons, past the old Peacock Inn.

'You all right, love?' an old woman with a headscarf asked him, peering underneath him as he held on to some railings, trying not to retch.

As he walked down Chapel Market, past where the mission used to be, where his mother'd go to have her face dressed after his father had kicked her or hit her with the pan or held a coal to her face or . . . whatever else he did, the images in his mind's eye grew stronger and he couldn't stop the sweating, the agony of his stomach cramping. The sounds in his ears. And he was back there again, running home towards the hell of his home life, that freezing clear night, January 1945.

He'd seen his dad at the pub and knew he was drunk already, but he didn't know where else to go. It was always the same: should he go home when the siren sounded, to make sure his mother and the baby were safe? Because it was always there, the fear that his dad really would get him this time. So he'd run along the street with the sirens sounding, caught up in the rush inside to be ready, and then getting to the front door, creeping in, hearing the sobbing, juddering screams as his father slammed his mother into whatever it was he was hitting her with that night. Tom Doolan wasn't scared of the fucking Germans. He wasn't fucking scared of anyone, not like that little drip of shit she said was his son.

The first time the bombs fell David was ten. He got used to the Blitz, got used to the shelters and the drama and the sobbing. He learned how to climb over rubble and pretend he wasn't scared. But in 1945, when everyone thought the war was coming to an end, it started up again. V2s. David didn't understand at first. Because D-Day had happened, we'd invaded France, wasn't it all over? But January, February, March, these new, infinitely more terrifying bombs hit London and you never heard them until it was too late and they smashed into you. And this time he really was scared.

His mum was so tired these days. The new baby took up all her time. She'd come out of the blue, she was a tiny little thing, and when David looked at her he felt no connection. He was fourteen, nearly fifteen. This mewling scrap of red skin and bone, she was nothing to do with him, was she? He was angry with his mum for having her, for being so sad, for letting his dad do this to her. Hadn't she learned how not to have any more babies?

The night she was killed they heard V2s over towards Shoreditch and the City. You heard them when they weren't for you, which didn't make it any less frightening. It just meant you might not hear the next one, and then it'd be too late. He'd run home from playing outside the Spanish Prisoners, the pub down the road from their house. There was a man there selling oranges if you gave him a fiddle, and one of David's friends had pulled him off, but David didn't want an orange that much. He'd hung around outside the pub, watching to see if his father was coming home, what temper he'd be in. He liked to do that, to warn his mother. He had to try to look after her. He'd always done it.

When he ran home and into the house, upstairs was having another row about something and his mother was playing her beloved piano – to block out the noise, he thought. Calm as you like, smooth hair coiled up around her long slim neck, and the little baby beside her, asleep in a drawer. Her tiny legs were waving. He thought she might be cold. Her blanket had fallen off.

'Ma,' he'd said. 'Didn't you hear the sirens?'

'No, I was singing, to cheer her up,' she said, turning round and smiling. 'Hello, my lovely boy. I suppose we'd best get off to the station then.'

'It's too late, Ma,' he'd said, half-angry, half-proud of her, playing her painted, dusty piano while the city exploded around her. 'No time. And, Ma, he's coming back. He's in a bad way.'

He remembered her face then. 'Oh, Davy.'

They hid under the piano, because he was sure

by now there wasn't time to get to the shelter, and David didn't know if they were hiding from the bombs or from his father. His mother's calm breathing, her hands smoothing his hair back from his head: he could still remember the feel of the tags and cuts on her red-raw fingers sixty years later. How small she always seemed, curled next to him.

They were quiet as mice for ten awful minutes. The baby didn't make a sound. And just when the silence had stretched to unbearable breaking point, the baby woke up and started crying, and just like that, there was a crashing sound, an explosion, a crunching, elemental force like the earth was cracking open. The piano buckled above them from the weight of the floor above collapsing, and David felt his mother's warm heavy body fall on top of him and the baby, as the house crumpled down around them all. It seemed to go on for ages, louder than anything. A great blow of something fell on to them, the baby was screaming, his back felt as though knives were stabbing him, and his mother was crushing him, hard, the weight of something above her like a battering ram.

Everything was white. David didn't remember crawling into a tiny shape, as small as he could possibly make himself go just like his mother had always said. But he must have done. He stayed there until he was sure there weren't more bombs coming, until he saw the sky, out of the corner of his eye, turn from black to grey. It occurred to him he couldn't usually see the sky from his home, and something was different.

It must have been a long time. He stank of his own urine and he didn't think he could move. He could hear voices, calling, and he crawled slowly out, from underneath his mother, blinking away the sharp dust in his eyes. One of her arms, and the side of her, had been ripped away. The ribs, like ribbons of flesh. David looked at her face and then looked away again, and was sick on the ground.

'Someone in there? Is that Emily's place?'

He forgot about the baby, till a little sound from beside his mother's body made him look over. There it was, this tiny little thing. Her mother had taken her out of the drawer. She must have had her on her lap and she'd rolled away on to the floor beside her mother. Her legs were still waving in the air. She was thick with dust. He pulled the blanket over her, wrapping it tightly round her, then picked her up carefully, clutching her to him, like girls with dolls he'd seen playing on the bomb sites. His legs almost buckled but he walked towards the voices. He couldn't work out where the door was, which way round he was.

'There's a kid in there. Oi, son! You all right? You hear me?'

'It's Emily's kid. Where's Tom Doolan?' he heard someone else say. 'Maybe he's under all that rubble.'

There was a hole at the edge of something. He

saw it and knew it had been the front door. He crawled through it, still clutching his sister. The light was bright, his eyes stung with the dust.

'It's all right, Cassie,' he said, to the tiny bundle, which barely seemed alive to him, or even human. 'It's just you and me now. But we're going to be all right.'

He hadn't been back there since – he knew well enough when. It was five years ago, and he wondered if she still worked round the corner. Perhaps that was what had pushed him up the hill. The hope of seeing her again.

Stumbling slightly, flashing lights in the corners of his field of vision blurring everything, David found himself standing outside the Spanish Prisoners, and without knowing what else to do, he went in. Before and during the war it had been a dark place, but not like this. Then at least you had a community, even if the community was poor and desperate and afraid. His mother had played piano there, and he'd sometimes sit along from her on the long worn wooden bench and sing the old songs with her. Everyone went in there, even if when they came out they were apt to be drunk and sometimes violent. It was just where you went.

Now, it was dirty, unloved, dusty. Full of memories. An old thin man behind the bar, bent almost double. Flies buzzing around the curling sandwiches next to the tills. Ashtrays full to over-flowing. A few mean-faced old timers, gazing into empty drinks. Only men. He wondered if one of them was his father. He'd no idea if he was alive or dead somewhere, under a railway arch, chucked in the river after a fight. Or waiting, just biding his time to come back and get his son, the bogeyman of his nightmares.

His stomach started cramping, unbearably now, and David went to the lavatory outside in the backyard. He emptied his liquid bowels, shaking and staring into space in the narrow, cramped privy, grateful that no one could hear him. Standing up at the bar he ordered himself a gin this time, and drank it whole, wondering what he should do, if he was brave enough to hang around, see if he could find her, just see her for a few seconds, make sure she was all right. Aunt Jem had said she was living here now, working a stone's throw away. That was why he'd come back, wasn't it? Even though half of him didn't even know if he should walk along the market, in case he bumped into her. He was sure she didn't want to see him.

That silly cartoon again . . . he sketched out another picture of Wilbur in his book, tearing out the page, marooning it on the dirty old wood. He stared at the dog, his head spinning. What had he agreed to, back in that office? And why on earth had he come here?

He finished his drink and walked slowly down Chapel Market, picking up an apple on the way, hoping that might make him feel better, and as he bit into the sharply sweet juice his sense of self, the story he believed about himself, returned a little. He'd got out, he'd got his sister out. He'd gone to the Slade, got his degree. He'd met Martha, and that had saved him, he was sure. She was his angel, his great love, his muse, his friend, he did everything for her, for her first, and then the children. He sometimes wondered what would have happened to him had he not gone out and met her that day.

Somehow, he'd managed to escape his father, and the life that had nearly sucked him in. But that didn't mean he forgot. He couldn't forget, much as he wished he could.

In another minute he was going past Cassie's work. A framer's, now that was funny too, when you thought about it, him an artist. The shops were mostly hidden from view by the market stalls in front, and the framer's had an old chap selling a pile of shoes right outside it, so David couldn't see in. He stopped behind a fishmonger's stall and peered over, to see if he could spot her bright hair through the window. She wasn't there, and it was a good thing. What would he say to her, anyway?

'Davy! *Davy*, is that you?'

He froze.

Instantly, David knew it had been a mistake to look for her. Stay calm, act like nothing's happening. He began walking casually away.

'Davy!' The voice bubbled in and out of the crowds. 'Davy! It's him, I know it is . . .' There was a muffled sound. 'Let me through! Oh, please stop! It's me, Cassie!'

Then, David wished he had the guts to just walk on. But he couldn't, there was something in her tone that drove right through him.

'Hello, Cassie,' he said. He wheeled round so swiftly that she almost bumped into him.

'It is you! I bloody knew it was.' Cassie hit him on the arm. 'You bloody deaf, or something? I was yelling all the way back down the market.'

He glanced at her, and his heart started thumping in his chest. He wished he could feel nothing, wished she seemed more like a stranger, but she didn't. She was smiling at him awkwardly, tall as ever, slim and gangly. Still so young, how old was she? Twenty-four? He thought of the last time he'd seen her, terrified, tired, her pale face determined.

'How you doing, Cass?' he said.

'All right,' she said, and then she shrugged, and he knew she was regretting calling out to him. She crossed her arms, her bobbed hair shaking as she said, 'Terry's got some work up the reclamation yard off the Essex Road. We're living back here now. Funny how things work out, ain't it? How . . . how are you, Davy?'

'I'm not too bad.' He almost couldn't bear to meet her gaze. His little sister, who sucked her thumb so hard there was a red welt on the joint, who had thick black lashes and funny little scrunched-up toes, who screamed like a rat in a

371

trap if you put a slide in her hair. His sister, who looked so much like his mother. 'It's been a long time, hasn't it?'

'Bloody right. I saw you in the paper, one of them exhibitions. Hark at him, I said to Terry! Who the hell does he think he is!'

'What do you mean?' He shrugged. 'It's my work, isn't it? Can't help that.'

'You had a flowery sodding neck-tie on, you big Jessie.'

'It's what I wear to . . .' He trailed off. It sounded so stupid. She laughed.

'I'm only having a go at you, Davy! I'm your sister, ain't I? I can do that? I'm the only family you got.'

That wasn't true any more, though. She realised it as she was speaking, he saw it. 'How's everyone? Your lot?'

'They're all good.' He could feel his heart pounding in his chest, painful.

'How is she, Davy? My little girl?'

He realised this was why he was so scared. He was terrified she'd want her back again.

'She's really well. She's ever so bright, Cass. Into her books, she loves history. I read to her every night.'

'You tell her where she comes from?' She shifted, moving away from him and he thought she might suddenly run off again.

He shook his head. 'No. Never. Like you wanted.'

Then Cassie gripped his wrist, her thin face pale

in the afternoon sun. 'You don't ever tell anyone. You promised me, all right? I know I was a mistake. Dad hated me. I know what it's like. I couldn't have another mistake round here. She's better off with you.'

'You can come and visit her whenever you want, Cass.' He wished he could share just a tiny piece of the joy her daughter, *his* daughter, brought him. 'She's wonderful. We come up to London together, she and I, we visit a gallery, have lunch, and she always—'

'Don't talk to me about her,' Cassie said, and she lowered her head, looked away, curling her face into an expression of agony. 'I don't want to know. I want to start over, see? Me and Terry, I'm sure we'll have our own kids, some time soon. That little one, she was a mistake, I was too young.' Her face darkened. 'That piano poof, eh? All that time Aunt Jem thought it'd be nice for me to learn like Ma, and all the time he was just waiting to get into my knickers.'

It was Aunt Jem who'd called him. From a phone box, outside the tube station. He'd picked up, thank goodness. 'Cassie's in trouble.' Just like that, after – how long had it been? Ten years? And he'd known right away who it was, what the problem was, known exactly what they wanted.

She was nearly nineteen. It was her piano teacher. Like her mother, she'd always loved the piano. Sentimental Jem had given her lessons every year as a birthday present. A moony-eyed, thin-faced, hungry boy in London with no money, come down from Edinburgh to study music, passionately in love with her, he said. Angus was his name. He wanted to marry Cassie; Cassie, out of her mind with fear and shame, had said no. She was seeing Terry already. And she couldn't bear the idea she'd be the girl at secretarial college who'd have to leave because she got knocked up. She'd got the measure of Angus too, got him to agree to pay for the backstreet abortion and Aunt Jem, full of surprises, had known just the woman. But Angus had done a bunk the day before, never turned up with the money. Aunt Jem didn't have it, and then Cassie started saying she'd run away. Have it, then ditch it. That's when Jem called her nephew. 'I don't know what to do,' she'd said, her voice breaking. 'I think she might hurt herself. Or the baby. Can't you – come and see her?'

That was the last time he'd been back here, one of several visits that summer, culminating in the final time, when he came to collect his new daughter. For though things were changing on the King's Road and elsewhere, in working class Walthamstow where Cassie lived with Aunt Jem, a nineteen-year-old unmarried mother would have found herself alone and friendless fairly soon. Terry wouldn't stick around, Cassie was sure of that. She'd lose her place at the secretarial college.

They told everyone Cassie was spending the summer in Ireland, helping a sick aunt. In fact she came back to the old neighbourhood, to Penton Street with Aunt Jem, took a room by the market, had the baby at the University College hospital down the road.

When Cassie handed the ten-day-old baby girl over to David, he took her gently, cradling the soft wrinkled head in one hand.

'Now, listen,' Cassie told him. 'I don't want to see her again.' She was very calm. 'I don't want nothing to do with it. I want to go on and forget all about it.'

He remembered her face when she said it. Only children who'd had a childhood like theirs would understand the need to start again, put the past entirely behind them. He'd done the same thing, after all, hadn't he?

'Of course,' he'd said, and he'd leaned over and kissed her forehead. 'Don't worry, Cass. Don't worry any more.'

He thought about that now, and Florence growing every day at home, and the leaks and the money pouring down the Winterfold drains.

'I'm not sorry I did it,' she said. 'Maybe I should be but I'm not.'

And David said the first heartfelt thing all day. 'I'm glad you did it too, Cassie. I love her more than—' he began. 'I love her more than if she was my own.'

She gave no sign that this pleased her but he knew it did. 'What d'you call her in the end?'

'We named her Florence. We call her Flo most of the time.'

'Flo.' She said it a few times. 'It's nice. She like me?'

'Yes, she is,' he said. 'Really like you. She's very clever.'

'Oh, sod off.'

'Her language is better than yours anyway.' She'd laughed. 'She's very gangly, but very charming.'

'That's her dad, the weirdo.'

'I think it's us, too. Mum.' They moved out of the way, to let two shuffling old ladies pass.

'I was right, wasn't I? To give her to you? Tell me I was right?'

'I think you were right.' He wished he didn't feel so sick, so apprehensive, being back here. He'd throw his arms round her, squeeze her tight. 'I know you were right, Cassie. Don't you want to come and see her one day?' He thought of Florence, kneeling on her bed that morning, trying to make a flower out of paper, tongue sticking out in concentration. 'She's lovely.'

Cassie closed her eyes briefly and gave a bitter little smile. 'No, Davy love. I don't want to ever see her again, all right? Please don't ask me again. You said you weren't ever coming back. What you doing?'

'I don't know,' David said.

His father hadn't seen the point of Cassie, but her being born meant he didn't bother David's mother for a while, and that was a good thing. He kicked David around instead. Balanced him on the mantelpiece once, so he sat there, legs dangling, the coals from the fire burning his bare feet, while his father ate supper and laughed, and when his mother came back and scooped him back on to the floor he hit her across the face. That time he broke her nose.

So every time he thought of her, something would remind him, lead him back to something else. David couldn't see that the memories were important, that he shouldn't bury them deep in his heart, that he might do himself more injury that way. He could only see how much it hurt him, and his sister, and the damage it could do to Florence. He was sure Daisy knew the truth, he didn't know how. And he sometimes felt Martha didn't understand Florence the way he did.

He shivered. Cassie put her hand on his arm. 'Listen, Davy. I'd best be off. They'll be wondering where I went. I only said I was going to the post office. You get back home to Molly and those kids.'

'Martha.'

'All right then.' She tossed her hair and he knew she knew what Martha was called. It was just bravado, what they did to get by, the Doolans of Muriel Street. 'Good to see you, Davy. Honest.'

It occurred to him she was called Bourne now; that was Terry's name. And he'd changed his name to Winter. Aunt Jem was dead, a heart attack last year. In a generation, there'd be nothing left of their old family, or their father's name. Just their children, being brought up in the same place. David took out his little sketchbook, scribbled down his address, tore out the page and pressed it into her cold fingers. 'Here. In case you ever need me.'

Cassie shook her head, her mouth clamped shut, her grey eyes swimming with tears. 'Don't ask me again,' she said, after a minute. She looked down at the paper, then shoved it into her pocket. A gesture just like Florence, full of confidence and strangely awkward. 'Got to get back to work now. Good seeing you again, big brother.'

'You too.' He kissed her cheek. 'Terry treating you well?'

She waggled her head. 'So-so. He's all right. I'm all right. Hoping to have our kids next year. That's what Terry wants. Suppose I do too. Anyway, bye then.' She raised her hand like a signal, and then she was gone.

As he walked through the crowded backstreets, the old roads he knew so well, past the past the mission hall and Grimaldi's churchyard and the old fishmongers, Cally Road towards King's Cross, he knew he wouldn't tell Martha he'd seen Cassie. And afterwards, on the train going back to Winterfold, David flicked through the bomb site drawings again, his eyes taking in every last detail, as if there might be some salvation in it. He knew he'd put them away when he got home, maybe never look at them again. Perhaps it was right they stayed in the past. Perhaps Cassie was right. For the remainder of the journey he practised drawing

Wilbur, as the coal-black steam threw smuts against the carriage windows, taking him further and further away from hell and back to his own home.

When he came into the kitchen that evening, teatime was over and the children were outside. He could hear them chanting, some strange game. Martha was slicing up onions for supper. He stood in the doorway watching her, her slim fingers sliding the moon shapes into the red pot. She wiped her eyes on her forearm at one point, her hair falling in front of her face, then she looked up and blinked, laughing to herself, and saw him.

'Hello there,' she said, and he knew he loved her more than anything and anyone in the whole world.

'Hello,' he said, coming towards her. 'I'm sorry for this morning. I'm sorry for everything. I didn't sell the drawings, but I've had an idea. A wonderful idea.' He gripped her shoulders, and kissed her. 'Everything's going to be great.'

She stepped back, holding the knife, still smiling. 'Careful, I'm armed. Well, that's good news. What's got into you?'

'Just as I say.' He threw his hat on to the table. 'Everything bad is in the past. Everything good is in the future.'

Martha stroked his cheekbone, tracing the line of his eye sockets. 'You look exhausted.'

The onion scent on her fingers made his eyes water. He kissed her again and she leaned back in his arms, her back curving away, arms outstretched, then she flung herself around him again, and hugged him.

'Oh, I'm sorry,' she whispered in his ear, head lying on his shoulder. 'I hate arguing with you. I love you, darling.'

'Em, Em . . .' He breathed in the scent of her, closed his eyes. 'It's in the past. I'm getting us a drink. I love you.'

When he'd made them both strong, lime-scented gin and tonics, Martha threw the thyme from their garden into the pot with the chicken, and they went outside and sat on the lawn, watching the children chase the dancing dragonflies, their rainbow wings catching the summer light. Martha sat back in her chair, humming, occasionally calling out to one of them. David gulped his drink down like a dying man. He knew he had seen his past today, in all its forms. And now he had to remake the future.

MARTHA

March 2013

Bill, Daisy, Florence.

In the weeks after David died, Martha realised that she did not see things clearly any more. She had lost all sense of what was normal and what wasn't. She could see the fear in people's eyes if she walked into the village, when she went to the shop, or to church. The horror of grief. She felt marked, like a leper. They wanted to shy away from her because of what she had done, and what had happened in her house that day.

She had to change several aspects of her day-to-day life. At first some were difficult, but it was much better this way.

She didn't go in the study. There was time to go through his papers, his sketches, the documents of their family. Not yet.

The night it happened she had found Florence in there and something about her face, her searching eyes, was like a warning signal. There was too much in the study, it was all him. She couldn't be going

381

in there, and neither could anyone else. Martha saw that quite clearly.

'I need to use the study,' she told Florence. 'Papers in there I need to find.'

'I was just looking for something.' Florence's eyes were red raw. Her fingers flapped uselessly: she had beautiful hands. She swallowed, about to speak. 'Ma . . .' Then she started crying. Martha stared at her daughter's sunken, heart-shaped face and knew she couldn't tell her anything. She stroked her lightly on the arm.

'Just give me a couple of minutes in here, please, darling. The police need some information.'

The next day, Florence left. Left the house less than twenty-four hours after he'd died. Something about a manuscript on loan in London only for one more day. It was a lie, of course.

'If I don't go now . . . I can't explain.' She'd rushed forward, briefly embraced her mother, and just as Martha inhaled that familiar Florence smell of coffee, something spicy, her soft hair brushing Martha's cheek, Florence gave a soft cry, which seemed to stick in her throat.

'I don't know what else to say to you,' she'd mumbled; Martha wasn't sure, afterwards, exactly what it was she'd said. For how could she know? How could her baby girl, the one she didn't choose but had been handed on a plate, the one she hadn't loved to begin with, not at all, how could she know? Was it a memory, the truth of the years rolling back like a stone to reveal the emptiness at the beginning, the huge lie at the heart of it all?

When you were little, you loved to chew my finger. Your long, white, slim little fingers, gripping mine, your tiny hard pink gums, your mouth sucking my knuckle, your huge blue eyes as clear as a summer sky. The solid small heft of you in my arms. You in your place with us. And I loved you, even though you weren't mine.

And then she was gone, like that.

She came back for the funeral, that awful, cold, icy day when everyone except Martha cried, and the earth was frozen so stiff that the men took twice as long to dig the plot, and the ice seemed sewn into the mud, glittering underfoot, as the family gathered around the open grave and watched the coffin lowered in. Martha saw him there, saw the earth she was handed scattering on to the wooden lid, saw the faces of her family – Bill's eyes hazy with grief, Florence's red with weeping, hands in front of her mouth, Lucy's hunched shoulders, flushed cheeks, mouth turned down like a clown, Cat, biting her woollen-glove-clad finger.

Martha didn't cry. Not then.

Since the funeral, Florence, like Daisy, had vanished. She was fighting this court case. She always busy: *I have to meet my barrister tomorrow. I have a paper to finish.* She'd say she was coming back and then she didn't. *I'm staying with Jim in London. I'll call you.* She never did. *The trial's in May.*

And in December or January, May seemed so far in the future as to be ridiculous. He would have come back by then, this was all like the episode in the kitchen, when she had felt herself slipping away. He had gone but he would come back. It seemed perfectly logical to her.

Bill, Daisy, Florence.

This is what Martha kept remembering: how it was when they returned from hospital, nearly five years ago. A hot summer's day, the hills beyond the house golden and lazy with late afternoon heat. David was limping, his knee still bandaged. She'd helped him from the car, and then walked with him through to the garden.

'I need to show you something.'

His arm was heavy around her neck, as she helped him along the rocky path towards the daisy bank. When they reached the scar of the freshly milled brown earth, he had stared down at it.

'What's been going on?' he said in a strange voice, and she knew he understood.

'Daisy,' she began. 'Darling . . . she's gone.'

His hand gripped the metal crutch the hospital had given him. It pressed into the wet soil. 'Oh, Daisy,' he said. He scrunched his face up and looked at her. His eyes were dark. 'What happened, Em?'

'She . . . did it herself.' She couldn't say 'killed herself', it was so brutal. 'She . . . I buried her.'

He gazed at the crumbling earth, at the crushed

daisies around the long rectagular grave. He didn't speak for a long time, but eventually he said, 'Don't you want to tell someone, Em?'

All Daisy had asked for was to be buried here, to not be bothered any more. And Martha had felt she had to give her that. She could have rung the police, yes, of course. But since it had happened, she realised, she didn't care about other people. She never had. She cared about the fact that her daughter, who hadn't ever felt at home in this place, had wanted to stay here, at last.

Don't you want to tell someone, Em?

'I thought I wouldn't,' she said. 'I thought I'd just let everyone think she's gone away again.'

'Yes,' he said gently.

'I . . . I think she's happy here now. Do you . . .?' And Martha faltered, the fatigue and sadness swamping her. She sobbed, stumbled against him, so that he supported her for a moment. 'Does that make any sense to you?'

'Yes. Yes, of course.'

They'd dug Daisy up, of course. Three policemen and forensics and a pathologist, a big white tent around the daisy bank and the light of huge arc lamps flooding the side of the house, the earth churned into new banks of brown mud. She'd sat at the window, watching them, with her usual cup of tea, gingerbread, trying to tell herself they couldn't hurt her, no one could, any more. She stood up and drew the curtains that looked out on to the daisy bank and the garden from the dining room. She kept them drawn from that moment on. She left the garden well alone.

Bill, Daisy, Florence.

He was eighty-two. Not young. By the New Year, Martha couldn't bear to see anyone other than close family or strangers because someone would say again, 'It was a good innings, eighty-two,' and the fear that she would turn on them in rage and lose control grew to possess her.

He didn't tell me he was ill. I could have helped him and he didn't tell me. I saw how he suffered. I watched him die.

So she stopped going into the village. Karen did her shopping and then when Karen moved in with Joe in the New Year, Bill did it, Bill and Lucy.

Karen was there that day they took Daisy away, two or three weeks after the birthday lunch. She sat with Martha in the dining room, watching the men do their job. She had her laptop with her and pretended to be working, but occasionally she'd look up and ask Martha a question, get up to make some more tea, fetch a book.

There was something restful about Karen, something calm and logical about her in those days after David went, when Christmas was approaching, and everything was supposed to carry on as normal. Martha was glad of her company.

But come the New Year Karen had left Bill, moved in with Joe. David, Daisy, Florence, Cat, now this little one, another grandchild, gone. Bill had known his father was ill. She knew it, she didn't know how. To see him and think of the skinny, muddy, serious, joyful little boy he'd been, nearly, but not quite, brought her down. It would if she thought about Bill then. The little boy who'd thrown himself into her arms, who'd run along the lane with her, jumping up with questions like a kangaroo, who'd left for medical school and said, in the doorway, an awkward, acned eighteen-year-old, 'Thanks for a great life so far, Ma, really wanted to just say that,' then got into the car with David, waved once and driven off.

Bill, Daisy, Florence.

Through the long, cold nights of late winter, Martha lay awake, staring at the blue-black ceiling, listening to the silence outside. Though it was never silent, not really: the owls, the dreadful sound of night murder in hedgerows, a lone dog barking somewhere and, always, a blackbird, throughout it all, in the tree outside.

One night she was lying, eyes fixed on the ceiling as though a movie reel were playing there when she suddenly turned to look at David's side of the bed. It had been cleared, but the book he had been reading still lay there. *The Day of the Jackal*. The tatty green woven bookmark that Cat had made at Brownie camp when she was nine marked his place: only halfway through.

Suddenly, Martha saw grief, like the sky, covering

everything, all over her, around her, impossible to permeate. That feeling again, the one she'd had before. The grey mist seemed to fill up the room, it slid along the floor, up the bed, sluicing over her now like water.

He's never coming back.

He is. Don't think about it.

He's never coming back, Martha. You threw the earth on the coffin. You cleared out his cupboard. He's dead. David's dead.

She fought it, literally, wrestling with the bedclothes, scrambling out of the room, pulling the door shut behind her. Memories, like a vortex. David in only a pair of pants, painting the kitchen. Lying on the grass with Bill by his side, listening to the cricket on the radio. His sweet hopeful face, staring at her as they lay in bed. The long, sad day they took Florence from Cassie for the last time, and his suddenly joyous expression back at their hotel as he peered at the small bundle, clasped tight in Martha's arms. His screams at night, when the bad dreams came and he'd moan and sob so loudly, sometimes wetting himself, sometimes curling up in a ball so tight she had to wake him to free him.

He needed her, wherever he was. She wasn't there and he needed her. Who would hug him tight and comfort him, who would be there wherever he was to smooth his hair, to hold his hand and whisper those words, who would help him draw, help him cook, help him make a house, a home, a family together? He was alone. He had never been without her and she needed him, now more than ever. Just to see him once more, to tell him once more, one more evening together . . . Tears poured down Martha's cheeks. She retched, her throat swelling up so much with the power of grief that she thought, then and there, she was losing consciousness. She leaned against the wall, panting, sobbing, gasping for breath. But there was no one to hear her in the empty house. No one.

Eventually her breathing returned to normal. She put her hand on her throat, wishing this thickness, this lump would go away. She leaned in and listened through the bedroom door. As though she were trying to hear something.

All was quiet again.

'He's somewhere round here,' Martha said to herself. She clicked her tongue.

In the darkness, she smiled to herself. She understood now. She thought she wouldn't say anything to anyone about it, but she knew she was right.

She just had to put a few plans in place, then, and she would see him again, when things were ready. She didn't go back to her room at nighttime. She started sleeping in Cat's room, hugging the old patchwork cushion, with Cat's name spelled out in blue, and which smelled faintly of Cat, close to her. She avoided Lucy's calls: because Lucy wanted to come over, to look after her, to boss her around and pry and get into things, to find out things. She mustn't let her do that.

She couldn't go into the village, so she went into Bath or Bristol to do her shopping. She would walk through the supermarket, pushing a trolley, thinking about what he would like for supper and sometimes see another person like her. Eyes blank. Face smooth, unlined, frozen. And Martha would think: I know why they're like that. They are waiting for someone too. I hope they come back soon.

She stopped cleaning the house, opening the post, answering the phone. She read and reread her old gardening books. She learned the name of every plant, its soil, its situation, its family. Memorising them so that, if someone started talking about him and how sad it was, or what she should do, or how plans should be put in place, she could just nod and smile and not listen, recite different varieties of forget-me-nots in her head to shut out the words, so she couldn't hear what they were telling her. Because if she couldn't hear them, she couldn't let them in. Since the first day, the day she'd met him and he'd worn that silly hat on his head, since the two of them walked away from the past and into their future, he had always been nearby.

KAREN

'Easy now,' said Dawn, as Karen heaved her shopping bag over her shoulder. 'Let me get the door for you. Where's that Joe, then?'

'He's up on the Levels, meeting some meat guys,' said Karen. 'Thanks, Dawn. I'm fine now.'

Dawn stared at Karen's vast, domed stomach, hidden by her coat. 'Look at you. That's a big baby in there, isn't it? Sure it ain't twins?' She roared with laughter.

Karen smiled, and hitched her bag up again, unlocking the front door. 'See you later.'

'You're sure you're all right up here?' Dawn persisted, peering inside at the nondescript carpeted hallway and the stairs that led up to Joe's flat. Trying to collect information about the adulterous love nest, Karen knew, because no matter how many times she said, 'We're not together. I'm just staying with Joe for a bit,' no one believed her. That wasn't how the story went, was it?

'Oh, yes. Till I work out what I'm doing next. It's very kind of Joe to have me.'

'Hmph.' Dawn said. 'You must be lonely, what

with Joe and Sheila and everything that's going on at the pub these days.'

'I don't mind. He deserves it. They both do.'

'It's mad, though, isn't it?' Dawn folded her arms and leaned against the door.

'Yes, it's great. Please, Dawn – I hope you don't mind if I just take that bag and . . .' Karen began, trying not to snap. Her feet ached more each moment she stood on them, and she felt if she didn't sit down soon she might just have to slump on to the stairs, wait for Joe to finish work so he could haul her up to his flat in a sack.

'All right, Karen?' Sheila appeared from the pub. 'I'll help you upstairs with them bags, shall I? Bye then, Dawn, good to see you. Len's all right?'

'Oh, he's fine these days,' Dawn said. 'Ever since the varicose veins got done he's a new man. All thanks to Dr . . .' She trailed off. 'Well, bye then.'

'She's a nice girl but she needs more to do with her time, now Bill's fixed Len's legs.' Sheila huffed upstairs, into the tiny kitchen, dropping the bags down on the worktops, as Karen followed behind. 'Only thing keeping her going before that, running around after him. Now, shall I put the kettle on? You look done in.'

Karen sat down slowly, and eased her swollen feet up on to the coffee table. 'That'd be great.'

'How long you got to go now?'

'I'm due end of May. I wish it was over, Sheila. Those celebrities they interview in *Hello!* or whatever who go on about how they've never felt better – what are they on about? And I've still got two months to go.'

'Those magazines conspire against women to keep them in their place. It's the patriarchy at work,' Sheila said grimly, and Karen looked at her in surprise. 'Oh, the last bit's the worst,' she added, in a normal voice. 'Everyone knows that. You got all your baby gear ready?'

The same questions, twenty times a day. *How long have you got to go? Have you got everything ready? Is it a boy or a girl? How are you feeling? You look well!* Karen knew from her fellow mothers-to-be on the parenting course they were doing that there were just as many questions she wasn't being asked. Whether they were going to stay in their current home or move somewhere with more space, for example. No one in Winter Stoke asked Karen that.

'I've bought some things but I don't want to go overboard till it's here. I'm superstitious. Joe had some journalist down from London last week – she swears by IKEA. He's obsessed with it now, keeps trying to buy stuff online only there's so much you have to go in the stores to buy. That's how they make their money, isn't it?'

'Those bloody wine glasses. Ten pounds for twelve, they do them, and those patterned cardboard storage boxes.' Sheila leaned on the counter, laughing. 'Every time I go in there I promise it's just to get a desk for the office or whatever, and every time I come out with a pile of those patterned cardboard boxes and a lorry-load of glasses and they smash on the way home and I never use those cardboard boxes, never.'

'Well, maybe you should go mad and treat yourself, Sheila.' Karen tried to reach her foot but her bump prevented her. 'Take Joe. He's desperate to go. I can't face IKEA, walking round like a beached whale in flats. No way.'

'You look beautiful,' Sheila said. She poured from the teapot. 'Honestly, you do. Suits you, being a bit more . . .' She stopped. 'Well, never mind.'

'Now you've got me worried.' Karen smiled. She hadn't ever really cared about her appearance. She knew she was attractive – it was part of her pragmatic nature that she accepted it as fact – and often it was boring, men coming on to you because you were short and had big boobs. It was one of the things she'd liked about Bill. He hadn't minded much about her clothes or nails or hair, or the fact she was seventeen years younger than he. He'd liked *her*.

It was Joe she'd tarted herself up for, almost like she knew she had to play the part of the scarlet woman to make sense of what she was doing and the irony was, he didn't like it. They'd only slept together four or five times, but they'd met a few more than that. In summer, going into September . . . before he'd found out she wasn't just Karen Bromidge, the lonely girl two years older than he, who was new to the area and from the north and sexy as hell and lots of fun, whom he could talk to about his son, and the weirdness of the village, and starting over again, and then have sex with – intense, heated, silent sweaty sex that matched the wet, humid summer. He didn't know her married name was Karen Winter, and she lived down the road with the doctor who'd sewn up his finger. She was married, and Joe – Joe was a damn prude, she was starting to think. He'd ditched her faster than a rubbish truck at full speed, and he'd been so angry with her, so bloody furious!

'You should have told me, Karen,' he'd said, gently, but his voice was cold. It was early October, and chilly in his small flat, where they'd had their secret summer. But summer was definitely over now. 'It changes everything.'

'What's the difference? You weren't into me,' she'd yelled, not caring who heard them, how mad she sounded. She'd have been pregnant then, two or three weeks, how weird to think of it. 'You didn't want to go out with me. I know you didn't. I'd have thought you'd have been glad, no strings attached, what's wrong with you?'

'What's wrong with *you*?' he'd said, angrily. 'Karen, you can't just go around lying to people like that. I really liked you. I'd – if I'd have known, then . . .'

It had been hard enough to get him to sleep with her, she'd thought. Then she found if she just kept playing the part of the bad girl, she'd start to believe it, and somehow she'd be OK. But it hadn't worked out like that. She'd engineered this whole sorry mess, and there was nothing to do but make the best of it.

The memory of it made her shiver. She took a biscuit from the tin and dunked it in the tea Sheila handed her. 'This is lovely. Thanks, Sheila.'

Since Karen had moved in with Joe, just after Christmas, Sheila had been nothing but kind to her. It couldn't have been easy, her star chef suddenly lumbered with a hormonal homeless pregnant ex, four weeks after that review in the *Daily News*.

It was funny, when she thought about it. How Lucy had babbled on for weeks about this guy at work, how he was old and sad and keen on her, how he kept saying he'd review the Oak Tree, and Karen just hadn't believed her. She was too worried about Lucy's obvious crush on Joe to see any further than that.

Karen sometimes wondered if Lucy knew how profoundly she had changed everything, really. The review had run the week after David's funeral, Saturday 1 December. A copy of it had been framed, and hung above the bar.

. . . In the cooking of Joe Thorne, the young, gentle chef who spent two years under Jean Michel Folland at Le Jardin in Leeds, we have the very best of British cuisine today. The apparent simplicity of the names of dishes belies the extreme complexity with which they are created.

396

Pressed ham hock, salmon roulade with beetroot relish, goat's cheese ravioli – they all sound straightforward, and they are, for this is no snob's menu, designed to dazzle and intimidate. Rather it is a menu for a neighbourhood restaurant, which happens to be situated in a pub, one that is as old as the Civil War, in an idyllic little slice of Somerset just outside Bath. The food is locally sourced – in an unpretentious and sympathetically realistic way, none of your foraging for borage nonsense here. The execution is perfect. The atmosphere – under the eagle eye of landlady Sheila Cooper – is welcoming, laidback, and yet with just a touch of magic: witness the rosehips on the table and the complimentary damson vodka offered to me after my meal. I booked another table for the following week when I left. I have now been back twice since that first magical visit. I cannot recommend this wonderful place highly enough.

It had happened fast. Bookings started coming in that day for dinners, and Christmas parties. Tables of six, eight, ten. Then weekend lunches, then requests for birthday parties, private room hire, the works. By New Year's Eve the restaurant had been booked out for two weeks, and though Sheila and Joe both fully expected the slump in January, it never came. There were mutterings from some of the villagers about cars blocking the High Street, and not being able to move for Londoners up at the bar now, and there'd been some defections to the Green Man but as Joe told Karen, he was sure he'd win them back. If necessary, they'd buy the field behind Tom and Clover's, turn it into a vegetable patch and a car park. Maybe institute a locals-only night, where you had to have a council tax bill with you to claim your table and all you can eat for £40 for two, including wine.

He was full of plans. So was Sheila. Karen went along with them, smiling at their enthusiasm, even as the endless winter passed and the days grew wetter, and longer, and her body grew bigger and began to drag her down. She had no idea what the future might hold. She was too terrified to ask herself the question, so she avoided it from anyone else.

She had left Bill after Christmas. Since his father died he was a robot, a man who put on his overcoat every morning, went to the surgery, solved his patients' problems, and in the evening came home and either went up to the house to be with his mother, or sat in an armchair listening to old episodes of *Hancock's Half Hour* and staring into space, square fingers drumming on the arms of the chairs. She tried to help: she ran errands for Martha, she fielded calls, answered letters. But Lucy wasn't talking to her, Florence had vanished off the face of the earth, and Cat was back in Paris. Karen was worried about Martha, more than merely concerned she wasn't coping. There was something strange about her, about the language she used. Karen didn't believe some of the things she said, didn't think she was quite well.

She tried to talk to Bill, to ask him what he thought, what he wanted for tea, what he wanted to watch on TV, but every time he'd just say, 'I don't know, Karen. You do what you want.'

On New Year's Eve, he sat in front of the television, gin and tonic in hand, a plump quarter of lime trapped under the ice cubes. He always had lime, not lemon, just like Martha and David. It was a Winter thing; there was always a pile of jewel-like limes in a brown glazed bowl on the table at Winterfold, even in the depths of winter. Karen stood behind him, twisting her fingers together over and over.

'Bill. Bill?'

He'd turned round, and she saw the tears in his eyes, the glazed expression. He hadn't really been watching anything.

'Yes.' He'd cleared his throat, and stood up, with the sofa between them.

'I think I should move out,' she'd said. 'I just wondered what you think about it.' There was a pause and, because she was terrified of his answer, she rushed ahead, and said, 'I think we need some time apart. So you can work out what you feel about all of this. You've got so much to deal with at the moment.'

He'd shaken his head. 'No, it's not that, Karen.'

He'd moved the empty glass on to the shelf, carefully. She loved how precise he was with everything, how neat and modest his movements were, how he inhabited his space so comfortably, how being with him was to feel safe, and secure, and . . .

Karen had put her hands in front of her eyes so he couldn't see her tears.

He'd said gently, 'I think you should move out because you have to work out what you want. I can't make you happy, that's clear. I loved you. If you want to go I think it's best you go. We got it wrong, didn't we?' He'd looked up, his eyes puckering together, his mouth creased into an awkward smile. 'It was always going to be a risk, wasn't it? Suppose it was worth it . . .' And then he'd come round the sofa and squeezed her arm. 'Do you have somewhere to go?'

She'd gritted her teeth, so he wouldn't see how ill-prepared she was. She hadn't booked a hotel, rung a friend . . . she had no friends here, anyway, now. 'Oh, yeah. I thought I'd . . . I'll . . . Yes, I'm staying with a friend,' she lied.

'Really?'

Bill picked up his keys. 'Well, then,' he said, quietly. 'I'll leave you alone to get your stuff together. I'll go and see Ma.'

He'd stood a couple of metres from her and they'd nodded, trying to keep the conversation alive. The distance between them . . . Then Bill had pulled on his coat.

'We'll talk soon, then. Let me know . . . how you are.'

And he left, leaving her alone in the little house. Karen packed her bags, tears falling on to the duvet cover. She could see every stepping stone on the path that had taken her to this point, every wrong turn, every mistake. She was completely alone, and there were no fireworks that signified the end of her relationship with Bill. He'd made her chicken Kiev sandwiches. Suddenly that was all she could think about.

Joe met her at the bottom of the street and helped her with her bags. He didn't ask any questions but that first night, he gave up his bed for her.

'I'll sleep in Jamie's room. It's absolutely fine.'

They were very formal with each other. 'Thank you,' she'd said, looking at his short, curly hair, the dark hairs on his arms, his strong hands gripping her bag. Trying to remember how it felt to be naked with him, to feel him inside her. She couldn't remember it at all. 'I won't be here long. I'll start looking for somewhere.'

He'd hung in the doorway. 'Please, Karen. Stay as long as you want. I know it must be difficult for you. It's my responsibility too.' Then, he cleared his throat. 'Isn't it?'

'I suppose it must be,' she'd said. 'All the evidence would suggest it is.'

Joe had swallowed, and for a split second he looked terrified. But it was so fleeting she might have missed it. He'd hugged the towel he was holding to his chest. 'I love kids, Karen, you know that. I won't let you down. I'll be there, I promise.'

Four months ago. Karen heard the thundering footsteps on the stairs, and her heart lifted. 'There he is,' Sheila said, smiling. 'He'll make it all all right, just you see if he doesn't.'

'You've already done that, Sheila,' Karen said, raising her mug as Joe came in.

'Sheila! We got Brian to commit to becoming our supplier, and we'll sell his meat through the pub.' Joe vaulted over the back of the sofa, landing next to Karen, who was jolted into the air, spilling her tea.

'Oh!' Karen mopped at her dripping lap.

He cupped his hand under her mug. 'I'm so sorry, Karen. How are you?'

'I was tired, but that's woken me up.' She smiled at him. 'Let me get you a cup of tea.'

'I'll get it,' he said, standing up again. 'I can't stay long.'

'I thought you weren't working tonight?' She tried to keep the disappointment out of her voice. After all, they were flatmates, and he was absolutely adamant he was going to do right by her – they'd talked seriously about her buying the dilapidated cottage two doors down, Karen pulling up Excel spreadsheets on her laptop and tapping figures into her computer, going through the motions of some plan that, frankly, alternately depressed her and terrified her. All so that when the baby was born he could come and help most days, and even stay over there instead when Jamie was down – the cottage was bigger, it had a garden, and Jamie and this new little thing, his half-brother, or -sister, would have room to grow.

When they sat on the sofa to watch TV on the rare evenings Joe spent in, there was at least two feet between them. They couldn't ever agree on what to watch anyway. She liked documentaries about people with bodily disorders. He liked US TV series. He thought she was prurient for recording programmes about men with engorged testicles or Siamese twins; she thought he was bloodthirsty for enjoying the spectacle of a fantasy king murdering a prostitute and someone being made to wear their own severed hand round their neck. She knew all this, but she couldn't say it, couldn't joke about it, the way she used to tease Bill about his love of Ealing comedies.

'I am working, I'm so sorry,' Joe said, peering through the hatch in the kitchen. 'But I'm going to quickly make you some bubble and squeak on a tray. I brought most of the ingredients up with me. Sheila—' he threw her a balled-up piece of paper – 'here's the receipts for the fishmonger. He says we're his best customer, now. Can you do me a favour? Start running Karen a bath?'

Sheila unfolded the receipts and put them into her pocket, watching Joe affectionately. 'Hot baths and tea on a tray? Ooh, you're a lucky woman, Karen.'

Karen watched Joe's head moving backwards and forwards in the kitchen, and she felt the baby move, shifting and sliding around inside her. All she could think of was that bubble and squeak was Bill's favourite meal, the one he'd cook singing along to his Northern Soul albums in his tuneless, awkward bass.

'I must be, mustn't I,' she said.

CAT

Cat had sold the red Lanvin shoes on eBay eventually, for one hundred Euros. Back in October she had taken out a credit card too, and both of these helped pay for the Eurostar for them both to go back to Winterfold in early April to see her grandmother. They arrived very late on the Friday, and the plan was to leave before lunch on the Sunday.

Staring out of the train at the still-freezing English spring she told herself coming back was the right thing to do, though Gran had told her not to. Everything had changed, that day in November. So there was no point in fearing what might come, as she had always done: it had already happened. No point in hanging on to memories. No point in fearing a debt when the people who needed you needed you now.

That first night back she lay next to Luke on one of the high twin beds in Lucy's room and wondered if she'd been right. Martha was sleeping in Cat's room. Something about damp in her own room. Cat didn't believe her. She'd said she had to go somewhere the next morning, to get some milk. When Cat asked her where, Martha said: Bristol. Cat had laughed, thinking it was one of her grandmother's impenetrable jokes, but she had been quite serious.

Everywhere she looked, the house seemed to be covered up, like shrouds over the dead. Curtains drawn. Dust on surfaces. Doors shut. Locked. Shawls and blankets she'd never seen before covering chairs and sofas, and when Cat asked why, Martha said simply: 'They're dangerous. They can't be touched.'

'Of course,' Cat said carefully, trying not to show Luke how much this scared her. It was because they were the pieces of furniture Southpaw had sat in, the things in the house he had used most frequently. His chair in the kitchen, a heavy oak thing with arms and carved feet: Martha said it had woodworm and might have to be thrown away.

On the Saturday morning, they sat in silence, Luke pushing cereal around his bowl, Cat eating some toast, Martha quite still, staring at nothing, humming very slightly. It was a cruelly cold day. A grey sky, no sign of spring.

'I have to go in a minute. The traffic into Bristol will be poor.' Martha stood up.

'Bristol?' Cat had forgotten, momentarily. She rubbed her eyes. 'No, Gran. Don't be . . .' She trailed off.

Her grandmother's tone was even. As though Cat were being hysterical. 'I need some milk, and

I don't get it from the shop any more. Problems with supply.'

'Gran – you really don't have to go into Bristol, honestly. I'll walk into the village in a little bit, get some milk, some things for you.'

'No, thank you.' She collected up the plates, though Cat and Luke hadn't finished.

Luke climbed on to David's chair, pulling an old green shawl to the floor. He rocked it back and forwards, against the table.

'Luke, stop it,' Cat said.

Martha, at the sink, turned. 'Don't do that,' she said, but Luke ignored her. The old chair creaked as he teetered backwards, his full weight on it.

Cat said, 'Luke. Stop it now.'

'I want to sit in it,' said Luke. 'I miss him. I miss Southpaw.'

Martha crossed the kitchen. Her expression remained unchanged. With one firm movement she grabbed Luke's skinny arm and yanked him out of the chair. As though he were a rag doll. She staggered a little, catching the weight of him against her, and his legs flailed, wildly in the air, then she let go, and Luke fell to the floor.

'I said, don't do that.'

Luke lay crying on the floor, looking at his great-grandmother with a bewildered expression. Cat helped him up, with one hand.

'Darling, she asked you to stop.' She hugged him close to her. 'I'm sorry, Gran. He was cooped up in the train all yesterday and now . . .'

'I don't care.' Martha was facing away from them, then she turned and draped the shawl over the chair again. 'Perhaps you'd better go out now, then.'

Cat, who was used to being in control of everything, felt helpless. She couldn't remember being at Winterfold and wanting to escape. She didn't know how to talk to her grandmother. Lucy, with whom she spoke regularly on the phone now, had warned her, but Cat realised she hadn't really grasped it.

They walked down the lane, Luke happy again, running in zigzags, Cat holding the list Martha had given her. It gave her a shock to see Gran's strong, elegant sloping handwriting again.

Milk
3 limes
3 potatoes
Bombay Sapphire gin. From the pub. <u>Not from the post office. They only sell Gordon's gin.</u>

Pushing the scrap of paper into her pocket, Cat ran to catch up with Luke. She didn't want to go into the pub. She didn't want to see Joe. I mean, she'd tell herself, when he came into her mind on those dark winter nights in Paris, lying in the chilly, tiny *chambre de bonne* in the Quai de Béthune: it's almost comical, the first man I allow myself to

408

like, the first man I kiss for years, whom I think: for once, you might actually be a good guy, a nice man . . . ha.

Compared to what had happened after that, she supposed her encounter with Joe was the light relief of the weekend. She was no judge of men, that was clear, and she thought she had probably had a lucky escape. Olivier, Joe – silver-tongued and black-hearted, both of them. And when she thought about his lips on hers, their bodies meeting in the chill damp, the way he'd pretended to understand, worming his way in, when Karen, his pregnant girlfriend, her *aunt*, was lying low at home less than a mile away . . . Cat, arriving at the village shop, shook her head, surprised at the power the thought of him still had, five months afterwards, to make her this angry. She'd have to lie to Gran. Tell her the pub was all out of Bombay Sapphire.

After they'd done their shop at the post office, Cat waved goodbye to Susan and chivvied Luke along the high street, towards the playground. It occurred to her that by now for all she knew the Oak was so famous there'd be hordes of people outside, food bloggers and critics and liggers waiting for Lily Allen or whoever it was who was supposed to love it there and she was possessed by a curiosity to see how different it was now. On the pretext of looking at the new cul-de-sac of ugly executive houses that were being built right at the end on the fields she walked them briskly to the end of the High Street, and as they passed, she glanced hurriedly in the windows of the Oak. But it was late morning and the lights were still off, the stools and chairs on tables. No other signs of life. She glanced up at the rooms above the pub. Karen was living there with him now, she knew.

As they turned back and crossed the waterlogged village green towards the playground, Cat felt more cheerful. Like she'd exorcised some silly teenage crush and now it was over she could admit she'd liked him. She'd enjoyed kissing him. Joe Thorne was cute, he was handsome, funny, shy, he loved *Game of Thrones*, and he'd told her about *The Gruffalo*. So it turned out he was bad news. So what? He was just someone she'd kissed after a long day and too much wine. It was done now. She'd been living the life of a nun on an island the last few years. She needed more experiences like Joe.

'Mum, swing me?' Luke said, leaping up at her side, his face flushed with cold, his huge eyes imploring.

'Sure.' One of the many little pinpricks you felt about being a single parent was that there weren't two of you to swing your child along in each hand. So instead Cat did her special thing, which was to loop her arms under Luke's shoulders and spin him around and around on the boggy grass till they were both dizzy and stumbling. She did it three or four times, then pretended to stop. 'OK, all done.'

'But that was hardly any spin! No! Again! More spin!' Luke laughed, jumping up and down, and she laughed back, the happiness at being alone with him in this huge expanse of green, away from the dark dusty house, the feeling of fresh country air in her lungs, in his little lungs too, making her almost drunk with sensation.

'OK. One more.'

'OK! OK! OKOKOKOKOK!!' Luke shouted, bouncing up and down.

'Spin!' Cat shouted, staggering around in a crazy circle, as Luke's shrieks of ecstatic excitement grew louder and louder, and the more they both laughed, the unsteadier she became, going faster and faster. Suddenly, one of her wellingtons squelched, suctioned in by mud and water, and she began to topple. She slid on to the ground, Luke on top of her.

'Oh, no,' she said. 'I'm covered in mud.'

'Joe Thorne!' Luke screamed. 'Mummy, it's Joe, he hit me with the car!' He scrambled to his feet and pointed, as though seeing a miracle. 'Mummy! He's got a boy with him. A BOY!'

Luke broke out of Cat's grasp and ran towards the two figures on the other side of the cricket field, his little legs drumming on the hard ground.

'Luke!' she shouted. 'Come back.'

When she caught up with him she was panting

hard. 'Hello,' she said, not looking at Joe. 'Luke, you don't *ever* run off like that, do you hear me?'

'I wanted to see Joe, Mummy, don't be strange.' Luke was jumping up and down, almost beside himself to see not only Joe but a big boy as well. 'Don't you want to see him? Who are you? Who is this? Is his jacket blue, or green? I can't tell.'

Joe pushed the little boy forwards. 'This is Jamie. He's five, Luke. Luke's three, Jamie. He likes *The Gruffalo* too.'

Jamie nodded, shyly. He had thick blond curly hair, which hung like a messy halo around his head. His skin was dark caramel, his eyes a warm grey.

'Hello, Jamie, I'm Cat.'

'Hullo.' Jamie had a deep voice. 'Does he like Moshi Monsters?'

'I love them! I really do love them!' Luke bounced up and down, as though he was on an invisible pogo stick and Joe put his hand on his arm, laughing.

'All right, Luke. Eh, you silly lad, it's good to see you.'

At the warmth in his voice Cat involuntarily smiled at him and their eyes met. He was exactly how she remembered him. Bit thinner. Stubble on his firm chin, his thick hair curly. Disappointment shot through her, taking her by surprise.

Joe's eyes were fixed on her, his gaze steady. 'I didn't know you were back.'

'Just for the weekend,' Cat said.

'I wondered . . .' he cleared his throat, '. . . I've been wondering how you were getting on.'

'I hate Madame Poulain. I used to like her. Joe, can we watch *Ratatouille* again?'

'He's talking to me, Luke.'

'I live in France, Jamie, do you? Can you speak French?'

Stoic, silent Jamie looked up at his dad with something like alarm.

'What's he like, Dad?' he said quietly, and Cat covered her mouth, trying not to laugh.

Joe bent down, resting his hand lightly on the back of his son's head. 'Listen, Jamie, why don't you show Luke the swing? He won't have seen it. It's new, isn't it?'

'Yes,' Jamie said, his serious eyes meeting his father's. 'Are we still having lunch soon, Dad?'

'Course,' Joe said. 'Can you pick some bay leaves off the tree over there, too? That'd be great. You know what they look like, don't you?' He lifted Jamie up, then pretended to drop him, and Jamie gave a shriek of laughter and ran towards the playground, Luke following him, one red jacket, one blue, maybe green.

They stood together watching them go. Joe cleared his throat.

'I won't ask how you all are. It must still be very hard.'

Cat shoved her hands in her pockets. 'We're OK.' The waves that hit her during the day at the market stall, staring out of the window of

Madame Poulain's sitting room, tears pouring down her cheeks, Luke saying, 'Come here, Mummy! Maman! Why are you crying?' Of her grandfather's jumper he used to wear to keep warm in his study, navy wool, eaten by moths to a cobweb. His smiling, shining eyes, his darling hands, so swollen and painful. And her mother – she hadn't even been able to think about her mother properly, yet. Not at all. As for Gran, and the family and all of it – there wasn't a place to start, a place to begin, a thread that would lead them out of the maze. Cat turned her head so he wouldn't see the tears in her eyes. 'That's not true. We're not OK really.'

He nodded, and he didn't try to hug her, as Susan Talbot had done, or grip her hands with tears in her eyes, like Clover, or shake his head, pityingly. He just said, 'I'm so sorry, Cat.'

'Me too.'

'How's Mrs Winter?'

'She's not great. I don't know. Sometimes I'm not sure she really understands what's happened.'

'What do you mean?'

Cat found she couldn't explain it. 'I think she is . . . I think she thinks he's coming back.' She spoke softly. 'Gran's always right. She's always had a plan. I don't know what to do.'

'I don't think you can do anything,' he said. 'Just be there for her.'

'I'm not, though, am I?' She thought it was a peculiarly insensitive thing to say. 'I'm in Paris.'

414

She tried to keep her voice steady. 'I can't do anything for her.'

'I'm sorry. It's none . . . none of my business.'

'Too right,' Cat said, and he stiffened, and she instantly regretted it: she hadn't meant to get into it, not now, it was so childish. One of the things that felled her constantly since Southpaw's death, since Daisy's body was found: the struggle to think of anything else, anything that was normal. She had this idea that she should only be concentrating on them, grieving for them, and not small, silly things, like how much she hated the way Madame Poulain's lipstick bled out of her lips, thin red veins reaching up to her wet nose. How endless the winter seemed that year on the stall, and how useless her thermal socks were. How her rage at Olivier gathered new strength every day, so that she wished she could find him, grip his neck like he used to grip hers, watch the veins bulge in his face, see the fear in his eyes. *You nearly finished me off. But I have our son, I will find a way out, and you can't do that to me any more.* How angry she was with Joe, the memory of them that night, talking together under the porch, the dripping rain surrounding them like a curtain. She shuffled. 'Look, forget it. Sorry.'

'What – what happened with us, Cat—' Joe turned to her. 'I don't do that kind of thing normally.'

'Normally! What does that mean?'

He closed his eyes and shrugged. 'I shouldn't have. It was wrong.'

'You knew she was pregnant when we kissed.'

'Yes.'

'Exactly.' He opened his mouth but she cut him off. 'How's Karen doing?'

'She's doing well. She's tired, quite heavy. Still a way to go but already she's slowing down. She finds it hard.'

'Right.'

'She's living with me.'

'Yes, I know.'

Cat thought of Lucy's voice, when she'd rung her to break the news.

'She just moved in with him, upped sticks and walked out, right after New Year! The brass neck! Apparently they're thinking of renovating Barb Fletcher's old cottage together.'

More than ever, Cat had been glad no one else knew she'd kissed him. 'No. The one with the old hearth and the massive garden? It's got an outside loo, right?'

'Well, Joe can afford it. He must be rolling in it soon. I can't believe I got him that restaurant review. I cannot believe it.'

'He deserves it, though,' she'd said, trying to be fair. 'He's really good.'

'Well, yes,' Lucy had said. 'But I still can't believe the way he's behaved. To think I fancied him! Oh my God. All that time he was shagging Karen. All that time . . .'

All that time.

Standing there in the wide open air with him,

416

everything out in front of them, Cat knew it was time to leave. 'I'd better get back to Gran,' she said.

'I'm sorry, Cat. Really sorry. I wish it hadn't happened like that.'

Cat leaned forwards: he spoke so quietly she wasn't sure she'd heard right at first. Luke was running around Jamie in a circle with a couple of bay leaves stuffed in his hands, shouting out pieces of information he thought Jamie would want to know. 'I'm a fish in the play at school . . . I had a beef burger with Gabriel . . . We are reading a book about cars.'

'Right, thank you.' She sounded like a prim schoolmarm.

He'd looked down at the bag of supplies he'd been carrying, then up at her. 'Screw it. Can I just say one thing?'

'What?'

'Cat, listen. I keep thinking . . .'

Often, afterwards, she wondered how he'd meant to finish that sentence, but he'd just stopped. No yelling children, no interruptions, no random acts of God, such as in a rom-com. He'd just stopped and said, 'You know, I think it's time we went.'

'What's in your bag?' she asked him suddenly.

'Oh.' He peered into the blue plastic. 'We've been foraging. On our walk. Dock leaves, wild rocket, some rosemary . . . and some roots. We're going to try a few things back at the pub.'

'You know where the wild garlic grows? Up over the hill, past Iford? Miles of the stuff. Not long now. And there's Bath asparagus everywhere in the hedgerows in May too.'

'I didn't know that. Any of it. Thank you.'

'Yes. I used to pick it, with – never mind. Luke! Come on! We need to get home.'

'Home?' Luke stood still, looking stricken. 'You said we were here for the weekend.'

'I mean to Gran's.' She corrected herself. 'We need to walk back and see Gran and make lunch.'

'OK!' Luke shouted.

'See you, then,' she said to Joe, wanting to part on a friendly note. 'Good luck with everything.'

Joe nodded. 'You too. Thanks.' Jamie ran over to him and buried his head in his dad's stomach. Joe pulled him towards him, and covered him with his coat.

Jamie stayed perfectly still for a few seconds, then opened the coat, looked up at his father and shouted, 'Boo, Dad!'

As Joe threw his head back and laughed, Cat realised she'd never really seen him grin before. Properly, like his face was made for it. He picked his son up and gave him a big kiss, then turned, to see Cat and Luke still standing there, watching like children waiting to be picked up at school.

Cat set off down the field towards the north exit. She walked briskly, a harsh spring wind on her cheeks. Luke scrambled to keep up with her. 'We see Joe later?' he kept asking.

'No,' Cat told him. 'We're going back home. Tomorrow.'

Back home.

The train the following day was crowded. Luke had to sit on her knee for most of the way, squashed up against a Moroccan lady who gave him pitta bread and pieces of apricot. Cat thought about her grandmother. How being with her was almost worse than leaving her, because it was clear they couldn't help her, no one could, and she didn't know what would happen.

They'd all, all of them, mocked Lucy gently over the years, for being so sentimental about Winterfold: the awards ceremonies at Christmas, her lists of favourite things about the holidays that she had pinned up on her walls. But they were no better, any of them, were they? Lucy was the most straightforward member of the family. She told the truth, at least, always had.

They went into the Tunnel, the sudden dark rushing past them, and Luke settled his head against the window, watching the single lamps that lit up their route. Cat made her plans. She would keep ringing Lucy and Gran up, and writing and emailing, even if Gran didn't want to hear from anyone. She'd go back to Winterfold twice a year at least, even if Gran didn't want to see anyone. And she would remember Southpaw, and try to remember her mother's life, and the mistakes she, Cat, had made before and mustn't make again.

419

She told herself summer would come soon, and then things would be different.

But in the following weeks Cat was almost glad when it became cold again, and the rain started. She had the excuse she wanted to feel as miserable as she liked.

MARTHA

Natalie, the lawyer, was a dark-eyed, brisk sort of person, Karen's friend. She reminded Martha of Karen, in fact.

'We have good news,' Natalie said, spreading out the paperwork on to the dining table. 'So, to explain briefly—'

'Could I open the curtains before you start?' Bill stood up. 'It's rather close in here.'

'It's fine,' Martha said. 'Leave it.'

'It's very dark, Ma.'

'Bill, she said leave it. If she wants it like that she can have it like that.' Florence drummed her fingers on the table.

Natalie looked at Martha, unsure how to react, and Bill came back to his seat, jaw set. The sun was shining brilliantly outside, the first splash of spring. It flooded through the curtains, into the lamplit room. Birds sang in the eaves of the house.

Martha knew what the daisy bank should look like by now, on a day like this. But after nearly six months she had still done nothing about resowing the grass and daisies. She thought she would leave it, for when he came back. They could do it together, perhaps, remember Daisy together. She liked to think up little things like that for them to do. When he was here.

'Ma!'

Martha realised someone was talking to her. 'Yes?' she said. 'Sorry, Natalie. Go on.'

'We've been lucky,' Natalie said. She took a sip of water. 'We've got the court date through. I think in other counties or under different circumstances we'd be looking at a trial or at least some kind of arrest, but here I'm pretty sure you'll merely be summoned to the Magistrates' Court and given a conditional discharge.'

'That doesn't sound very mere to me,' said Bill, looking carefully at his mother. Florence sounded incredulous.

'Nothing else? After what . . . happened?'

'No.' Natalie looked from mother to daughter. 'You sound surprised, Florence. Is there a reason for that?'

'No. None at all.' Florence crossed her arms.

Martha didn't know what to say to Florence. Her eyelids were still red, as though she had eczema. She'd had it when she was little; so had Bill. Not Daisy. David had eczema when he was worried, or overworked. She had bought him special cream, from the old pharmacist in Bath, the one that Jane Austen had used. It had always worked. She wondered if there was any left, and made a note to check upstairs. He'd need some more soon.

'There'll be a small fine and, Mrs Winter, you'll probably have to pay the court costs, too, but that's all.' Martha nodded, staring into space, thoughts swirling in confusion around in her mind. She heard Bill muttering something to Natalie, who turned to her and said, 'Foul play can't be proven either way, and there's no case to answer. Plus we have enough evidence that suicide was the likely cause of death to satisfy the police. More importantly, we have testimony from several witnesses – which I'm sure you'd back up – that Mrs Winter was under a great deal of psychological stress in the weeks leading up to her elder daughter's death and much of that was due to the behaviour of her daughter. The balance of her mind was disturbed.'

'*Daisy's* mind was disturbed,' Florence said, kicking her legs out under the table. 'She was crazy.'

'No, Florence,' Martha rapped her fist smartly on the polished wood. 'She wasn't.'

Natalie cleared her throat. 'With respect, it's Mrs Winter's state of mind that is relevant here. And we are able to suggest that it played an important part with regard to her uncharacteristic behaviour.'

Bill's arms were crossed. He leaned forward, trying to move things along. 'So – that's it?' Karen was a friend of Natalie's; it occurred to Martha that perhaps she should have asked someone else? This business with Karen, and all of that. But Bill was being so strange lately, bossing everyone around, butting in where he wasn't wanted, acting as though he owned the place. The trouble with Bill was he'd always been convinced he was a disappointment. That he wasn't enough like David. And it made his mother want to laugh. No one could be like David, absolutely no one in the heavens above or on the earth beneath, or whatever it was the bit from the church service always said.

'That's what?' Florence said sharply.

Bill glanced at his sister. 'I suppose – this whole business. It's over?'

'You really think that's it?' Florence laughed. She leaned forwards and tapped on the table close to Natalie. 'Natalie, is that really all there is to discuss? Nothing else you want to bring up?'

'Florence, whatever axe you have to grind . . .' Bill said sharply, and Florence whipped round, glaring at him.

'Shut up,' she said fiercely. 'Just – just shut the hell up, Bill. You have no idea what you're talking about.'

'I do actually, I'm the one who—'

Florence hissed, as though it were just the two of them, 'I said shut up. For God's sake, Bill, you pathetic little man. You don't even know, do you?' She turned to her mother. 'He doesn't know, does he?'

Martha didn't know how to reply to this. This poem she kept thinking of, they had been made to learn it at school and that was a long time ago, a very long time. It was in her mind all the time now. The first line made her think of the way up to the house.

Does the road wind up-hill all the way?

But she couldn't remember the rest of it. She stared at Bill and Florence, who looked back at her and it was as though they were all three of them strangers, meeting in this room for the first time. They hate each other, don't they? she found herself thinking. This pulled-in, tight-lipped man, this unhinged, wild woman – they're supposed to be my children. Supposed to be: isn't that funny?

She stood up. Her hips ached; her knees clicked. She felt old, lately. Old and fragile, made of bones, not flesh. She nodded at Natalie.

'Thank you so much, my dear. Will you stay for lunch?'

Natalie was tucking the papers into her plastic wallet, and she didn't meet her eyes. 'That's very kind of you, but no. I have to get back. I'll be in touch when I've spoken to the CPS again.'

'The CPS?'

'Crown Prosecution Service.' Natalie picked up her coat.

'Oh, of course.' Martha twisted her fingers together. She said, flatly, 'A biscuit? Some more tea?'

Natalie shook her head. 'You're always so hospitable, Mrs Winter. I wish I could, but I won't, thank you again. As I say, I'll be in touch.' She looked at her watch. 'I am hopeful we'll have a satisfactory conclusion soon.'

'What about the body?' Florence said, standing up too. Martha jumped; her voice was loud. 'What happens with that?'

Natalie looked quizzical. 'Daisy's, you mean?'

'Of course. Unless there's someone else in the garden we don't know about.'

Bill thumped his palm on the table. 'For goodness' sake, Flo, why on earth are you being such a b-b-bitch today?'

The stuttering word fell into the heavy atmosphere of the room and Florence, for the first time that day, looked taken aback, vulnerable. 'I – suppose I wish we'd all been honest with each other.' She turned to Martha. 'I'll ask you again. Is there anything else you want to say to me? Anything?'

'Like what?' Martha said, shaking her head in bemusement. She knew that, whatever idea Florence had got into her head, she had to act the part. This, this was the real secret she couldn't ever give away, because she knew by now if she did then something would alter for ever. David was adamant about it and he would be very cross. Florence must never find out. The door of the study would remain locked. She just had to stick to their story. 'What is it, my darling?'

Florence glared at her, and then her expression softened, and she said, sadly: 'Nothing. It doesn't matter.'

The younger Florence had delighted Martha, because in so many ways she was not her creation, she was like an exotic creature come to stay in the house, to be cared for, looked after. And in all other ways she was a mini-David, with her lanky limbs, her big smile, her sweetness and her earnestness. She knew the names of Persian queens and obscure butterflies, of symphonies on the radio and the different types of Greek columns. And here she was now, a stranger.

Martha's mind, starved of sleep, of emotion, was blank. She couldn't seem to see things clearly any more. The thought she kept hold of was: I have to carry on like this.

Florence rolled the edges of her folder over and over again, eyes fixed to the table. Martha wondered why she had a folder – what was in it? – and suddenly, without warning, Florence pushed her chair out and stood up.

'I have to go now,' she said. 'I'm needed in London. I don't know when I'll be back here. If that's all. Natalie, will you need me again?'

'No.' Natalie clasped her files to her body, obviously uncomfortable. 'That's all. Thank you, all.'

'I have to fetch something upstairs before I go,' Florence said loudly. 'Something I want. I won't be long. I'll say my goodbyes now.'

'Are you going into the bathroom?' Martha asked, perfectly politely.

'What?'

'The bathroom. Can you check in the cabinet,

and see if there's another tube of your father's eczema cream? I might buy some more if not.'

Florence shook her head. 'I don't know what's wrong with you, Ma. Honestly I don't. Thank you, Natalie. Goodbye, Bill.'

Bill didn't even look up as Florence stalked out of the room. Less than a minute later they heard her feet on the upstairs corridor, heard her rummaging around in the bathroom, opening cabinet doors, shutting them again.

'What the hell is she looking for?' Bill muttered. 'I'm so sorry,' he said, turning to Natalie. 'She's – upset. We all are. I shouldn't have been so unkind to her, but she . . . oh, never mind.' He sat down again, his hands covering his face.

'Of course,' Natalie replied, awkwardly, as Florence thundered downstairs. Martha waited in silence. Surely she would come in, tell her? But the door slammed shut without another word. A minute later the car roared off down the drive.

A hazy, fuzzy sort of buzzing sounded in Martha's head. As though the edges of some soundproofing were coming unstuck and the sound was leaking out of them. She clasped her hands over her ears, trying to shut it out.

'Right then,' Natalie said after a brief pause. 'Florence asked about the body. I'll be in touch with the coroner's office. We will have to apply for a burial order and permission for your daughter's reburial or – or cremation, whichever you choose.'

The buzzing grew louder. If they all knew about

428

Daisy then it had happened. He was gone, and she would never hear him chuckling over the TV, or listen to his soft, kind voice talking to someone on the phone, or look up from a book to see his soft brown eyes resting on her, late in the evening when the two of them sat up alone in the cosy drawing room. She would never turn to him as evening fell and smile and say, 'Another day, David darling.'

She would never take his still-warm pen in her hand and do his work for him, never have him lean on her, never ever walk into a room and know he was in there, waiting for her. Never hold him close in her arms at night when the dreams seized him and he screamed and cried aloud in his sleep, calling out hoarsely, waking up sobbing, sweating so much his pyjamas were soaked, when only she could tell him it was all right. Her boy, her man, her darling husband.

The sound was really loud now. Like the wasps in Florence's room. Martha could feel a ball pushing against her throat, pain welling up in her heart. She fixed her eyes on the garden, counted the blossom on the trees behind Natalie's head.

'Ah – they may say no – given the circumstances. But once we have cleared that up and you've completed the procedure that'll be that.'

'That'll be what?' Bill asked.

'Well, she'll be reburied or the ashes interred, and the case will be closed,' Natalie said, moving towards the door as if she felt the poison in the air of this house, didn't want to stay here another minute. 'You can all get on with your lives.'

Bill and Martha looked around the empty table, then at each other, and nodded. 'Fine,' said Bill. Martha watched him, wishing she could see. But suddenly all she could see was blackness. She sat still, hoping it would pass.

LUCY

'The India Club. The Strand. It's just before Waterloo Bridge. After the Courtauld.'

Lucy listened to the message again, and stared around her, bewildered. Buses and taxis shot past at an alarming speed, and pedestrians crossing from the Strand on to Lancaster Place pushed past her, buffeting her. The first days of warm weather had foxed her, as they seemed to every year – she was in a navy wool-mix long-sleeved dress and it clung to her back, now slick with sweat. 'I can't bloody see it,' she muttered, standing back and staring up at the shops in front of her. 'Arrgh,' she said, letting out a low groan. 'Oh, Florence.'

'Florence?' An amiable-looking, middle-aged man standing in a doorway stepped forwards. 'Are you – I'm sorry to interrupt. Must seem a bit odd. You're Lucy, aren't you? I'm Jim Buxton. I – I know your aunt.'

He held out his hand and Lucy shook it, uncertainly. 'Good day,' she said crisply, thinking if she sounded like a heroine from a BBC war drama she might somehow deter this strange man from mugging or murdering her, if that was indeed his intent. 'I'm looking for the India Club. I'm supposed to be meeting—'

'I've just left her here. It's upstairs,' Jim said, with a smile. He pushed his phone into his pocket, and opened a scuffed black door. 'I'll show you.'

Two floors up, Lucy found Florence in the small restaurant, which had murky yellow walls and was almost empty. She was seated at a large table, papers strewn everywhere, scribbling furiously, an uneaten dosa at her side.

'Hi, Aunt Flo,' Lucy said, loudly. She wasn't sure if Florence would hear her or not.

'Florence,' Jim called. 'It's your niece. I found her on the street.' He said tentatively, 'It's . . . Lucy.'

Florence looked up then, pushed her glasses up her nose, and broke into a smile. 'Hello, darling.' She enveloped Lucy in a big, messy hug. Pieces of paper flew to the floor. 'So you know Jim?' she said, slightly confused, scrambling to pick them up.

'No, Florence,' said Jim, patiently. 'I bumped into her, outside.' He pulled at the arm of his glasses, slightly like Eric Morecambe, and then hugged the Daunt Books cloth bag he was carrying closer to his chest. 'I forgot to ask. Are you in for supper?'

'No, Thomas wants me for a conference call with the lawyers.'

'Well, Jesus wants me for a sunbeam.'

'Bully for you,' said Florence, shovelling poppadum into her mouth. Jim slung the bag over his shoulder.

'I'll leave you some casserole out, that suit?'

'That'd be marvellous. I left the *LRB* review on the kitchen table, by the way. Do look. Utterly wrong about Gombrich, but it's a good piece.'

Lucy, not understanding a word of this conversation, sat down, glancing longingly at the dosa.

'Is Amna back tonight, by the way?'

'No, she's not,' Jim said. Something in his tone made Lucy glance up, curious. 'She's gone till May, I'm sure I told you that, didn't I?'

'The lawyers need to talk to her.' Florence slid the menu over. 'Pick something Lucy, it's all wonderful.'

'What do they want to talk to her about?' Jim asked.

'Oh, it's rubbish. Peter's lot are saying you and I are having an affair. That you're not a credible expert witness. Et cetera.' Florence rolled her eyes. 'Bloody idiot. I think it makes him sound pretty desperate, I must say.'

Jim pulled at his tufty grey hair. 'I see. Florence – maybe we should discuss this all later.'

'Of course,' Florence said heartily. 'I am living with you, it must look rather odd. But we need to be clear on the matter. I hoped Amna could clarify, or provide some kind of statement . . .' She shuffled through some papers. 'It's here somewhere.

Ah. Now, I'd forgotten about this passage.' She pulled out a cracked Biro and started writing furiously.

'Goodbye. Nope, she can't hear me.' Jim smiled at Lucy. He put his hand on Florence's shoulder, gently, then turned to Lucy. 'Goodbye. It's very nice to meet you. Very nice to meet any of Florence's family, in fact. I was starting to think she was a Water-Baby or something. Have the pakora, it's jolly good.'

'Oh—' Lucy began, but he'd gone. Florence waved vaguely behind his back, and carried on, her huge, looping handwriting covering the paper.

'Just a moment.' She scribbled one more line, and put down her pen. 'Sorry, Lucy. Thank you for coming.'

'My pleasure. It's so good to see—' Lucy began, tentatively.

Florence interrupted. 'I wanted to ask you something.'

Lucy glanced at her aunt, curiously. Florence wasn't the kind of aunt who took you to the ballet, or to tea at Fortnums. She was the kind of aunt who'd spend hours playing battles or making up stupid songs with you. But she didn't generally confide, or expect you to confide in her.

There was something else, too. Something that, since that awful day, had been pushed to the back of Lucy's mind. The evening Southpaw died. Bursting into his study to fetch her for supper, she had found Florence sitting in Southpaw's chair, glass of wine next to her and a postcard of a painting in her hand.

She was sobbing her heart out. When Lucy moved in the doorway and Florence saw her, she wiped her nose and gave a great, huge, galloping sigh.

'It's true,' she said, staring right through Lucy, her swollen eyes glazed, and she'd pushed away a piece of paper lying on the blotter, crumpling it up. 'Oh, no.' Her face collapsed again. 'Oh, no. It's really true.'

Lucy had reached to her across the desk. 'Oh, Flo. What's true?'

'Nothing.' She'd wiped her nose. 'Absolutely nothing. I'm coming now,' she'd said, folding the postcard up and putting it into one of her capacious pockets, but she didn't move, didn't move at all, until Gran went in and got her out.

Now she said carefully, 'What's up, then?'

'Why don't you order,' her aunt said. 'Then I'll tell you.'

When Lucy's pakora arrived – and it was delicious – she ate in silence for a few moments. She was ravenous. Lately, all she seemed to want to do was eat.

'You're in Hackney, aren't you?' Florence said. 'Not that far from Jim and Amna.'

'Of course.'

'Jim's a clever fellow. Very astute. Known him since Oxford, we rub along nicely together.'

'He seems lovely.' Lucy looked at her watch.

'You should come over one evening. It's a great place. Stuffed with books. Jim is—'

'Flo, what's this about?' Lucy interrupted. 'I don't want to be rude. It's just I have to be back by two.' Her aunt looked startled and Lucy said hurriedly, 'Work's horrible at the moment. I can't be away too long.'

Florence picked at the uneaten dosa. 'Oh. Why's it horrible?'

'I'm not right for it. And my boss is gunning for me.' *Especially now Southpaw's dead*, she wanted to say, but couldn't. The article about Daisy was of course not possible. There was no talk of promotion, and last week Lara had left to join *Vogue* and Deborah had looked at Lucy and said, 'Not to be brutal but it'd be a waste of your time. I don't want to sound negative, though, Lucy. I'm just being honest. OK?'

Lucy told Florence this.

'Oh dear. What would you like to do instead?'

The question caught Lucy unawares. It hadn't occurred to her that she could do something else. She squirmed on her chair. 'Oh. Well, I'd like to be a writer.'

Florence didn't laugh, or look amazed, or cough in embarrassment. She said, 'Good idea. Pleased to hear it. You can help me out, you know.' Lucy looked blank and Florence waved her hands. 'Luce, it's a good idea. You can write. Remember those funny stories you used to tell Cat. What are you doing about it?'

'Oh. Nothing.' Lucy laughed, self-consciously. 'Well . . . I write down bits and bobs.' Lately, she had taken to writing at all hours, on her laptop, late at night. About Dad, and Karen, about Gran and Southpaw. 'I had an idea, about us – it's . . .' She clamped her suddenly sweating armpits by her side, before remembering that Flo simply didn't care about things like that, and relaxed. 'Don't ask me yet. I don't think I'm quite there.'

'No time like the present,' Florence said grimly. 'What do you want to write?'

'Stories,' Lucy said, vaguely. Now it was out there, now she'd said to someone, *I want to be a writer,* she wished she could pick up the string of words, floating on the air between them, and cram them back in like a jack, out of its box. She shrugged and said, brightly, 'I'll get round to it, one day. So – um, how long have you been in London then?'

'Oh, over a month,' Florence said abruptly. 'Had to go home – to Winterfold for the night last week. But I'm staying with Jim till June, I think. Have you heard about this court case I'm involved with?'

'Of course.'

'It opens next week,' said Florence. 'I'm suing Peter, for a share of the royalties of his book and a co-author credit.'

'Golly. Is he the TV bloke? Didn't you once—'

Florence interrupted. 'Oh, yes. I've been a total idiot. And I didn't want it to get this far.' She gave a grim smile. 'I'm a bit afraid about what they'll drag out, actually.' She laughed nervously, and pushed her glasses up her nose. 'Embarrassing stuff.'

'Like what?'

Florence said quietly, 'Oh, Luce. I'm a solitary person. I've spent a lot of time in my own head, all these years. You get used to it in there. It's rather nice.'

'I know what you mean.'

'You do, don't you? One gets these ideas about things . . . Anyway, I made a fool of myself over him.' Florence swallowed. 'When I think about it for any length of time I feel quite sick. And I feel quite al . . .' she stumbled over the word, '. . . alone.'

'You're not alone.' Lucy put her hand over her aunt's, but she pulled it away.

'I am. Believe me. Now that Pa's gone and the rest of it—' She bit her lip, and pulled her hands in front of her face.

'You don't have to go through with it,' Lucy said. 'You could always pull out, couldn't you?'

A change came over Florence's face. She sat up straight, and put her hands together. Her expression was determined, her chin stuck out. 'All I have is my reputation, Lucy. Middle-aged men are seen as being in the prime of life. Middle-aged women are dispensable, my darling girl. Just wait, you'll see.' She paused, and Lucy thought she was trying to convince herself as much as anyone else. 'Look. I wanted to ask your help.'

'What do you need my help for?'

'Can you write an article? For your paper? A little bit of, I suppose one would call it persuasive PR on my side, would do me the world of good.' Florence leaned forward, brushing her hair in some chutney. 'I don't – want to look ridiculous. A nice piece about how respected I am – your – your paper would do that, wouldn't they?'

'Oh.' Lucy put her fork down, and dabbed her mouth with a napkin, buying some time. She caught Florence's hair in her hand, brushing a blob of chutney off.

'Um. I'm your niece, Flo. That would look a bit ridiculous. "Why Florence Winter is great, by Lucy Winter (No Relation)." They'd buy something on our family history – they wanted to do a piece on Daisy and Southpaw, but I couldn't bring myself to, and then – everything else happened.'

'Well, can't you now? With me in it?'

Lucy stared at her aunt, rather helplessly. 'Well, no. You can't just write articles about your relatives without some sort of angle. That's why I wouldn't do it before.'

'What sort of angle did they want?'

'Oh, Southpaw's sad early life, Daisy the missing daughter . . . etc. But it was too hard and now, obviously, I'm not going to do it.'

Florence reached over and took a piece of Lucy's chicken. 'What if I could give you something else?'

Lucy looked at her aunt's hands. They were shaking.

439

'What?' Lucy said, not really believing her.

Florence whispered, 'I – well. *Come on, Flo, come on,*' she added, under her breath. 'Look. Lucy. I'm – I'm not your aunt.'

'You're not – what?'

Florence's heart-shaped face was grey with misery. 'Oh dear.'

'Flo – what do you mean?'

'I'm adopted. That's what I mean.'

Something stuck in the back of Lucy's mouth. She coughed. '*Adopted?* Oh, no, you can't be.'

'I am, I'm afraid.' Florence gave a twisted smile. 'Daisy told me, when I was younger. I didn't believe her, I thought it was one of her little games, but at the same time you never knew with Daisy.' She swallowed. 'In fact, she was right. It's true. I . . .' she stopped, and looked down at the congealing food on her plate, '. . . I found my birth certificate. The night Southpaw died.'

'I saw you—' Lucy began.

'Yes. I was looking for Daisy's passport, the police wanted it, your grandmother said it was there and I went to look for it. I was going through this old folder of his drawings, of Pa's . . . Pa's East End drawings and there it was. Just tucked in there, thin as tissue. I almost threw it away.'

'Oh my goodness. Flo . . .'

'I've – I've always known, really. Known I wasn't like them. It's just, finding out like that was rather a shock.' Her eyes brimmed with tears again. She pushed her glasses furiously up her nose. 'Anyway!

I thought you could help me. Write an article, it doesn't matter if you say you're my niece or not. I just want some coverage that doesn't make me sound like a crackpot. It's become rather important to me now, winning this court case. I have to have some reputation afterwards, don't I?'

'Florence,' Lucy said. 'Please, wait a minute. Does Dad know? Who knows? Do you know who . . . who your mum was?'

She shook her head, furiously. 'Some eighteen-year-old girl. No idea of the father. Somewhere in London. I wrote her name down. Cassie something. Irish name.' She pressed her long hands over her face, and her shoulders shook. 'I've always known my mother didn't love me the way she loved the rest of you. I couldn't work out why.' Her voice was muffled. 'You can blow the whole thing right open, if you wish.'

'Oh, Flo, I couldn't do that.' Lucy reached over the table. 'Gran loves you, of course she does! She's always going on about you to us, how amazing you are, how there's nothing you can't do.'

Florence sat back, and said very softly, 'Look, it's true, Lucy. I used to think I was happy. Used to think it didn't matter I didn't fit in, that I had my dad to talk to, and that our home was a safe place, and now I see that was all a lie.'

'It was a safe place. It still is.'

'It's not. We've all gone our own ways, and why? Ask yourself that. Look, I just thought you might

441

want to help me. If you can have a word with someone on the newspaper, get them to write an article if you won't . . .' Florence stood up, stuffing sheets of writing and newspaper cuttings into a battered red folder as Lucy sat back in her chair, her head spinning. She felt dizzy. 'Does that make sense? Did you hear what I said?'

'Yes, I heard you, Flo. I just don't know what to say.'

'You don't believe me.'

'I do. Oh, Flo, I wish you'd talk to Gran about it.'

'I've tried to but she's like a brick wall.' Florence's mouth creased into an awful rictus smile, and she gave a great heaving sob. 'Lucy, I've tried. If Pa were around maybe but – I can't get through to her. I've realised that it's easier not to try, at the moment.'

Lucy squeezed her eyes shut. 'She needs you.' Her heart ached for Flo, for Gran. 'Oh, Flo, you know you're still one of—'

'Don't say it. Don't say "one of us", Lucy, I swear, I'll – just don't say that.' Florence put the folder under her arm, and cleared her throat. 'So you won't help me.'

'Write an article saying you were adopted? Just to get you some good PR? Absolutely not, Flo – come on, can't you see it's a terrible idea? You're just – you're just terribly upset, you're not thinking.'

It was all wrong, talking to your aunt like this. Florence's mouth was pursed, her expression pinched. Lucy frowned. *How can we not be related?*

She's just like Dad. Her mind was still whirring; the idea of these various shards of family china that lay shattered on the floor was overwhelming, and she felt as though she was the only one of them who wanted to start to put the pieces back together.

'I've had enough of this,' Florence said. 'I told myself, you see, it actually makes everything easier, now I can get on with my life. Without all of you.' She pulled some money out of her coat pocket, scattering receipts and coins on to the floor, and threw a couple of notes on to the table. 'Bye, Lucy.'

'Flo – don't go.'

Florence strode out of the restaurant, knocking a chair across the floor. Lucy sat still, not knowing what to do. A waiter came over, apologetically, and gave her the bill, then started cleaning up the mess Florence had made.

I've got this all wrong, Lucy kept thinking. This idea I had of this perfect family Gran fed me over the years, it was obviously not true. Because these terrible things have happened to us all and we can't seem to help each other. We fold like a pack of cards.

The waiter brought her change, and as it clunked into the bowl beside her Lucy stared out of the window at the pale blue sky, the faint roar of London buzzing outside. She wished someone would pick her up, pull her out of the city, put her in her bright, warm room at Winterfold, with the sound of Martha singing below, and Southpaw chatting about something, the radio on, dog barking . . . people talking . . . But that world was gone for ever and Florence was right. She picked up her change and lumbered slowly down the stairs, out into the warmth of the London spring sunshine.

DAVID

The previous day he had been drawing in Limehouse, where he'd watched four children wrestling over a doll. China face, pink blush dots on her cheeks. Nose smashed off, cracked inside her head so she rattled as they tugged at her and wrestled in the cobbled street.

'Givithere, you little sod, it's *mine*.'

'Won't, so fuck off.'

'I'm gon tell your mum how you're speaking to me, Jim.'

'Don't care.'

The doll was from a bombed-out house at the end of a short road, a Victorian terrace. They had gone in and excavated – not much, though. No one had survived, he knew that much from the Public Records Office. He'd tried to forget their names. Who knew what was still there? That doll had belonged to someone. A little girl had received it, maybe last Christmas, never thinking it would belong to someone else soon.

David hadn't been able to bear it, then. He'd made

445

drawings he'd never show anyone. He'd seen things, noticed details too many had overlooked. Like there were bits of people still, everywhere. He'd found a finger once, in a cave of rubble, right by where the children were playing. An old person's finger he thought, knobbled at the joint, the skin wrinkled.

Now he and his dad and Cassie were waiting, like so many others, for the housing that was supposed to come after the war. They were building along the City Road and behind the market, and then, David supposed, then they'd have their new family home. What a joke. The idea that they were family.

Aunt Jem and Uncle Sid had moved out to Walthamstow. Aunt Jem came for her tea sometimes, to see little Cassie, she said. Make sure she was being looked after properly. But she never stayed more than an hour; other than that they avoided Islington. Too many bad memories. They'd seen Angel bombed, seen the looting, the way people changed. Uncle Sid had a cousin banged up for stealing lead after a raid. They said it was too hard, coming back. But David knew it was also because they didn't want to see Tom Doolan. They sent Cassie little presents, knitted cardigans, a ribbon for her hair, that kind of thing, but they didn't send David anything. He was nearly seventeen now. He'd be all right, he was going to that posh art school, near them in Bloomsbury, wasn't he? Mr Wilson, the art teacher at school, had written to them, and they'd asked to see him and his work, and offered him a full scholarship. Aunt Jem was alternately proud and bewildered at the idea of a nephew who didn't do anything . . . just drew. 'Emily'd be so proud of you if she knew,' she'd said. 'You'd have made her so happy, love.'

The hottest Saturday so far in the year, she came for her tea. They didn't have anything to give her beyond tea from day-old tea leaves, briny and bitter, and she brought some shortbread a neighbour had given in exchange for some curtains she'd made. David and his aunt sat on the floor either side of the old chest that served as a table in the first room of the flat, while Cassie crouched next to them playing with the doll she always had by her side. Her mother had made it for her, the winter before she died, a patchwork girl carefully sewn from the tiniest scraps of discarded material.

Though a bright blue sky could be seen at the far corner of the small window, the flat was dark. It never really grew light no matter how much sun there was outside. Bluebottles buzzed loudly, crashing at the windows, hovering above the little tea party.

Aunt Jem was uneasy, rushing through the meal, starting at every sound on the street. 'You get paid to go to them classes, sit there and draw?' she asked, dotting her fingers with shortbread crumbs from the floor, licking them off, as if nervous of leaving a trace behind.

447

'Don't get paid, do I? I got a scholarship that covers tuition and all that. Everything else I got to pay for. They say sundry expenses. That means shoes and that.' David looked hopefully at his aunt. 'I need a job, Aunt Jem.' Uncle Sid's other brother, Clive (not the one that was in prison), had a fish-monger's off the Cally Road. Before the war his mother used to take him there, let him pick a piece of fish for tea, when times were good. Clive'd give him a bucket of eels to play with. David thought it was the best thing he'd ever seen, sticking his hand in a bucket of shiny slippery, snake-like crea-tures the colour of tar. 'Is Clive looking for anyone, you know?'

Jem shook her head. 'No, love, he ain't, and if you want my advice you won't ask him.'

'Why?'

'Just the way it is, love,' she'd said, and she'd leaned forward and stroked his cheek.

'Aunt Jem?' Cassie looked up at her aunt. 'Can I come and stay with you?' She fingered her aunt's shawl.

Jem laughed, and glanced at the door again. 'Me? Oh . . . we'll see. That'd be nice.' She said it in a vague way that adults had of saying no without you noticing.

'But I don't like it here any more.'

'Why not, little Cass?' Jem said, feigning surprise, and David wanted to slap his aunt's face, or punch her on the arm. *You know why. We live with our dad and he's a monster.*

'Dad's horrible,' Cass said quietly, looking around. 'Smacked me on the head for noise.'

Jem's eyes filled with tears. 'Oh, love, no.'

'He hits Davy and he shouts.'

'Just – hitting?' Jem leaned forward, took her young niece's wrists. 'He don't . . . try anything else on, does he?'

But Cassie looked at her blankly. 'What's it?'

She'd say that all the time to David. *What's it?* Like there was all these things she didn't understand. He hated the fact they were bad things and he didn't know how to explain them, like Dad smacking them, or the flies everywhere, or the old man who'd died in the street outside that last freezing winter, or the women you saw crying to themselves as they walked through the market. *What's it?*

'It's fine,' David said, cutting across them. 'No, he don't. Don't put disgusting ideas like that in her head. Don't ask her things like that.' He stood up. 'You'd better be off if you're to catch your train, Jem. Thanks a lot for coming. It's been a real tonic.'

His aunt scrambled to her feet, pulled on her hat, and she gripped his shoulders. 'Oh, Davy.' He stepped away from her. 'I don't like to leave you.'

He hated her guilt; it was fake. She didn't mean any of it. 'Thanks again, Aunt Jem.'

'I ain't done right by you. Neither of you. It's just Sid's so funny about it. He don't like me having anything to do with . . . with your father.

He thinks I'm well out of it now we've left the Angel. I wish I could . . . If I think about Emily – oh dear.' The tears came to her eyes again. 'The state he'd leave her in sometimes.' She gave a big sniff. 'God, I wish things was different. You don't think he'd . . . proper hurt you, either of you?'

He was going to say it, tell her what she wanted to hear. *Yeah, course. We're fine, me and Cassie! Don't you worry about . . .*

But something stopped him. The stifling heat, the buzzing flies, Cassie's bruised face. How quiet she was these days. 'Not sure any more,' he said flatly. 'He's . . . he's drinking all the time. He don't care if it's day or night. He hit Cassie so hard she couldn't hear the rest of the day. Still can't sometimes. I . . . I don't know.'

'What you mean, you don't know?' Jem said, clicking her tongue against the roof of her mouth, cold fear in her eyes.

David said, staring at the floor, 'He knocked out two of her baby teeth. It's not . . . it's not right, Jem.'

'Oh God. Oh, no,' Jem muttered.

Every old street had a dad like that. Since the war, every house had someone affected by what had happened. A daughter killed in a raid. A son missing somewhere in Burma or France. A father banged up for bashing his kids. A mother on trial for stealing from a bombed-out house. The war had changed everyone. You walked past a dead dog on the street and you kept on walking now.

Perhaps they'd get back to like it had been . . .
only David couldn't remember life before the war.
More and more he couldn't remember his mother,
only the feeling of her hair as she sat next to him
at the piano and the sound of her voice when she'd
sing to him at night. She loved Gilbert and
Sullivan.

> Ah pray make no mistake,
> We are not shy,
> We're very wide awake,
> The moon and I.

He was trying not to think about his mother, trying
not to remember what she'd been like, when there
came the sound of shouting in the street, and
someone swearing, a woman calling.

'Damn you, damn you to hell, Tommy Doolan!
You—'

'He's back,' Cassie whispered, sitting up ramrod
straight on the floor, her eyes like saucers. 'He's
comin' back now.'

And Aunt Jem swallowed, and breathed in. She
muttered something to herself; David heard his
mother's name. Then Jem's nostrils flared, and she
stood up. 'Listen to me, Davy, you hear? You get
out of here.'

'What do you mean?'

'Clear out.' She put her hands on his neck, held
his head steady. 'I can't take you both. I'm sorry,
I can't. You understand?'

He didn't understand, but he nodded. Now she had made up her mind, Jem seemed more resolute.

She said quickly, 'Sid won't go for it. Lord knows how I'll get Cassie past him but I'll do it. He'll have to like it, he'll come round to her. But if I turn up with both of you he'll kick me out, sure as eggs are eggs. Oh, Emmy, darling. I'm sorry.' She glanced up, gave a little sob, and patted Cassie on the shoulder. 'Come on, Cassie, sweetheart. We're going.'

Cassie stared up at her. 'What's it?'

'I'm taking you home. To my home. Only we got to move quickly and be quiet. I don't want your dad hearing us.' She crouched down on the ground. 'Fancy coming to live with your aunt and uncle?'

Cassie looked at him. 'What about Davy?'

'I'll be fine,' he said. 'I'm going to college, aren't I? I'm not going to be here much longer.'

Tom Doolan had stopped in the street to argue with someone. David could see him, swinging on some railings, his punching arm flailing, like a sheet in the wind. I'm going to get that if someone else doesn't, he thought.

Cassie crossed her arms and turned to her aunt. Her grey eyes were steady. 'Want to stay here with Davy.'

'No, Cassie, love,' Jem said weakly. 'You gotta get out of here. It's time to leave, all right?'

'Cassie,' David interrupted, 'I'm off to college soon. I got plans. I don't need you, you got that?

452

She stared at him and put her hands in her pockets, a sign she meant business. 'I don't want to go.' Her lip trembled. 'I want to stay here with you, 'cos you said we're together, you and me, you said you and me 'gainst everyone else. You said it.'

He'd say that to her all the time: when the bombs fell, when the looters came, when Dad rolled back late and they hid in the passage where David's bed was, when they didn't have enough food, when they were scared and cold and lonely. He said it all the time.

David shut his eyes tightly. He told himself it'd be easier just looking after himself, so he'd believe it. Repeated it in his head, a few times. Then he gripped her wrist.

'Listen, Cassie. I don't want you around no more. I'm sick of you. Best you piss off and live with Aunt Jem. They'll look after you.'

Her small hands caught his ragged shirt, and her thin face was blank with confusion. 'But you said we was our family, Davy.'

'Well, I didn't mean it. It's OK, so off you go.' He stretched one arm nonchalantly, and touched the soft curls that bobbed around her head. Just one more time. *We were our family.*

She stared at him, her small face pinched with misery, then turned away. 'Let's go, Aunt Jem.'

'How'll we get out?' Jem said softly, urgency in her voice. 'He'll be here any minute.'

David flung open the door, avoiding his sister's

gaze. He didn't think he could bear even to catch a glance of her. 'Come with me.'

'Clothes for night-time?' Cassie said. She looked around the sparse, mildewed room that had been their home these past two years.

'No time, sweetheart,' Jem said. 'We'll get you new things. It's all right.'

Cassie bent down. 'I take Flo,' she said, and picking up her patchwork rag doll she hugged it tight to her small body.

'Yes, take Flo.' David scuttled along the corridor and banged on the last door. 'Joan?' He hammered, frantically. 'Joan, let me in, he's back again.'

An old lady, hair tied up in rags, neat silk scarf snug over her head, opened the door cautiously. 'Oh, look at you, little one,' she exclaimed, pinching Cassie's cheek. 'It's all right. Come in with me till he gets over it. He don't mean it. He's just angry. Oh, hello, Jem. What you want?'

'Let them in, Joan.' Footsteps sounded on the staircase behind them. 'Show Jem the fire escape. Bye, then.' He squeezed Jem's arm. 'It's the right thing, Aunt Jem, you know it is.'

His aunt pushed Cassie through the door but she lingered on the threshold for a moment. 'You're a good boy, Davy. Come and see us, all right?'

His sister's face appeared under Joan's armpit. 'Davy?' Tears ran down her cheeks. 'Want Davy.'

David tried to keep calm. He swallowed. He could hear his father, boots tramping loudly on the cracked old boards. Swearing. 'Where's that little streak of shit, that fucking boy? Why the hell don't he come when I tells him to? Some git trunna swindle his dad and he don't even fucking give a toss. He don't even wan hear it, I'm going to – I swear . . .'

David crouched down. 'Listen to me, Cassie,' he hissed. 'You gotta go with Jem. You can come back here when you're older, when Dad's not here. But you'll have a better life away from him. All right? If you ever need me, you just come back here, and you ask for me at the pub or down the market, someone'll find me. I promise. I'll always be there if you need me.'

He gripped her thin shoulders. 'You understand that? Promise?' She nodded. 'But that's for when you're older,' he said, and swallowed. 'Anyway. You'd better fuck off now, I ain't got time.'

The serious grey eyes fixed on him for a clear second and he felt like his heart was being cut right in two. Then she nodded again. 'Yes.' And she turned, and disappeared, Flo clutched under her arm. The smell of Joan's armpit flowered under David's nose. He stood up.

'Bye, then,' he said. Aunt Jem kissed his cheek, squeezing his arm so hard it hurt.

'Bye, Davy. I'll come and see you soon. Get out of there soon as you can, eh? Work hard, be good, all right?' The words caught in her throat. She turned, and then she shut the door in his face, as the footsteps grew louder, and David turned round to face his father.

Tom Doolan was feared before the war, but things were different then. He'd fought in the Great War, after all. Got some shrapnel in his knee and it gave him pain. So he was a hero, once, albeit with a violent streak. There were worse men than he – at least he had a job and a wife and some outside respect, even if he did knock his wife to the floor with the vase she'd bought at the Sainsbury's grocers, or punch his boy in the face after one too many, and even if David heard screams and sobbing late at night when he should have been sleeping. At least there was a home, a roof.

Now Tom Doolan was a wreck. He'd always been a drunk – now he was drunk all the time. David was properly afraid of him, the three of them in the tiny one-bedroomed apartment the council had found for them off the Essex Road. Sometimes he'd wake up and see his father watching him, or Cassie while she slept, in the corner of the room, rolling imaginary tobacco between his fingers, his black eyes glittering. Last week, he'd woken Cassie up, dragged her by her thin arms and banged her head against the wall until she screamed, and that was why she couldn't hear properly, still. All for saying she was hungry that afternoon when there was no tea.

Course she was hungry. He didn't work and he did nothing to provide. They lived on handouts from neighbours and Aunt Jem, and what the welfare could give them, and they were lucky to have this flat, David knew – thousands of families didn't; were instead crammed into other people's houses. David wished they were living with someone else, though, because then Dad wouldn't be able to use his children as punchbags.

It was when their father called Cassie 'Emily', not once, but a couple of times, that David realised the danger was real. If the bomb hadn't killed their mother he was sure their father would have done soon afterwards. He'd murder one of them, David knew it.

'What are you doing, skulking round like a sneaking little thief?'

His father grabbed his arm and yanked David against the wall, dragging him back along the corridor to their flat. A tearing, hot pain in his shoulder made David scream. His father threw him in through the open door, then slammed it shut behind them. He looked around, and David looked up at him.

He was blond and tall; before the war people had said he looked like a matinée idol. Now he was flabby and red-faced, his teeth nearly all gone, his wide mouth permanently set in an ugly grimace, and his bloodshot eyes always open, darting around, looking for trouble.

'Where's Emily?'

'Cassie, Dad.' David crawled backwards and then pulled himself up. His shoulder and neck felt as though they were on fire. The first thought that crossed his mind was, at least it's not the arm I paint with. 'Not Emily. Cassie. Your daughter.'

Tom Doolan took one step towards him, and punched him hard, in the face. David staggered back, as his father kept walking, pushing him up against the wall.

'She's gone. She ain't coming back,' David said. 'I got her out of here. The police took her away and they said if you came looking for her, they'd have you arrested.'

And he spat in his father's face. 'They're going to put her with a family that wants her, and can look after her, like she deserves. She don't deserve a father like you. Hitler don't deserve a father like you.' He pushed him away, his heart thumping so loud in his chest he thought it might explode. I'm for it now, he thought. Bye world.

'You little shit,' Tom Doolan said, and he grabbed his son by the neck, pushed him over towards the range in the corner, and held him down against the hot iron, and as David yelled, and called for help, his father banged and banged his head on the surface, his fingers a vice around his neck where Jem's had been, firm and loving, only minutes before.

'No one leaves me. No one walks out on me, you hear? You get that, you fucking pansy?'

David struggled, writhing like mad, flailing out his arms and legs, kicking at his father, and when the grip tightened and he couldn't speak, he stared into Tommy Doolan's face, his red eyes, and he spat at him again, and kept on kicking. He could not articulate any particular thought, but a deep, primeval sense told him to keep fighting until his father killed him, and even though he couldn't see any more, couldn't think straight, with every last drop of strength he had he just kept on writhing, kicking, rasping out, doing everything he could until at last, his father simply let go and David sank to the floor, heavy as a chain. His father gave him a sharp, hard kick in the stomach, then dropped into the armchair.

'I'll kill you one day soon,' he said. 'You won't get away with it. You hear me?'

David stayed still, just kept on breathing, and he focused on Cassie, and Jem, the door shutting on them, where they'd be now. On the bus together, heading out north-east. Cassie'd get home with Aunt Jem, to that nice new house David always dreamed they had. He'd never been there, but he liked to picture it. Tiles on the path to the front door; stained glass in the window. A knocker in the shape of an owl – he'd seen that on one of those smart houses down the road; he liked it. Maybe even some honeysuckle, growing up the wall. Uncle Sid would open the door. He wouldn't be cross, or look suspicious with that weaselly stare, like *What are those brats doing here?* which was his normal expression when he saw Emily's kids. He'd say, with a smile, 'Well, hello, Cassie! What you doing up this way, sunshine?'

'She's coming to live with us,' Jem would say. 'Come in, sweetheart, let's get you something to eat.'

And they'd go in, hang their coats on the hook, go into the kitchen, which would have one of those tables with panels that slid out, to make room for visitors, like David. Maybe he'd spend Christmas with them. He'd drawn a picture of a Christmas meal he'd seen the previous year through a window over on Thornhill Square, the house that had the owl door knocker on it. David liked owls. He liked drawing them from pictures in books.

He'd stood looking up into their front room, clutching the railings so tight his palms were covered in rusted dust afterwards. Paper chains in bright colours hung from the ceiling, and there on a chair was a little girl singing 'Noel Noel' over and over again to herself. She was bouncing up and down on her chair with excitement, at the whole thing, the whole day, and David knew exactly how she must feel. That was what was strange. He knew how lovely it would be to be that girl.

As he stared in, a man appeared carrying a glistening brown Christmas pudding, electric blue flames shimmering round it, and the people at the table all clapped. None of them noticed him, face at the window.

Jem and Sid would have a Christmas pudding. And there'd be a lovely parlour with proper sofas and chairs to sit and read in all day long. A proper wireless – Cassie loved the radio.

All this for his sister, safe now, in someone else's house. David closed his eyes, playing dead and waiting for his father to fall asleep. Then he could go out again and draw some more. And hopefully not get killed, today at least.

LUCY

'Have some gingerbread.' Martha slid the plate towards Lucy, who took a piece, peering down as she always used to at the scene that opened up each time someone removed a biscuit. As she popped a square of gingerbread in her mouth she squinted to make out the familiar image of three Chinese men crossing a tiny ornate bridge, then sighed loudly. Martha's gingerbread was like nothing in this world: crumbly, spicy, thick with juicy, sweet flavour. This batch was stale, but it was still delicious.

'Hungry, Luce?' her father said, a faint smile on his face.

'Mmm,' she replied, saying what she thought her grandmother would want to hear. 'Lovely. It's still the best, Gran.'

Martha nodded. 'Glad to hear it.' She gazed out of the window, fiddling with a piece of wire tag fastening.

The paraphernalia of the house, once charming,

now threatened to overwhelm it. Bowls full of old pre-Euro coinage, scraps of paper, leftover Christmas cracker toys and wooden clothes pegs spilled on to the dresser. A mug with a broken handle sat forlornly on the table in front of them, covered in a light film of grey dust.

Summer hours had started again at work and though Lucy had left early the weekend traffic meant she hadn't arrived until teatime. It was dark and drizzling when she arrived, rain spread out like a cloak covering the valley. Gran said she was busy with something upstairs when Lucy arrived, and left her in the sitting room, unsure whether to touch anything, move the scarves away, clean up. She wished she was staying with Dad. She kept pushing herself at Gran, and Gran didn't seem to notice whether she was there or not. Lucy didn't know what to do. She found she couldn't seem to fix on anything at the moment: work was making her miserable. She was eating too much, not sleeping: she found she was either at the *Daily News* and hating it, or at home, dreading the next day. She worried about everything, kept making stupid mistakes, couldn't seem to get anything right: change for a coffee, matching socks, remembering to charge her phone. She felt as though she was starting to lose experience, as though everything she'd learned was slipping away, and that she was slipping away too.

Lucy put the gingerbread down on the plate,

and stared sadly around the dark, messy room. Martha followed her gaze.

'As you can see I'm not quite up to speed with everything. I haven't had a chance to get your room ready. Cat slept in there. I didn't realise you'd want to stay here. I thought you'd be at your father's.'

'I can do it, it's fine. I only wanted to see how you are.' Lucy knew her voice was too loud. 'It's wonderful news that they're not prosecuting.'

'Yes,' Martha said blankly. 'It's simply *wonderful*, isn't it?'

Lucy folded her arms uncomfortably. 'Sorry, I didn't mean it like that.'

Bill tapped the table. 'Well, Ma, as I was saying to Lucy, at least we're all set.'

Martha poured some more tea. 'All set for what?'

Bill's fingers drummed a steady, almost jaunty rhythm. 'Just that – good news there's nothing further to be done. You – you could have gone to prison, you know.'

'Yes, I know that.'

'We can talk about what you want to do now. About Daisy.' Martha didn't seem to be listening. 'Her funeral. They say we can rebury her now. Not here, but we should think . . . think about what you want to do. Ma?' Martha folded her arms. She gave a brief smile.

'I suppose so.'

Lucy watched her father, patiently wrestling with Gran. 'It's awfully dark in here, Ma. Mind if I turn the lights on?' Bill got up, flicking the switch. 'Oh.'

'They've blown.' Martha poured herself some more tea. 'One by one. I keep meaning to fix them and somehow . . . I never get round to it.' She shrugged. 'I've got this one here.' She flicked on an old bedside lamp she'd plugged in next to the Aga. 'It's fine.'

'I'll pop to the hall and get some bulbs . . .'

'I said it's fine.' Her voice was sharp. 'You know, Bill, I've been thinking. I'll probably sell Winterfold this summer, anyway. Move out of here.'

Lucy looked up, and Bill twisted round in his chair, awkwardly.

'Are you sure, Ma?' he said. 'Isn't that a bit soon?'

'Soon? What, leave it a year and I'll be ready to move on then?' She laughed. 'Listen, we can't be sentimental about this house. Not any more.'

Lucy swallowed, something hurting her throat. 'I think that's a good idea at some point, but Gran—'

'At what point?' Martha said, accusatory, swivelling round to face her granddaughter. 'I ask you, at what point?' She stared at Lucy, like she wanted an answer and Lucy, tired, sad, didn't know what to say. She simply shrugged.

'Well, let's discuss it later. I can get an estate agent in to value it, if that's what you'd like,' her father said. 'Maybe it's a good idea. Just let me know what you want to do.'

'I will,' said Martha, and Lucy saw the panic flitting across her face. Her father changed the subject.

'You know, I think Flo's case must be over by next week. I read something about it in the paper today. I don't think it's going that well for her.'

'Oh, really?' Martha gave a weary smile. 'I don't know. She's said nothing to me.'

'I think she didn't want to bother you,' Bill said.

'Right. When do you suppose we'll know?'

'When she calls, I guess. She's so funny about mobiles. She's staying with Jim and his wife in Islington but I don't have his number.'

'Islington,' Martha repeated again, blankly. 'I see. I didn't know she was there. That's funny, isn't it?'

Lucy didn't understand what she meant. 'He's nice, Jim,' she said. 'Met him the other day at lunch with her. He—'

'You had lunch with Flo?' Martha said, amazed.

'Yes, she asked me.'

'Why?'

Oh, she found out the night Southpaw died that she's adopted and I suppose she wanted to talk to someone about it as no one seems to have mentioned it to her before. 'Um. Well, she wanted me to do a puff piece. I wouldn't. I said I didn't think the *Daily News* would go for it.' Lucy shrugged. 'She's pretty . . . worried about everything at the moment.'

Martha began collecting up the tea things

smartly. 'Florence has always been in her own world. It's hard to get her to listen.'

'Gran, she needs your—' Lucy began, and then stopped. It wasn't for her to tell Gran that Florence knew. She didn't even know for certain it was true, anyway – these days, she was barely certain of what was real and what wasn't.

'Don't make me feel guilty. I'm too hard on her, I know it.' Martha shook her head; it was as though she was talking to herself. 'I can't help it.'

Lucy twisted her skirt around her finger. She looked at her dad, but he said nothing. Outside, rain dripped into a bucket by the back door.

Suddenly, her grandmother said, 'We've gone wrong, you see. I've done it all wrong. I thought when all this was out in the open it'd be better. He wanted a family home. A place we could all be safe, a unit. And we tried so hard, but it went wrong somewhere.'

'No, you didn't, Ma.' 'All families have problems.' Bill and Lucy spoke simultaneously.

'You would say that. You're the only ones left.' There was spite in her voice, something Lucy had never heard before. 'His wife ran off.' She jabbed a finger at Bill. 'Both of his wives, in fact. Florence has run off. Daisy ran off. I raised her daughter and then she ran off.'

'Not *both* of my wives. Clare didn't run off,' Bill said lightly, trying to make a joke of it. 'We decided it was for the best. And Karen . . . she hasn't run off. She's just moved out. We agreed she should.'

Dad, Lucy wanted to cry, *stand up for yourself!*

Her grandmother turned to him, her green eyes glinting. 'Oh, Bill, you live in a dream world. You didn't even notice your wife was having an affair under your nose for the best part of six months.'

Her father got up and took some plates over to the sink. 'Actually, I did know. I knew all along.'

'What?'

'Susan Talbot. She told me. Saw them kissing once.' His face twisted. 'But I'd already worked it out. I'm not stupid. I know her so well, you see. I've always known her, since . . . anyway I – I thought she'd come to her senses. I thought we worked because of what we didn't say to each other, not the other way round.'

'What an odd way to conduct a marriage,' Martha said. She blinked, too hard.

'So it would seem.' Lucy's father sat down and swiftly drained his tea. 'OK, well, I'll be off then.' He stood up, moved towards the door then looked back at his daughter. 'Luce – I'll see you tomorrow. You'll pop in for a coffee or something?'

'Absolutely.' She wished she was going with him, now, throwing her arm round his thin shoulders, bringing some noise and life back into the cottage. Suddenly, she really didn't want to be alone with Gran. 'Let us know if you hear from Florence, won't you?' she asked. 'Tell her we all hope she's OK.'

'Yes,' said Martha. 'Do let us know . . .' She reached out her hand as her son passed by and he bent down, so she could kiss his cheek, and then she whispered into his hair, 'Oh, Bill, my love. I'm sorry. It's bad at the moment.'

He hugged her, squeezing his eyes shut. 'It's all right, Ma.'

She clutched his wrist and stared up at him. 'Bill.'

'Ma?'

Her green eyes were clouded. She wasn't focusing on him but on something behind his head. 'It's beginning. It's here. I can't shake it. I keep putting it away and it keeps coming back.' She turned away. 'No. No.'

'Ma, it's fine,' Bill said calmly. He put a hand on her shoulders. 'That's good.'

'I don't think you understand.'

'Of course I do.' Bill bent down to look his mother straight in the eyes. 'You're in denial, Ma. It's normal.'

'I'm not,' Martha said, very softly, 'I just . . . I hate him sometimes.'

He crouched in front of her, as though she were a young child, and tucked a piece of hair behind her ear. 'Look. Ma, can I give you some advice?'

'Of course.'

'Don't force it. Any of it. Stop trying to control it.'

She looked straight at him. 'I want to stop it all,' she said. 'I want to be able to put it away.'

'But you can't, Ma. OK?'

Lucy watched, in agony. 'Ma,' Bill said softly, 'he's gone. He's not coming back.'

To Lucy's horror her grandmother's face buckled, her mouth slumping into a slack hole, her jaw thrust out. 'He said he would. Just for a while. He lied to me.' Her voice shook. 'I wish I'd known. I'd have helped him, I'd have made him feel better—'

'No.' Bill's voice was steely. 'Ma, I knew, and I couldn't help him and I'm a doctor. There is absolutely nothing you could have done. Please, please believe me. He lasted a lot longer than I thought he would. He'd been so ill for so long, you have to understand. He lived to meet Luke, and see Cat again, didn't he? He had the exhibition coming up. He'd have wanted us to be proud of it, to celebrate it. And he knew you were OK, and that you'd be OK. You have to remember all of this.' He put his hand on his mother's cheek and she nodded, the rictus smile of her face ghastly. 'Yes? Do you believe me?'

She stared at him. 'I don't know.'

They walked to the hall and stood on the threshold, the three of them glancing at each other, until Martha broke the silence. 'Well, goodbye,' she said, and turned and went into the study, shutting the door behind her.

'Are you OK on your own?' Lucy asked her father, as they walked down the drive together. 'Are you sure you don't want me to come back with you?'

The rain had stopped, and heavy drops fell through the newly green trees on to their heads.

'Absolutely not, but thank you,' Bill said, brushing the glistening blobs away from his jacket with precise fingers. 'I'll see you in the morning.'

'Yes, Dad,' she said. She wished she could ask him what came next, what they should all do – but his bowed shoulders and heavy, sad eyes told her he couldn't help. 'You should be more like that, you know,' she said.

'More like what?'

'More direct. Action-taking, Dad, you're really good at it.'

He gave a helpless laugh. 'I'm afraid I'm not, Lucy.'

'Yes, you are, you just think you're not. She needs you to tell her the truth.'

He laughed. 'I've never really understood the truth. Proves my point, all of this.' He hugged her. 'Goodbye, Luce. You're so grown up, lately. I barely recognise you.'

She stared curiously into his face. 'Dad, I'm still the same.'

'Nothing's the same, Lucy,' he said. 'The sooner Ma gets used to that idea the better.'

Walking back up the drive, Lucy stared up at the house. The wooden gables were grey in the dusk and moss coated the window casements. Weeds had sprung up on the gravel driveway. As if confirming the gloom of Lucy's mood, it started to rain again, heavy, like mist. She rubbed her eyes. It was as though the house was disappearing in front of her and she wished she could click on the carousel and move the image, replace it with . . . her tenth birthday party, when the house became a pirate ship and Cat gave her her old Benetton T-shirt. Or the time Florence was so enraged by some critic's interpretation of her reading of some old painting that she threw the book through the study window, where it landed out on the lawn, hitting Dad on the head, and Southpaw, Cat and Lucy laughed so much that lemonade came out of Cat's nose. Or the time she kissed her French exchange Xavier, in the woods full of wild garlic, the taste of his salty, plump lips, the smell of garlic and fresh earth. Any memory but this one, the present day.

Opening the study door carefully, she found Martha sitting behind Southpaw's desk and the sight jarred, as it always did. She was holding an itemised phone bill, and on the side was a scrib-bled drawing of Wilbur, scampering along the margin.

Lucy let out an – *Oh!* at the sight. She'd avoided Wilbur as much as possible because to look at him made her cry. But now, as she watched, Martha ripped the paper in two, slowly, one end to the other, all the time her eyes fixed on her granddaughter.

'Don't do that,' Lucy said furiously.

'You don't understand,' Martha said. 'I drew that one. It's my Wilbur. I can't ever draw him again. Now he's gone, Wilbur's gone too.'

Lucy slammed her hand on the desk. 'Wilbur's not yours to draw. What are you talking about? What the hell's *wrong* with you?'

Martha looked up in shock, her green eyes wary. 'What's wrong with me? Nothing. You're all wrong, not me.' She laughed. 'God, I really am going mad, aren't I?'

'Gran, what is it we're all wrong about?' Lucy asked, folding her arms.

'This idea of us all, in this place.' Her grandmother tore the paper up, into smaller and smaller pieces. 'It was all a lie. I thought I'd make it better by telling everyone about Daisy and I didn't.'

'No,' Lucy said, suddenly. 'It's not true. We were strong enough. We are.'

Martha gave her an almost sweet smile. 'Oh, Lucy, no, we weren't. Look around you.'

'That's you, that's you thinking like that because everything seems so grim, and sad, and I can understand why,' Lucy began, twisting her fingers together. 'No one's happy all the time. I'm not Pollyanna. I know everything wasn't perfect but, Gran, it wasn't a lie. We *were* happy. I used to love coming here more than anything else. I loved growing up here, being with Cat . . . being your granddaughter.' She swallowed. 'Seeing you and Southpaw all the time, and making coffee and reading books with Florence and all of that. It happened, Gran, it's not made up.'

Her grandmother shook her head. 'Wake up, Lucy. It's not a fairy story. Name me one person who's still standing after this and . . . Oh, I can't do this. Go away. Leave me alone, for God's sake.'

Lucy put her hands on her hips. She was trembling. 'No. I won't.'

Suddenly Martha shouted at her, her voice hoarse with anger.

'Go *away*.' She pointed at the door. 'God, Lucy, you have no idea. You've never woken up wondering if this is the day you'll be kicked to death by your father, like Southpaw, or been put on a train, sent away from your family for four years, like I was, so that by the time you go back to them you're so different no one knows you any more. You float around saying you want to write and saying you love it here and how wonderful this family thing is and – you're wrong.' Her voice softened. 'I know you idealise it here, I can see you must because of the divorce, and your parents but – but you're wrong.'

Lucy willed herself not to cry. She nodded. 'OK.'

'I'm sorry,' Martha began, but Lucy backed away, out into the hall, away from her.

She ran upstairs to her old room and shut the door. It was above the sitting room, and the other side of the L shape from Gran and Southpaw's room, so often Cat would creep in here late at night and get into bed with Lucy, so they could chat and laugh until the golden moon shone high like midnight sun through the thin floral curtains. The tall twin single beds were like shrouds, covered in the same worn woolly coverlets. This was the room where Lucy had had her first period; it was where she'd written her first short story, 'The Girl Who Ate the Moon'. Where she'd painted her hair with nail varnish and had to cut it off into a disastrous side fringe. She'd shown Cat her breasts and vice versa; though there was three and a half years between them, Lucy blossomed early, Cat late. The long window with its wooden casement was lined with her favourite books from childhood: *The Bell Family*, *Lanterns Across the Snow*, *The Magic Box*. The Christmas after her parents split up, she had spent the whole holiday here, lying on her bed, reading. No one bothered her, tried to make her 'join in'. She felt sorry for families who were always having to join in. You just did your own thing here, and sometimes that involved everyone, sometimes just you. Martha made her Scotch eggs, just for her, and she and Cat went into Bath on the bus by themselves and watched *The Fellowship of the Ring* and then there was that Christmas when . . .

Lucy stared out of the window at nothing, clutching her notebook, wondering about Martha, about Florence, about all of them. Then she sat on the bed and crossed her legs. It was very quiet; the only sound was the ticking of the old clock in the hall. She took out a pen from the bedside table and calmly and clearly, she began to write.

You say we weren't a happy family, Gran. But I remember the Christmas I was nine. Our car broke down on the way to Winterfold, on the A-road just outside Bristol, and Mum stormed off and went into a pub, and we called Southpaw and he came and picked us up, only Mum was kind of pissed by then, so she wouldn't leave the pub and she and Dad stayed there drinking and I went back with Southpaw, snuggled up in the back of the car in the big car rug (the orange one Joan Talbot knitted with the patch of purple in the middle because of her bad eyes).

I remember really clearly how great it was to leave them both in that pub. Because, you know, it wasn't a terrible secret that their marriage was disintegrating. It was obvious to me. I worked it out much earlier than they did. I just wanted **them** to work out they weren't right together. Just wanted them to get on with it and stop trying to pretend we were a happy family. We **really** weren't – you forget, Gran, I've lived in an unhappy family before; it's obvious. And it's awful being the only child in between these two people who are lying to you because they think it's for the best.

So I think of that Christmas a lot because, really, it was the first time I realised children are often right, but no one listens to them. Southpaw whistled all the way as he drove us home, incredibly slowly, because the roads were slippery with that two-day-old packed-down ice, and by the time we got nearer to Winterfold it was dark, we thought because it was night, but in fact it was because snow was coming. We sang 'Jingle Bells', and 'Blue Christmas', and 'Let It Snow' from Southpaw's Rat Pack tape in the car, and Southpaw did his Dean Martin impression, which was absolutely, as ever, terrible, and we wished you were in the car singing too, because you always knew all the words, and you loved singing. It's funny. You love singing, so does Dad, so does Southpaw. And Florence. You all sing, all the time.

You heard the car drawing up as we arrived, and you were standing in the doorway, and I remember this Christmas best of all because of that moment. You had your Christmas apron on, the one covered with berries, and you'd covered the door with holly, and ivy, glossy green leaves that shone in the porch-light. And it had started to snow by then, like someone had unzipped the clouds and it was just pouring out like feathers from a pillow. We jumped out and ran towards you, and I can still smell it as we came close, that delicious, woody, piny smell, wood smoke, spice, Christmas trees, earth, snow, cold, all mixed up together as I hugged you.

And you said, 'I'm so glad the travellers have returned.' Returned, like we were supposed to be here.

That day the snow fell, and we watched out of the window as it settled freshly over the valley like a drift of white on the grey trees. When it was dark, Mum and Dad appeared, and you always knew how to make Mum more cheerful. You gave her some camomile tea and asked her about her patients and we had your gingerbread, and we decorated the Christmas tree, but Cat and I were in charge of the decoration scheme, only you and Southpaw kept moving things around and putting strange things on the tree when we weren't looking and we all got hysterical with laughter. Like the packet of tissues, or one of Cat's socks, or your reading glasses, or whatever. That night, Cat and I worked out a play to 'She's Electric' by Oasis, which was so stupid we knew we couldn't show it to anyone. Cat said she wouldn't do plays any more, which was fair enough, but I was pretty upset about it, until we watched **Romancing the Stone** on the new TV and video player until about 3 in the morning. I loved **Romancing the Stone,** because Kathleen Turner's a writer, and really square, until all these wonderful adventures happen to her and her hair gets better, as does her blusher and the cut of her silk shirts.

The next day it was Christmas Eve, and the snow was inches thick. We made a snowman using one of the buckets we'd got on holiday in Dorset for his head, so he had a strangely machine-like yet sandy appearance. Our faces were red and our knees and hands were soaking with melted snow. We turned him into a proper robot. An old plug for his mouth, some fuses for his eyes, wire coat hanger as a kind of metallic carapace indicator and rusting tiny seedling pots on his hands, all to make him look as mechanical as possible. He was five feet tall! As tall as I was then.

We got the Christmas cake ready to eat, and I made Welsh rarebit with Flo (who always, always burns toast, even to this day) and you filled the old brown teapot to the top, as by then not only had Florence arrived but also Gilbert Prundy had popped in to fetch the extra heater from the shed (I remember him really well, the old vicar with his embroidered waistcoats, and his signet ring with the weird masonic symbol on it. We were convinced it opened the door to another dimension like in an Indiana Jones film). In the kitchen, you dropped a plate, one of the willow-pattern blue platters, shattered it to bits, and as we swept it up together you said, 'Easy come, easy go,' and shrugged, and I thought then, that's the way I want to live. It struck me then, that's a different way to see the world. I was always a worrier, always concerned about something in the back of my mind. And you made me see then that everything was perfect as it was, in that moment. Because we were happy there, sweeping up the pieces, you singing Dean Martin songs, and Southpaw joining in from his study. So that's what I remember, when I try to think about all of us. That Christmas. And it's not the beautiful house or the lovely table arrangements or the food you'd probably spent days preparing. It was all of us, the fact that we were together. Singing. Southpaw's voice, warbling and terrible. Like Dad's is now, Flo's too. Isn't it funny that she sounds just like them, Gran? Cat's voice, very low. Your voice is beautiful. It used to remind me of a clarinet. We always sing and I think that's so funny.

I am crying as I write this now. I can still see the sandy robot snowman. The fire, and the tree, and the warmth of all of us together. The sense of breathing out and letting everything go, because we were safe, together, with the door closed and the windows shut against the rest of the world. It is always there, even though he's gone. It won't go away.

MARTHA

They stood at the bottom of the stairs, facing each other. Martha's hands shook as she read the thin piece of paper. After a few minutes she put it down on the hall table, and went into the sitting room, not looking at Lucy. She stood by the French windows, gazing out over the lawn, the sky above. She felt her breath, coming, going, in out, in out, shoulder blades, rising and falling. She was here.

It was very quiet. She knew she had to say something.

'I don't remember it like that,' she said eventually.

'Right,' said Lucy. 'How do you remember it, then? Because, Gran, I was happy. It's not some fantasy in my mind. I knew my parents weren't getting on. I knew so many things in the world were terrible. But when I came here I was happy.'

Martha looked at her granddaughter. Lucy's heart-shaped face was flushed pink. 'I remember it being . . . I suppose I remember . . .' She stopped. 'I don't know. Maybe I've got this all wrong. I remember Daisy, wishing Daisy was there. For all of us, but for Cat most of all.'

481

'She was never there, though – how could Cat miss her?' Lucy scratched at her neck, upon which a rich red blush was creeping. 'We didn't like it when she was there, it was tense, and a bit strange. You'd all be on tenterhooks. And her breath always smelled.'

Martha flinched in surprise. 'What?'

Lucy blinked, mortified. 'I shouldn't have said that.'

'Her breath smelled?'

'Yes. Like she'd eaten . . . something rotten. I hated it. Didn't like hugging her and all that.'

'Did Cat think that too?'

Lucy nodded, slowly, not meeting her eye. 'Oh . . . yes, Gran. She wished she'd go away. It wasn't nice when she was there.'

'Because of . . . the breath?'

'No, because she was fake. She made me uneasy. She was too nice to Cat, you know what I mean?' Lucy watched her grandmother. 'No, you don't. Just – over the top. And she was horrible to Florence. You'd see it, these tiny little ways. Snide remarks and things like that, and Flo just took it . . . You know what she's like, just gets on with it, she's miles away . . .'

Martha's stomach clenched at the memory of a seven-year-old Florence, coming up the drive with her red plaits covered in mud, her too-long school skirt torn, sucking her thumb and crying, then saying, phlegmatically, 'Oh, I think I fell over.' The wasps that nearly killed her, the stuck door. When

Hadley had bitten her, way before he went mad, but Florence couldn't say how, or where. Her books, pages ripped out, that she just sellotaped in and carried on reading. Martha knew all that, yet she knew Daisy had needed someone to defend her, and . . .

Florence. She looked at her watch, then outside, as though she might suddenly be arriving, though she knew she wasn't. She desperately wanted to see her then, hold her fierce, angular daughter in her arms, tell her the truth, tell her how sorry she was, how silly she had been. The light poured in through the windows. She rubbed her eyes, tired.

'We liked it when it was just us, people popping round, everything normal,' Lucy was saying. 'Southpaw doing silly drawings. You singing. You helping us do plays. Helping us make weird drinks.'

Martha stared at her granddaughter's face. Lucy, sweet Lucy, her honesty, her openness. Lucy who had told her the truth because she had never learned to lie. Lucy, who loved this house and everything about what Martha had created, despite the secrets and untruths that Martha felt, for decades now, had spun Winterfold up into a web, skeins of silken spider thread covering everything over.

So something I did worked. Lucy believed it all. One person alone couldn't bring that down, one person against the rest of them. She hated to think of Daisy as the enemy; she wasn't. But Martha suddenly knew she had shielded her for too long, carried her. Maybe . . .

Her heart started to beat faster. A strange, metallic taste swept her mouth. It was frightening simply to consider that one might think differently about this. Try a new way of thinking.

Yet she had to. She blinked and shut her eyes, forcing herself to think about what Lucy had said.

'Apple . . . what was it called, your favourite drink?' she asked, eventually. 'We used to have to make it every time you came over.'

'Yes.' Lucy nodded. 'I liked Apple Mingo and Cat liked—'

'Banana Bomba,' Martha said. She could feel her chest opening out again, as though some invisible weight that had been sitting on her breastbone had been lifted away. All this love that she had to give, buried so deep. *Cat, oh Cat, my sweet, sweet girl, what did I do, why have I let you go like this?* 'Banana bomba was my favourite.'

'No, Apple Mingo was the best, only Cat wouldn't ever tell us what was in it,' Lucy said seriously. 'Wow, I still think she put maple syrup in it. Which is bloody cheating because we weren't supposed to use sugar. And some – Oh!'

Lucy jumped as Martha stepped forwards, and brushed her granddaughter's hair away from her forehead. 'Sweet Lucy.' Martha cupped her chin, staring at her flushed cheeks, her beautiful hazel eyes, the round, sweet face. 'Thank you.'

'For what?' Lucy laughed. 'Are you all right, Gran?'

Martha hugged her. 'Apple Mingo.' Then she squeezed her, tight, till Lucy gave a muffled yelp.

'You're strong, Gran, blimey.' She pulled herself away. 'What do you mean? Do you believe me now?'

'Yes, I do,' Martha began, then corrected herself. 'Only – yes, I do. But listen, Lucy. No one's happy all the time. We weren't living in this golden kind of cage of lovely memories. It's important you remember that, too.'

Lucy gave a rueful smile. 'Well, of course I do, Gran. I said that to you, remember? You keep forgetting I had Mum and Dad's divorce when I was thirteen. That was pretty awful, even if we were all glad it happened. Hell, I remember Dad's wedding to Karen. That certainly wasn't some lovely memory I'm writing up as a keepsake.'

'I like Karen.'

Lucy raised her eyebrows as if to say something, then relented. 'Actually, you know what? The sad thing is, I did too.'

'She's not dead,' Martha said, and they were both silent for a moment in the gloom of the room.

'I'll never stop missing Southpaw,' Lucy said after a while. 'But I've been thinking about it a lot.' She threaded her fingers through her grandmother's, and took her hand in both hers. 'I say to myself, it's dreadful you're gone, but we're so so glad you were even here. That we knew you and you were in our lives. I'm sad but I can't help be glad I had him for so long. That's what I think.'

Martha put her head on Lucy's shoulder. 'Yes,' she said, quietly, thinking about all the stories Lucy didn't know, how her grandfather had suffered to get to here, and how much happiness he'd brought people, how strong his spirit was. How he had saved Cassie, taken Florence, how they had found each other . . . But that was all for another day, she knew. 'Yes, you're right.' Then she gave a big, deep sigh and nodded. It had happened, and she saw it now, and it would be hard but she could see the way out, the way she had to start again.

She said: 'All right, then. It changes. Everything changes here.'

'What do you mean?'

'I mean, enough of this. I'm in charge now. Let's put the kettle on and work out what we do now. What I do now.' She said, quietly, 'I have to do everything differently now.'

She went to the huge cupboard in the hall and took out some light bulbs. 'A light bulb moment,' she said, and Lucy, who was in the kitchen, called through, 'What?'

'Nothing, nothing.'

As the kettle boiled, Martha pulled a green scarf off Southpaw's sturdy old chair and Lucy climbed up on to it, standing on tiptoe to fix the bulbs in. But halfway through the chair gave an ominous creaking crack, and buckled to one side. The first creak was enough warning for Lucy, who jumped off, just as it collapsed to the ground. She landed heavily on the tiled floor, rubbing her bottom, and looked up, her face already burning red with mortification, at Martha.

'Southpaw's chair. Oh, Gran. I'm so sorry. I'll get it mended.'

Martha merely stared at the chair. 'Goodness! Are you OK?'

'I'm fine,' said Lucy. 'But I know he loved it and—'

Crouching down, Martha ran her hands over the smooth warm wood, pricking the pads of her fingers on the cracked, broken back legs, one of which had simply buckled. 'It had a lot of wear and tear,' she said, patting her granddaughter's leg. 'Please, don't worry. It's my fault.'

Lucy tried to laugh. 'I'm sorry your lardarse granddaughter broke one of your chairs.'

'It was very old. I think we should go into Bath and get a new one tomorrow, hmm? We can burn this old friend,' said Martha, pushing the carcass of the chair to one side and standing up again. Then she helped Lucy off the floor, gripping her arm in her strong hands. 'Easy come, easy go, darling. Now. Let's see about booking some tickets.'

PART IV

THE END AND THE BEGINNING

I think that just now we are not wanted there. I think it will be best for us to go quickly and quietly away.

E. Nesbit, *The Railway Children*

FLORENCE

It was strange, coming out of the Royal Courts of Justice. It was so near to the Courtauld, in the one bit of London she knew really well. The sun had broken through the purple-grey rain clouds of the morning and, as Florence made her way through the great hall of the Victorian Gothic building, buffeted by swarming men and women in black, she found she had to squint as she emerged on to the pavement. A huge din greeted her, a mass of yet more people calling out, shouting. She felt completely bewildered. She still wasn't even sure she'd heard the judge right.

Outside, crowds and TV cameras thronged the pavement and she stopped still, in shock. Protesters were waving placards. Florence peered at one of the signs: did they all hate her that much? 'FRACK OFF', one of them read. She remembered brushing her teeth this morning at Jim's, frowning at herself in the mirror while listening to the *Today* programme: yes, of course. Some judgment was expected today at the Court of Appeal on a fracking company's right to drill in Sussex.

One of the signs of paranoia is the belief people

are out to get you. Not today. Florence gave a shaky laugh, walking with relief into the furious crowd, almost touched at the strength of their belief, the passion on their faces. She had been like that once and it wasn't real, she knew it now. It was fake, a comfort, something for her to cling on to alone at night, like the cloth bunny she'd had when she was small . . . and now she'd taken it away, exposed herself, everything about her own sad, strange life . . . and she didn't know what on earth she'd do.

Florence shook her head, trying to stay calm, and looked wildly around her for an escape.

'This is not a matter of "passing off" or of academic judgement for the court to decide upon . . . This is a matter of deception and of income fraudulently obtained on the basis of character assumption. You led the general public to believe you were an art historian who not only wrote and presented his own television documentary series, but also produced a tie-in book to accompany this series, for which you received a not inconsiderable advance of £50,000 from Roberts Miller Press. You have heard from the managing director of that company. Ms Hopkin says she believed, as did the public, that you were the author of this book, which was so well researched and written as to attract not merely favourable reviews in the academic world but to have been a word-of-mouth success, thanks to an endorsement from a television book club, and so on. And as a result of that belief you received a further £100,000 for a new book, not to mention substantial royalty payments on your first book. Professor Connolly, this case brought against you by Professor Winter is one of credibility. She is possibly the foremost expert in her subject in the world and your cynical attempt to exploit that, your arrogance and your sheer deceit is frankly breathtaking. I find her credible, and you to be liable for the costs of this case. The plaintiff's complaint is upheld.'

She wasn't crazy, she hadn't misheard, had she? She had won. She had done it, this weird, unlike-her thing. Hadn't she?

Florence had stood in the narrow wooden pew after the judgment, not sure what to do next. Her barrister, a florid young man called Dominic, had patted her on the shoulder and disappeared. She'd seen Jim earlier, but he was teaching that afternoon and hadn't been able to come. Lucy wouldn't be there, of course, or Bill, or Ma; she'd deliberately pushed them all away.

Before all this happened she'd always thought she was close to her brother. She and Bill weren't usually in daily contact, but they'd talk occasionally, amusing, low-key chats when he'd tell her about the village and what she was missing, ask about her job, that sort of thing. Bill was dry, and funny and kind. He was *very* kind. He was calm, too, always putting things in perspective. He *had* been calm, rather. Now, he seemed to be pitted against her, on Ma's side. But against her too, somehow . . . And there was no one she could talk to about the night Pa died . . . And that was . . . well, that was fine, because she was on her own now. So best get used to it.

Yes, get used to it. So much to get used to. Florence blinked and closed her eyes, longing for a moment of quietness in the bright, loud street. When she opened her eyes, she saw a rather strange man with a notebook standing nearby. In an effort to ignore him she fiddled with her new grey suit jacket, which she'd bought the day before the trial began. 'You have to wear something vaguely businesslike, Flo,' Jim had said, laughing at her discomfort. 'You can't show up in tie-dye skirts with mirrors on, or that dress with the pockets. Even I think so.' This was indeed strong stuff coming from Jim, who was usually in creased cheesecloth from March to September, so Florence had gone to a charity shop on Upper Street and come home with this. She'd been very pleased with it.

Today, though, Florence wasn't quite sure whether she'd bought a man's or woman's suit jacket. It had been on the women's rail but it looked really awful, like she was a tycoon in some programme like *Dallas*. She undid the button again, and began to look along the street for the bus that'd take her home to Jim's house, when a voice called:

'Happy now, then?'

Her heart leaping, Florence turned round. 'Oh.

494

Peter,' she said. 'I thought you were – never mind. Yes, I am. Thank you.' The *Thank you* sounded more jubilant than she intended.

Peter Connolly stood a few metres away on the edge of the crowd. His jowls were grey-black, as they always were by mid-afternoon, dark with stubble. He really was very hairy. Hair in his ears, in his nose – it was actually not at all pleasant, when you thought about it.

He nodded a farewell greeting to his lawyer and came towards her, slowly, and when he reached her he said, 'Well, you've proved your point, I suppose. You really are a bitter, dried-up old coot, aren't you.'

'It's over now, Peter. Come on.'

He was spitting, he was so angry. 'Living in your sad little apartment with your sad little mementoes, waiting like a spider in her web to trap me.' He shoved his hands in his pockets, made a gormless face and loped round in a circle in exaggerated imitation of her, as the anti-fracking protesters looked on, curiously, and one or two of them, recognising him, nudged each other.

'Peter.' Talitha Leafe appeared, and put one pale hand on the crumpled arm of his blue linen suit, the kind he always wore on television. Florence knew that one: he'd had it on the day she'd seen him eating in Da Camillo with a couple of students and she'd 'pretended' to walk past and popped in to say hi and they'd had to ask her to stay, of course . . .

'No,' she whispered to herself. 'Not any more.'

'God,' he said, his large face looming over her. 'I – I – you have no idea how much I *wish* I'd never laid a finger on you.'

Talitha said quietly, her lips curling in cold rage: 'Peter, for God's sake shut up! The press are everywhere.'

'"*Is* everywhere",' Florence muttered under her breath. She was amused to see the slightly untidy-looking chap with a notebook ambling up to them.

He stood in front of the awkward group and said, mildly, 'Hello, I'm from the *Guardian*. Any comment on the court's ruling today?'

'Um, well . . .' Florence could feel perspiration forming under the jacket, between her shoulder blades. She had no idea what the right thing to say was. 'I'm delighted.'

Peter shook his head and said under his breath, 'You'll regret this, you know that, don't you? I mean, it's the end for you, one way or another. You've burned your boats. George isn't going to want—'

Someone called his name and his expression changed, the whole cast of his face. He turned round and said in his most mellifluous voice: 'I say, hello! Kit! Hello there, Jen!'

'Hello, Peter,' said the first woman, in a neutral voice. Florence suddenly recognised her: she was the producer of his TV series.

'Yes! Thank you for coming. Wondered if you'd

be here, if you'd come – thanks for your support, Kit—'

Kit said, 'We had to come. We were subpoenaed, Peter.'

Peter spoke loudly. 'I need to come in for some dubbing, I know, for the last section outside Santa Croce.' Florence thought for the first time how like the snobbish English vicar in *A Room with a View* he was, how that had been part of his charm for them – and her too. And it was an affectation, of course. The real Peter was simply a mediocre person.

As the two women walked away, nodding farewell politely, the older one stopped suddenly, and whispered something to the younger one, then ran back towards Florence, avoiding Peter's gaze.

'Here,' she said. She thrust a small card into Florence's hand. It dug into her palm and Florence looked down at it in surprise. 'Take my card. We'd love to talk to you about a project we have in mind – now's not the right time, I know. But you'd be fantastic. I'm Kit. I'm the commissioning editor. Give me a call because – well, yeah. You really were terrific in there. I was really proud . . . anyway.' She avoided Peter's incredulous, shell-shocked expression and dashed off down the road to where Jen was waiting.

Peter and Talitha stalked off in the opposite direction without another word, Talitha's heels clicking angrily like tap shoes on the pavement. Florence was left holding the card in the middle of the street, feeling dizzier than ever. The noise from the fracking protestors grew louder. She didn't want to be on TV, did she? What would happen with Peter's next TV series? With his new book deal, his villa near Siena, the flat in Bloomsbury, his lecturing role on the *Queen Mary*? She had ruined it all for him, and for what?

'So,' said the *Guardian* journalist. She'd forgotten he was still there. 'What's next for you? I mean, do you think this kind of case is reflective of the current state of academia, of television commissioning policy?'

'Oh,' Florence said. 'I don't know. I just had to do it. I had to tell the truth. Everything out in the open.' She could feel her throat constricting.

'Right.' He scribbled furiously on a tiny pad. 'Of course. Right . . .' He scanned his pad with his pen. 'And is this correct, you're David Winter's daughter, right?'

Florence found, to her horror, that she couldn't speak. Her eyes filled with tears, her fingers clutched at her handbag strap. She opened her mouth.

No, actually. No, I'm not.

'You must miss him,' the journalist went on. 'He was very well loved, wasn't he? It's not long since he died, is it?'

How could he ask her questions like this? She stared at him, blankly, not sure what she was about to do, and then someone took her arm, gently.

'Come on, Flo.' She looked up, to find Jim

standing in front of her, puffing hard, out of breath. 'Let's go and get a drink.'

'Oh, Jim.' She wanted to throw her arms around him.

Jim leaned against a wall, wheezing. 'God, I'm unfit. I only just made it. They wouldn't let me miss the lecture. It's all anyone's talking about in the common room, I can tell you.' He turned to the journalist. 'Goodbye then,' he said, in his firm but awkwardly shy way, and took her arm. 'Shall we go back to the Courtauld?' he said, shepherding her across the street. 'There's a bit of a hero's welcome there for you, if you fancy it?'

'Oh, no, absolutely not, I'm sorry. I want some peace and quiet.'

'Right. Want me to leave you then?'

'No, please don't.' She clutched his hand so ferociously that he laughed.

'All right, of course. Come on, we'll go to the pub.'

In Ye Olde Cheshire Cheese, a tiny, warren-like pub off Fleet Street, Florence found a table deep in the vaulted cellars, while Jim went to the bar. She sat waiting for him, blinking hard, clutching her handbag on her lap and wishing everything wasn't so loud in her head, the clamour of too many voices all shouting to be heard.

Jim appeared, and handed her a stiff gin and tonic. 'Congratulations!' he said, clinking her glass. 'How do you feel?'

Florence gulped down her drink. 'Relieved, I suppose,' she said. 'Glad it's over.'

Jim watched her. 'Are you going to call your mother? Your family?'

'Oh. Maybe later.' She shook her head. 'They won't care. I haven't told them much about it. Anything, really.'

'Come on, Flo. They'll be over the moon. We all are.'

Florence couldn't tell him what she wanted to, what she'd told Lucy. She couldn't bear to say it again. *They're not my family. I don't belong to anyone.* She just shrugged.

Jim said softly, 'Flo, the way those lawyers tried to bring you down in there was horrible. You could sue Peter for defamation.'

Florence felt her eyes twitching, with tiredness, with mortification at the memory of what they'd said. She rubbed them. She couldn't really bear to think about the last four days of the trial, how Peter's barrister had, in his opening statement, exposed in five short minutes the sad, pathetic nature of her outer life. 'My suing days are over.' Florence downed the rest of her drink. She didn't feel triumphant. Just reckless, and quite mad. 'Maybe I shouldn't have done it. I wish everything hadn't come out like this.'

'Come on, Flo!' Jim looked appalled. 'You can't say that.'

'It's mortifying.' She looked almost with surprise at her empty glass. 'They made me look so – so pathetic. I haven't had that since . . .'

Since Daisy.

'Let me remind you, Flo,' Jim said, 'when you took this on, you were very clear to me. You wanted to prove your point. You wanted to show them they couldn't push you around.'

'Yes. Yes . . . I suppose so. I can't remember why now.' She brushed her forehead with her hand, bewildered. 'Peter – he and George, they were trying to get rid of me. And I'm better than both of them. I didn't know what else to do.'

'But you know you could have moved back here.'

'And do what?' She looked up uneasily, as the door swung open.

'Flo, you've just won a plagiarism case that says you wrote the biggest-selling book in recent memory on the Renaissance. Students come from all around the world to the Courtauld just to hear you lecture. You know, admissions to your course rose by nearly sixty per cent after you joined us?' She shook her head. 'You've written three other books. You're – you're about to be in demand. Get used to it. Stop thinking you're not part of the rest of society.'

'Sure. OK.' Florence picked at the worn trim of the stool. 'Sure. It's just . . .'

Jim said gently, 'Just what?'

She glanced up, and caught his kind grey eyes staring at her. She thought how well she knew him, how lucky she was that, in all this, she still had a friend, one friend.

The fact that she'd kept in a special bag a tissue

Peter Connelly had left at her apartment. The lists she'd kept of things they'd done, found in one of the manuscripts he still had. The stories, repeated over and over to colleagues, the notes she'd written him . . . The mug he used that she never washed. A piece of pink paper stuck to the fridge, a flyer advertising a joint lecture at the College: *Professor Connolly and Professor Winter*. Seeing their names printed together had continued to give her a thrill long after the paper grew faded and crinkled in the sun.

Florence had always told everyone that she didn't care what they thought of her. She had told Daisy she didn't care about the notes left on the bed, the wasps' nest, the constant pinches and bruises her sister gave her that no one ever seemed to notice. Only once had she cracked and told Ma, creeping into the kitchen while Daisy was out with Wilbur, silent tears running down her grubby face. And Ma had kissed her, and said, 'Oh Flo. You have to learn to get on with other people, birdie, instead of telling tales. Like I say. Fight back.'

And Florence was left with her mouth open, her tongue dry, wanting to speak next but too frightened. *I think she might kill me if I fight back.*

It had always been easier and safer to retreat into her own mind. And who was there who could help her, who would listen? She had burned her boats with everyone, really, except Jim. As she smiled awkwardly into his kind face she knew she couldn't talk to Jim about it. She liked him too much. She could feel the doors sliding shut, feel herself pulling the trapdoor in, retreating back. The fact was she'd been living in her own world for so long she wasn't sure if she could ever live anywhere else again.

Jim interrupted her thoughts. 'What will you do now?'

Clearing her throat, Florence tried to sound businesslike. 'I think I might go back to Florence next week. Get on with some work. A new paper for the *I Tatti Studies* Harvard journal on the relationship between Lorenzo de Medici and Gozzoli and how the latter controlled Lorenzo's public image, you know, not only the frescoes but—' She saw Jim was staring at her with a slightly glazed expression and she stopped. 'Anyway, I need to work. Most of the summer, I suppose.'

'What about the TV people?'

'Oh, they were just being nice, don't you think?'

'They're not charity workers. You should call them.'

'Listen, Jim,' she said, wanting to change the subject. 'Thank you. Thank you for everything the last few months. I don't know what I'd have done without you. Gone mad, probably. Thanks for having me to stay, too. It's great Amna doesn't mind me clogging up the house.'

He laughed. 'I don't think she'd be bothered one way or the other.'

'When's she back?' Jim had said something about Istanbul for a conference, but conferences didn't last a month. Florence had been so wrapped up in herself lately, it only occurred to her now that this was unusual.

'Oh. Well, she's back. Back a couple of weeks ago, in fact. It went well.' Jim nodded, then looked into his glass.

'Is she?' Florence didn't understand. 'Oh. Where is she then?' She wondered if, in her self-obsession, Amna had been eating breakfast with them every day, chatting about history or academic gossip in the evenings whilst making pasta in the kitchen and she simply hadn't noticed.

'Florence, we've split up.'

'Who?'

'Good grief, concentrate. Me! I mean, me and Amna.'

She shook her head, blindsided. 'I didn't know that.'

'You didn't ask.'

'You should have said.' She felt embarrassed. 'I wouldn't have stayed if—'

He laughed. 'What, like a Victorian maiden? You don't think it's appropriate for us to be in the house alone without Amna as a chaperone?'

'Don't laugh at me,' she muttered, flushing.

'I'm not, sorry.' His nice old face grew serious, and he said, 'I never saw her. She was away three weeks out of four. The house is too big for one person waiting for the other person to come home. And – well, no big surprise, but there's someone else.'

'Oh. Oh my goodness.' Florence impulsively put her hand on his, which was wrapped round his glass. 'I had no idea, Jim. I'm so sorry. I feel I've been no friend to you, while it's been going on and you've been . . .' She could feel herself, wanting to cry again, and dug her hands into her thigh. *For God's sake, stop feeling sorry for yourself. Wait till you get home. You can indulge it then. You can do what you want with your life, then.*

And a seed took root in her thoughts then, a seed that sprouted and grew rapidly, and which she realised then was, really, the only solution to all of this. But she didn't say anything to Jim, who was watching her intently.

'I'm fine about it,' he said. 'It's been over for years, really, and now I can get on with life. Leave it behind me.' He cleared his throat. 'Do you understand what I mean?'

They stared at each other. 'Yes,' she said. 'Perhaps I do.'

'Everything's changed,' Jim said, and he shifted a little closer towards her, but Florence's knees knocked against the stool that was in between them and, impatiently, she flung it away so it rolled on the floor. As Jim picked it up and set it right again she watched him and knew, of course, that she wasn't in any state for this, not now, probably not ever.

Dear Jim. With a monumental effort she plastered a smile on her face and said, 'Let's change the subject. I want to know what you thought about Talitha Leafe. I heard from someone at the Academy that she asked David Starkey out before she went for Peter. She's apparently a well-known TV historian stalker. Have you come across her before?'

Jim was silent for a moment, and then gave one of his delighted chuckling laughs, and shifted his weight on the stool, and she was glad to have made him smile, to leave everything else behind, to be gossiping and talking about someone else, for once. When she got back to Florence, that's when she'd take the next step, the final one. Not today.

CAT

Since they had come back, all Luke could do was ask when they'd be seeing Southpaw again. When they would be going back to England. He still cried when Cat left him at crèche, though nearly five months had passed. He was four, and naughty now, when during the supposedly terrible twos and threes he had been sweet-natured and gentle. She had braced herself, and contacted Olivier to ask if they could come and visit him in Marseilles. Now she was stronger, perhaps it was time to loosen the reins a bit, let Luke get to know his father, though her every fibre screamed that this was not what she wanted for him.

But Olivier had completely vanished. She'd emailed him several times, even called him, though she dreaded speaking to him. All to no avail. Cat even went back to Bar Georges and asked Didier if he'd heard from him. Didier thought he'd left Marseilles and gone to live in La Réunion. A new girlfriend who owned a jazz club on the island, in Saint-Denis, had offered Olivier a regular gig, Didier said. He had given Cat a café cortado on the house while Cat stood at the bar, shaking with rage and then relief. Pure, sweet, relief, at the idea that Olivier might just not be her problem any more, that the guilt she felt, and the worry she had that he might, like a bogey monster of her childhood nightmares, appear under the bed and snatch her son away had gone, that that might all be over.

So now it really was just her and Luke, and he was more difficult every day. He seemed to have grown nearly a foot since Christmas. He was too big for the small, intricate apartment. He was rude, and so badly behaved Madame Poulain now refused to look after him when Cat went to the doctor about her swollen toe. She had stubbed it on a treacherous cobblestone, dodging a group of Italian schoolchildren by Notre-Dame, two weeks ago, and it had grown huge, and turned an angry red, like a cartoonish injury in an Asterix book. She couldn't sleep, and every time she moved in bed, pain shot through her like a bolt of fire. It was waking Luke up too.

'I'm not taking care of that child. He is *mechant*, a horror. He is a bad child. He draws disgusting animals.'

'I know – I apologize . . .' The dragon in green pen on the bathroom wall still hadn't come off, despite Cat scrubbing it twice a day for the past week.

'And he sticks his fingers in his eyes and calls me rude names.'

Cat, clasping her hands in the doorway, had paused.

'What does he call you?'

Madame Poulain had shaken her fist. 'A troglodyte. He says—' she had cleared her throat – 'that his great-grandfather taught it to him. Disgusting that he does this, puts lies in the mouth of your dear dead *grand-père*.'

Cat's shoulders had started to shake, almost involuntarily. It kept happening to her, this feeling when she didn't know whether she was about to laugh, or burst into tears. 'I'm so sorry,' she had managed to say. 'So sorry. Please, if you could just—'

But Madame Poulain had refused, and Cat had had to drag Luke out with her, screaming and crying, 'No! Stop trying to snatch me!' across the bridge towards the Boulevard St-Germain and the doctor.

This afternoon, two days later, it was still pouring with rain. As Cat hobbled along uncertainly, one bandaged toe now encased in a cartoon-like plastic boot, she slipped on the cobblestones again, and nearly knocked over a smartly dressed old man. She grasped him by the shoulders. '*Excusez-moi, monsieur.*'

He had turned to her. 'It's quite all right,' he'd said, in a voice so like Southpaw's it made her heart stop. 'Don't apologise. It's treacherous out there.'

She went on her way, trying not to cry, though

as it rained harder and harder she gave in to it. How did he know she was English? That she didn't belong here, less so than ever?

'Luke, please will you clear away your pens, and help me set the table?'

'I can't, not yet.' Luke answered. 'I have to finish . . . this . . . Gruffalo . . . very carefully. It's very impotent.'

'Important. No, you can finish it later. After supper.'

'He is a monster,' said Madame Poulain, into her vermouth.

'That's right,' Cat said absently. The rain dripped through the tiny crack in the steamed-up kitchen window. The stench of drains and rubbish from the tiny galley kitchen hung in her nostrils. Her broken toe ached more than ever – she was sure now that going to the doctor had been a mistake. They'd strapped it so tightly to her second toe that now all of her foot, rather than just the big toe, throbbed with pain. Suddenly Madame Poulain screeched at Luke.

'Put these things away. Away! It is my house, my rules, you dirty, naughty boy.'

'Madame Poulain—' Cat said, wearily.

'No!' shouted Luke. He picked up the felt-tip pens, like candy-coloured plastic sticks, and threw them, all of them, at Madame Poulain. 'I hate you! I hate you! I hate being here! You are horrible, you keep us here like a witch, you should let

Maman go! I hate you! I hope that you turn into a bird and fly away into an electricity pylon and zzzzzzzap! You get fried and you die and it's really horrible!'

As Cat watched, frozen in horror, Luke picked up the nearest pen, a bright acid green, and ran over to the white wall. Her phone rang, buzzing loudly on the table beside her and jerking her into consciousness. She ran over to him and scooped him up from behind, swinging him around away from the wall.

'Luke! No! You don't, you *don't do that!*' She plucked the pen out of his hand, and slapped his wrist – she felt it was a pathetic action, and he gave her a strange, almost humorous look, and that half-sob, half-laugh wave of emotion swept over her again. She swallowed it down. Her phone rang again and she knocked it off the table, in fury.

'Take the child upstairs, and leave him there. And then . . .' Madame Poulain hesitated, and Cat saw that she didn't know what to do next, and neither did she, Cat. They had no formal arrangement, no ties that bound them together. They were not family.

As Cat stood there panting, holding a screaming Luke, her phone rang again, on the floor. She released him too suddenly, and he jumped on to her foot, stamping on her strapped-up toe. Cat screamed too, a great big howl of pain, and Luke looked up at her, his dark eyes huge. She stroked his hair. 'Sorry. It's my toe. I'm – I'm fine.'

Madame Poulain did not move, so Cat very slowly hobbled over to the dining table, reached down and picked the phone off the floor. She put her arm around Luke's shoulder. 'Please, Luke. Say sorry.' Ignoring the searing pain in her foot, she answered. '*Allô?*'

'Is someone being murdered in there?' came a clear voice. 'It sounds like it.'

'Who's – who is this?' Cat said, slowly. 'Is that you?'

'It is, darling.'

'Gran?' Cat whispered into the phone. 'What are you doing here?'

'I'm downstairs,' said Martha.

'*Where?*' Cat swallowed.

'I'm downstairs. Waiting outside. You said I should come and visit. Well, I'm here. Is now a good time? I heard the most awful sounds. Even with the rain.'

'Now . . . now's a very good time,' said Cat, laughing. She didn't know what else to do. 'I'll buzz you up.'

She looked around the crowded, bright apartment, like an antiques shop. At Madame Poulain's cold, furious face. At Luke, scared and cross, arms folded, looking at the floor. 'No. Stay there. I'll come down. I don't want you to come up here.'

'What, darling? You cut out for a second.'

'Wait a moment.' It seemed clearer and clearer, by the second, like the sun coming out.

'When will you be back?' Madame Poulain said, icily. 'I need more Vermouth, and some ice. Who is that, Cat? Who's downstairs?'

'My grandmother,' Cat said. She pulled Luke on to her lap. 'Luke, let's put on your shoes.' She looked up at the thin, lined face. 'I don't know when I'll be back, Madame Poulain. Don't wait for me. I'm going to call Henri. He'll come over and help you. Luke, put on your coat, please.'

Madame Poulain's eyes seemed to grow entirely round, her eyeballs bulging from her sunken skull. 'Don't you dare to say that. You said you would clean the bathroom this evening. I need it done tonight and before my wash.'

Cat opened the drawer of the bureau, and slid two passports into her jeans pocket. She didn't know why, just that the card file of her mind was flipping over and over, the thoughts that constantly raced through her head of what needed to be done, what she had to take here, or there, what she could afford, what she owned, all neatly, precisely itemised, and she realised then that all she needed was Luke. And the means to get Luke away from here, away from this overheated glass menagerie, away from the shadow of Luke's father, who hadn't even been in touch since their return, away from this strange, beautiful little island living that was, day by day, slowly torturing them both to death.

Her heart was thumping so loudly in her chest she thought it might burst. 'Goodbye,' she said, buttoning Luke's coat up. 'Thank you.' She pulled on her old mac and grabbed her handbag, opened the door, and, hobbling down the steps as fast as she could, calling to Luke to follow her, she eventually reached the bottom of the stairs.

She flung open the front door. There, in a great yellow mackintosh with a hood, stood Martha, her green eyes ringed with dull brown circles. She was smiling.

Cat said nothing, just flung her arms around her, sobbing into her squeaky yellow chest. Martha pulled Luke into her embrace and the three of them stood on the narrow little pavement, clutching hold of each other.

'Gran!' Luke shouted, breaking the grip first, and leaping up into his great-grandmother's arms, so that she staggered back and nearly stumbled. 'Gran, you're here! You are here!'

Cat caught her grandmother, felt how thin she was. She hugged her again, tears flowing along with the rain down her face, and she realised then what it was, this feeling of half sadness, half happiness that stalked her all the time lately. It was love.

'Let's go and get some hot chocolate,' she said, steering her grandmother away from the apartment. 'I think we could all do with it.'

Martha took Luke's hand. 'Of course. Do you – need an umbrella? What about your fearsome-sounding landlady? Does she need to know where you've gone?'

'I'll call her in a while and tell her we'll be back later,' Cat said. Up above she could see the thinnest seam of silver in the sky. She breathed in, and then she said, 'But we might not. We might just never go back there again.' She gripped Luke's other hand. 'What do you think about that?'

She was asking Luke, really, not entirely serious, half-acknowledging that it was clear now that their situation had to change, but Martha said, 'I think that's a very good idea.'

Cat glanced at her. 'I was joking really,' she said.

'I know, but – do you have to go back? No. I mean, pack up and get your things, of course, or I could do that, or, you know what?' Martha squeezed Cat's hand, and crouched down next to her grandson. 'I could go back to the flat now, get your passports, and we could all go home tonight. Back to Winterfold.'

Cat's hand was shaking as she took out the passports. 'I've got them here.'

'Why?' Her grandmother laughed.

'I really don't know. Just that – I heard your voice.' She started crying. 'And I thought we need to be able to not go back there. I'm always trying to think of a way out. All the time.' She hiccuped. 'I've got used to it.'

'What else do you need?' Martha said quietly.

Cat looked at her son. 'Nothing else.' she said. 'But we couldn't do that – so rude to Madame

Poulain, and . . .' she trailed off. The idea of walking away from here – it was intoxicating, like drinking champagne. Knowing this bit was over, these years of living this thin, sad, lonely life. She felt almost light-headed. And then she looked at Luke's face.

'Look, my darling girl, it seems fairly simple,' Martha said. 'I need you, Cat. You need me. Luke needs more than this.'

Cat hesitated, then said, 'Yes. We do. Yes.'

They hugged again, squashing against a wall to let a chic elderly lady walk past with her little dog. She stared at them from under her umbrella: Cat's hair, swinging in wet black strings around her smiling face, Luke jumping up and down and Martha, her hands over her eyes, trying not to cry. Her small, Gallic shrug said it all. *Crazy English people.*

Cat picked up Luke, and hugged him tight, and she put her arm round her grandmother as they walked along the road.

'Why are you here, Gran?' she said. 'I mean, what made you come?'

'Something Lucy said,' Martha replied. 'I'm not sure I can explain, not yet. Not till I've finished it all.'

The rain thrummed on the pavements, the swollen grey-blue Seine churned below them, the golden spires of Notre-Dame black in the afternoon gloom. 'You don't have to explain.'

'I do. To you, and to Florence, you see. I've got

things all wrong.' Cat tried to speak but Martha said, 'I have to put it right. I was always trying to be in control, you know. I was wrong to try and protect you from the truth all those years. You, and Florence.'

Luke was fiddling with the toggles on his raincoat, twisting them round and round so they spun out in a corkscrew, the tension released. Cat watched him. 'What's it got to do with Florence?'

'I'm going to see her after you, if she'll let me. She's won her court case. I'll tell you then.' She shivered. 'This really is appalling weather. Where's that hot chocolate place, then?'

'Yes, appalling,' Luke agreed, cheerfully. 'Appalling weather!'

'It's just around the corner,' Cat said. She shook her head, water flying everywhere. 'Do you – I should go back and get some of Luke's things, afterwards, shouldn't I?'

'Of course you should, and I'll come with you. You don't need to run away like a thief in the night, you know, Cat. And I would like to see where you spent all this time. I'd like to meet Madame Poulain. Then we will leave, and I promise you won't ever have to go back there.' Martha nodded to herself. 'Right. That's . . . that's you done.' She gave a little shiver. 'And it was easy! Wasn't it?' She looked down. 'Would you like to go home after that, to Winterfold, Luke? Would you like to come and live with me for a bit?'

'Thank you, Baby Jesus and the Holy Mother,' Luke said solemnly, putting his hands together in prayer, and looking up at the sky. 'At least you did listened to me about that, for once.' He pushed open the door of the crowded, cosy café and stood looking at his mother and great-grandmother as they gripped each other's arms, caught somewhere together again between laughter and tears.

FLORENCE

Her sandals slapped loudly on the cold marble as Florence heaved her suitcase up the stairs, sweating silently in the late afternoon heat. She had been away from Italy for nearly two months, and summer had arrived in her absence.

As she unlocked the door a cloud of stale warmth hit her. A pile of post lay scattered on the floor, the printed names on the envelopes leaping out at her: Oxford University, Harvard, BBC, Yale University Press. She was in demand, as they'd all predicted.

Everywhere else a light film of dust sat on the surfaces, on the little wooden table she ate at, on the tumblers by the French windows. Florence dropped her bag on the floor and opened the door to the balcony. A faint breeze blew softly in through the apartment. She ran her hands through her hair, looking out over the rooftops, trying to feel glad to be home. But being back here was curiously mortifying, after the things that had come out about her life in this place over the last couple of months.

The flight had been delayed. She was dirty, and sticky, and tired, that kind of dazed weariness you get from travelling. She made herself a coffee and began to unpack, and as she did the phone rang. She ignored it. Her mobile rang next, as she sorted out her clothes, put on a load of washing, slotted her books back on to the shelves in her study. The phone rang again. She put the papers from the case into a box file and shut the lid, firmly. She didn't ever want to see them again. Sometimes, when she thought about what had come out in that courtroom, she thought she'd sink to the ground, pass out. With the momentum of the case carrying her along, it had been bearable, but in the intervening weeks the memories – the notes, the mug, the strange behaviour, the witness statements – had burrowed into her brain. They haunted her so that it was all she could think about now. Florence had gone to court to stand up for herself, and she'd made herself a laughing stock in the process. Before, she'd been merely mildly risible.

And that was what they wanted, all these people who kept calling and writing to her. They wanted a slice of her notoriety, not her mind, and it wouldn't stop. The hammering in her head about not knowing who she was, what she should be doing: it wouldn't stop.

'All my own work,' she said, as she sat down with her coffee to go through two months worth of post. Three letters from publishers who wanted to 'have a chat' with her about her next project. Two TV companies aside from the BBC who wanted to meet her. Endless letters of support or abuse from strangers, who didn't know her, and she didn't know how they'd found her address. She read them with a weary kind of acceptance: they either wanted to tell her she was great, or that she ought to be ashamed of herself. One of them even said, 'It's women like you who are responsible for the mess we're in today.'

Florence thought about writing him a letter back. A really beautifully crafted, exquisite riposte that would put him in his place so firmly he'd never write another cruel letter to another person again.

But she told herself there was no point.

And then she found his letter. Postcard, really. The Sassetta St Francis, taming the wolf of Gubbio. A very small, dog-like wolf with his paw in St Francis's hand, and a plethora of severed limbs and savaged bodies lying behind him. It was, she knew, one of Jim's favourite paintings.

> Dear Flo
> A little card to welcome you back and to say
> I HOPE YOU BREAK AS MANY OF YOUR MUGS AS YOU DID MINE
> and also
> COME BACK SOON
> because I'm writing this and you've just left

and well – dammit, why not just write it down? I miss you. I really miss you, Flo.
Jim x

She pressed the card to her heart, feeling her pulse racing. Darling, kind, sweet Jim. But as she did she remembered doing exactly the same with Peter's communications, such as they were. She'd overlaid each one with some ridiculous symbolism. In this very room she had done it.

As though she'd conjured his spirit up, as she put Jim's card down she caught sight of Peter's handwriting, black, spidery and difficult, on a small white envelope.

Florence's hands shook as she opened it. She glanced anxiously around, as though she wished someone else might appear, a friendly ghost to battle the demon, alive with her in the apartment.

Dear Florence
I shouldn't be writing this letter I'm sure. Am sure it'll get me into more trouble. I just want to make one thing clear:
I really regret everything I did.
Really regret it.
I regret ruining my career because of you and your second-rate mind. You think you're an expert, but you don't expose yourself to anyone else. How you swung that Courtauld job is a mystery to me, and George. You are not an expert in your field. You are the

worst an academic can be: you're trenchant, and ignorant.

Having sex with you and seeing you déshabillé is one of the great regrets of my life, too. Again, it has cost me a lot, and it wasn't worth it.

I'm writing for two reasons: I will ask you for the final time now that this case is over, please leave me, and Talitha, alone. I think you are a very strange, sad woman with many problems, the greatest of which from my point of view is that you have no concept of real life. I am very sorry I met you, sorrier still that we live in such close proximity. Secondly, that in the light of this unfortunate case, and speaking as a member of the same institute as you, even though it be beyond my jurisdiction as your line manager, I strongly advise you seek psychiatric help.

With many regrets,
Peter Connolly

Florence put the letter down, as though it were very heavy. She frowned, thinking about her last night with Jim at his home in Islington. How she'd looked up from grating the Parmesan while they were making pasta one last time, found his gaze resting on her. His kind grey eyes, his sweet face, long, lean and still handsome, even though he had a few years on him now.

She wished she'd reached over, taken his hand, kissed him. Just once.

She wished he was here. So simple, she could see it now that she was back, but it was almost certainly too late. Florence flapped Peter's letter between her fingers, wondering if she ought to keep it.

Then she saw the bottle of pills again on the wedding chest, and it suddenly seemed as though it would be so easy to do it now. It was simply a gentle idea but it grew, like a breath growing into a gust then a storm, the butterfly effect.

It would be very easy to go now. No one would really miss me. Not really – Pa's dead.

There was a list that she kept running through in her head. *The way I feel, all the time. The court case. Getting up tomorrow and going on. Home. How awful I was to Lucy, to Bill, to Ma . . . Pa is dead. Pa is dead, he's dead and I don't know who I am.*

It was the truth; she didn't. The knowledge of this had been forcing its way to the front of her mind for ages now. Before David's death, really. When the invitation to the party arrived nearly a year ago, now. Maybe even longer ago than that – all her life, perhaps. Florence saw that it had all been building towards this moment, this reckoning, this first night back at home. She bit her tongue, so hard she tasted blood. *Don't think about Pa.* If she thought about Pa properly she'd cry, and if she started crying, she'd never do it.

★   ★   ★

She didn't know how long she stayed there for. It was quiet up on the top floor of the old palace. As the evening came and the sun started to slide over the roofs Florence sat still, not really thinking. The phone rang again; she ignored it. Moths crashed into the glass of the French windows, ambulances raced by. She felt frozen to the spot, only her clicking tongue reminding her she was still breathing.

Eventually, when it was quite dark, Florence stood up, and went over to the chest. She heard her feet clacking on the ground, thought how strange it was. Sound, sensation, taste. How hard would it be, to stop them, to take them away from herself?

She picked up the bottle, and shook a handful of the pills out on to her palm, stared at them. A church bell rang out over towards the river, a loud arrhythmic clanging. She remembered, suddenly, the story of Lorenzo de Medici's doctor, who was so upset after the prince died that he jumped into a well. She smiled, thinking perhaps that was a good way to go. Brave, if nothing else.

The phone rang again. Florence reached down and pulled the cord out of the wall. She stood, staring with surprise at the flex in her hand, the hole where the plaster had crumbled.

'Now,' she said, brushing away a tear.

She looked at the bottle in her hand, properly, for the first time. She read the label. And then Florence looked again, and laughed and laughed.

JOE

It all started because Joe wanted to collect some nettles. To make nettle soup. It was a beautiful May day and he was going mad, cooped up here. He wanted to feel the stretch on his legs and the blue sky above him. Back home he'd be up on the moors first thing on a day like this, feeling the turf underneath him, the sound of his mother's voice still ringing in his ears: 'You be back here before lunch, Joe Thorne, or I'll come fetch thee and then tha'll be sorry!'

'I'm just going up to the woods. I won't be more than an hour.' He hesitated, scrunching the plastic bags together in his hands. 'Do you want to come with me? It's a beautiful day.'

Karen looked up from the sofa where she was reading a magazine, eating some crisps. 'Joe, do I look like I want to come with you?'

'I don't know. I thought perhaps you'd like a walk.'

She gave a short, sharp bark of laughter. 'I'd love a walk, but since going more than a hundred metres makes me feel I've run a marathon I'll pass, thanks.'

'Right. Sorry.'

This only seemed to irritate her more. 'I'm not saying it's your fault. I'm saying I just don't want to go. Don't take it personally.'

'Of course not.' He grinned at her.

But that wasn't true. There were still three weeks till her due date, and a kind of sullen acceptance hung over the room. Lately, whenever they were together Joe had the sense Karen was angry with him, and he didn't know what to do about it. It wasn't like he could tease her into acquiescence, or give her a hug, or massage her feet. They were strangers, he knew it now, living in a tiny flat, bound by four or five nights together.

Sheila had tried to ask him about it, a few weeks ago. 'But this – you two. Everything OK? You all right about it?'

'Of course I am. I'm responsible for that baby.' Joe wanted to tell her to mind her own business.

'No, she is,' Sheila had said, sharply. 'I know you finished it when you found out she was married. I know the truth, my love. So do you. You had no idea who she was when you started it. It might not even be yours, Joe.'

He shrugged. Joe couldn't tell her that the only part of it that made sense was the fact that he knew he had to do the right thing. She was having his baby. A person to hold in his arms, to look after, to help into the world. He was going to do it right, this time. This baby would have a proper dad, they'd see him every day, he'd make it the best packed lunches in the whole country, he'd live next door, so close he could hear if they woke in the night. Maybe it wasn't the most conventional way to bring a child into the world, but they'd make it work.

She shifted on the sofa, not looking at him. Joe saw her purplish, bloated ankles, the yellowing rings under her eyes, saw her hand shift under her back to knead the aching muscles that supported her huge belly. Sympathy flooded through him. He couldn't screw this up, not again.

He put his hand tentatively on her shoulder.

'Go on, Karen. It'll do you good to get out of the house.'

'I'm just worried about bumping into . . . anyone.'

She didn't want to meet Bill, or any of the others, for that matter. That lot.

'I know. But it's going to happen at some point. I'm here, aren't I? Come on, Karen, love. I'll walk slow. It'll help. And I'll run you a bath when we get back and make you your tea. You'll sleep much better and you'll wake up feeling much better. I promise.'

'Oh, Joe. Thank you.' Karen's eyes filled with tears. 'I don't deserve you, I really don't . . .' She gave a big, juddering sigh. 'Sorry.'

'Don't start that up again,' Joe said lightly. He came round towards the sofa. 'Listen. I know it's not ideal, but we're going to make this work, aren't we?'

'Dead right we are.' She swung her legs off the

sofa. 'OK, I'd love to come for a walk with you. Let's go.'

It was the first really warm weekend of the year. As they went slowly up the High Street, the faint smell of blossom and barbecue hung in the air. He sniffed, and she laughed.

'Two nicest smells in the world,' she said. 'I could murder a hamburger right now.'

'I'll make you one, later.'

Karen hesitated. 'That'd be lovely. Thanks, Joe.'

He kept trying to make her things, to feed her up, to give her what she wanted so she'd be happy and he wouldn't have to listen to her stifling her sobs in the bathroom at night, radio right up, water draining. But his first macaroni cheese had truffle oil in it, which made her sick. His passion fruit cheesecake was too 'passion-fruity', she'd said. 'I just like it plain. Sorry, love.' He made her pizza, but she didn't like peppers and thought it was too thin. They'd at least laughed about it then.

He touched her arm, softly. 'Hey, I know you don't like talking about it, but what else do we have to get, do you think?'

'It's OK. I'm on it now. I've even done a spread-sheet.' They both smiled. 'I think we just need a few more babygros and then we're set. Mum's got some stuff back in Formby – she'll bring it down after it's born.' She looked up at him. 'By the way, it is OK if she stays for a while? I mean, the pair of us have no idea what we're doing, have we?'

'Well, with Jamie—' he began, then stopped. 'But yeah, it was probably all completely different.'

She shook her head. 'Of course. I always forget you know all this already. Sorry.'

'I don't mean that, no, it's great if your mum wants to come down.'

Karen stopped in the middle of the street, by the war memorial. She stood up on tiptoe and kissed him on the cheek. 'Oh, Joe. You know, you're a good man. A lovely, good man.'

Her bump was in the way and they laughed, as he twisted around and pecked her cheek back. 'You too. A lovely good woman. You're going to be a great mum.'

She smiled, and sank down on to the bench by the memorial. 'My back's killing me, Joe. I might just stay here for a bit.'

'Joe Thorne!' someone called, and Joe and Karen froze, as though caught in the act of doing something wrong. A little boy was racing towards them. 'Joe Thorne, hello! Hello!'

Joe squinted. 'Luke?'

Luke's hair was long, and crazy from running in the wind. He stood in front of them both, panting. 'Hi! Hi, Karen,' he said, looking at Karen. 'You have a baby in your tummy.'

His inflection was slightly French, and it sounded like a question. 'Yes,' Karen said. 'It's going to come out in a few weeks—' She stopped as she saw Joe's face, and followed his gaze as it traced the two figures who'd appeared in the bend down the hill.

Martha was carrying a string shopping bag containing an open carton of eggs, smeared with muck and straw, and she was telling a story, her hands animated. Beside her walked Cat. She held a bunch of wild flowers, frothing cow parsley, yellow cowslips, bright red campion. She was covered in goose grass, stuck to her blue jumper, in her hair, on her jeans. Martha reached the punchline, knocking her fists together, and Cat threw her head back with a loud, throaty laugh.

Joe stared, transfixed, as the two women caught sight of them and halted by the bench.

'Hello, Joe,' Martha said, politely. 'Karen, my dear. How are you? You look well.'

She had such a graceful way about her, a kind of calmness. He'd seen her in the village lately, face knitted all wrong, mouth pursed, eyes tight with anger, glazed like she wasn't there. Now she looked – looser. Like someone had released the strings that had kept her tight, like a puppet.

'I'm fine thanks,' Karen said politely. 'Not long now . . .' She trailed off awkwardly.

'Yes,' said Joe, staunchly. He could hardly tear his eyes away from Cat, though he knew he had to; it must be obvious to everyone else, mustn't it? This juddering, wild sensation of coming alive at seeing her again. When they'd met at the playground she'd been so pale, so thin, so sad. A bare tree in winter. He'd pushed her firmly from his mind since. How he wanted to fold her into his arms, feed her, take her for long, hearty walks that put the pink back into her cheeks.

He was ashamed of himself, then, and now, for thinking like that. With a huge effort, he shut his eyes briefly, turning to Karen. 'We're very excited,' he said, nodding at her.

'That's wonderful,' Martha said. Her tone was entirely neutral, though she smiled at Karen in a friendly way.

'I heard Florence won her case,' Karen said, resting her hands on her bump. 'That's great. She coming down soon?'

Martha's calm expression clouded momentarily. 'I – I don't know. Her friend Jim says she flew back to Italy yesterday. I need to get hold of her. I keep trying her and she doesn't answer.' She smiled. 'But yes, she won, and we need to get her back here.'

'He sounded like a right berk, that bloke.'

'Yes, indeed, I think he was,' she said, smiling. 'She was awfully brave, wasn't she? It's just like Florence.'

'Florence! Florence!' Luke chanted, then stopped and looked at Karen. 'When are you having the baby?'

'In about three weeks,' said Karen. 'Supposedly.'

'Where's Bill?'

Hastily, Cat stepped forward. 'You look great, Karen.' She kissed her on the cheek and said, frankly, 'Look, I'm sorry I haven't been over yet. I've felt a bit awkward and wasn't sure what the deal was, and whether you'd want to see any of us.'

Karen swallowed. 'Oh – Cat. Thanks. Of course I – it's . . .' she looked nervously at Martha. 'It's difficult, and I can appreciate that – I'm so . . .' Her hand flew to her throat and then she said, 'I didn't know you were back.'

'Been back over a fortnight now,' Cat said. 'We've decided to move in with Gran, haven't we, Luke?'

Luke smiled. 'Yes. We live here now! I don't ever have to see François again. He had smelly feet and he bites people. He bit me, and he bit Josef.'

'Well, but that's not why we left.'

'Why did you leave?' Karen asked politely. 'Quite sudden, wasn't it?'

Cat grimaced. 'When you know you can do something, you have to go for it.' She shrugged, and then smiled again. 'Sounds mad, I know. I sound like a hippy when I start trying to explain it.'

'No, it makes sense,' Karen said slowly. Joe looked at her curiously: Karen was the least likely hippy in the whole world. 'What are you going to do, then? For a job, I mean.'

'No idea.' Cat grimaced. 'I have to find something soon, though. I want to open a nursery garden eventually. Herbs and greens for eating, lavender and roses for oils, that kind of thing. A café, soft play area.' She smiled. 'Anyway, it's a pipe dream, but one day. Gran and I have talked about doing it at Winterfold maybe. I just need to find some work first.'

Martha said: 'I keep telling you, you don't need

to work for a while, Cat. Take a few months, relax, decide what you want to do.'

But Cat replied, firmly, 'I've always worked. I can't leech off you for ever. I couldn't just sit around not doing anything. For Luke's sake. I have to plan.'

He heard himself say, 'There's a job going at the pub, if you've waitress experience.'

'Yes, absolutely.' She looked amazed. 'You serious?'

'We're pretty busy. Yeah. Are you sure? What about the gardening, market stall thing?'

'All in good time. I want to get Luke settled in at school, work out what we do, before I plunge in. Why, do you want advice on a kitchen garden? You should do it, that's my advice.' She put her head on one side, looking at him. 'Joe, this job sounds perfect. Thank you. Should I ring—'

'Yeah, ring Sheila,' Joe said, too loudly. 'But I would like your advice on a kitchen garden too, though. That's our next—'

But he stopped, unable to say more. It was true, but it sounded too neat.

'Look, I'm not going to make it much further,' said Karen. She stood up, leaning on Joe. 'Why don't you two go and find Sheila and talk about it, and I'll go back and have a nap? How's that sound?'

'I can take Luke back, if you like,' said Martha.

Luke jumped up, grabbing Joe's other hand. 'Joe,

we slept in the woods last weekend. Mum and I built a tent.'

'It was awful,' Cat said. 'I didn't sleep a wink. I'd forgotten how sad the owls sound. And there were all these rustling things around us. And bats. Everywhere.' Her lips parted in a big easy smile. 'I love being in the garden more than anything in the world, but I'm not cut out for camping in the woods. Never was. Poor Luke.'

Joe said, 'Hey, Luke – I love camping. I'd go with you.' Karen looked up at him, and he felt himself blushing. *No. You have a son. They don't need you. Karen needs you.* 'I mean – some time. I'd love to.'

'Next weekend? How about next weekend?'

Cat bent down. 'Luke, Joe's going to be very busy because he's having a baby soon. Maybe later this summer he'll take you, or when Jamie's down? Remember Jamie? You could all go together.'

Luke nodded. He smiled at Joe. Joe wanted to cry then, to hug Luke close to him, just to feel his slim frame and small boy smell, to have one small moment when he might just believe it was Jamie he was hugging, Jamie who was here with him. He swallowed, looked up and met Cat's eyes. She was staring at him, squinting in the sunshine, a flush on her cheeks, but she glanced away immediately, pulling another string bag from her pocket.

'We were going to pick some elderflower for cordial but it's too early. Stupid of us – I've forgotten my country ways. Well—' she glanced at Martha – 'if you're sure Gran.'

'Very sure,' said Martha. 'I'll try Florence again. See you later. Good luck!'

'I think it's going to work out very well,' Sheila said. She threw a tea towel over her shoulder. 'I'm so glad you came in, Cat. Honestly. I never knew you had waitress experience.'

'I've done it all,' said Cat, sitting down at the table by the bar. 'Thanks for this.' She took a gulp of the large glass of white wine Sheila had given her. 'There's something truly wicked about drinking for no reason in the afternoon.'

'There's a reason,' said Joe. 'No more Sheila trying to waitress, which is an extremely painful process to watch, I can tell you.'

'Leave it, Joe Thorne. Just you try it.' Cat laughed loudly, and Sheila smiled at her. 'It's lovely to have you back, my dear. I'll leave you two. Let me know when you want to talk about the kitchen garden, Cat. I'd love to think some more about it.' She walked off, almost abruptly, leaving Joe standing beside the table.

Cat gestured. 'Aren't you going to join me? I can't sit here drinking alone.' He glanced at his watch. 'Oh. You've probably got loads to do before dinner service.' She shuffled along the bench. 'I'll leave you to it.'

'No – no.' Joe put his hand on the table. 'I'm good for a while. Please, don't go.' He poured himself a

536

glass from the fridge behind the bar and sat down opposite her. 'Cheers,' he said. 'To new beginnings.'

'In more ways than one,' she said, clinking his glass. 'Good luck with . . . with baby Joe or Karen.'

She tucked her hair behind her ear and then held the glass by the stem, looking into the yellowy-green liquid. It was very quiet in the bar, warm sun streaming as far as the floorboards behind them but not making it all the way to their table, next to the kitchen. He let his gaze rest on her, for a moment. Her thin fingers, short stubby nails, the faint lines around her eyes. She had a few freckles on her nose, he'd never noticed them. He didn't really know her. At all. He cleared his throat.

'We're excited. Both of us.'

'I thought you were an item, you and Karen,' she said, frankly. 'Gran says you're not.'

'Oh. Well – no. She's living with me.'

'Of course.'

'And I'm helping her with the baby.'

'Yes.'

Joe said steadily, 'We're in it together. We'll probably buy the cottage down the road and knock through so I'm next door but I'm there all the time. You know . . . I can pick him or her up from school when she's working late, that sort of thing.'

'That sounds like a very good plan,' said Cat. She nodded, then she smiled. 'You know – oh, I shouldn't say it.'

'Go on,' Joe said, intrigued.

She drank some more wine. 'This is going

straight to my head. Last time I drank a bit too much I ended up kissing you.'

'Well – I liked it,' he said. 'For what it's worth.'

'I did too.' Their eyes met over the wine and they both smiled. 'I just wanted to say . . . I'm sorry I was so rude to you. I thought you were a bit of a sleazebag. And maybe you're not.'

He shrugged. 'I've let so many people down. It's not great.'

'How so? Who?'

Joe shook his head. He didn't want to get into it. 'Never mind.'

He wished he could be the man who said what he was feeling. He looked at her, imagining saying the words. *I'm sorry I dicked you around. I was a total idiot. Karen's gorgeous and funny and we had fun and we really were a comfort to each other, before I found out she was married. I like her. But I like you even more. I like everything about you, your smile, the way you think, the way you frown because you're afraid of all these things. How you are with Luke, with Jamie. How brave you are.*

He wouldn't ever say it, though. He liked making things, but he wasn't good at explaining things. He rubbed his chin and looking straight at her, said, 'I'm not that kind of person. But there's no reason on earth you should believe me, I know that. And with Karen . . .'

Cat leaned across the table. She said, 'Don't take this the wrong way, but I have to do this,' and she kissed him.

CAT

She'd forgotten how good he tasted, how lovely the feel of his mouth on hers was, the connection like memory foam, leaning into him again in exactly the right way.

Across the table, Joe kissed her back, pushing into her, a strange soft sound in his throat, and then just as suddenly pulled away from her. 'What the hell did you do that for?' he said, startled.

Cat shrugged back at him, and twisted her hair up into a ponytail. 'Listen. I just wanted to . . . to wipe the slate clean. That injured pride thing. I've been rude to you. You were stupid to kiss me, but I've kissed you too now. We're not kids.'

'We're not kids? So what the hell, Cat – anyone could have walked in, Karen—'

She interrupted. 'We've both been through some rough times, OK?' She could feel her heart thumping high in her chest, in her throat almost. *Just say it, just get through it.* 'I like you, you like me, the timing isn't right, that's all there is to it.' She nodded, and sat back against the settle. 'OK?'

'OK?' He started laughing, softly, then almost helplessly. 'Cat, you're bloody crazy. That's an insane way to neutralise a situation, can't you see that?'

She shrugged again. 'I have been crazy. I'm not now. Clean slate, like I say.'

He was watching her, still laughing. She said, 'With everything else that happened, it just feels like years ago. I don't want you thinking of me as some victim. Or you feeling bad about what happened with us, carrying this guilt about so we have to shuffle around each other and it's awkward every day at work. Oh, she's damaged goods. Oh, he's a terrible person. Treading on eggshells.'

'Well, that's for me to decide.' He was still looking shell-shocked, and Cat's stomach lurched. 'Like I say, if someone had come in . . .'

'No one cares about your own life as much as you do,' Cat said frankly. 'Most important thing I've learned, over the last few years. It's really just you.' She leaned across the table again. 'You know the thing about men and women? You know what's completely crap about relationships?'

'What?' he said cautiously.

'People start playing roles. All that's bullshit. You and Karen should just do what you want.'

'What do you mean?'

'Before I started going out with Olivier, I was this confident person. I knew how to put up a shelf, how to argue with a gendarme, how to order

540

steak right. And then because of him, because of the way I felt when I was with him . . . how worthless he made me feel . . . I changed. I wasn't that person but I became that person, and he treated me like shit, so everyone else did too. I became shy, pathetic, afraid of everything. Just content to let it happen to me. Anyway . . . all I mean is . . . I wasn't like that to start with. And that's what relationships are about. Good ones, I mean. You have to be flexible. It's not about someone being in charge and someone following, or someone being the star and someone the applause. Gran and Southpaw, they were everything, the whole package. He was better at some things, she was better at other things, but they were both in charge.' Cat smeared the wine glass with her fingers, frowning into it. 'They led from the front, they were a partnership, because they knew what mattered to them, they knew what was important, and they worked everything else around that. Sometimes he was the star, sometimes she was.' She knew he was watching her, but she was too embarrassed now to stop and look at him. 'I've always thought it, that's when bad stuff creeps in, when you start having roles and suddenly you can't break them.' She nodded, and stood up. 'That's all I wanted to say. It's about being flexible. Rolling with the punches. Good times and bad. When I think about Olivier, I don't think there was a day with him I was ever actually myself.'

'That's the same as me and Jemma,' Joe said. 'We were pretty mismatched. I'd been the spotty fat kid a year before, I wasn't in her league. I couldn't believe she went for me.'

'But you weren't with her because she was some stunning model. You liked her, too.'

'I did, but it was more I thought I could look after her. Prove I wasn't a bastard like my dad. Save her from these sleazy blokes who'd treat her badly.' She watched him work his cheek, rough with stubble, with his fingers.

'And where is she now?'

He leaned on the bar, facing her. 'Oh, living with *Ian Sinclair.*'

'Who's Ian Sinclair?'

'He's got everything, hasn't he? He's a lawyer, got a nice pad in York, drives a big Subaru, buys her everything she wants, Jamie's going to private school . . . all of that.' Joe said, 'Her mum's got her own flat now, too; he's bought that for her. He's a wizard.'

'Well, aren't you happy for her? For Jamie?'

'Yes, of course I am,' he said impatiently. 'Of course.'

'And don't you stop to think if she hadn't been with you and had Luke she might have ended up somewhere worse? She might have gone off with one of those blokes, and who knows what might have happened to her?'

'Jemma's pretty tough,' Joe said.

Cat said, 'I was pretty tough, too, when I met

Olivier.' Her mouth was dry. 'You know women often don't have choices. They get sucked into things. My mum left when I was a few weeks old.' She touched his hand to try to make him understand. 'I don't know how she did it, it must have hurt her and I never thought about her, only me. She felt she didn't have any other option and that's awful. We live in a sexist world. We make girls think they'll be rewarded for being decorative, and then they think it's fine when they get treated like crap.'

'Your grandmother never did that to you.'

'Of course she didn't. But I grew up without a mum and a dad.' Cat's voice was soft. 'And it meant I really wanted people to like me, all my life. I wanted my mum to come back and say she loved me and she was going to look after me, and she never did. I think that makes you into someone who's a bit desperate for approval, that's all.' Tears clouded her vision; she blinked them back. Daisy still had the power to overwhelm her, but she knew that power was fading. 'Look, Joe, all I'm saying is, you might have saved Jemma from something worse. You came in and loved her, and you gave her Jamie. You had a son. And Karen . . . she and my uncle were always an odd fit. She was using you a bit, I think? You know?'

'I used her, too,' Joe said. 'It's been strange, living down here. Without Jamie.' He brushed something off his forehead; she saw the spasm of emotion crossing his face. 'I was so lonely. I mean, I was up for it. You can imagine, Karen's pretty determined when she sets her mind to something.'

Cat didn't want to hear about how great Karen was in bed. She didn't want to think about anyone touching Joe, wrapping their arms round him, having him all to themselves. She wanted to stay like this, in this deserted warm room, sun setting, the two of them leaning on the bar, in their own, perfectly sane world.

Already the spell was fading, though. She drained her drink. 'Well, Karen's lucky. Lucky you're such a good guy, Joe. You really are. I'm sure it's going to work out really well.' She pushed the glass to one side. 'Shake on it?'

She was appalled at what a big lie it was. She wanted him to shrug off his responsibilities, right here right now. Say, I want you, Cat. I want you now. I'm leaving Karen to do it by herself, she'll be fine. It's right with you, I know it, you know it too. I'm going to lock the pub door and pull down the blinds and make love to you on the floor, and it's going to be the best sex you've ever had, Catherine Winter. Hair-messing, earth-shaking sex, and then we'll move in with Jamie and Luke and make even more babies and grow plants and cook and love each other every day, in our own place.

She smiled a little to herself, then held out her hand. He shook it, vigorously. 'Thanks so much, Cat,' he said. His smile was ironic. 'It's good to have a friend. I mean it. Thanks for . . . for understanding.'

'Of course,' she said, nodding.

She walked back up to Winterfold feeling flushed with shame and attraction. The shadows were lengthening across the newly green fields. The evening was coming, and the warm breeze soothed her. Dog roses bloomed in the hedgerows, and stalks of Bath asparagus waved softly. She picked a small bunch to take in to work the next day. She imagined Joe's face, the pleasure it would give him to see it, and she smiled. She knew they weren't going to be together. It was fine, she understood why. After everything else that had happened, just to have him in her life as a friend was more than she'd counted on. It was getting better, every day.

Luke and Martha were having tea outside as she walked up the drive. Luke was kicking a ball over to his grandmother, who was alternately dead-heading flowers, drinking from her mug, and pacing up and down. When she heard Cat she turned.

'Darling. So great you're back. Luke, run inside and fetch your mum a mug for tea. And some more cake.'

Luke ran off, and Martha came towards Cat. 'How did it go?'

'It was fine,' said Cat. 'It was . . . good.'

Martha watched her shrewdly. 'He's nice.'

'He's very nice,' said Cat, robustly. 'Isn't it great?'

She noticed her grandmother's expression was drawn. 'Everything all right?'

Martha shook her head. 'I can't get hold of Florence. Neither can Jim,' she said. Her lips were thin. 'She's not answering her mobile and the number at her flat has been disconnected. No one's heard from her.'

FLORENCE

T he day after her return home, Florence slept as though she had been knocked unconscious, and when she was woken by the sound of a car horn and someone shouting in the street below, she felt muzzy. Hungover, like her head was filled with wet sand. She looked around, her bleary eyes taking in the lines of her tiny, nun-like bedroom.

Then she saw the small scratched bottle, full to the neck with tiny little white pills. Remembered the previous night, the inscription on the label.

Martha Winter
Magnesium tablets
Two a day when constipation occurs
Use before 09/12/12
DO NOT EXCEED THE STATED DOSAGE

The poster of a Masaccio exhibition on the opposite wall was faded over the years so that the figures looked like greenish-yellow ghouls.

A pile of typewritten pages splayed across the

cold stone floor; the transcript of the judge's ruling. Florence rolled on to her side, blinking. *'She is one of the foremost experts in her subject in the world and your cynical attempt to exploit that, your arrogance and your sheer deceit is frankly breathtaking.'*

Florence rolled back, sat up slowly, staring cheerfully at the ghouls opposite. 'Good morning,' she said, trying to sound happier than she felt. 'I'm talking to you,' she said to the figure of Adam. 'Yes, you. How rude. Fine, ignore me then.' She sat on the edge of the bed, wiggling her toes and stretching, then got up and made some coffee.

Peter's letter lay, along with the rest of the post, on the wedding chest. It had curled up in the night, as if trying to fold itself back into an oblong. Florence gathered up the post, the letters, the periodicals, the invitations, the prying, all of it except Jim's postcard. She threw the whole pile into the rubbish bin.

'If you could see me now, Professor Connolly,' she said aloud, as she waited for the coffee-maker to bubble, smelling the old, familiar, comforting scents of her home. She glanced at her desk, almost delirious with the thought of losing herself in some work again. 'Yes, I talk to myself. Yes, I'm crazy. And I don't bloody care.'

She didn't have wireless internet in her flat, so Florence had no way of knowing who'd been trying to contact her, which she rather enjoyed, but she knew she had to check her landline and her mobile, which had both rung consistently since she arrived back. Her mobile seemed to be crammed with missed calls, but the only thing she noticed, with a leaping heart, was a text from Jim. Florence took a deep breath, and read it.

Did you get home OK? Rather lonely here without you.

She was feeling so brave, she replied, tapping laboriously with many mistakes and much cursing.

Absolutely. Long dark night of soul but it's over. Thank you for your lovely postcard. I miss you too Jim. Can I come over and stay soon? Will bring new mugs to break.

After she'd sent this message, she was terrified of what she'd done and threw the phone on to the sofa, where it slid down behind the cushions. She couldn't bear to hunt around for it, already certain she'd made a terrible *faux pas*. She felt like a teenager.

The demons of the night before seemed far away now, but she knew enough to know they might come back and this tempered her cheerfulness, for she did feel surprisingly cheerful, considering. Would she laugh at this, one day? How she tried to kill herself with her father's sleeping pills, but accidently snatched her mother's constipation prescription instead? She thought it was maybe symbolic of something: she knew Daisy had killed herself with pills purloined from that same cabinet, but Daisy had taken the right pills, and heroin, too. In short, Daisy had known how to kill herself.

And now Florence, who had felt for the longest time as though the last few months were leading up to that night, that moment alone with these pills and the decision to end her life, was now faced with the question of what came next.

She let her mind drift. Either she changed something, went forward in a different way, or she continued upon the same path and accepted that, at some point, she would go around in a circle, come to this bend in the road again. Florence had trained her brain over the years. She had nourished it, exercised it, treated it with respect. She had to listen to it now, to feel there was some point to the very clear conviction she'd had that last night was the night everything changed. Coming back gave her some clarity of thought. She tried to pin it down, but perhaps the whole couldn't be seen yet and she accepted that too.

'It was the right thing to do,' she said aloud, as she picked up the pages of the transcript and filed them away. 'It was the right thing to do,' she said, as she pinned up Jim's postcard. 'It was the right thing to do,' she said, as she took a deep breath, and reached for the landline, to call her mother, before remembering she'd pulled the phone cord away from the wall.

She tried to plug the socket back in, but it

wouldn't work. So she hunted around down the back of the sofa, and pulled her mobile out from deep inside the frame. In addition to Jim's text, there were two voicemails from Martha. Florence kneeled on the sofa, the frame creaking underneath her, and listened intently to the last one.

'Listen, Flo – please call me? I don't know where you are. *Are* you back in Italy? Your phone doesn't seem to work. Darling, please call me. I'm – Cat's here. She's back. I need to talk to you. I need to tell you something and we need to talk. I want to see you. Call me back, sweetheart.'

Florence looked at the postcard on the wall. She took a deep breath. She felt as though she were staring out of the plane, parachute on her back. She said softly to herself: 'Yes.'

She made another coffee and rang her mother.

'Hello?'

'Hello? Who's that?'

'It's me, Ma. Flo.'

'Florence!' Martha's voice was joyous with relief. 'Oh, my goodness, darling, how are you? I've been . . . I've been trying to get hold of you. I was getting rather worried.'

'Worried?'

'Oh, I had a . . . a silly feeling.' Her mother laughed. 'It's silly.'

Florence said slowly. 'Oh. I'm back now. Got in last night.'

'Ah. How are you?'

'I'm good,' Florence looked at the bottle of pills

and smiled to herself. 'I'm really well. How – how are you?'

'Yes. I'm really well too. Flo—'

She interrupted, suddenly terrified of what came next. 'Ma, I was just ringing to say I forgot something when I was last over. My old notes on Filippo Lippi, I need them for an article I'm supposed to be writing.'

'Well, tell me where they are and I can post them for you.'

'They're in Dad's – the study. With all my other papers, on the shelf below the encyclopaedias. It's a cloth folder, kind of red and black.'

She could hear her mother walking through the house. 'Fine, well, then. I see it. So you want me to send them to you?'

'Yes please, Ma.'

'Grand.'

There was a pause. Small, expectant pause.

'And – I wanted to say something too.'

'You do? Oh – well, I – OK. You go first.'

Florence blundered on. 'I'm sorry about how I was when I was over. The court case and everything else. It made me rather lose the plot for a while. I've been very unhappy. Very selfish. I wasn't . . . Anyway, I am sorry.'

'You're sorry?' Her mother laughed. Florence stiffened. She wondered if she should just put the phone down, but then Martha's voice softened. 'You're not the one who should be sorry.'

'Oh.'

'Darling Flo, this is ridiculous . . . When are you coming back? I really would like to see you. Talk to you properly. Just us two.'

With one finger, Florence slowly pushed the pill bottle across the kitchen countertop. 'I'm not sure – I've just got back here. I can't leave for a while, there's various things . . . Probably August?'

'Right.' Martha's voice sank.

'Ma, do you need me to come back?'

'No. Yes.'

'What's going on? Are you OK?'

'I'm absolutely fine. I need to tell you something.' Martha gave a small sigh. 'It's about you, Flo, darling. Something you need to know.'

Florence stepped out of the sunny kitchen, into the darkness of the large sitting room, her heart beating like a drum. She put her hand on the bureau, to steady herself, glad that she was alone and no one could see her face. She had been waiting for this moment for most of her life, since she was ten in fact, and now it was here she didn't want it to happen.

'I know,' she said.

'You know what?' Martha's voice was close to the receiver.

'I've always known, Ma.' The word fell heavy out of her mouth. 'I know I'm not your child. I know my mother left me on the street and you adopted me from some orphanage. Daisy told me, Ma. After Wilbur died, and she got really nasty. She used to whisper it in my ear at night.'

There was silence but for one small sob.

'Ma?' she said, tentatively, after a long pause.

Eventually her mother said, 'Oh. It's not even ten in the morning.'

'What?'

'I'm sorry. I don't know what to say. That's . . . that's awful, sweetheart. Is that really what she told you?'

'Well, yeah, Ma. You never believed me when I'd tell you about her, so – so I stopped after a while.'

'Oh, Daisy.' Martha's voice was low. 'Florence, sweetheart . . . You're not from some orphanage. You're Pa's niece. His sister was your mother – she, she was only nineteen.'

Below her, a car trundled too fast down the narrow street; someone cursed, a dog barked, backing out of its way. Florence sat very still.

Eventually, she said: 'I – I'm Pa's – I am his . . . his niece?'

'His niece, you were always part of him, oh darling, yes of course.'

'His sister?' Florence turned around, slowly, kept turning. 'She was my – my mother?'

'Times were different then, she was engaged to someone else. She – we agreed – we wanted to take you. You became ours.'

Florence had stopped revolving. She stood with her hand over her face, eyes covered, as though terrified of what she might see. 'Why didn't you tell me?'

Martha's voice was hoarse. 'Cassie begged us not to tell anyone. Your father promised her. They had an awful childhood and – I can't explain it all now. Oh, Daisy. What did you do?' Martha gave a sob. 'Daisy lied, darling. I don't know how she found out but she must have heard us talking – you know what she was like.'

'I do, Ma,' Florence said.

'Well, she was wrong, it's not true. You're not Daddy's daughter, you're his niece, but – oh, you were the one he really loved. My angel. That's what he used to call you.'

'Who was – the father?' She didn't want to say 'my father'.

'I don't know. A music teacher. Older than her. He did a bunk, but I'm sure we can find out, I don't want you to – oh dear! Oh goodness.' And Martha started to laugh, a weak, silvery rattle. 'This is all wrong. Get you and Cat back, that's what I wanted to do. I wanted to do this face to face, not for you to find out like this.' She took a deep breath. 'Telling you over the phone. It's just not right.'

'I knew all along, Ma.'

'And you knew all along.' Martha was breathing hard. 'I'm sorry. I think I'm going mad.'

'Where is she?' Florence said, trying not to sound as scared as she felt.

'Who?'

'My – my real mother.'

'Your – Cassie. Cassie, of course. I – oh, love. I don't know. We hadn't seen her for years.'

'Really?'

'Yes.' Martha wrung her hands. 'I wish – I've just started going through the study, all your father's papers. There must be something there. Last thing I heard she was in Walthamstow.'

'When was that?'

There was a pause. 'Twenty years ago.'

Florence bowed her head. 'Didn't Pa ever—'

'I called her number, darling. She doesn't live there any more. I . . . but we'll see, OK? We'll find her. Cassie Doolan. But she was married, and I don't know her husband's name. I'm sure she'd have changed her name. But, darling, she didn't want to stay in touch. She was quite adamant about that to your father.'

'Really?'

'Yes. I'm so sorry. But we'll start looking for her. We will find her.'

'Ma, I need to think about it all. Take it all in.'

'Of course, darling.'

The sound of nothing, crackling over the phone line. Florence imagined the cables running under the sea, through the land, carrying this weight of silence between them, and still she didn't know what came next, and then Martha cleared her throat.

'Right. That's enough time. Flo, darling, can I come and see you? I'll be there by teatime. Would that work?'

She picked at the worn wicker chair. 'Ma – I think you're getting confused. I'm in Florence. I'll come and see you soon. I will, I promise.'

The voice down the line was amused. 'I know

where you are, darling. I haven't lost my marbles. I want to come and see you.'

'What? Come today? Ma, you can't just jump on a plane and . . .' Florence trailed off. Why couldn't she?

'I've been looking at flights with Cat. They had availability this morning, there's a flight in a little while leaving from Bristol. I wanted to sit opposite you, tell you all this in a sound and sane way. Look you in the eye, my darling.'

'But that doesn't mean you have to . . .' Florence looked around. Her mother, here? 'It's so far.'

Martha broke in. 'No, it's not. I'll see you later. Yes. I'll be with you for a drink this evening. Gin and tonic. Make sure—'

'Of course, Ma. Lime. Of course, who do you think I am?' Florence smiled, her throat tight.

'I know who you are, my darling. Right, then.' Martha sounded crisp, efficient, as though this was completely normal. 'I have your address, and I'll get Bill to call you with my flight details. I'm perfectly capable of getting a cab from the airport. You have that drink ready. Goodbye, my sweet girl. I'll see you soon.' And with that, the phone went dead, leaving Florence staring, open-mouthed, into her receiver.

KAREN

May 2013

The pain started in the morning, right after she booked the taxi. But she'd had these pains before, the midwife had said it was false labour. So she carried on packing. It didn't take long – she knew what she needed. The list said nighties, but who wore those these days? She had her Juicy tracksuits, three pairs, loads of vest tops, Uggs, flip-flops, breast pads, nursing bras and that was basically it. Some knickers. Her iPad loaded with seasons two and three of *Modern Family*. And some growys, nappies, vests, a very, very small hat, and some socks that made her want to cry when she looked at them, they were so tiny. All the rest of that beautiful new gear for the baby, it could be sent on to her mum's, or Joe could keep it, if he needed it. Whenever that might be.

Karen wasn't a stubborn woman, she was just determined. She was used to knowing what she wanted in life and going for it. Men got rewarded for being bold, women didn't. She knew that and sometimes it meant she had to step back and restrategise. But on this day of all days, things had to go exactly the way she wanted.

Joe had left early that morning, thinking everything was normal.

'Bye, Karen. See you later,' he'd said, halfway out of the kitchen, mind already on the restaurant and the day ahead. Then he'd turned and faced her. 'You all right? Yeah?'

'I'm grand.' She'd looked at him. 'Thanks, Joe. Thanks a lot.'

'OK.' He'd smiled, sort of uncertain, like he didn't know what that meant. 'Call me if you need anything, won't you?'

She'd waited till she heard the door slam, then pulled the little suitcase out from under the bed and, moving slowly as a hippo, she packed the last of her meagre possessions. She left out *Project Management for Dummies,* then put it back in. It had been a present from Bill. Sort of a joke, really, because he knew how much she loved business books. How much she loved planning, getting it right. Three pages of that and she was calm again. 'Like a hit from a bong,' he'd say.

Part IV: Steering the Ship: Managing Your Project to Success. She'd been planning for a while, really, ever since they'd met Cat in the lane that day. Did they know it, each of them? They must do. Something had happened with them, something before that. He'd run over her kid; it was hardly a rosy start, was it?

She'd asked him about Cat that evening, and Joe had said, 'Yeah, she's great, isn't she? Really glad she came back.'

Karen knew when people were hiding their feelings. She wasn't stupid. And Joe wasn't. She was stumped. She bumped into Cat the following week on the green.

'Joe? He's brilliant. I'm so glad it's all working out,' Cat had said, happily, and Karen had scanned her expression, searching for cracks in her demeanour, but she could see none.

Suddenly she had felt sick, like she'd throw up there and then. She blinked, and lurched forwards, and Cat had caught her, and Karen had to excuse herself. *I'm tired. Blood sugar low. I think I'd better get back.* Moving slowly back to the flat above the pub, she chewed her nails. Now, now she knew this was all wrong, this brotherly living arrangement with Joe – all wrong. She knew what she wanted, but it was too late.

How could she leave Joe, when he'd done so much for her, when he was so excited about this baby? When it was almost certainly his kid? Karen knew she was cornered. She had no idea what to do, and the one thing she knew was, you didn't start making major life alterations with a tiny baby on board. Unless you were Daisy, and she was no role model. Time was running out. Then the next week, in the pub, Karen saw something magical. She saw a tea towel being thrown.

She was sitting in a window seat, in the snug,

having a blackcurrant and soda, and wondering whether this would be the highlight of her post-baby social life, when a tea towel sailed through the air towards her. She turned, and saw as though in slow motion, Joe's hands raised as he threw it, Cat catching it and hugging it to her, eyes shining, that wide mouth with its huge smile.

'You're a rubbish thrower, Joe Thorne,' she said. 'I can see why you got kicked off the cricket team. Jamie's better than that.'

'You have the co-ordination of a day-old lamb, Cat Winter. Your legs wobble. And your arms look like a faulty windmill.' Cat's mouth dropped open, in outrage. 'It's true. You're a crap fielder, now get back to work.'

It wasn't even so much that they were flirting. She really didn't think anything was going on between them – it was just that they were completely happy, totally absorbed in each other's company.

Two days later she'd walked into the post office to see them there together at the counter, picking out seeds from a catalogue. Their heads were bent over the pictures, talking intently about this variety of thyme versus was there room for sorrel – who ate sorrel, she'd thought. What the hell even *was* sorrel?

Feeling like Miss Marple, cracking the village mystery, Karen had cleared her throat, and they'd turned round to apologise for being in the way, and seen her.

'Hello!' Cat had said, beaming. 'Wow, that kaftan

561

is great. Wish I'd been that stylish when I was pregnant.'

'Oh, hello, Karen love,' Joe had come over to her. 'Everything all right?'

'Fine, fine, I just saw you two in here and thought I'd come in . . .' She'd nodded coldly at Susan. Susan shifted behind the counter, awkwardly.

Suddenly Karen wanted to be on the sofa, under a blanket, crying her eyes out. She told herself it was the hormones. She felt completely surplus to requirements. 'I'll be off then. I don't want to stand around too long.'

'See you later,' Joe had said. 'I'll – get you what you want for tea, yes? Cat, I'd like to try some of those verbena plants. It may be the wrong time to get them, though.'

'I think they can be the first thing we put in the greenhouse, if we ever get round to building it.' She laughed. 'I'm sure it'll collapse at the first gust of autumnal wind. Susan, do you think Len would help us? He built that greenhouse up at Stoke House, didn't he?'

'Oh, he did, a girt big one. They're ever so pleased with it.'

'Well, maybe that's it.' Cat leaned on the counter. 'I might go over and ask him later. Then you can grow marrows and suchlike to your heart's content, Joe.' She turned to Karen. 'And the baby can eat all home-grown food. It'll be wonderful. A girt big greenhouse!'

Oh God, home-grown marrows. I hate marrows. And

I'm not going to be one of those mums who spends her time puréeing foods. That's what supermarkets are for, aren't they, convenience?

But she smiled at Cat, unable to resist her infectious, happy enthusiasm. 'Grow some bacon butties, Cat, my love, and I'll help you dig them up.'

'Deal,' Cat nodded, as Joe tapped her on the arm.

'The verbena, Cat. What about it? I'd like to try flavouring something like a lamb stew with it. Very delicately, see if it takes.'

She shrugged, smiling at him, and Karen felt a bit sick again.

'Yes, you're right. Let's do it.'

'OK.' He scribbled on the form.

He didn't even look at Cat when he was talking to her, the way he carefully, solicitously, nervously stared at Karen when asking her how she was or what she wanted, like she was a Chinese firework with indecipherable instructions and might suddenly explode. Karen left the silly little village shop, the flimsy door banging behind her, the jaunty bell drilling into her tired head.

Karen didn't know lots of things. She didn't know if Joe knew he was in love with Cat. Or if Cat knew either. She didn't know, if she went back home, where she'd end up having this baby – she assumed she'd have to go up to the hospital at Southport. She didn't know what she'd do afterwards, or how she'd care for the baby on her own. She didn't know if Bill would ever want to speak to her again, and whether it was worth trying. She was pretty certain the answer to that was no. She wanted him to fight for her. He wanted to let her go. She didn't know why, and she didn't know how to ask him, any more. Even as the days seemed longer and longer, and she thought of more and more things she wanted to say to him.

I thought we couldn't have kids.

I thought you didn't love me any more.

I'm so, so sorry about your dad, I loved him too.

She was certain of two things: one, she wasn't in love with Joe, nor he with her, and it wasn't fair, any more. He'd been good to her, and it was time she grew up and took responsibility.

Two, she had to get out of here, and set them both free because he was never going to do it. If she didn't go now when there was just one of her, she'd be trapped here until they made other plans, sitting upstairs above the pub with a screaming baby night after night listening to the noise of happiness, of life going on below her. It was time to leave.

The pain got worse as Karen rang the cab company again.

'Could you tell the driver I'll need a hand with the bag? And—'

She gave a strangled cry and bent over the bed, breathing hard and trying to moan into the pillow, sweat running down her forehead into her hair.

'Ma'am? Are you all right, ma'am?'

'Yes. I'm pre – aaah.'

Karen rested the phone on the duvet. She took a deep breath, trying to calm herself. This couldn't be it; there was no other sign, nothing. It had come on so suddenly, and she wasn't due for another two weeks, no matter what they'd said at the scan about her due date being earlier than she reckoned. She knew the last time she and Joe had slept together, of course she did. It was false labour, she'd had it for days now. She looked at her watch.

'Ma'am? The cab driver is just outside now.'

It was do, or die. She had a few minutes to get downstairs in case it started again, and she wanted to be in plenty of time for her train. Karen gritted her teeth. 'Thank you,' she said, and she put the phone down.

In the centre of the coffee table she carefully placed the note she'd written. She'd spent days composing it in her head, setting down carefully and concisely the reason for her departure, and then, at the last minute, writing it out this morning, had suddenly scrawled at the bottom:

> PS. I think you're in love with Cat. I don't know if you realise it but you ought to do something about it. She's in love with you, too. I want you to be happy, Joe. X

She eventually got herself downstairs, and as she appeared in the bright sunshine the cab driver stared at her. Karen realised she must look a sight. Her hair was tied up on top of her head, her shapeless brown maxi-dress looked like potato sacking, and she was bright red, sweating, mascara running down her cheeks. But she straightened herself up and smiled at him. 'Thanks. We're going to Bristol Parkway. I need to catch a twelve p.m. train.' And she buried her head in her handbag, leaning over the seat to check she'd got everything, buying herself a few seconds' time to stop panting.

'I don't know, ma'am,' the taxi driver said, doubtfully. 'I don't know if you should be travelling. I heard you screaming upstairs – are you – in some kind of trouble?'

Karen faced him, hoping that one day, when this was all a long way in the past, she'd be able to look back and laugh at that moment. *In some kind of trouble.* 'I'm fine,' she said firmly, shielding her eyes from the sun. 'I just need—' she stopped. 'I just need you to take me to the station.'

'Are you going to have the baby?'

'At some point, love,' she said in her sharpest voice. 'That's why I don't want to stand around chatting. OK? My bag's upstairs, could you be very kind and fetch it for me?'

He disappeared upstairs and reappeared with her suitcase but it was all done with a bad grace. Heaving it into the car, and staring at her again, he said,

'Look, I need to call the office again. 'Cause I don't think we're insured – health and safety . . .' he said vaguely.

Karen closed her eyes, trying to stay calm, trying not to burst into tears. 'Listen. I booked you and asked you to take me on a job. Are you going to do it or not?'

'I'll take you,' said a cool, quiet voice behind her, and Karen froze, as though caught in the act. 'I'll take you, Karen,' and she turned round, and there was Bill.

Slowly, Karen stood up straight.

'Hello,' he said.

'Bill. Hi.'

He patted the back of his neck, awkwardly. 'How are you?'

Karen swallowed. 'I'm – not too good. This idiot won't take me to the station.'

'How strange.' He was eating an apple, and he wrapped it carefully up in a paper napkin – it was a very Bill gesture, and the calm familiarity made her head spin. 'Where do you want to go?'

'Bristol Parkway,' she said, trying not to sound panicked. 'I just want to go home.'

She hadn't seen him for weeks. He'd kept himself to himself and she heard he'd been away too, to join his mother visiting Florence in Italy, the trip he was always trying to get her to take. He was tanned, and smiling slightly. Karen stared at him, as though he were a long cold drink, something icy and sweet.

The cab driver had got off the phone with his head office. He jammed his hands awkwardly on his hips. 'Listen, my love. I can't take you. Insurance won't cover it. Sorry.'

'Hey . . .' Karen looked wildly around her, at the quiet High Street, baking in the late morning heat. 'But I need to go now!'

Bill said again, 'I'll take you.'

'Don't joke with me,' she said, almost crying. She pulled her suitcase out of the back, so swiftly Bill didn't have time to get it, and she nearly hit him with it as he leaped forward to try to take its bulk. The car engine revved and she stepped back, exhausted.

'Screw you! You jerk!' she shouted at the taxi driver, as he sped away, tyres screeching. He beeped his horn, aggressively and long, as he passed out of the village and up the hill, and Karen turned to Bill. 'Look,' she said, brokenly. 'I'm going home to Mum. I have to get there, soon. Otherwise . . .' She paused, wincing.

'Otherwise you're going to have the baby in the street,' Bill said.

'It's not that,' Karen said. 'It's not coming just yet.'

'I wouldn't be too sure of that,' he said.

'How the hell do you know?'

'Well . . . I'm a doctor. I do know some things, Karen.' His arm tightened gently on hers. 'Look, come ho— Come back to New Cottages.'

'No, Bill!' she said, raising her voice. 'I'm not coming back with you! I'm not!'

An old man, passing slowly on the other side of the narrow street, looked over curiously, then stared straight ahead.

'I'm not trying to kidnap you. I just mean so that you can sit down, have some ice. I'll check you over and we'll see what to do next. OK?'

He held out his arm. Karen stared at the pub, at the long, narrow stairs leading up to the flat. Maybe she should go back up there again, plonk herself down on the sofa for the rest of the day and wait for Joe to finish work this evening, then act like none of this had happened.

She couldn't. No matter how mad it seemed, now she had decided upon this course of action, she had to keep moving. 'I'm leaving Joe,' she said, taking Bill's arm, and they set off, Bill pulling her suitcase. 'I know this isn't the best way to have this conversation but it's not going to work out, us living together like that.'

She didn't know what he'd say to this and she supposed he had the right to say anything, but he stopped and said mildly, 'Well, good that you realised it now, I suppose. What does he think?'

Karen ignored this. 'I think it's best if I go back to Mum's. Then see what's what.'

'Right,' Bill said. 'That seems sane.'

'Don't make fun of me,' she said quietly. A tear rolled down her cheek.

Bill stopped pulling her case. He stood in front of her on the narrow pavement, and wiped the trembling tear away with one finger and said, softly, 'I'd never do that, Karen. I'm sure you've made the right decision. You always were good at rational thinking. Most of the time. Keep walking.'

She remembered why she'd liked him so much at the start – that he'd never been threatened by her, where so many men were. That she could work out the tip on a bill faster, could drive better, drink more, strategise better. That first year they'd been dating he'd bought her *The 7 Habits of Highly Effective People* and read it out to her on holiday in the Seychelles while she sunbathed with the dedication of a pro.

And she remembered too how much they had both loved her tanned, glowing body, slick with cream, and the hot, lazy afternoons with cool wind blowing in through the room as they made love for hours, both as surprised as each other by how close, how good it felt to be together, how right it was. His kind, steady gaze on her, his huge smile that broke over him after they'd finished, his boyishness. He really was a little boy in so many ways, pretending to be old and grown-up, but really wanting approval, wanting to make people feel better.

He'd asked her to marry him in Bristol, at the top of the Cabot Tower, overlooking the whole of the city. And afterwards they'd walked down past a playground, and he'd sat on a swing while she'd fastened her shoe, and seen him there, clutching the cold chains of the swing, feet scuffing the ground, watching her with this look in his eyes, so happy and smiling and warm, swaying gently back and forwards. So hopeful. So glad.

Karen blushed, pushing the thoughts away. 'So, how have you been, Bill?' she said, as they progressed slowly up the street, Bill carrying her small case.

'I'm well, thanks. Been busy.'

'How was Italy? You were there, weren't you?' She leaned on him, grateful for the strength of his right arm.

'Yes, four days. It was great, actually. Didn't do very much, just pottered around. Flo's flat is wonderful.'

'Is she glad about the court case?' Karen asked.

'Oh, she's much more pleased than she lets on. Some TV producers want to make a pilot with her. Don't you think she'd be wonderful on TV?' Bill smiled. 'I can just see her, waving her arms around in front of some painting.'

One foot in front of the other, slowly and surely. Already Karen felt calmer. 'Yes,' she said. 'She'd be absolutely great.' She added, 'Good for Florence. I'm so happy for her.'

'Me – me too. We've just worked out Skype, you know. It's great. She's coming back for a visit in August and Ma's already worked up about it.'

'Is she? Why?'

Bill hesitated. 'Long story. Daisy . . . you know. Dad . . . all of it.' He looked at her, and a sweetly sad look came into his eyes. 'Some other time.'

She didn't have the right to hear any more about his family, about Winterfold, she knew. 'I think Flo pretends to like being alone, but she doesn't, not really.' He stopped. 'I don't think anyone does.'

They were silent for a few minutes. As they passed the church Bill cleared his throat, delicately.

'So, does Joe know you've left him?'

'No.'

'Shouldn't you tell him?'

'I've left him a note.'

They were back at their old home. 'I'm sure you're right, Karen. But I don't know why you have to leave today, this very minute.' Bill opened the door and she went in, grateful for the front room that had always seemed so poky, and was now welcomingly cool, and fresh.

She heaved herself on to the sofa. 'I have to get to Mum's before the baby's born. Otherwise I'd have been there – be trapped there, above that pub. I wouldn't have been able to get away.'

Bill stood in front of her, chewing a finger, and he said, quietly, 'Of course you would. Do you really think that?'

'Yes,' she said, sharply. 'Look, Bill, thank you, but can you just get me a glass of water and the keys and we'll go. Oh. *Oh* . . .'

She turned on the sofa, sliding herself slowly on to the ground until she was on all fours, eyes squinting, trying to focus on the shelves, counting anything she could in an effort not to scream at the splitting pain that seemed to twist her in two. She didn't care where Bill was, whether he was watching her. It seemed to last for an age, and when it was over, she sat back on the sofa again, light-headed, pale, legs sticking out in front of her like a child.

Bill put a glass of water in front of her, on the cool glass table.

'Karen, will you let me examine you?'

'What?' she blinked. 'No! No way.'

He grinned. 'Why do I keep having to remind you that I'm a doctor, Karen? You were always complaining about me working too hard, you'd think you'd remember why I wasn't around.'

'I don't care. You're not . . .' She stifled a moan of pain.

'Oh, my love.' He looked at her with concern. 'I really do think you're in labour, you know. I've seen plenty of contractions in my time. That was a contraction. Have your waters broken?'

She shook her head, miserably. 'No. It's all fine. I just need you to—' But her voice cracked into a whisper.

He crouched down in front of her. 'I'll take you there.'

'To Mum's?'

'No. To the hospital. Here. The RUH. And after that, I'll drive you to your mum's. Promise. If that's what you want, I'll pack up your stuff, I'll collect you and the baby and drive you over. It's two hours, three hours. Please, don't keep worrying about that.'

'Why would you do that?'

'You're my wife, Karen,' he said, and there was a catch in his voice.

'You mean because this is your kid according to the law.' Karen buried her head in her hands.

Bill shrugged. 'No, because we're not divorced yet and I promised to love and protect you. That's why.' Karen looked up, and thought she'd never realised before how much he looked like his father. 'I still love you. Don't worry, it's not a big deal, I'll get over it at some point. But I want to look after you because you need some help and you're – you're having a baby. It's a wonderful thing, whatever the circumstances.' He picked up his car keys. 'Will you trust me?'

'Why are you doing this?' She wiped the clammy nape of her neck.

'Because . . . well, what I just said.'

'Oh.'

'And because I – I didn't do enough when we were together. I was too . . . too stiff. Not enough like my dad, you know.' He rolled up his sleeves. 'But don't let's think about that now. You've got enough on your plate.'

'That's nice of you, Bill.' She wanted to tell him how sorry she was. How she'd got them all wrong, called them snobs, and she was the snob. How much she wished she could be a part of it all again, only – she shook her head, waiting for the next wave of pain.

'Come on, then,' he said.

'Just give me a minute. Let me sit still, for just a moment.'

He smiled, and sat down next to her. 'You know,' he said, conversationally. 'I've been thinking of moving back to Bristol anyway,' he said. 'I always liked it there.'

'I like Bristol too . . .'

She thought afterwards she'd heard a soft, high *pop*, but she must have been mistaken. But suddenly there was water everywhere, gushing on to the floor, coming out of her like a torrent. She rubbed her tired eyes, tried to stand up. 'Look, oh! Oh, no, I'm so sorry. Oh God. I've peed all over the sofa. Oh my God! Oh my flaming God!'

Bill looked down. 'No. But now your waters have broken. I told you you were in labour. Let's go.'

She sat still for a moment. 'The sofa's ruined! I loved this sofa!'

'I hated it,' he said.

Karen glanced away from her stomach. 'What? We bought it at the leather workshop sale! You said you loved that colour.'

'It's slippery, and it doesn't fit in here. Nothing really fits in here.' Bill put his jacket on, and jangled his keys in his pocket. 'Come on then,' he said calmly. 'I'm making no promises but I'd say you'll be a mum by teatime.'

'Bill . . .' Karen looked down at the mess of her waters, the immaculate sofa and floor awash in sticky gloop. 'Thanks.'

She wanted to say more, she wanted to tell him how he'd broken her heart, slowly driven her away, how she'd loved him so much. But of course she couldn't, not right now. 'I – I never meant to hurt you,' she said, and then she smiled. 'You know? That's crap. I did want to hurt you. I wanted you to notice me.'

He was bending over to pick up her bag and at that, he straightened up, his expression tight. He said, in a small voice, 'I always noticed you.'

'You didn't, Bill. I'm sorry. I'm so sorry, but you nearly sent me mad. You did!' She was laughing, through her tears.

'Oh.' Bill swallowed. He closed his eyes briefly, as if in pain, and nodded. 'I expect I did. I got used to doing my own thing when I was growing up, as Lucy keeps pointing out to me. I had to. I've changed, anyway. Hope so.'

She put her hand on his arm. 'Bill. I shouldn't have said it, now's not the time, let's—'

'It's the perfect time.' His sad, sweet face broke into a smile. 'Karen, come on, stand up, otherwise I'll carry you to the hospital myself and very likely you'll have to give birth in a hedge. I won't leave you. Let's worry about the rest of it all later. Deal?'

'Deal,' Karen said. They nodded, smiling at one another, and then Bill heaved her to her feet, and slung her bag over his shoulder, and they left the house, shutting the door on the ruined sofa, the immaculate front room and the plastic gerberas, the home that never quite worked for them.

CAT

July 2013

'I think a surprise party's a terrible idea,' said Cat, finishing her coffee. 'Isn't it a bit much, having a party that says basically "We love you even though it turns out you're adopted and you don't know where your mother or father are"?'

'No!' said Lucy, outraged. 'Cat, where's your sense of soul?' She leaned across the kitchen table, and pulled the butter dish towards her. 'Listen, it'll be great.' She began vigorously buttering her toast. 'A welcome home party, you know? A big banner and everything. For you, and Luke, too. Dad can come, with Bella and Karen. Everyone together.'

'What would it say? "Welcome Home, Everyone"?' Cat said, trying not to laugh at Lucy's enthusiasm. '"Again."'

'Exactly.' Lucy looked at her. 'Oh, you're taking the piss.'

'I'm just not sure . . . does Florence want a big banner saying hi you're adopted? What about Karen?'

'Hmm,' said Lucy. 'Karen doesn't notice anything these days other than Bella.'

Cat knew from Facebook that two-month-old Bella Winter (she had Bill's name, and Bill was certainly featured prominently in all the photos) was a gorgeous little thing, although according to Lucy she didn't sleep and was already showing signs of taking after her mother, in that she was extremely determined and spent a lot of time when her eyes were open glowering at you.

'I bet your dad doesn't mind.'

'He doesn't, actually. You know Dad. But—' Lucy lowered her voice – 'they're doing a paternity test.'

'Really?'

'He's said he has to know if she's his or not. I don't think he'll mind if she's not his. I mean . . .' They looked at each other. 'Ugh, well, let's not get into the merits of my father's . . . reproductive stuff versus Joe Thorne's. It doesn't bear thinking about. Oh! Completely ick. Let's move on. So I thought a nice welcome back home party for Florence and at the same time we can all say hi Bella, et cetera.' Cat put her head on one side. Lucy said, 'Well, I like it. Maybe we make it a christening party instead. I'm going to suggest it to Gran when she gets back from London.'

'How long's she there for?'

Lucy shrugged. 'She said two days. She has to approve the exhibition, she said. I don't believe her, though.'

'What do you mean?'

'Don't know. Sure it's nothing serious. She's so different now.'

'Yes, she is,' said Cat. 'Even from before, when Southpaw was alive. It's strange, isn't it? I can't think of the word.'

'So . . .' Lucy buttered her toast, and gazed out of the window, '. . . light-hearted. That's what it is. Poor Gran.' They were both silent, and then she said, 'Look how lovely it is outside. I think it was a great idea of mine, having a staycation here.'

'Brilliant,' Cat said. 'Oh, Luce, it's lovely to see you again.'

She dipped the last of her bread into her coffee, to hide the tears that sprang to her eyes. Everything made her cry these days, these last few months. As if she was making up for the years of control. She cried at the news, at a dead bunny rabbit by the road. She cried when the teacher at Luke's new nursery said he was a 'sweet kind boy'.

'Me too, Cat. Do you miss anything about Paris?' Lucy said, thoughtfully, chewing her toast.

'Proper croissants. And Petit Marseillais shower gel. That's it.' She hesitated. 'Not really. I do miss it I suppose. I miss – something in the air. The feeling of walking through the streets first thing in the morning, there's something about it that's magical, you could sense it, even on the worst days.'

Lucy said, 'Well, we should go back there, some

day. I'd love to go to Paris properly. You could show me the sights.'

Even though she was younger, Lucy always knew what to do, always had since they were little. There was such comfort in that. 'That'd be a great idea, actually. I don't want Luke to forget that part of his life.' Cat hesitated, her mouth suddenly dry. 'I want him to remember he's half-French, even if he never sees Olivier again.' It was the first time she'd said his name in a long time, and it surprised her, how little weight it carried. She was strong now.

She glanced into the window and smiled. The two cousins sat opposite each other, in the same position as they had done all their lives: Lucy hunched over her food, feet on the bar of the chair, licking the crumbs off her fingertips, Cat in the worn blue chair she always sat in, her elbows spread-eagled on the table, fingers pressing into her cheeks, watching her cousin, younger, brighter, irrepressibly more alive than she.

'Do you know,' she said, suddenly, 'Luke asked me what my favourite song was yesterday, because Zach's favourite song is "Firework" by Katy Perry, and everything Zach does is apparently perfect. And I didn't know what to say. I had to go upstairs and look through an old box of CDs to remember what music I used to like. It's as though . . . Oh, I blame myself, but he really did strip me down to nothing, Olivier.'

'Why on earth do you blame yourself?' Lucy

demanded. 'It was an abusive relationship, Cat. Don't smile and shake your head. It was. How on earth can you blame yourself?'

Cat felt a red flush rising up her neck, and she crossed her arms, and gave a twisted smile that she hoped didn't look as bitter as she felt. 'You always do, Luce, no matter what everyone tells you. You just do.' There was a gentle breeze at the window, honeysuckle and roses, and she stood up. 'I have to go to work. Are you sure you don't mind picking Luke up from Zach's?'

'Absolutely not,' said Lucy. 'I'm going to go back to bed for a while. Read the paper. Stretch out and think about what I'm going to do with the rest of my week.'

'Find another job?'

'I don't think anyone'd have me, to be honest,' Lucy said.

'Write a bestselling novel about our family?' Cat saw the look that flashed across her cousin's eyes. 'Oh! Oh, I'm so right. What a guess! You are. You're going to write a novel. Can I have a good name?'

'Don't be ridiculous.' Lucy took her plate over to the sink, grumpily. 'I'm not, and even if I were to, I certainly wouldn't tell anyone about it.' She dropped the cutlery into the dishwasher with a clatter.

'OK,' said Cat, disbelieving. 'Well, good for you. Can I be called Jacquetta? I've always wanted to be called Jacquetta.'

'Look, for the last time, stop going on about it.'

583

Lucy was bent over the dishwasher. 'I'm not going to. Anyway, I've got enough on at the moment, what with Dad and Karen. I've said I'll help out with Bella when they're back from her mum's.' She rolled her eyes. 'Wherever they end up. And I said I'd help Gran field everything for Southpaw's exhibition. It's moved to October now and already people are asking me about it. Then find a new job that I don't hate.'

'You know, no one likes their job when they're starting out. Or, loads of people don't. I think you're too hard on yourself.'

'Believe me, I'm not.' Lucy poured herself some more coffee and stood in the doorway. 'Honestly. Don't worry about me. I just have to figure it out. I know what it is, I just need to wait a bit. Like Liesl in the *Sound of Music*. I know I want to be a writer but I'm not sure how I'll do it yet. Some people are born knowing what they want to do, like Dad being a doctor. Or Southpaw being an artist.'

'Southpaw told me once that he absolutely hated his job at first. He wanted to be a serious artist, and he kept getting asked to do these cartoons to go with theatre reviews of some bedroom farce or pictures of ladies waiting at the vet with their sick parrots. And he wanted to tell the story of where he grew up, and no one was interested. And then he came up with Wilbur, out of the blue.'

'Well, he owned him already, he was his dog,' Lucy said.

'Yes, but he had the idea to make him into a

cartoon, I suppose. All I mean is, he got a bit sick of Wilbur over the years. I remember him in tears when his arthritis was bad, saying he couldn't do it any more. But he kept on, didn't he? He loved it because he knew how much other people loved it. He was a real people pleaser, Southpaw.'

Lucy opened her mouth to say something.

'What?' said Cat.

'Doesn't matter,' said Lucy. 'It was about Wilbur. I think he had a trick to get by towards the end. If that helps. Anyway, what's your point?'

'Oh. Well . . .' Cat felt as though there had been an eddy in the conversation that she'd missed and she wondered if she had gone too far, teasing Lucy. 'I just mean we don't all have our dream jobs. Someone to love and someone to love you and enough to eat and enough to drink, isn't that how the saying goes? That's all you can hope for, that's more than most people.'

'OK, thanks, coz.' said Lucy, solemnly, and she nodded. 'Deep.'

'Very deep,' said Cat. She slung her bag across her body. 'See you later, coz.'

Cat loved the walk to work. Down the winding lane from Winterfold to the village, the hedgerows heavy with summer green, wood pigeons cooing in the midday haze. She cut through the field at the bottom, swinging her long legs over the stile, glancing at the blackberry bushes fringing the road.

The fruits were still tight and green, but a few showed a hint of pinkish-purple. Joe had said they'd go out to pick blackberries in a few weeks, for crumbles, jam, coulis. He was supposed to be coming up to Winterfold next week to look at the apples – Martha had told him he could have as many as he wanted when they were ripe. Not for a month or two now, but soon. Autumn was coming. Not now, but it was coming. Nearly a year since Gran had sent out the invites. A whole year, and everything had changed.

Much as she loved working at the pub, she knew she needed a project, something that gave her a future here. Apart from anything else, she didn't want to live off her grandmother for ever. Lovely as it was at Winterfold, it wasn't her home, though to wake up in that old room every morning, to come down to breakfast and look out over the hills and touch the warm wood, to watch Luke run himself ragged with whoever was around in the garden, was a dream she never wanted to wake up from. But she wanted her life to feel real again, for the first time in years. She wanted a stake of her own, because she knew she and Luke belonged here, in these comforting, green hills.

Her mother's ashes had been scattered here, too. Perhaps a scintilla of her was in the air she breathed. In her, in Luke, on the leaves of the apple trees, in the daisy bank, settling over the house. Daisy had been cremated a week after the magistrate's court had fined Martha and released her. They had scattered the ashes in the garden. Cat had been home a week when the ceremony, if it could be called that, had taken place. She'd been weeding the vegetable patch when Martha had stood at the kitchen door and called out, 'I think we should do it now.' So Cat had gone up to her room, her mother's room it had been too, and changed out of her jeans into a dress. Silly, but she felt she ought to. Some kind of observance for Daisy, who'd chosen this way out, but who'd never had a proper goodbye. And when she came downstairs again, Natalie, the lawyer, Kathy the vicar, and Bill were all in the garden too.

'I asked them,' her grandmother had said. 'I thought it would be right.'

They stood quietly, and Bill smiled at Cat, and squeezed her arm as she passed him, and she was suddenly very afraid of the whole thing. Because Gran asked her to, Cat took the first handful, fumbling fingers feeling the cold metal and then the grey powder, throwing it gingerly out into the breeze. So little ash for a whole person.

She'd handed the urn to Martha, and seen her grandmother's unreadable expression. Grim, her mouth clamped shut in a straight line. She stayed still, not moving, and Cat didn't know what to do, but Bill had reached forward, taken the urn and said quietly, 'Goodbye, Daisy. Rest well now.'

He shook the contents of the urn into his palms, and then ran forward. They were facing the orchard, down towards the valley. Bill threw his arms up in the air, and the afternoon sun picked up the motes of ash as, like a swarm of bees or wasps, it glided, almost golden, airborne for a few seconds, then sank into nothing.

Now, there was nothing to show Daisy had ever been here. It made Cat sad, in a way, and in another way she finally understood the truth, which was that Daisy hadn't really every existed properly in this place anyway. She hadn't ever really been Cat's mother, or Bill's sister, or Gran's daughter. Had she ever been herself somewhere else, or not? And still it terrified her, though she couldn't say this to anyone. Was she like her mother? Was there something, something stopping her? She thought often of how successfully she had convinced Joe that she was over him. How easy it was to push him away, suppress her feelings. Because it was easy to keep yourself covered up, and very, very hard to peel off that layer, the one that smarted in the sun, shrank from touch.

Cat leaped over the final stile and crossed the lane towards the pub. It was quiet when she entered, no one in the bar except for the radio, playing 'Call Me Maybe'. She could hear Sheila, out in the garden at the back, singing along. Cat followed the noise.

Sheila was on the tiny pub terrace, bending over and snipping rosemary off a tiny plant, slipping the sprigs into her apron pocket, all the while miming a 'call me' motion with her hand as a substitute phone. 'Hello, my love. We're short-staffed again. John's off again. Says it's his varicose veins but I don't believe it. He's twenty-eight, he don't have varicose veins. He heard it off Dawn complaining about hers, I bet you. He's hungover. The little tinker.' She suddenly yelled out, '"Call Me Maybe"!' There was a long pause, the music playing in the background, then she bellowed again, '"Call Me Maybe"! I don't know the words,' she said, as Cat watched her, laughing.

'You know *some* of the words,' Cat said.

'Oh, what a song. What a song. Better than "Blurred Lines", all that nasty talk in the rap.' She tunelessly hummed the chorus, making it into complete gobbledegook. 'What can I do you for, my dear?'

Cat looked round for Joe, but he wasn't in the kitchen, and she peered into the bar, but couldn't see him there either. She took the scissors out of Sheila's hands, playing for time. 'You shouldn't be doing that with your back. What else do you need?'

'Very kind of you, my dear. What did I do before you came along? We need some thyme. Parsley, big bunch of it. And some tarragon.'

'Oh.' Cat started cutting. She looked up at the fence. 'Hey, Sheila, I was thinking something.'

'Oh, dance here,' Sheila said. 'I love this bit. She's got a great way about her with a song, hasn't she? I love dancing.'

'Me too,' Cat said, beaming. 'Me too!'

They danced round the garden a bit, clapping their hands and singing, laughing together and Sheila eventually leaned against the windowsill, and turned the radio down. 'Ooh, my sides. You have brightened this place up, Cat, you really have.'

'Oh, right.' Cat shrugged, trying not to show how much this pleased her, and pulled her cardigan off. 'I wanted to ask you, Sheila. I've talked about this with Joe but it was a while ago now. Have you ever thought of extending the garden? Making a vegetable patch down the back, putting some tables out under an awning?'

'Well, we were going to, this summer. But it got away from us, what with one thing and another. Now I'm off to Weston tomorrow, and he's ever so cross with me. Doesn't understand why I want a holiday.' Sheila crossed her arms. 'Ooh, the way he is at the moment, it's work, work, work. He wants everything yesterday, that's his trouble. Well, he'll have to wait.'

'Joe's lucky to have you.'

Sheila chuckled. 'My dear, I'm lucky to have him. Bless his heart. For all his moods, and he's a right pain at the moment, isn't he?'

'How do you mean?' Cat kept her voice level.

'Oh, Cat, you know. He's like a bear with a sore head lately.'

'Karen?'

'Of course. He's devastated. Never known him like this.'

Cat moved on to the tarragon bush. 'I just – I thought maybe he'd be glad. I never knew – right, that's . . .' She knew Sheila was watching her curiously and she swallowed, trying to sound normal, any earlier jollity all gone. 'It must be very hard for him.' As she handed Sheila a bunch of herbs, she was alarmed to feel her cheeks flaming red. She changed the subject. 'What about the herb garden, kitchen garden, then? Should we put a time in when you're free to talk it over properly?'

Sheila nodded, watching her. 'Good idea.' She leaned against the window ledge and banged on the window, which Cat now saw was open. 'He's back. Hey, Joe! Get out here! Cat's telling us how we ought to do the garden. You should have a chat with her. I'm sure she's right.'

A few seconds later Joe appeared in the doorway. 'Hello, Cat.' He nodded at her.

'Hi,' she said. Their easy friendship of early summer had vanished with Karen's departure, and the past fortnight, he'd barely spoken at all. The one time Cat had stopped him and ventured to ask him how he was, in the dark passageway out to the garden, Joe had stopped, fists clenched, and stared at her. 'Fine, thank you for asking. Why?'

'Oh. No reason. Just – been a while since we talked.'

'Yes. I'm in the middle of something, Cat, I'm sorry. Best get on.' Then he'd pushed open the door to the Gents, leaving her standing outside in the passageway feeling like an unwelcome smell.

Now he stood in front of them, his arms crossed. 'Sheila, the portobellos weren't in the veg box this morning. Can you call the suppliers and find out what's happened to them? Otherwise we've only got two main courses today.'

591

'I'll murder them, I will. That's the third time this month.' Sheila heaved herself off the window ledge. 'Cat, you come and find me later,' she called. 'Joe, get her to tell you her idea. It's a good one, it is. Stop this from happening again.'

The two of them were left standing in the shaded patio, where the sun hadn't yet arrived. 'Excuse me, will you? I need to check the soup,' Joe said, and turned back inside.

Cat followed him into the cluttered white kitchen. She watched a buzzing fly, dangerously close to the ultraviolet insect killer, high up on the wall. 'It's quiet today for once,' she said, wishing she was better at small talk.

'It's July. I've got two people away and a reviewer and a party of ten in for lunch. You'll be busy I should think.' He said it with almost grim satisfaction. 'So, what's up then?'

Cat looked around for a place to stand. She felt in the way, and she didn't want to talk to him if he was going to be like this. She'd thought he wasn't the type to be moody, the kind who liked watching others squirm because he dictated the atmosphere – she was wrong, though. How could he be acting like this?

'Joe – it's about the garden – but it doesn't matter today.'

'Not today?'

'No. Another time.'

His tired eyes narrowed to a flinty stare. 'Have you been talking to Lucy?'

'Lucy? Yes, why?' Cat said, surprised.

'You Winters. You stick together, don't you? I should have remembered.' He looked at her angrily, something like disgust on his face.

'What's Lucy got to do with it?'

'You know perfectly well, Cat. You waltz in here making a racket dancing round the garden with Sheila, trying to get her into your little gang too. Hi, I'm one of them, everyone loves us, we're better than the rest of them.'

Cat felt as if he'd slapped her. 'What the hell does that mean?' she demanded. 'You've got totally the wrong idea about us. We're not glued together like some clan.'

'Clan. Very posh.' His expression was ugly.

'Oh, shut up,' Cat said, fury suddenly uncoiling inside her. 'It's all in your head, whatever it is. These past few weeks, the way you blow hot and cold. Stop going on like you've got some chip on your shoulder about—'

'Chip on my shoulder?' he shouted, and she stepped back, astonished. 'That's funny, Cat. I could almost laugh at that.' He looked away and covered his eyes with his arm, then looked back. 'You should all be glad to kiss my boots, that baby'll grow up and one day she'll wish it had been the other way. That I was her dad. But I'm not, am I? She's stuck with you lot. What a life.' He turned his back on her, and began grinding garlic cloves with the head of a wooden spoon.

'Oh, Joe.' Cat cleared her throat. 'Is it little

Bella?' She bit her tongue. 'Joe? Did they get the tests back?'

He didn't move, just carried on pounding the garlic, pulling the skins off and smashing them to pulp. Cat watched his curved back slump. Her eyes stung. She could hear his breathing.

'She's Bill's, isn't she? Joe, I'm so sorry.'

She couldn't see his face. 'Why are you sorry? I've not met her, I don't know her.'

'I thought it'd be nice for you if she was—' That sounded completely wrong. 'I – I just wanted you to be happy.' The atmosphere was excruciating. She wiped her hand across her brow. 'Look, I shouldn't have asked. I'm sorry.'

'No.' Joe put the spoon down, back still to her. 'I'm the one who's sorry. I'm sorry for yelling like that.' He stared out of the window. 'I shouldn't have taken it out on you, you . . . Never mind.'

'You really wanted her to be yours, didn't you?'

He shrugged. 'Maybe.'

Cat reached forward, and gave him a tiny pat on the back, then stepped back. He hung his head, hand up to his eyes.

'It's silly things. Seeing Luke . . . every time I see him around I think of Jamie. And I think, oh well, Jamie's met Luke, they played together, so at least when I'm looking at your son there's a connection to mine even if he's . . . he's two hundred miles away. 'Cause I miss him that much. Does that sound mad?'

When Daisy came home when Cat was eight,

594

for a week, Cat had memorised everything she'd touched in the house. The William Morris print book. The orange casserole dish. The phone. The chair on the right of Southpaw's in the kitchen, painted blue many years ago, worn at the edges. She still sat in that chair out of habit, every time. That was why. It occurred to her only now that was why. 'I know what you mean, Joe.'

'I thought it'd be different with this one. And there it is, I'm not even her dad.' He turned round, and gave her a small smile. 'I only found out this morning. Came in the post. Old-fashioned . . . and I wasn't expecting it. Just a bit of a shock . . .' He trailed off, his head hanging. She thought he might be crying and moved towards him, patting his arm, softly.

'It must be really hard.'

This time he didn't stop her. He said quietly, 'I went to work one day and I said bye to her before I left, and she looked at me and said, "Thanks, Joe". And I thought it was weird. "Thanks, Joe" . . . I get back and she's gone. Nothing left of her.'

'Do you want to see her? See Bella, anyway? I'm sure she'll be back. You never know, this thing with Bill . . .'

But he gave her a strange look. 'They'll be all right together. I knew it all along. Always.'

'Really?' Cat said.

'She needs an older man, Karen does. She needs someone who's a different pace from her. He can look after Bella and she can take on the world.'

595

'I never really understood them, to be honest,' Cat said. 'I like her, I love him, he's my uncle. I just don't get them together.'

'Don't you? I do. More than she did, I think. Look, I have to get on, Cat. Sorry again. I really didn't mean to bite your head off.'

Cat nodded. 'Honestly, Joe, it's fine.' She dared to reach out and pat his arm, wondering if maybe he'd start yelling again, but he didn't. 'I wish it didn't make you so sad. Look – if you need to chat to anyone, OK?'

'OK,' he said. 'Thanks. You're a good friend.'

She wished there was something else she could do: wrench that baby away from Bill and give her to Joe, for just a couple of hours, so he could at least see her, say hello. Cat shut the kitchen door quietly behind her and went out into the pub.

'Cat, can you fold the napkins?' Sheila said from behind the bar. She pointed at a basket of gleaming snowy linen.

'Sure. Need to hurry now, I suppose.'

She was talking to herself really, not to Sheila. Though it was still a beautiful day, she shivered in the cool of the bar. Trying to ignore the old voice that shouted, that tried to panic her, bring her down again. The voice that said she was like her mother, that Luke was in danger, that relationships were trouble, that life was better small and cosy, not loud and scary and exhilarating, like the Looping Ride at the fairground they'd been to last week on the Bristol Downs.

She hummed 'Call Me Maybe' as she folded the napkins. She had almost learned to ignore the voice. Almost.

'Did you talk to him, then?' Sheila asked. 'Joe?'

'Now's not a good time,' Cat said, pressing down on the pile and feeling the cold smoothness of the linen beneath her skin.

MARTHA

T hat morning, her eyes flew open, and she realised she had barely been asleep. She had been dreaming again. It was happening a lot, lately.

As she lay in bed staring at the beams on the ceiling Martha's dream came back to her. The disastrous summer party: was it 1978, or '79? Such a long time since she'd thought about it and there it was, a fully formed memory, like a settled snow globe.

It had been a terrible summer. It rained for weeks. The lawn was a bog, so bad that Hadley (their dog after Wilbur, a tough act to follow), who was of a nervous disposition, sank into it whenever he went outside for a run around and had to be unplugged, like a suction cup. The iron-with-plastic-carapace DIY gazebo did not exist then, and so Martha, helped but mostly hindered by David, constructed her usual awning out of a shaky combination of bamboo sticks, two iron poles and plastic sheeting, which was folded away neatly each year and shaken out on to the lawn in August once again, rampant with spiders that scuttled across the lawn. The action of taking the awning out, spreading it across the grass – it was summer, for her, just like Studland Bay, and David's hat, which he wore every day the sun shone.

This year, though, despite the ceaseless rain, Martha and David put up the awning, decorated the tables, organised the food and waited for evening. Secretly, she hoped some of the guests might cry off but no, they tramped up the drive in wellies, in long floral floating dresses, in kaftans and jeans, in suits and ties. Martha watched them crowding under the awning with a kind of bemused despair. There they all stayed, for the rest of the evening, staring out at the drizzling, misty garden, which she'd worked so hard in all summer, so that it would look perfect for this one night. The *High Society* album was playing on the gramophone in the sitting room, the window ajar so that Louis Armstrong and Bing Crosby floated out across the garden. The women sank further into the grass, all except sixteen-year-old Florence, who took immense pride in pointing out to everyone that she was wearing flip-flops. Bill, on holiday from medical school, all Adam's apple and legs, dutifully handed round drinks, chatting politely, asking after people's holidays, people's children, people's health. Daisy was, as ever, nowhere to be seen. She'd been out all day. Shopping, she said. She was off to polytechnic in Kingston in the autumn, to study sociology. But her plans didn't seem quite real, with Daisy they never did.

Usually Martha loved parties: the ideas, the little touches, the food. The bringing together of people, the delicate social tasks often required. Not tonight. She just wanted it to be over. To be inside, dry and warm. To stop having to keep an eye on Hadley, who was more hyperactive than ever, circling and wheeling around the tent, shaking wet grass and mud all over the guests. The party wasn't working, everyone was cold and formal and annoyed: with her, maybe. She wished she were tucked up in bed with a hot toddy and even a hot-water bottle too, David next to her, the pair of them chuckling over the worst parts of the evening.

She could still see it now: the moment when Hadley, out of nowhere, suddenly stopped chasing his tail around on the lawn and turned, snarled at the assembled crowd and dashed into the awning, catching a dancing piece of twine with him, crashing into the outermost pole. He made for Gerald Lang, who lived up at Stoke Hall, and whom the Winters loathed: Bill said he was a cheat, Florence said he was a sex pest who put his hand down her top at the church fête. Now Gerald was flung to the ground, as Hadley went for him.

The tent began collapsing around them and the guests fled, screaming. Martha could see Hadley's yellow teeth, tearing into Gerald's thigh. Patricia, Gerald's formidable new wife, tried to pull the dog off him, but something had flipped inside

Hadley's always slightly confused brain and it was almost impossible to detach him.

Bill, clamping his hand around Hadley's muzzle and his knees around the snarling dog's trunk, eventually managed, with one hard yank, to jerk Hadley away. The guests looked on, in the rain, some screaming.

Daisy came running on to the lawn. 'I've called an ambulance,' she said. Then she stopped, and smiled down at Gerald. 'Hope he's ripped your cock off, you disgusting man.'

'Daisy!' Martha said, as David came forward with a lead and took Hadley by the collar, and locked him up in a shed at the back of the orchard.

The next day when the vet told them Hadley had been destroyed – 'He has to be, I'm afraid. No saying he won't do it again, now he's done it once' – Daisy was furious. She said Martha must be mad, that she hated the dogs, always had, and they had a blistering, white-hot row. Daisy went to London the day after, to stay with some schoolfriends. She returned for a week before poly started, but only to pack. It was never really her home again.

But they didn't know any of that, that evening. Didn't know Hadley would have to die, that Daisy would leave and not really come back, that Gerald and his new wife would never have any children and the rumour would always be that Gerald, who was to be avoided at drinks parties, as the polite parlance had it, wasn't the man he used to be. It became something of a terrible, black joke between

David and Martha, a couple's private jest, which, if anyone else were to hear it, would sound utterly appalling.

After the ambulance had taken Gerald Lang away, Martha sought a moment's sanctuary in the kitchen, where she leaned on the sink, head spinning. Then she opened the kitchen door and found her son, vomiting into a bucket.

'Bit green still,' he said, wiping his mouth, looking wholly ashamed. 'It wasn't pretty, I'm afraid. Poor Gerald.'

'You were wonderful, Bill.' She gripped his shoulders. 'You're so grown up! I can't believe it. You are, aren't you! You're going to be a wonderful doctor. So brave.' She kissed his hand, unbelievably proud of him. Gilbert Prundy, their old vicar, had appeared in the kitchen doorway.

'The hero of the hour. William Winter. I say, well done, old chap. Well bloody done.'

The strange thing about that night was: the party went on. In fact, it went on rather late. Gilbert Prundy fetched his Oscar Peterson albums from the vicarage and he and David sang along and danced. Kim Kowalski, the new owner of the cottage down the hill, played his guitar. They stayed outside, amongst the ruins of the party, the torn awning muddied on the floor, useless, the old trestle table buckled and broken. The moon didn't come out, that night, but after enough wine and enough Pimm's no one really cared. The rain grew heavy at around midnight, so the guests moved inside and the party went on until dawn. And Martha, relaxed for the first time that evening, enjoyed herself. Because it had been pretty much the worst party you could have, and yet they were all still there, when even the rabbits, which scampered constantly across the lawn in summer, stayed out of the rain.

She thought about that party constantly as she prepared the lunch, the first proper entertaining she'd done since David died. Poor Hadley. What was it that had set him off that day? Afterwards they had wondered constantly. Was it something they'd done? Eventually David had just said, 'Put it down to flipped switch syndrome.' But he hadn't drawn Wilbur for about a month afterwards.

She said out loud, 'What did you draw during that month instead? I can't remember.'

The lunch was all ready: cold cuts, pie, salads and burgers. She moved around the kitchen, touching her familiar things, feeling very calm. *What's the worst that could happen? You've arranged it now.*

She thought about Florence and Jim, somewhere on the motorway. Lucy, singing in the shower upstairs. About Luke and Cat, down by the river. Karen and Bill, out for an early morning walk with Bella, having driven over last night from their newly rented flat in Bristol. And she thought about Bella, her newest granddaughter, whom David would never meet.

More time. All she wanted was a little more time.

603

Not much: one more week, one more day, just even one more hour with him. That was all. Just a little more time, to sit in the kitchen as she sat now, her hands wrapped around the same old mug, gazing out of the window, to know that he was in the house too. Upstairs, shaving, singing. In his office, laughing at something. Calling out into the hallway. 'Any chance of some tea, Em?'

His voice. She could hear it so clearly it might have been real. Not in her head, just this once. She breathed, feeling the tight ball of pain that, ever since he died, seemed to sit above her lungs. It made her breathless, it made her cry, it made her throat swell with sadness. It was always there.

Any chance of some tea, Em?

What would happen if, for just one minute, she believed he was here, in front of her? Really believed it? Martha relaxed and closed her eyes, letting the sun warm her face.

The room was still, noises off, as though her ears were stopped up with wax. She sat, waiting. She felt something cold brush over her and found she couldn't open her eyes, didn't want to.

Then she knew he was here. That he was waiting for her, that he was here.

Martha froze. Very slowly, she opened her eyes and he was in front of her, in the doorway. Without his stick.

'Any chance of a cup of tea, Em?'

'Yes,' she said, and she smiled at him, and it was as though nothing had happened. As though he'd always been there, waiting to walk in through the door. 'It's a bit thrutchy. It's been in the pot a while.'

'Fine by me.' David sat down, in his chair. 'What's happened to this? It feels different.'

'Lucy stood on it, and it broke.' Martha poured him some tea, unable to tear her eyes away from him. The crease in his shirt, it was real. His eyes, his chin, his chest. He really was here again, really was. She missed the mug, and tea splashed on to the table. 'I fixed it.'

'Of course you did,' David said, and he slid the Rochester Castle tea towel over to her, his eyes crinkling, his wide smile. He was there, he was in front of her. Somehow she kept looking at him, and he didn't disappear. Somehow, she kept on talking.

She said, 'It's amazing what wood glue and some tape will do.'

'Not amazing. You can fix anything, darling,' he said, and they both drank their tea, together in the warm kitchen, nothing remarkable about it at all, really.

Suddenly, Martha didn't know what to say, and the ball of grief seemed wedged so high in her throat she thought she might choke.

'I miss you, David,' she said eventually, tears in her eyes.

'I know you do, Em.' He couldn't smile, now.

'I did it all wrong, all of it. I shouldn't have had that lunch.'

'No, darling. They had to know. We had to tell the truth.'

'But I lost you.'

'I would have gone anyway.' He seemed to be altering before her eyes. Was his hair less grey, more brown, was he younger, every time she looked at him? 'Em, I was dying. Nothing you could have done to change it. You do understand that, don't you? You had to tell them the truth about Daisy. I had to die. Those are the facts. They had to happen in their own time.'

In their own time. For the first time, she believed it. 'Yes.'

The table was too wide, she couldn't reach over and touch him. She hesitated.

'Good,' he said.

'I hate it here without you.'

'I know. But before that . . .' David said. 'Before that . . . we loved it. We loved it here. We were happy. We *are* happy.'

Martha wiped her eyes. She cleared her throat and said, 'Is it right, what I'm doing today? Is it the right thing to do?'

'Of course it is,' he said.

'I don't know any more. I don't seem to be able to fix on anything these days. They think I'm much better but I'm not. I – we – we . . .' She broke off with a sob, her head bowed, rubbing at her chest.

And he said, 'I'm here, you know that. I'm with you always. I won't ever go away.' He stretched his hands out to her, across the table. The hands.

She stared down at them. They were strong and supple, almost as good as new.

Martha tried to touch his fingers, to stretch towards him but he didn't move.

'I can't reach you.' Tears were blinding her eyes. 'David, I can't—' She stood up, stumbling, and when she looked up he was gone.

There was a knock, a tiny knocking at the back door, and she started, looking around. *I was here. He was here.*

'Martha?' The door creaked open. 'Ma?'

Karen came in, carrying her tiny daughter, Bill behind her.

'Everything all right?' Karen said, staring at Martha. 'You look as – you're very pale.'

Martha looked around, wildly. He was still here, wasn't he? Behind the door, perhaps just next door.

'I – did you see someone?'

Bill looked at his mother. 'Who?'

'I. . .nothing.' Martha shook her head. 'Nothing.' She kissed her daughter-in-law's cheek, and stroked her granddaughter's dark hair. As though it was normal, everything, all of it, the same, as though he wasn't there with her, but then she saw that of course he was. She looked behind them, and thought perhaps she glimpsed him there, by the doors that led to the dining room. Perhaps it was only the wind from the open casement, blowing in fresh air from outside.

She looked down at the table, and saw the mug of tea she'd given him. It was only half-full now.

'Is it all ready, then?'

'What?'

'Florence's lunch?'

'She's not here, not yet. Everything else is ready.' She blinked, trying to concentrate. 'Bill, I was thinking about that summer party today.'

'The one when Florence got drunk on gin and sang "Luck Be a Lady" out of the bathroom window?'

'No. The terrible one.'

'Oh, my goodness. I must say . . .' Bill rubbed his eyes, '. . . that was a great party.'

Martha said, 'Not for Gerald, of course.'

He looked contrite. 'Course. Poor Gerald. I always forget about him.'

'What happened?' Karen said.

'Well,' Bill began, and then he stopped. 'It was a long time ago. Past history.'

The kitchen door slammed, with a force so great they all jumped. Martha whirled round, but there was nothing there. Bella woke, and started crying and Karen said, 'I might give her a feed if she's awake. Bill, have you got my . . .'

They disappeared into the hallway, consulting in low voices.

And then someone said, 'Well, I didn't expect to sleep so late. What on earth was that bang?'

A figure in the doorway, so like David that Martha started again, and her hands felt instantly clammy.

Their face was the same shape, their eyes were

the same. But she was younger, her face less lined, her skin smooth. She was slightly portly – stately was perhaps a better word. Reserved, a little shy maybe: when she'd arrived last night, Martha had struggled to talk to her. She hadn't seen her for nearly fifty years, and they acutely felt the absence of David and his easy conversation. She was elegant, her silver-and-gold hair twisted neatly up into an old-fashioned chignon. Like her brother, she had remade herself.

'Cassie,' said Martha, looking up. She came forward. 'Did you sleep well?'

'I did, and I've been up for a while, I had a bath, had a nice read of some of David's old Wilburs.' She advanced into the kitchen. Martha took her hands, and held them.

'I'm so glad you came. Thank you.'

'Well. He wanted me to. He wanted me to come up before he died. I . . . I'm so sorry. I wish I had.'

'He hadn't told me he'd even met up with you . . .' Martha tightened her grip on Cassie's hands. 'I didn't go into the study for months, you see. I didn't see your letter.'

She had been up to London three times, looking for her. She had been to the Public Record Office, in Kew, sat poring over parish registers and censuses, and could find nothing. She had even been to the Angel, walked the streets David knew so well, searching for a woman who looked like him, like Florence. But there was nothing, and she had begun to despair.

It was only three days ago when, hunting around for something the gallery wanted for David's Muriel Street exhibition, she had finally opened the little drawer of his desk, and seen it lying there. On top of old rubbers, pencils worn to stubs, blotting paper and ink cartridges. David opened that drawer each morning to get his materials out; he must have seen it every day after it arrived. But after his death, no one else, much less her, had thought to look in there.

Dear Davy

I'm sorry I haven't been in touch since our drink. It was nice to see you, it really was.

I have been thinking about what you said. About family, and how we're the only ones left who remember. I'd like to come up and see you all some time. See Florence. I'd like to meet her. Could I come to your posh house and drink tea like a lady one day? I'll be on my best behaviour. How does that sound?

My phone number's on the back.

Maybe it's a bad idea. Not sure. Just thought I'd ask.

Love Cassie

Your sister x

'I heard he died,' Cassie said when Martha, shaking, rang her. 'But I didn't know how to call you. I didn't know if it'd be what anyone wanted.'

Florence was due home this Saturday. She was coming here, and she was bringing Jim who had been out with her in Italy for most of the summer. Ostensibly she was just here for the night (Florence had given some excuse about how Jim needed to go to the Holburne Museum in Bath to check out a Joseph Wright of Derby portrait but even she hadn't sounded wholly convincing about it) but it was really a much bigger event than that. Bill was bringing Bella and Karen home. Lucy, and Cat and Luke would be there.

So they would all be back. It was supposed to happen. Martha kept thinking of the wasted couple of months she'd spent looking for Cassie. She thought of how, the night of David's death, when Florence, unbeknown to her, had found her own birth certificate. She'd asked Florence to leave the study, and if she'd only left her in there a while longer, she might have opened the drawer, found Cassie's note.

But what if she had done? Wasn't David right? It had to happen in its own time. She, Martha, had to be ready to change things, to alter their family's script.

Cassie said: 'I'd have written right away if I'd have known.'

'I know, and we should have found you sooner. It's my fault.'

Cassie shook her head. 'It's all fine. Listen, Martha, I'm kind of nervous about all this,' she said frankly. She sat down in David's chair. 'It's so fast. Not sure, what if she freaks out? It's a big shock to land on someone.'

'I know.' Martha's mouth was dry. 'I know. But it has to happen. She wants to meet you, I promise you. She knows I'm looking for you, that I couldn't find you anywhere.'

'We liked being able to blend into a crowd, me and Davy,' Cassie said. 'Think we got that off our mum. We had to. Well, it had to happen some time, didn't it?'

'Yes. It did.' Martha stared at her sister-in-law, in David's chair, and something settled within her. She felt quiet, for the first time in a long while.

'I don't know what I'll say to her.' Cassie was fiddling with her buttons, slim white fingers fluttering. 'I'm not a mum, I don't know how to be a mum.'

Martha took her hand. 'You are a mum,' she said.

The sound of car wheels on gravel. The sound of Bella, crying, of Lucy clattering down the stairs, noise and chaos. Cassie sat still, clasping her hands together.

'Yes.'

Martha left her alone in the kitchen, hurrying through to see the front door open.

'Flo! Jim!' Lucy was advancing towards the pair at the front of the house, with Bella in her arms. 'Look, my new sister! Your new niece, Flo, look at her! Isn't she gorgeous? Look at her schmoochy cheeks.' She kissed the black-haired, black-eyed

Bella, who stared at her aunt, then Jim, unimpressed. 'Well, come in!' Lucy said, a little too loudly.

'Thanks,' said Florence, hugging Karen and Bill. 'Bill,' she said, gripping his elbows. 'Wonderful to see you, dear brother. This, this is Jim.'

With one finger pressed into his back she propelled Jim forwards and Jim, swallowing, held out a hand. 'Bill. Good to meet you. Hello, Martha.' He gave her a kiss and Martha, who had been out with him in Italy at the same time, smiled, and threw her arms around him.

'It's awfully good you're here,' she whispered. 'It really is.' Then she turned to Florence. 'Hello, my darling.'

'Ma.' Florence kissed her cheek. 'Hello. Look, I brought you that almond cake you liked.' She thrust a large waxy packet awkwardly into Martha's hands. 'Right.'

There was a sort of silence. Lucy said, 'You should come inside.'

'Yes, please,' Jim said, in his mild tones, and they all laughed nervously.

Lucy led the way. 'Everyone's here. And Gran's got a surprise for you, Florence.'

How did you do it? How did you do the next part?
You simply took a deep breath and kept on going.

She put her arm through Florence's. Lucy opened the sitting-room door. Martha saw them through the crack in the open door, Bill lying with his head on Karen's shoulder, Karen with her feet up on the footstool, looking exhausted. She smiled as Lucy came in, reaching her arms out for her daughter. Lucy laughed quietly at something and closed the door. 'She just . . .'

Her voice was a low murmur as the door shut.

'Jim,' Martha said calmly, 'Flo needs to go into the kitchen first.'

'Why?' Florence, looking through the open door, towards the table, the figure sitting sedately, head turned towards them. 'Who's in there?' she said. She froze. 'Ma? Who . . .?'

She looked at Martha and Martha blinked, and nodded. She wanted to say something, to beg her not to love this new mother more. She wanted to run in there now, ahead of Florence, pave the way. Call out to Cassie: *Be kind to her, tell her how wonderful she is! Ask her about her new book. Don't make her feel awkward, or stupid. Don't tease her, she mustn't be teased. She loves the sunshine. She loves coffee, like her father. Like David. Please don't take her away from me. Please don't hurt her.*

Florence looked back and lightly touched her mother's cheek. 'Oh, Ma,' she said. 'That's quite a coup. Well done.' She handed Jim the car keys. In the kitchen, framed by the door, they saw Cassie stand up, stiffly, as Florence walked towards her.

'Hello, Florence, my dear.' she said simply. 'I'm . . . I'm Cassie.'

Florence stood very still. As though she were hesitating.

'Hello, Cassie,' she said eventually, her hand on the door, in a small voice.

Martha wished she could hold her hand, push her forward, but she knew she couldn't. This was, maybe, the last thing she could do for her. For any of them. 'It's lovely to meet you.'

Florence turned back, and smiled at Martha. Then she closed the door, and there was silence in the dark hall, only the sound of Lucy's voice and Karen's soft laugh and then, nothing else, really.

Jim and Martha were left facing each other. He put his hand on Martha's. 'Shall we go for a walk? Would you show me the garden, Martha?' he said. 'I'd love to see it.'

'I'd love to show it to you,' Martha said. She tucked her arm through his, and on the way out of the door, picked up her garden pliers. The wisteria was too wild, and the honeysuckle would strangle everything one day. There was always something to do, there always would be. They walked outside, into the sunshine, down the lawn, towards the daisy bank, away from the house and the people inside. Just for a little while.

'Goodbye, my love,' she whispered, and she looked up at the sky. 'Thank you. Goodbye.'

CAT

At the bottom of the hill but before the village was the edge of the wood, and a web of streams that had flowed down from the hills around and converged on this shallow spot overhung with trees, babbling loudly and full of tiny, clear fish. It swept into one stream around the side of Winter Stoke and ran beside the green.

Cat sat on the side of the bank, dangling her feet in the water, trousers rolled up, wearing a piece of paper folded into the shape of a hat on her head. In one hand, she held a wooden spoon and in the other a plastic trumpet.

'Where are you?' a voice called from the other side of the river, and Luke's face, black with burned cork marks, popped up between the reeds.

'I'm here,' said Cat.

'You stay there. I am still building my boat. If you try and escape my men will beat you and kill you with sticks,' said Luke, and he disappeared again.

'Oh, no,' said Cat. 'Well, I'm going to escape anyway. I've got special powers. I've turned into a monster and I'm going to cross the bank and come and eat you.'

'No!' Luke shouted. 'You can't eat me.'

'Oh, yes I can!' Cat yelled, advancing slowly across the stream. 'I'm going to – oh, darling, I'm sorry,' she said, as Luke's face crumpled into terrified tears. She splashed across the rest of the stream towards him and took him in her arms.

'I don't like monsters, Mum.'

'Me neither. But they're not real, are they?'

'Well, sometimes they are. Zach says when you die you go to hell, and a monster eats you every night, and then the same bit grows back again in the day. His mum is a vicar. She told him.'

'Right.' Cat kissed the top of his head. 'Well, Zach's telling you porkies. That's not true.'

He shivered against her. 'I'm still scared.'

'Oh, Luke, I really am sorry,' Cat said, hugging him close again.

'Let's go back home.'

She hesitated. 'We can't. Not just yet. Gran's visitor wants to meet Florence and I said we'd go and play while they talk.' She didn't know how to explain the real reason. 'Now,' she said, 'have I shown you this?' She took some string out of her pocket. 'Real pirates, they stab their fish in the water. Trainee pirates, they catch their fish like this.'

'Where in the world?'

'Oh, all around the world. The Amazon, mainly.'

617

Cat fixed the bread she'd bought on to the string and tied it to a stick. 'That's yours.'

'When can we go back?' Luke said, staring at the stick in concentration as he lowered the string carefully into the water.

'Later. After we've caught a fish.'

'Jamie doesn't eat fish. We won't give him any fish.'

'Jamie? Right.' Cat wasn't really listening.

'Jamie's dad likes fish. He likes eating fish. He told me there are small fish you can eat all of them, including their heads.' Luke nudged Cat. 'Mum! Why don't you listen to me? Why are you always thinking about something?'

'I'm a busy pirate,' Cat said.

'What are you thinking about?'

'Never mind. Oh, look. There they are.'

She could hear their feet, crunching on the dry leaves and twigs of the undergrowth.

'Hey there,' called Joe, advancing towards them. 'Hi. Hi, Luke. How's your frog?'

'What frog?' Cat said, surprised.

'I got a frog in a box,' Luke said. 'When we camped, me and Jamie and Joe.' He waved at Jamie. 'How's your frog?'

'Dead.' Jamie fished around in his satchel, as Joe sat down and opened the coolbag. 'Dad made some sandwiches. Do you want sandwiches?'

Luke looked at Cat. 'Do pirates eat sandwiches? Do they?'

'Yes, they do,' called Joe. 'Big pirates eat them

with bones and eyeballs.' Luke's eyes grew huge, and he added hurriedly, 'But that's just in films. Not really.'

'OK, Joe,' said Luke, happily.

'You're a pirate too, Luke,' Joe told him. 'You can't be scared of other pirates. That's like . . . one of your toes being scared of the other toes.' He sat down next to Cat.

'What's up?' he said.

'Nothing, why?'

'You look like you haven't slept,' he said.

'I know we're friends again,' she said, 'but word of advice: don't go around saying that to people.' He said nothing, but she saw him glance again at her out of the corner of his eye. Cat took the sandwich he offered and took a huge bite, the fluffy sourdough, the crunch of the crust. 'That's so good. What is it?'

'Leftover beef slices from yesterday, bit of mayo, some watercress from down the way. You like it?'

'I've said it before, Joe. You make the best bread alive.'

'It's my pleasure,' he said. 'Honestly. You and Luke are my best bread customers.'

The boys were advancing further into the wood, shouting with joy. Luke looked back at Cat, waving, his eyes alive with excitement. 'See you later. If I don't come back . . . please don't be sad, Mum, OK?'

'Sure,' Cat said. 'OK. Roger. Jolly roger.'

Joe and Cat sat in silence, Cat swinging her legs

in the water again. Even in the cool of the trees it was hot, still. Two dragonflies danced above the stream. She watched them, the dappled light catching their wings.

'Thanks for meeting up. There's a thing up at the house and I wanted to clear out for a bit.'

'Right,' said Joe. 'Family gathering?'

She looked at him. 'All of them, yep.' She swallowed a bit more sandwich. 'Karen's there, with Bill. And Bella.'

'Of course,' he said, mildly.

'Just in case you – you know.'

'I heard he's looking to buy into a practice in Bristol then,' Joe said.

'Yes.'

'It's a shame.'

'Oh, Joe.'

'I mean, he's a great doctor, we'll miss him round here.' He ate some sandwich. 'There's not enough pepper on this, Cat. I'm sorry.'

She ignored him. 'You're very circumspect about it. About Bella.'

'I'm happy for them, that's why.' He wrinkled up his nose. 'I'd love to meet her some day. The little one.'

They were both silent for a few moments, and Cat remembered yet again with gratitude how easy it was to be with him. He understood.

'It's Florence,' she said eventually. 'She's meeting her mother. Her real mother. Florence is Southpaw's niece, they adopted her. His sister couldn't look after her, they had a very difficult childhood and he wanted to help her – something like that. Southpaw was always so cagey about his past.'

'Why?'

'I've seen the pictures he drew, the ones going into that exhibition. It was awful,' she said sadly. 'Anyway she's here, now. I thought I might take Luke out. Enjoy the sunshine.' She took a deep breath.

He smiled at her. 'Cat, is that why you didn't want to be up there this morning? Because of your mother?'

She reached for an apple. 'Maybe.'

'Why?'

'Mothers and daughters. Still makes me sad.' To her horror, Cat's eyes filled with tears.

Joe immediately pulled her towards him, stretching his arm around her. 'Oh, Cat. Hey. Don't cry.'

She leaned against him. 'Sorry. I didn't mean to.'

He patted her back. 'You poor girl. It's still hard, is it? I'm so sorry.' Cat nodded. She turned into him, and he wrapped both his arms around her. 'You cry if you want,' he said, his voice muffled by her hair.

She held on to him, thanking her lucky stars she had a friend like him, that they had found their way through. 'All those years,' Cat said, sitting back and wiping her nose on her hand. 'I spent so many years thinking one day we'll get close again, that she'd come and find me, take me home, you know.' She sat up, sniffing, and pushed her hair out of her face. 'I'm so sorry, Joe. I just always had this idea of her, even after I knew she was always going to let me down. But I think a part of her might have wanted me . . . might have missed me. Oh goodness. This is the eight-year-old in me. Forgive me.'

He leaned towards her, and touched her cheek. 'Nothing to forgive, Cat. Never, ever.'

She stared at him. At the sprinkling of freckles on his nose, his blue eyes. He held her gaze.

'Gran told me this morning it's been a year since she wrote the invitations to her party,' she said eventually.

'I heard the food at that party was amazing.'

'I heard the chef was a liability, he nearly mowed down her great-grandson and slept with her daughter-in-law.'

'*But* his miniature toad-in-the-hole canapés were sensational.'

'It's been good, hasn't it?' she said, after a while. She spread her arms wide. 'All of – this. This year.'

'Oh. Yes, of course.'

They smiled at each other again. The way she could stare into his eyes, see nothing hidden there at all except honesty, truth, kindness. Herself, and him, and all of them. And she was terrified, suddenly, as though a bubbling river had risen up and was about to sweep them away. She couldn't do it.

She just couldn't. She touched his hand, gently,

and stood up. 'I have to go. Would you mind watching Luke for an hour or so?'

Joe got up, and looked at her in confusion. 'Where are you going?'

'I have to go back to the house.'

'Why?'

'Just need to,' she said. She had to go. 'Is that all right?'

'We have to collect Jamie's hat so I'll drop them off in a while. I think it'd be good to say hello to everyone, anyway.'

Everything was straightforward about him. No silly petty games, no overthinking. He was as clear as the water in the stream.

'Sure, good idea,' Cat said. She tried not to look like she was backing away from him. She wished there was dust, something she could kick up, anything to create a cloud of something that would enable her to get out, run away. 'Thanks. Bye.'

She ran out of the wood, yanking at her top, as though it were covered with brambles that would pull her back in, and as she ran back up the hill, she swallowed back tears, already disgusted with herself.

At the top of the lane was a gentle curve and as she turned into it, Cat started. There was a figure, on the bench, holding a baby, her long hair falling over her face, both of them apparently sleeping. Cat slowed down, her head still spinning. The sun shone on the woman's hair and Cat found herself thinking again of her mother's ashes, scattered over the garden, still flying somewhere in the breeze around the hills. She stopped, and shook her head, smiling at herself. It was Karen, and Bella. She paused a few metres away, not knowing what to do. Her legs twitched; she felt quite mad, like she ought to just keep on running, past the house, up the hill.

The inscription on the bench was: 'Seek rest, weary traveller.'

Bella was in Karen's arms, her body almost entirely wrapped up in an old shawl of Martha's. Her chest went up and down. Cat had forgotten how quickly babies breathed, how alarming it had seemed to her at first. She watched her, suddenly transfixed. The tiny fingers of one hand waved involuntarily suddenly, like a magician's flourish, and Cat laughed softly.

'Hello,' said Karen, suddenly raising her head and opening her eyes. Cat had thought yesterday, when they'd arrived, how different she looked, especially without her make-up. Much younger. 'I'm getting good at catnapping. Sorry. Just went for a little post-feed stroll and sat in the sunshine and fell asleep. I bet you thought we were tramps.'

'You both looked very peaceful,' Cat said, smiling. She sat down next to her, trying not to fidget.

'Thought it might be good to clear out for a while.' Karen pushed her hair away from her face. 'The sound of a baby crying isn't necessarily the most appropriate . . . erm . . . vibe they want right now, do you know what I mean?'

'Totally agree,' said Cat. 'You're very wise.'

'Where's Luke then?'

'He's with Joe and Jamie. They're just by the river, actually. They're so happy down there.' Cat hesitated, and shifted on her seat. 'Joe'd love to see you and Bella, I know he would.'

'Really? I never heard back from him, I've emailed. And called.'

'He was pretty upset. You know Joe, he loves kids. Loves a family.' She laughed, already feeling exasperated with herself for running off like that. 'That's why I've given him mine.'

Karen stared at her, then her face cleared. 'That's so brilliant, Cat! I really hoped he'd go for it. I didn't realise. You two, at last! Fantastic.'

'Oh,' said Cat, hurriedly. 'No, Karen. I meant – not that. I meant I've given him . . . No, he's just looking after Luke. For an hour or so.'

Karen shifted the sleeping Bella under her arm. 'Oh.'

'There's nothing going on with me and Joe,' Cat said, mortified. 'It's not – we're friends. We're really good friends. Actually. It's great.' She nodded. 'Great.' The sun flickered in her eyes.

Karen stared at her, and then she laughed. 'Bollocks!'

'What?'

'I said that's bollocks. Cat, he's in love with you.'

Bella slowly opened her eyes, glaring sleepily at her mother.

'Joe,' said Cat, as though Karen just hadn't understood her.

'Yes, Cat. I know who you mean. Joe Thorne. Six one, blue eyes, black hair. Got a scar on his finger, loves *Game of Thrones*, makes nice bread.' She spoke slowly, as though Cat was a bit deaf. 'He is in love with you.'

Cat stroked Bella's hair, her heart thumping. 'He's not, honestly. We don't have that kind of relationship. Once . . . you know. We sort of once . . . anyway . . .'

'Cat, it's obvious. I've watched the two of you together. I'd see the way he looked at you. That's why I left. Wasn't fair on him, on you. On me, on Bill.' She gave a funny smile, then took Bella and clipped on the baby's sling. 'Look, Cat, none of my business, but I think you need to stop looking to the past. Forget about what's happened. I think we all need to.'

'Yes,' said Cat, looking at her. She stood up. 'Yes.' She looked down the drive, towards the old house. She could hear laughter through the open windows and peered forwards, to see what she could make out. Blurred figures, distorted by the leaded diamond panes of glass. She couldn't see who it was, who was there.

She could go back to the house now. Walk in, say hello to the reunited Cassie and Florence. Be part of that family, the niece, the granddaughter, the cousin, and then Joe would bring Luke back and say hello to everyone and it would be fine, of course it would be, and then he would leave, and she'd see him the next day and the next day . . .

But she didn't want to be part of that family, not in that way. She wanted her own family. She wanted her own life. She wanted him. She wanted them, together. She wanted his baby inside her, his food, his life, she wanted to make him feel so safe and secure he never got that look of desolate loneliness that puckered his brow, she wanted him to have a home that Jamie felt was as much his as anyone's.

I want our life. Our family. Our home.

What if it was too late?

'Karen, tell them I'll be back later, will you? I have to – I have to collect Luke.'

'Yes,' Karen said, and she nodded. 'Of course.'

'I'm – fine,' Cat told her, unnecessarily. 'I need to go now.'

It might be too late already.

She knew what she needed to do now, but what if it *was* too late, what if in one of the infinitesimal ways that the earth moves and millions of tiny changes happen, the world had altered and the path they were on could now never be reversed? What if she had missed her chance? She ran, feet thudding so hard on the bone-dry road her body juddered in time, one foot in front of the other, each stride longer than the last, longer, faster than she had ever run before.

Cat turned off through the woods, taking the short cuts, the old paths she knew so well. She jumped across the stream, and kept on running, as though someone was chasing her.

She saw him at the edge of the wood, at the bottom of the lane. Right by the bridge that crossed over into the village.

'Hey!' he shouted. She could see Jamie and Luke, in Zach's front garden, swinging on a rope hanging from a tree. Joe gestured back towards them, with his thumb. 'Luke's there! He's OK.'

'Joe!' she yelled back, almost terrified he might vanish, disappear into thin air before her eyes. She saw his boots on the ground, the sandwiches sticking out of his pocket, the sticks poking out of the bucket he was carrying. His eyes, so warm when he looked at her, and he was smiling; he smiled all the time now. He came forward to meet her at the foot of the hill.

'What's the hurry?' he said, clutching her arms to make her halt as she ran towards him, almost unable to stop. 'Hey! Are you OK?'

She looked around, panting, unable to speak. The boys were paying no attention. A car wound round the corner, and they stood to one side.

Cat took Joe's hand. She stood close to him. Her finger stroked his palm. She smiled into his eyes.

'I had to come back,' she said, her breath short, her cheeks flushed, mouth dry. 'I had to tell you, before it was too late.'

'Cat,' he said, his voice low. He knew, she could tell. She had to say it.

And she was still so scared, fear and adrenalin

pumping through her body. She was terrified, in fact, because this was life, falling in love, loving your children, fearing the worst, wanting the best. She had been away from it for so long. She had kept Luke away from it, too.

'I have to say it,' she said. He put his hand up to her cheek, his fingers stroking her face, palm to skin. They were inches apart. 'Let me say it.'

They stayed there, fixed together, smiling at each other.

One of the boys called out from the garden but they ignored him.

'It's like home, with you,' Cat said. 'Just like home. For the first time. Ever.'

He nodded. 'I know,' he said.

'I don't want us to be friends,' Cat said urgently. 'Please, can we not be friends?'

His face clouded over and then he relaxed. 'Yes.'

'I want you,' she said, and she leaned towards him, that final gap that separated them, and she kissed him, feeling how warm he was, how solid, how well she knew him, then broke away. 'I've been so scared, of stupid things,' she said.

'No, they were real. And you're not stupid.' He pulled her closer, cupping her face. 'Cat, I've been in love with you since November, you know. I didn't know what to do about it. I tried to pretend it wasn't really real either.'

'Me too,' she said. The release of emotion, of tension, of the build-up of years and years of running away from this, and here she was, and

629

she was holding him, kissing him, and he loved her, though she didn't believe he could love her nearly as much as she loved him. 'We can't do this now,' she told him eventually. 'Not out here, can we?'

'We can if it's for the rest of our lives,' Joe said, and he untangled their fingers, put his hands gently on her cheeks and kissed her.

The sky above them was clear, no clouds, nothing, the woods beyond dark green, the last burst of summer. She knew the house would be there behind them, if she turned. Over towards the vicarage garden the boys carried on playing, oblivious, and she kissed him again, laughing. It was just them, the two of them.

EPILOGUE

That morning when he opened his eyes, the stench of shit and something else, something rotting, hung in the stale air. He realised a noise outside had woken him and kneeled up to look out of the window. There was his father, slowly descending the steps. He stopped and looked up as if he knew he was being watched. David hid behind the moth-eaten green curtain, praying he wouldn't see him, praying it wouldn't move.

After his father had disappeared around the corner, David sat up, and looked around him. The bare room, with two mattresses, a chest that the local church had provided, a jug filled with water, a bowl. Flies gathered around the bowl, and he saw that his father had, once again, used it as a chamber pot. When he was drunk he couldn't be bothered to go outside to the privy.

As he was pulling his filthy trousers on, David caught sight of a childish scribble of green pencil on the wallpaper and remembered the last time he'd seen Cassie. It was the previous summer, three months after she'd gone to live with Jem. He'd caught a train out to Leigh-on-Sea and gone to the beach with them. Cassie was three, as she kept telling him, a lovely little thing, bouncing curly hair, a wide smile, just like his mum. In three months she'd already changed. She still knew who he was, but Jem was her favourite person now. It killed him, just a little bit, to see her curling into Jem's lap, running to her when a tiny crab got in her bucket, shouting information at her at the top of her voice. But that was the choice he'd made, and he knew it was the right one.

'She's the spit of Emily, isn't she, love?' Aunt Jem stretched out on the sand, pulling her cotton dress demurely over her shins.

David had nodded. He couldn't yet talk about his mother. He'd stared at his little sister, determinedly hacking at some seaweed, laughing with some children, and felt more alone than he'd ever been. He knew it wouldn't do any good to see more of her. It'd just hurt him. He knew she couldn't ever come back to London with him. Time would move on and he had to, as well. The Blitz had taught thousands of London children that. Things got broken, destroyed. You lost your friends, your parents, your siblings. But you got on with it. You played in the ruins, you got a new house, maybe a new baby brother or sister, maybe not. That had been a year ago. Jem sent a postcard now and then to keep in touch, but that was it and that was how he'd wanted it, wasn't it? His plan had worked. He just had to keep on reminding himself: Cassie was all right. She was out of there.

Suddenly, David felt a lightness steal over him. He looked out of the window again, to make sure his father wasn't coming back, then he scrambled into a shirt, grabbed his sketchbook, his photo of his mother, the locket she'd been wearing the night she was killed, and he checked under the brick for his father's cash, and took it, all of it. He didn't write a note. His father couldn't read. And he didn't want to leave any trace. He might come and find him.

He wasn't really sure where he was going, he just wanted to go away, somewhere unlike here, unlike this little patch of London that was all he really knew. At first he got on a bus thinking he'd head towards Buckingham Palace, but he fell asleep, and ended up at Paddington station and they turfed him out. He thought about walking down to the Park, but that wasn't far enough. He told himself now he'd started, he had to keep going. It was still early, not even nine thirty. He didn't want to go back home.

And then suddenly it occurred to him that he didn't ever have to go back, if he didn't want to. He had his scholarship, he had a room near the school from September. That was two weeks away now. The same teacher who'd sent his stuff off to the Slade, Mr Wilson, he'd given him a spare room in his house, down towards the Cally

Road, and the rent was subsidised by the council. He had the money he'd stolen from his father, and he'd the promise of a couple of week's work from Billy from school's dad down at Covent Garden, moving veg around. He didn't ever have to go back, did he? Did he?

The knowledge wasn't frightening. It was the most glorious feeling he'd felt for a long time. He could sleep in hedgerows. He could draw wherever he wanted. He could even get the boat train from Victoria, go to France!

But no, he wasn't going to do that, not just yet. But he was going to go away from here, today.

A loud, piercing whistle shrieked right beside him, and David jumped. He turned to see the train behind, its engine puffing gentle balls of steam into the smoggy station.

'Where's it going?' he said.

The guard jerked his head. 'West,' he said, gnomically.

West. Well, he had to go somewhere, didn't he? This wonderful feeling of freedom was still with him, and he didn't want to think about it, just enjoy it. David climbed on to the train, with the vague idea he might go to Bath, see the bombsites there and do some more drawings to add to his collection. Maybe he'd have some lunch at a pub in the country. Maybe he'd do all sorts of things. The day, and indeed time, stretched out ahead of him, splendid, never-ending, like the perfect blue sky.

★   ★   ★

634

He sat on the train, watching the buildings stream past, the rows of houses with bombed-out gaps, the men at work rebuilding the city. The empty warehouses, the vanished streets. All those stories in their spaces, of loss and devastation. He didn't feel jingoistic, he didn't feel pride in his country. He only felt numb, a quiet sense of gladness that he and Cassie had survived.

When he disembarked at Bath Spa station he looked around him, wondering what the noise was, a little engine bolt clanging against something, an organ? And then he realised it was birds singing, so beautifully it made tears spring to his eyes. You didn't heard birdsong these days in London.

David stood outside the iron-girdered ticket hall, looking this way and that, at the empty square of land where buildings had once stood. He crossed through a tunnel, over a road, not really caring where he was going. And he walked.

He walked and walked, up a hill lined with gracious villas and leafy gardens, until he could see countryside, sweeping away from him. And he carried on walking. At the top of the highest hill the land levelled out, and he stopped for a drink at a quiet pub, the Cross Keys. The landlady gave him some bread and cheese and told him, in a broad accent he'd hardly heard before, that he was in the most beautiful part of the world. He'd forgotten his hat, so before he continued he rolled up his trouser legs and put his handkerchief, tied in knots, on to his scorched head, bid her farewell and set off again.

He could see the Georgian town curved like a gold and cream seashell, tucked into the wide valley below. Perfect puffs of cloud now circled above him, but otherwise the sky was still a deep, kind blue. So David kept walking, as the road swooped down again, into another fold of land, until he came to a river, and fields, and long-distant woodland. He looked at his watch – he had been walking for nearly two hours, and it occurred to him only now that he would have to walk back to the station, unless he didn't go back at all, just stayed here in this beautiful place. Who would miss him? He was a half-person, that was what you became if no one else cared whether you came home at night. Living in the shadows of other people's lives.

So he lay down on the grass that had only just emerged from the shadow cast by the dark woods and was deliciously cool and damp. And he chewed a ripe ear of corn, staring up above him at the sky, at nothing whatsoever at all.

When he got up to walk again, the hill above him was steep this time, the going arduous, and he began to regret the absence of a hat more and more. But he fell into an easy rhythm. His limbs were strong, his heart was light and, when he found two apples the landlady must have sneaked into the bottom of his knapsack, he ate one, grateful,

636

smiling. After walking uphill again for half an hour he reached the crest of the valley, turning towards the north again, and then he saw it. A dark driveway, framed with heavy oaks, and a bench in front.

'Seek rest, weary traveller.'

He sat down on the bench, panting, and ate the second apple, staring out at the view. The still, heavy trees. The curling road, leading to the river. Homes dotted here and there in the plush landscape, a line of white rising up from some. Swallows swooping wildly about his head, darting in and out of hedgerows. The scent of wild roses and wood smoke.

When he'd finished, he wandered down the drive, ready to run if need be – his months of clambering around the ruined capital had given him a quick eye and a fleet foot, as well as a sense of danger.

There was a house behind a circular driveway. Low, quiet, tucked against the hill. Toffee-coloured stone and leaded windows on the first floor, soaring giant wooden clapboard gables on the second, a moss-tiled roof. Purple flowers scrambling along the golden exterior, the windows glinting in the late afternoon sun. A riot of pink, red, yellow flowers – Jem would know their names – hugging each side of the house, and behind to the right side he could see rows of vegetables. Like Rapunzel's mother in the storybook his own mother used to read to him then, he thought he might die if he didn't taste one of the lettuces, cool and green in the black earth. He could hear laughter, shouts of glee inside the house.

David did not know why, but he kept on walking towards the front door. He lifted the knocker. It was a great big owl. It made him smile; he knocked, hard.

A lady answered, grey hair dressed in a bun, a lace-covered blouse, a stiff back, and a battered straw hat. She stared at him enquiringly.

'May I help you?' Her hazel eyes were huge, flecked with blue and brown.

'Ma'am, I apologise for disturbing you,' said David. 'I've walked all day and I'm afraid I'm extremely thirsty. Could I trouble you for some water?'

She opened the door wide. 'Of course. That hill does tire one out, I know. I'm Violet Heron.' She held out her hand and he shook it, a little stunned. 'Please, come in.'

He followed her into the hall. Someone was screaming with pleasure, and he looked to his left to see two children wrestling on the floor, one a young girl in a torn pinafore, the other a boy whose shorts were covered in some kind of black creosote-like substance.

'Is that Em?' one of them yelled. 'Where is she? She said she'd come and play with us.'

'Ignore my embarrassing grandchildren. I do apologise,' said the lady, but she didn't look embarrassed.

'But where is Em, do you know, Grandmother?' the girl asked.

'She's upstairs, reading. She said she'd be down soon. Hush, children.' She turned to David. 'One of our old evacuees from London has been visiting us.'

She opened a door, which led into the kitchen. A red-faced woman stood tackling something in a brown earthenware bowl. 'Dorcas,' said Mrs Heron, 'this young man wants some water.'

Dorcas heaved a mound of glistening, rubbery dough on to the marble surface and pushed her hands down on to it. She glanced him over, appraisingly. 'From the looks of him he'll be needing a lot more than water. You want some bread and stew?'

David nodded, mutely. He stared out of the kitchen window at the valley. He'd never been anywhere so beautiful in his life.

'They say on a clear night, when the bombs were coming down over Bath, you could hear the bells over at Wells Cathedral in the opposite direction, in the silence.' Mrs Heron shrugged. 'I don't believe it, but it's comforting to think it, somehow.' She watched him for a moment then stood up again. 'Dorcas, bring the tray out on to the terrace, would you?' She gestured to David. 'Follow me.'

As they opened the door, the afternoon sun hit them in the eyes and Violet put her hat on. She gestured to a stone terrace, beyond which the garden ran riot, turning into woods. 'Sit down.'

David sat. The sun seemed to be bleaching his bones and a great feeling of peace stole over him.

Time seemed to stand still. The only noise was the hum of bees, birds singing in the woods ahead and occasionally, the scream of children echoing inside the house. It was like being in a dream. He still didn't really know why he was here. He couldn't explain why he'd walked down that drive.

'Their father went missing at Monte Cassino,' Mrs Heron said suddenly. 'Those children. They still believe he's coming back.'

David sat up. 'I am so sorry. Where – where's their mother?'

Mrs Heron looked out of the window. She said flatly, 'She died in London. One of the last bombing raids.'

David wanted to say, *Mine too*, but the words wouldn't come. Dorcas appeared with a tray of bread, cold stew, water, and he thanked her, resisting the urge to gulp it all down. The stew was thin and more like soup – meat was scarce still – but to David it was the most delicious meal he'd ever had. He felt as though he'd been away from London for months. With every step out of the train station he had walked away from the war, from the sound of his father's threats, his sister's howls, his mother's dying scream.

Mrs Heron crossed her hands neatly in his lap while he ate and when he had finished she said, 'So what do you do?'

'Nothing, at the moment,' said David. 'But I'm going to art school next month. The Slade,' he added, proudly.

'Goodness, you look older than that. Where are your people from?'

'Islington.' David didn't elaborate.

'I grew up in Bloomsbury, very near the Slade,' she said. 'I miss the shops. And the buildings.'

He gave her a big smile. 'How can you miss anything, in a place like this?'

'Oh, you miss some things.' She smiled at him. 'But you're probably right. I don't, really.'

'How long have you been here?'

'Fifty years. As long as the house.'

David scooped up the last of the stew with his bread. 'You . . . you built this?'

'My husband built it for me. Winterfold was my wedding present. He died ten years ago. I'm glad he didn't live through the war, it would have broken him. He'd fought in the Great War and . . .' She trailed off and looked away, and David saw the beautiful hazel eyes were brimming with tears. 'Everything must go on.'

He changed the subject. 'Winterfold? That's the name of the house?'

'Yes. The village is Winter Stoke, and we are here in the fold of the hill. It's a fine name, I think.'

His mother's maiden name had been Winter. He sat up. 'It is a fine name.'

'What's your name, my dear?' Mrs Heron said, kindly.

'It's David,' he said, and his youth betrayed him. 'David Winter.'

Her mouth twitched. 'Is it, now.'

David's father had fought in the Great War, too. He'd come back with a hand that didn't quite work, screaming nightmares and an iron strength he deployed nearly every day in some way. He could have told Violet Heron that. He could have given her his name, been a real person, one whom she could trace if she'd wanted to. His father's son. His father who, the previous week, had beaten his new girlfriend, Sally, from the butcher's, so hard she'd been put in the hospital. His father who, when he found David's cloth-backed folder crammed full of drawings of London children, of bombed-out houses, of rubble and decay and hope and experience, had kneed him against the wall, forced his arm across David's neck and pinned him down while he ripped every piece of paper into precise, inch-wide ribbons that fell on to the floor into nests of colour.

'Yes. My name's David Winter,' he said. 'For my mother. It was her maiden name.' He stuck his chin out and tipped his head back, because he didn't want to cry. 'Don't believe me if you don't want to.'

She nodded, her eyes kind. 'Of course I believe you.'

He regretted it now, and felt young, stupid. He'd told this woman too much and he shouldn't have come here. David fished his handkerchief, still in knots, out of his pocket. He was suddenly uneasy.

'Thank you for your kindness. I should probably

leave now. I have a long journey back.' He wanted to go right away. He felt embarrassed as if coming here had released something within him, that he shouldn't have knocked on the door, should merely have stared at the outside and turned back down the hill. They walked around the front of the house in silence. 'Well, thank you again,' he said. 'Goodbye.'

Violet Heron paused for a moment, as if wanting to say something, and then she took off her hat, gave it to him. 'Take it. For the walk. It was my husband's. I have my own and I'd like you to have it. It'll fit you.'

It was battered, frayed around the edges, the straw soft to the touch and pliable. He put it on, with a smile. 'That's very kind of you. It's more than I deserve. I—' He stopped, unable to speak. 'I mean it.'

Then a voice called out, 'Mrs Heron! I'm going now. I have to make that train.'

And a girl appeared, flying limbs, cramming a hat on her sleek head. She was his age, or maybe a year younger. 'Thank you so much, it's been absolutely lovely – oh.' She stopped, and stared at him. 'Sorry. I didn't know I was interrupting.'

Her voice was husky; South London, he thought. Mrs Heron stood up. 'You're not interrupting, my dear. The children were looking for you. I hope they didn't spoil your work.'

'It's fine. I have everything I need, I think. Thank you so much. Hello. Who are you?'

She held out her hand to him, and he took it, gazing at her.

'I'm David Winter,' he said, and it sounded perfectly, totally right and normal when he said it. 'That is my name.'

What an idiot, why had he said that then?

She looked at him as though he were a simpleton. 'Right then.'

'Em was evacuated here during the war,' Mrs Heron said, putting her arm around the girl. 'Four lovely years. We do miss her terribly. She's come back for the weekend to see us.'

Em looked uncomfortable, but pleased. She slid a sketchbook into her bag and ran a hand over her gleaming bobbed hair. 'Bye, Mrs Heron,' she said, gruffly. 'I'll see you soon, I hope.'

'You'll pay us a visit in the autumn?'

'I don't know about my classes yet. I'll write to you.' Her smile grew warm as she kissed the older woman's cheek. 'Thank you again, for everything.'

She was so self-possessed; how had she learned to be like that? He wiggled a finger through the hole in his stinking, grubby trousers, aware as never before that day how dirty and ragged they were. She must think he was a tramp.

'Any time it suits you, please come and stay, my dear girl.' Mrs Heron smiled at her. 'We do miss you.'

'I miss you. And I miss Winterfold. How could I not?' She turned to David. 'It was my home, you know. Only home I wish I'd ever known.'

He wanted to give it to her then, to pluck it out of the land like a wizard, shrink it down, hold it out to her in the palm of his hand. *Here.*

'Look, I have to make this train and I'm walking to the station. So I'd better go.'

'I'm going to the station too, yes,' he said, hearing his own voice, shrill and silly. 'Where are you going? Bath?'

'Yeah,' she said, squeezing Mrs Heron's hand and setting off at a pace down the drive. 'Well?' she added, over her shoulder. 'You coming or not?'

He ran after her, waving goodbye to Mrs Heron, who called after them, 'Goodbye, dears, goodbye . . .'

He pulled on the worn hat. It fitted like a glove, the weave cool against his forehead. David looked back and smiled at her, tipped the brim, in a comic fashion, and she nodded, pleased.

He never saw her again, but he never forgot her. The large, looping wave she gave them, as they turned the corner and she disappeared from sight.

When they reached the top of the lane, by the sign that said Winterfold, the girl stopped and faced him. 'What's your name again?'

'David,' he said.

'Ah. Well, I'm Martha. That's my name, but I like to be called Em for short. Just want to be clear in case you attack me and I have to report you to the police.'

He wasn't sure if she was joking. He was unused

to any kind of light-hearted conversation, much less flirting. 'I wouldn't – it's not—'

'I'm just being funny. Don't look so alarmed,' she said, smiling at him. 'It's a nice place here, isn't it?'

'Yes. Didn't know there were . . . places like this in real life. I want to sketch it.'

'You like drawing too, then?' she said, curiously, as if registering him for the first time.

'I do. You?'

'I love it,' she said, clutching the bag with the sketchbook. 'I'm going to try for a scholarship next year. Chelsea School of Art, or the Slade. I'm going to be a famous artist, I reckon. Paint anything you want, have a stand up on Sundays in Hyde Park and make all my money in one afternoon. I can copy all sorts, see? I copied this last month.'

She pulled out a picture. 'That's *Bubbles*!' David was amazed. 'Right there! You did that? Is it pastels? Where'd you get them from?'

'Joint birthday and Christmas present. My dad saved up for ages. My birthday's in November, you see. Early birthday present.' She rolled the sketch back up. 'Told you I was good. You any good?'

'Not like that,' he said. 'More . . . I don't know.' He shrugged. 'S'difficult to talk about.'

'Oh, he's a proper artist.' She walked alongside him, head bowed, lip drooping, in imitation. 'Oh, he's too good for all that. He can't talk about his art!' She laughed. 'Deary me.'

646

He stopped and smiled, pushing the hat back off his face. 'Oh, get off. Don't really talk to other people much about it.' About anything. About anything at all.

'All right, I get it.' Somehow he knew she did, without having to say more. 'I came down here to sketch. I love it. Get all the best ideas down here.'

He stared into her dancing eyes again, thinking that he'd never seen anyone so beautiful. 'I can see why.'

'It suits you, that hat,' she said, suddenly, and then added, 'You'll have to come back here one day too.'

'Yes, I think I will,' he replied, trying to sound nonchalant, though his heart was hammering. They walked on together, the afternoon heat shimmering in front of them, golden shafts of light falling on to the hazy, leafy road that lay ahead.

INTRODUCTION TO HUMAN RESOURCE MANAGEME

Introduction to Human Resource Management

theory and practice

Linda Maund

palgrave
macmillan

First published 2001 by
PALGRAVE MACMILLAN
Houndmills, Basingstoke, Hampshire RG21 6XS and
175 Fifth Avenue, New York, N.Y. 10010
Companies and representatives throughout the world

PALGRAVE MACMILLAN is the new global academic imprint of St. Martin's Press LLC Scholarly and Reference Division and Palgrave Publishers Ltd (formerly Macmillan Press Ltd).

ISBN 0–333–91242–X hardback
ISBN 0–333–91243–8 paperback

PB 9780333912430
HB 9780333912423

This book is printed on paper suitable for recycling and made from fully managed and sustained forest sources.

A catalogue record for this book is available from the British Library.

Library of Congress Cataloging-in-Publication Data

Maund, Linda.
    Introduction to human resource management: theory and practice / Linda Maund.
        p. cm.
    Includes bibliographical references and index.
    ISBN 0–333–91242–X — ISBN 0–333–91243–8 (pbk. : alk. paper)
        1. Personnel management. I. Title.

    HF5549 .M3392 2000
    658.3—dc21

                                                00–066867

Editing and origination by
Aardvark Editorial, Mendham, Suffolk

10 9 8 7 6 5 4 3
11 10 09 08 07 06 05

Printed and bound in Great Britain
by Ashford Colour Press Ltd, Gosport

Dedicated to Charlotte, Becky and Emma
and in memory of Pam – my lifelong guiding star

Contents

List of figures

List of tables

Introduction to Human Resource Management

Plan of the book

Part I HUMAN RESOURCE MANAGEMENT: CONTEXT, CONTENT AND DEBATE

Chapter 1	Chapter 2
Characteristics of human resource management	Strategic human resource management

Part II PLANNING, RECRUITMENT AND SELECTION

Chapter 3	Chapter 4
Human resource planning	Recruitment and selection

Part III INFORMATION PROVISION

Chapter 5	Chapter 6
Communication and employee involvement	Technology, information and knowledge management

Part IV EMPLOYEE RELATIONSHIPS AND ESSENTIAL EMPLOYMENT LAW

Chapter 7	Chapter 8
Employee relationships	Essential employment law

Part V DEVELOPING THE WORKFORCE

Chapter 9	Chapter 10
Rewards and remuneration	Employee development and performance management

Part VI CONTEMPORARY CONCERNS

Chapter 11	Chapter 12
Key issues: globalisation, ethics and workplace diversity	Human resource management in an international context

Preface

There is no best way to manage or to lead human resources. The human resource management (HRM) specialist and the line manager, in whatever country or organisation, must search for a true balance in the management of human resources if they are to compete in the global market. The field of HRM is full of competing and conflicting models and theories, wherein there are very few absolutes that dictate how people should behave in the workplace and how they should be managed. It is recognised, in theory if not always in practice, that the role of human resources is to assist in the long-term viability of a business or a non-profit making enterprise, is substantial and does not occur by chance. While it is recognised that other resources are essential to the efficacy of an organisation's business, for example finance and production, it is the human resources that remain virtually limitless in their capacity to make an impact – both positive and negative – on an organisation,

The principal objectives of this book are to provide some insights necessary to the comprehension and analysis of the nature of HRM and how people, the environment and situations interact to contribute to the long-term survival of business. The text is grounded in a firm foundation of research in the field and on new developments that apply to daily situations within organisations and their environment.

This book explores the issues related to HRM and seeks to define the shape of the organisation of the 21st century. The study of contemporary issues related to HRM shows that, at the level of the individual organisation, the problem is to overcome the barrage of legislation and appreciate that it is the workers who will bring the profit – both in financial and personal terms. At both national and international levels, countries may become laggards if, for example, they fail to provide an infrastructure which is sufficient to enable their organisations to take advantage of the contemporary ways of carrying out HRM that, in their totality, will shrink the effects of time and distance.

The book is contemporary in its topics, examples, research and readability. I hope that my enthusiasm for the field of human resources is contagious and will motivate all who use it to learn more about the dynamic nature of the management of people in the workplace.

ORGANISATION AND COVERAGE

The organisation and coverage in this book represent continuous fine-tuning within an ever-evolving field of study and the comments made by the numerous anonymous reviewers have been taken into account – their contribution is gratefully acknowledged elsewhere.

The content of *Introduction to Human Resource Management* is divided into six parts that emanate from the characteristics of the field:

- human resource management: context, content and debate

- planning, recruitment and selection

- information provision

- employee relationships and essential employment law

- developing the workforce, and

- contemporary concerns.

Chapter 1 discusses the basic concepts to be found in the field of HRM, showing its development over time and the similarities and differences between it and personnel management (PM). Chapter 2 develops these themes by focusing on the strategic role of HRM. The two chapters in Part II concentrate on human resource planning (HRP) and its link with recruitment and selection.

Part III contains two chapters concerned with information provision, with Chapter 5 analysing the issue of communication and employee involvement and Chapter 6 continuing with these themes within technology, including information technology (IT), data, information, knowledge and the increasing importance of the role of knowledge workers and knowledge management.

Part IV comprises two chapters that are also closely linked: the issue of employee relationships in the contemporary workplace and the legal meaning of 'employee', with an evaluation of the role of partnerships as they contribute to effective employee relationships (EI). Chapter 8 develops this theme with an investigation into what is understood by 'employment law' and an assessment of the key issues incorporated in the major Acts of Parliament and European Union Directives. Equal opportunities is a key linking issue between these two chapters.

Part V looks at how managers and organisations can enhance individual performance through reward systems, remuneration and performance measurement.

Part VI analyses some key contemporary issues incorporated in the text but in more detail. The choice of the themes for Chapter 11 – globalisation, ethics and workplace diversity – were not arbitrary but selected after a careful analysis of the issues raised in the professional and business environment. The final chapter develops the themes of the book into an investigation of the role of international human resource management (IHRM), with analysis of the position in different countries such as Eastern and Western Europe, African, Caribbean and Pacific countries, North America, Latin and Central America, China, Australia and New Zealand.

The author recognises that the future belongs to those individuals who are transculturally competent in that they can recognise, respect and reconcile differences and thus motivate themselves and their employees to work better.

FEATURES OF THE BOOK

ACCESSIBILITY AND PEDAGOGICAL FEATURES

One of the foremost aims of the book is to make it as accessible as possible. The language is aimed at the student with an attempt to avoid patronisation yet to engage the intellect and make the whole understandable. It contains a variety of pedagogical features designed to guide students through the text and help them to gain a complete and thorough understanding of the key concepts of HRM. These include:

- **Learning Outcomes** – what the student will be able to do after s/he has studied the chapter and carried out the activities within and at the end of the chapter

- **Framework Case Study** – a look at applications of the theory for that chapter, providing an interesting way to lock the student's attention and impart crucial theoretical content in a digestible format

- In-chapter **Activities** – peppered throughout the text

- **Points to Ponder** – challenging the student to think more analytically and critically about key issues presented

- **Scenarios** – case vignettes to help illustrate the theory

- **Thesis + Antithesis = Synthesis** feature – to encourage consideration of both sides of an issue to give the student an opportunity to unify ideas and thus assist and enhance the learning process

- **Chapter Summaries** – to enable the student to synthesise the key issues from the chapter

- **End of Chapter Case Study** and **Questions** – to consolidate the theoretical implications drawn from the chapter

- **End of Part Case Study** and **Questions** – of an international flavour to consolidate the key issues from the two chapters which comprise that part

- **Self-test Questions, Class Discussion Questions** and **Projects** – to stimulate further learning and interaction between students, for all of which model answers are provided on the lecturers' zone of the companion website

- **Recommended Reading** – to direct the student to wider reading sources

■ **URLs (uniform resource locators)** – to direct the student to wider research on the Internet

■ Running margin **Glossary** – to provide on-page definitions for quick reference of key concepts (complete **Glossary** also at back of book)

■ **Thematic Cross-referencing** – to assist the student in tracing the thread of an essay theme throughout the book.

CONTEMPORARY FOCUS

The theory, research and analysis of each topic represents the thinking at the time of writing. Popular and topical issues are interwoven within the text with examples to illustrate the current use of these ideas and concepts. For example, globalisation, ethics and diversity are discussed in several chapters but are given an in-depth discussion in Part VI, Chapter 11.

APPLICATIONS

Throughout the book the organisations cited in examples, case studies, scenarios, and points to ponder represent a blend of well-known international and national firms and less well-known small organisations in order to show the applicability of HRM to all organisations. Each chapter starts with a framework case study which incorporates the key themes for that chapter and gives concrete examples. Each chapter also comprises true-life scenarios and points for further consideration. All the examples and pedagogical features of the text combine to give the student both an understanding of how the concepts apply to the real world and also an opportunity to practise the concepts through activities.

SUPPLEMENTARY MATERIALS

The text is accompanied by a complete package of teaching and learning support materials which can be found at its companion website:

http://www.palgrave.com/business/maund

This is also available as hard copy on request. The companion site, divided into a lecturers' zone which is password protected and a students' zone, will include:

■ *Virtual guided tour of the text*

■ *Lecturers' zone*
- model answers to activities
- teaching notes for case study
- model answers to case study questions

- teaching notes for thesis/antithesis/synthesis feature
- model answers for self-test questions
- model answers for class discussion questions
- model answers for project questions
- overhead transparencies
- contact the author feature

- *Students' zone*
  - revision notes (these differ from the end of chapter summaries by fleshing out the key concepts for the student)
  - further reading to direct the student to wider reading sources
  - links and resources to direct the student to wider research on the Internet
  - discussion forum to encourage students to exchange ideas and initiate and foster discussions
  - contact the author feature.

Acknowledgements

Although this book bears the name of one author, a number of people have contributed to it. Over the years I have been able to work with students, academics and business professionals who have helped me to sharpen my thinking and thus enabled me to attribute analysis and evaluation to what is a complex field of study.

A number of key reviewers have been important and their contributions have been essential to the development of the text.

Every effort has been made to trace all the copyright holders but if any have inadvertently been overlooked, the publishers will be pleased to make the necessary arrangements at the first opportunity. However, any and all errors of omission, interpretation and emphasis remain my responsibility.

I would like particularly to acknowledge the outstanding team of professionals at Palgrave, particularly my publisher, Sarah Brown, who has made vital contributions while supporting me throughout the project.

In particular, I would like to thank the following for their invaluable comments: Paul Stokes at Sheffield Business School, Sheffield Hallam University; David Taylor at the Faculty of Management and Business, Manchester Metropolitan University; Rysia Reynolds at Southampton Business School, Southampton Institute; and Paul Hill at Newcastle Business School at the University of Northumbria at Newcastle.

Thanks also go to: Jane Thompson (Lincs & Humberside); Dr Len Holden (De Montfort); Laurie Lomas (Canterbury Christ Church University College); Peter Fenwick (UEL); Paul Frimston (University of Central Lancashire); Sue Bathmaker (Luton); Sue Simpson (Nottingham Trent); Susan Kirk (Nottingham Trent); Suki Manak (Coventry); Moira Calder (Dundee); Alison Alker (University of Central Lancashire); Professor John Leopold (Nottingham Trent); Chris Rees (Kingston); Graham Tomlin (Salford); Dr Keith Randle (Hertfordshire); Allan Blackburn (Oxford Brookes); Professor Henrik Holt Larsen (Copenhagen Business School); Richard Pullen (Middlesex); and Joanne Duberley (Sheffield).

Last, but by no means least, I must acknowledge the love and support of my beloved husband, Richard, without whom the many crises that occurred during the project period would not have been overcome.

LINDA MAUND

Abbreviations used in this book

ACAS	Advisory, Conciliation and Arbitration Service
ACP	African, Caribbean and Pacific countries
AGM	annual general meeting
AI	artificial intelligence
AMT	advanced manufacturing technology
BA	British Airways
BBC	British Broadcasting Corporation
BCC	British Chambers of Commerce
BIM	British Institute of Management
BMA	British Medical Association
BPR	business process re-engineering
BT	British Telecommunications
CA	Contribution Agency
CBI	Confederation of British Industry
CD	continuous development
CECLR	Centre for Equal Opportunities Combating Racism (EU Flemish translation)
CEO	chief executive officer
CIM	Chartered Institute of Marketing
CIPD	Chartered Institute of Personnel and Development
COD	*Concise Oxford Dictionary*
CPD	continuous professional development
CRE	Commission for Racial Equality
CWU	Commercial Workers' Union
DPR	Data Protection Registrar

DRC	Disability Rights Commission
DTI	Department of Trade and Industry
DVD	digital versatile disc
EC	European Commission
ECJ	European Court of Justice
EI	employee involvement
EOC	Equal Opportunities Commission
ERA	Employment Rights Act 1996
ESB	electricity supply board
ESOP	employee stock ownership plan
ET	employment tribunal
EU	European Union
EVA	economic value added
EWC	European Works Councils
FEDA	Further Education Development Agency
FT	*Financial Times*
GATT	General Agreement on Tariffs and Trade
GDP	gross domestic product
GLC	government-linked corporation
GMB	General Municipal Boilermakers union
GSP	generalised system of preferences
GWT	Great Western Trains
HKPU	Hong Kong Polytechnic University
HPM	human potential management

HRM	human resource management		MP	manpower planning
HRP	human resource planning		MSFU	Manufacturing Science Finance Union
HSC	Health and Safety Commission			
HSE	Health and Safety Executive		NACRO	National Association for the Care and Resettlement of Offenders
IBM	International Business Machines			
			NAFTA	North Atlantic Free Trade Association
ICT	interactive communication technology			
			NCVQ	National Council for Vocational Qualifications
IDS	Incomes Data Services			
IFG	International Forum on Globalization		NHS	National Health Service
			NP	new pay
IHRM	international human resource management		NSAP	non-specific arm pain
			NVQs	national vocational qualifications
IiP	Investors in People			
ILO	International Labour Organization			
			OB	organisational behaviour
IMDC	International Management Development Consortium			
			PCP	personal construct psychology
IMF	International Monetary Fund		PM	personnel management
IOD	Institute of Directors		PR	public relations
IPD	Institute of Personnel and Development (now CIPD)		PRP	performance-related pay
IPM	Institute of Personnel Management (now CIPD)		RIBA	Royal Institute of British Architects
IQ	intelligence quotient		RSI	repetitive strain injury
IR	industrial relations or Inland Revenue (depending on context)		SAS	Strategic Air Services
			SAYE	Save-As-You-Earn
IT	information technology		SC-SAC	Southern California Size Acceptance Coalition
JCC	Joint Consultative Committee		SEM	Single European Market
LSQ	learning styles questionnaire		SHRM	strategic human resource management
Ltips	long-term initiative plans			
			SMART	simple, measurable, achievable, realistic, time related
MBA	Master in Business Administration			
MBO	management by objectives		SMD	strategic management development
MCI	Management Charter Initiative			
MD	management development		SMEs	small and medium-size enterprises
MIS	management information system			
			STABEX	stabilisation of export earnings
MNC	multinational corporation			

STEEEP	social, technological, economic, environmental, ethical, political
SWOT	strengths, weaknesses, opportunities, threats
SWT	South West Trains
Tecs	Training and Enterprise Councils
TP	traditional pay
TQM	total quality management
TUC	Trades Union Congress
TUPE	Transfer of Undertakings (Protection of Employment) Regulations (1981)
UFHRD	University Forum for Human Resource Development
UfI	University for Industry
UNHCR	United Nations High Commission for Refugees
UNI	Union Network International
URL	uniform resource locator
USDAW	Union of Shop, Distributive and Allied Workers
VDU	visual display unit
VIE	Valence, Instrumentality, Expectancy (theory)
WERS	Workplace Employee Relations Survey (1999)
WHO	World Health Organization
WTO	World Trade Organization
www	World Wide Web

Human resource management: context, content and debate

Characteristics of human resource management

1

After studying this chapter, you should be able to:

- EVALUATE the development of human resource management (HRM) from the early 19th century to the millennium.
- CONCEPTUALISE the 'person as resource' and 'person as person' view surrounding HRM.
- COMPARE and CONTRAST personnel management (PM) and HRM as ways of managing people.
- SUMMARISE the contemporary views of HRM.
- ANALYSE the theoretical issues surrounding the HRM field of expertise.

Framework case study

The chocolate billionaire who terrorised his staff: Forrest Mars (1904–99)

Forrest Mars, the inventor of the Mars Bar, was one of the USA's most eccentric entrepreneurs. Obsessive, reclusive and notoriously bad-tempered he tyrannised his staff and his family to force a billion-dollar business empire which today employs some 30 000 people worldwide.

Born in Washington in 1904, the only son of a candy (sweet) maker, Mars was scarred by an unhappy childhood. His parents divorced when he was six and Forrest was sent to live with his strict grandparents in Canada. In 1923, however, he was reunited with his father, and began a partnership which would eventually make the Mars family the richest in the USA.

Frank Mars had just launched a chocolate called the Mar-O-Bar. It had achieved only a limited success when, over a malted milkshake, Forrest suggested that he 'put the milkshake in a candy bar'. The Milky Way – or Mars Bar as the sweeter British version was known – was an instant success, garnering sales worth US$800 000 in its first year. But money divided father and son. Where Frank adopted a champagne and caviar lifestyle, Forrest became a skinflint. At the Mars headquarters in Virginia, USA, even top executives were denied perks and had to clock in and out like factory workers. Father and son squabbled bitterly until 1932, when Forrest moved to England with his new wife – and with the foreign rights to the Milky Way. At the British base in Slough, Berkshire, his temper was legendary. Workers were fired for having the tiniest stains on their overalls and poorly wrapped chocolate bars were hurled around the factory floor. But by 1935 such attention to detail had made him a fortune three times the size of his father's, and he returned to the USA 'in triumph'. But Frank was by then dead and control of the firm rested with his second wife. Forrest's vicious campaign to win it back led to him being known as the 'Monster from Mars'.

In 1964, his stepmother finally gave way, and Mars descended 'like a wolf on well-fed lambs'. He called a meeting of executives, and told them he was a religious man, before sinking to his knees and chanting 'I pray for Milky Way, I pray for Snickers…' and so on through all 26 Mars products. He then ripped out their dining room, fired the chef and gave away the company helicopter. One executive who protested was reassigned to the pet food division. Later Mars visited the factory and told the executive that it was his duty to sample the products. Terrorised, he promptly ate a chunk of Pedigree Chum (a dog food).

Mars was equally harsh with his children. There was plenty of work, it was said, but little rest or play. When his son John once asked to be excused a sales meeting to attend his wife's birthday, Mars flew into a rage and ordered him to pray for the company. For two hours, the 29-year-old knelt on the floor as the meeting went on around him. But in 1973, Mars unexpectedly gave the firm to his sons to set up a new chocolate business in Las Vegas, USA. There he installed a two-way mirror to check on staff and lived in a flat above the factory. When his sons bought it from him in 1990, it was their turn to penny-pinch. Mars asked to stay in his flat, and his sons insisted he pay rent.

Adapted from: The chocolate billionaire who terrorised his staff, Obituaries, *The Week*, 10 July 1999, p32.

The above Framework Case Study may appear in today's climate to be rather extreme yet it epitomises the working conditions of some people in relatively recent history. However, the organisation is now more in tune with modern HRM concepts that are based on the firm traditions of its early history.

1.1

Activity

Make a list of the behaviour which you think is within the realm of PM and/or HRM.

Now, make two separate lists under the headings 'PM' and 'HRM'.

Make comments on the difficulties you had – if any.

Human resource management (HRM) is not dissimilar to ▶ **organisational behaviour** ◀ (OB) in that both are concerned with the individual members of an organisation's workforce. However, OB is directly concerned with a set of behaviours, for example attitudes, perceptions and motivation, whereas HRM recognises that people must be effectively managed if an organisation is to achieve its objectives and thus be 'ahead of the rest'. This is an important distinction. However, it is not a simplistic, or generally agreed, distinction and therein lies the paradox.

▶ The study of the impact that individuals, groups and structures within an organisation have ◀·····▶ **Organisational** on meeting the goals of an organisation. **behaviour**

Dawes (1995) believes that the view of managers and textbook authors is that people are the key resource in many organisations but goes on to state that:

there is little evidence to show that managers *behave* as though this is true. (p8)

This is a serious indictment of HRM. The statement that 'people are the greatest asset of an organisation' may be a ubiquitous organisational cliché yet it has within it some truth. In today's market one dominating factor makes the difference between success and failure – people.

A review of the literature on HRM treats it as either *hard* or *soft* although some writers attempt to take the middle line. Table 1.1 gives a commonly held view on the difference between the two.

Individuals who believe in the *hard* approach to HRM consider members of the workforce to be a resource, which can be hired, used and dispensed with without any thought to their feelings. Decision making concerning human relations issues is taken on a rational basis as part of the overall strategy for making a profit. Managers who adopt the *hard* approach pay little attention to the needs of their employees and emphasise the statistical and quantitative sides of their businesses. The *soft* approach is the other side of the coin where managers consider their workforce to comprise individual human beings who contribute to the organisation.

Table 1.1 'Soft' versus 'hard' views of human resource management

Hard	Soft
Resource	Human beings
Rational	Investment in continuous development
Business strategy and HRM strategy	Commitment strategies
Little attention to needs	Competitive advantage through people
Emphasis on quantitative	Emphasis on qualitative

see Chapter 9

Such organisations use commitment strategies, for example reward packages ■ *see* Chapter 9 ■ to maintain their competitive advantage through their workforce. Unlike the *hard* approach, there is an emphasis on qualitative and behavioural aspects of working life.

Whichever approach a manager takes, Bickerstaffe (1997) believes that:

> The effective management of human resources is a major consideration for all general managers. (p250)

The responsibility for managing aspects of the human resource elements of business has increasingly fallen upon the shoulders, in varying degrees, of ▶ **line managers** ◀. It is this line relationship which charts the authority of one person over others in the organisation's structure. This is one of the reasons why all managers – be they, say, specialists in marketing, accountancy or production – need to know how to manage people. Such managers call on the expertise of HRM specialists who provide a ▶ **staff relationship** ◀ function. An example here would be where an organisation has a separate department whose task it is to deal with

see Chapter 6

information technology and information management issues ■ *see* Chapter 6 ■ for all departments within the organisation.

Line managers ◀┈┈▶ Individuals who have direct responsibility for other employees and their work and duties. The line relationship charts the authority of one person over others in the organisation's structure.

Staff relationship ◀┈┈▶ A relationship where individuals provide a purely advisory support service to others and where there is a limited element of authority or control.

PricewaterhouseCoopers (Conoley, 1998) reported in their European HR benchmarking survey that:

> HR departments are the life-blood of organisations. They recruit, train, reward and manage all employees. They are a vital part of the economic process and as such, many companies are now examining the performance of their HR department in relation to that of their competitors. If people give an organisation a competitive edge, can the way in which we manage those people provide us with an even greater advantage? (p2)

Whatever the individual view on human resources, the purpose of HRM is to add value to an organisation and in doing this managers need to concentrate on the organisation's objectives. This might seem obvious, but if an organisation is aiming to, say, reduce its overheads and introduce ▶ **downsizing** ◀, a manager should, perhaps, be considering issues such as redundancy rather than recruitment and selection. The PricewaterhouseCoopers' (1998) business briefing report highlights that HRM strategy ■ *see* Chapter 2 ■ is paramount if human resources are to be used to achieve success.

see Chapter 2

> ▶ Sometimes called downlayering or rightsizing, and means a reduction in staff numbers ◀┈┈▶ **Downsizing**
> throughout an organisation.

To appreciate the views held on HRM it is essential to have a clear understanding of its growth and development. HRM did not just arrive – it has an important history and its current, and future, importance sits strongly within this historical framework.

HISTORY OF HRM

Fashions come and go and the same applies to ideas about ▶ **management** ◀ not least of all to the management of people. There is, however, a consistent view which has prevailed for over 20 years – those organisations which are the leaders in their fields always make effective use of their people.

> ▶ A distinct subsystem which is responsible for directing and coordinating all other subsys- ◀┈┈▶ **Management**
> tems in an organisation.

1.2

Activity

List five leaders of modern industry who are perceived to make effective use of their people. What else do they have in common?

The discussion on the historical perspectives of people management commences with the ▶ **Industrial Revolution** ◀, and then follows its evolution through significant events to the current era.

> ▶ Generally believed to refer to the development of industry through employment of ◀┈┈▶ **Industrial**
> machinery, which took place in England in the early 19th century. **Revolution**

THE INDUSTRIAL REVOLUTION

The Industrial Revolution saw the introduction of fundamental changes in the relationships between individuals and groups in communities and brought with it a new order to life and new sources of wealth. Accompanying this was a growth in both population and output. Some individuals, such as factory owners, developed considerable personal power and the combination of these factors forced organisations and communities to revisit the very nature of their activities and their interrelationships. The combination of large-scale migration – from the country to the town, from one workplace to another – and changing societal values, inevitably changed the nature of social relations within, and between, communities and, thus, workplaces.

Is the Industrial Revolution over?

Some individuals feel that it is not since there are still developments in, and in the use of, machinery.

Economic life increasingly became dominated by developing organisations which needed increasing numbers of skilled workers and individuals who were able to manage both the production line and the people concerned with it. Such owners and managers were expected to show ▶ **leadership** ◀ and the community looked to them to do just that. There were no trained experts in the management of people. There were external threats to the autonomy and authority of owners and managers – war, ▶ **recession** ◀ and political change. The combination of these external threats became a hazard to those in power – the owners and managers.

Leadership ◀┄┄▶ The process of guiding and directing the behaviour of followers within the workplace.

Recession ◀┄┄▶ A decline in economic trade and prosperity.

In the 1870s a recession arrived and lasted to the 1890s when the additional pressure for changes in the way organisations were owned, run and managed became important. There developed demands for a more sympathetic approach to the members of the workforce in response to their individual needs. Gradually, individual ▶ **entrepreneurial** ◀ and ▶ **corporate** ◀ responses to the needs of the disadvantaged became evident in practice.

Entrepreneurial ◀┄┄▶ The activities of an owner/manager of a business who attempts to make a profit by using her/his initiative and taking risks.

Corporate ◀┄┄▶ Belonging to a united group.

By the early 1880s industrialists began to become interested in the social welfare of their workforces and met to form such bodies as the Newcastle or Manchester

Library and Philosophical Societies. Such august groups addressed social issues of the period and tried to offer ideas within areas of concern – such as long working hours and the poor health of their workers ■ *see* Chapters 7 *and* 8 ■. Personnel management (PM) was beginning to take shape. Many of these industrialists moved on to play very important roles in establishing the English civic universities such as Manchester, Liverpool, Newcastle and Birmingham – areas where activities were centred on industrial concerns.

see Chapter 7 *and* Chapter 8

Booth (London) and Rowntree (York) studied the conditions under which people had to live by concentrating on diverse issues such as parliamentary reform, standards of education, aspects of health and the development of science. All these issues were concerned with an individual's competence in expressing a sense of ownership and responsibility to the wider community and set the foundation for human relations which was, therefore, projected into the workplace.

POINTS TO PONDER

In the mid-1860s a philosophy of self-help was posited and communicated through sermons, lectures, books, pamphlets and tracts. Free will involved choice because, according to him:

Nobody adulterates our food
Nobody fills us with bad drink
Nobody supplies us with foul water
Nobody spreads fever in blind alleys and unswept lanes.

It might do to consider whether this 'ditty' applies in contemporary society considering the issues of genetic modification of food, water pollution and the revised threat of biological warfare.

NONCONFORMIST CHALLENGES IN BRITAIN

Religion played a pivotal role in shaping the attitudes and actions of both owners and workers in Victorian Britain and such beliefs still have a place in contemporary HRM. The Christianity that was practised was ▶ **eclectic** ◀ – from the Catholicism of the Irish migrant and High Church Anglicanism to Quakerism and the Congregationalist beliefs. However, it was the actions of the ▶ **Nonconformists** ◀ (especially the Quakers) which played an increasingly important role in shaping the values of the upcoming entrepreneurial groups. Many leading entrepreneurs (with names which continue to exist in business today) were practising Noncomformists – some are given in Table 1.2.

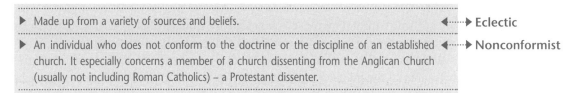

▶ Made up from a variety of sources and beliefs. ◀┈┈▶ **Eclectic**

▶ An individual who does not conform to the doctrine or the discipline of an established ◀┈┈▶ **Nonconformist**
church. It especially concerns a member of a church dissenting from the Anglican Church
(usually not including Roman Catholics) – a Protestant dissenter.

Table 1.2 Industry and great names

Brewing	Whitbread, Truman
Banking	Lloyd, Barclay
Confectionery	Cadbury, Rowntree
Glass	Pilkington
Tobacco	Wills, Player

The Nonconformists believed that through the very nature of their religious beliefs and training came the strength of character which led each of them to pursue an outlet in trade and commerce. They were actually forced to become entrepreneurs if they wanted to be viewed by others to be 'successful'. Their foundations and roots in religion were exceptionally strong and this enabled them to maintain the important links with the wider community which was encompassed by their various churches.

However, this state of affairs did not continue for long because the various churches began to soften their beliefs and activities. This was first seen in the USA where Rockefeller (1839–1937) made a large fortune from petroleum in his role as a financier. He did not appear to have any problems reconciling proactive membership of the Baptist church with what was a ruthless determination to build the most powerful Trust in the USA – Standard Oil. However, he was known as a ▶ **philanthropist** ◀. He established and endowed four charitable foundations – including the Rockefeller Foundation which was established in 1913 with a mission to promote the well-being of mankind throughout the world, a mission that could be seen as pompous in the current age. He also founded (1901) the Rockefeller Institute for Medical Research in New York. This example shows that working management practices were ruthless, yet in the wider community such individuals practised philanthropy.

Philanthropist ◀┅▶ A person who perceives her/himself to be a lover of mankind and who actively exerts her/himself for the well-being of her/his fellow beings.

Religion introduced further dimensions to the approach to the ownership of wealth and the management of industry and, by definition, the management of the workforce. The feeling of community was very strong and this was derived from the nature of the religions – the chapel or communal meeting places where there developed a tradition of community and support for others. Perhaps this was the start of teamworking! This developed into an emphasis on the responsibilities which were associated with increasing wealth and success. Some examples of these are prudence, thrift, enterprise and abstinence from alcohol and sexual intercourse (except for the purpose of procreation within marriage).

However, the church did not have a monopoly on the control of an individual's behaviour in the home or at work. At the same time as the church was influencing

SCENARIO 1.1

Port Sunlight

Port Sunlight is the picturesque 19th-century garden village built by William Hesketh Lever for his soap factory workers and named after his famous Sunlight soap. Lever employed 30 different architects to create Port Sunlight's unique style. His plans for the village included attractive, good quality housing and plenty of open spaces for recreation. Port Sunlight also boasted two schools, its own hospital, shops, two village halls, social clubs, the Bridge Inn and the majestic Christ Church, Lever's personal gift to the village.

The heritage centre explores the fascinating story of Port Sunlight and its community. A scale model of the village and copies of the original plans illustrate Port Sunlight's importance as a model for town planning. Old photographs and early film footage depict a quality of life for residents unimaginable in most 19th-century industrial communities.

Lever's celebrated use of marketing can be seen in the displays of packaging and advertising for his soap products.

Adapted from: Ship to Shore, onboard magazine for Norse Irish Ferries & Merchant Ferries, Spring/Summer 2000, p25.

1.3 Activity

Carry out a search of the archives of your university.

Identify its origins to see if they lie in industrial, commercial or religious philanthropy.

ownership and management, parliamentary reform (especially in the widening of the ▶ **franchise** ◀) was an ongoing theme of radical action. Direct intervention was used in an attempt to eradicate the worst abuses within factories, mines and private homes – abuse of children, lack of adequate health and safety, malnutrition, long working hours are just a few examples. However, in the final analysis, it was the dominance of the Nonconformists and ▶ **utilitarians** ◀ which created the opportunities for self-employment, and advocated changes in behaviour. It could be said that they were the first managers of human resources.

▶ The right to vote at a public election, especially for a member of a legislative body such as ◀····▶ **Franchise** central government.

▶ A principle of ethics; people who believe that the highest good lies in the greatest good for ◀····▶ **Utilitarians** the greatest numbers.

There developed a view that it was the responsibility of the owners and managers to show the underprivileged the error of their ways and/or to provide them with golden rules for self-improvement. It was believed that the labouring classes (the workforce) were all ignorant, debauched and brutal and in order to find a reason for such perceived behaviour, the entrepreneurs blamed drink, idleness, immorality and violence. Some employers, for example the Wedgwoods (owners of pottery works in Stoke-on-Trent), penalised all workers who were found to be carrying alcohol into the factory during the hours of work. Other entrepreneurs extended their sphere of influence outside the workplace – owners of the silk mills at Macclesfield actually sacked girls who made a 'single mistake' in their personal lives and they did so with considerable advertisement and pride.

Threats and fear tactics by the owners and managers of industry and commerce were commonly used in an attempt to gain the compliance of the workers. This Victorian notion that in self-improvement lay the key to all success was at the heart of their approach to the management of the workforce – in and out of the actual place of work.

TAYLOR (1911) AND THE SCIENTIFIC MANAGEMENT APPROACH

In the early part of the 19th century the work of Taylor (1911) stimulated the enthusiasm of entrepreneurs. Maund (1999) reports that Taylor was 'The founding father of scientific management' (p94). Taylor's views were based on the model of rational, economic man. The ▸ scientific management ◂ belief was that if an individual was given precisely defined tasks with clear objectives and if there were a clear economic reward for carrying out each task, then s/he would calculate the benefits of improving output to increase productivity. Entrepreneurs initially omitted to consider that this would probably only work if the processes and resources were available to the worker and that s/he was able to do the job – if s/he was trained to be competent. However, scientific management techniques did not prove to be the panacea expected by industrialists. They discovered that economic reward, as a driver to improve productivity, was not always an intrinsic motivational factor. However, the industrialists still hung on to the Victorian viewpoint that they had the threat of removing economic rewards as a way of punishing and correcting low productivity and managing their human resources.

Scientific ◂┄┄▸ management
A classical approach to management where the underlying belief was that decision making (particularly when related to organisational decisions and job design) should be based upon rational scientific procedures.

POINTS TO PONDER

Have things changed?

Although current management philosophy espouses a more human and integrated approach, do you think that there is evidence that the scientific management approach is still in use?

The paternalistic model was still in fashion in the early 1900s (Cadbury at Bournville, Rowntree at York) but it was in the USA that the fashion continued the longest with Henry Ford (1863–1947) setting the fashion for worker support in the automobile industry. His factories had departments comprising individuals whose sole responsibility was to administer aspects of managing the members of the workforce – the personnel issues.

SCENARIO 1.2

German entrepreneurs

German entrepreneurs were also paternalistic in their management of individuals – it wasn't a model only to be found in Britain.

The early 1900s also saw the evolution of specialists in personnel issues – mostly related to administrative matters such as wages payment rather than policy, procedures and strategy. They were also concerned with the welfare of their workers ensuring that they had their basic needs satisfied, that is, food, water and housing.

WORLD WAR I AND AFTER

World War I (1914–18) propelled the role of support for the workers into a welfare arena – particularly when women began to join the workforce to replace the men who were being sent to the war zones.

Between 1918 and 1935 there was a severe worldwide economic depression. This brought with it increasing unemployment and hardship for a significant proportion of people. This depression posed a considerable threat to the existing order – to society in general and to the workplace in particular. Such challenges were made more severe because the actions of entrepreneurs were perceived as being largely responsible for the problems that were facing the industrial nations. They were attempting to maintain the paternalistic, narrow approach to people management within a climate of depression.

At this time Hoover (1874–1964), Baldwin (1867–1947) and Mussolini (1883–1945) were heads of state (USA, Britain, and Italy respectively) each with very strong business connections. Other industrialists were active in international affairs – Kellogg (1856–1937) was US Secretary of State from 1924–29 when he piloted the Kellogg Pact which was a treaty signed by representatives of 15 nations in Paris (1928) renouncing war as an instrument of national policy. Kellogg was a leading light in the agriculture industry and is a name frequently seen on breakfast tables today. The organisation still has a strong non-confrontational approach to its business management.

During the 1920s and 30s there was recognition that the cyclical depression was coming to an end and recovery was in sight. Governments on both sides of the Atlantic were taking action, such as Macdonald's (1866–1937) £42m public works programme. Macdonald was a significant force during this time being the British Labour Prime Minister in 1924 and 1929–33 and of National Government in 1931–35. At the same time Hoover was heading a federal construction programme in the USA. Individual entrepreneurs such as Ford (1863–1947) and the economists who supported national initiatives – with a very high wage rise for his workers in November 1929 – were also attempting to manage people in a more positive way than in previous eras. However, there was a decisive shift towards the government being the key agent of change in the western world rather than individual entrepreneurs. This was reflected in the management of the workforce since the personnel role began to move towards a more central place in the organisation rather than being on the fringes.

HUMAN RELATIONS MOVEMENT

This attempt to rationalise employment and the increased use of scientific management (Taylor, 1911) was paralleled by the rise of the human relations movement within the workplace setting. Greater attention was increasingly being paid to the social factors concerned with the workplace and how individual members of the workforce behaved – human relations.

A major and significant piece of longitudinal research (the Hawthorne Studies) led by Elton Mayo was carried out in the 1920s. The results:

> suggested that favourable attitudes in employees result in motivation to work even harder.
> (Maund, 1999, p95)

The results of these experiments posited the view that there were things other than money – probably social interaction – that motivated individual workers. The prevailing view at the time was that if a worker was adequately rewarded for her/his work in the economic sense, s/he would be satisfied and thus her/his production and performance would rise. The human relations school attempted to improve on this view.

WORLD WAR II

World War II (1939–45) brought about an increase in the demand for raw materials for manufactured goods and for more workers to join the labour force being depleted by men going to serve their country. In the light of this women again joined the workforce. Accompanying this was the demand by organisational leaders for more experts in human resources – particularly for trainers who could bring the novice workers up to standard. Organisational leaders at this time had to make the most of their available workforce and maximise the resource so that productivity increased. This was a time of commercial and industrial stability. The PM sector became well established.

POST-WAR STATEISM

The end of World War II prompted a universal investigation of the relationship between industry, the state and the individual. There was reliance upon the state to take action to maintain the success of industry during the war. A commonly held view was that since the state had brought success in the war against Hitler (1889–1945) it could, according to Cannon (1994), also:

> fight the wars of poverty, unemployment and social injustice. (p26)

PM per se continued to rise in importance with practitioners banding together in 1945 to form their own professional organisation – Institute of Personnel Management (IPM) – in order to share visions and ideas related to the management of people. The IPM was the former Institute of Labour (IOL) and was reformed to take account of the increasing range of personnel practices. At this time, PM as a subject began to develop within college courses for business students and to take an increasingly important role in business.

The 1950s and 60s saw a growth in the labour market and during this time the various governments continued to support the rise of PM and industrial relations (IR) issues – PM was now a fact of working life.

During 1957–63 the British Conservative Prime Minister, Harold Macmillan, stated the British 'had never had it so good'. However, this image gradually diminished as the lack of continuity in economic policy hurt British industry and in less than a decade the UK's share of world trade slipped badly. A Labour government was elected in 1964, which attempted to get people to believe in qualitative rather than quantitative state intervention. However, state intervention actually increased in most aspects of life from housing, education and health to employment. It was back to ▶ **rationalisation** ◀ and increased efficiency. The late 1960s and early 1970s brought about an increase in state intervention in employment through legislation. The key legislation related to employment conditions and discrimination in the workplace is shown in Table 1.3. Discussion on legislation and HRM is covered further in ■ Chapter 7 *and* Chapter 8 ■.

see Chapter 7 *and* Chapter 8

▶ The reorganisation of, say, industry on scientific lines, with the elimination of waste of ◀┈┈▶ **Rationalisation**
  labour, time and materials and the reduction of other costs.

Between the mid-1950s and the late 1980s the number of people specialising in PM increased and HRM became established. However, the term 'human resource

Table 1.3 Legislation and associated documents of the 1960s and 70s

Contract of Employment Act	1963
Industry Training Act	1964
Redundancy Payments Act	1965
Equal Pay Act	1970
Health and Safety at Work Act	1974
Rehabilitation of Offenders Act	1974
Sex Discrimination Act	1975
Employment Protection Act	1975
Safety Representatives and Safety Committee Regulations	1977
Employment Protection (Consolidation) Act	1978

management' aroused considerable interest in academia because it had the potential to give a new perspective to replace the traditional (and fast becoming outmoded) IR – which was actually under attack from the Conservative government of the time. Industry itself preferred the new terminology because it was more fitting to the developing management ethos of the time.

However, Guest and Hoque (1993) reported that in 1990 less than 1 per cent of managers having a responsibility for human resources had taken on the title of 'human resource manager'. The larger organisations were similar – Marginson et al. (1993) reported that 9 per cent used Human Resource Management as a job title.

Final recognition of the strategic importance of HRM came when the IPM merged with the Institute of Training and Development (ITD) in July 1994 to form the Institute of Personnel and Development (IPD) and changed the name of its fortnightly professional journal to *People Management*. In early 2000 the IPD was awarded chartered status and in July 2000 officially became the Chartered Institute of Personnel and Development (CIPD) thus placing HRM firmly in a strategic framework ■ *see* Chapter 2 ■.

see Chapter 2

HRM IN THE VOLUNTARY SECTOR

It is not only private and public organisations that have to be concerned with the management of human resources. The voluntary sector has to ensure that its workers are similarly protected. For example, no fewer than 182 agencies have

SCENARIO 1.3

The UNHCR training strategy

The UNHCR training strategy aims to establish a link between training, staff development and the achievement of organisational goals, and to measure the effects of the US$4 million annual training budget. The programme is expected to take between seven and ten years to show a result. The strategy falls into six parts:

■ **Resources and structure**

■ **Career management system**
This involves agreement between staff and supervisors on competencies required to meet objectives, an appraisal process and an annual individual training plan for all staff. Management training was introduced and is being implemented from the top downwards. There are three kinds of competencies:

core competencies; management competencies, which are mainly aimed at professional staff; and functional competencies, which apply to specific technical or specialist jobs.

■ **Mandatory training requirements**
The aim is to deliver consistent levels of knowledge and minimum standards of operation. Although still under discussion, this is expected to include induction briefings, training for new postings, security awareness and stress management, refugee law and protection, communications, presentation, negotiation, advocacy and training skills.

■ **Flexibility and training approaches**
The agency is pursuing ways of moving away from formal workshop-based training to more flexible and

SCENARIO 1.3 cont'd

cost-effective methods, including coaching, shadowing, self-study, computer-based training, and distance learning. This strategy is being actively pursued at headquarters and in the field.

■ **Training for operational partners**

This process is now becoming more systematic. UNHCR is also using a database to keep track of all the training provided, not only for its own staff, but also for partner agencies.

■ **Monitoring and evaluation**

Improved reporting criteria are needed, for example, on who has been trained. Currently, the only information that is consistently monitored comes from post-workshop evaluations, but the agency is setting up systems to assess learning achieved and to quantify the impact of training on individual performance and operational effectiveness.

Adapted from: Johnson, R. (1999) Humanitarian resources, *People Management*, 15 July, p37.

been involved in the aid effort for Kosovo. Apart from coping with huge numbers of refugees, they have had to develop strategies for improving their own field workers' safety, well-being and effectiveness.

The United Nations High Commission Work for Refugees (UNHCR) provides support for its workers. The Red Cross is also involved, believing that there has been an accumulation of experience and a lot of professionalism and that they need to recognise this and capitalise on it. This has been done by the provision of a UNHCR training strategy as shown in Scenario 1.3.

HRM AS A CONCEPT

It is vital not to underrate the value of the ▶ **conceptual** ◀ understanding of the disparity in the views concerning the nature of HRM.

▶ Of, or characterised by, concepts, that is, abstract ideas. ◀┈┈▶ **Conceptual**

HRM is a ▶ **philosophy** ◀. It comprises a number of themes and concepts which have developed from over a century of management theory and research in social science.

▶ The love, study, or pursuit of wisdom or knowledge, especially concerned with the most ◀┈┈▶ **Philosophy** general causes and principles of things.

It is believed in some circles (Storey, 1995) that the utilisation of HRM practices has been the result of the work of line managers and non-specialist managers – a viewpoint which a historical perspective tends to support. Such managers have

POINTS TO PONDER

Few people can study the area of HRM, work in and with organisations and their managers without unconsciously picking up other people's views and having an appreciation of how they can amend their own opinions. The original sources of many of the ideas related to HRM have been lost in time. The evidence for some new insights may be recalled but its provenance forgotten.

HRM theory seeks to substitute a coherent set of conceptual frameworks for these collections of assumptions. In his landmark study, Handy (1993) wrote that concepts used properly and understood should:

> Help one to *explain* the Past which
> in turn
> Helps one to *understand* the Present
> and thus
> To *predict* the Future which leads
> to
> More *influence* over future events
> and
> Less *disturbance* from the Unexpected. (p16)

It is a good idea to continue to bear this in mind when studying the theory and practises of HRM.

very often been at the forefront of changes within the workplace relating to members of the workforce – often despite the obstruction of HRM specialists who became very precious about their perceived field of expertise.

Some of these specialists are uncomfortable with the use of the term 'human resource management' and such people rarely refer to members of the workforce as 'resources' but as 'people'. Kalra (1997) supports this view and argues that human potential management (HPM) should replace the concept of HRM – even though her definition of HPM is similar to the aims of HRM:

> An integrative and continuous process of enhancing human capabilities and capacities by enriching human beings' existing potential. (www p4)

She believes that by considering human beings to be a resource to be used and manipulated as other resources, for example raw materials, demeans individuals. She goes on to argue that the contemporary workplace houses an increasing number of very highly skilled ▶ **knowledge workers** ◀. Such people could well take offence at being labelled a 'resource' and could respond in a hostile or

see Chapter 6

unhelpful manner ■ *see* Chapter 6 ■.

Knowledge ◀┈┈▶ workers
Members of the workforce who are erudite, highly educated and informed in matters which will enhance the objectives of the organisation.

Digital age dilemmas

The apparent convergence of communications in the world through the rapid growth in the ownership of personal computers, mobile phones and other information technology equipment as well as the spread of satellite, cable and other networks is making a massive impact on forms of employment in the media and entertainment industries.

We are in the global information society and the digitalisation of information – its compression, storage, manipulation and transmission – is increasing at an extraordinary pace and not only in the English-speaking parts of the developed world.

The impact of the information revolution on employment and how work is organised is profound since many new job opportunities have arisen for geographically mobile, well-educated, multiskilled and adaptable people. However, more and more jobs are likely to be unstable, temporary assignments without fringe benefits or social security coverage and some job losses or downgradings are inevitable.

The multiplicity of job opportunities in a bewildering diversity of employment relationships makes it dangerous to generalise but there is no point in playing King Canute* in the face of remorseless change. But there is a need to try to establish some coherence and regulation, however limited, in the face of deregulation and liberalisation. The 'survival' mechanisms of the past – such as collective agreements, employer-provided job training and jointly funded social security – have all been weakened.

There need to be more training programmes for those employed only temporarily or part time in media and entertainment to make lifelong learning more than a well-intentioned slogan. In the USA, the Workforce Investment Act (1998) has given USA media workers more opportunity to improve their skills via individual training accounts, integrated one-stop career centres and a shift in the resources from low income to dislocated workers.

There is a recommendation that there be more 'social dialogues' between companies and employees in general covering much more than protection and including agreements that deal with the wider effects of the impact of information technology.

Adapted from: Taylor, R. (1999) Digital age dilemmas, *Financial Times*, Appointments Section, 10 February, pxi.

* The legend of King Canute (c.995–1035) states that he disenchanted his flattering courtiers by showing that the sea would not retreat at his command. It was a story first told by Henry of Huntingdon in 1130.

While this view is understandable, it is necessary in a competitive environment to make the best use of all resources and this includes the members of an organisation's workforce. It does not mean that individuals are depersonalised, but that they are as important to the organisation as are the finished products or services they provide – they are part of the accounting formula. Identifying people as resources *raises* the importance of people, and therefore, by extension, human relations in the workplace.

To help in the understanding of this view, and any other concept, the following formula is useful:

$$\text{thesis} + \text{antithesis} = \text{synthesis}$$

That is, by taking a proposition, opinion or belief and considering the opposite opinion, a whole fresh viewpoint comes to the fore. This is similar to taking regard of two sides of an argument except that there is a synthesis – another creation. This is what one has to do all the time in studying aspects of HRM because there is no common view of the concept of HRM.

1.4

Activity

Taking the view of people as being a 'resource' as the *thesis*, and people being dehumanised if they are referred to as a 'resource' as the *antithesis*, develop a *synthesis* for these opposing views.

In the contemporary knowledge- and service-based business environment, recruiting and maintaining a talented, educated, ▸ **empowered** ◂ and effective workforce is paramount to success.

Empowered ◂┄┄▸ When an employee has the right to take executive decisions within specified parameters; such an individual is accountable for her/his actions.

Mayo (1999) believes that an organisation's added value – its true value – lies in its intangible assets. The challenge for HRM, he believes, is how to measure these assets with the accuracy that senior management expects and demands. In order to do just that he states that:

> HR is more successful influencing management if it starts with what is on the manager's agenda and uses its expertise to help them achieve it. (p33)

see Chapter 2

He is of the belief, therefore, that HRM is a strategic issue ■ *see* Chapter 2 ■ rather than a provider of skills.

PERSONNEL MANAGEMENT

Personnel management (PM) is strong in its historical context and is often considered to be the aspect of management that is concerned with individuals within the workplace and their relationships within the organisation. Like the view of HPD propounded by Kalra (1997), the aim of PM is to ensure that individuals continually develop. However, its key agenda is with the development and application of policies which form the basis of this book. Such PM applications govern a number of key areas, which are shown in Table 1.4.

Graham and Bennett (1999) identify other areas of PM responsibilities as shown in Table 1.5.

It can be seen from the historical perspective of HRM that PM has been in place during periods of intense and often continuous change. It has had to survive during

Table 1.4 Key applications of personnel management

Planning, recruitment, selection and termination of employees.

Education and training.

Conditions and terms of employment.

Remuneration.

Communication with professional bodies and trades unions.

Negotiation of pay agreements and settlement of disputes.

SCENARIO 1.5

Falling demand hits soft landing

Demand for personnel skills continues to fall, according to the latest PM/Park Index.* Overall, the market for personnel skills was down 13 per cent on the comparable January–March period last year.

But the downturn is not universal. Decline in the private sector is now at 21 per cent (compared with a fall of 14 per cent in the final quarter of 1998), while demand in the public sector rose by 5 per cent. Also up is the number of personnel jobs advertised with salaries of more than £50 000 – 30 per cent higher than in the same period last year. Encouragingly, and for the first time since the Index started, demand in Scotland rose by 17 per cent.

The term 'personnel' seems to be becoming outdated as 'HR' now dominates. This is most notable in the private sector where there were 425 'HR' job titles advertised and only 149 'personnel' roles.

There is a distinctly cyclical feel to these figures. Previous downturns in demand have tended to see Scotland both suffering and recovering first, the private sector dipping steeply, with the public sector continuing to grow before eventually slipping into decline. Even with the private sector showing a 14% followed by a 21% quarter-on-quarter decline, this is beginning to look like a soft landing.

Market share of HR job advertisements (1 January–19 March 1999)

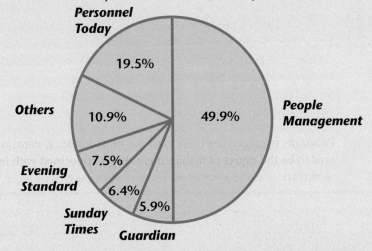

*The PM/Park Index monitors all recruitment advertisements in *People Management, Personnel Today, Sunday Times, Evening Stan*-dard, *Guardian, Daily Telegraph, The Times,* the *Herald* and the *Scotsman,* using data from Media Monitoring Services (MMS).

Source: Howard, S. (1999) Falling demand hits soft landing (PM/Park Personnel Jobs Index), *People Management,* 6 May 1999, p17.

Table 1.5 Further applications of personnel management

Carrying out research to ensure rewards and remuneration are competitive.

Devising rewards and remuneration, which will be motivators.

Keeping records of workers and workplace statistics.

Implementing health and safety legislation.

Administering pension and entitlement schemes.

Preparing detailed job descriptions and recruitment enhancers.

Managing training and development.

Informing employees of personnel matters.

changes in central government policy and the rise – and fall – of the influence of the trades unions. PM has been part of policy making but its principal activity is to put policies in action – reactive rather than proactive. Its principal interest has been in taking responsibility for that specific part of management which Graham and Bennett (1999) call *utilisation*, *motivation* and *protection*.

They characterise these as being:

1   *Utilisation*

see Chapter 4

see Chapter 10

All issues involved with recruitment and selection ■ *see* Chapter 4 ■ of staff and those issues which concern the worker's basic work life (for example transfers, promotion, performance appraisal) and development ■ *see* Chapter 10 ■.

2   *Motivation*

see Chapter 9

see Chapter 5

see Chapter 7

Issues which intrinsically motivate workers, for example job design, rewards and remuneration ■ *see* Chapter 9 ■, involvement ■ *see* Chapter 5 ■ and justice ■ *see* Chapter 7 ■.

see Chapter 10

More and more organisations are looking to the HRM function to find critical, on-demand information about employees and applicants, as well as the capability to use and distribute that information throughout the organisation. New government initiatives, national standards of performance and cross-organisational working mean that organisations have to support staff in achieving their very best on a daily basis ■ *see* Chapter 10 ■. To achieve this, strategies and programmes that meet the organisation's business objectives need to be developed. HRM requires

1.5

Activity

Under the separate headings of *utilisation*, *motivation* and *protection*, order the PM responsibilities given within Tables 1.4 and 1.5.

management to be aware of the demands of jobs and the abilities of people, identifying and addressing development needs, and to ensure that the manager has a talent pool to meet the organisation's needs. The working world is constantly changing – as is the concept of HRM.

SCENARIO 1.6

Is this the way the American dream ends?

A watershed of American history has just occurred in Portland, Oregon. Town officials have told the computer-chip company Intel that it will be fined US$1000 for every new job it creates. What Portland wants is to curb 'sprawl' and traffic congestion. 'We aren't just interested in jobs, jobs, jobs,' says a local director of economics. Imagine saying that any other time in the twentieth century. For generations, our overriding goal has been to employ as many people as possible and to extend prosperity and decent housing to the working class. But now we seem to have reached the point where middle-class people regard economic growth as a threat to their own 'personal growth'. The fact that home ownership in the USA is nearly 70 per cent is seen by them not as an economic triumph but a personal disaster, responsible for turning the dream of a leafy suburban existence into the nightmare of urban sprawl. But can our cities, in the name of 'personal space', be indifferent to those without jobs or workers who aspire to move up? In Portland, alas, the answer appears to be 'yes'.

Source: Hayward, S. (1999) Is this the way the American dream ends? *The Week*, 3 July, p11.

HRM AND MANAGEMENT

Clark (1994) states that there has been much critical and evaluative work carried out on the nature of HRM but that it did not say much about how its practice and rationale helped with the management function. While he agrees with the researchers and writers in the field that HRM can be studied theoretically, practically and holistically, he considers that it should be a tool to push management. He states that HRM's:

> point of departure centres on a distinction between the spirit and the substance of HRM. (www p1)

Human resource management, according to Clark (1994), is about empowering individuals, while it is the job of managers to:

> square the circle of increased competition, improved productivity/efficiency and financial stringency. (www p1)

He continued to say that HRM is about the:

> reconfiguration of existing management structures in an effort to recreate an entrepreneurial philosophy in management practice. (www p1)

Clark's (1994) view is therefore that there should be a distinction between entrepreneurism and the traditional style of management with HRM initiatives sitting within the entrepreneurial function.

see Chapter 7

see Chapter 2

see Chapter 7
and Chapter 8

HRM – THE DEBATE

A review of the prevailing literature in the field of HRM indicates that while the debate is healthy, there is divergence about what HRM actually *is* and what it *represents*. It is a highly complex issue.

Garavan et al. (1998) consider that HRM has become influential in the management of the relationship between employer and employee ■ *see* Chapter 7 ■. Beardwell and Holden (1997), who reported that HRM has become a pervasive and influential approach to the management of the relationship between employer and employer, supported this. Others believe that it is merely a renaming of the personnel function (Armstrong, 1996) while others consider it to be an amalgamation of PM and IR (Guest, 1987). However, there are two further views worth considering: the first stresses the role of the *individual* within the organisation and the second considers the strategic function of HRM ■ *see* Chapter 2 ■.

Both of these approaches have led some researchers to distinguish between 'traditional personnel' and HRM. Fowler (1987) and Legge (1995) take the view that PM and HRM are dichotomous models for managing people – the human resources. What is clear from the literature is that there are as many definitions for it as there are people researching in the area. However, they have in common the belief that such models provide a conceptual framework to aid in the understanding of HRM.

Monks (1996) explored the roles carried out by what she called 'personnel managers' revealing that the findings of her research indicated that the role has remained the same for some time – especially the management of employment relationships ■ *see* Chapter 7 *and* Chapter 8 ■ which has remained particularly constant. Her view is that the name given to the individuals responsible for managing the 'people' function is 'not necessarily important' but goes on to state that:

> it is however critical to give recognition to the complexity of the task that faces those who have to take responsibility for this function. (p1)

The new century is bound to provide a number of serious challenges for HRM and Monks (1996) believes that:

> The reporting and measurement of human capital is certainly a longer term issue but is one we should be discussing now. (p25)

In coming to this conclusion she believes that it is the growing realisation that people are the key factor in achieving organisation success and she highlights three areas of change which have been significant to the transformation of the HRM role:

1   Other disciplines use the term HRM and, therefore, understand that strategy is all very well, but that it is changing this into action which matters.

2   The recognition that a resource is not necessarily confined to a building or business.

3   A fundamental change is taking place in the way businesses operate in relation to the move towards greater ▶ **pluralism** ◀ and deeper ▶ **individualism** ◀.

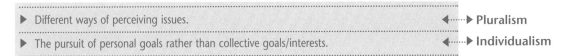

▶ Different ways of perceiving issues.	◀·····▶ Pluralism
▶ The pursuit of personal goals rather than collective goals/interests.	◀·····▶ Individualism

POINTS TO PONDER

HR extension

I was walking back from a working lunch (honest) through Soho when I happened upon an advertisement in Old Compton Street that advertised itself as a 'Human Resource Centre'. Having spent a few moments diligently investigating the premises, I realised that it specialised in hair extensions and various other fashionable additions to the human anatomy.

Is this an indication of where the HR profession is headed or where it has come from?

Source: Howard, S. Letter, *People Management*, 8 April 1999, p31.

As can be seen, HRM is often seen as being vague and elusive. This is understandable since writers rarely consider the area with like minds, and this confusion is reflected in texts and articles, which give different interpretations. This is a healthy situation because it means that there is an ongoing debate among managers and specialists, which can only help HRM – the thesis, antithesis and synthesis discussed earlier. It is through HRM that an organisation's future is shaped by bringing together all the aspects of managing people and organisational development to deliver the organisation's objectives.

The heart of HRM lies in its strategic role and integration into corporate strategy. This is a complex issue discussed in ■ Chapter 2 ■.

see **Chapter 2**

Note

In line with the modern convention, dates in the text are given, where applicable, as BCE or CE to mean 'Before the Common Era' or 'Common Era'. These religiously neutral letters replace the more usual 'BC' or 'AD' respectively.

- HRM is similar to OB in that both are concerned with the individual members of an organisation's workforce.

- HRM recognises that people must be effectively managed if an organisation is to achieve its objectives and thus be 'ahead of the rest'.

- A review of the literature on HRM treats it as either *hard* or *soft* although some writers attempt to take the middle line.

Chapter summary

- To appreciate the views held on HRM it is essential to have a clear understanding of its growth and development. HRM did not just arrive – it has an important history and its current, and future, importance sits strongly within this historical framework from the Industrial Revolution in England in the early 19th century to the contemporary age.

- There have been significant contributions to the care of workers through the nonconformist challenges, scientific management (Taylor, 1911), the two world wars (1914–18, 1939–45) and the post-war situations.

- HRM is a philosophy that comprises a number of themes and concepts which have developed from over a century of management theory and research in social science.

- Legislation has affected the development of HRM.

- The attention given to understanding people as a resource highlights the importance of people and, therefore, by extension, human relations in the workplace. It is helpful to use a formula here: thesis + antithesis = synthesis. That is, by taking a proposition, opinion or belief and considering the opposite opinion, a whole fresh viewpoint comes to the fore.

- PM is strong in its historical context and is often considered to be the aspect of management that is concerned with individuals and their relationships within the organisations. However, its key agenda is with the development and application of policies, which have been strategically defined elsewhere.

- More and more organisations are looking to the HRM function to find critical, on-demand information about employees and applicants for jobs, as well as the capability to use and distribute that information throughout the organisation.

- While it is healthy to debate the nature of HRM, there is divergence about what HRM actually is and what it represents.

- The heart of HRM lies in its strategic role and integration into corporate strategy.

Focus switches to the human factor

The focus within management buy-outs is now increasingly on getting the human assets to perform.

The Centre for Management Buy-Out Research at Nottingham University, England, has done a preliminary study on HRM issues in buy-outs.

It found that many companies 'renewed attention on managing employees' after they had completed a buy-out. In more than half of the 174 buy-outs examined, this resulted in employees becoming more flexible, workers 'taking more responsibility for their jobs', and the level of trust increasing between managers and workers.

In the past, buy-outs were about squeezing the most out of the physical assets but there is a growing realisation that the people assets can be as important.

Because a business going through a buy-out is in a state of flux, it is a good time to make other changes. It is the time to empower people throughout the organisation, and introduce flexibility. Cash may be tightly controlled but, in theory at least, decision making should be quicker and there should be more of a 'can do' culture.

Across the study 41% of companies said personnel and industrial relations matters were the full-time responsibility of an executive main board director.

Buy-outs were much more likely to operate profit-sharing schemes for non-managerial employees – 68% compared with a national average of 30%. Share ownership schemes were in place in 33% of buy-outs in the study compared with 15% across all companies in data compiled by the Department of Trade and Industry (DTI). Meanwhile 79% had individual performance-related pay schemes for non-managerial employees compared with 11% for the national average.

At the same time, buy-out managers generally had little time for the many 'softer' management practices such as teamworking, staff attitude surveys or problem-solving groups. A buy-out may also make life more uncertain for existing employees. There was a shift towards putting employees on flexible as opposed to fixed-term employment contracts, and there appeared to be less commitment to 'guaranteed job security'. Only 1% of buy-outs surveyed said internal promotion was 'preferred' because people no longer get promoted just because 'they are there'.

Adapted from: Campbell, K. (1999) Focus switches to the human factor, *Financial Times*, 15 August, p19.

END OF CHAPTER 1 CASE STUDY QUESTIONS

1 What is meant by the terms 'buy-out' and 'buy-in'?

2 This case study introduces a number of key concepts to be found in HRM and which are discussed throughout the text. Select *four* and briefly discuss what the terms mean.

3 Discuss the view hidden within this case study that 'People are our best asset and the best way to release an asset is by way of disposal'.

4 The case highlights the way that organisations can reshape their culture. Is there anything that other organisations can learn from the results of this survey?

THESIS + ANTITHESIS = SYNTHESIS

Explore the view that the term 'human resource management' is just a fad.

SELF-TEST THE KEY ISSUES

1 Extrapolate the parallels and differences between the ways in which a newly appointed manager of an organisation's workforce might develop her/his views on PM and HRM.

2 Does the history of PM and HRM teach us anything about the long-term impact of contemporary human relations initiatives, such as the Working Time Regulations (which came into force in October 1998) and the Fairness at Work White Paper (May 1998)?

3 Why is it important to understand the conceptual framework that surrounds PM and HRM?

4 Outline the steps needed to build an HRM ethos within an organisation.

TEAM/CLASS DISCUSSIONS

1 Debate the issue that an understanding of the historical perspectives of work is important if one is to appreciate the role of HRM in the contemporary world of work.

2 'PM and HRM are one and the same thing.' Discuss.

PROJECTS (INDIVIDUAL OR TEAMS)

1 Gather information from as many sources as possible and use these data to discuss the style of HRM adopted by a named international organisation. Explore the extent to which the company had any choice in their human resource decisions and outline practical ways in which the negative effects of their practices might be lessened.

2 Using the personnel and/or HRM statements from five named firms (available directly from firms or other public sources – including the Internet), write a business report which draws out the common features and which identifies any key omissions. Offer suggestions for the rectification of such omissions.

Recommended reading

Armstrong, M. (1999) *A Handbook of Human Resource Management Practice*, London: Kogan Page

Bratton, J. and J. Gold (1999) *Human Resource Management: Theory and Practice*, Basingstoke: Macmillan – now Palgrave

Graham, H.T. and R. Bennett (1999) *Human Resources Management*, London: Financial Times/Pitman Publishing

Legge, K. (1995) *Human Resource Management: Rhetorics and Realities*, Basingstoke: Macmillan – now Palgrave

O'Reilly, C. and J. Pfeffer (2000) *Hidden Value*, Boston: Harvard Business School

Sisson, K. (1994) *Personnel Management*, Oxford: Blackwell

Sisson, K. and J. Storey (2000) *The Realities of Human Resource Management: Managing the Employment Relationship*, Milton Keynes: Open University Press

Storey, J. (1992) *Developments in the Management of Human Resources*, Oxford: Blackwell

Storey, J. (ed.) (1995) *Human Resource Management: A Critical Text*, London: Routledge

Torrington, D. and L. Hall (1998) *Human Resource Management*, London: Prentice Hall

URLs (uniform resource locators)

www.peoplemanagement.co.uk

Online version of *People Magazine*, the two-weekly journal of the Chartered Institute of Personnel and Development.

www.enterprisezone.co.uk

Marketing Advisory Board, part of the Enterprise Zone. Essential advice for small and growing UK businesses.

www.businessbureau-uk.co.uk

Business Bureau for UK e-commerce. Resource for business entrepreneurs.

www.thepaperboy.com

Global views and news. Information and access to over 2000 papers in 60 countries.

www.shrm.org

Society for Human Resource Management. USA site with useful information and news. A useful site which can assist HRM managers with news, sample book chapters and a coverage of some international issues and trends.

www.ahri.com.au

The Australian Human Resource Institute. A comprehensive site with articles on HRM in Australia. Help with professional development. Knowledge Centre.

www.hrhq.com

Workforce-Online. Information on HRM issues. Useful background on topical issues with a USA bias. However, very useful on such issues as termination of employment, harassment, interviewing, outsourcing and training.

www.openhouse.org.uk/nsqt

National Society for Quality Improvement through Teamwork (NSQT). Information on, for example, how to carry out employee surveys.

Bibliography

Armstrong, M. (1996) *A Handbook of Personnel Practice*, 5th edn, London: Kogan Page

Beardwell, L. and L. Holden (1997) *Human Resource Management: A Contemporary Perspective*, 2nd edn, London: Pitman

Bickerstaffe, G. (1997) *Mastering Management*, London: Financial Times/Pitman

Campbell, K. (1999) Focus switches to the human factor in *Financial Times*, 15 August, p19

Cannon, T. (1994) *Corporate Responsibility: A Textbook on Business Ethics, Corporate Governance, Environment: Rules and Responsibilities*, London: Pitman

Clark, I. (1994) HRM – The reinvention of modern management? in *Personnel Review*, **23**(5) (http://www.hr-expert.com/members/data/rc_articles/01423EB1.htm)

Conoley, M. (ed.) (1998) *Human Resource: Business Briefing*, London: PricewaterhouseCoopers

Dawes, B. (1995) *International Business*, Cheltenham: Stanley Thornes

Fowler, A. (1987) When the chief executive discovers HRM in *Personnel Management*, **19**: 6–9

Garavan, T., M. Morley, N. Heraty, J. Lucewicz and E. Suchodolski (1998) Managing human resources in a post-command economy: personnel administration or strategic HRM [sic] in *Personnel Review*, **27**(3) (http://www.hr-expert.com/members/data/rc_articles/01427CC1.htm)

Graham, H.T. and R. Bennett (1999) *Human Resources Management*, 9th edn, London: Financial Times/Pitman

Gratton, L. (1999) Future shock in *People Management*, 16 December, p25

Guest, D. (1987) Human resource management and industrial relations in *Journal of Management Studies*, **24**: 503–21

Guest, D. and K. Hoque (1993) The mystery of the missing human resource manager in *Personnel Management*, June, pp40–1

Handy, C. (1993) *Understanding Organizations*, Harmondsworth: Penguin

Hayward, S. (1999) Is this the way the American dream ends? in *The Week*, 3 July, p11

Howard, S. (1999) Falling demand hits soft landing (PM/Park Personnel Jobs Index) in *People Management*, 6 May, p17

Johnson, R. (1999) Humanitarian resources in *People Management*, 25 July, pp34–9

Kalra, S. (1997) Human potential management, time to move beyond the concept of human resource management? in *Journal of European Industrial Training*, **21**(5) (http://www.hr-expert.com/members/data/rc_articles/00321EC1.htm)

Legge, K. (1995) *Human Resource Management: Rhetorics and Realities*, Basingstoke: Macmillan – now Palgrave

Marginson, P., P. Armstrong, P. Edwards, J. Purcell and N. Hubbard (1993) The Control of Industrial Relations in Large Companies: An Initial Analysis of the Second Company Level Industrial Relations Survey, Papers in Industrial Relations, Coventry: University of Warwick

Maund, L. (1999) *Understanding People and Organisations: An Introduction to Organisational Behaviour*, Cheltenham: Stanley Thornes

Mayo, A. (1999) Called to account in *People Management*, 8 April, p33

Monks, K. (1996) Roles in Personnel Management from Welfarism to Modernism: Fast Track or Back Track? Research Paper Series, No 17, Dublin: Dublin Business School (www.dcu.ie/business/research_papers/no17.htm)

Ship to Shore, onboard magazine for Norse Irish Ferries & Merchant Ferries, Spring/Summer 2000, p25

Storey, J. (1995) *Human Resource Management: A Critical Text*, London: Routledge

Taylor, F.W. (1911) *Principles of Human Resource Management*, New York: Harper & Row

Strategic human resource management

After studying this chapter, you should be able to:

■ ANALYSE the relationship between business strategy models and strategic human resource management (SHRM) models.

■ CRITICALLY DISCUSS the role of goals in SHRM.

■ COMMENT on the key dimension of SHRM: business process re-engineering (BPR), leadership, workplace learning/knowledge management, trades unions, workplace performance, restructuring and flexibility.

■ ANALYSE the importance of change strategy to SHRM.

■ EVALUATE the importance of the environment to SHRM.

Framework case study

The renaming of personnel

In the good old days it was called the Personnel Department. Everyone knew what it was and why it existed. And then somebody decided the name did not sound exciting or strategic enough, and it was renamed Human Resources.

Now it is changing again, but no one can agree what it should be called. At Air Miles they call it 'People and Culture', at CDW Computer Centres it is known as 'Co-worker Services'. Other companies are coming up with other names – all of which share one thing: they give you little clue as to what the department actually does.

It is as if they feel that by renaming personnel they will somehow demonstrate that their employees matter to them more than ever before. Indeed, most companies have gone further and renamed the employees, too. Only the most old fashioned companies use the word 'e' any more. No one talks of 'staff', either. Instead, they refer to their wage slaves variously as people, colleagues, co-workers, partners and, most recently, as job-owners. (Which is particularly contrived, as you do not strictly speaking 'own' your job at all.)

All this seems quite pointless as there is a perfect term that is sadly out of fashion: worker. It is plain, accurate and unpretentious, which explains why it stands no chance of making a comeback.

Source: Kellaway, L. (2000) Fun, fun, fun, till the FT took our e-mails away, *Financial Times*, 17 January, p13.

As has been seen in the previous chapter, there is considerable rhetoric about human resource management (HRM) and its involvement with personnel management (PM) – even Kellaway's (2000) tongue-in-cheek view in the Framework Case Study has more truth to it than some specialists might wish to admit. Some writers seek to distinguish HRM from PM (Boxall, 1992, 1994) on the grounds that HRM implies specifically a move away from seeing employees as a cost, towards an investment orientation and a more innovative and ▶ **strategic** ◀ view of the management of people in the workplace ■ *see* Chapter 1 ■. There is also debate about the position of HRM in an organisation's ▶ **strategy** ◀. When referring to such an implication, the prefix 'strategic' is used and HRM thus becomes SHRM. Although there is no general agreement on the characteristics of SHRM, there are some demanding claims about it. These emphasise, among other things, links with business strategy and organisational change as shown in the training which is taking place in Scenario 2.1.

see Chapter 1

Strategic ◀┈▶	Characteristics of a strategy – the tactics.
Strategy ◀┈▶	The practice or art of using plans (strategems).

SCENARIO 2.1

Up to speed

Modern and traditional techniques are being combined to enhance the development of personnel officers at Rolls-Royce. The company's shared learning programme started this autumn on an assault course.

'It was freezing and we got soaked, but it certainly helped to bring us together as a team,' says Jacqueline Waddell, one of the 12 participants.

The group has drawn up its own schedule of events and speakers. Each member will research and contribute topics for discussion. They draw up their own agenda and take turns at hosting events.

The programme has been designed within the framework of objectives provided by the company. These are to: share knowledge about, and learn from, best practice; work as a team; manage a budget and resources; develop an appreciation of the organisation as an international business; develop networking skills; and develop organising and project management skills.

Waddell, an HR officer who joined the company as a graduate two years ago, is fairly typical of the group. She has worked in the HR department at East Kilbride, Scotland for a year and is halfway through the Institute of Personnel and Development's qualifications at Strathclyde University, Scotland.

Waddell is hosting the final module of the programme, which focuses on HR's role in managing organisational change.

'The programme is supporting the theory I am learning on the IPD course really well, and vice versa,' she says. 'It's a great opportunity for professional development.'

Source: Boyle, K. (2000) Up to speed, *People Management*, 6 January, p5.

STRATEGY DEFINED

When boards of companies meet to discuss strategy, the key issues are sure to be:

- finance
- the organisation's position in relation to its principal competitors
- market development of the product/service.

It is not usual for issues relating to members of the workforce to be high on the agenda – unless that agenda is about cost cutting. However, there is more centrality in the positioning of HRM in organisations which believe that investment in the quality and enthusiasm of the workers will bring about increased:

- competitiveness
- quality
- overall business performance

which are features of a strong leadership in organisations as shown in Scenario 2.2.

Momentum for modernisation

When the British Labour government came into office (1997) it was firmly focused on delivering results in the community. It wanted to tackle pressing social problems including homelessness, teenage pregnancies and troubled housing estates.

Frustrated by the slow pace of working in the civil service, Tony Blair (Prime Minister) and Jack Cunningham, the former Cabinet Office minister, put their names to the Modernising Government White Paper.

Its central purpose was 'to make life better for people and business'. That was underpinned by three aims – joined-up and strategic policy making, a shift in focus from public service provides to users and delivering high-quality, efficient public services.

The aims were to be met by five key commitments, including forward-looking policy making that delivered results and a new information-age government that used the latest technology.

Whitehall reform had been simmering away long before Labour won power, but the White Paper put it on a more organised footing, setting targets for change to be met by specific deadlines.

Sir Richard Wilson, head of the Civil Service, set up four committees to look at performance management, diversity, bringing in and bringing on talent, and vision and values in the Civil Service.

Their reports were presented to the much-publicised meeting of permanent secretaries at the Civil Service College in Sunningdale in September 1999 within which environment there was a commitment to make change happen.

The meeting resulted in *Civil Service Reform*, Wilson's report to Blair, which was a direct response to the White Paper. It outlines a programme for change involving 27 key actions, all to be delivered by September 2002.

The actions are based on six key themes: stronger leadership with a clear sense of purpose; better business planning from top to bottom; sharper performance management; a dramatic improvement in diversity; a Civil Service more open to people and ideas and which develops talent; and a better deal for staff.

Adapted from: Rana, E. (2000) Open-plan government, *People Management*, pp34–8, 40, 41.

Taylor (2000) believes that organisations in the UK need to follow the example of organisations in the USA where most boards of directors have the HRM director as part of their team. He goes on to say:

> In order to avoid costly internal power struggles and [public relations] disasters, British companies must involve HR professionals in the personnel management and training for their boards. (p7)

see Chapter 3

Strategy is about planning ■ *see* Chapter 3 ■ and is variously defined by researchers and writers. In general terms, this means that the management of any organisation must carefully devise a plan of action in order to achieve their objectives. Strategy is also about the art of developing and carrying out such plans.

A common view is that strategy needs to be enduring and acceptable to all stakeholders. However, with this comes an implication that strategy should be all things to all people and inflexible over a fixed timescale.

According to Fombrun et al. (1984) strategic management concerns itself with three key issues:

- *Mission and strategy*
  The identification of the purpose and plan of the organisation and an indication of how that can be achieved

- *Formal structure*
  In order to meet the ▶ **mission statement** ◀. This is the formal organisation of people and activities within the workplace

▶ A written statement by an organisation which encapsulates the purpose of its activity, as much as the direction it wishes to take. ◀········▶ **Mission statement**

- *Personnel systems*
  Recruitment ■ *see* Chapter 4 ■, development ■ *see* Chapter 10 ■, evaluation and reward of members of the workforce ■ *see* Chapter 9 ■.

  see Chapter 4

  see Chapter 10

  see Chapter 9

Gunnigle and Moore (1994) define strategic management as:

concerned with ▶ **policy** ◀ decisions affecting the entire organization, with the objective being to position the organization to deal effectively with its environment. (www p1)

▶ Plan of action adopted/pursued by a business. ◀········▶ **Policy**

Contemporary writers tend to avoid actually defining 'strategy' in managerial terms, preferring, like Browne et al. (1999), to state that it:

encompasses a very wide variety of perspectives and approaches. (p269)

However, there is a difference between the traditional framework given above and that seen in contemporary organisations because the latter incorporates HRM considerations as an integral component of strategic management rather than – at best – a token mention of 'workers'.

STRATEGIC HUMAN RESOURCE MANAGEMENT (SHRM) DEFINED

If organisations are to achieve and retain effective performance in the current turbulent environment it is vital that policy decisions are drawn up in line with the activities of every member of the workforce – the human resources.

The use of strategy in HRM is not new as the theory-in-literature implies. Galbraith and Nathanson (1978) and Fombrun et al. (1984) argue that organisations would find it hard to implement strategies if they were not intertwined with the appropriate human resource policy.

SHRM is the development of strategic planning within an organisation and concentrates on the relationship between the former and HRM. Armstrong (1999) defines SHRM as 'the overall direction the organization wishes to pursue in achieving its objectives through people' (p247).

A strategic plan is implemented by people and, therefore, this very fact has to be considered seriously by those individuals who actually develop corporate strategy. HRM is part of that strategy – hence its title, strategic human resource management – and is, therefore, a constituent aspect of the organisation's overall strategy. Its role is to address any issues within the corporate plan which will affect the people within the organisation and it is, therefore, concerned with most of the activities of a business, such as:

- organisational culture

- change and the management of change

- performance ■ *see* Chapter 10 ■

  see Chapter 10

- motivation ■ *see* Chapter 9 ■

  see Chapter 9

- planning for future staffing

- employee development ■ *see* Chapter 10 ■.

  see Chapter 10

In general terms, that involves anything which concerns the workers within the organisation. It is SHRM which provides the context within which HRM will work and will include the resourcing to carry out the plans, for example, in relation to employee development the HRM specialist will consider training and development ■ *see* Chapter 10 ■.

see Chapter 10

Therefore, SHRM is concerned with assisting the organisation in achieving its objectives and gaining (or maintaining) the competitive edge through its objectives. These are informed by the mission of the organisation – its purpose, what it wants to achieve for the ▶ **stakeholders** ◀ – as well as by the internal and external business environment. Tyson and Witcher (1994) believed that the role of HRM was to

Stakeholders ◀┈┈▶ People who have a legitimate interest in the activities of an organisation, for example customers, shareholders and employees.

indicate what the plans and intentions were in the use of people to achieve the aims and objectives of the organisation. That is, the purpose of SHRM is to provide the organisation with guidelines which can be successfully activated and thus reinforce the success – or lack of success – of the original guidelines.

In order to understand the role of HRM in corporate strategy, it is necessary to appreciate strategy in general. Mintzberg and Lampel (1999) investigated strategic management from theory to practice and came to the conclusion that:

> scholars and consultants need to get beyond the narrowness of [current theory]… and to [aim] for better practice not neater theory. (www p1)

Beinhocker (1999) believes that it is a waste of time for managers to rely on traditional and historical views in order to develop a strategy for the future – in his view it is an unreliable activity. However, for business students, theory and models need to be in place before its practice can be appreciated. Traditional organisational systems have failed to resolve fundamental business problems and have led to a development of a new approach to the strategic planning process. As can be seen in Figure 2.1 plans and performance are often consistently not achieved and this is called the *hockey stick effect*.

However, organisations often adhere to the traditional process comprising an ultimate goal which may be met if subgoals en route are met. This can be seen in Figure 2.2.

Such a traditional planning process utilised what was termed the rational model where the ultimate objective (goal) is broken down into sub-objectives (small goals), and the process thus implemented. This traditional corporate planning was effective in the past when the business environment was more stable, for example, in organisations which knew who their competitors were, where customers were predictable and where pricing structures were stable and understood by all.

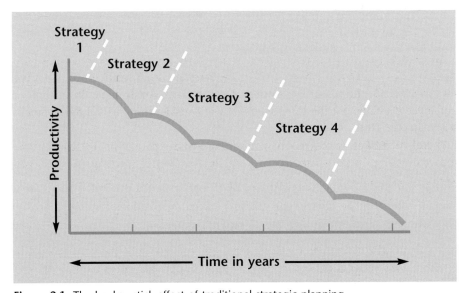

Figure 2.1 The hockey stick effect of traditional strategic planning

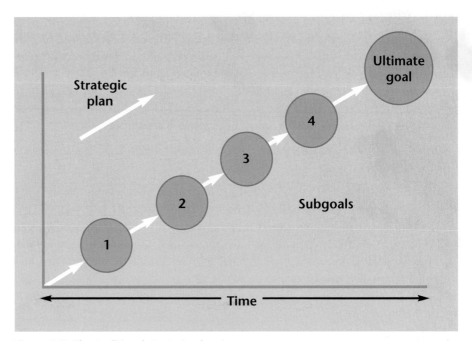

Figure 2.2 The traditional strategic planning process

Nowadays, a revised approach to strategic planning can provide organisations with a powerful tool for creating and sustaining profit growth. The focus has changed to a more volatile environment where the emphasis has changed from planning to the implementation of action programmes which in the short term produce visible results against which the long-term strategic vision may be refined. This can be seen in Figure 2.3.

In the contemporary environment organisations are highly complex enterprises comprising numerous interconnecting parts. However, according to Beinhocker (1999), these parts are impossible to predict because they show ▶ **punctuated equilibrium** ◀ and ▶ **path dependence** ◀.

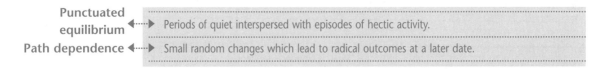

Punctuated equilibrium ◀┈┈▶ Periods of quiet interspersed with episodes of hectic activity.

Path dependence ◀┈┈▶ Small random changes which lead to radical outcomes at a later date.

He suggests that organisations should use multiple strategies, selecting the most appropriate for the situation and time – the ▶ **contingency theory** ◀ – in order to remain robust in the competitive market. Often organisations rely too much on their strategic plans which they have based on forecasting. Williamson (1999) and

Contingency theory ◀┈┈▶ The most effective way to establish power/dependence relationships that exist between the focal organisation and other actors in the network.

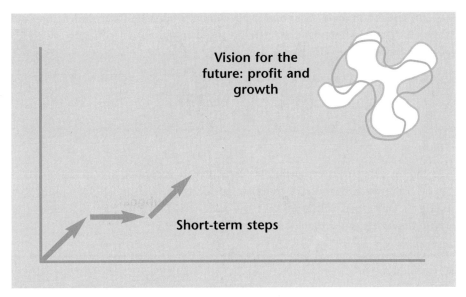

Figure 2.3 The volatile strategic planning approach

Beinhocker (1999) agree that no matter how carefully strategic plans are constructed they will probably not work if they are based on forecasting – especially if they concentrate on one specific strategy, for example, vehicle assets. It is typical for managers to attempt to plan strategy by assessing the areas their competitors do better than they themselves do. Using this method of ▶ **benchmarking** ◀ takes a considerable amount of effort and time for what can be minimal return. This is called *imitation* (copying) rather than *innovation* (▶ **modernism** ◀). Organisations that have sustained high growth and profits usually pursue a single strategy and value innovation very strongly. Organisations using such a paired strategy render their competitors irrelevant because they usually offer unique products and added value in their existing markets or by making very large leaps in value for the purchaser.

▶ A comparison point for judging some aspect of the firm's performance, sometimes referred to as *best practice*. ◀┈┈▶ **Benchmarking**

▶ The adoption of modern thoughts and ideas, that is, modern tendencies, thoughts or support of these. ◀┈┈▶ **Modernism**

However, it is very difficult to choose a distinctive strategic position because it involves, according to Markides (1999), in-depth analysis of three issues:

■ identifying the target customers

■ deciding what products and/or services to offer

■ choosing how to carry out efficiently any related activities.

It is also difficult to make clear and explicit choices on these three dimensions and Markides (1999) states that the inability to do just that is a common source of failure in business.

POINTS TO PONDER

The essence of strategy lies in deciding what *not* to do.

As can be seen, strategy is a complex issue, which, according to Mintzberg (1990) can lay claim to a number of different perspectives. Watson (1994) argues that strategy is concerned with managing the relationships within the environment to ensure the long-term survival of the organisation.

Activity 2.1

Analyse your study habits.

Outline how a study strategy may either help or hinder your study.

The debate lies in the issue of the extent to which strategy is deliberately planned or allowed to emerge and evolve. If strategy is planned, then it must be as a result of rational processes using the best available statistical methods and be open to implementation accompanied by details as to how to implement it. The latter – evolution – is the opposing view stating that the rational model and its accompanying decision making are themselves the result of compromises and resolutions of competing interests.

According to Slack et al. (1995):

> A strategy [is there] to provide the overall direction for decision making in the operation but it does not [usually] answer the more detailed or specific questions. (p6)

However the strategy is decided, the acceptance of it is deliberate and is said by Johnson and Scholes (1999) to have three stages:

- strategic analysis
- planning
- implementation.

The three stages are applied at three levels to produce a corporate strategy concerned with the organisation as a whole, a business strategy focused on significant elements or units within the organisation and a functional strategy for each of

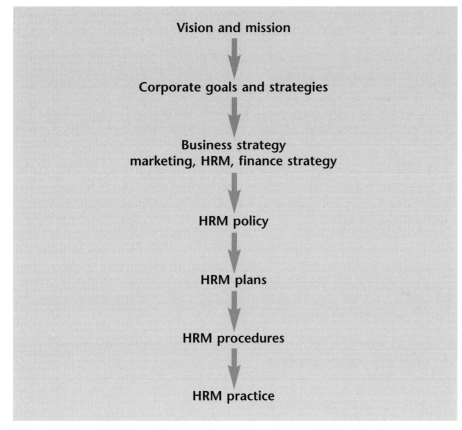

Figure 2.4 A model of strategic management after Stewart (1999, p7)

the specialist functions. According to Stewart (1999) it is possible to show the functions as having a linear relationship (as shown in Figure 2.4) which is derived from and contributes to business strategies.

All strategies – at whatever level – are derived from and enable achievement of the organisation's mission.

Miles and Snow (1978) posited some strategies which they said could be fitted along a continuum ranging from low to high in terms of environmental change and uncertainty. If one follows the logic of this theory, the more uncertainty and change that the organisation forecasts, the more it would move to the right along the continuum as shown in Figure 2.5.

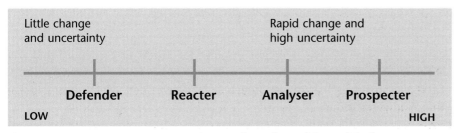

Figure 2.5 Environment–strategy continuum after Miles and Snow (1978)

Similarly, as strategies move to the right along the continuum, the organisation's structure should be modified or redesigned to be increasingly flexible and adaptable.

THE FORM OF SHRM

The form of SHRM used is represented by the management's commitment to the:

■ objectives

■ policies

■ practices

related to all employees within the organisation. It is not simply a matter of rhetoric. Objectives and policy are formalised within the framework of a corporate strategy as reinforced by the seminal work of Tilles (1969) who was in at the start of formal discussions on SHRM. He believed that strategy must be explicitly stated rather than be a philosophical mission because only then can organisations develop and balance planned action with entrepreneurial effort. A SHRM is as essential as other strategies for two reasons:

■ individual members of the workforce need to be able to cooperate in order to achieve mutual reinforcement

■ individuals (who comprise the organisation) need to be able to cope with changing environmental conditions.

Johnson and Scholes (1999) delve deeply into strategic matters stating that a strategy is the lifeblood of any organisation. They make some key points which are relevant to SHRM:

■ if there is not an *explicit* strategy individuals may work at cross-purposes

■ the top management must clearly communicate the strategy to those whose job it is to implement it – usually employees at the bottom

■ individuals are creatures of habit and tend to be suspicious of new patterns of working

■ change must be part of overall strategic planning

■ strategy statements are creative and thus an art

■ strategic planning requires individuals to change their attitudes and thus behaviour.

Strong, deliberate analysis is critical in order for SHRM to be defined and well documented. It will not happen accidentally – there has to be a proactive desire to make policies integral to the realisation of objectives defined by the other key strategies, which include:

■ finance

- production

- customer quality

- marketing.

HRM managers have to strongly articulate their developmental and employment strategies among those already strongly recognised within the organisation because, otherwise, the achievement of the totality of the business objectives may be vulnerable.

As can be seen strategy is a complex issue – a contemporary writer, Von Maurik (1999), believes that it is:

> an elusive concept. (p1)

He is right since the current debate takes the view that strategy is contentious and not simply about the traditional view of referring to decisions about long-term goals which would drive future actions within the organisation.

As Hunt (2000) states:

> Complaints are very, very rarely about HR strategy (p18)

but are more about the HR function.

Even though the role of HRM has been improving steadily over the last few years, its standing is still very weak and it may, according to Hunt (2000):

> disappear as a senior function, to be rolled either into a general resources or a strategy function. (p18)

The function of HRM ■ *see* Chapter 1 ■ can be described as the 'what' aspect which includes, among other things:

see Chapter 1

- the finding of staff ■ *see* Chapter 4 ■

see Chapter 4

- motivating ■ *see* Chapter 9 ■

see Chapter 9

- employee development ■ *see* Chapter 10 ■

see Chapter 10

- performance assessment ■ *see* Chapter 10 ■

see Chapter 10

- reward and remuneration ■ *see* Chapter 9 ■ and

see Chapter 9

- retaining those workers whose skills and talents will help the organisation to achieve its objectives.

It is this very talent which helps the organisation to formulate its strategy and cope with the management of change.

Hunt (2000) suggests that the change of title from 'personnel' to 'HRM' came about because neither personnel professionals nor employees thought that they were delivering what was actually required. The HRM specialists are still receiving criticism about their function and are continually redefining their role. This could be a dangerous way to go when determining the role of SHRM because in the constant redefinition and changing of role description, the HRM specialists could be, according to Hunt (2000):

> in danger of exposing divisions among themselves. (p18)

However, there is a strong view from Turner (2000) when he states that:

> Business leaders and personnel professionals are increasingly challenging the raison d'être of the human resources department. (p56)

Because his organisation (BOC UK):

> needed a radical departure in focus to transform HR from a supporting function into a strategic partner in the business (p59)

investigations resulted in the human resource services becoming a dedicated HR service centre where the fitter HR team was:

> well-placed to deliver strategic support to the business. (p59)

Therefore, there is still this division between the old school of thought 'personnel' and the new 'HRM'. It is the latter view which is urging the need for taking a strategic view of what HRM needs to offer and they want to discard the old basics and move into the strategic arena.

POINTS TO PONDER

The Chinese word for crisis, *wei ji*, is made up from two components, one meaning 'danger' and the other 'opportunity'.

It seems an appropriate image to describe the state of the HRM profession.

Adapted from: Hall, P. (2000) Feel the width, *People Management*, 6 January, p23.

In her review of the professional role and standards of HRM specialists, Whittaker (2000) states that it is vital that they:

> be equipped to develop into valued contributors at a strategic level, whether they work in the organisation, as external consultants or as service providers. (p29)

STRATEGY AND TACTICS – MAINTENANCE AND IMPROVEMENT

SHRM involves a certain amount of ambiguity because it deals with matters which are not run of the mill. It is also very complex with organisation-wide implications comprising changes which could be significant rather than small scale. The circumstances are driven by:

- pressures within the organisation's environment

- changes imposed on the organisation

- the perceived position of the organisation within its environment.

Strategic needs have to be analysed with objectives being agreed and then translated into everyday programmes which are devolved to line managers for implementation. Thus they must be communicated, resourced and controlled.

When market turbulence and competitive forces are so intense, policy and programme forming and reforming can be so rapid as to make tactical and strategic levels delineated. Receiving good ▶ **feedback** ◀ about progress of tactical (operational) programmes is essential and programme results must be evaluated with components being adjusted. As time frames become shorter, plans may be half completed before a reworking or U-turn is needed. Therefore, the best strategies could well be a framework comprising only objectives with specific programmes changing to fit circumstances.

▶ Information received by an individual, as a result of carrying out a task, concerning the ◀······▶ **Feedback** effectiveness of her/his work performance.

Activity 2.2

Search the Internet for a non-European organisation which includes HRM in its organisational strategy.

Strategy is often discussed metaphorically as a *game plan* which involves particular tactics whose form is mostly represented by operational programmes and projects – *doing*. Departmental arrangements and programmes of work are manifestations of tactics in playing the game. Each business unit has its budget, that is, its allocation of money and staff, organised to secure satisfactory day-by-day results.

Tactics can be either:

- maintenance (keeping the things going) or

- improvement (ensuring that performance does not slide)

and, therefore, they require organising and resourcing.

Organisations will have to pay attention and address a number of projects, that is, tactics for improvement. A sales campaign, market research project, a training course or a quality control programme are examples. An organisation's project or projects represent tactics that contribute to the strategic objectives of the business.

STRATEGY AND GOALS

Organisations use strategy as a scheme for competing in the marketplace and use tactics to carry out planned activities while continuously adjusting to the competitive situation as it unfolds. The objective of this is to block, or take over, a competitors' market share without losing any of its own. Hatch (1997) states that:

> In modernist organization theory, the concept of strategy refers to top management's planned efforts to influence organizational outcomes by managing the organization's relationship to its environment. (p101)

While a model of strategy is useful, it is often not long lasting because all organisations have to work in a complex and ever-changing environment which is influenced by, for example:

see Chapter 7 *and* Chapter 8

see Chapter 11

■ new legislation ■ *see* Chapter 7 *and* Chapter 8 ■

■ globalisation ■ *see* Chapter 11 ■

■ declining industry

■ fluctuating economy

■ war

■ departure of key staff.

However, the organisation has to be able to deal with all eventualities because it has to do more than maintain its position but needs to be 'ahead of all the rest'. It is not good enough nowadays to be as good as the market leader, the organisation has to be the market leader if it is to prosper.

SHRM AND THE ENVIRONMENT

People and management within organisations cannot take place in isolation – as Hollinshead and Leat (1995) stated:

> HRM does not exist within a vacuum. (p7)

The Harvard model posited by Beer et al. (1984) understresses the inclusion of outside stakeholders. Kotchan and Dyer (1995) argue that, despite the obsession with strategy, theories of HRM have a fundamental weakness:

> a myopic viewpoint which fails to look beyond the boundary of the firm. (p343)

Human resource practitioners must have the ability and interest to locate their activities in the wider environmental setting or they will be lose contact with practice and thus change and so their organisations will have lost any market placement – let alone be market leaders. They need to widen their perspectives beyond their own organisations to function in a globalised and competitive world. The essence of HRM lies in the competitive advantage to be gained from making the most of an organisation's human resources. However, the availability of suitable people is heavily dependent upon environmental variables, including:

- implications of world and national economic conditions for business growth

- effect of inflation on perceived value of wages

- traditions of local business culture

- particular nature of national employment markets.

Therefore, these variables have a macro effect on the utilisation of human resources. There is also the need to consider the other effects which can be caused by the activities of external stakeholders:

- competitors, utilisation and demand for human resources

- multinational organisations and strategic alliances leading to restructuring or integration on a global basis

- economic and legislative actions by government

- resistance or cooperation from trades unions

- pressure on senior managers to cut costs and maximise shareholder value.

D'Aveni (1999) goes further in attempting to indicate the importance of a positive business strategy by stating that supremacy can be gained by trying to appreciate the relationship between the changing environment within which the organisation sits and the choice of strategy that has been – or is being – made. By doing this he believes that:

managers can develop better strategies that lead to and maintain strategic supremacy. (www p1)

If an organisation has strategic supremacy it can then move to dictate the market within which it trades and form the basis upon which its competitors have to compete – that is, it sets the benchmark. However, in order to do this an organisation has to be successful in two areas:

- analysing the current competitive environment

- understanding the rules and regulations.

D'Aveni (1999) believes that if an organisation finds that it cannot do this – that is, it cannot find its 'fit' in the marketplace – it can gain strategy supremacy by changing the environment so that it *does* fit. His work was carried out in hyper-competitive markets and his findings suggest that where there is turbulence there will be competitive environments which are distinctive in their patterns of disruption determined by their frequency and their ability to destroy or enhance competence.

The goal of top management is to control the degree and pattern of the turbulent environment which their organisation works in and attempt to change it. However, it has to be remembered that competitors and existing customers are never content with the status quo – the war for strategic supremacy in every market is ongoing.

ORGANISATIONAL STRATEGIES AND MODELS

Strategy is not just an annual event or one carried out when organisations perceive that they are not competing in their specific market. Neither is it always decided at the top of the organisational hierarchy where the chief executive officer (CEO) and her/his colleagues make powerful decisions affecting lesser mortals. It takes place at all levels but particularly at middle management level, where it is all-pervasive and a critical aspect of organisational management. It is a highly complex area and a discipline which is studied in its own right. They are not all deliberate actions designed to produce a specific outcome or outcomes. It is usual to find that the processes are accidental and they result in unintended, emergent outcomes.

HRM does not differ significantly from the functional departments within an organisation. Even within a department such as production, it is still necessary to prove worth and value to the organisation – the same applies to HRM. HRM's new strategic role has given HRM executives unprecedented access to the CEO to whom the former should report and this indicates the CEO's level of commitment and interest in HRM.

As much as HRM professionals value accessibility to the CEO, they also place similar value on true empowerment – the freedom and latitude to make the hard choices and crucial decisions that shape HRM. However, empowerment also gives the power to disagree and, consequently an atmosphere where creative and independent thinking is encouraged.

SCENARIO 2.3

The short stay at the top

A chief executive taking on a new job can be sure of only one thing: he is unlikely to hold onto it for long.

The average stay at the top of the FTSE 100 companies is four years, and falling. In the USA, the picture is the same: almost two-thirds of chief executive officers spend less than five years in the job.

The main reason is that the duds are being kicked out ever more quickly. Every week, it seems, there is a new addition to the club: failed executives must be one of the fastest growing socio-economic groups in the western world.

The reason has nothing to do with shortcomings in strategy, vision, or any of the supposedly difficult stuff. These executives are all bright experienced people. No, the reason they screw up is that they cannot implement.

This strikes me as remarkably sensible and in need of underlining. Implementing is dead dull. The things that matter are decisiveness, follow-through, delivering on commitments. They are important, small-picture, blatantly obvious in theory. They are also extremely difficult to pull off.

And yet the execution side of the chief executive's job hardly ever gets a public hearing. We write about them as if they were super-brain heroes who beat the competition with their brilliant strategies.

How grey the reality is. What we should concentrate on is the nitty-gritty of implementation. But that is as dull and difficult to write about as it is for chief executives to achieve. The difference is that by stressing the glamorous bits we do not lose our jobs. And when CEOs lose theirs, it's another great story for us.

Adapted from: Kellaway, L. (1999) The short stay at the top, *Financial Times*, 14 June, p20.

The access to the executive office of the CEO by HRM specialists has brought added responsibility of being a confidante of the CEO. Often the HRM specialist is in post longer than is the CEO as can be seen in Scenario 2.3. It has presented human resource professionals with some interesting challenges as they try to balance the concerns and interests of employees with those of senior management. Individual confidences must not be betrayed and neither should the organisation itself. Some HRM professionals believe that the job is like walking a tightrope between being the employee advocate and also a member of senior management. This is often seen as a contrary view and some HRM specialists do not like to use the term *employee advocate*. HRM is part of management, and every decision made should be done so with the organisation's best interest in mind. The CEO has a responsibility as well to envision the direction of the organisation and then effectively to communicate that vision. Her/his most crucial task is to set the tone and expectations for the workforce. The HRM role is to find out what the CEO believes is important to the organisation and then direct efforts along these lines. The role of HRM is then to take that vision and mould it to the CEO's vision and goals. It is not HRM's role to convince top management to concentrate on what they – HRM – believe is important. Where management action is required it is important that HRM professionals maintain accurate records – if only to prove that they have taken action and are in command of the situation.

There is a simple choice here – if HRM specialists do right by the business, then ultimately they will do right by the employees. If the business prospers and succeeds, then employees will prosper along with the business. The HRM responsibility is to represent employees' interest but the organisation's objectives and the employees' goals usually go hand in hand.

Mintzberg (1987) stated that strategic actions have widespread, long-term consequences that establish *organisational posture*, that is, the internal shape and capability of the organisation. It also establishes the *organisational position*, that is, its relationship with its stakeholders. The posture and position determines the organisation's performance as can be seen in the formula below:

$$Posture + Position = Performance$$

This can be taken one step further to read:

$$Posture + Position + Performance = Action$$

That is, the strategy comprises the action. The source of the strategy is the circular feedback process of strategic management which the organisation uses.

Strategy, according to Von Maurik (1999), is about seeking to legitimise and understand all the actions and happenings that have already taken place.

Von Maurik (1999) takes on board the view that strategic decision making is not reserved for the people at the top of the ▶ **hierarchy** ◀. He believes that every

---

▶ A development of horizontal organisations where there are multiple centres with subsidiary ◀┈┈▶ **Hierarchy**
managers who initiate strategy for the organisation, with coordination and control being
achieved through the corporate culture and shared values.

2.3 Activity

Find five European organisations that actively market their products/services through advertising the competencies of their employees.

member of an organisation has acted strategically at one time or another and cites the examples of planning vacations or thinking about future careers. The model he posits suggests that in order to redefine strategy it is necessary to think in a new way by taking a helicopter view of the situation and then concentrating on one target before proceeding to making choices that will affect that target choice.

Daft (1995) defines a strategy as:

a plan for interacting with the competitive environment to achieve organizational goals. (p49)

Some managers think that goals and strategies are interchangeable. However, goals define *where* the organisation wants to go and strategies define *how* the organisation will get there.

One way of linking business strategy with SHRM is to develop a comprehensive and coherent model. The theory-in-literature does not seem to provide one and since HRM is still evolving and developing it might yet be too early to do so. However, a model would be useful in helping to synthesise the discussion on SHRM and would be particularly useful because of the increasing complexity and turbulence within the business environment. Some people might argue that models are not only useful, but that they are essential if the inconsistencies in the field are to be contended with. Figure 2.6 gives an overview model of the elements of strategy showing the differentiation between context, content and process.

POINTS TO PONDER

Goal
To achieve a 20 per cent increase in business studies undergraduates at a university.

Strategies
These are used to achieve the goal and could include:

- aggressive advertising to attract new students
- increasing the size of classes
- investigating non-traditional entry routes into higher education.

Strategies can include any number of techniques to achieve the goal.

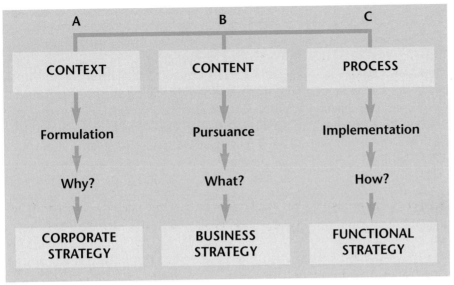

Figure 2.6 The elements of strategy

Context (A) corresponds to corporate strategy and formulates the strategy by trying to answer the question *Why?* All organisations have to operate within a framework which is externally dictated by factors such as:

■ environment

■ culture and climate

■ legislation ■ *see* Chapter 8 ■.

see Chapter 8

Because of these considerations, organisations must have a framework within which to operate.

Content (B) corresponds to business strategy and pursues it by finding answers to the question *What?* Consideration is given to:

■ the type of information available and being used

■ origin of the information available

■ rationale of the business.

Process (C) corresponds to functional strategy and implements the strategy by answering the question *How?* This means that attention needs to be given to:

■ the people involved

■ putting the plan into action.

While this is not a unique approach it does provide a sound starting point because it gives a theoretical foundation from which further analysis can be made. The model is ▶ **mechanistic** ◀. Such a model can be used to evaluate current strategy

Mechanistic ◄┈┈► A system of organisation which is characterised by bureaucratic systems encompassing roles, regulations, a clear hierarchical pattern of authority and centralised decision making.

within an organisation – especially if it appears to be floundering. With this in mind, care should be taken not to consider the three elements (context, content, process) as independent sets of issues – they are interdependent. In managing any strategy it is essential to pay significant attention to any combination of the three elements. This would depend upon the situational factors at the time. If there are difficulties in the mechanisms of strategy, it may well be because too much attention is being paid to one element at the expense of others. Or, the interventions between the three elements are not being either recognised or effectively managed.

There are three recognised models for formulating strategies that can be used to provide a framework for competitive action:

1   Miles and Snow (1978)

2   Porter (1980)

3   Miller (1987).

1 Miles and Snow (1978)

This is a popular model which Daft (1995) describes as:

> typology [is] based on the idea that managers seek to formulate strategies that will be congruent with the external environment. (p50)

Organisations are always trying to find a fit among the:

■   external characteristics

■   strategy

■   external environment.

Miles and Snow (1978) posited four strategies (see also Figure 2.5) that might be developed by organisations which they labelled:

1   prospecter

2   defender

3   analyser

4   reacter

with each having a close link related to their internal characteristics, strategy and external environment.

1   *Prospecter*
    This strategy has the need to:

    ■   innovate

- take risks
- seek out new opportunities
- grow.

It is suited to any organisation which is dynamic and creative – usually within a growing environment where efficiency gives way to idea creation. The internal organisation is organic and decentralised. The advertising and fashion industries could be examples here.

2   *Defender*
This is the counterbalance to the prospector because this strategy concentrates on stability and, to its extreme, ▶ **retrenchment** ◀. Such organisations want to hold on to current clients and not try to innovate and/or grow. The defender concentrates on:

- internal efficiency
- control, to produce reliable, high-quality products for regular customers.

▶ To take action to reduce costs, that is, to economise.   ◀┈┈▶ **Retrenchment**

It might be a successful technique to use if the organisation is part of a stable environment or part of a declining industry.

3   *Analyser*
This strategy involves an attempt to maintain a stable business while attempting to innovate on the periphery. It lies between the prospecter and defender and could be considered to be a safety mechanism. Some products are probably targeted towards stable environments in which an efficiency strategy designed to keep current customers is used. Others will be targeted towards new, more dynamic environments where growth might be possible. The analyser tries to balance efficient production for current lines of products with the creative development of new product lines. For example, Bill Gates, who developed Windows software, has shifted to analyser strategy in the core business but moved aggressively into the developing of innovative products/services in order to keep the organisation going.

This type of fit can be valuable to organisations but there are questions about its simplistic nature in the contemporary environment. It does not give consideration to factors related to the workforce which have emerged in the last 20 years, such as:

- strengths
- weaknesses
- potential
- motivation.

It also depends considerably on a rational strategy formation more than on an emergent strategy because of the nature of the one-way relationship with

Table 2.1 Strategy typology (after Miles and Snow, 1978)

STRATEGY	ENVIRONMENT	ORGANISATIONAL CHARACTERISTICS
Prospecter		
Innovate	Dynamic	Creative
Find new markets	Growing	Innovative
Grow		Flexible
Takes risks		Decentralised
Defender		
Protect turf	Stable	Tight control
Retrench		Centralised
Hold current market		Production efficiency
		Low overheads
Analyser		
Maintain current market	Moderate change	Tight control and flexibility
Plus moderate innovation		Efficient production
		Creativity
Reacter		
No clear strategy	Any condition	No clear organisational approach
React to specific conditions		Depends on current needs
Drift		

organisational strategy. It also has ▶ **unitary** ◀ assumptions because there is no recognition for employee interests and their choice of whether or not they want to change their behaviour.

> Unitary ◀┈┈▶ A whole unit or units – employers and employees share a common goal/mission with all differences resolved rationally.

4 *Reacter*

It could be argued that this is not actually a strategy because reacters respond to environmental threats and opportunities in an ad hoc fashion. In such organisations, top management will not have defined a long-range plan or given the organisation an explicit mission, so the organisation takes action as each situation arises – a reactive role. It can be successful, but more often than not it results in the demise of the organisation because it is unable to compete. Table 2.1 gives an overview of Miles and Snow's (1978) typologies:

2 Porter (1980)

Porter's (1980) model comprised three components:

1 low-cost leadership

2 differentiation

3 focus.

1 *Low-cost leadership*

When using this strategy, managers are attempting to increase the organisation's market share by emphasising low cost compared to that of its competitors – that is, they try to emphasise that their goods/services are cheaper. It is an aggressive strategy particularly during the period when the organisation is trying to:

■ seek efficient facilities
■ pursue cost reductions
■ use tight controls to produce products/services more efficiently.

2 *Differentiation*

The utilisation of this strategy means that the organisation is trying to make its products/service different from those of its competitors. There are numerous strategies to use to do this, the most usual ones being:

■ advertising
■ distinctive product/service features
■ exceptional service
■ new technology.

The organisation is trying to make a unique product or provide a unique service.

3 *Focus*

Here the organisation is concentrating on a specific geographical area, territory, or specific group of customers. The organisation has two choices it can take, being:

■ low-cost advantage or
■ differentiation advantage.

There are advantages and disadvantages of these three techniques which are shown in Table 2.2. A summary of Porter's (1980) model is given in Table 2.3.

For these strategies to be successful they have to be supported by certain employee role behaviours. These behaviours are shaped by the HRM practice of the organisation. Firms following focus strategy require an accumulation of HRM philosophy because they need adaptable employees to enable them to serve the very specific

Table 2.2 Advantages and disadvantages of Porter's (1980) competitive strategies

COMPONENT	ADVANTAGES	DISADVANTAGES
Low-cost leadership	Effective	Difficult to do in a high-cost organisation
Differentiation	Can be profitable if target customers are not particularly concerned with price	Costly to implement e.g. research and development, advertising costs
Focus	Quick returns	Takes time to identify area/group

Table 2.3 Key characteristics of competitive strategies (after Porter, 1980)

Low-cost leadership	Very tight control of costs
	Process engineering skills required
	Labour needs close and continuing supervision
	Products designed with easy manufacture in mind
	Frequent reports needed on control and progress
Differentiation	Needs powerful and sustained marketing abilities
	Strong coordination between functional departments
	A flair for ingenuity and creativity
	Strong flair for research and development
	Recognition in the fields of quality and/or technological leadership
Focus	Concentration on low-cost leadership and differentiation policies on a stated and named strategic target

needs of their customers. Concern for cost minimisation among firms following a cost-reduction strategy will lead them to follow the utilisation HRM philosophy.

Firms following differentiation strategy require facilitation HRM philosophy. Organisations following this strategy emphasise innovation to differentiate themselves from competitors. Specialists from a variety of areas work together to design and produce a product/service. Employees need to be able to work collaboratively.

A summary of HRM practice and competitive strategy is shown in Table 2.4.

Table 2.4 HRM practice and competitive strategy

Differentiation strategy	Focus strategy	Cost-reduction strategy
High participation	High participation	Low participation
Implicit job description	Explicit job description	Explicit job description
External recruitment source	Some external recruitment source	Mostly internal recruitment source
Broad career path	Narrow career path	Narrow career path
Process and results appraisal criteria	Mostly results appraisal	Results criteria
Long-term appraisal criteria	Mostly short-term appraisal criteria	Short-term appraisal criteria
Same group criteria	Same group criteria	Mostly individual criteria
Some employment security	Some employment security	Little employment security
Many incentives	Some incentives	Few incentives
Egalitarian pay	Egalitarian pay	Hierarchical pay
Cooperative labour–management relations	Cooperative labour–management relations	Traditional labour–management relations

The ability of the HRM practice of an organisation to lead to improved corporate performance is contingent on achieving a fit between strategy and HRM practice. However, empirical evidence to support these propositions is still not substantial.

3 Miller (1987)

A decade later, Miller (1987) reported his work and put forward an integrative framework for business strategy on four dimensions:

- innovation
- marketing differentiation
- breadth
- cost control.

This idea uses the concepts of Porter (1980) and Miles and Snow (1978). Table 2.5 summarises Miller's (1987) framework and predicted structural characteristics. He divides his into two sections:

- marketing differentiation
- product differentiation (innovation).

Table 2.5 The integrative framework attributed to Miller (1987, pp55–76)

Strategic dimension	Challenge	Predicted structural characteristics
INNOVATION	To understand and manage more products, customer types, technologies and markets	Scanning of markets to discern customer requirements Low formalisation Decentralisation Extensive use of coordinated committees and task forces
MARKET DIFFERENTIATION	To understand and cater to consumer preferences	Moderate to high complexity Extensive scanning and analysis of customers' reactions and competitor strategies Moderate to high formalisation Moderate decentralisation
BREADTH Breadth innovation	To select the right range of products, services, customers and territory	High complexity Low formalisation Decentralisation
Breadth stability		High complexity High formalisation High centralisation
COST CONTROL	To produce standardised products efficiently	High formalisation High centralisation

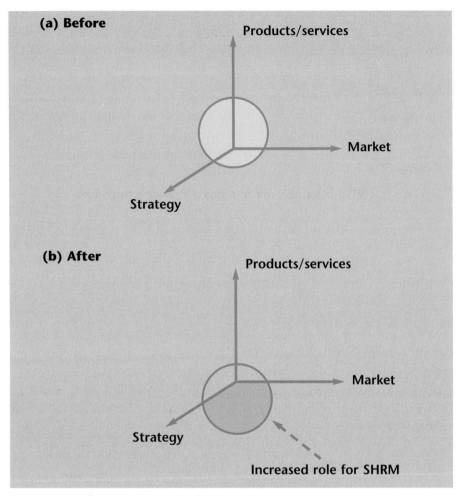

Figure 2.7 Business strategy redefined: shifting the business strategy using HRM

He also assumed that the breadth required for a satisfactory strategy could be achieved in two ways:

■ moving into a market segment by innovating more

■ moving into a more stable and placid setting.

That is, they all add value as can be see in Figure 2.7(a) and (b).

Figure 2.7(a) and (b) depict the shift in the business scope caused by the inclusion of HRM in strategic decision making. A major task for strategists is to make sure that the functionalities offered by their core activities do not obscure the potential of emerging newer roles. SHRM can provide improved functionality and cost-performance economies by using members of the workforce more efficiently and effectively.

Ulrich (1998) proposed a new mandate for human resources by arguing that HRM has never before been more necessary in achieving organisational excellence.

In his view HRM enables the organisation to address all the stakeholder issues in a positive way. He argues that the prime responsibility for transforming HRM into SHRM lies with the CEO and goes on to point out that HRM must play a leadership role in the competitive challenges which face organisations, for example:

- globalisation ■ *see* Chapter 11 ■

- technology ■ *see* Chapter 6 ■

- knowledge capital ■ *see* Chapter 6 ■

- change.

see Chapter 11

see Chapter 6

see Chapter 6

This means that HRM has a new role in terms of it being a partner in:

- executing strategy

- expertise in administration

- representing the employee

- acting as a ▶ **change agent** ◀.

> ▶ An individual or group who undertakes the task of introducing and managing a change ◀ ┈┈▶ **Change agent** within an organisation.

Senior management can make the HRM focus on outcomes rather than activities, for example, investment in innovative human resource practices as part of the overall business strategy.

Leonard (1999) interviewed seven human resource executives in a variety of industries, company sizes and locations. They all agreed that the role of human resource specialists had expanded and the strategic nature of HRM had changed significantly in recent years. He reported that human resource specialists achieved inclusion in strategy formation in different ways:

- their CEOs took the initiative to expand the role

- they themselves had to push for recognition to become a strategic partner

- external forces pushed them into the role (tight labour market, the change in stakeholder demands).

2.4

Activity

Under the headings of *planning, expertise, employee representation* and *acting as a change agent*, draw a model SHRM for a hypothetical company/activity.

All organisations have access to capital and equipment and the only distinguishing factor is the people who comprise the workforce. The market conditions in play will give organisations an opportunity to differentiate the organisation through its people and this has driven the change to include HRM in organisational strategy. It is an opportunity for HRM to provide leadership and guide the organisation through the new expectations and challenges of the globalised and turbulent work environment ■ *see* Chapter 11 ■. If HRM does not seize the challenges, it will remain in the background. It is essential that HRM ensures that top management understands its role.

see Chapter 11

However, if it is not possible for a human resource specialist to think strategically then critical business decisions will evade the area – managing the human resource used to be an administrative role but it has now moved to SHRM with the need to provide concrete evidence of its actual contribution to corporate strategy.

This is supported by Campbell (1999) who states that every company should have an action plan – if it does not it will not survive – and that most managers are used to creating strategic plans. He states that the root problem is that too many organisations benchmark their processes and therefore overlook what is unique to their own company. In common with other contemporary writers, Campbell (1999) believes that good planning processes are not generic ones – that is, they are ones which employ both analytic techniques and organisational processes to tailor carefully to the individual needs of both the organisation and the skills of the people. It is about adding value and each manager has her/his own views of what ▸ **added value** ◂ comprises and it will, also, differ from one organisation to the other. Bad planning can actually destroy added value because it can:

■ waste time and money

■ send incorrect signals to managers

■ lead managers to follow poor advice.

Added value ◂┄┄▸ The measure of organisational success.

It might be necessary for managers to put in more effort and re-examine the process by which their organisations plan and decide upon strategy.

Middle managers translate the strategies of top managers into goals and activities at the operational level as is shown in Figure 2.8.

The purpose of strategy is to link the organisation with its environment and it therefore reflects the intentions of those who formulate strategy – as can be seen in Figure 2.9. Here the middle managers take the strategies decided at the top and transform them into operational goals and tasks.

This model depicts strategy as a top-down process. However, strategy is both planned and unplanned elements as part of the strategy process as seen in Figure 2.10, where the intentions of those who are responsible for formulating strategy are reflected.

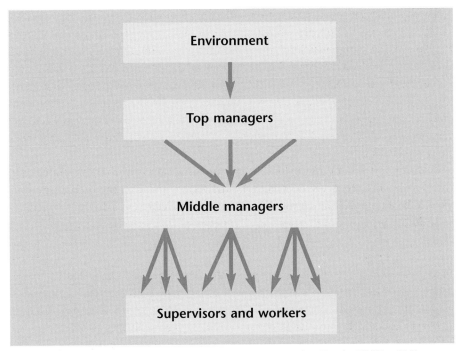

Figure 2.8 Translation of strategies by middle managers after Hatch (1997, p111)

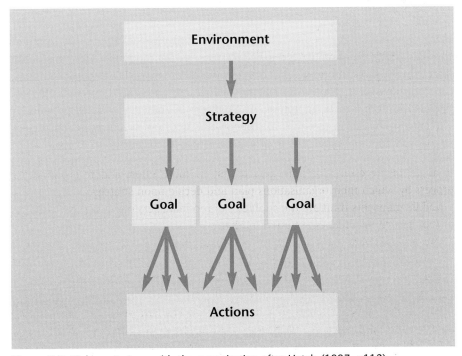

Figure 2.9 Linking strategy with the organisation after Hatch (1997, p112)

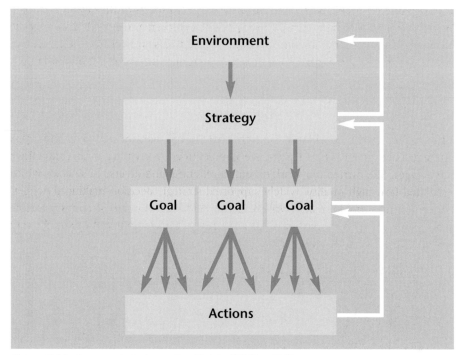

Figure 2.10 Emergent strategy after Hatch (1997, p112)

In this model there is added a bottom-up process to the top-down view of strategy showing the concept of emergent strategy.

A view that is often taken by organisational theorists is that strategic management provides an important link between the organisation and its environment through which information and influence pass. In the modernist view this occurs largely in the direction of the environment which is influencing the organisation at the time. However, the environment itself is also influenced through the link between itself and the organisation. The concept of emergent strategy provides an explanation for this in that, just as strategy emerges from organisational processes, so that environment emerges from the actions and interactions of the organisation. This explanation is then extended by enactment theory to include the symbolic meaning that organisations project onto the environment during the course of their deliberations about the environment and how the organisation should respond to it. In the enactment view, top management projects are an image of the environment based on a variety of analyses, and it is this projection to which the organisation responds. Strategy, in this view, is the label organisational members attach to the process of responding to the projection process.

Goals are often implicated in discussions of strategy because they form points of contact between stakeholders, top management and employees of the organisation. The channels of communication through which goals are developed and responsibility taken guide strategy implementation but also influence further strategy formulation by providing upward communication about what the organisation's capacities and desires are. Thus, following the discussion of goals as it travels around the organisation provides insight into the emergent aspects of the strategy process. It is in this sense that strategy and goals present a chicken and egg dilemma to those wanting to give priority to one over the other. Goals provide the link between strategy and everyday work activities as these occur throughout the organisation.

STRATEGY AND DECISION MAKING

Eisenhardt (1999) considered that the traditional methods of deciding upon strategy have given way to proactive competition by creating fluid competitive advantages. She carried out work on entrepreneurial and diverse businesses which exhibited fast, high-quality, widely supported strategic decision-making processes, concentrating – unlike many writers in the field – on the use of teams to create strategies. She reported that for success in strategy formation it was essential not to overlook the human resource input:

- management teams build collective intuition

- diverse teams are creative

- decision making is better in teams

- collaborative decision making.

Eisenhardt considered that the above approaches would direct executive attention towards strategic decision making as the cornerstone of effective strategy.

Hout (1999) reports on the same theme by suggesting that managers should stop trying to plan and prepare for change and instead build companies into self-organising teams which are ready to adapt to whatever opportunities emerge. However, there are limits to flexibility and self-organisation. Such organisations are information driven and they may be too quick to jump into a superficially attractive market – taking opportunities that more experienced rivals would ignore. Teams, for all their virtues, cannot manage themselves and it is the individual which makes the decision and not the team (teams comprise individuals). The combination of fast growing entrepreneurial organisations and mobile, ambitious people, the knowledge workers, ■ *see* Chapter 6 ■ has created workplaces that may actually be more fragile than their industrial predecessors. Solutions to workplace problems are more likely to come from good managers, suggests Hout (1999), than from the teams themselves.

see Chapter 6

A strong, easily accessible knowledge base empowers personnel and improves business performance. People need knowledge to perform at their best and companies need knowledge to perform effectively. Experience and organisation in partnership is needed to develop and deliver knowledge-based solutions that allow people and organisations to reach their true potential.

Most organisations move slowly and so the components of traditional strategy – the elements – no longer build business value. Such elements include:

- foresight

- commitment

- pre-emption

- deterrence.

Even in the faster industries, effective managers can still add value by creating the right conditions to spur creativity. Management, according to Hout (1999) matters a lot – even in the new economy.

HUMAN RESOURCE STRATEGY AND CHANGE STRATEGY

An organisation's change strategy tends to drive its HRM strategy rather than vice versa. Corporate and change strategies are generally initiated by HRM departments, and then implemented by supervisors and line managers. It is important to formulate a more integrated understanding of how various management choices interrelate – particularly so in relation to organisational change and HRM strategies, which are introduced into some enterprises in ways that are mutually contradictory. This view states that non-profit organisations, particular in education, health and religion, are the growth sector of the 21st century.

Drucker (1999) believes this is where management is most needed and can yield the greatest results most quickly. He argues that free enterprise cannot be justified as being good for business, only as being good for society. It follows, he argues, that management must be a humanist undertaking and a liberal art.

Tensions are being provoked by the needs of the knowledge worker (people whose asset is their intellect) as shareholder and future pensioner on one hand, and those of the knowledge worker as employee on the other.

It is necessary to learn how to balance short-term results – which is what the present emphasis on shareholder value amounts to – with the long-range prosperity and survival of the enterprise. His belief is that employers and employees will therefore have to learn to develop new concepts of what 'performance' means in an enterprise, but at the same time, performance will have to be defined non-financially so as to be meaningful to knowledge workers and to generate commitment from them ■ *see* Chapter 10 ■.

see Chapter 10

Just as the greatest triumph of 20th-century management has been, with the aid of computers, to make manual work so productive that only a minority need to do it, so the challenge of the next millennium is to do the same for the knowledge worker and the managers themselves.

Drucker (1999) explains that this requires a different managerial calculus: different information, measures, attitudes to people and accounting methods to include HRM.

Ghosal et al. (1999) stated that:

> The corporation has emerged as perhaps the most powerful social and economic institution of modern society (www p1)

and attempted to encourage managers to replace the narrow economic assumptions of the past and recognise that:

- modern societies are organisational economies in which organisations are the chief actors in creating value and advancing economic progress

- the foundation of organisation's activity is a new 'moral contract' with employees and society.

Firms that seem to proliferate new products and technologies continuously, for example Hewlett-Packard, Disney and Microsoft, have adopted a different management model based on a better understanding of individual and corporate motivation. They have moved into SHRM by:

> switching their focus from value appropriation to value creation, facilitating cooperation among people. (www pp1–2)

Ghosal et al. believe that a manager's primary tasks are:

- embedding trust

- leading change

- establishing a sense of purpose within the organisation.

The last task allows strategy to come about from the inside of the organisation, from the energy and alignment created by that sense of purpose. Here there is a close alignment with SHRM – the core of the management role has given way to the three Ps:

Purpose
Process
People

and has replaced the traditional 'strategy–structure–systems' trilogy that worked for organisations in the past. Figure 2.11 gives a general guide to the strategic process. From this model can be seen the importance of keeping control of the strategic direction, by recognising all the outcomes and analysing them according to the contribution they make to the overall strategic success of the organisation: to the context, content and process of the organisation in question.

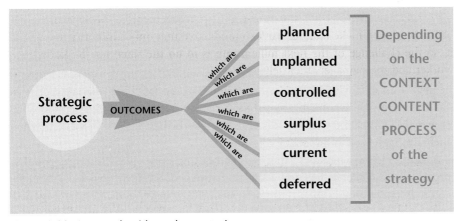

Figure 2.11 A general guide to the strategic process

HRM AND BUSINESS STRATEGY

It is believed under resource-based theory that organisations simply comprise a number of capabilities which need to be matched with the needs of market forces. This thesis is central to effective strategic management. An organisation's strategy must comprise a perfect match between its internal capabilities (what it can do) and its external relationships (what it has to achieve). A business will only be successful if it gives added value to its stakeholders (added value is the measure of organisational success). This is created by a competitive advantage based on the organisation's distinctive capabilities. The difficulty is that there are very few capabilities that are distinctive from one organisation to the next. Therefore, each organisation must have effective systems or regulations and relationships within them that are based on mutual trust and commitment in one significant area. The added value component could be the expertise of the HRM specialist.

Such expertise can contribute significantly to the development and implementation of the organisation's context, content and process. It is not sufficient for HRM specialists to have this added value – they have to be proactive and gain the respect of senior management who will value the edge that this expertise is giving to their place in the market. When this is so, the HRM function will become part of the organisation's strategic group.

Strategy requires long-term goals, broad programmes and allocation of resources designed to achieve such goals and objectives. Crisis management is not a part of well developed strategy. Every activity carried out by an organisation requires a policy for action to take place. For example, every activity must be resourced: money, time, people... every time a member of the workforce is hired s/he needs to be resourced.

Even if an organisation does have state-of-the-art human resource systems it is not sufficient if that organisation wants to be the market leader. There must be an alignment between human resource systems and the organisation's strategic focus. HRM needs to raise the profile of all employees but especially those in the key areas of the business by developing career streams and investing more in their development ■ *see* Chapter 10 ■. For example, if an information technology system is used to manage the learning process, the sharing of new ideas for core employees would allow innovation to take place more quickly and with more ease. There is a need to invest in knowledge management ■ *see* Chapter 6 ■ in order to ensure that the human resource system lines up strategically with what the business is trying to achieve – as is shown in Scenario 2.4. Grooming future senior managers may be the correct human resource priority for a service business that competes strongly on service quality and cost, but it is probably not the best for one in markets where there are high rates of product evolution.

Becker (1996) believes that implementing the best human resource programmes available will not have the degree of strategic impact as would a correctly configured human resource system. His research indicates that organisations need very carefully to evaluate their decisions to take advantage of

see Chapter 10

see Chapter 6

Are you making a strategic contribution to your company?

You could argue that the most important role of a HR professional is the *strategic impact* they have in their company, but of course this isn't possible without accurate and comprehensive reporting to base your opinions on.

At Propath Sense we understand the importance of strategic input, that's why we offer a total solution that can enable you to cut down on time spent on administration and increase the time you have for analysing and reporting company data.

Source: Propath Solutions (2000), *People Management*, 2 March, p7.

▶ **outsourcing** ◀ the human resource responsibilities. Routine administrative functions can be outsourced, but acquiring, developing and retaining the right people for a given strategy needs to be an integral part of the strategy and not an add-on service. This research noted that an effective human resource system can add anything from £30 000 to £50 000 per employee to a firm's market value.

> ▶ Where many of the activities of a once complex organisation are moved outside the organ- ◀┄┄▶ **Outsourcing**
> isation's boundary and brought in when required.

Human resource practitioners need to work closely with line managers to determine how best to align their offerings with the strategic direction of the organisation. State-of-the-art practices are of little value if they are not in direct support of the firm's business strategy. However, it is difficult to see if human resource specialists are not already active within the organisation. Theory-in-literature suggests that many organisations are too slow to see the human resource function strategically rather than as an overhead or an addendum.

Executives who are sceptical of the strategic value of human resource systems will only be convinced by hard facts. For example, organisations headed by financial executives tend to resist investing in people, preferring to cut costs to enhance short-term results. An effectively designed human resource system can enhance an organisation's long-term competitive advantage. HRM executives need to marshal all the evidence they can to make the case for a strategic approach to HRM and they also need to take the lead in arranging benchmarking visits to other organisations so that top executives can see firsthand how other organisations manage their human resources strategically.

HRM AND STRATEGY

The link between strategy and human resource practice has been discussed by a number of experts. Schuler (1989) reflects on an argument that the form of HRM practice of an organisation is contingent on the strategy it adopts.

This strategy has to be supported by a coherent set of HRM practices which are distinct and form a specific typology of HRM practice. Schuler (1989) proposed that the HRM practice of an organisation be categorised into three types which he terms 'HRM philosophies'. These are:

■ *Accumulation model of HRM*
This model emphasises careful selection of good candidates based on personality rather than technical fit, with employees being expected to adapt to changing skill requirements. Organisations practising this HRM philosophy put considerable emphasis on:

see Chapter 6
and Chapter 10

see Chapter 12

■ training and development ■ *see* Chapter 6 *and* Chapter 10 ■
■ egalitarianism
■ lifetime employment ■ *see* Chapter 12 ■.

■ *Utilisation model of HRM*
Organisations practising this philosophy of HRM select individuals on the basis of their technical skills. By putting minimal emphasis on training and development, such organisations seek to utilise new employees very quickly. They also take the short-term view of HRM and emphasise cost minimisation.

■ *Facilitation*
Organisations indulging in this approach engage in HRM practices that emphasise the ability of employees to work together. A high level of cross-functional and cross-unit cooperation is expected and these organisations put considerable
see Chapter 10 emphasis on employee development and enhancement ■ *see* Chapter 10 ■. However, instead of providing employees with training to impart new knowledge and abilities, these organisations achieve the development of employees by creating an enriching and stimulating work environment.

Firms that have strategically integrated HRM practices will have HRM practices that reflect the demands of the strategy when compared with those not strategically integrated. Evidence does not indicate the presence of strategic integration.

Othman (1996), working in the Irish food industry, examined HRM involvement in strategic planning and HRM practice for each strategy. A firm is considered to be involved in strategic planning if it participates in the process or at least provides input to the process. The HRM practices associated with respondents with HRM involvement in strategic planning for each strategy type were few and did not suggest any distinct form of HRM practice. The hypothesis that strategically integrated firms are associated with distinct HRM practices reflecting the demands of their strategy, when compared with those not strategically integrated, appears to be unsupported.

The findings show that the existence of trades unions has an influence on the HRM practice of respondent firms. The use of ▶ **performance appraisal** ◀ for all

Performance appraisal ◀┈┈▶ The process of assessing the development of an employee.

employees is more widespread among non-unionised firms ■ *see* Chapter 10 ■. They are also associated with the use of short-term performance periods to appraise their non-managerial salaried workers. Non-unionised firms are also associated with employee participation ■ *see* Chapter 5 ■ in decision making and showed that the presence of unions is associated with certain HRM practices. Either management's discretion in shaping HRM practice appears to be affected by union position or the adoption of certain HRM practices have been able to forestall unionisation.

see Chapter 10

see Chapter 5

The results of Othman's (1996) study suggested that the impact of strategy on HRM is less pervasive, if it exists at all, than suggested in the HRM literature. Instead, the evidence shows that none of the strategies associated with HRM practices can be considered distinct. Other variables, especially the presence of a HRM department, appear to exert more influence over the form of HRM practices within organisations. This suggests that the presence of HRM competencies in an organisation may explain the form of HRM practice adopted by that organisation. The background and competence of human resource managers and top management in HRM can colour an organisation's HRM practice.

Hilltrop et al. (1995) observed that human resource managers in the Netherlands and Italy tend to focus on cost control. They attribute this to the predominantly financial background of human resource managers in these countries. By the same token, human resource managers in Germany are from a legal background and thus more concerned about interpreting rules and regulations.

Other studies in HRM (Guest, 1990; Storey, 1992) also raise doubts about the strategy–HRM fit thesis. These studies found that the adoption of HRM techniques tend to be fragmented, opportunistic and driven by pragmatic considerations. Some studies (Pfeffer and Cohen, 1984; Osterman, 1994) found that the form of HRM practice adopted by organisations is shaped by multiple contingencies. At times some of these contingencies may make conflicting demands on the organisation's HRM practices (Bamberger and Phillips, 1991).

It can be said that the strategic HRM theory presents a very rationalistic view of organisations and it was even suggested by Boxall (1992) that such a view is probably simplistic and politically naive. What is certain is that empirical findings are beginning to cast doubt on the strategy–HRM fit thesis. For example, while Gratton (1997) makes a strong argument for aligning HRM with business strategy, she has found that research carried out by the London Business School showed that 'few companies succeed in linking the way they manage their overall business strategy' (p251). However, she goes on to suggest that this need not be so – when the way people are managed is linked with corporate strategy the results can be significant. According to her, there are explicit links between:

■ individual performance

■ human resource processes

■ business strategy.

Such specific links can become a central feature of SHRM as shown in Figure 2.12.

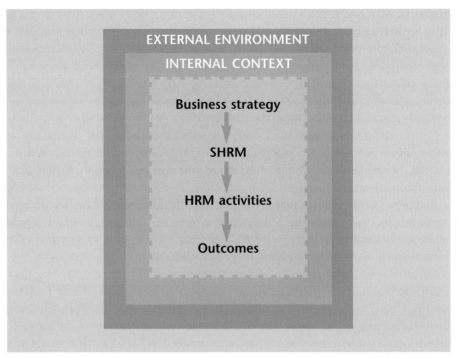

Figure 2.12 Some key contextual variants of SHRM after Gratton (1997, p252)

Theory-in-literature and research shows that there are different views related to SHRM strategies. There is a belief that a particular set of human resource practices depends on their strategic 'type' or stage in the organisational lifecycle, while another view is that the concept of 'fit' can cause rigidity and inflexibility. Human resource strategy can either be planned or emergent. Its design and implementation can be affected by external variables such as the number of young people entering the job market, an increasing level of education, or new employment laws, and by internal variables such as corporate culture, leadership style and the 'dominant coalition' (or most powerful group) phenomenon.

An important issue for companies is to identify human resource strategies that link business strategy to performance. HRM practitioners need to be mindful of the limitations of the prescriptions often found in strategic HRM literature. Their ability to shape the HRM practice of their organisations in a particular direction will be influenced by various internal and external factors and the ability to deal with change.

SHRM AND CHANGE

Skinner and Mabey (1998) report on a longitudinal research project carried out over a five-year period with 723 managers studying for the Masters in Business Administration (MBA) at the Open University. The results showed that while most human resource changes are organisation wide and are intended to enhance organisational performance and support the achievement of primary business objectives, with a clear board-level involvement at the initiation and planning stages, the responsibility for implementation is unclear.

There appeared to be an absence of clarity, together with the citing of poor communications as the main reason for the failure of change initiative ■ *see* Chapter 5 ■. This raised a number of questions about leadership, vision and direction, often involving inappropriate criteria and is perceived as having few links with the business strategy. From the perception of their managers, it appears that organisations are still not effective in managing human resource change and continue to make the same mistakes, despite the theories and prescription available in the literature.

see Chapter 5

Kamoche (1994) believes that the role of HRM within organisations and its relationship with organisational performance and business strategy has received lots of attention in last decade. He viewed the three most common reasons for the introduction of change in an organisation's human resource strategy as being: structural reorganisation, to increase competitiveness and the meeting of business objectives.

Very frequently management's actions belie what they say their SHRM is. The danger is that declarations about human resource intentions are only lip-service statements. Employees may see a disparity between what is said and managerial action (or inaction as is more likely). An example here would be when management offers training programmes within a participative organisational climate and in the same breath redundancies are declared.

HRM AND THE UNITARY PERSPECTIVE

HRM commitments are evident within their organisations by:

- methods of recruitment and selection ■ *see* Chapter 4 ■

see Chapter 4

- induction of new employees

- interaction between supervisors and subordinates

- team relationships

- methods of reward and remuneration ■ *see* Chapter 9 ■

see Chapter 9

- continuous development ■ *see* Chapter 10 ■

see Chapter 10

- mentoring and coaching

- the sharing of values.

This is an ideal picture and reflects McGregor's (1960) ▸ **Theory Y** ◂ model of managerial action which is the integration of the needs of the individual with the

▸ A group of assumptions of how to motivate people as individuals who are motivated by ◂·····▸ **Theory Y** higher order rewards such as autonomy and responsibility.

see Chapter 9

needs of the organisation ■ *see* Chapter 9 ■. Such organisations are characterised by being:

- unitarist, even though managers need to have policies and practices in place which minimise the potential for disruption and dysfunctional conflict

- having a strong HRM input into organisational strategy which is harmonious and characterised by high performance work teams and individual commitment

- displaying loyalty with clear managerial vision and leadership towards a common mission

- having a number of interests in use, however, the managerial prerogative means that the managers (who represent the owners) take charge and make the decisions

- working towards unity which has to be worked for and invested in

- management's right to manage which requires:

  - professionalism
  - sensitivity to the needs of others
  - social responsibility

- employees who are:

  - invested in
  - informed
  - consulted
  - communicated with
  - empowered

see Chapter 9

- employees who are given rewards – material and non-material – that satisfy ■ *see* Chapter 9 ■.

However, not all employers are positive in their relationships with their staff. Relationships can be separated – and possibly exploitative. For example, a hire and fire approach is very typical where an employer only employs casual labour or treats employees as horsepower showing no interest in them as individuals. Such an employer believes in the cash nexus – s/he has regarded her/his obligation to employees as satisfied once the wage has been paid and when the minimum conditions of employment are provided and no more.

MODELS OF SHRM

The models discussed earlier in this chapter originated from writers and researchers whose principal interest was business strategy. A number of other writers have commented and offered models related to SHRM – most of which have their foundations in the business strategy frameworks. There are five key models which each provide a base from which to show how SHRM has developed and also give an indication of appropriate strategy content:

1   Selznick's (1957) resource-based model

2   Matching model of Fombrun et al. (1984)

3   Harvard model of Beer et al. (1984)

4   Warwick's model   } both adapted from the

5   Guest's (1989) model } Harvard model

1   *Selznick's (1957) resource-based model*
    Selznick (1957) draws attention to the strategic value of the workforce and the key issues of workplace learning ■ *see* Chapter 10 ■. This is a soft view of HRM ■ *see* Chapter 1 ■. He suggested that organisations each have a distinctive competence that allows them to perform better than their competitors. Such an organisation usually comprises productive resources which distinguish between physical and human resources.

see Chapter 10

see Chapter 1

2   *Matching model of Fombrun et al. (1984)*
    These writers proposed the framework shown in Figure 2.13. It is an extension of what is known as the 'fit' model which idealistically aligns organisational strategy and SHRM. This model shows how the activities within HRM can be unified and designed in order to support the strategy of an organisation. It has its strength in that it is a simple framework which shows how key

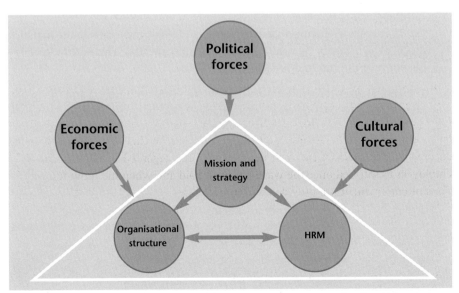

Figure 2.13 Strategic management and environmental pressures after Fombrun et al. (1984, p34)

HRM functions can fit with organisational strategy. For example, the HRM components could be:

see Chapter 4
see Chapter 10
see Chapter 10
see Chapter 9

- selection ■ *see* Chapter 4 ■
- performance appraisal ■ *see* Chapter 10 ■
- continuous development ■ *see* Chapter 10 ■
- reward ■ *see* Chapter 9 ■.

It can be mutually agreed to produce the required cooperative work team behaviour with mutual sharing of information and support. It relies very much on all members of the workforce recognising that HRM has a place in strategy formulation and is thus idealistic in nature.

Taking the examples of the HRM function given above, Table 2.6 shows the broad implications of each when incorporated in the strategic model attributed to Fombrun et al. (1984).

While this type of tidy fit is valuable, its weakness lies in its reliance upon a simplistic interpretation of strategy. Its success will rely upon a rational approach to strategy and the stability of the business environment which is not a feature of contemporary business. Also, it ignores individual behaviour as Torrington and Hall (1998) in their discussion of this model, point out:

> what if it is not possible to produce a human resource response that enables the required employee behaviour and performance? (p36)

This would need an investigation into such issues as motivation and dealing with dysfunctional conflict.

3 *Harvard model of Beer et al. (1984)*
Unlike the model discussed above, Beer et al. (1984) moved on to an analytical model which has been readily adopted within the UK. Figure 2.14 gives an overview of the Harvard model.

This model gives recognition to stakeholders and their interests and the impact on people's behaviour and performance – which was missing from the

Table 2.6 Implications of key functions of HRM within the model of Fombrun et al. (1984)

HRM FUNCTION	BROAD IMPLICATIONS
Selection	Successful experience of teamworking and sociable cooperative personality rather than an independent thinker who likes working alone.
Performance appraisal	Based on contribution to the work team and support of others rather than individual outstanding performance.
Continuous development	Based on individuals taking responsibility for their own learning and development rather than relying on the employer to dictate training and development.
Reward	Based on team performance and contribution rather than individual performance and individual effort.

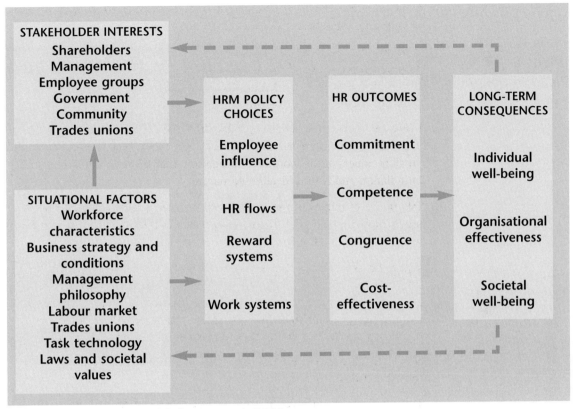

Figure 2.14 The Harvard model after Beer et al. (1984)

Fombrun et al. (1984) matching model. It also gives greater emphasis to the factors in the environment which help to shape SHRM choices.

Although this is primarily an analytical model, it does comprise some ▷ **prescriptive** ◁ elements which can lead to confusion. Fombrun et al. (1984) prescribed a matching fit with organisational strategy and proffered a process for engaging what are identified as the key human resource activities. In the Beer et al. (1984) model the prescriptive nature lies in the human resource outcomes box where the specific outcomes are identified as desirable.

▷ The making or giving of directions, rules or injunctions that are normally sanctioned by ◀┈┈▶ **Prescriptive** long-standing custom or based on legislation.

4 *The Warwick model*

This is a development made by researchers at the University of Warwick, England and is an adaption of the Beer et al. (1984) Harvard model and is shown in Figure 2.15.

The prescriptive elements of the Harvard model are absent and there is greater emphasis on an analytical approach to SHRM. This recognises the changing

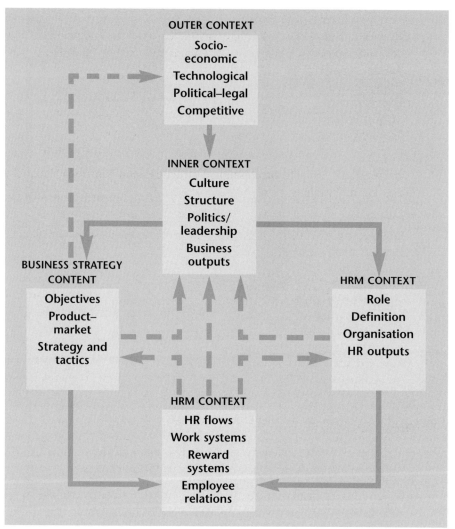

Figure 2.15 Model of strategic change and HRM after Hendry and Pettigrew (1986, p139)

nature of the business environment from a stable one to a more turbulent environment in an increasingly globalised marketplace. The model gives full recognition to the external context of SHRM and identifies a two-way rather than a one-way relationship with organisational strategy – it has become interactive. It is also useful to recognise from this model that the role of the personnel function has had an impact on the content of the SHRM. However, Hendry and Pettigrew (1986) offer a warning stating that to treat the design of HRM systems from a purely rational view would be a mistake. The Warwick model recognises emergent strategy rather than a purely rational, top-down planned approach.

5   *Guest's (1989) model*
Like Beer et al. (1984), Guest (1989) adapted the Harvard model but in a very different way. His model is a prescriptive one and is based on the four human resource outcomes which he developed into:

1 *Strategic integration*

This is ensuring that HRM is fully integrated into strategic planning, that HRM issues are coherent and that line managers use HRM practices as part of their everyday work.

2 *Commitment*

Making sure that employees feel bound to the organisation and are committed to high performance through their behaviour.

3 *Flexibility*

Ensuring an adaptable organisational structure, and functional flexibility based on multiskilling.

4 *Quality*

Developing high-quality goods and services through high-quality, flexible employees.

Guest (1989) sees these goals as a package – they all need to be achieved to create the desired organisational outcomes. Such policy goals are related to HRM policies and are expected to bring about organisational outcomes as shown in Figure 2.16.

Figure 2.16 A theory of HRM after Guest (1989, p49)

HUMAN RESOURCE PROFESSIONALS IN A STRATEGIC ROLE

Wamser (1996) believes that the role of human resource professionals has changed from:

■ controllers to consultants

■ architects of large, one-size programmes to smaller, tailor-made solutions for specific situations.

She writes that the human resource function is being transferred from behind-the-scenes staff work to leadership in change management. With such changes, the salaries of human resource practitioners are moving out of the lower ranges for professions in UK industry and into the higher ones.

The human resource function has probably never been in a better position to market itself in the organisation. Most companies are now actively exploring the use of core business competencies to leverage the capabilities, behaviours and outcomes of the workforce. The human resource manager is the natural partner of line business leaders in making that happen.

The key roles of the generalist and the training and development professionals are well known. Other specialists and human resource managers are also in a position to create significant value for their employers.

The corporate spotlight is on the human resource function: CEOs and other senior executives are increasingly looking to human resource for help in:

see Chapter 4
■ recruiting and selecting the right people ■ *see* Chapter 4 ■

see Chapter 10
■ continuing to improve capabilities and competencies of all members of the workforce ■ *see* Chapter 10 ■

see Chapter 9
■ managing and paying for results ■ *see* Chapter 9 ■

see Chapter 10
■ maintaining vital succession of management, professional and vocational talent as business grows and succeeds ■ *see* Chapter 10 ■.

A human resource system along with organisational structures and cultural norms has exceptional power because together they comprise the dimensions that

2.5

Activity

You have been asked to explain what it means when the role of human resource professions has changed from 'controllers to consultants'.

Write a simple paragraph to explain this.

are the most difficult for competitors to copy. Three critical factors of organisations can control the drive for productivity:

- employee competencies

- manner of supervision

- quality of leadership.

Research discussed by Wamser (1996) explores how to make the most of human capital and provides a blueprint for human resources work in the 21st century. Wamser believes that those employers who are willing to utilise their workforce in order to construct solutions that add value to their organisations will find the times ahead exciting. However, there is no one model of SHRM and no universally agreed components.

ADDITIONAL DIMENSIONS AND THEMES OF SHRM

It is possible to identify a number of additional themes associated with SHRM:

1   Business process re-engineering (BPR)

2   Leadership

3   Workplace learning/knowledge management

4   Trades unions

5   Workplace performance

6   Restructuring and flexibility.

1   *Business process re-engineering (BPR)*
    ▶ **Business process re-engineering** ◀ (BPR) is a label given to the redesign of an organisation and was first articulated by Hammer and Champy (1993) as being a:

    fundamental rethinking and radical redesign of business processes to achieve dramatic improvements in critical, contemporary measures of performance, such as cost, quality, service, and speed. (p32)

▶ A label given to the redesign of an organisation; it may include breaking away from outdated rules and assumptions that underlie how tasks should be performed. A key principle is the elimination or prevention of barriers which could themselves create a distance between employees and their customers. ◀··▶ **Business process re-engineering**

BPR has come a long way from its original inception – the term actually appeared in the world of academia in the early 1980s.

One of the first things to happen is that the organisation is 'flattened' – made leaner. This process entails ▶ **delayering** ◀. There is also a reduction in the number of hierarchical levels in the organisation. Re-engineering is about re-engineering the work that individuals do – not re-engineering a function. It concerns rethinking the whole of the business. Its popularity lay in the belief held by many CEOs that if a business was to be successful it needed to get the process flow right. The traditional organisational design with its hierarchical and structured frameworks restricted creativity and proactive change. It was not always a successful policy – where BPR failed, it tended to be as a result of one or more of eight reasons:

1 leadership at the top
2 unrealistic expectations
3 resistance of middle management
4 wrong change agent leading the project
5 task delegated totally to technical consultants
6 failure to consider the human resource implications
7 paralysis by analysis
8 fear of failure.

Delayering ◀┄┄▶ The taking away of a complete level of management with the idea of improving vertical communication and shortening the chain of command.

On a more positive note, the preconditions for success are sixfold:

1 total commitment from the top
2 realistic expectations
3 a realistic timescale
4 shared vision
5 staff involvement
6 cultural change to match the process change.

BPR has cost many jobs because of its radical nature – the need to go back to the root of the process rather than merely improve what exists. It is about the *process* – the redesigning of the organisation from a function-oriented structure to a process-organised structure. The search needed to be dramatic – the search for quantum leaps and not just incremental improvement. Failure in this procedure has been because the implementers ignored the human factor – Champy is currently continuing his research working in the area of re-engineering management. He is concerned about overcoming the less pleasant side of BPR to allow concentration on the positive side.

2 *Leadership*

This is a difficult concept bringing with it a number of definitive works. However, there is not one agreed definition among researchers and writers and there is often confusion between *management* and *leadership*. As Maund (1999) states:

The term 'management' implies 'leadership', yet they are not the same – the success or failure of managers will depend upon their individual leadership qualities. (p383)

Even though a definition is elusive because of the subjective nature of the concept it is necessary to understand that it is about a capacity to transform a personal vision into action and sustain it. This transformational style is required in contemporary organisations. The key is the ability of a manager to interact effectively with others – wherever they fit within the organisation and its environment.

The concept is particularly central when addressing the *soft* aspects of HRM ■ *see* Chapter 1 ■. Guest (1987) relates the debate of contemporary leadership styles to the prerequisites of the resource-based SHRM model.

see Chapter 1

Since managers want staff who are committed to the organisation, they need to be able to develop the human aspects of the organisation. The transformational leader has a vision and s/he relies on her/his followers to put the vision into action. This requires an ability to effectively communicate the vision. This is a distinct shift in emphasis to the importance of an individual member of the workforce working in self-managed, high-performance teams.

3   *Workplace learning/knowledge management*
All managers need to understand how an individual learns and develops if the organisational goals are to be effectively achieved ■ *see* Chapter 10 *and* Chapter 6 ■. Morgan (1988) stated that managers must:

see Chapter 10 *and* Chapter 6

find ways of developing and mobilizing the intelligence at every level of organization... become increasingly skilled in placing quality people in key places and developing their full potential. It will become increasingly important to recruit people who enjoy learning and relish change and to motivate employees to be intelligent, flexible, and adaptive. (p7)

Over a decade later, this view has not changed. According to Barrow and Loughlin (1993) all employees will have to own a number of abilities and skills, for example:

■ *A high level of education*
Up to at least first degree level so that they can use technology and appreciate their own contribution to the decisions they have to make.

■ *The ability to learn new skills and adapt to changing circumstances*
Through continuous development individuals must take personal responsibility for their learning and ensure that their skills remain current within an ethos of an ability to learn new skills.

■ *The ability to work in organisations with flatter structures and few levels of management*
Requires setting of personal objectives, working in self-management teams and making decisions.

- *The ability to interface with people at all levels*
  Including customers, superiors and team members.

- *The ability to problem solve*
  Through creative thinking.

A central theme of today's organisation is learning to learn and self-development through active learning. Pettinger (1996) incorporates the fundamental aspects of learning in his definition:

the process by which skills, knowledge, attitudes and behaviour are formed and developed. (p82)

He believes that learning and development are also a result of conditioning which he states are situations:

whereby the individual is persuaded to adopt, and ultimately accept, guidance, regulation, conformity and compliance in particular situations. (p82)

see Chapter 6

Effective knowledge management ■ *see* Chapter 6 ■ depends on harnessing experience and more senior managers are taking on the responsibility for the intellectual capital of their organisation. However, Donkin (1997) reports that organisations have not yet decided how to best manage their knowledge workers – let alone how to meet the need for the emotionally intelligent employee. Further discussion on the importance of learning in the workplace can be found in Maund (1999).

Kanter (1997) believes that it is imperative that all employees are developed to become key components within their organisation because it is through its employees that an organisation survives.

4   *Trades unions*
A trade union is an association of employees who have common interests based on their occupation or employment. Its role is to protect and advance its members' interests as employees, particularly in respect of terms and conditions of service. They are also concerned with improving the skills of their members.

This implies that the contemporary SHRM model assumes that employers and employees share a common goal/mission with all differences resolved rationally. Thus, by giving employees responsibility and autonomy they will be committed and loyal to their organisation based on the traditional adoption of contemporary HRM practices. However, trades unions, for example through the Trades Union Congress (TUC), have taken a proactive role in training employees and thus a partnership between employer and employee is seen positively by most trades unions and professional bodies.

5   *Workplace performance*
Pfeffer (1999) constructs an interesting and useful model for generating and sustaining workforce performance. He supports the model on two pillars comprising practical research and powerful examples.

He also proposed a high-performance work system which includes six key factors:

- *Employment security*
  Fundamental to winning employee commitment without fear of working themselves out of their jobs
  Employees freely contribute to improved productivity
  Guarantee of a job which promotes long-term thinking and actions

- *Selective hiring*
  Placing the right people in the right places requires a disciplined approach to employment process
  Selection is competency based
  Selection turns on identification on critical skills and attributes of jobs
  Calibre of employees has direct impact on business effectiveness and market success

- *Self-managed teams and decentralisation of decision making*
  Peer control replaces traditional supervisory processes
  Large proportion of workforce accepts accountability and responsibility for organisational performance
  Employees understand how their work affects the work of others
  Ideas are pooled and layers of unnecessary hierarchy removed

- *Training*
  Well-skilled front-line employees are more flexible, initiate change, predict and solve problems and take responsibility for product quality

- *Reduction of status differences*
  More egalitarian workplace promotes open lines of communication
  Commonality of purpose is enhanced

- *Sharing information*
  Trust of, and commitment to, the organisation both grow when financial information is shared
  Employees are able to prioritise multiple and conflicting goals.

Pfeffer (1999) also provides a formula for aligning business strategy with HRM practices. He believes that if the skills and behaviours needed to support the firm's strategy or strategic intent are plotted against the organisation's employee practices, the value of those practices becomes apparent, and a gap between intention and actual effectiveness can be measured. Assessment of the organisation's practices can then be made to ensure external congruence and internal consistency.

6 *Restructuring and work flexibility*
Mayne et al. (1996) used evidence from both quantitative and qualitative research carried out across Europe and showed that, while the profile of high and low users of part-time and short-term employment is country specific, it

is concentrated in the service and public sectors and is correlated with growth and unionisation. However, there is a link between these forms of flexibility and a strategic approach to HRM. Early writers argued that there is no such link, often used unrealistically restrictive models of strategy formulation and believed that a more comprehensive view indicates that flexibility is being used strategically.

As can be seen from the discussions of strategy on the flexibility of wider industrial relations (IR) and HRM, literature often assumes that strategy formulation is a rational, deliberate process instituted and controlled by senior management; this is what the strategy specialists Bourgeois and Brodwin (1987) termed the 'commander model'. The classical view of strategy was intellectually destroyed by Lindblom's (1959) seminal article. Current debates are more about the relationship between deliberate and enacted strategy and the ways in which incremental decisions coalesce within an organisational culture to define direction. The counterpoising of 'strategic' and 'reactive circumstances' in some of the flexibility literature leads to questioning the reality of a view of strategy that implies that it should not be responsive to developments in the real world.

see Chapter 11   Global competition ■ see Chapter 11 ■ has forced downsizing and restructuring, producing a shortage in many organisations' managerial talent base. This deficit has highlighted an important need to integrate management development into the competitive strategy formulation process. However, many organisations lack the commitment to adopt the concepts of strategic management development (SMD), fail to understand fully its long-term value and/or lack the knowledge to take the steps necessary to develop it as a component of their competitive strategy. McClelland (1995) presents a conceptual framework for adopting and integrating SMD into the competitive strategy formulation process as a means of ensuring the continued availability of trained and experience managers. Stressing the need for the realignment of resources, a rethinking of organisational culture and the need to shift focus from individual to organisational growth, he emphasises that SMD will provide the catalyst for the organisation to anticipate change, expand channels

see Chapter 5   of communication ■ see Chapter 5 ■, provide for a more effective allocation of

see Chapter 5   human resources and promote 'people involvement' ■ see Chapter 5 ■.

Global competition, including increased competition from expanding third-world economies, forced organisations to rethink competitive strategies. This needs experienced and adaptable managers. HRM assumed a more significant degree of importance as organisations attempted internal alignment of resources and functions. Downsizing and restructuring put many experienced managers (particularly those employed in middle management positions) out of work and thus introduced acute shortages in many organisations' human resource base.

Few argue that downsizing and restructuring as a means of reducing overheads to maintain profitability was – and is still – necessary. There are many who believe that the long-term negative effects, some of which we are already feeling, will inject even greater instability into the remaining managerial ranks. Implications associated with this take on a strategic dimension. With organisations facing potential shortfalls in managerial ranks, increasing pressure is being applied by corporate boards, investors and others to contain costs while increasing profitability. Under the present scenario 'doing more with less' is certainly applicable.

Throughout the past decade, HRM development professionals have been advocating the position that management development (MD) ■ *see* Chapter 10 ■ should have a more strategic role and be incorporated as an integral part of the competitive strategy formulation process. There is still a great deal of resistance and apathy. Many executives still review MD as simply training – a cost centre from which little or no tangible returns are produced. There is a need to realign human resources across the organisational spectrum.

see Chapter 10

Within this dimension SHRM has taken on a more significant degree of importance. Similarly, increasing significance is placed on the role of MD specialists to forecast appropriately and project strategically MD requirements that will most certainly be needed for the organisation not only to gain but also to maintain a competitive advantage.

Research has been carried out in this field and *The Employment Trends Report* (1999) was based on active research with 328 senior managers and executives between 3 and 14 December 1998 of which one-third worked in organisations that employed 500 or more people and a quarter had an annual turnover in excess of £100m. The Institute of Management (IOM) (1999) and the recruitment agency, Manpower, reported on the key businesses-related issues including restructuring and flexibility. The jointly authored report revealed that restructuring was an important part of contemporary corporate life stating that more than two-fifths (42 per cent) had reviewed their operations during the course of 1998. When it came to the drivers of change, the survey found that a clear majority of employees reported improved corporate performance, particularly in respect of:

■ strategic planning

■ productivity

■ teamworking.

However, the participants recounted that many firms reported that there had not been any change and, in some cases, a deterioration. This does not reflect well on business considering the amount of time and effort which goes into restructuring programmes, for example, BPR. Employers who expend considerable time and energy on such issues have a right to expect a successful outcome. The report highlights a substantial number of respondents who have stated that their organisations failed to gain improvement in profitability and internal communication, stating that it was of considerable concern. Three-fifths of the participants (60 per cent) had some form of flexible working. Almost one-third (29 per cent) reported that in 1998 there was an increase in the number of 'flexible' employees in the workplace.

The business leader participants were asked to specify which flexible working practices their organisations employed. Part-time working and the use of flexitime were well-established working practices with the newer forms of flexibility such as annual hours contracts, key-time working (used to provide seasonal and part-time cover) and job sharing were becoming well established. Another common practice was the use of outsourcing where 63 per cent of respondents reported that their firms had at least some contracted-out non-core activities – usually related to information technology. Customer care tended to remain a core activity within the firm. According to Hunt (2000):

> For some critics of HR, sub-contracting basic personnel services to consultants has confirmed HR's parlous condition. (p18)

However, according to strategic management expert Hall (2000):

> Judicious outsourcing may turn out to be an opportunity – losing some administrative responsibilities will free up HR people to spend their time in other departments. (p23)

TMP Worldwide (1999) surveyed 785 employees in 22 major private and public sector organisations. Eight out of ten respondents were female and half of the respondents were under 35 years of age. Three-quarters of employees chose to use flexible working. Two-thirds liked the added freedom and three-quarters of parents said that flexible working gave them more quality time with their family.

Overall, the collective results of the research have given a positive report on flexible working hours. Half of the respondents believed that it had improved their working lives over the last five years, and two-thirds stated they were lucky to be able to have the flexibility. However, they did report some worrying issues for flexible workers. The majority stated that they saw no reason why more people should not practice flexible working hours, but they could perceive two reasons for not doing so: first, a quarter believed that their employers did not actually trust them., and second, two in five said their promotion prospects were adversely affected, in that opportunities for career advancement were more likely to be given to those who followed traditional working patterns.

STRATEGIC FIT/CONGRUENCE/MATCH

This defines a successful strategy as one that brings what the organisation can do (its competencies) into alignment with the needs and demands of its environment. When the competencies of the organisation fit the demands of the environment, the organisation is selected and retained (the population ecology view), provided with resources (the resource dependence view) and legitimised (the institutional view). Strategy is concerned with actively managing fit in order to achieve competitive advantage which will ensure the organisation's survival, profitability and reputation.

In order to do this, that is, to match the competencies of the organisation with the demands of its environment, it implies that strategists are expected to be aware of a possible fit, and to do something about it. Thus attention to strategy introduces self-awareness and intentionality into the discussion of organisations.

According to resource dependence theory, being dependent upon a customer or supplier leaves an organisation vulnerable to its environment, even if management is unaware of its dependence. Likewise, institutional theory does not demand that management deliberately develop the organisation's social legitimacy, and population ecology theory claims that environments are indifferent to organisational attempts to strategise because the outcomes of selection and retention processes are largely a matter of chance or luck.

Because of their emphasis on intentionality, strategy researchers develop their own interpretations of organisation–environment theories. Their aim is to discover what these, and other theories, can tell strategists that will improve their changes of developing and maintaining a successful fit between the organisation and its environment. This is a difficult assignment with respect to population ecology theory, which can leave managers feeling a little helpless. Nonetheless, some strategists insist that, by becoming aware of the patterns of selection and retention processes, they can learn to manoeuvre their organisations into positions of competitive advantage and thus become more likely to be selected and retained. A few, accepting that survival can be a matter of luck, focus on how some organisations seem to inherit luck (Barney, 1986) – but this is an unusual view.

The resource dependence perspective is the most natural for the strategist to assume. This is because resource dependence theory is written from the viewpoint of the organisation, rather than the environment, and this is the perspective of the strategist. For example, the list of implications of resource dependence theory (for example, to engage in co-optation, joint ventures, or vertical integration) is a set of alternative corporate strategies for achieving and maintaining fit.

The institutional perspective suggests that strategy is a symbolic question. That is, does the organisation look successful? Does it conform to external expectations about its products and its practices? The establishment of public relations (PR) departments is one obvious way in which organisations respond to institutional demands for social legitimacy. But many other more subtle signs of institutional effects are apparent in organisations, right down to the decor of offices and the style of dress worn by employees.

A strategic interpretation of the institutional perspective suggests that the symbolic aspects of organisations can be managed, for instance, through imitation of successful firms. By using the practices of successful firms as a benchmark (a comparison point for judging some aspect of the firm's performance, sometimes referred to as best practice), organisations can signal to their environments that they are also successful, thus securing the social legitimacy required to attract resources. From the perspective of population ecology theory, imitating the best practices of other organisations can also be interpreted as a strategy for enhancing the likelihood of selection and retention through adaptation to environmental demands.

A strategist's concern with transforming theoretical knowledge into competitive advantage forces strategy research into a modernist perspective, regardless of the perspective from which the theory was originally developed. The reason for this is that the concept of competitive advantage objectivises organisations and environments. That is, in order to see firms in competition for scare resources, it is necessary to adopt a view of firms as tangible entities operating in a real world: that is, the objectivist stance.

see Chapter 6
and Chapter 11

It is the elements of excitement, energy and passion which increasingly play a central role in SHRM. It cannot be denied that business is now taking place at an increasingly fast pace because of increased technology and globalisation ■ *see* Chapter 6 *and* Chapter 11 ■. This is resulting in the classic use of the strategic plan being less organised because by the time it has been written and agreed, the world will have moved on. It is the energy and passion of the organisation which provides the lead in the contemporary world. It could well be argued that action in HRM is more important than analysis yet it is vital that the HRM specialist ensures that the people are better than those employed by the competition and, even if they have passion, excitement and energy, they are also skilled in key areas such as planning, recruitment and selection ■ *see* Chapter 3 *and* Chapter 4 ■.

see Chapter 3
and Chapter 4

Chapter summary

- There is a debate about the position of HRM in an organisation's strategy. When referring to such an implication, the prefix 'strategic' is used and HRM thus becomes SHRM. Although there is no general agreement on the characteristics of SHRM, there are some demanding claims about it. These emphasise, among other things, links with business strategy and organisational change.

- Organisations in the UK need to follow the example of organisations in the USA where most boards of directors have the HRM director as part of their team (Taylor, 2000).

- Strategy is about planning and is variously defined by researchers and writers. In general terms, this means that the management of any organisation must carefully devise a plan of action in order to achieve its objectives. Strategy is also about the art of developing and carrying out such plans.

- Contemporary writers tend to avoid actually defining 'strategy' in managerial terms, preferring, like Browne et al. (1999), to state that it 'encompasses a very wide variety of perspectives and approaches' (p269).

- There are a number of strategy planning approaches ranging from the traditional to the volatile contemporary approach.

- SHRM involves a certain amount of ambiguity because it deals with matters that are not run of the mill. It is also very complex with organisation-wide complications comprising changes which could be significant rather than small scale.

Chapter summary *continued*

■ Three recognised seminal models for formulating strategies and which can be used to proved a framework for competitive action are provided by Miles and Snow (1978), Porter (1980) and Miller (1987).

■ Strategic management provides an important link between the organisation and its environment through which information and influence pass.

■ An organisation's change strategy tends to drive its HRM strategy rather than vice versa. Corporate and change strategies are generally initiated by HRM departments, and then implemented by supervisors and line managers.

■ The thesis that organisations simply comprise a number of capabilities that need to be matched with the needs of market force (the resource-based theory) is central to effective strategic management.

■ An important issue for organisations is to identify human resource strategies that link business strategy to performance.

■ There are other models of SHRM that have developed from the seminal ones: the resource-based model (Selznick, 1957), the matching model (Fombrun et al., 1984), the Harvard model (Beer et al., 1984) and the Warwick model and that of Guest (1989) which both adapted the Harvard model.

■ The role of HRM professionals has changed from controllers to consultants, and from architects of large, one-size programmes to smaller, tailor-made solutions for specific situations (Wamser, 1996).

■ There are a number of additional themes associated with SHRM, including: BPR, leadership, workplace learning/knowledge management, trades unions, workplace performance and restructuring and flexibility.

■ Human resource practitioners must have the ability and interest to locate their activities in the wider environmental setting or they will lose contact with practice and thus change and so their organisations will have lost any market placement – let alone be the market leaders.

■ There has to be a strategic fit/congruence/match that defines a successful strategy as one that brings what the organisation can do (its competencies) into alignment with the needs and demands of the organisation. Strategy is concerned with actively managing fit in order to achieve competitive advantage that will ensure the organisation's survival, profitability and reputation.

■ The form of SHRM used is represented by the management's commitment to the objectives, policies and practices related to all employees within the organisation.

■ HRM specialists have to articulate strongly their developmental and employment strategies among those already strongly recognised within the organisation because, otherwise, the achievement of the totality of business objectives may be vulnerable.

■ Strategy is a complex issue and an 'elusive concept' (Von Maurik, 1999).

END OF CHAPTER 2 CASE STUDY

A real step change

Gratton (2000) worked on a seven-year project during the London Business School's Leading Edge Project and concluded that human capital has replaced finance and technology as the main source of competitive advantage which, in itself, presents both an opportunity and a threat to HRM practitioners.

Over the last ten years Gratton (2000, 2000a) has advised a number of large organisations about how they could put their people at the centre of the purpose of their business. Initial discussions were usually about techniques – how pay or benefits can produce certain behaviour, how training can develop particular skills. Certainly, these processes set the context and are crucial levers for change. But she believes that organisations will gain advantage primarily through the process by which they create and embed an HR strategy.

In her own work, Gratton (2000, 2000a) used as a guide a six-step process. She worked, among others, with teams from Philips Lighting to create what the organisation calls a 'living strategy', to support its goal of becoming the world's number one lighting

company. Their experience illustrates the six steps which Gratton (2000, 2000a) believes to be the major elements of success at the organisation.

1 Building the coalition

Bucking the trend, taking the unconventional approach, stretching performance, exposing the unexposed – all require a shared, articulated view of the current reality, what the future could be and the steps that could lead from one to the other. The energy to start and sustain the journey develops from all functions and levels in the business – a guiding coalition. The journey began, for Philips Lighting, in 1993. The then chief executive had a vision of what the company could be and set his team the challenge of delivering that. During the next six months, he involved 60 people from all over the world in elaborating this vision.

2 Imagining the future

For three months the researchers worked with each of the groups that had been set up, imagining what Philips Lighting could be in five years' time. In the sessions, the groups visualised the senior management team, the structure, the culture, the key HR processes, the skills and attitudes of the people.

When the groups' ideas were synthesised, a number of areas of strategic importance emerged: the structure of the business world would be focused on the global markets; the experiences of the senior team would be gained in these markets, particularly in Asia; high-performing, cross-functional teams would play a key role in anticipating customer needs; there would be global recruitment processes capable of identifying and retaining world-class skill sets in product design, miniaturisation and integration; and a culture of innovation and entrepreneurship would flourish. The creation of this shared vision was at the heart of the people-centred strategy and was an exciting process for the participants.

3 Understanding current capabilities and identifying the gap

The team at Philips Lighting now had to understand the organisation and that involved auditing global recruitment processes, surveying employees' perceptions of teamwork capabilities and analysing development plans for existing and future skill sets.

From this, it became clear that there were factors that were crucial for the future, but for which current alignment was poor. In particular, the way the business was structured according to function into research and development, manufacturing, marketing and sales worked against the market focus that would be essential for the future. Similarly, teams were primarily working within, rather than across, functions.

4 Creating a map of the system

The move was now into viewing Philips Lighting as a dynamic system which is important because, by constructing a map of the organisation, it is possible to see how individuals will view it. It is here that the parts are fit into a meaningful whole.

At Philips Lighting, three future themes were identified: globalisation, innovation and customer orientation. Then began the construction of a map of how the elements of the organisation could be aligned to these three themes. For example, innovation would be reinforced through cross-functional teamworking – using the performance management process to identify and encourage innovative work.

Each of these levers needed reinforcing. Cross-functional teamworking has implications for the structure of the business and how career paths are crated. Rewarding innovation would require a more rigorous method of encouraging and measuring innovation. Over time, the groups worked separately and then together to create a shared understanding of the dynamics of the future business, the key themes, the levers and the relationships.

5 Modelling the dynamics of the vision

The map created in step four is, in essence, static. In reality, systems are dynamic – for instance, one element can have unintended consequences that can destroy the desired results. At Philips Lighting, one of the unintended consequences of a system rewarding individual creativity was that it discouraged teamworking. The Philips Lighting team also modelled the forces for and against change in each of the key themes and levers. By doing this, it saw how the processes would play out over time and anticipated some of the resistance.

6 Bridging into action

There is no great strategy – only great execution. The challenge is to implement the ideas. The

END OF CHAPTER 2 CASE STUDY (CONT'D)

systems mapping creates the chance to agree about the broad themes for action and the specific issues that address these themes. The strength of the journey rests on a number of guiding principles. The foundation is to continue to build the guiding coalition by involving line managers.

At Philips Lighting, task forces were created around six global themes and these multi-functional groups drove the implementation for some years. The critical success indicators became crucial to measuring the extent of change. By following these steps, Philips Lighting built a momentum that has allowed it to realise its aspirations to become one of the world's greatest lighting businesses.

Adapted from: Gratton, L. (2000a) A real step change, *People Management*, 16 March, pp26–30.

 ### END OF CHAPTER 2 CASE STUDY QUESTIONS

1 What does the phrase 'levers for change' mean within the case of Philips Lighting?

2 What does it mean by people being at the centre of Philips Lighting's purpose?

3 Identify the key stages the organisation went through in its efforts to become 'one of the world's greatest lighting businesses'?

4 Why is it important that HRM specialists identify what is unique about the people who work for them?

END OF PART I CASE STUDY

TROUBLESHOOTER SETS OUT HIS STALL

Luc Vandevelde does not look like a man with the weight of huge expectations on his shoulders. A month after taking a job widely regarded as a poisoned chalice, the Belgian executive chairman of Marks & Spencer [M&S] is surprisingly upbeat.

M&S is not your average retailer. It is an icon of the UK retailing scene and a City blue-chip stock, but it has fallen on hard times, losing its way in a fast changing market where newer, nimbler competitors have been calling the shots. For any outsider, coming in to take over the top job would be a tall order.

Just to add to the challenge for Mr Vandevelde, the role of executive chairman is not straightforward. It is contrary to UK corporate governance guidelines, which prefer the roles to be split between a chief executive and a non-executive chairman. The last incumbent – Sir Richard Greenbury – is the man blamed by many for M&S's currently debased reputation.

But Mr Vandevelde, who joined the group from French retailer Promodès, is not letting expectations weigh him down – he says he is keenly aware of the retailer's special nature.

END OF PART I CASE STUDY (CONT'D)

His antennae are turned firmly inwards. 'I will be looking forward to much more internal appreciation of what I do and don't do than I would look at the external appreciation. I understand that the outside world is expecting to see some signs of change. I would hope that the signs would be the performance rather than dramatic changes in the board or in organisational structures.'

Like most retail bosses he has to cope with the fact that everyone he meets thinks they know just what is going wrong or right with a business that is part of the national psyche.

'People's views of the business or strategy are always influenced by the personal relationship they have with M&S as a company,' he says. 'If a journalist hasn't found the right size suit the first thing he will do is complain.'

Mr Vandevelde does not pay too much attention. 'Each is only one opinion out of many,' he says. 'But I think I find it fascinating in the sense that it probably explains something of the overreaction to the good things and the bad things that M&S may be doing.'

Adapted from: Campbell, K. (1999) Focus switches to the human factor, *Financial Times*, 15 August, p19.

END OF PART I CASE STUDY QUESTIONS

1 Luc Vandevelde is not a British national and is, therefore, not immersed in the culture of a British institution – M&S. How can his European experience head a strategy to bring M&S into a globalised marketplace?

2 The case study states that Luc Vandevelde will have a difficult job to turn round M&S. What are the key HRM issues he needs to address?

3 Why do you think that Luc Vandevelde considers one complaint not to be so important when M&S has prided itself in the past on dealing with complaints as a key activity?

4 What is 'the special nature' of M&S which Luc Vandevelde refers to?

THESIS + ANTITHESIS = SYNTHESIS

Explore the view that there is no such thing as strategy in HRM.

SELF-TEST THE KEY ISSUES

1 What is a business strategy and how does it differ from a strategy in HRM?

2 What contributions can a line manager make to SHRM?

3 Describe four SHRM models and list the key components of each.

4 Brainstorm the key issues related to SHRM.

TEAM/CLASS DISCUSSIONS

1 'There is no such thing as strategy in HRM. ' Debate this issue.

2 A line manager is continually faced with lateness from a member of his staff who otherwise works very well. Discuss the ways that this problem might be resolved by the manager.

 PROJECTS (INDIVIDUAL OR TEAM)

1 Obtain a copy of your faculty/school/department's strategic plan. Identify the areas therein which are related to SHRM both (a) explicitly and (b) implicitly. Explore ways by which you can inform the producers of the strategy of any shortcomings.

2 Conduct an attitude survey among students in an attempt to elicit their views of SHRM in either (a) public or (b) private industries.

 Recommended reading

Armstrong, M. (1999) *A Handbook of Human Resource Management Practice*, London: Kogan Page

Beardwell, I. and L. Holden (1999) *Human Resource Management: A Contemporary Perspective*, London: Pitman

Bratton, J. and J. Gold (1999) *Human Resource Management: Theory and Practice*, Basingstoke: Macmillan – now Palgrave

Graham, H.T. and R. Bennett (1999) *Human Resources Management*, London: Financial Times/Pitman

Gratton, L. (2000) *Living Strategy: Getting People at the Heart of Corporate Purpose*, London: Financial Times/Prentice Hall

Legge, K. (1995) *Human Resource Management: Rhetorics and Realities*, Basingstoke: Macmillan – now Palgrave

Pickard, J. (2000) Experts vie to define 'S' word in *People Management*, 9 November, pp10–11

Torrington, D. and L. Hall (1998) *Human Resource Management*, London: Prentice Hall

 URL (uniform resource locator)

www.mcb.co.uk

MCB University Press. Details of academic and professional titles of books in English speaking worldwide. Links to other relevant sites and over 100 journals. Topical news and resources, for example, HRM journal titles which cover a wide area of SHRM issues.

Bibliography

Armstrong, M. (1999) *A Handbook of Human Resource Management Practice*, London: Kogan Page

Bamberger, P. and B. Phillips (1991) Organizational environment and business strategy: parallel versus conflicting influences on human resources strategy in the pharmaceutical industry in *Human Resource Management*, **30**(1): 153–82

Barney, J.B. (1986) Organizational culture: can it be a source of sustained competitive advantage? in *Academy of Management Review*, **11**

Barrow, M.H. and H.M. Loughlin (1993) Towards a learning organisation in Great Metropolitan Foods Europe in Willis. G. (ed.) *Your Enterprise School Of Management*, Bradford: MCB University Press, pp195–208

Becker, B. (1996) The impact of human resource management on organizational performance in *Academy of Management Journal*, **39**(4)

Beer, M., B. Spector, P. Lawrence, R. Quinn, D. Mills and R.E. Walton (1984) *Managing Human Assets*, New York: Free Press

Beinhocker, E.D. (1999) Robust adaptive strategies in *Sloan Management Review*, Reprint 4039, Spring, **40**(3)
(http://mitsloan.mit.edu/smr/past/1999/smr4039.html)

Bourgeois, L.J. and Brodwin, D.R. (1987) Strategic implementation: five approaches to an elusive phenomenon in *Strategic Management Journal*, **5**(7): 109–42

Boxall, P. (1992) The significance of human resource management: a reconsideration of the evidence in *The International Journal of Human Resource Management*, **4**(3): 645–64

Boxall, P. (1994) Placing HR strategy at the heart of the business in *Personnel Management*, July, pp32–5

Boyle, K. (2000) Up to speed in *People Management*, 6 January, p35

Browne, M, R. Banerjee, E. Fulop and S. Linstead (1999) Managing strategically in Fulop, L. and S. Linstead (1999) *Management: A Critical Text*, Basingstoke: Macmillan – now Palgrave

Campbell, A. (1999) *Thinking About… Tailored, Not Benchmarked: A Fresh Look at Corporate Planning*
(http://www.hbsp.harvard.edu/products/hbr/marapr99/99202.html)

Chan Kim, W. and R. Mauborgne (1999) Strategy, value innovation, and the knowledge economy in *Sloan Management Review*, Reprint 4034, Spring, **40**(3)
(http://mitsloan.mit.edu/smr/1998/smr4034.html)

Daft, R.L. (1995) *Organization Theory and Design*, St Paul, MN: West Publishing

D'Aveni, R. (1999) Strategic supremacy through disruption and dominance in *Sloan Management Review*, Reprint 40313
(http://mitsloan.mit.edu/smr/past/1999/smr40312.html)

Donkin, R. (1997) Value and rewards of brainpower in *Financial Times*, 11 June, p14

Drucker, P. (1999) *Management Challenges for the 21st Century*, London: Butterworth-Heinemann

Eisenhardt, K.M. (1999) Strategy as strategic decision making in *Sloan Management Review*, Spring, **40**(3)
(http://mitsloan.mit.edu/smr/past/1999/smr4036.html)

Fombrun, C.J., N.J. Tichy and M.A. Devanna (1984) *Strategic Human Resource Management*, New York: John Wiley & Sons

Galbraith, J.R. and D.A. Nathanson (1978) *Strategy Implementation: The Role of Structure and Process*, St Paul, MN: West Publishing

Ghosal, S., C.A. Bartlett and P. Moran (1999) A new manifesto for management in *Sloan Management Review*, Spring, **40**(3)
(http://mitsloan.mit.edu/smr/past/1999/smr4031.html)

Gratton, L. (1997) The art of managing people in Bickerstaffe, G. (ed.) *Mastering Management*, London: Financial Times

Gratton, L. (2000) *Living Strategy*, London: Financial Times/Prentice Hall

Gratton, L. (2000a) A real step change in *People Management*, 16 March, pp26–30

Guest, D.E. (1987) Human resource management and industrial relations in *Journal of Management Studies*, **24**(5): 503–21

Guest, D. (1989) Human resource management: its implications for industrial relations and trade unions in Storey, J. (ed.) *New Perspectives on Human Resource Management*, London: Routledge

Guest, D. (1990) Human resource management and the American dream in *Journal of Management Studies*, **4**: 377–97

Gunnigle, P. and S. Moore (1994) Linking business strategy and human resource management in *Personnel Review*, **23**(1): 63–84
(http://www.hr-expert.com/members/data/rc_articles/01423AE1.htm)

Hall, P. (2000) Feel the width in *People Management*, 6 January, p23

Hammer, M. and J. Champy (1993) *Re-engineering the Corporation*, New York, Nicholas Brealey

Hatch, M-J. (1997) *Organization Theory: Modern, Symbolic, and Postmodern Perspectives*, Oxford: Oxford University Press

Hendry, C. and A. Pettigrew (1986) The practice of strategic human resource management in *Personnel Review*, **13**(3)

Hilltrop, J., C. Despres and P. Sparrow, 1995, The changing role of human resource managers in Europe in *European Management Journal*, **13**(1)

Hollinshead, G. and M. Leat (1995) *Human Resource Management: An International and Comparative Perspective on the Employment Relationship*, London: Pitman

Hout, T. (1999) Are managers obsolete? in *Harvard Business Review*
(http://hbsp.harvard.edu/ products/hbr/marapr99/99207.html

Hunt, J.W. (2000) Untapped resources in *Financial Times*, 9 February, p18

Institute of Management (1999) *UK Corporate Employment Strategies and Trends*, London: Institute of Management

IRS Employment Trends, April 1999, Nos 677/678

Johnson, G. and K. Scholes (1999) *Exploring Corporate Strategy*, Hemel Hempstead: Prentice Hall

Kamoche, K. (1994) A critique and proposed reformation of strategic human resource management in *Human Resource Management Journal*, **4**(4): 29–43

Kanter, R.M. (1997) It's a people thing in *Financial Times* ('The Management Interview') by Griffith, V., 24 July, p20

Kellaway, L. (1999) The short stay at the top in *Financial Times*, 14 June, p20

Kellaway, L. (2000) Fun, fun, fun, till the FT took our e-mails away in *Financial Times*, 17 January, p13

Kotchan, T. and L. Dyer (1995) HRM: an American view in Storey, J. (ed.) *Human Resource Management: A Critical Text*, London: Routledge

Leonard, W. (1999) What do human resource executives want from CEOs? in *Human Resources Magazine*, Society for Human Resource Management, December
(http://www.shrm.org/hrmagazine/articles/1298leonard.htm)

Lindblom, C.E. (1959) The science of muddling through in *Public Administration Review*, **19**: 79–88

Markides, C.C. (1999) A dynamic view of strategy in *Sloan Management Review*, Spring, **40**(3)
(http://mitsloan.mit.edu/smr/past/1999/smr4035.html)

Maund, L. (1999) *Understanding People and Organisations: An Introduction to Organisational Behaviour*, Cheltenham: Stanley Thornes

Mayne, L., O. Tregaskis and C. Brewster (1996) A comparative analysis of the link between flexibility and HRM strategy in *Employee Relations*, **18**(3), MCB University Press
(http://hr-expert.com/members/data/rc_articles/0198CA1.htm)

McClelland, S. (1995) Gaining competitive advantage through strategic management development in *American Journal of Management Development*, **1**(1): 4–10

McGregor, D.M. (1960) *The Human Side of Enterprise*, New York: McGraw-Hill

Miles, R.E. and C. Snow (1978) *Organizational Strategy, Structure and Process*, New York: McGraw-Hill

Miller, D. (1987) The structural and environmental correlates of business strategy in *Strategic Management Journal*, January/February

Mintzberg, H. (1987) Five P's for strategy in *California Management Review*, Autumn

Mintzberg, H. (1990) Strategy formation: schools of thought in Frederickson, J. W. (ed.) *Perspectives on Strategic Management*, New York: Harper & Row

Mintzberg, H. and J. Lampel (1999) Reflecting on the strategy process in *Sloan Management Review*, Spring, **40**(3)

(http://mitsloan.mit.edu/smr/past/1999/smr4032.html)

Morgan, G. (1988) *Riding the Waves of Change: Developing Managerial Competencies for a Turbulent World*, San Francisco: Jossey-Bass

Observer, 9 May 1999

(http://www.newsunlimited.co.uk.Observer/Story/ 0,3879,48737,00.html)

Osterman, P. (1994) How common is workplace transformation and who adopts it? in *Industrial and Labour Relations Review*, **47**(4): 173–88

Othman, R.B. (1996) Strategic human resource management: evidence from the Irish food industry in *Personnel Review*, **25**(1)

(http://www/hr-expert.com/members/data/rc_articles/ 01425AC1.htm)

Pettinger, R. (1996) *Introduction to Organisational Behaviour*, Basingstoke: Macmillan – now Palgrave

Pfeffer, J. (1999) *The Human Equation*

(http://www.shrm.org/hrmagazine/srticles/ 0298book.htm)

Pfeffer J. and Y. Cohen (1984) Determinants of internal labour markets in organisations in *The Administrative Science Quarterly*, **29**: 550–72

Porter, M.E. (1980) *Competitive Strategy: Techniques for Analysing Industries and Competitors*, New York: Free Press

Propath Solutions (2000) in *People Management*, 2 March, p7

Rana, E. (2000) Open-plan government in *People Management*, pp34–8, 40, 41

Schuler, R. (1989) Strategic human resource management in *Human Relations*, **142**(2): 157–84

Selznick, P. (1957) *Leadership and Administration*, New York: Harper & Row

Skinner, D. and C. Mabey (1998) Managers' perceptions of strategic human resource change in *Personnel Review*, **26**(6)

(http://www/hr-expert.co/members/data/rc_articles/01426FC1.htm)

Slack, N., S. Chambers, C. Harland, A. Harrison and R. Johnston (1995) *Operations Management*, London, Pitman

Stewart, J. (1999) *Employee Development Practice*, London: Financial Times/Pitman

Storey, J. (1992) *Developments in the Management of Human Resource: An Analytical Review*, Oxford: Basil Blackwell

Taylor, B. (2000) Turning the top tables in *People Management*, 20 January, p27

Tilles, S. (1969) Making strategy explicit in Ansoff, H.I. (ed.) *Business Strategy*, Harmondsworth: Penguin

TMP Worldwide (1999) *The Flexible Workforce*, London: TMP Worldwide

Torrington, D. and L. Hall (1998) *Human Resource Management*, 4th edn, London: Prentice Hall

Turner, A. (2000) Central preservation in *People Management*, 2 March, pp56–7, 59

Tyson, S. and Witcher, M. (1994) Getting in gear: post-recession HR management in *Personnel Management*, August, pp20–3

Ulrich, D. (1998) New mandate for human resources in *Harvard Business Review*, **76**(1): 124–35

Von Maurik (1999) *The Effective Strategist*, London: Gower

Voyle, S. (2000) Troubleshooter sets out his stall in *Financial Times*, 4 April, p17

Wamser, P. (1996) Pay growth reflects human resource's shift to a strategic roll [sic] in *Human Resource Magazine*, November

(http://www.shrm.org/hrmagazine/articles/1196cov.htm)

Watson, T.J. (1994) *In Search of Management*, London: Routledge

Whittaker, J. (2000) Standard deviations in *People Management*, 20 January, p29

Williamson, P.J. (1999) Strategy as options on the future in *Sloan Management Review*, Reprint 40311, Spring, **40**(3)

(http://mitsloan.mit.edu/smr/past/1999/smr40311.html)

Planning, recruitment and selection

Human resource planning

After studying this chapter, you should be able to:

- DEFINE the concept 'manpower'.

- EXPLAIN the importance of planning in general and its importance to the human resource management (HRM) specialist.

- SPECIFY the components of strategic, operational and action plans within the framework of planning processes and planning procedures.

- DISCUSS the planning process and its position in the manpower planning framework.

- APPLY the planning cycle to personal and organisation-related activities.

- EXPLAIN the role of senior, middle and lower-level managers in the planning process.

- ASSESS the value and importance of mission and vision statements.

- UNDERSTAND the role of management by objectives (MBO) (Drucker, 1973) in the human resource planning (HRP) process.

- APPLY the planning techniques of STEEEP, SWOT and forecasting.

- SET objectives using the SMART system.

- PRACTISE the scheduling techniques of critical path analysis, flowcharts, network analysis and Gantt charts as they relate to HRP.

- APPLY the principles and formulae related to the demand and supply of labour: labour productivity, absenteeism, labour turnover and levels of wastage.

INTRODUCTION

Framework case study

Jobs growth in call centres

More than 1.3m Europeans will be working in call centres by 2003 – a compound growth rate of 12% a year – in spite of fears that the Internet will destroy telephone-based jobs, a new report forecasts.

Datamonitor, the market analyst, believes the Internet will slow down call centre employment growth but not halt it. Call centres have been the biggest job-creating phenomenon in the USA and Europe over the past decade.

Up till now, call centres have been places from which companies offer goods and services by tele-phone. Increasingly they are being transformed into multi-media cen-tres handling all forms of contact with customers, including e-mail, fax, cash machines, Internet kiosks and digital television.

Integration is being accelerated by 'customer relationship man-agement' – the fashionable theory that companies organised on func-tional and product lines should restructure themselves around customers' needs.

Datamonitor bases its forecasts on more than 1000 interviews with managers in seven countries.

It says the UK will continue to have the most jobs – 426 000 by 2003, compared with 335 000 now – but growth will slow from double-digit rates to 6% a year.

Germany, the second largest, will grow fast from 175 000 to 263 000. Italy and Spain will expand rapidly, but Ireland and the Netherlands will see more sluggish growth.

Call centres have been accused of being sweatshops, with staff having to handle call after call using repetitive formulae.

Adapted from: Groom, B, (2000) Jobs growth in call centres too slow, *Financial Times*, 21 January, p7.

see Chapter 11

Lack of appropriate ▶ **manpower** ◀ is serious because it is a major limiting resource. In some countries, for example Singapore, it is the only resource. As a consequence, manpower can be a limiting factor to a country's growth and busi-ness expansion as is exampled in the Framework Case Study above. Countries and organisations have to develop their manpower resources in order to have a competitive edge and remain relevant in an increasingly competitive global envi-ronment ■ *see* Chapter 11 ■.

Manpower ◀····▶ The total supply of persons available and trained/educated for employment.

see Chapter 11

see Chapter 2 *and* Chapter 6

Therefore, a critical area in the business environment which needs attention is the development of a globally competitive ■ *see* Chapter 11 ■, knowledge-based (skilled) workforce ■ *see* Chapter 2 *and* Chapter 6 ■. To achieve this – the vision of a knowledge-based workforce with core competencies – it is important that organ-isations have a manpower strategy that will contribute to the enhancement of their economic competitiveness. This means that organisations need to look at their manpower issues in a total international perspective and adopt an integrated and comprehensive strategy for meeting the national and international manpower needs in both numbers and quality. An integrated approach ensures that manpower planning, development and management remain well coordinated and relevant to the needs of the economy.

By adopting an integrated approach, an organisation can develop a world-class workforce with capabilities and skills to succeed in the globalised knowledge economy ■ *see* Chapter 11 ■. This requires total commitment and effort on the part of the government, trades unions, workers and employers. Organisations have to draw on the resources and participation of the labour movement, employers' organisations and international partners in the formulation and implementation of manpower policies. This participation ■ *see* Chapter 7 ■ is a central part of manpower success.

see Chapter 11

see Chapter 7

see Chapter 2

Manpower planning is thus a vital part of an organisation's strategy ■ *see* Chapter 2 ■ and can be reviewed in a three-step process:

1   planning in general

2   manpower planning (MP)

3   human resource planning (HRP).

PLANNING IN GENERAL

Without a thorough and practical understanding of planning techniques, the HRM specialist cannot address the issues of MP and/or HRP with confidence or with any degree of accuracy.

A central job for the manager is that of planning. Every manager spends a large proportion of her/his time drawing up ▸ **plans** ◂ and communicating them to members of the workforce and then, when the plans have been activated, reporting on their progress and evaluating their success. Plans are a very important part of business and have a number of uses:

■   they give an opportunity for individuals to give serious thought to what they actually want

■   they allow people a better opportunity to achieve what they want

■   they give managers an opportunity to calculate the resources available to achieve the plan; for example financial, equipment, supplies and manpower.

> ▸ An account of how an individual intends to get from her/his current situation to one where ◂┈┈▸ **Plan**
> s/he wants to be, that is, to get from A to B.

Therefore, plans can help to ensure that all resources are used to maximum effect.

THE USE OF PLANS

It is not only managers who can make the best use of planning – it can help anyone who wants to focus on what s/he is supposed to be doing from the chief executive officer (CEO) to the telephonists in the call centre. For all users, plans can give motivation to achieve and allow individuals to gain a sense of purpose in their activities. They also allow individual employees an opportunity to see how they fit in within the larger scheme of things and help to give them self-esteem because they lose the sense of isolation which comes about if individuals are not part of 'the big plan'.

The same skills are required from all individuals who wish to plan – regardless of their place in the hierarchy. The CEO will use the same ways and means to plan as the student working part time in the lower levels of the organisation. With the acquisition of planning skills, an individual employee will gain a deeper understanding of the priorities and concerns of managers who have to make plans at a more senior level. Junior members of staff will also begin to collect information on how the organisation formulates its long-term plans and, thus, her/his role within the achievement of these plans.

Therefore, an understanding of the basic planning processes and procedures is essential before there can be an analysis of the more refined process of manpower planning (MP) and human resource planning (HRP).

THE PROCESS OF PLANNING

The planning process will be the same regardless of the type of venture or the individual carrying out the planning – whether an individual is deciding on how to sort out her/his studies or the drawing up of a manpower plan for an organisation.

There are five key components to any planning process:

1   identification of the goal

2   clarification of the present position

3   consideration of the range of strategies that could be used to achieve the set goal

4   choice of the most appropriate strategy

5   the breaking down of the chosen strategy into smaller, more manageable, steps.

Activity 3.1

Choose any simple activity that you will soon have to carry out – preferably related to your employment.

Apply the five stages of the planning process to it.

Directors and senior managers of any organisation will have to go through the same sort of process as was carried out in the above activity, regardless of the complexity of the situation or the level of the employee involved.

THE PLANNING CYCLE

The planning cycle constitutes four distinct parts as shown in Figure 3.1.

Drawing up the plan

This is made up of the five steps mentioned above.

Implementing the plan

This is when the plan has to be communicated to those who will activate it and it is at this stage that the resources, for example money, human resources and time, are committed.

Monitoring the plan

Consideration of the procedures which will be adopted for monitoring the plan at the start is very important because monitoring will take place throughout the activation of the plan from start to finish. Most organisations will use one or both of two tools – budget and/or schedule:

■ *Budget*
   This is a list of monetary amounts which are expected to be spent or received and which are presented under a number of headings appropriate to the project.

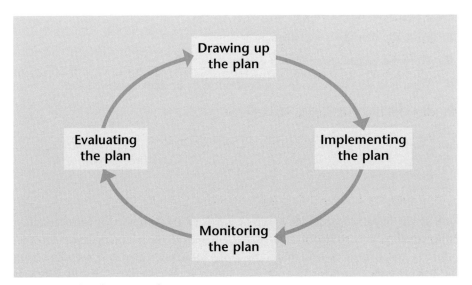

Figure 3.1 The planning cycle

During the activation of the plan, these figures will change with amounts being added and detracted. It is the ▶ **variance** ◀ which is the most important figure to keep an eye on because by doing this, a worker can see whether the activity is more costly (or less costly) than was originally planned. It is important to keep an eye on the dates to ensure that the activity is moving to schedule.

Variance ◀┄┄▶	The difference between the budgeted and actual figures being spent on a planned project.

■ *Schedule*

A list of dates at which/by which specific events should have happened. These are usually in the form of charts, diagrams and/or graphs. They are very important during the monitoring stage because they give the worker an idea of the speed of process.

Not everything can be monitored so it is important at an early stage to identify exactly what is going to be monitored and how much information is required. These indicators are used to decide whether the activity is going according to plan – as anticipated – or if it needs to be adjusted. In order to be good a plan has to be flexible.

Evaluating the plan

An ▶ **evaluation** ◀ needs to take place when the activity has been completed in order to decide what went well and what did not. However, for long-term and repetitive activities it is a good idea to carry out evaluations formatively, that is, as an ongoing activity. It is also a good time to consider, for example, what could have been done differently to achieve a better product/service with fewer resources. The best way to evaluate an activity is to answer a few simple questions:

■ Were the objectives achieved?

■ Were the objectives set worth achieving?

■ Were the objectives ambitious enough?

■ What mistakes were made and how can they be avoided next time?

■ How could we more effectively and efficiently use our resources?

Evaluation ◀┄┄▶	The assessment of the total value of a system, project or programme in social as well as financial terms.

A single employee could very well be involved in a number of projects and so s/he could find her/himself at a different stage in the planning cycle for each project – not all projects start and finish at the same time. Likewise, a student could be involved in a number of courses/modules each covering different issues, at different times and at different paces.

POINTS
TO
PONDER

Evaluation of courses/modules differs in application, design and efficacy, with feedback – the key feature of evaluation – often ignored.

Most courses/modules have a summative evaluation comprising a survey questionnaire at the end of the course/module. However, there should be formative evaluation as well which could take the form of direct questioning, focus groups and/or the use of small questionnaires at times throughout the course/module.

Formative evaluation is more useful because it gives the participants immediate feedback so that they can develop, whereas summative evaluation has only the potential to help those who follow – and then only slightly since each course/module is different for each cohort of students.

Course/module participants may not be aware that formative evaluation is taking place!

3.2

Activity

Reflect on a plan which you were responsible for, say, organising your time to achieve a number of deadlines for university essays/projects.

1 List the mistakes that you made.

2 What did you do to overcome these mistakes?

3 What did you learn?

4 Draw up a revised plan for the same activity which shows the lessons you have learned to improve the quality of the plan.

HOW ORGANISATIONS PLAN

Levels of plan

Although planning takes place at all levels of the hierarchy within an organisation, the plans made by managers at each level have different characteristics as shown in Figure 3.2.

All plans have to be based within a framework of the aims and objectives of the organisation which are set out in a mission statement. Such statements usually contain the following parts:

- a description of the business the organisation is in

- what the organisation is trying to achieve

- a very general indication of how the organisation intends to do that

- some mention of the values of an organisation.

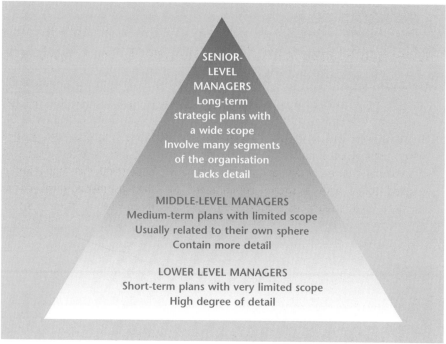

Figure 3.2 Different characteristics of plans at different levels

Sometimes a mission statement is labelled a ▶ **vision statement** ◀. Belgard et al. (1998) state that it can be likened to:

> an organizational dream – it stretches the imagination and motivates people to rethink what is possible. (p135)

Vision statement ◀┈┈▶   An attempt to articulate what a desired future for a company would look like.

It is generally believed (Jack, 1989) that Martin Luther King's most famous speech is literally labelled 'I Have a Dream' because he elucidated his vision of a non-racist USA.

see Chapter 2   Mission statements ■ *see* Chapter 2 ■ are all very different in style and can vary in length from a single line or phrase (as above) to a number of paragraphs. All kinds of organisation use them, for example international organisations such as the Microsoft Corporation and even cross-stitching enthusiasts, as shown in Scenarios 3.1 and 3.2.

Should organisations find it difficult to compose their own mission or vision statement, the Internet provides them with an opportunity to generate their own, although it might be tongue in cheek – just look at the Dilbert Zone website:

> We assertively build world-class infrastructures and completely initiate high standards in deliverables while promoting personal employee growth. (http://www.unitedmedia.com/comics/dilbert/career/bin/ms2.cgi, p1)

SCENARIO 3.1

Mission statement for Microsoft Corporation

What We Do

Since its inception in 1975, Microsoft's mission has been to create software for the personal computer that empowers and enriches people in the workplace, at school and at home. Microsoft's early vision of a computer on every desk and in every home is coupled today with a strong commitment to Internet-related technologies that expand the power and reach of the PC and its users.

As the world's leading software provider, Microsoft strives to produce innovative products that meet our customers' evolving needs. At the same time, we understand that long-term success is about more than just making great products. Find out what we mean when we talk about Living Our Values.

Source: Microsoft – corporate information on http://www.microsoft.com/mscorp/.

SCENARIO 3.2

Cross-stitching mission statement

We recognize and value the stitchery community as it exists in all facets of our lives. Our goal is to actively participate in that stitchery community through weekly stitchery features pertaining to cross-stitch and historical stitchery.

We value the free exchange of information on the Internet between interest groups and seek to direct stitchery enthusiasts to stitchery information sites, designer sites, other stitchery groups and communities through an ever-growing list of Net Links.

We recognise the importance of a dynamic Internet site and are committed to adding timely and interesting stitchery information, contests, free patterns, chats, bulletin board and newsletters as an ongoing development goal.

We believe that perhaps the global exchange of stitchery information on the Internet may be one of the most significant contributions of our generation to the legacy of our craft.

Most of all, we value the friendship and feedback from visitors to our stitchery website.

Source: http://crossstitch.about.com.

3.3

Activity

Look up the mission statement for your work organisation or for your university. For the latter it should be in your student handbook, university prospectus or on the Internet. Or see if there is one for your particular interest. Alternatively, carry out a search on the Internet using the key words 'mission statement'.

Does it contain the four elements that comprise a mission statement?

Strategic plans

Strategic plans are the long-term plans made by the senior executives within an organisation and while they do not give much detail, they do give an overall and general indication of what the organisation intends to do so that it can achieve its objectives. There are a number of strategies available to senior management. A strategic plan would, therefore, state in outline terms how a stated objective could be achieved ■ *see* Chapter 2 ■.

see Chapter 2

Operational plans

After the strategic plan has been decided, managers can work on it and decide on the operational objectives that will detail what each unit or department has to do within the overall strategic plan. For example, an organisation that wants to increase its outlets in continental Europe (its strategic plan) might well set the following operational objective for the HRM unit:

> Within the next twelve months, double the number of staff on the management trainee programme who can speak either German and/or French and/or Spanish.

An operational plan, therefore:

■ is a description of *how* an operational objective is to be achieved

■ is achieved usually within one year

■ includes information on the resources that will be required

■ details how such resources will be used

■ provides the basis for more detailed planning at a supervisory stage.

Action plans

This is the type of planning which most people are likely to be involved with in the workplace. It generally takes place at team leader level and is concerned with weekly and day-to-day activities of the workplace. An action plan:

■ is a description of how team objectives are to be achieved

■ is based on the operational plan.

Table 3.1 gives an example of an action plan for the HRM unit and, as can be seen, each action is accompanied by the initials of the person who is to be responsible for completing it and a date by which the task must be finished. To avoid confusion, both the start date and the completion date for each activity may be given and where only one set of dates is given, as in Table 3.1, that date must be stated clearly as the start or finish date. Dates are extremely important and so they have to be clearly stated. From Table 3.1, it can be seen that three activities (3, 4 and 5) are to be completed by one person (EF) and so s/he has been given completion dates within her/his overall task specification.

Table 3.1 Example of an action plan

Required: **To send out a revised version of the leaflet describing the management trainee scheme by the end of April**

	ACTION	BY WHOM	BY WHEN
1	Write the draft	AB	20.01
2	Proofread for accuracy	CD	22.01
3	Design leaflet	EF	30.01
4	Photographs for leaflet	EF	06.02
5	Desktop publishing of leaflet	EF	13.02
6	Proofs checked	AB, CD	16.02
7	Leaflet printed	GH	25.02

Management by objectives (MBO)

All the planning stages are linked to each other and so every manager knows exactly what s/he ought to be doing in order to help the organisation achieve its long-term mission – its objectives. Too much concentration on the day-to-day objectives can often allow employers to overlook the long-term perspective.

Management by objectives is a method that was developed by Drucker (1973). It links the personal goals of individual managers with the goals of the organisation as a whole. Every manager will have a discussion with her/his own immediate supervisor/manager and together they will draw up a list of key tasks. Using this list, the manager will then prepare a short list of objectives on which the manager should concentrate all efforts. Each objective is presented in the form of a standard that can be measured; for example:

Reduce the time for answering the telephone to a maximum of four rings.

Reduce the time period for responding to letters from customers to five working days.

3.4

Activity

Is your job performance or are your university studies assessed by the use of objectives?

1 If so, how useful is the process to you?

2 If not, what objectives would you set for yourself?

Management planning techniques

During the planning process, an individual can utilise one or more techniques to ensure that the plan is given the best chance of success in activation. The individual needs to choose a method which is appropriate and will give her/him an understanding of the current situation and the ability to predict what might happen in the future. There are two key planning techniques:

1   STEEEP factors

2   SWOT analysis.

■   *STEEEP factors*
Regardless of the type of business, every organisation will be affected by its environment and STEEEP factors are the:

Social
Technological
Economic
Environmental
Ethical
Political

forces which can affect an organisation.

The *social* factors include changes in the attitudes and behaviour of society and the way that the population as a whole, both nationally and internationally, is made up. For example, if there is a fashion for individuals to retire earlier than the statutory age, this would be a social change. Such a fashion changes the nature of an organisation's products/services because those individuals would have more available finances to take advantage of the products/services. It could also affect the way that employers treat their employees.

Technological factors are difficult to identify because technology itself is difficult to define ■ *see* Chapter 6 ■. Like other people-related issues, for example culture, it is different things to different people depending upon their individual perceptions. Maund (1999) posits an all-encompassing definition of technology:

see Chapter 6

> the intellectual and mechanical processes used by an organisation to transform the inputs into outputs such as products and/or services in order to meet the objectives of the organisation. (p148)

Such technological factors could affect the quality of goods/services which customers expect and the costs which the organisation has to meet in order to supply them. For example, a restaurant may well find that a competitor is using the Internet to advertise its services and decide it was likely, itself, to lose business (or, indeed, go out of business) if it did not adopt the same technology ■ *see* Chapter 6 ■.

see Chapter 6

Economic factors concern the monetary aspects of the organisation and include the money which customers have available, the rewards and remuneration ■ *see* Chapter 9 ■ expected by employees, the changing levels of ▶ **inflation** ◀, interest rates and international exchange rates. The last items have a very strong impact on the funds that an organisation will have available.

see **Chapter 9**

▶ In economic terms, this is a progressive increase in the general level of prices brought about ◀····▶ **Inflation**
by an expansion in the demand or the money supply or by autonomous increases in costs.
In general terms, it is the rate of increase in prices.

The *environmental* factors are related to the organisation's need to ensure that they in no way harm their environment. That is, not to damage their stakeholders in any way and to ensure that they do not cause damage to their physical environment, for example not polluting the rivers with effluent from factories or the air with air-borne pollutants. The organisation has to ensure that the physical and social environment remains pure.

Linked to this is the organisation's need to retain a high level of corporate responsibility and this is related to ▶ **ethics** ◀.

▶ A code of moral principles or values that a person holds for making judgments about what ◀····▶ **Ethics**
is right or wrong.

Since organisations are made up of individuals, the combined effect is that of corporate responsibility that is highly important in the modern business. Therefore, an organisation's view and practical example of ethical issues has to be included in its planning process ■ *see* Chapter 11 ■.

see **Chapter 11**

Political factors are often related to the laws of the national legislation and, in the case of organisations within countries which are members of the European Union (EU), Directives of the EU ■ *see* Chapter 7 *and* Chapter 8 ■. In the USA, for example, there is the national law (federal) and state laws with the former outranking the latter. Additionally, local government policies and actions have an effect as does the state of international relations. For example, if a local council within the UK decides not to permit the building of a factory then this

see **Chapter 7** *and* **Chapter 8**

3.5

Activity

Make a list of the STEEEP factors that could affect the organisation for which you work or the university which you attend.

would be classified as a political issue – as would a war. However, it could well be perceived by some to be social and/or economic.

STEEEP factors are very difficult to predict, although large organisations find the process very useful as a way of keeping a close eye on any emerging trends in the six areas.

■ *SWOT analysis*

A SWOT analysis is a tool which can be used to audit the internal and external business environment of an organisation. The initial letters stand for:

Strengths	}	Internal
Weaknesses		review
Opportunities	}	External
Threats		review

An *internal review* looks at:

- what the business is doing well (**S**trengths)
- what the business could be doing better (**W**eaknesses).

While the emphasis of a SWOT analysis is usually in the marketing area, it is a useful tool that can be applied to other aspects of the business of an organisation. For example, any organisation that has an inefficient HRM strategy will have high costs in the form of labour disputes, turnover of staff and high rates of absence ■ *see* Chapter 2 ■. Therefore, the organisation will lose its competitive edge to those organisations that are efficient in that area. However, each business will have its own problems and areas of excellence so it is not always possible to compare like with like.

see Chapter 2

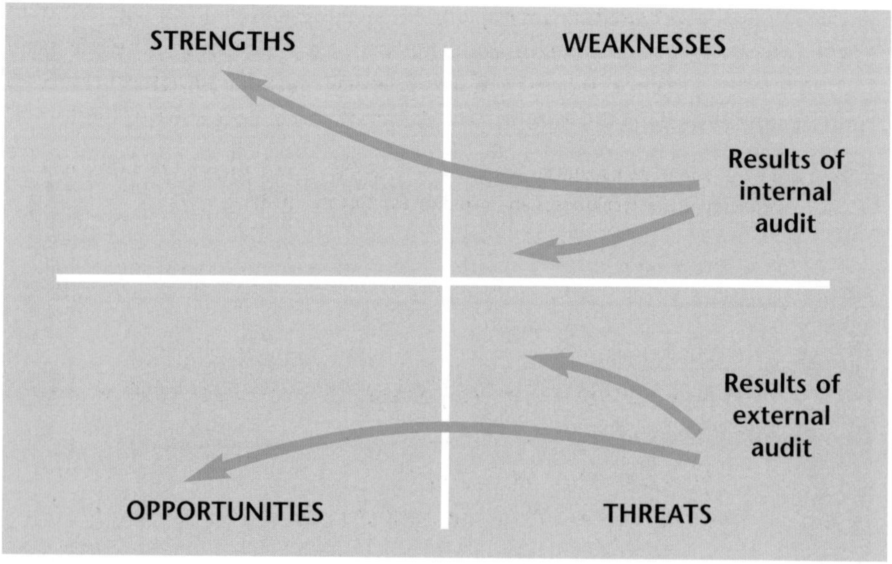

Figure 3.3 An example of a SWOT diagram

Table 3.2 Subdivision of internal and external audit information

INTERNAL AUDIT	EXTERNAL AUDIT
Factors that are positive relative to competitors are recorded as Strengths	Factors that have the potential to bring benefits to the organisation are recorded as Opportunities
Factors that are negative relative to competitors are recorded as Weaknesses	Factors that have the potential to cause a negative effect on the organisation are recorded as Threats

An *external review* looks at the business environment as it might affect the organisation itself, that is:

- the state of the economy
- position of the market
- technological situation
- demographic trends.

A large amount of information will accrue as a result of an internal and external audit of an organisation and these facts have to be organised by the managers into some semblance of order so that they can be understood by all who have to use the information in order to make decisions. The most widely adopted method used for such presentation of facts is the SWOT diagram as shown in Figure 3.3. The results of the internal and external audits are then subdivided as shown in Table 3.2.

The SWOT diagram should focus on the relevant key factors in each case. A brief outline highlighting the reasons for good or bad performance needs to accompany the diagram for the latter to be sensible. In order to be effective, the SWOT diagram and its accompanying narrative has to be relevant to those managers who are to use it. There is room for creativity in the interpretation of the diagram of both the internal and external audit data but not so much as to distort the findings. According to Lake (1999), the key purpose is to:

find a way forward that maximizes the opportunities that are available to the organization while correcting major weaknesses and avoiding the threats. (p38)

3.6 Activity

Using the organisation for which you work, or the university within which you study:

1. Make notes for a SWOT analysis.
2. Draw an appropriate SWOT diagram.
3. List the recommendations you would make for the way it should develop in the future.

SETTING OBJECTIVES

▶ **Objectives** ◀ can be set for:

- ▪ individuals
- ▪ teams
- ▪ departments
- ▪ organisations.

Objective ◀····▶ A statement of what is to be achieved (Lake, 1999).

Objectives should be SMART, that is:

Simple

Measurable

Achievable

Realistic

Time related.

Objectives have to be *simple* because they need to be fully understood by all the people they concern – ambiguity must be avoided at all costs.

If they are not **measurable** it will not be possible to test whether the objectives have been achieved or not, and to what extent.

Based on what is estimated that the people concerned are likely to be able to do, it is essential that the objectives are *achievable*. However, objectives must form some sort of challenge because if they are too easy they would not be worth working for. Conversely, if they are too hard, an individual would not even try to achieve them.

Objectives have to be *realistic* taking into account the internal and external factors which may influence the situation.

It is also important that objectives are *time related* so that an appropriate timescale against which to measure the progress made is in place.

3.7

Activity

Reflect on an objective or target which you have *not* met.

List the reasons why it was not achieved.

It is quite difficult to write an objective that meets all these requirements. In practice, many people draw up objectives that are too ambitious, or which are phrased so vaguely that it is difficult to know whether or not they have been achieved. Resource utilisation is one of the key areas in which most organisations set objectives.

THE REALITY OF PLANNING

Planning helps to decide how a project will be carried out to ensure that customer requirements are met cost-effectively. One way to achieve this is by using network analysis to show the order in which activities must be undertaken. Then, by identifying the ▶ **critical path** ◀, it is possible to show those activities that require the most careful management scrutiny.

> ▶ The activities that must be completed on time to avoid the delaying of a project.　◀┄┄▶ **Critical path**

Most managers operate at a level where the day-to-day work of the organisation actually gets done. Such individuals are given objectives and targets by their managers, but it is probably up to the individual to decide exactly how s/he and the rest of the employees are going to achieve them. The practical issues which have to be taken into account are:

- How long will it take?

- What are the conflicting priorities?

HOW LONG WILL IT TAKE?

When tasks are being assigned to individual people who have performed them before, it is possible to be able to make a reasonable estimate of the time the work will take. Sometimes, individuals will be asked to carry out tasks with which they are not familiar. Performance improves with practice. The first time an individual carries out a task, it is essential to find out what needs to be done and how to do it. The second time it will be done faster and so on. It has been calculated that, for most tasks, people improve their speed by between 80 and 90 per cent each time the number of repetitions doubles. So, if it takes one hour to do a task the first time, it will take, on average:

1×0.8 hours to do it the second time

$1 \times 0.8 \times 0.8$ hours to do it the fourth time

$1 \times 0.8 \times 0.8 \times 0.8$ hours to do it the eighth time

which can be charted as in Figure 3.4.

The line which joins up the dots is called the *learning curve* ■ *see* Chapter 10 ■.
There is at first a rapid improvement in the time it takes to complete the task but

see Chapter 10

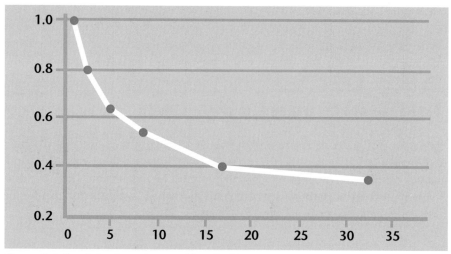

Figure 3.4 Graph to show the repetition doubles

the curve very quickly plateaus. The learning curve, however, is based only on mean values and individual performance will vary; therefore, it can only be a guide. For a very difficult task the curve will not drop very dramatically after the first few repetitions.

Conversely, if there is a short task which has to be repeated constantly it might well be worth a manager giving it to inexperienced individuals and allow them time to improve their performance. A longer task, which only needs to be performed once or twice, may not have the time in the schedule for an individual to move along the learning curve and it might be better to find someone already experienced in the work to carry out the task.

In estimating how long a task takes, a manager may be tempted to base her/his timing on the speed at which other people work when they are performing at their best. If a manager knows, for example, that it takes her/him 15 minutes to analyse an order form, s/he may expect her/his staff to complete 4 forms in one hour and then 28 forms in one working day. However, it is idealistic to expect any individual to perform at the peak rate all the time.

In practice, it has been found that, in the first 20 per cent of time that a job takes, people work up from doing nothing to their peak rate of activity in a linear manner. The same phenomenon happens in reverse during the final 30 per cent of the time a job takes. Figure 3.5 represents what happens.

3.8 Activity

Think of a situation when you were a member of a team, or are currently a team member:

1 Identify two tasks that are performed by your team where it would be worth allowing someone to move along the learning curve.

2 Think of two tasks which it would be advisable to give to a more experienced individual.

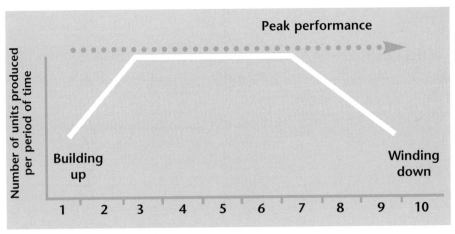

Figure 3.5 Peak rate of activity

People only achieve half their peak output in the first 20 per cent and last 30 per cent of a task. Over the whole period they are working they will only achieve 75 per cent of what they could do if they were working at their most efficient rate all the time. It is more realistic to take into account the fact that people need to build up to their peak performance and will wind down at the end of a period of work.

CONFLICTING PRIORITIES

When individuals make their own plans, they have to balance different priorities and may have to make some difficult decisions. It is likely that individuals will experience conflicts between the following areas of priority:

- *Work:* the task has to be completed and done to a certain standard by a particular time and so the work is a priority consideration.

- *Money* comprises a part of the resources available and it is important how this is used.

- The *people* with whom an individual works and the individuals s/he comes into contact with.

However, these three areas could work in conflict as shown in Scenario 3.3.

Reflect on a team you have worked in – or one within which you are currently a member. How long do the other members of the team take to build up to (and wind down from) what you perceive to be their peak performance?

SCENARIO 3.3

Prioritising conflicts

A   A conflict between work and money

'The HR manager has told me to train line managers in personnel record keeping, but s/he has not offered to pay for this training and its cost will take me over my annual budget.'

B   A conflict between work and people

'No one wants to work the Saturday morning shift, but it is a job which has to be carried out and got on with.'

C   A conflict between money and people

'I would love to be able to provide mobile phones for all my team members in order to make life easier for them, but I do not have the resources.'

see Chapter 1
and Chapter 2

The human resource function has been devolved to line managers yet the latter have minimum control over the objectives that are set for them ■ *see* Chapter 1 *and* Chapter 2 ■. They will, naturally, have some leverage on how they spend their budget, but it is not likely that they will have the power to increase the total amount that is assigned to them. However, line managers often have quite a bit of control over the people who work in their teams.

Dysfunctional conflicts have to be overcome and turned into functional actions. Some individuals attempt to resolve dysfunctional conflicts by asking more of the people who work with them. Other managers find this approach difficult – particularly if they have been an ordinary team member themselves, and so they try to resolve dysfunctional conflicts in other ways. One way could be by asking for an increased budget allowance or taking the responsibility personally for the team not being able to reach the objectives set for it. Such dilemmas have no easy answer but what has to be remembered is that an individual manager needs to reflect on her/his own preferred way of handling dysfunctional conflict – and to consider whether the priorities are set right.

3.10 Activity

Think about the times when you have faced – or are likely to face – dysfunctional conflicts between work, money and people.

1   What do you usually do?

2   In what other ways could you resolve these dysfunctional conflicts?

COMMUNICATING WITHIN THE TEAM

When a plan has been drawn up, it has to be effectively communicated to those people who have to carry it out. The type and amount of information that is passed on will depend upon several factors, including:

■   the complexity of the task which has to be explained

■   the current information level of the individuals who have to do the task

- issues of health and safety and security

- whether the employee has to put thinking time in or just follow instructions.

The two most popular ways of briefing individuals are team meetings where all people meet in person or by briefing individual team members in writing.

SCHEDULING TECHNIQUES

In all planning – be it for a basic project, for manpower planning (MP) or for HRP – it is essential that schedules are prepared so that the plan can be activated effectively. Three key ways which are used in business today are:

- ▶ **flowcharts** ◀

- network diagrams and

- Gantt charts.

▶ A diagram that shows a sequence or a series of interdependent activities.   ◀┈┈▶ Flowchart

Flowcharts

When planning a process or an event, it is often the case that one activity cannot be carried out until another task has been completed, for example:

- you cannot have a tattoo removed until it has been applied

- you cannot put in a nose ring until the hole has been pierced

- you cannot have a team briefing until the team members have been assigned.

When looking at each of the above examples individually, these dependencies are usually obvious. However, in the complicated environment of the workplace where there are often numerous people, teams, departments and organisations involved, there must be some sort of sequence of when things must happen.

In a number of processes, there will also be points at which decisions have to be made and if the decision goes one way then one set of actions is taken and if it goes another way, a different set of actions takes place.

A flowchart is a way of displaying such dependencies giving the alternative courses of action. It consists of a series of closed boxes of differing shapes, each of which is connected by arrows showing the chronological order in which activities must be completed. The shape of the boxes is also significant and standard to all flowcharts:

Shows the start   ◯

Shows a process   ▭

Shows a decision   ◇

Question   ◇ ? ◇

End   ⬭

Figure 3.6 gives an example of a flowchart to show what happens to an invoice when it comes into a university accounts section.

3.11 Activity

Study the flowchart in Figure 3.6 and then answer the following questions:

1 In what circumstances should the invoice be sent back to the head of department?
2 In what circumstances should the invoice be given to the supervisor?
3 Are there any circumstances under which an uncoded invoice could be filed?

3.12 Activity

Draw up a flowchart for a simple process that is performed by your team.

Is it possible to make the process more logical or efficient?

Network diagrams

▶ **Network analysis** ◀ identifies the activities that must be completed on a path to avoid delaying the whole project – the critical path. The latter comprises the activities which take the longest time to complete. They determine the length of the whole project and are activities which must never be delayed because if they are, the whole project will be late. Managers have to ensure that the key activities are completed on time and, thus, the less important activities can be completed in a more flexible time frame. The object is to ensure that there is a minimum wastage of resources and that includes the efforts of all workers who are the principle resource for an organisation.

Network analysis ◀┈┈▶ A way of showing how a complex project can be completed in the shortest possible time.

Most network analysis diagrams in the business environment are clear and utilised by trained employees and so the technique works effectively.

A network shows:

■ the order in which the task has to be undertaken

■ the length of time it will take to carry out each stage

■ the earliest date at which the later stages can be started.

The HRM specialist can predict with confidence that it will be ready to employ graduate management trainees after the time the previous ones have completed their in-house training, so the recruitment process ■ *see* Chapter 4 ■ can start.

see Chapter 4

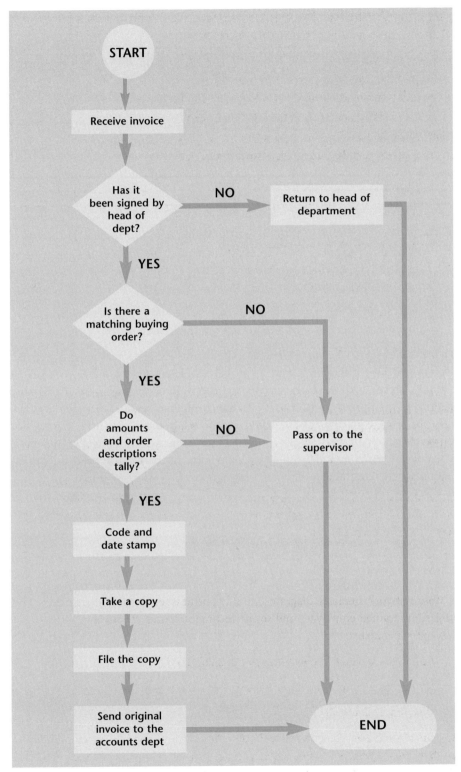

Figure 3.6 A flowchart to show the process of an invoice after its arrival at a university

3.13

Activity

You will probably have put together a piece of flat-packed furniture from, say, IKEA or MFI. Reflect on this activity.

The success of correct completion depended upon following the manufacturer's instructions to the letter, for example, A and B slot together, and then this inserts into C and so on.

These instructions follow the principle of network analysis.

However, did you experience difficulty at any stage of the assembly? Why?

A network consists of two components:

1. An *activity* is part of a project that requires time and/or resources. Therefore, waiting for application forms from potential graduate trainees is an activity, as is production. Activities are shown as arrows running from left to right. Their length has no significance.

2. A *node* signifies the start or finish of an activity and is represented by a circle. All network diagrams start and finish on a single node.

Figure 3.7 gives an example of what part of the graduate recruitment exercise would look like. Although A and B can be completed in 10 minutes, C takes 15 minutes, so the final 4-minute activity (D) can only occur after the 15th minute. Therefore, the duration of this part of the recruitment exercise is 19 minutes.

In the workplace, employees would not normally draw network diagrams for processes which are very simple – such as the production of the leaflet. However, if the overall planning is difficult, as it would be in the recruitment process for graduate management trainees, network diagrams can be extremely useful.

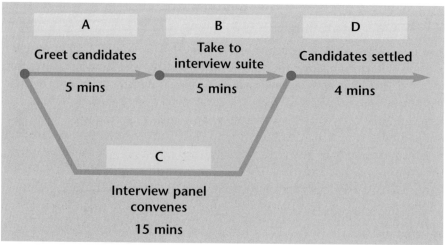

Figure 3.7 An example network of part of a graduate recruitment exercise

3.14

Activity

Using the example of the production of a leaflet shown in Table 3.1:

1 Draw up a table which shows the activities to be performed and the dependencies between them.

2 Draw a network diagram of the process (the notes below will help).

3 Which tasks lie in the critical path in the network diagram?

NOTES

How to draw up a network diagram

1 Sketch out the boxes. Each activity needs one box. Use arrows to show which tasks are dependent on each other.

2 Name the tasks.

3 Start at the left-hand side of the diagram and fill in the earliest time an activity can start and its duration.

4 Add the duration to the early start time and work out the earliest time the activity can finish.

5 Go to the next box and repeat (4) above. The earliest start time is always the same as the earliest finish time in the preceding box. If two boxes lead into one, select the later time.

6 When the box at the right of the diagram is reached, copy the figure for the early finish time into the late finish time box. The late finish time is the same as the late start time in the box connected by an arrow on the right. If there are two latest start times, select the earlier time.

7 Fill in the slack time by subtracting the early finish time from the late finish time in each box. Identical figures means 'no slack'.

3.15

Activity

Draw a network diagram for a simple process that you are responsible for either at work, or as part of a team assignment.

Gantt chart

This is a simple technique which allows an individual to represent a plan. Its effectiveness lies in its simplicity. They can be drawn by hand and presented on specially designed wallcharts with magnetic/adhesive tape or prepared on a computer. The basic framework is a chart in which time is measured along the horizontal scale and activities listed vertically. Figure 3.8 gives an example of a completed Gantt chart for the leaflet preparation exercise. Each column represents a day and they are numbered sequentially. The activity 'Check copy' is going on at the same time as the leaflet is being designed.

It is often a good idea to draw up a chart similar to the one used earlier to gather information for the network diagram. A flowchart can help show the dependencies.

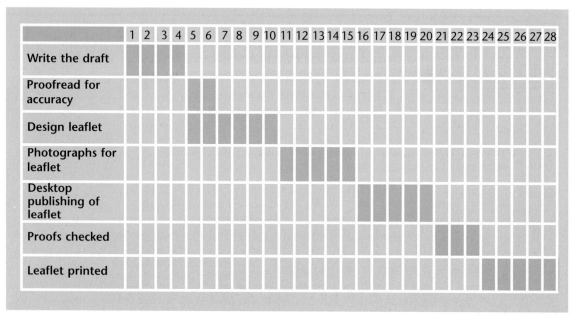

	1	2	3	4	5	6	7	8	9	10	11	12	13	14	15	16	17	18	19	20	21	22	23	24	25	26	27	28
Write the draft	█	█	█	█																								
Proofread for accuracy					█	█																						
Design leaflet						█	█	█	█	█																		
Photographs for leaflet											█	█	█	█	█													
Desktop publishing of leaflet																█	█	█	█	█								
Proofs checked																					█	█	█					
Leaflet printed																								█	█	█	█	█

Figure 3.8 Gantt chart for leaflet design and preparation

A Gantt chart can be converted into a schedule that can be universally understood. In Figure 3.8 the figures at the top have been replaced by dates and weekends have been inserted. This is because the time period is made clearer and can help to show exactly what has to be carried out.

The dates in such a schedule are based on an understanding that each worker will complete her/his task in the expected time. Unfortunately, real life does not deliver this and so a good planner will factor some extra time into the schedule to allow for potential delays. S/he can do this in any one of several ways:

■ add a little time to every activity

■ add time to the activities which might take longer

■ keep extra time for the end of the schedule.

Understanding the planning process is essential for all line managers and is exceptionally useful for those involved in MP and HRP. Without the skills of planning, it is not possible to deal effectively and efficiently with human resource issues.

3.16

Activity

Draw a Gantt chart for the process of completing a task at work or carrying out a university assignment.

MANPOWER PLANNING

▶ **Manpower planning** ◀ sits well in the general arena of planning because it enables an organisation to move steadily towards the achievement of its goals. It is through the plans of an organisation that its strategy is expressed ■ *see* Chapter 2 ■. *see* Chapter 2 The users of manpower planning are attempting to estimate their existing and future employment needs. According to Bratton and Gold (1999), manpower plans:

> can be expressed in a way that matches the overall business strategy and plan. (p168)

> ▶ The integration of human resource planning to ensure that the right numbers of the right people will be available for the right jobs at the right time. ◀┈▶ **Manpower planning**

Theoretically, this means that a manpower plan could:

> show how the demand for people and their skills within an organisation can be balanced by supply. (Bratton and Gold, 1999, p168)

The Department of Employment (1994), now the Department for Education and Employment (DfEE) broadly defined manpower planning as a:

> strategy for the acquisition, utilisation, improvement and preservation of an organisation's human resources. (p1)

Manpower planning is a highly complex area of work and requires specialised skills. However, it is linked very closely to the supply and demand of labour with the purpose of bringing about an equilibrium of manpower within an organisation. Because of its very complexity, organisations – especially large ones – tend to have specialist manpower analysts on the staff who are able to deal with such complexities.

The approach to manpower planning needs to be flexible so that plans can be developed as time and situation dictate. This requires analytical and diagnostic skills from the planners who attempt traditionally to seek to calculate manpower needs in the short, medium and long term. In the contemporary organisation issues of manpower planning have been devolved to line managers and often to the individual employee. This is in line with the devolution of human resource matters to the line manager, yet in the case of manpower planning it has tended to fragment the policies and undermine cohesion in a strategic way.

In order to carry out manpower planning in the traditional way, organisations relied upon familiar statistical techniques. Steady organisations and (usually) public ones did not need to be proactive in the marketplace as do those organisations which are affected by market competition. It is the latter organisations that do not have the time to carry out the luxury of constant statistical analysis of manpower.

However, now that HRM is a key strategic issue ■ *see* Chapter 2 ■, the matter of *see* Chapter 2 the relationship between manpower planning and strategy is high on an organisation's agenda – this has been labelled 'human resource planning' (HRP) and is discussed below. Some writers and researchers do not delineate between MP and HRP, considering that the latter has absorbed the former in theory and practice – the planning for people in organisations. However, such a delineation is an aid to the understanding of what is a complex issue.

HRP

see Chapter 2

Individuals enter, move through and leave an organisation and this should be done, as near as is possible, within that organisation's overall business strategy. Within this corporate strategy is an HR strategy ■ *see* Chapter 2 ■ and within top management's selection of an HR strategy it is essential that the workers are required to meet the corporate objectives. Put simply, HRP is about addressing the question:

How many employees do we need – immediately and for the future?

It is an activity that attempts to analyse what the likely influences are on the supply of, and demand for, people, with the intention of carrying out an organisation's mission.

Graham and Bennett (1999) define HRP as:

an attempt to forecast how many and what kind of employees will be required in the future, and to what extent this demand is likely to be met. (p163)

ASSESSING AN ORGANISATION'S DEMAND FOR AND SUPPLY OF LABOUR

Not only has an organisation to assess its demand for labour it also has to consider its likely availability. Both will depend upon the type of business and its future plans; however, it can be divided into two key areas, the factors which influence the:

1 demand for labour and

2 supply of labour.

Factors influencing the demand for labour

There are a number of factors that need to be taken into account, including the:

see Chapter 2

■ organisation's strategy and objectives ■ *see* Chapter 2 ■

■ demand for the goods/services offered by the organisation

see Chapter 6

■ type of technology used ■ *see* Chapter 6 ■

■ product range and/or numbers of products made or services provided

■ rate of production by each employee

■ amount of products and/or services bought from other organisations

■ level of stock.

Factors influencing the supply of labour

Likewise, a number of factors needs to be taken into account when an organisation considers the supply of labour:

- organisation's policies as they might concern selection and recruitment, including the level of staffing, retirement and redundancy ■ *see* Chapter 4 ■

see Chapter 4

- attractiveness of jobs available within the organisation

- available skills within the labour market

- cost of accommodation within the area

- demographic profile of potential recruitment area

- national legislation, for example employment law ■ *see* Chapter 7 *and* Chapter 8 ■.

see Chapter 7 *and* Chapter 8

An organisation will need to take into account its internal state and that of the local and national economy before it can carry out any detailed planning exercise. However, the key aspect of the demand for labour depends upon the demand for the products and/or services which the company provides. However, this is not always the case in business. For example, if one considers the National Health Service (NHS) in the UK, the demand for its services will be infinite – there is no way of measuring actual demand related to staffing because the latter will depend entirely on how much money the national government gives to the NHS. The same applies to education and the number of, say, teachers there are. This will depend not upon the number of students, but the amount of money that central government gives to the organisation – although this can, of course, be linked to student numbers in some cases. It could well be that each educational establishment can choose how to spend that resource (within stated boundaries) and could well decide that larger classes are better that employing more teaching staff – or vice versa.

However, in both cases (NHS and educational institutions), staff will be recruited locally and thus recruitment and the maintenance levels will depend upon the local labour market conditions. For example, prices of comparable houses are generally more expensive in the south-east of England than in the north-east and that factor is, therefore, a key contributor to the supply of staff. Therefore, all organisations – be they local, national or international – have to undertake local HRP.

Not all factors are short term in character, for example the number of unemployed nurses seeking employment in a particular geographical area at a particular time. Some could be medium term, for example the number of student nurses following a training course, or even long term – the birth rate and the age at which individuals are retired or choose to leave the workforce.

HRP is, therefore, more complicated than the definition of manpower planning stated earlier. It is more involved than this and tries to obtain:

- the right people

- in the right numbers

- with the right knowledge, skills, training and experience

- in the right job

- in the right place

- at the right time

- at the right cost.

Thus HRP comprises the balancing of the demand for employees with the number of suitable individuals available. This gives the view that HRP is all about number crunching and is thus a quantitative exercise. However, it is also about the qualitative side of employment such as the need for employee development ■ *see* Chapter 10 ■.

see Chapter 10

In order for every organisation to stay healthy it must have a steady supply of employees with individuals available to fill vacancies left by those who have left employment. However, there is also the need for organisations to consider whether they actually want to replace the leavers since new positions created by organisational changes and organisational expansion will also need to be filled. In order to carry out an effective job in recruiting those people, careful planning is essential. As Cascio (1987) states, such plans have to include a consideration of the organisation's needs for people and the supply of possible people for hire.

Forecasting human resource demands

The most common forecasts of human resource demands are usually in the simplistic form of the number of people needed in each job category – such as the number of nurses or teachers. However, it is essential that all organisations plan for the reduction in one specific type of employee and the increase in another or others, for example a reduction in nurses trained in intensive care procedures and an increase in those expert in accident and emergency procedures.

An organisation has the potential for taking a number of actions to deal with this shift between the nature of a job and the requirements of a job by:

- *the recruitment and selection process*
  Choosing more individuals who have the knowledge and expertise which is required. This is the less expensive option because costs are minimum when providing training to employees who continue to get paid while they are learning a new job ■ *see* Chapter 4 ■.

see Chapter 4

- *training and development*
  Retraining and re-educating existing staff. This has the distinct advantage of doing the least harm to existing employees while providing considerable benefits to those individuals who are given a new and more marketable skill. If there is an inadequate supply of people with the necessary skills, say, in intensive care techniques, then the training and development approach is essential ■ *see* Chapter 6 ■.

see Chapter 6

THE LABOUR MARKET

The supply of individuals available to hire from the labour market can be estimated in a variety of ways:

- an organisation can keep track of the number of people who apply for the various available positions

- government agencies provide information about the number of available workers.

The comparison of demand and supply of people for various jobs is an equally important component in choosing between a selection or training approach to the meeting of human resource needs. The globalisation of the world economy ■ *see* Chapter 11 ■ and the rise in technological advances ■ *see* Chapter 6 ■ has produced a tremendous shift in the demand for people who have various job-related skills. For example, the demand for semi-skilled and unskilled assembly workers in factories has been declining in industrialised countries such as Australia, Canada, the USA and western Europe while the number of jobs requiring high technological skills and intellectual ability has increased. Demand in manufacturing and mining are already showing a significant decline whereas there has been an steady increase in the demand for health-related fields, in the leisure and hospitality industries and within tourism.

see Chapter 11

see Chapter 6

POINTS TO PONDER

Ninety per cent of those included in the 1999 edition of Fleming's *Who's Who in Central Banking* list no leisure pursuits at all.

Source: Weekend Financial Times, the business, 13/14 November 1999, p9.

Is this healthy for the individual or for the organisation for which s/he works?

PERFORMANCE MEASUREMENT

For planning purposes, it is necessary for management to be able to measure the performance of the human resources within the organisation ■ *see* Chapter 10 ■. This is called ▶ **performance measurement** ◀.

see Chapter 10

▶ The process of monitoring employee performance in an objective way. This measures the success or failure of initiatives such as new working or payment methods (Marcousé et al., 1999). ◀┅▶ **Performance measurement**

However, in HRP it is necessary for the organisation to consider four key performance indicators:

- labour productivity

- absenteeism

- labour turnover

- levels of waste.

Labour productivity is repeatedly seen as the most important measure of how well an organisation is doing – or, more precisely, how its employees are achieving the goals and objectives of the organisation. It compares the number of workers with the output that they are producing and is expressed by way of a formula:

$$\text{Labour productivity} = \frac{\text{Output per period}}{\text{Number of employees per period}}$$

For example, if a hairdresser employs 20 people who will normally, in one day, work on the heads of 160 clients, then the labour productivity is:

$$\frac{160}{20} = 8 \text{ 'hairdos' per hairdresser per day}$$

If this is taken at its simplest level, then the higher the productivity of the employees then the better the workforce is performing. If there is an increase in the productivity figure, for example each stylist is carrying out, say, 10 'hairdos' in a day, then there is a suggestion that efficiency has improved. In order to be efficient, the organisation will want to maximise its productivity by ensuring that it gets the highest level of production (outputs) with the least number of employees (inputs).

This is the key to an organisation's competitiveness because if it can produce more for the minimum number of members of the workforce, then it will gain a cost advantage in the saving of wages/salaries and allied expenditure. Organisations which have employees as their major cost will find this particularly true but even those organisations with capital tied up in forms other than people, for example bricks and mortar, will find that productivity improvements can make them more competitive.

▶ Absenteeism ◀ – it is possible to calculate the number of employees who are absent from work as a percentage of the total number of employees using a formula.

$$\text{Absenteeism} = \frac{\text{Number of workers absent}}{\text{Total number of workers}} \times 100$$

Absenteeism ◀┈┈▶ The number of workers who miss work.

Therefore, in the hairdressing firm mentioned above, if two of the workers (out of 20) are away on one day, then the absentee rate for that day would be:

$$\frac{2}{20} \times 100 = 10 \text{ per cent}$$

Organisations work out their absentee rates for a yearly period which means that they need to know the total number of absences for the year in question as a percentage of the total number of days that should have been worked. For example, if the hairdresser has the shop open for six days of the week for 50 weeks of the year, then the total number of days each employee *could* work would be $6 \times 50 = 300$ days. For 20 members of staff, this would give a total number of possible dates to be worked as 15 000 days. If the total number of absences for the year were 800 days, the absentee rate for the year would be:

$$\frac{800}{15\ 000} \times 100 = 5 \text{ per cent}$$

However, it is not even that straightforward, because the organisation has to factor in statutory holidays and vacation time as well as flexible working arrangements which will all vary from organisation to organisation and from individual to individual.

SCENARIO 3.4

Council considers crackdown

Employees of the London Borough of Wandsworth may be made to pay for undertaking excessive sick leave under proposals designed to improve performance levels.

The proposed scheme would see employees penalised for taking more than five single-day absences – or a total of 10 days in three or more periods – over 12 months.

Potential penalties could include the deduction of a day's salary, or staff being forced to work extra hours or take the time off as holiday. Employees who can prove they are genuinely ill will not be penalised.

The council says the measures are being considered to reduce absenteeism and increase efficiency. But it has been criticised by unions as an unnecessary stunt, because disciplinary measures already exist to deal with staff suspected of dodging work.

Wandsworth already boasts one of the lowest levels of staff absenteeism of any London council.

Source: Council considers crackdown, *People Management*, 30 September 1999, p11.

Since ▶ **labour turnover** ◀ is a *measure* of the rate of change of an organisation's workforce, by definition it must involve a formula for such measurement:

$$\text{Labour turnover} = \frac{\text{Number of staff leaving per year}}{\text{Average number of staff}} \times 100$$

▶ A measure of the rate at which individuals leave the organisation. When high the figure may ◀┈┈▶ **Labour turnover** reflect an ineffective human resource strategy (Marcousé et al., 1999, p296).

Therefore, a firm which has experienced, say, 10 people leave out of its workforce of 200 has a labour turnover of:

$$\frac{10}{200} \times 100 = 5 \text{ per cent}$$

Taken on its own, this figure is meaningless. However, if it is compared with the figures of previous years and note is taken of how it has changed, it would be possible to search for the reasons why the turnover is as it is – especially if the figure is rising.

3.17

Activity

Using the figures presented below for an organisation:

1 Calculate the labour turnover for each year given.
2 Comment on the comparison of the labour turnover from year to year.

Year	Workforce number	Employees who have left
1998–99	250	5
1997–98	150	10
1996–97	100	20
1995–96	50	2
1994–95	30	1

The causes of labour turnover

SCENARIO 3.5

Staff turnover on the rise

Low unemployment and improved job opportunities are contributing to higher levels of staff turnover across all sectors, according to the Institute of Personnel and Development's (IPD) annual labour turnover survey.

Average rates of turnover for full-time employees rose from 16.6 to 17.6 per cent, but fell from 29.2 per cent to 26.1 per cent among part-time employees. Levels of turnover were highest in professional and skilled manual occupations.

Adapted from: Staff turnover on the rise, *People Management*, 6 January 2000, p12.

If the rate of turnover is increasing this could well be an indication that employees are demotivated and dissatisfied with their employment. However, it is only one indicator. The other could be a deliberate policy of the organisation which might have decided to downsize. An increasing rate of turnover could be the result of either internal factors (those within the organisation itself) and/or external factors (those outside the organisation itself). Tables 3.3 and 3.4 give the internal and external factors respectively.

Table 3.3 Some internal causes of an increasing labour turnover

- The recruitment and selection procedure is inadequate and incorrectly matches individuals to jobs.
  Employees will leave the organisation in order to find jobs which better match their skills and interests.

- Employees are not intrinsically motivated and feel that they are not being led in the direction that they think they, and the organisation, should go.
  In this case, the employee will feel that s/he does not 'own' the organisation and thus owes no loyalty to it. S/he will investigate promotional opportunities outside the organisation and will lack any interest in how s/he might be able to contribute to the organisation.

- Non-equity in wages and salaries with competitors.
  If wages and salaries do not meet the levels of organisations in a similar business, then individuals will find employment where the rates are competitive or the rewards are better.

Table 3.4 Some external causes of an increasing labour turnover

- There is competition for individuals with similar skills.
  Perhaps there are organisations in the same locality requiring similar skills of their employees and, therefore, there is competition for a scarce labour supply.

- Improved transport infrastructure.
  With the improvement in transport infrastructure and the rise in wages/salaries has come the ability for individuals to move away from their local community to find work.

Consequences of a high labour turnover

As will have been seen in the completion of Activity 3.16, a high labour turnover can have both positive and negative consequences which are shown in Tables 3.5 and 3.6 respectively.

Waste levels give an organisation an indication of its efficiency. In the competitive marketplace the key organisational objective is that of *zero wastage*. With a lean

Table 3.5 Positive consequences of a high labour turnover

- By importing workers from different organisations, localities and ethnic backgrounds, a business can bring in fresh ideas, enthusiasm, experience and creativity.

- The organisation can scout for individuals who have the specific skills that the organisation requires, rather than relying upon the 'best fit' and/or training people.

- New employees bring with them a new perspective and, therefore, a new approach to the decision-making process while long-standing members of the workforce tend to rely of the existing ways of carrying things out – even if it does not work effectively.

Table 3.6 Negative consequences of a high labour turnover

■ In order to be effective, recruitment and selection procedures can be expensive.

■ It is expensive to train and retrain.

■ The induction of new employees into the organisation and the absorbtion of its culture and climate is time consuming.

■ New workers tend not to be as productive as the experienced skilled workers.

production system related to the outputs of the firm, it is necessary for the organisation to eliminate wastage. The undermentioned formula gives an indicator of waste levels:

$$\text{Indicator of waste levels } = \frac{\text{Quantity of waste materials}}{\text{Total production}} \times 100$$

For example, if an organisation produces 100 000 units in a year and has had to scrap the equivalent of 1200 items every year, its waste level will be calculated by:

$$\frac{1200}{100\,000} \times 100 = 1.2 \text{ per cent}$$

The cost of waste materials

All wastage is a cost to organisations and needs to be reduced to *zero level*. However, there are costs associated with wastage being, according to Marcousé et al. (1999):

■ the actual cost of the unused or scrapped materials

■ the cost of reworking damaged goods

■ the loss of reputation caused by faulty products being sold or delivery dates being missed. (p301)

Reasons for waste production

No matter how careful an organisation is in its planning – either for production units or human resources – there will inevitably be some level of wastage. Some causes related to HR issues are:

■ *Lack of effective employee development*
  If employees do not have the required level of skill and/or knowledge, then they will not be able to perform at a high level and, therefore, there will be wastage.

■ *Organisation is badly designed*
  This is a physical issue. If employees have to move their products from area to area or if employees themselves have to move considerable distances, then

there is a greater possibility that goods will be damaged and the quality of services reduced.

■ *Reduced commitment*
Employees who lack intrinsic motivation ■ *see* Chapter 9 ■ and who do not recognise their place within the culture and climate of the organisation are likely to produce slipshod goods and/or provide low levels of service.

see Chapter 9

3.18

Activity

Reflect on your job of work or on some activity you have carried out while at university, say, a presentation or a report.

Other than the three issues given above (lack of employee development, badly designed organisation and reduced commitment), how else did wastage come about?

There are no easy solutions for the reduction of wastage but they do tend to be centred on the human resources within an organisation – the staff. Therefore, it is part of the HRM function to deal with these issues because it is their responsibility – in line with line managers – to ensure that workers are efficiently trained ■ *see* Chapter 6 ■.

see Chapter 6

AN HRM STRATEGY

The personnel performance indicators of:

■ labour productivity

■ absenteeism

■ labour turnover and

■ waste levels

combine to inform the management of the organisation of how it is performing. Although the individual results have little use, if they are considered in a comparative way such figures can be useful. Such comparisons can be taken:

■ *one year with another/others*
By comparing the results of one year against other years.

■ *benchmarking*
The process whereby an organisation attempts to find out how a competitor does things better than it does and then measures itself against these findings. In this case, the organisation would see what labour productivity, absenteeism, labour turnover and waste levels were for the best competitor in its market.

■   *with targets*

The organisation gives itself a target for each of the performance indicators and measures its results against this.

Such comparisons will indicate how the organisation is performing against a stated ▶ **yardstick** ◀. From these comparisons, the organisation investigates how it can improve on its results ensuring that it looks at the reasons for such performance before it addresses the human resource function – a shortfall is not necessarily the fault of employees. These comparisons are often called ▶ **ratios** ◀.

Yardstick ◀┈▶	A measure or standard used as a means of comparison.
Ratio ◀┈▶	The relating of one figure to another in order to identify relative performance.

Performance measurement is a key aspect of HRP and while it can assist an organisation it cannot supply all the answers. This is particularly true about ratios since these are only triggers and need to be followed up by other forms of measurement. For example, if the absentee ratio is high then the management might need to carry out investigations among its workforce using research tools such as surveys and interviews so that specific issues and concerns can be brought to the surface. However, such performance measurements can only indicate the state of affairs but they are very useful when compared with the corporate strategy and objectives of the organisation.

DETERMINING AND COSTING STAFFING NEEDS

An organisation has to determine and cost its staffing needs and in order to do this will take into account recruitment and selection, and career and succession planning ■ *see* Chapter 4 ■.

see **Chapter 4**

In relation to HRP, there are other areas in which organisations have to concern themselves:

■   staffing audit

■   skills audit

■   changes in working methods and practices

■   flexible staffing

■   staff retention

■   costing human resource requirements.

STAFFING AUDIT

Because HRP is part of an organisation's strategy and is integral to its planning and budgetary procedures, it is essential that organisations ensure that they consider all aspects of HRP. Since HRP is about making sure that the organisation attracts and keeps the quality and quantity of staff it needs to meets its corporate objectives, it is also essential that the workforce is flexible and able to adapt to the changing environment within which it operates.

Elements to be covered within a staffing audit include the identification of the number of jobs which exist within the organisation and the skills and knowledge which the job holders are required to have. Therefore, a skills audit needs to be conducted.

Such an audit will include an analysis of the labour turnover percentage and wastage levels which will give an indication of the potential wastage of staff and the subsequent staffing requirements. It is by using the labour turnover index that an organisation can gain an indication of its potential wastage of its staff and the future requirements for employees.

SKILLS AUDIT

A skills audit consists of a review of the skills and expertise of existing employees. The results of the analysis enable an employer to fill vacancies internally because s/he has knowledge of, and access to, the available expertise currently within the organisation. Skills audits need to be carried out on a regular basis in order to ensure that the organisation is aware of the qualifications as well as the experience of all its current workers.

A skills audit can also be used to assess employees for promotion, or as a means of identifying alternative positions within the organisation for those workers whose skills have become redundant because of a change in working practices or a change in the type of skills needed. The skills audit can also be useful in career and succession planning ■ *see* Chapter 10 ■.

see Chapter 10

The skills audit should not be carried out in isolation because it is only useful if compared with the organisation's corporate plans. By doing this, the employer will have a much better picture of where the skills shortages lie, or will lie in the future.

CHANGES IN WORKING METHODS AND PRACTICES

As part of its business planning procedures, employers need to consider not only what particular skills are needed to perform specific tasks, but they also have to ensure they appreciate the alternatives which are available. By so doing, employers will ensure that the output is maintained. This can be done by taking on board new technology or revising the current working practices within the organisation ■ *see* Chapter 6 *and* Chapter 10 ■. By reviewing the current organisational practices, employers may find that there is a need to move, say, from the principles of scientific management to the use of high-performance work teams and the introduction of 24-hour, seven-days-per-week shift working. Other considerations could be related to the methods of reward and remuneration in operation within the organisation ■ *see* Chapter 9 ■.

see Chapter 6 *and* Chapter 10

see Chapter 9

see Chapter 9

The essential requirement is that all workers need to be flexible in their working practices yet still retain a high level of intrinsic motivation ■ *see* Chapter 9 ■.

FLEXIBLE STAFFING

see Chapter 10

It is no longer possible to have a job for life within an organisation because the changing social and economic factors have brought about essential changes to working practices and the expectations of employees ■ *see* Chapter 10 ■. In the contemporary, competitive market, organisations must have their skilled staff to hand when required and thus the employment of individuals of temporary, casual, and fixed-term contract to support the core workforce is standard practice.

People management systems with the gift of perfect pitch

Until recently, whatever type of business an organisation was in, job classifications and career paths were fairly standardised; there were relatively few variations that an individual could play. Today things are very different!

Now, HRM professionals have to be capable of tuning in to an almost limitless and continuously changing variety of job and employee categories.

Returners, re-trainees, part-timers, home workers, job sharers, hot-deskers, life-long learners... these can present a real challenge to conventional HRM specialists.

Adapted from: Compel, *People Management*, 6 January 2000, p9.

Temporary employees are usually recruited to carry out tasks for either:

■ a fixed time period or

■ a defined completion point.

The benefits of employing temporary staff are given in Table 3.7.

Outsourcing is where many of the activities of a once complex organisation are moved outside the organisation's boundary. Many of an organisation's activities can be performed more efficiently by individuals outside the organisation – by subcontracting the work. This frees the organisation from the need to implement expensive training and development for short-term requirements ■ *see* Chapter 6 ■.

see Chapter 6

Table 3.7 Benefits of employing temporary staff

■ *Budgetary*
It is possible to control overhead costs.

■ *Reduction in employee benefits*
Because individuals are hired as and when the work is needed to be done, the employer does not need to provide employee benefits such as redundancy payments, pensions, paid holidays.

Outsourcing has grown dramatically in recent years as more and more businesses are forced to focus on their 'core' competences and buy in services in non-core areas. If employers do not consider outsourcing now they put the future of their organisations at risk. By outsourcing, an organisation can overcome distraction from its core activities and it can also assist in the reduction of employment over-heads – as for temporary staff.

POINTS TO PONDER

Judicious outsourcing may turn out to be an opportunity – losing some administrative responsibilities will free up HR people to spend time in other departments.

Source: Hall, P. (2000) Feel the width, *People Management*; 6 January, p23.

SCENARIO 3.6

Huge outsourcing hits HR jobs

Nearly half of BP Amoco's personnel staff will be affected by one of the world's biggest outsourcing operations.

The $600m (£370m) contract will see all administrative elements of the company's HR function – including employee relations, payroll, benefits, training, performance management, employee data and legal compliance – outsourced to Exult.

While Exult will need to employ up to 350 existing staff, BP Amoco admits that many of its employees will not want to transfer to Exult's two headquarters, which will be based in the UK and the US. Job losses are expected.

Many of those who retain their jobs within BP Amoco will have different roles. 'This is the biggest outsourcing of its kind, but it is only the data-handling aspects,' said a spokesman for the firm.

'Clearly, a computer can't help if an employee needs to talk to someone,' he said. 'We expect the HR staff who remain with us to be able to focus on that, and on the strategic and policy aspects of the job.'

Source: Huge outsourcing hits HR jobs, *People Management*, 6 January 2000, p13.

The use of *part-time* workers is on the increase. Part-time workers are those individuals who work less – and get paid less – than the full-time employees. It is particularly popular among those who have family commitments such as one-parent families or carers because, by working part time, an individual can combine work and family responsibilities. It is also very common among students. Organisations tend to use their part-time workers to cover the increased requirement for continuous shift working and for those tasks which are contained and repetitive in nature.

There has been an increase in the use of *job sharing* which is an arrangement in which two or more people share the responsibilities of one full-time job between them. However, it is more than, say, two people sharing a job because they also share the rewards, remuneration and responsibilities for that job ■ *see* Chapter 9 ■.

see Chapter 9

In order to be successful, it is imperative that the employer draws up a formal job-sharing policy which is designed to eliminate potential problems.

3.19 Activity

Find one person who works part time and another who is a job sharer.

What are the principal differences between these two types of flexible staffing?

see Chapter 6

The impact of new technology on HRM is discussed later ■ *see* Chapter 6 ■. However, aspects of this have concerned HRP in the form of working from home. The latter is now a viable option and is becoming the norm rather than the exception because of the rapid advancements in new technology. Facilities available through technology have increased the job opportunities for an increased number of individuals whose personal circumstances would have previously excluded them from the normal job market, for example carers and single parents. An increasing number of people choose to work from home even though they are able to work in a conventional office. There is considerable time saving for individuals working at home because of the lack of travelling and the absence of the need to hold meetings face to face – the latter being possible through video conferencing. Social considerations apart, as far as HRP is concerned, the home-working option reduces overhead costs, eliminates attendance problems and gives opportunities for organisations to adapt to changes in workloads. New technology has brought about a decrease in the need for secretaries since other individuals, at ease with the computer environment, are now competent in the skills of report generation and correspondence.

see Chapter 6

Organisations that are faced with an increasing number of short-term projects can now plan for the recruitment of external experts who are employed on fixed-term or specific-task contracts. This is similar to temporary staffing except that it tends to be concerned with individuals on the higher level management scale and those with specific knowledge-management skills ■ *see* Chapter 6 ■. This method of HRM is called *interim management*. Individuals engaged in this way are expected to provide the full management role including the identification of the strategy which will resolve the problem at hand as well as implementing the appropriate solutions, monitoring them and carrying out the evaluation processes. The interim management approach is becoming increasingly popular to employers because it is particularly useful for managerial work where permanent employment is not a viable option for the organisation, because of, say, its size, structure or overhead restrictions.

Individuals who take up interim management positions are usually those who have experience as managers and who have decided to ▶ **downlife** ◀. It is ideal for senior appointments within an organisation and can offer advantages to both the holder and the organisation. The individual can still have work responsibilities yet have time to spend on alternative life events and the organisation gains the experience and knowledge from individuals from very different environments. It is a very good HRP activity because it has the added advantage of the associated savings in respect of organisational benefits which do not need to be offered to those taking up interim management positions.

> ▶ When individuals have personally decided to reduce their workload by finding alternative, ◀┈┈▶ **Downlife**
> more flexible employment. It is not the same as downsizing which is the compulsory reduction of staff levels.

STAFF RETENTION

HRP has within it the responsibility for retaining staff – especially those who are intrinsically motivated, work effectively and who are loyal to the organisation's mission ■ *see* Chapter 9 *and* Chapter 10 ■. However, many organisations feel that in return for giving an individual a job, they have the right to expect perfect attendance at work and unquestioning loyalty. However, this is not the case. The planning involved in recruiting ■ *see* Chapter 4 ■ new employees must be progressed into plans for retaining them – for terms and conditions of employment, career progression and employee development ■ *see* Chapter 10 ■. If employers do not do this, staff are likely to become demotivated with a resultant increase in the organisation's labour turnover.

see Chapter 9 *and* Chapter 10

see Chapter 4

see Chapter 10

COSTING HUMAN RESOURCE REQUIREMENTS

Individuals who realise the importance of people within organisations ■ *see* Chapter 1 *and* Chapter 2 ■ consider that the employees are the most important resource available to organisations. While this statement can be debated among organisational theorists, there is no doubt that the full costs of human resources will provide all managers with a very clear and tangible indication of the importance of getting HRP right the very first time and *every* time. Mistakes made in HRP cost organisations very dear and can result in the demise of the business. Typical costs involved are:

see Chapter 1 *and* Chapter 2

- ▮ recruitment
- ▮ reward and remuneration
- ▮ employee development
- ▮ termination of employment.

Since mistakes are so expensive, it is often the case that managers are afraid to make decisions. This is particularly so in modern business where it is essential not to fall foul of the need to be an equal opportunities employer utilising policies of fairness in the workplace ■ *see* Chapter 8 ■.

see Chapter 8

POINTS TO PONDER

Are you too soft to be a manager?

According to one leading business training company, too many managers are afraid of falling foul of political correctness and as a result have developed 'grey and soggy' personalities that fail to offer leadership to the workforce. The research claims that managers' personalities and true characters are rarely turned up to full power. When asked why not, the managers' reply is consistently that this would be unacceptable. One result of this is that decision making is shunted from one person to another and no one is prepared to accept responsibility. Too often, as a result of this soggy managerial attitude, decisions become little more than a fudged consensus of what needs to be done. This quality of managerial greyness is infiltrating many companies and affecting their business abilities. Too few managers are prepared to make mistakes and even fewer to admit that they have made mistakes. The power of the individual needs to be harnessed. The individual, rather than the fudged committee decision, can make a crucial difference to a business. Unfortunately, that individual spark is being lost in too many companies.

Adapted from: Sunday Times, Appointments, 13 December 1998 on http://www.hr-expert.com.members/data/rc_articles/14129815.htm, p1.

The contemporary workplace holds both opportunity and challenges for all organisations and one of them is that of making the most of the skills and knowledge of the human resources – the people who comprise the workforce. In order to do this it is necessary for an organisation to adapt its traditional HRP practices so as to maximise its profit, minimise its risks and extend the boundaries of its business. It is, therefore, essential that employers carry out effective HRP within a framework of available tools to enhance this decision making.

HRP is linked very closely to the issues of the recruitment and selection of staff *see* **Chapter 4** as discussed in ■ Chapter 4 ■.

Chapter summary

■ Manpower is a vital part of an organisation's strategy and can be reviewed by using a three-step process: planning in general, MP and HRP.

■ Being able to plan is a central skill for all managers, but particularly those who are HRM specialists.

■ The use of plans (strategic, operational and action) requires specific skills within a framework of planning processes and procedures.

■ The planning process comprises the key components of goal identification, clarification of the present position, consideration of strategies available, choice of an appropriate strategy and breaking it down into more manageable segments.

■ In order to facilitate a plan, it is necessary to follow the planning cycle: drawing up the plan, implementing the plan, monitoring the plan and evaluating it.

■ Organisations plan in a hierarchical fashion with senior managers making the long-term, strategic plans, middle managers the medium-term plans with limited scope, and the lower-level managers working on short-term plans that are limited in scope.

■ Mission and vision statements are used to state what a desired future for an organisation would look like.

■ MBO (Drucker, 1973) is used to link the personal goal plans of individual managers with the goals of the organisation.

■ The management planning techniques used include STEEEP (social, technological, economic, environmental, ethical and political) factors and SWOT (strengths, weaknesses, opportunities and threats) analysis, as well as that of forecasting.

■ Planning requires the setting of objectives by individuals, teams, departments and organisations using the SMART (simple, measureable, achievable, realistic, and time-related) system.

■ Effective communication is vital in the implementation of HRP with the use of scheduling techniques such as critical path analysis, flowcharts, network analysis and Gantt charts.

■ MP is the integration of human resource plans to ensure that the right numbers of people will be available for the right jobs at the right time and must be part of a corporate strategy.

■ HRP is about deciding how many employees an organisation needs immediately and in the future – it is about forecasting.

■ Organisations have to assess their demands for, and supply of, labour and understand the movements in the international labour market by use of such tools as labour productivity, absenteeism, labour turnover and levels of wastage.

■ All organisations need an HRM strategy and within this the determining and costing of staffing needs. This involves techniques such as staffing audits, skills audits, changes in working methods and practices (temporary employees, outsourcing, part-time workers, job sharing, interim management and staff retention).

Staff loyalty in rude health

A scheme to provide healthcare to employees of a textile company has reduced absenteeism and promoted staff loyalty.

The quiet, provincial town of Baja, nestled by the Danube on Hungary's Great Plain, is an unlikely setting for innovative good   corporate governance   in the former Socialist bloc.

Until two years ago, management at Danube Knitwear had concerned itself mainly with ensuring that the 1600 employees – mostly female sewing machine operators – produced sufficient numbers of T-shirts to meet high levels of quality demanded by western brandname outfitters. By then Danube Knitwear – founded in 1993 and the brainchild of two US textile experts and a Hungarian economist and engineer, Janos Farkas – was a corporate success story, bringing badly needed jobs to a depressed agricultural community north of the Croatian-Yugoslavian border.

But when in 1997, Jim, the 56-year-old US sales manager, suffered a heart attack in the office and, in spite of the prompt arrival of an ambulance, died soon afterwards, the company began to rethink its policy on office healthcare.

Facilities in Hungary's health service vary from excellent to extremely poor and the supposedly free service is bedeviled with cash fees to poorly paid doctors to secure good treatment.

In the face of such difficulties, the management of Danube decided to implement a preventative healthcare programme throughout the company, working with its employees and local health authorities.

In view of the number of women at the factory, it chose a screening programme for breast and ovarian tumour as the pioneer project. Most of the 1000 female employees took up the scheme. Two or three cases of cancer were diagnosed at an early stage which, without medical attention, would probably have caused the death of the women concerned. Some of the women had not had a gynaecological check-up for 20 years.

The whole operation, planned in such a way as to minimise lost production time, cost the company very little and, flushed with the positive feedback from staff, it arranged further screenings. Modern DNA diagnostic tests were introduced to detect three complaints: the human tappilloma virus, which causes 90 per cent of ovarian cancers, chlamydia, a hidden venereal disease which causes infertility in women, and so-called Leiden mutation, a genetic problem which makes sufferers susceptible to thrombosis.

When management found that the test for osteoporosis – the thinning of bones – was not covered by national health insurance, they arranged for a pharmaceutical company to provide the testing equipment free as part of an awareness campaign for the condition. This was a very popular test with individuals even coming in from their vacations to take it.

Danube has also financed an emergency equipment package with the local hospital and arranged for a doctor and nurse to be on 24-hour call for any emergency at the factory.

As a result of the scheme, staff turnover and absenteeism, once causing serious problems for the company, have fallen sharply, and staff are more willing to work overtime. There has been an increase in loyalty and a more positive attitude towards the organisation.

The pioneering work at Baja has inspired similar programmes elsewhere. Danube Knitwear, the Hungarian Post Office, and the Dunaferr Steelworks have recently founded the 'Caring Employers Club', an association dedicated to expanding employee healthcare programmes. Before any company can join and display the trademark logo, it must undergo a

END OF CHAPTER 3 CASE STUDY (CONT'D)

quality assurance audit to ensure employee healthcare is up to standard.

Meanwhile, management at Baja has turned its attention to the psychological as well as the physical concerns of its staff. A culture of heavy drinking in Hungary – as elsewhere in the region – means cases of family disharmony and violence are common and this takes its toll on the workers.

A trained counsellor now visits Danube for two or three days a week at company expense. Whatever the problem, employees are encouraged to talk to the counsellor. A psychiatrist and lawyer are available free of charge for advice.

The purpose of these services is not as a wage compensation but to keep people healthy so that they can work and increase worker loyalty. The improvements to the management–staff relations over the two years the scheme has been in operation cannot, according to the vice-president for human resources at Danube, be accounted for in money terms.

Adapted from: Eddy, K. (1999) Staff loyalty in rude health in responsible business, *Financial Times*, Guide, June, pp22–3.

▶ The sum of those activities that make up the internal regulation of the business in compliance with the obligations placed on the organisation by legislation, ownership and control. ◀┈┈▶ **Corporate governance**

END OF CHAPTER 3 CASE STUDY QUESTIONS

1 What would Danube Knitwear have had to do prior to implementing their healthcare schemes related to HRP?

2 What relationship is there between the introduction of healthcare schemes, as discussed in the case study, and HRP?

3 What performance measurements would Danube Knitwear need to have taken before they introduced a healthcare scheme to ensure that there was a need for it?

4 Danube Knitwear believes that the purpose of healthcare services is not a wage compensation. How does this compare with the private healthcare services provided by organisations in other parts of the world such as Europe, the USA, Australia and Canada?

THESIS + ANTITHESIS = SYNTHESIS

There is no way that an organisation can plan its human resources because the nature of the contemporary competitive market makes it impossible to plan ahead.

SELF-TEST THE KEY ISSUES

1 What is a mission statement and what is its purpose?

2 How can the management of an organisation control all the factors affecting the demand for, and the supply of, labour?

3 What alternatives to overtime can an employer use to provide support to employees – especially those in teams – and ensure that production schedules do not suffer disruption?

4 How can the use of benchmarking help an organisation in its HRP?

TEAM/CLASS DISCUSSIONS

1 'Organisations never make big plans. They make small ones that eventually add up to a big plan.' Debate the logic behind this statement.

2 Discuss the view that it is the responsibility of top management to plan the organisational strategy and direction and, thus, to do all the human resource planning.

PROJECTS (INDIVIDUAL OR TEAMS)

1 Choose an organisation with which you are familiar or about which you can gain information either directly or through, for example, the Internet. Write a report as to why the attractiveness of jobs in that organisation is an important influence in the supply of labour for that organisation.

2 The music industry appears to be determined to benefit from the rapid growth in the online music market. It is expected that most of the increase will be accounted for by orders made via the Internet and CDs delivered by post, and an increase in downloading of music is expected to take off in the long term. Investigate the truth of these statements and suggest how HRP will need to adapt.

Recommended reading

Armstrong, M. (1999) *A Handbook of Human Resource Management Practice,* London: Kogan Page

Beardwell, I. and L. Holden (1999) *Human Resource Management: A Contemporary Perspective,* London: Pitman

Bramham, J. (1989) *Human Resource Planning,* London: Institute of Personnel Management

Bratton, J. and J. Gold (1999) *Human Resource Management: Theory and Practice,* Basingstoke: Macmillan – now Palgrave

Graham, H.T. and R. Bennett (1999) *Human Resources Management,* London: Financial Times/Pitman

Rothwell, S. (1995) Human Resource Planning in Storey, J. (ed.) *Human Resource Management: A Critical Text*, London: Routledge

Torrington, D. and L. Hall (1998) *Human Resource Management*, London: Prentice Hall

URL (uniform resource locator)

www.spinet.gov.sg/aboutus/org/man/man2.html

Forecasting of recruitment targets and the profiling of manpower trends and analysis. Helps with the development of information systems to support decision making in career development and the formulation of manpower.

Bibliography

Belgard, W.P., K.K. Fisher, and S.R. Rayner (1998) Vision, opportunity and tenacity: three informal processes that influence transformation in Kilman, R. and T. Covin (eds) *Corporate Transformation*, San Francisco: Jossey-Bass

Bratton, J. and J. Gold (1999) *Human Resource Management: Theory and Practice*, Basingstoke: Macmillan – now Palgrave

Cascio, W.F. (1987) *Applied Psychology in Personnel Management*, Englewood Cliffs, NJ: Prentice Hall

Department of Employment (1994) Company manpower planning in *Manpower Papers* **1**, London: Department of Employment (now Department of Education and Employment)

Dilbert Zone: Mission Statement (http://www.unitedmedia.com/comics/dilbert/career/ bin/ms2.cgi, p1)

Drucker, P. (1973) *Management: Tasks, Responsibilities and Practices*, Oxford: Butterworth-Heinemann

Eddy, K. (1999) Staff loyalty in rude health in responsible business, *Financial Times Guide*, June pp22–3

Graham, H.T. and R. Bennett (1999) *Human Resource Management*, London: Financial Times/Pitman

Groom, B. (2000) Jobs growth in call centres too slow in *Financial Times*, 21 January, p7

Hall, P. (2000) Feel the width in *People Management*, 6 January, p23

Jack, T.D. (1989) The vision thing in *Harvard Business Review*, Boston: Harvard Business School

Marcousé, I., A. Gillespie, B. Martin, M. Surridge and N. Wall (1999) *Business Studies*, Abingdon: Hodder & Stoughton

Lake, C. (1999) *Activities Management*, Oxford: Butterworth-Heinemann

Maund, L. (1999) *Understanding People and Organisations: An Introduction to Organisational Behaviour*, Cheltenham: Stanley Thornes

Microsoft Corporation (1999) *What We Do* (http://www.microsoft.com/mscorp/)

People Management, Compel, 6 January 2000, p9

People Management, Huge outsourcing hits HR jobs, 6 January 2000, p13

People Management, Staff turnover on the rise, 6 January 2000, p12

People Management, Council considers crackdown, 30 September 1999, p11

Spector, P.E. (1999) *Industrial and Organizational Psychology: Research and Practice*, Chichester: John Wiley

Sunday Times (1998) Appointments, 13 December, on http://www.hr-expert.com.members/ data/rc_articles/14129815.htm p1

Weekend *Financial Times*, the business, 13/14 November 1999, p1

4 Recruitment and selection

LEARNING OUTCOMES

After studying this chapter, you should be able to:

- DISTINGUISH between recruitment and selection.

- EVALUATE the role of recruitment in organisational strategy.

- DISCUSS the importance of recruitment and selection within a contemporary organisation.

- EXPLAIN the procedure for the recruitment of new entrants to an organisation.

- DEBATE the use of the systems approach to recruitment.

- EVALUATE and DRAFT key recruitment and selection documents including the job description, person specification and the job analysis.

- DISCUSS the place of economic factors within an organisation's recruitment and selection strategy.

INTRODUCTION

Framework case study

Wanted: 2000 Dome guides

Recruitment for the first 2000 jobs at the Millennium Dome began yesterday with pay rates between £13 700 and £17 100 on offer, and double pay on New Year's Eve.

The 'hosts', who will guide visitors around the Dome in Greenwich, south-east London, will be selected on personality and attitude rather than formal qualifications.

Sarah Henwood, marketing director of the recruitment company Manpower, said: 'We are looking for self-confident people. They need to be able to remain calm under pressure and have leadership abilities. There is no age bar.

'We are not looking for detailed knowledge of the religious significance of the millennium, for instance.'

About 1000 workers will be in place by the end of this year when the Dome opens for the first time.

Another 1000 will be hired next year, in addition to the 3000 catering and other jobs being created at the Dome.

The Dome's operator, the New Millennium Experience Company, has made an agreement with two of the country's biggest unions, the GMB and the Transport and General Workers' Union, which have combined forces to offer a joint, one-rate membership to workers.

Source: Bale, J. Wanted: 2000 Dome guides, *The Times*, 11 June 1999, p7.

▶ **Recruitment** ◀ is the term given to the overall activity of choosing suitable applicants for job vacancies. Included in this process is ▶ **selection** ◀. As can be seen from the Framework Case Study, it is no simple activity to find the most appropriate employees.

▶ The process of finding and employing individuals to carry out the tasks that need to be done within an organisation. ◀······▶ **Recruitment**

▶ The last part of the recruitment process when the organisation decides who to employ from the candidates available. ◀······▶ **Selection**

The recruitment activity is often treated as an experience-based activity with members of the recruiting organisation knowing more about the practice/process of recruitment rather than treating it as a body of knowledge. For example, such people generally have the following mindset:

■ because of the need for a replacement for a leaver or an entirely new job, a vacancy occurs

■ that is, the organisation is short of knowledge and a pair of hands

■ the matter is purely functional – it is necessary to fill a vacant post

■ decision making – what is the best way to fill the vacancy?

However, for the process to be successful there is a need for the recruiters to be:

■ able to understand the recruitment process

■ skilled in the recruitment activity

■ able to take a systematic approach.

Therefore, the ideal recruiter would be an individual who had experience in the field as a practitioner yet had been able to keep up to date with the knowledge-in-theory, say, on the development of the ▶ **competency** ◀ approach discussed later in this chapter.

Competency ◀┈┈▶ The knowledge, skills and personal qualitites needed to carry out a task, and how such attributes are applied.

▌ THEORY-IN-LITERATURE

The theory-in-literature on recruitment tends to concentrate on the selection process itself rather than the practice of recruitment, that is, the:

■ systems

■ procedures

■ advertising

■ shortlisting

■ organisation of selection and

■ overall administration of the process.

It provides the reader with *how to do it* guidelines which are very prescriptive in nature and offer what the writer perceives to be the best approaches. Such guides typically recommend:

■ a common, logical sequence to follow when carrying out recruitment

■ methods for evaluating the requirements of the job

■ skills and understanding associated with the process of selection, for example, how to carry out traditional one-to-one interviews

■ further methods and techniques for ascertaining the suitability of candidates – may even offer substitutes for the interview and include tests of ability, aptitude and intelligence

■ policy frameworks which will satisfy the legal side of the recruitment issue.

While these prescriptive guidelines may offer sensible pointers on *what* (methods) to do and *how* (skills) to do it, it is necessary for readers to be careful in their interpretation and activation on such information. By reviewing a number of these guidelines, it can be seen that recruitment and selection work has been given a pseudo-scientific veneer through advice which recommends that the processes and outcomes of recruitment and selection can be improved by the use of particular systems, procedures and psychology-derived methods. Such a package of 'dos and don'ts' can become too prescriptive if there are too many rules and regulations which stop individuals dealing with specific contingencies as they arise.

4.1

Activity

Investigate who is usually involved when a new member of staff needs to be found at your place of work or in your university faculty/school/department.

Therefore, for the recruitment process to be effective, organisations must use a strategic approach: often they adopt the ▶ **systems approach** ◀.

▶ A logical, analytical approach to the carrying out of an activity or the solution of a problem. ◀┄┄▶ **Systems approach**

SYSTEMS APPROACH

If a recruitment procedure is to be based on a systems approach it is necessary to carry out an analysis of the inputs, processes, outputs and environmental contexts of recruitment. A systems approach helps in the understanding of the strengths and weaknesses of the propositions of a prescriptive approach. Generally, such guidelines recommend that, when recruiting and selecting, systematic care is taken with the use of the right methods and the application of specific expertise, with attention being given to detail. By doing this, the organisation should make more reliable selection decisions.

While the latter is a sensible approach, the aim of recruitment is to maximise the critical concepts of:

■ the ▶ **validity** ◀ of decision-making criteria and testing methods. In the case of recruitment, this would mean that the advertised job description should contain criteria against which the interviewers and selectors can measure – that is, they are measuring what they set out to measure.

▶ The extent to which completed research actually measures what it sets out to measure. ◀┄┄▶ **Validity**

- the ▶ **reliability** ◀ of the whole process. If an organisation is recruiting over a period of time, the way that the competencies are measured must be the same each time.

Reliability ◀┄┄▶ The extent to which a measure is consistent over a period of time.

- decision making, giving due attention to ▶ **utility analysis** ◀, for example group interviews measured against individual interviews.

Utility analysis ◀┄┄▶ An estimation of the financial expenditure and benefits of the various techniques used in the selection of employees.

see **Chapter 8** *and* **Chapter 9**

By ensuring that these three concepts are faithfully adhered to there would be less likelihood of discrimination against candidates for other, non-job-related reasons, for example, skin colour, ethnicity, religion and/or sexual orientation ■ *see* Chapter 8 *and* Chapter 9 ■.

The use of tests is a contentious issue and can include testing any combination of the following:

- *Intelligence quotient (IQ):* used in an attempt to measure the learning capacities and general capabilities of the candidate.

- *Performance:* aimed at testing the professional skills of the applicant. Such tests also investigate the problem-solving and decision-making ability based on simulated or real situations.

- *Job ability:* testing the individual's use of professional language and her/his ability to handle tools and equipment required to do the job effectively.

- *Aptitude:* these tests lay emphasis on the individual's capacity to learn specific requirements related to the job.

- *Personality:* research is carried out into the personal characteristics of the applicant in an effort to secure a person-to-job match.

Together these tests do not offer an absolutely sure way of getting the right candidate in the right job, but they may provide help and support for the recruiters.

The availability of relevant knowledge and skills is of importance to the selection procedure, so it can be determined whether candidate A knows more than candidate B, or if B is more skilled than candidate A. By this stage it is more or less known whether a candidate has the qualities to perform well in a function and thus will be able to conduct a reasonable minimum performance in the type of work being advertised.

There is, however, a need to take care because any systems approach to recruitment requires a careful definition of a number of system-related issues, such as the purposes, elements and relationships between the component parts. It is also essential to have an understanding of the inputs, processing mechanisms and outputs.

That is, the transformational process of ensuring that the new entrant is able to carry out the job required and to the standard expected.

It is also important that recruiters remember that recruitment systems interact with their environment (other systems) and this needs to be adaptive. However, the whole process is open to human frailty.

STAGES IN THE RECRUITMENT PROCESS

The recruitment process is usually divided into three distinct stages:

1 *Definition of the requirements of staffing*
   By using a business planning process ■ *see* Chapter 3 ■ an organisation can work out:

   see Chapter 3

   - ■ the number of new people needed
   - ■ clear roles for each individual.

   Both of the above can be carried out by using human resource planning methods such as ▶ **job analysis** ◀ and ▶ **person specifications** ◀ which are discussed later in this chapter. A more recent development has been the use of competencies as discussed earlier.

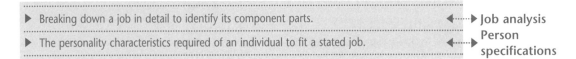

▶ Breaking down a job in detail to identify its component parts. ◀······▶ Job analysis

▶ The personality characteristics required of an individual to fit a stated job. ◀······▶ Person specifications

2 *Attracting candidates*
   Before the external resources are implemented, for example advertising, agencies and consultants, it is essential that a review of suitable internal candidates is made. The external resources used will depend entirely upon the number and level of the vacancies.

   Job vacancies must be communicated to the group of people who may be interested in applying for the job and making a good contribution to the performance of it. Organisations can, for example, target a special group of individuals such as ethnic minorities and/or women. There is also the opportunity to advertise in specialised media such as advertisements for, say, human resource assistants in *People Management* – see Scenario 4.1 – which is the Chartered Institue of Personnel and Development's (CIPD) professional magazine for those working in HRM.

3 *Selecting the employees from the candidates*
   This is considered to be the most crucial stage and is where the applicants are matched against the requirements of the job. There are a number of techniques for doing this, for example face-to-face interviews and selection tests. An offer of employment is made to the successful candidate at this stage.

SCENARIO 4.1

HUMAN RESOURCES ASSISTANT

Starting salary £13,443 per annum

2 Year Fixed Term Appointment with the possibility of Extension

The Natural History Museum is looking for an enthusiastic, hard working individual to join their Personnel team.

The Human Resources department is accountable for over 770 employees within the Museum. It will be your responsibility to provide and promote a professional service to managers and staff, as well as assist employees with guidance, advice and information on employment law, relations and general personnel matters.

You will have two A levels, or equivalent, and have had one years experience in an administrative role. You will be responsible for approximately 220 staff which requires excellent communication skills, confidentiality and the ability to organise your workload under pressure without compromising the quality of the service. You will also have experience of Microsoft Office and data processing.

The HR department would like someone who displays an interest in Human Resources and has had previous experience in a Personnel environment. A degree, or equivalent, is desirable as is experience in Excel or a similar spreadsheet package.

Application is to be made by covering letter and CV.

For further details, please send an A4 SAE to: Sarah Furlong, Personnel Section, The Natural History Museum, Cromwell Road, London SW7 5BD.

Closing date for applications is: 30 March 2000.

THE NATURAL HISTORY MUSEUM

 The Natural History Museum is working towards Equal Opportunities.

Source: People Management, 16 March 2000, p124.

POINTS TO PONDER

'Taking the rap' took on a new meaning for Scotland Yard as the Metropolitan Police launched a recruiting campaign for black officers using the rap artist MC Mo Reef.

In an attempt to increase ethnic recruiting in the aftermath of the Stephen Lawrence inquiry, the Yard released the £160 000 CD and video called *Taking Care of Business*, which exhorts youngsters to consider a career in the police. The nine-minute video will be shown in schools and clubs. The CD is being given away in London newspapers for ethnic groups and will later go on commercial release.

It was put together by Charles Bailey, Brixton-based songwriter who put up the idea after hearing Sir Paul Condon, Commissioner of the Metropolitan Police, talking on the radio about the need for more officers from ethnic groups.

The song tells the story of a black suspect wrongly arrested for a murder in south London. Released on bail, he tracks down the real killer and shows how black and Asian officers could have solved the case.

Adapted from: Tendler, S. (1999) Public upset by rude and arrogant police, *The Times*, 11 June, p16.

It is often perceived that selection is a simple process of matching what is wanted (the job description and person specification) against what is offered (information about individual applicants) and then deciding where the match (best fit) lies. This is the ideal but care should be taken not to make a premature decision during the interview itself. Neither should the appointment be decided on individual applicants between a series of interviews of different people as this pre-empts later interviews of other candidates.

The selection criteria describes the:

- qualifications
- skills
- knowledge
- abilities and the
- personal qualities

required to successfully perform the duties of the position. These may well vary in importance and can be classified as either mandatory (essential/must have) or desirable (preferable/optional). The applicant who best meets the essential selection criteria should become the successful applicant.

Applicants must address all selection criteria in their applications so that the selector/s can obtain the relevant information required to shortlist suitable candidates. The interview questions should be based on the selection criteria for the position with the wording of each criterion telling the applicant the ideal level of knowledge and skill needed for the job. For example: 'A candidate must have the potential to learn a skill or knowledge.' 'Knowledge', or 'provenability' means that the candidate possesses the knowledge, has performed the activity successfully or has used the skill in the past – s/he has the actual experience. The words 'thorough', 'detailed', 'good', 'sound', 'high level' are used to indicate that advanced skill, knowledge and ability is required. This is done under the auspices of a job analysis.

IDENTIFYING JOB REQUIREMENTS

There are a number of areas concerned with the identification of job requirements, including the key ones of:

- job analysis
- job evaluation
- job description

JOB ANALYSIS

Job analysis is an analytical exercise which provides the information needed by the organisation for them to develop job descriptions which are of fundamental importance not only in recruitment but also in ▶ **job evaluation** ◀ and the design of pay structures. They are also a vital tool in helping employees to understand what is expected of them. The outcomes of job analysis include:

■ preparing performance tests

■ writing position job descriptions

■ identifying performance appraisal criteria

■ job restructuring.

Job evaluation ◀····▶ A process designed to measure the demands of the job, not the job holder's performance.

The above characteristics require *information gathering*. The elements of the job need to be taken into consideration. However, information on the following is usually gathered:

■ *overall purpose:* an explanation of why the position exists and how the holder is expected to contribute to the achievement of the organisation's objectives.

■ *content:* the clarification of the nature and scope of the job in terms of the duties which will need to be performed.

■ *accountability:* a measure of the outcomes from the job when it is performed correctly.

■ *key performance criteria:* the levels of performance expected of the person in the post – usually expressed in terms of outputs which can be measured by the organisation ■ *see* Chapter 10 ■.

see Chapter 10

■ *competencies:* there are lists of competencies abounding in the theory-in-literature stemming from those proposed by Boyatzis (1982):

■ goal and action management
■ directing subordinates
■ HRM and
■ leadership

to those of Roberts (1997):

■ personal attributes
■ knowledge
■ skills and
■ values

required from the appointee in order to achieve the required level of performance in the job.

- *responsibilities:* a measure of the level of responsibility held by the post holder and the amount of authority s/he has in terms of decision making.

- *organisational factors:* this is a record of to whom the job holder reports, or those reporting to the post holder – her/his ▶ **span of control** ◀.

> ▶ The number of employees that a person in an organisation supervises. ◀····▶ **Span of control**

JOB EVALUATION

The job evaluation is a process designed by the organisation to measure the demands of the job. It is not a measure of the actual performance of the job holder. In order to be effective a good evaluation must have the support of the management of the organisation and also the trades unions and professional bodies, for example the CIPD, represented within the organisation. Usually, there is a job evaluation panel which has on it representatives of all the above bodies because the job evaluations form the basis of any ▶ **collective bargaining** ◀.

> ▶ The process of setting pay and conditions of employment through negotiation between the employer or group of employers and employee representatives acting on behalf of a group of employees. ◀····▶ **Collective bargaining**

Job evaluation is used to rank all the jobs within an organisation in order of their worth. Grades are established and attached to these jobs. Once this has been done, salaries and wages can be developed and linked to the various grades. The important point here is that the process compares jobs and not people and can, therefore, avoid any potential equal pay disputes. There are three principal areas which can be used to guide the evaluation process:

- *Non-analytical schemes:* these evaluate the whole job.

- *Analytical schemes:* rating scales are used to analyse the job against factors which have been predetermined, for example responsibility. These are then classified by their level of complexity.

- *Competency-based schemes:* the competencies required to do the job are identified and these are used as the basis of evaluation.

Job evaluation is not an assessment method but comprises a conversation between the job holder, supervisor and management that can clearly define the circumstances under which the job is conducted and the possibilities for the job to be enriched and offer career prospects. Such discussions can also cover issues on how any perceived future problems can be dealt with. Its success lies in its open character although it makes considerable demands on the style of management used. An

▶ **autocratic** ◀ management style will not be as effective as, say, a transformational one. However, so long as it is remembered that the dialogue is concerned with:

see Chapter 5
■ exchange of information ■ *see* Chapter 5 ■

see Chapter 5
■ effective communication ■ *see* Chapter 5 ■

■ creativity

see Chapter 10
■ continuous development of all employees ■ *see* Chapter 10 ■ and

■ future function and organisational development

the process will be successful and aid future recruitment.

Autocratic ◀┈┈▶ A style of leadership in which the leader makes decisions and communicates them to subordinates using strong, directive, controlling techniques.

Organisations are working in a time of significant change and this means that HRM specialists are in the forefront dealing with recruitment strategy. The IPD (1999) reported their third annual research exercise on recruitment. The key findings can be found in Table 4.1.

SCENARIO 4.2

The graduate's promise

Good-quality training and development and career management are likely to be more effective in attracting and recruiting graduates than pay, according to research carried out by Jane Sturges of the Open University Business School.

Sturges' study, based on research in five organisations and in-depth interviews with 50 graduates with three years' work experience, identified influences on individuals' decisions to stay or leave.

A common cause of dissatisfaction and lack of commitment was 'unmet expectations' in terms of development, career management and motivating work. Pay was not seen as adequate compensation for shortcomings in these other key areas.

Graduates looked to line managers, HR staff and mentors to help them in managing their careers, with line management playing a particularly important role.

Sturges' message to graduate recruiters, based on her research findings, is that they must be honest and tell it as it is. Organisations need to provide graduate careers, not just a job, or they will face retention problems as recruits become disillusioned with their lack of progress.

Adapted from: Crofts, P. (2000) The graduates' promise, *People Management*, 20 January, p57.

JOB DESCRIPTION

Where a vacancy has been created by the loss of an employee, the ▶ **job description** ◀ may already be in place. However, before seeking a replacement, it is good

Job description ◀┈┈▶ A statement which gives the purpose, scope, responsibilities and tasks which make up a stated job.

Table 4.1 Key findings of the IPD (1999) research on recruitment issues

Cohort	▪ 269 interviews ▪ all the most senior person responsible for recruitment	▪ broad sectoral comparisons ▪ establishments of 50+ employees	▪ from the sample of organisation, by workforce size

1 *Recruitment difficulties*

Nearly three-quarters of employers have experienced difficulties in filling one or more of their vacancies over the year to March 1999 compared to 60% of employers in 1998.

2 *Reasons for recruitment difficulties*

a Lack of required experience on part of applicants.

b Lack of technical skills.

c Applicants wanting more money.

3 *Recruitment methods*

a Advertising in the press or specialist journals.

b Internet growing in popularity.

4 *Most effective methods*

a Specialist trade press ⎫ for managerial and

b Employment agencies ⎭ professional posts

c Local press for unskilled workers.

5 *Identifying job requirements*

a Almost all employees use formal job descriptions to identify the tasks and duties of the post to be filled.

b Ninety per cent of organisations prepare formal person specifications.

c Competencies have entered the mainstream of recruitment – over one half of employers in the survey used a framework of competencies to inform their recruitment process.

6 *Devolving responsibilities*

In almost all organisations line managers either take a leading role or act as an equal partner in determining job requirements.

7 *Graduate recruitment*

a Just over one-third of organisations surveyed have had vacancies for new graduates over the year.

b Establishing links with universities is the most common method used by organisations recruiting graduates.

c However, recruitment fairs and the 'milk round' are now used by only a minority of graduate recruiters.

8 *Selection methods*

a Interview.

b Sifting techniques: application forms
curriculum vitaes
covering letters.

c Cognitive testing for some vacancies.

d Personality tests for sizeable majority of organisations surveyed.

e Assessment centres rated very highly.

9 *Recruitment and selection priorities*

a For managerial and professional vacancies, drawing up priorities in advance of recruitment and categorising relevant experience is seen as most important.

b Less emphasis on personal qualities.

c Some order of priority remains when actual recruitment decisions are made, but with a shift in emphasis.

d Relatively more organisations found that personal qualities were a prime determining factor in the choice of candidate than had set out to do so.

10 *Evaluating the recruitment and selection process*

a Almost all organisations attempt at least some form of evaluation of the effectiveness of their recruitment process.

b Informed assessment is by far the most common approach taken.

c More formal approaches are less common.

d Most prevalent is the analysis of labour turnover figures.

e Next an analysis of employee performance data.

f Considerable scope for quantitative, business-related techniques to be adopted more widely.

11 *Building a diverse workforce*

a Most employers taking appropriate steps to meet their legal obligation to accommodate diverse applicant needs.

b In public sector majority of organisations adopting additional measures that will help to achieve a workforce reflecting the composition of the local community or customer base.

c However, not the case in private sector.

12 *International selection*

a One-quarter of organisations in survey sent employees to work abroad over past 12 months.

b Half of these from existing workforce.

c Did not use formal recruitment techniques.

d Most common selection criterion is that the individual should have relevant job experience.

e Additionally, most organisations require technical skills and want individual to show resilience to enable them to function well in foreign cultures.

f Less important are 'good awareness of cultural issues' and 'can speak a foreign language'.

practice to review this document to ensure that it is still relevant to current working practices and organisational needs.

Regular reviews of job descriptions should be conducted to embrace changing working practices and organisational development. This is particularly important when the job description is being used as part of the recruitment process. Using an out-of-date job description may result in an individual being recruited who may not have the skills or experience to perform the duties required of the job.

There are consultancy firms that can carry out this analysis for organisations. Its main purpose is to find the answers to three key questions:

■ What tasks are involved in the job?

■ How should these tasks be performed?

■ What are the requirements of the successful candidate?

Methods of job analysis

The main methods, which are parts of the process of job analysis, used to collect information include the following:

■ questionnaires

■ checklists

■ individual interviews

■ observation

■ focus groups

■ use of diaries

■ work participation observation

■ critical incident analysis

■ personal construct psychology

■ hierarchical tasks analysis.

Questionnaires: The job holder is given the opportunity to describe the job activities in her/his own words. This procedure can be very effective if it is used when there are a large number of jobs to be covered. However, it is time consuming, both at the questionnaire design stage and at the evaluation stage. It is very important that the questionnaires are related to specific jobs because if they are over-generalised the results would be vague and useless.

Checklists: The job analyst gives the job holder a long list of possible tasks to be undertaken and the job holder is required to mark those which s/he perceives as relevant to the effective performance of the job. This method is a development of the questionnaire and is, therefore, subject to the same limitations and the need for careful design.

Individual interviews: Interviews are held with the job holder so that the interviewer can gain an understanding of all the tasks which need to be carried out to ensure the effective completion of the job. Such a procedure can be of limited value because bad habits may well have become established practice and this will distort the true activities required of the position.

Observation: The job analyst will observe the job holder while s/he is carrying out her/his job in an attempt to identify the activities which are considered necessary for the effective completion of the job. This can be an effective and accurate technique but it is seldom used because it is particularly time consuming for the analyst to observe all the behaviours and aspects of the job. It is specifically useful, however, for the preparation of training specifications for manual or basic clerical jobs.

Focus groups: A number of individuals – in addition to the job holder – meet with an interviewer in an attempt to gain an understanding not only of the tasks to be performed and the requisite standards but also the implications of the tasks for related activities.

Use of diaries: Job holders complete a diary on a daily basis recording all the tasks they have been required to undertake. This frequently results in inconclusive data because of the time taken to complete them. Additionally, the varying narrative styles of the writers often makes data analysis invalid.

Work participation observation: The job analyst actually does the job her/himself. This is a very limited technique in a complex organisation because the job will have to be one which can be learned very quickly by the analyst.

Critical incident analysis: This method is increasingly being used. It requires the analyst to develop two lists – one of statements indicating those tasks which contribute *positively* to the completion of the job and another of the tasks which *inhibit* satisfactory conclusion of those tasks. This method will clearly identify those tasks which are genuinely required to ensure the satisfactory completion of the job. It is essential to involve the job holder in the process and only appropriately trained and skilled assessors should be used.

Personal construct psychology (PCP): PCP was propounded by Kelly (1955) and is based on the belief that an individual can only understand her/his real world by constructing her/his own version of it. By using, for example, the ▶ **repertory grid technique** ◀ the dimensions which distinguish good from poor standards of performance are identified. It is a way of getting an individual to see her/his own world as s/he sees it. The method provides insight into attitudes and opinions about job performance factors. However, it can be an elaborate technique requiring considerable skill from the administrator. It is also time consuming. However, the quality of the results is high.

▶ A research technique (related to personal construct psychology) that is used to compare one set of constructs (ideas, thoughts) in relation to a given set of elements (things). ◀┈┈▶ **Repertory grid technique**

Hierarchical tasks analysis: Tasks are broken down in terms of the objectives needed to achieve the task and the task is analysed. This technique provides a helpful structure for job analysis in terms of output, plans and relationships. It can be used when analysing the data obtained by interviews or other methods.

The outputs of job analysis include:

- a list of the tasks involved in the job
- details of how each task should be performed
- clear statements describing the:
  - responsibility
  - job knowledge
  - mental application
  - dexterity and
  - accuracy in carrying out the task

  required of the successful candidate. It also gives a list of the:

  - equipment
  - materials and
  - supplies

  used to perform the job and its component tasks.

In order to be effective a job analysis must generate:

- the job prospectus information which is needed by the applicants
- a recruitment process which will attract suitable candidates (including the task of advertising)
- a better understanding of how the applications are received because they must be handled and processed in order to evaluate the candidates
- a shortlist of candidates to invite for further assessment
- quality information so that the selection decisions can be as objective as possible and attempt to avoid:
  - subjectivity
  - ▶ **stereotyping** ◀ and
  - premature judgments

Stereotyping ◀┈┈▶ The judging of another individual on the basis of one's own perception of the group to which that individual belongs.

since the soundness of decisions can be readily undermined by the:

- perceptions

- attitudes
- values
- arrogance and
- ignorance of what the job is about

on the part of the selector/s

- clear decision-making criteria for the selectors to use which must be relevant and valid for the performance of the job in question.

If these criteria are not kept in mind ▶ **discrimination** ◀ may creep in and thus the recruitment process could run counter to equal opportunities legislation. Such organisations are without a proper definition of the job requirements, performance criteria and competencies required. If this is so, then the recruiters may fall into the trap of selecting a candidate on the basis of false assumptions. Recruitment and selection involves discriminating between people through their applications but care should be taken to ensure that such discrimination is fair and just – ethically and at law (this is not necessarily the same thing). All recruiters have a social responsibility in relation to equal opportunities. They may well behave prejudicially by being blind to their own behaviours. Often recruiters simply make false assumptions about the requirements of the job and they may apply invalid, irrelevant criteria that applicants from, say, female or particular ethnic groups, are unable to satisfy. Such discrimination can be either direct or indirect ■ *see* Chapter 8 ■.

see **Chapter 8**

▶ The unfair treatment of individuals on account of their race, colour of skin, religion, nationality, gender, marital status or disability. ◀┄┄▶ **Discrimination**

SCENARIO 4.3

Ford pays damages to black drivers

The Ford Motor Company agreed to new selection procedures for a highly paid group of truck drivers yesterday after allegations that black and Asian workers had been frozen out.

In settlement of an industrial tribunal case brought by the Transport and General Workers Union seven months ago, Ford said it would adopt revised recruitment and training practices for truck drivers based in Dagenham, Essex, who earn about £30 000 a year, two-thirds more than assembly workers.

The company also agreed to pay undisclosed compensation to the seven union members who had alleged that they had been barred from jobs in the 300-strong truck fleet on racial grounds. More than 40 per cent of Dagenham workers are black or Asian, but they make up only 2 cent of truck drivers.

The TGWU claimed that vacancies among the drivers, who transport components between Ford's plants in the UK and Europe, tended to be passed on to friends and family of retiring staff, keeping down numbers from ethnic minorities.

Source: Marston, P. (1997) Ford pays damages to black drivers, *Electronic Telegraph*, Issue 613, 28 January.

An equal opportunity employer will select employees on the basis of their merits. That is, an individual appointed to a job will be the one who has been judged to be most able to perform the duties of the position.

Every job analysis has its advantages and disadvantages because of the difference in the jobs which make up the organisation. Because of this, there are different techniques or combinations of techniques which are appropriate to different situations. For example, an organisation could use a combination of on-site observation and individual interview.

Managers involved in recruiting can be complacent because they actually believe that they know all about the job vacancy and they fully understand the requirements needed for filling it. However, all too frequently such people apply stereotypical views about what they consider to be 'the ideal candidate'. Sometimes they have not even thought of a candidate profile at all but merely recruit on some personal vagary of their own. However, both the HRM specialist and the line manager must not ignore each other's opinion if they are to gain the right new entrant for the job. The job applicant does not hold the corporate values of the organisation and s/he needs to quickly absorb these during induction. Recruiters could do worse than keep the saying 'do unto others as you would be done by' in their minds throughout the process. It is not a one-sided decision – it is a buyer's and seller's market – although nowadays, in the higher level jobs, it is often a market which favours the knowledge worker. Recruitment is also part of the public relations of the organisation and should, therefore, be included as such within the organisation's recruitment policy. There should be consistency between the organisation's perception of itself and those it projects and this can be done through the media and the current workforce.

According to Donkin (1999) organisations often exhibit the wrong brand of message related to recruitment:

> Employers will not attract staff by taking the language of the marketeers seriously. (p32)

An organisation's reputation can influence recruitment and retention. However, Donkin (1999) makes the point that:

> it is a worrying sign when marketeers and public relations experts get hold of something as simple as the job. Once there were good jobs and there were bad jobs. Now there is the employer brand. (p32)

That is, job advertisements should be put together by the HRM specialist and not left to the marketing people who may not fully appreciate the specific requirements of the job or the target audience for the advertisement.

While it may be said that this latter statement could refer to the recruitment process, it is also relevant to the process of job analysis where the competencies are often identified.

While it might be obvious that recruiters need to comprehend the job requirements fully this is not often the case and so job analysis is essential. Combined with ▶ **exit interviews** ◀ they can confirm the nature and contribution of the job role which may often turn out to be more complex than was first thought. The information from a job analysis and sources such as exit interviews can help the organisation to restructure the job and thus resolve potential difficulties in the areas of:

- scope and authority

- demands of the job (overload, underload), choices and constraints

- ambiguities and uncertainties

- complexity and technical challenges

- incompatibility (person-to-person organisation)

- ▶ **dysfunctional conflict** ◀ and stress.

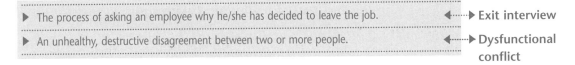

▶ The process of asking an employee why he/she has decided to leave the job.   ◀······▶ **Exit interview**

▶ An unhealthy, destructive disagreement between two or more people.   ◀······▶ **Dysfunctional conflict**

Coleman (1999) reports that in sectors where employee turnover is worryingly high, organisations need to start pooling their data. He believes that exit interviews could be the answer to keeping key staff because:

> Staff recruitment and retention have become key business issues for companies, perhaps more so than cost-cutting. (p32)

It can also identify the need for supervisory support and developmental opportunities for the appointed person. It might be necessary to carry out ▶ **job redesign** ◀ in order to hire the right candidate if there is a poor fit between the job and the capacity of a new starter. The latter could be because of a poor job description and the hired individual is not capable of doing it or the job turns out to be ill-suited to their needs and interests. It is not uncommon for someone to commence work and then leave within a week saying 'This is not the job I expected.' While this is part of the recruitment issue, it is still something which is highlighted in the job analysis exercise.

▶ An exercise that focuses on how existing jobs can be changed.   ◀······▶ **Job redesign**

Job analysis schedule

Campbell (1989) proffered a job analysis schedule which would be used to report the job information obtained through observation and individual interviews. Such an analysis provides a framework in which to arrange and describe the important job analysis information. He reported on 12 items, divided into 4 sections, as outlined in Table 4.2.

Table 4.2 Outline of a job analysis schedule after Campbell (1989)

Section	Items	
One	1, 2, 3, 4	Identifies the job within the organisation in which it occurs.
Two	5	Work performed. Thorough, complete description of the job. Describes what the holder: does how s/he does it why s/he is doing it.
Three	6, 7, 8, 9	Requirements placed on the job holder for successful performance. Detailed interpretation of basic minimum acceptable. What is required by the job holder in terms of: responsibility job knowledge mental application dexterity accuracy.
Four	10, 11, 12	Provides background information on the job relating to: equipment definition of terms general comments and information.

4.2 Activity

Reflect on a job you have had or the one you have at present.

List the steps and action you took/would take when considering a job application from the time you saw the advertisement to your behaviour at the interview.

REFERENCES AND INTEGRITY

The obtaining of references requires a security device to be in place so that honesty and integrity can be verified. It is naive to always assume that the person:

■ is who they say they are

■ has done what s/he says s/he has done

■ has been fully open about her/his background.

A number of organisations now require potential employees to carry out an ▷ **integrity test** ◁ to measure their level of honesty and integrity.

> ▶ Test which is designed to predict whether or not a member of the workforce is likely to ◀┈┈▶ **Integrity test**
> engage in behaviour which will lead to dishonesty on the job or be counter-productive to
> the interests of the organisation for which s/he works.

Maund (1999) reports that:

> There has been a development in the use of tests to recruit and select staff – especially honesty
> or integrity tests. (p25)

There are a number of approaches to the testing of integrity including:

- *Use of a written test*
  An integrity test seeks to measure the willingness of candidates to conceal or
  falsely declare their position. The design, validity and reliability of such tests
  needs critical examination. The use of such testing is a highly controversial issue.

- *Story telling*
  Questions and questioning strategies at interviews need to be fully developed
  and thorough in order to identify any inconsistencies in answers, that is, 'cock
  and bull stories'. A candidate may filter out the negatives in order to present
  her/himself in a positive light – non-disclosure of inadequacies. Some people
  would not consider this to be dishonest in itself because in terms of the individual's construction of themselves, the candidate's self-image might be said to
  be strong in integrity. As s/he sees it, her/his interpretation of self is entirely
  honest. The use of such narratives is a PCP approach discussed earlier.

- *Corroboration of references*
  When a selection decision is made there ought to be some corroboration by
  taking up references of key facts revealed by the applicant. Customarily, applicants who do not wish current employees to know of their attempts to find
  other employment ask for proceedings to be kept confidential – so corroboration can only take place after the offer has been made.

For certain jobs it is essential that references are checked to ensure that they
have actually come from a verified referee. Examples here would be:

- an industrial nurse who practises on the basis of a fake qualification
- the university senior manager whose stated qualifications on investigation
  were exaggerated
- the applicant for a post working with young people who has a criminal
  record (Rehabilitation of Offenders Act 1974), whose job qualifications have
  been falsified.

An application form may reveal, say, a 20-year employment history for an
applicant but some of the organisations will have disappeared, merged or been
taken over by other organisations. Personnel records might have been
expunged or staff who work in the firms who may have known the applicant
may have left.

In selection terms, the exploration of recent biographical experience is generally the most fruitful – even though an applicant may have been unemployed for several years. It is simple to exaggerate the period spent in most recent jobs and the responsibilities and successes in those jobs.

The question needs to be returned to – is it worth going through the reference process? With such low validity measures it seems that it is not always true that a reference will yield better information if the request is structured or unstructured – it does not seem to make any difference. What is clear is that the referee must be someone who has observed the performance of the individual concerned and even then semantic rating scales such as:

- excellent
- good
- satisfactory
- poor and
- unsatisfactory

can prove to be unhelpful to recruiters.

Some organisations permit applicants to nominate relatives and family firms as referees but this is likely to be of negligible value.

POINTS TO PONDER　Is there an obligation to give a reference?

There is no obligation on an employer to provide an employee with a reference. However, unwillingness to give a reference – the ominous silence – may itself be perceived to communicate something. Those giving references must not be defamatory or misrepresent. However, a reference may be *thickly worded* to help someone move on or *thinly worded* to evidence difficulty in being positive. The latter sentence is an example of this. Many organisations have a policy of not permitting members of staff, other than the HRM officers, to give personal references for past employees. Such organisational references will only give basic information – facts of past employment rather than criticise the performance of past employees. An example is given in Scenario 4.4.

SCENARIO 4.4

The [*employee name*] worked for [*name of organisation*] between [*dates*], in the post of [*position and grade*]. Her/his basic pay and average earnings at the point of leaving the organisation was [*amounts*]. In the last year s/he had [*days*] of absence. The employee concerned left of her/his own accord.

There were no disciplinary warnings outstanding. While in our employment s/he was a member of the trade union recognised by the organisation. S/he attended three training courses in health and safety, customer relations and basic food hygiene.

While such a reference gives useful facts, it may not give sufficient information for the potential employee to recruit the applicant. This is especially so in high level jobs – especially in the contemporary world of turbulence in the workplace and the need for knowledge workers.

RECRUITMENT STRATEGY

It may be obvious that an organisation will only be as effective as the quality of the members of its workforce, but it is still a truism that some organisations neglect this aspect of their business by hiring people who are unsuitable and who they end up wanting to get rid of because of their unsuitability.

Effective contemporary organisations use a strategic approach to the recruitment, selection and development of their staff. Their human resource strategy is linked to their overall strategic objectives so that they can utilise their people as a sustained source of competitive advantage ■ *see* Chapter 2 ■. This in itself requires an analysis of needs strategy which could take the form given in Table 4.3.

see **Chapter 2**

Such a strategic approach to recruitment has two key assets:

1 it ensures that the organisation:

   ■ identifies
   ■ develops and
   ■ utilises

   the potential of *every* member of the workforce.

2 it uses its finances on its people who directly contribute to the achievement of strategic goals.

STAFFING PLANS

It is the capacity of the individual which contributes to a high level of organisational performance and which identifies the difference between individuals. It is,

Table 4.3 A possible HRM recruitment strategy

Stage	Activity
1	Identification of the organisation's required competency profile.
2	Assessment of the organisation's existing competency profile.
3	Design of staff and management development programmes (to close the gap between existing and required competency profiles).
4	Design and implementation of organisation-wide policy on: ■ staff selection ■ career development ■ staff retrenchment.

therefore, essential that an organisation has a ▶ **staffing plan** ◀ in order to support the business goals of the organisation. In conjunction with this plan, the skills and expertise currently retained within the organisation should be analysed and compared against future requirements in order to identify future needs.

Staffing plan ◀┈┈▶ A strategy that identifies the business objectives and the quantity and quality of people required to support them..

Sir George Mathewson, CEO of the Royal Bank of Scotland, stated:

'My father always said to me, "First-class men hire first-class men. Second-class men hire third-class people." I have never been afraid to hire people who are better than me.'

Source: Garfield, A. (1999) Ambition! The Scotsman who's banking on buying Barclays, *The Independent*, Business Review, 2 June, p1.

As was discussed in Chapter 1, there are numerous organisations which state that their employees are the most important of their resources. Organisations that actually practise this belief show that they clearly understand the importance of strategic planning for the:

■ identification

■ selection

■ introduction and

■ continuous development

of every member of their workforce as central to the organisation's long-term growth.

To achieve this end, it is essential that the staffing plan is developed and continuously reviewed to ensure that it supports the goals of the organisation – short, middle and long term. The plan should be detailed and clearly identify the objectives of the organisation giving the quantity and quality of individuals who will be required to support them. Additionally, there needs to be consideration of the policies which will have to be continuously developed for attracting employees who have the skills to help the organisation meet its objectives and the experience to support those skills to satisfy the operational needs of the organisation.

The staffing plan alone is not sufficient for a recruitment policy to fit within the organisation. Employees need to know what skills and expertise are required of them at all stages of the organisation's strategy. Current skills need to be compared with future requirements and the gap can be closed by training. This ▶ **training needs analysis** ◀ is discussed in ■ Chapter 6 ■. Any planning needs to be linked

see **Chapter 6**

Training needs analysis ◀┈┈▶ A sequence of comprehensive analyses used to identify where current skills need to be developed to achieve future organisational strategy.

with the timescales the organisation has set for the achievement of organisational goals and the employment contracts which are used within the organisation. Such contracts may be full time and permanent or may include more flexible conditions, such as part-time working and teleworking, as discussed in ■ Chapter 2 ■.

see Chapter 2

RESPONSIBILITIES FOR RECRUITMENT

An employer uses the recruitment process to source the employees s/he requires to satisfy the organisation's staffing needs – it is about enlisting specific candidates for identified functions. In some organisations recruitment of employees for the 'lower' organisational functions, for example clerical and cleaning, are carried out by the personnel department in consultation with the department within which the successful candidate will work. Recruitment of 'higher' order staff, such as managers for key functions in the organisation, does not usually take place through the auspices of the 'personnel department' but by senior management within the organisation. Sometimes, if the position is a key one at a high level, the organisation may use external recruitment agencies or ▶ headhunters ◀ to advise them on available people for the job.

▶ A specialist consultant (executive search consultant) employed to recruit key staff. ◀····▶ **Headhunter**

SCENARIO 4.5

Pooled resources

The recruitment market in the retail sector is very competitive and so stores at the Lakeside shopping centre in Essex, near London, found it even more difficult to hire and retain workers when the vast Bluewater shopping centre opened nearby. Littlefield (1999) reports that the managers at Lakeside felt that the local job centres submitted too many unsuitable candidates for job interviews and that the services of the recruitment agencies were proving to be prohibitively expensive.

Lakeside set up their own recruitment bureau called People Point whose job it is to find, and then screen by interviewing and testing, all applicants for employment in any of the stores within the Lakeside complex. Jobs are advertised on notice boards in the People Point centre itself. Management then interviews each successful candidate and because of this can spend longer on each one of them.

By using this new bureau sudden demands from individual stores can be dealt with quickly and the bureau has found that it now needs to enter into recruitment at management level.

The People Point also provides open days for school leavers who experience how to complete an application form and cope with tests and interviews. Additionally, the bureau has regular monthly induction courses for all newcomers to the Lakeside complex where they train new entrants in the routines, places and faces of Lakeside.

Adapted from: Littlefield, D. (1999) Pooled resources, *Personal Management*, 3 June, pp52–3.

ASSESSMENT CENTRES

Garavan and Morley (1997) carried out an empirical investigation into the effectiveness of graduate ▶ **assessment centres** ◀ reinforcing the important fact that they are not specific places but:

> a structured combination of assessment techniques that are used to provide a wide-ranging, holistic assessment of each participant. (www p2)

Their results indicated that there were fundamental questions as to the value of the assessment centre as an approach to graduate selection. Organisations now make more of a direct approach to universities for graduates to enter their organisations by means of, for example, recruitment fairs held on university premises, direct mailing, or the Internet.

Assessment centre ◀····▶ An organisation within which a structured combination of assessment techniques is used to provide a wide-ranging, holistic assessment of each participant.

However, the theory-in-literature indicates that when organisations want to review the development and potential of a group of staff, such as junior managers, they often have interviews and assessments carried out at the same time by a group of trained and experienced evaluators in an assessment centre. In the area of recruitment, the system is used to evaluate a number of applicants simultaneously, for example management trainees. Candidates are given the opportunity to demonstrate their talents and the organisation gains a clear view of how each applicant might behave, say, under tension. Such an assessment will provide more useful information than might a short interview. During the assessment procedure, candidates are expected to carry out a number of disparate activities designed to assess a range of abilities and behaviour, for example written and oral communication skills, decision making, problem solving, leadership and the ability to work in a high-performance team.

SCENARIO 4.6

Graduates have to be wooed

Engineering and manufacturing firms must work harder at recruitment if they want to attract the best graduates, according to a recruitment consultancy whose blue-chip clients include Rolls-Royce and Honda.

Emma Powers, a consultant at Jonathan Lee recruitment, said, 'There is an increased demand for engineering graduates with industrial experience or specific training, as firms become more concerned with adding value through their people.'

Powers said that companies needed to approach good candidates quickly and sell themselves before applicants were snapped up by competitors. 'Graduates need to be sold the benefits of taking a job and offered positions with a variety of projects,' she said.

Source: People Management, 17 June 1999, p21.

The climate of an organisation will determine who actually has the overall responsibility for the process of recruitment. In some organisations, the responsibility will be with the HRM specialist yet in others it will be the responsibility of the line manager requiring the new member of staff. In the latter case, the line manager will work in conjunction with the HRM specialist to ensure that s/he is given professional advice, guidance and support to ensure that the right person to fit the job is employed and the whole process is in line with the strategic objectives of the organisation. A recruitment policy is important here because it provides a defined procedure and guides managerial action.

RECRUITMENT POLICY

As mentioned earlier, a recruitment policy reflects the prescriptions of literature on recruitment which themselves provide an implementation checklist covering, for example:

- use of interviews of a given order and composition

- adoption of educational qualification standards

- use of limited sources for recruits

- strict regulation of references and vetting of candidates

- use of ▶ **psychometric tests** ◀.

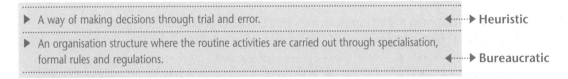

▶ Sometimes called occupational tests, or psychological testing, these are sophisticated tests used to measure an individual's capacities in areas such as intelligence and ability.   ◀┈┈▶ **Psychometric tests**

The steps involved can provide a ▶ **heuristic** ◀ and sensible outline which can be used to guide people through the recruitment maze. This is a standardisation approach and although somewhat generalised it does serve to reduce risk and allow the sharing of experiences. In a highly ▶ **bureaucratic** ◀ framework such a procedure could act to circumscribe discretion and behaviour related to the decision making within the organisation.

▶ A way of making decisions through trial and error.   ◀┈┈▶ **Heuristic**

▶ An organisation structure where the routine activities are carried out through specialisation, formal rules and regulations.   ◀┈┈▶ **Bureaucratic**

POINTS TO PONDER

'You have the qualifications, but not the experience. Sorry, we therefore can't employ you.'

Is this a truism?

DECISION-MAKING PROCESSES

There will be a number of individuals involved in the preparatory, shortlisting and interviewing/testing stages but the final decision could be the responsibility of one or more individuals. The question of 'who will make the decision' will reveal information about the line manager's authority over staffing and how far policy and intervention by others could well limit the discretion of the line manager who will supervise the appointed applicant.

The competency of the recruiter and selector is a key issue. Managers, school governors, members of university faculties and local politicians all participate in recruitment and selection without any particular training or practice. This raises the issue that it is conventional wisdom that recruitment does not extend beyond the business acumen held by such individuals and the assumption that they all have the repertoire of abilities required to make an effective appointment.

The systematic approach suggests otherwise and that unless the guidelines/techniques are used, the process of recruitment is bound to be less reliable and carry a higher risk of poor decision making. The latter can be exhibited by a number of behaviours as shown in Table 4.4.

The contemporary business environment is highly competitive with organisations vying for the best employees in order to gain/maintain market leadership and quality audit – they yearn for the best applicants. The best people could well be scarce or difficult to reach in a less than efficient labour market and the task of the recruiters becomes increasingly uncertain and demanding. Those involved in the recruiting process need:

■ *to review vacancies critically and redesign posts extensively to improve organisational performance*
A job can be targeted for elimination with tasks delegated to others who have the capability and capacity to do the job more effectively. Where an organisation is pursuing a policy of downsizing, a manager with a vacancy may face a struggle because other employees might think that an employee will have to be sacked before a new post can be advertised. In the contemporary working environment there is an increase in the termination of employment.

Table 4.4 Some behaviours exhibited as a result of poor decision making

■ Unsuitable staff will be appointed.

■ Stakeholders will be upset and frustrated when they encounter someone who cannot do the job.

■ Recruitment mistakes are expensive.

■ May fail to attract the right candidates and the best may turn the job down.

■ May be in breach of employment regulations and liable to litigation from individuals who feel that the decision-making process was discriminatory.

Keuning (1998) discusses the relationship between ▶ **demotion** ◀ and function relief. He notes that demotion has increased in organisations and can be used as a positive step within the recruitment procedure. Demotion could be part of an organisation's strategy in order to allow an individual to step down to make place for a new employee but it must be part of the open policy of the organisation ■ *see* Chapter 2 ■. The availability of demotion allows individuals to step back and function at a lower level within the organisation. This can be due to a number of factors, such as family responsibilities, involvement in the community, or by older workers who want to spend more time outside the workplace. The tendency to be willing to accept a lower level of function increases with age with the acceptance that further promotion is not probable. However, with demotion comes the tendency to reduce individual effort in some way and the will to work harder to gain promotion has disappeared. When younger managers look for higher level jobs, they tend to find them occupied by older workers. This can demotivate them and encourage them to seek promotion elsewhere resulting in a loss of skills and knowledge for the organisation.

see **Chapter 2**

▶ Reducing the rank/position of a worker involving removal from a higher to a lower function. ◀┈┈▶ **Demotion**

In order to have a satisfactory policy on demotion, the organisation must ensure that there is an open atmosphere related to the issue so that members of the workforce appreciate the position about future posts and, for example, the role of outplacement – a programme of help offered to such individuals to help them to cope with demotion or redundancy. Such a programme, usually provided by an external agency, is designed to help employees facing any career change. It is important that the organisation does not increase the pressure already on such workers who can sometimes adjust to the reduction in status, but certainly not a reduction in salary. Organisations can help here by ensuring that the demoted employee keeps her/his salary and by offering to freeze it. There are also other ways of compensating an employee – designed to meet the needs of the individual worker. Careers follow rising and falling curves and demotion could help the individual and the recruitment policy of the organisation ■ *see* Chapter 10 ■. However, in western organisations it is not yet a matter of course but is on its way through flexible working, such as job sharing and early retirement.

see **Chapter 10**

Flexible retirement is another way of increasing the recruitment potential of an organisation. This is when retirement is not fixed on a specific year in which an employee reaches a given age, say 65, but one in which the employee is permitted to make a choice to work a shorter or longer period. This system gives justice to the diverging vitality of different employees – not everyone wants to be a salary/wage slave until they reach the age of 65.

If the atmosphere around demotion and flexible retirement is open and sincere and respected by all members of the organisation from the CEO down, then the organisation will have increasing clarity in its recruitment policy.

■ *insight into the effect of recruitment on the organisation and implications of poor practice*

- An organisation's pool of expertise could be reinforced with fresh talent brought in to stimulate business improvements. However, newcomers could prove to be a disaster. It is necessary to identify existing talent within the organisation and nurture the organisation's own internal labour market.
- Communication weaknesses when recruiting new staff may lead to later arguments about job roles and terms and conditions of employment. Legal requirements for equal opportunities may be breached by inappropriate managerial behaviour.

■ *avoidance of over-prescription*

There are poor swimmers, poor drivers, poor chefs... there are also poor recruiters. Such individuals display the following behaviours:

- ad hoc, arrogant behaviour, narrow perceptions and whimsical reference when selecting
- poor ability to analyse
- less than effective coordination of a complex process
- incur expenditure with poor returns and, perhaps, no appointment when good candidates refuse the job (they decide they do not like the job, the organisation or the recruiters). The whole experience may have to be repeated.

Typical stages of recruitment and selection are summarised in Table 4.5.

4.3

Activity

Investigate the way you might be able to get a job as:

1 a bar person   3 a teacher or police officer
2 a construction site labourer   4 an actor.

Compare and contrast the formality and procedures you would expect to experience as they relate to the management of recruitment and selection.

CONSEQUENCES OF INEFFECTIVE RECRUITMENT PROCEDURES

The whole recruitment procedure is subjective and mistakes are compounded when an organisation does not follow the recruitment procedures laid down by the organisation. A wrong selection decision can prove to be very costly to the organisation in such areas as:

■ the lessening of productivity because of increased recruitment activities

■ a constant turnover of staff can bring about a low morale in the remaining staff which, in turn, can lead to:

Table 4.5 Typical stages of recruitment and selection

Stage		What is involved

1	*Response to the vacancy*	When vacancy arises identify: impact on staffing plan
		                                                need for job redesign
		                                                requirements for job shuffle.
		Decide whether or not to use an exit interview.

2	*Job analysis*	Ensure the post is understood by participants involved in the process. Identify the priorities, demands and competencies required. Carry out a job analysis. Produce an up-to-date job description and personal specification. Define target groups, their locale and what will attract people to apply.
3	*Employment terms*	Define the terms and conditions of employment. Agree a rewards package. Anticipate anomalous relationships within the job. Consider aspects of equal opportunities.
4	*Communicate vacancy*	What are the sources of our candidates? Should the vacancy be offered openly? Is there scope for: internal promotions? job transfers? What will be the ongoing effects of internal appointment? External sourcing. Confidentiality issues. Determining budgets. Placement of advertisements. Preparation of copy and placement of advertisement/s. Ethical standards.
5	*Process applications*	Ensure the administration procedures are ready to deal with the process. Prepare the job documentation for the candidates. Log applications and curriculum vitaes and compare with person profile. Follow up references and carry out security checks. Decide on and organise recruitment programme. Shortlist and invite candidates to the selection activity. Send out courteous rejections or stand-by letters.
6	*Carry out selection programme*	Organise candidate accommodation, tour of the organisation and arrangements for testing. Provide reception for candidates. Finalise briefing of selector/s and training and interviewer preparation and strategy. Implement selection programme. Conduct interviews, exercises and tests. Review candidate data and make the selection.
7	*Make job offer/s and finalise contract*	Advise unsuccessful candidates of rejection or stand-by. Process the job acceptances. Complete the reference investigations. Confirm the terms and conditions of employment. Design the new entrant induction programme.

8	*Evaluate effectiveness of:*	Recruitment process and methods: validity
		                                                        reliability
		                                                        utility.
		The recruitment service – internal or external agency.
		Identify whether costs of the activity were worthwhile.
		Selection decisions: is the new employee suitable?
		If unsuitable – how was the recruitment process at fault?

- increased workloads
- falling standards of work
- higher absenteeism

- less time for managers to actually do their job because of the time they have to spend on recruitment activities

- an unsettled organisational climate which might encourage staff to leave

- a change to the organisation's image – internally and externally.

Any combination of the above factors could seriously damage the organisation in the marketplace, resulting in non-achievement of strategic goals.

Apart from the costs involved in the recruitment process itself, there are other hidden costs which are often overlooked when the organisation assesses the true cost of any recruitment exercise. Such costs can be direct or indirect and would include:

- *direct costs:*
  - advertising the vacancy
  - preparing application forms
  - printing supporting recruitment literature, for example information about the organisation itself
  - interview expenses
  - consultancy fees

- *indirect costs* (time taken by managers in):
  - reviewing applications
  - conducting interviews
  - evaluation of candidates.

When procedures are poorly designed and executed with insufficient or inappropriate applicants coming forward, the recruitment exercise has to be carried out again and thus the implications become increasingly significant. While recruitment budgets might assist in controlling costs they do not eliminate the need to monitor the effectiveness of the recruitment process itself. It is possible to do this, for example by assessing the average cost per applicant and then monitoring this on an ongoing basis in order to identify the most cost-effective way to source any future applicants.

EVALUATION OF THE RECRUITMENT PROCESS

While a continual review of the performance of a successful candidate is vital, it is just as important to evaluate the recruitment process itself. Any mistakes which are made during the process need to be identified and remedied in time for the next exercise. However, the difficulty here is that what is appropriate strategy for one position may be unsuitable for the next which might be in very different circumstances. However, indicators could be used during the evaluation process and could include the following:

Quantity and quality of the applicants

The number of applicants is not a satisfactory measure of the success of the effectiveness of the recruitment process. A large number of replies could indicate that the advertisement had been too general in its wording and thus resulted in a number of candidates who do not fit the requirements of the position advertised. However, this technique (trawling) can be useful if the employers want to know what sort of people are available in a general, non-specific area. However, what is more important is the quality of the applications where the profiles of the applicants match the requirements identified by the organisation.

Sometimes it is difficult for organisations to closely match the requirements, for example when there is a shortage of high-quality applications. In this case, the organisation has to be prepared to revise the job description and person specification to ensure that their demands are realistic. A fresh recruitment process will then need to be implemented.

Review of the job description and/or person specification

A job description can be prepared by the organisation. Should there already be one in existence, it can be revisited and amended as felt necessary. The job description will state what needs to be done in the role and will give a definition of the principal responsibilities, tasks and priorities connected with the job. Such a document is useful to both the recruiter/s and the applicants because once the job has been described it can then be understood and given the attributes required of the person who is likely to be able to do the job effectively (the person specification). It is a way of finding a template or model for identifying those candidates who are most likely to be successful in the job. Such attributes will include:

- education

- skills

- experience

- competencies.

It will be necessary to repeatedly revisit the job description and/or person specification if performance targets are consistently not being achieved. In doing this, it will be possible to make sure that the appropriate questions have been asked of the applicants. It might also be necessary to review the rules used during the recruitment and selection process to make sure that the appropriate competencies and aptitudes are being sought.

Acceptable level of performance

Once a perceived suitable applicant has been appointed to the job, s/he should achieve the required performance level within an appropriate and acceptable time period. In order to be able to do so, new entrants need the organisation to provide:

- support

- information

- training.

If this is not in evidence, then the organisation will need to look at the nature of the ▷ **induction** ◁ programme provided for the appointed applicant. The way in which new entrants in an organisation are received is critical in not only ensuring that they reach the desired standard of performance as quickly as possible, but it is also important in forming their attitudes.

Induction ◀┈┈▶ The period of time when a new entrant to an organisation makes initial contact with the organistion until s/he has reached the desired standard of performance.

Operational improvements
Organisations are continually trying to increase the quality of their products and/or services, that is, make operational improvements. If they fall short on this, organisations need to review the level of improvements and determine whether they need to be re-evaluated. This view is essential to the process of recruitment. If the targeted operational improvements are well established and acceptable to other employees, it will not be necessary to return to the recruitment process to see whether there is any information available which shows that the appointed person is not actually capable of doing the job to which s/he has been appointed. However, they will have to be revisited if the individual is not doing the job satisfactorily.

Retention of new employees
Sometimes, although the operational activities are being carried out to the required

see Chapter 9

standards and the ▷ **remuneration** ◁ package ■ *see* Chapter 9 ■ is acceptable to the new entrant, the employee leaves very shortly after joining the organisation. There is usually a personal or social reason for this departure. However, sometimes an individual will leave early in her/his employment because there has been a failure in the development of positive working relationships with a manager or with fellow workers. It is important that this sort of problem is tackled and a review of the interview process and/or the interpersonal skills of managers to equip them to help the new employee to adjust to the changes required when commencing a new appointment.

Remuneration ◀┈┈▶ A reward, pay for services rendered; includes benefits such as pensions.

Stability of the workforce
It is no longer possible to have a job for life yet employers must retain their core workers to make sure that there is always a pool of experienced workers to train, develop and educate other employees so that there is stability for the stakeholders as well as for the operational activities. An effective communication system will cover all terms and conditions of employment as well as the social aspects of the

workplace and will help to build loyalty and secure long-term commitment from key members of the workforce.

DETERMINING AND COSTING STAFFING NEEDS

Determining and costing staffing needs is a complex activity yet it can provide organisations with information which will help the organisation to meet its objectives. Such analysis includes:

- staffing audit

- skills audit

- career and succession planning

- external factors affecting recruitment

- changes in working methods and practices

- flexible staffing

- staff retention

- costing human resource requirements.

STAFFING AUDIT

HRP ■ *see* Chapter 3 ■ is about continually analysing an organisation's human resource needs under changing conditions and then developing human resource policies which are appropriate for the long-term objectives of the organisation – it has to be part of the strategic planning of the organisation. The practical application of this strategy is to make sure that the organisation attracts and keeps the quantity and quality of people needed to meet its organisational objectives. In order to achieve this the workforce has to be well trained and flexible so that the organisation can adapt to a contemporary, changing environment.

    The elements of a staff audit will be peculiar to each organisation. However, the common components would be the:

see Chapter 3

- number of jobs existing/will exist in the organisation

- skills of job holder

- knowledge required and held.

An important aspect of a staff audit is an analysis of labour turnover ■ *see* Chapter 3 ■. The latter will give some indication of the potential wastage of staff and subsequent staffing requirements. To review, labour turnover comprises an elementary formula which measures the ability of the organisation to keep its employees:

see Chapter 3

$$\text{Labour turnover} = \frac{\text{Number of leavers}}{\text{Average number of employees}} \times 100$$

For example, if in 1998 an organisation had 50 people leave and the average number of people employed during that same year was 150 then:

$$\text{Labour turnover} = (50/150) \times 100$$
$$= (0.33) \times 100$$
$$= 33 \text{ per cent}$$

The percentage (33 per cent in the example above) gives an indication of the percentage of employees that the organisation will need to recruit in the period just to retain the same staffing level. Where there is a requirement to recruit individuals to fill newly created posts, these individuals will be needed in addition to the number of projected leavers.

Standing (1999) has reviewed the history of the labour market and believes that it helps the recruiter to understand the process of recruitment at the present time. He detected signs of what he regarded as an inevitable swing back to a concern for employment security. He does not believe that there will be a return to the labour market regulatory approach of the post-war golden age. Looking forward, Standing (1999) pins his hopes on the introduction of a basic minimum income security guarantee which he calls 'human development enterprises' to stabilise the workplace. This is accompanied by new forms of employee association based on community as well as worker profit sharing. These proposals, he believes, would redress the social fragmentation associated with flexible labour markets ■ *see* Chapter 3 ■ and globalisation ■ *see* Chapter 11 ■. This is a very ambitious hypothesis.

see **Chapter 3**

see **Chapter 11**

Whitehead (1999) supports this view by reporting that there is a drastic shortage of skilled labour and that more flexibility is required from organisations in their approaches to attracting applicants. He reported that one in three faced an absolute labour shortage (not one person applied for the job). The most common reasons given by employers for difficulties in filling vacancies were, in rank order:

1   lack of experience on behalf of the applicant

2   lack of technical skills

3   problems with the applicants wanting more remuneration than was offered ■ *see* Chapter 9 ■.

see **Chapter 9**

Employees are not paying enough to attract the skilled people required and are making the jobs on offer far too inflexible. Whitehead (1999) continued to report that employers are simply not prepared to pay the required rates that people with the required skills demand and they are also reluctant to be flexible with the working conditions offered.

Walsh (1999) reports that Ireland is a case in point where recruitment problems caused by record employment levels could stifle economic progress. The skills shortage is very severe there, so much so that the economy is suffering under spiralling wage demands. The official unemployment figure is 6.4 per cent and although this is the same as the UK, only 90 000 of those out of work are actively seeking employment. Irish firms cannot fill their posts and this is exacerbated by a shortage of housing and rising property prices. Harney, the Enterprise, Training and Employment Minister for Ireland, believes that there is a need to have an ongoing emphasis on re-education and upskilling but that organisations must take on this responsibility and not continue to expect central government to do all the education and training.

There could well be bullish areas of recruitment, that is, confidence and optimisim, and one of the principal ones is in management consultancy where demand is outstripping supply. Welch (1999) reports that entire teams are being lured away by rival consultancy groups.

SKILLS AUDIT

The skills audit, discussed earlier, also needs to form the centre of any staffing plan which aims to provide effective career and succession planning for all key personnel. By carrying out a regular skills audit, an organisation will keep abreast of the qualifications and the experience of existing staff. It can also be used to identify individuals for promotion as jobs become available. Regular reviewing of the skills audit against the strategy of the organisation can produce an indicator of potential skill shortages.

CAREER AND SUCCESSION PLANNING

The skills audit also has another important role in that it forms the centre of any staffing plan which aims to provide effective career and succession planning for key personnel. Career planning ■ *see* Chapter 10 ■ can be used as an incentive for all employees who have the capability and ambition to progress in their career. Additionally, a staffing plan will provide a framework for succession planning, which in turn provides a contingency strategy for identifying appropriately trained and experienced personnel who could move into key positions of those who are leaving the organisation or who are progressing through the organisation.

see Chapter 10

Wherever possible, clear succession plans need to be drawn up over a three- to five-year period. However, it is not always appropriate to disclose the details of such plans because individuals not appearing to be important to the plan, or who do not agree with it, may well decide to move to some other organisation to seek promotion. With performance appraisal now being an open activity, this is difficult ■ *see* Chapter 10 ■.

see Chapter 10

POINTS TO PONDER — What about freedom of information when considering the disclosure of planning details?

Any comparison of the skills and experience required with the skills and experience available internally will help to identify the ▶ **transferable skills** ◀ available to facilitate internal appointments or to identify potential vacancies requiring external recruitment.

Transferable skills ◄····► Skills which individuals have that can be used in more than one job.

EXTERNAL FACTORS AFFECTING RECRUITMENT

External influences are also important and should be considered as likely to affect its ability to recruit new staff. This is especially so in the contemporary knowledge-based economy. These could include economic, demographic and social factors.

Economic

see Chapter 9

The remuneration packages offered by competitor organisations both nationally and locally and resulting staff expectations may create difficulties for the organisation ■ *see* Chapter 9 ■. Additionally, the location itself may be a contributor to the difficulties in attracting individuals with the appropriate skills and experience. However, Gribben (1999) reports that:

> organisations are continuing to cut back on recruitment despite growing confidence about the economy. (p29)

Marks & Spencer announced in May 1999 it was to shed 700 jobs as a result of its worst decline in total profits, which fell to £546 million for the year to March 1999 from £1.26 billion the previous year. Following this devastating fall in profits, Marks & Spencer has withdrawn all offers of places on its graduate recruitment scheme. They have given each appointee £1000 – equal to one month's salary – to satisfy breach of contract and as a goodwill gesture and have passed on details of their management trainee recruits to other organisations such as Boots and Waitrose, while other organisations have contacted them direct offering to employ the graduates – Unilever advertised that it would welcome these graduates.

Marks & Spencer used to offer 250 trainee management places to graduates in the autumn of each year and they are no longer to do this. It is an unfortunate fact that appointed graduates have now missed the opportunity to work for other high-ranking employers and it will do nothing to enhance the image of Marks & Spencer, since the action is bound to have a wider effect on its profile as an employer.

However, the recruitment process in a deregulated labour market means that an employer seeks flexible staff. That is, individuals can be hired in a more flexible way – job sharing, part time or casual labour. There has been an increase in the formal use of work experience and voluntary work among young and older people available for work. At least such individuals can enter the work environment and therefore:

■ become known

■ have a chance to contribute

■ gain continuity in employment

■ build self-esteem

■ gain recognition

■ re-establish work routines

and are thus retained in the labour market ■ *see* Chapter 3 ■.

see Chapter 3

There are other economic factors which could be considered, for example competition and exchange rates, but these are beyond the scope of this text.

Through these processes decision makers in the workplace can get to know the competencies and abilities of such volunteers and they may, therefore, be inclined to offer them a post. However, a vulnerable volunteer may be exploited as nothing comes of the attachment.

Demographic

These factors dictate that the number of older people is increasing, while younger people are becoming a minority. The indications are, therefore, that there will be a future skills shortage resulting in organisations having to recruit employees from alternative sources and work harder to retain the employees they do have.

Social

The ability to source suitable applicants may be influenced by the social mix of the local labour pool and this may limit the types of skills available.

CHANGES IN WORKING METHODS AND PRACTICES

When employers consider the recruitment strategy for their organisation, they must take into account the skills which are required from the workforce in order to perform the recognised tasks and the alternatives which are available to ensure that the current output is maintained. This could be done, perhaps, by:

■ embracing new technology ■ *see* Chapter 6 ■

see Chapter 6

■ revising working practices.

A review of existing practices might show a need to move from, say, production lines to more integrated cell structures or changing to continuous processes and the introduction of continuous shift working. Alternatively, the review may well signify a change to the performance bonus schemes or retraining of individuals to become more multiskilled.

FLEXIBLE STAFFING

Changing social and economic factors have brought change to working practices and the expectations of employees and the concept of jobs for life no longer exists. Such flexible practices are related to the recruitment process and might result in a move from standard working to a system of shift working. Recruitment strategies have had to be amended to cope with this erratic working environment. The employment of people on temporary, casual and fixed-term contracts to support the core workforce is now standard practice in a large number of organisations and can include one or more of the following methods.

Temporary staffing

Temporary employees are usually employed to work in jobs which are for a fixed period of time or have a well-defined completion point. The principal benefits of employing temporary employees include:

■ the ability to control overhead costs

■ relinquished responsibility of providing employment benefits, for example redundancy payments.

Just because the appointment is temporary does not mean that the new entrant should not have a clearly defined contract from the outset. This is important in order to avoid any disputes over the work situation or when individuals are let go. It should also be clarified if the worker is not being employed on a regular basis.

Outsourcing

Many specialist activities may well be best performed by subcontracting the work and thus releasing the organisation from expensive training and development requirements. By outsourcing, an organisation may well become less distracted from its core activities and can, therefore, reduce employment overheads ■ *see* Chapter 3 ■. It is important for organisations to ensure that in respect of the employment relationship the subcontractor is retained solely to provide a service and is not an employee of the organisation. Such arrangements can often be expensive and the cause of friction and uncertainty among permanent employees, particularly if the organisation is considering outplacement in other areas of its activities. Table 4.6 gives some customised services offered by such recruitment agencies.

see Chapter 3

Therefore, the outsourcing agency will conduct and coordinate all the recruitment activities in an effort to reach as diverse a population of available candidates as possible. Organisations often initiate and develop relationships with outsourcing agencies and other appropriate specialised areas of potential applicants (for example Jobcentres) in order to always have a reservoir of potential employees when a position becomes available.

Table 4.6 Examples of customised services offered by recruitment agencies

- Application processing
- Occupational/specific aptitude testing:
  - Basic mathematics
  - Reading skills
  - Writing skills
  - Literacy skills
  - Mechanical abilities
- Collaborative recruitment for new employees with job service offices that have available applicants
- Assessment of employee leadership skills and reliability
- Analysis of performance and training needs
- First-line (initial) interviews
- Checking of references
- Verifying applications
- Carrying out individual test reports
- Final interviews
- Developing specific job descriptions
- Assessing candidates' levels against the job requirements

Organisations do not have to use the full menus of services offered by an recruitment agency since they may well have in-house experts of their own. However, certain parts of the recruitment process can involve a considerable amount of time and are thus better outsourced. Examples of these are:

Screening process

Outsourcing agencies will take the responsibility for carrying out this task in accordance with the criteria/guidelines established by the organisation and submitted to the agency in writing. The agency will provide guidance and technical consultation in the establishment of any pre-screening criteria. Only the candidates meeting the minimum requirements during the pre-screening process will be further tested for employment.

The screening process has to be formalised because it is critical to describe (in writing) what will exclude the candidate – such issues *must* be related to the job. Also, a comprehensive, written employment screening policy for use by both the organisation and individual members of the workforce will reduce the inconsistencies that could lay the framework for legal action.

Vocational and personality assessment

The agency will conduct group assessments at a site mutually agreed upon and maintain the individual results.

First-line interviews

These take about 30 minutes and involve the asking of special questions that have been developed by the organisation and the agency. Interview-rating criteria are used so that the process serves as the second step in the screening process. All applicants who score at the designated level for all areas of consideration have their details forwarded to the hiring organisation with written reports of:

■ applicant assessment

■ first-line interview ratings.

Checking of references

The agency will conduct telephone contacts with all the listed professional and/or personal references provided by each applicant. They will also provide written reports designating the source of references and the content of all telephone contacts will be documented and provided to the organisation.

Most employers ask for references and correspondingly give information on ex-employees and staff who have secured (or are seeking) jobs with other employees. Cooper and Robertson (1996) reported on a study on the use of references as part of the selection procedure questioning the validity of their use. They found that validity measures were low (averaging 0.14 and seldom more than 0.20) and asked why organisations should bother with them.

Reference seeking and writing is an administrative chore which includes:

■ letters of request (including stamped addressed envelopes)

■ preparation of job descriptions

■ preparation and analysis of cover questionnaire

■ ex-employer and personal referee/s have to go to the effort of replying.

The use of references is a cheap tool which is purely about capturing information by the most appropriate means – the referee/s provide free assessment data on the applicant. The referee's honesty and integrity is normally trusted and it is assumed that references bring in more information about the candidate–job fit (provided that the referee has an insight into the job performance criteria). The referee offers an opinion about whether or not the candidate will perform the job well.

POINTS TO PONDER

A potential employer has received a glowing reference for an applicant for a post. Does this mean that the applicant is as good as the referee reports or that the referee wants to see the back of her/him?

A reference – if it is to be trusted – confirms facts about the applicant. All it should do is confirm that the person is who they say they are and they have the experience and qualifications that they have claimed on their application form.

Part-time work

Part-time work – characterised by having fewer hours and less pay than full-time work – is becoming increasingly popular, particularly for single-parent/guardian employees who wish to combine work and family responsibilities. It is also a way of ensuring shift cover and filling 'small' jobs as well as making cost-effective use of labour.

Job sharing

This is an arrangement in which two people share the responsibilities of one full-time job. They also share the work, pay, holidays and rewards. It differs from part-time work in that it includes factors such as:

- teamwork

- joint decisions

- higher status

- better conditions

- better career progression

- more responsibility

- greater commitment

- job satisfaction.

Job sharing enables organisations to recruit skilled and experienced workers who may not be able to work a full working week. It allows one post to be filled by two people with differing but complementary experience. Continuity is maintained should one of the sharers be absent or leave the job.

New technology

Working from home has become a genuine option for many workers because of the rapid advancements in new technology ■ *see* Chapter 6 ■. The facilities available through technology have increased the job opportunities for many individuals whose personal circumstances would previously have excluded them from the job market. Major time saving can now be achieved by reducing the need to travel and hold face-to-face meetings. While there may be instances where home workers feel isolated and lose touch with the organisational identity and aims, the benefits of home working in terms of:

see **Chapter 6**

- reduction in overhead costs

- elimination of many attendance problems and

- opportunities to adapt to changing workloads

far outweigh the disadvantages and potential problems.

Interim management

Organisations faced with short-term projects can opt for the recruitment of external experts employed on fixed-term or specific-task contracts. Managers engaged on fixed-term or specific-task projects will differ from consultants, because they will be required to provide the full management role including the identification of the strategy used to resolve the issue at hand and the implementation of appropriate solutions. This type of appointment is particularly effective for managerial work where permanent employment is not a viable option for the organisation because of, say, its size or overhead restrictions.

Managers who fill interim positions have usually occupied senior appointments elsewhere, and thus offer many benefits in terms of experience and knowledge of many differing environments. Additionally, because the managers are recruited on a temporary basis, there may also be associated savings in respect of organisational benefits which do not need to be offered.

4.4 Activity

Investigate how your place of work/university provides for teaching staff who wish to work outside the hours of 0900 and 1800.

STAFF RETENTION

Many organisations are of the opinion that, once employed, individuals will remain with them unquestioningly believing that a wage or salary secures their loyalty and long service. However, the strategy involved in recruiting new employees should be progressed into plans for their retention, and failure to do so is likely to result in demotivated staff and a high labour turnover ■ *see* Chapter 3 ■.

see Chapter 3

There are three particular areas that organisations must monitor in order to ensure that they retain motivated and loyal staff ■ *see* Chapter 9 ■:

see Chapter 9

see Chapter 7 *and* Chapter 8

■ terms and conditions of employment ■ *see* Chapter 7 *and* Chapter 8 ■

see Chapter 10

■ career progression ■ *see* Chapter 10 ■

see Chapter 10

■ continuous development ■ *see* Chapter 10 ■.

Terms and conditions of employment

As well as remuneration, working conditions must be such that individuals feel that they are valued by the organisation ■ *see* Chapter 9 ■. Individuals may well compare the way they are treated, and whether their achievements are recognised,

see Chapter 9

with the experience of colleagues within the organisation, as well as benefits offered by competitors and other local employers. Organisations who fail to take note of this ▶ **equity theory** ◀ (Adams, 1965) will lose their key personnel ■ *see* Chapter 9 ■. Using this approach, the organisation will seek to create conditions under which all persons will have an equal opportunity to seek and obtain employment.

see **Chapter 9**

▶ A justice theory which asserts that members of any workforce wish to be treated fairly and ◀┈┈▶ **Equity theory**
have a desire to perceive equity in relation to others and avoid inequity with them.

Career progression

At the initial stages individuals will gain recognition from settling in and reaching the appropriate standards of performance. However, they will later expect to see their efforts being rewarded with promotion or transfer ■ *see* Chapter 10 ■.

see **Chapter 10**

Continuous development

To support their aspirations and to ensure competence in performing their required tasks to the expected levels, individuals will search for planned training and development activities, probably originating from regular review meetings (appraisals) with their managers. Individuals will wish to develop a portfolio of continuous development to demonstrate their continued knowledge and skills and thus participate in continuous professional development (CPD) ■ *see* Chapter 10 ■.

see **Chapter 10**

There is often a temptation at job interviews to make promises interspersed with misleading statements to potential employees in order to entice a particular individual to join the organisation. However, if such promises are not kept, the individual will lose trust in the organisation and start to look elsewhere for employment. There is a fine line when interviewing perspective employees because if a recruiter digs too deeply s/he might find later that s/he has invaded the privacy of the candidate yet if the employee later turns out to be unsatisfactory, the recruiters may well have failed to investigate the background of that candidate thoroughly. Both can be seen as negligent and result in charges of negligent hiring practices.

To make sure that all the elements are in position to retain staff, it is essential that the organisation has formal policies that have been developed to ensure that the processes which are needed to meet the requirements of that strategy are in place. Such policies have the key aim of ensuring the long-term retention of staff and include:

■ human resource planning ■ *see* Chapter 3 ■

see **Chapter 3**

■ career planning ■ *see* Chapter 10 ■

see **Chapter 10**

■ recruitment and retention

■ induction

■ continuous development ■ *see* Chapter 10 ■

see **Chapter 10**

see Chapter 9
■ rewards and benefits ■ *see* Chapter 9 ■

■ flexible working practices

see Chapter 5
■ effective communication ■ *see* Chapter 5 ■

see Chapter 10
■ performance appraisal ■ *see* Chapter 10 ■

see Chapter 8
■ equal opportunities ■ *see* Chapter 8 ■.

COSTING HUMAN RESOURCE REQUIREMENTS

Employees are not only the most important resource available to organisations, but more often than not they are the most expensive. A consideration of the full costs of human resources should provide managers with a clear indication of the importance of getting the recruitment planning and process correct first time, every time. Typical costs include:

■ remuneration costs

■ recruitment costs

■ continuous development costs

■ termination costs.

Remuneration costs include:

■ salaries

■ additional allowances

■ performance bonus schemes

■ company cars

■ National Insurance contributions

■ sickness payments

■ maternity/paternity payments

■ pension schemes.

Direct recruitment costs include:

■ advertising

■ preparation of application forms

■ recruitment literature

■ interview expenses

■ consultancy fees.

Indirect recruitment costs, in terms of:

■ time involved in reviewing applications

■ conducting interviews

■ evaluating candidates.

Sometimes there are additional costs incurred because of the need to relocate employees although this is usually in senior management posts ■ *see* Chapter 12 ■.

see Chapter 12

Continuous development includes the costs of:

■ attending training events

■ accommodation

■ preparation time

■ evaluation of events.

Termination costs would include the direct costs incurred in payments for:

■ redundancy and

■ severance

as well as the indirect costs, such as poor performance during notice periods, rescheduling of work tasks.

UTILISING THE COMPETENCY CONCEPT

The level of competence demanded for the effective performance of different jobs is a measure of the relative value of those jobs. Properly researched competence criteria enable selection testing of individuals to be more closely related to the characteristics required for successful job performance. Furthermore, potential high achievers can be more easily identified. Fletcher (1991) believes that competency is about the application of knowledge rather than the knowledge per se. In other words, it is what a worker does with her/his knowledge than actually having it that is important.

Competence analysis is normally achieved through interviewing a number of job holders. The questions focus on what is done, the situations job holders face and, importantly, what distinguishes performers at different levels of competence in terms of behaviour.

This enables an assessment to be developed of the particular skills, knowledge and abilities needed to behave appropriately at these levels and thereby deliver the required performance levels.

Once the required competencies have been defined, they can be incorporated into person specifications and job description which can be used as part of the recruitment and selection process. Differing levels of competencies may be identified indicating perhaps the differing levels of the job holders within the organisation.

The concept of competency is very difficult because it is perceived to be different things by different people. It is not a matter of semantics, but more one of perception. Armstrong (1999) states that it is:

a useful term for describing the sort of behaviour (the behavioural dimensions) that organizations are seeking in order to attain high levels of performance. (p275)

He goes on to state that the concept provides a common language and:

the notion of competency can be used to describe what people are expected to know and be able to do if they are to carry out their roles effectively. (p275)

4.5

Activity

1 Make a list of the competencies which you already have.

2 Make a separate list of those you wish to gain/achieve.

3 Note how you can meet the required competencies.

Some organisations have a formal person specification which they use to help them when faced with the actual applicants. The most common are:

1   Seven-point plan (Rodger, 1952)

2   Fivefold grading system (Munro-Fraser, 1954)

3   Competency frameworks

4   Competency maps

5   Competency profiles

6   Competency lists and clusters.

Seven-point plan (Rodger, 1952)

The seven-point plan is still commonly used in organisations – particularly in job interview situations – even though it is more complicated than the fivefold grading scheme. Its popularity lies in its design which places more emphasis on the active and dynamic aspects of an individual's development and career progression.

1   *Physical characteristics*
- health
- appearance
- height
- build
- eyesight
- general health
- general appearance
- voice

2   *Qualifications and experience*
    - qualifications required to do the job
    - experience in a particular type of job

3   *Intelligence*
    - general level
    - power of reasoning
    - analytical ability

4   *Special aptitudes*
    - individual skills
    - presentation skills
    - ability to be self-motivated

5   *Interests*
    - particularly those helpful to the job

6   *Personal disposition*
    - personality
    - loyalty
    - dependability

7   *Circumstances*
    Any special circumstances that apply to the job such as the need to work away from home at times.

The fivefold grading system (Munro-Fraser, 1954)

Also still commonly used in interview situations, as its title suggests, there are five components to this system:

1   *Impact on other people*
    Appearance, speech, manner, physical make-up.

2   *Acquired qualifications*
    Formal education, vocational training, work experience.

3   *Innate abilities*
    Inherent quickness of comprehension and aptitude for learning.

4   *Motivation*
    The level of intrinsic motivation within the individual and her/his reliability, consistency and determination in seeing them through to successful achievement.

5   *Adjustment*
    This is emotional intelligence and concerns the individual's emotional stability, ability to cope with tension and positive stress and the ability to interact positively with others.

The issue of competency is at the centre of SHRM because it is the purpose of the latter to recruit highly competent people who will, through continuous develop-

see Chapter 2

ment, achieve their personal objectives and those of the organisation for which they work ■ *see* Chapter 2 ■.

Competency frameworks

This is a contemporary term used to define the competency requirement that includes all the tasks within an organisation. They are put together into what is often called a 'job family'. Such frameworks will usually comprise what are known as 'generic competencies' – they apply to all individuals who work within a specific occupation, for example management, teaching or bar tending, where they apply to all staff or to a group of staff sharing the same type of job. For example, they can relate to the whole of Virgin Atlantic or just to cabin crews.

Specific competencies relate to a particular role, for example, that of a manager. Examples here are the Management Charter Initiative (MCI) (1988) which saw a move away from the more traditional roles and qualities of a manager towards the requirement for more sophisticated skills such as knowledge management and creativity. The MCI (1988) was developed as a result of investigation into the education, training and development of managers ■ *see* Chapter 10 ■. There were two key inputs into the development of the MCI (1988):

see Chapter 10

■ *The Constable and McCormick Report* (1987) was initiated by the British Institute of Management (BIM). This work investigated the development of British managers and concluded that many of them needed a broader professional training and education if their organisations were to be competitive. It was this report that brought continuous professional development to the fore, where the individual manager is responsible for continuing to maintain her/his professional knowledge and expertise.

■ *The Handy Report* (1987) was a result of Charles Handy's international investigation where he attempted to find out if there was something special about what each nationality offered to the role of the manager. His report highlighted the fact that expertise in functional and technical skills was insufficient in the modern business world and that managers must have considerable business knowledge, and human and conceptual skills.

As a result of such investigations, managers have now moved into the competencies arena whereby they are assessed against national standards in key management functions and skills. Such competencies are broken down further into specific activities that managers need to undertake on a daily basis. This continuous professional development is formally and professionally recognised through such organisations as the CIPD and the BIM.

Competency maps

These describe all the different activities and/or categories of the behaviour which is considered to be competent against a measure of competency dimensions.

Competency profiles

A profile is a written specification which details the competencies which are required for a specific job, task or role.

Competency lists and clusters

These describe the main competency dimensions required for an individual in the form of written frameworks, profiles or in diagrammatic form by the use of charts or maps. They can be clustered according to type or description, for example leading the team requires motivation ■ *see* Chapter 9 ■, interpersonal skill and vision.

see Chapter 9

As long as organisations revisit their recruitment strategy and maintain a dialogue with their stakeholders and the wider environment and keep abreast of available information, they should be able to maintain a labour force that is capable of meeting the eventualities of the complex business world.

- Recruitment is the term given to the overall activity of choosing suitable applicants for job vacancies. Included in this process is selection, which is the latter part of the process when the organisation decides who to employ from the candidates available.

- The theory-in-literature tends to concentrate on the selection process itself rather than on the practice of recruitment which comprises: systems, procedures, advertising, shortlisting, organisation of selection and overall administration.

- A systems approach to recruitment requires an analysis of the inputs, processes, outputs and environmental contexts of recruitment. Such an approach helps the organisation to understand the strengths and weaknesses of the propositions of a prescriptive approach.

- It is necessary to identify the requirements of the job vacancy which include the key ones of job analysis, methods of job analysis, competence assessment, job descriptions and person specifications.

- The obtaining of references requires a security device to be in place so that honesty and integrity can be verified.

- It may be obvious that an organisation will only be as effective as the quality of the members of its workforce but it is still a truism that some organisations neglect this aspect of their business by hiring people who are unsuitable and who they end up wanting to get rid of because of their unsuitability.

Chapter summary

■ It is the capacity of the individual that contributes to a high level of organisational performance and identifies the difference between individuals. It is, therefore, essential that an organisation has a staffing plan in order to support the business goals of the organisation. Such a plan identifies the quality and quantity of individuals required. In conjunction with this plan, the skills and expertise currently retained within the organisation should be analysed and compared against future requirements in order to identify future needs.

■ There will be a number of individuals involved in the preparatory, shortlisting and interviewing/testing stages, but the final decision could be the responsibility of one or more individuals. The question of 'who will make the decision' will reveal information about the line manager's authority over staffing and how far policy and intervention by others could well limit the discretion of the line manager who will supervise the appointed applicants.

■ While a continual review of the performance of a successful candidate is vital, it is just as important to evaluate the recruitment process itself. Any mistakes made during the process need to be identified and remedied in time for the next exercise.

■ External influences are important and should be considered as likely to affect the organisation's ability to recruit new staff. This is especially so in the contemporary knowledge-based economy. These could include: economic, demographic and social criteria.

■ When employers consider the recruitment strategy for their organisation, they must take into account the skills which are required from the workforce in order to perform the recognised tasks and the alternatives available to ensure the current output is maintained. Two key ways of doing this are by embracing new technology and revising existing working practices.

■ Many organisations are of the opinion that, once employed, individuals will remain with them unquestioningly believing that a wage or salary secures their loyalty and long service. However, the strategy involved in recruiting new employees should be progressed into plans for their retention and failure to do so is likely to result in demotivated staff and a high labour turnover. Areas which organisations need to monitor in order to ensure that they retain staff are:

terms and conditions of employment, career progression and continuous development.

■ At the centre of recruitment and selection is the issue of competencies which forms the backbone of SHRM. The level of competence demanded for the effective performance of different jobs is a measure of the relative values of those jobs.

Chapter summary *continued*

END OF CHAPTER 4 CASE STUDY

Energy efficient

An innovative project to recruit disabled people and their carers has switched energy supply and home services company Centrica on to a previously untapped source of skills.

Roy Bleackley works in customer metering services at a call centre in Manchester, England, using sophisticated computer packages to sort out problems with customers' bills. He enjoys the work and his prospects with the company are good.

It was not always so. Bleackley is profoundly deaf and, before starting at Centrica in September last year, spent two years out of work. He had been made redundant from his previous job checking engine components and inspecting goods for export and, in his early forties, was finding it impossible to get back into the engineering industry. 'I expected to have a hard time finding a new job because of my deafness,' he says. 'It really felt as if – because I was not able to communicate like Joe Bloggs – people were intimidated, and that was a disadvantage when looking for work.'

Many employers are still not willing to take a chance on employees like Roy. But he is now one of 47 disabled people who have been recruited by Centrica.

Centrica employs a large number of staff at its two call centres in Manchester and at its bill-processing departments in Oldham and Hattersley, and often finds it quite difficult to recruit the right people to work in them. Managers realised that there was an untapped pool of potential recruits among disabled people who were not applying for jobs, probably because they assumed they would be unsuitable. And there was a further pool of potential recruits among their carers. This amounted to a reservoir of unused talent. These people, given the right encouragement and conditions, might be interested in entering the workplace.

It was quickly realised, too, that work in a call centre might suit those people who found it difficult to commit themselves to regular nine-to-five, five-days-a-week work.

A benefit to the company was that employing people with disabilities would create more diversity in the workforce, better reflecting the customer base. Jill Shedden, group HR policy manager, admits that the company had previously overlooked the potential of a large number of people who had been generally ignored by employers.

'Our recruitment process wasn't encouraging these people to apply for jobs,' she says. 'We were missing potentially high-performing employees, and that was a loss to us as well as to them.'

END OF CHAPTER 4 CASE STUDY (CONT'D)

So far, progress is encouraging. The most important test of all must be whether the people recruited to the company – who may never have been given a similar opportunity anywhere else – are making a go of it. The signs are good. By all accounts, the new recruits are doing well and proving themselves to be valuable members of the workforce.

For people like Roy Bleackley, the future is much brighter than it might otherwise have been. 'It has allowed me to return to work more quickly and to a suitable job,' he says. 'I've made a big change in my life and I hope I will be able to stay here and develop myself even further.'

Adapted from: Whitehead, M. (1999) Energy efficient, *People Management*, 11 November, pp60–2.

END OF CHAPTER 4 CASE STUDY QUESTIONS

1 The Centrica project appears to have been a success since local managers have been asking for more recruits of the same calibre. How important is strategy to the success of such a recruitment policy?

2 How would Centrica approach the issue of equal opportunities?

3 Do you think that changes in working methods and practices has enabled Centrica to employ disabled individuals?

4 Do you think that Centrica uses a systems approach to recruitment?

END OF PART II CASE STUDY

ADVERTISING AGENCY GEARS UP FOR WORLD DOMINATION

The world's largest recruitment advertising company, TMP Worldwide, has undergone a major restructuring programme in a bid to stay ahead of its competitors.

The reorganisation, designed to give the company a more global outlook, has seen job changes for key members of the group's senior team. With the continued growth in Internet recruitment, TMP is keen to retain its clients as they migrate from paper-based media to online advertising.

If what the organisation has done turns out to be right, it will be able to alert a classified advertising client in, say, the UK of likely changes, such as the move towards online advertising, based on what is happening in other countries.

This will allow clients to make the best recruit-

END OF PART II CASE STUDY (CONT'D)

ment advertising choices for their companies. Strategically, this is a big step forward for the organisation, and something that their competitors cannot do.

Industry commentators have confirmed that, on a global scale, TMP has no real rival. But its rivals in the UK acknowledge that globalisation is crucial if they are to compete for the most lucrative clients.

The organisation cannot compete in its own right but recent acquisitions should help. They will be able to develop partnerships in Europe, the USA

and elsewhere. This will allow them to compete for pan-European business and become a reactive business, competing at the top.

TMP's rapid growth, which has seen the company acquire 100 recruitment businesses in 6 years, means that companies such as TMP's competitor, Riley, do not have time to develop independently into global competitors. The new TMP (monster.com) will help people to find work throughout the world.

Adapted from: Rana, E. (1999) Advertising agency gears up for world domination, *People Management*, 19 August, p16.

END OF PART II CASE STUDY QUESTIONS

1 Why are organisations vying to take control of the Internet as a recruitment mechanism?

2 What problems might TMP's monster.com meet?

3 What public persona is TMP trying to give?

4 Why did TMP restructure itself?

THESIS + ANTITHESIS = SYNTHESIS

Explore the view that recruitment is just a matter of relying on one's gut feelings.

SELF-TEST THE KEY ISSUES

1 If you or one of your staff is being accused of discriminatory recruitment practices, what sort of questions would you expect from the lawyer representing the disgruntled applicant?

2 How can line managers be convinced of the importance of job descriptions and person specifications for each post within the organisation, as a tool to increase the prospects of recruiting individuals better suited to working for the organisation?

3 You come across the following advertisement:

> ## BESTSHOP
>
> BESTSHOP is setting the pace in retailing – it is Europe's fastest growing business sector. The organisation is investing non-stop to make shopping a better experience for its customers and to create more opportunities for staff. New stores and super-stores – with masses of parking places – are being opened every week. Inside them are new products and ideas. And behind the scenes there's first-class management training and staff development to back up these exciting developments.

As a new graduate about to enter the job market, would the above descriptions inspire you to inquire after a job vacancy with BESTSHOP? If so, why; and if not, why not?

4 What recruitment and selection methods are available for:

a   unskilled jobs

b   skilled jobs

c   administration

d   sales representatives

e   professional knowledge workers

f   managerial jobs.

 ## TEAM/CLASS DISCUSSIONS

1 Debate the view that the only way to keep key staff is to pay them more money.

2 Where there is low staff morale due to poor developmental opportunities resulting in employees with two to three year's experience choosing to leave the organisation, discuss what an employer can do to address the problem.

 ## PROJECTS (INDIVIDUAL OR TEAMS)

1 The American Pizza Company runs 14 Domino's Pizza outlets, but its efforts to capitalise on the boom in home delivery sales are being hampered by two classic problems for growth firms in the consumer sector: staff recruitment and sharp swings in orders. Their daily sales volumes vary enormously and are often unpredictable and customer service suffers when sales are above or below average. Particularly, there is a huge turnover among part-time staff and network expansion plans are hindered by difficulties with recruiting full-time managers.

Len Woodhouse, Managing Director, is keen to expand but planning delays and the difficulty of recruiting new managers have held him back.

Investigate ways in which Woodhouse might overcome his recruitment difficulties and write a report for his consideration.

2 Your firm has recently opened a new production unit ten miles outside the local town where your head office is situated. Unfortunately, despite advertising nationally, you have had major problems recruiting both shop floor operators and support staff, the management team of supervisors and the works manager having been appointed through internal promotions.

Due to the difficulties in making these appointments, the factory opening has been delayed. You have been engaged to complete the recruitment exercise and prepare for a second site for next year.

Write a report that offers a remedy for the situation and avoids the pitfalls faced during the exercise.

Recommended reading

Armstrong, M. (1999) *A Handbook of Human Resource Management Practice*, London: Kogan Page

Beardwell, I. and L. Holden (1999) *Human Resource Management: A Contemporary Perspective*, London: Pitman

Bratton, J. and J. Gold (1999) *Human Resource Management: Theory and Practice*, Basingstoke: Macmillan – now Palgrave

Butt, V. and T. Butt (1992) *Invitation to Personal Construct Psychology*, London: Whurr

Dalton, P. and G. Dunnett (1992) *A Psychology for Living: Personal Construct Psychology for Professional Clients*, Chichester: John Wiley & Sons

Graham, H.T. and R. Bennett (1999) *Human Resources Management*, London: Financial Times/Pitman

Roberts, G. (1997) *Recruitment and Selection*, London: Institute of Personnel and Development

Torrington, D. and L. Hall (1998) *Human Resource Management*, London: Prentice Hall

URLs (uniform resource locators)

www.monster.com

Job search. Help with the preparation of curriculum vitae.

www.employmentservice.gov.uk

British government agency responsible for helping unemployed in England, Scotland and Wales.

www.bbc.co.uk/jobs/jobnow.htm

British Broadcasting Corporation (BBC) World of Opportunity. Gives, for example, a list of jobs available in international organisations.

careermosaic.com

CareerMosaic. International job search in comprehensive areas, including human resources. Gives help on producing curriculum vitae and preparation for interviews.

www.answers-recruitment.com

Answers to recruitment questions in the interactive and multimedia markets.

www.pricejam.com

Pricejamieson – one of the UK's foremost recruitment agencies specialising in multimedia, new media and the Internet.

www.ipl.co.uk/recruit.html

⎰ Recruitment information for the UK.⎱

www.international.recruitment.co.uk

International recruitment site.

www.graduate-recruitment.co.uk

Graduate recruitment site.

www.thomasint.com

Thomas International. Gives information related to research in careers, for example the use of benchmarking to reduce cost of selection, training and management.

Bibliography

Adams, J.S. (1965) Towards an understanding of inequity in *Journal of Abnormal and Social Psychology*, November, pp422–36

Armstrong, M. (1999) *A Handbook of Human Resource Management Practice*, London: Kogan Page

Bale, J. (1999) Wanted: 2000 Dome guides in *The Times*, 11 June 1999, p7

Boyatzis, R. (1982) *The Competent Manager*, New York: Wiley

Campbell, C.P. (1989) Job analysis for industrial training in *Journal of European Industrial Training*, **13**(2)

Clark, S. (1999) Tall order for pizza company in *Enterprise Network*, June (http://www.enterprisenetwork.co.uk/clubs/entnet/entnet/case/c—dominos-d.fhtml)

Coleman, A. (1999) Why exit polls could be the answer to keeping key staff in *Sunday Business*, Recruitment, May, p32

Cooper, D. and I.T. Robertson (1996) *The Psychology of Personnel Selection*, London: Thomson International

Crofts, P. (2000) The graduates' promise in *People Management*, 20 January, p57

Donkin, R. (1999) Wrong brand of message in *Financial Times*, 19 May, p32

Fletcher, S. (1991) *Competence-Based Assessment Techniques*, London: Kogan Page

Garavan, T.N. and M. Morley (1997) Graduate assessment centres: an empirical investigation of effectiveness in *Career Development International*, **2**(4)
(http://www/he-expert.com/members/data/rc_articles/13702DC1.htm)

Garfield, A. (1999) Ambition! The Scotsman who's banking on buying Barclays in *The Independent*, Business Review, 2 June, p1

Gribben, R. (1999) 'Wait and see' companies cut back on recruitment in *Daily Telegraph*, 18 May, p29

Institute of Personnel and Development (1999) *Recruitment, Survey Report*, May, London: Institute of Personnel and Development

Kelly, G.A. (1955) *The Psychology of Personal Constructs*, Vols 1 and 2, New York: Norton

Keuning, D. (1998) *Management: A Contemporary Approach*, London: Pitman

Littlefield, D. (1999) Pooled resources in *People Management*, 3 June, pp52–3

The Making of British Managers (The Constable and McCormick Report) (1987), London: The British Institute of Management

The Making of British Managers: A Report on Management Education, Training and Development in the United States, West Germany, France, Japan and the UK (The Handy Report) (1987), London National Development Office

Marston, P. (1997) Ford pays damages to black drivers in *Electronic Telegraph*, (613), 28 January
(http//:www.telegraph.cp.uk/et?ac=001626673941233&rtmo=gZYGwlju&atmo.../nfor28.htm)

Maund, L. (1999) *Understanding People and Organisations: An Introduction to Organisational Behaviour*, Cheltenham: Stanley Thornes

Munro-Fraser, J. (1954) *A Handbook of Employment Interviewing*, London: Macdonald & Evans

Rana, E. (1999) Advertising agency gears up for world domination in *People Management*, 19 August, p16

People Management, 17 June 1999, p21

Roberts, G. (1997) *Recruitment and Selection: A Competency Approach*, London: Institute of Personnel and Development

Rodger, A. (1952) *The Seven-Point Plan*, London: National Institute of Industrial Psychology

Standing, G. (1999) *Global Labour Flexibility: Seeking Distributive Justice*, Basingstoke: Macmillan – now Palgrave

Taylor, R. (1999) Work in progress in *Financial Times*, 2 June, p33

Tendler, S. (1999) Public upset by rude and arrogant police in *The Times*, 11 June, p16

Walsh, J. (1999) in *People Management*, June, p19

Welch, J. (1999) in *People Management*, 3 June, p15

Whitehead, M. (1999) Employers face a drastic shortage of skilled labour in *People Management*, 20 May, pp20–1

Whitehead, M. (1999) Energy efficient in *People Management*, 11 November, pp60–2

Information provision

Communication and employee involvement

After studying this chapter, you should be able to:

- APPRECIATE the importance of effective communication in the workplace.

- EVALUATE the various methods of communication available.

- DESCRIBE contemporary information technologies used by members of the workforce.

- SELECT the most appropriate methods of communication for any situation.

- APPLY the different models of communication.

- COMPARE and CONTRAST the concepts of presence, participation and involvement in the workplace.

- IDENTIFY the principal aspects of employee involvement.

- COMPARE and CONTRAST the roles of work councils and employee representative bodies.

- EXPLAIN the concept of consultation.

- APPRECIATE the position of employee involvement in human resource management (HRM).

INTRODUCTION

Framework case study

Addressing the issue of good communication

In July 1996 *People Management* carried an article written by an experienced business communicator, Octavius Black, wherein he looked at how different definitions of communication competency affected managerial effectiveness. He wrote:

> What is a communication competence? Definitions vary widely and the line between 'competency' and 'skill' is often blurred.

> Knowing how to use email is a communication competency in one major public-service organisation (see below). This is a stage ahead of organisations that simply have a competency labelled 'communication'. Others merely include communication as a vital element within

other competencies, such as team building, influencing, and coaching.

The definitions should be clear. Black describes communication competency as 'the ability to understand the choices involved in communication and to choose appropriately [in order] to influence outcomes and achieve desired objectives'. He sees communication skills as 'the ability to execute the communication in the chosen way'.

The Electricity Supply Board (ESB) in the Republic of Ireland has developed a new approach. Its definition of communication competencies for its managers is closely aligned with leadership competencies. Separate categories

reflect three different roles: as a manager of the organisation, as the manager for a district or department and as a team leader.

Competencies in the first category include 'communicating national messages in an effective way by taking collective responsibility and ownership for the content, ensuring recipients' understanding of the messages and knowing the organisation's position on difficult issues and rational for decisions'. Managers can no longer pass on company messages while distancing themselves from unpopular decisions. To be competent, managers need to create the right impact on their audience.

Adapted from: Black, O. (1996), *People Management*, 25 July, p44.

If all employees are to meet the objectives of the organisation for which they work they have to be effective and active communicators – as discussed in the Framework Case Study above. Managers need to promote collaboration, enlist support and provide clear expectations if they want to mobilise the commitment, intelligence and creativity of their employees by being effective communicators. They also need to be able to improve the skills of their colleagues, through training and appraisal, in the workplace ■ *see* Chapter 6 *and* Chapter 10 ■. It is through the process of communication that individuals interact and human and physical resources are amalgamated to produce outputs and to attain individual and organisational objectives.

see Chapter 6 *and* Chapter 10

In order to provide quality products and/or services, organisational members must fight against ineffective communication. When organisations grow profitable, they often become complacent and lose the ability to respond quickly to changes in the marketplace. Effective communication increases understanding about the need to reduce such complacency, thus allowing the employees to become more proficient communicators so that, as a result, the organisation can become a leader in its field. The way to prevent ineffective communication is to make positive changes and improvements while the organisation is still financially strong and to encourage organisational members to become effective communicators in order that the goals of the organisation may be met.

In her study of six British organisations (including British Aerospace and Ferranti) Cruise O'Brien (1999) investigated the link between achieving quality and the contribution of employee involvement (EI) and commitment. Her findings indicated that employees generally agreed to be cooperative and had a desire to take part in new process and improvement programmes. However, when they did become involved – at whatever stage their role allowed – they gave more of themselves in terms of intellectual and affective contribution, although this was not always maintained. This could well be because, in order to be committed to quality or any form of process improvement, the individual worker has to exhibit a high degree of personal involvement and increased levels of trust between the employer and the employed.

PRESENCE, PARTICIPATION AND INVOLVEMENT

Effective communication is brought about only when it is understood fully by all members of the workforce. Thus, communication requires individual involvement and participation on behalf of all organisational members. Communication, participation and individual involvement are very closely aligned as shown in Figure 5.1.

The *presence* of an individual simply means that s/he is physically there – s/he is in the immediate proximity.

When there is *participation* on behalf of the individual, then that individual raises the level of her/his physical activity and actually becomes engaged and shares in the events surrounding her/him.

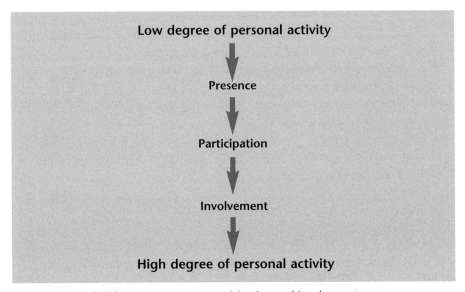

Figure 5.1 The link between presence, participation and involvement

The highest level of activity is that of *involvement* and is when the individual is not only participating but her/his behaviour and actions are making a difference to the situation – s/he is having an effect.

Employees will activate all these in a situational way; however, the common factor is that of communication because it is through the effective use of this that individuals can move from mere presence to the change agent role of involvement.

DEFINING COMMUNICATION

Communication ◄┈┈► The transference and understanding of a shared meaning.

Defining communication might appear to be simple; however, it is difficult to find a definition which is acceptable to all. Marcousé et al. (1999) define it as:

> The process by which information is exchanged between one group or person and another. (p242)

Maund (1999) states that communication is:

> the process by which two or more people exchange information and share meaning. (p58)

The Advisory, Conciliation and Arbitration Service (ACAS) (1982) in the UK takes a more organisational view by stating that communication is:

> the provision and passing of information and instructions which enable a company or any employing organisation to function efficiently and employees to be properly informed about developments. It covers information of all kinds which can be provided; the channels along which it passes; and the means of passing it. (p2)

Whether defined as interpersonal or organisational, communication is a process that involves interaction between people. Successful interpersonal communication in the workplace involves reading, listening, managing and interpreting information and interacting with all stakeholders of the organisation.

Thus, effective communication is vital to the survival of an organisation and acts as a coordinator of all activities within the organisation. Communication is a medium by which information can be shared because it is through communication that individuals express and share their individual emotions. It can be seen, therefore, that communication is not just about facts and figures but more about being a catalyst for the expression of individual emotions such as fear, displeasure, confidence and happiness.

POINTS TO PONDER

The meaning of communication is its effect.

Source: Anonymous.

It is important that an organisation is seen to be communicating as openly as circumstances allow, that employees feel they are being listened to and that their feelings, opinions and suggestions are taken into account. According to Thornhill and Saunders (1997):

> Communication will undoubtedly be more effective if it is designed to be 'two way'... to encourage individual involvement. (p87)

AREAS AND OBJECTIVES

Organisations can only carry out their business with the cooperation of individuals working together. However, most people are able to make independent decisions and take independent action. Whether working in a team, or as an individual, there is the potential for all to ignore the aims and objections of the organisation and, as a result, the organisation will go out of business. Therefore, it is essential that there is coordination among all employees so that they communicate in such a way as to work together towards meeting the organisation's mission ■ *see* Chapter 2 ■.

see Chapter 2

Effective communication is also about the passing of information from one person to another and managers are responsible for keeping employees informed about all matters which affect them. This is incorporated into what has been termed 'the theory of good communications' which is based upon three key assumptions as shown in Table 5.1.

Armstrong (1999) has some sympathy with these views but makes the valid point that they are:

> too sweeping, particularly the belief that the ultimate objectives of management and workers are necessarily identical. (p758)

That is, some employers believe that just by keeping their employees informed they can expect them to be loyal and committed. This is a simplistic approach, because an individual will have different groups to which s/he is loyal, for example family, sports team and religious affiliation. These groups compose the individual's

Table 5.1 Assumptions upon which management problems are dealt with

■ A corporate strategy will mean that all employees will know towards what objectives they have to work ■ *see* Chapter 2 ■.
Just because senior management has produced a corporate strategy with objectives and aims, there is an assumption that all employees own it and will work towards it.

see Chapter 2

■ All disagreements between employer and employee have come about because communication has been ineffective ■ *see* Chapter 2 ■.
This overlooks the issue, for example, that it may well be because the employer and employee do not own the same mission and vision and, therefore, the same objectives.

see Chapter 2

■ All dysfunctional conflict is a result of ineffective communication.
It could be because of other factors, such as poor work conditions or a lack of intrinsic motivation on behalf of the employee.

▶ **reference group** ◀ and each one affects the attitudes and beliefs of the individual in significant ways. For example, the beliefs of an atheist will affect her/his view on life in, perhaps, a different way to a Muslim (although, perhaps not). The important thing is that membership of such reference groups will affect an individual's perception of the groups with which s/he comes into contact in the workplace – management, employer, trades union, for example. The membership of reference groups will thus influence the commitment of an individual in a stronger way than might the exhortations of employers and their managers. The difficulty that employers have is that their employees might well disregard issues and information because they believe that it has nothing to do with them because it does not agree with their existing beliefs as influenced by membership of various and differing reference groups.

Reference group ◀┈┈▶ The group with which an individual identifies.

It is here that the difficulty arises with the linking of communication with involvement and participation at work. However, it is essential that employers continue to keep their employees informed on matters that concern them and to permit those employees to state their views on such matters. This needs to be done in an atmosphere of information sharing without information interpretation and is particularly difficult when change is needed – especially in areas which affect individual employees, for example legislation ■ *see* Chapter 9 *and* Chapter 10 ■. Such information has to be carried out within a communication strategy which will allow the recipient to be informed in such a way as s/he can understand the message.

see **Chapter 9** *and* **Chapter 10**

Organisations are changing their views about what information is necessary for employees. If organisations want workers to act like owners then they must have exactly the same information as employers.

COMMUNICATIONS STRATEGY

Far too often communication focuses on overcoming immediate problems – a strategy which contains too many obstacles, such as it:

■ is short term

■ incurs expense

■ falls on 'deaf ears', that is, those who do not *want* to hear.

In the contemporary workplace, organisations have moved towards perceiving communication as an integral part of all activities aimed at achieving the organisation's objectives in a stakeholder environment. Because all stakeholders differ, all communication has to be developed for different parts of the business, different niches and even for different individuals. With the new interactive communications technologies (ICTs) ■ *see* Chapter 6 ■, organisations have to consider not only how they communicate with their stakeholders, but also how the stakeholders can communicate with the organisation.

see Chapter 6

The communication process should, therefore, commence with an audit of the actual and potential interactions with all stakeholders. By doing this, there will be an assessment of the steps which everyone needs to take in order to ensure effective communication at all stages of business activities – including planning, monitoring and evaluating the activities ■ *see* Chapter 3 ■. Thus, understanding will help all employees to allocate their communication resources in a more effective way. It is through audit and analysis that organisations can make their communications more effective. Weaknesses and strengths are identified and development can be made through training ■ *see* Chapter 6 ■. However, bringing about effective communication is a complicated matter. Internal communication falls within the same strategy – it is necessary to analyse, according to Armstrong (1999), three areas:

see Chapter 3

see Chapter 6

■ what management wants to say

■ what employees want to hear

■ the problems being met in conveying or receiving information. (p759)

ORGANISATIONAL COMMUNICATION

The very heart of a business lies in its ability to exchange information and transmit meaning. The definitions given above all consider behaviour as a key aspect of effective communication and individuals do this in all environments – including their workplaces.

Therefore, organisational communication has a specific role. Bratton and Gold (1999) discuss the role of organisational communication, citing the importance of communication to both managers and employees. They discuss the work carried out by writers from the USA which strongly supports the view that:

80 per cent of the time of managers is spent on interpersonal communications. (p307)

EMPOWERMENT

There has been an increasing link between the internal nature of an organisation and its ability to effectively communicate. The more that individuals are empowered, that is, when an individual is given more autonomy, discretion and unsupervised decision-making responsibility, and encouraged to be creative and autonomous, the more important it is that communication is effective. With the latter comes more devolved decision making and, thus, an increased need for effective interpersonal communication.

According to Welch and Leighton (1997):

> The concept of HRM emphasises the enhancement of employee efficiency and productivity through the empowerment of the individual employee. (p50)

Changes in legislation and policy have made employee involvement more of an issue, for example works councils and the use of employee representatives. With this has come an increasing use of individualism – that of empowerment – through the introduction of systems for employee development. It is more likely that empowerment will be evidenced within a framework where employees work together, that is, individual and collective rights and interests in the workplace are more likely to complement rather than conflict with one another ■ *see* Chapter 10 ■.

see Chapter 10

With HRM now taking a more central role in organisational strategy ■ *see* Chapter 2 ■, the issue of communication and communication systems has increasingly become a responsibility of the HRM specialist. Naturally, the size of the organisation is a contributing factor to this specialisation and also to the sophistication of communication systems.

see Chapter 2

5.1 Activity

In a small organisation with which you are familiar, for example your corner shop or university union shop, find out what sort of communication system they use.

When organisations are small in size it is usual for communication to be very informal with verbal communication to the fore. The owner tends to become involved and intervene frequently and does not allow any employee to be autonomous – they want to have a finger in every pie.

In larger organisations there is an amalgamation of both informal and formal methods but the larger the organisation, the more likely it will be that communication systems will include the use of regulated methods, for example e-mail, notice boards and memoranda. The larger the organisation, the more likely will be the use of technological communication systems ■ *see* Chapter 6 ■. However, most larger organisations use a mixture of informal and formal communication systems.

see Chapter 6

5.2 Activity

Consider a large organisation – one which is national or international. What do you think their communication system is like?

Whatever systems are used within an organisation – from informal, ad hoc to the use of organisational communications specialists – a key understanding is that if communication in organisations is to be effective it has to:

■ take place frequently and regularly

■ be ▶ **dyadic** ◀

■ include all employees.

▶ Communication between two people.   ◀┈┈▶ **Dyadic**

A study of the theory-in-literature highlights some key issues related to communication in organisations which are shown in Table 5.2.

Writers in communication – as in other areas of HRM – have their own agendas and will concentrate on those areas which specifically either interest them or with which they specifically relate as researchers and experts. However, as Bratton and Gold (1999) discuss, there are three identifiable approaches to organisational communications:

■ *Functionalist*
  The ▶ **functionalist approach** ◀ stresses the purpose of communication. This is a view that considers communication to be simply a means by which information is sent from a transmitter (sender) to a receiver (recipient).

▶ An approach which stresses the purpose of something, that is, its purpose is determined by its use.   ◀┈┈▶ **Functionalist approach**

Table 5.2 Key issues related to communication in organisations

  ■ Communication is a basic component of all organisational activities

  ■ When considering corporate strategy, communication should be a key component

  ■ If top management is not committed to organisational strategies, then communication will not be effective – they have to take the initiative

  ■ There is a strong link between communication strategy and effective management

  ■ The most effective leaders are strong communicators because they have followers

  ■ The most effective communication is face to face combined with written follow-up

  ■ All messages should be in the appropriate medium to be understood by the recipient

  ■ The information contained in the message must be of relevance to the employee

  ■ Communication systems can be made more effective if individuals are trained in communication systems and skills

  ■ The message must be consistent with the action taken by the sender

■ *Interpretivist*

The ▶ **interpretivist approach** ◀ attempts to give meaning to the communication. It involves the intervention of a human being who does not act in a stated or conventional way and, therefore, the interpretation of the communication cannot be predicted.

Interpretivist approach
An approach which attempts to give meaning to something by clarifying or explaining the intention of the issue.

■ *Critical*

The ▶ **critical approach** ◀ is a later view which takes into account that views propounded by a capitalist environment are usually present in the business world.

Critical approach
An approach which takes the view that there should be an exposure of the often hidden, and highly persuasive, power that contemporary organisations have over their employees.

MODELS OF COMMUNICATION

No single model of communication takes into account all the elements that may be involved in a specific situation – regardless of the chosen communication medium. Communication models are simplified attempts to show how the complex concept of communication is carried out. All models have three components:

■ the *source*, which can be individual or group

■ the *message*, which may be written, a gesture or electronically processed

■ the *receiver*, which could be an individual or a group.

There are a number of communication models posited by researchers in the field each of which evolved from its predecessor. The key ones are:

■ Shannon and Weaver (1949)

■ Schramm (1954)

■ McLuhan (1964)

■ Jablin et al. (1987)

■ Clampitt (1991).

SHANNON AND WEAVER (1949)

The first, and most simplistic, model of communication was designed by Shannon and Weaver (1949), given in Figure 5.2. It tends towards the mechanistic, as was

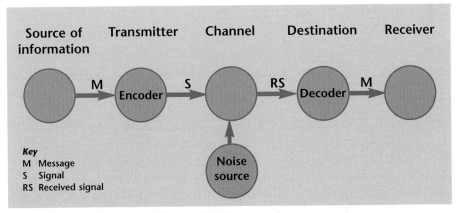

Figure 5.2 The Shannon and Weaver (1949) model of communication

common in the 1940s and 50s when scientific management was still to the fore in organisations ■ *see* Chapter 1 ■.

see Chapter 1

Shannon and Weaver (1949) developed the model having been asked to work with the Bell Telephone Company in the USA. Telephone engineers at this time were not able to understand how to transmit the electrical impulses required for the message to be transmitted and how they could be sent most efficiently from one place to another. This explains the mechanistic nature of the model. However, it began to be accepted as a suitable model for all communication processes.

In any communication process there are four key factors:

- message transmission
- encoding and decoding
- communication channels
- feedback.

Message transmission

The individual sender has some sort of concept concerning the message which is to be shared with others and such information has to be ▶ **encoded** ◀. Such an idea can be in the form of words, symbols, sounds or expressions that can be transmitted through an appropriate medium. Such transmission may involve face-to-face inter-action, written messages, drawings, digital formats or any other method of getting the information to the receiver.

▶ To convert words or ideas into symbols or code to form a message. ◀┄┄▶ Encode

The message is received through the human senses, and is ▶ **decoded** ◀ by the receiver. However, the receiver may interpret the message in a different way from

Decode ◀┈┈▶ The process by which the receiver of a message interprets the symbols contained in the message and determines what such symbols refer to.

that which the sender wished. This would result in ineffective communication, that is, the message has not been interpreted by the receiver as the sender wished it to be.

Therefore, for the communication to be effective, both the sender and the receiver must understand the code system being used. The sender can encode, and the receiver can only decode, according to the experience each one has. That is, they must have had similar experiences for the communication to be effective. If the sender uses information related to the receiver's past experience, then it is likely that the message will be encoded accurately.

However, such shared experience does not guarantee that the message will produce the desired response: the message is more than the code system. For example:

■ if the sender does not have adequate or accurate information the message generated has little chance of producing the desired response/s

■ it is the receiver, not the sender, who determines that the message is encoded efficiently

■ the attitudes, experiences and motivations of the receiver determine whether the message is decoded in a way that corresponds to the intentions of the sender.

Encoding and decoding

Both parties to the communication encode and decode. Inputs always affect outputs because individuals are constantly encoding information from the environment, interpreting it and decoding it. As information passes through an individual, it is changed by the interpretation which, in turn, changes the individual.

Communication channels

The channel is a vital part of the communication process in that the choice of an inappropriate channel may mean that the message is not acted upon in the manner the sender would wish. For example, in face-to-face communication it is considered by some that the non-verbal cues are as important as the verbal message itself. That is, facial expressions, gestures and intonation give the verbal message more meaning – this is discussed later on in this chapter.

Channels of communication gain importance because of two issues:

■ the increased experience of a particular individual

■ the increased sensitivity of non-verbal communication.

Single-channel communications are seldom used. In a speech communication, sound may well be the primary channel but non-verbal communication adds other

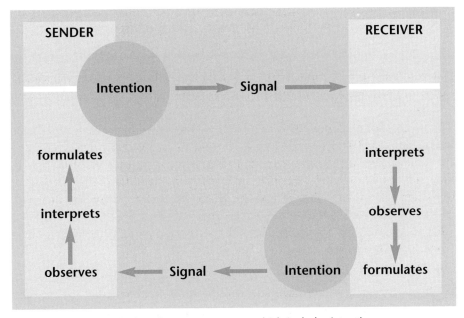

Figure 5.3 Communication shown as a process which includes intention

channels as do environmental factors such as ventilation, lighting, chair placement and the nature of the audience.

Feedback

A key criticism of the Shannon and Weaver Model (1949) is that it does not consider the role of feedback. The receiver's response to the message constitutes the ▶ **feedback loop** ◀ of the communication as portrayed in Figure 5.3. The receiver verifies the message through feedback to the sender which indicates that the message has been understood – usually by carrying out the action requested.

▶ The pathway that permits two-way feedback. ◀┈┈▶ Feedback loop

Figure 5.3 shows the communication process as it interfaces with the intentions of both the sender and the receiver.

SCHRAMM (1954)

This model, shown in Figure 5.4, concentrates on the principal participants in the communication process, highlighting the place of both the sender and the receiver as senders of messages – this is the first, although implied, consideration of feedback.

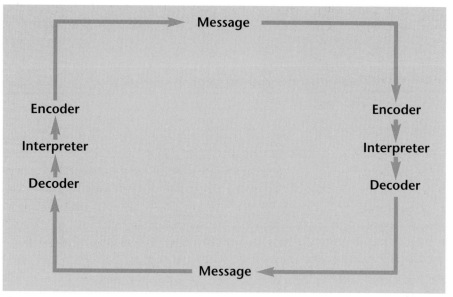

Figure 5.4 The Schramm (1954) model of communication

MCLUHAN (1964)

Most communication models indicate that all messages are prone to disturbance and distortion and theory-in-literature tends to concentrate on the issue of noise distortion, that is, the message can be upset by the surrounding noise. McLuhan (1964) has called this model 'the medium is the message'. As can be seen from Figure 5.4, the message is very much dominated by the kind and type of channel and/or medium used. For example, in the political arena when party political broadcasts are shown on the television, it is often the physically attractive who gain the support – this is visual imagery and it has a very powerful effect on the success of the message. It can influence the behaviour of the observer more than the message itself.

JABLIN ET AL. (1987)

As time went on, the basic communication process model began to be developed into something a little more complicated. However, there was a move away from the drawing of visual models to an attempt actually to define the complexity of the communication process. Until the 1980s, the communication models were based on ▸ **empirical** ◂ studies and thus lacked the stringent theoretical base required for rigorousness. Krone et al. (1987) were the first to make a significant contribution to this gap. They focused on four factors which, although comprehensive, were

Empirical ◂┈▸ Derived from or related to experiment and observation rather than theory.

rather sparing in content. However, this does not detract from the influence that their work had in this field. The four areas they concentrated on were:

■ mechanistic

■ psychological

■ interpretive–symbolic

■ systems–interactive

and were reported in detail by Jablin et al. (1987).

The *mechanistic* perspective concentrates solely on the actual channel of communication and the transmission of the message – it supports the Shannon and Weaver (1949) model. They discussed this as a linear model stating that A actually causes B, that is, there was a causality in the communication. The view was that the message would be distorted because of surrounding influences, for example noise. An example here would be when an employee is attempting to take down a message over the telephone while colleagues are having a team meeting around her/him.

The mechanistic form of communication is found in organisations where there is a strong hierarchy and a tradition of communication where orders and information are passed down from the top to the bottom.

The *psychological* perspective considers how the individual's characteristics – such as her/his personality, attitude, mood and physiological condition – impact on the receipt and consequent interpretation of the message. An individual will filter out those parts of the message which do not fit her/his psychological state. This is particularly apparent when the message is being encoded and decoded. How an individual perceives her/himself within the organisation, for example her/his role in the hierarchy, and power base, will affect how s/he receives and interprets messages.

Theory-in-literature frequently highlights the area of management communication. Managers appear to think that they communicate very well with their subordinates and that it is the latter who are unable to construe the meaning of such messages. Not surprisingly, the subordinates have the opposing view considering that their managers and supervisors are poor communicators and that they, as subordinates, feedback more to their superiors than vice versa. This has to do with the perceptual differences of individuals because no two individuals see, and thus interpret, the same event in the same way.

5.3 Activity

Reflect on a situation when you have attempted to communicate but have found this difficult because of interference. What did you do to avoid the interference?

Individuals bring with them a ▶ **perceptual paradox** ◀ to the process of perception. Individual perceptual sets provide a necessary framework for selecting, organising and interpreting experience, and without them there would be no benchmarks against which to measure and understand, in this case, communication. However, they can also serve to distort and limit what is perceived and how it is interpreted. Perceptual sets may set up strong barriers against experience which challenges the individual's key values and the strength of these barriers is dependent on the degree to which those perceptual sets sustain the fundamental sense of identity and meaning. Experience which threatens this fundamental sense of self is likely to be ignored or rejected.

Perceptual paradox ◀····▶ Arises from the fact that individuals bring with them a host of prior assumptions and expectations to the process of perception.

An example here would be if the top management decided that the workforce had to carry out a certain activity. The manager who has to pass the information on to her/his subordinates might well distort the message from the senior management in order to match it with the anticipated perceptions of the subordinates so that there is likely to be less dispute and they will receive the required strategy.

The *interpretive–symbolic perspective* is when there is a consideration of the social aspects of communication. Jablin et al. (1987) believe that the more able a communicator an individual is, the more s/he will create her/his own social reality. This means that such individuals will have shared meanings of what is a common event or action. Thus, individuals do not just respond to the information but develop it in a social environment and because of this, the social context will change.

The comment here is related to the importance of culture in the process of communication because it will make a difference to how an individual will interpret messages with a shared meaning and, thus, impact on the culture of the organisation as a whole.

When a new employee starts work, s/he will quickly learn 'how things are done' and construe how to become one of the workers. Should s/he carry out a function in a different way or have different ideas than those of her/his fellow workers, this could result in hostility and be perceived as threatening to the other workers because it does not fit in with the pervasive culture.

Messages which are passed from one person to another tend to get distorted.

5.4 Activity

When you are with a group of friends, play the game Chinese Whispers. You think of a message and whisper it into the ear of the person to your right who then whispers what s/he hears to the person to her/his right and so on until the final message comes back to you.

Is it the same message you sent at the beginning?

SCENARIO 5.1

The *Challenger* space shuttle disaster

The causes of most publicised disasters such as the *Challenger* space shuttle crash can be traced to organisational factors such as failure in management process, as well as (if not contributing to) technical problems. The *Challenger* disaster is a case in point.

Challenger was launched on 28 January 1986 from Cape Canaveral, Florida, USA and 73 seconds into its flight it exploded. All seven members of the crew, including a civilian school teacher (Christa MacAuliffe), were killed.

The post-accident inquiry evidenced that the physical cause of the explosion was an O-ring rubber seal that failed to do its job because of the freezing overnight temperatures at the launch site.

The president of the USA, who was leading the Congress, established a commission whose job it was to investigate the causes of the accident. It found that one of the causes of the accident was flawed decision making. There had been concerns about the safety of the shuttle and this information had not adequately been passed from the launch base engineers, who worked for Morton Thiokol, to the NASA controllers. The Thiokol engineers argued for the cancellation of the launch because they felt that the O-rings would not stand the pressure at the launch time temperatures. However, they were pressured by their superiors to keep their dissent quiet.

Everyone concerned with the launch wanted it to be successful because the future programme budgets from Congress hinged on it and the past record of success led to overconfidence, and various pieces of information were withheld from key individuals. Consequently, the launch had to be seen to be successful in all respects – including lift-off at the time arranged because the world's media were watching and the programme could not lose face in an international arena. The latter factors overrode those of safety and the resulting disaster certainly put an end to the abiding objectives and those of the programme as a whole.

So while the physical cause of the accident was an O-ring seal, the actual disaster was a result of flawed communication and decision-making practices.

There is a very well-known and well-documented story which is said to have taken place during World War I (1914–18) where there was a platoon of officers and men settled into a trench in France when the captain asked the soldier next to him to pass on the following message to the soldier next to him and then on down the line to headquarters:

We're going to advance. Send reinforcements.

By the time the message had passed along the line of soldiers in the trench and was given to the staff at headquarters, it had become distorted to:

We're going to a dance. Send three and fourpence!*

[* Pre-British decimalistion (1971) worth 19 pence; that is 'old pence' in pound, shillings and pence.]

At first investigation, the *systems–interactive perspective* has similarities with the mechanistic perspective discussed above. Like the latter, it has its emphasis on the external behaviours of the communicators by investigating the frequency and manner in which communication is carried out. However, an individual does not *do* communication, s/he actually participates in it.

Table 5.3 Alternative perspectives to organisational communication (after Jablin et al., 1987, p33)

PERSPECTIVE	WHERE IT OCCURS	CHARACTERISTICS AND/OR IMPLICATIONS
Mechanistic	Channel and message transmission	Focus on: ■ Conveying of information and accuracy of message reception ■ Sending and receiving is linear ■ Lack of meaning in the communication means it does not have the human touch ■ Simplistic
Psychological	Conceptual filters	■ Receiver actively interprets the message ■ The emphasis is on the intentions and the human aspects of the communication
Interpretive–symbolic	Role taking	■ Consideration is given to the individual's role regarding self and the rest of the team ■ There is a cultural context ■ Emphasis on symbols and 'shared' meaning
Systems–interactive	Sequences of communication behaviour	■ Patterns of feedback ■ Management of conflict ■ Development of work teams ■ Communication has become an evolving system ■ Focus is on types of message function, sequence and behaviours

This particular approach is used in organisations in an attempt to deal with dysfunctional conflict because it examines what individuals *do* in response to communication.

The four perspectives put forward by Krone et al. (1987) are summarised in Table 5.3.

CLAMPITT (1991)

A further key study is that of Clampitt (1991) who has put together a model of communication based on the assumptions made by managers within organisations. This model comprises three approaches:

■ arrow

■ circuit and

■ dance.

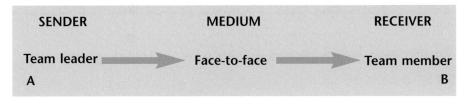

Figure 5.5 An example of the arrow approach

The *arrow approach* aligns with Shannon and Weaver's (1949) approach to communication because it is concerned with the transport of messages that have clarity and, as such, are unhindered by disturbances such as noise. Figure 5.5 gives an example of the arrow approach.

In Figure 5.5 the team leader (A) puts together instructions which s/he wants a team member (B) to receive. This is sent by a medium (in this example face-to-face) to the team member. The arrow is the direction of the communication from (A) to (B). Clampitt (1991) holds the view that every form of communication has within it a number of assumptions – the team leader's assumptions are given in Table 5.4.

It is possible that there could be considerable differences between the effectiveness of the communication as perceived by the team leader and the team member. It will have any number of underlying assumptions within it and the team member will also have her/his own perceptions and assumptions. An example here would be when the team member does not share the underlying assumptions of the team leader (either knowingly or unknowingly) and this results in a communication breakdown. It is usual in this situation for the team leader to blame the team member.

The *circuit approach* forms a cyclical model by extending the arrow to the circle. Individuals who utilise this sort of communication use feedback to form a loop and in doing so stress the importance of:

- feedback over response

- relationship over content

- connotation over denotations

- understanding over compliance.

Table 5.4 Evaluation of arrow team leader's assumptions (after Clampitt, 1991, p3)

COMMUNICATION EFFECTIVENESS	UNDERLYING ASSUMPTIONS
Being able to put precisely and clearly thoughts into words	What happens to be clear and precise to one person is clear and precise to another
Speaking with credibility and authority	Credibility is something the speaker possesses and not something given to the speaker by the audience
Getting the results I want by talking to my people	Communication is essentially a one-way activity

5.5

Activity

Give an example of how a manager can verbally apportion blame to a subordinate for incorrectly interpreting an instruction.

In the circuit approach, communication is considered to be a dyadic process involving both the sender and the receiver in an active way.

This approach aligns with the Schramm (1954) model of communication discussed earlier because both emphasise the two-way process of communication. It is also in line with the contemporary methods of management such as ▶ **total quality management (TQM)** ◀. TQM is a philosophy which makes continuous improvement a responsibility for all employees – hence it is closely linked with effective communication. It requires of all the workforce (including the CEO and her/his executive team) a dedication to meeting stakeholder's needs and expectations. Along with the introduction of BPR, which is a label given to the redesign of an organisation, it may include breaking away from outdated rules and assumptions that underlie how tasks should be performed. A key principle is the elimination or prevention of barriers which could themselves create a distance between

see Chapter 2

employees and their customers ■ *see* Chapter 2 ■.

Total quality management ◀┈┈▶ A philosophy that brings about the integration of techniques and quality control in line with an organisation's corporate strategy with the intention of providing continuous high-quality goods and/or services.

An individual who uses the circuit approach recognises that there will, inevitably, be occasions when communication is not successful, that is, the receiver does not behave in the way that the message sender wanted her/him to.

The circuit approach user will bring with her/him – as with other systems – baggage and perceptions. These assumptions are shown in Table 5.5.

5.6

Activity

List four examples of why communication might break down between a team leader and a team member.

Table 5.5 Evaluation of circuit team leader's assumptions (after Clampitt, 1991, p3)

COMMUNICATION EFFECTIVENESS	UNDERLYING ASSUMPTIONS
Listening to team members in order to keep them content	The goal of organisational communication is job satisfaction
Being sensitive to team members in order to adapt messages to each member	Messages are exclusively interpreted in the context of interpersonal relationships
Being open and understanding	Openness is useful in all circumstances Understanding is always more acceptable than ambiguity

Like all the models of communication, the circuit approach has the potential weaknesses given in Table 5.5. However, it is a live model because it concentrates on the interaction between individuals and the key aspect of empathy. This will bring about communication success in the workplace because empathy works only in a culture of high trust. Difficulties will arise, however, if organisations who have a culture of low trust and lack of empathy believe that they can use these approaches just to bring about change.

The *dance approach* is the final approach to communication put forward by Clampitt (1991) and is the one into which the other two have evolved. As a consequence, it is the best approach to effective communication in the workplace. Clampitt (1991) is fond of using ▶ **metaphors** ◀ in his writings and makes no apologies for using the word 'dance'. The word dance suggests many activities.

▶ A figure of speech in which a word or phrase is applied to an object or action that it does ◀····▶ Metaphor
not literally denote in order to imply a resemblance, for example 'S/he is a tiger in the boardroom.'

5.7

Activity

List as many descriptors as you can for the word dance – the first one is given as an example:

1 involves patterns

Although dance has many parts to it, one of the key things is that, according to Clampitt (1991), it is central to the happenings of all generations – it is a community activity. No dance can ever be captured in its entirety ever again and like communication, it can be a high or a low level of human expression.

Clampitt (1991) is very fond of the dance metaphor because it helps to illustrate how complex and diverse communication and the communication process are and, therefore, trying to simplify the explanations of communication is foolhardy. Communication will only be successful of the sender has goals but there is no one way of measuring if the communication has been effective – to state that the receiver does what the sender wants is simplistic because other factors come into play.

Within the workplace a person can be an effective communicator by telling, for example, the employees what s/he feels they want to hear when, perhaps, the state of the business contradicts the message.

Talk to any professional dancer and they will tell you that dance is governed by rules – they have to obey the choreographer and the rhythm of the music and certain steps and movements are not acceptable – or, conversely, acceptable. Clampitt (1991) will argue that it is the same with communication – as identified in the rules for effective listening discussed below.

Therefore, communication is active and behavioural since its success will depend upon the intentions of both the sender and the receiver – intention is feedback. As such, effective communication depends upon the interaction between the sender and the receiver. However, this interaction is further complicated by other elements in the communication process. To communicate effectively an individual needs to

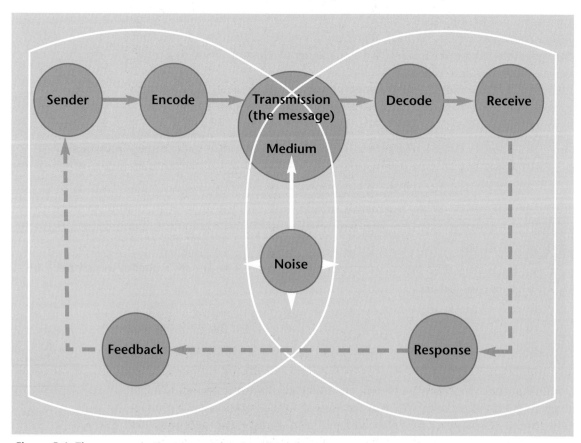

Figure 5.6 The communication process showing all its elements

SCENARIO 5.2

Motorola Wings

understand how communication works and the whole process has nine elements to it as can be seen in the model development in Figure 5.6.

As can be seen from Figure 5.6 there are two distinct aspects to the communication system (the sender and the receiver). The next identifiable aspects are the major tools used in the communication process (the message and the medium). The four other key communication functions come into position (encoding, decoding, response, feedback) which are then affected by noise. These various aspects can be exampled by looking at an advertisement for Motorola Wings in Scenario 5.2.

- the *sender* is Motorola

- *encoding* has been done by putting the thoughts into a symbolic form; the Motorola advertisement has an assemblage of words, pictures and illustrations which have been put together to produce an intended message

- the *message* constitutes the set of symbols which is transmitted by the sender; the Motorola logo, the Motorola WINGS and the mobile phone v3688

- the *medium* comprises the communication channel used and in this case it is *Cosmopolitan* magazine

- *decoding* is the way that the receiver assigns meaning to the message and in this case the consumer will read the Motorola advertisement and will interpret the words, illustrations and pictures it contains

- the *receiver* is the person getting the message from the sender – in this case it is probably a young woman who is reading the Motorola advertisement

- the reactions of the receiver (the *response*) could comprise any number of permutations, for example the consumer is more informed about the product, s/he remembers the symbols – or some of them, or particularly likes or dislikes the advertisement in general

- the *feedback* is what the receiver will send back to the sender; in this case, the number of sales which come about as a result of the advertisement, or consumers will correspond with Motorola and inquire about the mobile telephone or other products

- *noise* is an example of some unplanned distortion to the message; in this case, the receiver may have been distracted while reading the magazine and turned over the page before reading it.

The best message will result in action and so will consist of words and other symbols which are familiar to the receiver. In the case of the job advertisement you will choose for the activity below, the ability to highlight the elements will depend upon the familiarity the activist had with the words and symbols contained within the advertisement. The broader the experience with job advertisements, the more effective was the advertisement.

However, the receiver may not always share the sender's field of experience, for example the advertisement may be couched in unfamiliar jargon. However, to

5.8

Activity

Find an advertisement for a job which you might like to obtain. Identify the nine key components of the communication message and give an example of each.

communicate effectively, the sender must understand the receiver's field of experience. The model given in Figure 5.6 is an effective model since it indicates several key factors to effective communication. Senders must know what audiences they wish to meet and what responses they want to receive and, therefore, they have to be very good at encoding messages that take into account the target audience which has to decode them. The messages have to be sent through media that reach the target receivers, and they must also develop feedback channels in order to assess the receiver's response to the message.

METHODS OF COMMUNICATION

There are three primary methods of communication used in the workplace:

- written
- oral
- non-verbal.

Frequently, these methods are combined to provide reinforcement of the message and the choice of method depends on the:

- audience
- nature of the message
- urgency (or confidentiality)
- costs of transmission.

WRITTEN COMMUNICATION

There are many kinds of written communication used within business organisations:

- the *letter* is a formal communication with an individual outside the organisation
- the *memorandum* (memo) is usually addressed to one person within an organisation and normally addresses a single recipient
- the *report* generally summarises the progress/results of a project and often provides information which supports decision making
- *manuals* tell staff how to operate machines and give information about organisational processes and procedures
- *forms* are standardised documents on which information is reported
- *notices* which appear on strategically placed notice boards
- *newsletters* which are circulated to staff and contain information about the organisation and its activities

see Chapter 6

■   *electronic transmission* through digital methods, for example e-mail ■ *see* Chapter 6 ■.

POINTS TO PONDER

It is not difficult to get hold of reports and computer printouts. The difficulty lies in getting summarised information that an individual can use.

ORAL COMMUNICATION

This is the most common form of communication and is pervasive within most organisations. Conversations can be formal or informal and take place in, for example:

■   informal situations

■   the process of carrying out tasks

■   formal speeches and presentations.

Oral communication is a powerful medium of communication because it includes not only the speaker's words but also the changes in pitch, volume, tone and speed. These are the cues to the listener so that s/he can interpret the message. The receiver also interprets oral messages in context, taking into account any previous communications and, maybe, the reactions of other receivers of the oral transmission. Frequently it is the top echelons of management who set the tone for oral communication throughout the organisation.

POINTS TO PONDER

An individual who does not want to relinquish her/his turn in talking to other individuals never puts full stops at the end of sentences. By doing this, s/he is able to control the conversation itself and the responses to it.

Such people may also interrupt other people's responses that disagree with their own viewpoint.

NON-VERBAL COMMUNICATION

Most forms of communication are accompanied by some sort of non-verbal communication that includes all the elements associated with human communication not expressed orally or in writing. These are key issues and are dealt with in detail later in this chapter.

ELECTRONIC INFORMATION PROCESSING

Kanter (1997) confirms that the use of technology has brought about changes in communication methods in the world of work ■ *see* Chapter 6 ■. She states that by:

see Chapter 6

linking everyone up by computers, you encourage the flow of ideas from the margin. In opening up the lines of communication, the centre is saying 'Hey, we want to hear from you'. (p20)

She believes that, although times have changed, the core of her message has not, stating:

I think we already know a lot about what should be done. Now managers just have to go to it. (p20)

However, changes in the workplace are happening so rapidly that it is often difficult for members of the workforce to keep abreast of innovations – particularly those based on new technologies, such as computerised information processing systems, new types of telecommunication systems and combinations of these. Individuals now send and receive communications to their computer terminals. Additionally, a whole new industry is developing in the long-distance transmission of data between computers.

The 'office of the future' is now here. Most offices have a facsimile (fax) machine, a photocopier and personal computers linked into a single integrated system with access to numerous databases and electronic mail (e-mail) systems. There is now in existence what is known as the 'intelligent office' – incorporating into ever-changing patterns of job design such concepts as ▶ **hot desking** ◀, ▶ **hotelling** ◀ and open plan offices. According to Brown (1996) workers are being weaned from the territorial need to have a desk of their own while managers are making economic savings through such systems. With the rise of electronic communication systems, people have much less need to be together in a central location.

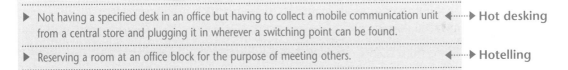

▶ Not having a specified desk in an office but having to collect a mobile communication unit ◀·····▶ Hot desking
from a central store and plugging it in wherever a switching point can be found.

▶ Reserving a room at an office block for the purpose of meeting others. ◀·····▶ Hotelling

The electronic office links managers, clerical employees, professional workers and sales personnel in a communication network that uses a combination of computerised data storage, retrieval and transmission systems. New information processing and transmission technologies have created new media, symbols, message transmission methods and networks for organisational communication. Such methods of communication have made a radical change to work and personal relationships and have disrupted the familiar ways of accomplishing tasks. There are the potential hazards of information overload, loss of records in a 'paperless' office and the dehumanising effects of electronic equipment.

The fully integrated communication information office system (the electronic office) links people in a communication network through a combination of computers and electronic transmission systems. The effects of such systems have not yet been fully realised and developments are still continuing to bring about different systems of electronic communication. Such changes have had a considerable impact on organisational behaviour and managers have to appreciate that there are individuals who have a specific viewpoint on the matter which may affect effective communication. These views are likely to fall into one of two camps. First, there are the ▶ **technophiles** ◀. The view here is that everyone will benefit because information and communication technology (ICT) has the potential to:

- enhance the speed and quality of organisational decision making

- increase transparency, thus making information available to more people

- facilitate the free flow of information

- increase the accuracy of information.

Technophiles ◀┈▶ Individuals who believe that all new technology must be an asset to management.

Second, there are ▶ **technosceptics** ◀ who believe that ICT can:

- increasingly formalise the organisation's culture

- being about a reduction in face-to-face communication

- increase the centralisation of power and control.

Technosceptics ◀┈▶ Individuals who identify any number of organisational problems each time a new technology is introduced into the workplace.

The new commonly used ICT is e-mail which, at its inception, was considered to be the answer to all ills related to communication in the workplace. Reasons given included that it:

- permits the free flow of communication

- makes information available at the press of a key

- provides easy and quick contact with individuals and groups.

E-mail lacks the intimacy and powerfulness of face-to-face communication but users have developed compensatory activities for this by using jargon and abbreviations (smilies) to express emotion on the computer screen, including, for example, :-) to represent happiness, :-(for unhappiness, and :-O for shock. Nowadays, these are only used by new users of e-mail or text messaging on a mobile phone.

It is e-mail's lack of intimacy which has brought about difficulties for managers. This psychological distancing has evolved into distrust by users in the information received because individuals tend to seek verbal verification of information, reply to e-mails less promptly than to messages received over voice mail and senior managers tend to disseminate bad news, such as dismissal notices, rather than good/positive news through e-mail.

While there are these two views on the role of ICTs, most users consider that e-mail is not suitable for any communication which relates to coaching, mentoring, appraisal or discipline.

Corbett (1997) reports that e-mail has brought about an increase in gossip in the workplace. Verbal gossip might have a positive role within the workplace, for example in providing new members of the organisation with an induction into organisational culture as well as acting as a means of allowing team members to stay together by providing a means for the alleviation of stress. It follows, therefore, that e-mail gossip has increased in popularity as e-mail itself has become more popular. The advantage to managers of e-mail gossip over the conventional grapevine is that it can be technically monitored.

COMMUNICATION NETWORKS

Communication is about the satisfaction of an individual's felt needs, and it uses available tools to affect the behaviour of others and also to achieve objectives – the individual's and the organisation's. Regardless of the behaviour required from a receiver, the individual is attempting to gain a behavioural response in order to satisfy her/his felt needs. Consequently, effective communication will only be brought about if the receiver knows what the sender means and thus reacts (behaves) in the way the sender requires.

Therefore, communication is a social system. What were once simple communications systems, for example individuals used to be given the information they needed to work with others within the same system, have now developed into more complicated social systems composed of small group communication networks within a larger organisational network. Such systems allow for the structural flow and content of communication and also support the organisational structure itself. Communication also supports the organisational culture, beliefs, attitudes and value systems that enable an organisation to operate.

MANAGING COMMUNICATION

Messages are not always understood because the feedback from the receiver was not as the sender desired – this is indicated in Figure 5.6 with the introduction of 'noise' to the model. The degree of correspondence between the message intended by the sender and the message understood by the receiver is called ▶ **communication fidelity** ◀. Fidelity can be diminished anywhere in the communication process, from source to feedback. Additionally, organisations have characteristics that impede the flow of information such as their culture or belief system.

> ▶ The degree of correpondence between the message intended by the sender and the message understood by the receiver. ◀┈┈▶ **Communication fidelity**

Such barriers to communication block or significantly distort successful communications. Effective managerial communication skills help to overcome some, but not all, barriers to communication in organisations – such barriers may only be temporary and can be overcome. The first step is to be aware and recognise this fact. Managers should always remember that it is estimated that individuals only remember 20 per cent of what they hear, but probably more than 50 per cent of what they see *and* hear. Worse, managers tend to make assumptions if there is no communication. Five significant barriers to effective communication are:

- physical separation
- status difference
- gender difference
- cultural diversity
- language and meaning.

Physical separation

The physical separation of people in the workplace poses a significant barrier to effective communication. The rise of the technological capacity of allowing an ever-increasing percentage of the workforce to carry out its responsibilities away from the workplace is not in itself a barrier to effective communication, but the resistance to such a change is. Such technology is not as information rich as face-to-face communication. Periodic face-to-face interactions can help physical separation problems because interactions such as these give more clues in the form of non-verbal cues. The richer the communication, the more the chance that the message will be correctly understood.

Status difference

Status differences are related to power and thus affect the effectiveness of communication. Effective interpersonal communication skills may make managers and supervisors and their subordinates more approachable and reduce the risks of problems related to status differences. The move towards flatter, leaner organisations may indicate fewer hierarchical differences but new information technologies and the rise of teamwork and ▶ **cell structures** ◀ provide another way of overcoming status difference barriers because they encourage the formation of non-hierarchical

see Chapter 4

working relationships ■ *see* Chapter 4 ■.

Cell structure ◀····▶ A small team which makes entire products or provides an entire service from conception to after-sales service.

Technology used in communication and employee involvement tends to incorporate status differences. For example, this book, like most texts in business, refers to employer/employee and manager/subordinate.

Gender difference

Communication barriers can be explained in part by differences in conversation styles. Some believe that women benefit from approaches and techniques for communication different from those used by their male colleagues. For example, women tend to prefer to converse face to face, whereas men are comfortable sitting alongside and concentrating on some focal point in front of them, for example a report or visual display unit (VDU). Hence, conversation style differences may result in a failure of communication between men and women. Male–female conversation is really cross-cultural communication. It is important for all to appreciate that an understanding of gender-specific differences in conversational style is a key to effective communication. The latter can be improved further if each seeks clarification of the other's meaning rather than freely interpreting meaning from one's own frame of reference.

Cultural diversity

Cultural diversity and international patterns of behaviour can confuse effective communication ■ *see* Chapter 12 ■. There are important international differences in work-related value which have implications for motivation, leadership and teamwork in organisations. People work to habitual patterns of behaviour within organisations and outsiders working to a different cultural pattern of behaviour are outside effective communication. Such differences can be overcome by increasing awareness and sensitivity. This is dealt with later on in this chapter.

see Chapter 12

Language and meaning

Meanings are in the minds of individuals. Language is central to effective communication and can pose a barrier if its use obscures meaning and distorts intent – it is a highly developed and complex system. Most of the desirable and undesirable qualities of language result from that characteristic. No necessary connection exists between the language symbol and what it symbolises, for example it might be said that something is beautiful when the opposite is what is actually what is believed. The use of jargon and technical language can convey precise meaning only if all parties to the communication are familiar with the meanings of such techniques. Physical things have both a functional value and a symbolic value. The latter is often what leads the individual to accept or reject a specific object. For example, when choosing a new car the decision is not always based on economic and/or functional grounds – one also needs to take into account the symbolic value of a 'prestigious image' car.

TOWARDS EFFECTIVE COMMUNICATION

In today's flatter organisations with their increased use of groups, teams and cell structures, there are now more people in supervisory roles and with such roles comes an increased need to be effective in the communication process. Effective communicators tend to have expertise in common skills and tend to be:

- expressive speakers

- empathic listeners

- persuasive leaders

- sensitive to the feelings of others

- managers of information.

Expressive speakers tend to speak accurately and clearly and are not afraid to express their thoughts, ideas, and feelings in public. They tend towards ▶ **extroversion** ◀, and their subordinates know exactly where they stand with such people.

Extroversion ◀····▶ Behaviour which indicates that the individual is energised by interaction with other people. An extrovert is an outgoing or sociable person.

Expressive speakers tend to be *empathic listeners* because they use reflective listening skills (see later section) to the limit and are thus responsive to all. Apart from hearing the words of others, they tend to be able to hear the feelings and emotions of the actual message being transmitted and not just the content and ideas of that message. Such people are very approachable and listen to suggestions – and complaints.

POINTS TO PONDER
Certain nationalities, for example North Americans and the British, are not happy with silence because they feel uncomfortable and sometimes find it a source of embarrassment. Such gaps are often filled up with chatter.

The most effective managers and supervisors are *persuasive leaders* because they can exercise power and influence over others in order to achieve the organisation's objectives. They encourage others to do their best and achieve results; they avoid autocratic styles and instead favour allowing their team members to decide for themselves. There is a situational exception to this – when there is an emergency, for example a life-threatening event – such people are directive and assertive. Followers obey without question because it is not that individual's normal style of leadership.

Effective managers and supervisors are *sensitive to the feelings of others*, avoiding any situation which might reduce the self-esteem of their team. They give criticism and feedback in a positive and supportive manner and with confidence. There are no public reprimands and they work to enhance the self-esteem of all.

The more efficient communicator is also an efficient *information manager*. Such people ensure that they are disseminators of information through the widest possible range of communication media. They are also effective managers of gossip, which is, according to Waddington and Fletcher (1997):

an important feature of organisational communication. (p33)

EFFECTIVE LISTENING

Effective communication is essential within the contemporary workplace and in order for it to be so, all employees need to be able to be active reflective listeners. This is a skill that can be learned and practised and by the use of it the sender and the receiver can fully understand the message sent. The key emphasis is on the receiver, who through effective reflective listening can clarify the meaning within the message. It is characterised in three ways:

- an emphasis on the personal elements of the communication message – that the sender is animate

- a concentration on the feelings communicated within the message – the thoughts and ideas of the sender

- an understanding that the concentration is on the sender of the message and not on the person receiving it.

Hamilton and Kleiner (1987) offer a number of hints to individuals who wish to improve their listening skills – to get them to hear rather than to just listen – which are given in Table 5.6.

Table 5.6 Are you an effective reflective listener?

You might think that you are a good listener – after all, don't your friends ask you to 'Listen to this...? However, how much do you hear of what they say to you? It is possible to become an active listener through practice – here are ten tips to help you to be a better listener. How many of them do you actually adhere to now?

1 *Stop talking*
   If your mouth is moving you cannot possibly be listening.
2 *Put the speaker at ease*
   Be friendly – put the speaker at ease. Smile, but do not use a fixed, inane grin.
3 *Show the speaker you want to listen*
   Move your papers away from you. Put anything you have in your hands aside, for example a coffee cup. Keep your eyes off your watch and on those of the speaker.
4 *Remove distractions*
   Close your door and turn off the telephone and computer screen, for example.
5 *Empathise with the speaker*
   Try to put yourself in the speaker's position and consider how s/he must be feeling.
6 *Be patient*
   No two people deliver a message at an identical pace – give the speaker time to get the message across to you – do not anticipate the contents of the message.
7 *Keep control of your temper*
   Be patient and do not lose your cool.
8 *Keep criticism at bay*
   Do not criticise too much – even if you think it is constructive in nature. Any form of criticism can stifle discourse.
9 *Ask questions*
   Paraphrase the speaker's message as a means of clarification.
10 *Stop talking*
   Do not talk until the speaker has finished – even though it will be a temptation to do so.

Adapted from: Hamilton, C. and B. M. Kleiner (1987) Steps to better listening, *Personnel Journal*, January.

CROSS-CULTURAL COMMUNICATION

Cross-cultural communication is a topical issue in management development and according to Blum (1997):

> Employees in culturally diverse organisations are increasingly demanding appropriate management and communication. (p4)

Blum (1997) went on to say that in order to ensure communication is effective across national cultures, it is essential that a manager understands the importance of culture. By understanding different national behavioural norms managers can better manage across national cultures and it is through the manner of their communication that understanding is expressed ■ *see* Chapter 12 ■. Blum (1997) defines cross-cultural communications as:

see Chapter 12

> the ability to interact verbally and non-verbally by sending, receiving and decoding messages appropriately. (p5)

As has been discussed earlier, all aspects of communication are dominated by an individual's perception of the situation: it is about how the communicators *feel* about each other. An individual's perception is dominated by her/his interpretation of the behavioural signals according to her/his own national identity, and, therefore, its cultural norms. Blum (1997) suggests that the use of translators is dangerous because:

> nationally biased reference points can obscure what is actually being said, either verbally or non-verbally. (p5)

She goes on to say that when an individual communicates across national culture boundaries, there are certain issues which must be taken into account, such as the:

■ different reference points

■ sensitive nature of such issues

■ need to adapt communication style and strategy accordingly.

Taking these three issues into account, the individual must then consider what is involved in any cross-cultural communication. Blum (1997) suggests the following:

■ understanding the expectations of the audience

■ selection of appropriate channels of communication

■ identification of appropriate communication styles

■ the articulation of messages in a sensitive way

■ recognition of the values within which the communication is taking place.

It could well be argued that communication across national boundaries does not differ from that within local boundaries. However, effective cross-cultural communication requires:

5.9

Activity

Check your university classes and see whether there are any fellow students who are from other countries.

1 Within what framework do you operate when communicating with them?

2 Upon what factors do you base your communication technique?

3 Answer the following questions which will help you with cross-cultural communication in the future:

a What is the reference point/cultural 'dimension' of those students?

b How is this reflected in your behaviour, style and values and those of your fellow students?

c What impact do you want your communication to have?

d Is the communication appropriate, given the culture within which you are working?

e Are your communication objectives relevant, realistic and culturally appropriate?

f What are the appropriate communication channels for the culture within which you are working?

g How will you measure your success?

Adapted from: Blum, S. (1997) Preventing culture shock, *Review*, London: Smythe Dorward Lambert, Winter/Spring, pp4–5.

a deeper awareness of what is important to your audience and what additional factors you need to consider when planning your communication approach. (p5)

NON-VERBAL COMMUNICATION

Non-verbal communication includes all elements of communication that do not involve words or spoken language. There are six basic kinds of non-verbal communication:

■ proxemics

■ kinesics

■ facial and eye behaviour

■ paralanguage

■ chronemics

■ object language/artifacts.

Proxemics

▶ The study of an individual's perception and use of space, including territorial space.   ◀┈┈▶ **Proxemics**

Figures 5.7 and 5.8 show two aspects of proxemics, territorial space and seating dynamics. As shown in Figure 5.7, the bands of space extending outward from the

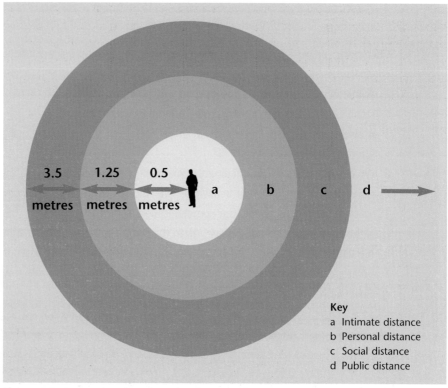

Figure 5.7 Zones of territorial space in UK culture

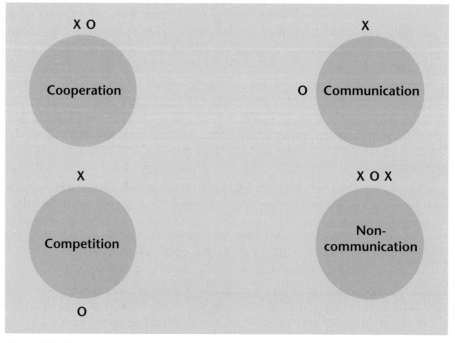

Figure 5.8 Seating dynamics

individual are called 'territorial spaces'. Each band constitutes comfort zones within which different cultures prefer different types of interaction with others. Territorial space varies greatly across cultures. Individuals often become uncomfortable when operating in territorial spaces different from those in which they are familiar. Relationships shape the use of territorial space – the more familiar individuals are with each other, the nearer they will invade the other's territory.

Seating dynamics is an aspect of proxemics and is the art of seating people in certain positions according to the purpose of the communication.

Kinesics

▶ The study of body movements, including posture.   ◀┄┄▶ **Kinesics**

SCENARIO 5.3

When in Rome...

The Italians are charming, intelligent people to whom Europe owes a great cultural debt. They are excellent communicators and combine ultra-keen perception with ever-present flexibility. Their continual exuberance and loquacious persuasiveness often produce an adverse reaction with reserved Britons, factual Germans and taciturn Scandinavians. Yet such northerners have everything to gain by adapting to the Italians' outgoing nature, meeting them halfway in their idea for dialogue. There is plenty of business to be done with the Italians, who export vigorously in order to survive.

Italians may appear to be disorganised, but don't forget Italy is the fifth largest industrial nation in the world and has outperformed even the Germans and Americans in such areas as domestic appliances and some categories such as cars. On top of that they have an enormous hidden or black economy, synonymous with shady dealings. While Italian business dealings may feel dishonest – businesses frequently get round rules – remember that this is the way they do business and you may well be able to benefit from the flexibility. They will regard your rather rigid, law-abiding approach as short-sighted or even blind. They do not consider their own approach to be in any way corrupt.

Italian negotiators often seem to proceed in a roundabout manner and will discuss things from a personal or semi-personal angle, while a northerner tries to concentrate on the benefit for his company and stick to the facts of the particular deal. Italians will also jump ahead to later points on the agenda or will rediscuss points that you think have already been settled. If you are in the chair, you have to create some kind of order, but you can only do this by establishing firm rules in advance. One German... used yellow, red and green cards to discipline people at meetings. This humorous but firm approach achieved the desired result.

A lack of self-discipline is also demonstrated by poor time keeping. Italians have a different concept of time from that of northerners and Americans. They do not arrive for appointments on time. Punctuality in Milan means they are 20 minutes late and in Rome half an hour. It is not possible to change them, so you have to adapt and be prepared to wait 15–45 minutes before an Italian counterpart arrives. Alternatively, you can deliberately turn up half an hour late.

Italian wordiness versus north European succinctness is a constant pain in internal company communication. Both sides wish to achieve clarity but one is doing so through many words and the other

SCENARIO 5.3 cont'd

through short messages and memos. A compromise must be reached. The northerner must teach himself to be more explicit in his explanations, but also encourage his Italian colleague to be more concise and economical with words and ideas, and, when practical, to put them in writing.

Overall then, a northerner should approach business deals with Italians with adequate time for the exercise and a store of patience. He must be prepared to discuss at length and maintain calm. An Italian may get overheated on some point, but changes a moment later. Italians also quarrel among themselves at the table, but are solid colleagues thereafter. In the course of doing business, you may speak much more freely with Italians than with most other Europeans, but do not exaggerate directness or bluntness. Remember that their communication style is eloquent, overdramatic for you. Do not be led into the belief that waving arms and talking with the hands denotes instability. They think you, by contrast, are rather wooden and distant.

Source: Lewis, D. (1996) When in Rome...? *Management Today*, August, pp77–8.

Facial and eye behaviour

The face is the richest source of non-verbal communication and, together with eye behaviour, gives cues to the receiver. The face often gives unintended clues to emotions that the sender is trying to hide. Eye contact can enhance reflective listening and it varies by culture – a direct gaze indicates honesty and forthrightness in the UK and in the USA, but this may not be true in other cultures. For example, in some Asian cultures it is considered good behaviour to bow the head in deference to a superior rather than look the manager in the eye.

SCENARIO 5.4

Those little white lies: new lie detectors use children's faces

You don't have to have watched many USA cop shows to know that the polygraph has had its day. Measuring the breathing and pulse rates of potential villains within the stressful environment of a police cell is to be updated. Researchers have developed a high-speed computer program that spots liars by analysing their faces.

Every emotion we feel produces an involuntary facial expression, sometimes for just a split second, and it is often invisible to the human eye. Researchers at the Institute for Neural Computation in San Diego have developed a computer program that works by superimposing a grid pattern over a photograph of the subject's face when it is devoid of expression. The computer then analyses a video of the subject, and every change of his or her expression, no matter how subtle, is recorded on the grid.

The system was developed using children's faces, including babies'. Theirs are the simplest faces to read because the facial muscles are tighter, the skin smoother, and because they don't disguise their emotions – the very thing that might necessitate you taking a lie detector test in the first place.

Dissembling, of course, comes later on in life.

Source: Those little white lies: New lie detectors use children's faces, *Financial Times* Weekend, 5 February 2000, p8.

Paralanguage

Individuals make ▸ **attributions** ◂ about the sender by deciphering ▸ **paralanguage** ◂.

▸ When someone pinpoints the causes of the behaviour of themselves and others. ◂┄┄▸ **Attribution**

▸ Variations in speech, such as pitch, loudness, tempo, tone, duration, laughing and crying. ◂┄┄▸ **Paralanguage**

5.10

Activity

Can you use paralanguage effectively? Read the following sentences aloud, making a strong verbal emphasis on the word which is highlighted in bold type.

How did she do that?

How **did** she do that?

How did **she** do that?

How did she **do** that?

How did she do **that**?

What difference did this use of emphasis make?

Chronemics

▸ The use of time as an element of non-verbal communication. ◂┄┄▸ **Chronemics**

Time is often viewed as a commodity that can be spent, saved, earned or wasted. European society is very time consuming, as reflected in the dependence of Europeans on clocks and time schedules. It is expressed everywhere in the workplace through completion dates for projects, specific pay periods and working hours.

Object language/artifacts

▸ The communication that results from the display of material things, for example curtains, carpets and furniture. ◂┄┄▸ **Object language/ artifacts**

Some of the objects that frequently influence communication are clothes, furniture, methods of transport and architectural arrangements. Individuals attempt to enhance their personal object language by purchasing items such as clothes and trinkets. Office furniture and its arrangement can affect communication patterns and this object language is linked closely to proxemics discussed earlier. Physical settings convey information about the kind of activities that are to take place and the kind of behaviours that are acceptable.

Non-verbal communication is important for managers because of its impact on the meaning of the message. However, the manager must consider the total message and each medium of communication. People's confidence in their ability to decode non-verbal communication is greater than their accuracy in doing so.

THE EVOLUTION IN COMMUNICATION

Over the last few decades, organisations worldwide have realised the importance of effective communication – it has to be accurate and fast. However, with the 21st century have come some issues that organisations have to address:

- more focused

- rise of information technology ■ *see* Chapter 5 *and* Chapter 6 ■

- social responsibility.

see Chapter 5 *and* Chapter 6

In the contemporary business environment, there has been a breakdown in mass production for more focused, specialised markets which means that organisations are now in closer contact with their customers. In this stakeholder environment, there is a need for individuals to be versatile in their communication techniques and all individuals should be able to communicate effectively at all levels and using all media.

The use of information technology has sped the movement of goods and the speed of the provision of services and it is easier to keep track of customer requirements. There is now more information available about stakeholders at both the international and domestic levels. These new technologies are providing increased communication avenues so that organisations can reach a wider and more specialised market – they can tailor their message to each client ■ *see* Chapter 5 *and* Chapter 6 ■.

see Chapter 5 *and* Chapter 6

see Chapter 7 *and* Chapter 8

see Chapter 11

There has been a considerable growth in the awareness of the legal ■ *see* Chapter 7 *and* Chapter 8 ■ and ethical ■ *see* Chapter 11 ■ matters surrounding communication issues. It is hoped that most individuals in the workplace work in an open and honest environment and treat their stakeholders in a similar way. However, there will always be abuses of this social responsibility and legislation has been developed to govern workplace activities, for example the time spent in the workplace, equal opportunities policies and other Directives from the EU ■ *see* Chapter 7 *and* Chapter 8 ■. The key issue here is that all members of the workforce should keep communications open and clear so that they deal agreeably with their fellow workers and their stakeholders.

see Chapter 7 *and* Chapter 8

Knowledge of communication will always be important to anyone who wishes to function more effectively within the workplace. It is a vital link between people and it makes it possible for organisations to function – a skill which is imperative to success and which, if deficient within any worker, will result in a non-profitable organisation. Hence, it is owned by individuals and is an integral part of individual involvement and participation within the organisation.

SCENARIO 5.5

Hanson: different systems, but a common bond

Hanson's two brick plants in the UK and Belgium produce the same product with the same technology. But the UK plant has a trade union-based system of consultation and information sharing, while the Belgian plant's system is based on a works council, albeit with a strong trade union presence.

Despite this difference, communications in the two plants are remarkably similar. Direct communication with managers, either one-to-one or through meetings, is the most important source of information for employees in both plants.

The proportion of employees who feel that they are well informed, are satisfied with the quality of the information they receive and can influence management decisions is also similar on both sites, as is the level of trust between employees and management.

Source: Hanson: different systems, but a common bond in Wood. S. and M. Fenton-O'Creevy (1999) Channel hopping, *People Management*, 25 November, pp44–5.

It is through employee involvement (EI) that both the employer and the employee can express opinions, views, interests and concerns about the operation of the workplace and the decision-making processes of the organisation.

More direct methods of EI tend to centre on the employee's tasks as a means of increasing and improving individual work performance. Cully et al. (1998) carried out a survey of 30 000 employees and 3000 organisations and highlighted the need for employers to concentrate on worker *participation* even though their remit was to investigate employee *involvement*. It is notable from the literature in the area that a number of writers and researchers tend to use the word 'involvement' synonymously with that of 'participation'. It may well be argued that it is a matter of degree, but as stated earlier in this chapter:

> When there is *participation* on behalf of the individual, then that individual raises the level of her/his physical activity and actually becomes engaged and shares in the events surrounding her/him. (p4)

> The highest level of activity is that of *involvement* and is when the individual is not only participating but her/his behaviour and actions are making a difference to the situation – s/he is having an effect. (p4)

There is a distinction between the two.

Cully et al. (1998) reported that 11 per cent of workplaces within the study stated that they did have employee representation and, where it was in place, it was at the top of the management hierarchy. The report indicates that there has been a limited take-up of ▶ **European works councils** ◀ ■ *see* Chapter 7 ■.

see Chapter 7

▶ A group of organisations and employee representatives who have established rights to both information and consultation. ◀┄┄▶ **European works councils**

The researchers found that where this representation was in place it dealt only with a narrow range of workplace issues such as health and safety factors on the factory floor or in the office ■ *see* Chapter 7 *and* Chapter 8 ■.

Guest and Peccei (1998) researched in the area of union and management partnerships ■ *see* Chapter 7 ■ and their findings appear to suggest that where there are representatives there is also greater employee participation in the decision-making process – especially concerning:

see Chapter 7 *and* Chapter 8

see Chapter 7

■ pay

■ hours of work

■ basic work conditions

■ levels of staffing.

At the higher echelons of the organisation, it appears that consultative systems were set up with a specific brief – usually to consider such issues as:

see Chapter 6

■ new technology ■ *see* Chapter 6 ■

■ reorganisation (BPR)

■ development of new products and/or services.

Guest and Peccei (1998) were not alone in their findings because Gallie et al. (1998) emphasised the lack of employee representation in the workplace – an issue which might well go towards explaining the very low levels of commitment among workers. The issue of employee representation is discussed in ■ Chapter 7 ■.

see Chapter 7

CONSULTATION

It is through ▶ **consultation** ◀ that employers and employees communicate with each other and so effective communication and consultation within an organisation are critical to the success of that organisation in achieving its objectives.

Consultation ◀┄▶ Taking counsel, asking advice and seeking an opinion.

The word 'consultation' has taken on a specific meaning within the workplace because of the increase in employment legislation related to employee relations which relates, primarily, to employee participation. Regardless of whether consultation within an organisation is formalised or is more informal, employers are seeking the opinions of their workers about aspects of the workplace which will directly affect them ■ *see* Chapter 7 *and* Chapter 8 ■.

see Chapter 7 *and* Chapter 8

The statutory obligations ■ *see* Chapter 7 *and* Chapter 8 ■ throughout most of Europe means that organisations have had to elect individuals both at the top hierarchical level and workbench level before taking any decisions that will affect the organisation and its business and day-by-day HRM. What exactly has to be

see Chapter 7 *and* Chapter 8

consulted on depends entirely upon the rights and the level of participation applicable to every country – it varies considerably. For example, in some countries, such as Germany and the Netherlands, an employer cannot act without the consent of the elected employee representatives. In Germany, this is called *Mitbestimmung* which means 'participation in decision making' as described in Scenario 5.6.

SCENARIO 5.6

Mitbestimmung

Mitbestimmung is a German term which means 'participation in decision making' and is usually confined to those made in the workplace. It is a term used to describe Germany's various statutory systems for employee information, consultation and involvement in decision making.

Probably the best known, but the least influential on a day-to-day basis, is employee representation on the supervisory boards (*Aufsichtsrat*) of companies. These supervisory boards appoint the management board (*Vorstand*) and monitor the overall policy of the organisation – including the annual report and accounts.

In organisations with 500 to 2000 employees this is one-third representation. In organisations with more than 2000 employees, the *Aufsichtsrat* consists of equal numbers of employee and shareholder members, although the chair (who is usually elected by the shareholders) has a casting vote in the event of a tie and managers (who usually support the shareholders) also have a separate representation within the employee arena.

In the large organisations within the coal, iron and steel industries, the so-called Montan industries,

there is also a 50:50 representation. However, the chair in this case is neutral and the director of human resources cannot be appointed without the agreement of employee members.

More important to the day-to-day management of an organisation is the structure of elected works councils which may be set up, if the employees choose, in any organisation with five or more workers. In practice this happens in the larger first: around two-thirds of all private sector employees work in an organisation which has a works council. Trade union representatives account for about two-thirds of all elected works council members. They have extensive rights to information, consultation and, on certain issues, codetermination.

In the narrow sense, this means that the employer cannot proceed with an action without the agreement of the works council or, if it refuses, the decision of an independent arbitration panel. Issues dealt with include the organisation of working time, health and safety factors, job design, organisation benefits, the hiring, transfer and regrading of workers and the right to negotiate on severance schemes.

Adapted from: Adkin, E. et al. (1997) *Pocket Employer*, London: Economist Books, pp128–9.

The use of consultation often slows down the pace of decision making within organisations to a speed that a UK- or USA-based employer would find tiresome. However, such consultation procedures can help to give a broader basis for the legitimacy of the decisions because individuals have contributed and will, therefore, own the decision and be positive in their actions related to the final decision rather than prevaricate and obstruct decision making. European Union (EU) Directives oblige member nations to ensure that employers consult with their elected employee representatives or the representatives of the recognised trades unions when redundancies or a transfer of the whole, or parts, of the business are proposed. Organisations are also expected to provide in their annual reports details of any actions taken to improve communication and consultation with members of their workforce ■ *see* Chapter 7 *and* Chapter 8 ■.

see Chapter 7 *and* Chapter 8

The effectiveness of consultation depends on the extent to which senior management are willing to share information, and whether employees believe they have the opportunity to contribute their opinions.

It could be believed that EI is a new phenomenon because of its link with modern working practices such as teamworking, TQM and BPR, yet it has been around for some time and is a part of modern organisational practices. Literature tends to concentrate on the semantics, but this apart, it is clear that EI is central to HRM. This is based in the belief that if employers involve their workers in the workplace – especially in any new initiatives – they will become empowered and, consequently, become autonomous and take responsibility for their work.

While EI is in popular usage it is often not understood in its entirety and is commonly used as a concession or bribe in order to mollify workers. It is rather an ▶ **oxymoron** ◀ because it is questionable that employees can be involved when an organisation, for example, is based on a design which concentrates on making workers just 'obey and do'. There are other considerations regarding EI which need to be taken into account. Beardwell and Holden (1997) propose these areas to be:

■ How much responsibility can be given to employees?

■ What are the boundaries between creativity and responsibility?

■ Is it about new ways of reinforcing management control?

■ What other factors impinge on the process? (p612)

Oxymoron ◀┈┈▶ A contradiction in terms, for example bittersweet, business ethics and military intelligence.

EMPLOYEE INVOLVEMENT AND HRM

The direct involvement of workers in organisational issues is seen by some to be a mark of a progressive and caring employer and key to satisfactory employee relations and participation ■ *see* Chapter 7 *and* Chapter 8 ■. Such direct involvement is closely associated with HRM because of the link between legislation and high performance ■ *see* Chapter 10 ■. It has long been the case that the direct involvement of employees in matters that directly affect them is both relevant to the needs of the individuals themselves and to those of the organisation – neither could meet their objectives without involvement. However, as has been mentioned earlier, such involvement is often included in discussions on participation through representative systems such as works councils and trades unions – especially in continental Europe.

see Chapter 7 *and* Chapter 8

see Chapter 10

In the UK, employers rely more on direct methods of involvement and show that these can be just as effective as methods used in, say, Germany and the Netherlands. It is believed by employers in the UK that such direct methods are more effective that works councils or union-based methods and so they justify the increased legislation (discussed in ■ Chapter 7 *and* Chapter 8 ■).

see Chapter 7 *and* Chapter 8

Legislation apart, EI is in play in most UK organisations. Wood and Fenton-O'Creevy (1999) carried out a study with 25 large multinational countries that all had headquarters in the UK and were all in the Times 100 list of organisations. This cohort was investigated to see whether direct employee involvement was better than, or equal to, that carried out through works councils and trades unions. The results:

> demonstrated that, in companies that use only direct methods, the overall level of employee involvement is in fact lower than it is where some form of representative channel is used either alone or in combination with direct methods. (p42)

They also found evidence that the productivity of organisations utilising formal employee representation and, thus, involvement, such as works councils and trade union representation, had a lower level of productivity.

EMPLOYEE INVOLVEMENT AND COMMUNICATION

Wood and Fenton-O'Creevy (1999) found that organisations, regardless of whether they used direct or indirect methods of EI, all used direct communications, usually by means of:

■ team briefings

■ notice boards

■ memoranda

■ meetings in canteens/staff restaurants.

In the UK, however, employers were more likely to rely totally on such methods although the researchers did note that such methods were not solely limited to the UK.

Respondents distinguished between different levels of employee involvement as set out in Table 5.7.

The research of Wood and Fenton-O'Creevy (1999) shows that the most frequently used systems by far in the participating organisations was direct involvement and then the combination of direct and representative involvement systems. They did not report on any organisations that solely used the trade union representative model.

Table 5.7 Different types of employee involvement (after Wood and Fenton-O'Creevy, 1999, p44)

- *Direct involvement*
  The direct channel predominated.
  Thirty-two per cent of the sample.

- *Representative involvement*
  The representative committee or works council predominated.
  Twenty-one per cent of the sample.

- *Union-based involvement*
  The trades union channel predominated although some use was made of representative committees.
  Four per cent of the sample.

- *Multi-channel involvement*
  In which direct, representative and union-based involvement was utilised.
  Eleven per cent of the sample.

Notes about research
25 large multinational organisations.
All with headquarters in the UK.
All in the Times 100 list of organisations.
Total of 108 country operations covering all EU countries.
29 per cent in the UK.
Further 46 per cent in Germany, the Netherlands, France or Spain.

SCENARIO 5.7

Nissan (UK)

When Nissan (UK) experienced its first drop in demand in 1993, the car maker immediately involved all its employees in deciding how to deal with the surplus labour problem.

The management could have unilaterally decided on redundancies, negotiating with union representatives to agree on voluntary packages or relying, as it could have done, on consultation with elected members of the company council. Instead, it spent two weeks talking in small groups with just about every employee.

Adapted from: Wood, S. and M. Fenton-O'Creevy (1999) Channel hopping, *People Management*, 25 November, p42.

SCENARIO 5.8

Commercial Union and General Accident

Commercial Union and General Accident behaved in a similar way to Nissan (UK) when designing the new organisation after they had merged, although trade unions were also involved.

Adapted from: Wood, S. and M. Fenton-O'Creevy (1999) Channel hopping, *People Management*, 25 November, p42.

The major findings of the work carried out by Wood and Fenton-O'Creevy (1999) appear to show that those organisations that relied solely on direct involvement actually involved the employees far less than those that used other systems. This might seem to be a paradox, but it came about because these organisations involved the workers in fewer issues than did the other combinations (see Table 5.7). When they did involve the workers, they were less likely to consult and/or negotiate rather than informing them. The behaviour shown by both Nissan (UK) and Commercial Union and General Accident (Scenarios 5.7 and 5.8 respectively) seemed to be rare. It seems that there was no significant difference in the level of involvement between the other combinations.

This significant finding:

> that exclusive reliance on direct involvement is likely to lead to lower levels of overall employee involvement and poorer productivity (p45)

has considerable implications for employers. This is because if direct involvement is used in isolation it does reduce levels of productivity, then institutions such as works councils and trades unions do matter. However, it may be the form that such representation takes that does not matter.

While the partnership between employers and employees implies employee involvement, the difficult part, according to Wood and Fenton-O'Creevy (1999), is to:

> marry cooperative relationships between managers and employees and their representatives in a constructive way with employee involvement in operational and strategic issues. (p45)

Chapter summary

- If all employees are to meet the objectives of the organisation, they have to be effective and active communicators and be involved in the meeting of the organisation's aims and objectives.

- There is a distinction between presence, participation and involvement.

- It is difficult to define communication but a central tenet is the interaction between two or more people.

- Communication is an integral part of all activities aimed at achieving the organisation's objectives in a stakeholder environment.

- Organisational communication has a specific role (Bratton and Gold, 1999) rather than being something that 'just happens'.

- Empowerment is a key issue with changes in policy and legislation making it increasingly active.

- There are three identifiable approaches to organisational communication (Bratton and Gold, 1999): functionalist, interpretivist and critical.

■ There is no single model of communication which takes into account all elements although each has in common: the source, message and receiver.

■ Communication models have evolved from Shannon and Weaver (1949), Schramm (1954), McLuhan (1964), Jablin et al. (1987) and Clampitt (1991).

■ There are three primary methods of communication: written, oral and non-verbal (proximity, kinesics, facial and eye behaviour, paralanguage, chronemics, object language/artifacts).

■ In order to manage communication, feedback is essential and lack of this is due to physical separation, status differentiation, gender differences, cultural diversity, language and meaning.

■ Effective communicators tend to be: expressive speakers, empathic listeners, persuasive leaders, sensitive to the feelings of others, and managers of information.

■ Cross-cultural communication is an increasing part of a diverse workplace (Blum, 1997).

■ Communication is evolving and, therefore, organisations have to be more focused, use more information technology, for example e-commerce and social responsibility.

■ Employee involvement is on the increase with direct involvement being to the fore (Guest and Peccei, 1998).

■ Consultation in the workplace has become very important because of increased legislation.

■ Employee involvement is closely linked to teamworking, the search for quality (TQM) and organisational redesign (BPR).

■ Employee involvement is central to HRM.

END OF CHAPTER 5 CASE STUDY

Performing arts

Business people are communicating in a fresh and exciting way. Lively Arts is a company that allows people to connect more effectively by bringing words to life. Participants leave its bespoke events with a full understanding in their hearts and their heads of the messages being conveyed.

Lively Arts is the result of a dynamic partnership between two highly creative individuals, performer and writer, David Pearl, and Jeremy Stuart, one of the United Kingdom's most sought-after producers. They created the excitingly unusual company, which devises bespoke events for blue-chip clients.

Lively Arts' projects are fresh and custom made for each organisation. If a company needs to communicate with its personnel, its customers or its markets in an inspirational way, Lively Arts can achieve this by creating an interactive event during which the participants do not just hear the relevant message but actively experience it. The hallmarks of a Lively Arts' event are a powerful business theme, mind-opening creativity and total participation.

Their insightful and deceptively entertaining approach has earned the company a formidable portfolio of clients worldwide. David and Jeremy were brought together by their first project, a revolutionary programme they conceived to use performing arts to enhance professionalism in business.

David explains: 'Lively Arts was founded in 1995 when we were least expecting it. One of the world's most eminent business organisations called out of the blue, wanting some creative outsiders to inspire them. Like most successful organisations they felt there was more within their business and its people than they had yet seen. They were right.

'But rather than us inspire them, we suggested it would be more effective if we created a way for them to inspire themselves with everyone participating in every aspect of their own project. Creating rather than consuming and drawing on skills that businesses have in abundance but don't always take full advantage of.'

Since then, Lively Arts has become involved in business development, brand building, internal communications, motivation, interactive conferences and product launches. The company is now looking to a future which will continue to challenge both grey matter and traditional grey suit thinking, by embracing projects for the business community and theatre audiences alike.

Source: Performing arts, *Success Now*, April/May/June 1999, Issue 12, p8.

END OF CHAPTER 5 CASE STUDY QUESTIONS

1 Lively Arts offers an integrated experience for its participants. Why is non-verbal behaviour so potent a method of communication?

2 What is the link between 'communication' and 'thinking'?

3 Why does Lively Arts provide bespoke courses?

4 What is the connection between communication and 'business development, brand building, internal communications, motivation, interactive conferences and product launches'.

THESIS + ANTITHESIS = SYNTHESIS

There is no link between effective communication and employee involvement.

SELF-TEST THE KEY ISSUES

1 How can communication models be used to improve the effectiveness of employee involvement?

2 Why is it important in employee involvement to be aware of the importance of situational factors?

3 What is the importance of the statement 'meanings are in people, not in words'?

4 What is the difference between *presence*, *participation* and *involvement* in the workplace?

TEAM/CLASS DISCUSSIONS

1 'In most cases one-way communication is about power and authority.' Discuss.

2 Think of the most recent defensive form of communication that you have had to handle. Discuss how you handled it.

PROJECTS (INDIVIDUAL OR TEAMS)

1 Research eye contact in various cultures and compare it with eye culture within your indigenous population, for example Britain.

2 Write a report for your manager which highlights the importance of theory and practice in linking effective communications with an increase in employee involvement.

Recommended reading

Armstrong, M. (1999) *A Handbook of Human Resource Management Practice*, London: Kogan Page

Beardwell, I. and L. Holden (1999) *Human Resource Management: A Contemporary Perspective*, London: Pitman

Bell, A. (2000) *Transforming Your Workplace*, London: Institute of Personnel and Development

Bratton, J. and J. Gold (1999) *Human Resource Management: Theory and Practice*, Basingstoke: Macmillan – now Palgrave

Graham, H.T. and R. Bennett (1999) *Human Resources Management*, London: Financial Times/Pitman

Legge, K. (1995) *Human Resource Management: Rhetorics and Realities*, Basingstoke: Macmillan – now Palgrave

Nether, W. (1997) *Organizational Communication*, Boston: Allyn & Bacon

Maund, L. (1999) *Understanding People and Organisations: An Introduction to Organisational Behaviour*, Cheltenham: Stanley Thornes

Storey, J. (ed.) (1995) *Human Resource Management: A Critical Text*, Routledge: London

URL (uniform resource locator)

www.bbc.co.uk/education/archive/war

British Broadcasting Corporation (BBC) site for tackling the downside of work, for example impossible targets and getting sacked.

Bibliography

Adkin, E., G. Jones and P. Leighton (1997) *Pocket Employer*, London: Economist Books

Advisory Conciliation and Arbitration Service (ACAS) (1982) *Workplace Communications,* Advisory Booklet No 8, London: Advisory Conciliation and Arbitration Service (ACAS)

Armstrong, M. (1999) *A Handbook of Human Resource Management Practice*, London: Kogan Page

Beardwell, I. and L. Holden (1997) *Human Resource Management: A Contemporary Perspective*, London: Pitman

Blum, S. (1997) Preventing culture shock in *Review*, London: Smythe Dorward Lambert, Winter/Spring, pp4–5

Bratton, J. and J. Gold (1999) *Human Resource Management: Theory and Practice*, Basingstoke: Macmillan – now Palgrave

Brown, M. (1996) Space Shuttle in *Management Today*, January, pp66–74

Clampitt, P. (1991) *Communicating for Managerial Effectiveness*, Newbury Park: Sage

Corbett, M. (1997) Wired and emotional in *People Management*, 26 June, p26

Cruise O'Brien, R. (1999) Employee involvement in performance improvement: A consideration of tacit knowledge, commitment and trust in *Employee Relations*, **17**(3): 110–20

Cully, M., S. Woodland, A. O'Reilly, G. Dix, N. Howard, A. Bryson and J. Forth (1998) *The 1998 Workplace Relations Survey: First Findings*, London: Department of Trade and Industry

Financial Times (2000) Those little white lies: New lie detectors use children's faces, 5 February, p8

Gallie, D., M. White, Y. Cheng and M. Tomlinson (1998) *Restructuring the Employment Relationship*, Oxford: Oxford University Press

Guest, D. and R. Peccei (1998) The partnership company: benchmarks for the future in *The Report of the IPA Survey Principles, Practice and Performance*, London: Involvement and Participation Association

Jablin, F., L. Putnam, K. Roberts and L. Porter (eds) (1987) *Handbook of Organisational Communication: An Interdisciplinary Perspective*, Newbury Park: Sage

Kanter, R.M. (1997) It's a people thing in *Financial Times* in 'The Management Interview' by Griffith, V., 24 July, p20

Lewis, D. (1996) When in Rome...? in *Management Today*, August, pp77–8

Marcousé, I., A. Gillespie, B. Martin, M. Surridge and N. Wall (1999) *Business Studies*, Abingdon: Hodder & Stoughton

Maund, L. (1999) *Understanding People and Organisations: An Introduction to Organisational Behaviour*, Cheltenham: Stanley Thornes

McLuhan, M. (1964) *Understanding Media*, London: Routledge & Kegan Paul

Motorola Wings in *Cosmopolitan*, October 1999, p5

Putnam, I. and T. Jones (1982) Reciprocity in negotiations: an analysis of bargaining interaction in *Communication Monographs*, **49**: 171–91

Shannon, C. and W. Weaver (1949) *The Mathematical Theory of Communication*, Urbana: University of Illinois Press

Schramm, W. (1954) How communication works in Schramm, W. (ed.) *The Process and Effects of Mass Communication*, Urbana: University of Illinois Press

Success Now (1999) *Performing Arts*, April/May/June (12): 8

Thornhill, S. and M.N.K. Saunders (1997) Downsizing, delayering, but where's the commitment? The development of a diagnostic tool to help managers survive in *Personnel Review*, **26**(1/2): 81–98

Waddington, K. and C. Fletcher (1997) Oh I heard it on the grapevine in *Professional Manager*, July, p33

Welch, R. and P. Leighton (1997) Individualizing employee relations: the myth of the personal contract in *Personnel Review*, **25**(5): 37–50

Wood, S. and M. Fenton-O'Creevy (1999) Channel hopping in *People Management*, 25 November, pp42–5

Technology, information and knowledge management

After studying this chapter, you should be able to:

- DISCUSS the meaning of technology, information technology (IT), data, information, knowledge, knowledge worker and knowledge management.

- ASSESS the role of electronic learning and training within an organisation.

- UNDERSTAND the key developments which have taken place in technology.

- ANALYSE the role of technological change as it relates, specifically, to: telecommuting, expert systems/knowledge systems, automation and robotics and artificial intelligence (AI).

- EVALUATE the opinions held by the technological determinists.

- UNDERSTAND the importance of information sharing and knowledge management.

- EXPLAIN the changes in the working environment, such as: hives, cells, dens and clubs with hot desking and hotelling.

- DEFINE IT.

- DISTINGUISH between IT and computing.

- DESCRIBE the effect that technology, information sharing and knowledge management have on organisation structure and design.

- DISTINGUISH between information, IT and knowledge.

- ASSESS the need for planning in an information-sharing environment.

- IDENTIFY the key aspects of frustration and stress as they affect technology, IT and knowledge management.

INTRODUCTION

Framework case study

Students net a £10 million deal at the click of a button

Like many of the best ideas, Student-Net came to Peter Atalla in a flash. Brushing his teeth one morning, the university student pondered the difficulty of finding a new flat for himself and his friends.

Wouldn't it be useful, he thought, if all the information they needed was on one site on the Internet?

Later, over a few beers in the student union bar, he put the concept to three of his friends.

Now, six months on, Peter Atalla, 21, John Boardman, 22, Mik Haycock, 23, and Alan Edmondson, 22, have just sold their Internet company for £10 million.

Student-Net, a guide to accommodation, college courses and bars, pubs and clubs, has been snapped up by a firm in the USA.

The four friends were living in shared digs, caught the bus to classes and scrimped to enjoy the odd night out.

The idea came one morning in June 1999, hours before one of the students was due to sit his physics exam. He suggested the site to his three friends in the student union bar and within weeks Student-Net was born.

The friends' intent was to make the company a global concern after they agreed the deal with International Media Products Group of Nevada.

They will be kept on as directors and the firm will remain in Nottingham, UK.

Adapted from: Powell, A. (2000) Students net a £10 million deal at the click of a button, *Daily Mail*, 26 January, p5.

Effective communications and employee involvement (EI) are very important if the objectives of the organisation and those of the individual worker are to be met. However, this can be greatly enhanced by the careful use of technology – including information technology (IT), information sharing and the productive management of knowledge.

Writers sometimes, for convenience, amalgamate these three terms under the one heading of 'technology'. However, although closely aligned, they are not the same. This chapter will review technology and then consider the role of IT within it. Following this there is a discussion on information and its input in the role of knowledge and knowledge management.

Technology is very difficult to define because it is different things to different people depending upon their individual perceptions. A number of writers have attempted a definition of technology but each one has concentrated on a different approach that tends to mirror their own life experiences and the year of their research and writing. For example, those writing in the pre-1980s tended to have a broad approach while the later writers leant towards the more narrow. Such definitions provided by writers tend to sit on a 'broad' to 'narrow' continuum with the former concentrating on the traditional, mechanistic approach; such an approach takes the view that it refers to machinery and equipment which is used to carry out the transformational process within production. For example, Perrow (1967) stated that:

Technology is... the actions that an individual performs on an object, with or without the assistance of mechanical devices, in order to make some change in that object. (p194)

Others tend to take the narrower and more concise view that technology applies to the members of the workforce and therefore they take a more organic approach to the appreciation of technology.

For the purpose of this text, an all-encompassing definition of ▸ **technology** ◂ is proposed.

> ▸ The intellectual and mechanical processes used by an organisation to transform the inputs ◂┈┈▸ **Technology**
> into outputs such as products and/or services in order to meet the objectives of the
> organisation.

DATA, INFORMATION, KNOWLEDGE AND WISDOM

In its simplest terms, ▸ **information** ◂ is the result of the ▸ **processing** ◂ of data for use and the making of meaningful decisions. However, in the age of information this is extended to include the consideration of information which is used for the making of decisions. Once that information has been obtained, it can be further refined to provide ▸ **knowledge** ◂ and with the advances in technology, knowledge may well provide eventual ▸ **wisdom** ◂. This is shown in Figure 6.1.

> ▸ The result of the processing of data for use and the making of meaningful decisions. ◂┈┈▸ **Information**
>
> ▸ Conversion of raw data into information that has meaning. ◂┈┈▸ **Processing**
>
> ▸ A parcel of concepts and cognitive frameworks which individuals use to collect, store, ◂┈┈▸ **Knowledge**
> process, organise and communicate understanding.
>
> ▸ The ability or result of an ability to think and act using knowledge, experience, under- ◂┈┈▸ **Wisdom**
> standing, common sense and insight.

IT has impacted heavily on:

■ how information is processed

■ how information is handled

■ the provision of knowledge for decision making.

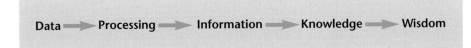

Data ⟹ Processing ⟹ Information ⟹ Knowledge ⟹ Wisdom

Figure 6.1 The progression from data to wisdom

KNOWLEDGE MANAGEMENT AND KNOWLEDGE SHARING

Dixon (2000) believes that an organisation cannot just 'do' knowledge management – it has to consider the types of information that members of the organisation need to share with each other. Often, within organisations, there is the knowledge required to allow the organisation to become a market leader, however there is often a problem of how to take advantage of that knowledge.

One solution put forward by Dixon (2000) is for an organisation to provide some sort of knowledge repository where employees can place their innovations and ideas. Any team that needed help could utilise such a repository to bring them up to speed and to help them move onwards – it is a form of shared creativity. However, organisations that used this idea, for example the high-tech multinational communication company FasTech, found that the ideas were not being fully utilised and that there was minimal use of the system. It was only when it was linked to performance-related pay ■ *see* Chapter 9 ■ that the idea took off – albeit minimally and operationally close to the period when pay was being reviewed. As it turned out, FasTech decided that the organisation's culture was so competitive anyway that knowledge sharing would not work and abandoned the idea.

see **Chapter 9**

However, in her research, Dixon (2000) found many success stories, for example Lockheed-Martin's best practice initiative set a goal of £1.6 billion in cost savings and had no difficulty reaching it. However, the best example of success is that of Ford – the international vehicle manufacturer.

There are a number of reasons why Ford succeeded while FasTech failed. A number of people conclude – as did FasTech – that the organisational culture worked against knowledge sharing. However, Dixon (2000) refutes this stating that the unsuccessful organisations implemented a transfer system – in FasTech's

SCENARIO 6.1

Ford's focus group

Over the past two years, shopfloor workers at Ford's body plant in Dagenham, Essex, England, have come up with 51 ideas for improvement, which have been beamed around the world to other Ford factories via their intranet-based Best Practice Replication system.

Robin Hay, a production engineer and one of five 'focal points' responsible for ideas transmission at Dagenham, says the figure puts his team second in the company's global 'good ideas' league.

'It certainly encourages pride in their ideas,' he says. 'And, if they are successful, there's a cost reduction.'

One of their proposals, for a sealant application to make Ford Fiestas quieter and drier, is projected to save the company £250 000 (USA$150 000) a year after being taken up elsewhere.

'I get about half a dozen best practices sent through from other plants each week. And we put up an idea of our own about once a fortnight,' Hay says.

'We have had e-mails and telephone calls from other plants in response. It's really encouraging.'

Adapted from: Dixon, N. (2000) The insight track, *People Management*; 17 February, p34.

case a database – that bore no relation to the kind of knowledge it was trying to transfer. That is, there was a mismatch between the software used and the knowledge the organisation was trying to harvest. Ford was successful – as was Lockheed-Martin – because the system was designed to match the type of knowledge with the right type of method of transfer. Dixon (2000) states that there are three conditions where this can take place:

- whether the task is routine or non-routine

- whether the knowledge related to it is tacit or explicit

- the similarity between the originator and the receiver of the information.

It is the above that determines the method through which the transfer of knowledge can be effective. Unfortunately, many organisations have resorted to trial and error when building a knowledge transfer system and have, as a result, expended valuable resources in achieving nothing of benefit.

It is possible to avoid the mistakes of trial and error mechanisms by taking a more systematic approach by looking carefully at:

> the type of knowledge, matching it to the most effective transfer method and using a set of coherent and internally consistent design principles to produce an effective transfer system. (Dixon, 2000, pp38–9)

LONG-DISTANCE LEARNING

Successful transfer of information is an aspect of learning ■ *see* Chapter 10 ■ with the four key principles being shown in Table 6.1.

see Chapter 10

Accompanying the four principles of learning are five ways that transfers can take place and these are shown in Table 6.2.

Table 6.1 Long-distance learning

The four key principles of successful transfer are:

1 *The system is designed as a reciprocal exchange between peers*, as opposed to methods that aim to identify the 'best' and provide it to the 'less capable'.

2 *People, rather than electronic methods, transport the knowledge.* The knowledge is largely tacit – it resides in the heads of colleagues who may not even be aware of what they know until faced with a problem that calls on the knowledge. So they must 'be in' the situation in order to recall and apply the knowledge.

3 *The source of the knowledge makes the translation to the new situation.* Elements of the new situation can trigger people's memories so that they can call up ideas and solutions from other situations they have experienced. They can bring together seemingly unconnected ideas to form a new response.

4 *The system has a name.* In all firms, peers have informal networks to call upon in difficult situations. But a sanctioned process broadens the network and is a recognised way of using knowledge so that people don't feel they are 'asking for a favour'.

Adapted from: Dixon, N. (2000) The insight track, *People Management*, 17 February, p39.

Table 6.2 Transfer protocols

1 *Serial transfer*

A team performs a task and then the same team repeats the task in a new context. For example, a generator producer, Bechtel, replaces a steam generator in a chemical plant over a period of two to three months. At the end, it will hold a meeting to consider what was learnt and work out how to do it better next time. The team then moves on to, say, a refinery to replace a generator there. Much of the knowledge gained at the chemical plant can be reused at the refinery because the team made explicit much of that tacit knowledge that its members had learnt.

Of course, not all the knowledge can be used because every situation is going to be different. Serial transfer offers a way to prevent the repetition of mistakes and to increase speed and quality.

2 *Near transfer*

Knowledge is transferred from one team to another doing a similar task, in a similar context, in a different location. A task involving largely routine work in Chicago can be reduced by 15 seconds by employing a best practice generally used in Atlanta, for example. The knowledge is explicit and the company intranet is an ideal transfer method. The potential for cost savings is enormous.

3 *Far transfer*

Knowledge about a non-routine task, which affects a specific part of the operation, is transferred between two teams. An example is the Peer Assist scheme developed and used widely at BP Amoco. An oil exploration team might invite four or five peers from around the world to meet them on site for a day to help them through decisions at a critical point.

The knowledge to be transferred is primarily 'tacit' – that is, it isn't written down, but exists in the heads of visiting peers. Because the interpretation of seismic or geological data is a task that is emergent and variable, those who hold the knowledge must themselves be immersed in the new situation in order to draw on and transfer what they know. Far transfer makes possible the application of specialised, critical knowledge to problems (as seen in Table 6.1).

4 *Strategic transfer*

Very complex knowledge, such as how to launch a product or make an acquisition, is transferred between two teams that may be separated by both time and space. It differs from far transfer in that it has an effect on large parts of the system. The cross-functional teams that are the source of the strategic knowledge will have learnt important concepts that could save money and effort the next time around. For instance, the receiving team may be responsible for acquiring a company that is larger and less friendly than the company the source team was dealing with. Yet there will be some part of the knowledge, both tacit and explicit, that is valuable in the new situation.

The method must be able to retain the complexity of the knowledge and the multiple voices that represent various options.

5 *Expert transfer*

Explicit knowledge about a task that may be done infrequently. An example is a technician who e-mails his network to ask how to increase the brightness on an out-of-date monitor and gets back knowledge that allows the team to complete their task in a timely manner. But their expertise can be offered in a formula or a procedure. The situation does not have to be interpreted.

TECHNOLOGICAL CHANGES

Technological changes in the workforce have been continuous for generations – they are nothing new. Throughout history people have been developing mechanistic methods of improving the ways of doing things. It is the term 'new technology' that has evolved from the early 1980s and, more recently, according to Rana (2000), there has been a growth in the use of new technology as shown in Table 6.3.

The two forms of new technology which have had a particular effect in the workplace are:

- advanced manufacturing technology (AMT) and

- office technology.

AMT includes a wide range of equipment that adds to the manufacturing process while what is commonly known as *office technology* concentrates on storage, retrieval, presentation and the manipulation of data. It does not interpret those data and give them meaning – only human beings can do that, although there is evidence that this state of affairs is debatable.

During the latter half of the 20th century social scientists have researched the key issues concerned with the new technology. For example, some ▶ **ergonomists** ◀ have attempted to improve the compatibility between humans and technology.

▶ People who study the relationship between workers and their environment. ◀┈┈▶ **Ergonomists**

Jobs are frequently designed/redesigned to minimise the requirements for specific skills, to reduce the need for decision making from operatives and to reduce labour costs. Along with such a scientific view comes a potential for human dissatisfaction and a lack of continuous development – discussed in ■ Chapter 10 ■. The introduction of new technology has meant that there has been the potential for deskilling even further. However, this is not always the case because when incorporated into job design/redesign with the balance of process and people in mind, new technology can maintain and even enhance existing skills. It is the *nature* of the skills which tends to change. Unfortunately, new technology is often introduced piecemeal without a holistic investigation and this brings about the need to rely on technical experts. When introduced with the wider organisational implications in mind, new technology can enhance the nature of the work.

see **Chapter 10**

Table 6.3 Growth in the use of 'new technology' from 1998 to 1999

	1998 %	1999 %
No. of organisations training staff through the Internet and ▶ intranet ◀	25	28.5
No. of organisations making use of ▶ extranets ◀	9.7	11.35

▶ A network of computers, especially one which uses www conventions, that can be accessed ◀┈┈▶ **Intranet**
only by an authorised set of users, for example those working for a particular organisation.

▶ An intranet which is only accessible by selected individuals. It can be worldwide or ◀┈┈▶ **Extranet**
organisational.

While technological change has been more an evolution than a revolution, there have been considerable innovations over the past few years which particularly affect how individuals work. Employers and employees face increasing challenges related to rapidly changing technology with the responsibility of putting that technology to good use within the organisation. The slower that they are at doing this, the more slowly the economic advantage will accrue to the organisation for which they work.

Any change that affects the way people work is a technological change – it is not purely related to IT – discussed below. Some of the more familiar relate to:

■ ▶ **telecommuting** ◀

■ expert systems/knowledge systems

■ automation and robotics

■ artificial intelligence (AI).

Telecommuting ◀┈┈▶ Transmitting work from a home computer to the office by the use of a modem or cable.

One of the first companies to experiment with telecommuting was IBM, which installed computer terminals at key workers' homes. However, there are advantages and disadvantages to telecommuting as shown in Table 6.4.

Another technological change is the use of ▶ **expert systems** ◀. Thomas and Ballard (1995) define them as 'computer packages designed to mimic the decision-making processes of experts in a given field' (p155).

Expert systems ◀┈┈▶ Computer-based applications that use a computer representation of the expertise attributed to humans in a specialised field of knowledge in order to solve problems.

By using such expert systems a non-expert in a specified field can perform as expertly as an expert in that same field, because the system has within it the required information framework, rules and regulations of the stated topic and it is also able to adapt to new rules as the program is being used. As the user works through the program, the latter will adapt its knowledge as a result of that interaction and thus make inferences that will then allow it to make the most appropriate decision and offer alternatives on the information given to it. There are limitless applications of this use of expert power from investment analysis, human resource *see* Chapter 7 *and* Chapter 8 ■ to the preparation of an academic paper or company report.

see Chapter 7 *and* Chapter 8

Table 6.4 Advantages and disadvantages of telecommuting

ADVANTAGES	DISADVANTAGES
Flexibility	Distractions
Time saved not commuting	Lack of socialisation with colleagues
Enjoyment of home comforts	Lack of communication with supervisor/subordinates

POINTS TO PONDER

Story overheard at a conference:

The storyteller works on a computer manufacturer's help desk in London, England. He had just spent an hour with a purchaser who knew nothing about the computer he had just bought and nothing about them in general – he even had to be told how to switch it on.

Shortly after that telephone call, the customer rang back: 'It says here that I should visit your website. What's the nearest underground station?'

▶ **Automation** ◀ and ▶ **robotics** ◀ are also changing the way jobs are designed but are primarily concerned with how existing jobs can be redesigned. There is a growing reliance on automation and robotics with their accompanying advantages and disadvantages as suggested in Table 6.5.

▶ Where mechanical or electronic machines or processes replace/minimise human labour. ◀┈┈▶ **Automation**

▶ The use of computer-controlled mechanical devices. ◀┈┈▶ **Robotics**

Table 6.5 Advantages and disadvantages of automation and robotics

ADVANTAGES	DISADVANTAGES
Eliminates boring, routine and hazardous jobs	Dehumanises jobs
Workers can be moved to more interesting and challenging jobs	The worker has less to do
Speed of process	The worker becomes an adjunct to the technology
Accuracy in completion of tasks	
No illness requiring time off	

SCENARIO 6.2

Automation and robotics in the supermarket

Tim works as a checkout operator in a large supermarket. In one of his rare quiet moments he is reflecting on the components of his job – how much is automated and how much this affects him personally.

He feels that automation has dehumanised his job because optiscan technology reads the prices from the barcodes attached to the products as he passes them over the scanner. While he has become more efficient because of this process, he has much less to do and his task has become boring and repetitive.

However, he has been promised a new checkout unit which will be able to call out the prices, total the bill and tell him the customer's change. Tim has been told that his till will also be able to speak to the customer by saying 'Thank you for your custom – have a nice day.' He is not very keen about that idea because it takes away one of his only opportunities to interact personally with his customers.

Tim feels that he is merely an adjunct to the technology and, with the use of the Internet increasing and automatic scanning devices already in store, he will become obsolete.

SCENARIO 6.3

What about *my* feelings? Robots get all emotional

The trouble with robots, it seems, is that they are just too, well, robotic. Scientists are now convinced that robot technology has been slow to get widespread consumer acceptance because we can't be persuaded to love and cherish something so unfeeling.

The latest creatures to emerge from the depths of the research lab at Tokyo's Waseda University are distinguished not so much by their technical capabilities as by their ability to mimic human behaviour.

Shine a light in these robot eyes and the silicon-and-steel monsters will squint coyly, blink their CCD-camera-controlled eyes and turn their head away. Motors contained in their faces allow them to respond to commands with one of six different expressions, and if you hit them they don't bruise but they will recoil.

Wearing their feelings proudly on the outside is one thing, but researchers are confident that they are closing in on the next big thing: robots that not only nod and smile, but also have conversational skills.

Source: What about my feelings? (2000) in the business, The Financial Times, 19 February, pp13–14.

Artificial intelligence (AI) consists of three separate fields:

- senses systems

- language systems

- expert systems/knowledge systems.

The *senses systems* are concerned with interpreting and retrieving as much information as possible from two-dimensional pictures.

Language systems are more directed to interpretation, for example of English, French or Swedish as it is spoken.

As discussed earlier, *expert systems* (otherwise known as knowledge systems) are programs that solve the most difficult of problems which demand specific and specialist knowledge. It is this area that will continue to have a dramatic effect. For example, applications exist in diagnosis, medical information systems, process control, planning and industrial processes.

TECHNOLOGY, QUALITY AND ORGANISATIONAL DESIGN

Technological advances have given organisations the opportunity to alter the structure of their organisation and the jobs within them. There has been a development in the way in which people communicate at work – ■ *see* Chapter 5 ■ for an in-depth discussion on communication. Through total quality management (TQM), programme managers have sought to alter the traditional communications systems to complement the newer approaches to work design, for example teamwork. Communication and information theory comprise an area of management theory that concentrates on the key role of communication and information systems.

see Chapter 5

Some important work has been carried out by Juran and Gryna (1970) both of whom are termed ▶ **technological determinists** ◀. This belief takes the view that there is no discussion possible between humans and technology and because of this there will be a loss of quality. Simply, they cannot communicate as do humans-to-humans. Therefore, there is no treatment of the human resources issues involved or the role of interpretation with respect to either IT or the idea of quality.

> ▶ Individuals who see human beings as the recipients of technology rather than the shapers of it. ◀┈┈▶ **Technological determinists**

However, Juran and Gryna (1970) do not actually go on to seriously consider the role of the human being in the work process because they see human resource issues as being peripheral to those of process control, tools and techniques. That is, in their opinion the human being is not part of the work process and has no effect on the end product. It is important for individuals who are convinced that people comprise an organisation ■ *see* Chapter 1 *and* Chapter 2 ■ to appreciate that not all individuals hold this view. What Juran and Gyrna (1970) seem to imply is that people cannot be simply dropped into a set of beliefs and slavishly accept procedures and applications, for example TQM and IT. They actually subsumed the human resources issues into the product itself and in doing so they separated the 'soft' and 'hard' aspects of HRM – discussed in ■ Chapter 1 *and* Chapter 2 ■.

see Chapter 1 *and* Chapter 2

see Chapter 1 *and* Chapter 2

Through some technological systems it is possible to disseminate information to everyone within the organisation and, especially, downwards. Increasingly, organisations are sharing with the entire membership of the organisation information which once used to be secured at the organisational apex.

The four technologies discussed earlier (telecommuting, expert systems, automation and robotics and AI) – although not so much AI – are standard practices in organisations today. The challenges now facing employees concern the more advanced technologies and the practices which have come about as a result of such innovations. They all continue to reshape the working environment – some will be passing fashions – but others will remain part of the work environment and the way jobs are carried out. Some of the key developments are:

- ■ information storage and processing

- ■ communications

- ■ advanced materials

- ■ superconductivity

- ■ biotechnologies.

Improvements in information processing and storage continue to increase. Currently desktop computers' capability is measured in gigabytes (billion words) and some computers have a capacity measured in terabytes (trillion words). Megabyte capacity (million words) is obsolescent. There continue to be improvements in the price:performance ratios of equipment which means that it is becoming less expensive to apply machine intelligence to jobs currently being performed by human beings, that is, AI. Data are only data to human beings and not to the computer, which works by the use of ▶ **logarithms** ◀ to carry out tasks.

Logarithms ◀┈┈▶ A mathematical system used, particularly, to simplify multiplication and division.

Most developed countries have a digital telephone communications network that uses fibre optic technology which utilises laser beams to send data along minute fibre tubes. Such a system is smaller, cheaper and more reliable than a wire cable and because it uses lights to send data, the resultant transmission is highly accurate. Since the data are in digital form, modems and cables can turn analogue to digital (and vice versa) extremely quickly.

Smaller quantities of raw materials are now required in the processing industries and this has meant a significant decline in jobs within the extractive industries, for example coal mining. There have also been considerable developments in new materials such as ceramics and reinforced plastics which has meant that manufactured products now last longer. Thus the skills required of workers have changed, as has the design of their jobs.

The development of *superconductive materials* is having a rapid effect on industry. Such materials are able to carry electrical currents without any loss of energy and thus the efficiency of electric motors is improved.

It is not only in the manufacturing industries that developing technology has changed the nature of work. The agriculture and health service industries, for example, are continuing to change dramatically because of the considerable advances in ▶ **biotechnology** ◀, especially in the ability to manipulate life forms at the cellular and sub-cellular levels. This is apparent in the debate on genetically modified foodstuffs and the modification of animal – including human – genes.

Biotechnology ◀┈┈▶ The technology of biological processes.

TECHNOLOGY AND THE WORKING ENVIRONMENT

Many of the predictions concerning the influence of technology have proved to be correct, for example the use of the microchip and how it has revolutionised the way individuals work. However, there have been others which have not lived up to expectations and a principal one here concerns the so-called 'face of the future'. There was a considerable amount of literature on the subject in the late 1990s. Brown (1997) reflected on such predictions which came to the fore in the 1990s, stating that for a significant section of the working population:

the traditional office would soon become a thing of the past. Wage slaves would become teleworkers, beavering away at home, attached to their offices by an electronic umbilical cord (telephone and personal computer) but otherwise free to organise and carry out their work as they choose. (p77)

He went on to state that it was estimated that by the mid-1990s there would be more than 2.5 million teleworkers using modern technology to do their jobs – regardless of where they were geographically situated. This estimate initially seemed rather ambitious yet in 2000 the figure has nearly been met. Brown (1997) sourced statistics which showed that in the UK just 5 per cent of the total number expected were actually teleworking and that the situation was the same in other countries and there was no evidence that the proportion of teleworkers to the working population was on the increase.

Colin Jackson, managing director of the business consultancy Organisation and Technology Research (OTR), did warn people in the early 1990s that the estimation of the demand for teleworking was grossly exaggerated – indeed, he himself over-estimated the market by a factor of ten, according to Brown (1997). Jackson stated there were three factors that had to be met if teleworking were to become as important as was anticipated:

- the jobs had to be suitable for teleworking

- the individuals had to be suited to teleworking

- organisations had to have staff who were capable of managing such tele-workers.

Organisations found it difficult to meet just one of the above criteria and to secure all three turned out to be impossible for most organisations except for those which were small scale, such as journalism and the writing of computer software. Jackson stated that to secure all three key premises was:

> a bit like the chances of finding a one-legged accordion player who was a fighter in the Second World War. (Brown, 1997, p79)

Teleworking has been overestimated as a means of designing jobs because there are now some further developments based on that premise which can be given the overall term *the virtual office*.

The virtual office has been in place for some time and affects the way individuals' jobs are designed – many workers work in this environment without fully realising that it is a virtual office. As Brown (1997) says:

> a grand-sounding term simply denotes an ordinary office complemented by fairly everyday equipment like mobile phones and laptop computers which mean that office workers don't need to be in the office itself to get on with their job. (p79)

As Colin Jackson of OTR believes, the virtual office is for those workers whose jobs are designed such that they normally work in an office but are in and out of the office, either in the outside environment (to see customers) or in other offices or branches of the same organisation, that is, they are away from their desks. Such workers require support and, to put this in economic terminology, demand and supply is there for the virtual office that was not present for teleworking. The

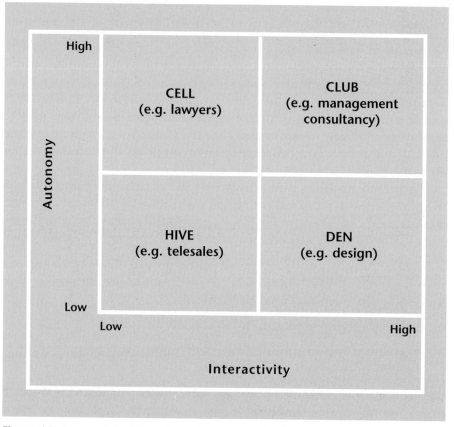

Figure 6.2 Four models of the office, after Brown (1997)

evolution in digital technology (see above) has meant a growth in speedy and accurate communication that allows individuals to work away from their desks.

Architect Francis Duffy (former president of the Royal Institute of British Architect (RIBA)) has stated that the key to office design, and thus the design of individuals' jobs and the way they work, is:

> understanding the relative importance of interaction and autonomy in job functions. (Brown, 1997, p84)

and he has proposed an office design which is divided into four models as shown in Figure 6.2.

The hive

In this design the workers have a low level of autonomy and low interaction and the hive works best for working on repetitive tasks which need little consultation with others. Examples here are data entry or call centres. Hives are open plan with standard workstations containing a personal computer (which may be networked) and a telephone.

The cell

Individuals here have a high level of autonomy and a low interaction and the cell is for those who have a limited need to talk with colleagues and who operate mainly at an independent level. Examples here would be lawyers and accountants. A cell is usually heavily partitioned and may well be a separate office.

The den

Employees here have low autonomy and high interaction where jobs are designed to have an element of decision making which often involves group activity and which draws on a range of skills. Dens are best suited for creative activities such as the production of a magazine or the design of a fashion layout. They tend to be open plan rooms separated from other groups.

The club

This is for those whose jobs require high autonomy and high interaction. Examples would be university lecturer and management consultant because both of these involve considerable communication with colleagues and a high degree of independence. Clubs can incorporate desk sharing and many modern elements of office design such as sofa areas with coffee tables and the use of mobile furniture, for example trolleys and wheeled workstations.

6.1

Activity

Observe the working environments of the various people who are employed at your university. Do not forget the non-teaching staff, such as the registrar's office, learning resources and deans.

Which ones exhibit the characteristics of a:

1 hive

2 cell

3 den

4 club?

Does any individual carry out a task or tasks within an environment that does not match any of the above categories? Why do you think that this is so?

The virtual office is the ultimate minimalist office and is now beginning to become popular. However, there are intermediate practices common in organisations that are affecting the design of jobs. Two of these are hot desking and hotelling where the point of the systems is to wean workers away from their territory – the instinctive need to have and to hold space which is their own. Through hot desking and hotelling, staff who are not permanently based at the office cease to possess their own desk. Through effective organisational planning and job design, such people are able to commandeer a workstation/desk whenever they need to come into the host organisation. Through hotelling or hot desking the right to have one's nameplate on a door or desk is taken away – the retention of such a culture is very expensive since an office building is typically unoccupied for 15 out of 24 hours and is occupied for only a fraction of time, if at all, at the weekends. Hotelling is depersonalising the workstation, that is, removing all the personal bits and pieces which people tend to use to territorise their work area.

Thus a smaller space can produce the same or a better output than before and some organisations are changing work design by introducing shift working to offices.

SCENARIO 6.4

How the creative use of office space can avoid relocation costs

When management consultants Andersen Consulting realised three years ago that continued expansion would mean it might soon outgrow its headquarters in Arundel Street it hit on a radical solution. Instead of searching for another building it looked around for another way to organise the present one that would allow for growth.

The solution, now fully implemented, was to turn the headquarters into a sort of hotel, only in this case the guests booked in to work rather than to sleep the night. Since a lot of its fee-earning consultants were, by the nature of their jobs, peripatetic, spending more time in the offices of clients than in Andersen's office, the organisation decided that they didn't need offices and desks of their own. They could simply book in, just as they would in to a hotel, when they needed an office.

The offices now have several different types of workstation, designed for anything from a transitory touchdown to a stay of a day or more. The booking system is PC based. Consultants who want a workstation can either book in person, by telephone, by voice mail or by e-mail. The request is acknowledged and fed into the system; then each morning the floor administrator gets a readout with the day's bookings. Andersen's Paris organisation has gone further than the London one. All staff have moved from their outer Paris building to one right in the centre of Paris where everyone, up to and including the partners, will have to use a workplace booking system. This is a sort of 'just-in-time' office. As well as bookable work spaces the office has a complete floor designed to look rather like an executive lounge at an airport.

Instead of booking in, people who are coming to the offices for a very short period will use this club lounge. They might be meeting people, collecting their mail or just touching base at the office to get a sense of belonging. It is here that workers can sit and rest, read the papers, discuss things with their peers. They can also use compact workstations in the lounge without having to book them.

The partners accept that there is a trade-off between privacy and comfort. They are losing their rights to space but getting instead one of the most magnificent and best equipped offices in the centre of Paris. Another thing which appeals to the partners is that the building makes a statement about Andersen. What they are actually saying to the outside is that most of their senior partners spend their time at clients' office and not at HQ. They are also stating that their mission is to help them become more successful and the building in Paris (located where the Champs Elysées meets the Avenue George V) is a living demonstration of what Andersen can do for their clients: they are able to make their people change – even the senior partners – in order to achieve a strategic goal in their business.

Source: Brown, M. (1997) Design for working, *Management Today*, March, pp77–84.

While there are economic arguments in favour of new technology and new designs for making the work environment and work more technologically efficient, it is essential that the feelings of the workforce are considered. Since work is an important part of the organisational member's life, it needs to be borne in mind that individuals need a psychologically secure base. Technology is continuing to dissolve distance and location is becoming irrelevant to the conduct of work, thus affecting how the jobs of individuals are designed and, particularly, redesigned to cope with technological innovation.

The age of electronic interconnection – the *knowledge age* wherein human beings work in tandem with smart machines – is in its infancy. Alongside this is the demise of mass production and the industrial concentration.

DEFINITION OF IT

Elliott and Starkings (1998) highlight the opinion that computing and IT are not interchangeable concepts stating that:

> Computing is part of information technology, but not the same as information technology. (p15)

They go on to say that IT:

> includes all aspects of computing, integrated with technological developments in networking and telecommunications technology. (p15)

Information is often defined in terms of a convergence of telecommunications and computing technologies and thus IT assumes an important role in the act of communication (discussed in ■ Chapter 5 ■) and the creation of information. Nurminen (1988) wrote that knowledge and information always exist in relation to a subject, that is, an individual who 'knows', or possesses, that information – a knowledge worker. This is a humanistic point of view because it emphasises the role of the individual in the communication process. As was discussed in ■ Chapter 5 ■, the individual, through processes of interpretation and reinterpretation, is essential to the production of information. It is the interpretation that produces the information because, otherwise, it would simply be data. It therefore follows that any definition of IT must have within it a human element or it will fail to be more than a concern for data handling.

see Chapter 5

see Chapter 5

POINTS TO PONDER

The Department of Trade and Industry in the UK has defined IT as:

The acquisition, processing, storage and dissemination of vocal, pictorial, textual and numeric information by an microelectronics-based combination of computing and telecommunications.

Source: Elliott, G. and S. Starkings (1998) *Business Information Technology: Systems, Theory and Practice*, London: Longman, p15.

STRATEGIC ADVANTAGE OF IT

In the globalised marketplace managers have increasingly to consider the role of information management in their constant search for the right combination of:

- strategy

- motivation

- technology

- organisational design.

According to Broderick and Boudreau (1992) it is only by doing this that they can maintain their competitive edge.

IMPACT OF IT ON ORGANISATIONAL STRUCTURE

The use of fast developing technology is causing an explosion in information. Traditional manual systems for storing, retrieving and disseminating information have been overtaken by high-speed communication links. Accompanying this has been the change in organisational structure from horizontal to lateral design which has brought about a differing in working patterns, for example outsourcing, and project teams where individuals have never worked with each other before and are from different backgrounds, with varying work habits and ethos. The impact of technology on organisational structures can be acute because organisations change as they grow and their approach to information technology can develop, or lag behind, that of their competitors. In the early years of an organisation, its structure evolves in a relatively unplanned way and this is usually accompanied by the inability to meet the broader strategic requirements. It is at this time that organisations tend to neglect the positive exploitation of information technology – particularly in relation to information and communication technology (ICT).

SCENARIO 6.5

ICT signals transformation in HR styles

The growing impact of information and communication technology (ICT) on traditional working patterns is one of the biggest challenges facing HR managers, according to a leading economist.

Duncan Campbell, senior economist in the employment strategy department of the International Labour Office (ILO), believes that ICT will lead to profound changes in the way companies are organised.

Teleworking, outsourcing work to remote locations and the move to network-based and virtual organisations will put pressure on traditional HR practices, Campbell said.

SCENARIO 6.5 cont'd

'These increasing ambiguous organisations are likely to be complemented by less defined occupational boundaries, because they need employees who are multi-disciplined, flexible and teamworkers', he said.

'These pressures will probably create new forms of industrial relations that will pose challenges, as well as opportunities, to both employers' and workers' organisations. These groups will be called upon to provide a new and extended range of services to members'.

Campbell believes that ICT will help to empower workers. And it will be mainly up to the individual to be disciplined and take responsibility for their working practices, he said.

'The greatest advantage of teleworking is that you can work any place, any time, and the greatest disadvantage of teleworking is that you can work any place, any time', he said.

'This is an HR issue. You can no longer have people clocking in and clocking out. You have to ask: "Did you produce or not?"'

Source: 'ICT signals transformation in HR styles' in *People Management*, 23 November 2000, p12.

SCENARIO 6.6

Hong Kong Polytechnic University Library

The Hong Kong Polytechnic University Library (HKPU) wanted to evaluate its management structure in the light of the need to make quicker responses to what was demanded of the library system in a period when there was an information revolution.

Until the introduction of the new library system, HKPU used a method that was very traditional and run on old-fashioned lines. Organisation was based on functional/subject lines until the demands of continuous and rapid development of global networking became increasingly important.

At this stage, the library staff agreed a strategy. A team approach to library services was essential if they were to respond quickly and proactively to the users' request for help in navigating the complexities of information retrieval. Such an approach would need to be activated across all the services provided by the library. This approach took the place of the previously very structured one and, consequently, brought with it a different sort of emphasis.

There was more dependence upon interpersonal relations with effective and continuous communication systems in place. There was also a need to increase the levels of trust between all the members of the library team. This informality and lack of reliance on rigid rules and hierarchies was difficult for some to adjust to.

The emphasis was on providing a fast, end-user service and resulted in the library encompassing all facets of learning support, for example computer services, multimedia production units, audio visual centres, books, journals.

Adapted from: Farrow, J. (1997) Management of change: technological developments and human resource issues in the information sector, *Journal of Managerial Psychology*, 12(5): 319–24.

Again, there is the problem of aligning specialist staff with the need, as in the case of the HKPU library, where staff were expected to become multiskilled and multi-tasking. This can increase the ▶ stress ◀ levels of staff because they are constantly working at high tension. Negative stress can be brought about by any force that pushes a psychological or physical factor beyond its range of stability, producing a strain within the individual – this is discussed in detail below.

Stress ◀┈▶ Any force that pushes a psychological or physical factor beyond its range of stability, producing a strain within the individual.

IT AND CHANGE

It is through IT that knowledge can be shared through discussion and the use of creative ideas which are then developed. This is the arena of the knowledge worker. IT allows the creation of a potentially problem-free organisation – an interesting view since the application of any aspect of behavioural science, for example leadership, conflict resolution and motivation, has not yet been able to create this. However, Adams (2000) states:

> A constraint on behaviour which information technology cannot remove is the number of hours in a day. (p27)

This view is useful because it fits in better with the now common flatter and leaner organisations with their associated pay-related systems and employees who are multiskilled and multidisciplined. It is through these procedures that employees are more able to self-actualise and achieve their highest goals. Interestingly enough, teamworking provides these behavioural environments and results in personal empowerment.

The use of IT within organisations is fraught with difficulty. This is particularly brought to the fore when reviewing past failures in the application of computerised systems in various organisations. In the UK such failures have been the ineffective implementation of the system at the London Ambulance Centre, the Taurus system at the London Stock Exchange and the system at the UK Passport Offices.

Organisational practices are highly complex yet it is vital that employers understand what an important role employees play in adapting and moderating the effects of computer technology – often in order to make it work.

The strength of socio-technical approaches is in how it stresses the importance of variations in organisational contexts of IT applications and the need to take notice of employees' social and work needs.

Users of IT should own the systems they interact with and, thus, the organisations in which they are employed. There should not be any losers because any interaction is a positive basis for challenging the theoretical and ethical assumptions and practical implications of the implementation of IT.

SCENARIO 6.7

Sounds of silence

Twenty people – specialists, experts, thinkers – sit around a seminar table. They might be discussing education or the US stock market. Although people are speaking, no one is saying anything.

At least half of the participants have an original idea at the front of their mind. But they do not share it because it is too valuable. They are afraid that one of the others will steal the idea and use it, publish or sell it before they do. Their intellectual property is at risk. So received wisdoms are recycled.

Images of the new economy are of speed, complexity, hubbub. You get the sense that it will be a noisy place. In fact, such is the fear of being intellectually gazumped that the new economy may echo to the sound of silence.

There has always been some caution about sharing ideas in a profession like journalism. But this caution seems to be spreading, especially into the world of policy – into thinktanks and government departments. On an individual level, hoarding and hiding make good sense. But collectively it impoverishes conversation – potentially to the detriment of good policy making.

This new intellectual coyness highlights the peculiar quality of information and ideas in a market economy. The essential problem is this: you cannot know the value of a piece of information until you know what the information is, and you cannot then give it back. You cannot feel the quality of an idea before you make the decision whether to buy it or not. This means that ideas make bad commodities.

Many of the best ideas come out of a conversation between at least two people. Who, then, do they belong to? The danger of legally based approaches is that they will make us more cautious, not less.

The argument that we are becoming intellectual scrooges flies in the face of current trends. Isn't the Internet democratising knowledge? And what about the free software at the heart of cyberspace? Far from living in monastic silence, aren't we being bombarded with ideas and information?

Well, yes. But most of the information we receive is of limited value. How many people who have a truly innovative idea will broadcast it on the Web? Some, but not many. With so much guff all over the place, the value of an original idea is worth guarding.

All this means that intellectual generosity is becoming rarer and much more precious. Suppose that Helen Wilkinson, writer on family issues and e-commerce, gives me an idea through conversations or in print, it is critical that I 'tag' the idea as hers, rather than succumbing to the temptation to pass it off as my own. Tagging means that Helen continues to reap the rewards of her intellectual labour. And tagging means that she will be willing to share other ideas in the future, that our conversations will be free of the fear of theft. In short, she will trust me, and vice versa. Trust becomes critical to the free flow of information.

There are issue for employers here, too. When someone's ability to add value rests on their ability to come up with ideas, how do you ensure they are working as hard for you as they should be? How do you know they are not storing up the best stuff for the online consulting firm they run from home?

In most cases, the desire of workers to be seen to be talented, to win promotion and greater financial reward is sufficient incentive. But as brighter, younger people tire of corporate hierarchies and become less willing to wait for their reward, the danger of staff leaving their brains at home can only grow. Managers have to become taggers too – ensuring that a breakthrough idea or killer phrase generated by one of their staff is credited properly to them. This means losing the fear that promoting the idea of your subordinates will threaten your position, which is not always easy.

Adapted from: Reeves, R. (2000) Sounds of silence, *Prospect*, March, p13.

MANAGEMENT IN THE INFORMATION ERA

Information is increasingly becoming the lifeblood of all organisations and the management of information and the use of new information technologies such as management information systems is a vital part of any manager's job.

According to Earl (1997) the concept of management is going out of date because:

> Information is the new resource and all companies are information companies and all managers are information managers. (p552)

He believes that organisations are energised by information because it is through the latter that products and services are developed and new ones come into the market. Along with this has come a new way to manage.

6.2

Activity

Review Scenario 6.7 and while doing so reflect on a time when you worked as part of a team, perhaps on a university project.

1 How did you deal with your own ideas and those submitted by others? Did you use the 'tag' method?

2 Consider using the 'tag' method in future situations where you share ideas.

Technology has to be part of an organisation's strategy and accompanying this there must be plans for action and policies which will combine to ensure that information is utilised to the full and not wasted. The success of an organisation will depend on its ability to link information strategy and business strategy which includes that of human resources as discussed in ■ Chapter 2 ■. The historical development of IT and business strategy is shown in Table 6.6.

see Chapter 2

Daft (1995) discusses the important aspect of the evolution of IT – the delineation in Table 6.6 is not as clear as expressed here. In Figure 6.3 this evolution is shown in diagrammatic form.

First-line management is usually characterised by well-defined, programmed problems about operational issues and historical events. This is in contrast with those at the top of the apex because they are concerned with uncertain and ambiguous issues, for example strategy, planning and other events which cannot be programmed yet about which decisions have to be made.

Table 6.6 Historical development of IT and business strategy

THE PAST	Business strategy took precedence with IT in a supporting role.
RECENTLY	While IT still supported business strategy it began to become important in providing opportunities for growth and development.
THE FUTURE	The *information age* will be common with IT taking the lead role and business strategy absorbed within it to become *information business strategy.*

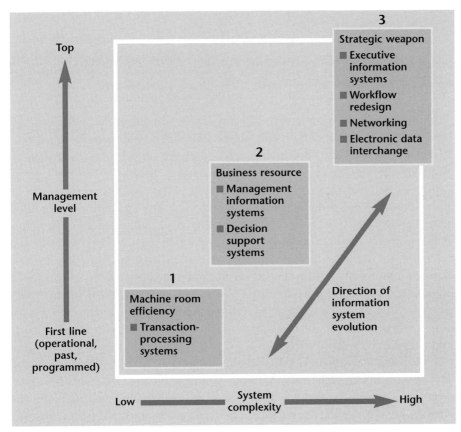

Figure 6.3 The evolution of organisational applications of IT, after Daft (1995, p301)

Wightman (1987) agrees because he states that the complexity of computer-based IT has increased and along with this applications have grown to include non-programmed issues at the level of top management. The unfortunate thing is that top management often misapplies this evolving technology.

In a large number of organisations these two factors are distinguishable, yet success will depend on an organisation being able to merge them into one factor – they have to be indistinguishable. Consequently, managers have to become:

> as skilled at managing information as at managing conventional resources. (Earl, 1997, p556)

INFORMATION AND KNOWLEDGE

It is common for individuals to use the words *information* and *knowledge* inter-changeably yet they actually refer to entirely different and distinct things.

Information is the product of a filtering process where raw data are turned into a form which has the potential of being useful. Knowledge, contrariwise, comes from the analysis of information within an expert frame of reference so that it incorporates actual meaning. This can be seen in Figure 6.4.

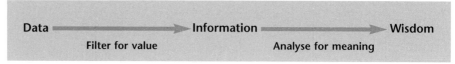

Figure 6.4 The relationship between data, information and knowledge

To use an example, a supermarket loyalty card is scanned at the store checkout. The information on that card provides the retailer with a continuous stream of *data*. In themselves, these data are useless unless they are turned into information by means of analysis. This is a filtering technique and is carried out automatically by a computerised management information system (MIS). Such information will be in the form of sales figures by checkout, product line, store position – or any other desired category such as the age, sex and buying habits of the card user. This information will only have meaning when it is reviewed by the retailer so that s/he can determine the status of business operations. It could well be that only, say, two items of information actually impact significantly on the retailer's knowledge of her/his store's continuing performance, for example most popular product lines and time of use. The extraction of information from data is automated by a computerised system but the translation of that information into meaningful knowledge requires human expertise.

Some individuals might argue that this distinction between information and knowledge is unimportant and very subtle. Some would also argue that it is situational and contextually sensitive, that is, it depends on the time and place of use and interpretation. However, the distinction is of increasing importance and is closely aligned to the increase in the number of knowledge workers and knowledge-based industries.

When you start up a business, potential clients say that you haven't the experience.

And when you are established in your business, they say they want someone new and cheap!

Adapted from: Pyne, K. (2000) Mr Smee, *The Times*, 22 February, p36.

IT AND KNOWLEDGE

In the 1990s the development of computer technology and telecommunications had the effect of 'making the world smaller' because information from all corners of the world was easily available. Such technology has allowed multinational organisations to control the production of their products on a global, rather than a local or national, scale. For example, in the field of fashion, it is common for the raw material, such as cotton, to be grown in one country, sent to another for the fabric to be woven, to another for manufacture and to another for sale. Therefore, the components will have visited several countries before the finished article is finally sold at a major market. IT has allowed huge markets to gain ▶ **economies of scale** ◀ because they can standardise and specialise their processes.

> ▶ The ability to benefit from being a large organisation, for example by buying in bulk. ◀┄┄▶ **Economies of scale**

There has been an ongoing and relentless change in expectations of the markets with consumers continually requiring new products and services. This has been accompanied by the gradual replacement of capital as it was known, for example buildings and machinery, and the use of high levels of labour. In its place have come the knowledge-intensive organisations and, according to Starbuck (1992), 'routine work by knowledge work' (p79).

It is not a new phenomenon. Drucker (1988) reported that researchers in the field of knowledge-based organisations were stating that most organisations in the service, industrial and government sections were increasingly becoming more knowledge intensive.

POINTS TO PONDER

In a few score* years there will be thousands of workers at this business of ordering and digesting knowledge where you now have only one.

* One score = 20 years.

Source: Wells, H.G. (1938) *World Brain*, London: Adamontine Press.

TECHNOLOGICAL DEVELOPMENTS AND KNOWLEDGE WORKERS

The amount of time spent by employees – particularly by staff and line managers – on analysis and document handling has been reduced by the inroads of automation. Accompanying this is a decrease in the time spent on non-productive tasks. With the increasing efficiency that increased automation brings comes more job satisfaction for employees whose jobs, as a result, become less repetitive and routine.

The new telecommunication technology is bringing about techniques which are making the physical work some employees have to do less important. With the increased use of personal computers, extensive use of e-mail and access to a central database or the office automation network of the organisation, some employees can become ▶ **telecommuters** ◀.

> ▶ Individuals who work away from the office, for example at home, and transmit their work ◀┄┄▶ **Telecommuters** from a home computer to the office by the use of a modem or cable.

It is the layer of middle management that is affected most by automation and telecommuting because their traditional functions of, for example supervising staff, is now redundant because of the increase in autonomous knowledge workers, the use of high-performance work teams and telecommuting. Thus organisations have become flatter and delayered so that they can speed up decision-making processes and influence the markets within which they stand.

Such technological developments – which include IT – have gradually become management tools. The areas are so sophisticated and powerful that some people believe that all decisions will be taken by computers. Others say that this is pure fancy because the human brain is far too complex to be completely simulated by digital technology.

In organisations today the emphasis is on the accurate timing of such decisions because they are crucial to the success of the organisation in the meeting of its objectives.

POINTS TO PONDER

People pose the problems.

People interpret the information.

People set priorities.

Technological innovation affects the nature of most jobs within an organisation but has had a specific impact on those members of the workforce who process information – the knowledge workers. With the increased use of self-managed teams has come the ability to access information at all levels of the organisation through all sorts of technological systems.

In the past, individuals often tended to extend their breaks whereas nowadays it is more likely that knowledge workers take more frequent breaks although they are not at the traditional times of mid-morning, lunch and mid-afternoon.

SCENARIO 6.8

The irritations of modern life: desktop lunches

Once upon a time, lunchtime meant just what it said: a time for lunch. It might be a large lunch, a small lunch, a snack or just a quick drink. But it didn't mean sitting hunched over your desk – not, at least, unless there was a crisis which needed sorting *right now*.

These days, lunch hours are strictly for wimps. Even among those Britons who still do take a break, few take as much as half an hour. According to a survey by Nimble, the breadmakers, one in four Britons takes no break at all; among women, the figure is even higher.

The refusal to leave the office for lunch leaves everybody feeling grumblingly virtuous and irritably unproductive. Worse, staying in doesn't just mean failing to eat, which would at least be a matter only of private grief. Instead, millions have succumbed to the alternative: the smelly box of lunch.

Once, office canteens existed so that employees could get away from their desks for a few minutes for a simple bite to eat. Nowadays, only skivers eat away from the computer screen. Dedicated workers know that they must bring back a polystyrene box.

The advantages are clear. The meal is not pleasurable and the employee can demonstrate that he or she is not relaxing (relaxing at lunch is a capital crime under the lunchtime working regulations, section 6 paragraph 3). The merged smell of various polystyrene lunches – chicken curry on one side, beef stew on the other, fish and chips wafting from across the room – is so dodgy that it proves the infinite loyalty of desk eaters.

Theoretically, desk eating is necessary because of work. In reality, when you are *really* under pressure, there is not time to queue for food. No, we are talking here about image.

An unpleasant lunch hour is proof of infinite virtue. The Bible taught us that those who suffer on earth shall be rewarded in heaven; in the office, similar rules apply (although the reward is deemed closer to hand).

Adapted from: Crawshaw, S. (2000) The irritations of modern life. Desktop lunches in The Wednesday Review, *The Financial Times*, 23 February, p7.

Working with a computer having a keyboard input can encourage repetitive strain injury (RSI) and there is the chance that, without careful monitoring, individuals will suffer eye strain, neck and back strain, headaches and depression as a result of sitting at a computer terminal for too long. Individuals are also now so used to technology giving them a response very quickly that they are becoming very short tempered and aggressive with co-workers who, because they are human, may take longer to reply and may not be as accurate as the computer.

SCENARIO 6.9

Finger of suspicion

Early 19th-century typewriters were large and cumbersome and wholly impractical. The first functional typewriter was invented in the USA, in 1867, by Christopher Latham Sholes (typically, it was based on a British prototype) and went into production in 1874.

Almost everything has changed since, except the most obvious; the QWERTY keyboard. This was not invented to boost typing speeds, as you might suppose, rather to slow them down.

Early typewriters were prone to jamming when character keys were pressed in quick succession. QWERTY solved this problem by making it difficult to type fast enough to cause a character pile up. (The makers of the first typewriters, however, wanted their salesmen to be able to type one word very quickly to impress the people to whom they were selling. That's why all the letters for 'typewriter' are on the top line, along with q, u and o.)

A few years later, when manufacturers had sorted out the jamming problem, they toyed with the idea of introducing a rational keyboard. But by that time an entire industry had grown up around the QWERTY system: typing schools and secretarial courses were all based on it. So they decided it would be better to leave things as they were.

Perhaps another reason for not bothering to change the keyboard was that QWERTY users were mostly women. The typewriter had an enormous social effect: the first jobs respectable young ladies could hold outside the home were positions as typists and, later, telegraphists and telephonists.

Naturally, all work involving typing became a female preserve. Male bosses made a point of not knowing how to type at all, while senior male journalists wilfully dictated their copy to a secretary or wrote it out in longhand to be typed up later by an

SCENARIO 6.9 cont'd

underling. Rumour has it that some still do.

But then along came the computer and the ability to type became a necessity. So men finally got into the typing lark and immediately came up with a computer keyboard using the same QWERTY system but including a plethora of other keys of very dubious provenance.

There are 101 keys on the average PC keyboard: about 25 per cent of them are redundant or serve no practical purpose. To take but one example, what is the point of the 'insert' key? (Or keys – there are actually two of them.) On most computer keyboards, one of them lurks beside the 'delete' key, and so is easily activated by mistake. Only too late do you discover you're overtyping all the stuff you wrote before.

And why has the 'caps lock' key, which was the same size as any other key on typewriters, mutated into a megakey on computer keyboards, making it all but impossible to miss as you're fumbling for the 'A', and ENSURING YOU'LL TYPE THE REST OF THE LINE IN UPPER CASE? We should be told.

Adapted from: Mungo, P. (2000) The full picture: anatomy of a keyboard in Finger of Suspicion, the business, *Financial Times*, 19 February, pp24–5.

It is now possible to use computerised monitoring to check on employee performance but with this has come the potential for misuse.

POINTS TO PONDER

An employer can listen in to any telephone conversation which is made by an employee and also track the use of the Internet – reading e-mail received and sent and websites surfed.

In a recent survey of human resource managers, 64 per cent said it was an acceptable thing to do but only if the employer was investigating a financial loss. If the purpose of monitoring was for updating the quality of services then the response was 'No' for 66 per cent of the respondents. Most of the resource managers surveyed (94 per cent) stated that if the employees were advised in advance that their conversations and use of the Internet *could* be monitored, then it was in order to do so.

Source: Human Resource Magazine (1992) September, p21.

The growth of the use of the internet in the space of just a few years has transformed how employees work and how they can transmit or acquire information at a fraction of the speed at which they could previously. (p30)

So writes McKinnery (2000) who goes on to stress that with these huge benefits have come some legal issues. Many employers have already encountered problems with employees in connection with the misuse of their computer and have been seeking advice of the legal experts in relation to such issues.

In late 1999 a case was publicised in the British national newspapers in relation to an employee who was fired because he had used his office computer to access the Internet and book himself a holiday. An employment tribunal in Liverpool ruled that the employee was guilty of misconduct and his dismissal was justifiable because he had used the computer at work to make 150 searches on the Internet.

This is the first reported case where an employment tribunal has judged that to use an office computer to gather information constitutes grounds for dismissal. The employer argued that the employee stole time from them, by using it to look at the Internet, so depriving the employer of at least 30 minutes of each day in surfing the Internet for entertaining material (it is estimated that British companies 'lose' £2.5m annually because of employees surfing the Internet for non-work-related material). The employee lied at the tribunal when asked how long he had spent using the Internet. The employing organisation was able to provide evidence in documentation form as to what the employee had actually accessed, and when, over four different days. The tribunal upheld the claim for breach of contract and awarded the ex-employee one month's salary in lieu of notice.

Amphlett (2000) also warns that there are pitfalls in such activities and that organisations should have a clear policy on the use of the Internet and e-mail:

> Employers will want to monitor the use of the Internet and e-mail to ensure compliance.
> (Amphlett, 2000, p24)

She makes the point that a policy alone may not be sufficient. In the past monitoring has been unregulated but with the implementation of the Data Protection Act 1998 in March 2000 has come protection. The Code of Practice on the Act – drafted by an independent consultancy, the Personnel Policy Research Unit, and approved by the Data Protection Registrar – has been implemented. Since it has statutory backing the ▶ **employment tribunals** ◀ and courts will have to consider it. More discussion on employment legislation can be found in ■ Chapter 7 *and* Chapter 8 ■.

see Chapter 7 *and* Chapter 8

▶ Panels which deal with minor bureaucratic issues related to employment disputes such as redundancy, unfair dismissal, deductions from pay, discrimination and breach of contract. ◀┈┈▶ **Employment tribunals**

McKinnery (2000) believes that legal action – on either side – can be avoided if the employer has a set of ground rules in the form of an 'acceptable policy'. In addition to describing the acceptable uses, she says, it is always necessary for policy to specify the prohibited uses, rules of online behaviour and access privileges. She recommends that employers clearly define the penalties for breach of an agreed policy and that this should include security violations (such as downloading pornography, ownership of domain names and defamation of other individuals) and vandalism of the system (computer rage). Such a policy should be incorporated in the staff handbook or other written agreement given to all employees.

KNOWLEDGE AND IT PLANNING

see Chapter 1
and Chapter 2

It has been suggested by Rockart and Short (1991) that IT planning and design recognises the need for supporting integration among differentiated sub-units in contemporary organisations. For example, departments which used to specialise in one activity, say, personnel, now integrate their activities across all departments within the organisation (■ *see* Chapter 1 *and* Chapter 2 ■ for information on the changing role of personnel).

However, Tenkasi and Boland (1996) argue that it is traditional that information systems lack the integration of differentiated knowledge and expertise and are unable to facilitate mutual learning. That is, they are not able to marry the need for individuals to continue to become experts in their own specialist fields and become members of a team with shared interests and specialisms. Tenkasi and Boland (1996) propose that:

> Exploring diversity in knowledge intensive first is... a new frontier for the development of information technology. (p80)

MANAGING TECHNOLOGY: FRUSTRATION AND STRESS

Some commentators believe that stress is a fashionable way of 'swinging the lead', others report that their research indicates that a certain amount of tension at work is healthy. However, there is still evidence that individuals having to use technology become very stressed.

There is a story going round about a new computer user who rang the help desk of the company from which he had purchased his computer system. He had read on the screen:
'Press any key.'
His question: 'Where is the "any" key?'

In the case of the library staff at HKPU library (Scenario 6.6), they found that they used a tremendous amount of energy (Mendelsohn, 1994) in increasing quantities, as shown in Figure 6.5.

In the past, library staff were able to plateau after a period of activity during which time they could reflect on what they had done and regenerate their batteries. Now, the periods of activity where they are using maximum energy have increased dramatically and, as the plateaux become shorter, the library staff become exhausted. This behaviour is now common in most workplaces. More and more employees are becoming multiskilled and multitasking and so their activity levels are high with plateau times reducing. This is further compounded with the increase in downsizing staff.

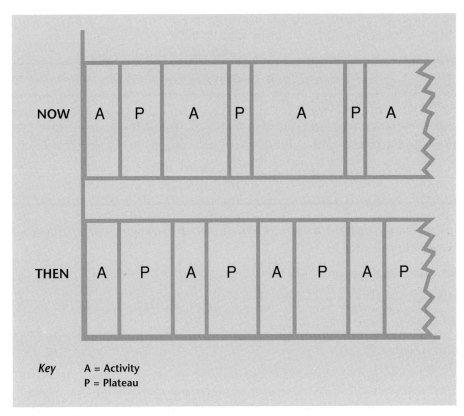

Figure 6.5 The increased use of activity over plateau

Such a work pattern can result in high levels of negative stress and with it the objectives of the individual and, therefore, the organisation will not be met. A key point related to stress in the workplace is that stress, like change, is self-perpetuating, so raising the awareness of frustration and stress could well result in negative stress for the manager. However, there is no doubt that workplace stress is a part of the life of employees today – particularly those who are knowledge workers. Apart from having to cope with the intricacies of managing their own work, they often have to manage other people in the workplace and so operate in a complex environment – one made even more complicated by increased work diversity, technological innovation, ethical factors and ▷ **globalisation** ◁ (all discussed in ■ Chapter 11 ■).

see Chapter 11

▶ When something, especially a business or company, becomes international or starts oper- ◀┈┈▶ **Globalisation**
ating at an international level.

A consideration of frustration and stress, therefore, can help to link all the factors related to the behaviour of people as employees in the workplace. Stress can also be seen as an excess of perceived demands over an individual's ability to meet them – as in the case of the librarians at HKPU library.

6.3 Activity

Reflect on the times when you have felt stressed.

Were the periods of time spent on activity increased at the expense of plateauing?

What effect do you think this had on your performance, say, in the preparation of a piece of work for university?

With this in mind, the Institute of Management Foundation (1997) recommends that individuals need to:

- recognise the symptoms of stress

- search out the sources of the pressure

- identify coping strategies.

This is because:

> Successive waves of downsizing, closures and reorganisations [have] put pressure on managers and employees alike. Additionally, technological changes to improve the speed of communications... have created twenty-four hour accessibility. This is a potential recipe for disaster. The detrimental effects of poorly managed pressures can be measured in terms of the cost to organisations and society as a whole. It has been estimated that 40 million working days or £7 billion are lost annually due to stress. The cost to individuals is less easy to measure but it affects the quality of life and relationships and can be enormous. (p1)

While managers dream, as do others in the workplace, of reducing the strain on the complex working environment brought about by, for example, IT, the reality is that they are not able to do so – the result is frustration and stress.

FRUSTRATION

When individuals are unable to achieve their objectives because something hinders, disturbs or thwarts their progress, for example the need to learn new software programs, they will become frustrated. Such barriers could be situational or environmental, thus they are external to the individual and beyond his/her control. An example of this could be a computer software-assisted presentation which 'crashes' during a session. They could also be internal such as the tendency to talk incessantly when s/he is unable to carry out an activity or deal with a person who is perceived as behaving in a difficult way. It is an individual condition which is based on individual perception and not on the external environment, as is often believed.

POINTS TO PONDER A computer should be called Tomasina/Tom because it is a Totally Obedient Moron.

When discussing motivation ■ *see* Chapter 7 ■, it can be seen that needs are not always satisfied. As a result frustration, accompanied by tension, occurs. This is an increasing phenomenon as the complexity of the work environment and the demands made upon individuals within it result in more barriers being raised to frustrate personal ambition (the move to leaner and flatter organisations and its effect on promotion opportunities). Lack of knowledge and continuous development opportunities (the technological revolution) also frustrate individuals. A young person who has career goals that require a university education but who lacks the intellectual aptitude for university work has overestimated her/his abilities. This principle applies also to a manager already on the career ladder in that s/he may be capable of carrying out the job specification but s/he has erected an individual barrier by undermining her/his own self-esteem. Individuals at work continually strive to achieve personal goals and are frequently frustrated by such internal factors as well as by external barriers erected by the organisational design and its environment.

see Chapter 7

An organisation is not composed of bricks and mortar but of people and it is the actions of others that can frustrate the achievement of personal goals. For example, a manager who wants to ensure that a report gets to the CEO swiftly could well be frustrated because the finance department has not provided the financial analysis required to accompany the report. Most on-the-job frustrations tend to result from dysfunctional conflict related to the dynamics of organisations and the restraints of organisational practices. As an organisation comprising human beings attempts to meet the needs of individual employees, there is a move from externalising to internalising individual needs.

Frustration can be perceived as dysfunctional and it is in this state that individuals allow it to affect them. Managers need to appreciate that frustration can be functional and can be used to help them achieve personal and organisational objectives by means of:

■ *Strengthening effort*
Sometimes frustration can act as a catalyst which stimulates the effect required to achieve the required objective. However, the goals must be achievable by a recognised procedure. If the latter is not provided, frustration could lead to the abandonment of the initial goal, which will be replaced by another which is seen to be achievable, but may well not be appropriate to meeting the needs of either the individual or the organisation's goals.

■ *Evaluating other methods*
When a person is frustrated a common action is to choose a different method of achieving the desired objective. When tension is increased because a barrier (internal or external) cannot be eliminated, then an individual will find an

alternative objective. For example, if the worker wants to achieve a high-quality report but the financial department cannot be relied upon to produce the data in time, the individual may well decide to do the research into the financial matters her/himself.

■ *Trying another objective*
When frustrated an individual could choose a different objective which s/he knows s/he can achieve. Such a change in direction is very often attractive because the worker cannot remove the perceived barriers to her/his initial goal.

However, it is not always possible for a worker to eliminate the barriers which block the achievement of personal and/or organisational objectives. Whether these are real or not is irrelevant – *they are perceived as real by the individual.* In such a case the tension and frustration might well reach such a high level that the effects of it disrupt objective-directed activities. At this stage an individual will usually become highly emotional and thus lose the ability to make rational decisions or deal positively with the situation. For example, when an employee has been working steadily towards an attainable objective and finds that such work results in frustration, s/he may become emotional and actually cause physical and psychological damager to her/himself and others in the process. It is, therefore, vital that frustration is avoided, yet a certain level of frustration can act as a springboard to effective achievement of objectives. The level of frustration an individual can control is a matter of individual toleration, some people being able to tolerate high levels of frustration and others not so much. Some tasks involve more pressure than others but all employees must be able to tolerate some frustration. Employees need to be able to recognise in themselves and in their colleagues when a tolerance level has been exceeded and this is usually exhibited by the onset of aggressive behaviours and/or a withdrawal from the situation through stress behaviours and depression.

SCENARIO 6.10

Stressed managers complain of e-mail overload

E-mails have piled additional stress of Britain's managers, who say that having to cope with their overloaded 'inboxes' is damaging their work performance and home lives.

In a study of more than 8000 managers, published in February 2000 by the Institute of Management, keeping up with e-mails has entered the top 10 stresses of modern working life for the first time. Nearly one-quarter of people interviewed said it has caused them stress in the past 12 months.

Previous research conducted by the Institute showed that in 1993 'new technology' was not a stressful subject for managers in Britain, who were more concerned about office politics and incompetent senior management.

However, the new technology in general seems to be increasing stress in people's working lives. E-mails are an interruption and, because people are having new technology foisted on them by IT professionals with little training, it is causing high stress. New technology may not be the new panacea it once appeared.

The research report *Taking the Strain*, shows that British managers are failing to heed the warning signs of stress and that many are failing to survive and thrive in today's pressured work environment.

The top 10 sources of pressure cited by managers include constant interruptions, lack of support, poor senior management and time pressure. Nearly three-quarters of those surveyed said that stress adversely affected their performance at work, as well as their home life, health and enjoyment of life in general.

Most managers experienced a range of stress symptoms, including excessive tiredness, disturbed sleep and lower sex drive. The most popular ways of coping with stress are physical exercise, talking to friends, drinking alcohol and shopping.

Constant change has become a part of working life and two-thirds of the managers said that they now had increased responsibilities because business restructuring had led to the loss of staff in key positions.

Adapted from: Norton, C. (2000) Stressed managers complain of e-mail overload, *The Independent*, 24 February, p9.

STRESS MANAGEMENT

Occupational health and organisational effectiveness are closely aligned and it is in the interest of the employer and employee that the workforce is in good health. The Institute of Personnel and Development (IPD) (1996) issued a keynote statement with a viewpoint, based on field research, which highlighted their belief that stress in the workplace has to be properly managed if it is to be controlled. They believe that:

■ people work more effectively within a participative management style

■ people are better motivated when work satisfies economic, social and psychological needs

■ motivation improves if attention is paid to job design and work organisation. (p1)

In the same document the IPD addressed stress in a work setting, stating that it had become one of the principal health issues of the contemporary workplace. The point was made that stress was more common among manual workers than managers. With the flatter organisational structure has come increased pressure for the organisation to remain competitive in a globalised market. Change should make them more flexible and the combination of both places the employees under considerable stress. The IPD (1996) acknowledges the fact that it is not always possible to prevent stress associated with job insecurity, but employers should be able to monitor and control the known causes of stress, which are:

■ autocratic and erratic management

■ ineffective communication processes

■ overwork

■ lack of autonomy over work practices.

The Health and Safety Executive recognises that occupational stress is within their remit and employers should appreciate this factor as well since guidance can be obtained from the Executive. In order to alleviate occupational stress a problem-solving approach needs to be adopted. Such an approach should take into account other key organisational concepts such as the culture of the organisation, individual circumstances and personality and the work itself.

There is a significant amount of literature available about occupational stress. However, it is vital that employers and employees – particularly those responsible for human resources development within the organisation – recognise that their responsibility stops with an appreciation of the relevant factors associated with stress and its management and that they are not qualified to intervene in cases of serious disorder or potential disorder. Such workers should be referred to the relevant practitioners through the organisation's occupational health system.

RECOGNISING OCCUPATIONAL STRESS

Arnold et al. (1997) define stress as:

> any force that pushes a psychological or physical factor beyond its range of stability, producing a strain within the individual. (p359)

It can be described as any experience which is unpleasant which either over- or under-stimulates an individual and which, in turn, has the potential to led to ill health. Additionally, individuals can feel threatened by knowing that stress constitutes a threat to them. Cummings and Cooper (1979) summarised a way of understanding stress in their schema shown in Figure 6.6.

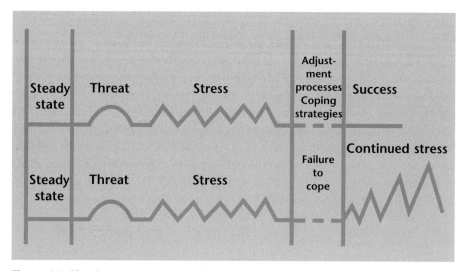

Figure 6.6 The Cummings–Cooper scheme (1979)

ORGANISATIONAL EFFECTS OF STRESS

Individuals exhibiting high stress within the workplace will affect the organisation and the achievement of organisational goals. There are four key areas where the consequences of high stress can be exhibited:

- *physical*
  headaches, chronic indigestion, tiredness, ulcers, heart attacks

- *psychological*
  anxiety, chronic depression, aggression and bullying, low self-esteem

- *behavioural*
  eating disorders, abuse of drugs (including nicotine and alcohol), emotional outbursts, sleeplessness

- *organisational*
  absenteeism, high job turnover, accidents, dysfunctional conflict, low productivity.

Occupational stress is a dynamic force that interacts with a number of key organisational issues. Arnold et al. (1997) identify five categories which are found to be causally responsible for work stress and common to all jobs:

- factors intrinsic to the job

- organisational role of the individual

- work relationships

- career developments

- organisational structure and climate.

Arnold and his co-writers (1997) developed a model (Figure 6.7) to explain the interaction of the above factors.

Any change will cause anxiety and stress among some staff, but not all. There will always be some individuals who will welcome the break from their daily routine and who want to learn new skills. However, there can be problems where individuals have, for example, joined an organisation to do a particular job but find that as the use of IT pervades all jobs and they begin to view its import into their job as deskilling and a threat to their position and their way of working. As was discussed in ■ Chapter 5 ■, technophobes and technosceptics have an even more difficult time. This is stressful, because instead of being an experienced and competent staff member, the individual is out of water because he has to learn alongside the newest, most junior member of staff.

see **Chapter 5**

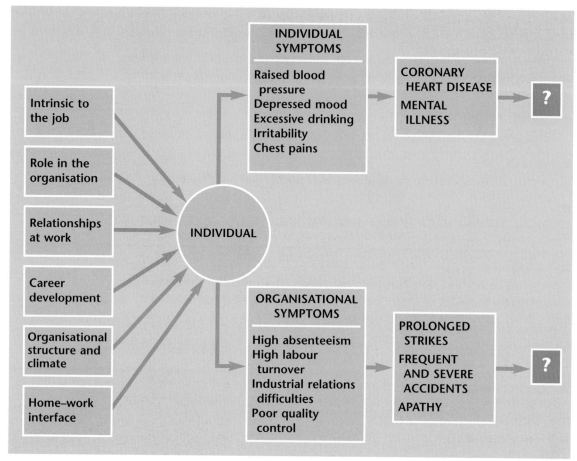

Figure 6.7 The dynamics of occupational stress, after Arnold et al. (1997)

CONTROLLING STRESS

In order to control stress it is desirable for individuals to identify what is a bearable level of stress of them. Therefore, employers need to appreciate that they and their employees can each cope with differing levels of tension. As mentioned above, the control of stress should be placed in the hands of the professionals. However, there are some basic strategies that individuals can use to control stress by controlling their individual behaviour. Such strategies include:

■ avoidance of high-pressure situations

■ managing situations in such a way that tension and frustration are both controlled

■ reacting to potential stress areas less intensely.

Employers should attempt to minimise stress in their organisations and should understand that the effectiveness of any specific action will depend on the situational factors and the nature of the individuals involved. A certain amount of tension and frustration can be positive yet managers can provide the foundations for aiding stress reduction by:

■ aiding subordinates to recognise and analyse the sources of occupational stress

■ making informational material available to employees

■ providing professional counselling

■ offering stress-management training

■ listening to what employees say rather than superficially hearing them ■ *see* Chapter 5 ■

see **Chapter 5**

■ avoiding telling the subordinate what to do.

Regardless of the tools available to employers, they should not try to practise psychotherapy or psychiatry unless they are qualified to do so. As in all organisational contexts, managers should deal only with areas in which they are competent, which are usually work-centred decision making and problem solving. Unfortunately, particularly in a large organisation, senior managers get so far removed from the front line that they have no idea of the impact of their decisions on the workforce. Hence the introduction of such fora as works councils and representative bodies.

Managers need to reassess their attitudes to work practices and understand the importance of how individuals behave and are managed in the workplace. People need to perceive that they have a say over what they do and when they do it and that being told what to do all the time can be destructive. Positive stress programmes in the workplace can assist but senior management must be committed to them, no matter what level of staff they are eventually provided for. There are dire consequences for firms that choose not to reassess their negative attitudes towards workplace stress because it will show up in the form of a lack of cooperation, less creativity, lower productivity, high turnover or employees not meeting their targets.

The way forward is to look at human relationships in the workplace and understand that employees are individuals and work more effectively in very different ways.

KNOWLEDGE WORKERS

Knowledge workers comprise individuals who are involved in the creation of new information or knowledge, as distinct from those individuals who are categorised as ▶ **data workers** ◀.

▶ Individuals who use, manipulate, process and disseminate information. ◀┄┄▶ **Data workers**

According to Adkin et al. (1997) knowledge workers are those individuals who deal with ever-changing information so complex that only they can understand it. These are the individuals with the specialist knowledge and because of this it is not possible to tell them what to do. They cannot be directed and are very difficult to manage in the traditional sense. Because of the nature of contemporary business, its complexity and need for expertise, these people are on the increase in organisations and have taken the place of the more traditional labour force. Such knowledge workers have to be led by being shown the mission and vision of the organisation and to understand and appreciate its goals. Linked with this is the need to motivate them intrinsically to use the knowledge they have in a way only they know how.

POINTS TO PONDER

Denying all knowledge

The new generation of knowledge workers could be keeping precious information from employers, according to researchers at Birkbeck College, London, England.

More companies are asking their staff to share their knowledge, which they increasingly see as a vital weapon.

But less rigid employment contracts and the pressure to manage one's own career is leading to knowledge hoarding. Individuals realise that their marketability depends on their knowledge. They are not going to give that away if it means they cannot realise their full value in the labour market.

Adapted from: Denying all knowledge (2000), *People Management*, 20 January, p18.

KNOWLEDGE WORK, LEARNING AND TRAINING

According to Boland and Tenkasi (1995) knowledge work is about creating fresh understanding of the nature of organisations, markets and how the application of these factors and their application within an organisation and their effect on technologies – particularly IT – within the organisation.

Knowledge work requires expertise across all disciplines, for example HRM, economics, marketing, finance and IT. Not only is such multidisciplinary expertise required but so also is ▶ **mutual learning** ◀. Only in this way can organisations work successfully in a business environment which is highly complex and where specialist, state-of-the-art technology is used.

Mutual learning ◀┈▶ Common or shared learning.

There is no doubt that ▶ **open learning** ◀ and technology-based ▶ **training** ◀ are now part of an organisation's daily life, yet the potential they offer are not yet fully being met. It is vital that IT is successfully integrated into the development programme of all organisations.

> A system whereby individuals can access learning materials such as computer programs, CD-ROMs, DVDs, books and videos. ◄····▶ **Open learning**

> A planned process to modify attitude, knowledge or skill behaviour through learning experience to achieve effective performance in an activity or range of activities. ◄····▶ **Training**

According to Carnall (1999):

> The emerging evidence... does appear to show that properly integrated electronic learning has a role to play. (p57)

It is important that employers integrate ▶ **electronic learning** ◄ (e-learning) into the workplace so that there are alternatives available to employees and they are able to access information and, therefore, develop ideas more completely and soundly.

> Learning through the use of technology. ◄····▶ **Electronic learning**

According to Maisie (1999):

> The world of learning is changing and learning is changing the world. (p32)

E-learning is now globally used in most sectors of business but especially in the financial sector. It also has an increasing alignment with ▶ **electronic commerce** ◄ (e-commerce). For example, an individual can download information from the Internet on, say, a product and this information can be learned from. Organisations are increasingly concentrating on delivering knowledge and competencies to their stakeholders in this way. Time is saved in the decision-making process because, for example, by purchasing a new product or taking advantage of an Internet service and even by communicating and implementing that decision, learning is taking place throughout the organisation – it is being shared.

> Carrying out transactions through electronic information systems such as the Internet. ◄····▶ **Electronic commerce**

All new developments need new knowledge and learning and, as discussed in ■ Chapter 10 ■, learning is about bringing a change in behaviour and is one of the most difficult areas to speed up. This is a key advantage of e-learning because it has that speed. Work carried out by Maisie (1999) in the USA, Asia and the Middle East shows that organisations tend to take on board online learning primarily because the data are available when the learners are available and wishing to learn. Individuals have to want to learn – it cannot be forced upon them. The UK government is embarking on the validation of degrees provided entirely through the Internet.

see Chapter 10

At present there is a huge change in how learning and development (discussed in ■ Chapter 10 ■) are to be achieved. The people who will benefit the most are

see Chapter 10

those who effectively integrate learning and development to add real value. This can only be achieved if the workers who are engaged in the real problem-solving and decision-making situations are able to access information immediately they require it. Training courses are redundant – there is now no time because organisational problems have to be sorted immediately if the organisation is to remain in the competitive arena.

SCENARIO 6.11

A word of warning

In small and medium-sized businesses (those with up to 500 employees) most employees feel unprepared to deal with new technology. Despite this, most believe that it is important to invest in new technology, with 60 per cent believing that the Internet will be key to business survival.

According to a MORI survey of 900 workers in 316 firms (carried out on behalf of Compaq and One2One):

- Half of men and three-quarters of women in small and medium-sized firms feel they can't cope with new technology. Firms with fewer than 50 employees admit to the greatest concern.

- A quarter of respondents think that new technology is likely to be a waste of time and money.
- A further 20 per cent would prefer to go back to using older methods such as typewriters and faxes.
- Over 90 per cent think that it's important to invest in new technology.
- Businesses in the south of the UK are more technology friendly than those in the north or Scotland, although the north-east is less prepared for technological change than the north-west, and the south-west in less prepared than the south-east.
- Even in London, a quarter of workers are anxious about using new technology.

Source: Johnson, R. (1999) A word of warning in Maisie, E. (1999) Joined-up thinking, *People Management*, 25 November, p35.

Technology gives workers access to knowledge and allows the learning achieved to be more readily shared. In the UK the University for Industry (UfI) has been developed – see Scenario 6.12.

The principal aim of the UfI is to deliver online learning opportunities by endorsing material that already exists and enhancing what it is able in order to make it suitable for the needs of the learners. Where there are gaps in that provision, the UfI intends to commission new packages. The aim of the UfI is to identify courses, enrol, charge for the course (through smartcards and online financial transactions), provide the learning material and give support – all electronically.

In its developmental stages, the UfI was criticised for its lack of relevance to business and difficulties in attracting interest – particularly from smaller organisations. Now, the UfI has designed its services in consultation with employer bodies such as:

- Training Enterprise Councils (disbanded April 2000)
- British Chambers of Commerce
- Confederation of British Industries
- Trades Union Congress.

Current development is in the field of services for the small and medium-sized organisations which need packages specifically tailored to their individual needs. According to Carnall (1999) a key factor in organisations is to 'bring the relevant knowledge to the workplace [and] has the need to focus training programmes on real organisational issues' (p57).

SCENARIO 6.12

Centre stage for the University for Industry (UfI)

Churches, community centres, sports clubs and supermarkets were among the first organisations signing up to run local learning centres as part of the UfI. Even a funfair put in a bid to host one of the first centres which were launched in the UK on 24 November 1999.

The new centres are fast-track development projects designed to further test the UfI concept. Some will have only one computer terminal; others are fully equipped with a range of technology and libraries of support materials.

From small beginnings, UfI will become, perhaps, the ultimate in online learning service providers, networking the entire country together, as well as bringing learning to local communities through around 1000 local learning centres. It went 'live' across the country in the autumn of 1999. Up to one million learners are expected by 2004, with 2.5m people logging on to the advice service. The programme will have received £44m of government funding by the end of its first year.

For the first time these centres will have run a limited number of online training packages in seven areas where chronic skills shortages have been identified. These are: small businesses, automotive components, environmental services, retail and distribution, IT, multimedia and basic skills. These are backed up by induction courses for technophobes and those with little experience of using computers. Training is supported by online and face-to-face **mentoring** and Internet discussion groups.

The first centres are assessing demand and testing the learning materials, support systems and technology on offer. They are also offering the UfI advice service, Learning Direct, by phone and Internet. Learning Direct points customers in the direction of appropriate courses for their needs, with information on funding sources and other means of assistance, including childcare.

Most of the courses are delivered by new technology, including interactive digital TV and video and CD-ROM as well as Internet.

Adapted from: Johnson, R. (1999) Centre stage for the UfI, People Management, 25 November, p36.

▶ The act of being a teacher and protector to a junior colleague. ◀┈┈▶ Mentoring

SCENARIO 6.13

Knowledge vision understood

The UK government's goal of a knowledge-based economy could be threatened by a dearth of information literacy skills. Many businesses lack the information management skills needed to fully explore the knowledge they have access to. Unless there is a substantial investment in information literacy, the knowledge economy is likely to pass the UK by.

Adapted from: Knowledge vision understood, People Management, 20 September, p12.

Technology gives employees access to knowledge and allows what they learn to be shared with others in the organisation. This will only be truly successful, however, when the technology is fully integrated into all learning activities and the development of business. New technology is a powerful tool which not only enables learning to take place but also adds observable – and demonstrable – value to the organisation's activities.

Schank (1999) agrees, stating that there is no doubt that online training has the potential of being truly effective but emphasises that this will not be fully integrated until the traditional teaching and training methods are abandoned, for example lectures. The point is not that computers, multimedia and the Internet can provide the answers – it is about how they make up a toolbox to add to the process of education. Just because the medium is new does not mean that the message is successfully received and understood.

Training managers see the new training technology skills as more important to their jobs than they did in 1998 (Rana, 2000). The study highlighted the fact that the workload of trainers had increased – and shows signs of continuing so to do. Despite this, they report a high level of job satisfaction among HRM professionals because they are increasingly being allowed to contribute to an organisation's busi-

see Chapter 2   ness strategy (discussed in ■ Chapter 2 ■).

Businesses are now very complicated and have to rely on the integration of knowledge and expertise. For example, the pharmaceutical industry does not rely solely on the skill and knowledge of chemists to produce drugs, but also, according to Tenkasi and Boland (1996), on the expertise of individuals with knowledge and experience in molecular biology, physiology and pharmacology.

The concept of knowledge work is an integral part of the organisation as a

see Chapter 10   ▶ **learning organisation** ◀. There is more on this in ■ Chapter 10 ■. In his ▶ **seminal** ◀ work, Senge (1990) stated that it is such organisations that can create the necessary systematic knowledge by integrating their various interdependent parts.

Learning ◀┅▶ **organisation**	An organisation which encompasses an attitude that has developed the continuous capacity to adapt to the environment and to change. Such an organisation also supports the self-development of members of the workforce towards this end.
Seminal ◀┅▶	A piece of writing or something of a similar nature that is highly original and important.

However, a difficulty arises here: the specialists have to keep their expertise up to date, that is, keep their knowledge base separate so that they maintain an understanding which is unique to them.

6.4

Activity

Find out if any of your lecturers at university experience the difficulty related to the separation of their knowledge base from that of their role as a team member within a department/school/faculty. See if they will tell you how they cope with this.

SCENARIO 6.14

Most large US corporations boast an employee with the job title chief knowledge officer – yet there does not appear to be any convincing explanation of what such people actually do. It is, perhaps, obvious to say that they manage knowledge (whatever that involves) and give complex speeches at conferences concerned with knowledge management.

At the Deutsche Bank in Frankfurt, Germany, there is a job entitled 'head of fundamental issues' which appears to be even more difficult to analyse. For example: who is responsible for non-fundamental issues? What about having a job for 'head of trivial pursuits'?

In today's workplace, individuals are members of teams. Organisations are much leaner with a reduced hierarchy, and so these two factors require integration of members knowledge to give multiple and differentiated fields of expertise.

THE ROLE OF TRAINING

The use of technological developments can move employees away from the humdrum and routine tasks to those requiring more knowledge-based techniques. Accompanying this is the need for training and development for all members of staff. The training, development and education of all employees at all levels within an organisation is a vital component in maintaining the competitiveness in an international arena. The issue of training is a complex one and a detailed investigation is beyond the scope of this text, yet it is important in the field of technology, IT and knowledge management.

POINTS TO PONDER

Tell me and I will forget;

Show me and I will remember;

Involve me and I will understand.

Source: Chinese proverb.

LEARNING ASPECTS OF KNOWLEDGE MANAGEMENT AND TECHNOLOGY

Technology has brought about shorter innovation cycles and, in tandem with increasing competitive pressures with the need for more flexibility in an uncertain business environment, there is a need for more efficiency and effectiveness in education and training. Computers can provide an added degree of freedom that can be used both within and external to the traditional classroom environments and can be coupled with new as well as traditional structures and techniques in the field of training.

Petrovic et al. (1998) carried out a survey of Austrian and German enterprises and universities into the learning aspects of knowledge management and new technologies. Their findings support the view that:

> The evaluation of new technologies... should be embedded in a systematic approach of controlling training and education measures. (p288)

see Chapter 10

This is linked very closely to the issue of learning (discussed in ■ Chapter 10 ■).

IT presents considerable challenges and opportunities to businesses and to society. The manner in which the organisation and the country meet the challenge of IT will largely shape their economic and social future well into this century.

THE USE OF IT BY HRM SPECIALISTS

Theory in research suggests that the potential use of IT by HRM specialists is still largely unfulfilled. According to research carried out by Kinnie and Arthurs (1996), most uses of IT by HRM specialists concentrates on transaction processing, reporting and tracking. They found very few uses of expert systems or decision-support applications. The general use of IT has been explained, according to Kinnie and Arthurs (1996), by reference to the influence of:

■ the structure of the personnel function

■ the knowledge, skills and attitudes of personnel specialists and

■ their exercise of political power. (p15)

However, HRM specialists are being made to change their attitude to IT by managers working in other functions, for example finance and production, because they are impatient with the unambitious use of IT throughout the organisation and recognise the importance of the HRM specialist in promoting innovative and advanced uses of the computer.

It is important for organisations to have a good fit between users and suppliers of technology. By understanding suppliers it is possible to become even more successful.

It is only by being thorough in perusing the advertising literature and talking to the providing organisations that a better fit between the supplier's idea of HRM practice and the organisation's own strategies can be met. This is an important consideration because suppliers of HR systems are selling their customers ideas, not just software.

It is vital that the supplier has the implementation and support expertise to match the HR strategies the organisation wants to implement. HRM has traditionally been administrative but it has moved towards being more aligned to the needs of business and is now central to an organisation's strategy. This change has raised the profile of the HRM function immeasurably.

Whitehead (1999) stated that:

> The key for the HRM professional is to be able to provide high-quality information to the decision-makers by using the best technology. (p12)

Employees could well worry about their own competences, that the technology was too complex and that they would never understand it. Accompanying this is a fear that they would never have sufficient time to learn. The only way to manage the fears that individuals have in coming to grips with information technology is through effective communication (discussed in ■ Chapter 5 ■) and training. Through training sessions employees will begin to open up a dialogue with their trainer and other participants. However, Farrow (1997) says:

see Chapter 5

> The importance of training cannot be over-emphasised but equally the opportunity for staff to talk in a relatively informal manner with someone who listens and cares is the key to success. (p323)

KNOWLEDGE INTEGRATION AND PERCEPTION

see Chapter 10

It is only through learning (discussed in ■ Chapter 10 ■) that knowledge-intensive organisations can gain a competitive advantage. Success will depend upon how effectively individuals can develop their own skills and knowledge and the efficacy of how both can be synergised within the organisation. Contemporary organisations exist in very complex environments and because of this individual experts, and the teams of which such individuals are members, will only be successful if they work in an atmosphere of collaboration and mutual learning.

It is the increase in the need for problem solving within organisational activities which utilises the integration of individual knowledge competences. Problem solving needs a creative approach and thus the insight from the varying perspectives of members of the workforce is essential. In their seminal work Duncan and Weiss (1979) summarised this process as:

> The overall organizational knowledge base emerges out of the process of exchange, evaluation and integration of knowledge. Like any other organizational process, it is comprised of the interactions of individuals and not their isolated behaviour. (p86)

This means that there is a process whereby the unique knowledge held by each individual member of the workforce is exchanged, evaluated and integrated with that of other workers.

Developing a comprehensive knowledge base in an organisation where the individuals are highly differentiated yet dependent individual specialists needs an ongoing approach. Individual knowledge and the understanding of meaning are:

■ surfaced

■ reflected upon

■ exchanged

■ evaluated

■ integrated with others.

see Chapter 10 This can be seen in the theory of learning discussed in ■ Chapter 10 ■ because it is about developing individual workers and the management of their performance. It is important to realise that the development of a knowledge base within an organisation is not about data but about what knowledge an individual employee possesses, then giving it meaning and finally sharing it with others. It is through *see* Chapter 5 effective communication (as discussed in ■ Chapter 5 ■) that this takes place.

Because of this knowledge, the membership in teams of such knowledge workers is difficult. If managers try to manage these people by attempting to dominate them, they will find that the knowledge worker will revolt. Coercive management and the use of dominance and fear are totally inappropriate forms of management because the knowledge workers will rapidly vote with their feet and move to another organisation where their need to work autonomously is appreciated. Such workers perceive themselves as being professionals and expect to be treated with respect. In today's organisation, such workers appear at all levels of the hierarchy – from the shopfloor upwards and it is a mistake to assume that they only appear at the top end of the staffing tree.

6.5 Activity

1 What standard of education do you think knowledge workers have in comparison to data workers?

2 List ten occupations which are carried out by knowledge workers.

MANAGING HUMAN RESOURCES

There is considerable change taking place in organisations because of the drive to implement new technology. Most knowledge workers are confronted by a number of key human resource issues which need to be assessed and managed.

It cannot be argued that contemporary information technology is moving rapidly and, therefore, such changes have to become part of the manager's framework. Even though many of the developments in technology are sophisticated, there appears to be little change in the related human resource issues as they were 10 to 15 years ago. As Farrow (1997) states:

> Maintaining the balance between technology and the individual must be the key to success, both in staff management and end-user services. (p324)

It can now be seen that it is important for organisations to remain 'ahead of the rest' if they are to survive in the contemporary business environment and employers and employees alike have to be aware of what these contemporary issues are. Those key issues – ethics, globalisation and workplace diversity – are considered in Part VI.

- Technology is difficult to define because it means different things to different people.

- Information is the processing of data and it is the human being who turns data into knowledge through the use of her/his wisdom.

- Members of organisations need to share their knowledge if the organisation is to achieve its objectives and maintain a competitive advantage. This can be done through knowledge transfer systems.

- Technology can assist in learning if it is designed as a fair transfer system (Dixon, 2000).

- Technological changes are not new – it is the speed of development into AMT and office technology which has developed quickly with telecommuting, expert/knowledge systems, automation and robotics and AI revolutionising the workplace.

- The HRM specialist needs to be aware of the technological determinists (Juran and Gryna, 1970) who do not see the human being as part of the technology/work interface.

- The working environment is advanced by the development in information storage and processing, communications, advanced materials, superconductivity and biotechnology.

- There are four key work environments – hive, cell, den and club – all of which now use hot desking and/or hotelling to various degrees.

- Computing is part of IT but is not the same since IT includes all aspects of computing, integrated with technological developments in networking and telecommunications technology (Elliott and Starkings, 1998).

- IT has had a considerable impact on organisational structure and design allowing telecommuting and the multiskilling and multitasking of employees through training.

- The role of management is now concentrated on the management of information (Earl, 1997).

- IT is central to the strategy of an organisation because organisations are now central to the information age.

Chapter summary

- IT is closely aligned to knowledge and can provide economies of scale.

- All areas of business need to be knowledge intensive with the potential for employers to monitor their employees' electronic activities.

- The increase in the use of technology has brought about a rise in frustration and negative stress which can become proactive if carefully managed by professionals.

- There has been an increase in knowledge workers with their need to work autonomously and independently.

- Learning is now more flexible and efficient through e-learning.

- The role of the HRM specialist has changed because s/he now has to implement the new technology and be part of the business strategy.

END OF CHAPTER 6 CASE STUDY

IT drives car parts maker into higher gear

Investment in computer-aided design (CAD) packages and more PCs has paid off for one small company.

When Morgan's new aluminium-based car was unveiled in Geneva in February 2000, two companies got their day in the sun.

Morgan Motors, one of the few remaining independent sports car manufacturers in the UK, was one of them. The other was Radshape Sheet Metal, a small Birmingham, England, automotive components supplier.

The latter are trying to move away from low-value to high-volume, high-end design and that is why they invested in IT.

Previously Ford and General Motors, the two giants of the automotive industry, have dominated discussions of e-business in the sector by announcing plans to link suppliers via electronic trading exchanges.

But the use of e-mail, computer-aided design software packages and Internet conferencing have begun

to filter down to companies as small as Radshape Metal, which has 50 employees.

Over the last year, the company has invested about £80 000 in more personal computers and CAD packages and increasing its server power.

The sum is small by absolute standards, but it represents about 3.5 per cent of annual turnover. By comparison, a recent survey by KPMG, the professional services firm, of FTSE 350 companies found half planned to invest 3 per cent or less of turnover in IT.

The move has fundamentally changed Radshape's core business: producing small auto components to exact specifications laid down by upmarket manufacturers such as Morgan Motors and Rolls-Royce Motors.

These designs have traditionally been sent in the form of dense print drawings by post or express courier. E-mail has become a quicker, cheaper and more flexible alternative.

CAD packages allow designs to be rotated,

END OF CHAPTER 6 CASE STUDY (CONT'D)

expanded and broken down into individual measurements on screen. Electronic drawings from various stages of the production process can be superimposed on top of each other.

Approved designs can be networked electronically to precision laser-cutting equipment on the factory floor.

If during the production and assembly process, a component is discovered to be the wrong size, the mistake can be traced back through the information trail. The company has added real value to the process and produced a new way of conducting business.

Adapted from: Grande, C. (2000) IT drives car parts maker into higher gear, *Financial Times*, 12/13 February, p14.

END OF CHAPTER 6 CASE STUDY QUESTIONS

1 Radshape Sheet Metal has introduced CAD. What is this and how can it help the organisation?

2 Radshape Sheet Metal is said to be in the manufacturing sector. Discuss the issue that it is also part of the service sector.

3 How can Radshape Sheet Metal be classified in the framework of a manufacturing technology?

4 Is it likely that the change to the use of IT at Radshape Sheet Metal will have created uncertainty and ambiguity in the workforce?

END OF PART III CASE STUDY

IS YOUR BOSS REALLY READING YOUR E-MAILS?

If you are sitting in the office, bored, underpaid and overworked and would like to entertain yourself by sending a few e-mails to your best mate or a CV* to your potential new employer, then think again. Apparently the bosses think it is OK to snoop on your e-mail, store it and retrieve it at their leisure. Perhaps they are underworked and have nothing better to do in their spare time, but clearly reading the e-mails of their not-so-diligent flock is

something of a favourite pastime among the upper echelons of corporate UK.

A recent survey publish by National Opinion Polls has indicated that over 59 per cent of UK employees suspect that their boss monitors their e-mails. As a result of those fears, a huge majority (70 per cent) of workers avoids using e-mail from work for private communication.

Are we paranoid or is there a real threat to our

privacy at work? The technology sadly works against us. E-mail is easy to record and monitor, as it only requires a little bit of memory on the system to archive and record all the messages and a not too sophisticated key word search to find out the juicy bits at a touch of a button.

Seeking an answer to the question of whether Big Brother is watching us, I have found strong evidence that there are people in the UK who have been fired as a result of using e-mail for private purposes. Even more clearly, over 27 per cent of US companies freely admit that they store and retrieve employees' e-mails, considering that it is the legal right of a boss to have access to what people write or receive on their corporate e-mails. Infuriating as it may be, the companies claim that cyberspace with their signature on it (that is, the company name on your e-mail address) fully entitles them to the ownership of the e-mail message and therefore the right to snoop if they wish to do so.

There are other implications when using an e-mail address that belongs to KPMG, Oracle or any other corporate body. For example, some retailers use the information from your corporate e-mail address to analyse data about your private shopping behaviour and publish them on their website. The most annoying case of that must be Amazon with their highly dubious practice of 'purchase cycles'. The analysis derived from the correlation of the e-mail addresses with the titles of purchased books allows them to publish on their website information on what employees of certain companies are reading. For example, you can find out what the people employed at Oracle read. I strongly suspect that the poor souls at Oracle haven't been asked if they agree to be the subject of a public survey, but hey, according to Amazon, if you use your work address to buy books, you have only yourself to blame.

To make matters worse, even the British government is jumping in on the act of surveillance and somewhat legitimising the behaviour of the employers by leading the way in cybersnooping. The new legislation in the UK indicates the new, widespread power of the government to tap, bug and monitor our e-mail communication. Although it is rolled out in the name of 'national security', the veil is pretty thin and the legislation seems to be wide open for abuse. It is unfortunate that despite the long campaign of civil rights activists, the government has chosen a rather aggressive monitoring strategy and went further than was necessary with the new proposals.

One of the most controversial aspects of the proposals is that the government appears to expect Internet providers to pick up the tab for implementing the storage and monitoring devices that will be necessary for the surveillance operations. It seems bizarre, as the bill will run into millions if not more, and will undoubtedly be passed on to the users in some shape or form, resulting in higher usage charges or higher telephone charges. It also runs against the declaration from Gordon Brown (UK Chancellor of the Exchequer) who, in early February 1999, indicated his intentions to make Internet access cheaper, not more expensive.

On the other hand, financing the new surveillance devices on the Internet providers' systems shouldn't be covered by taxpayers' money. The Internet is still a sport of the top 30 per cent élite of the country and, as such, should not be subsidised by the wider population, even on such an important issue like cybersnooping by the government.

E-mail ownership must be properly debated and considered before any legislation is passed through the House of Commons. Similar debate is necessary

END OF PART III CASE STUDY (CONT'D)

on the rights of companies to monitor and retrieve employees' e-mails. The ownership of the service shouldn't automatically transfer the ownership of the contents of e-mail messages to the employer. The civil rights issues here must not be glossed over.

In the long term, the civil rights people have a job on their hands to stop companies assuming the right to snoop and to quash the government's enthusiasm for cybersnooping without a mandate from us all.

* CV = curriculum vitae
An outline of a person's educational and professional history, usually prepared for job applications.

END OF PART III CASE STUDY QUESTIONS

1 How can the more enlightened organisations treat the issue of staff using the Internet and sending e-mails from company systems?

2 How can employees avoid getting into trouble for making private e-mails?

3 What is the long-term solution?

4 Why should there be a problem if only 30 per cent of the population is using cyberspace?

THESIS + ANTITHESIS = SYNTHESIS

IT is all about control.

SELF-TEST THE KEY ISSUES

1 What is the difference between a *knowledge worker* and a *data worker*?

2 What is information and how does it differ from data?

3 Analyse the view that employees need information that is independent of computers.

4 How can IT be used to give an organisation a strategic advantage over its competitors?

TEAM/CLASS DISCUSSIONS

1 Discuss the extent to which technology can meet the needs of top managers for rich information and consider whether technology will ever allow managers to do their job without face-to-face communication?

2 A manager of a computer processing department has informed his staff that it is important that all top managers have a need for the same control data that everyone else has.

However, he also believes that his staff should aggregate those data for the organisation as a whole. Discuss the pros and cons of this viewpoint.

PROJECTS (INDIVIDUAL OR TEAMS)

1 Information and communications technology provides a series of tools that can be used to help businesses operate more effectively. Select *one* and analyse its effect on the consumer and the business.

2 Choose *three* different applications that a computer of your choice can access. Analyse its use in the workplace as regards reaching an organisation's objectives.

Recommended reading

Beardwell, I. and L. Holden (1999) *Human Resource Management: A Contemporary Perspective*, London: Pitman

Graham, H.T. and R. Bennett (1999) *Human Resources Management*, London: Financial Times/Pitman

Hogg, C. (2000) *Pros and (dot)cons*, London: CIPD

Maund, L. (1999) *Understanding People and Organisations: An Introduction to Organisational Behaviour*, Cheltenham: Stanley Thornes

van Adelsberg, D. and E. Trolley (2000) *Running Training Like a Business – Delivering Unmistakeable Value*, Maidenhead: McGraw-Hill

Williams, M. (2000) *The War for Talent: Getting the Best from the Best*, London: CIPD

URLs (uniform resource locators)

www.brint.com/km/whatis.htm

Information on knowledge management.

www.dti.gov.uk

Department of Trade and Industry. Documents and lists of publications – lists those related to human resources within trade and industry.

www.lib.uchicago.edu/~llou/forintlaw.html

Legal research on international law regarding the Internet.

www.ozemail.com.au

Oze-mail. Australian site which covers the international spectrum. Search facilities on comprehensive topics, such as business and finance, information technology, business education, business professionals, economic research, jobs and careers and small business issues.

Site for the British Department for Education and Employment.

www.iipuk.co.uk

Investors in People. National quality standards which sets the lead of good practice for improving an organisation's performance through its people. Library, international, articles and news.

www.idc.com

International Data Corporation (IDC). E-commerce assistance and information on the formulation of business practices using the Internet.

www.datanetworking.co.uk

Data Network Association (DNA). Assistance and information on carrying out business on the Internet.

Bibliography

Adams, J. (2000) Hypermobility in *Prospect*, March, pp27–31

Adkin, E., G. Jones and P. Leighton (1997) *Pocket Employer*, London: Economist Books

Amphlett, J. (2000) Caught in the web in *People Management*, 3 February, pp25–6

Arnold, J., C.L. Cooper and I.T. Robertson (1997) *Work Psychology: Understanding Human Behaviour in the Workplace*, London: Pitman

Ball, K. (2000) Interface value in *People Management*, 6 January, pp40–2

Boland, R.J. and R.V. Tenkasi (1995) Perspective making and perspective taking in communities of knowing in *Organization Science*, **4**(3): 456–75

Broderick, R. and J.W. Boudreau (1992) Human resource management, information technology and the competitive edge in *Academy of Management Executive*, Part 6, No 2, pp7–17

Brown, M. (1997) Design for working in *Management Today*, March, pp77–84

Carnall, C. (1999) Positive e-valuation in *People Management*, 2 September, pp54–5, 57

Crawshaw, S. (2000) The irritations of modern life. Desktop lunches in The Wednesday Review, *The Financial Times*, 23 February, p7

Cummings, T. and C.L. Cooper (1979) A cybernetic framework for the study of occupational stress in *Human Relations*, **32**: 395–419

Daft, R.L. (1995) *Organization Theory and Design*, Minneapolis/St Paul: West Publishing

Dixon, N. (2000) *Common Knowledge: How Companies Thrive*, Boston: Harvard Business School Press

Dixon, N. (2000) The insight track in *People Management*, 17 February, pp34–9

Drucker, P. (1988) The coming of the new organization in *Harvard Business Review*, Jan/Feb, pp45–53

Duncan, R. and A. Weiss (1979) Organisational learning: implications for organizational design in Cummings, L.I. and B.M. Staw (eds) *Research in Organizational Behaviour*, Vol. I, CT, Greenwich, CT: JAI Press

Earl, M. (1997) Management in the information era in Bickerstaffe, G. (ed.) *Mastering Management*, London: Financial Times/Pitman, pp552–6

Elliott, G. and S. Starkings (1998) *Business Information Technology: Systems, Theory and Practice*, London: Longman

Farrow, J. (1997) Management of change: technological developments and human resource issues in the information sector in *Journal of Managerial Psychology*, **12**(5): 319–24

Human Resource Magazine (1992) September, p21

Institute of Management Foundation (1997) Stress Management: Self-First in *Checklist* 034, undated, issued January, Corby: Institute of Management Foundation

Institute of Personnel and Development (1996) *Occupational Health and Organisational Effectiveness, Key Facts*, September (published 19 December)

Johnson, R. (1999) Centre stage for the UfI in Maisie, E. (1999) Joined-up thinking in *People Management*, 25 November, p36

Johnson, R. (1999) A word of warning in Maisie, E. (1999) Joined-up thinking in *People Management*, 25 November, p35

Juran, J.M. and Gryna, F.M. Jr (1970) *Quality Planning and Analysis*, London: McGraw-Hill

Kellaway, L. (2000) Business jargon is pants in *Financial Times*, 21 February, p14

Kinnie, N.J. and A.J. Arthurs (1996) Personnel specialists' advanced use of information technology in *Personnel Review*, (3): 3–19

McKinnery, K. (2000) Misusing e-mail and Internet could mean dismissal in *The Business Magazine*, February, p30

Maisie, E. (1999) Joined-up thinking in *People Management*, 25 November, pp32–6

Mendelsohn, S. (1994) Managing at sea in *Library Manager*, December, pp22–4

Mungo, P. (2000) The full picture: anatomy of a keyboard in Finger of Suspicion in the business in *Financial Times*, 19 February, pp24–5

Norton, C. (2000) Stressed managers complain of e-mail overload in *The Independent*, 24 February, p9

Nurminen, M. (1988) *People of Computers, Three Ways of Looking at Information Systems*, Sweden: Lund

Perrow, C. (1967) A framework for the comparative analysis of organizations in *American Sociological Review*, **32**(2): 75–80

People Management (1999) Knowledge vision undermined, 20 September, p12

People Management (2000) Denying all knowledge, 20 January, p18

People Management (2000) ICT signals transformation in HR styles, 23 November, p12

Petrovic, O., N. Kailer, J. Scheff and D. Vogel (1998) Learning aspects of knowledge management and new technologies in *Journal of European Industrial Training* 22/7: 277–88

Powell, A. (2000) Students net a £10 million deal at the click of a button in *Daily Mail*, 26 January, p5

Rana, E. (2000) Budgets grow as trainers turn to IT-based methods in *People Management*, 17 February, p14

Reeves, R. (2000) Sounds of silence in *Prospect*, March, p13

Rockart, J.F. and J.E. Short (1991) The networked organization and the management of interdependence in Scott Morton, M.E. (ed.) *The Corporation of the 1990s*, Oxford: Oxford University Press, pp189–210

Schank, R. (1999) Courses of action in *People Management*, 14 October, pp54–5, 57

Senge, P. (1990) *The Fifth Discipline*, New York: Doubleday

Starbuck, W.H. (1992) Learning by knowledge-intensive firms in *Journal of Management Studies*, **29**(6): 713–49

Tenkasi, R.V. and R.J. Boland Jr (1996) Exploring knowledge diversity in knowledge intensive firms: a new role for information systems in *Journal of Organizational Change Management*, **9**(1): 79–91

the business in *The Financial Times* (2000) What about *my* feelings? 19 February, pp13–14

Thomas, R. and M. Ballard (1995) *Business Information: Technologies and Strengths*, Cheltenham: Stanley Thornes

Wells, H.G. (1938) *World Brain*, London: Adamontine Press

Whitehead, M. (1999) 'Adapt, or be a victim of technology,' expert warns in *People Management*, 30 June, p12

Wightman, D.L. (1987) Competitive advantage through information technology in *Journal of General Management*, Summer (12): pp36–45

Employee relationships and essential employment law

Employee relationships

After studying this chapter, you should be able to:

- CONCEPTUALISE the role of the employer/employee relationship in the contemporary workplace.

- EXPLAIN the importance of law as it relates to employee relationships.

- DESCRIBE the legal meaning of the word 'employee'.

- ANALYSE the position of loyalty, trust and justice in the employer/employee relationship.

- EVALUATE the role of partnerships as they contribute to effective employee relationships.

- EXPLAIN the principles and practices of employee representation.

INTRODUCTION

Framework case study

Deregulation leaves cabin crews with high anxiety

Cabin crews working some of the UK's leading airlines are under pressure from increased workloads and long hours caused by the deregulation of Europe's airways, according to new research.

A study by Strathclyde University for the Transport and General Union claims that, far from a glamorous life of exotic travel, the reality for many airline staff is lack of sleep, unhygienic working conditions, poor health and high stress levels.

While shocking incidents of 'air rage' have recently hit the headlines and are clearly growing, they are only one of the many serious hazards cabin crew face, the report says.

The drive to increase competitiveness has had a direct impact on employees' jobs. It was found that the intensity, speed and volume of work had increased. Most respondents felt that their health had deteriorated since starting their jobs. And there were complaints of inadequate training in areas such as lifting heavy objects, contact with body fluids and dealing with disruptive passengers.

But long hours, lack of breaks and erratic shift patterns were the most common complaints. Cabin staff were not covered by the working time regulations, but there are industry rules that dictate minimum rest periods before and during flying.

Yet over two thirds of KLM UK respondents claimed they had received no crew break while on duty, although proportionately more Britannia and British Airways respondents reported an increase in the intensity and volume of work. Almost three-quarters of all respondents had flown with a reduced crew.

Management commitment to the quality of the working environment came in for strong criticism.

Adapted from: Walsh, J. (1999a) Deregulation leaves cabin crews with high anxiety, *People Management*, 8 April, p20.

From the above Framework Case Study it can be seen that the relationship between the employer and the employee covers a wide spectrum of issues from payment for work carried out to protection in the workplace. While the phrase *employment relations* appears to be self-explanatory, it might be better expressed as *employment relationships* since it is about the interaction between the hired worker and the organisation which employs her/him. It concentrates on their inputs and outputs as shown in Table 7.1.

7.1

Activity

A fellow student has asked you to distinguish between 'employment relations' and 'employment relationships'.

How would you respond?

Table 7.1 Examples of the interrelationship between employer and employee

	INPUT	OUTPUT
Employee	Hours of work	Productivity, for example volume, quality
Employer	Conditions of work	Reward and remuneration

In order for an organisation to achieve its objectives, the relationship between the employer and the employee has to be fruitful, which itself is achieved only if there is ▶ **equity** ◀ between the inputs and outputs of the employer and the inputs and outputs of the employee. If there is inequity there will be dis-relations – like any other relationship between two people it must evolve over time. Relationships between an employer and an employee have to be within a legislative framework ■ *see* Chapter 8 ■ which encompasses certain never ending truths, for example duties, rights, responsibilities and justice, which are discussed below.

see Chapter 8

▶ A position where the members of any workforce are treated fairly and have a desire to ◀┄┄▶ **Equity**
perceive equity in relation to others and to avoid inequity with them.

THE EMPLOYMENT RELATIONSHIP AGENDA

During the last decade the employment relationship agenda has shifted dramatically. In the early 1980s employment relationships were significantly influenced by 'keeping the lid on' industrial conflict and troubleshooting when that failed. Emmott (1997) reported that by the 1990s the whole issue of employment relationships became much more subtle. However, the relationship between the managers and employee representatives – such as trade union officials – is still very important. The concentration is now on the *relationship* between the employer and employee rather than on the employees themselves and the ways they can be controlled. This change of emphasis has presented managers with fresh questions that need answers, for example how can they:

■ find out what an employee is actually *thinking*?

■ deal with sensitive issues such as redundancy, demotion and hours of work?

■ gain loyalty and commitment from employees?

■ get that little bit extra from employees: that is, the willingness to act beyond the basic job role, use initiative and do something extra – to go the extra kilometre?

Armstrong (1999) states that employment relationships:

describes the relationships that exist between employers and employees in the workplace. (p185)

According to Kessler and Undy (1996) an employment relationship comprises four dimensions, each of which is interrelated to form a comprehensive whole. These components are:

Parties

Operation

Structure

Substance.

The *parties* are the individuals concerned in the employment relationship and comprises individuals such as the worker her/himself, the manager, the employees' representative and national government.

Operation consists of different hierarchical levels within the organisation, using different processes and procedures with different types of management style.

The *structure* comprises those factors that dictate the rules and regulations which have to be adhered to, that is, the bureaucracy. It also includes the informal views, perceptions and expectations of the employer and the employees.

Substance is the cooperation which each individual brings to the organisation as a whole and this can range along a continuum as shown in Figure 7.1.

Other writers such as MacNeil (1985), and Rouseau and Wade-Benzoni (1994) agree on their conception of the employment relationship by distinguishing between two types of contracts:

- transactional

- relational.

Transactional contracts are easy to identify because they are clearly written and are usually specified in financial terms. They are transient and detail the specific requirements related to the performance of a job.

Relational contracts are much more difficult to define because they are abstract and refer to non-specific issues with the performance requirements being ill stated, open ended and ambiguous.

Both types of contract are strongly related to the ▶ **psychological contract** ◀ which is discussed in detail later in this chapter.

Psychological ◀┈┈▶ An unwritten agreement which sets out what a member of the workforce wants from **contract** her/his employer and vice versa.

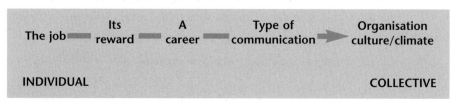

Figure 7.1 Substance as a continuum

SIGNIFICANCE OF EMPLOYMENT RELATIONSHIPS

The relationship between the employer and the employee governs a considerable amount of what organisations need to be aware of in order to develop and apply human resources related to:

- processes
- policies and
- procedures.

The chief consideration is to address the issues of what will and will not contribute to the organisation's desire to reward positive employment relationships.

Employment relationships is one of the most popular areas for social science researchers to investigate. A key piece of work was carried out by Gallie et al. (1998) when they used a longitudinal study to investigate employment in Britain. The results of the study indicated that while there were indications that changes had taken place in the way that individuals had actually been employed, there was minimal evidence to prove that there had been any significant changes in the relationship between employer and employee. What they did extrapolate from their data was a number of distinguishing features concerning employment itself – these are addressed in Table 7.2.

Table 7.2 Changes in employment (after Gallie et al., 1998)

FEATURE	EXPLANATION
Commitment	High levels of commitment did not affect the quality of the work although it did contribute to low absenteeism and labour turnover.
Discretion	While there was evidence of increased discretion for the employee there was no significant reduction in management control. In some cases there was an increase in such control.
Integrative forms of management policy	Concentrated in the area of non-manual employees.
Intrinsic motivation	Highly important to employees.
Involvement	The lower the level of skill required the less the workers were involved with their work.
New/revised types of management	Usually founded on HRM principles and practice with a reduction in the use of collective bargaining in favour of individual contracts.
Skill levels	The quality of work experience was highest where employees were given discretion in how to carry out their work.
Supervision	Even with the use of autonomous high-performance work teams there was still an importance placed on the supervisory role.

MANAGING THE EMPLOYMENT RELATIONSHIP

It is very difficult to manage the employment relationship because of its changing nature. It comprises a large number of ingredients all of which together, in their various forms, compound the problem. Some of these can be seen in Figure 7.2.

While there are numerous components that affect the employer/employee relationship, it is the human resource policies and practices of the organisation that tend to dictate the climate. The aspects of human resource management (HRM) and personnel were discussed in ■ Chapter 1 *and* Chapter 2 ■. However, they are central to:

see Chapter 1 *and* Chapter 2

- ■ the way the employees are actually treated

- ■ how they are required to do their various jobs

- ■ what the performance expectations are

- ■ how workers are managed.

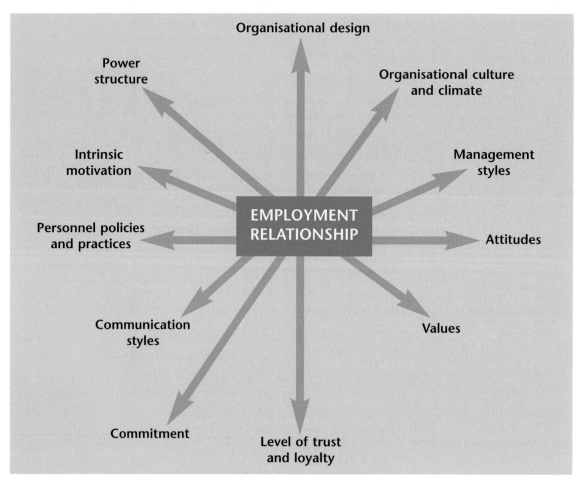

Figure 7.2 Some components affecting the employment relationship

SCENARIO 7.1

New ways to work at Remploy

Unions and management at Remploy are discussing new working practices as part of a deal to scale back on factory mergers and lift the threat to jobs.

The company, which is the biggest employer of disabled people in the UK, has launched a new strategy document entitled 'Remploy 21 – a vision for the future'. This states that factory mergers will no longer be 'the leading element' of the organisation's mission statement.

Remploy's proposals for closing nine factories have been on hold since September 1999. Unions have threatened industrial action if the plans proceed. The mergers would lead to around 1000 job cuts over three years, although Remploy promised that they would be achieved without redundancies.

The government has repeatedly refused to increase Remploy's annual grant to help it to modernise its factories, preferring instead to concentrate on funding for disabled people and the supported employment programme.

Adapted from: New ways to work at Remploy, *People Management*, 2 March 2000, p17.

It is the role of the human resource management (HRM) specialist to assist in a positive and productive employment relationship. Armstrong (1999) highlights some key approaches to a satisfactory employment relationship, reinforcing the point that a positive employment relationship is an ongoing process. These key approaches are given in Table 7.3.

Table 7.3 Ways in which HRM specialists can support a positive employment relationship

Recruitment	During interviews present the favourable and unfavourable aspects of the job.
Induction	Ensure new entrants are informed of the organisation's: ■ personnel policies ■ performance standards ■ procedures expected with regard to ■ core values quality and customer service ■ flexibility requirements
Employee handbook	Issue and update regularly to reinforce the information given in the induction sessions.
Performance management	Develop processes that make sure performance expectations are agreed to and regularly reviewed.
Personal development plans	By the use of self-managed learning encourage review of agreed performance expectations.
Training and management development programmes	Underpin the core values and define the performance expectations.
Manager and team leader training	To ensure they are aware of their roles.
Contact	Encouraging the maximum contact to achieve mutual understanding of expectations.

(cont'd)

Table 7.3 (cont'd)

Transparency	Everybody knows what is happening and understands the impact it will have on their: ■ employment ■ prospects ■ development
Personnel procedures	Must be developed in order to cover: ■ handling of grievances ■ promotion ■ discipline ■ redundancy ■ equal opportunities
Personnel policies	Develop to cover the major areas of: ■ employment ■ reward ■ development ■ employment relations
Reward system	Develop and manage to achieve: ■ equity ■ consistency ■ fairness
Employment procedures	Adopt those that foster positive collective relationships.

While the employment relationship is better effected by efficient HRM practices and policies, it is underpinned by ▷ **legislation** ◁ – particularly that derived from the European Union (EU). There is one significant difference between the new employment law and the old legislation, which strongly affects the employer/ employee relationship. Old employment law usually prohibited certain types of action and detailed the actual steps which had to be taken when specific problems arose, while the new employment law requires that employers take the initiative. The obligation and onus of responsibility has thus shifted from the ▷ **legislature** ◁ to the employers who have to ensure that they themselves are not breaking the law. With this comes the further difficulty of maintaining equity and ensuring that both the employer and employee are treated fairly – that is they are treated justly

see Chapter 8 ■ *see* Chapter 8 ■. This not only requires thorough HRM practices but also a competent understanding of the role of the law.

Legislation ◀┄┄▶ The act or process of making laws and/or the laws which are so made.

Legislature ◀┄┄▶ A body of individuals that has the power to make and repeal laws.

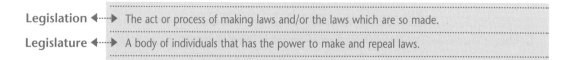

7.2

Activity

Find an article related to any legislation covering the employer/employee relationship and précis its key points.

UNDERSTANDING LAW

The study of ▶ **law** ◀ is very complex and it is a specialised area beyond the scope of this book. However, an appreciation of the role of law is essential in the understanding of employment relationships. Davies (1996) writes that:

> It is often said that Roman law is one of the pillars of European civilization. (p173)

> ▶ A rule or set of rules instituted by an Act of Parliament, custom or practice in order to ◀······▶ **Law**
> punish individuals who offend the conventions of society.

The Latin word *lex* means 'the bond', or 'that which binds'. The same principle underpins another key aspect of Roman law – the *pactum*, which is the contract ■ *see* Chapter 8 ■ agreed by two people whether it be for commercial, matrimonial or political purposes. It still forms the basis of a contract as it is known today – the conditions of the contract bind the parties to observe it. The Romans appeared to value the ▶ **rule of law** ◀ believing that such a law ensured that the government of the time was sound and because of this there would be commercial confidence and a society that was well regulated. However, Roman law did not continue uninterrupted as the legislation of Europe because most of their codes fell out of fashion as the Roman Empire collapsed. It was in the Middle Ages (*c*.750–1270CE) that the Roman laws came back into use within Europe – even so they had to compete with non-Roman (often contradictory) practices. Davies (1996) continues to suggest that some countries, for example France, balanced their customs with Roman law and in Germany the law of the Romans arrived even later. However, it was in England that the basis of Roman law was adopted and was adapted within the principles of equity to gain a virtual ▶ **monopoly** ◀.

see Chapter 8

> ▶ A formal order or regulation governing the procedure or decisions of a court of law and ◀······▶ **Rule of law**
> which forms part of common law.

> ▶ The exclusive possession, control or use of something. ◀······▶ **Monopoly**

Europe had diversified political systems yet the Roman legislation seemed to suit its development with ▶ **civil law** ◀ in most European countries being based on the codes of practice adopted by the Roman civilisation. Whatever their qualifications and experience, most educated European lawyers acknowledge their debt to Cicero (106–43BCE) and his successors, stating the importance of his writing was in emphasising that:

> *Salus populi supreme lex.*
> [The safety of the people is the highest law.] (Davies, p173)

> ▶ The law of a country relating to private and civilian affairs. ◀······▶ **Civil law**

In contemporary language this would be expressed by stating that the rule of law provides individuals with the highest degree of safety.

It has been popular in Europe, the USA and other parts of the western world (Australia, New Zealand and Canada, for example) to believe that employment law is intrusive and costly to legislate and implement and because of this there have been calls for ▶ **deregulation** ◀ of some employment legislation. The Framework Case Study is an example of this. In European countries (as in most countries) law is considered to be very important and so calls for deregulation are not too much in evidence – except perhaps in the UK with, for example, the Working Time Directive (1998) where there seems to be disagreement between trades unions, management and the government ■ *see* Chapter 8 ■. Relating this to the workplace, if law is to be looked at in a positive manner it is important that it provides a clear framework and is relevant to the issue it is seeking to address. All employers and employees should appreciate what the law is really saying, rather than relying upon what other people report that it is saying. The legal framework is not the same in every country in the nature of the rules themselves, how they are enforced, or in the remedies they provide. Such rules and their interpretation are developed through each country's legislation (▶ **statute law** ◀) and decisions made in their courts (▶ **common law** ◀) with each being equal in their importance within employment relations ■ *see* Chapter 8 ■.

see Chapter 8

see Chapter 8

Deregulation ◀┈▶	To remove any regulations which are encompassed in, say, legislation.
Statute law ◀┈▶	Law enacted by a legislative body, for example national government.
Common law ◀┈▶	The body of law which is based on decisions made in courts of law and customs.

Regardless of the legal system of each country, be it Britain, Sweden, Belgium or Australia, it is usually divided into two areas:

1 *Systems dominated by legislation*
   This comprises the codes, basic laws, statutes and acts which are typical of Europe, South America, Australia and North Africa, with the courts of law interpreting and applying the legislation. An example here is the National Minimum Wage Act 1998 in the UK and the Workplace Relations Act 1996 in Australia.

2 *Common law systems*
   This is where case law and decisions made by law courts have a significant role and is typical of the UK, Canada and Australia. It also includes statutes of the Commonwealth of Nations which is a free association of independent member states and their dependencies. It includes the UK, Canada and Australia as well as 52 other members including Pakistan, India, Singapore and Jamaica. In these cases new legal rules can be developed by the courts.

Both systems are based on traditions and they assist in bringing about more enterprising legislation covering aspects such as:

- smoking in the workplace

- repetitive strain injury (RSI)

- bullying, and

- ▶ **whistleblowing** ◀ (discussed later in this chapter).

> ▶ The use of writings on the practice of calling public attention to waste, mismanagement or corruption in government, industry and the military and so on. ◀·····▶ **Whistleblowing**

In these areas test cases have been brought in common law and have been incorporated into legislation. This helps to explain the difficulties experienced in the UK in the absorbing of complex and continuing employment law ■ *see* Chapter 8 ■.

see **Chapter 8**

PURPOSE OF BUSINESS, EMPLOYEE STATUS AND THE PSYCHOLOGICAL CONTRACT

Employment legislation is very complex and this is reflected in the difficulties involved in attempting to gain, and maintain, a well-balanced employer/employee relationship. The latter is intertwined with legislation and the very use of the word 'employee' is fraught with difficulties. The word is often used in general terms, but HRM specialists, line managers and workers need to be aware of its legal usage if they are to avoid ongoing difficulties. In view of this, there are three key issues which need to be addressed at this stage:

- purpose of business

- employee status

- psychological contract.

PURPOSE OF BUSINESS

The economist Friedman (1980) stated that:

> Something like three-quarters of all income generated in the United States through market transactions takes the form of the compensation of employees, with about half the rest going to the self employed. (p40)

An even more extreme view was taken by Drucker (1980) when he stated that:

> In every developed country between 85 and 90 per cent of the economy's product is being paid out in the form of wages and salaries. (p181)

Some might say that, over 20 years later, things have not changed with about 85 per cent of the UK economy's ▶ **product** ◀ being used to pay wages and salaries. Friedman (1980) believes strongly that organisations are in business purely to make a profit and labour is a cost to be kept as low as possible. Sherwin (1999) states that:

> Growth has to be achieved by a combination of service, quality, competitive pricing, people management, product development, capital investment, and cost control. (p9)

Product ◀┈▶ What is produced by the effort of a process of work.

He believes that growth by itself has no place in any organisation unless it is accompanied by profit and, therefore, there must be a never ceasing focus on margins and profit. In Sherwin's (1999) view:

> The really successful companies are those which can achieve sales growth combined with a continuous growth in net profit margin. (p9)

However, there is another perspective – that of the individuals who are employed within the organisation. From their viewpoint, the organisation is very much about providing them with jobs and they perceive that the business is not much good if it cannot do just that. Moreover, the better the jobs are that are provided, from the employees' point of view, the better the business is working. They also believe that the higher the pay, the more secure the job; and the better the conditions of work then the more they welcome the business.

Therefore, there is a different perspective which seems to contradict the opinion of those who run businesses. This is a view that sees labour not exclusively as a cost but rather as a source of income. This view is a prevailing one and is publicly expressed by some individuals. It gives the wages/salaries awarded to employees exactly the same status as profit for the owners and shareholders. That is, both are monies derived from the operation of the business. From the employee's perspective, if anything is a cost it must be the profit that diverts part of the income they generate into other hands – the owners and ▶ **shareholders** ◀, for example.

Shareholders ◀┈▶ The owners of one or more shares in a company.

Because they are directly involved in the workings of the organisation, employees are stakeholders and, often, shareholders as well and therefore they have an interest in the profits as well as the wages/salaries they receive. Because workers can have a financial interest in both wages/salaries and profits the two are considered to be economically interdependent. The key issue is in the attempt to find out where the prominent interest now lies – is it in profit or wages/salaries? Businesses provide people with goods and/or services but they also provide the wherewithal to buy goods and/or services. This is a fundamental concept in trying to understand the employer/employee relationship.

Theory-in-literature seems to take a social responsibility approach to this issue by indicating that society's view is that business is very much about providing jobs, but

Figure 7.3 The dyadic communication related to duties owed

preferably well-paid jobs combined with excellent working conditions. Some people would view this issue as an ethical one – and they would be correct if they believe that organisations have a responsibility for their staff – especially related to duty. That is, the duties which the people involved in a business owe to each other. This can comprise dyadic – two-way – communication ■ *see* Chapter 5 ■. Communication related to duties owed is shown in Figure 7.3.

see Chapter 5

This involves, for instance, being honest and keeping promises made with a concern for others. Since this means that a duty is owed to others it brings with it a responsibility and thus, the need to behave in a responsible way. Since this is behavioural there must be a consequence for every action taken by an individual and so there is a ▶ **causal relationship** ◀ between rights and duties. For example, the failure of employees to look at a new health and safety poster display may not be caused by apathy but by, say, a lack of opportunity.

▶ A situation where one happening may, or may not, have caused a different one.

◀·······Causal
relationship

7.3

Activity

Reflect on a workplace situation where you have been promised something from your employer or supervisor but that promise was not kept.
Was it part of their duty to do so and if so, what could you have done about it?

An employee has the right to expect that while at her/his workplace s/he will be safe from harm and so the employer has a responsibility to take all precautions that they can to provide a safe environment – it is their duty. By the same token, the employee has the responsibility, and thus the duty, to take due care and attention. More generally, however, it is the duties which these groups owe to the business as a whole – to the business as an organisation – which links their separate (and possibly conflicting) interests.

While the ideal situation would be where the employer and employee have equal rights and, therefore, responsibilities, the reality is that this will depend upon the balance of power that exists between them. In the early 1990s the balance of power lay with the employer – a view which appeared to be reinforced by legislation during the previous decade which was heavily influenced by traditional ▶ **industrial relations** ◀ trying to keep the lid on industrial conflict and troubleshooting when that failed. Such legislation decreased the powers of trades unions and at the same time unemployment increased and job security decreased. This was the period when there was considerable downsizing. Such events have had a huge effect on the relationship between employer and employee – particularly between members of the workforce – and their line managers and has exhibited itself in behavioural areas such as confidence, openness and cooperation.

Industrial ◀┈┈▶ The rules, practices and conventions that govern the relationship between employers and
relations their workers.

An imbalance of power will aggravate the employer/employee relationship and thus the working atmosphere will be unhealthy, resulting in negative energy being expended rather than a joint positive effort to achieve the organisation's objectives. It is the managers who have the driving role, because they have to ensure that their workers have a positive attitude and that they are full participants in the *see* Chapter 5 employer/employee relationship ■ *see* Chapter 5 ■.

EMPLOYEE STATUS

People use the words 'employee' and 'worker' in a general sense, however in the world of work it is essential that all employees understand that it is more complicated because when discussing employment relations the word 'employee' has a specific, and defined, meaning which is actually inscribed within legislation. Aikin (1999) attempts to clarify the issue by stating:

> You often hear people talking about 'employees' as if there were a universal definition of what the term means. This is not the case. (p25)

The Employment Rights Act 1996 (ERA) states that there are a number of specific rights which are restricted to 'employees'. These include:

■ written statements concerning the particulars of the job

■ itemised wage payments

■ time off

- maternity rights

- Sunday working rights and

- protection against unfair dismissal and redundancy.

In section 230, the common law definition of employee status is used to cover those individuals who have entered into, or worked under, an employment contract – regardless of whether this contract was oral, written or implied.

However, Aikin (1999) goes on to report that the second part of the ERA which deals with the way in which wages, deductions and repayments are handled, applies to 'workers'. This is not a case of semantics since in this section the term includes all employees and *any person* who undertakes to carry out work/services for another party to the contract who is not a professional client of the person. This includes the self-employed and people working for agencies.

The difficulty in identifying what an 'employee' actually is, is further compounded when moving to other active legislation such as the Trade Union and Labour Relations (Consolidation) Act 1992. Within this Act there are several terms used to described employee status. For example, in section 295 'employee' has the same definition as in the ERA and is used in section 146 in relation to dismissal and detrimental treatment for union membership and also consultations in relation to redundancy.

However, the term 'worker' is also used, for example in the definition of a trade union in section 1. Here the term includes all 'employees' and any self-employed people who fit the ERA definition of someone who personally does work for another person to the contract who is not a professional client. When addressing the issue of 'who is a worker', the Department of Trade and Industry (DTI) (1998) guide states that the Working Time Regulations 1998 consider an employee to be:

> someone to whom an employer has a duty to provide work, who controls when and how it is done, supplies the tools and other equipment and pays tax and national insurance. (p3)

They hasten to add that the definition of a worker is simply an indicator rather than an exhaustive or exclusive criterion. For example, the majority of agency workers and freelancers are likely to be workers.

Aikin (1999) goes on further to state that the provisions relating to any industrial action do not refer to 'workers' or to 'employees', but to 'persons', a word which has been given no definition whatsoever in the legislation. Other unexplained general terms such as 'persons', 'work' and 'their place of work' are also used. This action has avoided the need to identify the precise category of employment to which the law applies.

Therefore, what is often considered to be a simple word in general use, 'employee', is – in its legal sense – complicated. Help might have been expected from other statutes but the Working Time Regulations 1998 use the term 'workers' being defined in the same way as the ERA. Because of this, the Working Time Regulations 1998 include self-employed and casual staff. Under these Regulations, agency staff are given their own category because they could be employed by either an agency itself or the client's of an agency. For example, if an individual signs on at a temping agency and is assigned to a job at a named organisation, s/he could be employed by *either* the agency *or* the organisation that has paid the agency (client) to find a temporary member of staff.

In the case of the Working Time Regulations 1998 legislation where there is no contract under which an individual can be defined as 'worker', s/he is still covered by the regulations. Therefore, the person who actually pays such a person her/his wages has to comply with the legislation.

It would be expected that the National Minimum Wage Act 1998 would have clarified the situation because it contains the broadest coverage of all employment legislation. The Act includes both employees and workers as covered in the ERA and emphatically includes agency workers, homeworkers and volunteers even though they may already come within the definition of a worker.

Although volunteers who work for charities, voluntary organisations, associated fundraising bodies and statutory organisations (such as the National Health Service, local authorities and the police force) are included, only those who are paid are so covered. The point being made here is that expenses and subsistence allowances do not count as pay in these cases. An individual who is carrying out work for someone on a self-employed basis is not entitled to the rights enshrined in the ERA because that individual is not considered to be an employee in the eyes of the law. For example, if an organisation hires a tree surgeon to work on the organisation's site, then s/he is not considered to be an employee in the eyes of the law because s/he is self-employed or the employee of another organisation.

This review shows how complicated the legislation is and how easy it is for the untrained to become unstuck. However, it does illustrate the need for employees and employers to be careful in their use of words when it comes to employer/employee relationships.

By reviewing current employment legislation, it appears to be in order to consider an individual to be an employee if:

- the employee is assimilated into the design of the organisation

- the employer is entitled to control what the worker does and how s/he does it

- both the worker and the employer agree that they have to supply and accept work.

PSYCHOLOGICAL CONTRACT

Recent and ongoing legislation may well make the employer/employee relationship more equitable. In the contemporary world of work it is part of the business environment to fulfil the needs of the employees and this is related to what is commonly known as the psychological contract. The work of MacNeil (1985) and Rousseau and Wade-Benzoni (1994) on the transactional and relational contracts discussed earlier is contained within the domain of the psychological contract.

Warr (1996) states that the psychological contract:

denotes the informal and largely unwritten expectations of employees and employers about their mutual rights and obligations, and about expected inducements and contributions. (p177)

It comprises a reciprocal arrangement between the employer and the employee and implies an implicit (unwritten) contract which is based on a series of assumptions about relationships.

The psychological contract takes on a momentum because it incorporates the two key skills of communication ■ *see* Chapter 5 ■ and motivation ■ *see* Chapter 9 ■, and recognises that there is now a collective dimension to employment relationships. The psychological contract offers a framework for interpreting effective communication and motivation.

see Chapter 5

see Chapter 9

Employees expect to receive:

■ financial reward for their labours ■ *see* Chapter 9 ■

see Chapter 9

■ status

■ opportunities for promotion ■ *see* Chapter 10 ■ and

see Chapter 10

■ challenging work

to meet their individual needs. In return, the employer expects to receive:

■ time

■ energy

■ talents and

■ loyalty

from the employee.

While the employment relationship has become more of a shared experience over recent times, many managers and supervisors are uncomfortable with the role of trying to conceive and maintain a satisfactory collective relationship. Such a relationship is influenced by a range of circumstances of which managers feel that they are ignorant or over which they have little – or even no – control, for example employment legislation ■ *see* Chapter 8 ■.

see Chapter 8

Positive employment relations is centred round a climate of involvement that will itself depend upon the extent to which managers are successful in engaging the employee's total support. This must start immediately the individual is recruited by the organisation. There is a close relationship here between HRM practices and involvement because each affects the psychological contract, that is:

HRM practices + Involvement = Positive psychological contract

The psychological contract begins with the employee's entry into the organisation when social support is needed from as many sources as possible so that the new employee can settle in quickly and effectively. Modifications need to take place as the individual worker proceeds through her/his career ■ *see* Chapter 10 ■. This is the establishment phase when the newcomer begins to form attachment relationships with many people in the organisation, for example, her/his fellow line

see Chapter 10

Table 7.4 Newcomer–insider psychological contracts for social support (after Nelson et al., 1991)

TYPE OF SUPPORT	FUNCTION OF SUPPORTIVE ATTACHMENTS	NEWCOMER CONCERN	EXAMPLES OF INSIDER RESPONSE/ACTION
Protection from stressors	Direct assistance in terms of resources, time, labour or environmental modification.	What are the major risks/ threats in this environment?	*Supervisor* cues newcomer in to risks/threats.
Informational	Provision of information necessary for managing demands.	What do I need to know to get things done?	*Mentor* provides advice on informal climate in organisation.
Evaluative	Feedback on both personal and professional role performances.	How am I doing?	*Supervisor* provides day-to-day performance feedback during first week on new job.
Modelling	Evidence of behavioural standards provided through modelled behaviour.	Who do I follow?	Newcomer is apprenticed to *senior colleague*.
Emotional	Empathy, esteem, caring or love.	Do I matter? Who cares if I am here or not?	*Other newcomers* empathise with and encourage individual when reality shock sets in.

workers, supervisor, security staff and the head of department. It is very important that all individuals work out effective psychological contracts with each of their relationships. A common concern for new employees is whose behaviour should they model in order to gain cues so that they themselves are considered to be exhibiting appropriate behaviour. This is the role of senior colleagues – although it is only one type of support that newcomers need. Employers should help newcomers form relationships early and should encourage the psychological contracting process between newcomers and insiders.

Nelson et al. (1991) posit a model for newcomer–insider psychological contracts as shown in Table 7.4.

The psychological contract has been around some 40 years since it was first mooted by Argyris (1960). It was then developed by Schein (1988) and, more recently, addressed by Mayo (1995) who stated that:

> employees [should] be treated fairly and honestly, and that information will be provided about changes at work, so as to meet the need for equity and justice.

> employees can expect to have some degree of security and certainty about the jobs in return for their loyalty to the employer, thus fulfilling the need for security and relative certainty.

> employers can expect employees to recognise and value their past and future contribution, so as to satisfy the need for fulfilment, satisfaction and progression. (p229–65)

However, Herriot (1995a, b) believes that although the psychological contract may well have been in existence in the 1970s, by the late 1990s it had disappeared because the 1990s were characterised by ▶ **instrumentality** ◀ and uncertainty.

▶ The calculation of the number and degree of rewards resulting from achieving an outcome. ◀····▶ **Instrumentality**

Individuals were working within the theory of equity and thus calculating what rewards they would get for their efforts in a working environment of increasing uncertainty and instability. In the mid-1990s most employees were concerned with the issue of job security as organisations were downsized – flattened and made lean by the removal of hierarchical levels. As time moved on, the latter part of the decade saw a general reduction in anxiety and an increase in what is commonly called 'the feel good factor' which is linked to improvements in the labour market.

However, there is still an imbalance in what is offered by the employer and what is expected by the employee. Herriot (1995a, 1995b) states that in the 1990s individual employees offered:

■   flexibility

■   accountability and

■   long working hours

in return for a higher salary. There are still insecurities that characterise the psychological contract which are particularly felt by those occupying middle management positions, for example the fear of downsizing, redundancy or demotion. Marchington and Wilkinson (1997) believe that employees are in a no-win situation. Because of the recession with its resultant downsizing, organisations knew that managers were unlikely to complain, so they tended to increase the pressure on them. It is only with an improvement in the economic climate and its accompanying lack of oppression that the pendulum is likely to swing from an attitude of 'do it or else', to one of worrying about staff turnover and loyalty. Schein (1988) says that managers need to be flexible and accept:

> a variety of interpersonal relationships, patterns of authority and psychological contracts. (p16)

If an employer does not make encouraging sounds regarding the future structure and stability of the organisation, s/he will have indirectly promoted this apparent lack of ambition, mobility and general lack of trust which, according to Marchington and Wilkinson (1997), is now commonplace among long-serving and loyal staff.

The changing nature of the psychological contract has left many employees relatively powerless in relation to their employers and has also left them unsure how their legitimate concerns might be articulated and dealt with – unless by the 'conscience' of the organisation. Many employees feel that the psychological contract is too one-sided and, while they may lack the resources (or the will) to engage in industrial action, feelings of unfairness and inequity can easily translate into demotivation, lack of interest in quality and customer care and more serious problems in the community at large as they verbalise their negative feelings outside the workplace. Emmott (1997) reported that employment relations were not rated as being well carried out within most organisations.

However, a positive psychological contract reflects a healthy employer/employee relationship which is characterised by fairness, trust and the delivery of promises – on both sides. The psychological contract is very important because it is a key explanatory variable in contemporary employment relations. However, the involvement of the employee is essential – it is a key predictor of the success of a psychological contract.

7.4 Activity

Believing that a psychological contract is a positive part of an employer/employee relationship, check past issues of the Chartered Institute of Personnel and Development's (CIPD) magazine *People Management* and/or other business-related sources to see what the HRM specialists' view is on such relationships.

Write a 200-word review of one source you have found.

JUSTICE, LOYALTY AND PARTNERSHIP

Sometimes the relationship between employer and employee is inequitable. What is important is that employers and workers are not inherently hostile and they both understand that they each have mutual obligations. The current work environment should be that of mutual cooperation between the employer and the employee, between management and trades unions: in each case the two parties are perceived as being social partners each with mutual obligations. For example, the employer has a right to expect the employee to be honest, not to damage organisational property or cause any injury to her/his employer; while individuals have a right to belong to a trade union, although their right of assembly must not include violent or riotous behaviour.

JUSTICE

Justice can be defined as being what people deserve or what they have a right to. In the workplace this can be a matter of, say, receiving a particular type of treatment from others or being in receipt of payment for work carried out. When rights are part of the equation, it will almost certainly concern some sort of positive benefit – since there are few workers who particularly request to be harmed in some way! However, a worker's just desserts can be in the form of reward *or* punishment, credit *or* blame and therefore justice is really no more than the use of morality in relation to the things people at work feel that they *ought* to have. Individuals in the workplace will come across four types of justice:

■ *Procedural justice*

All workers are entitled to this – it has ▶ **universal eligibility** ◀. Procedural justice is about the rules and regulations that concern employees and that govern or control them in one way or another. An example here would be, say, the wearing of a uniform while at work. Such rules must be applied consistently and in a fair way and should not rely on ambiguity or arbitrariness. That is, all decisions should be made in a logical way, rules and regulations must be adhered to, agreed procedures should be followed and there should be no discrimination. Employers exercise power over people and, therefore, they have to give serious consideration to procedural justice.

▷ Common to all, everybody is entitled to it. ◀┄┄▶ **Universal eligibility**

POINTS TO PONDER

It is possible to adhere conscientiously to rules and regulations which are perceived to be unjust – an unjust rule can be applied even-handedly!

For example, take the issue of smoking in the workplace. A total 'No smoking' policy may be seen by some workers to be unfair, but the policy itself can be policed even-handedly even though some workers may not think that the original policy is just.

The other three types of justice are all types of *substantive justice* – its position can be seen in Figure 7.4. Substantive justice is what individuals actually receive under rules and regulations.

■ *Retributive justice*

This is the punishment given to workers when they do wrong – that is, they break the rules. For example, they smoke at a workplace which has a 'No

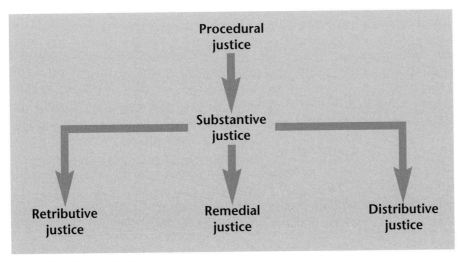

Figure 7.4 Types of justice

smoking' policy. Therefore, it is about what punishment is appropriate for what offence and the issue of how an employer can maintain the balance between severity and leniency. When a punishment is not equitable with the offence – being either too severe or too lenient – then this is retributive injustice. Retributive justice concentrates on the perpetrator, with a precondition for retribution being proof that the alleged offence has actually been committed.

■ *Remedial justice*
This can also be called *rectificatory* or *compensatory* justice and is the opposite of retributive justice because it deals with wrongdoing as it affects the victim rather than the perpetrator. It is about putting things right or, at the very least, compensating the injured party for the wrongdoing. In the workplace, it will involve issues such as awarding damages, costs or similar compensation. Remedial injustice is perceived to have taken place when an individual is inadequately compensated – or overcompensated – for a wrong done against her/him.

■ *Distributive justice*
Unlike the other forms of justice, distributive justice does not necessarily have any connection with wrongdoing. It is about the manner in which the benefits (and burdens) are to be shared among others, that is, the division of the points or the sharing of the penalties. Examples here could be power, property, work obligation, responsibility and accountability as a member of a work team.

While it might be tidy to distinguish between the types of justice, there is no clear delineation: taking a persistent latecomer to work as an example, retributive justice states that s/he must be guilty of that offence in order to be punished but this is also a procedural principle. A separate example would be in the payment of

SCENARIO 7.2

The Met fails inspection on race and recruitment

A damning report into the Metropolitan Police's efforts to erase racism has focused on HR management. Their mistakes were:

■ Local police stations are not setting recruitment targets for ethnic minority staff.
■ Line managers are insensitive to the needs of ethnic minority staff.
■ Staff lack faith in grievance procedures.
■ Job descriptions and person specifications vary too much.

■ There is too little monitoring of career progression among minorities.
■ The race relations training programme bypassed a thorough needs analysis, is unclear over who is responsible and lacks common standards and an inbuilt evaluation strategy.
■ Major policies on 'stop and search' and recording racist incidents are not reaching grassroots level. Local officers are not being brought on board.

Adapted from: Cooper, C. (2000) The Met fails inspection on race and recruitment: Metropolitan mistakes, *People Management*, 20 January, p11.

damages to a person who has had wrong done by them; there is a combination of retributive and remedial elements of justice. Also, the payment of awards is distributary – the sharing out of benefits and burdens (a benefit to the recipient and a burden to the organisation suffering the costs of payment).

Social justice and employment standards are closely linked. Walsh (1999) reports that the International Labour Organisation (ILO) has started what is perceived to be an ambitious programme in an attempt to ensure that workplace rights are global. In the past, the ILO has been seen as a remote organisation, made up of a clique of individuals who did not wish (or were unable) to integrate with the business community. However, the recently appointed director-general (Juan Somaria) is making a point of attempting to redress the inequity by raising the ILO's profile through establishing links with employers on a global scale. Somaria is the first non-western leader of the ILO in its 80 years (he is Chilean) and it is interesting to note that he is driving the modernisation.

Globalisation has brought with it prosperity for some and inequality for others ■ *see* Chapter 11 ■. Somaria realises that the changes made in employment patterns and labour markets have had a considerable influence on the work environment in all countries. Somaria and his team have four strategic objectives:

see Chapter 11

1   fundamental principles and rights at work

2   decent employment for all

3   improved social protection

4   strengthened social dialogue.

POINTS TO PONDER

What is the International Labour Organisation?

The ILO was born out of the economic and social chaos of World War I (1914–18) as part of the Treaty of Versailles (1919) signed between Germany and the Allies, which terminated the war. It was based on the principle that peace could last only on a solid foundation of social justice.

Its creation in 1919 was motivated by concern that 'conditions of labour exist involving... injustice, hardship and privation to large numbers of people', and by fear, following the Russian Revolution, of further uprisings. It was also thought that any nation adopting social reforms would be disadvantaged economically. The preamble of the ILO's constitution states: 'The failure of any nation to adopt human conditions of labour is an obstacle in the way of other nations that desire to improve the conditions in their own countries.'

The organisation's labour code consists of legally binding conventions and voluntary recommendations. These lay down minimum standards to be achieved in areas including the protection of the basic human right of freedom of association, the abolition of forced labour and the elimination of discrimination in employment, as well as focusing on technical aspects of the regulation of employment.

Adapted from: Walsh, J. (1999a) Incoming director-general strengthens the ILO break, *People Management*, 17 June, p15.

In this way the ILO has increasingly become a significant organisation in the globalisation of business. It is taking a highly constructive approach in the development of best practice within a strong framework of ensuring human rights for all.

However, as there is intense rivalry between national trades unions (and between trades unions which compete for members in one country), it will be hard for them to develop common trade union positions and organise effective international campaigns. With more coordinated union bodies emerging it might be easier for them to work together although it needs to be recognised that it will be very hard to reconcile diverse interests and cultures. The first steps were taken in January 2000 when an international trade union was inaugurated, to be centred in Nyon, Switzerland, which will cover 15 million workers from 140 different countries. The union is to be called the Union Network International (UNI) and will comprise a merger of the five existing international union federations for the:

- communications

- printing

- media and entertainment

- services

- professional

sections of work.

Taylor (1999a) reports that the head of the union (Philip Jennings) believes that:

> We need greater unity to ensure the new global village is not just for the super-rich and we need to use the latest technology ourselves to improve communication between 800 unions worldwide. (p5)

LOYALTY

see Chapter 8

The modern workplace prides itself on positive relationships between the employer and the employee with equal opportunities given to all potential and existing employees ■ *see* Chapter 8 ■. The latter has its focus on the duty of the employer to do what is right by her/his employees. However, when it comes to issues such as loyalty and trust it is the employee who becomes the centre of attention rather than the employer. An employer looks for a high degree of loyalty from her/his employees but it might be questionable if this means that a worker is expected to keep quiet about any malpractice within the organisation. Whistleblowing, mentioned earlier in this chapter, has become a central issue in the employer/employee relationships. A whistleblower is someone who does not remain silent about an issue – be it illegal, immoral or perpetrated against the organisation itself, for example what is known as 'white-collar crime' – stealing stationery goods from an employer. The latter is internal whistleblowing and such a behaviour will probably be dealt with by the organisation itself. External whistleblowing is when the malpractice is carried out by the employee's organisation against an outside party, such as another organisation, the local community or the public at large. The costs of whistleblowing can be very high because the whistleblower could become very unpopular with her/his own management and colleagues since both could well be disadvantaged by any external exposure. Whistleblowers take on the role of an informant, a 'grass', a 'dobber-in'.

SCENARIO 7.3

When group loyalty is dangerous

Japan has no word for a 'whistleblower', says Tom Crowell. That's because the concept simply doesn't exist in the Japanese mindset. If it did, Japan wouldn't be in so much trouble today. Consider the recent leak at a nuclear lab near Tokyo – Japan's worst-ever nuclear accident. The sloppy management practices which led to the disaster would never have been tolerated at the nuclear plant in Washington State where I work, says Cromwell. Someone would have exposed the plant's contractor, who for years had used an unauthorised operations manual that he himself had written. But in Japan, where group loyalty is seen as the supreme virtue, 'ratting' is anathema. Paradoxically, once things do go wrong, those responsible are expected to resign – or worse. In 1995, for example, a senior manager at the Monju breeder reactor committed suicide after an accident. 'There's something perverse about a culture that thinks it's okay, even admirable, to take one's own life to atone for an accident,' but shameful to reveal potentially fatal mismanagement. If Japan had a few more whistleblowers, three workers at the nuclear plant would not now be fighting for their lives.

Source: When group loyalty is dangerous, *Asiaweek* (Hong Kong), The Week, 27 November 1999, p12.

The most effective way to protect whistleblowers is through legislation which prevents the victimisation of whistleblowers and provides them with compensation for any suffering which might occur as a result of their actions. This is the purpose of the Public Disclosure Act 1998 which became law in the UK in July 1999. Some firms have their own procedures to deal with whistleblowing and these include:

- ASDA
- Barclays Bank
- The Body Shop
- Tesco
- WHSmith

as well as most local authorities/councils.

Stewart (1999) cites the case of when the UK Conservative Government (1979–97) made whistleblowers in the public sector subject to official sanction. He cites the example of the National Health Service (NHS) whose employees were forced to sign legal documents that meant in effect that if they blew the whistle about their concerns they would be sacked. Since the Act entered the UK Statute Book in July

1999 these contracts became illegal. Whistleblowers in the NHS are given specific protection from any attempts by managers to downgrade them or label them as troublemakers. There are some who believe that legislation is unwarranted government interference and consider that self-regulating practices are superior by arguing that it is in the organisation's long-term interest not to be involved in malpractice.

At the centre of discussions on whistleblowing is the issue of loyalty and trust. The normal presupposition is that employees owe a duty of loyalty to their employers and some believe that this is also a moral duty. Thus, in the case of whistleblowing, for example, there must be a conflict between the duty to expose the wrongdoing and loyalty to an employer. It is this very conflict which complicates the issue because whistleblowing moves away from something that really ought to be done into a moral dilemma.

POINTS TO PONDER

Fewer than two-thirds of private sector companies have a whistleblowing plan despite the UK Public Interest Disclosure Act 1998 which came into effect in July 1999. Why should this be so since employers risk heavy penalties and media attention if they discourage or make any attempt to cover up staff warnings about malpractice?

It could be because of the publication of Lord Nolan's report *Standards in Public Life* (1995) and the Government White Paper on modernising local government (1998), where it was recommended that every local authority/council should have a whistleblowing procedure.

Others, such as Duska (1990), will find this viewpoint questionable being of the belief that employers and businesses are not the sort of beings to which an individual owes loyalty. The belief here is that loyalty and trust are based on the relationships between individuals and depend upon no requirement for reward. It demands considerable self-sacrifice. This is not the case when it comes to organisations and businesses because they exist to make a profit (Friedman, 1980) and the employees' view tends to be that the organisation is there as a means to gain a salary or wage and if they are fortunate workers might get some job satisfaction. In this case, the employer/employer relationship is purely one of mutual self-interest which is the opposite sort of relationship required for loyalty and trust to be present. Duska (1990) believes that to have the opposite opinion is to be fooled and is a misplacement of emotions by the employer. He cites the example of someone who has been a very loyal employee and who has worked above and beyond what was required, only to find her/himself downsized during a company restructure. He believes, therefore, that no loyalty is owed by an employee to an employer and, therefore, in the case of, say, whistleblowing, there is no conflict between a moral duty to expose wrongs and loyalty to the organisation.

Whether one agrees or disagrees with this viewpoint, what is clear is that his observations set a severe limitation on the ideas behind employee loyalty. Such limitations may be overcome, according to Chryssides and Kaler (1996) by:

the reconstituting of businesses through participation. (p99)

Loyalty is allied to trust and both are a matter of perceptual differences. *The Concise Oxford English Dictionary* (COED) (1999) (Pearsall, ed.) defines trust as:

> acceptance of the truth of a statement without evidence or investigation

This leads to the link with loyalty which the COED uses to help define 'trustworthy' – the implication that others can rely upon an individual. Thompson (1998) takes an output viewpoint with the belief that if there is good management there will, naturally, follow the outcome of trust.

If the relationship between the employer and the employee is honest and individuals keep their promises then a climate of trust will evolve. Yet some organisations make such comments but ignore them and are thus low-trust organisations. Trust is very much related to justice, discussed earlier in this chapter.

PARTNERSHIP

Contemporary employee relationships are often referred to as *partnerships*. There is no agreed definition of this term as it relates to work, however, it applies a sense of common action and purpose.

SCENARIO 7.4

Enter the people dimension

With the twenty-first century on its way, Eila Rana asked key figures in the world of work for their predictions about the future of employment. She received the following response in the area of employee relations.

After 20 years of declining membership, the tide is finally turning for the trade union movement, according to Brendan Barber, the Trades Union Congress's (TUC) deputy general secretary.

We would like to see trade union membership grow by a million in the next five years. A particular challenge for the TUC in this area is to build approaches based on unions working together, not competitively.

As the UK moves into an era of statutory union recognition, partnership is the name of the employee relations game. And Barber is keen to see the development of many more partnership arrangements throughout industry. He sees a dual role for unions, not only 'battling with the bad bosses' but also playing a key role in the success of the firms that employ their members.

Whether employers play ball depends on which approach the unions take, according to Mike Emmott, employee relations adviser to the IPD. 'How far will trade unions use the recent tremendous burst of employment regulation to strengthen their appeal and support in the workplace?' he asked. 'Or how far will they retreat into the political scene and prefer to exercise their influence on EU committees?'

Emmott believes unions will try both strategies, but their success will depend on workplace support.

Source: Rana, E. (2000) Enter the people dimension, *People Management*, 6 January, pp16–17.

Monks (1999) believes that it is time for a new approach to the employer and employee relationship. In his position as general secretary of the TUC he has seen the use of both industrial militancy and macho management in the field of employment relationships and highlights the issue that the unions' approach has changed:

Our starting point is what our members want. (p29)

He goes on to suggest that partnership is essential if progress in employment relations is to be made. He makes no apology for not providing a model that organisations could adopt but he does offer six clear principles which he believes must be at work if a positive relationship is to be found – these can be seen in Table 7.5.

The procedure means that the unions do not respond to change by quickly saying 'No' and the employer has to permit the unions to influence decision making. All this takes time and effort but, as Monks (1999) states:

the cliché is true: employees are any organisation's greatest asset. (p29)

The HRM function is vitally important here because, with its help, partnership can provide the foundation of positive relations in order that the organisation can:

contribute to the competitiveness of the business and the nation. (p29)

Whether employers believe that 'partnership' is a buzzword, jargon or just a rebranding of the status quo, or, according to Crabb (1999), they are simply sceptical, it is essential that a new approach to employment relations is made in order to move forward.

Table 7.5 Principles for progress in partnership agreements between employers and trades unions

Number	Principle	Component
1	Both partners must be committed to the success of the enterprise.	Shared perception and understanding of goals.
2	Recognition by each side that both may have legitimate and separate interests and that each must be free to represent their respective bodies.	Trust. Respect. Willingness to resolve differences. Independent union.
3	Employment security.	Maximisation of security within the organisation. Improvement of employability through training.
4	Improvement in working life.	Creating opportunities for personal growth, both vocational and non-vocational.
5	Sharing of all information.	Genuine consultation. Commitment to listening to alternative ideas. Acceptance of confidentiality. Effective communication.

SCENARIO 7.5

Stagecoach and unions join forces at Waterloo

A unique partnership approach between Stagecoach Holdings and the transport unions has paved the way for employees to update their skills and qualifications.

The Open Learning scheme is being piloted among South West Trains (SWT) staff at London's Waterloo Station, where the company's first learning centre was opened recently.

Stagecoach set up the initiative with the TUC* and the transport unions ASLEF,* RMT* and TSSA.* All parties were involved in the scheme from its inception and will continue to steer its development. The scheme is part of the TUC's Partners for Progress campaign, which seeks to encourage progressive relations between employers and unions.

Stagecoach chief executive, Mike Kinski, says: 'To me, partnership is the way forward for any organisation. If you're going to be successful, you need to take your workforce with you. And to do that, you have to develop forward-thinking relationships with the trade unions.'

*	TUC	Trades Union Congress
	ASLEF	Associated Society of Locomotive Engineers and Firemen
	RMT	Rail and Maritime Transport
	TSSA	Transport Salaried Staff's Association

Adapted from: Rana, E. (1999) Stagecoach and unions join forces at Waterloo, *People Management*, 3 June, p13.

Taylor (1998) reports that it will not be easy to improve cooperation in the workplace believing that the only way to win workers' commitment is to involve them from the beginning.

Edmonds (1999), in his role as general secretary of the General Municipal and Boilermakers Union (GMB), stated that companies that sign partnership agreements with trades unions are going to have to guarantee interesting, quality work and job security as well as having to:

> address what their employees want. They will have to accept partnership means a commitment not only to the end of boring work, and employee security, but also acceptance that every worker has a right to quality training. (p8)

He argues that making recognition deals with trades unions will not be sufficient for companies if they wish to change workplace culture. The signing of an agreement is only the start of improved relationships because if it is to be successful it means that employers will have to come to terms with the needs of their workforce.

Partnership has become a fashionable word to describe those organisations that concentrate on their core business but who also work closely with their suppliers to ensure that they get the quality of materials and components they need in order to make their products and/or provide their services. The Institute of Personnel and Development (IPD) (1998) believes partnership is:

> essentially about particular processes of management, rather than about structures. (p8)

However, the CIPD also suggests that there is a longer term relationship in which the partners will be more concerned with maximising growth than with short-term negotiations over the sharing of the results. In positive partnership relationships each individual has absolute respect for the other as well as to the needs of all stakeholders – and this includes the relationship between the employer and the employee. It is very difficult in the turbulent and competitive contemporary workplace to balance the needs of all stakeholders and the partnership concept has gained influence within this increased level of competition when it is much more difficult to balance the interests of all.

HRM specialists tend to consider partnership to be more about the relationship between the employer and the employee, individually and in groups, than it has to do with bodies which represent employees, for example trades unions and professional bodies like the CIPD and the Chartered Institute of Marketing (CIM). More and more organisations are negotiating partnerships with trades unions because they recognise the value of such agreements to the success of their own businesses. Organisations which already have partnership agreements are diverse and include:

- Barclays Bank

- British Aerospace

- British Nuclear Fuels (BNF)

- British Telecommunications (BT)

- Gardner Merchant

- Group 4

- Imperial Chemical Industries (ICI)

- McGregor Gory

- National Grid

- North Sea Oil Industries

- Prudential

- Stagecoach Holdings (see Scenario 7.5)

- Tesco

- Unilever

- United Utilities.

The director-general of the Confederation of British Industry (CBI) is in favour of partnerships but states that not all organisations perceive that the inclusion of a trade union in a partnership agreement is necessary. He argues that partnerships should be based on direct communication with all the employees within an organisation or where there is shared ownership of an organisation. Examples of such partnerships are:

- ASDA

- Hewlett-Packard

- International Business Machines (IBM)

- Unipart.

Jones (1999) cites the particular example of the retail outlet, Tesco, where cooperation has helped staff and management. Communications between Tesco and the Union of Shop Distributive and Allied Workers (USDAW) brought about one key shared belief – the adversarial approach to employee relationships was not effective. While the union and the management were not actually at loggerheads, they were in an unproductive rut and backward-looking situation. In 1997 the old agreements and structures were replaced by shopfloor participation (with USDAW having gained the cooperation of its members) through the use of workplace forums at local, regional and national levels. The organisation retained only the existing representation for grievances or disciplinary matters. The higher participation level brought about by this new partnership has engendered a greater openness and discussions in the forums are based on sounder information. The partnership is still maturing and the signs are that it has brought about:

greater understanding and participation in corporate strategy. (p13)

However, the ongoing emphasis is on the partnership between the employer and the trades unions as representatives of the employees.

There is a steady and increasing number of organisations which are developing partnership arrangements with trades unions and the elements of good practice which have emerged with employment relations legislation ■ *see* Chapter 8 ■. It is probably best to consider that employers generally want to recognise that employee security is an issue and offer some reassurance, for example by undertaking that there will be no compulsory redundancies. Trades unions, for their part, commit themselves to working with management to improve business performance. These commitments are supported by mechanisms for communication and involvement ■ *see* Chapter 5 ■.

see Chapter 8

see Chapter 5

POINTS TO PONDER

Industrial action in the UK is at its lowest since records began and in Wales it is almost non-existent. Many people might be surprised that Wales also has the UK's highest union membership.

This could be because high union membership ensures better working environments and, therefore, less industrial unrest. However, whether good or bad, improved relations between employers and unions were the key to improving industrial relations in Wales. With the increase in the use of European works councils it might be expected that industrial action will be totally eliminated yet union membership is declining.

EMPLOYEE REPRESENTATION

With the decline in collective bargaining many organisations concentrate on ensuring effective involvement with individual employees. This is especially true at the higher levels of management or in high-performance work teams. However, *all* employees want to know that their individual interests are being taken into account when decisions are made that will concern them as members of the organisation's workforce. It is particularly difficult in the larger organisations to consult all members of the workforce individually on every matter that will, directly or indirectly, concern them as employees and so there has to be some form of machinery – whether procedural or structural – to represent the employees collectively. Whether collective representation is needed, or desired, depends upon the representation criteria used in each organisation and some individuals do not wish to be part of organised bodies that purport to represent them.

Employees have the legal right to elect an employee representative who is someone whose purpose is to be consulted about, for example, proposed redundancies or about a proposed transfer of ownership of the employing business; or who are elected for general purposes which embrace one of those specific purposes. The role was created by the Collective Redundancies and Transfer of Undertakings (Protection of Employment) Regulations 1995 as a result of a ruling by the European Court of Justice (1994) which stated that the UK was not complying fully with the European Community Collective Redundancy and Acquired Rights Directives. This was because UK law only required consultation with employees about proposed redundancy dismissals or, in the event of the sale or other transfer of ownership of an employing organisation, only applied if the employees were represented by a trade union. Employee representatives have special employment rights, which are:

- to be paid for time off work in order to attend to their duties

- not to be victimised

- protection against dismissal.

Employment law gives individuals certain basic protection against being penalised because they are, or are not, members of a trade union and these are given in Table 7.6.

In its annual survey of business (1999), the CBI reported that over 1500 organisations were concerned that they would be faced with claims for union recognition under the legislation. They also reported on the widespread anxiety concerning the impact of a whole range of employment legislation – including that concerning the limiting of working time ■ *see* Chapter 8 ■. The study shows that more than one in four organisations believes that the consequences of the new labour laws will be negative – among companies with more that 5000 workers this figure increases to two out of five. The survey found that about half the firms employing more than 500 workers assumed that they would be faced with a claim for union recognition –

see Chapter 8

Table 7.6 Basic protection for all employees regardless of trade union membership

- Unlawful for employers to select recruits on the basis of trade union membership

- Unlawful to choose staff for redundancy because they belong to a trade union or because they wish to join a trade union

- Employees have a right to belong to a trade union, irrespective of the views of their employer

- Unlawful to take any action to prevent, penalise or deter employees from belonging to a trade union, for example blocking promotion on the grounds of trade union membership (or lack of it)

- Employers must not oblige employees to join, or remain a member of, a trade union

- Employers are not obliged by law to recognise a trade union for bargaining purposes if their employees belong to a trade union; employers are free to decide for themselves whether they wish to recognise trades unions, irrespective of the number of members among their employees

- Employees, or job applicants, can complain to an employment tribunal if they believe that their rights to belong – or not to belong – to a trade union have been infringed – regardless of the individual employee's length of service with the organisation or hours worked

two out of five firms responding to the survey said that they had already recognised unions for collective bargaining.

There are two key areas of concern which need to be developed:

- the role of the trades unions

- the evolution of European works councils (EWCs).

THE ROLE OF THE TRADES UNIONS

Trades unions are disappearing from large tracts of the privately owned sector of the economy and they are finding it extremely difficult to win recruits within the new, more flexible labour markets. Official government statistics released on 8 July 1999 state that only 19 per cent of workers employed in the private sector are trade union members contrasting with 61 per cent of the public sector who are members of a trade union.

Taylor (1999b) reported on the European Trade Union Conference in Helsinki (1999) stating that the international trade union movement is to review its structure early in 2000 because it needs to create:

a strong unitary body to represent the world's workers in the age of globalisation. (p3)

National trades unions within the UK are each duplicating the work of other national trades unions and it is time that they reformed their structure to take into account increased globalisation. Like other organisations, unless the trade union sector organises itself internationally it will not succeed – the opportunity is there for national trades unions to participate actively in the Union Network International (UNI) body which came into being in January 2000.

THE EVOLUTION OF EUROPEAN WORKS COUNCILS (EWC)

In the past, employees in the UK have been represented by their trade union shop stewards and in continental Europe representation was, and still is, mostly through works councils. In the 1990s the trades unions and organisations within the UK started to become interested in the works council model which was to be found in continental Europe. This came about because of:

- a growing interest in the stakeholder approaches to corporate governance

- trade union interest in the legally secured rights following the decline in trade union membership and union influence in the 1980s

- the obligation on larger organisations with extensive operations in Europe to establish EWCs under the EU Council Directive (1994).

The Directive's principal aim was to get organisations to set up an EWC or other procedures on an EU scale which were to be used for the purpose of informing and consulting employees. Other items were to:

- require organisations with at least 1000 employees in the EU and at least 150 employees in two or more member states to establish an EWC

- set up EWCs on the basis of an agreement reached after the organisation had consulted its employees.

There are over 300 UK organisations which are required to set up EWCs and this comprises the largest single grouping in the EU. EWCs are expected to embrace over 50 000 employee representatives throughout Europe once all the 1500 or so organisations covered have established them. They could well be the means of bringing about European-level collective bargaining which might be the reason why most organisations and many trade unionists oppose them or are, at the very least, sceptical about the development of EWCs. One of the most difficult parts to deal with is membership of the EWCs. This is not such a problem when there is widespread trade union membership but it becomes more so with non-union staff who also need to be represented.

The European Works Council Directive (1994), which became law in the UK in December 1999, applies to organisations which have more than 1000 employees in the European Union and at least two establishments in different member states, each employing at least 150 people. Although around 1600 businesses are large enough to fall within its scope, only 515 EWCs had been set up by April 1999. An organisation is required to set one up only if 100 or more employees from at least two member states request it.

The TUC predicted in mid-1999 that 146 multinational organisations in Britain will be affected by the Regulations: 111 UK-based parent companies and 35 firms with headquarters in other countries. The number of non-UK-based firms that will be affected is likely to be between 35 and 100, according to its research.

EWCs normally meet annually and they report back to employees – this feedback is very important. In many organisations this involves using the existing systems of employee communications ■ *see* Chapter 5 ■. The key factors in the development of an effective EWC system have been identified by the Incomes Data Services in London who report that they are:

see Chapter 5

■ establishing clear and open two-way communication

■ working in a cooperative spirit

■ being sensitive to differing attitudes towards European integration

■ writing an agreement in terms that are easy to translate

■ setting up good translation facilities

■ keeping the agenda of the EWC to transnational issues

■ providing training for representatives.

The last point has been a key concern because an increasing number of officials, representatives and even more employers are claiming that there is so much complexity connected with the introduction and process of EWCs and they have ever-increasing matters to deal with. While this might be in the interests of relationships between employers and employees, there is minimal investment in the training of representatives so that they can cope with the work. Little time appears to be given to enable them to carry out their preparatory work and feedback to their colleagues. There is no current obligation for the communication of information to employees outside the EWC meetings. It would be in the interests of all employers to ensure that information reaches all members of the workforce. This could be brought about by a more effective use of technology with the availability of resources for representatives to talk face to face with the workforce ■ *see* Chapter 5 *and* Chapter 6 ■.

see Chapter 5 *and* Chapter 6

There is another problem with the use of EWCs in that they also have to cope with technical and legal jargon and although some training has been provided in this area, it is still very erratic. The skills required of EWC members are:

■ language

■ intercultural communications

■ confidentiality

■ reading financial statements

■ understanding organisational structures.

While it is expensive to release and train EWC representatives it does seem that some firms, for example Renault, are beginning to view the cost as an investment in employee relations and it is particularly cost-effective for organisations who are radically restructuring their enterprises ■ *see* Chapter 2 ■.

see Chapter 2

The use of EWCs is still in its infancy and even in France, Germany and the Netherlands – where works councils are well established – the EWCs are not the principal body for negotiating the basic terms and conditions of employment which is a right still reserved for the trades unions. However, the EWCs do have extensive rights to:

■ information

■ consultation and

■ participation in some decision making

and they can sign workplace agreements covering a wide range of issues, such as the health and welfare of members of the workforce.

Gollan (1999) states that:

> The benefits of giving workers a voice, through company councils, joining consultative committees, works councils and other indirect forms of worker participation, are increasingly being recognised by organisations whose renewed interest in such schemes has, perhaps, been sparked by legislative imperatives. (p17)

There is no doubt that legislation has driven the introduction of EWCs (particularly in the UK) but this has been accompanied by a reduction in trade union presence. It does seem that employees have less representation within the workforce and because of this perception the issue of the mechanisms for employee representation has been high. Another consideration has been the European Directives concerning forms of employee representation at European level which have renewed interest in organisation councils other than EWCs (where they are not legislatively required) – for example joint consultative committees (JCCs).

Through both direct and indirect process both the employer and the employee can express their opinions, views, interests and concerns about the operation of the workplace and, thus, all become part of the decision-making process of the organisation. Where executive accountability is to be participatory in the sense of involving employees in shopfloor decision making, then it tends to go against the conventional hierarchical power structures to be found within organisations. As can be seen from Figure 7.5(a) and (b), it would produce a downward flow of accountability (b) to be set up against the more usual upward flow (a).

An example would be the German works councils where managers need to obtain the agreement of an elected works committee before instituting certain sorts of changes in working practices as previously agreed. This is opposite to the more usual upward flow as shown in Figure 7.6(a) and (b).

The European Commission started a review of the Directives operation in September 1999 and consulted with the EU trades unions and employer bodies in an attempt to ensure that all organisations covered by the Directive activated their EWCs.

With an understanding of the key factors related to the employer/employee relationship it is necessary to understand the key legislation and Directives that underpin positive work relationships.

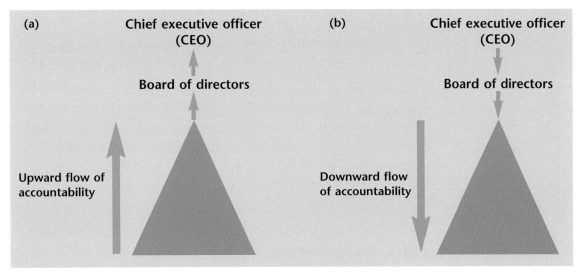

Figure 7.5 (a) Hierarchical power; (b) European Works Councils (EWCs)

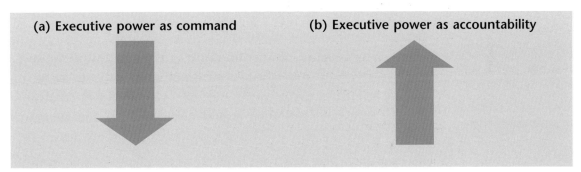

Figure 7.6 Pattern of power and accountability in organisations

7.5

Activity

One of the main aims for all types of union has been to counteract and protect their members from the power of the employer.

How have the trades unions come to grips with the introduction of EWCs?

■ Relationships between the employer and the employee cover a wide spectrum of issues from payment of work carried out to protection in the workplace.

■ In order for an organisation to achieve its objectives, the relationship between the employer and the employee has to be fruitful, which itself is achieved only if there is equity between the inputs and outputs of the employer and the inputs and outputs of the employee.

■ During the last decade the employment relations agenda has shifted dramatically. In the early 1980s employment relations were significantly influenced by 'keeping the lid on' industrial conflict and troubleshooting when that failed. In the 1990s the whole issue of employment relations has become much more stable (Emmott, 1997).

■ The concentration now is on the relationship between the employer and employee rather than the employees themselves and the ways they can be controlled.

■ The study of law is very complex and it is a specialised area of study. However, an appreciation of the role of law is essential in the understanding of employment relations.

■ Regardless of the legal system of each country it is usually divided into systems dominated by legislation and common law systems.

■ There are a number of specific rights which are restricted to employees such as written statements concerning the particulars of the job, itemised wage payments, time off, maternity rights, Sunday working rights and protection against unfair dismissal and redundancy.

■ The legislation does not have a common definition for the word 'employee' and so care must be taken when interpreting various legislative documents.

■ Recent and ongoing legislation may well make the employer/ employee relationship more equitable. In the contemporary world of work it is part of the business environment to fulfil the needs of the employees and this is related to the psychological contract. This is an unwritten agreement that sets out what a member of the workforce wants from her/his employer and vice versa. It takes on a momentum because it incorporates the two key skills of communication and motivation and recognises that there is now a collective dimension to employment relationships.

■ Sometimes the relationship between employer and employee is inequitable. What is important is that employers and workers are not inherently hostile and they both understand that they each have mutual obligations. The current work environment should be that of mutual cooperation between the employer and the employee, between management and trades unions: in each case the two parties are perceived as being social partners with mutual obligations.

■ Contemporary employee relationships are often referred to as partnerships. There is no agreed definition of this term as it relates to work, however it infers a sense of common action and purpose.

■ With the decline in collective bargaining, many organisations concentrate on ensuring effective communication with individual employees – especially at the higher levels of management or in high-performance work teams.

■ The EU Council Directive (1994) has brought about the setting up of works councils within organisations for the purpose of informing and consulting employees.

■ Justice features closely in the employer/employee relationship with individuals within the workplace coming across the four types of justice: procedural, retributive, remedial and distributive.

■ With an understanding of the key factors related to the employer/employee relationship it is necessary to understand the key legislation and Directives which underpin positive work relationships.

END OF CHAPTER 7 CASE STUDY

Second opinion

On the whole, I am not impressed by the power of compensation to compensate. Even where deserved in the strictly legal sense, it is either insufficient or totally irrelevant because the loss suffered was often not a financial one in the first place. The possibility of compensation encourages the cynical view that everything has a price. Of outright fraud I shall not speak, suffice it to say that there are many shades between

END OF CHAPTER 7 CASE STUDY (CONT'D)

truthfulness and mendacity. Let us not forget that what distinguishes man from the animals is his capacity for self-deception.

Those who receive compensation are inclined to spend it as they might spend winnings at roulette or on the football pools. I remember a man early in my career, the husband of a patient of mine, who was awarded what was then a considerable sum for an injury caused at work. He at once bought a lavender-coloured car of great power and Italian lizard skin shoes of the kind that wealthy Africans, grown rich by their association with the current dictator, are inclined to wear.

Naturally, he soon crashed the car; but on the day of his victory in court he brought his wife in hospital a present, the only tangible benefit she was to receive from his forensic triumph: a packet of cigarettes. He didn't even given them to her himself, but left them for her at the gate of the hospital, asking the porter to deliver them on his behalf. In a couple of weeks, he was dead broke again, as he had been before.

Since those days, the population has become even more compensated-minded. You can't do anything right for the public these days, nor can the public do anything wrong, poor lambs. For example, last week a man high on drugs came into our casualty department and started hurling himself around like a dervish. In the process, he crashed through a glass partition and cut himself on the face and arms, requiring stitches and not altogether improving his already unpleasant features. Lo and behold, the hospital received a letter from a solicitor alleging that the hospital, as a resort of whirling-dervish drunks and drug addicts, was negligent in permitting a glass door to remain on their potential trajectory.

The hospital legal adviser called me up and asked me what I thought.

'The patient ought to be taken to the front entrance of the hospital,' I said, 'and there be publicly flogged.'

'I wish there were judges like you,' he said. 'You wouldn't like to be a judge by any chance, would you?'

I asked what the likely outcome was.

'We haven't got a leg to stand on,' he said. 'I'm afraid it's down to quantum.'

'Are you telling me that we shouldn't have any stairs in the hospital in case drunks fall down them?' I said, rousing myself to a thoroughly gratifying pitch of indignation. 'Is everybody in this country to be regarded as helpless infants?'

Later, I calmed down. I was helped to do so by an old lady, a patient who told me that her son had died a few years ago.

'What did he die of?' I asked.

'He died of compensation, doctor,' she said.

If the drug addict gets compensation, the same fate awaits him. So there is justice in the world after all.

Source: Dalrymple, T. (1999) Second opinion, *The Spectator*, 23 October, p29.

 ### END OF CHAPTER 7 CASE STUDY QUESTIONS

1 Why is the issue of compensation part of the employer/employee relationship?

2 With references to the case study, what is the relationship between compensation and justice?

3 The final sentence in the case study states 'So there is justice in the world after all.' What sort of justice do you think Dalrymple is referring to?

4 Is there evidence from the case study that there is a partnership in practice?

THESIS + ANTITHESIS = SYNTHESIS

Explore the point of view that HRM specialists should welcome legislation relating to employment relationships.

SELF-TEST THE KEY ISSUES

1 What is the difference between statute law and common law?

2 Why is the psychological contract important for effective employer/employee relationships?

3 What are the advantages of having an EWC in place?

4 Why should organisations have a positive employer/employee relationship?

TEAM/CLASS DISCUSSIONS

1 Debate the proposition that employees owe loyalty to their employer.

2 Analyse the pros and cons of having legislation governing the employer/employee relationship.

PROJECTS (INDIVIDUAL OR TEAMS)

1 You are an EWC representative and you have been asked to talk to a group of sixth-form students on the Minimum Wage Act 1998 and how it will affect employee relationships. Prepare suitable overhead transparencies outlining the following:

a the main provisions of the Act
b the worker's rights in the event of a breach of the Act
c the sources of help and advice available to an individual with a minimum wage problem.

2 You are working part time in a trade union office while reading for your undergraduate degree. You have been asked to put together a basic information sheet describing the key legislation in the field of employment law and their main provisions. Design and produce the sheet.

Recommended reading

Armstrong, M. (1999) *A Handbook of Human Resource Management Practice,* London: Kogan Page

Beardwell, I. and L. Holden (1999) *Human Resource Management: A Contemporary Perspective*, London: Pitman

Bratton, J. and J. Gold (1999) *Human Resource Management: Theory and Practice*, Basingstoke: Macmillan – now Palgrave

Graham, H.T. and R. Bennett (1999) *Human Resources Management*, London: Financial Times/Pitman

Legge, K. (1995) *Human Resource Management: Rhetorics and Realities*, Basingstoke: Macmillan – now Palgrave

URLs (uniform resource locators)

www.unison.org.uk

Unison is the biggest trade union in Britain. Information on difficulties and disciplinary matters at work.

www.open.gov.co.uk

Details of all publicly funded Internet sites. Initial entry point to the finding of public sector information on the Internet. Has an index by organisation and topic. Opportunity to give feedback and search for information.

www.ei-ie.org/action/english/etrindex.htm

Information about trades unions and human rights. Globalisation issues.

www.irseclipse.co.uk

The Eclipse Group. One of the UK's leading providers of business information and services. An independent organisation. Covers equal opportunities, employment relations in Europe, health and safety issues, environmental issues, pay and conditions and human resource issues. Articles.

www.acas.org.uk

Advisory, Conciliation and Arbitration Service (ACAS). Statutory independent body in the UK whose aim is to promote the improvements of employee relationships. Articles, news, lists of ACAS publications and contact details, for example Codes of Practice, recruitment, disciplinary and grievance procedures, and the implications of change.

www.dti.gov.uk

Department of Trade and Industry.

www.tuc.org.uk

Trades Unions Congress (TUC) which coordinates member trades unions (70) and their activities. Section of information for students and an employment rights section.

Institute for Employment Studies. Information on employment policy, research, consultancy. Internationally related.

Citizens Advice Bureaux: advice guide on rights issues at work.

Bibliography

Aikin, O. (1999) Working Titles in *Personnel Management*, 3 June, pp25, 27–8

Argyris, C. (1960) *Understanding Organisational Behaviour*, London: Dorsey Press

Armstrong, M. (1999) *A Handbook of Human Resource Management Practice*, London: Kogan Page

Chryssides, G. and J. Kaler (1996) *Essentials of Business Ethics*, London: McGraw-Hill

Confederation of British Industry and William M. Mercer (1999) *Employment Trends Survey 1999, Measuring Flexibility in the Labour Market*

Cooper, C. (2000) The Met fails inspection on race and recruitment: Metropolitan mistakes in *People Management*, 20 January, p11

Crabb, S. (1999) Employers 'still sceptical' about partnership benefits in *People Management*, 15 July, p15

Dalrymple, T. (1999) Second opinion in *The Spectator*, 23 October, p29

Davies, N. (1996) *Europe: A History*, Oxford: Oxford University Press

Department of Trade and Industry (1998) *A Guide to Working Time Regulations*, September, London: DTI

Drucker, P.F. (1980) *Managing in Turbulent Times*, New York: Harper Row

Duska, R. (1990) Whistleblowing and loyalty in DesJardins, J.R. and J.J. McCall (eds) *Contemporary Business Ethics*, Wadsworth: Belmont pp142–7

Edmonds, J. (1999) in Taylor, R. (1999c) Union leader sets forms for partnership in *Financial Times*, 14 June, p8

Emmott, M. (ed.) (1997) Employee motivation and the psychological contract, Issues in *People Management*, Report No 21, London: Institute of Personnel and Development

Friedman, M. (1980) *Free to Choose*, Harmondsworth: Penguin

Gallie, D., M. White, Y. Cheng and M. Tomlison (1998) *Restructuring the Employment Relationship*, Oxford: Clarendon Press

Gollan, P. (1999) Business case for giving workers a voice in *Professional Manager*, London: The Institute of Management Foundation, May, pp17–19

Herriot, A. (1995a) The management of careers in Tyson, S. (ed.) *Strategic Prospects for Human Resource Management*, London: Institute of Personnel and Development

Herriot, A. (1995b) Why do people work? Presentation to the Institute of Personnel and Development National Conference at Harrogate, Yorkshire, England

Institute of Personnel and Development (1998) *Employment Relations into the 21st Century: an IPD Position Paper*, January, London: Institute of Personnel and Development

Jones, S. (1999) Quicker wins in store in *Financial Times*, 11 August, p13

Kessler, S. and R. Undy (1996) *The New Employment Relationship: Examining the Psychological Contract*, London: Institute of Personnel and Development

MacNeil, R. (1985) Relational contract: what we do and do not know in *Wisconsin Law Review*

Marchington, M. and Wilkinson, A. (1997) (reprint) *Core Personnel and Development*, London: Institute of Personnel and Development

Mayo, A. (1995) Economic indicators of human resource management in Tyson, S. (ed.) *Strategic Prospects for Human Resource Management*, London: Institute of Personnel and Development

Monks, J. (1999) Ready, willing and able in *People Management*, 20 May, p29

Nelson, D.L., J.C. Quick and J.R. Joplin (1991) Psychological contracting and newcomer socialization: an attachment theory foundation in *Journal of Social Behavior and Personality*, **6**: 65

Pearsall, J. (ed.) (1999) *The Concise Oxford Dictionary*, Oxford: Oxford University Press

People Management, New ways to work at Remploy, 2 March 2000, p17

Rana, E. (1999) Stagecoach and unions join forces at Waterloo in *People Management*, 3 June, p13

Rana, E. (2000) Enter the people dimension in *People Management*, 6 January, pp16–17

Rouseau, D.M. and K.A. Wade-Benzoni (1994) Linking strategy and human resource practices: how employee and customer contracts are created in *Human Resource Management*, Fall, **33**(3): 463–89

Schein, E.H. (1988) *Organisational Psychology*, New Jersey: Prentice Hall

Sherwin, B.J. (1999) Business must focus on profit first, *Professional Manager*, **8**(4) July

Stewart, S. (1999) Blowing the whistle at last in *Mail on Sunday* Review, 5 September, p57

Taylor, R. (1998) Dim view of EU vision in *Financial Times* Management, Fast Track, Autumn, p8

Taylor, R. (1999a) Staff 'increasingly want workplace rights enforced' in *Financial Times*, 5 May, p6

Taylor, R. (1999b) Unions 'vanishing' from the private sector in *Financial Times*, 8 July, p12

The Week (1999) When group loyalty is dangerous, 27 November, p12 (Originally in *Asiaweek*, Hong Kong)

Thompson, M. (1998) Trust and reward in Perkins, S. and StJ. Sandringham (eds) *Trust, Motivation and Commitment: A Reader*, Faringdon: Strategic Remuneration Research Centre

Walsh, J. (1999) Incoming director-general strengthens the ILO brand in *People Management*, 17 June, p15

Walsh, J. (1999a) Deregulation leaves cabin crews with height anxiety in *People Management*, 8 April, p20

Warr, P. (1996) *Psychology at Work*, London: Penguin

Essential employment law

After studying this chapter, you should be able to:

- ◼ DEFINE what is meant by 'employment law'.
- ◼ EVALUATE the importance of human rights as the foundation of all employment legislation.
- ◼ ASSESS the key issues incorporated in the major employment law Acts of Parliament and European Union Directives.
- ◼ DISCUSS the importance of equal opportunities within the workplace.

INTRODUCTION

Framework case study

Coping with the tide of red tape

ROC Recruitment is one of the *Sunday Times*/Virgin Atlantic Fast Track 100 companies within the league table of Britain's fastest growing unquoted companies. It is a growing and dynamic organisation which is central to the HRM field. They are facing so much red tape that it is threatening to give them last place in a three-legged egg and spoon race.

ROC has achieved considerable growth because of its lightweight framework and because of its ability to cope with legislation.

The organisation has its own mission statement which it calls its Recruitment Challenge and which channels its activities:

ROC Recruitment Challenge

■ Keep pace with the speed and complexity of new legislation.

■ Develop communication and training programmes to ensure that staff and clients assimilate regulatory changes.

■ Maintain focus on the core business while ensuring compliance with new legislation.

Joint owner and operations director Deborah Burke says that, like other business owners, she is not averse to a sensible boost to workers' rights but feels that it is happening so fast that there isn't time to assimilate it all. Her co-owner husband, Stephen Burke, is managing director of ROC Recruitment and states that when he tries to seek clarification from lawyers about the impact of new legislation, three different lawyers often give him three different answers.

Adapted from: Gracie, S. (1999) Coping with the tide of red tape, *Sunday Times*, 30 May, p13.

There has been a wave of employment legislation from Whitehall, London, and Brussels, Belgium, which is directed at the relationship between employer and employee and, because of its complexity, it can cause complications for companies. While organisations are trying to run their businesses in a dynamic way, some, as illustrated in the Framework Case Study, are finding that their livelihood is being threatened by the sheer volume of legislation coming from the British government and the European Union (EU). It is important that organisations do not allow such legislation to divert them from their business goals, yet it has to be implemented while at the same time attempting to maintain a positive employer–employee relationship so that all can work together to achieve the goals of the organisation

see Chapter 7 ■ *see* Chapter 7 ■.

Cridland (1999) reports that:

> There is a disturbing fuzziness about some current and proposed employment legislation, and this is leading to wasteful and damaging litigation. (p31)

Litigation ◀┈┈▶ The act or process of bringing or contesting a law suit. It can also refer to the actual judicial proceeding itself.

He believes that organisations are increasingly:

> trying to regulate matters that are poorly understood or hard to define, and where the statute begs as many questions as it answers. (p31)

As reported in the *Sunday Times* (1999) many employers will not realise that they have such obligations under the new legislation and the article further states that it is the smaller businesses which are going to find the onus the greater since they tend not to have in-house lawyers who are experts in employment law:

> it is only the large companies [who] will have the resources to study the legislation and put
> into proactive new procedures. Smaller companies will not be able to cope and just one, inad-
> vertent error could financially break the company. (www p1)

An employer survey carried out jointly by the Confederation of British Industry (CBI) and human resource consultants William M. Mercer (1999) reported that nearly three-quarters of employers in the UK believe that government regulations on employment matters will not have a significant effect on their own ability to compete. The survey also found that 27 per cent of respondents thought the new regulations would have a negative, or very negative, impact on their business competitiveness and 4 per cent said it would have a positive effect. Organisations which employed over 5000 workers (43 per cent) believed that the new Regulations would hit them negatively compared with only 20 per cent of companies with between 50 and 199 workers. At the same time workplace staff increasingly wanted their workplace rights enforced. There is an increasing number of employees who are demanding the enforcement of their workplace statutory rights.

Statutory rights are the rights of all employees enshrined in law ■ *see* Chapter 7 ■. There are an increasing number of statutory rights that are applicable regardless of the length of service put in by an employee – for example the right to opt out of working on Sundays. The legislation means that employers cannot carry out unilateral deals with their employees so that the latter are unable to exercise their statutory rights. General statements made by employees will be ignored by any employment tribunal (ET). For example, if an employee signs a document that says something like 'I agree that if there are not enough people at work, I will come in and work extra hours,' it will be ignored by an ET.

see Chapter 7

EMPLOYMENT LAW

Nothing is either simple, or clear, in the field of employment legislation and employment relationships are a minefield for even the most well-informed and trained lawyers. The human resource management (HRM) specialist – and, indeed, line managers as well – needs to have an awareness of legislation which affects employees (as it is defined in the legislation). However, they cannot be expected to know the details of all Acts and European Directives since organisations will need to have their own lawyers or buy in specialist legal help when required. It is beyond the scope of this text to cover all but the key employment legislation and there will always be amendments to existing legislation and new legislation in the pipeline.

EUROPEAN LAW

Organisations within member countries have Directives from the EU to cope with as well as legislation from their national governments and this adds to the complexity of issues. ▶ **European law** ◀ affects the legislation of the UK since it overrides domestic law. European law acquires its ultimate power from the various treaties that have been signed by the member nations. This started with the Treaty of Rome (1957) which was the document that embodied the formal contract between the then member states. The Single European Act (1987) established the single market (then known as the *Common Market*). However, it was the Treaty on European Union (1992) (known more commonly as the *Maastricht Treaty*), which came into being in 1993, that included the timetable for economic and monetary union. These treaties created and developed the various legal instruments of the EU – such as Directives and Regulations – and the procedures for arriving at their intentions.

European law ◀┈▶ European law comprises the legal rules of the EU and takes precedence over equivalent national laws of member countries.

The accumulated body of European community legislation is known by its French title, the *acquis communautaire* and it is to this that any new member of the EU must subscribe – it has absorbed the previous treaties. European Directives have clear policy objectives and they establish broad legal demands which the member states transpose into their own national law. All nation states must make sure that they give full effect to the purpose of the Directive because if they do not do so, or do it ineffectively, individuals can call on the European Court of Justice (ECJ) for redress or guidance. In some cases, members of nation states do not have to wait for their national legislature because where the ECJ believes an article of one of the treaties to be clear and precise, individuals have recourse to the treaty itself. A particular example here is application to the Treaty of Rome (1957), Article 119, which requires equal pay for equal work.

EQUAL OPPORTUNITIES

An attribute of contemporary society is a worldwide concern for ▶ **human rights** ◀ which according to Honderich (1995) are:

> justified claims to the protection of persons' important interests. When the rights are effective this protection is provided as something that is owed to persons for their own sakes. The upholding of rights is thus essential for human dignity. (p776)

Human rights ◀┈▶ Justified claims to the protection of persons' important interests.

An example is the right to equal treatment, that is, it is considered to be a universally recognised human right – although different cultures have different views on

Table 8.1 Examples of early human rights declarations

England	The Magna Carta	1215
England	The Bill of Rights	1688
France	The Declaration of the Rights of Man and the Citizen	1789
USA	The Bill of Rights	1791

this. Human rights are the backbone of equal opportunity legislation and various countries have declared this as shown in Table 8.1.

It is usual for any discussion on international protection of human rights to commence with the Universal Declaration of Human Rights (1948) which was passed by the ▶ **United Nations** ◀ (UN). The foreword to the declaration includes an explanation for the justification of human rights:

> recognition of the inherent dignity and of the equal and inalienable right of all members of the human family is the foundation of freedom, justice and peace in the world.

▶ An international organisation comprised of independent states, with its headquarters in ◀┈┈▶ **United Nations** New York, USA. It was formed in 1945 to promote peace and international cooperation and security.

In the early days of the UN, Britain was a particularly leading light, as was Australia, which was highly involved in the development of the UN itself and was also a key drafter of the Universal Declaration of Human Rights (1948). When the Declaration was adopted in 1948, an Australian, Dr H.V. Evatt, was the President of the UN General Assembly. Since 1948 the UN and associated bodies such as the International Labour Organisation (ILO) ■ *see* Chapter 7 ■ have put through a number of human rights documents. These have been used to formulate legislation in member countries such as the UK, Australia and Canada.

see Chapter 7

In the UK the Human Rights Act 1998 makes provision with respect to holders of certain judicial offices who become judges of the European Court of Human Rights (ECHR) (established 1950) and for connected purposes. The Commission's findings are examined by the ECHR, whose compulsory jurisdiction has been recognised by a number of states – including the UK.

SCENARIO 8.1

Human Rights Day is 10 December, commemorating the adoption of the Universal Declaration of Human Rights by the UN General Assembly. The declaration is not legally binding, and the frequent contraventions are monitored by organisations such as Amnesty International.

In 1988 the European Court condemned as unlawful the UK procedure of holding those suspected of terrorism for up to seven days with no judicial control, and in 1995 condemned the killing of three Irish Republican Army (IRA) suspects in Gibraltar (1988) by members of the British Special Air Service (SAS) regiment.

Equal opportunities in the workplace has been founded on the belief that human beings have human rights. It was the USA which made the first specific equal opportunities initiative when in 1941 the Democratic President (Franklin Delano Roosevelt) signed legislation outlawing discrimination on the grounds of race or sex in the USA Civil Service. It is usual in the industrialised world for countries to have legislation that protects individuals from unfair discrimination.

The USA introduced highly comprehensive ▶ **federal** ◀ laws. In the UK the Equal Opportunities Commission (EOC) was set up under the Sex Discrimination Act 1975 and the Commission for Racial Equality (CRE) under the Race Relations Act 1976. The EOC was inaugurated with the intention of removing ▶ **unlawful discrimination** ◀ and to bring about equal opportunities for all. The CRE has the role of doing the same in the areas of race and ethnicity. The Disability Rights Commission Act 1999 set up the third equality commission – the Disability Rights Commission (DRC) as shown in Table 8.2.

Federal ◀····▶ A form of government in a country in which power is divided between one central and several regional governments; for example, in the USA, central government is the federal government and then each state has its own additional and complementary laws.

Unlawful discrimination ◀····▶ Treating a person differently and less favourably on one of the grounds laid out in legislation, for example sex or race.

Its independent role is to take responsibility for rights investigation and enforcement, along with equality promotion and advice to employers. It is modelled on the Centre for Equal Opportunities Combating Racism (CECLR – translated from Flemish) in Belgium. This last group has had a steady increase in the number of complaints of racism with a sharp increase from the public sector. This may be because the CECLR is only four years old and is just becoming familiar to members of the public. It will take time for the DRC to become as well known as the EOC and CRE.

Individuals are protected by legislation against being unjustly treated because of their:

■ race

■ skin colour

■ religion

■ nationality

Table 8.2 Equality commissions in the UK

COMMISSION	SET UP BY	DATE
Equal Opportunities Commission (EOC)	Sex Discrimination Act	1975
Commission for Racial Equality (CRE)	Race Relations Act	1976
Disability Rights Commission (DRC)	Disability Rights Commission Act	1999

- gender

- marital status

- disability.

However, employers in the UK can discriminate on the grounds of age.

AGEISM

Walker (1999) argues that there is a need to:

> reverse the UK's ageist culture. (p7)

It is widely accepted that ▶ **ageism** ◀ is prevalent in the UK workforce and it is wasteful, according to Walker (1999), because it:

> creates a series of barriers to the achievement of individual potential. (p7)

▶ Discrimination on the grounds of age.   ◀····▶ Ageism

While ageism places a hurdle in the way of the best use of people it also represents a source of injustice and social exclusion. ▶ **Demographic trends** ◀ are affecting the numbers of people available for work. This is a reality facing all EU members and most industrialised countries, such as Australia and Canada. As society in general ages, so does the workforce and it is estimated that by 2015CE more than two-fifths of people of working age in the UK will be aged 50 or over. There is a trend for individuals to retire early and this trend needs to be reversed if human endeavour is not to be wasted.

▶ The statistics of births, deaths and diseases.   ◀····▶ Demographic trends

In May 1999 the UK government asked employers to sign an anti-ageist voluntary ▶ **Code of Practice** ◀ which was designed to provide a comprehensive plan to combat discrimination against older employees. The document contains advice only and does not carry any penalties for infringement of the recommendations contained therein. The Code of Practice on Age Diversity in Employment addressed ageist discrimination related to:

- recruitment

- selection

▶ Leaflets or booklets published by government agencies, for example the Equal Opportunities Commission, or by professional bodies or trade associations giving their procedures for good practice.   ◀····▶ Code of Practice

- promotion

- training

- development

- redundancy

- retirement.

The Code was widely circulated to trades unions, employers, employee bodies and other interested parties such as Age Concern. This last body considered it to be ineffective, believing that discrimination against older workers would only end if there were legislation to bring them into line. This was also the view of the Carnegie Third Age Programme which further believed that the lack of legislation would act as reverse discrimination since even more employers would adopt discrimination measures. Worsley (1999), writing as director of the Carnegie Third Age Programme, states that:

> employers, especially small firms, would be more likely to help with anti-discrimination policies if they did not fear 'the long arm of the law'. (p17)

He is also of the opinion that:

> The problem is that [the] government is neither doing enough, nor doing it with conviction, nor doing what it promised. (p31)

Another view was put by the Institute of Personnel and Development (IPD) whose director-general (Geoff Armstrong) was reported by Whitehead (1999a) to believe that heavy-handed ways of persuading employers of the benefits of a diverse workforce will never work because legislation would discourage them from seeking advice on best practice, fearing that action would be taken against them for carrying out illegal activities.

Worman (1999) takes on the CIPD banner as adviser on equal opportunities stating that the launch of the code was:

> a welcome step in the continuing drive to combat discrimination. (p59)

The CIPD has supported the battle against ageism on the grounds of the potential loss of talent as well as the harm such discrimination can do to both the individual and the organisation for which s/he works. The CIPD advised the government on the contents of the code so it is not surprising that they support the concept although they do recognise that:

> the law can help to achieve change in employment practice. (Worman, 1999, p59)

However, they have a stronger reliance on the ability – and desire – of senior managers to understand and implement the benefits of a fully diverse workforce.

Ageism in employment has already been tackled by the UK government's Code of Good Practice, but it is not statutory as it is in Australia, Canada, France, New Zealand, Spain and the USA where ageist practices are illegal. While the UK government states it is opposed to discrimination in employment on the grounds of age, it is not prepared to legislate against it. General opinion seems to be that the

UK government's campaign has been a failure, although the IPD (1999) argues otherwise. This might be because it is:

> committed to the removal of age discrimination in employment because it is wasteful of talent and harmful to both individuals and organisations. (p1)

However, not every organisation follows the model put forward by the CIPD.

SCENARIO 8.2

Door stays shut on older workers

A campaign aimed at persuading bosses to employ older workers has flopped. Tony Blair [British Prime Minister] unveiled a voluntary anti-ageism code three months ago. But according to a survey, three out of ten employers have not even heard of it and most of the rest are only vaguely aware of its existence.

The charity Employers Forum on Age, which polled 430 companies on their recruitment stance, found that 68 per cent had no intention of changing their policies. The organisation warned that failure of the voluntary code would lead to pressure on the government to bring in laws against age discrimination instead.

The Department for Education and Employment denied that the voluntary code had flopped. Copies had been sent to all major companies and the response was very good, said a spokesperson.

Studies have indicated that 40 per cent of the 5.6m aged between 55 and 65 want to work but cannot find a job. The do-it-yourself chain B&Q has been notable in actively recruiting staff in their 60s and older.

Adapted from: Door stays shut on older workers, *Daily Mail*, 7 September 1999, p15.

Walker (1999) believes that in order to combat discrimination because of age, there must be a contribution from both the government and the employer as shown in Table 8.3.

Table 8.3 Government and employer's contribution to combating discrimination (after Walker, 1999, p7)

GOVERNMENT	EMPLOYERS
Lifelong learning opportunities.	Create conditions in which the employer can manage better their own careers and the ageing process.
Public education to counteract negative images.	Developing 'age awareness'.
Active labour market policies.	Ensuring age is not used inappropriately in recruitment and training.
Promotion of quality working conditions.	
Removing incentives to make older workers redundant.	
Encouragement for employers to recruit and train older workers.	

Organisations that have a proactive attitude to ageism include B&Q, WHSmith, Sainsbury's and Littlewoods.

While there is no plan to legislate against ageism in the UK, it may well be required if all employers do not prescribe to the Code of Good Practice. However, Buggy (1999) makes the point that an age limit affecting more of one sex than another could be actionable under the Sex Discrimination Act 1975.

8.1

Activity

List four reasons why young people should take the issue of ageism seriously.

EQUAL OPPORTUNITIES POLICIES

▶ **Equal opportunity** ◀ is a concept that attempts to provide a concrete way of describing the absence of discrimination which itself can be defined as the difference between things or people. Individuals are provided with equal opportunity if they are not discriminated against because of irrelevant characteristics such as race, gender and disability. Equal opportunity legislation serves two purposes. First, it obliges individuals not to act in a certain way and, second, provides an antidote for individuals when people do behave unlawfully against them: that is, unlawful discrimination.

Equal opportunity ◀┄┄▶ Equal rights of both access to, and participation in, all areas of public life.

8.2

Activity

List five reasons why women are considered by some still to be disadvantaged in the workplace.

Most organisations have an equal opportunities policy which are of a similar nature. The University of York's Equal Opportunity Policy for Students (1999) states:

The University of York is committed to the active pursuit of an equal opportunities policy which addresses the need and right of everyone in the University to be treated with respect and dignity, in an environment in which a diversity of backgrounds and experiences is valued. It aims to ensure that no prospective or existing student should receive less favourable treatment on any grounds which are not relevant to academic ability and attainment. The University has a continuing programme of action to bring about the implementation of its policy. (p1)

It goes on to give details of its Code of Practice, which includes the statement that the:

equal opportunities policy should go beyond the avoidance of unfair discrimination, to the encouragement, wherever practicable, of academic activities which reflect a diversity of cultural experience. (p1)

The University of York is an example of good practice because it is explicit in its description of the areas where prospective or existing students should not receive less favourable treatment, which goes beyond legislation and Codes of Practice, citing these as:

- age
- race
- colour
- nationality
- ethnic origins
- creed
- disability

- HIV status
- sexual orientation
- marital status
- parental status
- social class
- economic class

or any other criterion accepted as unjustifiable by Council. (p1)

While some organisations publish their policy, they neglect, unlike the University of York, to monitor the policy or provide advice and training. The University of York does monitor and train in order to:

ensure the implementation of equal opportunities policies within [the University]. (p1)

POINTS TO PONDER

In Salt Lake City, Utah, USA, a 333-pound (150 kilo) man is seeking $3m damages from one of the nation's largest supermarket companies, claiming his boss violated anti-discrimination laws by calling him a 'fat slob'.

The employee has reports from the company that he excelled at his work and did an outstanding job, receiving excellent performance reviews, pay rises and bonuses prior to his promotion. Things changed when a new supervisor was appointed.

Would a European employee be similarly protected under EU and UK national law?

In Southern California there is an organisation called 'The Southern California Size Acceptance Coalition (SC-SAC) which has as its mission statement:

We, the members of the Southern California Size Acceptance Coalition, aim to break down stereotypes that promote size discrimination in our society. It is our goal to enlighten others through education and advocacy. We strive to provide support to each other by establishing a sense of community among fat people and allies regardless of age, ethnicity, gender, national origin, physical ability, race, religion, sexual orientation, or marital or socioeconomic status.

Perhaps this mission statement is itself discriminatory?

In London, Islington Council issues a statement of its policy on equal opportunities within a brochure that is sent to all job applicants. Its actual statement reads:

Who does equal opportunities apply to?

Everyone. The aim of the council's equal opportunities policies is to ensure fair treatment to everyone. People must not be discriminated against because:

- of their race, sex or marital status
- they have a disability
- of their religious beliefs or age.

Why do we need equal opportunities policies?

Because there is proof of high levels of discrimination. Our equal opportunities policies:

- acknowledge this discrimination
- identify who is most at risk from discrimination
- identify how the discrimination takes place
- set out ways of tackling this discrimination
- follow the legal requirements to promote equality. (p1)

When organisations have published policies it gives those concerned an opportunity to measure the actual behaviour against the promises. Some people living and/or working in the Borough of Islington felt that the Council fell far short of its commitment because it was perceived that the complaints procedure was:

subject to the same discriminatory pressure as the rest of its services. (p1)

Their Internet page states:

individuals who think that they have been treated unfairly because of their race, gender, marital status, sexuality, disability, age or religion, by any officer or member of the Islington Council at any time or in any manner [to] complain. [sic] (p2)

An organisation can refer to the Trades Union Congress (TUC) for advice on equal opportunities policy. The TUC advises its affiliates to take steps to make sure that all workers, including minority groups, are able to participate fully and actively in trade union structures. They make a general statement:

The TUC recognises that discrimination in society is widespread and that employment practices often discriminate against groups of employees, particularly women and ethnic minority workers. (p1)

The TUC actively campaigns for justice for all individuals who are facing discrimination at work and they act as an advisory service for trades unions and employers who want to achieve equal opportunities and briefs them on legislation changes by taking a practical approach in offering training courses on equal opportunities.

EQUAL OPPORTUNITIES LEGISLATION AGAINST DISCRIMINATION

POINTS TO PONDER

In an effort to tackle sexual harassment, army officers have been forbidden from touching a female recruit without first saying: 'I am about to touch you.' Women too have been given new instructions: they now have to say 'zero' instead of 'oh' because the latter is thought to be too sexual.

Source: The Week, 18 September 1999, p94.

The key legislation in the UK is shown in Table 8.4.

Table 8.4 Key legislation against discrimination

ACT	DATE	COVERAGE
Equal Pay Act	1970	Male and female to get equal pay for: ■ like work ■ equivalent work ■ work of equal value
Rehabilitation of Offenders Act	1974	Individuals having spent convictions
Sex Discrimination Act	1975	Gender and marital status
Race Relations Act	1976	Race, colour, nationality, ethnic origin
Disability Discrimination Act	1985	Disabled people
Asylum and Immigration Act	1996	Illegal immigration status
Data Protection Act	1998	Extending existing data protection under the Data Protection Act 1984
Public Interest Disclosure Act	1998	Whistleblowing
Employment Rights (Dispute Resolution) Act	1998	Reform and simplification of industrial tribunal system
National Minimum Wage Act	1999	Enforce statutory minimum wage
Working Time Directive	1999	Maximum hours of work
Employment Relations Act	1999	Employment tribunals; maternity leave; trade union representation; unfair dismissal claims
Disability Rights Commission Act	1999	Set up the Disability Rights Commission (DRC)

Table 8.5 Recommendations to employers by the EOC

- Inform all employees that their organisation is an equal opportunities employer

- All job advertisements to be accompanied by a statement mentioning that the organisation is an equal opportunities employer

- All recruitment is from all sections of the community

- Make sure that every employee has access to training and development

- Make work more accessible and thus flexible to all by the use of part-time, job sharing, teleworking and fixed-term contracts

- Have in place a well-advertised grievances procedure which should include how to deal with perceived harassment

- Regularly review its equal opportunities policy

Equality of opportunity is not really an option for employers in Britain, however it is different in Northern Ireland where racial discrimination is not legislated against.

Underlying all equal opportunities legislation is the belief that it is not fair to discriminate against individuals on grounds that are irrelevant to the job they are carrying out or intend to do. The EOC, CRE and DRC also have the power to investigate discriminating practices, jointly and severally, and will take action to make organisations comply with legislation. The EOC makes recommendations to employers, as shown in Table 8.5.

There are some exceptions to equal opportunities legislation. For example, those occupations which are called 'genuine occupational qualifications' which are mostly to do with catering for the needs of a specific age or race. Examples here are being an attendant in a single-sex changing room or the preparation of specific foods for ethnic groups. There are other exceptions, such as acting, working in ethnic restaurants, lifeguarding at single-sex swimming pool sessions and modelling. These are called 'genuine occupational qualifications'.

Equal opportunities works on the supposition that it is the merit of individuals that matters, not, say, their sex, race, ethnicity or sexual orientation. Most equal opportunity legislation is uncontroversial, but there are employers who believe that the prerogative of who is employed lies with them and, therefore, they have the right to decide who they want to work for them and if they do not want to employ women, the Irish, the English, a homosexual, that is their right. Conversely, potential employees can decide who they want to work for and it is a belief by some that employers should have the same right. Such a view relies solely on the belief that employment is purely a private arrangement between the employer and the employee and that to restrict the free choice of either, or both, is an infringement of human rights – employment at will.

As far as equal employment is concerned, it runs contrary to the idea of employment at will because it restricts employers' freedom to hire, fire and promote whomsoever they want. While people should be appointed to jobs on their merit and competence, there is a view that those sections of society that have been disadvantaged in the past should be positively helped to become able to compete effectively in today's job market. An example here could be women who have stayed at home to bring up their children and who want to enter, or re-enter, the workforce but because of their time away lack the skills or techniques required to be an effective employee. They are also less advanced in their careers than their counterparts who remained in the workforce and have made their way up the career ladder. It is argued that such disadvantaged people should be given special help to put them in a position to compete on an equal footing. Therefore, equal opportunities has to go beyond non-discrimination to positive action.

There are a number of approaches ■ *see* Chapter 7 ■ to equal opportunities which are reviewed in Figure 8.1.

see Chapter 7

1   *Traditional discrimination* is the position before equal opportunities is given any consideration and supports the 'employment at will' view.

2   *No discrimination* is the ideal where the individual who met the job criteria – or the nearest to them – was appointed to the job regardless of sex, ethnicity, race, sexual orientation or disability.

3   *Positive action with no targets* gives preferential treatment to individuals because of their race, sex or mental situation. It results in discrimination against another person on the same grounds and in some countries this is unlawful.

4   *Positive action with targets* is the use of targets related to the recruitment and promotion of underrepresented groups. Targets are seen to be legitimate by

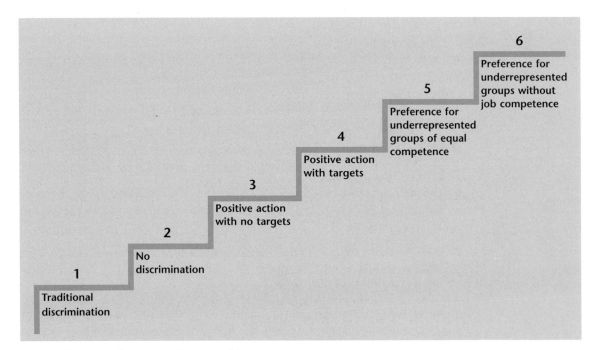

Figure 8.1 Approaches to equal opportunities

equal opportunities legislation because it is something to be aimed for. An example here would be Superdrug who in 1992 started targeting women in an aim to achieve an overall proportion of female lower to middle managers by 25 per cent and its senior management levels by 50 per cent. Both targets have been achieved. However, quotas are not acceptable because they can encourage what is known as 'affirmative action' (see 6 below).

5   *Preference for underrepresented groups of equal job competence* is the position where individuals of equal ability and experience who meet all the job criteria apply for the job, yet the person who is part of an underrepresented group (for example a disabled person over an able-bodied one, or a woman over a man) would be appointed. This is perceived as reverse discrimination because it discriminates against, for example, the able-bodied.

6   *Preference for underrepresented groups without job competence* is sometimes referred to as 'affirmative action'. Still in place in the USA, this is positive action which is intended to speed up the process of achieving equal opportunity for all. It is discrimination in favour of an individual on the grounds of race, sex or marital status – even if they do not meet the job criteria.

The above divisions can be simplified into two:

■   direct discrimination

■   indirect discrimination.

According to Lawrights (1999) *direct discrimination* takes place when:

an employee, or prospective employee, is less favourably treated because of their race or sex. (p1)

Most of the time such discrimination is easy to see as in 5 and 6 above. The law takes no account of an employer's intentions, that is, the process – it is only concerned with the end effect – the product.

Indirect discrimination is less easy to identify because it is less concrete and more intangible than direct discrimination. An ET would take into account three specific issues:

■   whether the number of individuals from, say, one race, or one gender, who can meet the job criteria is considerably smaller than the population at large

■   whether a specific criterion is actually needed to complete the task, therefore any candidate who cannot meet that particular criterion could do the job just as well as anyone else

■   because the individual cannot comply with one or more criterion s/he must have actually suffered in some way because of it. This means that an individual cannot lay a complaint unless s/he has lost out in one way or another.

An employer may well be able to put forward a view that, while s/he may be actively discriminating, such discrimination is a necessary component of the job. Such a view is rarely upheld by ETs but there are circumstances where it is acceptable under the terms of the Act as was discussed earlier: actors for certain characters and ethnic staff for the preparation of ethnic foodstuffs. A number of exceptions relate to sex discrimination in areas where it seems sensible to do so, for example where a job is in a single-sex situation.

The responsibility for acts carried out by an employee while s/he is present at the workplace belongs to the employer and this includes any acts of discrimination. This applies not only to those things that an employee does while carrying out her/his specific tasks, but also other behaviours done at the workplace which are not specifically related to the job. While this applies to all forms of discrimination, an employer can defend her/himself by pointing out that s/he has done all that was possible to prevent the discrimination from occurring.

POINTS TO PONDER

Indirect discrimination is justified, according to a long-awaited ruling by the House of Lords, UK.

The two-year qualifying period for access to an employment tribunal in unfair dismissal cases amounts to indirect sex discrimination, but it is justified because employers would otherwise be reluctant to recruit replacements (Case: Seymour-Smith and Perex, February 2000).

The two-year qualifying period was reduced to one year by the British government in October 1999, but many employers had claims against them put on hold while the Lords considered the case. The Court of Appeal had declared that there was no justification for the rule and that it indirectly discriminated against women, because a greater proportion of women than men were in short-term jobs.

Adapted from: Ruling on indirect discrimination, *People Management*, 2 March 2000, p11.

REMEDIES AND COMPENSATION

For an individual to bring a case of discrimination to an ET s/he has to be self-financing because there is no ▶ **legal aid** ◀ available for such cases. This is one of the reasons why a claimant is supported by a trade union or professional association because they will foot the bill but only in cases they judge to be just and right. If the ET refers the case to the Employment Appeals Tribunal (EAT), then legal aid could be available – although it is not an absolute right. In the case of an individual succeeding in the case, s/he will have the legal costs paid for by the opponent only if the circumstances are exceptional, for example when the defendant knows s/he had no chance of winning.

▶ Financial help which is made available to individuals who are unable to meet the full cost   ◀⋯⋯▶ **Legal aid**
of legal proceedings.

As in all law issues, the guidelines are very complex. For example, a person is permitted to make an application to the ET within three months of the sex or race discrimination yet each ET has its own discretion to decide at exactly which point the three-month period commences.

It is in cases of indirect discrimination where the ET has the right to decide whether the discrimination has actually taken place without actually having concrete evidence. While they will take a holistic view, the ET will still expect the applicant to prove their own case. An applicant gleans specific answers about the incident from the employer through the use of a questionnaire. While answers to questions contained therein are used by the ET, so are refusals to answer any of the questions. If there is documentary evidence, such as memoranda, notes and hard copies of e-mails then the applicant is able to disclose them. If both the applicant and defence agree, then the ET can judge on written evidence alone and if no defence has been put forward they can also make a ruling without a full hearing.

Normal practice is for the ET to appoint an official from the Advisory, Conciliation and Arbitration service (ACAS) in an attempt to work out an out-of-tribunal settlement between the two parties. It is also possible for the CRE to become involved if the applicant is, say, underrepresented or if the case has a high profile. The CRE has its own Code of Practice on race relations and an ET will look at issues which breach this. It is possible for the CRE to have their own investigation and ask the employer to provide the required evidence and relevant documents. In the case of a sex discrimination case the EOC can take similar action and they have a number of codes of conduct which, if breached, can be used as evidence at an ET. The DRC will advise on issues related to disability discrimination.

If the ET rules that discrimination has taken place, then it can make one or both of the following recommendations:

1   *Compensation:* The respondent can be ordered to pay compensation which sum will include interest. There is no statutory limitation to the sum and so it could be large. Such a sum can include compensation for hurt feelings, loss of self-esteem and loss of earnings on the side of the applicant and/or the loss of the chance of a job. In the last situation the damages could also be increased if the employer's behaviour was insulting or malicious.

2   *Corrective action:* The ET may also instruct the employer to take remedial action and correct the situation or, at least, limit the damage done to the application. However, they cannot force the employer to hire or promote the applicant.

Legislation in Britain has two forms of positive action:

1   *Straightforward encouragement:* It is legal to target recruitment and promotion at disadvantaged groups such as, say, women or ethnic minorities, but it is illegal to give them preference.

see Chapter 6 *and* Chapter 10

2   *Training and development:* ■ *see* Chapter 6 *and* Chapter 10 ■. Employers and training organisations are allowed to run courses designed for, and even restricted to, those groups that are underrepresented. For example, a manage-

ment development course on 'Leadership skills for women' where the participants have all to be women. Such courses are designed to let underrepresented people improve their skills to compete for jobs on an equal footing with like candidates. They can be run for individuals already in the employ of an organisation or for students within ethnic minority groups to encourage them to enter the workforce.

LEGISLATION AGAINST DISCRIMINATION

A particular problem with the issue of discrimination is that the laws that were designed to deal with it do not actually cover contemporary problems – it was legislation of its time. Javaid (1999a) highlights the issue of sexual harassment where there is no defined legislation to protect individuals, stating that this has meant that lawyers bringing a case to a court have to use:

> obscure arguments in attempts to prove or disprove the Acts' jurisdiction over situations that were not envisaged when they were passed. (p27)

In 1998 the EOC detailed its ideas for what it called a 'super law' which would combine the Sex Discrimination Act 1975 and the Equal Pay Act 1970 into one piece of legislation with the suggestion that it provides equal treatment between women and men as outlined in Table 8.6.

It is not only the EOC that takes the view that discrimination laws should be amalgamated into one statute. In early 1998, the CRE proposed radical changes to the Race Relations Act 1976. Racial discrimination, under the Race Relations Act 1976, refers to discrimination on grounds of race, colour, nationality or ethnic origin. Organisations need to ensure that there is no indirect discrimination in place where the conditions of work make it difficult for members of certain racial groups

Table 8.6 Likely developments in sex discrimination proposed by the EOC

- Expressly prohibiting sexual harassment as defined by the European Commission

- Making employers responsible for reviewing their pay systems in line with the EOC's Code of Practice on equal pay

- Employers would be required to publish its outcome and to propose a programme for dealing with any inequalities

- Putting employers under a statutory duty to monitor their workforces

- Placing a statutory duty on public bodies to promote equal opportunities, publish summaries of their equality programmes and to state their progress in annual reports

- Establishing a discrimination division within the tribunals to hear both employment and non-employment discrimination cases

Adapted from: People Management, 1999, Likely developments in sex discrimination, 6 May, p27.

Table 8.7 Recommendations by the CRE for changes to legislation

- Compulsory ethnic monitoring for all employers with 250+ employees

- A revised definition of indirect discrimination which aligns with EU Directives

- More investigative powers for the CRE

- An increase in the time limit for discrimination complaints for three to six months

to comply. That is, the conditions may be fair in principle but discriminatory in their effect.

Deliberate racial segregation and ▶ **victimisation** ◀ is unlawful. Victimisation is part of discrimination and includes the results of harassment in the form of bullying. An example would be where an individual faces disciplinary action or dismissal as a result of bringing a complaint under the Race Relations Act 1976. Whitehead (1999b) reports on a study, based on UK government statistics, carried out by Blackaby (University of Wales) which confirms:

ethnic minorities continue to suffer unjust treatment in the workplace. (p18)

Victimisation ◀┈┈▶ Where a worker is singled out for using a workplace complaints procedure or exercising their legal rights.

This is both in respect of the difficulty in securing jobs and, when in employment, earning less than their indigenous colleagues. The CRE reported that the findings did not surprise them as:

only limited progress has been made in tackling discrimination since the commission published its code of practice fifteen years ago. (p18)

Among its recommendations are those given in Table 8.7.

DISABILITY DISCRIMINATION

It is discriminatory to give a disabled person less favourable treatment than her/his able-bodied workplace colleagues. The Disability Discrimination Act 1995 records that an employer must not discriminate against anyone because of a disability they might have. Employers have to make adjustments and alterations to their premises and procedures so that disabled workers do not perceive themselves to be at a significant disadvantage to their able-bodied workers. The Act describes a disabled person as any individual who has an impairment that is physical and/or mental, long term or that stops them from carrying out daily activities in what is considered to be a normal way. A weakness here lies in the wide nature of the definition of 'disability'. It can be defined, albeit simplistically, as being the difference between individuals and people.

However, the Disability Discrimination Act 1995 defines disability as:

A physical or mental impairment which has a substantial and long-term adverse effect on a person's ability to carry out normal day-to-day activities.

By impairment the legislation means:

- physical
- mobility ⎫ impairment
- sensory ⎭
- learning disabilities
- mental health needs
- severe disfigurements.

However, it excludes alcoholism and certain personality disorders.

In the UK there are approximately four million disabled people of which less than 30 per cent are employed. If an organisation employs 20 or more people (including ▶ **atypical workers** ◀), it is required to make reasonable adjustments to:

- premises
- fixtures
- fittings
- furnishings and
- stairways

if any of these factors actually substantially disadvantage disabled job applicants or existing employees. The Disability Rights Commission Act 1999 was instigated by legislation and it has the following general functions:

- to work towards the elimination of discrimination against disabled persons
- to promote the equalisation of opportunities for disabled persons
- to take such steps as it is considered appropriate with a view to encouraging good practice in the treatment of disabled persons
- to keep under review the workings of the Disability Discrimination Act 1995.

▶ Any category of employee who does not have an ordinary full-time contract of indefinite ◀┈┈▶ **Atypical workers**
length – that is, a permanent job within the organisation.

With contemporary society come complex problems, for example the Ministry of Defence is currently reviewing its practice of genetically testing all its aircrew for sickle-cell anaemia. Such use of genetic testing in recruitment may well contravene the Disability Discrimination Act 1995 because the disease is most commonly suffered by individuals of Afro-Caribbean origin. The IPD is reported by Whitehead (1999c) as having warned that:

> genetic testing could lead to discrimination against people who are likely to become sick, and could create an 'unemployment underclass'. (p13)

Baron (1999), as the CIPD's adviser on employee resourcing, advises that:

> Genetic testing should be used only if there is a risk that an individual has a gene that puts them or others at risk. (p13)

The government is considering the setting up of targets in order to increase the number of disabled people who are leaving financially supported jobs to move into full-time work. However, the plans put forward by the Employment Service are being closely monitored by disability groups who, according to Welch (1999a), feel that:

> any changes to the funding of supported workplaces could threaten disability-friendly business and put jobs at risk. (p14)

The agencies want the disabled to move into mainstream employment as soon as possible while the government has to wait on its plans until employers accept that disabled individuals are regular members of the workforce – a 'chicken and egg' situation. The retail firm ASDA is keen to support the government's ideas so that it can move 500 people from its sheltered work programme (people who are undergoing rehabilitation after accidents as well as those with long-term difficulties). However, some employers are not so keen to move people from sheltered programmes into mainstream employment for reasons such as they lose the protectiveness of the programme and, thus, do not perform so well and/or are uncomfortable in the mainstream.

The British Chambers of Commerce (BCC) is the largest business network in the UK, having over 62 approved chambers throughout the country, representing over 11 000 business members. The BCC consulted with the various chambers and members concerning the issue of disability at work among all businesses with the result that there was little evidence to suggest that the Disability Discrimination Act 1995 has done much actually to improve the job prospects of people with disabilities.

Meager et al. (1999) monitored the Disability Discrimination Act 1995, reporting that there were a number of areas which needed clarification such as the discrimination among those who could financially bring a case and those who could not because of limited financial resources. Although the principle of equal opportunities for the disabled is universally accepted, there is still a perception that disabled workers carry a cost which legislation alone will not overcome. The BCC argues that if the UK government is serious about improving opportunities for the disabled, it should assist small firms to meet the financial costs incurred in making workplace adjustments. It states that smaller firms tend not to have HRM specialists who can help complement an increased awareness of the positive aspects of people commitment, and so overlook the positive role of disabled workers. The BCC (1999) also point out that the selection of a disabled employee can be dependent upon the type of disability, for example it is cheaper to:

> accommodate an employee that [sic] has a facial disfigurement compared to a wheelchair-bound individual. (p1)

The main issue is that employers need to be careful when carrying out recruitment, training and development and dismissal procedures.

Sexual orientation is a particularly difficult area because there is no compensation for individuals who are thus discriminated against, unlike, say, discrimination against a physically disabled worker. However, case law (*Smith* v. *Gardner Merchant Ltd*, 1998) suggested that discrimination had taken place on the grounds of sexual orientation – in this instance, a homosexual man was treated differently from a homosexual woman.

Unfortunately, there are still large numbers of jobs that are not regulated by employment legislation or policies and individuals are recruited for these jobs very casually by means of, say, word of mouth. Such recruitment methods allow for discrimination to creep in – employers themselves must take action to ensure that their own workforces are balanced. An example is Marks & Spencer where there is priority to ensure that the workplace reflects the communities which they serve.

However, while it is wholly laudable to have an anti-discrimination policy and then expect the minorities to apply for jobs because organisations need proactively to seek applicants from minorities, this means the use of specific measures so that certain sections of the community become employable and when they attend an interview they are equal to all other applicants.

EMPLOYMENT RELATIONS ACT 1999

While this legislation came into force on 27 July 1999, it is what is called ▶ **'enabling' legislation** ◀ because the provisions will be phased in over time as decided by the government. Like all legislation, its contents are complex but it has, according to Lawrights (1999), key parts as given in Table 8.8. Those sections of the Act that came into effect in September 1999 are given in Table 8.9.

▶ Legislation where the provisions are phased in over time, for example the Employment Relations Act 1999. ◀┈┈▶	**'Enabling' legislation**

NATIONAL MINIMUM WAGE ACT 1999

The National Minimum Wage Act 1999 became law in the UK on 1 April 1999. Its purpose is to enforce a statutory minimum wage, as shown in Table 8.10, thus making it illegal for any UK employer to pay less – regardless of the size or type of business. The types of workers covered by the Act are given in Table 8.11.

Table 8.8 Key parts of the Employment Relations Act 1999 yet to be effected

- Ceiling for compensatory award in employment tribunals rises from £12 000 to £50 000.

- Compensatory and basic awards will be linked to the Retail Prices Index (RPI) and will thus rise with inflation.

- Employment tribunals given discretion to make additional awards of compensation between 26 and 52 weeks apart.

- Right to maternity leave after one years' service.

- Maternity leave to be extended to 18 weeks and also the right to take additional maternity leave, with the employee's job still having to be kept open during this time.

- Entitlement to take a reasonable amount of unpaid time off to deal with domestic incidents.

- The right to be accompanied by a fellow employee or trade union representative during a grievance and disciplinary procedure. Colleagues will be allowed time off during working hours to accompany a fellow worker who is going through a grievance and disciplinary procedure.

- Any dismissal for taking procedural leave, leave for domestic incidents, extended maternity leave or accompanying a fellow worker going through a grievance and disciplinary procedure will not be automatically unfair and can form the subject of an unfair dismissal claim for an employment tribunal.

- Part-time workers will be given the same rights as full-time workers.

Table 8.9 Key parts of the Employment Relations Act 1999 that came into effect in September 1999

- Trades unions with more than 20 members can apply to the central arbitration committee for recognition, where an employer is failing to recognise that union, as long as they meet certain conditions.

- Dismissal or selection for redundancy will be automatically unfair if the main reason is connected to trade union recognition or collective bargaining. Tribunals can now make interim relief orders.

- Unions no longer need to give the employer a list of their members' names when holding industrial action ballots or calling strikes.

- The period between the ballot and the start of industrial action can be extended from 28 days to up to 8 weeks by agreement between the employer and the trade union.

However, the Act does allow for exceptions as shown in Table 8.12. It is illegal for employers to avoid paying the minimum wage by making a worker self-employed. The Act provides strict tests under employment law regarding who is judged to be self-employed and who counts as an employee ■ *see* Chapter 7 ■.

see Chapter 7

The Act itself is enforced by the Inland Revenue (IR) and the Contribution Agency (CA). The IR can serve an employer with an enforcement notice by itself or on behalf of the CA, instructing the employer to comply with the law within a given time limit. Should an employer fail to obey s/he has to pay a civil fine of £7.20 per day for every worker who is being paid below the minimum wage.

Table 8.10 Minimum wage rates covered by the Minimum Wage Act 1999

Standard minimum wage	£3.60 per hour
Minimum wage level for workers aged 18 to 21	£3.60 per hour
Minimum wage level for workers aged 22+ for the first six months in a new job if they are receiving accredited training	£3.20 per hour

Note
It is likely that these figures will be adjusted through time.

Table 8.11 Types of worker covered by the National Minimum Wage Act 1999

- Full time
- Part time
- Casual
- Home
- Freelance
- Temporary and agency
- Those of retirement age or pensioners (if working)
- Piece workers – minimum wage for every hour worked

Table 8.12 Types of worker not covered by the National Minimum Wage Act 1999

- Members of the armed forces
- Fishermen/women
- Volunteers
- Prisoners employed during their sentence
- Self-employed

Additionally, there is also a maximum criminal fine of £5000 for the following situations:

- refusing to comply with the Act

- failing to keep proper wage records or keeping false records

- obstructing an official from either the IR or the CA.

It is also an offence against the Act for an employer to allow an employee to agree, orally or in writing, with her/his employer to be paid less than the minimum wage appropriate for her/his status (see Table 8.10).

WORKING TIME DIRECTIVE 1999

The Working Time Directive 1999 came into operation on 1 October 1998. It is an EU Directive which applies to full-time, part-time and casual workers as long as they have been in their particular job for at least 13 weeks. Certain workers are exempt:

- transport workers

- doctors in training

- members of the armed forces

- police officers

- self-employed.

Those workers who are aged 18+ have a right to a 20-minute break if the working day is 6 or more hours long. They must additionally have a rest period of 11 consecutive hours between each working day as well as a two-day rest period in each of seven days.

Night workers have different regulations because their average 'daily' hours of work should be eight, averaged over a 17-week period. Night workers are also entitled to free regular health assessments in order to make sure that they are in good health for night work.

If an employee refuses to work more than the 48 hours maximum or during their entitled rest breaks and as a result s/he is chosen for redundancy or is sacked, s/he could have grounds for unfair dismissal.

POINTS TO PONDER

Legal sweatshops where trainee barristers are paid little or nothing will have to change their practices completely as a result of the Working Time Directive 1999.

It seems strange that the very people who are paid to expedite legislation themselves need legislation to guide their own activities. There are a significant proportion of barristers' pupils who are over 21 and so qualify for the national minimum wage under the National Minimum Wage Act 1999. Chambers will now have to pay each pupil a minimum of £8000 per year when, in the past, they would have been paid nothing.

KEY EU DIRECTIVES AFFECTING EMPLOYMENT

Key Directives that directly pertain to employment include those covering:

- equal pay and equal treatment

- health and safety

- protection of pregnant women while at work

- working time

- proof of an employment relationship

- transfer of undertakings

- collective redundancies

- European works councils

- parental leave

- rights for workers assigned for short working times abroad ■ *see* Chapter 12 ■.

see Chapter 12

Since these are common and key issues, it is important that employees, HRM specialists and managers understand the principal issues related to them, even if they have access to the services of an employment law expert.

EQUAL PAY AND EQUAL TREATMENT

The principle that individuals who do equivalent jobs should be paid the same, regardless of their sex, is still less widely applied than it perhaps ought to be. Equal pay was awarded to women in the USA in 1870, and by 1955 it had been introduced to 16 other countries. The Treaty of Rome (1957), Article 119, states that each member of the European Economic Community (now the EU) should apply the principle of equal remuneration for equal work for men and women. In the contemporary workforce this is now perceived as work of an equal value. However, it is difficult to quantify what work of equal value is. If two jobs have, for example, been evaluated without any sexual bias (using a job evaluation scheme) this will provide the necessary evidence. However, without such an evaluation, the jobs will need to be reviewed to take into account such factors as:

- effort

- skill

- decision making

as well as other characteristics that are pertinent to that particular job ■ *see* Chapter 4 ■.

see Chapter 4

Progress on equal pay has been mixed within the European states. In the Netherlands a national job evaluation scheme has successfully established work perceived to be of equal value while in France and Italy equal pay legislation has been in place since 1945 and 1947 respectively – long before the Treaty of Rome (1957) came into being. All EU member states – regardless of their own national legislation – are subject to the two equal pay and equal opportunities Directives passed in the mid-1970s. The key principles of the Treaty of Rome (1957) have been developed by the ECJ through clarification of the concept of pay to include pensions and pension ages.

In the UK equal pay legislation applies to employees of all ages, as well as part-time and full-time workers, temporary and permanent workers, homeworkers, contractors and apprentices. The Equal Pay Act 1970 states that a women is entitled to equal pay with a man who is 'in the same employment'. The Act defines this as being employed by the same employer, or any associated employer, at the same establishment or at establishments in the UK which includes the one in question and where there are common terms and conditions of employment for the group of employees being considered. This means that men and women must be treated equally in terms of pay and benefits, if they are employed in 'like work', work rated as equivalent under a job evaluation scheme or work judged to be of equal value.

Equal pay claims cut across different occupational groups, and jobs may be compared which are quite dissimilar in nature, for example a builder with a chef. In the event of an equal pay claim, the onus is on the employer to prove that the job evaluation methodology it has used has no sexual bias. Both parties to the case may call 'expert witnesses', who are recognised experts in job evaluation, to assist with their case.

HEALTH AND SAFETY

It is an employer's responsibility to make sure that all employees work in a safe and healthy environment. Most of the law relating to this is encompassed by the Health and Safety at Work Act 1974 which expects all employers to consider the welfare of their employees. Should they not do so, it is very likely that the result would be a criminal prosecution in the magistrate's court or a crown court. It could also result in an employee suing her/his employer for personal injury or, in certain cases, the employer being prosecuted for ▶ **corporate manslaughter** ◀.

Corporate manslaughter ◀┈┈▶ A group as a whole being responsible for the death of another person or persons.

The UK government is proposing to introduce a new offence of corporate killing with the Home Secretary (Jack Straw) putting forward a consultation paper within which he states that the manslaughter charge law should be replaced by three main offences. These would be, from the greatest to the lesser:

■ *Reckless killing:* Crimes close to murder, or in blatant disregard of the safety of other people.

■ *Killing by gross carelessness:* Cases of death caused by a bad mistake.

■ *Unintentional killing:* Killings that could not have possibly been foreseen.

The last is not popular with the UK Law Commission because they strongly believe that it is contrary to the laws of natural justice – discussed earlier in this chapter – and they are pushing for it to be abandoned.

It would be very difficult to prosecute directors of companies or employees on any of the above counts because it is very difficult to prove any direct responsibility ■ *see* Chapter 7 ■. Therefore, it is suggested that a company could be prosecuted as if it were an individual which would bring about the principal remedy of an unlimited fine. The Law Commission is in favour of this suggestion because:

see Chapter 7

> the test of guilt would be that a company's conduct was 'far below' what could reasonably be
> expected. (www.ft.com/corporate manslaughter, p1)

The reasoning behind this is that only through severe fines that would damage the company would organisations take notice.

However, the Home Secretary (Jack Straw) is not satisfied with this because he wants to identify an individual or individuals and make them personally responsible for the killing/s. He wants legislation to enable individuals to be charged so that they can be disqualified as directors or be charged individually under the corporate killing law. However, there is a problem here because 'corporate' and 'individual' are not synonymous.

Apart from the UK government's attempt to put legislation on the judicial books, a separate private bill is being put forward in an attempt to implement a law of corporate homicide. The Labour MP, Andrew Dismore, has become impatient, stating that the UK government has had the Law Commission's report in its possession since 1996 and has not acted on it. He is attempting to hold directors responsible for any systems failures in safety that lead to an accident. This is what happens in the USA where corporate manslaughter laws ensure that companies and executives can be liable to fines running into millions of dollars, in addition to any compensation claims that might accompany the incident.

The UK Deputy Prime Minister (John Prescott) holds an even more severe view – he is arguing for even tougher laws on corporate manslaughter. A start was made in 1987 when the Appeal Court ruling in the case of the *Herald of Free Enterprise* – which sank with her bow doors open in 1987 – established that a charge of corporate manslaughter could be brought against named individuals in organisations, but it is left to the prosecution to prove that such an individual or individuals actually have a 'controlling' responsibility.

Whatever the views held by individual ministers and members of parliament, it seems that there will be legislation to include the offence of 'corporate killing'. In this case, HRM specialists will need to be au fait with developments.

The fine for the Southall train crash (which will go to the UK government Treasury) eclipsed the previous highest of £1.2 million in February 1999 against Balfour Beatty Civil Engineering for its part in the collapse of the Heathrow airport express tunnel in London in October 1994. Poor risk management was largely to blame, according to the Health and Safety Executive (HSE) and the case judge.

SCENARIO 8.3

Record £1.5m fine for GWT after Southall HST crash

Great Western Trains (GWT) has been fined a record £1.5m for its part in the Southall rail crash in September 1997.

The crash left seven people dead and more that 150 injured when the 10.32 Swansea to London HST [high speed train] ploughed into a freight train crossing in front of it. The company, now owned by FirstGroup, was also criticised for not being represented in court.

The fine came after GWT pleaded guilty to an offence of failing to transport the public 'in such a way as to ensure they were not exposed to risks to their health and safety' under the Health and Safety at Work Act 1974.

Adapted from: West, L. (1999) Record £1.5m fine for GWT after Southall HST crash, *Rail,* 11–24 August, p4.

The Regulations concerning the health and safety of employees in the workplace are often seen by some as being tiresome, time consuming and expensive, resulting in a burden on businesses. However, if the workplace is unsafe and the employees are working in an unhealthy environment, accidents and absences because of ill health can cost employers dear. It is not only the lessening of productivity but, in the case of major accidents involving deaths and injuries – such as the high speed train crash in Southall, London, in September 1997 – it can cost organisations considerable adverse publicity.

It is not only large organisations that find themselves in court because of the lack of satisfactory safety procedures as is shown in Scenario 8.4.

The Health and Safety at Work Regulations 1992 require an employer to carry out a regular risk assessment of the workplace and then to put into place the neces-

SCENARIO 8.4

Company fined for workers' deaths

A demolition firm has been fined £200 000 over the deaths of two workers who fell 100ft after drilling a hole round themselves.

Together they cut through thick concrete apparently without realising they were standing in the centre of the circle. Neither was wearing a safety harness and they had no chance of saving themselves as they plunged through eight floors of an office block. They died instantly at the site in the City of London in January 1998.

The Crown Court judge who heard the case accused the employers (Kelbray Ltd) of breaches of safety regulations which amounted to the 'grossest negligence'. Kelbray Ltd pleaded guilty after the judge ruled that it was an 'absolute offence' meaning that it had no defence.

The judge ruled that although the two workers may have been experienced, he was satisfied that not only had the men not been supervised as they should have been, but that they had nowhere to fasten a safety harness had they been issued with one. The firm had been under a legal duty (Health and Safety at Work Act 1974) to prevent such a situation ensuing. It would have been 'so very preventable' if the site foreman had been carrying out his duties.

Adapted from: Company fined for workers' deaths, *The Times,* 8 September 1999, p7.

sary procedures and controls to comply with the Regulations. This was highlighted by the case of Beverley Lancaster, a former housing officer with Birmingham Country Council. She became the first person to be awarded damages for stress-related injuries received at the workplace. The Management of Health and Safety at Work Regulations 1992 require firms to conduct risk assessments for each employee. They must consider the risks posed by the employee's duties and environment, with regard to their individual characteristics. Firth (1999) cites the example of assessments for women which must:

take account of any special risks to both the woman and her unborn child if she were to become pregnant. (p24)

Actress Hunter Tylo has been awarded nearly $5m for emotional distress and economic loss after finding that she was fired from the television show *Melrose Place* because she became pregnant – she had not appeared in a single programme. The jury found that the show's procedures breached their contract with the actress and that she would have been able to perform her role as a 'vixen' on the programme even though she became pregnant after being hired. The makers of the programme argued that Ms Tylo's contract forbade her to make any 'material change' in her appearance.

Ms Tylo said she would make a substantial contribution to women's rights efforts 'to help pregnant women discriminated (against) on the job.'

A more common risk is that of the use of visual display units (VDUs) which is covered by the Health and Safety (Display Screen Equipment) Regulations 1992. There is the general need to ensure that the employee's workstation and chair do not cause muscle or tendon injuries, discussed later in this chapter, and employers must consider other risks such as eye strain or headaches. Problems are usually associated with poor-quality lighting and faulty screens. There is legislation is this field – the Health and Safety (Display Screen Equipment) Regulations 1992 require that employees have breaks or changes in activity throughout the day so that they do not work at a VDU for long periods. Table 8.13 gives the employers' liability on VDU use.

While risk management is a critical part of an organisation's activities, it has become principally a case of organisations protecting themselves from damaging legal action, rather than taking, as Walsh (1999a) says:

Table 8.13 Employers' liability on VDU use

- Carry out a workstation assessment and identify any special needs of the person using it
- Ensure the workstation is suitably lit and that it complies with legal requirements
- Ensure the employee takes sufficient breaks; this may involve a change of activity
- Give employees the opportunity to have regular eye tests
- Communicate health and safety requirements to employees and provide training in safe working where necessary

a 'holistic' approach in understanding and preventing the causes of injury and illness. (p18)

Such assessment requires an investigation into ▶ **occupational health** ◀ which is a key feature of organisations today and means that they are encouraged to consider the health of all employees. The government is not likely to consider legislation to force employers, particularly small and medium enterprises, to enlist the assistance of health experts such as occupational health therapists and work psychologists. It has relied on encouraging firms to commit to the Healthy Workplace Initiative which is a national information and education campaign designed to persuade – not force – employers to recognise the business benefits of good health and safety practice.

Occupational health ◀ ....▶ The physical and mental health of members of the workforce.

Any new employer setting up a business has to be aware of six vital Regulations – given in Table 8.14 – which came about as a result of membership of the EU and which are now incorporated into UK law.

The responsibility for enforcing the Health and Safety at Work Act 1974 and the various Regulations that followed it, lies with the HSE and the environmental health departments of the local authority/council within which the workplace lies. These bodies can, jointly or separately:

■ enter premises to investigate conditions

■ seize and destroy harmful substances

Table 8.14 Regulations incorporated into UK law as a result of membership of the EU

REGULATION	YEAR	AN EMPLOYER MUST...
Management of Health and Safety at Work Regulations	1992	Carry out a risk assessment of the workplace and make all necessary changes to bring property, practices and procedures up to the required standard.
Workplace (Health, Safety and Welfare) Regulations	1992	Maintain the property adequately.
Provision and Use of the Work Equipment Regulations	1992	Ensure all machinery is guarded and operators are provided with safety equipment for its use.
Manual Handling Operations Regulations	1992	Ensure safe manual handling of stock, materials and such like.
Personal Protective Equipment Work Regulations	1992	Ensure all workers are issued with protective clothing where necessary.
Health and Safety (Display Screen Equipment) Regulations	1992	Alert all employees to measures to offset repetitive strain injury (RSI), tiredness and eye strain related to the use of technological equipment.

Adapted from: Lawrights (1999) *Health and Safety at Work* on http://www.lawrights.co.uk.

- serve notices to improve workplace conditions

- serve notices to cease business altogether

- prosecute.

However, they would prefer to act in an advisory capacity by guiding employers on safe and healthy practices in the workplace.

8.3

Activity

Carry out a review on items you perceive in your lecture room which:

1 have been made safe and healthy

2 could be the cause of accidents or ill health.

There are numerous other contributors to adverse effects on employee health and safety which include, for example:

- high or low temperatures

- dusty and dirty environment

- high noise levels.

All individually or combined reduce the efficiency of the working environment and thus the workers will not achieve productivity with the final result of a loss in business efficiency and an increase in costs. Poor health and safety standards can cost organisations dearly (for example the case of Great Western Trains [now First Great Western Trains] and the Southall train accident) and although Regulations might be seen as tiresome and a burden to employers, they can, if correctly implemented, save the employer money that could be lost as a result of accidents, ill health, loss of productivity, high insurance premiums, disruption and adverse publicity. In 1993 Sir Robert Reid, Chairman of the then British Rail organisation, stated that people often seemed to see health and safety awareness as a sign of weakness within an organisation. Merrick (1999) reports that:

> Law reforms and potential changes to health and safety regulations mean that employers need to take a hard look at the way they behave after an accident has occurred. (p42)

Changes are being introduced to health and safety Regulations because the existing system is too expensive and unwieldy. In future, claims for compensation must be settled without the need for litigation. At the same time that the employers are trying to absorb reforms, the Health and Safety Commission (HSC) is considering additional proposals that would increase the obligation to investigate all work-related accidents. While existing Regulations dictate that employers must ensure the health and safety of their workers, record accidents involving ten or more individuals and report more serious accidents to the HSE, there is no explicit legal duty for the investigation of accidents and their causes with the aim of preventing a similar occurrence. The new Regulations might extend to this area by investigating any incident that causes injury to an employee, studying 'near misses' and looking at cases of work-related illness. There is a new duty on employers to be more self-critical.

Self-regulation by the employee in the area of health and safety is not reliable and, therefore, most countries have legislated for minimum health and safety standards. However, this has developed into a plethora of legislation, some of which are given in Table 8.14, dealing with issues ranging from the use of hazardous material to ▶ **repetitive strain injury** ◀ (RSI) which is also referred to as ▶ **non-specific arm pain** ◀ (NSAP). There are about 200 000 people in the UK alone who are thought to suffer from the effects of RSI. Absences from work because of RSI and back-related illness are considered to cost organisations around £2bn every year. The damage is said to be associated with the intensive use of a keyboard, however it can affect a wide range of people who carry out repetitive work, including musicians, checkout till operators and assembly line workers. There has been considerable debate about the affliction with medical and legal experts often dismissing complaints about RSI/NSAP, putting it down to stress. This is because there are no obvious signs of any physical injury. However, in July 1999 doctors at University College, London reported their findings that sufferers do have a loss of movement in a major nerve in the wrist. This is the first time that doctors have found out what is actually happening inside the arm of a sufferer of RSI/NSAP. In May 1999, record damages of nearly £100 000 were paid out to a women who developed RSI within a few months of starting to work on a keyboard.

Repetitive strain injury/ Non-specific arm pain

A recurring strain injury, normally of the wrist and upper arm, which is caused by prolonged repetitive activities such as working at a keyboard.

Europeans, in particular, have carried out a considerable amount of work in an attempt to identify potential hazards within the workplace and have tried to identify those individuals who are most at risk. Thus legislation has been introduced in an attempt to minimise the risks as effectively as possible. There are numerous statutes and Regulations that employers (see Table 8.14) need to be aware of, regardless of the issue, and which are beyond the scope of this text. European law has a basic and consistent approach as shown in Table 8.15 and Table 8.16.

In the contemporary workplace employers have a particularly difficult time because they are responsible not only for their own employees but also for those over whom they have minimal control, for example, atypical workers such as:

- contractors
- self-employed
- agency staff
- outsourced staff.

SCENARIO 8.5

Ye olde RSI

RSI is seen as the curse of the computer keyboard operator and was unheard of even a generation ago.

But now a former pit worker has reinvented the modern affliction as the bane of the life of a Victorian blacksmith at the Museum of Welsh Life* near Cardiff, Wales.

In period dress, he got to grips with bellows, hammer and anvil to forge one of the museum's most popular attractions.

But then, like countless typists and other office workers before him, the blacksmith began suffering from pains in his arm which were identified as repetitive strain injury (RSI).

Unlike his Victorian precursors, who would no doubt have had to grin and bear it, the blacksmith of today was able to fall back on the power of his union (the Public and Commercial Services Union) and modern-day employment law.

In August 1999 he accepted an offer of £10 000 compensation from the Museum which failed to carry out a risk assessment on the blacksmith's job and this was in breach of the Health and Safety Agency's manual handling regulations. There were also requests by the blacksmith to provide him with proper equipment which were ignored. However, the deputy director of the National Museums and Galleries of Wales stated that the agreement on the settlement did not mean that they had made an admission of liability or causation and that they were 'always mindful of the welfare of all our staff and follow current guidelines and health and safety legislation'.

* Part of the National Museums and Galleries of Wales

Adapted from: Woodward, T. (1999) Ye olde RSI, *Daily Mail*, 24 August, p19.

Table 8.15 Health and safety: what employers MUST do

- Assess all potential risks to employees and others within the workplace

- Do all they can to minimise risks by, for example:
  - improving maintenance
  - replacing old machinery
  - training staff to use equipment correctly
  - supervising staff effectively

- Regularly and frequently:
  - monitor
  - review
  - improve

  health and safety standards

Table 8.16 Health and safety: what employers CAN do

- Provide adequate and appropriate resources for the health and safety of employees and others

- Fully support all health and safety standards

- Use specialists to help in the initiation and development of health and safety policies

- Make sure that all managers and supervisors are aware of their health and safety responsibilities

- Ensure that when making organisational decisions, health and safety is included

These workers may well also be referred to as:

- contingent

- marginal

- flexible

- precarious

depending upon how badly the commentator feels they are being treated.

All employers have a legal duty under the Health and Safety at Work Act 1974 to take all reasonable care to ensure the safety of all their employees. This is not only an altruistic approach since accidents cost employers money through the absence of injured or ill workers and the possibility that victims may claim compensation (as in Scenario 8.5). The sum awarded is either prescribed by legislation or has been established by case law which is comparable to a similar situation. In the UK – as in the USA – compensation is normally in the form of a financial settlement.

In UK law, if an organisation employs ten or more people on its premises, every accident involving an employee must be recorded. All employers have a duty under the Occupiers Liability Act 1957, the Defective Premises Act 1972 and the Work-place (Health, Safety and Welfare) Regulations 1992 to make sure that all premises are safe for occupation. Employers are also responsible for the safety of all employees and visitors to the premises.

When an organisation has five or more employees it must publish a written state-ment of its health and safety policy and have staff who are trained in first aid on site. If there are more than 400 employees, an organisation must have a designated and equipped first-aid room.

Most countries recognise that leaving the employer to ensure that they take due care and attention is not sufficient to ensure adequate safety standards and so a large number of laws have been enacted throughout the developed world. A considerable amount of work has been done in Europe to identify hazards in the workplace and to identify those individuals who are most at risk from them with a view to frameworking legislation that will effectively minimise the risks. Regardless of the issue – machinery, buildings, visual display units, hazardous chemicals – European law has a basic and consistent approach stating that employees must:

- assess all risks at the workplace to employees and others

- take appropriate steps to minimise risks, for example by providing safety and protection equipment to staff

- regularly monitor, review and improve health and safety standards if required.

It is a full-time responsibility to address all these issues but the health and safety environment is enlarging for organisations which are now becoming increasingly responsible for the safety standards of not only their own employees but also of those over whom they have less control – such as atypical workers which includes contractors, agency staff, self-employed and outsourced staff.

Health and safety legislation does not stand alone – recent legislation also affects workplace health and safety. For example, the Working Time Regulations 1998 govern the maximum hours an employee may be required to work if they are not opted out and specifies minimum periods of daily and weekly rest. Another example is the Public Interest Disclosure Act 1998 which came into force in July 1999. This Act protects individuals who make disclosures on wrongdoing or malpractice by their employers. Employees who decide to whistleblow on a firm that is putting the health and safety of its workforce and visitors at risk are protected against dismissal or disadvantaged treatment as a result of their actions – ■ *see* Chapter 7 ■ for a discussion on whistleblowing.

see Chapter 7

8.4

Activity

Check past issues of the *Financial Times* either in paper form or on CD-ROM and see how many items refer to amendments to the Working Time Regulations 1998.

While it is sensible to protect employees and visitors while they are at the work-place, there is an increase in other forms of risk to which the employer needs to pay attention. When the introduction of tuition fees for university undergraduates came on line, it was not unknown for university tutors to be advised on how to counteract physical attacks from students who perceived themselves to be aggrieved. This would be part of a university's risk assessment procedure as required under the Health and Safety at Work Regulations 1992. Welch (1999b) reports that employees are:

> demanding courses in self-defence and conflict management to protect themselves from attack.
> (p17)

The retail chain ASDA is facing prosecution after a man died during a scuffle with security guards at one of their London stores, and the death in 1994 of John Penfold, a trainee assistant manager at Woolworth's – stabbed as he attempted to fend off a thief – raises the issue of employees' reactions to violent incidents. Increasingly, employees are becoming more proactive in asking for training in self-defence and conflict management. The implementation of satisfactory health and safety conditions in the UK workplace is overseen by the HSE. This body not only polices the regulations but also prides itself in encouraging good practice. It is always on the lookout for examples of good practice in all organisations – regardless of size – that can:

> demonstrate active employee involvement in health and safety. (*People Management*, July 1999, p15)

8.5

Activity

Look around your place of work or your university campus (or a section of it such as a branch or site) and see if there are any posted instructions related to health and safety.
Make a list of them.

They look for examples of effective employee involvement in health and safety from all employment sectors, being particularly keen to learn from the experiences of organisations that do not have all their employees on one site and/or who employ atypical staff.

PROTECTION OF PREGNANT WOMEN WHILE AT WORK

The rights to leave and benefits of employees who become pregnant vary enormously from country to country with, broadly, the Nordic countries in Europe offering the most generous provisions. Rights can vary from two years' leave on full pay after the birth to a few weeks' unpaid leave or sick pay. There is an ever-increasing number of women in the workforce and a large proportion of these are of child-bearing age. Therefore, there is an increasing number of women requiring time off for maternity reasons. This is a fact and it is one that employers have to be sensitive to – although a number of organisations find it inconvenient (real or perceived) and expensive. Employers need to anticipate and respond to such absence in a coherent and low-key manner. Any hostile or adverse treatment of a pregnant women is ▶ **sexual discrimination** ◀ if it is connected with her actual pregnancy. Maternity also covers women who have recently given birth, including a woman returning to work after maternity leave or a new employee with a baby. An organisation's maternity policy should include certain items of detail as shown in Table 8.17.

Sexual discrimination ◀┈┈▶ Discrimination between individuals because of their gender.

WORKING TIME

The trend in the contemporary working environment is towards more flexibility and open-ended working hours – especially for those within supervisory and managerial jobs. Workers in the UK, USA and Japan tend to work longer hours than those in other countries in the developed world ■ *see* Chapter 12 ■. There is a well-established link between long, unbroken hours and health and safety at work.

see Chapter 12

Table 8.17 Contents of an organisation's maternity policy

- Statement of the organisation's positive approach to maternity

- Links with other employment policies, for example equal opportunities

- Explanation of the individual's obligation to inform the employee when she is, or suspects she might be, pregnant; such an explanation should concentrate on the employer's responsibility for her health and safety requiring her to cooperate with decisions to, say, redeploy her or change her terms of work temporarily in order to comply with the Management of Health and Safety at Work Regulations (1992)

- Explanation of the women's legal and occupational entitlements and what she needs to do to comply with them

- Identification of the staff the women needs to inform or consult

- Explanation of the options she has after the birth

- Explanation of what help or support the organisation provides to women with children, for example subsidised childcare or workplace crèche

- Inclusion of a 'keep in touch' strategy to reassure women on maternity leave that they will not be sidelined or have their employment terminated

The UK government provided limits on working time and entitlements for employees in the Working Time Regulations 1998 which implemented the EU Working Time Directive. It is the employer who is responsible for ensuring that the worker receives the protection provided for by the Regulations. They will also need to make sure that the organisation's working practices need to be changed in the light of the rights which the Regulations confer upon employees. The Regulations do allow for flexibility that enable modifications to be made in certain circumstances, for example an individual can choose to agree with her/his employee to work in excess of the weekly working time limit. Table 8.18 gives the principal provisions of the Regulations.

The Regulations also give consideration to the implementation of provisions of the Young Workers Directive 1998 which relates to the working hours of adoles-

Table 8.18 Principal provisions of the Working Time Regulations (1998, p2)

- A limit on average weekly working time of 48 hours (although individuals can choose to work longer)

- A limit on night workers' average normal daily working time to eight hours

- A requirement to offer health assessments to night workers

- Minimum daily and weekly rest periods

- Rest breaks at work

- Paid annual leave

cents, defined as those over the minimum school leaving age but under 18 years of age. The Directive has also been implemented within other legislation such as:

- Health and Safety (Young Persons) Regulations 1997

- Children (Protection at Work) Regulations 1998

- Merchant Shipping and Fishing Vessels (Health and Safety) (Employment of Children and Young Persons) Regulations 1998.

The Working Time Regulations 1998 give adolescents rights that differ from those given to adult workers and these relate to:

- health assessments for night work

- minimum daily and weekly rest periods

- rest breaks at work.

It is important that employers are aware of the Health and Safety (Young Persons) Regulations 1997 because they require risk assessments for young workers.

A leading law professor (Leighton, 1999) denounced the government's attitude to employment edicts from Brussels arguing that the government only had a half-hearted approach to implementing the EU Working Time Directive and because of its attitude organisations will be confused and could probably act in such a way that would land them in court. She made the point that the Working Time Directive is not about interpreting the words but about understanding the policy objectives of the EU. The legislation, she said, is open to so many different interpretations and legal challenges and the legislation has not yet been interpreted properly. As was mentioned earlier under the section on health and safety – the Working Time Directive is more about health, safety and personal well-being than terms and conditions of employment. Leighton (1999) says:

> it is the *non*-working directive. (p13)

The very fact of forcing people to opt out of the 48-hour week will be difficult to operate and the ECJ will be concerned about the need to hear so many cases. This has turned out to be true because an increasing number of organisations are requesting opting out of the Regulations, for example RJB Mining and East Riding County Council. There have been so many that the Trade and Industry Secretary (Stephen Byers) has published guidelines that make it clear that all levels of employee can benefit from exemption and includes a sample 'opt out' form with the guidelines. Leighton's (1999) point is that proposed legislation is not being subjected to democratic scrutiny and the scrutineers are not lawyers and are, therefore, not used to determining the meaning of key phrases.

In July 1999 the UK government removed the need to keep time records for staff who had opted out. This was received warmly by the CBI and helped to alleviate the fears of red tape which threatened to swamp businesses. Eastham (1999) and Wighton and Taylor (1999) reported on the amendments to the Brussels Directive which would give more flexibility to workers who determined their own hours (such as managers and senior executives), in that if they voluntarily worked hours above their ▶ **contract of employment** ◀, such hours would not count towards the working limit of 48 hours. The second amendment stated that it was no longer necessary to keep detailed records of hours of workers who opted out of the Regulations.

▶ A legal agreement that governs the mutual obligations between an employer and an ◀······▶ **Contract of**
employee. **employment**

However, not all people were pleased with the early July 1999 amendments. Clement (1999) and Hibbs (1999) reported separately that the trades unions were unhappy because they rode roughshod over those workers who determined their own hours and the amendments undermined Brussels Directives. The general secretary of the UK's largest union (UNISON) said that it was galling to see the government chipping away at the Regulations and added:

> The Government talks about partnership but what sort of partnership allows one partner to exploit another? (*Independent*, 8 July 1999, p2)

Roger Lyons, general secretary of a white-collar union, complained that the proposals would 'ride a coach and horses' through the purpose of the Brussels Directive:

> Millions of salaried staff will have no protection against being forced to work dangerously long hours. (*Daily Telegraph*, 8 July 1999, p10)

Aiken (1999) reports on the continuing amendments made by the UK government and states that it is essential that the 'promised clear guidance' (p25) is quickly forthcoming.

The trades unions were considering asking the European Commission to intervene in the issue in an attempt to clarify the Directive which is being interpreted so differently by member states, for example a 35-hour working week in France and a 48-hour one in the UK, with the former being managed strongly while the latter is being eaten away at the edges to become almost meaningless. While the UK has adopted the European Directive on working time with so many opt outs, exceptions and exclusions as to make the measure almost irrelevant, the French have made a much more radical reduction in working hours and are reshaping organisational thinking. The *Loi Aubrey* (named after the French labour minister, Martine Aubry) limits the working week to 35 hours which is calculated on a yearly average. The legislation was introduced, primarily, in an attempt to reduce France's high unemployment rate (currently 11 per cent) but it is also having a dramatic effect on the nation's working culture. Altman and Bournois (1999) report on this fundamental change stating that the process of implementation is complex and prolonged, requiring exceptional time from the HRM specialists whose job it is to translate and implement the legislation. Graham (1999) noted that France's socialist government has permitted a one-year transition period for companies introducing a 35-hour week in the year 2000 – in an attempt to limit overtime payments.

There is another view in that it does put the HRM specialists into a high-profile situation. It will take some time before it is known whether the legislation has worked and in the meantime, according to Altman and Bournois (1999), this 'bold experiment in social engineering' (p56) will be monitored carefully by all members of the EU.

PROOF OF AN EMPLOYMENT RELATIONSHIP

The Employment Rights Act 1996 requires that a written statement of terms of work is provided but this is not the contract of employment since it simply provides evidence of the terms of a contract and it can be overridden by other evidence within the contract of employment. When an individual is newly hired, it is common practice for an employer to issue the statement of terms prior to the contract of employment. Surprisingly enough, about 40 per cent of employers believe that they are using binding written contracts of employment when they are actually using statements of terms.

The contract of employment is a legal agreement which governs the mutual obligations between an employer and an employee. Such a document should be written in appropriate language and signed by both the employer and the employee. This contract overrides any other pre-dated contract or statement and it also overrides any custom and practice evident in the organisation. For example, if management has provided all employees with an extra day off after each public holiday for the last, say, ten years it is likely to be perceived as a contractual entitlement. Thus, what is written in the contract of employment supersedes common practice. However, the contract of employment cannot contain any terms that purport to override an employee's common law or statutory rights – if it does, they are made null and void by such common law and legislation. It is important, therefore, that contracts of employment are regularly revisited by both the employer and the employee to ensure that they reflect the current employment relations position.

Therefore, in order to avoid difficulties in the future, it is advisable that an employee ensures that s/he is issued with a contract of employment that must contain the information given in Table 8.19.

Table 8.19 Mandatory information within the contract of employment

- Name and full address of the employer
- Normal place of work (if it differs from the address)
- Name of employee
- Job title
- Date of appointment
- Pay, interval of payment, method of payment, normal payment date
- Hours of work
- Holiday entitlement (including public holidays)
- Length of contract

Table 8.20 Optional information within the contract of employment

- Confidentiality
- Copyright and intellectual property rights
- Disciplinary rules and procedures
- Driving licence inspection
- Expenses while on organisational business
- Grievance procedure
- Health and safety policy
- Hygiene rules
- Smoking at work policy
- Period of notice for termination of employment
- Other benefits
- Arrangements for pension
- Notification of pregnancy
- Security of organisational policy
- Sick pay procedures and entitlements
- Undertaking of other duties
- Requirements for wearing a uniform

There is other information which can be included in the contract of employment which could well be part of the contract of employment – although some organisations place these within the staff handbook. Some of these items are given in Table 8.20.

If an employer wants to change any aspect of a contract of employment, s/he must give the employee written notice of the intended change and its implications – an employee does not have to accept changes to the contract of employment. Often, changes to conditions of employment are negotiated through the employee's trade union or professional body. If an employer tries to instigate new conditions without the employee's permission, the latter can take her/his employee to an employment tribunal claiming compensation. For example, if an employee is contracted to work the night shift, s/he cannot be expected suddenly to work the day shift – unless s/he agrees to the change in the contract of employment. However, care should be taken to ensure that the contract of employment, when agreed, is unambiguous in its wording.

TRANSFER OF UNDERTAKINGS

Following the EU Acquired Rights Directive 1977 the UK brought in particularly complex legislation in the form of the Transfer of Undertakings (Protection of Employment) Regulations 1981. This legislation comes into force if a business is acquired or if it merges with another business in that it protects the employees to ensure that they are fairly treated by the new employer and that all their contractual rights are safeguarded. If there are attempts to sack them or to reduce any of their employment rights, this will usually result in successful claims by the ex-employee for unfair dismissal. When an organisation outsources a particular function or service it must comply with the legislation.

The difficulty is that it is often hard to define what comprises a transfer or an undertaking and so employers need to seek professional advice. However, if an organisation acquires another company, it has to accept the current employees' terms and conditions of service even if they are different from the takeover organisation – at least for a year or so. While employees may voluntarily agree to changes within a shorter time, the law checks that such agreements are sincere and the terms are not worse than those originally held. The point to remember is that business mergers or undertakings do not provide a quick or easy opportunity for organisations taking over other companies to amend terms of work and save labour costs.

SCENARIO 8.6

Merged steel giants aim to sidestep HR policy pitfalls

Integration teams are working at British Steel and Dutch steelmaker Hoogovens to ensure that their merger does not flounder on people issues by ensuring that the merger includes a clear personnel strategy.

At least 2000 jobs are likely to be lost as a result of the £3.5m merger, but British Steel insists that plant closures remain unlikely, because the two companies are committed to growing the business. Although most of the job cuts will be among headquarters staff, they come as British Steel reaches the halfway point in its programme of delayering and job cuts. Almost 7000 jobs have gone since 1997.

Meetings between the Dutch and British trades unions and the companies' two personnel heads have assuaged early fears of mass redundancies. But the unions are unhappy that the merger was leaked to the media before employees had been informed, and came as British Steel shareholders learnt that they were set to rake in a dividend* of 35 pence per share.

Insecurity was an inevitable product of the rumours created by such major business decisions. British Steel emphasised the importance not only of preventing large-scale job losses, but of ensuring that those parts of the two businesses that do overlap were brought successfully into a single company ethos.

* A portion of the distribution from the net profits of a company to its shareholders.

Adapted from: Walsh, J. (1999b) Merged steel giants aim to sidestep HR policy pitfalls, *People Management*, 17 June, p12.

In her report, Walsh (1999b), believed that:

the creation of Europe's largest metals group has underlined the fact that mergers succeed or fail on their staff. (p12)

In the same report, Walsh (1999b) comments on a 1999 report by Right Management Consultants which estimated that only 30 per cent of the 23 000 merger and acquisition deals taking place worldwide over the past year were likely to achieve their aims, because they had mismanaged the people issues. The survey contacted 179 organisations that had been involved in mergers and they found that most were having employee relations difficulties. Only 34 per cent were deemed to have maintained employee morale and 30 per cent had integrated the workforce smoothly. The research highlighted the singular importance of ensuring that the HRM team is central in the merger planning because:

> If a merger is driven entirely by financial experts, it runs a high risk of failure. (p12)

COLLECTIVE REDUNDANCIES

Redundancy is a complex matter that requires careful handling in a sensitive and respectful manner. Most policies look to the future of the organisation and to the flexibility of the workforce and most members of the contemporary workforce understand this. It is important that all organisations have a redundancy policy that is fair and correct, being within legislation, and that is communicated to all members of the workforce.

EUROPEAN WORKS COUNCILS

This is a group of organisation representatives which have established rights to consultation and feedback within the organisation ■ *see* Chapter 7 ■.

see **Chapter 7**

PARENTAL LEAVE

The UK does not have any form of statutory or agreed provision for parental leave. Parental leave is time allowed to either parent to take off work, where maternity leave, or where applicable paternity leave, has expired, to take care of a young child. An EU Directive became law in the UK on 1 December 1999 and this gave all working parents a minimum of three months' unpaid leave that may be taken at any time until each child is eight years old, although each country can set its own lower cut-off points. National regulations are usually more generous than EU Directives. For example, in Germany either parent can remain at home until the child is aged three. During this leave time the parents can swap over, and there is a means-tested state benefit paid as part of the leave. Usually, parental leave is taken by the woman although the Swedes actively encourage men to participate. Swedish legislation additionally permits the extension of parental leave until the child is eight if it is taken on a part-time basis.

However, in the UK, employer representatives are concerned about the burden of implementing more regulations. The Chartered Institute of Personnel and Development (CIPD) is not in favour of supporting a voluntary approach to any policies which are 'family friendly'. The Institute of Directors (IoD) is also very concerned because they feel that the increasing number of comments and complaints they are receiving about the increasing amount of legislation coming out of Brussels and national government is showing that organisations are finding it highly disruptive to the way business is run.

Rana (1999) reports on the view that there is a fear that the UK will fall foul of the Directive as modelled by a similar system in the USA. The USA Family and Medial Law Act 1993 was introduced by the Clinton administration giving parents the legal right to have time off work in order to take care of their sick children – however, neither the employer nor the state was obliged to fund such leave. An investigation into the US law showed that while it was very popular and had no detrimental effect on organisational effectiveness or business competitiveness, the fact that it was unpaid leave meant that the take-up among low-income families was low. It is suspected that this is what would happen in the UK and suggestions are that low-income families should be compensated through financial social benefits.

The IoD is opposed to the Directive (whether leave is paid or not) claiming that the implementation will cost employers an extra £35m per annum. They further reported that 45 per cent of IoD members currently think twice about employing young women and claimed that the introduction of paid paternal leave rights would only serve to compound this already controversial issue. However, the IoD reported that employer members would not be willing actually to contravene the rules of the Sex Discrimination Act 1975 and Amendments (1986). Members believe it is not about breaking the law but more a matter of survival.

The BCC (1999) published a report which revealed that the majority of its members would, whenever they got the opportunity, choose to develop their own policy on parental leave. Nearly half the firms which responded to the survey currently allow fathers time off when their children are born and 94 per cent give time off for family emergencies.

Among the recommendations made by the BCC is for the government to compensate smaller firms that incur extra costs when taking on temporary cover for staff on parental leave. While the government became obliged to implement the EU Directive when it signed up to the Social Chapter, ministers are now consulting on the actual details of that Directive.

RIGHTS FOR WORKERS ASSIGNED FOR SHORT WORKING TIMES ABROAD

As a result of globalisation and the open market for jobs within Europe, there are many individuals who work outside their home countries. However, this is balanced with the use of local market workers linked with developing their individual management skills – particularly in multinational organisations. The organisation must ensure that the preparation for workers who are going overseas is thorough and sound because if there is not a smooth adjustment, there may be problems as a result – not least of which is the individual performing below

see Chapter 12

maximum ■ see Chapter 12 ■.

Table 8.21 Key areas for consideration when sending workers overseas

Pay	Are any adjustments required because of a higher cost of living in the host country? If so, a percentage pay rise or help with direct costs, say housing, should be forthcoming.
Culture	This includes the change in language. An intensive language course might be needed or education on the cultural aspects of the host country. Business methods and etiquette vary from country to country – especially for countries in the east, for example Japan.
Family	What are the potential difficulties regarding the spouse and children related to local customs, for example in Islamic countries, and education?
Health	Are there any particular health risks and, if so, how can they be prevented?
Safety	Are there any particular dangers such as a high crime rate, political unrest or the chance of kidnapping? What can be done to counteract these difficulties?
Social contact	What can be done to support the worker in her/his new environment so that s/he does not become isolated?

The Posting of Workers Directive 1996 requires organisations to ensure that employers sent to another member European state on a temporary basis receive some of the same terms and conditions that apply in the host country. It comes into play when an employee of a UK company undertakes work in another member state as part of a commercial contract between her/his employer and another organisation, for example a service engineer sent out to repair items under a maintenance contract (Reid, 1999).

Table 8.21 gives the key areas that organisations need to consider.

DATA PROTECTION ACTS 1984, 1999

Employees, through necessity, keep a large amount of personal information on all their employees in both paper and computerised formats. All employees have a right to believe that such data are accurate and kept confidential to those who have a need to know. The Data Protection Act 1984 provided this assurance with regard to the computerised details and the Data Protection Act 1999 went further. The Act has significant implications in the employer–employee relationship because it introduces further restrictions on computerised decision making and the processing of personal, confidential and sensitive information concerning employees.

Under the Act every employee has the right to ask her/his employer to inform them of what records of employment are being kept on them – whether it be in paper or computerised form – and they can also request a full description of such data and be given reasons why they are kept. Employers also, upon request from employees, have to state how the information is being used in any decisions being made within the organisation, for example plans for redundancy. Such information has to be provided in a way that the employee can understand without detracting from the actual information kept and the accuracy of it.

There are exemptions to this, which include confidential references given by an employer, but they do not cover references by a third party held by an employer. While employment legislation is a very complex issue and requires specialist study, its sheer complexity and size should not detract from the fact that HRM specialists and line managers ought to be aware of its presence and be able to go to others for specialist help and advice. The Act is another example of an 'enabling' Act because it is being brought into place in two transition periods to allow employers to obey the Act over a period of time and to give them the opportunity to bring their current documentation into line with the Data Protection Act 1999.

ASYLUM AND IMMIGRATION ACT 1996

This Act makes it a criminal offence for employers knowingly to employ anyone whose immigration status prevents them from working in the UK. It is possible for an employer to avoid any problems in this area if s/he ensures that a potential employee provides evidence of her/his right to work. This can be in the form of such documentation as:

- passport

- travel permit

- birth certificate

- residence or home permit

- Home Office letter

- document with a valid National Insurance number.

If an employer hires anyone who has not proved their legality to work, then the former is liable to prosecution and can be fined up to £5000 if found guilty. By September 1999 there had only been one prosecution brought on these grounds.

However, in 1998, the government appointed a task force called the 'Better Regulation Task Force' whose job it was to cut the government bureaucracy because the Act has proved to be a minefield for employers. Support has been provided by the CRE which believes that the Asylum and Immigration Act 1996 has resulted in considerable discrimination against ethnic minorities who were seeking work. The Conservative Party, led by John Major, brought in the law in order to combat illegal immigration and the Labour Party stated then that, if elected in the upcoming general election, it would scrap the law. However, now in power, it has no intention of doing this but, instead, uses a Code of Practice that advises employers on how to carry out the checks without discriminating between individuals.

Unfortunately, this means that employers are being forced to act as immigration officials and the Code of Practice will, according to Javaid (1999b):

reinforce the dangers for unwary, ignorant or careless employers. (p28)

REHABILITATION OF OFFENDERS ACT 1975

This Act was brought into assist those individuals who had served their sentences and wanted to return to or enter the workplace.

SCENARIO 8.7

Ex-offenders 'unfairly treated'

Unemployed offenders are twice as likely to reoffend on release from jail than those who find jobs, according to the National Association for the Care and Resettlement of Offenders (NACRO). They also face an 'alarming' level of discrimination.

In a report 'Going Straight to Work', NACRO urged firms to adopt equality policies based on the principle that only convictions that are directly relevant to the post will be taken into account when deciding who to employ.

Source: Ex-offenders 'unfairly treated', *People Management*, 25 March 1999, p12.

THE EMPLOYMENT RIGHTS (DISPUTE RESOLUTION) ACT 1998

The UK government's objective is to help in the resolution of disputes more quickly than has been happening in the past. They want a quicker, more efficient and cheaper system put into practice. Therefore, the Employment Rights (Dispute Resolution) Act 1998 is in place in order to reform the industrial tribunal system and to simplify the ways in which disputes in the workplace are dealt with.

Industrial tribunals were established in 1964 in order to deal with minor bureaucratic issues. Nowadays, however, their replacement, ETs, handle thousands of disputes involving such diverse issues as:

- redundancy
- unfair dismissal
- unlawful deductions from pay
- breach of contract
- discrimination.

The success rate of cases brought to tribunals varies and employees do not always win. Compensation is relatively minor – even though the media report otherwise by giving the impression that claimants have won the National Lottery. Industrial tribunal cases take considerable time to resolve and claims can be rejected if they are perceived to have been instituted without sufficient ground or are unworthy of serious treatment because of their puerility. More cases are now heard by the chair-

Table 8.22 Experience of industrial tribunals (after Adkin et al., 1997, pp106–7)

- There is no substitute for good personnel procedures that have been carefully and fairly followed. The strongest defence of a claim can be ruined by misuse of procedures. Even when outraged by an employee's behaviour, an employer should keep calm, follow procedures and do so with transparency.

- A successful outcome depends as much on careful preparation for a hearing as well as good grounds. All the relevant witnesses should attend the hearing because evidence must come from the people concerned.

- Allow time for the hearing and expect delays and disruption. Hearings rarely run smoothly.

- Do not patronise the tribunal or make assumptions, for example that the officials have knowledge of the workplace, its culture and its priorities.

- Be prepared for the other party to be aggressive or emotional.

- Be sensitive to the dilemma of other employees or ex-employees called to give evidence; few people are willing or enthusiastic witnesses.

- Do not count on others sharing your view of the world of work.

- Cooperate fully with the tribunal officials and ACAS – discussed below; both groups are highly professional and impartial.

person sitting alone and although this can speed the system up, it could mean that there is a lack of input from individuals who have experience of the world of work. Adkin et al.'s (1997) report on the experience of industrial tribunals is shown in Table 8.22.

The Employment Rights (Dispute Resolution) Act 1998 renamed industrial tribunals as employment tribunals, commonly referred to as 'tribunals'. They can come to a decision, in certain cases, without convening a hearing or hearing only one of the parties to the dispute. The chairperson has been given wider powers when s/he sits alone. ACAS has been given a further role.

POINTS TO PONDER

The Employment Appeals Tribunal (EAT) has reminded the London Borough of Hillingdon that it was obliged to recognise disabled employees' merits, after it ruled that the authority was 'supine' in its dealings with an employee suffering from myalgic encephalitis (ME).

ACAS

This is a statutory UK body whose principal aim is to promote the improvement of employee relations. It acts as a mediator by helping both employers and trades unions and also provides information in three key areas:

1   The prevention and resolution of dysfunctional conflicts in the workplace

2   Acts as conciliator in both potential and actual complaints in employment tribunals

3   Carries out and recommends good practice by publishing various codes of practice and advisory booklets.

For example, ACAS provides advisory information on the Disciplinary Practice and Procedures in Employment 1997 (revised February 1998) including:

- guidance to employers, stating that procedures should be designed to emphasise and encourage improvement in an individual's conduct

- a clear message from recent case law is that organisations consider the provisions of the ACAS code when disciplining or dismissing employees, therefore, an employment tribunal will do so.

The work is carried out in regional areas with each area having its own office. They also provide more participatory help, particularly to small organisations, in the form of, for example, conferences, seminars and self-help meetings.

The Employment Rights (Dispute Resolution) Act 1998 allows ACAS to take a more involved role by allowing them to draw up a voluntary arbitration scheme as an alternative to a tribunal in cases of unfair dismissal. The ACAS has equal powers with the ET when it comes to redressing the issues at hand. If the parties to the issue are able to make a compromise agreement, they will be allowed access to arbitration and this agreement is binding between those concerned. This means that the issue cannot then come before the employment tribunal. If both parties choose to go for arbitration they would use the services of an independent adviser. The Act has been extended to allow people other than lawyers to be such an adviser so trade union officials and advice centre workers can now represent individuals at an ET.

The Act has also given a flexibility to increase or decrease compensation to reflect the effort that both parties have taken to resolve the issue themselves. However, there is an opinion that the relaxed rules of membership of ETs could undermine the integrity of the system. The ability to use people with diverse backgrounds might bring to a dispute different views that could have a positive influence – yet it might have the opposite effect. It is the lack of legal knowledge by the ET's members and/or the parties' representatives that is at issue. Both the TUC and the IPD fear that mistakes could be made because of a lack of understanding of complex legal issues.

The Act loosened its strict ET membership rules in an attempt to broaden the membership of ETs and thereby encourage more women, ethnic minorities and the disabled to sit on the panel. It certainly increased applications with over 10 000 being made for 330 vacancies. Those appointed will be given the necessary training and a daily payment of £131 when they are sitting to hear cases. Under the pre-Act system, candidates were formally nominated by leading employment and professional bodies such as the CBI, CIPD and the TUC and as lay members they were au fait with workplace issues. Now, individuals can even nominate themselves. Whitehead (1999d) reports on the specific views of these bodies who are concerned that appointees may not have the expertise to sit on ETs. The Act has raised the maximum available compensation to £50 000 (from £12 000) and removes limits on compensation for whistleblowers.

The government's view is that ETs as amended would better reflect the diverse nature of the contemporary workforce than the previous ITs set up in 1964.

Perry (1999) (director of marketing with the Chartered Institute of Marketing (CIM)) believes that it is a good idea for different members of staff to be responsible for different aspects of the law and having an HRM manager would allow an enterprise to continue in their work without being sidetracked from their key business. However, Davis (1999) in his representative role for the Association of Manufacturing Excellence (AME UK) states that small business have a particular problem because they cannot afford to hire HRM professions. This view was supported by Eggleston (1999), the head of the owner-managed business unit of the consultants KPMG, who thinks that organisations, regardless of their size, ought to hire a lawyer (either part time or on a fixed-contract basis) as a cost-effective step. Also, employees need to have access to information and expertise and this is usually available through the services of their employer or their trade union or professional body – such as the CIPD or the CIM.

Employment relations form the backbone of a productive workforce and in order to help with this process it is essential that all workers are rewarded and have a well-developed career structure. This has to be done within the legislation that is related particularly to employment. Additionally, the workplace environment is ever-changing and has to compete in a contemporary framework. Issues such as globalisation ethics and workplace diversity are prominent, with HRM in an international context to the fore. While these issues have been referred to throughout the text, they are important enough to warrant their own chapters ■ *see* Chapter 11 *and* Chapter 12 ■.

see Chapter 11
and Chapter 12

Chapter summary

- There has been a wave of employment legislation from Whitehall, London, and Brussels, Belgium, that is directed at the relationship between employer and employee, which can, because of its complexity, cause complications for companies.

- There is an increasing number of employees who are demanding the enforcement of their workplace statutory rights.

- The field of employment legislation and employment relationships is a minefield for even the most well-informed and trained lawyers.

- Organisations within member states of the EU have Directives from the EU to cope with as well as legislation from their national governments and this adds to the complexity of employment law and employee relationships.

■ Equal opportunities has been founded on the belief that human beings have human rights.

■ Individuals are protected by legislation against being unjustly treated because of their race, skin colour, religion, nationality, gender, marital status and disability. In the UK there is no legislation covering ageism.

■ Equal opportunity is concerned with ensuring equal rights both of access to and participation in all areas of public life.

■ There is considerable legislation in the UK against discrimination from the Equal Pay Act 1970 to the Disability Rights Commission Act 1999.

■ Key EU directives which have directly encroached upon employment include those covering: equal pay and equal treatment, health and safety, protection of pregnant women while at work, working time, proof of an employment relationship, transfer of undertakings, EWCs, parental leave and rights for workers assigned for short working times abroad.

■ There are discussions in the UK government on the introduction of legislation for corporate manslaughter.

■ There are six key approaches to equal opportunities: traditional discrimination, no discrimination, positive action with no targets, positive action with targets, preference for underrepresented groups of equal competence and preference for underrepresented groups without job competence.

■ An individual can attempt to gain redress for discrimination through an ET where s/he might be awarded compensation or corrective action.

■ Assistance is available through the services of the EOC, the CRE and the DRC which have all been set up by their respective Acts of Parliament.

■ Employment relations forms the backbone of a productive workforce and in order to help with this process it is essential that all workers are rewarded and have a well-developed career structure. This has to be done within the legislation related particularly to employment.

END OF CHAPTER 8 CASE STUDY

Dyke calls for more ethnic diversity at BBC

Greg Dyke, director-general of the BBC, raised the BBC's three-year target for ethnic recruitment from 8 to 10 per cent and said he wanted the proportion of ethnic minority managers at least to double to 4 per cent by 2003.

Speaking at the Race in the Media Awards, organised by the Commission for Racial Equality (CRE), Mr Dyke vowed to make ethnic diversity one of his top priorities and said that financial bonuses would be provided to staff who helped the BBC achieve new targets.

With Afro-Caribbean and Asian people making up at least 40 per cent of the youth population of cities such as London and Birmingham within 15 years, the BBC had an obligation to become more multicultural, he said.

'From Marks & Spencer right through to the Metropolitan Police you find institutions which have been slow to react to modern Britain and as a result have had problems.

'The BBC is no different. We need a new vision, and central to that vision is that the BBC must serve Britain's broad and diverse population.'

Mr Dyke added that recent research had shown that although the overall proportion of ethnic minorities shown on BBC programming was a fair reflection of society as a whole, there was evidence of stereotyping.

In factual areas, ethnic minorities were more likely to be employed in or talking about sport and in fictional programming they, rather than white people, were more likely to be portrayed as unemployed.

Although the BBC had met its 8 per cent target, Mr Dyke said that with only 2 per cent of management coming from an ethnic minority, the corporation still had work to do.

'The top of the BBC is very white,' he said. 'I suspect many creative people from ethnic minorities still prefer to go to work for independents or other channels rather than the BBC.'

Adapted from: Sanghera, S. (2000) Dyke calls for more ethnic diversity at BBC, *Financial Times*, 8/9 April, p3.

END OF CHAPTER 8 CASE STUDY QUESTIONS

1 The director-general of the BBC is reported as wanting to increase the three-year target for ethnic recruitment from 8 to 10 per cent. What is a target and what comments have you to make about its use in business?

2 If, within 15 years, the youth population of cities such as London and Birmingham is due to be made up of at least 40 per cent Afro-Caribbean and Asian, what did Mr Dyke suggest he could do to harvest this potential labour force?

3 What approaches could the BBC take to its equal opportunities policy? Which one/s do you feel Mr Dyke could consider for the BBC?

4 How can employment law help those who belong to an ethnic minority who feel they have been discriminated against because of their ethnicity?

END OF PART IV CASE STUDY

EMPLOYERS UP IN ARMS OVER SHORTER WEEK

It is rare in any country for employment law to become the subject of discussion in a doctor's waiting room. But such is the controversy stirred by the French government's recent introduction of a compulsory 35-hour working week that, even in the tiny Aveyron village of Coupiac, ordinary people are at a loss to know whether it is a good thing.

In 1936, French workers undertook nationwide factory occupations to force the introduction of the 40-hour working week, together with two weeks' paid holiday for all. Since then, working hours have changed remarkably little.

Today, the average French employee works 39.7 hours a week, according to Eurostat. That compares with an EU average of 40.4 hours and variations ranging from 44 hours in the UK to 38.3 hours in Belgium. In Germany, the average working week is 40.1 hours.

No one is demonstrating for shorter working hours in France today. With an unemployment rate of 11.1 per cent, French workers are glad to have jobs at all.

Rather, the law on the 35-hour week, passed on 15 December 1999, is a job-creation measure. Martine Aubry, France's employment minister, has stated his objective to cut unemployment by sharing out the work available.

Companies will now be obliged to cut the number of hours staff work to fill the gaps. To encourage companies to comply, the government has promised to reduce social charges. Those that drag their feet will face extra taxes. Employees, in theory, will receive the same salary for working fewer hours.

The law fixes the maximum number of hours an employee can work at 1600 a year, plus 90 hours of overtime (compared with a potential maximum, including 130 hours of overtime, of 1963 at present).

It also sets out overtime rates, a variety of ways in which hours can be counted and curtailed and seven ways in which companies can qualify for reduced social contributions.

Companies with more than 20 employees will have until 2001 to make the adjustments without penalty; those with 20 or less employees will have until 2003.

French managers believe economic growth is the best means to cut unemployment and fear that tightening controls on working hours can only damage their competitiveness and stifle entrepreneurship. They say France is running against the international trend of liberalising employment practices, typified by the increased employment flexibility introduced in Britain. They argue the net effect on job creation will be negligible. Employment ministry calculations suggest the new law will only achieve pay falls of 2.5 per cent and hourly productivity rises of 4 per cent. It seems that 35 hours worked will be paid for 35 hours, and not for 28.

That is why the debate in the doctor's surgery is so inconclusive. Many people find the idea of working less hours attractive. But not if it means a three-year pay freeze and slows the rate at which the economy is creating jobs.

Adapted from: Tieman, R. (1999) Employers up in arms over shorter week, *Financial Times*, 21 December, p14.

END OF PART IV CASE STUDY QUESTIONS

1 Why has the introduction of a compulsory 35-hour working week prompted widespread controversy in France?

2 Why are those French in employment only too pleased to have a job regardless of the hours they have to work?

3 Given the evidence of the French case study, do you think that it has been easy for the French government to frame the law and if so, why, and, if not, why not?

4 The British Working Time Directive (1999) lays down a 40-hour maximum working week rather than the 35-hour week of the French legislation. Why do you think that there is this differentiation?

 THESIS + ANTITHESIS = SYNTHESIS

Explore the view that there is no such thing as equal opportunities in the workplace.

 SELF-TEST THE KEY ISSUES

1 What rights does an individual have under the sex and discrimination laws?

2 To what extent do the Directives from the EU infringe on UK legislation?

3 Why are laws to protect the employee felt to be necessary?

4 List some of the bodies which could help with advice on anti-discrimination in the workplace.

 TEAM/CLASS DISCUSSIONS

1 Debate the proposition that 'Employers should be able to employ at will'.

2 'The sporting world is full of inequality.' Discuss.

PROJECTS (INDIVIDUAL OR TEAMS)

1 Design a survey questionnaire on any aspect of equal opportunities in employment, for example racism, disability, sexual orientation. You are not expected to carry out the questionnaire itself but to prepare a written report on both the strengths and weaknesses of the design of the questionnaire.

2 As the equal opportunities representative for your university Student Union, you have been asked to design a single A4 page of information for students on equal opportunities for the disabled. Prepare the leaflet.

Recommended reading

Bratton, J. and J. Gold (1999) *Human Resource Management: Theory and Practice*, Basingstoke: Macmillan – now Palgrave

Farnham, D. (2000) *Employee Relations in Context*, London: CIPD

Jackson, T. (2000) *Handling Grievances*, London: CIPD

Suter, E. (2000) *The Employment Law Checklist*, London: Institute of Personnel and Development

Terry, M. (2000) *Redefining Public Sector Unionism*, London: Routledge

URLs (uniform resource locators)

www.networkwomen.org

Organisation for women to make professional and business contacts giving them an opportunity to network.

www.lawcrawler.com

Legal advice worldwide.

www.findlaw.com

Search on comprehensive legal topics.

www.leeds.ac.uk//hamlyn/european.htm

Information of European Union law. UK law line.

www.emplaw.co.uk

British employment law with professional notes.

www.ndirect.co.uk/~law/bentham.htm

Bentham Archive of British Law. Independent synopsis of criminal, roman, European and property law. UK legal themes.

www.incomesdata.co.uk/brief/wtime.htm

Implementation of the European Working Time Directive in the UK.

www.hmso.gov.uk/acts.htm

Acts of Parliament for the UK in full.

www.pcaw.demon.co.uk

Issues concerned with Public Concern at Work, for example whistleblowing.

www.gov.uk/cre

The Commission for Racial Equality (CRE). About the CRE, ethnic diversity, asylum issues and publications available.

www.gov.uk/eoc

The Equal Opportunities Commission (EOC). About the EOC, its work and role.

www.open.gov.uk/hse

Site for the UK Health and Safety Commission.

dibblupton.co.uk

Dibb Lupton Alsop. Employment law specialists. Legal assistance, advice and occasional articles.

www.sofcom.com.au

Australian site giving information on business including business guide and search facility.

Bibliography

Adkin, E., G. Jones, and P. Leighton (1997) *Pocket Employer*, London: Economist/Profile Books
Aiken, O. (1999) Cutting the red tape in *People Management*, 16 September, pp24–5
Altman, Y. and F. Bournois (1999) *Temps perdu* in *People Management*, 30 June, pp54–6
Baron, A. (1999) in Whitehead, M. (1999) MoD to back down over gene tests on candidates in *People Management*, 29 July, p13
British Chambers of Commerce (1999) *The Employment Provisions and Small Employers* on http://www.chamber.co.uk/newsandpolicy/employment/disabilitydiscriminationact.htm
British Chambers of Commerce (1999) *Parental Leave Survey*, July, London: BCC
Buggy, C. (1999) What's age got to do with it? in *Professional Manager*, May, pp28–30
Clement, B. (1999) Anger at working time opt-out in the *Independent*, 8 July, p2
Cridland, J. (1999) Courting confusion in *People Management*, 6 May, p31
Confederation of British Industry and W. Mercer (1999) *Employment Trends Survey: Measuring Flexibility in the Labour Markets*, London: Confederation of British Industry
Daily Mail (7 September 1999) p15
Daily Telegraph (8 July 1999) p10
Davis, R. in Gracie, S. (1999) Coping with the tide of red tape in *The Sunday Times*, 30 May, p13
Eastham, P. (1999) Bosses salute rethink over the 48-hour week in *Daily Mail*, 8 July, p34

Eggleston, J. (1999) in Gracie, S. (1999) Coping with the tide of red tape in *The Sunday Times*, 30 May, p13

Firth, J. (1999) Risky business in *People Management*, 19 August, p24–5

Gracie, S. (1999) Coping with the tide of red tape in *The Sunday Times*, 30 May 1999, p13

Graham, R. (1999) Paris to delay 35-hour week in *Financial Times*, 22 June 1999, p2

Hibbs, J. (1999) Union anger as working hours law watered down in *Daily Telegraph*, 8 July, p10

Honderich, E. (1995) *The Oxford Companion to Philosophy*, Oxford: Oxford University Press

Independent, 8 July 1999, p2

Institute of Personnel and Development (1999) Age and Employment, Key Facts, insert in *People Management*, 16 September

Islington Council (1999) *Complain About the Council: Equal Opportunities* on http://www.n52sn.demon.co.uk/equality.html September, pp1–2

Javaid, M. (1999a) Equal measure in *People Management*, 6 May, p27

Javaid, M. (1999b) Passport control in *People Management*, 3 June, p28

Lawrights (1999) in *Lawrights – Employment* on http://www.lawrights.co.uk

Leighton, P. (1999) in Walsh, J. Working time legislation 'not interpreted properly' in *People Management*, 8 April, p13

Meager, N. B. Doyle, C. Evans et al. (1999) *Monitoring the Disability Discrimination Act (DDA) 1995*, Research Report No. 116, Institute for Employment Studies

Merrick, N. (1999) Into injury time in *People Management*, 29 July 1999, pp42–3

People Management, Ex-offenders 'unfairly treated', 25 March 1999, p12

People Management, HSE seeks firms' input, 29 July 1999, p15

People Management, Ruling on indirect discrimination, 2 March 2000, p11

Perry, R. (1999) in Gracie, S. (1999) Coping with the tide of red tape in *The Sunday Times*, 30 May, p13

Rana, E. (1999) Parent leave rights 'will exclude low-paid families' in *People Management*, 29 July, p14

Reid, P. (1999) Restricted movement in *People Management*, 16 September, pp21–2

Sanghera, S. (2000) Dyke calls for more ethnic diversity at BBC in *Financial Times*, 8/9 April, p3

Sunday Times (1999) Flood of employment law brings chaos, in Small Business Section, 15 November on http://www.hr-expert.com/members/data/rc.articles/16119815.htm

Tieman, R. (1999) Employers up in arms over shorter week in *Financial Times*, 21 December, p14

Times, The (1999) Company fined for workers' deaths, 8 September, p7

Trades Union Congress (1999) *Equal Opportunities Policy* on http://bized.ac.uk/compfact/tuc/tuc10.htm September, p1

University of York (1999) *Equal Opportunities Policy for Students* on http://www.york.ac.uk/admin/aso/eqopps/code.htm 5 September pp1–4

Walker, A. (1999) Breaking down the barriers on ageism in *Professional Manager*, May, p7

Walsh, J. (1999a) Call for 'holistic approach' to health and work strategy in *People Management*, 25 March, pp18–19

Walsh, J. (1999b) Merged steel giants aim to sidestep HR policy pitfalls in *People Management*, 17 June, p12

Week, 18 September 1999, 94

Welch, J. (1999a) Sheltered workers face job losses in funding row in *People Management*, 2 September, pp14–15

Welch, J. (1999b) Rising violence puts focus on staff protection policy in *People Management*, 6 May, p17

West, L. (1999) Record £1.5m fine for GWT after Southall HST crash in *Rail*, 11–24 August, p4

Whitehead, M. (1999a) Anti-ageism protagonists divided on voluntary code in *People Management*, 30 June, p17

Whitehead, M. (1999b) Racial discrimination still denying equality at work in *People Management*, 8 April, pp18–19

Whitehead, M. (1999c) MoD to back down over gene tests on candidates in *People Management*, 29 July, p13

Whitehead, M. (1999d) Alarm raised over tribunal membership in *People Management*, 2 September, p12

Wighton, D. and R. Taylor (1999) Companies applaud red-tape cut in *Financial Times*, 8 July, p12

Woodward, T. (1999) Ye olde RSI in *Daily Mail*, 24 August, p19

Worman, D. (1999) Enter the age of diversity in *People Management*, 15 July, p59

Worsley, R. (1999) Third age of forgetfulness in *People Management*, 30 June, p31

Developing the workforce

Rewards and remuneration

After studying this chapter, you should be able to:

- DEFINE the key terms: benefits, compensation, disposable income, remuneration, reward, salary and wage.

- DISCUSS the difference between traditional pay (TP) and new pay (NP).

- EXPLAIN the relationship between motivation and reward.

- EVALUATE the advantages and disadvantages of performance-related pay (PRP).

- JUDGE the effectiveness of share ownership schemes for (a) knowledge workers and (b) other workers.

- ASSESS the different kinds of contemporary pay structure.

- STATE the role of *perquisites* (perks) for shareholders.

INTRODUCTION

Framework case study

Sports stars a race apart from fat cats

The claim that chief executives and sporting heroes are justifiably in the same pay league has one big flaw.

According to Stephen Byers, the United Kingdom Trade and Industry Secretary, sports stars and chief executives are much the same. Both operate in global markets, both are in high demand. We do not object to sporting stars getting paid so much, so we should not object to 'fat cats' getting so much either.

In fact, fat cats and sporting heroes are not merely as alike as Mr Byers supposes. The difference lies in performance. It is all very well saying that chief executive officers (CEOs) deserve a lot of money so long as their performance calls for it. But that is just the problem. It is extremely difficult to judge whether the performance of a fat cat calls for it or not.

By contrast, the performance of the sports person is there for all to see. They may play as part of a team, but it is easy to measure how they are doing as individuals. Game by game, it is clear to everyone.

The same is not true of a CEO. Measuring the individual performance of the top person who works in a team is very hard. It is possible that the force of inertia in large companies is so great that the CEO has very little impact at all.

Not only is it hard to single out the contribution of the CEO, but it is also difficult to assess her/his impact when results of her/his decisions may not be apparent for years later.

None of this means that chief executives should not be paid so much. One company has to pay a CEO a fortune because other companies do. And it follows that if everybody is prepared to pay over the odds, they must be worth it.

Mustn't they?

Adapted from: Kellaway, L. (1999) Sports stars a race apart from fat cats, *Financial Times*, 26 July, p10.

Previous chapters have emphasised that human resource management (HRM) is about enabling members of the workforce to carry out their tasks as efficiently as is possible within the best available environment. One of the ways in which this can be brought about is by utilising a suitable method of payment which will both encourage and reward each worker as indicated in the Framework Case Study. Druker and White (1997) believe that:

> Changes in reward management systems have been at the heart of development in HRM. (p128)

A reading of HRM literature shows that there has been a move towards the individualisation of the employment relationship within an increased emphasis on linking HRM policies and the proactive business strategy of the organisation and the performance of employees ■ *see* Chapter 2 *and* Chapter 10 ■. Bratton and Gold (1999) state that:

see Chapter 2 *and* Chapter 10

> Personnel management is to be directed mainly at the organization's employees, recruiting, training and rewarding them, and is portrayed as a 'caring' activity. (p14)

There has also been a change in emphasis relating to reward management. The specific literature on reward management makes issue of the shift from giving individuals short-term rewards using off-the-cuff approaches to management to a much longer term, strategic approach – remuneration and rewards are now part of organisational strategy rather than a necessary 'add-on'.

The management of rewards is a challenge for managers and all indications are that it will continue to be so for some time to come. HRM specialists will have to take on board the Directives from the European Union (EU) which become enshrined in legislation ■ *see* Chapter 7 *and* Chapter 8 ■. Walsh (1999) reports that despite the trend towards more integrated approaches, pay systems are retaining their national flavour. Over 50 per cent of European multinational organisations believe that economic and monetary union will encourage further pan-European pay agreements. She reports on the work carried out by the HR consultancy, Towers Perrin, which indicates that such a pan-European trend cannot be avoided.

see Chapter 7 *and* Chapter 8

Of 464 major organisations surveyed, while there were significant national differences, nearly 80 per cent of the respondents expected increased pay transparency across the nations to lead to more commonality in the types of remuneration systems in operation. Approximately 60 per cent said that they actually wanted their system to harmonise with those across the continent. However, this is an ideal and will not become practice for many years – national systems remain dominant ■ *see* Chapter 11 ■. There is a ▶ **cafeteria style** ◀ of remuneration packages. However competency-based pay has not taken off in Europe as it has in the USA. Brown (1999), as principal of Towers Perrin who carried out the research, stated:

see Chapter 11

> The overwhelming impression is of continuing country-based variations in reward management, with organisations borrowing from other traditions in a national context. (p11)

▶ The selection by an individual of what items s/he requires from those on display. ◀······▶ Cafeteria style

However, he believes that there is evidence in the research to show that pay harmonisation will eventually happen. He quotes the examples of Rover and Vauxhall where the need for competitiveness has forced comparisons with their European counterparts. However, organisations need to consider their strategy and make sure that they understand, according to Brown (1999):

> [that] strategy is not merely a nice plan, it has to work in practice, and communication is key to that. (p11)

DEFINING THE TERMS

In the contemporary workplace there are a number of words which are used to describe what an individual receives in return for her/his work efforts. Different people use different terminology, so it is important that all managers thoroughly understand the varying interpretations of such words which include:

■ benefits

■ compensation

- remuneration
- reward
- salary
- wages and
- disposable earnings.

All the above could be housed under the one word *payment* – some writers, for example Foot and Hook (1999), believe that:

> Payment is the most straightforward of... terms and seems to be the most appropriate term to use. It can include monetary or non-monetary payment. (p256)

While this might be true, in the field of HRM it is this very generality that is its weakness, because in use it can mean:

- the *actual* act of paying someone
- the *specific* amount of money being paid or
- something being *given* in return, be it a reward or a punishment.

It is, therefore, necessary to use specific words for specific situations as those listed above can show – each one is briefly defined below and is used accordingly within this chapter.

▶ **Benefits** ◀ comprise the second half of what is known as the 'compensation equation' – the first half is pay. While virtually every business has to offer some type of monetary compensation to employees, most benefits are optional.

Benefits ◀┈┈▶ The non-cash elements of a worker's reward package, for example a paid holiday.

Compensation = Pay + Benefits

see Chapter 8

The word ▶ **compensation** ◀ is often used to refer to an individual's payment for work performed, injuries received or loss of employment ■ *see* Chapter 8 ■. It goes beyond the simple payment for services rendered to refer to the making good of some sort of loss or injury the individual has incurred while working. It is additional to her/his regular payment for work. An example here would be as a result of a ruling by an employment tribunal (ET) ■ *see* Chapter 8 ■.

see Chapter 8

Compensation ◀┈┈▶ The sum of money awarded to the victor in any claim headed by an employment tribunal. It can be used interchangeably with the word remuneration meaning pay – including benefits.

Remuneration means reward or pay for work done and/or a service rendered – it shows the distinction between payment and reward. It is a word that can encompass the others, for example payment, benefit and compensation.

The word ▶ **reward** ◀ has come into more common use in the workplace because the systems used to reward individuals for their efforts increasingly include some aspect of ▶ **motivation** ◀ – encouraging individuals to work even harder and then to reward them for that 'extra kilometre'.

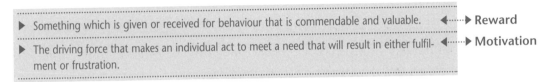

▶ Something which is given or received for behaviour that is commendable and valuable. ◀······▶ **Reward**

▶ The driving force that makes an individual act to meet a need that will result in either fulfil- ◀······▶ **Motivation**
ment or frustration.

Adkin et al. (1997) define wages as being:

Broadly, the money paid to employees by their employer for doing their jobs. (p196)

They also make the point that a ▶ **salary** ◀ is a ▶ **synonym** ◀ for ▶ **wages** ◀ (p165). It is traditional that weekly pay is referred to as a 'wage' while a monthly payment is a 'salary' – usually made to ▶ **white-collar** ◀ and managerial staff. A salary may be categorised into basic salary, and total salary, which contains more than one part, for example a bonus payment.

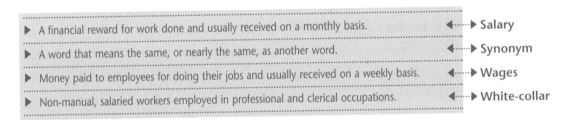

▶ A financial reward for work done and usually received on a monthly basis. ◀······▶ **Salary**

▶ A word that means the same, or nearly the same, as another word. ◀······▶ **Synonym**

▶ Money paid to employees for doing their jobs and usually received on a weekly basis. ◀······▶ **Wages**

▶ Non-manual, salaried workers employed in professional and clerical occupations. ◀······▶ **White-collar**

Most employees in continental Europe receive extra pay over and above their 12 monthly salaries. This is called the 13th-month salary, although in most cases it is not paid out in one lump sum but is divided into a summer and Christmas bonus. It may, or may not, be exactly equal to one month's pay, depending on the country and local custom and practice. Where they can, employers are trying to tie the payment into meeting conditions, such as good attendance and quality performance. In Spain employees also receive a 14th- or even a 15th-month salary.

An individual's earnings comprise his/her wages and/or salary including bonuses, commissions and pension contributions. His/her ▶ **disposable earnings** ◀ are the sum which remains after deducting those amounts required by law, for example National Insurance payments and income tax.

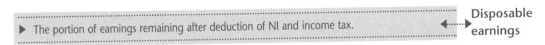

▶ The portion of earnings remaining after deduction of NI and income tax. ◀······▶ **Disposable earnings**

As with most business decisions, there are pros and cons to consider when offering benefits to employees. These have to be evaluated within the organisation's particular business environment because they can help the employer to determine

9.1

Activity

Look at the appointments section of any newspaper or professional magazine and list details of the advertisements that offer benefits in addition to a wage/salary.

List these benefits.

Identify the most common and the least preferred.

Table 9.1 Advantages in offering benefits to employees

Taxation	Plan contributions may be deductible from tax
Recruitment	Benefits packages can attract good employees and can be structured in such a way as to reward and retain them
Personal gain	Employers, especially in small and medium firms, may be able to get benefits for themselves for less money if they offer such benefits to all employees rather than getting them privately for themselves as the employer

Table 9.2 Disadvantages in offering benefits to employees

Health coverage	Higher rates have to be paid for group health coverage in small firms because there are fewer employees among them to spread the risk
Life insurance	More difficult in providing this coverage to an employee group
Retirement plans	High administrative costs can reduce design choices
Administration	Complexity may limit fringe benefits

whether to offer other benefits. Tables 9.1 and 9.2 give the key advantages and disadvantages of offering benefits.

SYSTEMS OF PAYMENT

In selecting a particular system of payment an organisation can bring about a specific behaviour in an individual employee – each will respond differently to the various methods of rewards. Keuning (1998) believes that it is important to examine the motives on which the choice of payment system is made. The functional salary comprises the basic amount paid to the employee, be this determined by seniority, merit and/or other considerations. It is necessary for the employer to calculate into the basic salary/wage the legal requirements for the payment of social security and income tax payments. As Keuning (1998) shows in Figure 9.1, the personal reward is also brought about by choosing a particular system of payment.

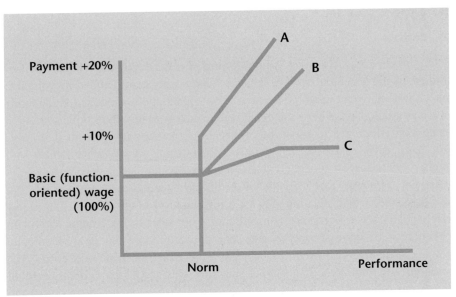

Figure 9.1 The principle of performance-related reward, after Keuning (1998, p414)

PAY SURVEYS

Successive pay surveys confirm a change in approach to pay by British employees. The most recent large-scale survey of pay practices in the UK was carried out in 1995 and jointly published by the Confederation of British Industries (CBI) and Hay Management Consultants. Their research incorporated 400 private and public sector organisations with an involvement of 1.3 million individuals. The conclusion was that there had been fundamental changes in reward and remuneration systems. For the period 1994–96 almost 50 per cent of the organisations surveyed stated that they had made some sort of change in their pay strategy concentrating on the principal areas of:

■ salary structures

■ salary progression practices

■ introduction of ▶ **profit-related pay** ◀ (discussed later in this chapter).

▶ That part of an employee's pay based on the profit which her/his organisation makes. ◀······▶ **Profit-related pay**

About 30 per cent of organisations reported that they were in the process of changing their benefit package, with:

■ company cars

■ pensions

■ maternity leave

- paternity leave and

- holidays

being the key areas of change. An interesting issue here is that there was minimal interest in the 'cafeteria style' of benefits – only 5 per cent planned to introduce such a system. Even though 50 per cent of the organisations already used some sort of job evaluation, a further 38 per cent were planning to introduce some sort of job evaluation which went against the principle of rewarding the individual and this was particularly evidenced in jobs lower than senior management. Druker and White (1997) suggest that the explanation for this may lie in the impact of the

see Chapter 8

equal pay for equal value legislation ■ *see* Chapter 8 ■ and the fact that a job that is constructed using evaluation may assist the employer in offsetting any equal pay claims. Sixty-seven per cent of organisations surveyed had a grading system in operation with approximately 20 per cent of organisations having a broad-band grading structure – a further 17 per cent were planning to introduce one. The research also indicated that competency- or skills-based pay systems were in the ascent.

THE 'NEW PAY'

According to Lawler (1995) these changes in pay and benefits have brought about a new term, referred to as 'new pay' (NP). The literature suggests that the change to NP has been swift but there is no recorded evidence that this is so. In the USA there has been considerable change, but less in Europe. What has been clear is the move away from collective bargaining towards a more individual performance-driven or skills-based system. This includes all attempts to link pay with organisational goals aligned with more flexible pay components such as reward packages for white-collar workers.

The term 'new pay' was coined by the US management writer Lawler (1990) and was later developed by Schuster and Zingheim (1992). 'New pay' may well be of US origin but the concept has been developed in Britain through adoption of its use by, for example, reward management researchers such as Armstrong and Murlis (1994) and Hewitt Associates (1991).

TP VERSUS NP

New pay (NP) is used in concert with 'traditional pay' (TP) which is typified by:

- a job-evaluated grading structure

- payment by time

- seniority-based pay progression

- service-related benefits.

The TP methods go back to the principle of Taylorism after Taylor (1911), who was the founding father of scientific management which was a relatively simple model of motivation, being labelled a theory of 'rational economic man' ■ *see* Chapter 1 ■. This model looked at ▶ **goals** ◀ and ▶ **extrinsic** ◀ factors as a key to reward and motivation. The idea was that if an individual were given a precisely defined set of tasks, clear objectives and the extrinsic increasing set of economic rewards related to performance, then s/he would calculate the benefits of improving individual output and thus productivity would rise. That is, deciding whether the effort required to do the job or task was worth the monetary reward. This was an acceptable theory in a working environment that was stable and not prone to changes as in the contemporary marketplace. Taylor (1911) believed that the only possible barriers to this traditional system would be the limitations imposed by the processes and resources available and the capacity of the worker to do the job. He also felt that threatening to remove the economic rewards would serve as a way of punishing and correcting any low productivity by the individual. As Taylor (1911) discovered, workers did not, in practice, respond in the way this motivational model predicted because it was shown that the driver of economic reward, for example money, was insufficient to improve performance.

see Chapter 1

▶ Aims or objectives towards which the employee is working.	◀┈┈▶ **Goals**
▶ Tangible outcomes for effort that derive externally, for example financial or non-financial payments.	◀┈┈▶ **Extrinsic**

Taylorism had significance in the early part of the 20th century because, in the USA, there were large numbers of immigrants at work in organisations and the principles of scientific management provided a simple approach to work issues, such as rewards, which was needed at the time. However, the scientific management theory does shed light on the principles of payment and rewards in the contemporary world because it identified the key ingredients in motivation (discussed further below), which were clearly defined tasks and objectives backed by some sort of reward structure that could provide a foundation for effective motivation.

NP AND TP IN CONTRAST

NP contrasts to the more stable TP environment because it is seen as being more suitable for the acute, fast-moving and performance-driven organisations of the 21st century. Because of the nature of contemporary business, NP meets the objective of increasing control over rewards and remuneration at organisational level by letting pay levels and structures fluctuate according to the circumstances of the individual business. As a consequence, pay systems have to be informed and supportive of the organisation's business strategy and its culture ■ *see* Chapter 2 ■. Lawler (1995) states:

see Chapter 2

The new pay argues in favour of a pay-design process that starts with business strategy and organizational design. It argues against an assumption that certain best practices must be incorporated into a company's approach to pay. (p14)

This view is supported by Heery (1996) who states:

For Lawler and other new pay writers, discrete business strategies require particular behaviours and attitudes from employees and strategic pay management involves selecting pay policies which will secure these behaviours and attitudes. (p3)

Brown (1995) believes that:

An organisation's reward system represents another powerful means of influencing its culture. (p137)

Kerr and Slocum (1987) report that their research indicates that culture plays a very important role when related to reward systems. They believe that it provides employees with stated instructions of what they have to do in order to receive pay rises, bonuses, promotion and other rewards. It follows, then, that an organisation's reward system can be seen as a statement of its values, beliefs and assumptions – its ▶ **culture** ◀. It thus likewise follows that organisations can tailor their reward systems to fit their culture. Organisations that are diversified can offer reward systems reflecting the demands of the differing business environments, products, services and stakeholders. This can be further fine-tuned by the use of multiple reward systems which will result in multiple cultures because they reinforce the differing cultural systems within a single organisation.

Culture ◀┈┈▶ The distinctive ways in which different human populations or societies organise their lives.

The NP writers (Lawler, 1990; Gomez-Mejia and Balkin, 1992; Schuster and Zingheim, 1992) state that the NP approach is facilitated by a move from the TP methods such as 'job-related pay' to 'person-related pay' structures. Kanter (1989) wrote earlier:

Traditional pay scales have reflected, largely, such estimated characteristics of jobs as decision-making, responsibility, importance to the organization, and number of subordinates. People's pay has been largely a function of the social and organizational positions they occupy... In traditional compensation positions each job came with an assigned pay level, relatively fixed regardless of how well the job was performed or the real value of the performance produced for the organisation. (p231)

In TP schemes, pay was job related and therefore had to be accompanied by job evaluation schemes which became cumbersome and time consuming to administer. It was through these job evaluations that attempts were made to maintain equity between the responsibilities of the job and the rewards allocated to it. That is, the *see* Chapter 7   adoption of the justice theory ■ *see* Chapter 7 ■ of motivation which asserts that members of any workforce wish to be treated fairly and have a desire to perceive equity in relation to others. Maund (1999) states that:

All people who work in a business will want a reward for their efforts in the form of, for example, the best pay and conditions that they can achieve. They will also want rewards which they feel reflect the value of their work and the market rate for the job compared to other workers in comparable jobs – they will search for equity. (pxix)

Mahoney (1992) put the view that:

the concept of job was the unifying concept in the Scientific Management approach to organization and management (p339)

and continues to say that such payment systems:

led to the development and application of a concept of job ownership expressed in the labour movement and collective bargaining. (p339)

Collective bargaining is not a major contributor to NP – if at all – but it seems that part of its philosophy remains because it involves a rejection of any concept of joint regulation of pay or collective bargaining. Heery (1996), in his evaluation of writers on NP, says that they stress the value of employee involvement in the design and operation of pay systems ■ *see* Chapter 5 ■. New pay followers have no time for TP 'job-related' pay systems and so NP is distinguished by its emphasis on 'person-related' reward and remuneration systems.

see **Chapter 5**

In his work, Lawler (1990) stresses that strategic pay systems must emphasise the person-related forms of reward; that is, paying individuals according to their value in the marketplace. He reinforces the belief that it is people who develop skills and are the most important assets of an organisation. It follows, therefore, that NP is an individualised approach to pay and is manifested in the use of individual ▶ **performance-related pay** ◀ (PRP). It can also be found in the competency-based model – where employees are rewarded for the acquisition of new skills, competencies or qualifications. This cannot be divorced from the range of benefits provided – the flexible or cafeteria approach discussed later in this chapter.

▶ Employees' pay which depends partly on their performance.

Performance-related pay

Keuning (1998) considered that the principle of payment required a balance of what is understood to be a usual and fair performance, that is:

a performance which, under average circumstances, can be delivered by suitable personnel members (selected, educated, with the necessary experience) and with normal effort. (p414)

The findings of the CBI/Hay (1996) research on pay practices in the UK, discussed above, put an interesting distinction with the NP views which have been imported from the USA. There is evidence that there have been fundamental changes in payment methods in the UK from job related to individual related and this is in line with the NP ideas. However, there are reasons why the NP systems are coming into play in the UK more slowly. This may be due to the increasing use of job evaluation grading systems and the nature of the legislation relating to the workplace originating from the EU ■ *see* Chapter 7 *and* Chapter 8 ■. Smith (1992) notes that

see **Chapter 7** *and* **Chapter 8**

the discussions on rewards within the USA have happened at a 'much higher plane' (p171) than in the UK and he suggests that the UK-based changes, particularly in the 1980s, were less extensive and coherent than those taking place at the same time in the USA. However, Kessler (1995) takes a different view. While he agrees to some degree that post-1945 history shows a move towards reward management in the UK, it has been unplanned and has 'just happened'. There is evidence that the use of reward systems in the current contemporary workplace has become part of the overall strategy of organisations and thus it can:

> reinforce the broader process of organizational transformation in a new and distinctive way. (p255)

CHANGES IN PAY PRACTICES IN THE UK

The key developments in UK remuneration and reward policies over the last 25 years have been in the shift to more flexible and variable reward systems and the decline of collective bargaining. Such a new pay flexibility has resulted from a number of developments in the economy, including:

- changes in business organisation leading to flatter, less hierarchical organisational structures

- greater emphasis on the individual organisation's internal requirements and the ability to pay

- a parallel decline in industry-wide pay determination systems

- changes in the balance of economic activity

- restructuring of the labour market

- the abandonment of most forms of government involvement in wage regulation

- clear government support for more employment flexibility.

The last point was emphasised by Smith (1993) who commented that:

> Linking reward management to the entrepreneurial spirit placed it on the political agenda. (p47)

The Department of Trade and Industry (DTI) (1996) confirms a move to greater pay flexibility. The DTI supports moves to any sort of greater pay flexibility stating that:

> Britain's deregulated labour market now allows employers considerable freedom to choose pay systems that meet their own needs and those of the workforce. (p3)

The foreword to the DTI Report (1996) has a comment by the president of the Board of Trade which states that 'flexible pay is an integral part of the wider business agenda' (unpaged). This is a view, some argue, that the UK Labour Party had when it was elected in 1997.

Employers find the area of flexible pay attractive because of the chance of tax relief, the aim of which, according to Her Majesty's Treasury (1993), has been to:

encourage employers to introduce financial participation... and... give employees a direct financial stake in the business they work for. (p2)

Such flexible payment schemes have included the Inland Revenue-approved profit-related pay scheme and employee share schemes, for example Share-As-You-Earn share option schemes, profit-sharing schemes and discretionary share option schemes. In November 1996, the government announced that its tax incentive scheme was to be phased out.

Such techniques cannot just come about in a haphazard way but must be included in the organisation's strategy ■ *see* Chapter 2 ■. Effective strategy implementation should occur when the individuals who are required to take action actually do so. Galbraith and Kazanian (1986) state that reward is one of the most powerful motivators in an organisation's reward system and this view is supported by Stacey (1996). These researchers believe that if the rewards are suitable and appropriate they will stimulate individuals to make the effort to take actions which are directly relevant to the strategy of the organisation. That is, the way in which their jobs are graded, and how pay scales are attached to those grades, will set the opinion that the individual has about her/job and the effort that s/he will make.

see Chapter 2

However, the system needs to be seen to be fair or it will adversely affect performance. There are many ways of tying monetary rewards to the actions that strategy implementation requires and these include:

■ bonuses

■ PRP

■ piecework

■ productivity.

There are non-monetary rewards which play a more important role in motivating people:

■ promotion ■ *see* Chapter 10 ■

■ career development ■ *see* Chapter 10 ■.

see Chapter 10

see Chapter 10

Whatever method of reward is used within an organisation it must be seen to be useful to that organisation in achieving its goals and also in the provision of greater self-fulfilment for each individual worker concerned. There are, however, simpler forms of reward which are very important:

■ praise

■ recognition and

■ thanks.

Training and development is a key implementation tool because, according to Hussey (1991) it:

- acts as a motivator

see Chapter 2   ■ provides skills required for strategy implementation ■ *see* Chapter 2 ■.

The aims of all training and development programmes should always be aligned within those of an organisation's strategy and those aims should consist of measurable changes in the performance of the organisation ■ *see* Chapter 1 *and* Chapter 6 ■.

see Chapter 1 *and* Chapter 6

9.2

Activity

List those things which motivate you to do a good job:

(a) at your place of work and/or

(b) in your studies.

REWARDS AND MOTIVATION

Maund (1999) defines motivation as:

> the process by which an individual wants and chooses to engage in certain specified behaviours. (p87)

It is a highly complex area of study which, in its detail, is beyond the scope of this book. However, there are aspects of it that underpin the rewards and remuneration of workers. The work environment is highly globalised and competitive and because of this organisations are having to exercise ever-tighter controls over their costs. Randle (1997) states that organisations should be:

> more productive and reduce escalating costs – minimise costs. (p187)

They also have to become quicker and more responsive to their ▶ **markets** ◀ and such pressures on costs, and the need to improve levels of service, have meant that organisations need to be flexible and efficient in their working practices. This, in turn, means that employees have to behave in such a way to add value to the final product and/or service they are engaged upon. All this means that individuals have to be motivated – an area of concern which management will always find difficult to come to grips with because of its complexity. However, it does form a foundation for most aspects of HRM.

Markets ◀┄┄▶ The actual and potential buyers of a product or service.

ESSENTIAL COMPONENTS OF THE MOTIVATIONAL PROCESS

The essential components of the motivational process are shown in Figure 9.2. The starting point to this motivational process is the identification of a ▶ **need** ◀. There is a distinction between a need and a ▶ **want** ◀. A need is something that an individual must have in order to survive and is, therefore, physiological in nature, for example water, food and shelter. In this case, the employee will need money in order to satisfy these basic needs. However, s/he may want money for items which are not essential for physical survival, for example a digital versatile disc (DVD) player would be a want. In this text the word 'need' has been used to encompass both needs and wants.

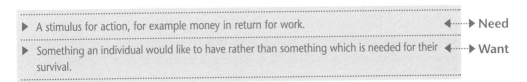

> ▶ A stimulus for action, for example money in return for work. ◀┈┈▶ Need

> ▶ Something an individual would like to have rather than something which is needed for their ◀┈┈▶ Want
> survival.

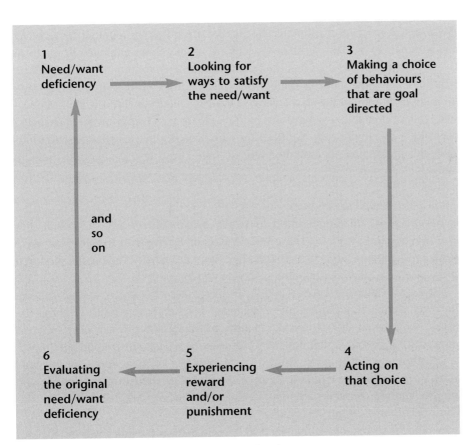

Figure 9.2 Essential components of the motivational process

Referring to Figure 9.2 a worker will first (1) experience a deficiency (or deficiencies) in a need and when these are strong enough s/he will then try to find a way to satisfy that deficiency (2), for example by finding a job which pays monetary rewards so that s/he can satisfy her/his physiological needs. The individual will then choose the best behaviour that will satisfy that goal (3), for example visit the job centre. However, while an individual may be directed in all behaviour to get a job, s/he will be faced with more than one option at the same time in order to achieve the desired end. For example, s/he may choose to follow a training course or visit various organisations personally in an attempt to secure a job. Whatever decision the individual makes, s/he will act on those choices (4) which will result in the experience of a reward (getting a paid job) or a punishment (maybe not getting a job because of lack of effort) (5). The final stage (6) is where s/he will assess the extent to which s/he has achieved her/his original need deficiency. If a job with enough financial reward to satisfy the required physiological needs has been secured, then the individual will have satisfied her/his particular need, remembering that it is an unsatisfied need that motivates an individual. The whole model becomes cyclical because an individual has many needs in play at any one time.

PRP and culture

Physiological needs are instinctive needs that are primarily required for survival and sustenance, whereas secondary needs are usually those exhibited in the form of psychological behaviours that are learned from the environment and the culture which the individual came or comes from. Theory-in-literature is mixed in its views on the suggestion that PRP has a place in bringing about the difficult, if not impossible, task of changing organisational culture. PRP is perceived as a way of changing the culture by emphasising the need for employee flexibility, willingness to innovate, the importance of customer service, only stressing the importance of the individual employee as opposed to the collective or disillusion with existing payment schemes.

It is a fact that all organisations have a culture and it is in many ways as much a characteristic of the organisation as is the personality of any individual. For example, Nike or Sony have characteristic ways of dealing with a problem or operating a procedure, which often strikes those who are new to the organisation and eventually impresses itself on a long-serving employee.

Just as individual personality is difficult to change so is organisational culture. However, change is not impossible to achieve – it is simply very difficult. This is the reason why, when PRP is introduced into an organisation, it can only function successfully either in a situation which already lays great stress upon the importance of the individual in the context of the organisation as a whole, for example Sony, or in a situation where it is one of a number of changes that reinforce one another and are conscious attempts to change the whole culture of the organisation, such as business process re-engineering (BPR).

It is the secondary needs that tend to be exhibited in the workplace and therefore they are very important when managers consider the motivation of their

SCENARIO 9.1

PRP for manual workers

A PRP scheme was introduced in Company A while attempts were being made to change the culture of the organisation under the title of 'Project 2000'. This project introduced:

- attitude surveys

- communication policies

- teamworking

- revised management methods

and thus the work culture which the organisation was trying to build was that of an OPEN system being:

Open thinking
Being creative in one's thinking and being bold enough to follow conclusions through with action.

Personal impact
Influencing others through personal example and recognition of their needs and aspirations.

Empowering
Getting others involved in teamwork and helping to build people's enthusiasm and skills.

Networking
Sharing items and information in order to get things done to the best of everyone's ability.

Adapted from: Brough, I. (1994) PRP for manual workers: issues and experience, *Employee Relations*, **12**, p29 (pp18–32).

workers and their level of performance – and thus their reward. Performance is a word which is very difficult both to define and to measure. Both motivation and performance are part of an employment relationship and by means of the psychological function a manager may well be able better to understand such a relationship ■ see Chapter 7 ■. The word ▶ **motive** ◀ comes from the Latin word for 'move' (*movere*) and it can vary in length and intensity. For example, the need to have a drink of water to satisfy a thirst when at work can normally be satisfied very quickly, yet a decision to find another job (maybe one with more financial reward) needs to be considered over a period of time. This is the reason why individuals act in one way or another. An individual's choice will depend upon her/his particular motive. Hence, there is a connection between needs, motives and behaviour:

see Chapter 7

- a *need* is a stimulus for action

- *motives* are the channels through which the individual thinks the need can best be satisfied

- manifestation of motives is actual *behaviour* – they are learned needs which influence an individual's behaviour by leading her/him to pursue goals because they are valued.

▶ The channel through which the individual thinks the need can best be satisfied thus ◀······▶ **Motive** reflecting the specific behavioural choices enacted by the individual.

This means that motivation can also be allied to ▶ **cognition** ◀ because through the process of knowledge acquisition and decision making an individual worker can choose her/his desired outcomes, and will thus set into motion the actions appropriate to achieving them. For example, if a worker decides s/he wants promotion it might be because s/he wants more money and/or more recognition – these are the needs. The individual will, therefore, decide to work longer hours and make all hours more productive so that s/he can attract the attention of the manager (benefits). The worker will then put in longer, more productive hours and work towards perfection (behaviours). This is what is called the goal-oriented aspect of motivation where an internal psychological process of:

■ initiating

■ energising

■ directing and

■ maintaining

goal-directed behaviour is brought about.

Cognition ◀┈┈▶ Individual thinking through which individuals decide to make changes in their lives.

Behaviour which is a purposeful activity is goal directed – it is very hard to find any behaviour which is not motivated. The underlying motives are conceptualised differently by different individuals because it depends upon their ▶ **perception** ◀.

Perception ◀┈┈▶ The process by which individuals interpret sensory impressions so that they can assign meaning to the environment.

DEVELOPMENT OF MOTIVATIONAL THEORIES

There are a number of theories put forward by many researchers but none of them is conclusive – there is no one theory which can be used as a model to motivate all individuals under all conditions. Although such theories do compete they all try to explain the nature of motivation itself. Some of them are partially true and comprise commonsense explanations of behaviour in the workplace but to identify a generalised theory of motivation would seem futile. However, an investigation of the key theories of motivation indicates a division into two contrasting approaches:

■ *content approaches* place the emphasis on *what* motivates

■ *process approaches* emphasise the *actual process* (or method) of motivation.

Because motivation is a complex area there is no one answer to what motivates individuals to work productively neither is there one to tell managers how to reward their employees. Different theories provide convenient frameworks within which attention can be directed to the issue of how to motivate individuals to work willingly and effectively towards the goals of the organisation. Since the complex and various theories are not conclusive, each having its own critics (particularly the content theories), or have been subjected to alternative findings claiming to contradict original ideas, it is essential that managers understand the different theories available with their accompanying implications for both the employer and the employee.

MOTIVATING INDIVIDUALS AND REWARDS

The issue of what motivates an individual to perform and how best to use rewards to bring out a higher performance from an individual is influenced by many variables. Each individual worker has a variety of changing (and conflicting) needs and expectations which s/he will attempt to satisfy in a number of different ways. There are three such needs and expectations that overlap as shown in Figure 9.3.

An individual expects to have:

- economic rewards
- intrinsic rewards and
- social relationships

as part of her/his workplace experience.

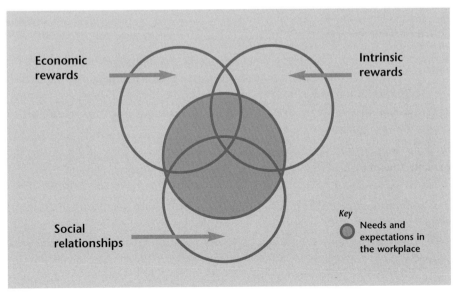

Figure 9.3 The overlap of individual needs and expectations

In addition to ▶ **economic rewards** ◀ and ▶ **intrinsic rewards** ◀, the aspect of ▶ **social relationships** ◀ is also important to every individual worker because each needs to be able to interact with other workers during their daily work. It is the lack of social relationships that is the key disadvantage of working from home rather than a shared workplace. These three components are not always equal, as Figure 9.3 might suggest, but they overlap to bring about a balanced working environment.

Economic ◀┄┄▶ A financial reward for work done which could include non-monetary benefits such as paid
rewards   holidays.

Intrinsic rewards ◀┄┄▶ Intangible rewards which derive from the experience of work itself, for example a sense of
                challenge and achievement, recognition and responsibility.

Social ◀┄┄▶ Interaction with other individuals.
relationships

When it comes to organisational rewards there are a few key theories that are of particular help to managers. These are all process theories, sometimes called *justice theories* of motivation because they concentrate on the cognitive process by assuming that individuals are conscious and active in how they learn, using past experiences as a basis for their current behaviour, because those individuals will make a decision about whether the ▶ **effort** ◀ is worth it. Such process theories suggest that an individual is motivated to gain what s/he feels is a fair return for her/his efforts in the workplace; that is, the role of justice theories as they relate to the employment

see Chapter 7   relationship ■ *see* Chapter 7 ■. However, as far as a reward for work is concerned, both *distributive justice* and *procedural justice* are important:

■ *Distributive justice* is related to an individual's belief that s/he has actually received a fair reward or anticipates that s/he will receive a fair reward.

■ *Procedural justice* describes a situation where an individual believes that the procedures for the allocation of rewards used within the organisation are fair. Folger and Konovsky (1989) started work in this area and their research indicates that distributive justice is becoming increasingly important to individuals in the workplace.

Effort ◀┄┄▶ A determined physical or mental exertion in order to achieve or create.

If an individual perceives that her/his pay is much lower relative to others doing a similar job in another organisation (or within the same organisation), s/he might well perceive distributive injustice. However, if s/he perceives that her/his own organisation is rewarding as much as is possible and the system for distributing such rewards is transparent and fair, s/he will probably perceive a situation of procedural justice. According to McFarlin and Sweeney (1992) such persons would be likely to have a low satisfaction related to pay but their commitment to their employer is likely to be high.

Equity theory of motivation (Adams, 1965)

A key theory having implications for managers when it comes to organisational rewards is equity theory, which is related to the potential rewards that are promised to an individual to fulfil her/his needs if s/he performs a given task. These act as a force to pull people into meeting the objectives of the organisation – hence the need for reward and remuneration issues to be part of the organisation's overall strategy within which managers should develop a remuneration policy that helps with the recruitment, retention and motivation of all employees. This justice theory was put forward by Adams (1965), who gave the name 'equity theory' to a simple assertion that members of any workforce wish to be treated fairly; in other words, it 'felt fair' to them as individuals. The theory centres on an individual's desire to be treated equitably in relation to others and to avoid inequality – the belief that s/he is being treated unfairly when compared with another individual. It is only one of the many facets of a social comparison process – Goodman (1977) stated that an individual evaluates her/his own situation in the context of the situation of another – the comparison-other. It is the most highly researched concept within the social comparison process, besides being a theory that is more plainly concerned with motivation in the workplace as related to rewards and remuneration.

An individual will tend to use a four-stage approach in the formation of her/his perceptions related to equity on, say, pay. For example, s/he will follow the following pattern:

1 evaluate what s/he is being paid by the organisation

2 evaluate how a comparison-other/s, for example someone in the same project team, is being paid by the organisation

3 compare the results of (1) and (2) above

4 experience equity or inequity.

The above procedure was supported by Huseman et al. (1989) who believed that an individual would thus balance her/his contribution to, and the reward for, a task by comparing their perceptions with those of others. Such an equity comparison is expressed in terms of an input–output ratio.

Inputs are what the individual brings with her/him, such as education, past experience, knowledge, loyalty and effort. *Outcomes* are what s/he receives in return (the rewards and remuneration), such as salary, social recognition and intrinsic rewards. Any assessment of input–outcome relationships will depend upon:

■ objective information such as salary, paid holiday entitlement

■ perceptive information such as the level of effort being made.

This comparison can be formulated as a psychological equation as in the four points above:

$$\frac{\text{Outcome (self)}}{\text{Input (self)}} \quad \text{compared with} \quad \frac{\text{Outcome (other)}}{\text{Input (other)}}$$

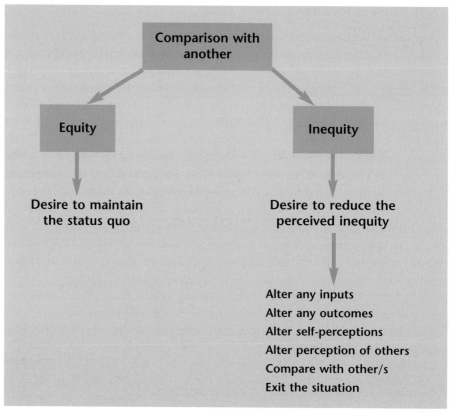

Figure 9.4 An individual's response to perceived equity and inequity

If both sides of the equation balance, the individual will then have experienced a sensation of equity. However, if there is an imbalance, then s/he will feel inequity. Adams (1965) makes the particular point that it really does not matter if the perceived outcomes and inputs are unequal because what is important is that the ratios are the same. For example, an individual member of the workforce may believe that the other person deserves a higher salary because s/he works harder – in this case, the individual has rationalised her view that the other person has an acceptable higher outcome–input ratio. If, however, s/he feels that her/his comparison-other has outcomes that are disproportional to her/his inputs, s/he will then perceive a level of inequality. This is shown in Figure 9.4.

If the individual perceives that there is an equity situation s/he will attempt to maintain that situation – to keep the status quo. Her/his input level will remain the same only so long as s/he perceives that her/his outcomes do not change and the inputs–outcomes of the comparison-other/s also remain constant. Should s/he perceive an initial inequality, or a situation of inequality occurs, s/he will be motivated to do something to bring about a state of equity by carrying out one of the following behaviours:

9.3

Activity

Identify a fellow worker or student with whom you are friendly and share a high degree of trust. Implement the equity theory of motivation as propounded by Adams (1965), that is:

$$\frac{\text{Outcome (yourself)}}{\text{Input (yourself)}} \quad \text{compared with} \quad \frac{\text{Outcome (your friend)}}{\text{Input (your friend)}}$$

What do the results tell you about the equity theory? How do you feel about the results – do you perceive them as equitable to you? What about your friend? If they are inequitable to both or either one of you, what could you do about it?

1 *Alter any inputs*

S/he could change any of her own inputs, for example by reducing her/his efforts. In this way, the ratio is altered and if s/he feels that the reward is insufficient then a further decrease in effort might be brought about.

2 *Alter any outcomes*

The individual may alter her/his perception of the current value of the outcomes and as a result s/he might well make a request for more pay or seek other areas where s/he can increase income. Some individuals even resort to activities such as theft and fraud in order to bring about a perceived equity.

3 *Alter self-perceptions*

This is a much more complicated response than (1) and (2) because when an individual has perceived the inequity, s/he may decide to alter the original assessment of her/his own input. In this way, it might be assessed that s/he is actually contributing less but receiving more outcome than was originally thought.

4 *Alter perceptions of others*

The individual may decide to amend her/his perception of the comparison-other's inputs and outcomes. For example, if s/he feels unrewarded for her/his own hard work and effort, s/he may well come to the view that her/his comparison-other is actually putting in more hours and achieving more tasks than s/he originally thought.

5 *Compare with others*

The individual can change the comparison-other. It could well be that s/he perceives that the original comparison-other has specific skills and talents and is not a fair person to use as a comparison. Thus another member of the workforce – who might give a more valid basis for comparison – is chosen.

6 *Exit the situation*

This is the last resort. An individual may feel that the level of equity perceived cannot be resolved and so the only way to gain equity is to leave the situation, for example by moving to another area of work within the same organisation or leaving the organisation altogether.

Huseman et al. (1989) found that some individuals were more likely than others to be sensitive to perceptions of inequality. Their research stated that some workers paid more attention to their relative value in an organisation than did their colleagues through the equity-based comparison process. Such others tend to be more personally focused on their own situation without regard to that of others.

Most of the research carried out in the field of equity theory has concentrated on a narrow band of concepts centred on pay compared with the quantity/quality of outcomes. Most of this work reinforces the view that people tend to resort to the practical use of equity theory when they perceive that they are underpaid.

Expectancy theory/VIE theory (Vroom 1964, 1970)

A second key process theory which relates very much to rewards and remuneration is expectancy theory wherein there are two principal researchers:

- Vroom (1964, 1970) – Expectancy theory/VIE theory

- Porter and Lawler (1968) – Expectancy theory.

The basic model was put forward by both Tolman (1932) and Lewin (1938). However, Vroom (1964, 1970) identified two key variables under the umbrella term 'expectancy theory', which is generally used for applying the theory to the workplace. These two key variables are:

- *Valence,* which is the anticipated reward from an outcome – the value or importance that an individual gives to a reward. It is concerned with what an individual expects from an outcome as opposed to the actual content and value of that outcome. The valence of an outcome may be directly related to the outcome desired – some individuals may desire higher wages because they like to accumulate money – or it may concentrate on the social standing that this outcome might confer: higher wages might bring an improved lifestyle and status.

- *Expectancy,* which is the perceived probability of performing sufficiently well to achieve the outcome and thus the reward – the belief of an individual that the more effort s/he puts in the higher her/his level of performance will be. Expectancy measures an individual's perception of the likelihood that his actions will be successful and lead, ultimately, to the rewards that meet his needs.

In measuring valence Vroom (1964, 1970) also introduced a third variable:

- *Instrumentality,* which is the calculation of the number and degree of rewards resulting from achieving an outcome – that is, the individual's performance is related to the rewards. It measures the degree to which performance of a task leads to the rewards that then fulfil the needs that first motivated the performance of the task. This measurement is determined by the relationship between first- and second-level outcomes.

The amalgamation of these three parts gives Vroom's (1970) theory the more usual name of the VIE theory (**V**alence, **I**nstrumentality, **E**xpectancy).

First-level outcomes are those related directly to the carrying out of the task itself, for instance its successful completion or an improved level of performance or productivity. Such outcomes must be related to organisational goals and be performance related, and can be contrasted with second-level outcomes, which are related to the benefits conferred by performance of the task, for example higher wages, promotion and recognition from superiors and colleagues. First-level outcomes are individual and needs related, describing the rewards conferred as a result of successful first-level outcomes.

The distinction Vroom (1964, 1970) makes between these outcomes is important. An individual would tend to be demotivated if either good performance (first-level outcome) does not lead to appropriate rewards (second-level outcomes) or such second-level outcomes do not seem to be related to quality of performance.

The overall calculation of motivational force needs to take account of the range of outcomes from a particular action, for instance, the possible isolation and unpopularity an individual might experience from colleagues as a result of being singled out for, say, promotion. Clearly, valence is dependent on instrumentality. If a person believes that good performance will not lead to the desired second-level outcomes, valence will be low.

The degree to which an individual is motivated to act is determined by a number of variables. First, the reward must be seen as appropriate and attractive in meeting a need. At the level of the individual, motivation is then determined by the ability to carry out the task required to achieve the reward and the perception of the effort needed to achieve that reward. If the effort required is seen as too great in relation to the ability to carry out the task and the attractiveness of the reward, the individual will not be motivated to act. Motivation, then, is based on the expectation that an individual has of the most favourable outcome.

Vroom (1964, 1970) consistently emphasised the distinction between performance of a task (first-level outcome) and the rewards that successful performance of that task might bring (second-level outcomes). Expectancy is focused on the achievement of first-level outcomes; instrumentality on the range of available second-level outcomes. He calculated the strength of individual motivation (M), the motivational force, as the sum of the products of the valences of all outcome (V) multiplied by the strength of expectancies that action will result in achieving these outcomes (E). He expressed this formulaically as:

$$M = (E \times V) \text{ where:}$$

M = motivation to behave

E = subjective probability or expectation that the behaviour will lead to a particular outcome

V = valence or strength of preference for the outcome.

Vroom (1970) later argued that while the strength or 'force' of an individual's motivation to act in a particular way can be expressed as a result of the above formula it did not take account all of the values involved. This is because in most situations there will be a number of different outcomes as a result of particular behaviours. For example, in the quest for more pay an individual may work harder and as a result this can affect, say, an individual's:

■ prospects for promotion

■ workplace friendships

■ status in the organisation

■ levels of personal fitness/tiredness and

■ social and family life.

Therefore, the equation needs to be summed across all these possible outcomes. Vroom (1970) amended his formula to read:

$$M \ = \ \frac{n \ (E \times V)}{\Sigma}$$

where Σ means 'summation – add up all the values (n) of the calculation in the brackets'.

It therefore takes into account all values: positive, neutral and negative.

POINTS TO PONDER

If behaviour depends on the outcomes that an individual personally values, and the expectations that a particular type of behaviour will lead to those outcomes, then it is possible to use expectancy theory to predict the answer to the question:

'Will I pass my HRM course?'

Expectancy model (Porter and Lawler, 1968)

Vroom's (1964) pioneering work was further developed by Porter and Lawler (1968) in their expectancy model which differs significantly from that of Vroom (1964) in that it considers the contribution of ▶ **roles** ◀, perceptions, abilities and ▶ **traits** ◀. At the start of the cycle of motivation, there is effort in one function of the value of the employee's potential reward (valence) and a perceived reward for that effort (expectancy). The individual combines this effort with her/his abilities, personality traits and role perceptions in order to determine actual performance. An individual's performance results in two kinds of rewards:

■ *Extrinsic rewards,* which are tangible outcomes. These are rewards that derive from the organisation itself and then act on individuals within the workforce. For example, the issue whether there should be parity of pay or individual

Roles ◀┈┈▶ Sets of expected behaviour patterns attributed to someone occupying a given position in a social unit such as an organisation.

Traits ◀┈┈▶ Characteristics, features or qualities that distinguish a particular person.

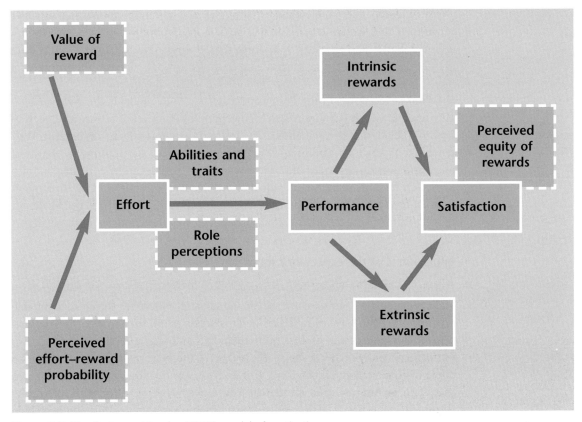

Figure 9.5 The Porter and Lawler (1968) model of motivation

bonuses based on performance, changes in the content and responsibility of duties, or the nature of management supervision.

- *Intrinsic rewards,* which are intangible. They derive from the experience of work itself for each individual. Examples here might be a sense of challenge and achievement, recognition and responsibility.

The Porter and Lawler (1968) model of motivation can be seen in Figure 9.5.

An individual judges the value of her/his performance to the organisation and then uses the social comparison process to form an impression of the equity of the rewards received. There is an effect on subsequent behaviour by the individual because actual performance following effort influences future perceived effort–reward probabilities.

Porter and Lawler (1968) argue that it is important to have both types of reward for effective motivation, but that intrinsic rewards are more likely to produce job satisfaction than extrinsic rewards. They recognise that the relative importance of the two types of reward is ▶ **contingent** ◀ on the job itself – if the nature of the

---

▶ Conditional or dependent upon. ◀┈┈▶ **Contingent**

work is varied and challenging, it provides the potential for strong intrinsic rewards. If not, extrinsic rewards will be a more important factor in motivation, although Porter and Lawler (1968) argue that, if this is the case, overall motivation may be weaker. They also suggest that extrinsic rewards do not often provide a direct link to performance – a significant issue when considering PRP.

A final key variable in the Porter and Lawler (1968) model is the *perceived equitable rewards,* which is an individual's perception of the level of reward s/he feels to be fair in relation to the demands of the job and the effort s/he has expended. They pointed out that, in awarding what they consider to be appropriate rewards, managers need to be aware of not just what they consider to be equitable but also how such rewards relate to individual and collective perceptions of fair treatment: if actual rewards fall short of perceived equitable rewards, individuals will be demotivated. Failure here could, therefore, invalidate the whole process of motivation.

Implications of the expectancy theory

The result of the intrinsic and extrinsic rewards measured against performance and mediated by a framework of individual and collective perceived equitable rewards is a given level of satisfaction. Satisfaction is not the same as motivation – it is the outcome of the process of motivation – and only affects performance if it informs the individual's sense of the value of the rewards that result from the effort to achieve a given objective. If it does so, an individual will be encouraged to sustain or improve that effort. The continued value of the reward, driven by sustained levels of satisfaction, must remain high compared to effort and perceived equitable rewards.

Expectancy theory is complicated and difficult to test: accurate measuring is very difficult and can thus invalidate the theory – especially if viewed as a scientific ▶ **paradigm** ◀. Also, it assumes that individuals are rational and objective whereas they are more likely to be irrational and lack objectivity. The very fact that expectancy theory is complex makes it hard to apply to the workforce and so implications and applications are complex to assess. A manager would need to:

- be aware of what rewards are wanted by each employee as an individual

- be aware of how valuable the rewards are to that individual

- adjust the relationships in order to create motivation.

Paradigm ◀┈▶ A pattern or model.

Regardless of such criticisms, the theory is valid according to researchers on work motivation such as Nadler and Lawler (1983) and Pinder (1984) who believed that some of the fundamental guidelines for managers include:

- determining the primary outcomes each employee wants

- deciding what levels and kinds of performance are needed to meet organisational goals

- making sure the desired levels of performance are possible

- linking desired outcomes and desired performance

- analysing the situation for conflicting expectancies

- making sure the rewards are large enough

- making sure the overall system acknowledges performance.

Reinforcement theory

Reinforcement theorists believe that the behaviour of an individual is caused by her/his environment; that is, behaviour is a function of its consequences. This behaviouristic approach takes the view that the internal, cognitive happenings of an individual are of no consequence but that behaviour is controlled by ▶ **reinforcers** ◀.

▶ Any consequence that, if immediately followed by a response, increases the probability that ◀····▶ **Reinforcers** the behaviour will be repeated.

This theory takes no account of the inner state of the individual but simply concentrates on what happens to the individual when s/he takes some kind of action. This means that, while reinforcement theory cannot strictly be called a theory of motivation, it can be used as a motivational approach and give an insight into how people learn. Take Activity 9.4 as an example – is the lecturer's response different when the answer is not correct or not what was expected?

Strict adherence to reinforcement theory means that the internal components of the individual, such as her/his feelings, attitudes, expectations, as well as other variables, will affect her/his behaviour. Looking at Activity 9.4 – will a student's response depend upon how s/he is actually feeling? Reinforcement theorists believe not. Some researchers (Locke, 1980) have reviewed experiments carried out by reinforcement theorists and then interpreted them within their own cognitive framework; that is, they used the experiments in an attempt to show that internal factors (feelings, attitudes, expectations) are present.

9.4
Activity

During a class session, a seminar or a tutorial observe how the lecturer reinforces correct responses to her/his questions.

Reinforcement has an important place when related to rewards and remuneration because how an individual behaves at work and the level of effort s/he puts to her/his job may well be affected by the consequences that follow after that particular behaviour has taken place. High-quality productivity could be reinforced by some sort of reward – financial or otherwise. However, it may not be quite that straightforward because if the individual is outperforming her/his colleagues, the likely response is that the individual will reduce her/his own productivity – although there are other considerations such as the goals the individual has in aiming for equity and, perhaps, her/his expectations.

Cognitive evaluation theory

The ▶ **cognitive evaluation theory** ◀ has considerable implications on how individuals are paid for their work. Over the years motivation researchers assumed that intrinsic motivators, such as pay or non-financial rewards, were the key to productivity. They thought that if one was stimulated it would affect the other. That is, if an individual was given extrinsic rewards s/he would be intrinsically motivated and vice versa. The cognitive evaluation theory suggests that the exact opposite is the case by arguing that when an employer uses extrinsic rewards, the intrinsic rewards, which come about when the worker is doing what s/he enjoys doing, are reduced. That is, when an individual is given extrinsic rewards for doing something that they enjoy doing, it results in the intrinsic interest in the task itself declining.

Cognitive evaluation ◀┈┈▶ theory

Allocating extrinsic rewards for behaviour that had previously intrinsically rewarded an individual tends to decrease the overall level of motivation.

The key here is to be able to appreciate *why* there is such an outcome. It is commonly believed that with the extrinsic reward for something the individual intrinsically enjoys doing comes a feeling that s/he has lost control over her/his own behaviour. This has the knock-on effect of reducing the original level of intrinsic reward. Conversely, the loss of extrinsic rewards can produce movement from external to internal in the way that an individual perceives s/he works at a task.

If the cognitive evaluation theory is to be believed then the implications in the field of rewards and remuneration are major. For many years experts in the field of reward and remuneration believed that if extrinsic motivators, such as pay, are

POINTS TO PONDER

Consider the reading of this textbook. Are you reading it only because your lecturer has told you to? If you are, then your behaviour might well be attributed to an external source.

If you find yourself reading similar books, then you could find you say 'I must enjoy reading HRM texts because I'm still reading them when I don't have to!' That is an internal source.

to be effective as motivators then they should be made contingent to an individual's performance, for example the payment an individual receives must be dependent on the level of performance achieved. However, a supporter of the cognitive evaluation theory would say that this latter view would be likely to decrease the level of internal satisfaction that the individual enjoys from doing the job. What has happened here is that an internal stimulus has been replaced by an external one. It follows then that it would be sensible to ensure that pay is not contingent on performance in order to avoid decreasing intrinsic motivation. These issues are of key concern to the issue of PRP which is discussed later in this chapter.

There are supporters and critics for all theories and the cognitive evaluation theory is no exception. Further research is required but the theory does guide the manager to the conclusion that the interdependence of extrinsic and intrinsic rewards is important. However, as time goes on, its impact on rewards and remuneration in the workplace may not be seen to be as significant as it might be now. The query lies over the manner in which the research itself was actually carried out – with students and not with those employed by an organisation – the study did not represent the real workplace situation.

The theory can only be helpful because in the world of work, if extrinsic rewards cease, it is usually because the individual has left the employment of the organisation. Arnold (1976) started his research in this area and concluded that very high levels of intrinsic motivation are strongly resistant to the detrimental impacts of extrinsic rewards – which is contrary to the central belief of cognitive evaluation theory.

Calder and Staw (1977), working in the same area, reported that when a task was dull, repetitive and boring, intrinsic motivation was stimulated and increased by the use of extrinsic payments. Staw (1977) also reported that even if the task was marginally intrinsically rewarding, extrinsic payments still appear to be a powerful feature.

The conclusion to be drawn here is that cognitive behaviour theory may well have a limited, yet important, application in the workplace because most low-level tasks are not intrinsically satisfying enough to bring about high internal interest and many managerial and professional positions do offer intrinsic rewards such as a sense of recognition or achievement. The theory, however, may have its key contribution to make when considering the rewards and remuneration for individuals whose jobs fall in between the two, that is, jobs which are neither extremely dull or boring nor extremely interesting.

Cognitive dissonance theory (Festinger, 1957)

Leon Festinger (1957) was the proponent of ▶ **cognitive dissonance theory** ◀, that is, an inconsistency between attitude and attitude, or behaviour and attitude.

> ▶ Any incompatibility between two or more attitudes or between behaviour and attitudes, that is, an inconsistency.

◀┈┈▶ **Cognitive dissonance theory**

While the theory is particularly concerned with behaviour and attitude, it does have a bearing on rewards. Robbins (1998) described cognitive dissonance as:

> any incompatibility that an individual might perceive between two or more of his or her attitudes or between his or her behavior and attitudes. (p144)

The important issue is that of perception since no two individuals will perceive attitudes and behaviour in the same way – their interpretation will be different. Festinger (1957) believed that an individual would try to reduce any form of such inconsistency which makes them feel uncomfortable because by doing so s/he will be more comfortable. In this way, the individual will search for a position which is stable so that there is as little dissonance as possible.

While this is the ideal it is not always achievable – it is the amount of influence that an individual feels s/he has over it that is important. Related to rewards, these influence the degree to which an individual is motivated. If there is a high level of dissonance – especially if it is of a type over which the individual has no control – an individual might find her/his tension reduced if the rewards are high. Thus, rewards can help to reduce dissonance because the individual is compensating for the disturbance s/he is experiencing – the rewards become a moderating factor.

Care should be taken when considering the use of reward schemes because reward schemes are not an end in themselves. The use of such schemes relies on the relationship between an employer and the employee and if this breaks down the reward system alone cannot repair the bridge. In other words, the use of employee benefits is not the key to securing staff loyalty and motivation.

RESPONDING TO REWARDS

There are a number of variables which determine how people respond to rewards. A key issue is the tension between an individual's ability and her/his perception of the effort needed to achieve the reward. If the required effort is seen as too great in relation to the individual's ability, s/he will be discouraged, especially, although not exclusively, if her/his need is not sufficiently strong. Such a perception may counterbalance both the need and the attractiveness of the reward, which will now seem unattainable.

All organisations have easily identifiable rewards in the formal sense: pay and the assignment of tasks. They also have more informal rewards (such as intrinsic satisfaction, self-worth, achievement) which are very difficult to identify – let alone measure. The difficulty is that it is the latter that are frequently at the core of an individual's perceptions when s/he comes to assessing her/his perception of equity. Such social comparisons are increasingly becoming a powerful feature of the workplace.

Moorhead and Griffin (1995) identify three clear messages for managers:

1   The basis of the reward system must be transparent in that it needs to be understood by everyone. If quantity is going to be rewarded rather than quality, that needs to be clearly communicated to all members of the workforce.

2   Rewards are perceived as being multifaceted because individuals get different rewards: some tangible (pay) and some intangible (achievement).

3   People have a differing understanding of what reality is – based on their perception. For example, a team leader may know that her/his team members are being fairly rewarded, but the members themselves may not agree.

Theories are often complicated when applied to the workplace. Dornstein (1988) reinforced this view by stating that individuals in the workplace have a wide choice of strategies by which to establish their equity and their comparison-other choice and although individuals often choose similar workers as a comparison, they do not *always* do so.

The equity theories put forward by Adams (1965) and Vroom (1964, 1970) together with the expectancy model of Porter and Lawler (1968) have been developed over time and have become much more difficult to measure. Organisations are now competing in a complex world with globalisation, work diversity and social responsibility being key considerations and so rewards and remunerations must take this into account.

REWARD SYSTEMS AND DECISION MAKING

The organisation itself can constrain decision makers, and the reward system is one case in point because it will influence them by suggesting to them what choice is preferable in terms of their own pay off, that is, which choice will be to their own personal benefit. An example here would be if an organisation rewarded those who avoided any risk taking, then an individual is more likely to make cautious decisions because the reward system favours those whose decisions preserve the established customs and values of the organisation.

SALARY INCREASES

This is a factor of organisational culture and two of the most popular criteria for deciding who should have a rise and when are:

■   length of service and

■   performance.

These two factors are evaluated by senior management and the organisation is often likely to end up with large numbers of long-serving middle and senior managers who may well be conservative and unadventurous because they have no reward for creativity and risk taking. There could also be a climate of dysfunctional conflict between the employee and the supervisor who makes the decision as to who gets what in the form of pay rises. The usual practice is to determine salary increases by means of a rigid and published pay structure that tends to become ingrained within the organisation. If pay increases are left to the discretion of senior managers, then the organisation is likely to comprise a culture of close personal relationships, the formation of cliques and an upsurge in self-serving activities related to the potential of gaining an increase in pay.

PROFIT-RELATED PAY

The Workplace Employee Relations Survey (WERS) (1999) reports that almost half of private sector workplaces receive some form of profit-related pay. Burt (1999) reports that DaimlerChrysler workers are seeking a boost in their profit sharing in the first challenge to the German–USA automotive group's new management team. Workers at DaimlerChrysler's Mercedes plants felt that the existing profit-sharing scheme was unfair because it only awarded rewards to employees according to profitability at the group's Mercedes division, that is, it was not organisation wide.

With profit-related pay part of an employees' pay is based on the profit which her/his organisation makes. In the UK the profit-related element of employees' pay, in schemes that satisfy the requirements of tax legislation and are registered with the Inland Revenue, gets favourable tax treatment, although this is being phased out. The percentage of profit to be allocated for profit-related pay has to be set up before an organisation starts a scheme. Individual employees are able to receive up to 20 per cent of their annual pay tax free up to a maximum of £4000. In January 1998 that maximum came down to £2000 and in 1999 it became £1000 ready for its abolition in 2000. This means that the government profit-related scheme has been phased out, the last year of its operation being 1999–2000, but employers can still devise their own schemes, although tax breaks will no longer be available.

The key argument against the scheme was that under the rules organisations have to give every employee in the scheme a share of the bonus regardless of whether s/he has been an excellent or a poor performer. It is because of this fact that most organisations prefer to use bonus schemes or PRP that can be more directly based on the contribution that an employee has actually made.

REMUNERATION PACKAGES FOR KNOWLEDGE WORKERS

see Chapter 2 *and* Chapter 6 *and* Chapter 10

One of the largest problems within organisations is the lack of individuals with the skills required to work in an environment which is increasingly based on ever-changing information technology ■ *see* Chapter 2, Chapter 6 *and* Chapter 10 ■. Organisations have to be even more creative concerning the way that they reward and remunerate workers who are highly skilled and talented – these people are called 'knowledge workers' and are highly educated, intelligent people who are not motivated by extrinsic factors such as money and cars. They are more concerned with the intrinsic returns for their work such as autonomy, flexibility and responsibility. Because such workers are in short supply all organisations have to work very hard at recruiting such staff and even harder at keeping them. In the past this was done by offering extrinsic rewards such as a car, or membership of a health or golf club, but this no longer works because organisations can continue to compete in this area and can always be outbid by someone else. Some sort of creative thinking has to be done by organisations in order to keep their knowledge workers who are the hub of contemporary business. Such individuals are not concerned with extrinsic rewards and are more excited by such things as personal satisfaction and values including the colleagues they have and the opportunity to take risks, make mistakes and learn from them.

REWARD PACKAGES

There is a wide continuum of rewards being used by organisations, which vary from the use of gift vouchers, for example Next store vouchers, luncheon vouchers, eyecare vouchers and childcare vouchers, to complex competence-related pay schemes that reward the employee for the skills and behaviours they bring to their job and thus to the achievement of the objectives of the organisation for which s/he works.

The most widely used reward strategy is PRP which started off as a simple system of rewarding individuals if they met the stated job criteria – usually through the ticking of a box on a form. Nowadays, it is much more complex and organisations are tending to adopt a broader definition of performance and more clarity around how performance is actually appraised. They are looking to create some sort of legitimate variability so that it is actually worthwhile for individuals to perform highly.

SHARE OWNERSHIP

Employees are often rewarded based on the performance of the organisation for which they work and two of the ways in which such organisations can reward their employees financially are:

- profit sharing
- employee stock ownership plans (ESOPs).

The first comprehensive survey of employee relations under the Labour government – the Workplace Employee Relations Survey (WERS) (1999) – reports that 30 per cent of workplaces have profit-sharing schemes for non-managers and 15 per cent share ownership for non-managers – this comprises about 2000 organisations in the UK – mostly large ▶ **blue chip** ◀. Share ownership has moved away from the provision of an 'extra reward' to a philosophy of being a central part of payment to workers. The UK Labour government has supported such a philosophy by offering tax breaks to those employees who participate in share ownership. The Chancellor of the Exchequer's 'shares for all' declaration in the March 1999 budget has, however, been received sceptically by those who have scrutinised the details.

▶ A stock considered reliable with respect to both dividend income and capital value. ◀┈┈▶ **Blue chip**

The principal concern is that the new scheme could well lead to the abolition of existing employee share schemes with which the government is not satisfied because they do not promote their objective of increasing productivity by encouraging wider share ownership and long-term shareholding by employees. This is because in most cases the employees sell their shares immediately and are, therefore, not exposed to risk.

Remuneration experts think that the government may well stop the facility for employees to participate in the Share-As-You-Earn scheme which is operated by a large number of organisations. While the risk is considered to be remote the new scheme commenced in April 2000 when the government still felt that organisations would use share ownership to reward productivity and performance effectively. The new system allows employees to buy up to £1500 worth of shares each year with the organisation matching them with a maximum of £3000 of free shares. The system offers tax incentives and payroll savings for employers so that they are encouraged to participate in the scheme – shareholders can avoid tax if they keep their shares for ten years before selling and tax breaks are given to employers if they match their employees' investments.

The government wants to double the number of organisations that offer shares to all employees but it is unlikely to meet this objective unless it can find ways of interesting smaller firms and those that are not quoted on the stock exchange. It is imperative that these small and medium-sized enterprises (SMEs) participate in the scheme because such firms comprise most of the UK's employers. The problem is that the scheme could be expensive to administer and SMEs do not have the resources. Administration charges could, therefore, become a disincentive to move into share ownership schemes. There is also the concern as to how share ownership could affect pensions since it has the potential to divert employees' savings away from company pension funds.

Most employee share ownership schemes have fallen short of their aims and the UK's rate of employee share ownership is half the level of the USA.

Larger firms, such as British Airways (BA), already have a scheme in operation. In BA, 88 per cent of employees joined the share scheme and the company is hoping, according to Walters (1999), performance management and reward consultant at BA, to:

> influence the legislation... pleased that the government is doing this, but the proposed framework is different to our scheme. We are still digesting its implications. (p16)

However, the poor financial performance of BA is threatening the value of the such shares.

A leading company in the business technology field, FI Group plc, is passionate about giving its employees a stake in the company. Ninety five per cent of its employees own shares in the business with over 40 per cent of their equity – the value of their ordinary shares – being held by members of the workforce and their associated companies. Lucas (1999) reports that employees can:

> choose from a menu of three different schemes which enable them to buy shares at special discounted rates and build up their stake in the company over time. (p11)

A share ownership programme has to be managed effectively if it is to provide a positive reward for employees. For example, at FI Group plc, before the annual general meeting (AGM), managers tour the various sites to explain all the resolutions to be discussed at the AGM and to encourage all the members of the workforce to vote.

There appears to be a strong link between share ownership and business success. The business at FI Group plc has grown 50 per cent per year for the last five years and in 1998 the company was top of the FTSE 500 'highest, fastest risers'. They have outperformed their competitors and as a result the employees have each had a maximum payout of ten per cent of their salary which they could take in the form of cars or additional shares in the company.

Those who support share ownership as a reward mechanism believe that when individuals are given a stake in the company in which they work, they have an increased motivation to succeed and their contribution to the company's performance is higher. Such improved performance results in a more competitive environment and increased business. FI Group plc also report that their staff turnover has decreased and is lower than the average in the information technology area.

London (1999) reports on employee share ownership in a contemporary arena. If employees want to buy shares in their company, all things being equal, they probably will not want to unless they have secure information as to the confirmed success of the organisation – and, thus, its shares. Individual workers rely on the organisation for their salary and bonuses and so there is care on behalf of the employee not to put all their eggs in the one basket – which could be rather unstable. However, the UK government has offered tax incentives to encourage employees to take the risk because they believe that share ownership is a good thing and is worth pushing – as shown in Table 9.3 – by offering some attractive tax breaks for the employee investor.

The 1999 proposals were put forward because none of the previous initiatives encouraged employees to become worker–shareholders. Some individuals who work for large organisations have benefited from the Share-As-You-Earn scheme

Table 9.3 History of UK government encouragement in share ownership schemes

TIME	GOVERNMENT ACTION	AIM
1978	Approved profit-sharing scheme	Lets employers give free shares to any employee at any level as a bonus.
1980	Share-As-You-Earn share option scheme	Employees able to take some of their remuneration in the form of shares in their company.
1984	Company Share Option Plan (CSOP)	Special plan for senior executives who wish to take out shares in their company.
1999	Employee Share Ownership Plan (ESOP) and Enterprise Management Incentive (EMI)	Proposed by UK government.

Table 9.4 Old versus new in executive option schemes

	MAXIMUM SIZE OF COMPANY	NUMBER OF OPTION HOLDERS	MAXIMUM LIMIT	INDIVIDUAL EXERCISE PRICE FOR TAX PURPOSES	HOLDING PERIOD
Company Share Option Plan (CSOP)	None	None	£30 000	Not less than market price on grant	3 years
Enterprise Management Initiative (EMI)	Gross assets of £15m	10	£100 000	Any price (including nil) but discount to price on grant subject to tax	No minimum period

but those who are employed by SMEs have not had the opportunity to participate. In fact, many organisations have not even offered share schemes that are UK government approved. Early reports seem to indicate that the Enterprise Management Initiative (EMI) will be attractive to senior executives, as shown in Table 9.4, but these are very few in number. It is the Employee Share Ownership Plan (ESOP) which is less likely to be effective.

see Chapter 2 The use of share ownership needs to be part of a strategic management move ■ *see* Chapter 2 ■. In May 1999 the US investment bank Goldman Sachs gave every worker, from chairman and chief executive down to the door guards, shares in the organisation. The sums involved were not miniscule with low-grade workers getting around £20 000 each and the banks 221 partner's sharing £20 million thus making the shareout £3.5 billion. What is unusual about this is the fact that such an action is unprecedented in that all members of the workforce received a windfall, not just the top management. It has been reported (Rana, 1999a) that the change from private partnership to employee ownership is based on the belief that staff motivation would be increased by the change. This, it is believed, will have the knock-on effect of maintaining the highest reputation of the leading investment bank in a market which is becoming increasingly competitive.

The employees of Goldman Sachs will not be able to sell their shares until the year 2002 but they can exchange a third of them for cash each year over the next three years. Employers believe that share ownership is an ideal way to secure and maintain employees' loyalty and commitment for the next three years because if an employee leaves the firm before the three-year period is up, s/he has to relinquish her/his shares.

However, there is another reason – other than motivational – why Goldman Sachs went public and introduced share ownership. Guest (1999) believes that it might well be concerned with:

appeasing the consciences of those at the top who are getting vast amounts of money. (p15)

This view could well be supported by the fact that staff at Goldman Sachs' Fleet Street headquarters in London were aggrieved because there was inequity between their payout and that of their partners. Rana (1999a) stated:

> While most employees received half their annual salary and bonus in shares, plus $1000 (£620) for each year of service, Goldman Sach's 221 partners netted breathtaking amounts. (p15)

A partner and government adviser in Goldman Sachs, Gwyn Davies, saw his £25 million worth of shares increase to £33 million on the first day of trading.

Guest (1999) believes that the initial resentment will not last long, relating this to equity theory:

> we tend to be much more annoyed over time by people who are close comparators to us. If the person working next to you gets more and you feel they don't deserve it then you're going to feel aggrieved. But it is unlikely to effect the way you perform at work. (p15)

Small organisations also use share ownership schemes for their employees. Such a scheme is used within recruitment and retention in a family-owned facilities management firm Williams Lea. They introduced the scheme in an attempt to give their 1300 employees a sense of belonging and to use employee ownership as a key driving force for the organisation. The firm had a problem in retaining workers in both low- and high-skilled areas and wanted to ensure a long-term commitment from both. They had an executive share option scheme in place and felt that it was unfair to have one reward scheme for the executives and nothing for the other workers.

In 1997 they offered their Share-As-You-Earn share scheme and made the first annual presentations to all workers on the scheme prior to the AGM – just as FI Group plc, discussed above. They also recognised that there needed to be small reward presentations to individuals or teams for their achievements. There has been a positive impact on retention and morale as a result of employee share ownership but management seems to want to ensure that things remain fair and equitable – a feeling that seems to be held by all organisations using share ownership.

In his pre-budget report, Gordon Brown, the UK Chancellor of the Exchequer, outlined proposals to offer the 'most generous' ever incentives for employee share ownership. He believes that it is an incentive for employees to have a share in their company and that the more tax efficient it is, the better. Critics believe that such incentives will be clawed back, but the system should give organisations flexibility to reward employees. What is important is that it is closely linked to organisational performance.

Beattie (1999) discusses the arguments for and against the UK government's proposals to encourage share ownership and states that:

> There is not much evidence that giving workers shares does much for productivity. (p6)

CONTEMPORARY PAY STRATEGIES

There are two other reward strategies which are becoming popular in the workplace:

- competence-related pay

- team reward.

Competence-related pay is very difficult to define and is different to all people. Maybe this is its attraction – its versatility. Such pay schemes are unusual and the definition differs from actual practice and between organisations. However, the common tenet is that the concentration is not only on rewarding individuals for how they do their job but also on the results which they achieve: that is, performance and production. Edelsten (1999) believes that competence-related pay is about looking at jobs as three stages: 'development, target and super performance' (p11). He also believes that it is essential to take into account the behaviour that is required from individuals at each of those stages. His example is:

[to move away from] this job involves managing five people

to

what kind of behaviours and social interactions do we expect from people in a particular job at a particular level. (p12)

Team reward

The use of team rewards is discussed a great deal in organisations although only about 8 per cent of organisations have attempted to use it in any formal way. Trist and Bamforth (1951) reported on their work with the then newly nationalised coalmines and highlighted the problems in applying tidy engineering theories to the ever-changing, real life interaction of high technology, social and pay variables which are involved in any team-based activity – in theory, production goes up yet, in practice, it goes down. It was the social factors which were crucial to the effectiveness of the reward system in this case.

Lucas (1999) cites AXA Sun Life as a pioneer of team reward systems, who introduced them in the early 1990s in order to underpin a major business process re-engineering (BPR) related to how the company provided customer support. The system has evolved into one of giving team bonuses that cover the 3500 clerical workers within the organisation. Team reward has to be measured against some sort of criteria and in the case of AXA Sun Life this comprises the use of measurement criteria such as:

- quality

- quantity

- turnround times

- feedback on customer service.

Each team is expected to relate these measures in the two key areas of:

- customer service and

- budgetary management.

In their research on team incentive schemes, Hoffman and Rogelberg (1999) state that:

> The arguments of compensation experts regarding team incentive systems are clear: team incentive systems, in some form, are generally necessary to facilitate optimal team performance. (p5)

Other theory in research seems to support this view (Geber, 1995; Gross, 1995; Team Pay Case Studies, 1997).

With teams comprising 8 to 12 people, the organisation uses a divisional and corporate element within the bonus element. When it comes to the annual payout to the teams the amount depends mostly upon how well the individual's team has done. However, also taken into account is how successful the division within which the team works has done and how well the organisation has performed overall. Such a bonus scheme can allow organisations to concentrate on focusing individual's efforts each year on those areas which actually need improving, that is, working towards organisational goals.

According to the IPD (1996):

> Team reward is a just and equitable way to acknowledge the contribution made by people as team members or individuals. (p1)

The IPD believes that organisations can use team rewards in order to recognise and demonstrate that they value their contribution to high performance and they can be concentrated on any priorities, such as:

- quality

- customer service

- innovation and

- cooperation.

Their research on team rewards in 98 organisations in the UK brought about 11 key conclusions, which are given in Table 9.5.

However, the IPD (1996) does make the important point that team performance will not depend on rewards alone but that the quality of teamwork depends upon:

- culture

- values

- structure and operating processes

- performance management and

- employee development programmes.

Table 9.5 Key points from research into team pay carried out by the IPD (1996)

- Formal team pay schemes exist in only 24 per cent of those surveyed.
- Team pay is being considered by 47 per cent of the respondents.
- It is not possible to prescribe a standard model or approach as there are so many different types of teams and schemes.
- There are stringent conditions for the introduction of team pay – this is thought to account for the small number of schemes in the survey.
- The mechanics of the team pay schemes are less important for success than management style, culture and the working environment.
- Teams are able to plan and implement their own improvement programmes if they receive feedback and meet regularly to discuss performance.
- Over 50 per cent of organisations with team pay believe it is improving performance.
- For many people, the extent to which team pay should replace individual performance-related pay is an unresolved issue.
- Alongside team bonuses, some organisations are considering or introducing, individual skills or competence rewards for personal contribution.
- Many organisations are including teamworker capability as a key 'input' factor in performance management systems.
- Some individuals expressed the opinion that team pay is either inadequate or inappropriate for performance improvement. Other forms of reward should be used instead of, or in conjunction with, team pay.

Source: IPD, 1996, Team Reward, *Key Facts*, September, pp2–3.

Table 9.6 The advantages and disadvantages of team pay

Advantages
- can encourage cooperative work and behaviour
- clarifies goals and priorities at team and organisational level
- emphasises flatter and process-based organisations
- acts as a lever for organisational change
- encourages flexible working and multiskilling
- collectively improves performance and team processes
- encourages the less effective to meet the team standards
- develops self-managed and directed teams

Disadvantages
- best applied to well-defined and mature teams
- diminishes individual self-worth
- masks individual team contribution
- compels individuals to conform to oppressive group norms
- results in low output which is sufficient only to gain a reasonable reward
- causes difficulties when developing performance measures which are fair
- shifts problems of uncooperative behaviour from individuals in teams to the relationships between teams
- prejudices organisational flexibility – cohesive and high-performance teams may be unwilling to change

Source: IPD, 1996, Team Reward, *Key Facts*, September, p3.

Like other writers the IPD (1996) does not believe that there has been proof that team pay is cost-effective for white-collar employees and supports the view that there has been more talk about team pay than there has been action on implementing it – it can fail because of the wrong time of implementation. However, they do believe that team reward, in principle, should not be dismissed because its success lies in the belief that it works, especially in situations where team pay is supported with non-financial rewards such as positive feedback, praise and recognition. Team reward schemes cannot be of one design because each scheme is unique and they are hard to design and manage. The advantages and disadvantages of team pay are given in Table 9.6.

The IPD (1996) recommends that organisations have an action plan before they implement team rewards, as shown in Table 9.7.

Within most organisations an individual will be paid a personal wage/salary. However, there are cases when a decision has to be made how to pay individuals when they are a member of a work team – especially when it comes to the payment of bonuses. If rewards are paid to individuals rather than the team as a whole, then the individual might well feel that s/he should behave in a manner which best furthers his/her individual interests rather than those of the team as a whole. Conversely, if the whole team is given the reward, there comes the difficulty of how that reward should be divided among the team members. Rewarding individuals is a very sensible idea if the organisation is based on sales, say the Ann

Table 9.7 Action plan for implementing team rewards

- Assess the need for and determine if the organisation is ready for team rewards. Identify teams, set objectives and consult employees.

- Consider the options, either team pay and/or non-financial rewards. Design the scheme with employees' help and communicate details.

- Conduct training in managing team rewards and in team building. Introduce team rewards, monitor and evaluate.

- It is essential to develop and introduce team pay with great care. The complementary impact of non-financial rewards should always be acknowledged. Good teamwork may be enhanced by the reward system but there are other ways of developing it too:

  - Describe and think of the organisation's functions as processes carried out by interlocking teams. Devise communications which develop identification. Emphasise the key values of constructive teamwork. Ensure the purpose and objectives of teams are clearly defined.

  - Create teams which are largely self-managed, where short-term objectives are set and performance is measured. Take care to appoint and train team leaders who will achieve results and develop the team.

  - Use training to improve team processes. Set overlapping or interlocking team objectives in the form of targets or projects to be completed.

  - Assess individual performance on results and team player effectiveness. Set up cross-functional teams with a brief to get on with the job.

Source: IPD, 1996, Team Reward, *Key Facts*, September, p3.

Summers organisation, where what is good for the individual is correlated to that of the organisation. However, in areas where creativity is required and teamwork is essential, the whole team has to be rewarded.

Bonuses

Bonuses can be used to reward both individuals and teams – or the entire workforce – for their achievements. They are paid when specified objectives, targets or standards are met or exceeded. They can be discretionary or contractual and are usually paid in a lump sum monthly, quarterly, half-yearly or annually. They can be restricted to particular teams such as high-performance teams, executives or members of the salesforce. Kerr and Slocum (1987) believe that:

> Issues such as how large a proportion of total compensation bonuses should be, who decides who should receive a bonus, and whether the size of the bonus awarded should vary with length of service or seniority. (p137)

Considerable thought needs to be given to the issue of how bonuses are used in organisations and their potential impact on the employees and the culture of the organisation.

In Germany and the Netherlands there is a preference for individual rather than team bonus schemes while in the UK and Scandinavia the reverse is true (Adkin et al., 1997, p37). Organisations in the Mediterranean rarely operate bonus schemes.

If an organisation is contemplating a bonus scheme there are certain principles, according to Adkin et al. (1997), that should apply which are given in Table 9.8.

Non-financial benefits

This is sometimes considered to be a solution in the retention of a happy and loyal workforce. In a rapidly changing world, it is vital to retain a highly motivated workforce and one way to help bring this about might be through the use of perceived high-value employee benefits packages which are low cost to the organisation offering them, for example through the provision of cash when employees need it most – when they are ill.

Table 9.8 Principles that should apply to a bonus scheme (after Adkin et al., 1997, p37)

- Based on clear, measurable, challenging and appropriate targets or objectives
- Designed to encourage employees to meet the needs of the business
- Acceptable to the employees
- Appropriate for the group(s) of employees it is covering
- Clearly communicated, so that all employees can understand how it operates
- Designed to produce payments that reflect the achievement of targets
- Paid on a regular basis

There are many different types of employee benefits and to make matters more difficult for the employer, for each type of benefit, there is a vast array of plans, companies and administrators that can offer employers benefits in different forms. The more employees that an organisation has the better off the employer is when it comes to benefits. The size of the organisation is important because it is expensive to offer a rich benefits package to employees if there are only two or three employees in total. In the latter case, there ought to be a focus on only one or two benefits that both the employer and the employee will value most and that are most cost-effective.

POINTS TO PONDER

Work Smart

If an organisation only has a few employees, the best bet is to join a consortium of other small organisations in order to become an alliance in purchasing benefits.

Evidence shows that the use of benefit schemes is growing relentlessly without regard to the outlook for each individual business. There are three key factors to be taken into account when deciding generally which benefits an employer wants to offer:

- what the employer can afford

- what other organisations are offering

- how the benefit can help the organisation to meet its objectives.

Druker and White (1997), in their work on reward and remuneration in the construction industry, cite the key rewards used and these are given in Table 9.9.

Table 9.9 Benefit provision in the construction industry (after Druker and White, 1997, p137)

- Company sick pay scheme
- Company pension scheme
- Company retirement scheme
- Industry retirement scheme
- Company private health insurance
- Industry private health insurance
- Tool allowances
- Working conditions allowances
- Travel and subsistence
- Essential use of cars
- Non-essential use of cars
- Company paid holidays
- Sabbaticals/career breaks
- Company maternity
- Company paternity
- Relocation
- Company redundancy pay
- Long service awards
- House purchase assistance
- Company loans
- Financial advice
- Sports and social club
- Season ticket loan
- Childcare allowance

Small and medium-sized enterprises (SMEs) should consider offering as many as possible benefits.

Retirement

Retirement benefits are very attractive to employees because they let them save for their own future in a relatively pain-free way and enjoy a tax advantage while they save. With those employees who are highly compensated, pension plans tend to have greater popularity. The most important thing in offering employees a retirement plan is that it allows the employer also to take advantage of the plan.

Employees must ensure that once they have decided to create a retirement plan, they:

■ understand the advantages and disadvantages of having a retirement plan

■ know the major characteristics of the various types of plans available

■ determine the goals for having an organisational plan.

Healthcare (including dental and vision)

Healthcare benefits are one of the most important and popular benefits to employees. This may not be reason enough for an employer to offer such benefits, but if the organisation is in competition for workers with particularly rare or valuable skills, it could play an important part in recruitment if the organisation offers them. There are a number of organisational schemes available which can include a range of covers, including dental and vision care.

UK organisations spend around £50 billion on benefit each year without any assessment of the real cost of such benefits, with managers only having a rough idea of the extent to which benefits are actually valued by employees. That is, there is no coherent view of the purpose of the different elements in any benefits package. However, there appears to be a steady change in this approach as businesses begin to relate benefit packages to organisational aims and incorporate them *see* Chapter 2 into organisational strategy ■ *see* Chapter 2 ■. Study of research in this area seems to bring about contradictory views with legislative changes on working time (Working Time Directive 1998) and parental leave meaning that for the first time certain benefits are guaranteed and are therefore not bonuses – they have become *see* Chapter 7 *and* Chapter 8 legislative rights ■ *see* Chapter 7 *and* Chapter 8 ■. At the same time, some employers are introducing flexible benefits but each with different purpose, for example to spice up their recruitment package. The key objective is to make the benefits on offer cost-effective. Whatever their intention, organisations have to investigate alternative ways of valuing benefits and what the pressures are in both the short and long term, with an overall need for greater attention being given to the cost of such schemes.

Some organisations use medical insurers to provide employees with a package that will pay them cash when they are in hospital or require new spectacles or dental treatment. The organisation gets the credit because the employee is considered to be grateful to them for a service which does not cost the organisation very much in financial terms, since it is administrated by the medical organisation and not the employee's organisation. Common benefits, according to Adkin et al. (1997) include:

> pension contributions, death and disability insurance, subsidised canteen meals, private medical and dental insurance, free or cheap company products, a company car, subsidised loans. (pp37–6)

Benefits used to be an extremely popular and tax-efficient way of rewarding workers but the trend is now for tax authorities to consider benefits as taxable income.

COMPANY CARS

Company cars account for more than 50 per cent of all car sales in the UK and is on the increase throughout the rest of Europe. The company car is second only to a pension as the most valuable employment benefit in Europe. There has never been a successful measure made of those cars which are 'status' or 'genuine need' cars, but the suggestion is that status cars account for over 30 per cent of the total. However, Unsworth (1999) reports that research carried out by the training company, the Aziz Corporation, does not support this as a general view – it is only held by poorly performing organisations.

The Aziz Corporation survey shows that there are stark differences between the attitudes of companies with growth in annual turnover of more than 20 per cent, and those with less than 5 per cent. Most organisations provide perks to their staff, the most popular being cars and fuel, worth up to £3500 a year before tax, and medical insurance, worth £390 before tax. However, 71 per cent of directors of the most successful companies said they believed training was more effective in boosting morale than benefits in kind ■ *see* Chapter 1 *and* Chapter 6 ■.

see Chapter 1 *and* Chapter 6

REWARD VOUCHERS

The purpose of reward vouchers is to reward employees by giving them the opportunity to have a 'good time' – for example Whitbread's Leisure Vouchers can be redeemed at over 3000 restaurants, hotels and leisure centres within the UK. Such vouchers are used either as part of a structured organisational strategy to support a particular aspect of the work, for example excellent communication with customers on the telephone, or as a one-off surprise reward for outstanding overall performance. A large number of organisations have a rewards catalogue from which those who have performed outstandingly can choose a gift. The problem with this is that the gifts are not always sufficiently attractive to motivate staff to work harder to get them.

There has been a move towards rewarding the individual rather than a group or team because it is felt that this is more motivating. Times have changed however, because – especially with knowledge workers – a subsidised evening meal at a chain restaurant is insufficient to retain them (and thus their skills). Nowadays, organisations are moving towards rewards which are seen as personally designed such as the possibility for a sabbatical or the gaining of a further qualification such as a Masters in Business Administration (MBA). However, some people still get a thrill when they see their name highlighted as having made a specific contribution to the goals of the organisation. Such things are personal motivators and managers require the skill of recognising what motivates a specific individual. For example, one person may be motivated by time off to take a long-haul adventure activity holiday while another may be happy with a new freezer. Most organisations, unfortunately, have not yet realised the need to identify and tap into such personal motivators. According to Lucas (1999), HRM specialists still tend to cite pay as the key factor that motivates their workforce. If one asks employers what they want, the high flyers will want challenge and interesting work with autonomy, while those lower down the hierarchical pyramid would cite money. This could well be because the people at the lower end are still trying to satisfy the physiological and social aspects of their life (house, family and car) while those at the top have achieved this and need more intrinsic motivators.

FLEXIBLE BENEFITS

Flexible benefits of an employee's reward package consist of items such as company cars and pensions which are non-cash elements. Such a system allows employees to choose which of the benefits on offer they want and whether they would prefer to receive a cash equivalent. In the USA this is often referred to 'cafeteria benefits' and in the UK as 'pic'-'n'-mix' because the individual worker is choosing her/his own items from those on offer just as in a cafeteria, sweet selection bar at the station or in the local branch of Woolworths. This is linked to the contingency theory, discussed earlier in this chapter, which is about the need to achieve fit between what the organisation wants – to achieve its goals and objective – and what the worker does.

Since flexible benefits offer employees the opportunity to influence the shape of their benefit packages, employers must ensure that they address some key issues:

■ Why are they introducing flexible benefits?

■ How can they communicate the scheme to all employees?

■ How will the benefits allowance be made up?

■ How can individual employees get enrolled?

■ How will the system be administered?

The Royal Bank of Scotland, in an effort to strengthen its 'employer brand', has addressed the above concerns and has developed one of the biggest flexible benefits plans of its kind in the UK. Banks have always offered the traditional rewards such as a subsidised mortgage, a non-contributory pension scheme and a car for the bank branch managers, but this is insufficient within a complex and contemporary work environment with increasing competition. The Royal Bank of Scotland wanted to be perceived by others as an 'employer of choice', that is, there would be a considerable demand by individuals to work for it and it would be able to retain a happy and highly motivated workforce devoted to providing the best service possible, thus maintaining a competitive edge.

The organisation destructured its complex grading system and benchmarked jobs for both pay and benefits against similar jobs in other organisations. Then they launched a total reward benefits package which gave all employees a wide choice of benefits and complete flexibility in how they allocated the overall value of their remuneration package. The flexibility lies in the fact that every individual knows the full worth of the whole package which no longer contained rewards that were not perceived as such by the employees.

All employees, from the CEO downwards, received information and were given the chance to make her/his own selections. The workers were informed of the total value of the benefits for their personal reward package and, knowing what each item is worth, they each put together a personal portfolio of benefits. Like most organisations offering such a flexible benefits scheme, no employee is permitted to forgo all the benefits in favour of cash. For example, most employers would consider it irresponsible to allow people to opt out of the pension provision – although this rule may be relaxed if the other partner in a relationship has pension arrangements elsewhere. Having made their choice they may have either under-spent on their personal benefit value, and would receive the balance in cash, or purchased extra benefits that must be paid for out of their salary. The benefits package has been adopted slowly by the employees, although they did recognise that the previous package was relevant only to a certain section of the staff and it tended to be paternalistic. Some of the new benefits offered proved to be universally popular, for example health schemes and critical illness insurance. The childcare option was little taken up – which was very surprising since the bank has a high proportion of female workers with children.

SCENARIO 9.2

Enumerating remuneration at the Royal Bank of Scotland

Branch customer service officer, aged 43, two children

Before	*After*
Basic salary of £13 800	Buys:
Christmas bonus worth 2.5 per cent of salary	a childcare vouchers worth up to £4000 a month (cost: £4320)

SCENARIO 9.2 cont'd

b two days' holiday to spend with children during school breaks (cost: £106)

Total remaining salary taken as cash is £9374, plus Christmas bonus of £345

Assistant IT manager, aged 29, single
Before
Basic salary of £28 000
Christmas bonus worth 2.5 per cent of salary

After
Buys:
a dental insurance (cost: £47.76)
b personal accident insurance worth £25 000 (cost: £6.84)
c critical illness cover worth £50 000 (cost: £38.40)

Makes additional voluntary contribution to pension fund of £7000 in place of Christmas bonus.

Total remaining salary taken as cash is £27 907

Business manager of branch network, aged 47, single
Before
Basic salary of £30 000
Company car entitlement worth £3120 a year
Private healthcare benefit worth £380 a year
Christmas bonus worth 2.5 per cent of salary

After
a smaller company car worth £2000 a year
b private healthcare (cost: £380 a year)
c Safeway vouchers (cost: £4200 a year)
d sells three days' holiday entitlement (gain: £450)

Total remaining salary taken as cash is £27 433 plus Christmas bonus of £750

The implementation of such schemes has been quite slow in both the USA and Europe. It is assumed by some employers that the schemes are difficult to implement, costly to administer and 'just a gimmick'. Organisations which have implemented such schemes, for example the Royal Bank of Scotland, dispute this view – they suggest that when employees who participate in such a scheme are asked for their opinion, their response is: 'It's great to have a choice.'

This is a key point in the potential success of flexible benefits. Murlis (1999) believes that it is essential that the employees are asked if the reward structure is working – to find out what makes the individual come to work, what motivates her/him and what they need out of their pay. This approach will enable organisations to be ahead of the rest – according to Murlis (1999):

> Reward can be a fashion business and there are always fads and you have to take a very shrewd look at what's right for you. (p12)

9.5 Activity

Look at recent copies of the Chartered Institute of Personnel Management magazine *People Management* and find three advertisements from organisations which provide employers with ways of flexibly rewarding their staff.

POINTS
TO
PONDER

What are you worth or what will you be worth?

To help put a cash value on the most valuable items in a benefits package, the *Financial Times* (1999) looked at the total compensation package of two employees:

	Mr Brian Bullion	Mr Gary Gold
Age	50	35
Marital status	Married, 2 children at university	Married, non-working wife, 2 small children
Job profile	Managing director of a medium-sized company	Middle manager
Basic salary	£95 000 per annum	£70 000 per annum
Annual bonus	25% of salary (£23 750)	15% of salary (£10 500)
Value of pension per annum	£11 400	£7000
Value of life assurance per annum	£1400	Cost of 4 times salary protection (£200)
Value of income protection per annum	£1700	£600
Value of private medical insurance	£2200	£900
Value of company car per annum	£17 000	£10 000
TOTAL VALUE OF SALARY AND BENEFITS PACKAGE	£152 450 plus share option of approximately 50% salary	£99 200

Brian Bullion's package is weighted towards non-salary benefits, raising the headline figure to over £150 000. Note the impact of the value of the pension scheme and stock option for this employee.

Gary Gold, who earns £70 000 per annum, actually receives the equivalent of almost £100 000.

Adapted from: *Financial Times* (1999) A huge salary isn't everything, 20 October, p19.

EXECUTIVE PAY AND COMPANY PERFORMANCE

According to Taylor (1999):

> Executive pay is rising at more than four times the average rate of increase in national earnings, in spite of government calls for boardroom restraint. (p1)

A survey by Incomes Data Services (IDS) (1999) – the independent pay research body – discovered that chief executives' pay in the UK's largest FTSE 100 companies rose an average of 17.6 per cent over the previous financial year – with individual remuneration packages bearing little relationship to company performance. This runs counter to the UK government's warnings against excessive pay awards and suggests that large companies may find it hard to put an end to the pay expectations of their employees.

Table 9.10 Annual remuneration according to sector (FTSE 100)

SECTOR	£ MAXIMUM	£ MINIMUM
Chemicals and pharmaceutical	3 640 000	426 000
Retail and distribution	2 039 000	439 000
Finance	1 465 543	278 000
Construction, property and construction materials	786 000	405 625

Source: Directors' Pay Report (1999), London: Incomes Data Services.

Table 9.11 Highest paid directors at privatised companies (ex-utilities)

Company	Salary at privatisation (£)	Salary, bonus and benefits (1994) (£)	Salary, bonus and benefits (1997–98) (£)
British Gas	50 000	492 602	427 245
British Telecom	94 000	663 000	1 101 000
Eastern	62 670	296 000	376 000
East Midlands	62 270	331 712	458 000
London	75 950	201 145	180 000
Manweb	62 270	240 509	487 345
Midlands	57 500	231 802	358 000
Northern	86 800	210 000	123 000
Norweb	62 270	215 274	238 400
Seeboard	65 100	184 000	407 000
Southern	62 270	258 000	297 148
Swalec	65 375	203 420	320 000
SWEB	70 525	213 000	269 000
Yorkshire	62 270	211 354	255 400
National Power	185 000	374 886	546 285
PowerGen	103 075	350 393	458 000
National Grid	N/A	330 000	355 000
Anglian	59 750	169 000	286 967
Northumbrian	54 800	135 000	175 000
North West	100 000	338 000	229 366
Severn Trent	75 250	224 200	239 800
Southern Water	100 000	169 000	487 345
South West	70 000	130 000	198 000
Thames	150 000	247 000	277 000
Welsh	59 125	139 000	325 000
Wessex	72 563	166 000	216 000

Source: Sunday Times, 25 July 1999, News Review, Section 2, p2.

There appears to be little relation between the total financial packages awarded to chief executives and the performance of the companies they run. Nearly one-third of the chief executives secured remuneration packages which increased their earnings to more than 20 per cent. Taylor (1999) reports from the research that:

- One fifth had basic 20 per cent salary increases.

- Chief executives in the FTSE 100 had a median basic salary almost double that of their board colleagues at £473 000 compared to £263 000.

- Just over 10 per cent of all directors received a long-term incentive plan payment.

The payouts by industry can be seen in Table 9.10. Tables 9.11 to 9.14 give details of payments received in different types of companies.

Table 9.12 Random list of directors reported to have earned over £1m in 1997–98

Director	Company		Reported earnings (£)
Jim Fifield	EMI	1998	6 900 000
Jan Leschley	SmithKline Beecham	1998	2 446 000
Rod Kent	Close Brothers	1998	3 400 000
Lord Hollick	United News and Media	1997	2 970 000
Martin Sorrell	WPP	1997	2 790 000
Martin Bandler	EMI	1998	2 700 000
Greg Hutchings	Tomkins	1998	2 150 000
Terry Green	Debenhams	1997	2 600 000
John Browne	BP	1997	2 470 000
John Ritblat	British Land	1997	2 400 000
Hugh Collum	SmithKline Beecham	1998	2 300 000
Charles Brady	Amvescap	1997	1 950 000
Richard Oster	Cookson	1997	1 700 000
Keith Oates	Marks & Spencer	1997	1 440 000
Robert Peel	Thistle Hotels	1997	1 400 000
Jean-Pierre Garnier	SmithKline Beecham	1998	1 300 000
George Simpson	GEC	1997	1 252 000
Lord Blyth	Boots	1997	1 250 000
Sir Richard Greenbury	Marks & Spencer	1997	1 250 000
Richard Brown	Cable & Wireless	1997	1 240 000
Sir Clive Thompson	Rentokil	1988	1 230 000
Sir Peter Bonfield	British Telecom	1998	1 101 000
Ann Iverson	Laura Ashley	1997	1 100 000
Sir Richard Sykes	Glaxo Wellcome	1997	1 127 000
Ken Hanna	Dalgety	1998	1 040 000
Sir Colin Chandler	Vickers	1997	1 070 000
Phil White	National Express	1997	1 050 000

Source: Sunday Times, 25 July 1999, News Review, Section 2, p2.

Table 9.13 Highest earnings at law firms

Firm	Gross fees (£m)	Earnings per partner (£m)
Slaughter & May	152.6	437–875 000
Allen & Overy	219	320–800 000
Freshfields	232	320–640 000
Linklaters & Pains	266	250–625 000
Clifford Chance	377	220–550 000
Herbert Smith	125	250–575 000
Macfarlanes	40	240–520 000
S J Berwin & Co	50	150–600 000
Lovell White Durrant	140	200–500 000

Source: Sunday Times, 25 July 1999, News Review, Section 2, p2.

Table 9.14 Partners' earnings at top accountancy firms in 1997

Firm	Fee income (£m)	Number of partners	Fees per partner (£k)	Profit per partner (£)
Andersen Worldwide	696.4	410	1 694	423 537
Deloitte & Touche	440.9	335	1 316	329 029
Coopers & Lybrand (now PWC)	766	596	1 285	321 309
Ernst & Young	525.1	411	1 278	319 404
Price Waterhouse (now PWC)	520	479	1 085	271 399
KPMG	576.2	561	1 025	256 328
Latham Crossley & Davis	12.5	18	694	173 611
Robson Rhodes	42	70	600	150 000
Grant Thornton	119.6	213	562	140 376

Source: Sunday Times, 25 July 1999, News Review, Section 2, p2.

In 1995 Richard Greenbury (then chairman of Marks & Spencer) reported on executive pay and this led to the complete replacement of share incentive schemes with long-term incentive plans (Ltips), long term being a minimum of three years which is a figure which has subsequently become the norm. Greenbury (1995) justified the endorsement of rich rewards on the basis of performance. Thus, any incentive scheme should align the interests of the individual executive with those of the shareholders, with the executive then having to produce an above-average performance to earn her/his bonus. This is idealistic and not possible in all cases because not all organisations can be above average and even the best of managers cannot deliver simply on demand. Success in business does not rely solely on judgement because there is always luck involved. Because of this there will be losers as well as winners (or both). Richard Greenbury himself found this out when he lost his job as chairman of Marks & Spencer!

While there may be acceptable reasons why it is not possible to expect a correlation between performance schemes and performance and between ▷ **fat cats** ◁ and high profits, it is the presence of one which ought to increase the probability of the other. If this is not the case then there is little point in having it. However, Hilton (1999) reports that there is little correlation between the two.

> ▶ Executives who are perceived to receive reward and remuneration that is excessively high ◀······▶ **Fat cats**
> for the work which they do.

Harper (1999) believes that professionals have created a business climate which no one trusts any more. Just as some fat cat company directors have lost touch with reality, so the modern professional has lost her/his sense of the goodness of human beings and of the moral habits and rules that govern their behaviour.

SCENARIO 9.3

Union bosses rake in pay rises worthy of fat cats

A new breed of fat cat is stalking Downing Street in search of beer and sandwiches. Union bosses have had pay rises three and a half times the rate of inflation.

The average package of pay and perks for a union general secretary has increased by 7.55 per cent and some remuneration deals are topping £125 000 for the first time.

Union bosses are taking home pay and perks worth up to nine times the wages of their members at a time when trade union membership is at its lowest since the 1940s. Some of the biggest earners are the very general secretaries who have accused company directors of being 'greedy bastards'.

A *Sunday Times* survey of the general secretaries of Britain's leading unions shows that the average package is £73 591. The largest rise last year was more than 22 per cent.

The figures, which sparked accusations of hypocrisy, are drawn from accounts for 1998 submitted to the UK government's certification office for trades unions.

Salary increases have given union leaders a 6.74 per cent rise, but they also receive generous perks and allowances, such as chauffeur-driven cars, mobile phones, dress allowances and help with mortgage payments.

John Edmonds, leader of the 710 000 strong General Municipal and Boilermakers Union (GMB), had an 11.27 per cent increase to £79 000. Edmonds attacked the 'politics of the tough' at last year's Trades Union Congress (TUC) and called for higher taxes on anyone earning more than £50 000.

Roger Lyons, secretary of the Manufacturing Science Finance Union (MSFU), had an 11.67 per cent increase to £81 979, although membership of his union fell by 20 000 between 1996 and 1998. In July 1999 he attacked the fat cat company bosses, saying: 'People are sick of being lectured on the need to work harder and accept lower pay rises while their bosses award themselves kings' ransoms for mediocre performances.'

The biggest earner in other unions is Dr Mac Armstrong of the British Medical Association (BMA), who receives £126 785, a 7.17 per cent rise.

Derek Hodgson of the Communication Workers' Union (CMU) received £92 141, five times the basic salary of postal delivery staff.

The unions defended the payments to their top officials. The GMB said Edmonds's apparent sharp leap was because a salary increase for 1997 was delayed and paid in the same year as his 1998 rise. It said his actual rise last year was 3.5 per cent. The MSF said Lyons was not receiving a pay rise this year (1999). Rodney Bickerstaffe, general secretary of UNISON, the health and local government union, said his £89 878 package, a rise of 7 per cent, included a £5788 car allowance.

Members of parliament are not convinced. Ann Widdecombe, the shadow home secretary, said: 'These are exactly the sort of people who encourage the politics of envy about other people's pay while quietly helping themselves. They need to practise what they preach, particularly when many of these pay rises are coming out of members' subscriptions rather than from company profits.'

Adapted from: Chittenden, M. and C. Dignan (1999) Union bosses rake in pay rises worthy of fat cats, *The Sunday Times*, 25 July, p26.

Hunter (1999) reinforces this view when he writes that:

> The government is proposing to curb final payouts to directors by regulating their periods of notice. (p1)

The consultative document has concerned itself with the issue of executive directors having too much control over how their pay is determined. Past experience has shown that shareholders have had little influence in the matter and companies did not use the services of independent non-executive directors enough when determining executive directors' remuneration packages. The matter became serious with directors giving each other increases willy-nilly. The three reports on the issue:

- Cadbury (1992)

- Greenbury (1995)

- Hampel (1998)

formed the basis of the government's code of good practice but Hunter (1999) believes that:

> the issue that probably causes most concern for HR professionals relates to the role of employment contracts in directors' termination arrangements. (p1)

In recent years the sums of money departing directors have been given has caused considerable concern but trying to limit the size of such payments is not easy. Directors are wary of contracts of employment which attempt to provide the company with the right to dismiss them immediately because of poor performance or incompetence – however defined and measured. The reason for this is that they do not wish to be the scapegoats for all the ills and failures of their company because this is beyond the control of any one individual. If they are expected to have to depart under such circumstances, they expect to be paid well for it.

The continuation of large pay-offs suggests that the bonus incentive schemes are offering directors the chance to earn sizeable amounts over very short periods of time. It is this very fact that has made the UK government suggest that shareholders require greater information and opportunities to vet directors' remuneration packages (Hunter, 1999).

The government's proposals themselves state that they do not anticipate that the code and other safeguards are strong enough to take tackle the directors being rewarded for failure but there is a question mark over how much further such controls can go.

POINTS TO PONDER

In granting excessive power to shareholders in deciding the level of directors' remuneration in every case could prove to be very cumbersome and thus counterproductive. This is because the UK lacks talented and innovative entrepreneurs and an unpalatable fact of commercial life is that the greedy are often the most effective.

Adapted from: Hunter, I. (1999) Goodbye to all that? on http://www.peoplemanagement.co.uk/editorial/law/hunter.asp?page_no=29&qu= 28 October, pp1–2.

The UK government's consultative paper proposes that:

- directors' notice periods should be one year or less, unless there are exceptional reasons for a longer period
- directors' compensation arrangements on termination should be explained to shareholders
- shareholders should vote annually on the remuneration for members of the board
- companies should be required to disclose how directors' pay is linked to performance.

It is the very fact that the reward levels of senior executives within companies have increased disproportionately to other employees in the same organisation which has caused controversy. Employees see that their executives are receiving very high salaries while, at the same time, severely restricting the incomes of other workers. However, such high payments pay little attention to market forces or accountability to shareholders – it is a short-term activity. There is considerable criticism where there are no clear relationships between executive pay and the performance of the organisation for which such executives work. Graham and Bennett (1999) suggest that there may well be a case for providing extremely high salaries to senior executives which are given in Table 9.15.

Overholser (1999) reported on one topic in the USA which was still taboo – the inflated pay of US bosses. In 1998 the average CEO of a large organisation earned $10.6m (nearly £7m). Her/his pay went up 36 per cent, compared with only 2.7 per cent for the average blue-collar worker. It appears that, if this 'grotesque disparity' is mentioned, people act as if the free enterprise system itself was under threat.

Table 9.15 Propositions which support the case for executives' high salaries

- Necessary in order to motivate individual executives, for example through performance-related pay.

- High remuneration implies high status and recognition of individual worth.

- Competent top-level managers are in great demand and likely to be headhunted, so that high wages are needed to secure their loyalty and long-term commitment to the organisation.

- Senior management involves taking risky decisions which, if wrong, have serious adverse consequences both for the organisation and the individual executive. A high salary is needed to compensate for the assumption of such high-level risk.

- Only a small number of executives possess the management skills, knowledge and contacts necessary to succeed in competitive situations and market forces of supply and demand naturally raise the remuneration levels of these people.

- Failure to attract the best management talent available will damage the firm in the long term.

- Senior management is at the top of the management pyramid, so that high salaries are needed to maintain differentials while enabling lower levels to earn a reasonable reward.

- High salaries generate a culture of effort and achievement within the firm.

Source: Graham, H.T. and R. Bennett (1999) *Human Resources Management*, London: Financial Times/Pitman Publishing, pp202–3.

　　The argument is that CEOs have huge responsibilities and an organisation will rise or fall because of them. While this might be true to some extent, Overholser (1999) makes the point that they do not get equally well rewarded when the company *does* fail. She cites Citigroup as an example stating that in 1998 the chairman took home $52m (£32.5m), plus $152m (£95m) – a total $204m (£127.5m) – yet the

Table 9.16 Earnings of the highest paid directors in relation to the average wage of their employees

COMPANY	HIGHEST PAID DIRECTOR	DIRECTORS' PAY (£)	AVERAGE WAGE OF EMPLOYEES (£)	RATIO
Kingfisher	Geoff Mulcahy	2 062 000	7 670	268.8
Northern Leisure	Nicholas Oppenheim	1 078 000	4 980	216.5
EMI Group	Jim Fifield	6 728 000	32 570	206.6
Lonmin	Nick Morrell	630 000	3 120	201.9
Bass	Ian Prosser	1 631 000	9 760	167.1
MEPC	David Gruber	8 291 000	38 830	162.2
New Look	Jim Hodkinson	1 005 000	6 410	156.8
Royal Bank of Scotland	Larry Fish	3 302 000	21 910	150.7
Rentokil Initial	Sir Clive Thompson	1 419 000	9 420	150.6
Hilton Group	Peter George	1 326 000	9 620	137.8

Source: Abrams, F. (1999) Pay gap grows in fat cat Britain, *The Independent on Sunday*, 21 November, p5.

company's return to its shareholders was *minus* 9 per cent. It does not matter how the organisation performs, the CEO's pay increases.

If the pay of clerks and cooks increased at the same rate over the last two years they would now be earning $110 000 (£68 750) a year instead of $29 000 (£18 125). Overholser (1999) questions why these workers do not earn the higher sums and suggests that they would, if:

they too were in control of how much they pay themselves. (p11)

Abrams (1999) reports that many of the highest flying directors have the worst-paid employees, as shown in Table 9.16.

PERQUISITES FOR SHAREHOLDERS

When organisations consider rewards and remuneration for their employees – especially in the form of perks (*perquisites*), they need also to remember that it is actually the shareholders who own the company. Hargreaves (1999), as CEO of Hargreaves Lansdown Stockbrokers Ltd, believes that:

The best companies in which to invest are run first for the benefit of the shareholders, with customers, employees and directors taking second, third and fourth places respectively. (1)

His view is that members of any board of directors need always to remember that it is the owners for whom the company is run and no one else. In light of this, his firm offers an annual booklet listing the names of those companies worth investing in:

not just for the perks, but for the long term capital growth that the UK equity market offers. (p1)

The perks are listed by category of business and range from one of the best-known companies to those which provide preferential arrangements, perks and discounts to certain shareholders, for example P&O, the giant shipping organisation. P&O has, over the years, allowed investors who have purchased P&O concessionary shares not only to benefit from the attractive income they earn, but also to benefit from the extremely advantageous channel crossing fares offered to shareholders.

Dolan (1999) outlines a number of different organisations which 'care enough about their private shareholders to offer them incentives.' (pB13).

Examples of companies and what they offer in perks and benefits for shareholders include those given in Table 9.17.

Other areas where discounts are offered are:

- Do-it-yourself
- Dry cleaning
- Electrical
- Engineering
- Financial
- Furnishing
- Health
- Jewellers
- Leisure
- Media
- Mineral extraction
- Restaurants
- Retailers
- Stores
- Telecommunications
- Textiles
- Transport
- Utilities

Table 9.17 Perks and benefits to shareholders

Company	Perk/benefit
Allied Domecq Fuller Smith & Turner Merrydown Scottish & Newcastle Whitbread	Discounted alcohol
Arcadia Austin Reed Coats Viyella Gieves & Hawkes Moss Bros Next Storehouse	Clothes at less than retail price
Friendly Hotels Granada Hilton Queens Moat Houses Regals Hotel Group Swallow Thistle	Cheaper hotel rates
Bank of Scotland Lloyds Woolwich	Various benefits including discounts on wine, holidays and travel
Iceland Group Bensons Crisps	Discounts on food product

Organisations have moved away from the minuscule strategy of what they make or the services they provide to, according to Hilton (1999), 'deliver enhanced value to shareholders' (p47). This means that managers have to provide ever higher share prices for their investors – a position which has developed sharply over the last ten years. Investors will only purchase shares after following the performance of their potential investment organisation and any drop in shares is attributed to competition from another organisation rather than the failings of specific managers. Individuals who manage the investments of others only invest in those organisations that have the senior executives of the organisation as their major shareholders. It seems that too many incentive schemes follow the point that the management can never lose. By owning shares outright – often as part of a share ownership scheme – rather than having them available on a promise is a key factor because it is only then that executives 'suffer on the downside' (Hilton, 1999, p51) and thus managers tend to manage the organisation with the mid-term in sight through share ownership.

Whatever form the perks take, their distribution within one organisation needs to be given careful attention by those members of the senior management stratum – especially if they wish to maintain an existing organisational culture. Employees are aware that factors such as:

- location of offices

- type of office furniture and fittings

- travel expenses

can all be important symbols of status and authority.

9.6 Activity

When you are visiting the various studies of university staff (for example lecturers, heads of schools, deans of faculties, registrar, rector, vice chancellor), see if the type of furniture and fittings varies among them.

If so, how does this relate to their position in the university hierarchy?

Try observing at your place of work – is the same thing happening there?

Some organisations, for example British Airways (BA), try to eliminate some of these differences in status by not having reserved car parking spaces, using hotel or hot desking, insisting that all staff travel standard class by rail and closing executive-only dining rooms. Others maintain the divisions, believing that they are integral to the organisation's traditional culture and are important in motivating the more junior staff. However, the key issue is not that one approach is right and the other is wrong, but that there should be a conscious strategy in operation so that perks can be distributed according to some transparent formula.

PRP

In the UK, PRP began to replace the ▶ **fixed incremental systems** ◀ in white-collar work during the 1970s. Even at this time the philosophy of relating individual performance to reward was not new – according to Swabe (1989):

> an individual's increase in pay is determined solely or mainly through his/her appraisal or merit rating. (p189)

▶ Fixed points on a transparent scale where employees can expect to receive an increase in wage/salary regardless of effort and productivity, and usually set at years of service. ◀┈▶ **Fixed incremental systems**

This started to increase during the 1980s with PRP increasing in the 1990s. Cannell and Wood (1992) found that almost half the private sector companies at that time relied on such schemes for all non-manual employees.

The specific details of PRP schemes will vary but overall they can be viewed as representing a shift in emphasis from rewarding job content and effort (inputs) to the rewarding of individual achievement and performance (output).

PRP is employees' pay that depends partly on their performance. It has grown in significance rapidly over the last decade and in 1992 was recorded as the main method for determining pay progression for non-manual workers and almost half of the schemes had been introduced in the ten years prior to 1991. It is certainly more limited in the manual worker sector of employment than at management level although there seems to be a gentle increase in its use within non-managerial sectors (Cannell and Wood, 1992).

The definition of PRP is not as simple in practice as it might appear to be. A wider definition given by Wright (1991) supports this view believing PRP to be that part of the financial, or financially measurable, reward to the individual that is linked directly to individual, team or company performance.

The Advisory, Conciliation and Arbitration Service (ACAS) gives a much narrower definition of PRP:

> pay based wholly or partly on the regular and systematic assessment of job performance. (Booklet undated and unpaged)

The term used by ACAS in its booklet title – *Appraisal-related Pay* – is useful but unfortunately has never been widely adopted and this has resulted in confusion as to whether PRP is related to ▶ **appraisal** ◀ or not ■ *see* Chapter 10 ■).

see Chapter 10

Appraisal ◀┈┈▶ The process of assessing the development of an employee concentrating on achievement and what needs to be done to improve it.

GROWTH IN PRP PROGRAMME USE

There have been a number of research studies carried out in this area and it seems that there is more than one reason for the growth in PRP systems within organisations. Armstrong and Murlis (1994) believe that the underlying philosophy is the concern for the need to increase the effort of all employees and to motivate them. This is more often than not tied in with the view that PRP would be more equitable to employees that other benefit systems, such as bonuses. Organisations also introduce PRP systems because they believe that they will help overcome labour market pressures by paying individuals who perform highly more than those who do not and thus increase the retention of high-performing staff. Some of the evidence from traditional pay incentive schemes is that money can act as an extremely powerful motivator in some instances (Armstrong and Murlis, 1994, pp250–4) and the idea of linking pay to employee performance became obvious.

Brough (1994) believes that organisations, like individual workers, demand flexibility to meet sudden changes in their environment. He suggests that this might be the reason why the introduction of PRP is often concurrent with the decentralisation of an organisation. There is then a completely altered role for the line management and supervisory staff because they gain increased autonomy and responsibility.

The difficulty lies in the fact that organisations have introduced PRP indiscriminately and have found that it does not always increase individual performance – as they hoped it would. The IPM's report of 1992 on a study of 1800 employers undertaken in the summer of 1991 concluded that there was no correlation between the use of PRP and the performance of the organisation: that is, the poor financial performers were as likely to be using PRP as were the better performers.

CRITICISMS OF PRP

There has been a wide range of criticisms from ones stating that PRP is divisive and demotivating to the opinion that it diverts the attention of organisations from the wider issues of managing employee performance in line with the objectives of the organisation.

Performance-related pay is complex and can take many forms and may or may not be linked to a performance appraisal system, the purpose of which is to assess the development of an employee, focusing on achievement and what needs to be done to improve it ■ *see* Chapter 10 ■. PRP can be based on individual, team or organisational performance or any combination thereof. Measuring the effectiveness of management initiatives on employee performance is difficult. Fletcher and Williams (1992) identified a link between a positive appraisal system and the performance of the workforce. However, their work was measured by the use of employee attitudes and commitment and did not measure job satisfaction, clarity of goals and the role of feedback which all affect individual performance. The overall objective is to improve the performance of the organisation and to reward employees for their achievements which contribute to that performance.

see Chapter 10

Research in the field of PRP does not confirm that it has a positive effect on motivation but, theoretically, such schemes do make management pay greater attention to the measurement of performance ■ *see* Chapter 10 ■. However, there is real skill needed to determine the performance criteria that trigger the extra payments. Such criteria must be challenging yet also reasonable and fair. For instance, there is no point in setting a target over which an employee has little or no influence or one that is impossible to achieve. Also, if an individual is set short-term goals, long-term interests may be forgotten. The underlying principle of PRP is to pay employees for performance rather than potential.

see Chapter 10

Even as far back as the 1970s issues were being debated about PRP, for example Friedman (1970) believed that managers should ask:

> important questions about the relationship between performance and reward in a function where there is a high degree of indeterminism in the work and a related high level of employee autonomy. (p188)

He was making the point that before introducing PRP, managers should ensure that they allowed workers a responsible level of autonomy within their work rather than direct control.

Another problem is that PRP can include traditional piecework as well as a whole variety of collective bonus and value-added schemes such as:

■ profit sharing

■ merit pay

■ individual incentive bonus

■ individual discretionary bonus

■ team bonus

■ company bonus

■ skills-based payments

■ shares

■ gifts

as long as they are all related to performance.

It is the link between the performance of the employee and the pay rewards which shows the weaknesses at the heart of PRP schemes. Some researchers believe that it is this very link between performance and reward which is basic to employees' feelings of equity which underlies the attractiveness of PRP for employees. Armstrong and Murlis (1994) believe that its strength lies in the belief that it is right and equitable to reward people according to their level of contribution to the desired ends.

However, in practice it is often easy to offend an employee's feelings of equity. The work carried out at the Inland Revenue by Marsden and Richardson (1994) highlighted that most employees:

■ basically agreed with the philosophy of PRP

■ felt that in practice the scheme would not work because the allocation of performance payments appears to them to be unfair

■ believed that a quota of bonus payments was in operation and this often overrode any assessment of performance

■ thought that the appraisal system was too distorted and tied to monetary decisions.

The research showed that PRP schemes could very well have the opposite effect to that envisaged – they could well be highly demotivating. Employees criticised their PRP scheme because they perceived that it:

■ undermined staff morale

■ caused jealousies among staff

- made colleagues less willing to help each other.

This is not an uncommon situation and the difficulty appears to stem from the fact that employees are rated as 'average' and, therefore, the amount of money which is available for bonus provision is usually very small and organisations may prefer to use that money in giving substantial bonuses – which are perceived as meaningful to the employees – to the few exceptional performers than spread it around all the workers. This might result in motivating the high performers but will succeed in demotivating the great mass of employees.

WHY ORGANISATIONS INTRODUCE PRP

There are a number of reasons why organisations introduce PRP systems and one study carried out by Kessler and Purcell (1992) reported that central to most of them was a desire to reward good performance and increase motivation with the former being perceived to be more important. The overall objective of PRP is to provide rewards that will prompt improvements to individual performance and, in turn, to the organisation as a whole. Armstrong and Murlis (1994) found in their work that there appeared to be moral grounds for the introduction of PRP. They claimed that organisations felt that it was right and proper for individuals to be rewarded in accordance with the contribution they had made to meet the organisation's aims. However, whether the individual PRP schemes achieve their specific purpose is very difficult to determine. There does not appear to be much in the way of objective evaluation of PRP schemes themselves. Organisations have a vested interest in the success of their PRP schemes and this means, according to Kessler and Purcell (1992), that the view of the organisations that practice PRP are uncritical and favourable. In the reviews that have taken place it is not the improved individual performance which seems to concern managers but the concern that the employee will stay with the company.

Managers themselves appear to believe that potential benefits are seen in terms of widening managerial control over wage determination and the commercialisation of the workforce rather than improved performance.

PRP has implications for all: the individual, the team, trade unions and staff associations. By definition, payment levels for an individual are determined by that individual's performance so the trades unions have to influence the design of the scheme and support the individual should there be any disputes. In Europe and the USA, PRP – although not widely used – is the most common form of variable pay but it is used mostly to remunerate managers, professional and technical staff and, to a lesser extent, factory workers and support staff such as technicians. However, it is not the same in all countries, for example in Germany managers are less likely to be participating in PRP schemes and in Sweden it is mainly the low-level workers who are covered by PRP schemes. Within the EU, it is Portugal which uses PRP the most widely across all levels of employee.

Another way of referring to PRP is *end-of-year claptrap*.

Armstrong and Murlis (1994) cite the case of British Telecom (BT) and Marsden and Richardson (1994) researched the Inland Revenue. Findings from both suggest that the use of individual performance pay demotivated some employees, although it might be expected that reward systems are designed to improve performance by promoting creative activity. They also found that the use of merit pay in certain jobs, for example those which contain a certain level of autonomy and responsibility and those where teamwork and cooperation are valued, bore no relationship to performance.

IN FAVOUR OF PRP

The case in favour of introducing PRP within an organisation seems to rest on unproven causal links between incentives and individual performance and between individual and organisational performance. Geery (1992) points out that the adoption of HRM mechanisms of both employee remuneration and appraisal generate new problems for management rather than solving those that already exist. It seems that organisations which are poor performers and those which perform effectively both have PRP schemes indicating, according to Bevan and Thompson (1991), that the introduction of a PRP scheme within an organisation does not automatically mean that the organisation will become more competitive. Randle (1997) continues to research the causal links based on the assumption that:

> attitudes of those on whom the system has been imposed may be the only measure of its effectiveness. (p197)

Kohn (1993) carried out research and found that the assumption of a relationship between incentives and improved performance was not supported. He argued that

SCENARIO 9.4

What's my motivation?

Katie Woolf, a 32-year-old personal assistant from Putney, south-west London, stated that if her employer wants her to give more in terms of workload and hours, then she wants rewards that correspond with her lifestyle.

She was offered a company car with her job but she has already got one of her own and could not get excited about an upgrade. She asked for funded training instead, explaining that it would be a long-term benefit to her employer and would cost a lot less than the car. They saw sense in this view.

Adapted from: Hilpern, K. (1999) What's my motivation?, *Independent*, Wednesday Review Section, 2 June, p12.

faults with PRP are often put down to implementational details rather than to the PRP philosophy itself. However, he believed that rewards succeed only in securing temporary compliance from employees. Even those who are in favour of individual PRP awards, for example Shapero (1985), accept that there can be negative effects which can be stronger than the positive ones. Kohn's (1993) results suggest that pay itself is not a motivator and that rewards punish employees through:

- the experience of being controlled

- the destruction of cooperation

- ignoring reasons for poor performance

- discouraging risk taking

- restricting creativity

- undermining intrinsic interest in work.

According to Beer (1994), if pay is made contingent on performance as judged by managers, management is in control. This links to the principal concerns listed above. If an individual has feelings of competence and self-determination which are associated with her/his autonomy over the management of her/his work, such control will mean a reduction in that highly prized autonomy and more management control. This is a serious blight when the contemporary workforce must comprise highly skilled knowledge workers who value such responsibility and autonomy and are intrinsically motivated by such factors.

THE USE OF PRP SCHEMES

The introduction of PRP schemes is likely to be more complicated for manual workers than for non-manual ones because the communication programme is likely to be protracted and involve some very difficult negotiations. The supervisors will need to be retrained in order to deal with what is a complex system of reward and will demand skills with which they are unfamiliar and are, therefore, alien to them. This is made even more difficult because of the pressure placed on middle management as organisations have delayered and flattened, thus increasing middle management's responsibilities even more (Kessler and Purcell, 1992).

Brough (1994) believes that it should be easier to base any PRP scheme for manual workers on objectives and criteria, because a considerable amount of manual work has traditionally been directed, and specific targets – in order to measure output and quality, for example. However, he goes on to state that his research indicated that at the lower levels of organisational workers, the degree of discretion accorded to individual employees to accomplish their goals is typically very limited.

DEVELOPING PRP

PRP is concerned with rewarding the individual employee – the better her/his performance the higher will be the pay. Such a principle is extremely basic and easy to understand but a problem arises when it comes to putting any PRP scheme into operation. The scheme falls or rises on the appraisal of the individual by her/his supervisor.

Appraisal interviews are difficult for all parties concerned. They are easier to deal with when they concentrate on training and development issues which relate to the individual and her/his job, because they are then more like counselling interviews with all parties benefiting from the discussion. However, as soon as the issue of remuneration enters the appraisal system, a situation arises that has the potential of being dysfunctional. Employees become much more concerned with the justification of a PRP reward than they are in thinking about the needs of personal development as indicated by their performance ■ *see* Chapter 10 ■.

see Chapter 10

This means that the pay element of performance management gets in the way of the vital development element. Brough (1994) found in his research that some organisations try to separate the award of pay from the appraisal by anything from three weeks to three months. Within this there are systems which use two interviews: one for performance and one for training and development. Others use information gathered at the appraisal interview for a later (and separate) salary review which considers:

■ the position of the employee in the salary scale

■ recent salary history

■ the scarcity of skills in the organisation.

It is unfortunate, however, that most organisations abandon the attempt of separating the reward aspect from the personal development one and, as a result, the reward element takes priority, leaving the potentially more valuable personal development and training element to drag on behind. Employees often believe that they are working to their maximum – or they perceive that they are – and so they feel that management has to do more than just offer cash rewards to them.

Maybe the solution – especially in the area of manual workers – is not to use PRP as a pay system because, in most situations, it does not promise much. Its importance actually lies in its contribution to an overall change either in the organisation's objective and/or how it achieves them. Particularly, although not critically, it has a part to play when an organisation is attempting to change its culture wherein the developmental process of an individual employee is critical, especially if the organisation is attempting to become more flexible in dealing with the contemporary and changing workplace. It is then that PRP can become an element in a total change process – but it is a small element and one which can be dispensed with in some situations.

Table 9.18 Advantages and disadvantages of commission payment as PRP (after Adkin et al., 1997, pp49–50)

Advantages
- Pay is linked purely to sales volumes or profitability.
- Sales representatives may be self-employed.
- Payments generally keep up with inflation and are therefore attractive to sales representatives.
- Only successful representatives stay with the company.
- Remuneration of sales staff is related to profits.
- Different commission rates can be paid for different products.
- Payments can be designed to be easy to administer and monitor.

Disadvantages
- Lack of security in respect of pay may cause stress to sales staff and make it more difficult to recruit and retain them.
- Badly designed schemes may result in managers having little control over earnings.
- Sales representatives may be tempted to overload customers with stock, promoting items they may not need.
- Non-selling activities take second place.

COMMISSION PAYMENT

This is a form of performance-related payment. Many staff who work in the sales section of their organisation are paid a commission, the amount of which is based on their performance. There are three key commission systems in operation:

- low basic salary and high commission
- average to good salary and low commission
- commission only.

Adkin et al. (1997) suggest that there are advantages and disadvantages in the commission method of PRP, as shown in Table 9.18.

SHARE OPTIONS

Executive share options and similar incentive schemes are, according to research carried out by Pensions Investment Research Consultants (Mackintosh, 1999), being set up to pay hundreds of thousands of pounds sterling for meeting undemanding targets. The report warned that the low targets for which payouts would be made to top executives failed to match the suggestions issued by the DTI in July 1999.

The research indicated that incentive packages did not provide an effective link between performance and bonuses by paying out for growth which was not better than the average. It seems that most of the uncovered performance targets did not represent world-class performance – which is what the UK government wants. Low-level performance thresholds give a message to directors that average is good enough.

The Consultancy looked at 92 share option and long-term incentive plans of which 25 per cent were from FTSE 100 companies. Their findings showed that of almost 100 new share option and similar schemes for directors of such listed companies, more than 50 per cent paid out to individuals who met the average. Additionally, findings showed that most of the schemes only considered the short term (three-year performance) and not the long term. About 66 per cent of the schemes researched pay out if earnings per share grew at just 3 per cent per annum a year after inflation had been taken into account, for example Securicor (transport and security) and Schroder (banking). The conclusions of the report suggested that such targets were not tough enough because they simply matched the predicted growth of the economy. The most demanding required 5 per cent and 6 per cent growth per annum (Singer and Fiendlander (financial sector) and Pizza Express (food)).

Mackintosh (1999) reports that plans set up in 1999 usually pay out a bonus equal to a quarter of salary simply by staying in the middle of a comparator group, and the full amount if the company is in the top 25 per cent.

As research director of Pensions Investment Research Consultants, Bell (1999) states:

> These schemes contribute little to incentivising individuals or enhancing competitiveness. (p3)

An additional, and important, point made by the report writers was that their investigations highlighted the secretiveness of companies concerning the makeup of their schemes and the complexity of measurement. The consultancy warned that:

> companies were using this [complexity] as a way of getting around corporate governance guidelines. (p3)

The report will be a disappointment to the DTI and could well increase the pressure on the UK government to take action over 'fat cat' executive pay. However, the government is not in favour of intervention because their view is that legislation could make it very hard for international companies to recruit executives.

ECONOMIC VALUE ADDED (EVA)

Globalisation requires a workforce that is flexible and able to make informed decisions and because of this they have the power to create enormous value ■ *see* Chapter 11 ■. The key to success lies in the increase of employee participation – especially in organisational decision making – thus supporting the TUC participation in partnership ■ *see* Chapter 7 ■. There has always been an effort made to find a secure link between financial reward and individual effort. These have moved from

see Chapter 11

see Chapter 7

the use of piece rates to the more recent use of PRP, share options and profit sharing. However, there has always been in the background, although prominent in the rest of Europe, the difficult concept of ▶ **economic value added** ◀ (EVA) which is now gaining prominence as a means of assessing takeovers and then as a remuneration scheme for senior executives.

▶ The net operating profit after tax, minus the profit required to justify the risk. ◀-----▶ **Economic value added**

POINTS TO PONDER

Active plc has a capital investment of £1m. The management uses £800 000 for buildings and equipment.

This leaves the organisation with £200 000 in cash.

The turnover of the business is £500 000, with costs of £300 000, leaving a pre-tax profit of £200 000.

After tax at, say, 40 per cent, there is a net profit of £120 000.

To calculate the EVA the organisation takes the bank interest payable on investing the £1m, say, 4 per cent (£40 000).

To this is added an element/figure/percentage to reflect the relatively greater risk involved in actually undertaking the business venture rather than simply taking the safer option of leaving the money in the bank.

This results in a figure of £100 000.

The £20 000 difference between this and the net operating profits is the EVA.

Pollock (1999) reports on Stern Steward Europe which is a European branch of the consultancy that developed the concept of EVA in the USA. Sirona, a German dental equipment manufacturer, shows that it can be applied beyond the top level of management. They claim that they are able to calculate EVA targets all the way through an organisation and then pay bonuses when such targets are achieved. This is not only at the highest level but right down to the factory floor – all by using economic incentives. It is the contribution that each team of employees makes which can be calculated and bonuses linked to the EVA for that team.

However, the system of EVA will only work if it can be added at every level of decision making. If, for example, a board of directors agrees to improvements at one factory, then thousands of lower level choices can also lead to improvements in value. Sirona, for example, makes such choices by including them in choices as to whether to make requests for additional staff or resources and finding ways of reducing stock levels.

Pollock (1999) states that:

The trick is to find areas where employees have some discretion in how they do their jobs. (p57)

However, it is essential that the EVA is linked closely with the bonus schemes which are used by the whole workforce.

While this use of EVA and bonus schemes has considerable benefits it will only prove to be so if all members of the workforce are willing participants and thus utilise a proportion of their wage/salary as an investment in the organisation. It is only when – and if – the EVA target is achieved that workers receive the original wage/salary back as well as the bonus that has been achieved by the organisation. Under the scheme the organisation adds a percentage to the part of the wage/salary invested and thus the final payment is higher than the originally earned wage/salary.

However, employees do not receive their hard-earned bonuses in full each year because a proportion is retained to offset those years when the EVA target is not achieved and this negative equity has to be cleared before any bonuses are paid out. Employees themselves decide what proportion of their earned salary is invested in the scheme and so contributions vary from individual to individual.

It is difficult within this scheme to link rewards with individual performance, although the EVA scheme is more beneficial in this way than other bonus schemes in operation elsewhere, for example benefit schemes. Whatever the scheme in use, a reward scheme on its own will not change an individual's behaviour because, as Tyson (1999) believes, that will only come about 'via the implementation of a "bundle of policies"' (p58).

This mirrors the view of the TUC relating to reward strategies. Williamson (1999), the TUC's policy officer, states:

> We do not see individual reward systems as being primarily a way to motivate staff. There is a place for them, but they are not key. (p58)

The use of EVA as a reward system throughout all levels of an organisation is a relatively new concept and because of its complex nature, it is not possible to come to concrete conclusions about its effectiveness. As Pollock (1999) says:

> A concept that seeks to reward and motivate both a top executive and a lathe operator will have to survive a long period of implementation before its claims can be verified. (p58)

EMPOWERMENT

Empowerment can be defined as:

> Organisational arrangements that allow employees more autonomy, discretion and unsupervised decision-making responsibility.

It encompasses the principle of participation and is relevant to all aspects of an individual's existence. Individuals cannot be empowered, but organisations can use their job designs and structures to empower people. This can apply to the issue of rewards and the way in which reward systems can support empowerment. Born and Mollman (1996) found that there was some support for the idea that rewards and empowerment were connected and their research supported the view that rewards can enhance the potential of the individual worker and through empowerment, an individual can be rewarded for her/his multifunctionality ■ *see* Chapter 5 *and* Chapter 10 ■.

see **Chapter 5** *and* **Chapter 10**

ETHICS OF REWARD AND REMUNERATION

Because of the interest over the last few years in executive pay and the so-called 'fat cats', increased attention has been paid to the ethics of remuneration. The concern has been over the disparity between executives and workers at the lowly end of the hierarchy related to their individual rewards and the way the decisions are made as to how organisational rewards are apportioned. Share options should be attached to measures of performance which are vigorously and equitably handled and packages paid to directors should be communicated to shareholders. Members of the board of directors should not sit on any committees which concern themselves with remuneration packages. Ethical issues are discussed in ■ Chapter 11 ■.

see Chapter 11

REWARD AND ENCOURAGEMENT

SCENARIO 9.5

Ringing true

Employers have gone to considerable lengths to offset the intense nature of work in call centres by using fringe benefits.

The Thomas Cook Global Traveller Service call centre in Peterborough, Cambridgeshire, England has a multicultural workforce with more than 30 languages being spoken. To retain its highly skilled employees, the company provides a subsidised restaurant, a workplace nursery and a gym with swimming pool, sauna and Jacuzzi. There are also travel discounts for staff, subsidised private health insurance and a flexible contributory pension plan.

This is a far cry from the clichéd image of 'dark, satanic mills'.

Adapted from: Hatchett, A. (2000) Ringing true, *People Management*, 20 January, pp40–32.

Encouragement for individuals and teams can be included in reward and remuneration strategy. This could be by managing the objectives of PRP where individual and team rewards are linked to the achievement of objectives which were established in the planning process which led up the strategy definition. In this way the attention given to planning and the commitment to it will increase. Numerous reward systems have been organised either formally or informally in this way, for example by the provision of a bonus, productivity pay or PRP attached to the meeting of such planned objectives.

However, Hatch (1997) believes that:

When performance criteria and rewards emphasise the distinct performance of separate units, they downplay the combined performance of the entire organisation and lead units to ignore the value of co-operation. (p311)

POINTS TO PONDER

Imagine a scenario when a large number of students have to sit the same examination paper but at different times. How can one make sure that after taking their paper, the first set of candidates do not inform the following ones what is on the examination paper?

One way to assure students in the first group of candidates is to tell them that all examination papers will be graded on the same standard and that if students in the later sittings get the questions and improve their own marks, it will be at the expense of the students who did not have this advantage.

Note here that the creation of a conflict of interest between students leads to the elimination of cooperation between them.

Also, while this strategy may increase fairness in the grading system, such strategies may be counterproductive from the viewpoint of encouraging information sharing and the formation of cooperative study groups which can benefit all students and the class which they attend.

Consider how would you feel if this strategy was adopted and you:

a were not in the first cohort of examinees

b did not get or were not given the questions by the first cohort

c scored an individual high score?

Adapted from: Hatch, M.J. *Organization Theory: Modern Symbolic and Postmodern Perspectives*, Oxford University Press p311.

Reward processes can be one of the greatest sources of leverage available to an organisation as it searches to increase its performance and effectiveness in the contemporary and globalised environment ■ *see* Chapter 11 ■. However, it is still one of the most underused and potentially complex tools for driving the performance of an organisation. As Gratton (1997) stated:

see Chapter 11

> The importance and complexity of linking reward strategies to business goals in a systematic manner has been a recurrent theme in... research. (p255)

Rana (1999b) reported that:

> Perks and bonuses may win loyalty and boost motivation, but even sweeteners can turn sour for some people. (p16)

This was in relation to new research carried out by Abbey National, which highlighted the importance of benefit schemes in keeping the loyalty of employees, yet emphasised the fact that an ET case revealed the pitfalls that such programmes can bring with them. In 1999 Marconi Communications (an international electronics giant) had to defend itself at an ET against a claim that it failed to adjust the bonus scheme targets of a former employee when there was a change in his responsibilities at work. This case highlighted the fact that employees have to take care that they do not unquestioningly trust employers to deliver on the promise of perks. In this case, without his knowledge, the employee's bonus scheme had not only not been adjusted but it had actually been temporarily frozen in his second year of employment with the organisation, when Marconi underwent a major reorganisation. The principle issue was that the organisation, thought that it was in order to wipe away a huge part of an employee's reward package without telling her/him or discussing it with her/him.

The ET found on behalf of the employee who had gone to them on a point of principle because he knew that he was not actually owed any bonus as he had not actually reached the targets. The ET reported that Marconi had failed to contact the employee: Catchpole (1999) states:

> There should be some implied duty of good faith on the employer to inform employees if their remuneration package is not going to be operated in any year, because people's expectations are such that they will expect it to be operated. (p14)

It is vital that the reward process in an organisation is linked strongly to its strategy and, therefore, it would be expected that they would enforce the behaviours that are crucial to that business strategy, for example customer service versus financial profit, long-term results versus short-term ones. A second key point for organisations to bear in mind is that the reward system will only be accepted by the employees if it is effectively communicated and performance measures are believable. As Hunter (1999) stated:

> a reward system must provide incentives rather than disincentives for the sorts of behaviours that the new work organization expects: problem solving, teamwork, contribution to organizational behaviour. (p270)

Chapter summary

- People need to be paid for their work and also encouraged to work efficiently for that pay. This chapter discusses the link between work and reward with attention being paid to international harmonisation.

- This leads to an explanation of the key definitions used in the discussions that follow and which are used in the workplace as they add to the understanding of a discussion on pay surveys.

- Within a framework of pay there is a distinction made between new pay (NP) advocated by Lawler (1995) and traditional pay (TP) which stems from the work of scientific management led by Taylor (1911). From this comes a discussion on the changes in pay practices within the UK as it relates to developments in the economy.

- Rewards are linked closely to motivation and its key components such as culture. It also affected by the developments in key motivational theories such as the equity theory (Adams, 1965), expectancy theory (Vroom, 1964, 1970; Porter and Lawler, 1968), reinforcement theory, cognitive evaluation theory and the theory of cognitive dissonance (Festinger, 1957).

■ Reward systems work hand-in-glove with decision making – especially when it comes to risk taking.

■ Salary increases are normally based on the length of service and performance of the individual worker which could result in an organisational climate which is based either on close, personal friendships and cliques or on one which is rigid and regulation oriented.

■ The use of profit-related pay can enhance an individual's remuneration package if the organisation's scheme is appropriately designed and managed.

■ This leads to the problem of how to reward the increasing number of knowledge workers through creative and imaginative schemes which will encourage their retention by giving them autonomy, flexibility and responsibility.

■ Valuing the employee involves rewarding them and there are many ways by which this can be done, for example reward packages, share ownership and contemporary pay strategies such as competence-related pay.

■ Contemporary organisations rely heavily on high-performance teamwork and such teams need to be rewarded. The discussion of pay variables within teams by Trist and Bamforth (1951) leads to the modern examples of equitable team reward with the dependence on culture, values, organisational structure, performance management and employee development programmes.

■ Share options are developing as a reward mechanism but there is concern that they are being paid out to individuals for meeting undemanding targets and that an element of secrecy on the part of organisations is inhibiting their development as a potent reward method.

■ Globalisation requires a workforce that is flexible and able to make informed decisions and because of this, they have the power to create enormous value. Economic value added (EVA) is gaining prominence in Europe as a means of increasing employee participation and it is the EVA of an organisation that is used to calculate bonuses for individuals and for teams.

■ Reward and remuneration process can be one of the greatest sources of leverage available to an organisation as it searches to increase its performance and effectiveness in the contemporary, globalised environment. It is vital that corporate strategy is borne in mind because rewards have to provide an incentive and not a disincentive to the employee.

Chapter summary *continued*

END OF CHAPTER 9 CASE STUDY

Perks that keep the workers in their place

With almost 3000 guest rooms and more than half a million square feet of meeting space, the Opryland Hotel outside Nashville, USA boasts of being the biggest hotel and convention centre in the world. So why is this highly acclaimed colossus currently renovating a second-hand motel with 300 beds half an hour's drive up the road? And why did it appoint a manager with experience of supervising student hostels to run it?

The answer lies in the acute shortage of labour that now afflicts many of the US's fastest growing regions. Quite simply, the Opryland Hotel needs to attract – and keep – qualified staff and to do that it is resorting to an extensive range of perks, including, for 300 of its more junior staff, cheap housing. As Todd Smith of Opryland puts it, the resort-cum-conference centre aims to be the 'employer of choice' in the Nashville area, and employee benefits – rather than higher pay – are the route it has chosen.

The hotel – if it can be called that – is a lavish and punctiliously maintained complex built almost 20 years ago and steadily expanded since, preserving the principle that it should remain under one roof. Keeping up the standards that made the Opryland Hotel one of the US's top ten convention venues – a massive and expanding US market – takes a cast of thousands: 4600 for the hotel, including 150 gardeners and a further 2000 if you include the real 'outside', maintaining the golf course, the showboat that plies the river (The Cumberland), and the Grand Ole Opry, the classic country music vaudeville house that moved out of central Nashville 25 years ago to what was then almost the country – and gave the hotel its name.

The 300 workers housed by the company are charged $47.50 (about £24.50) a day for rent and may stay only three months (there is a waiting list for places). They are predominantly workers, many from south-east Asia, Mexico and the Caribbean, who are just finding their feet in the United States.

The 'housed' workers are a small minority of the total, but other perks are open to all: a nursery on the premises; one free meal per shift in the company cafeteria, plus cheap meals to take away; continuing education and training programmes that include English as a second language (which also has a waiting list); and bus transport to and from work.

In Britain, such perks might be taken for granted. In the United States, where 'outsourcing' and 'buying in' are the rule, they are a welcome benefit for workers,

END OF CHAPTER 9 CASE STUDY (CONT'D)

whose most urgent complaint is how little time they have for their families. The manpower shortage has given workers a chance to turn the tables, just a little, on their bosses.

Nor is Opryland unique. From across the USA come reports of company-owned blocks of flats, on-site clinics, subsidised childcare, and even fully fledged schools, with after-hours activities. More and more companies sited in far-flung 'business parks' are introducing on-site shops or a supermarket ordering and delivery service.

With the unemployment rate nationally running at 4.2 per cent and still falling, the labour shortage has become an increasingly conspicuous problem in many areas of the country. But it is especially acute in the mid-west and central southern states.

In Tennessee, where the April jobless rate, at 4.1 per cent, was slightly below the national average, there are variations between the prosperous suburban areas and poorer rural and inner city districts, just as there are in other states. But so far as the Nashville area is concerned, the jobless rate for all practical purposes is, as Todd Smith puts it, 'pretty much nil'.

His observation is borne out in all manner of ways: in city cafés that must restrict their menus for shortage of staff, in poorly cleaned hotel rooms – 'we just can't get enough help' – in the stalling of house building for

lack of labourers and in the ubiquitous 'help wanted' signs in shop windows. The most vivid evidence is the number of advertisements in the free employment newspapers that promise 'signing-on' bonuses of hundreds of dollars for a commitment to stay at least 90 days.

One result of the boom in perks is a revival of something akin to the 'company town', but for other reasons. While enlightened 19th-century industrialists on both sides of the Atlantic provided education and housing out of a sense of paternalistic responsibility or social idealism, today's US proprietors are acting out of pure capitalist concern for the bottom line.

The irony is that in doing so, they risk replicating the model of the former communist economies, where the workplace was the provider of everything from nurseries to schools, clinics, canteens and shops – a model long denounced by North Americans as clumsy and irrational.

Strangely, perhaps, the one benefit that US employers are so far resisting – except for certain highly trained specialists – is substantially higher pay. This is a cause of considerable relief to economists, who fear a return of inflation. But it is scant consolation to the lowest paid: their perks, however welcome, bind them ever more tightly to their employer – which is just what the company intended.

Adapted from: Dejevsky, M. (1999) Perks that keep the workers in their place, *Independent on Sunday*, 20 June, p21.

   ### END OF CHAPTER 9 CASE STUDY QUESTIONS

1 Since the Opryland Hotel is one of the biggest recruiters in its area, why does it need to offer rewards other than a wage/salary?

2 With a considerable shortage of labour, why do you think that the management of the hotel only offer short-term rewards such as limited time stay at subsidised accommodation?

3 What suggestions could you make to the management of the hotel to increase the labour force?

4 Why does the Opryland Hotel resist paying higher wages/salaries in order to retain their staff?

THESIS + ANTITHESIS = SYNTHESIS

Explore the view that there is not such thing as PRP.

SELF-TEST THE KEY ISSUES

1 Why is it necessary for an organisation to offer benefits to its employees?

2 What are the advantages and disadvantages of flexible benefits? Consider your answer from the view of both the employer and the employee.

3 Of the theories on motivation covered in this chapter, which appeals to you the most? Which of the theories, if different, do you think is most relevant to the rewarding of employees?

4 List the key differences between new pay (NP) and traditional pay (TP)?

TEAM/CLASS DISCUSSIONS

1 'It is not possible to measure performance, so to link pay with performance is a dream.' Debate.

2 Debate the view that it is not possible to motivate knowledge workers by giving them an increase in salary.

PROJECTS (INDIVIDUAL OR TEAMS)

1 Find out the name of one public and one private organisation that offers share ownership to its employees. Write a report that gives the pros and cons of such a reward scheme for both the employer and the employee.

2 Using two CEOs from different organisations of your choice, investigate how their remuneration package differs from that of their employees.

Recommended reading

Armstrong, M. (1999) *A Handbook of Human Resource Management Practice*, London: Kogan Page

Beardwell, I. and L. Holden (1999) *Human Resource Management: A Contemporary Perspective*, London: Pitman

Bratton, J. and J. Gold (1999) *Human Resource Management: Theory and Practice*, Basingstoke: Macmillan Business

Storey, J. (ed.) (1995) *Human Resource Management: A Critical Text*, London: Routledge

Torrington, D. and L. Hall (1998) *Human Resource Management*, London: Prentice Hall

URLs (uniform resource locators)

www.rewardstrategies.com

Free published articles on compensation programmes for growing organisations aimed at increasing revenues, reducing expenses and focusing achievement profitably.

www.evanomics.com

Detailed information about EVA.

www.employersinc.com/seminars/altcomp.html

Alternative compensation and reward strategies.

www.remuneration.org

Remuneration Organization. Non-profit organisation dedicated to improving the world's workplaces through education and training of business professionals in remuneration and employee ownership strategies.

www.gronline.org

Global source for remuneration and benefits. Training and information.

Bibliography

Abrams, F. (1999) *Independent on Sunday*, 21 November, p5

ACAS (Undated) Appraisal-related pay in *Advisory Booklet No 14*, London: ACAS

Adams, J.S. (1965) Inequity in social exchange in Berkowitz, L. (ed.) *Advances in Experimental Social Psychology*, **2**, pp267–99, New York: Academic Press

Adkin, E., G. Jones and P. Leighton (1997) *Pocket Employer*, London: Economist/Profile Books

Armstrong, M. and H. Murlis (1994) *Reward Management: A Handbook of Remuneration Strategy and Practice*, London: Kogan Page

Arnold, H.J. (1976) Effects of performance feedback and extrinsic reward upon high intrinsic motivation in *Organizational Behavior and Human Performance*, December, pp275–88

Beattie, A. (1999) Taxing dilemma of an incentive for workers in *Financial Times*, 24 November, p6

Beer, M. (1994) Reward systems in Beer, M., B. Spector, P. Lawrence, D. Mills and P. Quin *Managing Human Assets*, New York: Free Press

Bell, S. (1999) Executive share options reward 'the average' in Mackintosh, J., *Financial Times*, 18 October, p3

Bevan, S. and M. Thompson (1991) Performance management at the crossroads in *Personnel Management*, November, pp36–9

Born, L. and E. Mollman (1996) Empowerment and rewards: a case study in *Empowerment in Organizations*, **4**(3): 30–3

Bratton, J. and J. Gold (1999) *Human Resource Management: Theory and Practice*, Basingstoke: Macmillan – now Palgrave

Brough, I. (1994) PRP for manual workers in *Employee Relations*, **16**(7): 18–32

Brown, A. (1995) *Organisational Culture*, London: Pitman

Brown, D. (1999) in *Euro Rewards 2000: Revolutionary, Realistic or Reticent?*, London: Towers Perrin, October

Brown, D.(1999) in Walsh, J., Pan-European strategies on reward are 'inevitable' in *Personnel Management*, 11 November, p 11

Burt, T. (1999) DaimlerChrysler workers to seek profit-share boost in *Financial Times*, 27 September, p2

Calder, B.J. and B.M. Staw (1977) Self-perception of intrinsic and extrinsic motivation in *Journal of Personality and Social Psychology*, April, pp599–605

Cannell, M. and S. Wood (1992) *Incentive Pay: Impact and Evolution*, London: Institute of Personnel Management

Catchpole, M. (1999) in Rana, E. (1999b) Marconi's communications fail over incentive scheme in *People Management*, 28 October, p14

Chittenden, M. and C. Dignan (1999) Union bosses rake in pay rises worthy of fat cats in *Sunday Times*, 25 July, p26

Confederation of British Industries/Hay Management Consultants (1996) *Trends in Pay and Benefits Systems*, May Survey Results, London: CBI

Cully, M., S. Woodland, A. O'Reilly and G. Dix (1999) *Britain at Work*, London: Routledge

Department of Trade and Industry (DTI) (1996) *Workplace Employee Relations Survey* (WERS), London: Department of Trade and Industry

Department of Trade and Industry (DTI) (1996) *The Rewards of Success. Flexible Pay Systems in Britain*, London: Department of Trade and Industry

Dejevsky, M. (1999) Perks that keep the workers in their place in *Independent on Sunday*, 20 June, p21

Dolan, E. (1999) Where to find the pick of the perks in *Sunday Telegraph*, Business Section (B), 11 July

Dornstein, M. (1988) Wage reference groups and their determinants: a study of blue-collar and white-collar employees in Israel in *Journal of Occupational Psychology*, **61**: 221–35

Druker, J. and G. White (1997) Constructing a new reward strategy: reward management in the British construction industry in *Employer Relations*, **19**(2): 128–46

Edelsten, M. (1999) in Lucas, E., Turning on the knowledge workers in *Professional Manager*, May, pp11–12

Festinger, L. (1957) *A Theory of Cognitive Dissonance*, Stanford, CA: Stanford University Press

Financial Times (1999) A huge salary isn't everything, 20 October, p19

Fletcher, C. and W. Williams (1992) The route to performance management in *Personnel Management*, October, pp42–7

Folger, R. and M.A. Konovsky (1989) Effects of procedural and distributive justice on reactions to pay rise decisions in *Academy of Management Journal* (32): 115–30

Foot, M. and C. Hook (1999) *Introducing Human Resource Management*, Harlow: Addison Wesley Longman

Friedman, A. (1970) Managerial strategies, activities, techniques and technology: towards a complex theory of the labour process in Knights, D. and H. Willmott, *Labour Process Theory*, Basingstoke: Macmillan – now Palgrave

Galbraith, J.R. and R.K. Kazanian (1986) *Strategic Implementation: Structure, Systems and Process*, St Paul, MN: West Publishing

Geber, B. (1995) The bugaboo of team pay in *Training*, **30**(8): 25–34

Geery, J.F. (1992) Pay control and commitment linking appraisal and reward in *Human Resource Management Journal*, **2**(4): 36–54

Gomez-Mejia, I. and D. Balkin (1992) *Compensation, Organizational Strategy and Firm Performance*, Cincinatti, CH: Southwestern

Goodman, P.S. (1977) Social comparison processes in organizations in Staw, B.M. and G.R. Salancik (eds) *New Directions in Organizational Behavior*, Chicago: St Clair, pp97–131

Graham, H.T. and R. Bennett (1999) *Human Resources Management*, London: Financial Times/Pitman

Gratton, L. (1999) in Bickerstaff, G. (ed.) *Mastering Management*, London: Financial Times/Pitman

Gross, S.J. (1995) Compensation for teams: How to design and implement team-based reward programs in *American Management Association*, New York: American Management Association

Guest, D. (1999) in Rana, E., Christmas comes early for Goldman Sachs employees in *People Management*, May, p15

Hargreaves, P.K. (1999) *Attractive Perks for UK Shareholders*, London: Hargreaves Lansdown

Harper, D. (1999) *The National Wealth*, London: HarperCollins

Hatch, M.J. (1997) *Organization Theory: Modern Symbolic and Postmodern Perspectives*, Oxford: Oxford University Press

Hatchett, A. (2000) Ringing true in *People Management*, 20 January, pp40–32

Heery, F. (1996) Risk representation and the new pay. Paper presented to the BUIRA/EBEN Conference Ethical Issues in Contemporary Human resource Management, Imperial College, London, 3 April 1996

Her Majesty's Treasury (1993) *Sharing in Success, The Government's Employee Financial Participation Schemes*, London: Her Majesty's Treasury

Hewitt Associates (1991) *Total Compensation Management, Reward Management Strategies for the 1900s*, Oxford: Blackwell

Hilpern, K. (1999) What's my motivation? in *The Independent*, Wednesday Review Section, 2 June, p12

Hilton, A. (1999) Weighing up the fat cats in *Management Today*, July, pp46–51

Hoffman, J.R. and S.G. Rogelberg (1999) *A guide to team incentive systems* on http://www.hr-expert.com/members/data/rc_articles/13504AB1.htm

Hunter, I. (1999) *Goodbye to all that?* on http://www.peoplemanagement.co.uk/editorial/law/hunter.asp?page_no=29&qu=, 28 October, pp1–2

Huseman, R.C., J.D. Hatfield and E.W. Miles (1989) An empirical examination of the antecedents of commitment to difficult goals in *Journal of Applied Psychology*, **74**: pp18–23

Hussey, D.E. (1991) Implementing strategy through management education and training in Hussey, D.E. (ed.) *International Review of Strategic Management*, **2**(1), Chichester: John Wiley

Incomes Data Services (1999) *Directors' Pay Report*, 27 October, London: Incomes Data Services

Institute of Personnel and Development (1996) *Team Reward, Key Facts*, September, London: Institute of Personnel and Development

Institute of Personnel Management (1992) *Performance Management in the UK: An Analysis of the Issues*, London: IPM

Kanter, R.M. (1989) *When Giants Learn to Dance: Mastering the Challenge of Strategy, Management and Careers in the 1990s*, London: Routledge

Kellaway, L. (1999) Sports stars a race apart from fat cats in *Financial Times*, 26 July, p10

Kerr, J. and J.W. Slocum (1987) Managing corporate culture through reward systems in *Academy of Management Executive*, **1**(2): 99–108

Kessler, I. (1995) Reward systems in Storey, J. (ed.) *Human Resource Management: A Critical Text*, London: Routledge

Kessler, I. and J. Purcell (1992) Performance-related pay: objectives and applications in *Human Resource Management Journal*, **2**(3): 16–33

Keuning, D. (1998) *Management: A Contemporary Approach*, London: Pitman

Kohn, A. (1993) Why incentive plans cannot work in *Harvard Business Review*, September–October, pp54–63

Lawler, E.E. (1990) *Strategic Pay*, San Francisco, CA: Jossey-Bass

Lawler, E.E. (1995) The new pay: a strategic approach in *Compensation and Benefits Review*, July/August, pp46–54

Lewin, K. (1938) *The Conceptual Representation and the Measurement of Psychological Forces*, Durham, NC: Duke University Press

Locke, E.A. (1980) Latham vs Komaki: a tale of two paradigms in *Journal of Applied Psychology*, February, pp16–23

London, S. (1999) Workers who take a share in *Financial Times*, 17 November, p22

Lucas, E. (1999) Turning on the knowledge workers in *Professional Manager*, May, pp10–12

Mackintosh, J. (1999) Executive share options reward 'the average' in *Financial Times*, 18 October, p3

Mahoney, T.A. (1992) Multiple pay contingencies: strategic design of compensation in Salaman, G., *Human Resource Strategies*, London: Sage/Open University, pp337–46

Marsden, D. and R. Richardson (1994) Performing for pay? The effects of 'merit pay' on motivation in a public sector in *British Journal of Industrial Relations*, **32**(2): 243–61

Maund, L. (1999) *Understanding People and Organisations: An Introduction to Organisational Behaviour*, Cheltenham: Stanley Thornes

McFarlin, D.B. and P.D. Sweeney (1992) Distributive and procedural justice as predictors of satisfaction with personal and organizational outcomes in *Academy of Management Journal* (35): pp626–37

Moorhead, G. and R.W. Griffin (1995) *Organizational Behavior: Managing People and Organizations*, Boston: Houghton Mifflin

Murlis, H. (1999) in Lucas, E. (1999) Turning on the knowledge workers in *Professional Manager*, May, p12

Nadler, D.A. and E.E. Lawler (1983) Motivation: a diagnostic approach in Hackman, J.R., E.E. Lawler and I.W. Porter (eds) *Perspectives in Behavior in Organizations*, Homewood, IL: Dorsey Press

Overholser, G. (1999) Company bosses should earn their pay in *The Week*, 13 November 1999, p11

Pinder, C. (1984) *Work Motivation*, Glenview, IL: Scott Foresman

Pollock, L. (1999) EVA believers in *People Management*, 16 September, pp56–8

Porter, J.W. and E.E. Lawler (1968) *Managerial Attitudes and Performance*, Homewood, IL: Dorsey Press

Rana, E. (1999a) Christmas comes early for Goldman Sachs employees in *People Management*, May, p15

Rana, E. (1999b) Marconi's communications fail over incentive scheme in *Personnel Management*, 28 October 1999, p16

Randle, K. (1997) Rewarding failure: operating a performance-related pay system in pharmaceutical research in *Personnel Review*, **26**(3): 187–200

Robbins, S.P. (1998) *Organizational Behavior: Concepts, Controversies, Applications* (International Edition), London: Prentice Hall International

Shapero, A. (1985) *Managing Professional People*, New York: Free Press

Schuster, J.R. and P.K. Zingheim (1992) *The New Pay: Linking Employee and Organizational Performance*, New York: Lexington Books

Smith, I. (1992) Reward management: a retrospective assessment in *Employee Relations*, **15**(3): 45–59

Stacey, R.D. (1996) *Strategic Management and Organisational Dynamics*, London: Pitman

Staw, B.M. (1977) Motivation in organizations: toward synthesis and redirection in Staw, B.M. and G.R. Salancik (eds), *New Directions in Organizational Behavior*, Chicago: St Clair

Sunday Times, 25 July 1999, News Review, Section 2, p2

Swabe, A.I.R. (1989) Performance-related pay: a case study in *Employee Relations*, **3**(2)

Taylor, F.W. (1911) *Principles of Scientific Management*, New York: Harper & Row

Taylor, R. (1999) Boardroom pay surging ahead in *Financial Times*, 27 October, p1

Team Pay Case Studies (1997), New York: Academy of Management

Tolman, E.C. (1932) *Purposive Behavior in Animals*, New York: Appleton-Century-Crofts

Towers Perrin (1999) *Euro Rewards 2000: Revolutionary, Realistic or Reticent?*, London: Towers Perrin, October

Trist, E.L. and K.W. Bamforth (1951) Some social and psychological consequences of the Long-wall method of coal-getting in *Human Relations*, **4**

Tyson, J. (1999) in Pollock, L., EVA believers in *People Management*, 16 September, pp58

Unsworth, R. (1999) Job perk that really has staff motoring in *Mail on Sunday*, Financial Mail on Sunday Section, 16 May, p44

Vroom, V.H. (1964/1970) *Work and Motivation*, New York: Wiley

Walters, R. (1999) Share plans create SAYE uncertainty in *People Management*, 25 March, pp15–16

Walsh, J. (1999) Pan-European strategies on reward are 'inevitable' in *People Management*, 11 November, p11

Williamsom, J. (1999) in Pollock, L., EVA believers in *People Management*, 16 September, pp56–8

Wright, V. (1991) Performance-related pay in Neale, F. (ed.) *The Handbook of Performance Management*, London: Institute of Personnel Management

Employee development and performance management

After studying this chapter, you should be able to:

- DEFINE the term 'employee development' (ED).
- DISCUSS the relationship between ED and performance management (PM).
- IDENTIFY the key concepts related to ED.
- EVALUATE the difference between learning, training and education.
- ASSESS the different learning theories and styles related to ED.
- STATE the connection between management development (MD) and ED.
- DISCUSS personal growth, career development and career planning.
- IDENTIFY the key aspects related to the concept of the learning organisation.
- EVALUATE the need for knowledge management, intellectual capital, talent and emotions in the workplace.
- APPLY the principles of performance appraisal.
- EVALUATE the relationship between participation and empowerment.
- ASSESS the evolution of MD.

INTRODUCTION

Framework case study

The Kalahari bushmen

For hundreds of years, the Kalahari bushmen were nomadic hunters and foragers in the harsh, unpredictable South African desert. They developed the skills to find water during drought, to live on reptiles and plants in the absence of game and to fashion bows and arrows from their limited sources. They travelled in groups bound together by ties of kinship and friendship. Their mobility and few possessions enabled the bushmen to switch easily to more successful groups, in this way capitalising on success wherever it was found over a wide geographical area. The flexible group system (known as the 'band system') was enhanced by values of equality, sharing and gift giving. A hunter's kill would be used to feed neighbours, who would later reciprocate. Gift giving meant that useful artifacts and utensils were widely shared. Hunting camps had grass huts facing the centre of a circle where the cooling hearths were hubs of continuous discussion and social exchanges. The bushmen of the Kalahari also bonded through a deep culture in their camps of shared mythology, stories and dances.

Then came along civilisation. In recent years, exposure to material wealth has fostered a transformation. The Kalahari bushmen have now accumulated possessions, which hamper mobility, thus forcing a lifestyle shift from foraging to farming. A new community structure has evolved, with families living in separate, permanent huts. Entrances are located for privacy and hearths have been moved inside. Survival skills have deteriorated, with bows and arrows produced only for curio shops. Without sharing and communication, a hierarchy of authority – the chief – is used to resolve disputes. Tension and dysfunctional conflict have increased and the tribe's ability to handle drought and disaster today is nonexistent. No longer are there shared stories and mythology that bind the tribespeople into a community.

Adapted from: Hunt, D.K. (1991) Cautionary tales from the Kalahari: how hunters become herders and may have trouble changing back again, *Academy of Management Education*, 3(5): 74–86.

The hunter–forager society of the Kalahari bushmen given in the Framework Case Study is a metaphor for the fluid learning organisation of today – an aspiration of all companies who survive in the contemporary business environment. It is through an understanding of the learning organisation that those involved in ED can integrate the various techniques and methods discussed in this chapter to become a practitioner of performance management.

If employees are to contribute competently to the achievement of their organisation's objectives, they need to be rewarded in a manner that they find intrinsically motivating. While reward and remuneration programmes are essential to the competitive ability of all organisations, and may go some way to intrinsically motivating an employee, it is also important for employers to appreciate the potency of the development of all employees in terms of their career development as it is linked to career planning – that is, for both the employer and the employee ■ *see* Chapter 9 ■. There has been a significant development in this area since the early 1900s when the Institute of Personnel Management (IPD) (1992) published their

see Chapter 9

study on the development of people at work. Even at this time, organisations reported that pay was significant in their developmental programmes but also that the programmes they used were development led with a key component being to identify the developmental needs of the organisation and the individual and then move on to filling them.

If ED is successfully designed and managed, it can contribute to the success of the organisation within the contemporary business environment. This issue cannot be underrated, according to the vice-president of human resourcing at Prudential Banking, Jean Tomlin (1999), who states:

> Ignoring people development and training is not an option for any business. To do so would be commercial suicide. If you want to bring the best out of people you must invest in them, believe in them and trust them to respond. (p14)

However, ED still appears to be treated as a novelty by many managers and leaders who do not perceive it as an employment benefit or perk – they still perceive ED as a cost in financial terms rather than an investment in the assets of their organisation. Some CEOs consider that the use of funding for long-term development of individuals is a waste of money because they believe that no sooner have they educated or trained individuals, they move on to other organisations or are ▶ **headhunted** ◀ by other firms. Such organisations tend to find that they have difficulty in attracting and keeping knowledge workers yet tend to overlook the link between the two situations.

▶ The name given to an individual who has been particularly recruited, or is being recruited, ◀┈┈▶ **Headhunted**
by another organisation in such a way that they are enticed away, usually by an increase in rewards and remuneration.

The maxim 'people are our best asset' is frequently used by managers, yet there is often no tangible evidence that this is actually the case. When designing their corporate strategy, organisations often overlook ED as a key factor ■ *see* Chapter 1 *and* Chapter 2 ■. McClelland (1994) found this to be so although there was evidence in his study that those organisations that did identify ED as a key aspect of their corporate strategy also reported that it helped in gaining and maintaining their competitive advantage – although this was principally related to the development of managers rather than all staff. Nowadays, employees and potential employees are more than ever keen to explore the opportunities for their own development – they want to translate cliché into action. It would be unfair to state that all employers have overlooked this change in attitude by their staff since some do state exactly what sort of development is on offer within their organisations and use it as a carrot to attract high quality staff who will stay with them. An example here is the Cap Gemini organisation whose motto is: 'We aim to take your career in the direction you choose.'

Organisations that do see the importance of ED as part of their organisational strategy tend to do so by identifying needs from the view of the organisation rather

see Chapter 1 *and* Chapter 2

than at the needs of the individual. In the best cases, for example Cap Gemini, Ford and Unilever, individual needs are not neglected.

DEFINING EMPLOYEE DEVELOPMENT (ED)

The development of people is essential and is not ▶ **altruistic** ◀ as is believed by some managers. The issue needs to be turned on its head: rather than considering the view that the purpose of an organisation is to develop its employees, the task of employers is to put people development first. ED is not just training. It has a much broader range of components that have a deeper impact on an individual that training alone does because it is not only the individual who is impacted upon but the organisation and the wider environment within which the organisation works, for example the community.

Altruistic ◀┈┈▶ An unselfish concern for the welfare and interests of other people.

Therefore, the definition of ED is not as straightforward as it might seem because it is more of an attitude which includes the concepts of:

- growth

- expansion

- improvement and

- education.

Armstrong (1999) states that:

> The employment development policy should express the organization's commitment to the continuous development of the skills and abilities of employees in order to maximise their contribution and to give them the opportunity to enhance their skills, realise their potential, advance their careers and increase their employability within and outside the organization. (p264)

ED is brought about through interventionist activities and the management of ED is an art specific to differing situations. It cannot be characterised by definitions, that is, it cannot be identified by terms that have unique meanings used to explain the same things. ED is therefore ▶ **contextual** ◀.

Contextual ◀┈┈▶ The real meaning depends upon the context within which the term is used.

It will also depend upon a number of criteria, for example the:

- context of the organisation, its: culture

  climate

structure

design

use of technology ■ *see* Chapter 6 ■

see **Chapter 6**

■ views of the stakeholders and

■ type of individuals involved in the organisation.

Because of this, the nature of ED is such that it is constantly on the move and evolving over time – it is beyond definition.

ED, according to Reid and Barrington (1999), is primarily about providing an arena for individuals to learn to do something that they could not previously do. It is usually related to the achievement of goals in the workplace although learning can take place in other contexts and places. ED is less about learning at random and more about the use of organised, planned and developed journeys.

Reid and Barrington (1999) do make an attempt to define ED:

> part of personnel (or human resource) management and involves the planning and management of people's learning – including ways to help them manage their own – with the aim of making the learning process more effective, increasingly efficient, properly directed and therefore useful. (p7)

Such a definition is based on generalised concepts – as indeed the nature of ED itself encourages. However, it is possible to discuss what ED is about and consider the concerns and processes of managing that development.

THE ROLE OF THE MANAGER IN ED

All senior managers should have direct responsibility for ED and it should, therefore, be part of their defined role – it is a key management ▶ **skill** ◀ that, if utilised effectively, will make all the difference in the success of the organisation.

▶ The ability to do something well, especially if as a result of experience. **Skill**

Hammond (1999) believes that there is a conundrum for all managers. In the past the personal goals of employees were closely tied to the achievement of the organ-

10.1

Activity

Search the appointments section of any broadsheet newspaper (for example Financial Times, The Times, Guardian) or a professional journal (such as People Management, Management Today) and find an advertisement for a manager (other than HRM specific) where the job description explicitly asks for the applicant to have experience in people development.

How difficult was it to find?

isation, while the ever-changing nature of the contemporary workplace means that individuals have become:

> more independent in their planning and seek development to support their own ambitions, not just those of their employers. (p14)

It may well be that the individual's aspirations will be fulfilled within the organisation but it is more often found that ED is, according to Hammond (1999), the:

> fair exchange for good work on the journey towards individual goals. (p14)

A discerning employer will recognise both instances and will see that the latter offers benefits to all members of the workforce, especially when the opportunities and choices are transparent to all.

ED IN ACTION

Organisations that consider ED as central to their corporate strategy recognise that most employees will start their formal learning experiences by studying anything related to their personal interests in, say, sport or hobbies which are then quickly followed by a desire to learn more about career-oriented development. Those organisations which are at the forefront of ED, for example Ford and Unipart, have devolved their ED budgets to departments and/or individuals so that they can manage their own development within the framework of the organisation for which they work. Where this has happened, the manager acts as a guide for the employee and works with her/him individually by challenging her/him to use their funds to support her/his careers decisions. This is usually done through the auspices of the performance appraisal system.

This is not a one-way street because managers themselves can gain self-development by this process. However, it cannot just happen because not all managers are able to advise wisely neither are all employees able to make positive choices. The process, according to Hammond (1999):

> calls for people who can judge how much they should determine the path or follow the aspirations of their staff. (p14)

It requires managers to be knowledgeable about personal development as well as having the ability to increase the skills and knowledge of their subordinates. Such managers have the adeptness to look at developmental experiences in such a way that they meet the objectives of both the organisation and the individual who works for that organisation so that the intellectual capital is of benefit to both parties.

Some organisations take a different view and attempt to shift the total responsibility for ED onto the shoulders of the individual employees, expecting them to keep up to date and fully equipped to compete in the contemporary environment. While this might be an attractive road to take, it is both unrealistic and too simplistic because employees cannot work in a vacuum and they need information, time, space, funds and resources to make decisions that will help them to gain the required skills and knowledge. While learning has become more accessible to individuals, it is the organisation that must set out the skills and attributes required for the future. There is a fine balance to be had here because organisations can help the employee out of what Hammond (1999) calls 'development isolation' by facilitating their self-development. That is, by assisting in the process of acquiring skills and knowledge, the manager can help the organisation and the individual to reach the required objectives.

ED FOR THE FUTURE

There is a considerable amount of rhetoric in organisations concerning ED, yet the time has come for a rejuvenation and fresh commitment to the developing of individuals. The workplace is an ever-changing environment that provides an admirable impetus for ED. Organisations such as Virgin Atlantic, Nike, Next and Carphone Warehouse, which are maintaining their market lead, use imaginative and resourceful approaches to the development of their employees and do so in a fresh way. They recognise that individual employees should be full partners in the process along with the employers, the providers of ED and sometimes with the support of the national government – as shown in the formula below:

$$Em + E + P + G = ED$$

where: Em   represents the employer
      E   represents the employee
      P   represents the providers
      G   represents the government
     ED   represents employee development.

The learning age is a reality and the true value of ED is that it has the potential to give all individuals a greater choice and enhance their performance for the benefit of their employing organisations and thus there is a knock-on effect in providing benefits for the wider environment, such as the community within which the employee lives and within which the employer carries out her/his business.

IDENTIFYING ED

There is no one way to finding success in ED. However, there are some areas, supported by the stages as shown in Table 10.1, which can be investigated in the achievement of this.

The continually changing nature of the business environment means that unique demands are constantly being placed on people because they must acquire new skills and resources in order to cope with those demands. It is an error to believe that this can be brought about by education and training alone. Alongside the latter must come initiatives that bring about changes in the attitudes – ED is attitudinal – of both employees and their managers. With such changes also comes a change in interpersonal relationships and identities.

Table 10.1 Some stages to finding success in ED

1 *Corporate strategy*
The need to connect ED with the overall strategy of the organisation.

2 *Full participation*
All employees need to participate fully in the identification of their own developmental needs.

Those who actually do the job are best qualified to do this but they also need managers to inform them of future developments within the organisation.

Unfortunately, line managers generally have a poor understanding of development aspects such as learning, training and needs analysis.

3 *Individual responsibility*
There has been a growth in individual's taking responsibility for planning their own continuous development, that is, work-based and longer term career-based training and development.

4 *Reward systems*
The recognition and reward system is important when individuals take responsibility for their own continuous development. Such rewards need to be suitably tailored to the individual employee by, for example:

linking bonus systems to indices of customer satisfaction or by the development of a top to bottom performance pay system. (IPD, 1992, p3)

5 *Organisational design*
With the leaner and flatter organisational design has come the necessity for individual employees to develop laterally:

- within their own organisation
- between organisations

in order to make the most of personal satisfaction related to both job and career.

6 *Flexible workforce*
A more flexible workforce comes about with more breadth and depth in individual development.

7 *Record keeping*
With the increased use of electronic data systems, it is now easier to store records of achievement for all employees. These systems keep track of the skills and knowledge accrued by employees.

8 *Diverse workforce*
There has been an increase in opportunity for utilising flexible temporary labour, for example outsourcing, job sharing, part-time working and subcontracting. Such practices allow organisations to maintain a highly skilled and specialised workforce with the competitive strengths required to meet the needs of the stakeholders. A diverse and decentralised workforce is essential.

Contemporary literature and practice has adopted the term 'performance development' to encompass:

the framework to identify, formulate and implement the best policies and practice in the management and development of people. (Armstrong and Baron, 1999, back cover)

If an organisation is to be successful it must develop its employees and, as has been mentioned earlier, this needs to be carried out in a flexible framework which empowers the managers to communicate effectively with their staff and through this develop and intrinsically motivate them ■ *see* Chapter 9 ■.

see Chapter 9

Armstrong and Baron (1999) state that:

> in our view, development is the prime purpose of performance management. (p51)

DIFFERENCE BETWEEN LEARNING, TRAINING AND EDUCATION

ED concerns itself with three specific concepts:

■ learning

■ training

■ education

each of which has its own meaning and there is also an interrelationship between the three.

Learning is the most critical of the three and is common to the others because without it training and education cannot take place. Since it is so important, it is dealt with in detail below. There is no universally accepted definition of learning and most writers discuss it as it relates to the acquisition of new information. Pettinger (1996) incorporates the fundamental aspects of learning in his definition:

> the process by which skills, knowledge, attitudes and behaviour are formed and developed. (p82)

In the context of ED, learning must allow the individual to do something s/he could not do before.

ED is about making learning happen and this can be done through training and education. Training is the use of productive and planned routes within learning and education is more about the general basis for living. That is, training modifies an individual's abilities towards a particular activity – it assists the individual in her/his learning.

All managers, and HR managers in particular, need to understand how an individual learns and develops if they are to achieve the goals and objectives of the organisation. Morgan (1988) stated that managers must:

> find ways of developing and mobilising the intelligence, knowledge, and creative potential of human beings at every level of organization... become increasingly skilled in placing quality people in key places and developing their full potential. It will become increasingly important to recruit people who enjoy learning and relish change to motivate employees to be intelligent, flexible, and adaptive. (p7)

It is essential that employees are developed as key components within the organisation because they are the only thing which will enable the organisation to survive. According to the Annual Report of the IPD (1998/99) the management and development of people is:

increasingly recognised as the key difference between sustainable success and failure. (p4)

The employees will require, according to Barrow and Loughlin (1993), a number of abilities and skills such as:

- *A high level of education*
  Up to first degree level so that they can use the technology and understand their own contribution to the decisions required in their jobs.

- *The ability to learn new skills and adapt in changing circumstances*
  Through continuous development individuals must take responsibility for their own learning and ensure that all their skills are current and that they have the ability to learn new skills.

- *The ability to work in organisations with flatter structures and few levels of management*
  Requires the setting of personal objectives, working in self-managed teams and making decisions.

- *The ability to interfere with people at all levels*
  This includes customers, superiors and team members.

- *The ability to problem solve*
  Through creative thinking.

Some of the most accomplished people in our time have failed the 11-plus, their GCSEs and A levels, as well as higher certificates, diplomas and degrees. Many of them still think of themselves as failures.

DEFINING LEARNING

As mentioned previously, it is difficult to define learning which can be ambiguous in its conceptual use. However, an appreciation of learning in context is essential to the understanding of ED, which is learning in action. Most writers – particularly those who take a psychological approach to learning – tend to agree that learning brings about a permanent change in behaviour. It is this aspect of a change in behaviour which is important because it distinguishes two different aspects which are pertinent to the workplace:

- *practice* which tends to be related to events which are deliberately planned and

- *experience* which may have been intentionally arranged – remembering that it is possible to learn unintentionally – or may have occurred spontaneously in the natural course of events.

A central theme in organisations today is that of 'learning to learn' and self-development through active learning. When workers come together they will learn spontaneously and because of that they will change their behaviour in a variety of ways.

10.2

Activity

Reflect upon the most recent time that you worked as part of a team either at university or in your place of paid employment.

List what you learned spontaneously.

In order for learning and development to take place, four factors must be in play:

- education
- training
- socialisation and
- experience.

According to Pettinger (1996), learning and development are also a result of conditioning and restriction:

> whereby the individual is persuaded to adopt, and ultimately accept, guidance, regulation, conformity and compliance in particular situations. (p82)

VIEWS OF LEARNING

When accepting the view that learning and development will bring about a permanent change in behaviour which has come about as a result of experience, it is possible to appreciate that it is not just a cognitive activity, that is, it is not merely thinking and collecting knowledge about a subject, for example HRM.

POINTS TO PONDER

By reading this textbook you are not necessarily learning. If you believe that you are doing so in a parrot fashion you are supporting the behaviourist approach, which is an assumption that observable behaviour is a function of its consequences.

All learning and development has as its base two theories:

- classical conditioning and
- operant conditioning.

Classical conditioning is the modifying of an individual's behaviour so that a conditioned stimulus is matched with an unconditioned stimulus and elicits an unconditioned response. The theory is based on the work of a Russian physiologist, Ivan Pavlov, who worked with dogs to support his views. His dogs secreted saliva (unconditioned response) when they were given food (unconditioned stimulus). When Pavlov presented the dogs with a conditioned stimulus (Pavlov rang a bell at the same time as the unconditioned stimulus (the food)) this caused the dogs to salivate (conditioned response).

Although some employers might think they are, employees are not dogs! However, they may well behave in the same way if classical conditioning methods are used by managers. For example, a keyboard operator may get lower back pain (unconditioned response) as a result of poor posture (unconditioned stimulus) in her/his office computer seat. However, if the operator becomes aware of the pain in the back only when the telephone in the office rings (conditioned response), then s/he might very well develop a conditioned response (lower back pain) as soon as the telephone rings.

10.3 Activity

Bring to mind one or two of your university classes or training events you have attended at your place of work.

Note briefly any experiences of classical conditioning which you have observed.

Operant conditioning happens when behaviour is modified by means of positive or negative consequences following specific behaviours. It is based on the belief that behaviour is a function of its consequences, which could be positive or negative. It is through this resultant behaviour that an individual influences or shapes future behaviour. There are three distinct strategies which help this process:

- reinforcement
- punishment
- extinction.

A number of organisations use the ideas within this theory in an effort to get employees to behave in a required way – this is called ▶ **organisational behaviour modification** ◀ ■ *see* Chapter 9 ■.

see Chapter 9

Organisational behaviour ◀┈▶ modification

The use of operant conditioning theory to get members of the workforce to behave in a required way.

Through ▶ **reinforcement** ◀ acceptable behaviour is enhanced and through ▶ **punishment** ◀ and ▶ **extinction** ◀ undesirable behaviours are extinguished. All organisations have a standard of behaviour which is acceptable and some behaviours which are not. Such behaviours are usually emphasised through the culture of the organisation. However, a specific behaviour in one context might not be acceptable in another.

▶ The attempt to induce required behaviour in others by the use of positive rewards or by ◀┈┈▶ **Reinforcement** withholding negative consequences.

▶ The attempt to eliminate undesired behaviours in an individual either by bestowing nega- ◀┈┈▶ **Punishment** tive consequences for that behaviour or by withholding the positive consequences (the rewards).

▶ Any behaviour which is used in an attempt to weaken behaviour in others by attaching ◀┈┈▶ **Extinction** some sort of consequence (positive or negative) to it.

An employee who is a member of the Reserve Forces will be trained to use sophisticated weapons designed to kill people. If s/he used these skills in the workplace in an attempt to downsize the staff and delayer the organisation, her/his behaviour would not be construed as contextually acceptable.

That is apart from the ethical considerations about what behaviour, here as a result of learning and experience, is desirable and undesirable.

It is management that uses reinforcement and punishment in an attempt to encourage acceptable behaviours. Positive consequences are brought about as a result of any behaviour that is found to be attractive or pleasurable, for example PRP or promotion. Negative consequences are the result of behaviour that an individual finds to be unattractive or aversive. Examples here might a forced attendance on a training course or disciplinary action. The consequences of an individual's behaviour – be they positive or negative – are defined for the individual receiving them. Like ED in general, they are person specific. It follows, then, that individual, gender and cultural differences may be important when considering positive or negative consequences of behaviour.

The use of positive or negative consequences follows a specific behaviour and therefore reinforces or punishes that particular behaviour. Research shows that when an individual's behaviour is followed by a positive consequence the original behaviour is reinforced and is likely to continue. Conversely, any behaviour which is followed by a negative consequence is unlikely to reoccur. Figure 10.1 shows how positive and negative consequences can be applied or withheld in the strategies of reinforcement and punishment.

An alternative to punishment is extinction, which is any behaviour used in an attempt to weaken the behaviour in others by attaching some sort of consequence (positive or negative) to it. The basic philosophy behind this technique is that by ignoring the behaviour it will disappear, but it does take patience and time. An example here would be when an individual ignores (no consequence) the bigoted comments (behavioural) of a colleague. It is more effectively used in tandem with

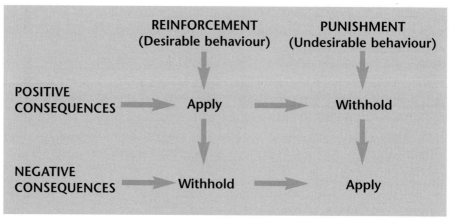

Figure 10.1 Reinforcement and punishment strategies

positive reinforcement of behaviour which is deemed desirable. In the above example, this would mean complimenting the bigoted colleague for any constructive comments (reinforcing desirable behaviour) while ignoring the bigoted comments (extinguishing undesirable behaviour). However, it is sometimes necessary to give a swift punishment and extinction procedures would not be suitable. Examples here would be in the case of theft from the organisation or unethical behaviour ■ *see* Chapter 11 ■. In learning and development, it is important that there is a concentrated effort to manage the consequences of behaviour.

see Chapter 11

SOCIAL LEARNING THEORY

Bandura (1977) offered an alternative to classical and operant conditioning in his social learning theory, which considered that learning happens because individuals observe the behaviour of others and model themselves upon them. Examples here would be a worker who models her/himself on the leadership style of a manager s/he admires. It is through the behaviour of superiors that individuals learn to pattern their own responses. Bandura's (1977) social learning theory has its central idea in the notion of ▶ **self-efficacy** ◀ which is part of the perception process. People who have a high level of self-efficacy tend to be effective learners – at least, more effective than those at the other end of the continuum. According to Bandura (1977) it is possible to enhance low levels of self-efficacy through any of four methods:

■ *Performance accomplishments:* getting on with it.

■ *Vicarious experiences:* modelling behaviour on someone else – watch someone else doing it.

■ *Verbal persuasion:* becoming convinced by someone else to get on with it.

■ *Emotional arousal:* getting excited by it.

Self-efficacy ◀┄┄▶ An individual's beliefs and expectations about her/his ability to accomplish a task efficiently.

10.4

Activity

Remember a skill that you have mastered, for example driving a car.

Do you think that you were a skilled driver when you passed your test? Are you one now?

Is your HRM tutor facilitating learning or using the traditional lecture approach?

What effect does the style being used have on your learning?

LEARNING AND INDIVIDUALS

No one employee learns in the same way as another since all individuals learn at different paces, at different times and life stages. This is why it is important that ED is a partnership activity. There are some who can acquire knowledge and skills easily while others find it more difficult. Investigations into learning theory suggest that learning is based on any, some, or all of the following:

- *Intrinsic motivation*
  The higher the level of intrinsic motivation individuals have the more likely they are to learn and thus bring about a permanent change in their behaviour. If, for example, they believe that learning something has a reward in a form they want, say increased esteem, they will learn ■ *see* Chapter 9 ■.

  see **Chapter 9**

- *Facilitating quality*
  If the learning environment and teaching quality are perceived by the learners to be good, they are more likely to learn.

- *Pressure*
  External pressure from others desiring the individual to learn will include the intrinsic desire to learn the norms of fellow workers and the culture of the organisation.

- *Specific drives*
  Intrinsic desires to keep abreast of expertise in their specific area through ▶ **continuous professional development** ◀ will drive individuals to learn.

▶ The ongoing self-development of an individual towards recognition in a particular profession or vocation; it is a purely personal definition.

Continuous professional development

- *Personality factors*
  If individuals have the attitude and disposition to acquire new skills and competencies, then they will improve their knowledge and qualities.

Pettinger (1996) believes that the result of successful learning is to:

increase the range, depth and interactions of thoughts, ideas and concepts, as well as skills, knowledge, attitude, behaviour and experience; to increase the ability to organise and reorganise these; and to order them in productive and effective activities (whatever that may mean in the particular set of circumstances). (p84)

Each learning event has its own learning curve showing the relationship between behaviour, action and experience. Such cycles highlight the importance of testing and experience and the need for the learner to be able to distinguish between abstract learning through practice and performance. Figure 10.2 shows the various learning curves that are dependent upon the matter to be learned.

LEARNING STYLES

Even though there appears to be no universally accepted theory of learning, the concept of learning ▶ **styles** ◀ is an important development for members within an organisation because it might help to illuminate how people learn from experience. When planning specific learning activities, it would be prudent that the training method allows for the fact that some people learn better by one style than another, and some may indeed reject certain styles altogether (Honey and Mumford, 1986). It is beneficial, therefore, if programmes are planned with a knowledge of learners' own preferences regarding learning styles, although it is not necessarily advisable that *only* the preferred style is adhered to by individuals. Kolb (1974) suggested that there were four stages in influencing learning:

- experience

- observation and reflection

- theorising and conceptualisation

- testing and experimentation.

Styles ◀┄┄▶ The ways by which something, for example learning, is done.

To be effective, the learner correspondingly needs four different but complementary kinds of ability which Kolb (1974) defined using the model represented in Figure 10.3.

Kolb (1974) suggested that this ideal is difficult to achieve and argued that, in fact, the required abilities might even be in dysfunctional conflict. He claimed that most people are better at, and prefer, some of the four stages than others. For example, an actuary might give preference to abstract conceptualisations and active experimentation while a manager may have greater concern for concrete experience and the active application of ideas. The essence of the theory is learning from experience, the nature of which is described as a continuous cycle or process. However, his *abstract conceptualisation stage* could well be more correctly described as *academic learning*.

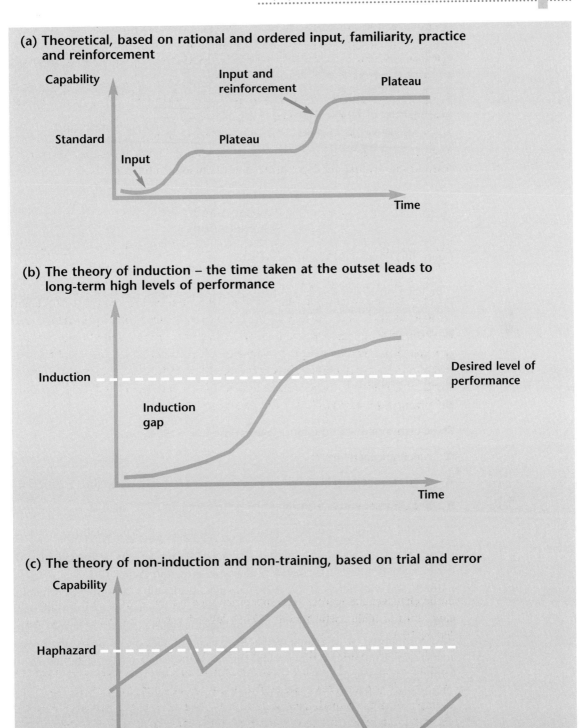

(a) Theoretical, based on rational and ordered input, familiarity, practice and reinforcement

Capability

Input and reinforcement

Plateau

Standard

Plateau

Input

Time

(b) The theory of induction – the time taken at the outset leads to long-term high levels of performance

Induction

Desired level of performance

Induction gap

Time

(c) The theory of non-induction and non-training, based on trial and error

Capability

Haphazard

Time

Figure 10.2 Learning curves

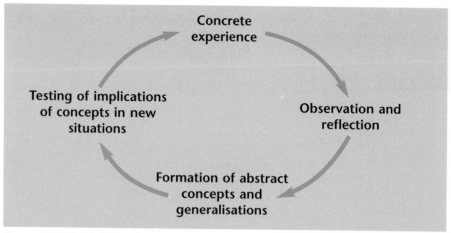

Figure 10.3 Kolb's (1974) learning cycle

Building on Kolb's theoretical base, Honey and Mumford (1986, 1992) defined four major categories of learning styles:

■ activist

■ reflector

■ theorist and

■ pragmatist.

These correspond with the four stages in the Kolb (1974) cycle:

■ concrete experience	activist
■ observation and reflection	reflector
■ formation of abstract concepts and generalisations	theorist
■ testing implications of concepts in new situations	pragmatist.

Hence, Maund (1994) suggests that Kolb's (1974) model can be integrated with Honey and Mumford's (1986, 1992) theory as shown in Figure 10.4.

Honey and Mumford's (1986, 1992) adaptation of Kolb's (1974) cycle is helpful to managers who assist employees in their personal development, and thus their learning, because of its potential utility for learning styles (activists, reflectors, theorists, pragmatists), which could well be seen as more relevant to the world of work and as significant aids for trainers and learners who want to develop an interest in learning and development.

Both models have a cyclical appreciation of learning strategies – learners may move around the cycle – and yet neither indicates an appreciation of the fact that it is not a staged cycle, therefore individuals may ignore or utilise one or more of the learning styles.

During the course of their continuing research and applications, Honey and Mumford (1986, 1992) developed a learning styles questionnaire (LSQ) on self-description, employing established norms for different types of people such as those

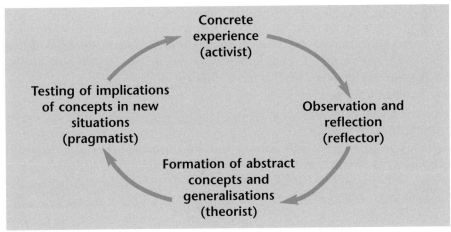

Figure 10.4 Merging Kolb's (1974) and Honey and Mumford's (1986, 1992) learning cycles

engaged in research and development, finance or production. Such a questionnaire is a useful measuring instrument for the manager who is responsible for assisting in ED and for the individual learner and could ultimately yield data which would constitute a valuable guide for, say, determining an optimum composition of groups within which individual members of a team can learn. While membership of project teams is selected by managers using criteria other than group dynamics and composition (such as experience and knowledge), the LSQ has the advantage in defining the composition of smaller groups within the workplace.

For the individual worker it provides a self-diagnostic tool which s/he can use as a tool to guide her/him on individual strengths (best learning styles) and over-coming weaknesses (least favoured learning styles), leading to the adoption of a richer variety of methods. Thus, the worker is more adaptable and flexible and is more likely to develop in a way that will assist in the meeting of the organisation's goals. To this end, Honey and Mumford (1986, 1992) gave advice on how to make the best use of individual learning strengths and how to improve and practise each of the four styles. Their work has been developed within organisations and is now a key measure of individual learning development.

Individuals will differ in the ways they prefer to learn, partly in reaction to the instructional models provided in the organisation, but more generally in terms of a distinction between ▶ **holistic** ◀ and ▶ **serialistic** ◀ styles of learning. Individual workers who adopt a holistic learning strategy want to see the 'whole picture' and how their present learning fits into the organisation's goals as a whole and what its

---

▶ Observing and analysing the whole rather than the individual parts which make up that whole. ◀┄┄▶ **Holistic**

▶ A person who tends to focus narrowly on the particular task or topic and who needs to ◀┄┄▶ **Serialist** learn step by step, concentrating first on the details and the connected logic and progressively building up skills and self-developing understanding.

purpose is. In learning, such workers thrive on everyday examples, illustrations, diagrams and anecdotes: they look for links with similar ideas and they also build up more idiosyncratic forms of understanding that are personally satisfying. In other words, they want relevance to their work. In contrast, employees preferring serialist learning strategies tend to focus narrowly on the particular task or topic and for them learning needs to be step by step, concentrating first on the details and on the connected logic, progressively building up their own skills and developing their understanding.

If workers are to own their learning and bring about a permanent change in behaviour they must use holistic strategies (relating ideas and developing a personal organisation) and serialist strategies (examining both the evidence and the logic); indeed, some members of the workforce will have such strong learning styles that their learning will be ineffectively incomplete, being dominated either by overgeneralisation or too narrow a vision. Through training and development workers can be encouraged to carry out the more complete forms of learning that lead to conceptual understanding and, thus, a higher level of competency.

Kroeger and Thuesen (1988) developed a further theory that linked personality functions with learning styles, believing that every employee has a preferred model of:

- gathering information

- evaluation and

- decision making.

Kroeger and Thuesen (1988) show this link between personality functions and learning as summarised in Table 10.2.

Each worker has a preferred model of gathering information, evaluation and decision making. For example, feelers will want to find out what other people think about a specific training course and look for a fair result, whereas intuitive thinkers are likely to want to observe a training event and use their hunches about attending one.

Therefore, learning styles actually refer to the characteristic ways of processing information and behaving in learning situations. An individual who has awareness of her/his individual learning style will be able to identify her/his own strengths and weaknesses. ED is about empowering individuals to enhance their thinking and problem-solving skills which are requisite in the modern information age.

10.5 Activity

List as many of the tools and environments required in order to work in the contemporary information age. Start each one with the statement 'The ability to work...' The first one has been given as an example.

The ability to work:

1 in an unstructured or highly structured environment

Table 10.2 Personality functions and learning

Personality preference	Implications for learning by individuals
Information gathering Intuitors	Prefer theoretical frameworks. Look for some sort of meaning in all materials. Try to make sense of the whole scheme of work. Attempt to find possibilities and interrelationships.
Sensors	Prefer facts and empirical information. Want to apply the theory. Attempt to master the details. Use what is realistic and possible.
Decision making Thinkers	Analyse data and information. Are fair minded and even handed. Seek logicality rather than direct conclusions. Like to remain at a distance from the work.
Feelers	Interpersonally involved. Usually fair minded and happy to keep the peace. Look for subjective and fair results. Dislike factual, objective analysis.

By delving into the acquisition of knowledge through learning strategies an employee will realise that s/he has gained many skills varying from mathematical theory to the ability to roller blade.

10.6

Activity

Take the list you made in Activity 10.5 and:

a group the different situations together using your own criteria

b record your preferred way/s of learning

c list your preferred learning environment.

No two employees will gain skills and/or knowledge in the same way and thus ED is an individual activity. Its success will depend upon the individual worker taking personal responsibility for their own learning and thus their own career development. This is best done with guidance from trained managers and specialists in training and development.

BARRIERS TO LEARNING

There are a number of barriers to learning, and thus to personal development, that a worker might face. For example, the fear of failure or the inability (or unwillingness) to expend time and effort on personal development. In the rapidly changing work environment it is not sufficient to *acquire* the standard knowledge and skills; the ability to *transfer* such knowledge and skills is paramount to the continuous learning process required of workers in today's world. The successful learning environment is one in which attention is paid to minimising demotivating factors by creating a supportive climate and developing workers' confidence in their ability to tackle and overcome barriers to learning; in other words, an environment which fosters and encourages the natural self-generating learning process. This is an important aspect of ED because employees who have grown as learners will continue to be competent at learning and will thus take the lead in self-development – they will be proactive rather than reactive. It is the role of the learning organisation (discussed below) to ensure that all employees appreciate the importance of learning because it takes place in a complex, interacting system. The outcomes of learning depend on the combined effects of the whole learning environment provided by the organisation and its design, as well as on the training and development provided.

GOAL SETTING

Within the workplace goal setting is closely linked to ED because it is the process of deciding on the required objectives of an organisation that will ultimately guide and direct the behaviour of individuals within the organisation. It originally surfaced in the work of the scientific management school, members of which believed that performance standards would lead to higher work performance.

It is not easy to identify work goals since they tend to be umbrella terms and workers tend to 'just do it'. Different organisations define their own goals in their own way. Some organisations use the SMART system to communicate their approach to the achievement of effective goals – be they for ED or for the organisation as a whole ■ *see* Chapter 9 ■.

see Chapter 9

If the goals are specific and challenging an individual will concentrate on them and s/he is, therefore, likely to be effective in learning what is required to achieve the goals – as can be seen in Figure 10.5.

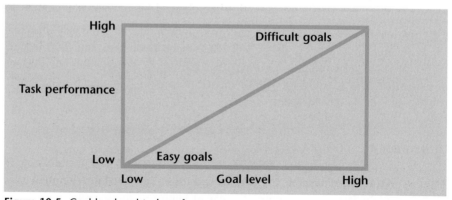

Figure 10.5 Goal level and task performance

Through these measurable and achievable goals comes feedback concerning goal progress. Not all goals are quantifiable and qualitative goals are extremely valuable in ED. They could include the desire to improve team member relationships; indeed, qualitative goals may be sufficient in themselves.

Time-bound goals help with measurability, whether the time is implicit or explicit. For example, without a time limit an employee will not be able to compare her/his goals with those of previous time periods. However, there is not always a finely tuned limit concerning the achievement of personal goals.

Overall, goal setting serves several functions, each of which is related to the way individual employees learn:

- increases intrinsic work motivation and thus the performance of tasks

- reduces high levels of stress by reducing dysfunctional conflict

- improves the validity and reliability of performance evaluation.

Employees learn from the consequences of what they do and, therefore, it is vital that managers and supervisors take care when they apply any form of positive or negative reinforcement. It is through these experiences that individuals are intrinsically motivated ■ *see* Chapter 9 ■.

see Chapter 9

FUSION BETWEEN MANAGEMENT AND DEVELOPMENT

The prevailing culture of organisations is that performance expectations are continually rising within a workplace environment in which it appears that everyone is working harder and taking more responsibility. According to Fonda and Guile (1999) organisations:

> need to transform their whole system of management and development, starting with a fundamental shift towards the partnership approach. (p38)

The New Learning for New Work consortium, comprising 50 affiliated individuals and organisations and using sponsorship from a number of sources including the CIPD, the Department of Trade and Industry (DTI) and the Further Education Department Agency (FEDA), is investigating the need for fundamental changes to performance management and, thus, ED.

The consortium started its work with the agreement that the responsibilities of members of the workforce had changed dramatically within an environment where change was rapid and individuals had increased expectations; that is, all members of an organisation have to take responsibility for its performance – or at least for part of it depending upon their individual role within the organisation. This means that all employees have to take responsibility for the added value of their organisation.

Organisations are using competency frameworks in order to allow individuals to manage the processes needed for positive results and they recognise that individual

10.7

Activity

If employees are no longer expected merely to do what they are told, with competence and commitment, what else are they expected to do in the contemporary workplace?

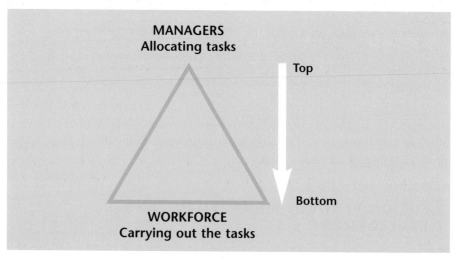

Figure 10.6 Top-down command-and-control model

behavioural habits are as important as their knowledge and skills. However, this is often rhetoric when organisations actually practise a control-based model, as shown in Figure 10.6.

The consortium's report (1999) gives four features, shown in Table 10.3, of the top-down system that harm ED and performance management and, therefore, do not allow employees to take responsibility for adding value.

Table 10.3 Features detrimental to the development of a workforce

- The belief that employees can offer nothing of value to decision making.

- If an individual needs to change her/his performance, all that needs to be done is to top up the worker with new skills or knowledge – like an empty bottle.

- The expectation that managers are accountable only for tangible issues such as achieving volume, quality and/or financial targets and not for the development and outcomes of the process by which their part of the organisation is managed.

- A misunderstanding of the meaning of 'partnership', believing that it is only about the relationship between the customer and its supplier. This view supports the perception that the managers are the customers with the employees and development specialists being the suppliers.

These views are no longer valid in the workplace if the organisation is to:

develop and sustain a workforce that is capable of taking responsibility for adding value (p41)

It is encouraging that the consortium has noted an increase in the number of organisations that are trying out new practices which encourage ground-level ED.

EMPLOYEE VIEWS

The consortium hopes to encourage organisations to adopt a system for managing learning which includes:

- respect for the views of individual employees

- transparency of the capabilities that the whole workforce will need

- a climate which will challenge yet support ED

- an individual approach to potential.

With these key principles in mind, the consortium has produced a list of six imperatives for people development, as shown in Table 10.4. This requires managers to work within a guiding framework drawn up by the consortium and shown in Table 10.5.

Table 10.4 Six new imperatives for development

1 Focus on the performance challenges for individuals and teams.

2 See performance challenges as encompassing tomorrow's employability as well as today's work.

3 Recognise that most development is the result of social interaction.

4 See development needs and pathways as contingent.

5 Assume that everyone has rights as well as responsibilities.

6 Collaborate to develop capabilities.

Source: Fonda, N. and D. Guile (1999) Joint learning adventures, *People Management*, 25 March, p40.

Table 10.5 Guiding principles for management

1 Managers should respect the views of the workforce. They should listen to what people say is required and seek to respond.

2 They should be clear about the kinds of capabilities expected of the organisation's whole workforce and make these public.

3 Managers should recognise that the development of these capabilities depends on creating an environment in which everyone focuses on results and on facing the challenges to be overcome to achieve them.

(cont'd)

Table 10.5 cont'd

4   Managers should work to the principle of subsidiarity – that is, moving accountability, authority and responsibility to wherever people in the organisation have the information needed for value-adding decisions and action.

5   Managers should understand that employees need competent support in identifying and responding to challenges.

6   Managers should be aware that everybody has their own talents and interests. It is pointless to expect them to take responsibility for situations that they are not interested in or good at handling.

7   Managers should be conscious that this 'challenge and support' environment will not happen on its own. It must be encouraged and regularly reviewed.

Source: Fonda, N. and D. Guile (1999) Joint learning adventures, *People Management,* 25 March, p40.

The impetus is on recognising that people are the critical stakeholders and that their views count and the system should operate as a partnership comprising joint ventures and strategic alliances.

SCENARIO 10.1

Where management and development become one

Roffey Park Management Institute used to offer separate programmes for managers and developers. Now it has realised that there is no real difference between the needs of the two groups.

'We found managers were coming on to programmes that we thought were for developers and the other way round,' says Val Hammond, Roffey Park's chief executive. 'So we now label them differently, and people can get out of them what they want.'

This is only one way in which the management educators at Roffey Park have found themselves responding to a change in their market. Hammond believes that this reflects the idea identified by the New Learning for New Work consortium, that there is a fusion between management and development.

'In the past, management's job was to manage people. Now it is to develop people,' she says. 'The approach being advanced in the consortium's report is not brand new. But the point is that the current climate is making a new approach imperative. It is becoming obvious to us that managers are realising that people will not accept the old methods of management any longer. Now, with a generation of young people who have been taught to question, I don't think managers can be in the business of browbeating them. It's about treating people as adults.'

Another way in which Roffey Park is reflecting the changing demands of the workplace is by offering weekend workshops for people not sponsored by their companies. 'We are always looking for ways to help people with the responsibilities being thrust upon them,' Hammond says. 'We have recognised that people have to take more responsibility for their own development.'

But she adds, 'A lot of organisations have bought into the idea that an individual's responsibility for their own development lets the employer off the hook. But it doesn't. There are various government initiatives to help people with their career planning, but employers and managers also have a key part to play.'

Source: Fonda, N. and D. Guile (1999) Joint learning adventures, *People Management,* 25 March, p41.

DEVELOPMENTAL PARTNERSHIPS

Partnership involves the use of a concept developed by Chan Kim and Mauborgne (1997) which involves looking for the input from everyone into decisions that concern development and change. In doing this, care must be taken to make sure that all those people who will be affected by the change actually understand why subsequent decisions will be made and informed of the benefits such a change or changes will bring about. It is also important that there is effective communication concerning the standards by which an individual's performance will be measured and judged.

This is similar to the Kolb and Frohman (1970) model of planned change which gives a sequence for initiating and managing change as shown in Figure 10.7. This model emphasises three key points related to any management of change:

- it is a sequential process

- each stage is equally important

- success will depend upon the manager's relationship with those who will be affected by the change.

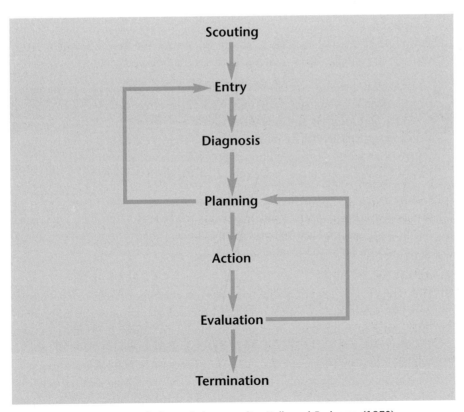

Figure 10.7 The process of planned change, after Kolb and Frohman (1970)

At the *scouting* stage managers will check that they have adequate knowledge about the matter in hand, for example ED and PM. Here the manager is making sure that s/he is ready for the change in current practice by:

■ identifying any obvious obstacles

■ observing what is currently happening.

It is a *passive* stage where the manager will size up the costs and benefits of the intervention. Her/his key task is to decide exactly:

■ where the change needs to be implemented

■ what permission is needed

■ who the people are who might help/be unhelpful.

During the *entry* stage there is negotiation among the interested parties and the development of an agreed contract of operation. This will probably be centred on power – the gaining of the required influence to implement the new development programme or method of operating it. French and Raven (1962) carried out research to determine the sources of power that the manager (the agent) uses to influence another individual (the target) – their work has become very influential in the field of employee behaviour. In their seminal study, they identified four forms of interpersonal power that managers use:

1   *Reward power*
    Power based on the manager's ability to control the rewards that a target wants, for example salary increase, bonuses, PRP and promotion.

see Chapter 9

    If a manager uses this sort of power in an attempt to increase the performance of an individual employee it will only work if the target perceives a correlation between performance and reward ■ *see* Chapter 9 ■. Therefore, a manager needs to be explicit with an employee concerning the required behaviours and targets that will be rewarded and then make the relationship between that behaviour and the reward very clear.

2   *Coercive power*
    This power is based on the manager's ability to cause an unpleasant experience for the employee and can be in the form of force, threats of punishment, verbal abuse and/or the withdrawal of support.

3   *Referent power*
    This is an elusive power because it is based on charisma – interpersonal attraction. The manager has power over her/his employee because the latter identifies with that manager or wants to model her/himself on that person. Transformational (or charismatic) leaders tend to have this sort of power. With referent power, a manager does not necessarily need to be superior to the employee but generally is. He/she is also individualistic and respected by that employee.

4   *Expert power*

This is similar to referent power and one individual could have both. Expert power is the power that exists when an agent has information or knowledge the target wants and needs. Such power can work well in ED when:

- the employee trusts that the given information is correct
- the information is of relevance to the employee
- the information is of use to the employee
- the employee's perception of the manager as an expert is understood to be crucial.

In most change projects, such as introducing alternative methods of ED, power from all four of these sources is brought to bear in the implementation of the change. However, changes to bring about a partnership require, by definition, the use of collaboration and it is often perceived that the formal power structure and experts are part of the problem that has to be solved. In other words, the management at the top are set in their ways.

When it comes to *diagnosis*, there ought to be as much of a collaborative process as possible, which involves as many of the affected parts of the organisation as possible. There is a focus here on three key areas:

- the perceived problem

- the defining of the required goals

- identification of resources.

The results of the diagnostic phase form the starting point for the *planning* stage. Depending on the findings, these results could well require a move back to the entry stage for renegotiations to take place. This, in ED, usually concerns an expansion to include members of the workforce who will be responsible for implementing any changes and/or who will be immediately affected by the change.

If the planning stage is securely reached, then the *action* stage can be implemented and this encompasses a wide range of activities such as ED, creation of new information systems and organisational structure changes. It does not matter what the changes are, but there is likely to be some resistance to them. Unfortunately, such resistance is often treated as an irrational negative force to be overcome by whatever means management can utilise, yet it can be positive because it creates new ideas and innovation. Therefore, any resistance to change should be identified at the early stages so that it can be positively utilised in the change programme.

With ED it is important that there is not a sudden imposition upon an individual employee. It is essential that the worker has prior knowledge of, and participation in, matters which are likely to change her/his environment and, thus, working conditions. If a manager does not communicate effectively with the subordinate, then the latter will take the naturally human response route and become hostile and resist any plans – even if they are intended to benefit the employee. If managers impose a change upon an individual, such an imposed change will only serve to stop the process of growth and maturation by denying the employee the opportunity to work in an environment that s/he can understand and control. If the top-down method (as shown in Figure 10.6) is used, then the employee will spend her/his life in an organisation that is managed by imposed change and s/he can become a helpless, passive victim of the system, cursed by management for her/his stupidity and lack of initiative.

Any dysfunctional aspects of resistance to change in an employee's development can be alleviated by careful preparation for the action phase. If the employee is involved at the appropriate stages of *scouting*, *entry*, *diagnosis* and *planning*, then s/he can take on changes which affect her/his ED and PM in a more intelligent way which is more appropriate to the needs of the organisation.

see Chapter 1

In the days of scientific management, the tradition was to separate the *evaluation* phase from the *action* phase ■ *see* Chapter 1 ■. All change programmes need to be evaluated – preferably at all stages of the process. In respect of ED, this means that appraisal systems ought to be carried out frequently – more than the once each year which is common practice.

The *termination* stage is when the change process, for example an individual has incorporated new processes into the work arena, has become a natural and integral part of the system.

If the above stages have been correctly managed with the necessary supporting evaluation, then there will have been considerable effort put into the change. Goals will have been met and the excitement of completing the change can lead to an anticlimax. However, in the modern work environment one change is always simultaneous with another and so planned change becomes very difficult. It is also very time consuming and, thus, the advantages of a quick change can be lost. For example, in the case of ED, skills are required immediately or in the very near future and Kolb and Frohman's (1970) model becomes idealistic. However, when a change is perceived to be 'finished' then an individual will need to have continuous development – there must be mechanisms in place in the ED arena that allow individuals to flex and change there skills and knowledge as situations demand.

In the fair process systems propounded by Chan Kim and Mauborgne (1997), there is a recognition of the Kolb and Frohman (1970) planned change process although the former do recognise the change in the business environment with its roller-coaster environment. Managers are now recognising that there is a need to communicate effectively through direct, face-to-face contact with encouragement being given to employees to be proactive rather than wait for their managers to intervene. However, this relies on all employees having access to the necessary information so that they can act independently and take responsibility for their actions.

It is only by working together and improving all members' ED that a business can become successful in its market. In this is the recognition of intellectual and human capital (discussed below) and the building of core competence. A significant number of organisations have outsourced their ED and PM to consultancy and training providers, with employees becoming more proactive and demanding (and discerning) over their own development. Successful organisations establish standards and work with those providers that reflect the imperatives outlined in Figure 10.8.

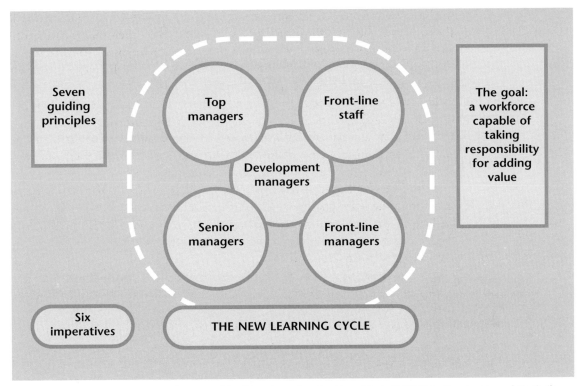

Figure 10.8 The development of partnership (New Learning for New Work (1999)) in Fonda, N. and D. Guile (1999, p44)

Such partnerships will be social, collaborative and engaging, requiring considerable communication concerning the nature of the organisation and how it uses teams and relates to its environment, as shown in Figure 10.8.

This is linked to the managing of learning in order that it can add value and gives a further dimension to the learning cycle models, as shown in Figure 10.9.

Fonda and Guile (1999) believe that the new learning cycle will increase at a growing rate as individuals 'learn to make capability development a "joint venture"' (p44). As this happens the role of development managers will change as they begin to acquire a strategic position becoming leaders because they will be acquiring, sharing and using the specialist knowledge they have with other executives. It also changes the role of HR specialists because they are now moving to centre stage as suppliers of advice and services to line managers. Consequently, they have moved into the leadership role of agents of change bringing with them:

> expertise in managing learning for added value... at the core, not the periphery, of successful organisations. (Fonda and Guile, p44)

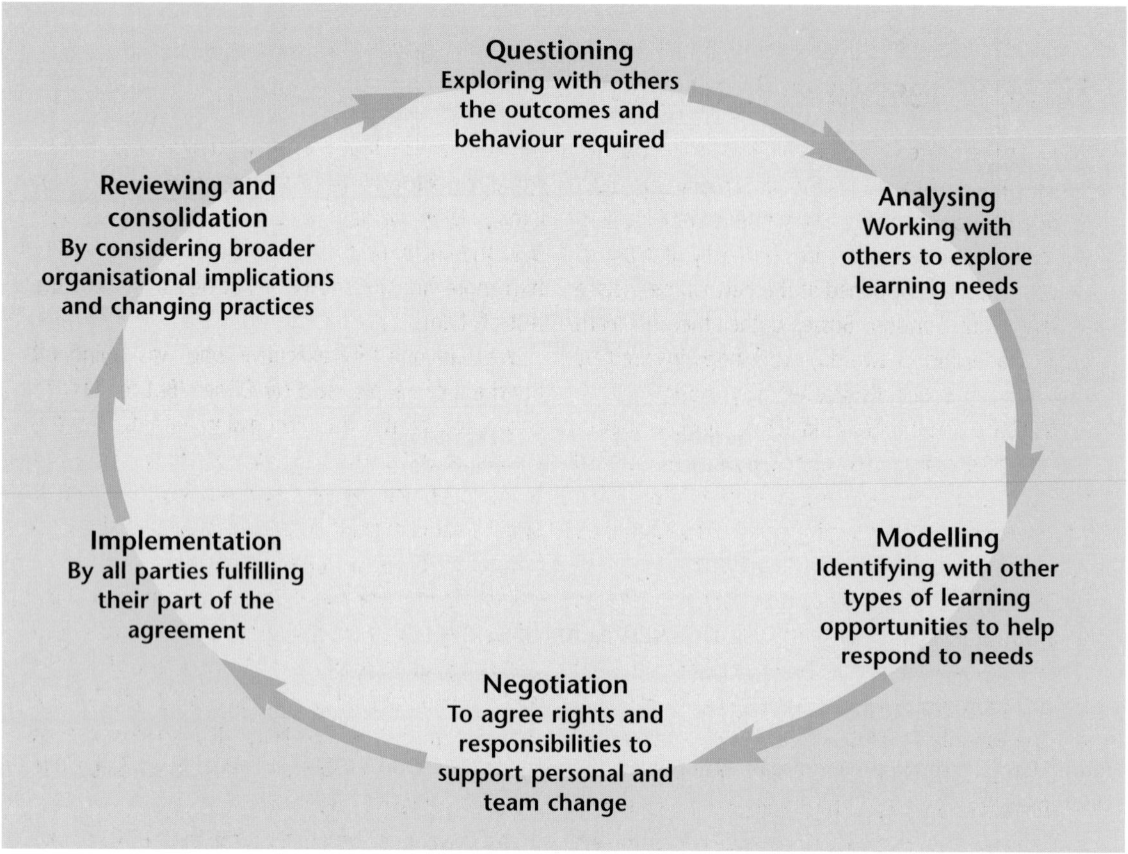

Figure 10.9 The learning cycle (New Learning for New Work (1999)) in Fonda, N. and D. Guile (1999, p44)

POINTS
TO
PONDER

Raftery (1999) states that:

> Rightly or wrongly, many HR professionals are being challenged on how investment in learning opportunities adds value to the business. (p23)

There is no evidence to show that HRM specialists have argued their case effectively and have relied solely on:

> our frustration that the issue is being raised all the time. (p23)

Such an attitude will do nothing to convince any doubters that there are benefits to be gained from investment in learning.

SCENARIO 10.2

Henry's lesson in leadership

When Shakespeare wrote *Henry V* he would not have expected senior executives to be among his most enthusiastic audiences. Peasants and nobility, yes, but corporate lovers of his work? Hardly. But that is exactly what has happened at the new Globe theatre in Southwark, London. Bosses gather there to learn about leadership in two-day workshops inspired by the stories of England's greatest playwright.

The Globe and the Cranfield School of Management have called on Laurence Olivier's son, Richard, to head the programme. His students examine the leadership of young King Henry in inspiring an ill-disciplined mob of soldiers to follow him against the French.

'This is not a Shakespeare class,' said Mr Olivier. 'Nor do we work with the text. It is an inquiry into the nature of leadership. Having pointed out that Henry's vision is to gain the territory he covets, I ask the participants to think of their own "territories" and the business dreams they want to fulfil.

'As the play progresses Henry suffers setbacks and his clear mission becomes muddled – just as in corporate life. Falstaff and the common foot soldiers can't see the point of the war. But in his speech before the Battle of Agincourt he convinces them of his cause with a powerful performance and faultless presentation.'

Before trying it themselves, students are shown some of the oratorical devices Henry uses – for example, by saying: 'Once more unto the breach, dear friends, once more.' The use of 'friends' makes him more human, showing that he's in it with the rest of them.

'We had one City executive who was laying off hundreds of people,' said Mr Olivier. 'But the task he chose for himself in the session was to let the remaining 200 or so know that they need not fear for their jobs. Of course, no one believed him. It wasn't until he came out with a rousing, honest, confidence-boosting, Henry-type speech that they responded.'

Role-playing workshops are far from new. But the added ingredient of Shakespeare brings creativity and imagination to the format. Getting Shakespeare to help with the education process dovetails with today's management thinking – that there is a need for 'emotional intelligence' [discussed below] in anyone's leadership skills.

'What we are seeing is the feminising of the work-place and this is forcing men to re-examine them-selves and how they see themselves in power,' said Mr Olivier. 'A lot more subtlety is called for than in the past.'

Adapted from: Nurden, D. (1999) Henry's lesson in leadership, *The Independent on Sunday*, 23 May, p1.

PERSONAL GROWTH, CAREER DEVELOPMENT AND CAREER PLANNING

One of a manager's most important jobs is to manage the ED of an employee which includes her/his personal growth and career development. Additionally, managers have the very personal responsibility for their own career planning. In previous business environments, career planning was handled in the main by the organisation which employed an individual, who was likely to be in that organisation's employment for life. However, nowadays the work environment is rapidly changing with increasing work mobility bringing about alternatives and potential for almost any worker.

The average European will change jobs seven times and careers three times during her/his actual working life, and with this increasing pattern of career change has come greater implications for how organisations and educational institutions manager career development. It is unfortunate that social responses to these changes have lagged behind the actual workplace changes. Organisations are now changing their structures and designs to respond to the non-traditional stable notions of career development although some still retain the traditional model described above. The latter organisations will lose their business to other organisations that are more flexible.

The career paths of many people will pass through two, three or four distinct phases, each of which requires major new learning of knowledge, skills and attitudes. Education and training programmes have moved towards retraining and not simply training for the start of a career.

Adult and continuing education used to have a low status with low-priority activities done half-heartedly in the name of community service. However, today they are geared more to individuals changing career direction and the development of transferable skills and re-entry into the workplace after a period of absence – for whatever reason.

In the past there was a failure to provide avenues for career change which produced great losses in social productivity and in human satisfaction. Employers now realise that they do not benefit by locking their employees into careers that long ago ceased to be rewarding and challenging to them. If individuals are barred from entry into new careers, society loses the creativity and productivity of such people.

Traditional adult developmental patterns for women have included a phase where marriage and family kept them from the job market in their early careers. Social norms have changed dramatically and the maintenance of careers throughout the family upbringing phase and re-entry after a short period out of the workplace are now the norm.

While organisations and the educational system have changed to ensure access to education and learning throughout the whole life span, it is equally important that individuals gain a greater awareness and insight into the problems and possibilities of adult development.

Individuals are now more responsible for managing their own lives and careers, while in earlier times, personal identity and continuity were sustained in relatively stable environments of expectation and demand where both career and lifestyle were set down and given by other than the individual concerned, rather than chosen by that individual.

Today's environment of complexity and constant change has denied employees what used to be that easy route to personal identity. Identity and continuity are now brought about by personal choices – the opposite side of the coin. These choices go beyond the computational selection of one alternative over another according to some predetermined values and beliefs because they required an individual to choose the basic values which they themselves ascribe to. For example, instead of asking, 'What is the right thing to do?' an individual has to ask, 'What do I believe is right?' However, the personal insight questioning does not stop here because an individual also has to find answers to the questions, 'Who am I'? and 'Who do I want to be?'

10.8

Activity

Complete the following sentence: 'Five years from now, I will be satisfied if...' at least five times. Then rank order your goal statements which will help to establish the personal importance of each of the goals for you.

COPING WITH INCREASING CHALLENGES

In order to cope with the increasing challenges of self-management, an individual has to develop her/his own skills for planning and guiding the direction of her/his life. There are four key themes that are important for effective career self-management:

1 *Focus on life rather than occupation*
   Any career development and planning for life should commence with a holistic analysis of the individual's life space and an examination of the relationship among, for example:

   ■ work
   ■ family
   ■ leisure activities and
   ■ spiritual/developmental needs.

   Therefore, the term 'career' needs to be used in its broadest sense, being the self-mediated progress through times of transaction between person and environment. If career planning places work/income in a central focus (that fits for many but not all individuals), other life interests are placed in ranked peripheral and compensatory role. With this bias there is a loss of any fundamental reassessment of an individual's own life and lifestyle and places in a secondary position the primary problem experienced by many individuals – that of integrating the many diverse elements of their lives.

2 *Career as a here-and-now issue*
   An individual's goals and interpretations of her/his own personal history represent attempts to make sense and meaning of her/his present life situation. One major task is in coping with change, the reinterpretation of her/his own personal life and the replacement of one goal for another because of changing life circumstances. In this sense, any previous accomplishments and developed abilities and life goals are as much determined by life experiences as they are the causes of such life experiences.

3 *Emphasis on choice as well as planning*

Implicit in (2) above is an emphasis on immediate personal choice in the context of longer range planning. Individuals need to manage their choice-making process which can be accomplished by increasing awareness of choice making and control over that choice-making process by shortening the time lag between choices and consequences. An example here would be when a new graduate sees a first-choice job in terms of its immediate consequences as well as a long-term determining decision.

Planning and goal setting are but one mode for achieving personal continuity and direction. Many individuals who are achievement-oriented prefer this mode but for others it is unpleasant and they find it unethical as related to their own lifestyles ■ *see* Chapter 11 ■. For example, an individual might find her/his sense of meaning in the present and finds that goals are simple abstractions and are, therefore, unreal.

see Chapter 11

4 *Emphasis on the learning process as opposed to outcomes*

The problem of managing and adapting is central to the ED task in contemporary society and is, at its most fundamental level, one aspect of the process by which people learn. Learning as a central force implies that individuals need to examine not only what they are as people, for example their abilities, aspirations, interests and needs, but also their self as a process; that is, the process by which an individual makes choices among various alternatives. When an individual focuses only on the outcomes, where s/he is going and what s/he wants to accomplish become more important than how s/he is getting there. Consequently, the individual may still be ill-prepared to cope with a future set of career and life choices.

10.9 Activity

Develop the goal statements you made in Activity 10.8 by thinking about and working on some strategies for getting where you want to go.

You might like to share this activity with a couple of other students. However, for each goal you have set write down three alternative strategies you could utilise to achieve that goal.

ACHIEVING A COMMITMENT TO PERSONAL GOALS

In ED the setting of prioritised goals and strategies for achieving them is important and it is a critical aspect of personal growth and career development. The ability to conceptualise life goals and to imagine future alternatives for living can free an individual from the inertia of the past by providing future targets that serve as guides for planning and decision making.

Commitment to clearly stated goals leads to achievement of those goals, yet achieving commitment is not as easy as it might sound – there are several factors that make it difficult:

1 *Reluctance to give up the alternative goals not chosen*

In order to choose one goal it is necessary to reject others. Unless an individual believes in the importance of the goal and its superior value, then other goals will, as time passes, dominate and overshadow the initial decision.

2 *Fear of failure*

Without any goals and ideals, an individual will never risk failure. In making a commitment to a future state, a worker is involving the risk to her/his self-esteem should the goal not be achieved. This fear of failure makes it very difficult for any individual totally to commit her/himself to a goal.

3 *Lack of self-knowledge*

If an employee does not know of the opportunities available to her/him within the environment, then confusion and an inability to define goals is brought about. It is important for individual employees to research the resources and opportunities available to them and use that information to discover any new goals and redefine the old ones.

4 *Insecurity and low self-esteem*

If an employee's circumstances or lifestyle lead her/him to feel as though s/he is a hopeless victim of circumstances, s/he will have difficulty in planning her/his future and becoming committed to future goals. To achieve goals implies having self-control over one's environment. To become committed to a goal, the employee must feel as though s/he has the ability to achieve it.

INCREASING COMMITMENT TO GOALS

Goal setting is a key part of ED and performance management and, therefore, it is not only the selection of goals which is important but the individual's commitment to them once chosen. There are some things than can be done to increase commitment to goals:

1 *Explicit examination of the value of the chosen goals and comparison with the rejected alternatives*

An employee can explicitly consider the alternative opportunities that may arise and by doing this s/he can avoid being swayed in a weak moment by an alternative which s/he has not considered before. A very useful technique here is to link short-term goals with long-term objectives. The awareness of the fact that a particularly difficult short-term goal is linked to a long-term objective can avoid its rejection for a more immediately gratifying but useless short-term pleasure.

2 *Committing oneself to a continuing process of self-evaluation and goal setting*

Individuals need to appreciate the fact that it is impossible to plan one's whole life at one sitting. Not only is it impractical, but everything is changing far too fast for any individual to anticipate clearly what the future will be. An individual's goals will change as her/his experiences change and increase. There is a risk of missing unforeseen circumstances if an employee insists of working blindly towards obsolete goals. This can be minimised by returning to the goals periodically and reassessing them in the light of new information and situations. If an employee accompanies this by seeking feedback from others about her/himself and by using these data for continuing self-evaluation, then the employee will achieve a much more accurate self-image and a clear conception of her/his values which underpin the goal selection and activation.

3   *Support from others*
Achieving goals on one's own is a lonely path and does not encourage ED – they are best achieved in a supportive atmosphere. An individual needs to include other people who are significant to her/his life and in this way s/he can build self-confidence and clarify thinking about the future – feedback about her/his behaviour is very useful in the achievement of goals.

4   *Future visions and here-and-now awareness*
Planning for the future implies a continuing awareness of ways that an individual can proactively shape her/his future. The goal-setting process means that the individual can acknowledge what s/he is doing at a particular moment and identify that s/he can do or be at some time in the future.

CAREER MANAGEMENT

Even though ED is best carried out by a positive interaction between the individual employee and her/his manager using goal setting, this would probably be within a framework that allows employees to move up the organisation through well-delineated ranks. This is called a ▶ **career ladder** ◀ of which the most obvious example is that of the armed forces where the lines between the ranks are well defined.

Career ladder ◀┈┈▶ A system within an organisation that gives employees the opportunity to move up through the ranks to even higher positions.

According to Spector (1996):

A progression of positions is established for individuals who acquire the necessary skills and maintain a good job performance. (p56)

Armstrong (1999) defines career management as:

the process of career planning and management succession. (p551)

His definition highlights the point that within modern society individuals are forging new pathways to professional and organisational success. This is being driven by demographic, economic and social realities of the contemporary world with work life mirroring the opportunities and obstacles of a workplace which has been reshaped by continuous and relentless change. In organisations, the pressures and priorities of internal and external change require doing more with less, while continuing to build a competent and committed workforce. For individuals who are trying to make their way through unfamiliar channels in search of professional fulfilment, they will experience complexity and uncertainty. The aim of ED and professional development is for the individual and the organisation (as a body of individuals) to bridge the separate but complementary ideals of work life and workplace. It is through career development that a balance of roles and responsibilities can be achieved alongside the bridging of work life and workplace.

This requires attention being paid to a number of aspects:

- skills and achievements

- knowledge and learning style

- values

- interests and

- entrepreneurism.

Skills and achievements

A skill can be considered to be the ability to do something well – especially if it is as a result of experience. Most of the skills which an individual has gained can be transferred to other situations in the workplace (and outside it). The skills possessed by one individual are numerous and various and to typify them all would be an impossible task. However, it is possible to group them in some way and one is to show the functional skills of the individuals, such as:

- working with others
- data and information ■ *see* Chapter 6 ■

see **Chapter 6**

- things and/or objects.

It is also possible to group them into different groups of skills:

- intellectual

- aptitudinal

- creative

- leadership

- problem solving.

An employer will want to know which skills a potential employee can bring to the organisation and also how existing employees are developing their existing skills. For the purpose of career development, and thus ED, it is essential that individual workers be given the opportunity to review their skills frequently.

When an employee is asked to consider the key skills s/he has and those s/he wishes to develop, the source is usually from past experiences. This is because an employee's future direction will often lie in her/his past experiences. For an

10.10

Note

Use the matrix given in the activity to help you with the organisation of the skills.

1 For each of the 3 skill types, list 6 that you possess (making a total of 18 different skills).

   a *Specialised skills*

   Those skills that are required in order to carry out a particular job, for example analysing statistics, debugging computer programmes, refereeing sporting activities, repairing cars or bikes... Do not forget to draw from your life experiences.

   b *Communication/interpersonal skills*

   Those skills that help you to communicate in some way and to interact with other people. Examples here might be: writing, mediating, training, liaising, hosting, motivating.

   c *General skills*

   Skills that might be required in most jobs, for example initiating, improving, resolving, compiling, organising, scheduling.

2 Place an x in the column if you would like (L) to use that skill in future work and another if you currently perceive that you have a sufficient level of proficiency (P) for employment.

Matrix

SPECIALISED			COMMUNICATION/ INTERPERSONAL			GENERAL		
My skills	L	P	My skills	L	P	My skills	L	P

10.11

Select 5 skills from the 18 you listed in Activity 10.10 and then:

a Give a good example of the circumstances when you used each skill.

b Explain the outcomes of your action.

employee to benefit from such an ED exercise, s/he has to recognise that positive experiences or accomplishments are considered because these are the ones which are likely to suggest the paths that the individual can take in her/his career development. They are also the ones which an employer will want to know about so that s/he can ensure that the individual is developing positively.

KNOWLEDGE AND LEARNING STYLE

Apart from working out the skills that an employee has, it is necessary to work out what s/he needs to know in order to develop. Individuals have learned in a variety of ways – as has been discussed earlier in this chapter – through their experiences such as attending classes, training sessions, working on projects, independent reading and travelling. If an employee is at the start of her/his career, an employer might well ask them to review their learning experiences through the form of activities such as those below.

10.12

Activity

a Review your formal education, for example school, college, university, training courses – situations where you gained a diploma or certificate or recognition from someone for whom you studied. Include points on, for example, university through your courses; school through your essays, projects and any other situations specific to you.

b Consider such areas as:
- specialisations
- options
- subjects you liked the least, and why
- marks/grades
- certificates, diplomas and other awards obtained.

This sort of activity will allow an employee to recognise that s/he has brought skills from her/his formal education which will be useful in the workplace.

10.13

Activity

List the knowledge which you have gained through any other educational opportunities.
Include dates, organisations and topics for both *formal* and *informal* training.
Include the training provided by employers on and off their premises and do not forget the training which you have received through any volunteer activities or other activities.

Matrix
Training provided by:

Employers	Volunteer organisations	Other ways

Individuals often do not appreciate that they have already acquired a number of skills from situations outside the workplace and that these skills are useful in the world of work and of value to a potential employer – or an existing one. Employees, however, also need to be able to analyse their own knowledge and learning.

10.14

Activity

It is useful at this stage to move on to the amount of knowledge that you feel you have gained on your own and may want to use in the working environment.

a List those things you have learned through travel, your own research and in other named ways.

b Review the list you made in (a) above and choose the five main areas of knowledge that you have and would like to build on in your career.

When employees are asked to consider their own career development, they often limit themselves to the skills that they have acquired because they are usually tangible and, therefore, easily measured. However, individuals do tend to overlook what actual knowledge they have acquired and how they have acquired it. This is closely related to learning styles (discussed earlier in this chapter). However, employees need to be able to put their learning into a strategic format.

VALUES

In the context of ED, the word 'value' refers to how you feel about work itself and the contribution it makes to society. Most individuals who pursue work that is congruent with their values feel satisfied and successful in their careers. The identification of personal values is a very important part of a career development

see Chapter 11

■ *see* Chapter 11 ■.

It is possible to divide work values into two functional categories:

1 *intrinsic values* relate to a specific interest in the activities of the work or task itself or to the benefits which the results of the work offer to society in general.

2 *extrinsic values* relate to the favourable conditions that accompany a choice of occupation, for example the physical setting, potential for earning and other external features.

Most employees need to have personal intrinsic value in their work if they are to be truly satisfied with their lot.

When working on their ED, it is important that individuals appreciate that their values will affect their acquisition of skills and knowledge as well as their choice of learning style/s.

10.15

1 Below is a list of personal values that some people consider important to them in their careers. As a start to exploring your personal work values, rate each value listed with the scale given and then add other values you consider essential.

1 Things which YOU VALUE VERY MUCH

2 Things which YOU VALUE

3 Things which YOU DO NOT VALUE VERY MUCH

AREA	DESCRIPTOR	RATING
Help society	Do something which contributes to improving the world I live in.	......
Help others	Be directly included in helping other people, either individually or in small groups.	......
Public contact	Have a lot of day-to-day contact with the public.	......
Work with others	Work as a team member towards common goals.	......
Work alone	Do projects myself, with limited contact with others.	......
Competition	Engage in activities that pit my abilities against others.	......
Make decisions	Have the power to decide courses of action and policies.	......
Work under pressure	Work in situations where time pressure is prevalent.	......
Influence people	Be in a position to influence the attitudes or opinions of other people.	......
Knowledge	Engage in the pursuit of knowledge and understanding.	......
Work mastery	Become an expert in whatever work I do.	......
Artistic creativity	Engage in creative artistic expression.	......
General creativity	Have the opportunity to create new programmes, materials or organisational structures.	......
Aesthetics	Participate in studying or appreciating the beauty of things and ideas.	......
Supervision	Have a job in which I am directly responsible for the work of others.	......
Change and variety	Have work activities that frequently change.	......
Precision work	Work in situations where attention to detail and accuracy are very important.	......
Stability	Have a work routine and job duties that are largely predictable.	......
Security	Be assured of keeping my job and receiving satisfactory compensation.	......
Recognition	Be publicly recognised for the quality of my work.	......
Fast pace	Work in circumstances where work must be done rapidly.	......
Excitement	Experience a high degree of (or frequent) excitement in the course of my work.	......
Adventure	Have work duties which require frequent risk taking.	......
Financial gain	Have a high likelihood of achieving great monetary rewards for my work.	......
Physical challenge	Do activities that use my physical capabilities.	......
Independence	Be able to determine the nature of my work without significant direction from others.	......
Moral fulfilment	Feel that my work contributes to a set of moral standards that I feel are important.	......
Community	Live where I can participate in community affairs.	......
Time freedom	Be able to work according to my own schedule.	......

Add others that are important to you.

2 List the top five from the list above.

Activity

INTERESTS

Every individual has developed personal preferences for certain types of activities and environments. Most people who enjoy their work have some sort of intrinsic interest in the activities with which they are connected. In ED it is important for both the individual employee and her/his managers to appreciate this because if a worker is employed in areas they intrinsically enjoy, then it is probable that quality work will be the result.

Employers can use a vocational interest test in an attempt to match:

either the interests or personality of the test taker to those of people in a variety of different occupations and occupational categories. (Spector, 1996, p116)

One of the most used vocational interest tests is the self-directed search devised by Holland (1994). This test gives scores on six personality types (see Table 10.6) and each type is associated with a particular family of occupations. Table 10.6 shows that the artistic type likes jobs that enable her/him to use her/his creativity and would probably prefer to be in an occupation such as artist, actor or photographer. The profile of scores on the six types can guide a person in choosing a career.

The match between an individual's vocational interests and those of people in occupations is supposed to give a high level of satisfaction with the occupation. It is likely that an individual who takes a job, or moves into one, which has a poor match has a high likelihood of being unhappy with it, whereas an individual who takes a job, or moves into one, that is a good match will probably like it.

The principle behind this test, and others like it, is to encourage an individual to select a career or move, within an organisation, to a job which matches her/his interests. They are frequently used in ED for guidance in career development and the development of a curriculum vitae.

Table 10.6 The six personality types and associated occupations as assessed by the self-directed search

The *realistic* type likes realistic jobs such as car mechanic, air traffic controller, surveyor, farmer, or electrician.

The *investigative* type likes investigative jobs such as biologist, chemist, physicist, anthropologist, geologist or medical technician.

The *artistic* type likes artistic jobs such as composer, musician, stage director, writer, interior decorator, anthropologist, geologist or actor/actress.

The *social* type likes social jobs such as composer, musician, stage director, writer, clinical psychologist, psychiatric case worker or speech therapist.

The *enterprising* type likes enterprising jobs such as salesperson, manager, business executive, television producer, sports presenter or buyer.

The *conventional* type likes conventional jobs such as bookkeeper, financial analyst, banker, cost estimator or tax consultant.

Source: Adapted and reproduced by special permission of the publisher, Psychological Assessment Resources Inc, 16204 North Florida Avenue, Lutz, Florida, USA, from Holland (1985) *You and Your Career*

10.16

The six general areas of vocational interests developed by psychologist John Holland (1985, 1994) are given below.

a Think about your past experiences and your current activities.

b Rank these work environments from (1) to (6) with the one that best describes you (1) to the one that least describes you (6).

c Rank the items on your list for (b) to find out where your interest lies.

GENERAL AREA	DESCRIPTOR	RANKING
Realistic	For people who like activities that are practical and concrete. They like to work in the outdoors and with tools and machines using their physical skills. Such individuals usually search for work that relates to nature and the outdoors, mechanics, builders or the armed forces.	......
Investigative	For people who like any scientific or intellectual pursuit. Such people like to gather information, uncover new facts or theories and analyse and interpret data. Such individuals look for work relating to academic research, medicine or computer-related industries.	......
Artistic	For people who value aesthetic qualities and like the opportunity for self-expression. They prefer to work in environments that are unstructured and flexible. Often they seek work which relates to art, music, drama, writing or in libraries and museums.	......
Social	For people who like to work with people. They like to inform, train or develop them. Such individuals enjoy working in groups, sharing responsibilities and tend to be good communicators. They also like to solve problems through discussions related to feelings and interactions with others. Often they seek work that relates to teaching, counselling, recreation or facilitating.	......
Enterprising	For people who like to influence, lead and manage others in order to achieve organisational goals or economic success. Such individuals enjoy persuading others to their views and tend to choose social tasks where they can assume leadership. They usually seek work relating to business management, sales or politics.	......
Conventional	For people who enjoy systematic activities which need attention to accuracy and detail – often associated with office work. Such people like to work for large organisations and are most comfortable with an established chain of command. They seek work relating to financial institutions, accounting firms or other large businesses.	......

ENTREPRENEURISM

For ED this is often thought to be the most important consideration. Self-responsibility has become a key term in the contemporary workplace. When individuals interact with others the style that they use can be described as 'enterprising'. People are constantly monitoring what is happening in the world, that is, globally, as well as nationally and locally. While doing this they are searching for opportunities and, when necessary, they are prepared to make a sacrifice. People have the ability to withstand setbacks.

Employers are constantly seeking ▷ **intrapreneurs** ◁ who demonstrate high-level leadership skills in:

- themselves

- situations and

- others.

Such people are prepared to take risks on behalf of their employers.

Intrapreneurs ◀┈┈▶ Employees who have the ability and confidence to work both independently and as a member of a high-performance team during a period of rapid change.

10.17

Activity

1 List those characteristics which you think are entrepreneurial. The first two are given as examples.
  a good organisational and time management skills
  b enthusiasm...
2 Give two examples of a time when you demonstrated each strength.
3 List the weaknesses you have and state how you would compensate for them.

ED will only be successful if the employer and employees are committed to it and are working in a learning organisation framework.

THE LEARNING ORGANISATION

A learning organisation is one where there is a prevalent attitude which is considered to be relevant to any organisation that has developed the continuous capacity to adapt to the environment and to change and which supports the self-development of members of the workforce towards this end.

The above scenario resembles a bureaucracy that provides a stable and safe environment, thus leaving the Kalahari bushmen (see the Framework Case Study at the start of this chapter) unable to cope with sudden environmental changes. However, the entrepreneurial and learning organisation of today is based on:

- a minimum of hierarchy

- equality of rewards ■ *see* Chapter 9 ■

- shared culture and

- a flowing, adaptable structure

see Chapter 9

which is designed to seize opportunities and handle crises.

Argyris and Schön (1978) believed that a mutual change in behaviour increases competence rather than purely relying on individual competence. They called this *theory in use*, explaining that this was the understanding (whether conscious or unconscious) that determined what an individual actually did. This counteracted the *espoused theory* being what an individual says s/he will do. Put simply, the rules of an organisation which are unspoken have actually changed. Even though the writers carried out their research in the early 1970s, in the 21st century, the issue of how the learning of an individual can be incorporated into transformational organisational learning is still in its infancy. The essence here is that the organisation has to be viewed as a process rather than as a single object.

Argyris and Schön (1978) described different levels (or loops) of organisational learning:

- *Single-loop learning* is about *how* an individual might improve on her/his current position. It is perceived as learning at the level of rules and regulations – the operational level.

- *Double-loop learning* is much more fundamental and is about asking *why* an individual is doing what s/he is doing. It is not about how things might be improved upon. Such a level is about developing knowledge and understanding due to insights, and it can result in strategic changes and renewal.

- *Triple-loop learning* is the most difficult to achieve because it is concentrated on the purpose or principles of the organisation for which the individual works. It challenges the situation by asking whether they are appropriate. It can sometimes be referred to as learning at the level of individual will or being.

In his seminal work, Senge (1990) puts forward an ambitious theory which states that a learning organisation is one which is continually expanding its capacity so that it can create its own future. He posited four basic management disciplines:

- personal mastery

- mental models

- building shared vision

- team learning.

His *fifth* discipline is called 'systems thinking' and he believes this is the one discipline that integrates the other four. According to him, the rewards of this integration are incalculable but, in essence, it creates the fusion that prevents the individual disciplines from becoming fancies and/or fads. It is through the five disciplines that organisations systematically become learning organisations without just allowing it to happen by accident or fortune.

However, Sloman (1999) believes that:

The concept of the learning organisation needs to be updated or dropped. (p31)

He identifies three key issues which need to be taken on board if an organisation is to truly be a 'learning organisation':

1   *Learning should be seen as a continuous process rather than a set of discrete training activities*
This means that learning has to be part of all the activities of an organisation. It would be necessary to produce evidence to show that this has occurred. Thus any reward systems ■ *see* Chapter 9 ■ would be linked to the contributions which individuals made to learning. Therefore, learning reviews would need to be taken after significant projects.

see Chapter 9

2   *Organisations should encourage employee participation*
This is as a consequence of (1) and means that every worker needs to participate in learning that is over and above what is required for narrow business needs.

3   *Policy to increase skills capabilities and knowledge application*
Through interactions that are designed to encourage learning come a policy that will increase the skills capabilities and application of knowledge workers.

Until recently the learning organisation has been rigorously defined as at the start of this section. However, not all organisations are able to define themselves as 'learning organisations' even though they might be participating in learning activities. As Sloman (1999) states, some may find that achieving points (1) to (3) above may constitute a legitimate aspiration and for others it could well be that they are currently activating them. However, the majority of organisations would find the approach beyond their capabilities and totally inappropriate to their organisation's goals.

The latter is a legitimate point of view – not all organisations can be defined as 'learning organisations' or indeed aspire so to be. This could be because of the need to use finite resources in the best way possible. Resources in the form of both time and money are needed to create the ideal learning environment and employers have to make choices in an environment where resources are difficult to control. The time has come for a less tightly defined learning organisation to one that demands continuing commitment to individual learning. This, in itself, provides a unique learning opportunity for employers and employees with the environment to become more self-critical.

BUILDING A LEARNING ORGANISATION

There are few organisations that use all the talents and creativity of their workforce and because of this, organisations are underutilising the skills and knowledge of their employees and employees are not developing their own skills and talents.

Some people view the concept of a learning organisation with a degree of suspicion considering it to be the latest fashion, which will pass on as something new comes along. However, there is evidence that some organisations are able to build on the skills and knowledge of their employees in such a way that their bewildered competitors have failed to understand.

Some people argue that it is only individuals who can learn. While this may well be true, an organisation is made up of a number of such individuals and, therefore, it could be said that an organisation learns. It will do so in a number of ways because of, for example, the differing businesses, culture and composition of the workforce. If an organisation is to do well, its rate of learning has to be greater than (or at least equal to) the rate of change that is taking place in its external environment.

POINTS TO PONDER

By the time you graduate from university much of what you have learned in your first year is out of date.

Therefore, surely it is better to 'learn how to learn' rather than learn facts and figures?

In the ever-changing environment of business it is impractical to expect any one single model of business or design of product to last more than a few years. The constant changes in both technology and taste can destroy what may appear to be a stable market in a matter of a few months. This rollercoaster of change has brought with it a shift from finance being the only type of business capital to the importance of knowledge as capital. Organisations have to move from thinking about investing only in physical assets to a mindset where they are also constantly trying to renew their knowledge capital ■ *see* Chapter 6 ■.

see **Chapter 6**

Competitive success now lies with organisations that have knowledge capital rather than financial capital – this comparison can be seen in Table 10.7.

An organisation needs to learn how to manage its own internal functioning, for example processes, structure and systems. It must also be aware of changes in its external environment and adapt to them. The internal and external functions of an organisation are closely related because, for example, a sudden shift in technology will clearly have a major impact on internal ways of operating.

Table 10.7 Comparison of financial capital and knowledge capital

FINANCIAL CAPITAL	KNOWLEDGE CAPITAL
Physical assets	Ability to learn
Number of staff	Quality of staff
Market share	Closeness to customers
Mass production	Constant innovation
Organisation's power	Organisation's flexibility

RECOGNISING A LEARNING ORGANISATION

Whatever the definition of a learning organisation, or an individual's opinion on its existence, there are four key facets that are essential to the development of an organisation wanting to develop its staff:

1 *Moving from a single- to a double-loop learning*

A learning organisation is very different to an organisation which is made up of highly trained staff because learning is aimed at being able constantly to assess whether what an individual is doing is right. With learning comes effectiveness and a professed learning organisation will continually try to improve its process while at the same time questioning whether the processes are the right ones by using double-loop learning, that is, the use of feedback as a check and balance.

2 *Perceiving change as continuity and not as an upheaval*

It is a truism that all organisations are capable of changing. A learning organisation will change in line with the changes in its internal and external environment, while a non-learning organisation will slip behind the rate of external change. Such organisations will go through a massive and very painful upheaval

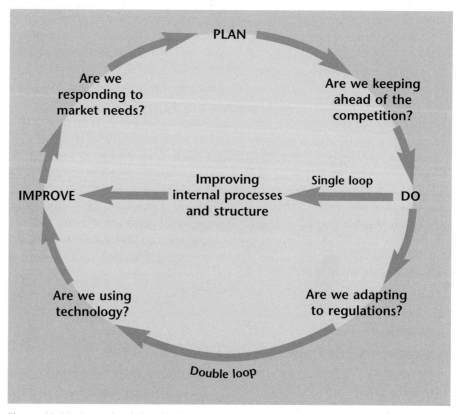

Figure 10.10 Example of the double-loop learning process

in order to catch up with their competitors. They will continue to slip, with all the associated upheaval and then follow this cycle until their demise. With upheaval will come such negative factors as lost jobs, closure of factories and offices while the staff will be obedient – although intimidated. In the western industrialised world individuals have become experts at coping with recurring upheaval but are considerably less capable of encouraging learning.

3   *Having a non-linear mindset*
    In order for ED to take place within an organisation it is necessary to view that organisation in a particular way, that is as:
    - a complex open system
    - an organisation which constantly reacts with its environment
    - one which uses predictable and unpredictable ways
    - an organisation which understands that simple actions can have unexpected results.

4   *Encouragement of diversity*
    Learning and creativity come about from a clash of opposites. If an employee has a uniform and repetitive job s/he will find it becomes monotonous. If employees are permitted to share their experiences this could well encourage ▶ **groupthink** ◀. However, it is in groups that individuals share ideas and can become creative and innovative. The challenge in a learning environment is to encourage a diversity of opinions even though this could well be threatening to the existing power structure within the organisation.

▶ The psychological drive for consensus at any cost that suppresses dissent and appraisal of ◀┈┈▶ **Groupthink**
alternatives in cohesive decision-making groups.

DEVELOPING A LEARNING ORGANISATION

In order to become an organisation within which the employees can develop, it is necessary for it to change the deep-rooted cultures and behaviours inherent within it. It is not possible directly to build a learning organisation. It is about radically changing the way people behave at work, that is, changing behaviours on concrete task-related issues and not attempting to instil what is sometimes termed a 'learning climate'.

Changing behaviour is very difficult, although there are two ways in which one can attempt to do so:

1   *External*
    The use of threats, rewards, and/or incentives ■ *see* Chapter 9 ■.

see **Chapter 9**

2   *Internal*
    Changing the way an individual sees her/his world and finding out the reasons why s/he acts in a specific way ■ *see* Chapter 9 ■.

see **Chapter 9**

To encourage an employee to consider ED or a change in career direction will necessitate a change in the mindset which drives that individual's behaviour. There are six steps to this procedure, each of which is important:

1   find out the original mindset

2   observe the original behaviour

3   test the new behaviour

4   gain positive feedback

5   now have a changed mindset

6   observe the new behaviour.

WHY ORGANISATIONS DO NOT LEARN

Learning ought to be a natural human activity and, therefore, it follows that organisational learning should be just as natural. In the workplace, individuals quickly understand that things have to be done in a certain way and no other – except in the most enlightened organisation, that is. Any deviation from the prescribed norm, however valid the reasons, usually brings about one or more of three behaviours from employers/managers:

■   disapproval

■   sanctions

■   expulsion.

This means that an individual employee has to leave the organisation or very quickly learn the behaviours required so that s/he can ensure her/his survival and success.

  While the forces for moving towards a learning organisation are theoretically very strong, as can be seen in Table 10.8, the practical arguments can appear to be insuperable.

Table 10.8 Forces against building a learning organisation

FORCES FOR	FORCES AGAINST
Rapidly changing markets	Fixed ways of behaviour
Change in technology	Existing power structure
Competitive pressures	Interests of key groups are threatened
Political and regulatory changes	Hierarchical organisation structure
Creative power of a motivated workforce	Difficulty in changing executive mindset
	Practical difficulties in implementation

THE LEARNING ORGANISATION OF THE FUTURE

There is an ongoing debate about the identification and role of the learning organisation and it is likely that this interest will continue to grow. The literature on the topic is increasing dramatically and thus shows that it is a matter of concern – to both HRM practitioners and to academics. It was one of the key areas of interest in the 1990s. While the learning organisation has recently been criticised as a piece of unachievable jargon, Burgoyne (1999) proposes a model for a learning organisation for the contemporary workplace. He disagrees with Sloman (1999) and states that it is not 'in terminal decline' but has become one of the most popular areas of study in business management. He also suggests (admittedly without empirical evidence) that:

> more and more companies are using the term to describe what they hope they are or aspire to
> be, or as an important guiding concept for their current change initiatives. (p39)

Where Burgoyne (1999) and Sloman (1999) do agree is in the confusion about what the concept of a learning organisation actually is and that there has been substantial naive thinking about the concept. Unlike Sloman (1999), Burgoyne (1999) believes that most learning takes place in a natural environment and not within a hothouse for professionally managed and expensively resourced learning as Sloman (1999) believes.

While there are a few case studies where organisations state that they are learning ones, for example the Open University and GEC, there is little evidence that this is on a large scale.

As mentioned above, changing an organisation into a learning organisation is not possible by the use of one large project. Burgoyne (1999) suggests that it is possible to use the concept of a learning organisation to:

> guide specific projects such as revising reward systems, reviewing appraisal schemes as a frame-
> work for internal training provision, or evaluating the accounting system. (p41)

Learning organisations used to comprise those that tried to adopt the theory of learning with its various styles and formats but this has now developed into a more developed process where there is vision. Burgoyne (1999) offers three ideas for what needs to happen in the development of learning organisations:

1   *Accumulated experience* of the last decade needs to be examined by researchers in order to identify any constructive ways forward in the development of a learning organisation formula.

2   *Concept needs to integrate with knowledge management initiative* by removing itself solely from the HRM arena and becoming integrated with information systems and to also take knowledge management from its technology mindset.

3   *Develop appropriate level of tools and technology* so that the concept of a learning organisation can be implemented.

SCENARIO 10.3

Bass taps into student power

Lancaster University Management School runs an in-company MBA* course for Bass, which is integrated with a mentoring scheme and a programme of continuous assessment and appraisal.

The learning organisation concept suggested viewing the participants as an inquiry team on behalf of the company, and not simply as a set of students on a course. So assignments are not only tests for marks, but for work that can make a difference in the company.

This led to a broadening concept of the role of mentors to help participants to identify key strategic issues and disseminate any interesting conclusions they might reach. This is in addition to the traditional 'personal coaching' element of the mentoring process.

The project, which is led by Bass, is continuously evaluated, which keeps alive the debate about how the programme is intended to be and is emerging as a contributor to corporate development. This exemplifies the principle of using the learning organisation to reframe, revisualise and reform what might otherwise be a relatively standard example of good practice.

*Master of Business Administration

Adapted from: Burgoyne, J. (1999) Bass taps into student power in Design of the times, *People Management*, 3 June, p41.

Burgoyne goes on to detail some ideas in each of these areas to open the debate and then finishes his views by stating that 'the learning organisation has not delivered its full potential or lived up to all our aspirations' (p44). Criticism is vital to any concept or development as long as it is constructive and it should, according to Burgoyne (1999):

> be treated, in the spirit of learning, as a resource with which to strengthen the idea and its application. (p44)

He finishes by saying that 'this is what defines the future of the learning organisation' (p44).

Just after Burgoyne (1999) suggested that a new model of the learning organisation was required, Miller and Stewart (1999) reported on work they had carried out with other academics and HRM professions within Unipart – they wanted to find out whether it was justified in calling itself a learning organisation.

Using their academic and professional research skills they investigated the organisation using criteria devised by the University Forum for Human Resource Development, as given in Table 10.9.

The investigations concentrated on five significant areas of activity in Unipart as they related to the definition of learning given in Table 10.9:

Linking learning to strategy: For Unipart, learning is about staying in business and, therefore, the organisation has set patterns for the sharing of information with learning as a key to its business strategy ■ *see* Chapter 2 ■.

see Chapter 2

Unipart U is a learning resources centre which is intended to represent a high-profile, creative corporate commitment to learning. Through this, the organisation

Table 10.9 Definition of a learning organisation according to the University Forum for Human Resource Development

- Learning and business strategy are closely linked

- The organisation consciously learns from business opportunities and threats

- Individuals, groups and the whole organisation are not only learning, but continually learning how to learn

- Information systems and technology serve to support learning rather than to control it

- There are well-developed processes for defining, creating, capturing, sharing and acting on knowledge

- These various systems and dimensions are balanced and managed as a whole

attempts to produce strategic advantages by encouraging faster learning than its competitors can.

Information systems are used to disseminate information to the workers on the shopfloor through empowering them into lifelong learning.

Critical incidents are used to encourage positive and real learning activities. An example here is that of reskilling where individuals had to be retrained.

Knowledge management is considered by Unipart to be 'the fuel that runs the business' (Miller and Stewart, 1999, p46) and it leads to improvements in all the processes carried out by the organisation with each one being linked to pay.

The researchers believed that Unipart was a model learning organisation although the difficulties in deciding upon this seemed to stem from the acceptance of the definition of a learning organisation.

It is important to remember, as mentioned previously, that individuals and *not* organisations learn and so the emphasis must be upon their ED rather than the cost of training per se.

The organisation which espouses to be a learning organisation will go much further forward than the limited imagination of a non-learning organisation. While learning cannot be taught to a whole organisation it can be gradually built on to a very firm base which has been well targeted and which is supported by the operational initiatives within the organisation – it is a strategic approach to success.

Therefore, organisations need to take a realistic period of time to:

- choose the key process to start on

- redesign the way employees work with that process

- protect them from inertia

- protect them from interference from the rest of the organisation

- prove the benefit of the 'new way'

- move to the next process.

KNOWLEDGE MANAGEMENT, INTELLECTUAL CAPITAL AND TALENT

Every organisation has a few skills that are critical to high performance being linked to how:

■ new products are developed

■ suppliers are managed

■ customers are dealt with.

While organisations may well comprise areas of best practice where success is the norm, it is too often the case that these areas of expertise depend upon a few individuals or groups. The ethos is not captured within the whole organisation and thus there must be, by definition, areas which are ill-performing. Consequently, it is essential that best practice is disseminated throughout the organisation.

This is all well and good but in some cases it is not always possible to disseminate best practice because, for example, personal or departmental rivalries prevent it. Any organisation which states that it is a learning organisation must have knowledge management processes for:

■ identifying existing best practice

■ developing new areas of best practice

■ ensuring that best practice is transferred to those people who should be using them.

Best practice exists in a time continuum – it does not last forever as the competitors establish better and more effective systems. Therefore, those that do exist must be continually upgraded in the light of new learning in order that they do not become restrictive and out of date.

Thus, knowledge management requires new:

■ roles

■ responsibilities

■ systems

■ cultures and climates

entwined in a framework of abundance thinking, that is, creativity and innovation ■ see Chapter 2 and Chapter 9 ■.

see Chapter 2 *and* Chapter 9

Measuring intellectual capital

There is an ongoing shift towards a knowledge economy, where work is increasingly knowledge based and organised around projects. Intellectual capital has become an organisation's most distinctive asset. According to Harrison (1999):

Collection time

The Post Office is one of the biggest employers in the UK and the knowledge required to keep the whole operation running smoothly is enormous in this most complex of organisations.

Individuals have considerable knowledge about everything from how to get mail from A to B, to how to use their people to get them through the Christmas rush. A considerable amount of that knowledge is contained in documents, manuals, reports and so on, but there is also a lot more that isn't written down anywhere – it's all in people's heads.

The Post Office has a knowledge management group whose aim is to find ways to capture as much of those vital data as possible. Referred to as 'tacit' or 'implicit' information, it is not written down and is often quite difficult to communicate clearly. This information comprises about 90 per cent of the knowledge. This knowledge is not a matter of simple facts and figures; it often involves understandings, assumptions and attitudes, which are far more difficult to convey. This latter factor is crucial.

Everything about the Post Office can be replicated by any other organisation except one thing – the knowledge that the employees have cannot be bought and it is that vital ingredient that makes the whole thing work. People who have worked for the Post Office for decades have built up a large amount of knowledge and while there may be fewer managers with MBAs than other organisations, they do have an enormous amount of information inside people's heads.

The knowledge management team has developed a range of techniques for capturing information, including 'after-action reviews', used when someone has completed a task or project. This poses questions:

- What were the aims of the project?
- What actually happened?
- Why did it happen in this way?
- What could be done better next time?

The most important development has been that of the 'knowledge interview' which is a process specially designed for collating an individual's knowledge and recording it for the benefit of others.

Knowledge interviews are most appropriate in three situations:

- *When a senior member of staff moves on*
  Unless a way is found of extracting what they know, most of their insights are likely to disappear with them.
- *When someone joins the organisation*
  They may possess all sorts of relevant experience from other organisations that could prove useful to the Post Office.
- *When someone is recognised as having particularly vital knowledge*
  This ought to be disseminated more widely.

The Post Office did try computerised knowledge capture packages but did not find them nearly as effective as the interview. They found that the technology got in the way because it broke the link in the conversation while the interviewer had to type in the answers to the questions. There was a loss of valuable eye contact and non-verbal communication.

The adoption of the one-to-one interview allowed individuals to develop their questioning technique and maintain a conversational link with the other person. They did admit that technology might work for other organisations, but not for the Post Office.

Adapted from: Whitehead, M. (1999) Collection time, *Personnel Management,* 28 October, pp68–9, 71.

> intellectual capital [has become] an organisation's distinctive asset. Knowledge is bought and sold... Knowledge is now seen as a key factor of production, products themselves are more 'knowledge-intensive' and, in some sectors, knowledge is almost all that there is. (p33)

With downsizing and the demographic trend towards an older, retired population, the knowledge workers are gone from the organisations. As the Post Office has recognised, these individuals have a considerable amount of information which can be harvested by the organisation, but not all organisations recognise this.

Bajer (1999) believes that:

> In a knowledge economy, businesses are wary of developing their talent pool for the benefit of others. (p27)

While employers are attempting to retain the talent they have in their organisations, they still do not recognise the importance of developing their people and so skills shortages will always be a problem in such organisations. Bajer (1999) believes that the more talent an organisation has, the less they invest in its development. In order to keep their talented staff, employers need to recognise the real costs of talent attrition and misuse when set against the benefits of investing, in the medium to long term, in their existing workforce.

According to Bajer (1999):

> Most organisations don't yet believe in the value of learning. (p27)

It is only those organisations that do which will benefit from recruiting and retaining talented staff because non-learning organisations will not be able to adopt learning techniques or identify the skills that will be needed in the 21st century.

EMOTIONAL LABOUR

see Chapter 1

In the past – particularly during the time of scientific management and bureaucratic management ■ *see* Chapter 1 ■ – emotional support for workers was expected to be provided by 'the wife at home', and not by employers, because the belief was that workers were carrying out routine operations within a bureaucratic environment.

see Chapter 1

With the rise of the human relations school ■ *see* Chapter 1 ■ came the view that there was some importance to the human side of people; and that included their emotions although this was more implicitly than explicitly expressed.

The study of ▶ **emotion** ◀ is a complex one, requiring an understanding of its psychological characteristics such as its definition, classification, levels and theories and is thus beyond the scope of this text. However, it is an area which is increasingly being referred to within the contemporary world of work and needs to be appreciated by all employees whatever their role.

Emotion ◀┈▶ A heightened feeling about, say, a subject or an agitation caused by strong feelings (Encarta, 1999, p615)

Every person has emotions, however, it is the way in which they express the emotion which constitutes the word ▶ **emotional** ◀. If a worker makes an exaggerated show of her/his emotions, for example by having a temper tantrum in the workplace, s/he is said to be emoting.

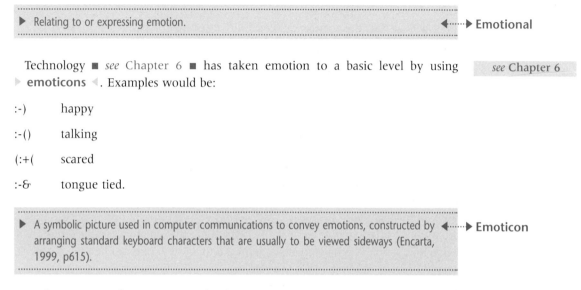

▶ Relating to or expressing emotion.   ◀······▶ **Emotional**

Technology ■ *see* Chapter 6 ■ has taken emotion to a basic level by using ▶ **emoticons** ◀. Examples would be:

see **Chapter 6**

:-)   happy

:-()   talking

(:+(scared

:-&   tongue tied.

▶ A symbolic picture used in computer communications to convey emotions, constructed by ◀······▶ **Emoticon**
arranging standard keyboard characters that are usually to be viewed sideways (Encarta, 1999, p615).

In order to use such emoticons individuals have to behave in a particular way – become emotional, which is relating to or expressing emotion. That is, the very use of an emoticon requires an emotional input from the individual who keys it in.

In the series *Star Trek*, Mr Spock repeatedly points out to Captain Kirk that human beings expend too much energy by having an emotional reaction to subjects or situations when, according to him, a more logical and rational approach would be more productive. However, it is the nature of human beings to react emotionally. Individuals should not 'be emotional' in the sense of losing control of their feelings or being unable to consider things in a calm and detached way. A psychological view is that it is the richness of an individual's emotions and her/his ability to have feelings as well as to think and reason which makes human beings unique. It is emotions which set the tone of an individual's experiences and give her/his life a vitality. According to Rubin and McNeil (1983) they are internal factors which can energise, direct and sustain behaviour. This applies to all aspects of life – both at the workplace and elsewhere.

Individuals will also react emotionally to happenings and situations that they think will make demands upon them that they cannot meet – either because they do not have the abilities, training or the resources required or because they force the individual worker to make very different choices and decisions. This is increasingly important in a workplace environment which encourages autonomy, for example the knowledge worker. Such negative sorts of happenings and situations are very stressful ■ *see* Chapter 6 ■.

see **Chapter 6**

see Chapter 5

Individuals in the workplace are not governed by the same needs because they are intrinsically motivated by different things ■ *see* Chapter 5 ■. Thompson and McHugh (1995) develop the human relations view by stating:

> managers and administrators could *become* rational, precisely because they can free themselves from social routines and the accompanying emotional involvements. (p50)

They believe that this view is rather curious because:

> any analysis of management shows that it has *its own* routines and 'illogicalities'. (p50)

see Chapter 3

This may well be true, yet systems are designed and implemented by individuals ■ *see* Chapter 3 ■ and thus they bring their emotional baggage with them. Everything that takes place in the workplace is tied up with the emotions of individuals. All stakeholders now demand a perfect service and all business activities work towards that end. With this comes an increasing demand for individuals to display their feelings in a standardised way through the use of smiles, forced pleasantness

see Chapter 5

and the use of verbal and non-verbal interactions and kinesics ■ *see* Chapter 5 ■. Most business operators answer a ringing telephone with a prescribed script and there are standardised responses. Individuals who physically deal with the public are trained to respond in a set way. By demanding that employees standardise their behaviour, employers have turned emotion into an item that can be traded, that is, something that can be bought and sold.

This used to apply only to raw materials or manufactured items. However, the interpretation has now broadened to include emotion as an extension of a commodity – anything that individuals find useful and, in this case, including individual emotions. This view is debated in the work of Putnam and Mumby (1993) who also considered that the increase in the need for individuals to act in a set manner is using emotion as a commodity.

see Chapter 9

Emotion is strongly linked to motivation ■ *see* Chapter 9 ■. Stress, rewards and punishments can reduce flexibility in thinking and may lead to irrational behaviour. For example, if an individual worker has been instructed to display feelings through forced smiles or pleasantness, then they could well act irrationally. The outward signs of a 'smile' and 'forced nice words' may not prevent irrational behaviour. The latter can have deleterious effects in the workplace for the employee. For example, if a worker is rewarded for 'smiling', the employee could well select only those activities which are easy and which need little negative action. Thus the individual will prevent themselves from reflecting on the general principles involved by just providing routine solutions. This would be increasingly true if the worker is rewarded in the form of praise from her/his supervisor. This will also result in creativity and is often too little regarded in this day and age, perhaps as a result of the mistaken views that creativity is linked totally to the ability to produce unusual but meaningless material. According to Sutherland (1992) in his seminal work on irrationality, true creativity is:

> the ability to solve new problems, to induce general principles and to construct sound explanatory theories... the ability to paint a picture that in some way or other moves the beholder. (p124)

Through their own personal development, individuals are assessing their own activities and controlling their behaviour and this continues to be encouraged by employers who utilise performance management ■ *see* Chapter 10 ■. While scientific management procedures tried to make a clear distinction between ideas and their activation, the contemporary workplace is an environment of team-working and interaction and this, by definition, means the expression of individual emotions.

see Chapter 10

There seems to be a depressing note in this area. Sutherland (1992) reports that a psychologist boasted that:

> there are now dozens of distinguishable theories of emotionality, hundreds of volumes devoted to that topic, and tens of thousands of articles dealing with various aspects of human affect. (p130)

There may be hope for the worker, however, since Sutherland (1992) goes on to state:

> psychologists know little more about emotion than does the layman. (p130)

However, there is little hope for the worker because management is still attempting to enlarge the rules which govern an individual's emotions although recognising that the established traditional rules still apply (Sutherland, 1992, p215).

This can be in the form of the monitoring of the activities of workers, for example the monitoring of e-mails and the use of closed circuit television ■ *see* Chapter 6 ■.

see Chapter 6

GENDER ROLES

On the whole women in employment do not enjoy the same job conditions, pay, status and career opportunities as their male counterparts. Generally, women are significantly underrepresented in UK management – even though Mukhtar (1997) states that:

> there was a dearth of data on the subject of women running their own businesses, even though their numbers had clearly increased. (p13)

Women are not only poorly represented in management positions but where they are to be found in management their role tends to be in what is commonly referred to as the 'softer' aspects of business – those which are traditionally considered to be within the 'female framework'. Examples here would be in HRM, retailing and customer services. That is, those areas where there is a high level of interaction with others. Herein lies the paradox – it is in these very roles that the emotions are more evident.

The majority of women are concentrated in a limited number of occupations and particularly those dominated by part-time workers. Despite the protection in law, women's advance into what have been traditionally men's jobs (especially the higher status roles) is still highly limited ■ *see* Chapter 7 *and* Chapter 8 ■.

see Chapter 7 *and* Chapter 8

APPRAISAL AND PERFORMANCE DEVELOPMENT

Appraisal is a key component of performance management. Organisations are now more focused on the need to get more from their employees if they are to achieve their objectives. When effective, the appraisal process reinforces the individual's sense of personal worth and assists in developing her/his aspirations. It is central to the ED process. Therefore, its central tenet is the development of an employee.

Individuals frequently make ad hoc judgments about others but are unable, or unwilling, to discuss the basis upon which such beliefs are made. Performance appraisal was introduced in the early 1970s in an attempt to put a formal and systematic framework on what was previously very casual. Appraisal is the analysis of the successes and failures of an employee and the assessment of their suitability for training and promotion in the future.

THE APPRAISAL PROCESS

Appraisal focuses on what has been achieved and what needs to be done to improve it. The problem is that too many employees try to make performance appraisal do too many things, at which point it becomes complicated and incoherent. It should be used to help to clarify what an organisation can do to meet the training and development needs of its employees.

It is a process intended to facilitate effective communication between managers and employees, and it should provide a clear understanding for both of them of four key components:

■ the work that must be accomplished

■ the criteria by which achievement will be judged

■ the objectives of the exercise

■ the process for giving the ▶ **appraisee** ◀ feedback on achievement.

Appraisee ◀····▶ The individual being appraised at an appraisal interview.

Part of the appraisal process is the potent aspect of self-appraisal because without this no profitable discussion can take place. Bandura (1977) stated:

> Self-appraisals of performance set the occasion for self-produced consequences. Favourable judgements give rise to rewarding self-reactions, whereas unfavourable appraisals activate punishing self-responses. (p133)

As a social learning theorist, Bandura (1977) argues that by self-reinforcing our activities and expectancies individuals will influence their own behaviour.

An appraisal system has a number of advantages and disadvantages as given in Tables 10.10 and 10.11 respectively.

Table 10.10 Advantages of an appraisal system

- The appraiser and the appraisee are forced to meet formally.

- The employee becomes aware of what is expected of her/him.

- The employee learns or reaffirms her/his exact status.

- Feasible targets can be set and agreed upon.

- Valuable feedback can be received by both employee and employer.

- Managers can learn what the employee is *actually* doing rather than what s/he *thinks* s/he is doing.

Table 10.11 Disadvantages of an appraisal system

- The appraiser could harbour favouritism, be biased and stereotypical when carrying out appraisal interviews.

- The criteria upon which the appraisee is being assessed could be interpreted differently by the appraiser.

- There may be limited information to hand.

- Any information that is available could be interpreted subjectively.

- The appraiser could be tempted to evaluate every appraisee s/he sees as 'average' or 'satisfactory' or 'fair'.

- An appraiser could well concentrate on isolated cases of excellence and/or bad performance without taking into account the appraisee's average performance.

- Appraisal requires extra work on behalf of the appraiser and the appraisee which both or either may not be prepared to do. If this happens, appraisal is an annual chore requiring a quick meeting and least comment from both appraiser and appraisee.

Schneier et al. (1991) believed that the issue of criteria was an important one. Whenever criteria are used to rate performance, even if all those involved help to put the criteria together, each one of them will interpret them in differing ways. Hence this is a key disadvantage for appraisal.

Performance appraisal is not a new event in the world of work. McGregor (1957) had his reservations some time back and these are relevant to appraisal today. He noted in his research that most managers were very reluctant to take on the role of ▸ **appraiser** ◂ because managers wanted to treat their subordinates as colleagues rather than as inferiors upon whom they could pass judgment. This was a comment on the 'top-down' style of appraisal (180° appraisal) which is, unfortunately, still *in situ* in many organisations. McGregor (1957) felt that most managers did not like to play the role of 'God' and, in recognising their own biases and prejudices, did

▸ The person carrying out an appraisal interview. ◂┄┄▸ **Appraiser**

not want them taken to appraisal situations. This was not a one-sided feeling – employees were also unhappy with their personal feelings being given a public airing, feeling that appraisal was patronising and had only one purpose – to humiliate and punish them because of the inadequacies of their work.

Kinnie and Lowe (1990) believe that through the appraisal system an organisation can incorporate valuable data into its career and management planning, the identification of training needs and its human resources plan and, as a consequence, help to avoid compulsory redundancies ■ *see* Chapter 1 *and* Chapter 6 ■.

see Chapter 1 *and* Chapter 6

The key feature of appraisal – regardless of which system is used – is that it is part of the ED process and has to be perceived, therefore, as useful to everyone concerned. It should never be used as a restrictive mechanism or as a form of punishment. Its purpose is to help individuals and the organisation in improving performance. With this in mind, there are three types of appraisal, as shown in Table 10.12.

Any form of appraisal requires skills from the appraiser and the appraisee and, consequently, each should be trained in the skills required for their roles. Managers cannot be expected to be able to act as an appraiser just because s/he happens to have subordinates. In the same way, the appraisee needs to know how best to get the most out of an appraisal – it is an opportunity for both to work towards their personal ED. Each one requires the ability to concentrate for some period of time, to carry out the preparation and the interview in a diligent way and also to be competent in their respective roles. Training alone is not sufficient, however, because application of the newly acquired skills is essential. This can only be done through substantial guidance from experienced appraisers and this causes an extra strain on appraisees who have to trust yet more people who are acting in the role of trainers. However, the use of role-playing exercises can assist here. McGregor (1957) pointed out two key facts which are still relevant 40 years or so later:

■ few managers receive any instruction in appraisal methods

■ even managers who are trained might not have all the information they need to undertake competent and impartial interviews, for example they may be out of touch with contemporary working practices or ignorant of the immediate working environment of the appraisee.

Table 10.12 Major types of appraisal review

TYPE OF REVIEW	COMPONENT
Performance	An analysis of the appraisee's past successes and failures within a positive framework, aimed at improving future performance.
Potential	An assessment of the appraisee's suitability for further training and/or promotion.
Reward	For determining the appraisee's performance related to set objectives and deciding the type and level of reward.

THE APPRAISAL INTERVIEW

The appraisal interview should take place once or twice every year. However, this does not mean that managers should not talk informally to employees about performance, training and development issues during the rest of the year. If the latter happened in a positive and fruitful way for both employee and manager, then the annual appraisal will be an open meeting which brings the pieces together. This annual interview should be a summary of the discussions that have occurred during the past year.

10.18

Activity

An annual appraisal interview between an employee and a manager has the potential for going very wrong for both parties.

List some reasons why this can happen.

A poorly conducted appraisal interview can be seen by the employee as being worse than not having an interview at all. Ideally, the record of the interview should be written on a special performance appraisal form that is signed by the manager, the employee and often the senior manager. It is good practice to allow the employee to see the completed form and add any comments.

The appraisal interview is a golden opportunity for the employee to take advantage of the occasion and sort out any issues s/he may want to raise and to make individual ambitions clear.

JOINT REVIEW

In the 1990s, traditional top-down style of performance appraisal scheme was still in use the involving unilateral judgments by managers of their subordinates. Lately, performance management has been seen as more of a continuous process where the individuals concerned talk with each other and try to share their perceptions in a mutual way. The annual appraisal is on its way out – especially in those organisations that have enlightened views on ED.

SELF-APPRAISAL AND PEER GROUP APPRAISAL

A top-down appraisal (180°) is sterile and biased and has limited use for either the appraiser or the appraisee and, hence, the organisation itself. One way of overcoming this sterility is to use self-appraisal and peer group appraisal. This method is still popular, having found its feet in the 1980s, and is seen by some as more

Table 10.13 Disadvantages of self-appraisal and peer group appraisal

- Many people cannot evaluate themselves because they lack the experience.

- Because the appraisal forms the basis for career development, the appraisee is tempted to overstate her/his strengths and understate the weaknesses.

useful to the appraisee in particular because it may lead to greater efficiency over time. Such an appraisal can be carried out by the employee her/himself or a chosen colleague of a similar status to the individual being appraised. With the fear of punishment being removed, an individual could well be more forthcoming and analytical with her/his ED.

Using this method, appraisees state:

- how they feel that they have performed

- the value of training they have received

- the effects of any amendments to the content of the job

- perceptions of what they see as the key objectives of the job

- future aspirations

- training and development required to meet those aspirations.

A key feature of this sort of appraisal is that the individual identifies her/his own strengths and weaknesses and accounts for them in a framework which lets her/him offer methods for overcoming weaknesses and working on the strengths so that her/his individual talents, skills and experience are put to good use.

However, like all methods of appraisal, the self-appraisal and peer group appraisal has disadvantages as shown in Table 10.13.

However, this approach does force individuals to consider very carefully how much they actually contribute to the achievement of the organisation's goals and how they are stopped from doing this by hurdles they perceive. They are also given the opportunity formally to consider their own ED, career development and the quality of their interpersonal relationships.

360° APPRAISAL

Armstrong (1999) and Armstrong and Baron (1999) give 360° appraisal creditable space in their work stating that it is 'the latest... the most exciting development in the field of performance management' (p313). Although small in number, more and more organisations are using 360° appraisals by gathering, usually through a questionnaire, the views of peers as well as the appraisee's manager; the purpose being to give a view of the employee's performance from a range of perspectives, while trying to eliminate bias. However, care needs to be taken when introducing such a scheme, as individuals may not be comfortable receiving feedback from their peers and subordinates.

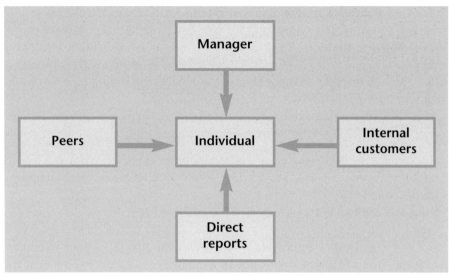

Figure 10.11 360° appraisal – before (after Armstrong, 1999, p466)

Armstrong (1999) devised a model shown in Figure 10.11, stating that 360° appraisal relied upon feedback which:

can be generated for individuals... from the person to whom they report, their direct reports, their peers (who could be team members and/or colleagues in other parts of the organization) and their external and internal customers. (p465)

It is interesting to note that Armstrong and Baron (1999) appear to have developed the model in Figure 10.11 to become more of a 540° appraisal by extending it to include other stakeholders such as external customers, clients or suppliers as shown in Figure 10.12, although they still refer to it as the 360° appraisal model.

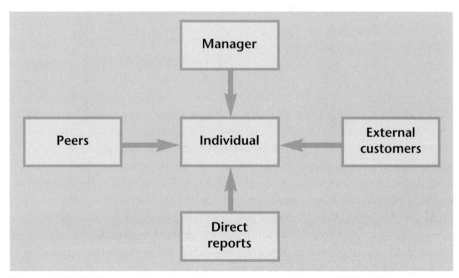

Figure 10.12 360° appraisal – after (after Armstrong and Baron, 1999, p314)

The form which an appraisal can taken is various and can include the use of 180° feedback upwards and downwards in the more traditional appraisal system discussed above. However, if the individual is part of a high-performance work team, the self- and peer group appraisal might be more appropriate with feedback being given by the team leader and/or the team leader and other members of the appraisee's team.

There is no doubt that 360° feedback has the most potential in bringing the best out of an appraisal situation. Armstrong (1999) and Armstrong and Baron (1999) are strong in their praise of the method, having carried out research as practitioners in the field of HRM.

PARTICIPATION AND EMPOWERMENT

Since appraisal requires individuals to reflect on their own ED, it empowers them and permits them to take responsibility for their own continuous development. The principle of empowerment is not new, is often considered to be a jargon word in the workplace and is:

> Related to the organisational arrangements that allow employees more autonomy, discretion and unsupervised decision-making responsibility.

Empowerment encompasses the principle of participation and is relevant to all aspects of an individual's existence and, therefore, is key to the development of an employee.

The Human Relations School (1930s to mid-1950s) made the assumption that if employees were happy and satisfied they would naturally work harder and thus increase their productivity ■ *see* Chapter 1 ■. Because of this premise, the movement encouraged a wider appreciation of the importance of worker participation within the organisation – not least with their own ED and career progression. The premise was that when given an opportunity to take part in organisational decision making (such as the nature of their own jobs) employees would be satisfied and this, in turn, would result in improved performance. Managers who adopted this view made the supposition that the participation of an employee would result in increased satisfaction and they paid less regard to the deprival of satisfaction from other inputs which could be valuable in meeting the organisation's goals, for example skills gained in the wider environment such as the individual's hobbies and interests. As time went on, managers began to realise that the input of an employee was a valuable entity in itself apart from the presumed effect on satisfaction.

see Chapter 1

The role of participation and empowerment in motivation can be expressed in terms of both the content- and the process-based motivational theories – particularly the expectancy theory ■ *see* Chapter 9 ■. When individuals are permitted to participate in aspects of their own ED, they 'own' the decisions made and are, consequently, committed to executing such decisions correctly. In seeing ED through all its decision-making processes (need for achievement, provision of recognition and responsibility, enhancement of self-esteem), individuals satisfy their own needs and are helped to self-actualise and thus meet their ED aims.

see Chapter 9

Through ED and appraisal in particular, managers can use job enrichment to make jobs more meaningful and challenging. They can hand responsibility to individuals through participation and empowerment. Participation can be brought about by giving individuals a voice in making decisions about their own work whereas empowerment goes one stage further by allowing workers to set their own work goals, make their own decisions and solve problems within their sphere of responsibility and authority. It is aligned closely with teamworking.

Empowerment is a broader concept which incorporates participation in a wide variety of areas, such as work itself, the context of work and the work environment. In its initial stages of recognition (1930s through to the 1950s) employers considered that participation was simply a means of increasing job satisfaction, while today it is recognised as having the potential as a valuable input into the ED arena.

Empowerment is about sharing power within an organisation: individuals cannot be empowered, but organisations can use their job design and structures to empower individuals. Modern organisations have grown flatter and leaner (some say meaner) through such concepts as downsizing, which, in turn, has eliminated layers of management and has increased the use of teamworking. As a consequence, empowerment has become more and more important in the development of employees. It involves the sharing of power in such a way that individuals learn to believe in their ability to do the job. Empowerment is driven by the idea that the individuals closest to the work and the customers should make the decisions and that this, in turn, makes the best use of employees' skills and talents. Empowerment is a concept which is easy to champion but very difficult to practise. Linked to empowerment is the concept of ▶ **open-book management** ◀.

▶ Giving employees all the information any owner receives if the latter wants employees to ◀┈┈▶ **Open-book**
   act like owners and care for the organisation.   **management**

EMPOWERING OTHERS

There are four key guidelines on how a manager can empower others through ED:

- by expressing positive confidence in their staff

- by creating positive opportunities for employees to participate in decision making

- by removing bureaucratic restraints

- by setting inspirational, yet achievable, goals in partnership with individuals.

There is also a risk of failure in attempts to empower employees: particularly when delegating responsibility the empowering authority must be prepared for the possibility of failure, which is something that managers do not tolerate well. To avoid failure or to learn from the experienced failure, it is vital that empowerment is accompanied by positive feedback through the appraisal process followed by the appropriate counselling and/or coaching.

MANAGEMENT DEVELOPMENT

Mayo (1999) believes that:

> The amount of time spent on management development seems to be constantly increasing, and it is only to be expected that questions are arising as to whether it will all turn out to be worthwhile. (p56)

The theory-in-literature on management development appears to take the consensus view that MD can only be good since all development is good development. It follows from this that all ED is good ED. However, there has been a steady rise in the number of individuals who are attempting to demonstrate its significance and effectiveness. One key study is that of Syrett and Lammiman (1999) which reflects on 20 years of MD within European organisations. However, they have used the term 'management education' as synonymous with 'management development' (MD), ignoring aspects of development that arise from an individual's experiences in the workplace. This is a common error in MD because transferable skills are central to ED of any kind.

Management development is about using programmes to support any change management within organisations by helping them to analyse the rationale for doing things in a different way. Managers must be constantly aware of themselves and their environment and broaden their thinking beyond the daily grind of work. Management development allows individuals to broaden their creativity and innovation which must, in the end analysis, be part of their strategy at work.

However, MD has a wider component which relates to issues covered earlier in this chapter – that of identifying what managers need to learn and how they can learn it. Each organisation will have different requirements from its managers (although some skills and knowledge will be common) but MD is also about the effects of education on individual and business performance.

Winterton and Winterton (1999) delved into the development of managerial competencies, believing that the evaluation of the benefits to be gained from education and training should be a key factor in deciding whether an overall management development programme deserves resources. While a ▶ cost–benefit analysis ◀ might be a well-reasoned approach, it is very difficult to use in the evaluation of management education and development. According to Hodgkinson (1999):

> in practice this type of evaluation [cost-benefit analysis] is hard to do and is all too often ignored, resulting in a culture of indifference about whether the money being spent is having a beneficial effect. (p65)

Cost–benefit analysis ◀┈▶ An evaluation of a project as to its benefits and costs with an attempt to put a monetary value to the process.

Management development should be undertaken as part of a systematic analysis of the ED programme of an individual – particularly as it relates to training and education. A number of key developments have highlighted the significance of MD:

■ IPM's Code of Practice on continuous professional development (IPM, 1984)

■ Charles Handy's (1987) report *The Making of Managers*

■ creation of training enterprise councils (TECs)

■ National Vocational Qualifications (NVQs)

■ National Council for Vocational Qualifications (NCVQ)

all of which have been discussed in ■ Chapter 6 ■.

see **Chapter 6**

Winterton and Winterton (1999) highlight the considerable difference between top managers in the UK and the USA by stating that in 1989 top managers in the UK comprised 24 per cent graduates while in the USA it was 85 per cent. They felt that this underlined a feeling that the UK was lagging behind in management training.

In order to make up the loss, the UK has introduced further approaches to management development and recognition, including:

■ Investors in People (IiP)

■ Management Charter Initiative (MCI)

again discussed in detail in ■ Chapter 6 ■.

see **Chapter 6**

Like all ED, in order to benefit from MD it must be linked to both organisational strategy and management standards ■ *see* Chapter 2 ■. This suggests that organisations working towards the IiP and MCI accreditations should increase the value added from their management development programmes.

see **Chapter 2**

In order for an organisation to survive in the contemporary business environment, it can be seen that it is essential to provide the most appropriate ED for all staff at all levels and this can only be done by means of effective interpersonal communication ■ *see* Chapter 5 ■. However, the workplace is no longer as simple and straightforward as it used to be and both employers and employees have to ensure that they are aware of the contemporary and international issues related to HRM.

see **Chapter 5**

■ The development of employees is essential and comprises any activity or situation whereby an individual's activities have a deep impact on her/him.

■ ED is attitudinal and is, therefore, difficult to define. However, it must be central to the strategy of every organisation.

■ Every manager has a direct responsibility for ED and should, therefore, be trained in the concept and be knowledgeable about

Chapter summary

personal development and how to increase the skills and knowledge of their subordinates.

■ ED is a partnership between the employee, employer, providers and the national government.

■ The term 'performance management' is used to identify and postulate best policies in the management and development of people at work.

■ Learning, training and education are different yet all are important to ED.

■ Learning is, however, critical to ED and every employer and employee must be able to understand how an individual learns and the barriers to learning. The key themes are operant conditioning, reinforcement and social learning theory.

■ The only way to bring about effective ED is by the development of partnerships.

■ ED is grounded in the power of the employer and particularly to the power bases propounded by French and Raven (1962): reward, coercive, referent and expert.

■ ED is also pertinent to change mechanisms, especially planned change and leadership.

■ Personal growth, career development and career planning are central to the process of ED, with individuals having to learn to cope with the increasing demands and challenges of self-management with the achievement of personal goals as they refer to personal values and interests.

■ Self-responsibility is key within the contemporary workplace and the required interaction means that individuals have to become more entrepreneur-like.

■ Success in the contemporary organisation relies upon the recruitment and retention of staff with high-level knowledge, intellect, creativity and talent which must be fostered by employers.

■ Performance appraisal focuses on what an individual has achieved and what needs to be done. The key method is 360° appraisal although self- and peer appraisal are both potent.

Chapter summary *continued*

- Since individuals have to reflect on their own ED, they have to take responsibility for their own continuous development (CD) and continuous professional development (CPD). Therefore, participation and empowerment becomes even more important.

- Management development has an increasing amount of time spent on it, yet there is little evidence to show that it is all worthwhile in a cost–benefit scenario.

END OF CHAPTER 10 CASE STUDY
Technology takes a back seat

Scientific Generics is an unusual organisation that, alongside its technology and business consultancy work, develops new products and sells them on as intellectual property rights to clients or commercialises them through spinoffs. The firm has produced a number of successful and important innovations, including a pen-input device for hand-held computers, a laser for ophthalmic surgery and software for modelling an organisation's skills and competencies.

The firm consciously integrates the different activities and types of people in one building at its main site in Cambridge, England. It has laboratories and meeting rooms on the ground floor and an open-plan office above. Although Scientific Generics has in place the usual IT systems, they are viewed as secondary rather than central to the way it manages knowledge. Groupware tends to be used only when physical distance limits face-to-face interaction, and the value of internal e-mail is limited by information overload – on a typical working day a consultant might receive between 100 and 150 messages.

Instead, much more emphasis is placed on creating the right environment for knowledge creation. This is partly about selecting people who will fit in with the hothouse culture. For instance, nearly all the consultants have science PhDs.* But equally important is a performance management system that links rewards to each consultant's contribution to projects. Projects are constantly starting all over the organisation and there are no formal rules for allocating people to them. As a result, every consultant has a vested interest in selling their expertise to their colleagues, creating an internal market for knowledge. The performance review process also includes specific reference to passing on skills and sharing knowledge.

*Doctor of Philosophy

Adapted from: Scarbrough, H. (1999) Technology takes a back seat in System error, *People Management*, 8 April, pp68–70, 73–4.

END OF CHAPTER 10 CASE STUDY QUESTIONS

1 Why, in an organisation which is a leader in the field of technology, does Scientific Generics concentrate on people rather than technology when it comes to knowledge management?

2 What are the limitations of technology?

3 At Scientific Generics they pay particular attention to rewarding their staff. What disadvantages are there in too much emphasis on rewarding those with knowledge and intellectual capability?

4 While it is easy to criticise Scientific Generics on its knowledge management ideas, what constructive contribution are they making, as a member of the IT community, to the general business arena?

END OF PART V CASE STUDY

TAKING THE BRAKES OFF THE LEARNING CONCEPT

Volvo has worked for two years on a set of initiatives to turn the idea of the learning organisation into reality. The core project involved cross-functional teams, with a mix of personnel, IT and line managers, in a series of meetings and projects that Volvo has called 'dialogue on learning'.

The main outcomes have been a number of principles defining a centre to facilitate learning across the organisation and to provide learning resources and facilities. The meetings have also evolved into a methodology for corporate learning. The essence of this is to have a cross-functional, cross-company and cross-level group of managers form a temporary 'inquiry team' to investigate and report back on a significant strategic problem.

A recent example has been the issue of doing more business in Eastern Europe. This was investigated by the kind of group described above, based temporarily in Prague. It passed back a much greater awareness of the diversity of developments in the region and the sophistication and speed of growth in certain regions.

Other projects have included feasibility studies of how the annual business planning process might be reformulated as an explicit contributor to organisational learning and how IT systems can make a balanced contribution in this area too.

Volvo has deep-rooted values and clear policies concerning quality, safety and the environment. Part of the project led to serious consideration as to whether corporate learning should become a fourth element of this set of guiding principles. The conclusion was that it should not, but instead be declared as a core process by which these values are pursued. This is a useful reminder that although learning is a crucial process, it is a means to an end.

Adapted from: Burgoyne, J. (1999) Taking the brakes off the learning concept in Design of the times, *People Management*, 3 June, p43.

END OF PART V CASE STUDY QUESTIONS

1 Why would Volvo want to become a learning organisation?

2 Why has Volvo decided not to make the corporate learning one of its stated guiding principles?

3 On what did the organisation base its decision to develop its corporate learning?

4 Why did Volvo consider the learning organisation to be important in the contemporary workplace?

THESIS + ANTITHESIS = SYNTHESIS

Analyse the view that there is no such thing as a learning organisation.

SELF-TEST THE KEY ISSUES

1 Explain the difference between a single-loop learning organisation and a double-loop learning organisation using either a quality problem or a drop in market share as an example.

2 Why would a one-to-one conversation about, say, knowledge capture, prove to be better than a technological approach?

3 Why is it essential that employers not only recognise but activate the knowledge, intellectual capability, creativity and talents of all their employees?

4 What is 'performance management'?

TEAM/CLASS DISCUSSIONS

1 Debate the issue that ED is a personal matter and is of no relevance to the achievement of the goals of an organisation.

2 'An organisation will not survive if it does not actively recruit and retain the most knowledgeable, intellectual, talented and creative people.' Discuss.

PROJECTS (INDIVIDUAL OR TEAMS)

1 a Write down any questions that have arisen as a result of your learning experiences from working on Chapter 10.

b From the questions in (a) above, what *key concepts* can you extrapolate for further learning? Write them down.

c Write a report on how you can now go about finding the answers to (a) and (b) above. Find a few suggested readings and/or exercises to facilitate the learning of these key concepts.

d Discuss your present learning goals and questions with other students, members of the faculty or persons outside your learning environment. Discuss further learning possibilities with them and document your findings.

2 'Learning how to learn' has been put forward as a key aspect of ED and performance management for individuals and organisations. To learn something is to 'know' it. Therefore, a crucial step in learning how to learn is to understand your own definitions of knowledge.

Your manager has asked your team to present a report to her which addresses the following issues:

a What does it mean to 'know something' and does it vary between individuals?

b Has an individual's knowledge base increased when they 'know' something? For example, that being dependent upon someone else makes you unhappy? What difference, if any, would there be if other people 'knew' the same things as other individuals, or they felt the same way?

c Does everyone have a common definition of 'knowledge' and if so, why and if not, how can a definition of knowledge be expanded? Would it affect an individual's learning style?

Recommended reading

Armstrong, M. (1999) *A Handbook of Human Resource Management Practice*, London: Kogan Page

Bratton, J. and J. Gold (1999) *Human Resource Management: Theory and Practice*, Basingstoke: Macmillan – now Palgrave

Graham, H.T. and R. Bennett (1999) *Human Resources Management*, London: Financial Times/Pitman

Halman, D., K. Pavlica and R. Thorpe (1996) Rethinking Kolb's theory of experiential learning: the contribution of social construction and activity theory in *Management Learning*, **4**(24): 485–504

Hartle, F. (1997) *Transforming the Performance Management Process*, London: Kogan Page

Heil, G., Bennis, W. and Stephens, D. (2000) *Douglas McGregor Revisited*, London: John Wiley

Institute of Personnel and Development (IPD) (2000) Success through learning: the argument for strengthening workplace learning, insert in *People Management*, 8 June

Pavlica, K., D. Holman and R. Thorpe, The manager as a practical author of learning in *Career Development International*, **3**(7): 300–7

Peipert, M., M. Arthur, R. Goffee and T. Morris (2000) *Career Frontiers: New Conceptions of Working Life*, Oxford: Oxford University Press

Randell, G. (1994) Employee Appraisal in Sisson, K. (ed.) *Personnel Management*, Oxford: Blackwell

Torrington, D. and L. Hall (1998) *Human Resource Management*, London: Prentice Hall

Walters, M. (ed.) (1995) *Performance Management Handbook*, London: Institute of Personnel and Development

URLs (uniform resource locators)

www.info@career-psychology.co.uk

Students, mid-career change, senior career change, staff career development. Free brochure.

www.learning-providers.org.uk

Association of Learning Providers. Skills transition questions and answers. Qualifications.

www.efa.org.uk

Employers Forum on Age (EFA). Promotion of good practice on ageism.

www.thirdageexperts.com

Third Age Experts (TAE). A professional association of mature experts available to assist businesses and commerce with project-related challenges. Includes section on human resources.

www.worklifeforum.com

National Work-Life Forum. Work-life strategies for the 21st century.

www.reed.co.uk

Reed Employment searchable job database.

www.charitypeople.co.uk

Information of work positions in the charity sector.

www.sirius.com

Career development process and guide to Internet resources.

www.careertrainer.com

On-line career resource for counselling and career development.

Bibliography

Argyris, C. and D. Schön (1978) *Organisational Learning: A Theory of Action Perspective*, New York: Addison Wesley

Armstrong, M. (1999) *A Handbook of Human Resource Management Practice*, London: Kogan Page

Armstrong, M. and A. Baron (1999) *Performance Management: The New Reality*, London: Institute of Personnel and Development

Bajer, J. (1999) Distressed flair in *People Management*, 16 December, p27

Bandura, A. (1977) *Social Learning Theory*, Englewood Cliffs, NJ: Prentice Hall

Barrow, M.J. and H.M. Loughlin (1993) Towards a learning organization in Grand Metropolitan Foods Europe in Wills, G. (ed.) *Your Enterprise School of Management*, Bradford: MCB University Press, pp195–208

Burgoyne, J. (1999) Design of the times in *People Management*, 3 June, pp38–41, 43–4

Burgoyne, J. (1999) *Develop Yourself, Your Career and Your Organisation*, London: Lemos & Crane

Chan Kim, W. and R. Mauborgne (1997) Fair process: managing the knowledge economy in *Harvard Business Review*, July–August

Encarta (1999) *World English Dictionary*, London: Bloomsbury

Fonda, N. and D. Guile (1999) Joint learning adventures in *People Management*, 25 March, pp38–41, 43–4

French, J.R.P. and B. Raven (1962) The bases of power in D. Cartwright (ed.) *Group Dynamics: Research and Theory*, Evanston, IL: Row & Peterson

Hammond, I. (1999) In my opinion in *Management Today*, May, p14

Handy, C. (1987) *The Making of Managers: A Report on Management Education, Training and Development in the United States, West Germany, France, Japan and the UK*, London: Manpower Services Commission, National Economic Development Office and British Institute of Management

Harrison, R. (1999) Called to account in *People Management*, 30 June, p33

Hodgkinson, D. (1999) Executive decisions in *People Management*, 6 May 1999, pp65–6

Holland, J.L. (1985) *You and Your Career*, Lutz, FL: Psychological Assessment Resources

Holland, J.L. (1994) Self-Directed Search Form R, Lutz, FL: Psychological Assessment Resources

Honey, P. and A. Mumford (1986 and 1992) *The Manual of Learning Styles*, Maidenhead: Honey)

Hunt, D.K. (1991) Cautionary tales from the Kalahari: how hunters become herders and may have trouble changing back again in *Academy of Management Education*, **3**(5): 74–86

Institute of Personnel and Development (1994) *People Make the Difference: an IPD position paper*, October, Institute of Personnel and Development

Institute of Personnel and Development (1996) *The Lean Organisation: Managing the People Dimension.* Consultative Document, October, London: Institute of Personnel and Development

Institute of Personnel and Development (1999) *People mean business: IPD Annual Report 1998/99*, September, London: Institute of Personnel and Development

Institute of Personnel Management (1984 and 1986) *The IPM Code: Continuous Development: People and Work*, London: Institute of Personnel Management

Institute of Personnel Management (1992) *Getting Fit, Staying Fit: Developing Lean and Responsive Organisations*, London: Institute of Personnel Management

Kinnie, N. and D. Lowe (1990) Performance related pay on the shop floor in *Personnel Management* (21) November, pp45–9

Kolb, A. (1974) On management and the learning process in Kolb, D.A., I.N. Rubin and J.M. McIntyre (eds) *Organisational Psychology: A Book of Readings*, Englewood Cliffs, NJ: Prentice Hall

Kolb, D.A. and A.L. Frohman (1970) An organization development approach to consulting in *Sloan Management Review*, **12**: 51–65

Kroeger, O. and J.M. Thuesen (1988) *Type Talk: The 16 Personality Types That Determine How We Live, Love, and Work*, New York: Dell Publishing

Making of British Managers: A Report on Management Education, Training and Development in the United States, West Germany, France, Japan, and the UK (The Handy Report) 1987, London: National Development Office

Maund, L. (1994) The Role of Conflict in the Teaching and Learning of Undergraduates: A Case Study (unpublished PhD thesis). Guildford: The University of Surrey

Mayo, A. (1999) Well worth the weight in *People Management*, 19 August, pp56–7

McGregor, D. (1957) An uneasy look at performance appraisal in *Harvard Business Review*, **35**(3)

McCLelland, S. (1994) Gaining competitive advantage through strategic management development in *Journal of Management Development*, **13**(5): 4–13

Miller R. and J. Stewart (1999) Opened university in *Personnel Management*, 17 June, pp42–3, 45–6

Morgan, G. (1988) *Riding the Waves of Change: Developing Managerial Competence for a Turbulent World*, San Francisco: Jossey-Bass

Mukhtar, H. (1997) Women who make a difference in *Financial Times*, 18 February, p13

New Learning for New Work (1999) *Managing Learning for Added Value*, London: Institute of Personnel and Development

Nurden, D. (1999) Henry's lesson in leadership in *Independent on Sunday*, 23 May, p1

Pettinger, R. (1996) *Introduction to Organisational Behaviour*, Basingstoke: Macmillan – now Palgrave

Putnam, L.L. and D.K. Mumby (1993) Organizations, emotion and the myth of rationality in Fineman, S., *Emotion in Organisations*, London: Sage

Raftery, T. (1999) Speak their language in *People Management*, Letters, 16 December, p23

Reid, M.A. and H. Barrington (1999) *Training Interventions: Managing Employee Development*, London: Institute of Personnel and Development

Rubin, Z. and E.B. McNeil (1983) *The Psychology of Being Human*, London: Harper & Row

Scarbrough, H. (1999) System error in *People Management*, 8 April, pp68–70, 73–4

Schneier, C.E., D.G. Shaw and R.W. Beatty (1991) Performance measurement and management: a tool for strategy execution in *Human Resource Management*, **30**(4): 279–303

Senge, P. (1990) *The Fifth Discipline: The Art and Practice of the Learning Organization*, New York: Random Century

Sloman, M. (1999) Seize the day in *People Management*, 20 May, p31

Spector, P.E. (1996) *Industrial and Organizational Psychology: Research and Practice*, Chichester: Wiley

Sutherland, S. (1992) *Irrationality: The Enemy Within*, London: Penguin

Syrett, M. and J. Lammiman (1999) *Management Development – Making the Investment Count*, London: Economist Books

Thompson, P. and D. McHugh (1995) *Work Organisations: A Critical Introduction*, Basingstoke: Macmillan – now Palgrave

Tomlin, J. (1999) *People Mean Business: IPD Annual Report 1998/99*, September, London: Institute of Personnel and Development

Whitehead, M. (1999) Collection time in *Personnel Management*, 28 October, pp68–9, 71

Winterton, J. and R. Winterton (1999) *Developing Managerial Competence*, London: Routledge

Contemporary concerns

Key issues: globalisation, ethics and workplace diversity

After studying this chapter, you should be able to:

Globalisation

- ◾ EXPLAIN the key concepts related to the concept of globalisation.
- ◾ DISCUSS the importance of globalisation strategies.
- ◾ CONTRAST domestic and global sourcing.
- ◾ DISCUSS the role of information technology within globalisation.
- ◾ IDENTIFY and DISCUSS the key features of global forces and the organisational lifecycle.
- ◾ ANALYSE the key stages in international development.
- ◾ SPECIFY how the design of an organisation is aligned with global advantage.
- ◾ DISCUSS what is meant by 'the new economy'.
- ◾ DESCRIBE the key aspects of global marketing.
- ◾ SPECIFY the key aspects of global competition.
- ◾ CATEGORISE the link between global management, leadership and training.
- ◾ UNDERSTAND the importance of global citizenship.
- ◾ UNDERSTAND the importance of the role of the human resource management (HRM) specialist in the field of globalisation.

LEARNING OUTCOMES (cont'd)

Ethics

- DEFINE ethics and business ethics.
- ANALYSE the role of the individual in ethics.
- UNDERSTAND the link between individual differences and ethical behaviour.
- EXPLAIN the ethics of employee empowerment.
- ASSESS the role of ethics in work teams.
- SPECIFY how ethics affects the activities of an organisation.
- DESCRIBE the role of ethics in training.

Workplace diversity

- ASSESS how an organisation can define diversity and implement a diversity policy.
- APPRECIATE the link between diversity issues and the role of the HRM specialist.
- DISTINGUISH between the narrow and broad descriptors of diversity.
- EXPLAIN the link between workplace diversity and ethics.
- ANALYSE the dimensions of workplace diversity.
- DISCUSS diversity in action.
- DESIGN and MEASURE diversity initiatives.
- IDENTIFY the business benefits of workplace diversity.
- EXPLAIN the link between workplace diversity and good management practice.

INTRODUCTION

Framework case study

Poor nations assert place in global trade

If nothing else, developing countries demonstrated that they still prize global trade talks as a mechanism for exerting leverage on the rich north, according to delegates attending the United Nations Trade and Development meeting in Bangkok.

In the absence of any actual trade talks, the meeting affirmed that developing countries' problems had moved to the forefront of multinational negotiations.

Some countries want to shake everything up and others want to ensure that subsequent discussions are not destroyed. However a delay in the World Trade Organ-

ization (WTO) negotiations is a delay in solving the problems of economies.

An action plan was agreed that gives pride of place to bringing 48 least developed countries into the economic mainstream, while a separate declaration on global dialogue and dynamic management strongly commended open trade and economic integration as the path for future development.

No country in its right mind could be against a multilateral trading system that puts checks on the powerful, but the WTO has to deliver as well.

The Bangkok declaration said

that it was essential that globalisation be managed through consensual solutions and that new trade talks should take into account the dimension of development of the developing world.

Critics say there was still a divide between the rich west and the developing world because the meeting was full of rhetoric but did not attempt to find solutions to things that really matter – like poverty.

The agreements may not be binding and the USA and the European Union (EU) were reluctant to agree unconditionally to drop, for example, all quotas and tariffs on the world's poorest 48 nations.

Adapted from: Barnes, W. (2000) Poor nations assert place in global trade, *Financial Times*, 21 February, p11.

Throughout this text there have been discussions on the aspects of contemporary business that affect HRM. This chapter concentrates on three of the key ones: globalisation, ethical behaviour and workplace diversity because each runs through all aspects of modern business yet each is often given scant consideration. A further important aspect of contemporary business is that of information technology ■ *see* Chapter 6 ■. These topics should be subsumed into the general discussions of business and HRM – as can be seen in the Framework Case Study – but are still new enough to warrant a definitive consideration. Organisations increasingly have to focus on such challenges because global challenges increasingly require employers and employees to consider ethical behaviour and cultural differences and to regard appreciation of the culture as vital for organisational survival. Cultural diversity encompasses all forms of difference among individuals, including age, gender, race, sexual orientation and ability. Globalisation and technological changes reshape jobs and the workforce, management is challenging and ethical issues are compounding that complexity.

see Chapter 6

GLOBALISATION

KEY CONCEPTS AND DEFINITION

According to Barnett (1997) the latter half of the 1990s saw:

> Nations and their organisations... forced to open themselves up extremely broadly to the world at large. So critical is this need today that 'globalisation' in all manner of forms has been argued to have [become a] key concept. (p152)

Another key writer on globalisation, Waters (1995), believes that it is the material exchanges of physical goods that localise, or domesticise, while it is the political exchanges that internationalise – hence communication exchanges globalise. Barnett (1997) argues that Waters (1995) ignores the need which human societies have:

> to command influence over increasing and/or more widely-integrated geographic spans simply in order to survive and progress. (p153)

This viewpoint means that globalisation is more than a function of an awareness of ▶ **global** ◀ issues that has been brought about by modern knowledge systems. It has the potential to bring about choice, however, globalisation per se is in its infancy.

Global ◀┈┈▶ What is happening throughout the world.

11.1

Activity

Think about a day in your life and consider how globalisation has impacted on you.

It is very difficult to define globalisation because it means different things to different people depending upon their culture. According to Encarta (1999), globalisation means:

> to become, or cause something, especially a business or company, to become international or start operating at the international level. (p794)

It is imperative that organisations constantly 'think global', that is, worldwide, if they hope to survive in the modern world. Many people want the world to become a ▶ **global village** ◀ with a totally integrated ecological, socioeconomic and political system where all the parts are dependent on one another (Webster, 1984).

Global village ◀┈┈▶ The world viewed as a totally integrated ecological, socioeconomic and political system of which all the parts are dependent on one another. That is, when the whole world is considered as a single community served by electronic media and information technology.

SCENARIO 11.1

The International Forum on Globalization (IFG)

The IFG, founded in 1994, is a non-profit alliance of over 60 activists, economists, researchers and writers formed to stimulate new thinking, joint activity and public education in response to economic globalisation. Most of them view the process of globalisation as the most extreme restructuring of the planet's social, economic and political arrangements since the Industrial Revolution, bringing with it profound effects on human life and the natural world.

In April 2000, the IFG held 'A Teach-in on the Devastating Effects of the International Monetary Fund (IMF) and the World Bank'. The IFG noted the momentum born of the activities around the WTO conference in December 1999 which was characterised by street battles in both London, England, and Seattle, USA, which is now focused on another key instrument of economic globalisation – the IMF and the World Bank.

Fulop and Linstead (1999) believe that the term 'globalisation' has become useful because it is 'captivating' (p401). By this they mean that it can be used in a number of ways, for example:

> used by its champions to promise a leaner, more efficient economy, one that will ensure growth and be beneficial to all the nations of the world. (p401)

However, in their study of theory-in-literature and applied research they found that 'the benefits of globalisation are unevenly distributed' (p401).

SCENARIO 11.2

What 'globalisation' denies the poor

The following is a copy of a letter sent by the CEO of Intermediate Technology to the editor of the *Financial Times* in response to an article that Professor Jagdish Bhagwati wrote (*Financial Times*, 17 August 1999). The letter read:

It seems strange that Professor Jagdish Bhagwati should claim that 'globalisation indeed has a human face' before launching into a polemic in which people barely appear.

He answers his own question, 'Does globalisation work for poorer countries?' by noting that Brazil is seeking inward investment. But the fact that any specific developing country seeks a larger piece of cake does not prove that the cake is either adequately proportioned or sufficiently nutritious to sustain the developing world. And it is certainly not evenly cut: in 1996 less than 5 per cent of all foreign

direct investment went to sub-Saharan Africa.

A better question would be, 'Does globalisation benefit the poorer people of the poorer countries?' Intermediate Technology, founded by the alternative economist E.F. Schumacher, has more than 30 years' direct experience in building the technical skills of poor people in developing countries.

We are not driven by uninformed fears and raging passions but by a determination to develop, with local communities in three continents, the hands-on, practical solutions that will secure sustainable livelihoods for small-scale producers at the margins of the global economy.

These are the entrepreneurial millions for whom activity in the informal sector of the economy is the only possible source of improved incomes and a better quality of life. In our experience some of them can make markets work to their advantage, but the majority are denied access to the requisite means to appropriate technologies, to skills, to credit and to market information and business support.

Our experience is that the current model of 'globalisation' does not provide the means because the policy and trade environment, far from being 'beneficial' to them, fails even to recognise their existence and contribution. A different model, which recognises and supports the productive capacity of poor people, is urgently required.

Source: Underhill, C. (2000) What 'globalisation' denies the poor, *Financial Times*, Letters to the Editor, 19 August, p14.

GLOBAL STRATEGIES

According to Perimutter (1997), the key importance of globalisation is not what kind of civilisation might emerge as a result of it – since this cannot be forecast – but that there will be:

> a vast and sometime turbulent mosaic of cultural differences and a great variety of global hybridisations. (p408).

It cannot be denied that there will certainly be a global civilisation but it is not possible to define it or describe its nature. It is becoming normal to talk of business dealings as being 'global'.

11.2

Activity

Peruse the quality newspapers for a couple of days and:

1 list the articles which are global in nature

2 note why you perceive them to be global.

A careful scrutiny of the performance of organisations in different markets will show that there are more organisations having difficulty with global issues than those who are finding it successful. This is often because the management of unsuccessful organisations lack the skills and capabilities needed to go beyond the domestic, national market. Perimutter (1997) gives a number of reasons why organisations cannot find their niche in a globalised market, highlighting the following as the key ones ■ *see* Chapter 2 ■:

see Chapter 2

■ unwillingness to update

■ inadequate products

■ vacillitating commitment

- sending the wrong people

- selecting the wrong business partners

- failure to manage the stakeholders.

Jolly (1997) believes that:

> Global strategies do not mean huge companies operating in a single world market... they are much more complex than that. (p572)

The complexity lies in the belief that an organisation which has a well-planned and genuine global strategy, rather than one that is hastily designed, will be able to compete in any market that they choose to enter. This means that globalisation is at the heart of their strategy and so they can utilise their worldwide competencies at any time, in any place and in any transaction. They have managed to organise themselves to be able to transfer their skills to become a fully fledged global organisation. That is, their strategy is integral to globalisation.

Jolly (1997) suggests that an organisation which is, or wishes to become, truly global possesses certain specific attributes, given in Table 11.1.

Ulrich and Black (1999) make the point that choices such as where the work will be done should:

> address how to identify and instil capabilities that sustain the global strategy. (p42)

It is through HRM strategies that such activities can take place.

However, there is the problem that global strategy will tend to cause conflict within the organisation and pull it in all directions. This is because organisations are trying to work towards global integration and also to act locally – it was in the mid-1990s that the phrase 'think global and act local' became part of business nomenclature.

The development of global integration comes about because of increased research and development with differences between countries and customer preferences being two issues that push organisations to consider localisation issues.

As Procter & Gamble found out, it is not always easy to change people's deeply held beliefs – in this case in the washing of their whites. Neither is it easy to get a nation to change from one sort of technology (front-loading machines) to another (top-loading machines). The transnational solution to the problem actually came in the

Table 11.1 Specific attributes of a global organisation

- Possession of a standard product which is marketed uniformly throughout the world.

- Sourcing of all assets, for example capital, software skills, products and components in the most desirable or favourable way.

- Generating a volume of sales that the local infrastructure demands.

- Ability to neutralise the assets and competencies of competitors when circumstances require.

- Internationalising all functions such as research and development and human resources.

Adapted from: Jolly, V. (1997) Global Strategies in the 1990s in Bickerstaffe, G. (ed.) (1997) *Mastering Management*, London: Financial Times/Pitman, p577.

SCENARIO 11.3

Procter & Gamble

In the late 1990s Procter & Gamble faced a conflict between 'thinking globally and acting locally' with a laundry detergent called Visor. They were developing the product for the European market with the aim of capturing the efficiencies of a single development, manufacturing and marketing effort across the continent.

But the company found that the Germans generally prefer front-loading washing machines and think that boil washing white clothes is the only way to clean them, while the French prefer top-loaders and do not believe that it is necessary to boil whites.

Visor was designed to work best when cleaning whites in cool water and it did not get distributed as well among the clothes when poured into front-loading washing machines.

Adapted from: Ulrich, D. and J.S. Black, 1999, Worldly wise, *People Management,* 28 October, pp42–3, 45–6.

form of a plastic ball that dispensed the detergent gradually as it bounced about in the wash and the matter of water temperature was overcome with successful advertising.

Organisations have to develop a global mindset, or as Ulrich and Black (2000) call it 'a matrix of the mind' (p43). In doing so organisations can begin to understand how they can realise the efficiencies of globalisation and, simultaneously, not overlook any local differences that there might be. It is a matter of careful judgment and balance but it does lead to complex organisational structures with a mixture of regional and centralised activities.

see Chapter 2

The turning of strategy into action is often very difficult and none more so than in the issue of globalisation ■ *see* Chapter 2 ■. Ulrich and Black (1999) suggest six capabilities that 'enable firms to integrate and concentrate global activities and also separate and adapt local activities' (p45). Each one of these capabilities (shown in Table 11.2) represents important tensions that organisations must manage because it is through management capability, as discussed later in this chapter, that individuals are enabled to think globally and act locally.

None of these capabilities is easy to bring about, and therefore the members of the organisation must ensure that considerable care is given to their decision making.

Table 11.2 Capabilities enabling organisations to integrate and concentrate global activities (after Ulrich and Black, 1999)

1 Ability to determine core activities from non-core activities.

2 Achievement of consistency while permitting flexibility.

3 Building of global brand equity while honouring local customs.

4 Sharing learning and creating new knowledge.

5 Engendering global perspectives while ensuring local accountability.

POINTS TO PONDER

Disney recently reviewed its alcohol ban throughout its theme parks and found that visitors in their park in Paris, France proved less acquiescent on the subject than those elsewhere in the world.

Source: Ulrich, D. and Black, J.S. (1999) Worldly wise, *People Management*, 28 October, p45.

GLOBAL SOURCING

Although domestic sourcing means that organisations can avoid problems of cultural uncertainty (remaining in familiar surroundings with their stakeholders), long distances in distribution channels, exchange rate fluctuations, political and economic risks and tariffs, it also means that organisations have less choice over the quality and type of inputs available to them. Not only is there an increased market in globalisation for the sale of goods and/or services but also an extended source of supply.

Global sourcing can provide an organisation with:

■ access to lower cost raw materials and components

■ access to raw materials and components which are not available domestically

■ access to higher quality inputs (which may include better technologies or more skilled workers)

■ less reliance on a small number of possible suppliers which reduces risks.

GLOBALISATION AND INFORMATION TECHNOLOGY (IT)

In the 1980s IT managers were asked to provide local PCs for their staff and ensure that they could access the current software packages. There was little use in the workplace for telecommunications as understood and recognised today ■ *see* Chapter 6 ■. The same managers – or those now occupying their posts – are now being called to serve their organisation's interests by reaching beyond geographic boundaries – they have to think locally but act globally. The input of the information highway has been enthusiastically adopted by tens of millions as the first many-to-many global channel for uncensored news and information.

see Chapter 6

This has been brought about as a result of the:

■ rise in integrated markets

■ common currencies (for example the ▶ **euro** ◀)

▶ The currency of most of the countries of the EU which was introduced in 1999 as part of economic and monetary union. It is planned that by 2002 the euro will have replaced the local currency in the participating member states.   ◀······▶ **Euro**

■ falling trade barriers

all of which are generally clubbed together under the umbrella 'globalisation'.

POINTS TO PONDER

Euro

Everything is not as we think it is and needs to be considered in context. For example, the wallaroo, a large, reddish-grey kangaroo (*Macropus robustus*), is also known as a *euro*.

Computers have become globally interconnected to serve as the primary business communications network. The IT systems connected to this growth are so inter-linked that they are, according to Barnett (1997), presenting organisations with continually challenging new frontiers to cross in which to find new markets, to sell and to distribute their products and/or services. He believes that too many people still 'debate global issues with a national mindset' (p180). He makes the point that Britain, for example, does not operate in a global economy but it constitutes part of the global economy. The difference is not one of pure semantics because Barnett (1997) makes the point that:

> if every nation *operated* in a global economy – rather than being *part of one* – then the global economy would not actually exist. (p180)

11.3 Activity

Whether you are a university student, an employee or a private individual, you probably have access to the Internet.

Reflect on how this is part of a global mindset – beyond the supply of the actual hardware and software.

However, the increased flow of goods and data among regions and countries and the standardisation of products and procedures worldwide have come at a high price. The impact of recent economic problems in several parts of the world attest to the interrelated nature of business markets and the need for an increase in the flow of information between countries.

Global IT systems have their own separate price which is measured in the consid-erable efforts made to overcome the manifold technical and cultural obstacles that increased globalisation brings. It is a continuing challenge to IT managers, yet they are coming up with innovative ways to unite the supply chains that cross national boundaries. The euro holds out some promise in the provision of a standard for international commerce but the IT to support it is not yet fully functioning.

Organisations which are just starting in business can find opportunities in the use of IT so that they can beat the larger organisations to the competitive international markets – or they are, at least, working with them to exploit those markets through the use of IT. Global IT is a challenge yet it defines how contemporary organisations need to work and it is the IT managers who exploit global IT who will bring about the true effects of globalisation ■ *see* Chapter 6 ■.

see Chapter 6

SCENARIO 11.4

The net really will change everything

Behind the hype, the dot.com has a solid base in reality. Not only is the Internet intensifying competition and producing benefits to customers in the form of lower prices, but it is also leading to wholesale restructuring of businesses – including giants such as Ford and Unilever.

About 80 per cent of the $150 billion of global e-commerce revenues in 1999 were transactions between businesses, and volume is mushrooming.

Adapted from: The Week, The net really will change everything, 4 March 2000, p34.

The right e-strategy

In the past, organisations were able to take a number of years to establish themselves gently in the market. However, businesses are now in the e-business era, where the pace of market development is very fast and the window of opportunity is minuscule. This has brought about collapsing timescales which means that the start-up of an organisation could take only a matter of weeks. The available space to grow is shown in Figure 11.1.

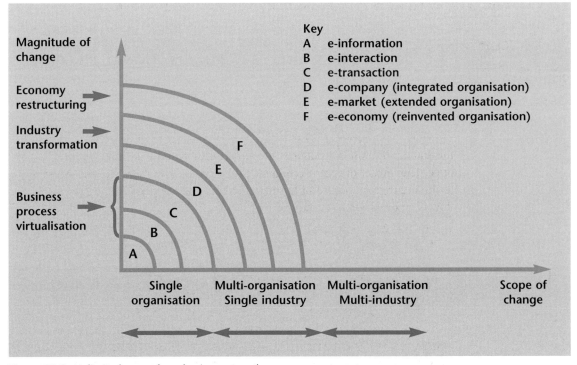

Figure 11.1 Unlimited space for e-business growth

It is essential that organisations have strategic vision when they consider business development and it is imperative that organisations establish and plan all key stages of growth from securing funding to defining an exit strategy.

Globalisation is nothing new. It is a process that has been going on for over 5000 years. However, it has considerably accelerated since the demise of the Soviet Union in the early 1990s. It is not possible to find a definition which will encompass all aspects of globalisation so for the purpose of this text there will be an emphasis on the general and contemporary use of the word as defined above, that is, to become, or cause something, especially a business or company, to become international or start operating at the international level (Encarta, 1999, p794).

Remicke (1999) states that there is a:

> tendency to perceive globalisation as something inevitable, as something that cannot be reversed, or even as the end of history. (p7)

He advocates that there should be a global public policy on the issue and this is not as remote – or as difficult – as it may appear.

Giddens (1990) defines globalisation as:

> the intensification of worldwide social relations which link distant localities in such a way that local happenings are shaped by events occurring many miles away, and vice versa. (p64)

For example, a local labour market in Stoke-on-Trent, England can be affected by decisions made in Japan and villages in the developing world can be affected by changes in the money market. All globalisation depends on rapid and simultaneous access to shared information on the part of individuals who are geographically apart from one another.

GLOBAL FORCES AND THE ORGANISATIONAL LIFECYCLE

At one time or another all organisations will feel the impact of global competition because the world is a vast potential market. It is a matter of evolution rather than revolution because no one organisation can instantly 'become global' – it comes about through gradual stages of development called 'the lifecycle' as shown in Figure 11.2.

This is similar to the organisational lifecycle propounded by Quinn and Cameron (1983) and Greiner (1972). While the lifecycle can indicate the stages through which an organisation grows and changes, it is also a good model for showing how organisations become ▶ **globalised** ◀. The model uses the analogy of a human being – s/he is born, grows older and eventually dies. Globalisation follows a fairly predictable pattern – although the speed through the stages tends to vary according to the nature of the organisation – with the stages being sequential in nature and following a natural progression. Greiner (1972) and Quinn and Cameron (1983) believed that the larger the organisation, the more likely its process through the

Globalise ◀····▶ To make global, especially to make worldwide in scope or application.

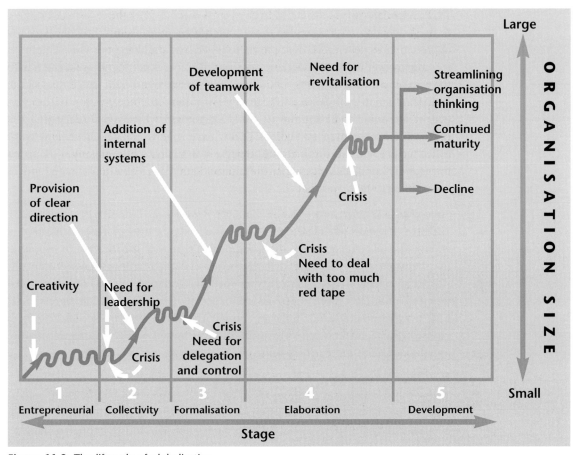

Figure 11.2 The lifecycle of globalisation

lifcycle would be formalised. In the area of entering the globalised market place this is probably still true.

It can be seen from Figure 11.2 that organisational growth is not easy to achieve, because each time an organisation enters a new stage in its lifecycle it enters a whole new arena with a new set of rules for how the organisation functions in relation to its internal and external environments. This is further complicated by the need to consider the issue of globalisation. As the organisation grows it will increase its position within the global marketplace.

Stage One – Entrepreneurial
At this young phase the emphasis is on creating a product and/or service and marketing it with the founders acting as entrepreneurs and devoting all their energies to production and marketing, that is, technical activities. The organisation is informal and non-bureaucratic and work hours are long and hard. Control is based on the owners' personal supervision and charisma and growth derives from the creation of a new product and/or service. Towards the end of this first phase comes a crisis of leadership which has to be resolved before stage two can be initiated. At this stage the owners are giving only token consideration to globalisation issues.

Stage Two – Collectivity

If any leadership crisis is resolved, the emerging strong leadership will allow the organisation to develop clarity relating to objectives and direction. For example, is it going to enter the global marketplace? At this stage, departments are created with their accompanying hierarchy of authority, job assignments and a beginning of the division of labour. Employees still identify with the vision and mission of the original organisation and continue to work long hours with a view of helping the embryonic organisation to succeed. They have a sense of belonging and work collectively, communicating and controlling informally. As the organisation grows through direction, this phase then culminates with a crisis of autonomy and moves into the third stage.

Stage Three – Formalisation

The organisation is just moving from a crisis of red tape into a new environment of teamwork and collaboration – there is growth because of the increase in coordination between activities. Bureaucracy reaches its limit of effectiveness during this stage and managers have gained experience in handling problems in a functional way and interacting more effectively. Managers tend to work with the bureaucratic system without adding to it and they simplify the formal systems by replacing them with project teams and cell structures. There is now a move towards the mature organisation with more action being given to globalisation issues.

Stage Four – Elaboration

This is the development of growth through collaboration and requires bold leadership so that the organisation can face the growth cycle and move into a new era. It is usually at this stage that established organisations feel secure enough to take on globalisation, although it depends on the nature of the organisation and the type of ownership. It is at this stage that the organisation needs to go through revitalisation, and globalisation of markets often gives established organisations a lifeline.

Stage Five – Development

As the organisation moves through each stage its life becomes increasingly difficult. Most organisations do not make it through the first stage (entrepreneurial) although with the rise in the use of e-commerce there are cases which dispute this view. Of those which do survive the first stage, 85 per cent will fail at some time through the rest of the lifecycle. As the survivors move onwards, the transitions become even more difficult. For organisations that fail to resolve their end-of-stage real crises, there comes, at best, growth restriction or, at worst, demise – this could well be – according to Greiner (1972) – a crisis of overload. It is tempting for contemporary organisations to try to take on all eventualities and all new business methods, and globalisation is one of these.

As a consequence of globalised markets, organisations are having to be innovative and flexible in their structure, design and practices, since they have to extend their markets beyond the domestic to the multinational organisation. This move means that the formerly domestic organisations are becoming more competitive and thus need to move away from the top-heavy, functionally operated structure towards the more horizontal structures where the focus is more on process than function, and the organisation uses a flat hierarchy with empowered self-managed teams that make the decisions needed to satisfy the demands of the customer. It is only by going through this procedure that an organisation can compete successfully in the globalised market.

An organisation needs to take into account how many opportunities it has for a globalised market because, if it is large, its products and/or services can be standardised to suit that market. It is important that a globalised organisation is in a position to compete on multiple dimensions simultaneously through ▶ **heterarchy** ◀ which is a development of horizontal organisations.

> ▶ A development of horizontal organisations where there are multiple centres with subsidiary ◀······▶ **Heterarchy** managers who initiate strategy for the organisation, with coordination and control being achieved through the corporate culture and shared values.

POINTS TO PONDER

Business guru, Professor Charles Handy, uses an 'elephants and fleas' metaphor.

The small e-commerce companies are the fleas, springing up everywhere, being innovative and providing the seed of the ideas that the elephants would develop.

The big companies are the elephants, developing ideas and giving them substance.

'It's no accident that the richest and fastest growing countries (respectively) in Europe are Luxembourg and Ireland,' he says, declaring that both are fleas feeding off the European Union which he considers to be an elephant.

Adapted from: People Management, 11 November 1999, p12.

STAGES IN INTERNATIONAL DEVELOPMENT

Herbert (1987), Adler (1991) and Rickey (1991) state that there are four stages that organisations go through as they evolve towards fully fledged global organisations:

■ domestic

■ international

■ multinational

■ global

as shown in Figure 11.3.

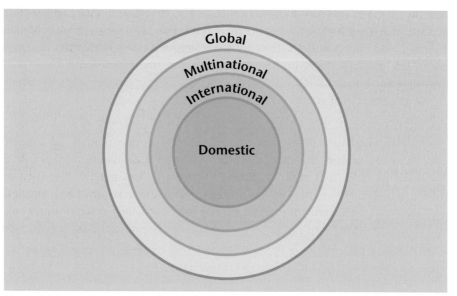

Figure 11.3 Four stages in the evolution towards globalisation, after Adler (1991), Herbert (1984) and Rickey (1991)

Stage One – Domestic

At this first stage the organisation concentrates its efforts in its domestic market, although the employer is well aware of the global environment. At this stage, managers are probably considering their organisation's involvement in the expansion of production and/or services. However, their market is primarily national and very limited. Any foreign sales are probably handled through a functional system – they are likely to have a separate department called 'export'. They use outsourcing – where many of the activities of a once complex organisation are moved outside the organisation's boundary – to handle any freight and foreign exchange matters, An example here would be Levi Strauss.

Stage Two – International/multi-domestic

The organisation now seriously takes on board the export situation and begins to consider a ▶ **multi-domestic** ◀ market. This means that the organisation recognises that competitive concerns within each country are independent of other countries. The organisation will concern itself with its international position in relation to other organisations in the same industry. The export department will disappear in favour of an international division and the organisation will employ specialists to handle sales, service and warehousing overseas. At this stage, the organisation will identify multiple countries as a potential market.

Multi-domestic ◀┄┄▶ The operation of a business, and thus its employees, in different countries.

Stage Three – Multinational

When an organisation matures to this stage, it has all its marketing and production facilities in numerous countries with a minimum of one-third of its total sales outside its own country. It is at this stage that there is intense activity with the organisation having business units scattered throughout the world. It is also likely that the organisation's suppliers, manufacturers and distributors are scattered worldwide.

Stage Four – Global

This is the final stage – the ultimate destination. The organisation has moved away from a collection of domestic industries to a position, according to Porter (1986), where the competitive position of the organisation in one country significantly influences its activities in other countries. When an organisation reaches a true transnational state, it is really 'homeless', because it does not perceive itself as having a single home country. Such organisations are actually called 'stateless organisations'. These are truly global organisations and they perceive the whole world as their marketplace. Examples of global organisations are Procter & Gamble and Unilever. Table 11.3 shows these four key stages in summary.

ORGANISATIONAL DESIGN FOR GLOBAL ADVANTAGE

In order to remain competitive, organisations have to think global because increasingly they are facing foreign competition. The global environment is a vast potential market and can provide a lifeline for those organisations that have fully utilised their national markets and/or are beginning to stagnate. Expansion in an international market can lead to:

- greater profits
- increased efficiency
- responsiveness.

Table 11.3 Organisational designs for global activity

STAGE	TITLE	DESCRIPTION
One	Domestic	Predominantly domestically oriented. Managers developing initial international involvement. Desire to increase market potential.
Two	International (multi-domestic)	Exports taken seriously. Organisation deals with competitive issues of each country separately.
Three	Multinational	Marketing and production facilities in many countries. Worldwide access to capital. One-third plus sales outside home country.
Four	Global	Organisation transcends any single country. Does not identify with any single home country: it is 'stateless'.

With this has come a dramatic redesign of organisations – particularly in the traditional industries, for example car manufacturing in the UK, where there have been, and still are, large numbers of leveraged buy-outs, mergers and break-ups; for example Vauxhall (General Motors in the USA) and Rolls-Royce to Volkswagen Germany.

Such organisations are attempting greater efficiency in an increasingly turbulent domestic environment within a highly competitive international environment – this turbulence must be accepted by organisations as the norm if they are to survive. This is especially true of some countries, for example the USA, which has developed and evolved the ethos that it is superior and invincible.

There is a considerable advantage in having turbulence in the workplace because it creates new winners. However, whenever there are winners there are also losers.

POINTS TO PONDER Someone has to lose a race if someone is to be a winner.

However, no organisation can become global overnight. The change from a domestic organisation to an international one goes through the stages similar to the lifecycle discussed above. There are also specific stages that organisations go through in their international development.

THE NEW ECONOMY

There are some people who believe that there is now what is generally called the ▶ **new economy** ◀, seeing it as a new revolution. According to Birchall (2000) the new economy has brought with it:

a whirlwind transformation to global business and economic systems... (p10)

New economy ◀┈▶ Where business dominates and is driven by technological change and innovation in an economic environment with flat inflation and interest rates.

Birchall also considers the other side of the coin – the new economy may just be part of a continuing and gradual change.

GLOBAL FORCES

For over 25 years nations have lost their discreteness and gone through political, cultural and environmental forces which have unified them to an increasing degree. However, it is economic globalisation which has been the most significant.

SCENARIO 11.5

Will the new economy reach Britain?

True believers in 'the new economy' – who believe new technology brings ever greater productivity increases, raising 'the economy's speed limit' – are mainly in the USA. Sceptics, still worried about 'old' inflationary forces, tend to be European and Japanese. If one accepts the idea of 'a positive IT shock' – boosting growth and quelling inflation – how long will it last and will it come to Britain?

It is estimated that only 10 per cent of the potential US productivity gains have been seen so far, suggesting that the new economy could have two or three decades left in it. In Britain there is scant evidence of a new economy effect so far – hence the urge to raise interest rates at the slightest hint of inflation – but labour shortages may soon start to boost productivity and Britain will gain from downward pressures on prices in global markets. With increasing rate rises it is time to give the new economy in Britain a chance.

Adapted from: The Week (2000) Will the new economy reach Britain? 12 February, p34, Commentators, from Smith, B. in The Sunday Times.

Ohmae (1995) puts this well by stating that it is economics, rather than politics, which provides the arena within which everything else has to operate – the borderless economy has arrived.

While some people, according to Ritzer (1993), have become 'McDonaldised' (or 'McDisneyised') as the huge transnational organisations 'reorder' consumption as well as production on a planetary scale, there is the opposing view that globalisation carries the surety that as many consumers as possible have access to the best product ranges available worldwide. For example, as one travels round the world, it is increasingly difficult to avoid 'internationalised' foods such as McDonald's and find local foodstuffs. One thing is assured, however, the quality (at whatever level) is standardised – a McDonald's hamburger is a McDonald's hamburger wherever it is bought. The global product range, as it is called, should allow each and every geographical region to specialise in just those areas of production in which it enjoys comparative advantage.

The impact of globalisation is felt by all members of society – its effects are difficult to avoid, for example, the choice of foodstuffs from different lands to be found in most supermarkets up and down the land. Uncertainty is caused by certain international ▶ **blocs** ◀ such as the EU and the North Atlantic Free Trade Agreement (NAFTA) – a free trade agreement signed between the USA and Canada in 1989, and extended in 1994 to include Mexico. These blocs uphold the aims of their own member countries which could work against those countries or states who are not members. It is these blocs who hold the power and, consequently, shape the economy now and well into the future.

▶ A group of countries with a shared aim. ◀⸱⸱⸱▶ **Bloc**

Such dominant economies, for example Japan (the 'Yen bloc') and Germany, have meant a decline in US company dominance and the end of US policies also holding dominance in the world market.

One outcome has been a rise in economic volatility because, for example, a country no longer knows how much oil is going to cost per barrel from year to year. Currency is also fluctuating in value because it is based on:

- inflation

- trade balances

- capital investments

over which no one country has total control.

Newly industrialised countries, for example Korea, Taiwan, Singapore and Spain have brought low-cost, high-quality commodities into the marketplace. No longer can products bought today say, 'British', 'Australian' or 'Swedish' because most will contain components from other nations. Neither can one country, or organisation, provide global economic leadership because every country and every organisation is now subordinate to larger economic forces. A shift towards ▷ **market economies** ◁ is bringing more and more sources of goods.

Market economies ◀····▶ Economies where prices and wages are determined mainly by the market and the laws of supply and demand, rather than being regulated by a government.

SCENARIO 11.6

Tetley tea/Tata: bagged

Ta-Ta Gaffer,' was how the *Daily Telegraph* (UK) greeted the news that Tetley, the world's second largest maker of tea bags – best known for their Gaffer, Sidney and the 'tea folk' in its advertisements – has been acquired by Indian conglomerate Tata for £271m.

It will be the first time that Tetley has passed out of British ownership in its 163-year-old history, reported *The Times* (UK). Founded in 1837 by the Tetley brothers, salt and tea peddlers from Huddersfield, England, it has been privately owned since a £190m management buy-in from Allied Domecq (now Diaggo) in 1995, in which 20 per cent of Tetley shares were distributed to management and staff. Many of Tetley's 1100 worldwide employees have received windfall payments for their shares.

Tata-Tea – India's second largest group – has promised that the 'tea folk' will be retained.

Adapted from: Tetley Tea/Tata: bagged (2000) in *The Week*, 4 March, p33.

PAN-EUROPEAN AND GLOBAL MARKETING

Many firms have attempted to exploit the fact that modern communications and methods of transport have created a situation where the consumers of all nationalities are developing common habits and wants. This is particularly true when it comes to international branding where brands such as Levi Strauss, Sony, McDonald's and Coca-Cola are available in most countries. This results in a global mass market for those products which are standardised. This global marketing approach involves selling the same product with the same marketing strategy the world over. McDonald's aims to create the same brand identity for its products the world over. This affects the people who work for such organisations because their way of working is also standardised – there is an organisational culture.

POINTS TO PONDER

Colgate-Palmolive's toothpaste did not sell well in Latin America until it started producing smaller tubes that the market could afford.

Source: Ulrich, D. and J.S. Black (1999) Worldly wise, *People Management*, p46.

European and Asian multinational organisations are particularly skilled at marketing their goods and services, for example Toyota, Nestlé, Sony and Samsung have consistently outperformed their US competitors – even in the latter's home market. However, a number of US organisations have successfully become global, for example IBM (International Business Machines), Coca-Cola and Motorola. This is not just marketing, but also making good abroad.

It is a two-way street, because these same organisations are buying components, services and staff from other countries.

SCENARIO 11.7

Skills crisis forces rethink on work permit restraints

The UK government is to 'streamline' the application for overseas employees to reflect the global market.

While the UK will continue to benefit from the imported skills of European footballers, skill shortages in other areas of the economy have prompted the government to look further afield.

Industry and government in the UK recognises that there is an acute shortage of certain workers in, for example, the IT sector and enterprising companies need skilled employees to create and sustain growth.

But employment law experts have seen a contradiction in these two elements because it has the potential to be controversial. The belief is that the EU is more concerned with excluding non-EU workers from its markets than importing them. The announcement made by the UK would have had agreement from the EU and it only serves to empha-

sise the skills shortage in certain sectors.

The problem was aired in 1995 with the Bosman ruling – which prevented football clubs charging transfer fees for out-of-contract players and lifted restrictions on the number of EU-based players that clubs could field. It sparked an influx of foreign players into the UK, leading to fears that homegrown talent would be stifled.

Changes in the rules governing the renewal of UK work permits are already making it easier for non-EU players to continue playing in the UK. In addition, a fast-track system has been introduced to extend the maximum length of work permits from one to three years. The approach is considered by some to be sensible because it still protects homegrown talent, but takes a more businesslike approach.

Adapted from: Lamb, J. (1999) Skills crisis forces rethink on work permit restraints, *People Management*, 16 December, pp14–15.

GLOBAL COMPETITION

Over the last 25 years the world economy has gone through radical change. Additionally, geographical and cultural distances have seemed to shrink because of developments in supersonic travel, facsimile (fax) machines, global computer and telephone connections, world television satellite broadcasts and other ever-developing technological and electronic advances ■ *see* Chapter 6 ■. Such developments have enabled organisations to increase their geographical markets, their purchasing power and their production facilities and capabilities.

see Chapter 6

In today's business world, most organisations have been touched by global competition – from the local greengrocer who gets her/his fruit from tropical nurseries to the tailor who get her/his cloth from Asia; from UK car manufacturers that compete with Korean car makers, to the organisation that hires staff from all parts of the world.

One of the key issues facing organisations is that of global competition, which is now on a unprecedented scale. While the principal players in the world's economy are international or multinational organisations, smaller organisations are still affected because the emergence of these global organisations creates pressures on them to redesign and, in turn, internationalise their operations. There is a global market for most products, but in order to compete effectively in it, organisations must transform their design, structures, operations and culture.

However, while people in some quarters – including the national government – believe that British industry is heading for a global renaissance, Heller (1996) states that 'the hard facts reveal a large gap between rhetoric and reality' (p24).

GLOBAL MANAGEMENT, LEADERSHIP AND TRAINING

Globalisation is one of the most important factors in the contemporary business world and global competition has become a central part of business activity – it demands a new way of thinking that incorporates global management. According to May (1997) a key issue that takes up the time of managers in the contemporary marketplace is how they can identify and develop the global leadership competencies required if their businesses are to compete in the global marketplace. It is a popularly held view that:

> global management will think strategically in a worldwide context, but act like a local organization in each national market. (May, 1997, p308)

Mobil Oil has funded the International Management Development Consortium and has designed a programme for top managers to follow so that they can develop their existing skills to include those required for the globalised market. This programme is open to other organisations and has itself become globalised, providing a unique approach for participants. One of the key components is the need for the participants themselves to examine the issue of which competencies are essential for global leadership.

As has been seen in previous chapters, training is a very positive aspect of organisational activity yet such acquired skills and knowledge have to be transferable within a market that is becoming increasingly global. Heise (1998) carried out research in Europe, the USA and Japan on the portability of qualifications between countries, that is, how did countries recognise and accept the qualifications awarded by other countries?

There is no doubt that in order to be competitive in a globalised market all members of every workforce need to be highly trained, flexible and mobile. Without these three qualities, an organisation will remain local. Some organisations, because of the nature of their business, remain such but will find the globalised market impinging increasingly on their domains, for example the supply of parts and labour.

It could be argued that the ability to recognise qualifications internationally could help to bring down high levels of unemployment – where they exist – and also to provide the key workers when and where they are required. However, by doing this, new jobs are not actually being created – individuals are just moving about to do the jobs. It is important that political and economic commitments accompany the need for lower unemployment and it is this aspect that expands the complexity of globalisation as discussed earlier in this chapter.

SCENARIO 11.8

Europe must get to work

Tackling Europe's unemployment problems has been a long and difficult struggle. In the early 1990s, the European Commission produced a White Paper on growth, competitiveness and employment. It put the economic, employment and wider structural change issues together on the same European agenda for the first time.

The paper has changed the policy focus by moving it away from the belief that unemployment problems were derived from, and solved by, the labour market alone and towards the view that more sophisticated changes were needed.

The belief was that growth was necessary although that was, in itself, insufficient and that what had to be done was to build cooperation across all policies if the EU was to be successful in creating jobs.

The changes agreed in the Amsterdam Treaty (1997) reflected the new balance and a new employment document was introduced that strengthened the political focus on employment and created new mechanisms for cooperation and support at EU level.

It includes strong policy guidelines and recommendations for reforms in member states.

But the EU's unemployment problems remain vast and multidimensional. The gap between the employment levels they have and those they could have – if they did as well as the USA or even their best-performing members states and regions – is around 30/35 million jobs. There are twice as many people in Europe who would work, if work were available, than there are people who are currently recorded as jobless. Fulfilling this potential would raise average living standards by 15 per cent or more. If most of the benefits accrued to poorer families, it would significantly reduce continuing problems of inequality and poverty. But the jobs gap is far from evenly spread.

Globalisation is increasing the pace of competition. Social change and economic change are creating new patterns of work, family and social life. At their summit in March 2000 the EU addressed these challenges in a comprehensive way. The EU has

SCENARIO 11.8 cont'd

entered an important new phase in its development. The demands and opportunities presented by the knowledge-based economy, combined with a healthy outlook for growth in the medium term, has given them a framework within which to integrate and reinforce their social and economic policies.

They are in the process of updating their European model by ensuring that not only economic and social policies work together, but also that they are relevant to their new social, family and work environments.

Adapted from: Diamantopoulou, A. (2000) Europe must go to work, *People Management*, 2 March, p31.

The next European Treaty is due to be ratified at the end of 2000/beginning of 2001 – to replace the Amsterdam Treaty (1997) – and it takes account of the increasing participation of the workers in the development of work and technology. This is important because training workers will not suffice on its own, the qualifications gained have to be accepted by other countries and therefore become portable. The UK has a government body – the ▶ **National Council for Vocational Qualifications (NCVQ)** ◀ – whose qualifications are recognised in Europe and are, therefore, portable, but this not the case throughout the world – there is not yet a globalised standard of competence although work is being carried out in the area. The latter is a difficult thing to do because it is still apparent that there are differences within each single system within one nation. In his work Heise (1998) states that:

> There is no point in 'comparing' systems with a competitive approach on the one hand or an approach towards formal standardisation on the other. There is enough room for improvements and development within each single system. (p299)

National Council for Vocational Qualifications (NCVQ) ◀·····▶ A UK government body set up to implement a national framework for the provision of vocational qualifications and to determine national standards of occupational competence.

However, research being continued in Europe shows that a cooperative and collaborative approach to training is increasing and that mutual learning is on the increase. The latter is opening a broader and deeper view to the system each nation uses and its implicit assumptions.

POINTS TO PONDER

Colleges with a mandate for training global leaders are leaning more towards market-related issues.

Source: Wendlandt, A. (2000) Elite courses learn to be the business, *Financial Times*, 28 February, p18.

There is no doubt that in order to be effective as a manager in the 21st century, an individual has to have the ability to perceive and evaluate the opportunities presented in a global perspective. While there is some training taking place, for example Mobil Oil, most programmes focus on the functional aspects of management such as international marketing or international finance. However, it is the important skills such as negotiation, adaptability, flexibility and communication that are essential and these are often overlooked in education and training programmes.

Chan (1994) reflects on the fact that managers are now desperately trying to equip themselves with:

> insights into new patterns of thinking, strategy, and management for the dynamic global business environment in the twenty-first century. (p38)

In order for management education to be effective it is important that there is a concentration on matching the needs of the future – too many courses concentrate on the past orientations of management and while this provides a framework, it must now encompass the ideas of the future. That is, the need to explore specifically the approaches and processes involved in the planning and implementation of international management development programmes. Research into postgraduate courses shows that there has been a swing in this direction and this can only be a good thing for organisations that hire the participants.

Managers should be able to present their actions as being necessitated by global business logics and distance themselves from the less admirable consequences of their actions: sweatshop conditions, health and safety violations, subsistence wages, discrimination and failure to feedback any of the profit to the community.

SCENARIO 11.9

Globalisation 'is bad for health'

According to two UN agencies, globalisation is bad for health. The WHO and the ILO said that the continuing shift of industrial production to low-cost sites in developing countries where worker protection is lower is likely to increase the global incidence of occupational disease and injury.

The WHO believes that, from the occupational health perspective, trends to globalisation of trade pose certain health risks. The ILO estimates that work-related injuries and diseases kill an estimated 1.1 million people worldwide each year, equal to the global total of deaths from malaria.

This figure includes about 300 000 deaths from 250 million workplace accidents, as well as deaths from occupational diseases such as respiratory and cardiovascular diseases and cancer.

Hazards include not only exposure to toxic chemicals, noise and dangerous machinery but also stress, which is associated with higher incidence of cardiovascular disease and mental illness.

The UN agencies put the cost of occupational disease and injury at 4 per cent of world output in 1997.

Adapted from: Williams, F. (2000) Globalisation 'is bad for health', *Financial Times*, 10 June 1999, p5.

Flexibility in production and vast leaps in the development of IT have freed up the world to manage production globally and challenges managers to seek new organisational forms to manage this situation. Managers no longer need to invest in production facilities if they can find other people, perhaps in other parts of the world, to take that risk. More important, they need to develop their own brands and be able to manage marketing rather than production: for example Adidas sports shoes are made in Asia but sought after all over the world.

The world is now as one, where production is separated from marketing and marketing is being described as global, that is, it is managed on a global basis although recognising local requirements and cultures.

GLOBAL CITIZENSHIP

Today communication and causes are sweeping the planet and these are starting to allow all people to share in a single global identity, for example when there are environmental tragedies such as the floods in Mozambique in February 2000.

Global citizenship can only be good for business and for world peace, yet as individuals become global citizens they have to cast aside the structures and regimes that constitute their local community spirit and patriotism. This brings a ▶ **paradox** ◀. While global citizens may, in time, become increasingly unified in totality, in a local context they are also likely to be increasingly alone.

Paradox ◀┄┄▶ A statement, situation or proposition that seems to be absurd or contradictory, but is in fact true.

As individuals spread themselves wider because of increased opportunities to travel and work in nations other than their own, it is necessary for them to spread themselves thinner. They spend more time interacting with people at a distance, and therefore, must spend less time with those closer at home. As individuals have contact with more people, they must devote less attention to each one. In ▶ **hypomobile** ◀ societies, everyone knows everyone else. The old-fashioned ▶ **hypermobile** ◀ communities have been replaced by ▶ **aspatial** ◀ communications of interest.

Hypomobile ◀┄┄▶ Small-scale pedestrian economies where everyone knows everyone else.

Hypermobile ◀┄┄▶ Old-fashioned geographical communities.

Aspatial ◀┄┄▶ Where individuals spend more time, physically, among strangers.

Just as workers are fast losing the certainty of long-term organisational membership, in future they are also destined to become less and less enshrined within the culture and values of a parent nation.

GLOBALISATION AND HRM

HRM is changing as a result of globalisation. Legge (1995) believes that such developments are acting to reinforce existing relationships in, say, the workplace and are moving away from being considered in isolation. She documents the development of market changes from the 1980s when the globalisation of markets and intense competition began to have an effect with the rise of the Pacific economies (Japan, South Korea, Taiwan and Singapore) and then the EU. Such globalisation of markets has been facilitated by the developments in IT, which has speeded up worldwide communications, and the reduction of trade barriers and the breakdown of international trade treaties have all forced many UK organisations to become more strategically aware.

Such developments have had an effect on HRM because organisations have been forced to adjust their businesses in order to become profitable in an increasingly competitive market. The UK economy has become *relatively* low skill with low hourly labour costs and low productivity (and, therefore, high unit labour costs).

In the UK the 'hard' model of HRM gives an important message to employers: they must tailor the management of the labour resource to the business strategy of each constituent business unit, that is, a contingency approach ■ *see* Chapter 1 *and* Chapter 2 ■.

see **Chapter 1** *and* **Chapter 2**

There has been a decline in the number of manual jobs relative to non-manual jobs which has had a number of effects in the workplace, shown in Table 11.4.

One model of HRM sees a less hostile environment than in the days when the workforce comprised predominantly male, young, single manual workers who were members of trades unions.

Nowadays, managers cooperate with rather than confront their core knowledge workers because they want commitment through cultural management and margin-alisation of trades unions, rather than compliance through collective bargaining.

As globalisation becomes increasingly part of an individual's daily life, no longer are people significantly bounded by the land of their nationality. This can only be a positive way forward because it empowers both individuals and organisations by allowing them to operate across what may well have been disruptive geographic divides. There is, however, a downside to this. Individuals may become lost because of a crisis of identity, for example Scotland and Wales becoming devolved from the central British government has meant that there is discomfort in the use of the word 'British'. 'British' was used as a descriptor for Scotland, England, Wales and Northern Ireland and now the term 'European' has come into play. Some people have become discomforted and the comfort and refuge they had in, say, England is not so easily found now.

Table 11.4 The effect of a loss of manual jobs

- Workforce increasingly polarised between those undertaking jobs requiring the skills of knowledge workers and consequently high levels of education and training and those performing routine, low-skilled service jobs, for example checkout operators, shelf fillers and fast-food workers.

- Workforce is becoming feminised. It has become the norm for women to work with only a minimal break for child rearing.

- By the beginning of the 21st century the workforce had become, because of demographic trends, increasingly middle aged.

Globalisation requires all organisations to move people, ideas, products and information around the world in order to meet local needs. New and important ingredients must be added to the mix when making strategy, for example a volatile political situation, contentious global trade issues, fluctuating exchange rates and unfamiliar cultures. There is a growing awareness that the failure of many international assignments is caused not by a lack of technical competence so much as a lack of adaptation to different cultures. As these traditional boundaries become more relaxed so all nations are having to adjust and re-engineer in the face of global economies, global media, global citizenship and the environmental problems that cross all national borders – such as global warming.

There are periods of quiet among the cycles of political upheaval and economic turbulence and many organisations have now finally committed themselves fully to global mindsets as well as to their operations. Consequently, at the start of the 21st century, there is a complex system of individualism and globalism in place. The 21st century may become dominated by a clan of global business organisations whose economy might well give them muscle to dictate patterns of citizenship – to programme tastes and cultures to their whim. A better way is to have a highly differentiated yet relatively consensual family of nations who will pursue a shared global agenda while punishing the deviant and protecting the defenceless.

Human resource professionals can engage in the global strategy (discussed above) by assessing the required strategies and ongoing flexibility so that the organisation can succeed and become successful in a global market. Globalisation should mean integration and worldwide standardisation with separation and adaptation. If individuals know how to standardise they will then be able to adapt as necessary. It is difficult for individuals to do both simultaneously.

According to Ulrich and Black (1999) it is important that HRM specialists go beyond attendance at strategy meetings because they need to add value by encouraging discourse on the capabilities which are required for globalisation and localisation, and:

> profiling which capabilities are critical and investing in HR practices that ensure these capabilities. (p46)

ETHICS

ETHICS AND THE INDIVIDUAL

One of the difficulties in defining ethics lies in the way in which they are learned. Most people learn expected standards of behaviour from their parents/guardians, religious affiliation, reading, school environment and peers. During a normal lifetime such ethics and morals are learned and changed as societal values change.

The forces of childhood experiences are particularly important in shaping an individual's ethical decision making. This is so important, in fact, that many people believe an individual would have no value system at all unless s/he had experienced strong inputs from parents/guardians and other closely affiliated adults. People who react in an 'instinctive' manner are those who have not examined the values they gained in their formative years. To be effective members of any society individuals have to build into their lives what they have learned in childhood related to the position of what is perceived by them to be right and wrong. It is in this way that individuals develop their own value systems and attitudes to their environment and situation. The judgment of peers and superiors about their actions will have a major effect on their future behaviour.

As individuals progress into early adulthood and on to positions of responsibility, the reactions from others will further work to modify their ideas of right and wrong and, consequently, their behaviour. These forces are very strong and often in conflict with each other – such is the situation that human beings find themselves in. Every decision made by an individual will produce an intrinsic force.

The *Concise Oxford Dictionary* (1999) defines ethics as:

> the moral principle governing or influencing conduct. (p490)

and

> the branch of knowledge concerned with moral principles. (p490)

Maund (1999) defines it in behavioural terms stating that ethical behaviour is:

> Behaving in a way that corresponds with one's ethical beliefs and in line with the beliefs commonly held by the organisation and society in general. (p417)

Individual differences and ethical behaviour

The issue of ethics and social responsibility is one of the key concepts for employers and employees and part of this attention focuses on the influence that individual differences might have on moral behaviour and individual social responsibility. A study carried out by Trevino and Youngblood (1990) suggested that ▶ **locus of control** ◀ and ▶ **cognitive moral development** ◀ are important in helping to explain whether an individual will behave ethically or unethically. People appear to pass through stages of moral reasoning and judgment as they mature, and judgment with regard to right and wrong becomes less dependent on outside influences (such as peers and colleagues). It also becomes less self-centred. At the higher levels of cognitive moral development, an individual develops a deeper understanding of the principles of justice, ethical behaviour and the balance between individual and social rights.

Kohlberg (1981) believes that individual moral reasoning is developmental and that individuals move from the more basic, primary stages to higher levels.

▶ The extent to which an individual believes that her/his behaviour has a direct impact on the ◀┈┈▶ **Locus of control**
consequences of that behaviour.

▶ An individual's level of moral judgment. ◀┈┈▶ **Cognitive moral development**

However, not everyone reaches the higher levels because some people do not develop the capacity to involve themselves in the more difficult moral reasoning of the advanced stage. His three levels of development translate into six stages of progression, with individual need being pre-eminent.

Stages One and Two

In these stages, individuals see only their own needs in a dysfunctional conflict situation. These are the levels children are at when they think they must have whatever they want whenever they want it. Some adults are stuck at this level throughout their lives and are seen by others as self-centred (although sometimes what others think is self-centredness may only be a healthy awareness of one's own needs – it is a matter of balance).

Stages Three and Four

This is when the individual has developed sufficiently to appreciate the idea of fairness based on society's idea of the same. Here an individual will be looking at how the collective group of people (society) has determined what is right and good. Moral judgments are based on such things as 'That's the way I was brought up'.

Stages Five and Six

This is a principled understanding of fairness based on the individual's conception of equality and reciprocity. In these final levels, which many individuals never achieve (some question whether an individual can ever get to Level Six), moral judgments are based on a thoughtful and analytical process which the individual has cultivated over a long period of time.

Maturity helps to bring about moral development and Kohlberg (1981) believes that involving people in discussion of ethical issues helps them to develop better moral reasoning skills and thus aid their moral development.

11.4

Activity

Reflect on those ethical dilemmas you have faced in your life.
What stage of moral development were you at for each?

Individuals with a mature attitude and with high ▸ **internal locus of control** ◂ appear to exhibit more ethical behaviour when making decisions within the work-

Internal locus of control ◂┄┄▸ The extent to which an individual believes that her/his behaviour has a direct impact on the consequences of that behaviour and that such behaviour is a result of her/his own actions.

place than those with a high ▸ **external locus of control** ◂. Furthermore, a person with higher levels of cognitive moral development is more likely to behave ethically than others. Individuals in the workplace need to appreciate the differences between values, integrity, morals and responsibility while also addressing ethics in the organisation and the responsibility of that organisation to its stakeholders.

> ▸ The extent to which an individual believes that her/his behaviour has a direct impact on the ◂┈┈▸ **External locus of**
> consequences of that behaviour and that such behaviour is a result of other people's actions. **control**

According to Mahoney (1996):

> individuals who invest a large part or a major proportion of their lives in a particular company are morally entitled to have some expectations about how they are treated by, and in, that company. (p9)

Ethics of employee empowerment

Empowering individuals in the workplace is now a common practice and is enveloped in the language of autonomy, responsibility and intrinsic motivation. It allows both the employer and the employee to be in a 'win–win' situation – the manager retains some control and the employee has some autonomy and responsibility. Empowering workers is also positive in the climate of competition and is often seen as a moral issue. This is because the words used to describe empowerment are termed in humanistic terms, namely that:

> as well as making good business sense, empowerment allows for self-direction, self-development and personal growth. (Claydon and Doyle, 1996, p13)

The empowerment of employees is viewed as a way of providing the organisational and personal needs of individuals and meeting their desire for autonomy and self-expression in the workplace.

However, empowerment has not met with a straightforward acceptance in the workplace since some employers believe that it is only a fad. However, time has proved this not to be so. Empowerment is here to stay and with it has come one of the key aspects of working life – that of trust ▪ *see* Chapter 5, Chapter 9 *and* Chapter 10 ▪.

see **Chapter 5,** **Chapter 9** *and* **Chapter 10**

ETHICS AND WORK TEAMS

As individuals develop ethical values, they are strongly influenced by the groups they associate with most closely and such reference groups have a profound effect on behaviour. There are two principal issues that relate to the role of an individual within a reference group. The first is geographic location, which can affect what is considered acceptable behaviour by different reference groups. For example, in the seaside town of Blackpool, England, a male entering a department store clad only in shorts and sports shoes is generally acceptable. Similar behaviour in Harrods,

London would be entirely out of place and such attire would certainly result in the individual being asked to leave the store. By the same token, cities in a number of countries, for example the UK, Sweden, Canada, Australia and Japan, have ordinances forbidding the drinking of alcoholic beverages in spaces exposed to normal pedestrian traffic, such as shopping precincts, yet most European cities consider as proper and civilised the provision of outdoor facilities for customers wishing to drink beer or wine at a table outside.

Second, the type of work undertaken by individuals influences what is considered appropriate behaviour. Chartered accountants, lawyers, scientists, physicians and university lecturers have different expectations of themselves and others than do general maintenance workers, machine operators, construction workers and forklift truck operators. What is right or wrong is established partly by the group with which each worker associates daily (the reference group) and partly by the lessons learned from childhood and adult experiences.

Ethics and group decision making

Ethical behaviour conforms to generally accepted norms, whereas unethical behaviour does not. Although some decisions made by employees have little or nothing to do with their own personal ethics, many other decisions are, in fact, influenced by the individual's own ethics. For example, decisions involving such disparate issues as hiring and firing employees, negotiating with customers and suppliers, setting wage rates and assigning tasks and maintaining one's expense account, as can be seen in Scenario 11.10, are all subject to ethical influences.

SCENARIO 11.10

The price of honesty

Hewlett-Packard has introduced a paperless expenses reporting system where employees enter their expenses through their computers onto an electronic form which they then electronically send to a financial services centre where reimbursements are paid electronically into the sender's bank account. This system has done away with the scrutinisation of hard-copy expenses sheets. While such a system might appear to have given a corporate licence to swindle Hewlett-Packard, it appears that the system has helped the company to reduce the number of sites that handle general ledger accounting from 56 to 2 in the USA and from 25 to 4 in Europe. The company believes that this has produced savings of £645 000 a year, more than outweighing any abuse of the system by unscrupulous employees. A less

tangible benefit is the goodwill that this trust in the honesty of employees engenders. The organisation is continuing to reduce its operating costs as a percentage of turnover from 40 per cent in 1988 to 25 per cent in 1995, so it would appear to be doing something right. But surely most employees are taking advantage of the lax expense reporting by making exaggerated claims?

Not so, the organisation reports. Senior management feels that people want to do the best for their company, so they are trusted and treated like adults and those who want to fiddle the organisation are in the minority. Perhaps the fact that Hewlett-Packard is a US-owned company has something to do with this. Like so many US businesses, it seems to arouse fierce devotion from its employees rather than the cyni-

SCENARIO 11.10 cont'd

cism that is often part of the European corporate psyche. The organisation does have one form of control, in that it keeps a record of the average living expenses in countries where employees travel and uses this as a measurement for expense claims. The management feels that the stricter the control the more people will find a way around it.

Adapted from: Cohen, A. (1996) The price of honesty, *Financial Times*, 2 September, p16.

It can be seen from the above scenario that whatever model of decision making and control is adopted by individuals and groups, a key criterion is the ethical implications of the decision. The way in which people make their decisions will depend upon many influential factors such as individual differences and organisational control. Blanchard and Peale (1988) suggested that before making a decision, three things should be taken into account:

- *ensuring that the decision is legal*
  That is, making sure that the laws of the country and company policy are kept

- *ensuring that the decision is well balanced*
  That is, making sure that the decision is fair to all concerned and that it fosters a win–win relationship

- *considering how it makes the decision maker feel*
  Ensuring that the individual is proud of the decision and is happy to live with it.

SCENARIO 11.11

Beech-Nut

Beech-Nut admitted that they had been selling millions of jars of 'phoney' apple juice that contained cheap concentrates and chemical additives. The organisation was running at a loss and managers were of the opinion that other companies were also selling fake apple juice. Beech-Nut were convinced that their fake juice was safe for consumers and that even if laboratory tests were carried out, they would not be able to come to the definite conclusion that it was different from real apple juice.

Adapted from: Sims, R.R. (1992) Linking groupthink to unethical behavior in organisations, *Journal of Business Ethics*, No 11, pp651–62.

The above case shows that teams can make decisions that are unethical. Beech-Nut was perceived to be a reputable company and there was no evidence to prove the opposite. However, possibly because of groupthink – the psychological drive for consensus at any cost that suppresses dissent and appraisal of alternatives in cohesive decision-making groups – the organisation ignored caution and morality in favour of immediate profits and by ignoring any dissent they suffered considerable damage to their reputation: a result of unethical practices.

It is possible to prevent unethical group decisions by avoiding groupthink. Groups can appoint a person whose role it is constantly to ask questions of the group related to what it is doing and who can also raise ethical issues for the group to consider. Another way is to place two groups together so that they can question the course of action being taken by the other group.

All decisions, whether made by an individual or by groups and teams, must be evaluated for their ethics. It is the responsibility of the organisation to reinforce ethical behaviour through praise and reward. All organisational members need to understand that effective and ethical decisions are not mutually exclusive.

In general, ethical dilemmas for employees may centre on direct personal gain, indirect personal gain or simple personal preferences. Consider, for example, a top executive contemplating a decision about a potential takeover of another organisation. Her/his share option package may result in enormous financial gain if the decision goes one way, although the stakeholders may benefit more if the decision goes the other way. An indirect personal gain may result from a certain decision that does not directly add value to a manager's personal worth but does serve to enhance her/his career. Or the employer may face a choice for relocating a company section where one of the options is closer to her/his home.

Whenever groups make decisions they should carefully and deliberately consider the ethical content of those decisions. The goal is for the person making the decision to do so in the best interest of the organisation, as opposed to the best interests of the individual. The use of teams within which to discuss potential ethical dilemmas is helpful because others can often provide an objective view of a situation that may help to deter individuals from making unintentionally unethical decisions.

Ethics deals with right or wrong in the actions and decisions of individuals and the organisations of which they are a part. Ethical issues are more common and complex than is generally recognised. According to Donaldson and Dumfee (1994), ethical issues do influence the decisions that employees make daily and some ethical issues involve factors that make the choice of 'right or wrong' muddy – thus many employees experience ethical dilemmas.

Trevino and Youngblood (1990) support the view that ethical decision making is extremely complex: thus there are no simple rules for coping with decisions that have an important ethical content. The best that can be done is to share ethical reasoning with others and that is encouraged by the use of high-performance task teams. Organisations must structure the decision-making process in ways that consider the range and legitimacy of ethical pressures, for example working as a member of a diverse project team. According to Pettinger (1996) this also means:

> understanding where the greater good and the true interests of the organisation lie, and adopting realistic steps in the pursuit of this. (p390)

Globalisation will help in understanding the needs of current parts of business, as well as future clients. Learning about various cultures enables organisational members to understand that other companies' missions and objectives are not vastly different from their own and that they need not surrender their company loyalty to interact and negotiate with others – neither need they compromise their ethical principles.

CORPORATE ETHICS

SCENARIO 11.12

The protection of reputation becomes a core concern

The days when companies could do as they pleased, fly in the face of public opinion, turn a deaf ear to the cries of staff, routinely give 'no comment' to the press and speak in the City only via their profit margins are long over. High-profile public relations debacles as varied as British Airways (dirty tricks), McDonald's (McLibel) and Shell (Brent Spar) clearly illustrate that the corporate reputation has become more important and more vulnerable than ever before.

Adapted from: The protection of reputation becomes a core concern (1997), *Management Today*, October, p6.

Since ethical behaviour is acting in ways that are consistent with one's personal values and the commonly held values of the organisation and society, they therefore underlie ethical behaviour in all aspects of one's life.

11.5

Activity

Look through a few different quality newspapers and journals and see how many references you can find related to the issue of ethics.

Note them down and make a comment on why you think that there are so many – or so few.

It seems to be part of our times that individuals' values are being scrutinised by others. The problem is now concentrated on how these moral conflicts are resolved. The cases reported in the press tend to be those of specific interest because they have resulted in, for example, large-scale pollution of the environment. However, not all ethical issues in business bring about public outrage. These are the problems faced by managers who have to manage responsibly and cope with ethical dilemmas of a less popular nature. Such situations are frequently intractable, for example if the safety of a product is suspect, a manager cannot close down the manufacturing facility immediately without immense cost being incurred. This in itself is an ethical consideration.

It is true to say that most managers will not meet such major ethical decisions but they do have everyday issues which arise and which can be interpreted from an ethical perspective. Some of these can be so trivial that they are not recognisable as ethical dilemmas while others are more significant.

11.6

Activity

List five workaday issues that a manager might face which may be perceived as being ethically related.

There will be little difficulty in identifying issues that affect a manager on a day-to-day basis and all will be within two areas:

1   the internal affairs of the organisation and/or

2   the external affairs of the organisation.

It is with these relatively minor issues that individuals find they have difficulty in handling ethical concepts – it is often much easier when considering major issues such as transport disaster or financial scandals. Maclagan (1994) makes the point that programmes aimed at raising an individual's level of ethical awareness are doomed to failure and it is when the:

> emphasis is on developing the *process* of ethical analysis and reasoning rather than imposing *substantive* views on clients and students (p3)

that success will be achieved.

ETHICS AND TRAINING

While it is essential that individuals are trained to cope with all aspects of contemporary business, including globalisation and work diversity (discussed below), there has to be some consideration given to the ethics of training itself. While trainers should have technical and educational qualifications, the profession should also have ethical normative competence.

Bergenhenegouwen (1996) is carrying out research in the Netherlands on this very issue stating that:

> Training implies certain dealings in which one has to make a choice among various options. (p23)

Trainers have to use value judgments about the available alternatives and such choices are based on ethical decisions. This could be said about most decisions made in the workplace, but in the case of a trainer it is important that there is a code of professional practice available. This responsibility lies with the training professionals and is incorporated in the qualifications provided by the professional body for HRM specialists – the Chartered Institute of Personnel and Development (CIPD).

Personal adjustment at work has been a major concern of management analysis for a number of years and is an increasing ethical dilemma for both employer and employee. Recently, greater attention has been paid to the causes of destructive forms of frustration and stress in the work environment. A major concern has been the need for a better understanding of the reactions of people in the work environment.

Conflict, frustration and stress affect individuals differently. What may be highly stressful to one person may be source of either satisfaction or indifference to others. Not only does the perception of conditions affect the ability to cope successfully with stress, but the degree of tolerance of stress helps to determine specific types of reactions. Many higher level managers seem to enjoy high-stress situations and see them as challenges, while others at lower levels in the organisation view the same conditions as major threats ■ *see* Chapter 6 ■.

see **Chapter 6**

Since ethical behaviour is about an individual's perception and understanding of what is right or wrong, good or bad, it is an ethical dilemma for managers when they come to demand consistently high levels of performance from their employees and similarly high standards from their employers.

BUSINESS ETHICS

In the discussion above, the emphasis was on the word 'ethics' and how it relates to the individual, groups and organisations. It was said that ethics comprised the moral principles that should underpin all decision making. However, Marcousé et al. believe that:

> A decision made on ethical grounds might reject the most profitable solution in favour of one of the greater benefit to society as well as the firm. (p495)

This leads to what is actually termed 'business ethics'. Business ethics simply provide moral guidelines for the handling of business affairs. It is set in the framework of ethics in general and is based on two key premises:

1   organisations comprise individuals

2   organisations consist of cultures that shape their corporate ethical standards.

Business ethics are about trying to find out what the role and function of business is in society and thus, according to Trezise (1996) it:

> explores the difference between ethical values in the private, economic and political spheres of human activity, and values in the private, economic and political spheres of human activity. (p86)

It is an area of study in its own right and, therefore, a detailed discussion is beyond the scope of this text.

There will be conflicting ethical expectations from both employer and employees within an organisation and the expectations of, say, managers and subordinates will be different. Sims (1998) carried out a study that explored the relationship between these conflicting ethical expectations. He used a sample of 107 managerial level employees and found that:

as the perceived difference between formal and informal ethical expectations increases… and job satisfaction, organisational satisfaction, and affective commitment decrease. (p386)

Such differences are related closely to the issues of globalisation and, particularly, diversity in the workplace.

WORKPLACE DIVERSITY

DIVERSITY AWARENESS

see **Chapter 7** *and* **Chapter 8**

Diversity awareness, like globalisation, is an issue which is sweeping the business world ■ *see* Chapter 7 *and* Chapter 8 ■. However, in many organisations the conversation continues to centre around the issue of what diversity actually *is*. It is imperative that all members of the workforce thoroughly understand what diversity is and are able to communicate the answer to all – understanding is essential. It is one of those issues which can be investigated from any number of places and from any angle.

POINTS TO PONDER

If you do not know where you are going, then any road will do.

POINTS TO PONDER

When asking for directions to, say, a particular nightclub, the answer could well be: 'I know where it is but I wouldn't go from here.'

If individuals just go ahead and 'study diversity' the result will be like the two Points To Ponder above – they won't know where they are going and they won't know when they have got there. According to Digh (1998) this means that if an organisation wishes to concentrate on diversity it has to:

articulate, clearly and simply, what it meant by diversity and what approach it is going to take. That is, are the members of the organisation going to tolerate, value, celebrate, manage, harness, or leverage diversity? (www p1)

The term 'diversity' is often used broadly to refer to many demographic variables, including, but not limited to:

■ race

■ religion

■ colour

■ gender

■ national origin

- disability

- sexual orientation

- age

- education

- geographic origin

- skill characteristics.

Care should be taken not to mix 'diversity' with 'discrimination' because they are not the same thing. Diversity is about variety and differences while discrimination concerns treating people differently through prejudice. This means that a worker can behave unfairly towards another person or group but it is usually because of prejudice about one or more of the components of diversity listed above ■ *see* Chapter 7 *and* Chapter 8 ■.

see Chapter 7 *and* Chapter 8

The diversity in such countries as, for example, the UK, Sweden and the USA has given them a unique strength, resilience and richness.

SCENARIO 11.13

Diversity means business

In April 1999 the Institute of Personnel and Development published its guide to workplace diversity (*The IPD Guide on Managing Diversity: Evidence from Case Studies*). This study investigated the experiences from a wide range of employers across a broad spectrum of businesses from local government activities (Bolton Metro, Greenwich Healthcare) to national government activities (the Inland Revenue) and to larger organisations such as Levi Strauss.

The report identified a number of components that are vital if diversity policies are to be successful. The key issue was that organisational policy needs to be designed to enhance overall business objectives. Senior level support was needed if things were to happen and to add credibility and recognition from the organisation that it was committed to the principles of diversity.

Adapted from: Pierce, N. (1999) Diversity means business, *People Management*, 22 April, p59.

DIVERSITY INITIATIVES AND THE HRM SPECIALIST

It is very easy to ask the question 'What is diversity'? However, that is only part of the issue as it concerns workplace diversity. It usually falls within the HRM specialists area of expertise to put into place an 'workplace diversity scheme' or some similarly titled initiative. The HRM specialist needs to ensure that s/he has clearly defined the terms and business reasons for concentrating on the issue of workplace diversity and in doing this must have involved all the staff in developing the definition and the focus of the initiative. It is an issue which has to be owned by all members of the organisation and not a policy which is imposed upon them.

As Digh (1998) puts it, there are two issues here: 'What is diversity? And the real question: What value does our company place on diversity?' (www p2). As can be seen above, it is not difficult to define diversity but it is more difficult to estimate its value. However, it is not the definition of diversity that is the key issue but what diversity means to an organisation and how it can maximise the benefits accrued by diversity. Individuals will want to know how they are valued in the workplace.

In order that an organisation can achieve the future state of being the dominant professional services organisation in the business, they need the people who can best serve their stakeholders. This should comprise a diverse group of people who are selected, developed and treated on the basis of merit and fairness. By valuing diversity through respecting and appreciating peoples' differences, the organisation will have the potential to be more innovative, to increase retention of their staff and provide their stakeholders with the best value in an environment that ought to be positive and motivating for all their staff.

SCENARIO 11.14

Ethnic minority graduates lured by equality policies

Employers must make sure they are seen to be free of prejudice and can offer a secure working environment if they want to attract graduates from ethnic minorities, according to new research.

The study, by Oxford, England-based occupational psychologists Pearn Kandola, showed that students from ethnic minorities are more likely to pick big-name companies with strong equal opportunities policies.

The study also found that ethnic minority students relied far more heavily on the media and word of mouth to find out about potential employers than on recruitment literature.

To make the most of the skills of the whole population and achieve a diverse workforce, organisations need to ensure they are seen as having a strong equal opportunities policy and that they use the right means to advertise career opportunities.

Adapted from: Whitehead, M. (1999) Ethnic minority graduates lured by equality policies, *People Management*, 29 July, p16.

Some organisations go further in their view of diversity and include not only the direct employees but their families and the community. The most important thing is that the workplace atmosphere is one of respect, openness and trust which should then build enduring relationships among all stakeholders.

Diversity, therefore, is at its best when it is actively promoted in a positive way so that the organisation uses that very diversity in the interests of each individual, and, therefore, the organisation. However, it is at this stage that diversity is often mixed with discrimination – discussed above.

A BROADER DIMENSION OF DIVERSITY

Diversity goes beyond a list of descriptors because it is about creating a workplace environment that maximises the potential of every individual member of the workforce and appreciates that every employee is diverse – not just those 'on the list', for example women, ethnic minorities and homosexuals. Unfortunately, it is still a truism that employers and employees consider diversity to be an issue related to minorities and this is really a difficult problem for those organisations who wish actively and positively to empower all their employees.

Perhaps it would be better to consider the issue as one in which it is necessary to find out all the ways by which individuals differ. This leads on to consideration of the barriers those differences pose to the full activity of all employees. It is all very well stating in vision statements that diversity is valued but rhetoric has to become reality.

The dimensions that an individual uses to define diversity – the way that co-workers differ – are filters to the way s/he sees the world and they can act as barriers to the acceptance of other people. It could be said to be a moral issue.

Ethics and workplace diversity

Today an understanding of individual ethical values is particularly important – more so than in the past – and it will continue to be so. One significant reason for this is increasing globalisation and its accompanying concept of work diversity.

SCENARIO 11.15

Individual ethics and work diversity

Everyone has different expectations of a company – particularly those who work for it. Many aspects of employment are covered by legislation, others depend on the observance of ethical values and norms.

Discrimination against someone is wrong where it is not job related – it is *individual* when practised unchecked by prejudiced members of an organisation, *structural* when it relates to job or promotion conditions and *occupational* when it reflects a common presumption that certain classes of people are only capable of performing certain tasks.

Positive discrimination has been a popular remedy in the past. But the effect can be disproportionate and carries the risk of creating new victims, low self-esteem and low workforce morale.

Affirmative action – planning and executing deliberate, institutional and ethical steps to remove imbalances – does not go so far and can involve actions in the recruitment, interviewing and training fields.

The dividing line between working life and private life is another delicate area. Information should be restricted to those who 'need to know' but a company is entitled to know the reason for adverse performance.

Source: Mahoney, J. (1996) Discrimination and privacy: summary in *Mastering Management*, (12): p9, insert in *Financial Times*, 26 January.

Loden (1995) takes up the issue of defining diversity within an acceptable framework stating that it is necessary to define it broadly in order to avoid considerable opposition. Whatever definition or description is used, it is essential that it is obvious to all employees who must be included and who will, therefore, value the diversity in others.

DIMENSIONS OF WORK DIVERSITY

It is all very well listing the components of diversity and making an attempt to define it in a way that is acceptable to employer and employee but not all these components are equal in nature. Some will make a greater difference to the operations of an organisation than others and therefore it seems logical to concentrate of some more than others. Digh (1998) makes the point that just because a broad definition is used, this does not imply that one component is more important than another. The important issue is that each organisation will have its own key diversity issues upon which it has to concentrate its resources.

SCENARIO 11.16

American School Food Service Association

The American School Food Association in Alexandria, Virginia examined the four layers of diversity at a conference of its leaders.

The diversity issues that emerged were not about race and gender but were organisational in nature. Cafeteria workers in elementary [primary] schools were not perceived to be treated with as much respect as those in high [secondary] school settings.

Such workers in satellite kitchens also were perceived to be at a disadvantage compared to those in central kitchens for school districts. As a result, school districts were losing good people.

Adapted from: Digh, P. (1998) Coming to terms with diversity, *HR Magazine*, November, unpaged or on http://www.shrm.org/hrmagazine/articles/1198digh.htm, p3.

DIVERSITY IN ACTION

Having decided on its definition of diversity and the dimensions that will have the greatest impact on its own organisation, employers and employees have to consider the most positive strategy to adopt. It is here that organisations put together their value statements. More than 70 per cent of Fortune 500 organisations have diversity initiatives in place that are accompanied by vision statements which include the definition and interpretation of diversity. Any vision statement related to diversity must:

see Chapter 2

- be linked to the organisation's own strategic business objectives ■ *see* Chapter 2 ■

- be linked to the overall belief that the organisation is the best there is

- include all employees

- acknowledge equitable employment.

In order to be effective, diversity vision statements have to reflect what the diversity is and also what it means to the organisation. The better ones give a clear signal that as an organisation they support diversity.

Organisations may well have goals in order to deal with diversity issues and employers look for ways in which they can make diversity an integral part of the

11.7

Activity

Draft a vision statement for your university or an organisation with which you are familiar.

culture of their organisations. Some of them attempt to link rewards to diversity while others consider it as a part of the culture of the organisation in general ■ *see* Chapter 9 ■.

see Chapter 9

MEASURING DIVERSITY INITIATIVES

Stutz and Massengale (1997) discuss the ways in which organisations can track diversity data and the difficulties they may face:

> It can be difficult to analyse and understand such data or communicate the trends they reveal to managers who handle transactional activities such as hiring, firing, promotions and transfers. (www. p1)

An 'equity continuum' is available for the measurement of diversity in an organisation. This is a tool for rating organisations on a scale from one to five concerning their orientation toward equity in the workplace. The values and labels attached to each of the five points are given in Table 11.5 and these labels suggest that organisations at each point on the continuum have distinct motivations guiding their approach to equity in the workplace.

Wilson (2000) identified eight diversity dimensions against which organisations could place themselves:

1   commitment

2   policy ■ *see* Chapter 2 ■

see Chapter 2

3   strategy and planning ■ *see* Chapter 2 ■

see Chapter 2

4   communication ■ *see* Chapter 5 ■

see Chapter 5

5   accountability

6   implementation

7   measurement ■ *see* Chapter 3 ■

see Chapter 3

8   review and realignment

with each one of the dimensions having its own continuum upon which the particular dimension sits at a particular time.

Table 11.5 The equity continuum

0 Think they are a five	1 Legislative fairness	2 Politically correct	3 They have business reasons	4 Levelling the playing field transition	5 Equitable employment systems
These organisations are rated as zero and are at the bottom of the equity continuum. They are not motivated to pursue equity in the workplace, and have not yet started to recognise the value of creating an organisational environment that supports a diverse workforce. Although these organisations may believe or send the message that they fully endorse equitable employment systems, in reality they do nothing actually to promote diversity.	These organisations are motivated to pursue equity in order to avoid negative consequences that may result from non-compliance with legislated guidelines. Such organisations recognise that ignoring equity legislation may be very costly in terms of litigation, settlements, fines or loss of government contracts. While these organisations comply with legislation, they do so in only a minimalist sense. Resources are largely focused on securing adequate representation of women and minorities. These organisations direct their attention to the letter of the law, but do not embrace it in spirit.	These organisations support initiatives that go beyond securing adequate representation. They are motivated by a sense of altruism and a desire to lend a hand to those who have been historically disadvantaged. They are likely to have one or more diversity initiatives in place, but typically these represent isolated efforts. There is no plan in place to integrate diversity into all aspects of HRM and the larger organisational culture.	These are organisations that appreciate that managing diversity can yield positive dividends. The motivation to pursue equity among these organisations reflects a value-added business perspective. Whereas once concerned with how failure to attend to diversity will influence costs, organisations at this level realise that diversity can be a source of competitive advantage that can positively affect the revenue side of business. They recognise the competitive advantage attached to diversity and are in the process of identifying barriers to diversity and developing human resource strategies that encourage and support a diverse workplace.	These organisations recognise that diversity is a positive issue and are acting in ways to encourage it. They are driven by a commitment, shared by workers at all levels of the organisation, to achieve a diverse workforce representing the most qualified people. However, unlike those who have business reasons (3), they have begun to break through the barriers that stand in the way of equity.	Organisations that have fully committed themselves to equity, and have been successful at removing all barriers to fair employment practices. These organisations are also involved in an ongoing process of monitoring and continuous improvement, aimed at maintaining equitable employment systems through the identification and elimination of emerging barriers. They are motivated by the merit principle, which dictates that the most qualified candidates will always be the individuals who are hired and promoted. These organisations recognise and have experienced the benefits of human resource practices governed by the merit principle. Such organisations are extremely rare.

Source: Wilson, T. (2000) The equity continuum in *Diversity in the Workplace*, Canada: Ivey Business.

BUSINESS BENEFITS OF DIVERSITY

A survey of 285 organisations, carried out in 1995 in the USA, was designed to identify:

- the most and least frequently implemented initiatives

- initiatives perceived to be the most and least successful

- initiatives least and most likely to be assessed

- reasons for taking action

- the degree of monitoring

- priority areas for future actions.

They highlighted the ten most frequently implemented initiatives in each of the above areas. Their results appear to indicate a high level of awareness in the area of diversity but only a low take-up in action, showing rather more rhetoric than reality.

The issue of diversity is important in a number of aspects of business, all of which have a predominant place in the role of the HRM specialist. These are:

- hiring and retention of employees

- the promotion and upward mobility of specifically targeted groups

- the organisational climate within which diversity policies are to be delivered

- the issue of human rights ■ *see* Chapter 1 ■

- flexible compensation and benefit programmes

- wage and salary adjustments beyond the basic levels.

see Chapter 1

IMPLEMENTING A DIVERSITY STRATEGY

Once the employer and employees within an organisation have decided to implement a diversity strategy, there are a number of steps to be gone through. In order to be effective it needs to be ▶ **iterative** ◀. There are seven key steps:

▶ Where each successive step builds on the accomplishments of the previous step.   ◀······▶ **Iterative**

1   carrying out a needs analysis with management

2   educating, communicating and consulting with all employees

3   gathering data (qualitative and quantitative)

4   checking the data

5   analysing the data

6   planning the implementation of the policy

7   implementation.

In order to ascertain that an organisation has implemented its policy, it is essential that it addresses eight key areas of its business – it is within these areas that a check can be made to ensure that diversity is in practice. They are, unranked and unrated:

1   marketing, sales and customer service

2   recruitment

3   retention of talent

4   enhanced productivity

5   management of teams

6   globalisation

7   adherence to legislation (and Directives if in the EU)

8   ethical and social factors.

Managers can mobilise their culturally diverse workforce to be at the forefront of business effectiveness and international competition. Countries such as the UK, Canada and Australia have a high ethnic mix in their workforces and can, therefore, use, according to Shaw (1999), productive diversity.

Organisations increasingly have to focus on such challenges as workplace diversity, technological change, ethical behaviour and global competition. Global challenges increasingly require employers and employees to consider cultural differences and to regard appreciation of the culture as vital for organisational survival. Cultural diversity encompasses all forms of differences among individuals, including age, gender, race, sexual orientation and ability. Technological changes are reshaping jobs and the workforce, management is challenged and ethical issues are compounding the complexity.

DIVERSITY AND GOOD MANAGEMENT

Diversity in the workplace is often approached with fear. Managers are aware that they have to do something about it, but they are wary about what that something should be. They are familiar with the rhetoric – usually in the form of a vision statement – but at a loss how to implement the positive aspects of such diversity in the workplace. There is no special way of managing diversity because, put simply, the management of diversity is about managing well. This captures the essence of managing in the contemporary, diverse work environment.

There are no set answers because there is no panacea for diversity problems. Diversity is not a single issue because it is intertwined with sound management practices, with an emphasis on creating an environment that allows all employees to relate as adults through respectful, empowering relationships. Mastering the diversity challenge requires leadership, sensitivity, influence and motivational skills – the very skills that all managers should have anyway.

The culture of the organisation is very important because this should bring about a more ▶ **egalitarian** ◀ workplace. Individuals should be included in the activities of the workplace and not excluded, thus becoming 'outsiders'. Effective communication practices are vital so that workers can be educated and sensitised to the 'outsider' and 'insider' feelings and issues – issues such as gender differences ■ *see* Chapter 5 *and* Chapter 7 *and* Chapter 8 ■.

see Chapter 5 *and* Chapter 7 *and* Chapter 8

> ▶ Maintaining, relating to, or based on a belief that all people are, in principle, equal and ◀┈┈▶ Egalitarian
> should enjoy equal social, political and economic rights and opportunities.

Diversity is a positive issue where information can be shared, commitments upheld and trust developed and it can be managed by using good management practices that apply to most work situations.

Diversity can affect all management strategies but particularly some of those which are used in business today, for example the formation of employee work teams. Ideally employers need to operate their businesses in a way that maximises productivity, however, this effort is frustrated by the increasing level of diversity found in the workplace, which often heightens the difficulty of getting individuals to work together effectively.

Organisations have to learn to understand and adjust to workplace diversity, because many of the specific assets and liabilities of modern business management practices, for example work teams, arise directly out of the diverse talents and perspectives of individual team members. This in turn shapes the internal team dynamics and the team outcomes.

The concept of diversity has three components, each of which is important, yet all three need to gel together to form a positive workplace environment. These are:

1 *traditional concept of diversity*
   ethnicity, gender, and age

2 *psychological differences*
   values and beliefs

3 *organisational differences*
   hierarchical level and occupation.

Organisations need to have a strategic plan for increasing diversity and a vision which highlights its value.

The issues of globalisation, ethics in business and workforce diversity underpin the human resource function and HRM specialists need to raise the subjects in the many areas associated with the employment of people. It is particularly applicable at the start of the new century when there has been a change of emphasis from PM to HRM and the need for proactive approaches to change in a turbulent business see Chapter 1 environment ■ *see* Chapter 1 ■. The HRM specialists must be responsible for raising awareness, facilitating learning and ensuring that issues such as globalisation, ethics and workplace diversity are practised within human resource policies and practices. It is particularly important now that the business world has 'shrunk' and the HRM specialist finds her/himself working in an international context.

Chapter summary

Globalisation

■ The issue of globalisation is central in the contemporary marketplace and must be at the heart of an organisation's strategy.

■ Globalisation is difficult to define because it is different things to different people.

■ What is important about globalisation is what might emerge from it (Perlmutter, 1997).

■ A global organisation has specific attributes (Jolly, 1997) and develops a mindset (Ulrich and Black, 1999) that appreciates the efficiencies of globalisation.

■ Global sourcing increases the market for goods as well as being an extended source of supply.

■ Computers and information technology (IT) are globally interconnected (Barnett, 1997) and present organisations continually with new frontiers to cross.

■ Globalisation evolves through an organisation's lifecycle (Quinn and Cameron, 1983; Greiner, 1972) and stages in international development (Herbert, 1984; Adler, 1991; Rickey, 1991).

■ The 'new economy' plays a significant role, being part of the continual and gradual move towards globalisation through the means of global forces into unification.

■ Global competition and marketing is now the norm and this necessitates training in global management and leadership.

■ HRM is changing as a result of globalisation because people are at the heart of global citizenship.

Ethics

■ Although definitions of ethics can be found, they are difficult to capture, particularly in the ways in which ethics are learned.

■ The issue of ethics and social responsibility is a key concept for employers and employees and it links closely with globalisation and workplace diversity. Attention focuses on the influence that individual behaviour has on moral behaviour and individual social responsibility (Trevino and Youngblood, 1990).

■ Individual moral reasoning is developmental and individuals move from the more basic primary stages to higher levels (Kohlberg, 1981).

■ Empowering workers is common practice in the workplace and is often perceived to be a moral issue because the terms used to describe empowerment are humanistic in nature (Claydon and Doyle, 1996).

■ Individuals are strongly influenced by their reference groups and the way in which decisions are made are related to the norms of such groups.

■ Organisations need to develop the process of ethical analysis among workers and use reasoning rather than the imposition of substantive views on others (Maclagan, 1994).

■ Trainers have to raise their awareness of the fact that training itself is full of ethical components. For example, trainers make value judgments based on ethical decision making (Bergenhenegouwen, 1996).

■ Business ethics provide moral guidelines for the handling of business affairs.

■ There will always be conflicting ethical expectations between stakeholders.

Workplace diversity

■ It is imperative that employers and employees know what diversity actually is, articulate it and then value it (Digh, 1998).

■ The term 'diversity' is often limited to any demographic variable when it is more about valuing individuality and is, therefore, an ethical issue.

■ Diversity has three key components: traditional, psychological and organisational.

■ Diversity is not the same as discrimination.

- HRM specialists are the activators and implementers of workplace diversity policies and are therefore central to organisational strategy planning.

- It is important to have a vision on diversity but it is the activation of that vision that is the key to effective management.

- Having a diversity policy requires that its effects are measured (Stutz and Massengale, 1997).

- Business can benefit from work diversity because it offers opportunities for growth in a globalised marketplace.

- A diversity strategy must be steadily implemented from a needs analysis to actual implementation.

- An individual who manages well within an organisation will also be able to manage diversity because the principles of good management apply therein.

END OF CHAPTER 11 CASE STUDY
Global learning power

SmithKline Beecham's worldwide purchasing organisation has a team of 500 people in 41 countries. Using the Internet to deliver part of the training and development programme means that employees worldwide have instant access to a consistent body of training material, reinforcing the global culture of the organisation.

Careful consideration was given to the subject matter to be included on the Internet, ensuring that it was able to sway everyone, wherever they were based. This means that it has to be a core success that is fundamental to at least half the role and should be specifically aimed at the purchasing environment.

The first part of the Internet programme was launched in January 2000 and is an online career and development planning tool known as Pinnacle. It combines paper-based references to activities that are already up and running, including the competency framework, job ladders and the development planning process.

Individuals are able to identify their competency requirements and their own gaps that are then directly linked to development activity suggestions, including everything from traditional and structure-led training through to a wide range of self-study resources.

Participants worldwide can order training material from a remote learning resources centre, which is then delivered to them direct.

The organisation plans to produce a multimedia induction programme that will be delivered through the intranet, and an intranet learning management system is also being developed to provide a personalised portal for everyone accessing the online content. This will provide competency assessment tools, individualised learning maps for participants' specific roles and online training activities that they can carry out at their desks.

END OF CHAPTER 11 CASE STUDY (CONT'D)

The flexibility of Internet delivery means that individuals will be able to plan their own development timetable around the working day. Ultimately they will be able to take a course while away from the office by downloading the material from the Internet.

The cost of going online involved an initial investment in a learning management system to link the programme content and track assessments. There were also the content development costs, although these are decreasing over time because the organisation uses a standard framework. It takes about 300 working hours to produce one hour of content and the developers charge about £100 an hour.

The main challenge in setting up the Internet programme was the technology. The organisation had assumed that the technology infrastructure was standardised throughout the company, but that wasn't the case and they needed to find solutions suitable for everyone, not only those with access to modern technology.

The variations in bandwidths worldwide meant that in some countries, including parts of Africa and the Far East, the computer lines had a very limited capacity for transmitting information. Many commercial training packages have elaborate technology that cannot be transmitted universally, so the organisations found simplified solutions.

Computer literacy varied from country to country. The UK workers were excited by the methodology, but far more cautious about IT than those in the USA.

The process of putting development material online took more time and effort than planned because they found that instructor-led material didn't convert automatically to effective online instruction. Interaction had to be more frequent and it needed to clarify the points that an instructor would make face to face.

The organisation advises others not to let the technology be the driver and remember that the aim is to make learning more accessible. They believe that if one loses sight of that point, then the technology will begin to take on a life of its own.

Adapted from: Finn, W. (2000) Global learning power in Procure-all, *People Management,* 2 March, pp44–5, 47.

END OF CHAPTER 11 CASE STUDY QUESTIONS

1 SmithKline Beecham has taken a global view on its provision of learning and training through the use of the Internet. How might this affect workplace diversity?

2 Why does the organisation have to ensure that it does not 'let the technology be the driver'?

3 What are the ethical issues involved in SmithKline Beecham's use of the Internet as described in the case study?

4 How might the use of technologically supplied learning power help to make SmithKline Beecham a truly global organisation?

THESIS + ANTITHESIS = SYNTHESIS

'Business ethics' is an oxymoron.

SELF-TEST THE KEY ISSUES

1 What are the consequences to organisations of no single organisation or country being able to dominate global business?

2 How can individual workers be empowered when an organisation becomes ethical?

3 If the management of diversity takes on board the same principles as good management, why is the issue being give so much attention?

4 How are the concepts of globalisation, ethics and workplace diversity linked?

TEAM/CLASS DISCUSSIONS

1 The Internet is the key to organisations becoming fully globalised. Discuss.

2 There is no need to have an organisational policy on workplace diversity. Discuss.

PROJECTS (INDIVIDUAL OR TEAMS)

1 Your manager has asked you to investigate how the organisation can raise the awareness of all its stakeholders in the issue of diversity in the workplace. Write a report to her/him making your recommendations.

2 Search the Internet to find out how any ONE organisation is dealing with the issue of globalisation.

Recommended reading

Black, J. et al. (1999) *Globalizing People through International Assignments*, London: Longman

Crainer, S. (2000) *The Management Century: A Critical Review of Twentieth Century Thought and Practice*, London: John Wiley

Donovan, P. (2000) Globalisation and the ethical credibility gap in *People Managment*, 12 October, p14

Fulop, L. and S. Linstead (1999) *Management: A Critical Text*, Basingstoke: Macmillan

Holden, P. (2000) *Ethics for Managers*, London: Gower

Maund, L. (1999) *Understanding People and Organisations: An Introduction to Organisational Behaviour*, Cheltenham: Stanley Thornes

Micklethwait, J. and A. Wooldridge (2000) *A Future Perfect: The Challenge and Hidden Promise of Globalisation*, London: William Heinemann

Torrington, D. and L. Hall (1998) *Human Resource Management*, London: Prentice Hall

URLs (uniform resource locators)

www.depaul.edu/ethics/ethb13.html

Institute for Business and Professional Ethics.

www.pbs.org/globalisation/home.html

Globalisation and human rights.

www.wiser-inoinc.com

Information concerning interactive self-directed study programme in understanding workplace diversity issues.

Bibliography

Adler, N.J. (1991) *International Dimensions of Organisational Behaviour*, Boston: PWS-Kent

Barnes, W. (2000) Poor nations assert place in global trade in *Financial Times*, 21 February, p11

Barnett, C. (1997) *Challenging Reality: In Search of the Future Organization*, Chichester: John Wiley & Sons

Bergenhenegouwen, G.J. (1996) Professional code and ethics for training professionals in *Journal of European Training*, **20**(4): 23–9

Birchall, D. (2000) The new economy: revolution or evolution? in *Henley Manager*, Spring, (4): 10

Blanchard, K. and N.V. Peale (1988) *The Power of Ethical Management*, New York: Fawcett Crest

Chan, T.S. (1994) Developing international managers: a partnership approach in *Journal of Management Development*, **13**(3): 38–46

Claydon, T. and M. Doyle (1996) Trusting me, trusting you? The ethics of employee empowerment in *Personnel Review*, **25**(6): 13–25

Cohen, A. (1996) The price of honesty in *Financial Times*, 2 September, p16

Concise Oxford Dictionary (1999)

Diamantopoulou, A. (2000) Europe must go to work in *People Management*, 2 March, p31

Digh, P. (1998) Coming to terms with diversity in *HR Magazine*, November
    http://www.shrm.org/hrmagazine/articles/1198digh.htm pp1–5

Donaldson, T. and T.W. Dumfree (1994) Toward a unified conception of business ethics: integrative social contracts theory in *Academy of Management Review*, (19): 252–84

Encarta World English Dictionary (1999) London: Bloomsbury

Fulop, E. and S. Linstead (1999) *Management: A Critical Text*, Basingstoke: Macmillan – now Palgrave

Giddens, A. (1990) *The Consequences of Modernity*, Cambridge and Oxford: Polity and Blackwell

Greiner, L. (1972) Evolution and revolution as organisations grow in *Harvard Business Review*, **50**, July–August, pp37–46

Heise, W. (1998) Portability of qualifications: an answer to the qualificational demands of globalisation? in *Journal of European Industrial Training*, **22**(7): 289–300

Heller, R. (1996) Drunk on misguided optimism in *Management Today*, August, p24

Herbert, T. (1984) Strategy and multinational organisational structure: an interorganizational relationships perspective in *Academy of Management Review*, (9): 259–71

Institute of Personnel and Development (1999) *The IPD Guide on Managing Diversity: Evidence from Case Studies*, Wimbledon: Institute of Personnel and Development, April

Jolly, V. (1997) Global strategies in the 1990s in Bickerstaffe, G. (ed.) (1997) *Mastering Management*, London: Financial Times/Pitman

Kohlberg, L. (1981) *The Philosophy of Moral Development*, San Francisco: Harper & Row

Lamb, J. (1999) Skills crisis forces rethink on work permit restraints in *People Management*, 16 December, pp14–15

Loden, M. (1995) *Implementing Diversity: Best Practices for Making Diversity Work in Your Organization*, New York: Irwin Professional

Legge, K. (1995) *Human Resource Management: Rhetorics and Realities*, Basingstoke: Macmillan – now Palgrave

Maclagan, P. (1994) Education and development for corporate ethics in *Industrial and Commercial Thinking*, **26**(4): 3–7

Mahoney, J. (1996) Discrimination and privacy: summary in *Mastering Management*, (12): 9, insert in *Financial Times*, 26 January

Management Today (1997) The protection of reputation becomes a core concern, October, p6

Marcousé, I., A. Gillespie, B. Martin, M. Surridge and N. Wall (1999) *Business Studies*, Abingdon: Hodder & Stoughton

Maund, L. (1999) *Understanding People and Organisations: An Introduction to Organisational Behaviour*, Cheltenham: Stanley Thornes

May, A.S. (1997) Think globally – act locally! Competences for global management in *Career Development International*, **6**(2): 308–9

Ohmae, K. (1995) Putting global logic first in *Harvard Business Review*, January/February, pp119–24

People Management, 11 November 1999, p12

Perimutter, H.V. (1997) Becoming globally civilised in Bickerstaffe, G. (ed.) (1997) *Mastering Management*, London: Financial Times/Pitman, pp408–13

Pettinger, R. (1996) *Introduction to Organisational Behaviour*, Basingstoke: Macmillan – now Palgrave

Pierce, N. (1999) Diversity means business in *People Management*, 22 April, p59

Porter, M.E. (1986) Changing patterns of international competition in *California Management Review*, **28**, Winter, pp9–40

Quinn, E.E. and K. Cameron (1983) Organisational life cycles and shifting criteria of effectiveness: some preliminary evidence in *Management Science*, **29**: 35–51

Remicke, W.H. (1999) Pre-UNCTAD Seminar on the Role of Competition Policy for Development in Globalizing World Markets, Washington, DC: The World Bank and the Brookings Institution

Rickey, L.K. (1991) International Expansion – US Corporations Strategy, Stages of Development and Structure, unpublished manuscript, Nashville, TN: Vanderbilt University

Ritzer, G. (1993) *The McDonaldization of Society*, Thousand Oaks, CA: Pine Forge

Shaw, J. (1999) *Cultural Diversity at Work: Utilising a Unique Australian Resource*, St Ultimo, NSW: Woodslane Pty Ltd

Sims, R.L. (1998) When formal ethics policies differ from informal expectations: a test of managers' attitudes in *Leadership and Organization Development Journal*, **19**(7): 386–91

Sims, R.R. (1992) Linking groupthink to unethical behavior in organizations in *Journal of Business Ethics*, (11): 651–2

Stutz, J. and R. Massengale (1997) Measuring diversity initiatives in *HR Magazine*, December http://www.shrm.org/hrmagazine/articles/1297div.htm pp1–5

The Week, Tetley Tea/Tata: Bagged, 4 March 2000, p33

The Week, The net really will change everything, 4 March 2000, p34

The Week (2000) Will the new economy reach Britain? 12 February, p34, Commentators from Smith, B. in *The Sunday Times*

Trevino, L.K. and S.A. Youngblood (1990) Bad apples in bad barrels: a causal analysis of ethical decision making behaviour in *Journal of Applied Psychology*, (75): 378–85

Trezise, R.K. (1996) Review article: An introduction to business ethics for human resource management teaching and research in *Personnel Review*, **25**(6): 85–9

Ulrich, D. and J.S. Black (1999) Wordly wise in *People Management*, 28 October, pp42–3, 45–6

Underhill, C. (2000) What 'globalisation' denies the poor in *Financial Times*, Letters to the Editor, 19 August, p14

Waters, M. (1995) *Globalization*, London: Routledge

Webster, M. (1984) *The Global Village*, London: Longman

Wendlandt, A. (2000) Elite courses learn to be the business in *Financial Times*, 28 February, p18

Whitehead, M. (1999) Ethnic minority graduates lured by equality policies in *People Management*, 29 July, p16

Williams, F. (2000) Globalisation 'is bad for health' in *Financial Times*, 10 June 1999, p5

Wilson, T. (2000) The equity continuum in diversity in the workplace, Canada, Ivey Business

Human resource management in an international context

After studying this chapter, you should be able to:

■ DISCUSS the complexities of an international role in human resource management (HRM).

■ SUGGEST steps that can be taken to develop internationalism in HRM.

■ COMMENT on the personal qualities and competencies required of international human resource managers.

■ DISTINGUISH between the HRM of techniques of western countries and countries in transition.

■ OUTLINE broader international issues relevant to HRM specialists.

INTRODUCTION

Framework case study

Global ambition

Tesco is exporting its special brand of retail philosophy to central Europe and the Far East. The retail giant believes that there is huge potential in central Europe, Ireland and South East Asia, all of which are regions where Tesco has made a strong start.

Tesco has moved into Slovakia, Poland, Hungary, the Czech Republic, Northern and Southern Ireland, Thailand and Korea and they are researching the potential of moving into Taiwan and Malaysia.

Central Europe is a fast-growing market and Tesco successfully opened six more hypermarkets there in 1998, and have opened ten more in 1999 in Hungary, the Czech Republic and Poland.

They have also taken over 13 hypermarkets in Asia and now have 14 stores there, with plans to double the number of stores by the end of 2002. A partnership has begun with Samsung in South Korea with a plan to take over 25 existing hypermarkets and build 12 more by the end of 2002.

Tesco is able to transplant its UK supermarket format into central Europe, Ireland and South East Asia because the style of their overseas operations is broadly similar. The philosophy appears to be the same, but it is tailored to local markets. The firm recruits staff locally and trains them and most of the products are locally sourced. All the central European stores' general managers are Tesco trained. In 1999 the company recruited 44 local graduates for its Excel training programme which encourages participants to take management responsibility at an early age.

Tesco's aim is to become a major retailer globally, or more precisely to be in the global food super league rising above their present 12th position.

Adapted from: Altmin, W. (1999) Global ambition, *Professional Manager*, July, **8**(4): 20–2.

All employers have to ensure that the HRM profession takes a proactive role in the international perspective of its specialism as does Tesco in the Framework Case Study. This means that the HRM role is even more integral to the strategy of an organisation ■ *see* Chapter 2 ■. With the advent of globalisation has come an increased international market with its accompanying opportunities and it is, therefore, essential that employers raise awareness that global responsibilities are now integral to the business of an organisation and not just added on. HRM specialists have to ensure that training is designed to distinguish between national (domestic) and international human resources ■ *see* Chapter 11 ■. The Institute of Personnel and Development (IPD) (1996) stated that this is a matter 'more of depth than difference' (p1).

All members of an organisation's workforce need to share their information and improve their international career development if the organisation is to exhibit what is considered to be best practice – the basis of benchmarking. Organisations that achieve 'world class' status are engaged continuously in benchmarking their products, processes and results against acknowledged best practice. Some think that benchmarking is only for large organisations but, in fact, in this day and age of

see Chapter 2

see Chapter 11

increasing competition and international markets, the concept is essential for the survival of even the smallest organisation. Benchmarking is a vital tool for establishing operational goals and discovering the best practices that will lead to superior performance. It is a discovery process that motivates everyone involved and it often produces excellent results. Many organisations, including Xerox, Barclays, Motorola, Rover Group, ICI and Shell as well as smaller organisations, have achieved significant breakthrough improvements using benchmarking methodology. This means that employers need to provide workers with the necessary opportunities for the assessment of needs and then to develop their international competence.

SCENARIO 12.1

Global business – male fashions

The great majority of French people are still turning up their noses at daringly cut clothes in delicate fabrics – in contrast to the Italians, who can't get enough of them. The French just don't get it and designers are furious. 'The market for men's clothes in France is the hardest in Europe,' says Jeff Sayre, an American stylist at Georges Rech. The German male spends twice as much on clothes as his French counterpart, who still shies away from bright and lively colours.

Nothing could make people happier beyond the banks of the Rhine and in Scandinavia. All the same, a big effort is being made to explain colour to the French. Gently. Lots of stores, such as the Daniel Cremieux chain, have altered the way they display their collections. Now everything is classed by colour and not by the type of clothing.

Source: Global business – male fashions from *Le Nouvel Economiste, Management Today,* July 1999, p21.

DEFINITION

International human resource management (IHRM) is very closely linked with globalisation ■ *see* Chapter 11 ■. However, it needs to be given its own space if HRM specialists are to manage in an increasingly global arena. Armstrong (1999) defined IHRM as:

see Chapter 11

> the process of employing and developing people in international organisations which operate in Europe or globally. (p79)

It is about carrying out all the HRM activities that specialists and line managers are familiar with in a domestic market but applying these to an international workforce, such as:

■ employee development

■ recruitment and selection

■ reward and remuneration

■ policies and practices

and so it means working across national borders.

12.1

Take a look at a professional journal, for example *People Management* or *Management Today* or the appointments section of a quality newspaper such as the *Financial Times*.

1 Calculate what proportion of the advertisements ask candidates for skills which are related to international business.

2 List the requirements, noting how commonly they are asked for.

It can include any type of worker, be they:

- an own country national working overseas as an ▶ **expatriate** ◀

Expatriate ◀┈┈▶ Someone who has left her/his own country to live and work in another country.

- an own country national working overseas for a short period on a specific project

- an individual of one nationality, who is working in another country for an organisation which is based in yet another country, for example an individual who is French, working in England for a Japanese-owned organisation.

Beardwell and Holden (1997) distinguish between comparative HRM and IHRM believing that:

> the latter exists primarily in multinational corporations (MNCs) and the former has a wider contextual setting. (p701)

For the purposes of this text, the issue will be discussed in a general international framework.

POINTS TO PONDER

Screen test

The organisation Swift assesses all external recruits against its 'international mindset' competency.

Source: Sparrow, P. (1999) Abroad minded, *People Management*, 20 May, pp43.

IHRM AND STRATEGY

All organisations now need to include a discussion of international issues and the matter of moving beyond national boundaries when considering their business strategy ■ *see* Chapter 2 ■. Even organisations which are small and do not buy any of their supplies from abroad, or do not sell any of their products and services abroad should, at least, be considering doing so. However, the issue of globalisation

see Chapter 2

has meant that this situation can no longer be maintained – all organisations are affected, to some extent, by globalisation. The environment for all businesses is now a global one and this is particularly true for the multinational organisations when they are making their strategic operations decisions ■ *see* Chapter 2 *and* Chapter 11 ■. According to Slack et al. (1995), these organisations have four types of strategic operations decisions to make:

see Chapter 2 *and* Chapter 11

1   Where should their operations facilities be located?

2   How should their operations network be managed across national boundaries?

3   Should operations in different countries be allowed to develop their own way of doing business?

4   Should an operations practice that has been successful in one part of the world be transferred to another? (p864)

INTERNATIONAL LOCATION

Where the organisation should be located is a strategic decision which has to be made within the framework of the whole of the organisation's business practices. Networks of operations can involve threads crossing numerous and distinct geographic regions and some organisations, for example Levi Strauss, IBM, Shell and Kodak, are truly globalised because they have branches all over the globe. However, it does not suit all organisations to design the configuration of their organisations on a geographical basis and they may choose a more appropriate method of location that is more useful to their individual businesses. There are, according to Du Bois and Oliff (1992), four configuration strategies identified in the location behaviour of those organisations which consider themselves to be international (see Figure 12.1):

Strategy One – Home Country Configuration
When an organisation has its business in its domestic environment and trades only nationally. By doing this, an organisation has no need to locate its business or its workforce anywhere other than at home. There are a number of reasons for this strategy which could include, for example, the nature of the business, such as fashion that is pertinent to the home nation or specialist work which is limited to the domestic environment.

Strategy Two – Regional Configuration
This is when an organisation decides to divide its activities into a small number of geographical regions, for example Europe, South America and Australia. In doing this, the organisation will attempt to ensure that each region is as self-contained as possible. Thus, the Australian region, say, would have its own complete range of operations capabilities so that it could produce the full range of products and/or provide all the services required in Australia. This model is usually confined to those businesses that have to provide a quick delivery of products and/or services

with a speedy after-sales service. While it is possible to have regional warehouses and local service centres, it is not as efficient as a regional configuration.

Strategy Three – Global Coordinated Configuration

This is the opposite of strategy one (home country configuration) because an organisation in this category is one that has locations worldwide. Such organisations tend to concentrate on a narrow group of activities, products and/or services and then distribute throughout the world. An organisation can, for example, use cheap labour in one country and distribute the finished products in another country where the organisation will get a high mark-up on its goods. This strategy will also allow organisations to take advantage of local specialisms. Therefore, such an organisation will exploit the specific advantages of specific areas and use a head office in one country to coordinate all its activities and act as the centre for all planning.

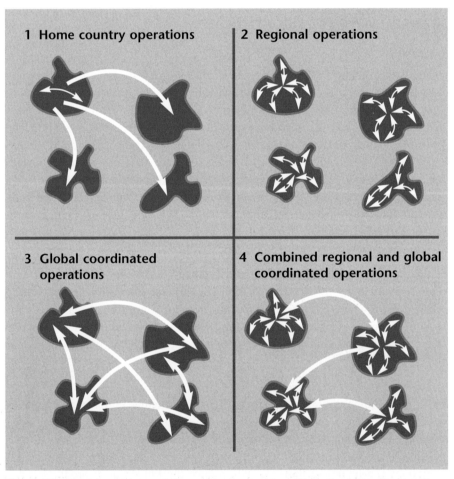

Figure 12.1 Four broad types of international network configuration, after Slack et al. (1995, p866)

Strategy Four – Combined Regional and Coordinated Configuration

By using this strategy an organisation attempts to get the best of both worlds: the advantage of organisational simplicity and clarity offered by the regional configuration (strategy two) and the global coordinated strategy of well-exploited international advantages. This is the ideal and organisations try to find a compromise between the two. This might mean that regions might be somewhat autonomous but certain products/services are moved between the regions to take advantage of particular regional circumstances such as cheap labour – MercedesBenz and Kodak are organisations which do this. In some cases many of the products are made in a number of locations worldwide while each regional market is served by more than the plants in that region.

DIFFERENT PRACTICES FOR DIFFERENT REGIONS

Each organisation will adopt its own individual way of running its organisation, dependent upon such factors as:

- culture

- economic conditions

- tradition

- market needs

- demographic trends.

Taking ethics ■ *see* Chapter 11 ■ as a working example, organisations have to be aware of the issues as they relate to, for example, differing cultures. Using Scenario 12.2, the issue here is whether the organisation that originates in Sweden, where involvement in any sort of bribery is considered culturally unacceptable, prevents its representative from doing what is culturally acceptable in the other country? Bribery in India is part of the culture and without it business cannot usually be carried out. It is a moral dilemma for members of the organisation and they can respond in a number of ways:

see Chapter 11

SCENARIO 12.2

A case of bribery

A small Swedish organisation specialising in helping children with AIDS wants to set up an office in a city on the Indian subcontinent. They have found an appropriate site for the office and have hired an architect to draw up the plans. Now the owner of the organisation is seeking planning permission to develop the plans into bricks and mortar.

However, the planning department has indicated that, in order to get planning permission, it is necessary to offer some sort of bribe to the officials responsible for passing the plans.

1   Argue that it is up to the individual as to how s/he acts. This approach takes the view that it is the individual who has to live with the decision and if giving and taking bribes does not bother her/him, then go ahead and bribe the officials in order to get the necessary permission. Ethical theorists call this approach 'subjectivism'.

2   Use the argument that everyone uses bribery – especially in India – and in order to get anywhere, the organisation's representatives will have to bribe the officials. This ethical theory is called 'cultural relativism'.

3   A view can be taken that it is wrong to use bribery under any circumstances – even if by doing it, the organisation will get planning permission. Even if the organisation will be able to carry out its work with children with AIDS, to use bribery to do this is not right. This is the 'non-consequentialist' viewpoint.

4   India is still a developing nation with its fair share of people with AIDs and malnutrition and disease are also highly visible. The organisation might take the view that helping children who have AIDS is so important that it transcends the issue of bribery; that is, it is the best of the evils presented to the organisation. This is the ethical theory of 'consequentialism'.

5   People who take the 'natural law/ethics of rights' approach believe that the Indian planning officials have no right to the organisation's money because it belongs to those who have earned it, for example, the workforce and other people who have actually done something to entitle them to it.

Another issue that faces organisations with a global image is that of marketing of their products. For example, the fast-food chain McDonald's has a highly standardised, rationalised way of carrying out its business, making its products and providing its services. While this approach has aided their success in the market, they have had to allow local managers autonomy to adjust processes and products to cope with local cultural conditions. For example, in Lyons, France it is possible to buy wine at McDonald's, while in Tokyo, Japan teriyaki burgers are on the menu. Such cultural differences have been positively used by McDonald's and it is now evident that their menu choices are being broadened in all outlets to cope with an increasingly internationalised clientele.

12.2

Activity

Use the Internet to access a broadsheet newspaper from a country other than your own. For example, if you are a Japanese national you can access the *Daily Telegraph* or *The Boston Globe*. Alternatively, get hold of a hard copy.

Find two articles which relate to the issue of ethics in business. Why are they of concern to IHRM and how would your home nation view the issues?

SCENARIO 12.3

Role playing in French business

'No, it can't be!' shouts Lionel, commercial director of a textiles firm, who can't believe the rude, angry man that he is watching is an accurate portrayal.

His company has been using role play for several years to shed light on dysfunctional internal relationships. 'The actors exaggerate what's going wrong in a real workplace situation,' says Beatrice Aragou from the Nantes Conservatoire. 'You don't attack anyone by name, but everyone knows who's being talked about.' There are some 30 theatrical troupes offering this widely accepted service in France. Where once role plays were used for technical issues, they now represent a kind of social catharsis. 'We all use the Mary Poppins strategy,' says one very senior (and anonymous) manager. 'A spoonful of sugar helps the medicine go down.'

Source: Global Business – *Le Nouvel Economiste* on role playing in French business, *Management Today,* June 1999, p23.

It is evident that successful global organisations need to be adaptable to local conditions. For example, Sweden is known to have a society which is liberal in its work activities and so non-national organisations involved in Sweden or using Swedish workers will have to develop working conditions and job designs that retain the staff – the role of the IHRM specialist.

CHALLENGE OF IHRM

There is likely to be an increased need for HRM specialists and line managers to accept the challenge of IHRM because with increased globalisation and workforce diversity has come a requirement to manage beyond domestic and national boundaries ■ *see* Chapter 11 *and* Chapter 12 ■.

see Chapter 11 *and* Chapter 12

Armstrong (1999) suggests four key areas where the demands are likely to be found:

1   *Managing the complexity of the workforce mix*
    In a workforce with employees from a variety of nationalities, there could be problems with employment practices as well as with remuneration and reward.

2   *Managing diversity*
    Between cultures, social systems and legal requirements. The IHRM specialist will have to be able to deal with non-conformity rather than conformity.

3   *Communications*
    Face-to-face communication is the most potent communication method and even a sophisticated electronic system cannot compensate for this ■ *see* Chapter 5 ■.

see Chapter 5

4 *People of the right calibre*

The problems of IHRM are far more complex than those in the domestic situation and so IHRM specialists have to be able to employ and retain staff who can keep the organisation competitive in a worldwide market.

SCENARIO 12.4

Le cyber challenge

In a scruffy cybercafé nestling between the Parisian landmarks of Les Halles and the Pompidou Centre, and reverberating with North African rap music, French youngsters are surfing their way around the world. But many of the pages flashing up on their screens are not written in French. This is, after all, a cyber-world dominated by English, in which French is used by only 1.2 per cent of the world's websites and even fewer of all international online forums.

More than any other medium of recent years, the Internet is challenging French attempts to control and protects its culture. Its pride in its culture is fierce. No other country, apart from Spain, has a body quite like the Académie Française, dedicating itself for the past 365 years to the defence of the national language. No other country has quite the same belief in linguistic solidarity; witness its ministerial department of *la francophonie* which spreads the word in over 50 countries (some of them not French-speaking) from Canada to Vietnam. No other country makes quite the same fuss in world trade talks over culture, demanding the right to keep minimum quotas of French-language pop music or films.

The Internet tests this instinct in two ways. The first is the weight of the English language on the web. In some ways, the French have not helped themselves. They were slow to 'get' the Internet. A government decision in the early 1980s to leapfrog France along the information superhighway landed the country with France Telecom's Minitel system – wonderful for looking up telephone numbers or booking train tickets, but incapable of matching the Internet's flexibility and range. The popularity of Minitel, however, stunted the growth of the personal computer. By 1998, only a fifth of French households had a computer, compared with two-fifths in the USA, and only 2 per cent of households were connected to the Internet.

Those figures are now surging. The French Association of Internet Service Providers calculates that, in January 1998, only 540 000 French residents were connected to the net, and for a collective total of 4 million hours. By January 2000, the connections had swollen to just over 3 million. Surfers spent a total of 25.3 million hours on line.

But will these *internauts*, as the culturally correct call them, surf *la toile* in French, or the web in English? The answer, despite the proliferation of French-language websites, will probably be both. For all the Académie's efforts to promote French translations of the new Internet vocabulary – *la messagerie électronique* for e-mail, for instance – most French surfers think it cool to sprinkle US geek-talk into their conversation.

The second challenge is the defiantly anarchic nature of the net, which, unlike Minitel, does not lend itself to the sort of cultural policing that the French have used in the past to fend off the US cultural invasion. The official idea now is to promote the spread of French sites on the net in order to advance the cause of 'cultural diversity and democracy'. But keeping control will be hard. A few years ago, when French judges banned a book about President Françoise Mitterand's last illness, an enterprising cybercafé in the eastern town of Besançon simply put it on the net.

Source: Le cyber challenge (2000) in *The Economist*, March 11, p. 53.

CHARACTERISTICS OF IHRM

It would be easy to say that IHRM is just a matter of extending domestic and national HRM issues in a globalised manner, because it is more than mimicking the practices from other countries such as, for example, those in the EU, Australia, Japan and the USA. This is obvious to those employers and employees who appreciate the complexities of culture and the difficulties involved in transferring culture across individuals – let alone across national boundaries. In the early days of globalisation organisations held training courses for those employees going to work overseas in the hope that they could be inculcated with the language and culture of their receiving nation. At this time, the 1980s, it was not really appreciated that national cultures are discrete and complex – even for the indigenous population.

The seminal work of Torrington (1994) is helpful to IHRM specialists when it comes to trying to refine the definition of what IHRM and in this he referred to the '7 Cs', given in Table 12.1.

While Torrington (1994) does say that IHRM is not just a matter of copying the practice of other countries, he seems to take the view that it is merely national HRM on a larger scale. While he does state that it is of a more varied nature and that it requires more coordination (see Table 12.1), this is a rather simplistic approach for the 21st century. The key is that adaptation must be within cultural limits and when dealing with, say, recruitment and selection, extra special care has to be taken.

Table 12.1 The '7 Cs' of IHRM

CHARACTERISTIC	TYPE	DESCRIPTOR
One	Cosmopolitan	Members of the elite group who are constantly on the move. Expatriates.
Two	Culture	Individual backgrounds differ considerably in relation to culture.
Three	Compensation	Specific arrangements for reward and remuneration for expatriates and nationals of host countries.
Four	Communication	Effective worldwide communication between all parts of the organisation.
Five	Consultancy	The bringing in of experts with local knowledge.
Six	Competence	Employees who have to work across political, cultural and organisational boundaries need to develop a wider range of competencies than those who work in the domestic sector.
Seven	Coordination	Integrating the widespread international business to work holistically.

SCENARIO 12.5

Expatriate games: tailored solutions for Marks & Spencer

Sara Beckett, Marks & Spencer's development manager, stepped off the plane in Dubai looking forward to the start of six months in the Gulf setting up a new franchise store. That same day, she was interviewing hopeful candidates for management positions in the new store.

Sara had an objective to achieve but a limited time in which to do it. Fortunately, she had been prepared for the challenge of working with a different culture by attending a business briefing programme on the Middle East at the Centre for International Briefing.

Sara felt that without this course she would have been ill-equipped for her task because it gave her an awareness of how business operates in a different culture, why people act in a certain way and how best to cope with difficult situations.

Sara's role involved establishing the commercial operations of M&S franchise stores in new countries and this involved coordinating all the disciplines from staff training to store management. The objective was to provide the store with all the support that it needed to run self-sufficiently.

The philosophy of Marks & Spencer stores is the same worldwide, ensuring that all the stores are recognisably M&S and providing the quality on which people rely. But every country is different and adaptations are made to fit the culture and needs of the people shopping and working in the store.

Sensitivity to the Muslim culture in the Middle East has resulted in the world's first prayer room for staff and customers in a Marks & Spencer store. In the Gulf countries M&S staff will always be wearing headscarves and long skirts. The company had opened four outlets in the Gulf by the end of 1999 and preparation for this included staff travelling to the country to train local staff, as well as local store managers being trained in stores in the UK.

The human resources director for M&S said that, in order to ensure that both M&S and the franchise partners gained maximum benefits from the investment, they provided all the preparation necessary for an effective transfer of skills, and intercultural training from the Centre for International Briefing played a key role in that.

Staff from both countries attended intercultural training sessions, one benefit of which was that everyone came away with a better understanding about each other – the similarities as well as the differences. The training helped to clarify the preconceptions and built upon areas of commonality. The staff at M&S stores in the Middle East represent many nationalities and have different styles of learning. Some may speak up and actively participate, while others are shy about speaking in groups. These differences were taken into consideration and M&S tailored their programme to meet the characteristics of the people they are training.

As in national HRM, there are no lists of 'tips for HRM specialists' because they can only really take the generalisations and develop them according to the international situation they find themselves in. However, organisations now have to include IHRM as a part of their core programmes in training and development and not make it an option for those employees who have a personal interest.

INTERNATIONALISM AND THE HRM SPECIALIST

Understanding and working with diverse national practices is essential for HRM specialists or line managers with international responsibilities. With increased globalisation and diversity in the workplace, such individuals have to know other countries arrangements in the areas of, say, recruitment, contracts of employment, national legislation and practices and procedures on the termination of a contract of employment ■ *see* Chapter 4, Chapter 7 *and* Chapter 8 ■. All managers need to take due diligence in international affairs, yet it is the HRM professionals who are:

see Chapter 4 *and* Chapter 7 *and* Chapter 8

- overseeing IHRM issues

- exercising the 'due diligence' as part of overseas acquisitions by their organisations

- undertaking strategic reviews of HRM policies in other countries.

Specifically, the HRM specialist has to concern her/himself with all the key issues of such a specialist, for example:

- recruitment

- contracts of employment

- training and development

- reward and remuneration

- working time

- equality issues

- representation and communication

- rules and procedures

- health and safety factors

- discipline and termination.

These issues have been discussed throughout this textbook and the principles apply to whatever country or countries the HRM specialist is concerned with. However, the issues will take on a national influence when related to specific countries. The IPD (1996) research showed that:

> given the complexity of working across borders, people need strong intercultural and communications skills, resilience, ability to handle diversity, knowledge of local employment conditions, an awareness of strategic business aims and understanding of international business environments. (p1)

Globalisation is becoming increasingly important and is causing an increase in the number of IHRM specialists required, because:

- many organisations are managing an international workforce

- many employees are employed by organisations that have branches in other countries

- there is an increase in the number of organisations that employ a workforce based overseas

- fast-growing international economies are proving to be attractive as business markets

see Chapter 11

- most organisations are conscious of the need to be interdependent and global ■ *see* Chapter 11 ■.

INTERNATIONAL DIMENSIONS AND MANAGEMENT

see Chapter 9

see Chapter 6 *and* Chapter 9

see Chapter 10

While some HRM activities are common to all organisations regardless of their location or national bias, for example motivating employees ■ *see* Chapter 9 ■, rewarding and remunerating them for work which leads to the achievement of the organisation's objectives (through appraisal) ■ *see* Chapter 6 *and* Chapter 9 ■ and employee development ■ *see* Chapter 10 ■, the way in which such management is carried out depends upon a number of critical factors:

- *Culture*

see Chapter 6 *and* Chapter 11

  The attitudes and beliefs that workers have, individually, collectively and nationally. This has been discussed above related to the issue of bribery. However, there are cultural issues connected to the perceptions that are held about work – teamworking, employment conditions and remuneration and rewards are just a few examples. There is evidence that, with increased globalisation and diversity in the workforce, work practices are becoming internationally harmonised and with the addition of high-tech worldwide communications, individuals are more exposed to cultural differences ■ *see* Chapter 6 *and* Chapter 11 ■.

- *Legislation*

see Chapter 7 *and* Chapter 8

  As was discussed in ■ Chapter 7 *and* Chapter 8 ■, nations have their own legislation related to employment practices, for example the UK has its own Acts of Parliament and Directives from the EU. Such legislation protects employees in the workplace in areas such as health and safety, working time and minimum wage.

- *The economic conditions*

  The prevailing national economic conditions will highlight the differences between countries, that is, such things as the level of unemployment, and the rate of economic growth.

- *Competition*

  In order to stay competitive in a changing market, organisations have continually to use working practices which are flexible and so they turn to the HRM specialist for techniques that will give the organisation the edge it must have.

■ *Employee relations*

The nature of employer/employee relationship has moved from the conflict-centred arena of trades unions versus the employer and collective bargaining to a more employer:employee partnership framework ■ *see* Chapter 5, Chapter 6, Chapter 7 *and* Chapter 8 ■.

see Chapter 5, Chapter 6, Chapter 7 *and* Chapter 8

■ *Training and development*

Organisations need to ensure that all their employees are skilled in the required areas and have the knowledge required to meet the organisation's objectives. In countries where little state assistance is given towards training and development – especially in the vocational field – organisations have to turn an increased level of their resources to this area ■ *see* Chapter 1 *and* Chapter 6 ■.

see Chapter 1 *and* Chapter 6

PEOPLE AND THE ORGANISATION'S GLOBAL ENVIRONMENT

Managers in business and writers in the field of HRM tend to say that the most important people in an organisation are its workers. However, in the UK there is little evidence to show that this is any more than rhetoric, while other countries do treat their people as a valuable resource ■ *see* Chapter 1 ■.

see Chapter 1

The advanced capitalist countries, for example the USA, Japan and Germany, are said to be in their 'post-career' phase. An organisation's needs for workers changes very quickly and because of this individual workers feel insecure in their current positions. Advanced capitalism is continuing to create more long-term unemployment with a growing disparity between those 'who have' (the rich) and those 'who have not' (the poor). This, however, is not confined to the workers but also to and between nations. The key areas of concern in this area are:

■ insecure employment prospects

■ deteriorating terms of employment

■ a weakening in the rights of employees

■ often lower wages and salaries for those in the lower echelons.

Such a situation is more apparent in the UK than in any other country. The national government is doing all it can to take restrictions off the responsibility of employers and putting them on to the employees ■ *see* Chapter 7 *and* Chapter 8 ■. The attitude to employment is different in other countries, for example Japan.

see Chapter 7 *and* Chapter 8

Staff employed by global organisations which have more enlightened attitudes are likely to find retraining an essential part of their working experience. Therefore, it is very important that governments provide their people with as good a general education as possible, as a basis for retraining in later life.

Organisations also need to give training a high priority; if they really want to invest in their staff in this and other ways, they are more likely to win their loyalty and increase their productivity.

POINTS TO PONDER

The recent graduate in business who applies her/his knowledge and skills to increase an organisation's productivity is considered to be part of the productive process.

However, the lecturers who taught the graduate those skills and imparted the knowledge to her/him are considered to be outside it.

Adapted from: Dawes, B. (1995) *International Business: A European Perspective*, Cheltenham: Stanley Thornes, p9.

TRANSBORDER DATA FLOWS

see Chapter 6
and Chapter 11

see Chapter 11

see Chapter 6

Information technology (IT) and the strategies of the multinational organisations are the integration of the global capitalist economy ■ *see* Chapter 6 *and* Chapter 11 ■. The ability to search for global resources and markets gives enormous power and control on those who are able to act globally ■ *see* Chapter 11 ■. Along with the high-tech economies has come knowledge that replaces raw materials as the source of wealth creation ■ *see* Chapter 6 ■.

It is generally believed that Britain is the most inventive nation on earth (Dawes, 1995, p9) but most of the inventions and discoveries attributed to Britain were made available to other nations without cost to them or were allowed to take a back seat because it was not known how they could be made economically viable. By the same token, the USA was able to patent and commercially exploit many British inventions and discoveries and now Britain finds herself in the position of having to buy back such ideas in concrete form. No country would even consider giving another its raw materials without payment, yet, according to Dawes (1995), multinational organisations:

> argue for complete freedom to transfer knowledge from one place to another without restriction or cost. (p9)

Numerous countries, including Australia, Austria, Brazil, Canada, Denmark, Finland, France, Germany, Japan, Luxembourg, Norway and Sweden have in place legislation which constrains transborder data flow and others are considering it. Britain has learned to its cost that making knowledge freely available to all other nations is not economically viable unless all those other nations are doing it too.

EMPLOYMENT AND DEVELOPMENT STRATEGIES

As was mentioned earlier in this chapter, it is essential for organisations to ensure that their workers are knowledge based, skilled and flexible. In order to achieve this, an organisation has to turn its attention specifically to international employment and development strategies. Armstrong (1999) believes that such concentration is warranted in three areas:

■ a strategy of centralisation

- the staffing of posts in management areas

- a strategy for management development.

A STRATEGY OF CENTRALISATION

Centralisation is about housing all policies and practices related to employment with its controlling factors from a headquarters. This would mean that all decisions related to staffing, for example recruitment and selection, remuneration and rewards and employee development, would be made at the centre ■ *see* Chapter 4, Chapter 9 *and* Chapter 10 ■.

see Chapter 4
and Chapter 9
and Chapter 10

12.3

Activity

Find out if your university or place of work has more than one branch. For example, are there buildings other than the one on the site where you study and/or work?

Does each site have its own human resource-related decision-making system or is it centralised at one of the sites?

According to Armstrong (1999), when an organisation does centralise it allows it to:

> be well placed to plan for management succession and to secure the availability of high quality staff to exploit new opportunities as well as to manage existing operations. (p81)

Centralisation encourages a systematic system that can cope with worldwide business but it could also generate a very different culture within which employees find themselves uncomfortable.

STAFFING OF POSTS IN MANAGEMENT AREAS

There are three key areas of staffing management positions, as shown in Figure 12.2.

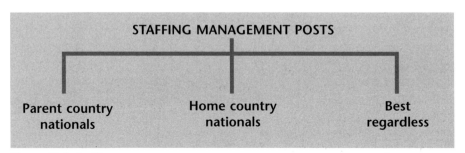

STAFFING MANAGEMENT POSTS

| Parent country nationals | Home country nationals | Best regardless |

Figure 12.2 Staffing management posts

By using *parent country nationals* an organisation will ensure that the posts are held by individuals who are steeped in the business. This is often done at the start of internationalism with the parent country's staff being qualified to develop the overseas organisation. This is a simplistic model and often one full of dangers. The managers were originally hired and developed for a domestic market with its own particular culture and they could well find it difficult to adjust to their new conditions. It is difficult enough to manage the indigenous staff, let alone expatriates with their additional problems.

Making tracks

EMI Music uses a database system to follow the progress of expatriate executives, such as the British managing directors of its Australian operation.

Adapted from: Sparrow, P. (1999) Abroad minded, *People Management*, 20 May, p43.

If an organisation uses *home country nationals* to manage its overseas business this does help overcome the difficulties of using parent country nationals, yet poses different problems. These could arise as a result of cultural differences or the lack of experience outside their own country – similar to the use of parent country nationals.

The ideal situation is to use the *best regardless* which means hiring the most appropriate person regardless of her/his nationality. This approach is a truly international one and allows the very best to be recruited without the local approach which could stunt growth and development of the organisation. However, it requires the organisation to be running a centralisation strategy and an ethos of risk taking because it is difficult to bring about. However, this strategy is particularly difficult in countries which state that in order for a business to operate in that country, local nationals have to be hired. This policy of discrimination makes globalisation of business even more complicated.

Scullion (1995) found that, while 50 per cent of the organisations which he surveyed did have in place formal policies favouring the hiring of host country nationals to management positions, actually 33 per cent of them did use expatriates to manage their overseas businesses.

STRATEGY FOR MANAGEMENT DEVELOPMENT

Any organisation which wishes to trade internationally has to give thought to how it is going to develop a truly international perspective. This can only really be done by making the best use of the knowledge, skills and talents of all the workers and developing this through the use of, say, international business schools and specialist management development courses ■ *see* Chapter 10 ■.

see Chapter 10

Whatever method is used, it is essential that an organisation concentrates on its international employee development if it is to compete in the world market. The principle of employee development (ED) applies to all employees, yet particular care has to be taken to allow international workers to be effective away from their national or home base ▪ *see* Chapter 10 ▪. Such workers have to be able to manage a quality, multicultural environment which is evolving rapidly in all areas of business.

see Chapter 10

There are three particular areas of ED that need to be addressed, and these are concerned with the increasing complexity of worldwide business:

■ *Cultural diversity*
  Cultural diversity factors and the impact of the different legal, political, social and belief systems of countries and of individuals ▪ *see* Chapter 11 ▪.

see Chapter 11

■ *Training*
  Organisations and their employee representatives need to maintain a dialogue with national government to decide which initiatives are to be centrally controlled and which are to be left to individual organisations ▪ *see* Chapter 1 *and* Chapter 6 ▪.

see Chapter 1 *and* Chapter 6

■ *Competencies*
  Attention needs to be given to the competencies required of managers working in an international environment.

INTERNATIONAL RECRUITMENT

As has been discussed above, it is possible that an organisation will need to recruit staff locally or from people willing to work for parent country branches overseas. The basis is the same as that of 'at-home' recruitment and selection ▪ *see* Chapter 4 ▪. However, there are some particular issues that need to be addressed.

see Chapter 4

JOB DESCRIPTION AND JOB SPECIFICATION

The job description is the key and it should carefully lay out what is required of the potential job holder. Scenario 12.6 gives an example of an advertisement for such a job.

Job descriptions and person specifications need particularly to address the international components of the job and they should give specific attention to the cultural factors required.

RECRUITMENT

Because the finding of staff appropriate for work in an international context is specialised, organisations are better off if they use the services of specialised recruitment agencies and/or consultants who have specific expertise in the area. Such people will be familiar with the market and will be au fait with the local customs, legislation, politics and so on of the country where the individual is to work. The IHRM specialist can be of assistance with some of the selection procedures to

SCENARIO 12.6

Newspaper Sales Manager

Frankfurt, Germany

The Economist is one of the world's leading international newspapers, specialising in business/finance, current affairs and new technologies. Founded in 1843 it has a strong reputation for its independence of ideas and defence of free trade.

Reporting to the European Circulation Director and working closely with the sales, distribution and marketing teams, you will be responsible for developing sales and promoting the Newspaper in Germany and central Europe, dealing with both direct clients and press distributors.

You will need a minimum of 2 years' sales experience preferably in the newsstand sector, and to be fluent in both German and English. Your experience and skills must include written presentations, telesales and face-to-face presenting at all levels.

Please apply in writing with a concise résumé, including current salary details and quoting ref. ENL/CCFF, to Adam Ellis, The Economist Group, Recruitment Office, 15 Regent Street, London SW1Y 4LR, United Kingdom. Email: adamellis@economist.com Fax: 44 (0)20 7839 2338.

The Economist

THE ECONOMIST GROUP

Source: Executive focus (2000), *The Economist*, 11 March, p16.

ensure the appointed individual is happy with the culture of the host organisation for which s/he will work.

INTERVIEWING AND SELECTION

Even if the candidates are being screened for work away from the parent organisation, they should still be interviewed by an executive from the host/parent organisation so that it can be established that the individual is competent to do the job and to ensure that s/he is mobile and has the potential to make a success of what is to be an international career.

As with the recruitment of national, domestic employees, it is imperative that the organisation retains a solid reputation for excellent employment practices because *see* Chapter 4 without this the good people will go elsewhere ■ *see* Chapter 4 ■.

TRANSFERRING OPERATIONS PRACTICES

Because different parts of the world, and hence, different countries, develop their own ways of doing things it is likely that the way in which the businesses are run will differ. For examples, the way of carrying out operations in an organisation in

Japan will differ to those in, say, Scandinavia. To some extent there will be similarities but the differences will comprise the larger part. A key industry in Britain that has experienced these difficulties is car manufacturing where management and manufacturing differences have led to the virtual demise of the industry in the UK.

SCENARIO 12.7

Nordic neighbours embrace the net

'Some pupils have no e-mail address,' scream bold front page headlines as Stockholm commuters scurry about Scandinavia's largest city. It is hardly the kind of headline you would expect to sell papers in most countries but in Sweden – where the Internet is now a national obsession – failure to link all children to the net is causing concern. The mass readership daily means newspapers can regularly splash the latest IT developments across their front pages and be sure of finding an audience and is the result of the huge surge in Internet use. This has turned Swedes into some of the world's most industrious surfers of the web.

High levels of automation in Swedish industry, in part due to high labour costs, have educated the workforce in the use of computers. But since 1998 home use has spearheaded the expansion of the Internet. A change in tax regulations allows employers to provide employees with computers for home use without individuals having to pay tax on them. This led to an explosion in PC sales, which jumped 56 per cent in 1998.

In Finland there is extensive use of the Internet in local schools and universities. There has been a long-standing competition between different telecommunications operators that has made Finland by far the cheapest place in the world to get online. The country also leads the world in the percentage of people using Internet banking. The region's biggest bank, the Finnish–Swedish owned MeritaNordbanken, had over a million Internet customers at the end of 1999, 20 per cent of its customers.

Adapted from: George, N. (2000) Nordic neighbours embrace the net, *Connectis*, March, (2): 54–5.

It is possible to follow the movement and development of how an organisation manages its operations as it responds to the conditions in one country and then see how it is adopted elsewhere worldwide. For example, the use of working practices such as ▶ **just-in-time** ◀ in the car manufacturing industry. Accompanying this was the practice of downsizing with the reduction in staff numbers so that the organisation can be 'lean', that is, there are no excess resources in the organisation. This is particularly true in the motor car industry. Slack et al. (1995) illustrate the progress of car manufacturing across nations as shown in Figure 12.3.

▶ A manufacturing and stock control system in which goods are produced and delivered as ◀······▶ **Just-in-time**
they are required with the purpose of eliminating waste and avoiding the need for the storage of large amounts of stock.

Cars were originally made through craft-based processes. Demand increased so much that it actually exceeded supply and so there was a development into mass production methods by individuals such as Henry Ford in the USA and, through

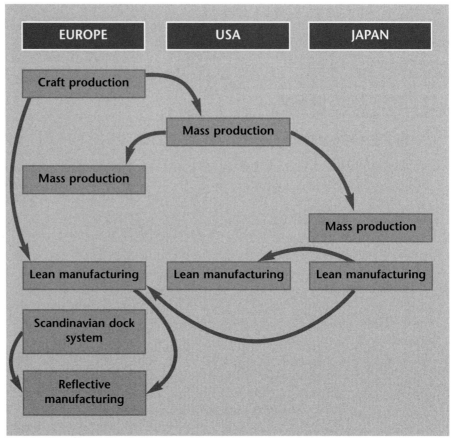

Figure 12.3 The transfer of operations practice in the motor car industry, adapted from Slack et al. (1999, p869)

this, the assembly line method of production came into being. It spread from the USA to Europe and Japan. However, the Japanese were using such management methods as 'just-in-time' and high-performance groups and so there was a further development in the industry which incorporated these methods of manufacturing and management. The methodology transferred back to Europe and the USA yet, particularly in Europe, the original craft-based systems still survived for the specialist market, such as Morgan Cars in Malvern, England. In Scandinavia the ▶ **dock system** ◀ minimises movement of people and parts. Organisations are now combining the economic effects of lean manufacturing with modern team-working and autonomous aspects of docking into a system known as ▶ **reflective manufacturing** ◀.

Dock system ◀┄┄▶	Where the manufacturing area of an industry has a short and fat layout.
Reflective ◀┄┄▶ manufacturing	The amalgamation of the economic efficiency of lean manufacturing with the social ideals of dock manufacturing.

IHRM AS A CAREER

The IPD (1996) published key facts for individuals who wanted to develop an IHRM career with a view to assisting individuals who were contemplating an international role. They highlighted nine different areas of concentration:

■ intercultural effectiveness

■ interpersonal and communications ability

■ language skills

■ managing complexity and diversity

■ flexibility

■ resilience

■ local country employment law and conditions

■ business understanding

■ understanding the international business environment.

MANAGING EXPATRIATES

Even if an IHRM specialist has all the skills outlined above, s/he has the most difficult task of managing expatriates. Theory-in-literature seems to paint a gloomy picture in this area showing that the failure rate of expatriates is high. However, there is a balance as shown in the work of Mendenhall and Oddou (1985) who stated that the failure rate in the case of US nationals between 1965 and 1985 moved between 25 per cent and 40 per cent. However, Scullion (1995) reported a different picture, stating that in a study of 45 British and Irish multinational organisations 90 per cent of organisations were satisfied with the overall activities of their expatriate managers. A more detailed investigation into these two studies would probably need to look into the difference in the time period and nature of the culture of the parent countries, in order to give a more detailed comparison. Suffice it to say that British multinational organisations appear to have lower expatriate failure rates than US organisations.

Scullion (1995) suggested that there were possible reasons for this difference in experience, pointing out that British multinationals had:

■ very effective HRM policies relating specifically to expatriates

■ taken care in the recruitment and selection of expatriates

■ placed a high value on workers with existing international experience

■ managers who were less parochial in their outlook than US managers.

It seemed that the British multinationals gave specific attention to the areas of recruitment and selection, preparation of individuals for their overseas placement, individual development and help when they return to the parent organisation in their home country.

HRM AND EUROPE

With the increase in globalisation and IHRM, it is essential that individuals have a thorough understanding of the political, economic and social policy of the European Union (EU) which is a unique, treaty-based, institutional framework that defines and manages economic and political cooperation among its European member countries. The EU is the latest stage in a process of integration begun in the 1950s by six countries – France, Germany, Italy, the Netherlands, Belgium and Luxembourg – whose leaders signed the original treaties establishing various forms of European integration. These treaties gave life and substance to the new concept that, by creating communities of shared sovereignty in matters of coal and steel production, trade and nuclear energy, another European war would be untenable. While the EU has evolved common policies in a number of other sectors since then, the fundamental goal of the EU remains the same: to create an ever-closer union among the peoples of Europe.

Due largely to the success of Europe's economic integration, there are 15 member states:

Austria	Germany	Netherlands
Belgium	Greece	Portugal
Denmark	Ireland	Spain
Finland	Italy	Sweden
France	Luxembourg	UK.

Membership is likely to increase to more than 20 with each one at different stages in their application.

For more than 3000 years, Central Asia and the Caucasus have been at the crossroads of civilisations. Now, freed from Soviet tutelage, they face the considerable task of restoring their identity, stability and economic growth. The Eurasia Economic summit held in 2000 looked at how they could assert themselves in the 21st century and onwards. The summit focused on Eurasia's core countries, from countries in Central Asia:

Kazakhastan	Tajikistan	Uzbekistan
Kyrgyzstan	Turkmenistan	

to those in the Caucasus:

Armenia	Azerbaijan	Georgia.

Close attention was paid also to the surrounding countries such as China, Iran, Russia and Turkey which all play key roles in determining the fate of the core countries – most of which wish to become members of the EU.

The EU plays a greater role in world affairs than it has ever done. With the collapse of communism in central and eastern Europe and the former Soviet Union, the EU was presented with new challenges and responsibilities on its doorstep. Far-reaching economic and political changes in other world regions call for new European responses. In the meantime, deeper EU integration over the last ten years has given the EU new statutory responsibilities in world affairs.

From its start, the EU (originally the European Community) had wide powers for shaping its trade relations with the outside world. It also undertook development aid and technical assistance programmes, initially in the former colonies and dependencies of member states and subsequently throughout the developing world.

Over the years, the EU has created a dense network of international agreements and relationships whose purpose extends well beyond the development of commercial ties and cooperation. These remain at the centre of the many ▶ **bilateral** ◀ and ▶ **multilateral** ◀ agreements that have been signed, but they have also launched regular high-level political contacts with many countries, cooperation between organisations and industries, as well as investment promotion and cultural exchanges.

▶ Involving or carried out by two groups, especially the political representatives of two ◀┈┈▶ **Bilateral**
countries.

▶ Involving or carried out by a number of groups, especially the political representatives of ◀┈┈▶ **Multilateral**
several countries.

The EU has always been a strong advocate of free trade and EU customs on industrialised goods are among the lowest in the world. The EU's capacity to play a leadership role in global negotiations to liberalise world trade over the last 35 years has been crucially shaped by its common commercial policy. They have had to speak with one voice during all the most important developments in international trade over the last 35 years and other countries have listened.

WORLD TRADE ORGANIZATION (WTO)

The EU has negotiated a series of trade packages under the General Agreement on Tariffs and Trade (GATT), most recently the Uruguay Round, which was implemented in 1995 and included the creation of the WTO ■ *see* Chapter 11 ■. The EU is implementing another round of liberalisation at the start of the 21st century while also taking the lead with the USA in helping to forge global agreements to liberalise telecommunications, financial services and technology trade (e-commerce). One of its key activities was to take on China as a member. There has been a decisive turn in the Chinese government's economic reform. During its fourth plenary session in September 1999, the Central Committee of the Communist Party relinquished the need for the state to dominate all sectors of the economy. This move, made in the face of possible high unemployment and growing social tension, indicates more than

see Chapter 11

ever the state's firm belief that China's continued growth and development depend on all forms of enterprise ownership, including private ownership, playing significant roles in the economy.

QUADRILATERAL TALKS

The EU meets with the USA, Canada and Japan to discuss trade problems and often to pave the way for global liberalisation, in the annual quadrilaterals, initiated in 1981.

Canada

Links between Europe and Canada have traditionally been very close. Bilateral trade exceeds $21bn and the EU is the second most popular destination for Canadian foreign investment after the USA. In 1976 a commercial and economic agreement, the first with an industrialised country, established mechanisms for cooperation in areas such as trade, industry and science. A Declaration on EU–Canada Relations, laying down the principles and framework for consultation and cooperation, was adopted in November 1990. There are also agreements on nuclear cooperation and medical research.

Japan

This relationship has been dominated for many years by the EU's trade deficit with Japan. Japan exports to Europe almost 50 per cent more than Europe exports to Japan. While keeping up the pressure on Japan to remove non-tariff barriers, the EU has also sought to deepen and extend cooperation beyond the field of trade. A joint Declaration on EU–Japan Relations in 1991 lists shared objectives in the political and economic fields and establishes a consultation framework including annual meetings between the presidents of the European Council and the European Commission and the competition policy, development assistance, environmental policy, industrial policy, industrial cooperation, macroeconomics and financial affairs and transport.

COOPERATION WITH DEVELOPING AND NEWLY INDUSTRIALISED COUNTRIES

The EU is strongly committed to providing aid and technical assistance for economic development. The EU member states are now by far the largest aid donors in the world. Trade relations are characterised by the Generalised System of Preferences (GSP) under which developing countries are allowed duty-free exports of a large range of finished and part-finished goods to the EU.

African, Caribbean and Pacific (ACP) countries

Under the Fourth Lomé Convention aid from the EU and its member states amounted to $15 billion for 1990–95 and will approach $19 billion for 1996–2000. The Lomé Convention, which links the EU to 70 African, Caribbean, and Pacific (ACP) countries, creates a stable legal framework for development cooperation involving negotiations between equal partners. It provides permanent dialogue through common institutions in which the ACP states act as a group. The Convention frees ACP countries from customs duties on 99.5 per cent of their exports to the EU, with no reciprocal concessions for EU exports. It has also set up systems for the stabilisation of export earnings (STABEX) and to help the ACP countries maintain their mineral export potential.

Asia

EU policy is embodied in a set of recommendations intended to stimulate a more coordinated, proactive strategy, published by the European Commission under the title *Towards a New Asia Policy* (1994) and endorsed by the European Council at Essen in December 1994. The priorities are to:

■ strengthen Europe's economic presence in the Asian market, assist former state-trading Asian countries to embark on economic reforms and promote scientific cooperation

■ generate political dialogue to bring Asian countries into the international community, control the proliferation of nuclear and chemical weapons and promote respect for human rights

■ combat poverty and improve primary education, healthcare and the environment.

The first 25-nation summit between EU and Asian leaders was held in Bangkok in 1996 to help implement the new strategy and broaden economic and political relations. A second summit was held in London, England in 1998 and the third was in the Republic of Korea in 2000. The EU is at the forefront of international efforts to resolve the Asian financial crisis and Europe's role increased after the euro was launched in 1999.

China

At the end of 1995 the EU issued guidelines for a strategy emphasising the importance of the smooth and gradual integration of China into the world economy. The strategy also included the promotion of democracy, structures based on the rule of law and respect for human rights. The legal framework for commercial relations and a programme of cooperation and development are provided by a cooperation agreement signed in 1985.

Association of South East Asian Nations (ASEAN)

A cooperation agreement covering trade, economic and development matters was signed in 1980 with the ASEAN countries – Brunei, Indonesia, Malaysia, the Philippines, Singapore and Thailand.

Latin and Central America

The EU is a leading trading partner and source of development aid to Latin and Central America. Taking 20 per cent of the region's exports, it has trade and economic cooperation agreements with several Latin and Central American countries and has instituted political dialogues to promote democracy, peace and economic development in Central and South America. In December 1995 it signed a framework agreement on trade and economic cooperation with Argentina, Brazil, Paraguay and Uruguay (Mercosur) for cooperation on science and technology, the environment, energy and telecommunications and to liberalise trade through dialogue on customs duties, market access, technical standards and rules of origin. The Mercosur region has 250 million consumers and $1000 billion worth of services and goods. With its associate members Bolivia and Chile it has the potential to rank third among the world's trading blocs and to be the first integrated market of the emerging economies. However, in 1999 the consequences of the Asian crisis and the devaluation of the real had a negative impact on the South American economies. In 1998 a trade cooperation agreement was signed with Mexico.

THE EUROPEAN SOCIAL CHAPTER

see Chapter 7 *and* Chapter 8

The role of the EU and workplace legislation has been discussed in ■ Chapter 7 *and* Chapter 8 ■. The position of HRM and the EU has been researched by a number of writers (for example Lockhart and Brewster, 1992, and Addison and Stanley Siebert, 1991) each of whom have made a useful contribution to the debate.

SCENARIO 12.8

Global business: *Manager* on Franco–German relations

All is not well in the Franco–German marriage. It is clear that if Paris and Bonn fall out, Europe's wheels stop turning. Germany should demonstrate commitment to their neighbours. Talking alone about a *ménage à trois* with the UK, without considering whether the Brits would sign up to such an agreement, was foolish. Dasa boss Manfred Bischoff could have warned Germany of the perils of ignoring the French. He tried to form an alliance with BAe [British Aerospace], without talking to the French, only to see the deal of the century slip from his grasp as BAe went off with Marconi. The British would have felt more comfortable if the Germans and the French had been side by side, not hinting at some future 'transatlantic alternative'. Germany's commitment to France must remain deep and strong.

Adapted from: Global business – *Manager* magazine on Franco–German relations, *Management Today*, August 1999, p23.

It is in the area of the social framework where the foundations for IHRM have been laid and this has been done for member nations of the EU through the European Social Chapter. This is a Chapter of the Maastricht Treaty on the European Union (1991) that relates to social policy. It required EU member states to adopt common social policies and was intended to implement the Community Chapter of the Fundamental Social Rights of Workers, adopted by 11 EU member states, but opposed by the British Prime Minister (Margaret Thatcher), at a summit meeting in Strasbourg in December 1989. In the face of continued UK opposition, member states were given freedom of choice over whether or not to adopt it: only the UK declined to sign up to it. However, the Labour government, led by Tony Blair, signed it in May 1997 having come out against any extension of EU laws that impair the competitive edge of UK producers.

The Chapter was originally proposed by the European Commissioner for Social Affairs and Employment (Vasso Papandreou) and presented at a summit meeting in Madrid in June 1989. At this event, the then British Prime Minister – Margaret Thatcher – described it as a 'socialist charter' believing that the European employment Directives damaged the flexibility of the UK labour market. The Institute of Directors claimed that the Social Chapter would mean increased power and influence for trades unions, higher business costs, more regulations and a loss of jobs. Rights to be guaranteed by it included:

- free movement throughout the EU

- equitable remuneration

- a maximum number of hours per working week

- free association in trades unions and collective bargaining

- professional training

- sex equality

- minimum health and security provision

- employer–employee consultation and participation

- a minimum working age of 16

- minimum pension rights

- protection for disabled workers.

In 1991 Margaret Thatcher's successor, John Major, spoke out against the Social Chapter (which embodied Papandreou's original Charter) and, after a prolonged debate, persuaded the other 11 leaders to make it an optional clause within the final version of the Maastricht Treaty, allowing member states to adopt it individually. It was on this basis that the British government finally ratified the Maastricht Treaty.

Social policy has taken a more important role as EU nations have deepened their economic integration. This has been controversial for the UK – not least because many business organisations argue that the European social legislation imposes unwelcome extra costs on employers with negative effects on job creation. However, it is becoming obvious that structural social problems within the EU caused by high unemployment and rising inequality must be given increasing priority. The newly established ▷ **Social Fund** ◁ will be an important vehicle for addressing these difficulties.

Social Fund ◀┈▶ A fund set up as part of the British social security system, from which people in need may receive money as a grant or loan for a specified purpose.

There is still debate on the issue of the Social Chapter, as it tends to be linked to the issue of labour markets and the movement of labour. A search of the literature shows that there is little discourse on the actual influence on organisations. The key works seem to be:

- Wood and Peccei (1990)

- Pricewaterhouse Cranfield Project (1991)

- Leblanc (1994).

Wood and Peccei (1990)

The research carried out by Wood and Peccei centred on the HRM needs for organisations who wished to trade within the Single European Market (SEM) – now known as the EU. The results indicated that most organisations did not think that there was any difficulty and where difficulties did erupt they were not considered to be critical. The organisations that had an active HRM strategy were those organisations which were already active within the EU, although they tended to be separate to the corporate strategy and, being 'add-ons', were often considered to be of less importance than domestic strategies.

Pricewaterhouse Cranfield Project (1991)

This was a major research project and one still used to assess the decision-making process related to organisational influences. The research team at Cranfield surveyed the human resource initiatives in business organisations across ten European countries. While organisations were concerned about the SEM, they had very few strategies in place to deal with human resource issues. While they seemed to have come to terms with the issues of the Social Chapter, they did not attend to putting together a specific HRM strategy – as part of the organisation's overall strategy or, even, as an add-on ■ *see* Chapter 2 ■. They seemed to be policies on organisational aspects already part of most organisation's strategy, such as health and safety and equal opportunities but this was because they were part of national legislation ■ *see* Chapter 7 *and* Chapter 8 ■.

see Chapter 2

see Chapter 7 *and* Chapter 8

However, the Pricewaterhouse Cranfield Project (1991) did find that there were common trends in HRM appearing in European organisations relating to HRM. The strongest one was the decentralisation of the HRM role to line managers especially in the areas of recruitment and selection and employee development ■ *see* Chapter 1 ■. However, there were still activities that had remained in the hands of the centre, such as pay negotiations and employee relationships. The study did report, however, that change was in the offing with organisations recognising that EU Directives would bring about centralisation for member countries ■ *see* Chapter 7 *and* Chapter 8 ■.

see Chapter 1

see Chapter 7 *and* Chapter 8

Leblanc (1994)

In 1991 a group of directors of human resources in European organisations banded together in an attempt to:

> identify the specific competencies required for companies to develop in Europe in the context of the Single Market. (p72)

They wanted to increase their understanding of the European market and the management of human resources. They identified and clarified the specific competencies that organisations and their managers needed to distinguish between those organisations which used expatriates and those which did not. That is, the competencies required when the organisation reached one or more of the stages in the organisation process. They identified three broad stages (Table 12.2) in what they called the 'internationalisation process', finding that each one also corresponded to a strategic choice of how to develop in Europe.

Table 12.2 The three stages in the European organisation process (after Leblanc, 1994, p73)

STAGE ONE – First Landings
■ strong national/domestic base
■ wants to enter the European market for the first time
■ gains a few acquisitions in different European countries
■ focuses on being successful in the preparation, implementation and management of these 'foreign' acquisitions

STAGE TWO – Go Native
■ well-established in Europe
■ uses a network of branches and subsidiaries
■ branches and subsidiaries have autonomy for day-to-day management
■ human resource policies encourage more national managers in each subsidiary
■ expatriate general manager responsible for medium and long-term career development of the high-calibre members of her/his local staff

STAGE THREE – Integration
■ truly European
■ has manufacturing facilities and a commercial presence throughout Europe
■ believes national boundaries must give way to a European perspective
■ seeks to organise and pursue its development on a continental basis
■ develops a pan-European strategy within a global one
■ generates awareness of a global policy within the organisation and finds practical ways of implementing it

Leblanc (1994) identified different competencies which were required at each of the three stages stating that:

> when it comes to real integration, European competencies of individual managers are not enough. The company needs to integrate European competencies at its different levels, and in its different areas of activity. (p79)

Leblanc (1994) also stated that:

> It is top management's responsibility to advocate and push through European goals and objectives and the role of he human resources function in developing the corresponding competencies are critical. (p79)

He believed that there were three key tasks which are shown in Table 12.3.

As part of the study, Leblanc (1994) and his team reviewed existing research in the area and found that the HRM function lagged behind the other management functions, such as sales, production and finance, when organisations set about developing a European perspective. Things had not changed since the early reviews of 1991 discussed above. Leblanc (1994) felt that by implementing certain recommendations, given in Table 12.4, human resources would be able to contribute to successful Europeanisation.

The developments within Europe since the Pricewaterhouse Cranfield Project (1991) appear to show that this centralisation has taken place and it could, therefore, be suggested that the initiatives and Directives of the EU have affected HRM within organisations and dictated the nature of organisational policies in that area. *see* Chapter 7 *and* Chapter 8 However, this could well be because of European legislation ■ *see* Chapter 7 *and* Chapter 8 ■. Beardwell and Holden (1997) suggest that:

> the reality seems to be that organisations are still more influenced by their own particular markets and global trends in HRM rather than by regional initiatives. (p735)

see Chapter 11 It is from the USA and Japan that trends have emerged to be adopted by European countries but the latter have adapted them to fit in with local factors such as organisational size, employment relations arrangements and geographical distribution of the organisation's market ■ *see* Chapter 11 ■.

TRANSITION ORGANISATIONS IN EASTERN AND CENTRAL EUROPE

Organisations in eastern and central Europe faced an unprecedented change in business conditions when the Soviet-dominated communist government fell. New managers were faced with daunting challenges to manage their organisations through the transition from central planning to competition. They had to change their organisations radically so that they would become capable of competing effectively in what was a very different type of market.

Newman (1998) analysed six longitudinal organisational cases and identified the key skills that the new managers needed and from where they were able to obtain those skills. She found that the seeds of current managerial expertise could often

Table 12.3 Implications for training and development (after Leblanc, 1994, p79)

Recruitment

- develop a European recruitment policy
- favour mobile, multilingual candidates
- develop selection procedures which identify European integration skills and behaviours

Career management

- systematically build expatriate experience into career development programmes
- centralise career planning information
- give national personnel functions European responsibilities in this area

Communication

- communicate the European integration message
- explain the importance of mobility for the organisation to achieve its integration goal

Table 12.4 Human resources that could contribute to successful Europeanisation, (after Leblanc, 1994, pp79–80)

- The skills and capabilities requirements of companies differ according to the stage of European development. They also differ according to the mode of European development – ownership of foreign subsidiaries or alliances, partnerships and joint ventures.

- There is a real need to develop training programmes focused around:
    - discovering the diversity of an organisation's national environments (economic, social, cultural) and developing the ability to tolerate and take into account that diversity in the fulfilling of individual organisational responsibilities
    - understanding the meaning and implications of developing and managing from a pan-European perspective rather than on a nation-by-nation basis
    - organising for transnational/European-wide work and cooperation
    - managing pluricultural teams
    - developing European strategies and organisations

  Training groups should include participants of different nationalities and facilitators from different countries. This helps the one-on-one or on-the-job programmes to develop internally.

- There is a clear need to redefine the organisation of the HRM function within organisations at a European level. Discussions between organisations with similar development objectives would be useful in moving this process forward.

be found in experiences under central planning, despite the fact that central planning more generally rewarded behaviours that were counterproductive in market-based competition.

In her discussion and conclusions, Newman (1998) notes that her data suggest that there are four leadership qualities for the managers under their new conditions which she lists as:

- strategic thinking
- willingness to make decisions
- willingness to take the initiative
- ability to manage costs. (p318)

As discussed earlier in this chapter, this is similar to the leadership qualities required from managers in the west. However, such qualities are lacking in the transition economies because of the nature of the structure of central planning. However, this does not mean that the skills cannot be found – not least in their emerging form. In the 1990s there was an acceleration in how top managers learned:

- requisite skills and abilities
- relevant role models
- constructive business partners
- rigours of the marketplace.

Newman (1998) contrasts this with the situation prior to 1990, as shown in Figure 12.4.

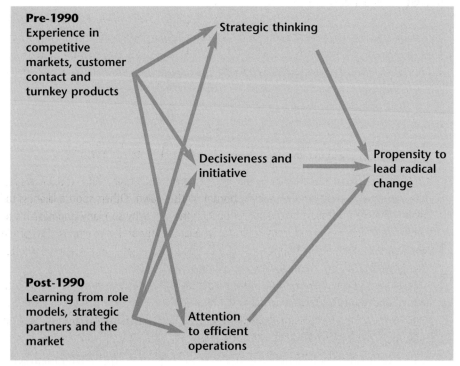

Figure 12.4 Leading radical organisational change in transition economies, after Newman (1998, p319)

Organisations in the transition areas are going through conditions of radical institutional change. They are also faced with changes in their competitive markets. With these two major changes, organisations are looking for new top management talent from whatever sources they can. However, these new managers must have knowledge that is relevant to the new business conditions in which the organisations find themselves. While the predictors given in Figure 12.4 are not universal, they have been found by Newman (1998) to be 'important and powerful in the generation after the change in governments' (p319). As central planning has become more and more dissipated in the transition organisations of eastern and central Europe, the predictors will become more varied and there will be more ways by which managers can become successful.

This has been supported by Garavan et al. (1998) who carried out research on strategic HRM in Poland. Their work suggested that HRM was very underdeveloped in Poland because:

> The communist system was not conducive to the growth of personnel activities, so there was significant ground to be made up. (p209)

The researchers found little evidence that Polish organisations adopt HRM as generally understood by those organisations that developed outside a command economy, for example the UK, the USA, Japan and Australia. However, Polish firms are trying to develop an HRM approach to the running of their businesses although, like western organisations, there is a difficulty in actually deciding what strategic HRM actually is ■ *see* Chapter 2 ■.

see Chapter 2

As a consequence, developments in Poland have been haphazard and managers have suffered considerable stress as a result of their post-command situation. As in other post-command countries, the approach to HRM is still entrenched in decades of personnel practices which concentrated on pure administration rather than decision making.

SCENARIO 12.9

Past the border into gnome man's land

It started as a tiny cottage industry, but gnomes are now big business along Germany's border with Poland. They can be found by the border post on the Polish side of the main road from Berlin to Szczecin. Whole armies of grinning hobgoblins and cherubic elves line both sides of the highway.

Stallholders do a roaring trade. 'They sell much better than wicker baskets or fizzy drinks,' said one trader. 'Gorbachev gnomes attract gardeners with an interest in world affairs.' One stall specialises in Helmut Kohl gnomes, some of which are as bulky as the original and would leave little room on a modest lawn. Others sport a likeness to Tony Blair.

Why so many gnomes? It's to do with the cost of labour: Polish workers can produce the hand-painted end result at a fraction of the cost of German gnome makers.

Meanwhile, in an apparently separate development, 32 stolen gnomes were found in a forest near Brussels. Police suspect the Belgian Garden Gnomes Liberation Front, given the message attached to several of them: 'I am free.'

Source: Foster, N. (2000) Big money, little people, the business, *Financial Times Weekend*, 26 February, p10.

There is evidence that strategic HRM issues is one of the paths and organisations in eastern and central Europe can benefit from the expertise of the IHRM specialist at the start-up of their major changes and thus be in more of an advantageous position than those attempting to 'add on' IHRM to an existing organisational strategy ■ *see* Chapter 2 ■.

see Chapter 2

HRM AND THE USA

It was in the USA that HRM, as it is known and recognised in the contemporary world, was conceived, even though it might generally be thought that the practices of HRM were imported from Japan. While both countries were putting HRM theories into practice, the issues were published internationally by the University of Harvard, USA, in their ubiquitous journal *Harvard Business Review* which has supported HRM as a discipline in its own right and given it both an academic and practical place in the business world.

SCENARIO 12.10

Global business: *Le Point* on America's Gulliver complex

America's global dominance as a superpower is unprecedented. In the last year of the century, the US has reeled off its ninth consecutive year of growth, in contrast to old Europe emerging joylessly from its welfare-state cocoon. But the US, deep down, mistrusts the old quarrelsome and ungrateful continent. They see Europe as all style and no substance. Right until the last moment they didn't think the euro would work. Like Gulliver, America is getting cross with the European Lilliputians.

They're pushing the Europeans around, not least at the WTO in the banana and hormone-stuffed beef wars. They've made the world in their own image with their advertisements, jeans, Disney and jazz and they're doing it again with the English language, on the Internet. But it's time for Europeans to stop whining about these problems. Only a truly united Europe will be prosperous enough to defend its legitimate identity.

Adapted from: Global business – *Le Point* on America's Gulliver complex, *Management Today*, May 1999, p27.

APPROACH TO HRM IN THE USA

HRM in the USA can be said to be based on an individualistic approach in that it concentrates on the individual worker and how s/he is concerned with such issues as:

■ using initiative

■ taking personal responsibility

■ selection, recruitment and career advancement on merit

■ loyalty to the parent organisation.

The employer, in contrast, is willing and able to dismiss those workers who do not perform to the standards set by their employers. This balance of responsibility and shared interest is brought about by a concentration on issues such as motivation with its accompanying rewards and remuneration ■ *see* Chapter 9 ■. The communication methods in US organisations, unlike those in most transition economies, are open and relatively informal, being based on interpersonal relationships and the development of a strong and owned organisational culture ■ *see* Chapter 5 ■.

see Chapter 9

see Chapter 5

However, the backbone of US HRM is the issue of strategy because organisations closely link their external strategies for competing in the global marketplace with the internal needs of the domestic, national organisational activities.

ATTRACTION OF HRM IN THE USA

Texts concentrating on how individuals behave in organisations, for example Maund (1999), include in their discussions the foundations of HRM as it developed in the USA through:

■ scientific management (Taylor, 1911)

■ human relations approach (Mayo, 1920s/Hawthorne Studies)

■ organic theories (Burns and Stalker, 1961).

Scientific management (Taylor, 1911)

The work of the founding father of scientific management, Frederick Taylor (1911), was based on a relatively simple model of management, that of 'rational economic man'. This model looked at goals and extrinsic factors as the key to motivating workers to produce more. It suggested that if individuals were given:

■ a precisely defined set of tasks

■ a clear set of objectives and

■ the extrinsic driver of increasing economic rewards related to performance

they would calculate the benefits of improving their output and their productivity would rise.

The only barrier would be the limitations imposed by the processes and the resources available and the capability of the workers to do the jobs. Conversely, the threat of removing such economic rewards would serve as a way of punishing and correcting low productivity.

As Taylor (1911) discovered, workers did not, in practice, respond in the way that the scientific model predicted because it was shown that the driver of economic reward was not sufficient to improve performance. He did, however, identify the key ingredients in the model, which were clearly defined tasks and objectives backed by some sort of reward structure and these are all key HRM concepts in the 21st century. Thus, the scientific model defined the fit between HRM policies and organisational strategy. The work of Taylor (1911) is discussed in detail in ■ Chapter 1 ■.

see Chapter 1

Human relations approach (Mayo, 1920s/Hawthorne Studies)

This view was based on the Hawthorne Studies carried out in the 1920s which suggested that favourable attitudes in employees result in the motivation to work even harder and thus raise productivity. Such a view posited that individuals are motivated by things other than money – probably by social interaction. It was assumed that if an individual was satisfied with her/his job, production and performance would rise. However, the approach proved not to have answers for the many questions that it raised.

Organic theories (Burns and Stalker, 1961)

There have been a large number of studies carried out in the area of the organisational environment which document the movement from the mechanistic organisation to the organic, but particularly Burns and Stalker (1961). A mechanistic organisation comprises one that uses a system of organisation characterised by bureaucratic systems encompassing roles, regulations, a clear hierarchical pattern of authority and centralised decision making. It is the classic bureaucratic organisation with a well-defined division of labour and is more often found in a stable environment within, usually, the principles of scientific management.

With the nature of the current markets being global and competitive, it is argued that organisations must be able to be reactive – preferably proactive – if they are to remain in business. Therefore ▶ **organic organisations** ◀ tend to do better than mechanistic ones. They are characterised by less rigid structures and are better able to deal with problem solving and decision making.

Organic ◀┈┈▶ A system of organisation that has free-flowing systems with adaptive processes, unclear
organisation   authority hierarchy and where decision making is decentralised.

Since HRM concentrates on the management of change in a rapidly evolving business environment, it is the organic organisation that tends to utilise modern methods of HRM management such as empowerment and cell groups.

SPREAD OF IDEAS AND TECHNIQUES IN THE USA

HRM became actively popular with managers in the USA and, although this might well have started simply by a change of name from 'personnel management' to 'human resource management', from the 1960s they developed it beyond this by using management techniques associated with HRM such as ▶ **quality circles** ◀ and cell structures ■ *see* Chapter 1 ■.

see Chapter 1

> ► An organisational system that attempts to empower individuals by allowing them to meet ◄·····► **Quality circle**
> periodically to discuss any concerns that they have and to assess solutions to meet the
> problem.

There are a number of key areas where the USA has individualised the HRM concepts:

■ employment legislation

■ cultural influences

■ employment relations

■ increase in globalisation

■ growth in bureaucracy

■ reduced growth in the home economy.

Employment legislation

As in the EU, the USA increased its legislation relating to fairness in the workplace to ensure that US organisations provided fair employment practices. With litigation being the norm in the USA, this made managers ensure that they were aware of, and practised, legislative issues in order to avoid expensive court cases.

The USA also practices a policy which is termed 'employment at will' which means that US organisations can hire and fire whoever they want to so long as it is within the remit of each individual's terms of employment. Consequently, except in unionised organisations, collective bargaining has given way to individual, often short-term contracts which have reduced the bargaining power of the workers. Most organisations in the USA have short-term contracts which are reviewed by both the employer and the employee every two to three years.

Cultural influences

The issue of culture and work diversity has been discussed in ■ Chapter 11 ■. The   *see* **Chapter 11**
USA has a tradition of being ethnically diverse and multidenominational. The USA is a vast country, extending from the Atlantic Ocean in the east to the Pacific Ocean in the west, bounded to the north by Canada and to the south by Mexico, and including the outlying states of Alaska and Hawaii. Its land mass is twice that of the EU countries combined with a total population of around 250 million. This means that the country has a diverse climate with its associate conditions.

The USA has two levels of legislation (federal and state) and, therefore, the employment legislation and practices differ among its 50 states and many of these impinge on HRM.

As in most parts of Europe and, particularly the EU, it is market forces that determine the economy of the USA and (with the exception of the defence and defence-related industries) there is strong and active competition. Because the country has experienced large numbers of organisations going out of business and engaging in mergers and takeovers, the workers are willing, prepared and adaptable to change and, therefore, the workforce is more mobile than other countries, such as Britain. The economic base of the country is also built up from migrants from numerous other countries, which has meant that the workforce is diversely skilled and any glitches in, say, demographic downturns have been compensated for by immigration. The USA also has a workforce composed of younger people than either Europe taken as a whole or Japan and while this might mean a greater ability to be mobile, for example, it will bring problems as these workers leave the workforce and retire at the same time bringing with it the difficulties experienced in Britain, for example, a 'grey population' that needs financing.

Employment relations

see Chapter 9

The USA has maintained collective bargaining to some extent at organisational level and US trades unions tend to have a wider area of influence than do unions in western Europe. The USA has a history of negotiating the fringe benefits for employees ■ *see* Chapter 9 ■. However, there are some industries and businesses in the USA that avoid having any union representation within their sectors and there has been a history of activity to ensure that trade union representation – or any employee representation – is kept out. Graham and Bennett (1998) document some measures that have been used with the intention of preventing trade union involvement in an organisation and these are given in Table 12.5.

Increase in globalisation

see Chapter 11

The issue of globalisation was discussed in ■ Chapter 11 ■. The USA has found that the increase in international competition has weakened its competitive status in

Table 12.5 Some measures used in the USA to prevent trade union involvement in organisations (after Graham and Bennett, 1998, p387)

■ *Use of the legal framework*
All labour and employment matters are referred to an organisation's lawyers which means that all issues have to be discussed with a lawyer rather than a line manager.

■ *Intimidation*
The identification and intimidation of those workers who support union philosophy and activity.

■ *Dismissal*
The unfair and unlawful sacking of trade union representatives because the employer knows that the incurred fines and compensation to the affected individuals will be lower than the effects of having a unionised workforce.

■ *The USA National Labour Relations Board (NLRB)*
This is a federal body that compels all employers to bargain with trades unions on a number of issues. Some employers encourage non-union employees of unionised businesses to file derecognition petitions with the NLRB with the aim of deunionising the whole organisation.

certain areas, such as the steel industry and car manufacturing. Because of this, the country has utilised further its HRM skills. This increase in international competition has been particularly evident with regard to the competitive success of Japan – discussed below. It seemed to the USA that Japan was better able than they themselves were to manage their workforces to retain global advantage.

Growth in bureaucracy

There was a tendency, particularly before the downsizing and delayering exercises of the 1990s, for US organisations to be very large and complex. This brought about more mechanistic management techniques which, in turn, were very costly in financial terms. Something foreign to the nature of the US workforce was also introduced, a barrier between the individual and the organisation for which s/he worked. This had a knock-on effect in that it reduced each individual's perception and appreciation on what the competitive pressures were on the organisation.

Reduced growth in the US economy

In the early and mid-1980s the US economy took a downturn and although in the early 21st century it is more buoyant, a slower growth has meant that the existing, well-practised methods of recruitment, selection, remuneration and reward were discarded. For example, there were limited promotion opportunities.

HRM in US organisations today

During the 1970s and early 80s, the developments in HRM in the USA tended towards the adoption of techniques which generated employee commitment, such as empowerment, rewards and teamworking. However, with the downsizing of the 1990s and the perception that there are fewer workers having to do even more for no extra reward has come a workforce that is less committed and increasingly disloyal. But, these aspects do not concern the employers because they do not perceive a change in their business success, feeling that when the labour market is weak, any disaffected workers have nowhere else to go. Also, the weakened powers of the trades unions in the collective bargaining arena have favoured the employer. Having downsized the middle management, the employers are receiving new entrants whose expectations – and demands – are less than those of previous workers. However, with the coming of the knowledge worker, there is a disaster waiting to happen. What is evident, however, is that the 'commitment-based worker' is gone, with employees being more exposed to the forces of external markets upon their organisations.

HRM IN THE FAR EAST AND AUSTRALASIA

Japan (in Japanese, Nippon) is a liberal-democratic country in north-east Asia composed of a group of islands, the four main ones being Hokkaido, Honshu, Kyushu and Shikoku, comprising 377 535 square kilometres and 125 351 000 people. Japan is situated between the Sea of Japan which is to the west and the north Pacific to the east and is to the east of North and South Korea. The geological variety of the country – mountainous and volcanic – tends to dictate its resources of coal, iron, zinc, copper, natural gas and (because it comprises over 1000 islands) fish. Its expertise lies in the key industries of motor vehicles, steel, machinery, electrical and electronic equipment, chemicals and textiles. Exports comprise motor vehicles, electronic goods and components, chemicals, iron and steel products, scientific and optical equipment.

Japan trades principally with the USA, exporting over 27 per cent of their finished products, and importing over 22 per cent from the USA – in the form of mineral fuels, foodstuffs, live animals, bauxite, iron ore, copper ore, coking coal, chemicals, textiles and wood.

It was after the Second World War (1938–45) that Japan began to become prominent in the global economy and thus opened itself to inspection by other countries concerning the way it managed its industrialised economy. Japan increased its trade value throughout the following years and despite political uncertainty in 1993–97 reached record trade surplus levels in 1992 and 1993, yet remaining in recession until the end of 1995. With the annual gross domestic product (GDP) growing to over 5 per cent in June 1996, the Bank of Japan officially announced the end of its long recession. However, in November 1997 Japan faced its biggest corporate failure since 1945, following the collapse of the country's fourth largest stockbroker (Yamaichi Securities). Yamaichi announced that it was closing down with debts of about £15 billion. The brokerage employed 7500 people at 117 domestic branches and more than 30 branches outside Japan.

SCENARIO 12.11

How much? Tokyo – no place for fruit fans

Our proud English nation took another body blow last week, when the latest *Lonely Planet* guide insisted that food in London was hugely overpriced. Prices were compared with Tokyo, traditionally the most expensive of the guide's capitals.

The results offered, at best, a partial triumph for London. The comparison was least favourable for Japanese staples such as rice and noodles (sushi rice: England: £2.50, Japan: £1.25) and there was little disparity between most household basics. Only in exotic fruits, such as the mango, did London start to look cheaper (England: 95p, Japan: £1.25). Finally, however, the one true tie-breaker emerged – the humble melon. To the English it is just another fruit, to the Japanese, this ball of fructose goodness, admittedly gift-wrapped from somewhere like the prestigious Kinyo Kunja store, represents an investment of at least £40.

Adapted from: How much?, the business, *Financial Times*, 19–20 February 2000, p8.

APPROACH TO HRM IN JAPAN

The western interest in Japan has come about because of close trading and has thus highlighted the key Japanese working practice interest in:

- employment for life/commitment

- payment by seniority

- quality and flexibility.

SCENARIO 12.12

Young Japanese losing interest in lifelong relationship with one employer

At 0900 sharp on Monday 3 April 2000, 550 new employees of NEC, the Japanese electronics company, bowed deeply and then burst into the company song.

The recruits, wearing nearly identical navy and grey suits, were among the one million Japanese starting work that week. For decades, such ceremonies have marked the beginning of a lifelong relationship between a Japanese company and its employees.

No longer. More than 20 per cent of high school seniors and about 18 per cent of university students failed to find jobs this year – both the highest levels ever, according to a recent government study. Nearly two-thirds of recent graduates leave their first company after four or five years, according to Recruit, the leading job search agency.

'The employment system is dead,' says Junichi Ishikawa, editor-in-chief of *Shushoku Journal*, a leading job search magazine. 'As global competition increases, companies can no longer afford to wait for their employees to develop over many years.'

The conditions underpinning lifetime employment – strong corporate profitability, easy bank lending terms and a steady supply of graduates committed to one company – are disappearing.

The change reflects a shift in the supply and demand for labour. Japanese companies' labour needs have changed, as deregulation and several quarters of declining demand force managers to shed excess workers and cut costs. As a result, companies are outsourcing accounting and other activities and relying on temporary employees.

Muneaki Ueda, vice-president of Pasona, Japan's largest temporary staffing agency, believes Japan is suffering from a severe shortage of IT workers – those who understand technology and are comfortable with computers. 'About 20 per cent of people employed now are no longer useful to their companies,' he says.

The economic changes have also transformed the supply of labour. New graduates, who watched the collapse of leading companies such as Yamaichi Securities, have lost interest in jobs for life. More than 40 per cent of Japanese graduates would consider joining a venture capital funded company, signalling a greater willingness to take risks in employment. The young are also flocking to technology groups.

The top three choices for graduates in 1999 were Sony, Nippon Telegraph and Telephone and NHK, the national television network. The favourite companies when their parents were entering the workforce in 1965, for instance, were Toray, the textile group, Taisei Fire and Marine and Marubebi, the trading company.

'My dad has tried to tell me about the benefits of life-time employment. But he also says that if I choose lifetime employment, I will fall behind in the world,' says Yasuhiro Kawahito, a recent graduate whose father, now 55, has worked for Hitachi for more than 30 years. However, despite the revolution in attitudes, it will take time for Japan to adjust. Executives complain that the country's universities fail to educate students about careers in industry. As a result, Japanese college students request information from nearly 100 companies before applying to about 20, says Recruit. Foreign managers are puzzled that young recruits can seldom describe why they are suited to a particular company.

SCENARIO 12.12 cont'd

In addition, the hiring procedure in Japan is still firmly rooted in tradition. Most companies hire full-time employees only once a year, in April, in order to guide new recruits through several months of training. And many companies rank candidates according to which university they attended, not on specific qualifications.

But this cannot last. There is a growing divide between traditional manufacturers and financial groups and younger, nimbler companies. 'The old Japan is not moving very quickly to really change,' says Brian Rose, senior economist at Warburg Dillon in Tokyo. 'A lot of these companies are in trouble, but they are not going to adjust fast enough and will be chewed up by the faster moving companies.'

Ultimately, the younger generations will determine how quickly Japanese companies adapt. Eri Miyagi, 24, who started work at NEC this week, feels this burden acutely. 'If we don't want to change the company, it will never change,' he says. 'It is our responsibility.'

Source: Harney, A. (2000) Young Japanese losing interest in lifelong relationship with one employer, *The Financial Times*, 8/9 April, p9.

There have been many attempts at explaining the secret of Japanese business success by writers such as:

- Ouchi (1981)

- Pascale and Athos (1981)

- Peters and Waterman (1982)

- Peters and Austin (1985).

In the 1980s a westerner, Ouchi (1981), noted that many of the most successful US organisations displayed organisational behaviour similar to that commonly found in Japanese organisations. This included emphasis on:

- collective decision making

- team responsibilities

- quality control based on quality circles

- lifetime commitment to the organisation.

However, Ouchi (1981) also commented on the fact that the Japanese style of management was based on Taylor's (1911) model of scientific management. He believed that management success would be brought about by an integration of both approaches, in that the scientific methods could be integrated into some kind of integrative management theory when combined with HRM. He felt that in this way the goals of an organisation could be achieved because the decision making was developed into a participatory and collaborative function, being a product of team processes. This integrative approach was given the label 'Theory Z' by Ouchi (1981) and has become the basis of contemporary management. His approached comprised three strategies and six associated techniques, as given in Tables 12.6 and 12.7 respectively.

Table 12.6 The Theory Z strategies (after Ouchi, 1981)

1 Employment should be lifelong and an organisation should be committed to this.

2 The philosophy and strategy of the organisation must be effectively communicated to each employee and every new entrant should feel that s/he belongs to a clearly defined corporate ethos.

3 Recruitment and selection must be in line with the existing value system of the organisation with new workers being socialised very intensively and quickly.

Table 12.7 The Theory Z techniques (after Ouchi, 1981)

1 *Seniority-based promotion system*
New entrants usually expect to spend their working lives with one organisation and therefore acquire extensive experience through job rotation. Movement is slow through the management hierarchy with limited opportunities for promotion. Therefore, people tend to move laterally rather than horizontally with the result that managers become generalists rather than specialists.

2 *Continuous employee development*
With job security and continuous training and appraisal comes the ability for an individual to plan her/his career. It is thought that managers might thus experience less stress than managers in the west.

3 *Team-centred activities*
The allocation of tasks to teams rather than to individuals.

4 *Open communications*
Within work teams and between management and subordinates. There is no delineation in perks, for example management and workers eat in the same restaurant.

5 *Worker participation in decision making*
Full consultation with all those who might be affected by any organisational change.

6 *Production-centred approach*
A combination of a production-centred approach aligned with concern for employees with no considerable social divide between workers.

Pascale and Athos (1981)

Pascale and Athos (1981) emphasised that the work team is the basic building block of organisations because they believe that group efforts are central to business strategy and are, therefore, highly sensitive to and concerned with group interactions and relationships. The researchers use the analogy of a worker's view of a group being like a marriage which rests on the issues of commitment, trust, sharing and loyalty. They perceive that management has the ultimate responsibility but that the leader of the group handles the interactions within the group in a careful manner. This is called 'participative assumption' and is closely linked to the lifetime employment assumption discussed above.

Peters and Waterman (1982) and Peters and Austin (1985)

The view that the best way intrinsically to motivate workers was to get their full commitment to the values and beliefs, that is, the culture, of the organisation by effective leadership and participative involvement. Such management is popularised by involvement management techniques, such as quality circles. Such was the developmental work of Peters and Waterman (1982) and later Peters and Austin (1985) when they stated that if employers trusted their workers and treated them like adults and balanced this with lively and imaginative leadership, the result would be quality, autonomy and total commitment.

JAPANESE HRM AS A MODEL

Like most concepts related to HRM, there are advantages and disadvantages in the claims made for the Japanese model of HRM which are given in Tables 12.8 and 12.9 respectively.

With the gradual demise of employment for life with one Japanese organisation, those individuals who are now forced to retire are experiencing difficulties about

Table 12.8 Advantages of Japanese HRM as a model

1 Since the employees participate in the decision-making process, they own them and thus implement them quickly and wholeheartedly.

2 Because employees devote so much of their lifetime energies in the organisation, they are totally committed to the survival of the organisation.

3 Employee development is long term with appropriate rewards and remuneration.

4 Loyalty, morale and trust are improved by having a single status for all workers – management and other workers dress alike and share the same toilets and restaurants.

Table 12.9 Disadvantages of Japanese HRM as a model

1 The very fact that there is an emphasis on conformity and obedience to authority may stop the organisation from dealing quickly with changes.

2 Because the pace of work in Japanese organisations is fast and intensive and workers are expected to give their all to their organisations, stress levels are high, but so is the level of job satisfaction.

3 Trades unions change their role from representing the workers to becoming an instrument of management.

4 The Japanese approach is to use brainwashing to make workers subservient and obedient to the wishes of their managers.

5 There is discrimination in all areas but specifically against women.

6 Young managers resent the fact that they cannot proceed as fast as they would like in the promotion arena and so often become the disruptive change agents.

what to do with themselves. These people are called *corporate warriors* and they feel that at one time they were part of the peoples who helped to make Japan a superpower yet they are now discarded. They used to work every day from dawn to dusk, having no interests or hobbies and no social life, seeing their families only rarely. Now they are retired they feel that they are of no use to anyone. In Japan, these retired workers are also called *sodai gomai*, the literal translation meaning 'big-scale garbage'. The latter term was originally used to describe broken pieces of furniture that individuals cannot be bothered to get rid of. However, things are improving in Japan because corporate warriors are now encouraged to participate in new pastimes such as cooking, computer literacy, environmental issues and painting. However, even then they tend to go to excess, taking on large numbers of classes and still labouring long hours to be the best of all the rest.

HRM IN THE PACIFIC REGION (EXCLUDING JAPAN)

The pace and scope of change are unprecedented – especially in the Asia–Pacific region where rapid growth has challenged the capacity of people and organisations to adapt. Researchers in the field (Blunt and Jones, 1997; Graen and Chun Hui, 1996; Haley, 1998; Haley and Haley, 1998; Hallinger, 1998; McDaniel et al., 1999) have all identified learning as being the key to bringing about individual and organisational change.

Other significant areas that are in the globalised marketplace and have come to the fore regarding their HRM practices including some in the Pacific region – with the exception of Japan which has been discussed above – are:

■ Australia and New Zealand

■ Singapore and Vietnam.

While it is not possible to give each one detailed coverage within this text, each deserves a mention because of the contribution they are making.

AUSTRALIA AND NEW ZEALAND

Australia and New Zealand are two distinct countries and it should not be assumed that they manifest the same characteristics as each other. However, Avery et al. (1999) carried out a study on Australian and New Zealand management development practices in the 21st century, and their argument for putting the two countries together is that both are 'among the world's wealthiest countries' (p94). However, according to Avery et al. (1999) both countries have over the last 25 years or so:

suffered a decline in relative wealth as their Asian neighbours' economies expanded rapidly. (p94)

Table 12.10 The '7 Steps' involved in redeveloping WestpacTrust

- Finding out how the bank was using training expenditure.

- Understanding the training and development value chain.

- Understanding the 'make or buy' decision.

- Segmenting learning, training customers and structuring the development centre to deliver accordingly.

- Restructuring supply contracts.

- Building supply contracts.

- Aligning with the brand and the business segments.

Source: Simmons, C. and E. Valentine (2000) Good mixers, *People Management*, 30 March, p50.

They attribute this to the fact that both Australian and New Zealand organisations, and thus their managers, are falling behind in world standards because they are not recognising:

> basic and continuing [management development] initiatives. (p106)

Both Australia and New Zealand have, like other western countries, experienced mergers which, although they can cause difficulties, can also, according to Simmons and Valentine (2000) 'create opportunities to improve HR management' (p49). For example, the creation of New Zealand's biggest bank (WestpacTrust) has led to a more strategic approach to one of HRM's central concepts – training and development. The bank worked on seven steps (given in Table 12.10) which were critical in the redevelopment of WestpacTrust's training function in an international banking market.

Avery et al. (1999) include in their analysis workplace-related activities, within the context of lifelong continuous development – a key component of HRM. Managers are unable to cope with the rapidly changing working environment and have been reluctant, overall, to take on board cross-cultural management skills. They have to do this more if they are to strengthen the position of both Australia and New Zealand in relation to their neighbouring Asia–Pacific and other major worldwide partners and competitors.

POINTS TO PONDER

Some advice for North Americans: down under, you are the ones with the quirky accent. Thanks to the pervasiveness of television and movies from the USA, we will readily understand you. However, to understand us, remember Crocodile Dundee and Babe do not live in Sydney, and that the last time a piano was delivered on a beach in New Zealand was over a century ago. Instead, our friendly shores offer willing markets for honest, localised, state-of-the-art (management development).

Adapted from: Avery, G. Emerging trends in Australian and New Zealand management development practices in the 21st century, *Journal of Management Development*, **18**(1): 106–7.

SINGAPORE AND VIETNAM

SCENARIO 12.13

DaimlerBenz in Ho Chi Minh City, Vietnam

In early 1996, the German car maker, DaimlerBenz, had been trying for a year for permission to build a car and light truck factory in Ho Chi Minh City, Vietnam.

Like other manufacturers, this multinational corporation (MNC) believed that most of its future growth would come from Asia's developing countries.

Several Vietnamese officials had collected DaimlerBenz's application fees – always in cash and in US dollar bills of small denomination; however, the officials would not grant this MNC a business licence. Frustrated, DaimlerBenz turned to Singapore for a surprising kind of government-to-business aid. At DaimlerBenz's invitation, two Singaporean government-linked corporations bought a 22 per cent stake in the proposed Vietnamese project. Then, Lee Kuan Yew, Singapore's Senior Minister, visited Vietnam's capital, Hanoi, and pressed DaimlerBenz's case. Within two weeks the Vietnamese government approved DaimlerBenz's application.

DaimlerBenz is investing about US $80 million over four years in Vietnam and will be turning out 11 000 cars a year by 2005.

Vietnam has an expanding economy with a location at the centre of the Asia–Pacific Rim. The country has discovered an increasing need to develop its managerial talents – as shown in Scenario 12.13. At all levels and sectors, government, state-owned organisations and the fast-growing private sector, organisations have to raise their management skills to the standards found elsewhere in the world. The country needs to develop its employment development programmes and would do well to outsource these tasks to organisations that are skilled in these areas. The level to which Vietnamese organisations can reach has no limit except that placed upon it by their own unwillingness to develop. McDaniel et al. (1999) offer the following advice to those considering offering their consultancy services to Vietnam:

> Pick the right local partner. Respect local culture and government. Get good translation assistance. Engage participants with your best content and presentation technique. Do not underestimate their capabilities and learning desires. Listen, stay flexible, and be wiling to learn as a program unfolds. And, importantly, do not forget to enjoy the Vietnamese culture, environment, and people while you are there. (p92)

These are the skills required of any individual concerned with employee development – wherever they are working.

It is desirable to encourage informed debate about the role of western HRM in developing countries. However, as Blunt and Jones (1997) state:

> The debate must be genuinely multilateral, and it should welcome differences of opinion. (p17)

HRM specialists have never been frightened of debate and should be aware that, as in other fields, the debate could be one-sided and, in the field of IHRM, too culturally and ideologically biased. For example, western views on leadership are not widely applicable in, for example, Africa and East Asia because of the different views placed upon the values concerning authority, group loyalties and interpersonal harmony.

Trompenaars and Woolliams (1999) believe that:

> Managers who can reconcile opposing values in a diverse organisation will be the best performers. (p30)

Blunt and Jones (1997) put the situation in context by stating that:

> there is no one best way to manage or to lead human resources. (p20)

And that has been the theme throughout this text – the HRM specialist and line manager, in whatever country and organisation, must search for a true balance in the management of human resources if they are to avoid relying on the models now popular in the west – other areas have cultural and institutional differences which can be incorporated to improve strategic human resource management (SHRM) so that it becomes, as a matter of course, strategic international human resource management (SIHRM) in a truly globalised way. The future belongs to those individuals who are transculturally competent in that they can recognise, respect and reconcile differences and thus perform better.

Chapter summary

- HRM is even more important in an international environment, where there is increasing competition in an increasingly market-led world economy. All organisations now need to include a discussion of international issues and the matter of moving beyond national boundaries when considering their business strategy.

- Each organisation adopts its own individual ways of running its organisation dependent upon such factors as, culture, economic conditions, tradition, market needs and demographic trends.

- Ethics forms a constituent part of IHRM, particularly because of the different value systems to be found in different countries.

- There is an increased need for HRM specialists and line managers to accept the challenge of IHRM, because with increased globalisation and workforce diversity comes a requirement to manage beyond domestic and national boundaries (Armstrong, 1999).

- IHRM has to be redefined beyond merely absorbing the national HRM issues. Organisations have to consider the '7 Cs' (Torrington, 1994): cosmopolitanism, culture, compensation, communication, consultancy, competence and coordination. Organisations have to include IHRM as part of their core programmes in training and development and not make it an option for those employees who have a personal interest.

■ Understanding and working with diverse national practices is essential for HRM specialists or line managers with international responsibilities, especially with the increased globalisation and diversity to be found in the workplace.

■ Globalisation is becoming increasingly important and is causing an increase in the number of IHRM specialists required, because many organisations are managing an international workforce, employing people in organisations that have branches in other countries. More organisations employ a workforce which is based overseas, fast-growing international economies are proving to be attractive as business markets and most organisations are conscious of the need to be interdependent and global.

■ Although a number of techniques used in HRM are universal, with IHRM the key areas of consideration will be those concerning the country/ies with which the parent organisation wishes to do business. These issues include culture, legislation, economic conditions, competition, employment relations and training and development.

■ The advanced capitalist countries, for example the USA, Japan, and Germany, are said to be in their 'post-career' phase. An organisation's needs for workers changes very fast and because of this individual workers feel insecure in their current positions. Advanced capitalism is continuing to create more long-term unemployment with a growing disparity between those 'who have' (the rich) and those 'who have not' (the poor). This, however, is not confined to the workers but also to and between nations. The key areas of concern in this area are insecure employment prospects, deteriorating terms of employment, weakening in the rights of employees and lower wages and salaries for those in the lower echelons.

■ It is essential for organisations to ensure that their workers are knowledge based, skilled and flexible. In order to achieve this, an organisation has specifically to turn its attention to international employment and development strategies. Armstrong (1999) believes that such concentration is warranted in three areas: a strategy of centralisation, the staffing of posts in management areas and a strategy for management development.

■ It is possible that an organisation will need to recruit staff locally or from people willing to work for parent country branches overseas. The basis is the same as that of 'at-home' recruitment and selection although there are some particular issues that need to be addressed: job description, job specification, international recruitment, interview and selection.

■ Because different parts of the world, and hence, different countries, develop their own ways of doing things it is likely that the way in which businesses are run will differ. For example, the way of carrying out operations in an organisation in Japan will differ to those in, say, Scandinavia. To some extent there will be similarities but the differences will comprise the larger part. A key industry in Britain that has experienced these difficulties is car manufacturing where management and manufacturing differences have led to the virtual demise of the industry in the UK.

■ Managers cannot simply go and work in other countries, they need specific skills which include: intercultural effectiveness, interpersonal and communications ability, language skills, ability to manage complexity and diversity, flexibility, resilience, knowledge of local country employment law and conditions, business understanding and of the international business environment. S/he will also need to know how to manage expatriates (Meddenhall and Oddou, 1985; Scullion, 1995).

■ With the increase in globalisation and IHRM it is essential that individuals have a thorough understanding of the political, economic and social policy of the EU and other European countries – both the advanced economies and those in transition. Examples here are Central Asia (for example, Kazakhastan), the Caucasus (for example, Armenia), the WTO, Quadrilateral Talks (Canada, Japan and the USA), cooperation with the developing industrial countries of Africa, Caribbean and the Pacific (ACP), Asia, China, ASEAN and Latin and Central American countries.

■ It is in the area of the social framework where the foundations have been laid for IHRM and this has been done for member nations of the EU through the European Social Chapter. While there is still debate on the issue of the Social Chapter, it tends to be linked to the issue of labour markets and the movement of labour, but a search of the literature shows that there is little discourse on their actual influence on organisations. The key works are those of Wood and Peccei (1990), Pricewaterhouse Cranfield Project (1991) and Leblanc (1994).

■ The origins of HRM lie in the USA, with its history of scientific management through to organic businesses, although the influence of union representation has had an impact on employment relations to a commitment-centred system of management.

■ Western organisations have searched for ways to improve their labour market performance and have turned to the Japanese for guidance. The more recent belief is that some of the Japanese methods, for example just-in-time and high-performance work teams, can be adjusted to work in a western organisation, although the key distinction is in the belief held by the Japanese that employment is for life and that the organisation owns an individual's life – the opposite to the individualism of western culture.

■ Avery et al. (1999) carried out a study of emerging trends in Australian and New Zealand management development practices in the 21st century. Although both countries are among the world's wealthiest, they have suffered a decline in relative wealth over the last 25 years or so as their Asian neighbours' economies expanded rapidly.

■ Other Pacific Rim countries such as Singapore and Vietnam are adapting to the new economy and providing specialised training and development courses for their workers so that they can adjust to the change from planned economy to a market-led one.

■ It is desirable to encourage informed debate about the role of western HRM in developing countries. However, the debate must be genuinely multilateral and it should welcome differences of opinion (Blunt and Jones, 1997).

■ HRM should continue to participate in the debate on IHRM and should be aware that, as in other fields, such a debate could be one sided, and in the field of IHRM, too culturally and ideologically biased. For example, western views on leadership are not widely applicable in, for example Africa and East Asia, because of the different views placed upon the values concerning authority, group loyalties and interpersonal harmony.

- There is no one best way to manage or to lead human resources (Blunt and Jones, 1997). The HRM specialist and line manager, in whatever country and organisation, must search for a true balance in the management of human resources if they are to avoid relying on the models now popular in the west. Other countries have cultural and institutional differences that can be incorporated to improve SHRM so that it becomes, as a matter of course, IHRM in a truly globalised way – SIHRM. The future belongs to those individuals who are transculturally competent in that they can recognise, respect and reconcile differences and thus perform better.

END OF CHAPTER 12 CASE STUDY

The Rover sell-off

What happened

With an abruptness that surprised the UK government, German car maker BMW announced that it was selling Rover, its loss-making British subsidiary. Up to 60 000 jobs in Britain's heartland were put at risk, beginning with 8500 at Longbridge, Birmingham. As the British government struggled to contain the fallout, British Alchemy (a ▶ venture capital firm ◀) agreed to buy part of the operation. This will be renamed the MG Car Company and based at Cowley, near Oxford. Ford is to buy Land Rover, based at Solihull.

BMW said the continuing strength of the pound sterling and Britain's failure to join the single currency were factors, on top of 1999's losses of more than £800 million. It was alleged by the British government that BMW had failed to consult with them. The unions promised protest strikes.

What the editorials said

The dumping of Rover was 'one of the darkest days for Birmingham since the Blitz', said Birmingham's _Evening Mail_. The 'opportunist' BMW had wrung endless sacrifices from the workers, while thoroughly mismanaging its British subsidiary. Certainly Rover's demise could not be attributed to the workforce, agreed the _Independent_, but Longbridge remained 'the least productive car plant in Britain'. This should be the close of 'a sorry chapter of British history'. At least Land Rover is being bought by Ford (USA), which has made such a success of Jaguar. And Alchemy might yet be able to do something with the MR ▶ marque ◀.

Venture capital firm ◀····▶ An organisation that uses money for investment in high-risk projects offering the possibility of large profits on the investment.

Marque ◀····▶ Brand or make of product, especially a make of luxury or high-performance item.

END OF CHAPTER 12 CASE STUDY (CONT'D)

Rover is 'dying of old age', said the *Sunday Express*. It will be painful for the people of Longbridge, but they will come out the other side – as others have – with the demise of heavy metal-bashing industry giving way to the rise of smaller factories and service-sector employers.

What the commentators said

BMW should never have bought Rover in the first place, said Karl-Heiz Büschemann in the *Süddeutsche Zeitung* [*South German Times*]. 'The English Patient, as Rover was known, had swallowed DM10 billion and absorbed the energies of BMW management without ever showing signs of the necessary improvements in productivity. BMW must be mightily relieved, and it would be no surprise to learn that Alchemy was being paid to take it off their hands.

Of course BMW was right to sell Rover, said James Bartholomew in the *Daily Telegraph*. It had secured all the available aid, and still couldn't make Rover profitable. The British government's outrage was thoroughly synthetic, playing on ancient anti-German feeling. But those who prefer to blame the government and the Bank of England for destroying Rover have got it wrong, said Anatole Kaletsky in *The Times*, True, the strength of sterling was one of the proximate causes of Rover's collapse. But that strength is not a British problem: it reflects the growing weakness of

the mark and the euro. Compared with the dollar [USA] or the yen, the pound is actually weaker today than it was when BMW decided to buy Rover. If anyone is to blame it is BMW, who snatched Rover from under the nose of Honda [Japanese], a company prepared to invest heavily in improving Rover's efficiency. By contrast, BMW's strategy was to bank on the continued devaluation of the pound. It was a ▸ **disingenuous** strategy and it didn't work.

Still, Labour [the British government] will have learnt one lesson from all this, said Mark Lawson in the *Guardian*. Like the Conservatives [the opposition] before them they now realise that however much you privatise, 'the market takes the credit while the [political] leaders take the blame'.

What next?

The people of Birmingham will not be impressed with the government's handling of this affair, said Alan Watkins in the *Independent on Sunday*. Unlike the British Prime Minister, they do not believe that modern capitalism is 'uniformly beneficent in its intention', and they will punish him 'as much for his foolishness as for his failure, if failure it was'.

Not only the British government's ten seats [parliamentary positions] but many others throughout the West Midlands will be at risk in the aftermath of the Rover debacle, warns Watkins.

Adapted from: The Rover sell-off, *The Week*, 25 March 2000, pp2–3.

▸ Withholding or not taking account of known information; giving a false impression of ◂┈┈▸ **Disingenuous** sincerity or simplicity.

END OF CHAPTER 12 CASE STUDY QUESTIONS

1 Why will workers who have been at the Rover factory for a long time have difficulty in getting new jobs?

2 How can legislation help the workers?

3 Why is there such a diversity of views on the issue?

4 How does culture feature?

END OF PART VI CASE STUDY

SINGAPORE TRAINS OLD WORKERS FOR NEW ECONOMY

Abdul Kadir is a product of the old economy. The 52-year-old father of three lost his job as a shipyard worker when his company restructured. Now, after 30 years in the same vocation, he is among Singapore's 63 100 unemployed.

He is of a breed known as 'heartlanders'. These are people the government is desperately trying to prepare for the new economy.

It is an enormous task and one carrying tremendous risk, for if Mr Abdul and other unskilled workers cannot find a role in the knowledge-based industries moving onto centre stage, the curtain could fall on the political stability upon which this thriving economy has been so carefully scripted.

That possibility was brought into sharp focus by the regional financial crisis. It revealed that Singapore had grown too expensive to compete with neighbours for labour-intensive manufacturing investments, which for decades had sustained workers such as Mr Abdul, and needed to develop a highly skilled services sector. Singapore decided to liberalise the financial, telecommunications, power and insurance industries and encourage the import of foreign talent to enable companies to compete. But that was the easy part. The real concern to the Singapore government was what to do with those left behind. The government has put the onus on the individual by propounding the message that learning is a lifelong process that Singaporeans must engage in to keep up. And it

built an adult training institution to retool those most at risk.

Mr Abdul is learning to become an electronic technician. Around him are 20 students bent over white circuit boards. They are given S$500 (£180) a month during the six-month course to cover basic living expenses. There is a keen sense of determination about the orderly classroom.

'Now is the chance for me to learn some skill to protect myself,' says 39-year-old Pang Chin Soon, who quit his job as a bus driver to enrol.

He is having difficulties absorbing the skills and logic being taught and does not know what he will do if he cannot pass. 'It's very difficult for me because year-by-year, the world is changing. You have nowhere to run. You have to face it.'

Not every Singaporean is up to the task. This is a nation built just decades ago by immigrants who arrived with nothing but the shirts on their backs. Those aged 45 and above have an aggregate third-world profile. Years of first-rate socialist planning have advanced the rest so those aged 35 and below have a first-world profile. The progression into the technology age will widen the gap between the two segments.

The government is trying to develop creative ways to contain a political backlash by the unskilled workers through giving them a stake in the society. This includes distributing national wealth by selling them shares in companies such as the government-

END OF PART VI CASE STUDY (CONT'D)

owned Singapore Telecommunications at a discount and providing schoolchildren with funds to enrich themselves with music lessons and other extracurricular activities. While the government is sure nobody will starve, it needs everyone to be patriotic. The idea is that the people must feel that they are getting something from society. This includes the 'cosmopolitans', who comprise those Singaporeans with a university education and who drive MercedesBenz cars and takes vacations in Australia, whom the government wants to feel committed to helping propel the new economy forward. This sense of duty is bred through national military service and subsidised housing which provides every Singaporean an opportunity to own a home. Those who venture overseas are reminded of their duty to the nation state in Singapore clubs established where there are 100 Singaporeans.

While some Singaporeans feel that the country is taking care of them, the maintenance of such social cohesion will become harder with the entrance of 'foreign talent', which does not benefit from the nation-building policies and feels no loyalty to the island state.

Foreigners also generate resentment as they are taking jobs away from Singaporeans. Yet the government feels they are necessary to enable its companies to compete in the global economy.

Adapted from: McNulty, S. (2000) Singapore trains old workers for new economy, *Financial Times*, 31 March, p11.

END OF PART VI CASE STUDY QUESTIONS

1 What does McNulty (2000) mean when she says 'Abdul Kadir is a product of the old economy'?

2 Why does the Singapore government feel it should do something for the 'heartlanders'?

3 How does the situation of the 'heartlanders' compare with that of the 'cosmopolitans'?

4 What future does the training course have?

THESIS + ANTITHESIS = SYNTHESIS

Examine the view that it is not possible to have an IHRM model.

SELF-TEST THE KEY ISSUES

1 What are the advantages of the European Social Chapter?

2 What are the main concerns about adopting Japanese HRM concepts?

3 What is meant by 'employment at will'?

4 Why is IHRM better than HRM?

TEAM/CLASS DISCUSSIONS

1 Prepare arguments and then debate the following statements in two teams. Try to persuade the members of the opposing team of your point of view.

Team One
The western model of HRM is the best.

Team Two
The countries in transition offer some good HRM models to the west.

2 Debate the issue that all HRM should be IHRM.

 PROJECTS (INDIVIDUAL OR TEAMS)

1 Write a report in which you assess the commonalities and distinctions between the development of HRM in a western country and one which is in transition.

2 Design a job description advertisement for a human resource manager required to work in a non-parent national country to that of the individual/team and then draw up the checklist for the interview panel.

 Recommended reading

Beardwell, I. and L. Holden (1999) *Human Resource Management: A Contemporary Perspective*, London: Pitman

Cooper, C. (2000) The people's republic opens its doors to people management, *People Management*, 26 October, pp16–17

Graham, H.T. and R. Bennett (1999) *Human Resources Management*, London: Financial Times/Pitman

 URLs (uniform resource locators)

www.voila.co.uk

France Telecom site for all EU countries with a view to promoting all countries.

www.usip.org

Ethics and human rights initiatives.

www.amnesty.org

Amnesty International news and comments.

www.shrm.org

Society for Human Resource Management. USA site with useful information and news. It can assist HRM managers with news, sample book chapters and coverage of some international issues.

Bibliography

Addison, J.T. and W. Stanley Siebert (1991) The Social Chapter of the European Community: evolution and controversies in *Industrial and Labour Relations Review*, **44**(4): 597–625

Altmin, W. (1999) Global ambition in *Professional Manager*, July, **8**(4): 20–2

Armstrong, M. (1999) *A Handbook of Human Resource Management Practice*, London: Kogan Page

Avery, G., A. Everett, A. Finkelde and K. Wallace (1999) Emerging trends in Australian and New Zealand management development practices in the 21st century in *Journal of Management Development*, **18**(1): 94–108

Beardwell, I. and L. Holden (1997) *Human Resource Management: A Contemporary Perspective*, London: Pitman

Blunt, P. and M.L. Jones (1997) Exploring the limits of western leadership theory in East Asia and Africa in *Personnel Review*, **269**(1/2): 6–23

Burns, T. and G.M. Stalker (1961) *The Management of Innovation*, London: Tavistock

Dawes, B. (1995) *International Business: A European Perspective*, Cheltenham: Stanley Thornes

Du Bois, F.C. and M.D. Oliff (1992) International Manufacturing Configuration and Competitive Priorities in Voss, C.A. *Manufacturing Strategy: Process and Content*, London: Chapman & Hall

Economist (2000) Executive focus, 11 March, p16

Economist (2000) Le cyber challenge, 11 March, p53

European Commission (1994) *Towards a New Asia Policy*, Strasborg: European Union

Garavan,T., M. Morley, N. Heraty, J. Lucewucz and A. Suchodoloski (1998) Managing human resources in a post-command economy: personnel administration or strategic HRM in *Personnel Review*, **27**(3): 200–12

George, N. (2000) Nordic neighbours embrace the net in *Connectis*, March (2): 54–5

Graen, G. and Chun Hui (1996) Managing changes in globalizing business: how to manage cross-cultural business partners in *Journal of Organisational Change*, **9**(3): 62–72

Graham, H.T. and R. Bennett (1998) *Human Resource Management*, London: Financial Times/Pitman

Guiler, R. (1999) Expatriate games in *Success* (13), July/August/September, pp54–7

Haley, U. (1998) Virtual Singapore: shaping international competitive environments through business–government partnerships in *Journal of Organisational Management*, **11**(4): 338–56

Haley, G.T. and U.C.V. Haley (1998) Boxing with shadows: competing effectively with the overseas Chinese and overseas Indian business networks in the Asian arena in *Journal of Organisational Change*, **11**(4): 301–20

Hallinger, P. (1998) Increasing the organization's IQ: public sector leadership in Southeast Asia in *The Learning Organization*, **5**(4): 176–83

Harney, A. (2000) Young Japanese losing interest in lifelong relationship with one employer in *Financial Times*, 8/9 April, p9

Institute of Personnel and Development (1996) Developing an International Personnel Career, Key Facts, September

Leblanc, B. (1994) European competencies – some guidelines for companies in *Journal of Management Development*, **13**(2): 72–81

Lockhart, T. and C. Brewster (1992) Human resource management in the European Community in Brewster, C., A. Hegewisch, L. Holden and T. Lockhart (eds) *The European Human Resource Management Guide*, London: Academic Press

Management Today (1999) Global business – *Le Point* on America's Gulliver complex, May, p27

Management Today (1999) Global business – *Le Nouvel Economiste* on role playing in French business, June, p23

Management Today (1999) Global business – male fashions from *Le Nouvel Economiste*, July, p21

Management Today (1999) Global business – *Manager* magazine on Franco–German relations, August, p23

Maund, L. (1999) *Understanding People and Organisations: An Introduction to Organisational Behaviour*, Cheltenham: Stanley Thornes

Mayo, A. and E. Lank (1995) Changing the soil spurs new growth in *People Management*, 16 November, pp26–8

McDaniel, D.O., J.R. Schermerhorn Jr and Huynh The Cuoc (1999) Vietnam: the environment for management development in the 21st century in *Journal of Management Development*, **18**(1): 79–93

McNulty, S. (2000) Singapore trains old workers for new economy in *Financial Times*, 31 March, p11

Mendenhall, M. and G. Oddou (1985) The dimensions of expatriate accumulation: a review in *Academy of Management Review*, (10): 39–47

Newman, K.L. (1998) Leading radical change in transition economies in *Leadership and Organization Development Journal*, **19**(6): 309–24

Ouchi, W. (1981) *Theory Z: How American Business Can Meet the Japanese Challenge*, London: Addison-Wesley

Pascale, R. and A. Athos (1981) *The Art of Japanese Management*, New York: Simon & Schuster

Peters, T. and N. Austin (1985) *A Passion for Excellence*, Glasgow: Collins

Peters, T. and R. Waterman (1982) *In Search of Excellence*, New York: Harper & Row

Pricewaterhouse Cranfield Project (1991) *Report on International Strategic Human Resource Management*, Cranfield: Cranfield School of Management

Scullion, H. (1995) International HRM in Storey, J. (ed.) *New Perspectives in Human Resource Management: Critical Text*, London: Routledge

Simmons, C. and E. Valentine (2000) Good mixers in *People Management*, 30 March, pp48–50

Slack, N., S. Chambers, C. Harland, A. Harrison and R. Johnston (1995) *Operations Management*, London: Pitman

Sparrow, P. (1999) Abroad minded in *People Management*, 20 May, pp40–1, 43–4

Taylor, F.W. (1911) *Principles of Scientific Management*, New York: Harper & Row

the business (2000) Big money, little people in *Financial Times* 25/26 March, p10

the business (2000) How much? in *Financial Times* 19/20 March, p8

The Week (2000) The Rover sell-off, 25 March, pp2–3

Torrington, D.P. (1994) *International Personnel Management*, Hemel Hempstead: Prentice Hall

Trompenaars, G. and P. Woolliams (1999) First-class accommodation in *People Management*, 22 April, pp30–4

Wood, S. and R. Peccei (1990) Preparing for 1992? Business-led versus strategic human resource management in *Human Resource Management Journal*, **1**(1): 63–89

Glossary of terms

Absenteeism
The number of workers who miss work.

Added value
The measure of organisational success.

Ageism
Discrimination on the grounds of age.

Altruistic
An unselfish concern for the welfare and interests of other people.

Appraisal
The process of assessing the development of an employee concentrating on achievement and what needs to be done to improve it.

Appraisee
The individual being appraised at an appraisal interview.

Appraiser
The person carrying out an appraisal interview.

Aspatial
Where individuals spend more time, physically, among strangers.

Assessment centre
An organisation within which a structured combination of assessment techniques is used to provide a wide-ranging, holistic assessment of each participant.

Attribution
When someone pinpoints the causes of the behaviour of themselves and others.

Atypical workers
Any category of employee who does not have an ordinary full-time contract of indefinite length – that is, a permanent job within the organisation.

Autocratic
A style of leadership in which the leader makes decisions and communicates them to subordinates using strong, directive, controlling techniques.

Automation
Where mechanical or electronic machines or processes replace/minimise human labour.

Benchmarking
A comparison point for judging some aspect of the firm's performance, sometimes referred to as *best practice*.

Benefits
The non-cash elements of a worker's reward package, for example a paid holiday.

Bilateral
Involving or carried out by two groups, especially the political representatives of two countries.

Biotechnology
The technology of biological processes.

Bloc
A group of countries with a shared aim.

Blue chip
A stock considered reliable with respect to both dividend income and capital value.

Bureaucratic
An organisation structure where the routine activities are carried out through specialisation, formal rules and regulations.

Business process re-engineering
A label given to the redesign of an organisation; it may include breaking away from outdated rules and assumptions that underlie how tasks should be performed. A key principle is the elimination or prevention of barriers which could themselves create a distance between employees and their customers.

Cafeteria style
The selection by an individual of what items s/he requires from those on display.

Career ladder
A system within an organisation that gives employees the opportunity to move up through the ranks to even higher positions.

Causal relationship
A situation where one happening may, or may not, have caused a different one.

Cell structure
A small team which makes entire products or provides an entire service from conception to after-sales service.

Change agent
An individual or group who undertakes the task of introducing and managing a change within an organisation.

Chronemics
The use of time as an element of non-verbal communication.

Civil law
The law of a country relating to private and civilian affairs.

Code of Practice
Leaflets or booklets published by government agencies, for example the Equal Opportunities Commission, or by professional bodies or trade associations giving their procedures for good practice.

Cognition
Individual thinking through which individuals decide to make changes in their lives.

Cognitive dissonance theory
Any incompatibility between two or more attitudes or between behaviour and attitudes, that is, an inconsistency.

Cognitive evaluation theory
Allocating extrinsic rewards for behaviour that had previously intrinsically rewarded an individual tends to decrease the overall level of motivation.

Cognitive moral development
An individual's level of moral judgment.

Collective bargaining
The process of setting pay and conditions of employment through negotiation between the employer or group of employers and employee representatives acting on behalf of a group of employees.

Common law
The body of law which is based on decisions made in courts of law and customs.

Communication
The transference and understanding of a shared meaning.

Communication fidelity
The degree of correspondence between the message intended by the sender and the message understood by the receiver.

Compensation
The sum of money awarded to the victor in any claim headed by an employment tribunal. It can be used interchangeably with the word remuneration meaning pay – including benefits.

Competency
The knowledge, skills and personal qualities needed to carry out a task, and how such attributes are applied.

Conceptual
Of, or characterised by, concepts, that is, abstract ideas.

Consultation
Taking counsel, asking advice and seeking an opinion.

Contextual
The real meaning depends upon the context within which the term is used.

Contingency theory
The most effective way to establish power/dependence relationships that exist between the focal organisation and other actors in the network.

Contingent
Conditional or dependent upon.

Continuous professional development
The ongoing self-development of an individual towards recognition in a particular profession or vocation; it is a purely personal definition.

Contract of Employment
A legal agreement that governs the mutual obligations between an employer and an employee.

Corporate
Belonging to a united group.

Corporate governance
The sum of those activities that make up the internal regulation of the business in compliance with the obligations placed on the organisation by legislation, ownership and control.

Corporate manslaughter
A group as a whole being responsible for the death of another person or persons.

Cost–benefit analysis
An evaluation of a project as to its benefits and costs with an attempt to put a monetary value to the process.

Critical approach
An approach which takes the view that there should be an exposure of the often hidden, and highly persuasive, power that contemporary organisations have over their employees.

Critical path
The activities that must be completed on time to avoid the delaying of a project.

Culture
The distinctive ways in which different human populations or societies organise their lives.

Data workers
Individuals who use, manipulate, process and disseminate information.

Decode
The process by which the receiver of a message interprets the symbols contained in the message and determines what such symbols refer to.

Delayering
The taking away of a complete level of management with the idea of improving vertical communication and shortening the chain of command.

Demographic trends
The statistics of births, deaths and diseases.

Demotion
Reducing the rank/position of a worker involving removal from a higher to a lower function.

Deregulation
To remove any regulations which are encompassed in, say, legislation.

Discrimination
The unfair treatment of individuals on account of their race, colour of skin, religion, nationality, gender, marital status or disability.

Disingenuous
Withholding or not taking account of known information; giving a false impression of sincerity or simplicity.

Disposable earnings
The portion of earnings remaining after deduction of NI and income tax.

Dividend
A portion of the distribution from the net profits of a company to its shareholders.

Dock system
Where the manufacturing area of an industry has a short and fat layout.

Downlife
When individuals have personally decided to reduce their workload by finding alternative, more flexible employment. It is not the same as downsizing which is the compulsory reduction of staff levels.

Downsizing
Sometimes called downlayering or rightsizing, and means a reduction in staff numbers throughout an organisation.

Dyadic
Communication between two people.

Dysfunctional conflict
An unhealthy, destructive disagreement between two or more people.

Eclectic
Made up from a variety of sources and beliefs.

Economic rewards
A financial reward for work done which could include non-monetary benefits such as paid holidays.

Economic value added (EVA)
The net operating profit after tax, minus the profit required to justify the risk.

Economies of scale
The ability to benefit from being a large organisation, for example by buying in bulk.

Effort
A determined physical or mental exertion in order to achieve or create.

Egalitarian
Maintaining, relating to, or based on a belief that all people are, in principle, equal and should enjoy equal social, political and economic rights and opportunities.

Electronic commerce (e-commerce)
Carrying out transactions through electronic information systems such as the Internet.

Electronic learning (e-learning)
Learning through the use of technology.

Emoticon
A symbolic picture used in computer communications to convey emotions, constructed by arranging standard keyboard characters that are usually to be viewed sideways.

Emotion
A heightened feeling about, say, a subject or an agitation caused by strong feelings.

Emotional
Relating to or expressing emotion.

Empirical
Derived from or related to experiment and observation rather than theory.

Employment tribunals
Panels which deal with minor bureaucratic issues related to employment disputes such as redundancy, unfair dismissal, deductions from pay, discrimination and breach of contract.

Empowered
When an employee has the right to take executive decisions within specified parameters; such an individual is accountable for her/his actions.

'Enabling' legislation
Legislation where the provisions are phased in over time, for example the Employment Relations Act 1999.

Encode
To convert words or ideas into symbols or code to form a message.

Entrepreneurial
The activities of an owner/manager of a business who attempts to make a profit by using her/his initiative and taking risks.

Equal opportunity
Equal rights of both access to, and participation in, all areas of public life.

Equity
A position where the members of any workforce are treated fairly and have a desire to perceive equity in relation to others and to avoid inequity with them.

Equity theory
A justice theory which asserts that members of any workforce wish to be treated fairly and have a desire to perceive equity in relation to others and avoid inequity with them.

Ergonomists
People who study the relationship between workers and their environment.

Ethics
A code of moral principles or values that a person holds for making judgments about what is right or wrong.

Euro
The currency of most of the countries of the EU which was introduced in 1999 as part of economic and monetary union. It is planned that by 2002 the euro will have replaced the local currency in the participating member states.

European law
European law comprises the legal rules of the EU and takes precedence over equivalent national laws of member countries.

European works councils
A group of organisations and employee representatives who have established rights to both information and consultation.

Evaluation
The assessment of the total value of a system, project or programme in social as well as financial terms.

Exit interview
The process of asking an employee why he/she has decided to leave the job.

Expatriate
Someone who has left her/his own country to live and work in another country.

Expert systems
Computer-based applications that use a computer representation of the expertise attributed to humans in a specialised field of knowledge in order to solve problems.

External locus of control
The extent to which an individual believes that her/his behaviour has a direct impact on the consequences of that behaviour and that such behaviour is a result of other people's actions.

Extinction
Any behaviour which is used in an attempt to weaken behaviour in others by attaching some sort of consequence (positive or negative) to it.

Extranet
An intranet which is only accessible by selected individuals. It can be worldwide or organisational.

Extrinsic
Tangible outcomes for effort that derive externally, for example financial or non-financial payments.

Extroversion
Behaviour which indicates that the individual is energised by interaction with other people. An extrovert is an outgoing or sociable person.

Fat cats
Executives who are perceived to receive reward and remuneration that is excessively high for the work which they do.

Federal
A form of government in a country in which power is divided between one central and several regional governments; for example, in the USA, the central government is the federal government and then each state has its own additional and complementary laws.

Feedback
Information received by an individual, as a result of carrying out a task, concerning the effectiveness of her/his work performance.

Feedback loop
The pathway that permits two-way feedback.

Fixed incremental systems
Fixed points on a transparent scale where employees can expect to receive an increase in wage/salary regardless of effort and productivity, and usually set at years of service.

Flowchart
A diagram that shows a sequence or a series of interdependent activities.

Franchise
The right to vote at a public election, especially for a member of a legislative body such as central government.

Functionalist approach
An approach which stresses the purpose of something, that is, its purpose is determined by its use.

Global
What is happening throughout the world.

Global village
The world viewed as a totally integrated ecological, socioeconomic and political system of which all the parts are dependent on one another. That is, when the whole world is considered as a single community served by electronic media and information technology.

Globalisation
When something, especially a business or company, becomes international or starts operating at an international level.

Globalise
To make global, especially to make worldwide in scope or application.

Goals
Aims or objectives towards which the employee is working.

Groupthink
The psychological drive for consensus at any cost that suppresses dissent and appraisal of alternatives in cohesive decision-making groups.

Headhunted
The name given to an individual who has been particularly recruited, or is being

recruited, by another organisation in such a way that they are enticed away, usually by an increase in rewards and remuneration

Headhunter
A specialist consultant (executive search consultant) employed to recruit key staff.

Heterarchy
A development of horizontal organisations where there are multiple centres with subsidiary managers who initiate strategy for the organisation, with coordination and control being achieved through the corporate culture and shared values.

Heuristic
A way of making decisions through trial and error.

Hierarchy
A development of horizontal organisations where there are multiple centres with subsidiary managers who initiate strategy for the organisation, with coordination and control being achieved through the corporate culture and shared values.

Holistic
Observing and analysing the whole rather than the individual parts which make up that whole.

Hot desking
Not having a specified desk in an office but having to collect a mobile communication unit from a central store and plugging it in wherever a switching point can be found.

Hotelling
Reserving a room at an office block for the purpose of meeting others.

Human rights
Justified claims to the protection of persons' important interests.

Hypermobile
Old-fashioned geographical communities.

Hypomobile
Small-scale pedestrian economies where everyone knows everyone else.

Individualism
The pursuit of personal goals rather than collective goals/interests.

Induction
The period of time when a new entrant to an organisation makes initial contact with the

organisation until s/he has reached the desired standard of performance.

Industrial relations
The rules, practices and conventions that govern the relationship between employers and their workers.

Industrial Revolution
Generally believed to refer to the development of industry through employment of machinery, which took place in England in the early 19th century.

Inflation
In economic terms, this is a progressive increase in the general level of prices brought about by an expansion in the demand or the money supply or by autonomous increases in costs. In general terms, it is the rate of increase in prices.

Information
The result of the processing of data for use and the making of meaningful decisions.

Instrumentality
The calculation of the number and degree of rewards resulting from achieving an outcome.

Integrity test
Test which is designed to predict whether or not a member of the workforce is likely to engage in behaviour which will lead to dishonesty on the job or be counter-productive to the interests of the organisation for which s/he works.

Internal locus of control
The extent to which an individual believes that her/his behaviour has a direct impact on the consequences of that behaviour and that such behaviour is a result of her/his own actions.

Interpretivist approach
An approach which attempts to give meaning to something by clarifying or explaining the intention of the issue.

Intranet
A network of computers, especially one which uses www conventions, that can be accessed only by an authorised set of users, for example those working for a particular organisation.

Intrapreneurs
Employees who have the ability and confidence to work both independently and as a member of a high-performance team during a period of rapid change.

Intrinsic rewards
Intangible rewards which derive from the experience of work itself, for example a sense of challenge and achievement, recognition and responsibility.

Iterative
Where each successive step builds on the accomplishments of the previous step.

Job analysis
Breaking down a job in detail to identify its component tasks.

Job description
A statement which gives the purpose, scope, responsibilities and tasks which make up a stated job.

Job evaluation
A process designed to measure the demands of the job, not the job holder's performance.

Job redesign
An exercise that focuses on how existing jobs can be changed.

Just-in-time
A manufacturing and stock control system in which goods are produced and delivered as they are required with the purpose of eliminating waste and avoiding the need for the storage of large amounts of stock.

Kinesics
The study of body movements, including posture.

Knowledge
A parcel of concepts and cognitive frameworks which individuals use to collect, store, process, organise and communicate understanding.

Knowledge workers
Members of the workforce who are erudite, highly educated and informed in matters which will enhance the objectives of the organisation.

Labour turnover
A measure of the rate at which individuals leave the organisation. When high the figure may reflect an ineffective human resource strategy.

Law
A rule or set of rules instituted by an Act of Parliament, custom or practice in order to punish individuals who offend the conventions of society.

Leadership
The process of guiding and directing the behaviour of followers within the workplace.

Learning organisation
An organisation which encompasses an attitude that has developed the continuous capacity to adapt to the environment and to change. Such an organisation also supports the self-development of members of the workforce towards this end.

Legal Aid
Financial help which is made available to individuals who are unable to meet the full cost of legal proceedings.

Legislation
The act or process of making laws and/or the laws which are so made.

Legislature
A body of individuals that has the power to make and repeal laws.

Line managers
Individuals who have direct responsibility for other employees and their work and duties. The line relationship charts the authority of one person over others in the organisation's structure.

Litigation
The act or process of bringing or contesting a law suit. It can also refer to the actual judicial proceeding itself.

Locus of control
The extent to which an individual believes that her/his behaviour has a direct impact on the consequences of that behaviour.

Logarithms
A mathematical system used, particularly, to simplify multiplication and division.

Management
A distinct subsystem which is responsible for directing and coordinating all other subsystems in an organisation.

Manpower
The total supply of persons available and trained/educated for employment.

Manpower planning
The integration of human resource planning to ensure that the right numbers of the right people will be available for the right jobs at the right time.

Markets
The actual and potential buyers of a product or service.

Market economies
Economies where prices and wages are determined mainly by the market and the laws of supply and demand, rather than being regulated by a government.

Marque
Brand or make of product, especially a make of luxury or high-performance item.

Mechanistic
A system of organisation which is characterised by bureaucratic systems encompassing roles, regulations, a clear hierarchical pattern of authority and centralised decision making.

Mentoring
The act of being a teacher and protector to a junior colleague.

Metaphor
A figure of speech in which a word or phrase is applied to an object or action that it does not literally denote in order to imply a resemblance, for example, 'S/he is a tiger in the boardroom.'

Mission statement
A written statement by an organisation which encapsulates the purpose of its activity, as much as the direction it wishes to take.

Modernism
The adoption of modern thoughts and ideas, that is, modern tendencies, thoughts or support of these (see Postmodernism).

Monopoly
The exclusive possession, control or use of something.

Motive
The channel through which the individual thinks the need can best be satisfied thus reflecting the specific behavioural choices enacted by the individual.

Motivation
The driving force that makes an individual act to meet a need that will result in either fulfilment or frustration.

Multi-domestic
The operation of a business, and thus its employees, in different countries.

Multilateral
Involving or carried out by a number of groups, especially the political representatives of several countries.

Mutual learning
Common or shared learning.

National Council for Vocational Qualifications (NCVQ)
A UK government body set up to implement a national framework for the provision of vocational qualifications and to determine national standards of occupational competence.

Need
A stimulus for action, for example money in return for work.

Network analysis
A way of showing how a complex project can be completed in the shortest possible time.

New economy
Where business dominates and is driven by technological change and innovation in an economic environment with flat inflation and interest rates.

Nonconformist
An individual who does not conform to the doctrine or the discipline of an established church. It especially concerns a member of a church dissenting from the Anglican Church (usually not including Roman Catholics) – a Protestant dissenter.

Object language/artifacts
The communication that results from the display of material things, for example curtains, carpets and furniture.

Objective
A statement of what is to be achieved.

Occupational health
The physical and mental health of members of the workforce.

Open-book management
Giving employees all the information any owner receives if the latter wants employees to act like owners and care for the organisation.

Open learning
A system whereby individuals can access learning materials such as computer programs, CD-ROMS, DVDs, books and videos.

Organic organisation
A system of organisation that has free-flowing systems with adaptive processes, unclear authority hierarchy and where decision making is decentralised.

Organisational behaviour
The study of the impact that individuals, groups and structures within an organisation have on meeting the goals of an organisation.

Organisational behaviour modification
The use of operant conditioning theory to get members of the workforce to behave in a required way.

Outsourcing
Where many of the activities of a once complex organisation are moved outside the organisation's boundary and brought in when required.

Oxymoron
A contradiction in terms, for example bittersweet, business ethics and military intelligence.

Paradigm
A pattern or model.

Paradox
A statement, situation or proposition that seems to be absurd or contradictory, but is in fact true.

Paralanguage
Variations in speech, such as pitch, loudness, tempo, tone, duration, laughing and crying.

Path dependence
Small random changes which lead to radical outcomes at a later date.

Perception
The process by which individuals interpret sensory impressions so that they can assign meaning to the environment.

Perceptual paradox
Arises from the fact that individuals bring with them a host of prior assumptions and expectations to the process of perception.

Performance appraisal
The process of assessing the development of an employee.

Performance measurement
The process of monitoring employee performance in an objective way. This measures the success or failure of initiatives such as new working or payment methods.

Performance-related pay
Employees' pay which depends partly on their performance.

Person specifications
The personality characteristics required of an individual to fit a stated job.

Philanthropist
A person who perceives her/himself to be a lover of mankind and who actively exerts her/himself for the well-being of her/his fellow beings.

Philosophy
The love, study or pursuit of wisdom or knowledge, especially concerned with the most general causes and principles of things.

Plan
An account of how an individual intends to get from her/his current situation to one where s/he wants to be, that is, to get from A to B.

Pluralism
Different ways of perceiving issues.

Policy
Plan of action adopted/pursued by a business.

Postmodernism
A belief that the contemporary world is so different to the past that there are very few connections between past, current and, possibly, future events.

Prescriptive
The making or giving of directions, rules or injunctions that are normally sanctioned by long-standing custom or based on legislation.

Processing
Conversation of raw data into information that has meaning.

Product
What is produced by the effort of a process of work.

Profit-related pay
That part of an employee's pay based on the profit which her/his organisation makes.

Proxemics
The study of an individual's perception and use of space, including territorial space.

Psychological contract
An unwritten agreement which sets out what a member of the workforce wants from her/his employer and vice versa.

Psychometric tests
Sometimes called occupational tests, or psychological testing, these are sophisticated tests used to measure an individual's capacities in areas such as intelligence and ability.

Punctuated equilibrium
Periods of quiet interspersed with episodes of hectic activity.

Punishment
The attempt to eliminate undesired behaviours in an individual either by bestowing negative consequences for that behaviour or by withholding the positive consequences (the rewards).

Quality circle
An organisational system that attempts to empower individuals by allowing them to meet periodically to discuss any concerns that they have and to assess solutions to meet the problem.

Rationalisation
The reorganisation of, say, industry on scientific lines, with the elimination of waste of labour, time and materials and the reduction of other costs.

Ratio
The relating of one figure to another in order to identify relative performance.

Recession
A decline in economic trade and prosperity.

Recruitment
The process of finding and employing individuals to carry out the tasks that need to be done within an organisation.

Reference group
The group with which an individual identifies.

Reflective manufacturing
The amalgamation of the economic efficiency of lean manufacturing with the social ideals of dock manufacturing.

Reinforcement
The attempt to induce required behaviour in others by the use of positive rewards or by withholding negative consequences.

Reinforcers
Any consequence that, if immediately followed by a response, increases the probability that the behaviour will be repeated.

Reliability
The extent to which a measure is consistent over a period of time.

Remuneration
A reward, pay for services rendered; includes benefits such as pensions.

Repertory grid technique
A research technique (related to personal construct psychology) that is used to compare one set of constructs (ideas, thoughts) in relation to a given set of elements (things).

Repetitive strain injury (RSI)/Non-specific arm pain (NSAP)
A recurring strain injury, normally of the wrist and upper arm, which is caused by prolonged repetitive activities such as working at a keyboard.

Retrenchment
To take action to reduce costs, that is, to economise.

Reward
Something which is given or received for behaviour that is commendable and valuable.

Robotics
The use of computer-controlled mechanical devices.

Roles
Sets of expected behaviour patterns attributed to someone occupying a given position in a social unit such as an organisation.

Rule of Law
A formal order or regulation governing the procedure or decisions of a court of law and which forms part of common law.

Salary
A financial reward for work done and usually received on a monthly basis.

Scientific management
A classical approach to management where the underlying belief was that decision making (particularly when related to organisational decisions and job design) should be based upon rational scientific procedures.

Selection
The last part of the recruitment process when the organisation decides who to employ from the candidates available.

Self-efficacy
An individual's beliefs and expectations about her/his ability to accomplish a task efficiently.

Seminal
A piece of writing or something of a similar nature that is highly original and important.

Serialist
A person who tends to focus narrowly on the particular task or topic and who needs to learn step by step, concentrating first on the details and the connected logic and progressively building up skills and self-developing understanding.

Sexual discrimination
Discrimination between individuals because of their gender.

Shareholders
The owners of one or more shares in a company.

Skill
The ability to do something well, especially if as a result of experience.

Social Fund
A fund set up as part of the British social security system, from which people in need may receive money as a grant or loan for a specified purpose.

Social relationships
Interaction with other individuals.

Span of control
The number of employees that a person in an organisation supervises.

Staffing plan
A strategy that identifies the business objectives and the quantity and quality of people required to support them.

Staff relationship
A relationship where individuals provide a purely advisory support service to others and where there is a limited element of authority or control.

Stakeholders
People who have a legitimate interest in the activities of an organisation, for example customers, shareholders and employees.

Statute law
Law enacted by a legislative body, for example national government.

Stereotyping
The judging of another individual on the basis of one's own perception of the group to which that individual belongs.

Strategy
The practice or art of using plans (stratagems).

Strategic
Characteristics of a strategy – the tactics.

Stress
Any force that pushes a psychological or physical factor beyond its range of stability, producing a strain within the individual.

Styles
The ways by which something, for example learning, is done.

Synonym
A word that means the same, or nearly the same, as another word.

Systems approach
A logical, analytical approach to the carrying out of an activity or the solution of a problem.

Technological determinists
Individuals who see human beings as the recipients of technology rather than the shapers of it.

Technology
The intellectual and mechanical processes used by an organisation to transform the inputs into outputs such as products and/or services in order to meet the objectives of the organisation.

Technophiles
Individuals who believe that all new technology must be an asset to management.

Technosceptics
Individuals who identify any number of organisational problems each time a new technology is introduced into the workplace.

Telecommuters
Individuals who work away from the office, for example at home, and transmit their work from a home computer to the office by the use of a modem or cable.

Telecommuting
Transmitting work from a home computer to the office by the use of a modem or cable.

Theory Y
A group of assumptions of how to motivate people as individuals who are motivated by higher order rewards such as autonomy and responsibility.

Total quality management (TQM)
A philosophy that brings about the integration of techniques and quality control in line with an organisation's corporate strategy with the intention of providing continuous high-quality goods and/or services.

Training
A planned process to modify attitude, knowledge or skill behaviour through learning experience to achieve effective performance in an activity or range of activities.

Training needs analysis
A sequence of comprehensive analyses used to identify where current skills need to be developed to achieve future organisational strategy.

Traits
Characteristics, features or qualities that distinguish a particular person.

Transferable skills
Skills which individuals have that can be used in more than one job.

Unitary
A whole unit or units – employers and employees share a common goal/mission with all differences resolved rationally.

United Nations
An international organisation comprised of independent states, with its headquarters in New York, USA. It was formed in 1945 to promote peace and international cooperation and security.

Universal eligibility
Common to all, everybody is entitled to it.

Unlawful discrimination
Treating a person differently and less favourably on one of the grounds laid out in legislation, for example sex or race.

Utilitarians
A principle of ethics; people who believe that the highest good lies in the greatest good for the greatest numbers.

Utility analysis
An estimation of the financial expenditure and benefits of the various techniques used in the selection of employees.

Validity
The extent to which completed research actually measures what it sets out to measure.

Variance
The difference between the budgeted and actual figures being spent on a planned project.

Venture capital firm
An organisation that uses money for investment in high-risk projects offering the possibility of large profits on the investment.

Victimisation
Where a worker is singled out for using a workplace complaints procedure or exercising their legal rights.

Vision statement
An attempt to articulate what a desired future for a company would look like.

Wages
Money paid to employees for doing their jobs and usually received on a weekly basis.

Want
Something an individual would like to have rather than something which is needed for their survival.

Whistleblowing
The use of writings on the practice of calling public attention to waste, mismanagement or corruption in government, industry and the military and so on.

White collar
Non-manual, salaried workers employed in professional and clerical occupations.

Wisdom
The ability or result of an ability to think and act using knowledge, experience, understanding, common sense and insight.

Yardstick
A measure or standard used as a means of comparison.

Index